# GENERAL MOTORS

## BUICK/OLDSMOBILE/PONTIAC
## 1975-90 REPAIR MANUAL

D1546802

**President, Chilton Enterprises** — David S. Loewith

**Senior Vice President** — Ronald A. Hoxter
**Publisher & Editor-In-Chief** — Kerry A. Freeman, S.A.E.
**Managing Editors** — Peter M. Conti, Jr., W. Calvin Settle, Jr., S.A.E.
**Assistant Managing Editor** — Nick D'Andrea
**Senior Editors** — Debra Gaffney, Ken Grabowski, A.S.E., S.A.E.
Michael L. Grady, Richard J. Rivele, S.A.E.
Richard T. Smith, Jim Taylor
R. Trevor Webb
**Project Managers** — Martin J. Gunther, Kevin M. G. Maher
**Production Manager** — Andrea Steiger
**Director of Manufacturing** — Mike D'Imperio
**Editor** — Will Kessler

## CHILTON BOOK COMPANY

ONE OF THE **DIVERSIFIED PUBLISHING COMPANIES**,
A PART OF **CAPITAL CITIES/ABC, INC.**

Manufactured in USA
© 1994 Chilton Book Company
Chilton Way, Radnor, PA 19089
ISBN 0-8019-8584-6
Library of Congress Catalog Card No. 94-071953
2345678901    4321098765

# Contents

310-A

# Contents

## SAFETY NOTICE

Proper service and repair procedures are vital to the safe, reliable operation of all motor vehicles, as well as the personal safety of those performing repairs. This manual outlines procedures for servicing and repairing vehicles using safe, effective methods. The procedures contain many NOTES, CAUTIONS, and WARNINGS which should be followed along with standard procedures to eliminate the possibility of personal injury or improper service which could damage the vehicle or compromise its safety.

It is important to note that the repair procedures and techniques, tools and parts for servicing motor vehicles, as well as the skill and experience of the individual performing the work vary widely. It is not possible to anticipate all of the conceivable ways or conditions under which vehicles may be serviced, or to provide cautions as to all of the possible hazards that may result. Standard and accepted safety precautions and equipment should be used when handling toxic or flammable fluids, and safety goggles or other protection should be used during cutting, grinding, chiseling, prying,or any other process that can cause material removal or projectiles.

Some procedures require the use of tools specially designed for a specific purpose. Before substituting another tool or procedure, you must be completely satisfied that neither your personal safety, nor the performance of the vehicle will be endangered.

Although information in this manual is based on industry sources and is complete as possible at the time of publication, the possibility exists that some car manufacturers made later changes which could not be included here. While striving for total accuracy, Chilton Book Company cannot assume responsibility for any errors, changes or omissions that may occur in the compilation of this data.

## PART NUMBERS

Part numbers listed in this reference are not recommendation by Chilton for any product by brand name. They are references that can be used with interchange manuals and aftermarket supplier catalogs to locate each brand supplier's discrete part number.

## SPECIAL TOOLS

Special tools are recommended by the vehicle manufacturer to perform their specific job. Use has been kept to a minimum, but where absolutely necessary, they are referred to in the text by the part number of the tool manufacturer. These tools can be purchased, under the appropriate part number, from your local dealer or regional distributor, or an equivalent tool can be purchased locally from a tool supplier or parts outlet. Before substituting any tool for the one recommended, read the SAFETY NOTICE at the top of this page.

## ACKNOWLEDGMENTS

Portions of materials contained herein have been reprinted with the permission of General Motors Corporation, Service Technology Group.

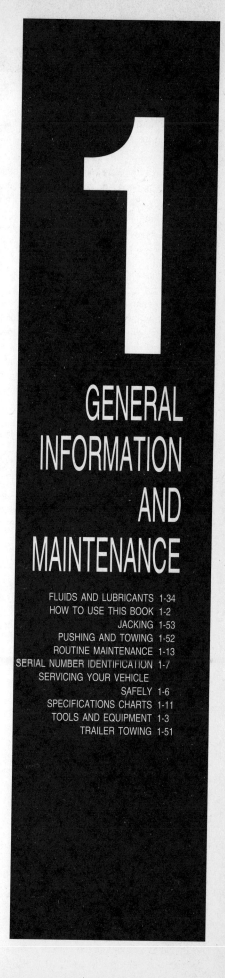

# 1

# GENERAL INFORMATION AND MAINTENANCE

## HOW TO USE THIS BOOK

Chilton's Total Car Care Manual for Buick, Oldsmobile and Pontiac full-sized cars is intended to help you with the care and maintenance of your car and save you money on its upkeep.

The first two sections will be the most used, since they contain maintenance and tune-up information and procedures. Studies have shown that a properly tuned and maintained car can get at least 10% better gas mileage (which translates into lower operating costs) and periodic maintenance will catch minor problems before they turn into major repair bills. The other sections deal with the more complex systems of your car. Operating systems from engine through brakes are covered to the extent that the average do-it-yourselfer becomes mechanically involved. This book will not explain such things as rebuilding the differential for the simple reason that the expertise required and the investment in special tools make this task impractical and uneconomical. It will give you the detailed instructions to help you change your own brake pads and shoes, tune-up the engine, replace spark plugs and filters, and do many more jobs that will save you money, give you personal satisfaction and help you avoid expensive problems.

A secondary purpose of this book is a reference guide for owners who want to understand their car and/or their mechanics better. In this case, no tools at all are required. Knowing just what a particular repair job requires in parts and labor time will allow you to evaluate whether or not you're getting a fair price quote and help decipher itemized bills from a repair shop.

Before attempting any repairs or service on your car, read through the entire procedure outlined in the appropriate chapter. This will give you the overall view of what tools and supplies will be required. There is nothing more frustrating than having to walk to the bus stop on Monday morning because you were short one gasket on Sunday afternoon. So read ahead and plan ahead. Each operation should be approached logically and all procedures thoroughly understood before attempting any work. Some special tools that may be required can often be rented from local automotive jobbers or places specializing in renting tools and equipment. Check the yellow pages of your phone book.

All chapters contain adjustments, maintenance, removal and installation procedures, and overhaul procedures. When overhaul is not considered practical, we tell you how to remove the failed part and then how to install the new or rebuilt replacement. In this way, you at least save the labor costs. Backyard overhaul of some components (such as the alternator or water pump) is just not practical, but the removal and installation procedure is often simple and well within the capabilities of the average car owner.

There are a few basic mechanic's rules that should be followed when working on any vehicle:

1. Left side of the vehicle means the driver's side; right side is the passenger's side.

2. Most screws, bolts, and nuts are right handed; they are tightened by turning clockwise and removed by turning counterclockwise.

3. Never crawl under a vehicle supported only by a jack. Jack up the vehicle, then support it with jackstands!

4. Never smoke or position an exposed flame near the battery or any part of the fuel system;

5. THINK AHEAD. Take your time and use common sense during ALL operations.

Safety is always the most important rule. Constantly be aware of the dangers involved in working on or around an automobile and take proper precautions to avoid the risk of personal injury or damage to the vehicle. Please refer to Servicing Your Vehicle Safely (located later in this section), and the SAFETY NOTICE on the acknowledgment page before attempting any service procedures and pay attention to the instructions provided. There are 3 common mistakes in mechanical work:

6. Incorrect order of assembly, disassembly or adjustment. When taking something apart or putting it together, doing things in the wrong order usually just costs you extra time; however it CAN break something. Read the entire procedure before beginning disassembly. Do everything in the order in which the instructions say you should do it, even if you can't immediately see a reason for it. When you're taking apart something that is very intricate (for example a carburetor), you might want to draw a picture of how it looks when assembled at one point in order to make sure you get everything back in its proper position. We will supply exploded views whenever possible, but sometimes the job requires more attention to detail than an illustration provides. When making adjustments (especially tune-up adjustments), do them in order. One adjustment often affects another and you cannot expect satisfactory results unless each adjustment is made only when it cannot be changed by any other.

7. Overtorquing (or undertorquing) nuts and bolts. While it is more common for overtorquing to cause damage, undertorquing can cause a fastener to vibrate loose and cause serious damage, especially when dealing with aluminum parts. Pay attention to torque specifications and utilize a torque wrench in assembly. If a torque figure is not available remember that, if you are using the right tool to do the job, you will probably not have to strain yourself to get a fastener tight enough. The pitch of most threads is so slight that the tension you put on the wrench will be multiplied many times in actual force on what you are tightening. A good example of how critical torque is can be seen in the case of spark plug installation, especially where you are putting the plug into an aluminum cylinder head. Too little torque can fail to crush the gasket, causing leakage of combustion gases and consequent overheating of the plug and engine parts. Too much torque can damage the threads or distort the plug, which changes the spark gap at the electrode. Since more and more manufacturers are using aluminum in their engine and chassis parts to save weight, a torque wrench should be in any serious do-it-yourselfer's tool box.

There are many commercial chemical products available for ensuring that fasteners won't come loose, even if they are not torqued just right (a very common brand is Loctite®). If you're worried about getting something together tight enough to hold, but loose enough to avoid mechanical damage during assembly, one of these products might offer substantial insurance. Read the label on the package and make sure the product is compatible with the materials, fluids, etc. involved before choosing one.

8. Crossthreading. This occurs when a part such as a bolt is screwed into a nut or casting at the wrong angle and forced, causing the threads to become damaged. Crossthreading is more likely to occur if access is difficult. It helps to clean and lubricate fasteners, and to start threading with the part to be installed going straight in, using your fingers. If you encounter resistance, unscrew the part and start over again at a different angle until it can be inserted and turned several times without much effort. Keep in mind that many parts, especially spark plugs, use tapered threads so that gentle turning will automatically bring the part you're threading to the proper angle if you don't force it or resist a change in angle. Don't put a wrench on the part until it's been turned in a couple of times by hand. If you suddenly encounter resistance and the part has not seated fully, don't force it. Pull it back out and make sure it's clean and threading properly.

Always take your time and be patient; once you have some experience, working on your car will become an enjoyable hobby.

## TOOLS AND EQUIPMENT

▶ **See Figures 1, 2, 3, 4, 5, 6, 7, 8, 9, 10 and 11**

Naturally, without the proper tools and equipment it is impossible to properly service your vehicle. It would be impossible to catalog each tool that you would need to perform each and every operation in this book. It would also be unwise for the amateur to rush out and buy an expensive set of tools on the theory that he may need one or more of them at sometime.

The best approach is to proceed slowly, gathering together a good quality set of those tools that are used most frequently. Don't be misled by the low cost of bargain tools. It is far better to spend a little more for better quality. Forged wrenches, 6 or 12-point sockets and fine tooth ratchets are by far preferable to their less expensive counterparts. As any good mechanic can tell you, there are few worse experiences than trying to work on a car or truck with bad tools. Your monetary savings will be far outweighed by frustration and mangled knuckles.

Begin accumulating those tools that are used most frequently; those associated with routine maintenance and tune-up.

In addition to the normal assortment of screwdrivers and pliers, you should have the following tools for routine maintenance jobs (your car uses both English and metric fasteners):

• Metric wrenches,sockets and combination open end/box end wrenches in sizes from 3mm to 19mm; $^{13}/_{16}$ in. and $^{5}/_{8}$ in. spark plug sockets.

If possible, buy various length socket drive extensions. One break in this department is that the metric sockets available in the U.S. will all fit the ratchet handles and extensions you may already have ($^{1}/_{4}$ in., $^{3}/_{8}$ in., and $^{1}/_{2}$ in. drive).

• Jackstands for support
• Oil filter wrench
• Oil filter spout for pouring oil
• Grease gun for chassis lubrication
• Hydrometer for checking the battery
• A container for draining oil
• Many rags for wiping up the inevitable mess

In addition to the above items there are several others that are not absolutely necessary, but handy to have around. These include absorbent gravel (such as cat litter), a transmission fluid funnel and the usual supply of lubricants, antifreeze and fluids, although these can be purchased as needed. This is a basic list for routine maintenance, but only your personal needs and desires can accurately determine your list of tools.

The second list of tools is for tune-ups. While the tools involved here are slightly more sophisticated, they need not be outrageously expensive. There are several inexpensive tachometer/dwell meters on the market that are every bit as good for the average mechanic as a more expensive professional model. Just be sure that the meter scale goes to at least 1,200  1,500 rpm on the tach scale and that it works on 4, 6 and 8-cylinder engines. A basic list of tune-up equipment could include:

1. Tach/dwell meter
2. Spark plug wrench
3. Timing light (a DC light that works from the car's battery is best, although an AC light that plugs into 110V house current will suffice at some sacrifice in brightness)
4. Wire spark plug gauge/adjusting tools
5. Set of feeler blades

In addition to these basic tools, there are several other tools and gauges you may find useful. These include:

6. A compression gauge. The screw-in type is slower to use, but eliminates the possibility of a faulty reading due to escaping pressure
7. A manifold vacuum gauge
8. A test light
9. An induction meter. This is used for determining whether or not there is current in a wire. This is handy for use if a wire is broken somewhere in a wiring harness.

As a final note, you will probably find a torque wrench necessary for all but the most basic work. There are three types of torque wrenches available: deflecting beam type, dial indicator and click type. The beam and dial indicator models are perfectly adequate, although the click type models are more precise and allow the user to reach the required torque without having to assume a sometimes awkward position in reading a scale. No matter what type of torque wrench you purchase, have it calibrated periodically to ensure accuracy.

## Special Tools

Special tools are occasionally necessary to perform a specific job or are recommended to make a job easier. Their use has been kept to a minimum. When a special tool is indicated, it will be referred to by the manufacturer's part number, and, where possible, an illustration of the tool will be provided so that an equivalent tool may be used. Special tools for GM cars can be purchased from a dealer or through: Service Tool Division Kent-Moore 29784 Little Mack Roseville, MI 48066-2298

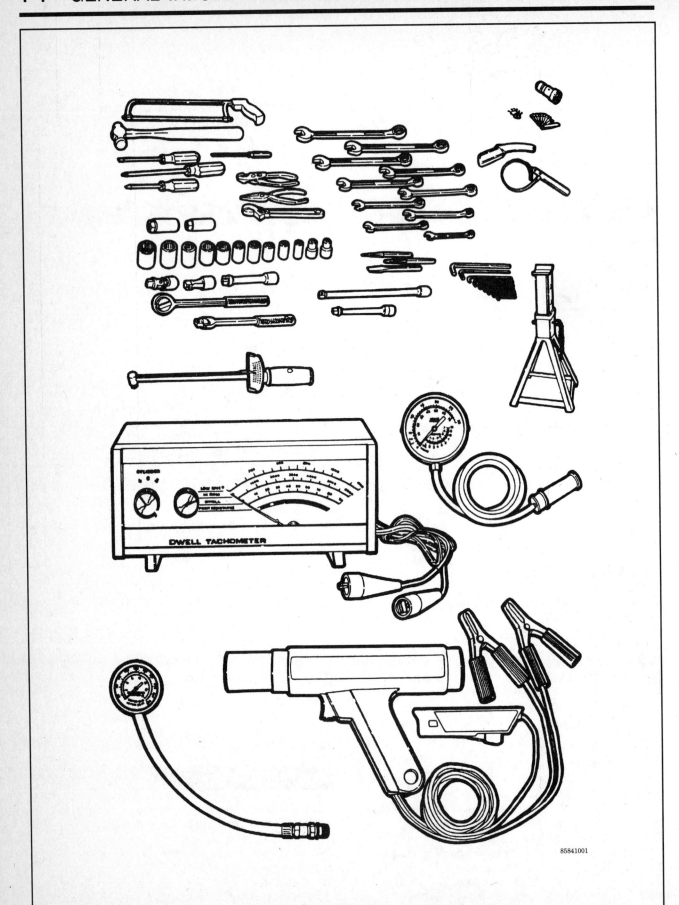

**Fig. 1 A basic collection of tools and instruments is all you need for most vehicle maintenance**

85841001

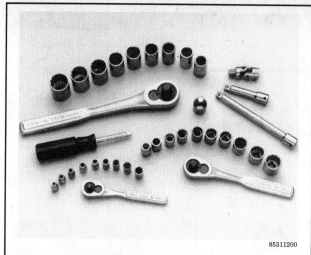

85311200

**Fig. 2 All but the most basic procedures will require an assortment of rachets and sockets**

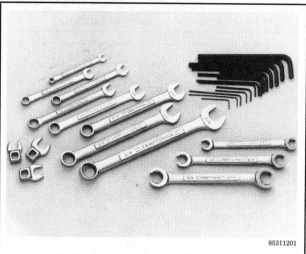

85311201

**Fig. 3 In addition to rachets, a good set of wrenches and hex keys will be necessary**

85311202

**Fig. 4 A hydraulic floor jack and a set of jackstands are essential for lifting and supporting the vehicle**

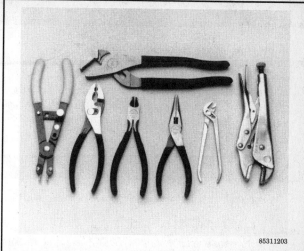

85311203

**Fig. 5 An assortment of pliers will be handy, especially for old rusted parts and stripped bolt heads**

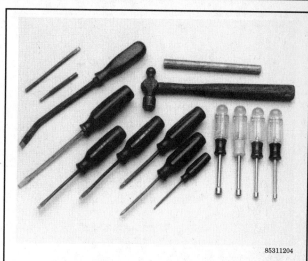

85311204

**Fig. 6 Various screwdrivers, a hammer, chisels and prybars are necessary to have in your toolbox**

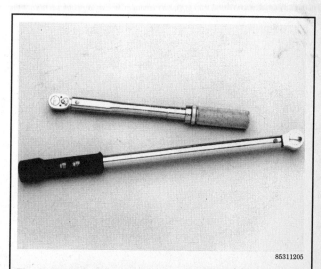

85311205

**Fig. 7 Many repairs will require the use of a torque wrench to ensure the components are properly fastened**

## SERVICING YOUR VEHICLE SAFELY

It is virtually impossible to anticipate all of the hazards involved with automotive maintenance and service, but care and common sense will prevent most accidents.

The rules of safety for mechanics range from "don't smoke around gasoline", to "use the proper tool for the job". The trick to avoiding injuries is to develop safe work habits and take every possible precaution.

### Dos

• Do keep a fire extinguisher and first aid kit within easy reach.

• Do wear safety glasses or goggles when cutting, drilling, grinding, or prying, even if you have 20-20 vision. If you wear glasses for the sake of vision, they should be made of hardened glass that can serve also as safety glasses, or wear safety goggles over your regular glasses.

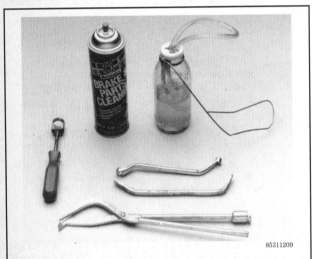

Fig. 8 Although not always necessary, using specialized brake tool will save time

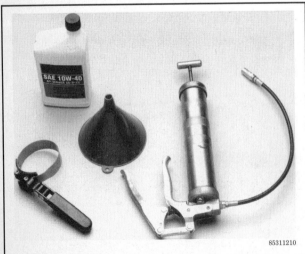

Fig. 9 A few inexpensive lubrication tools will make regular service easier

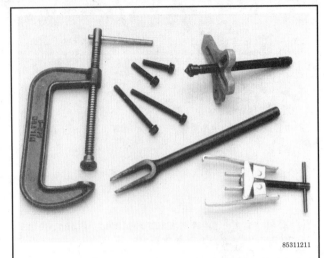

Fig. 10 Various pullers, clamps and separator tools are needed for the repair of many components

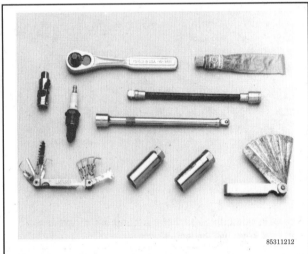

Fig. 11 A variety of tools and gauges are needed for spark plug service

• Do shield your eyes whenever you work around the battery. Batteries contain sulfuric acid. In case of contact with the eyes or skin, flush the area with water or a mixture of water and baking soda and get medical attention immediately.

• Do use safety stands for any under car service. Jacks are for raising vehicles, safety stands are for making sure the vehicle stays raised until you want it to come down. Whenever the vehicle is raised, block the wheels remaining on the ground and set the parking brake.

• Do use adequate ventilation when working with any chemicals or hazardous materials. Like carbon monoxide, the asbestos dust resulting from brake lining wear can be poisonous in sufficient quantities.

• Do disconnect the negative battery cable when working on the electrical system. The secondary ignition system can contain up to 50,000 volts.

- Do follow manufacturer's directions whenever working with potentially hazardous materials. Both brake fluid and antifreeze are poisonous if taken internally.
- Do properly maintain your tools. Loose hammerheads, mushroomed punches and chisels, frayed or poorly grounded electrical cords, excessively worn screwdrivers, spread wrenches (open end), cracked sockets, slipping ratchets, or faulty droplight sockets can cause accidents.
- Likewise, keep your tools clean; a greasy wrench can slip off a bolt head, ruining the bolt and often ruining your knuckles in the process.
- Do use the proper size and type of tool for the job being done.
- Do when possible, pull on a wrench handle rather than push on it, and adjust your stance to prevent a fall.
- Do be sure that adjustable wrenches are tightly closed on the nut or bolt and pulled so that the face is on the side of the fixed jaw.
- Do select a wrench or socket that fits the nut or bolt. The wrench or socket should sit straight, not cocked.
- Do strike squarely with a hammer; avoid glancing blows.
- Do set the parking brake and block the drive wheels if the work requires the engine running.

## Don'ts

- Don't run the engine in a garage or anywhere else without proper ventilation--EVER! Carbon monoxide is poisonous; it takes a long time to leave the human body and you can build up a deadly supply of it in your system by simply breathing in a little every day. You may not realize you are slowly poisoning yourself. Always use power vents, windows, fans or open the garage doors.
- Don't work around moving parts while wearing a necktie or other loose clothing. Short sleeves are much safer than long, loose sleeves; steel-toed shoes with neoprene soles protect your toes and give a better grip on slippery surfaces. Jewelry such as watches, fancy belt buckles, beads or body adornment of any kind is not safe working around a vehicle. Long hair should be tied back under a hat or cap.
- Don't use your pockets for toolboxes. A fall or bump can drive a screwdriver deep into your body. Even a wiping cloth hanging from the back pocket can wrap around a spinning shaft or fan.
- Don't smoke when working around gasoline, cleaning solvent or other flammable material.
- Don't smoke when working around the battery. When the battery is being charged, it gives off explosive hydrogen gas.
- Don't use gasoline to wash your hands; there are excellent soaps available. Gasoline may contain lead, and lead can enter the body through a cut, accumulating in the body until you are very ill. Gasoline also removes all the natural oils from the skin so that bone dry hands will suck up oil and grease.
- Don't service the air conditioning system unless you are equipped with the necessary tools and training. The refrigerant, R-12, is extremely cold when compressed, and when released into the air will instantly freeze any surface it contacts, including your eyes. Although the refrigerant is normally non-toxic, R-12 becomes a deadly poisonous gas in the presence of an open flame. One good whiff of the vapors from burning refrigerant can be fatal.
- Don't use screwdrivers for anything other than driving screws! A screwdriver used as a prying tool can snap when you least expect it, causing injuries.
- Don't use a bumper jack (that little ratchet, scissors, or pantograph jack supplied with the vehicle) for anything other than changing a flat! These jacks are only intended for emergency use out on the road; they are NOT designed as a maintenance tool. If you are serious about maintaining your vehicle yourself, invest in a hydraulic floor jack of at least 1½ ton capacity, and at least two sturdy jackstands.

## SERIAL NUMBER IDENTIFICATION

### Vehicle

▶ See Figures 12, 13, 14, 15, 16, 17 and 18

The Vehicle Identification Number (VIN) is important for ordering parts and for servicing. The VIN is a thirteen digit (1975-1980) or seventeen digit (1981 and later) sequence of numbers and letters visible on a plate fastened to the upper left instrument panel area, seen through the windshield.

➡Model years appear in the VIN as the last digit of each particular year (6 is 1976, 8 is 1978,etc.), until 1980 (which is A). This is the final year under the thirteen digit code. The seventeen digit VIN begins with 1981 (B), and continues 1982 (C) and so on, except letters which may be confused with numbers (I, O or Q are skipped). Because of this, 1987 is represented by (H) while 1988 is (J) and 1989 is (K).

### Engine

▶ See Figures 19, 20, 21, 22 and 23

Engine identification can take place using various methods. The VIN, described earlier in this section, contains a code indentifying the engine originally installed in the vehicle. In most cases, this should be sufficient for determining the engine with which your car is currently equipped. However, some older vehicles may have had the engine replaced or changed by a previous owner. In this case, the engine can be identified by an engine serial number stamped on the block or located on adhesive labels that may be present on the valve covers.

### Automatic Transmission Identification

▶ See Figures 24 and 25

All Buick, Oldsmobile and Pontiac models covered in this guide use various GM Turbo Hydra-Matic (THM) automatic transmissions. Transmission identification numbers are found on either side of the transmission case, depending on model.

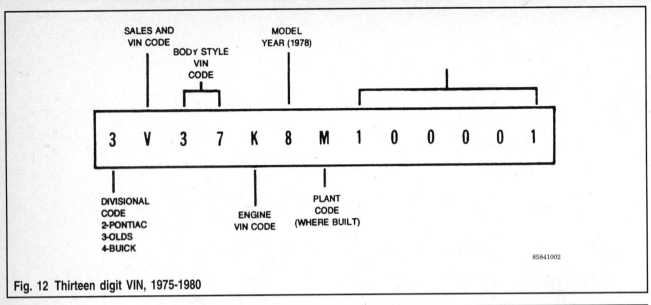

Fig. 12 Thirteen digit VIN, 1975-1980

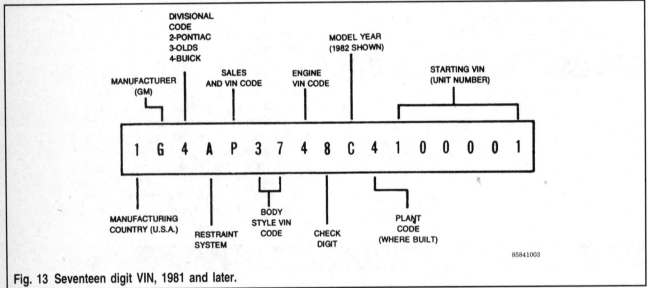

Fig. 13 Seventeen digit VIN, 1981 and later.

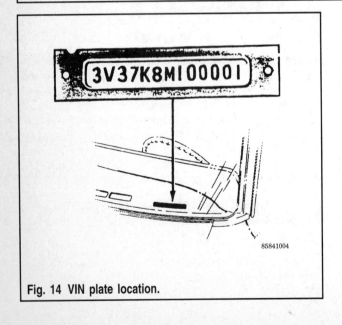

Fig. 14 VIN plate location.

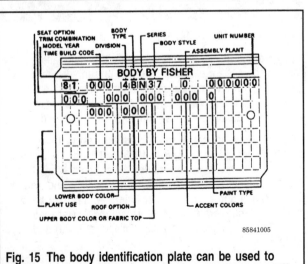

Fig. 15 The body identification plate can be used to determine the original paint and trim combinations. U.S. models is shown here.

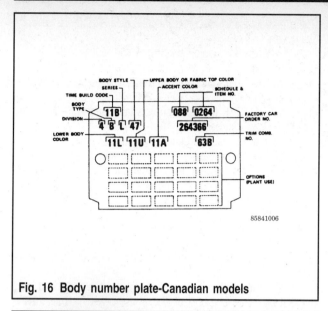

Fig. 16 Body number plate-Canadian models

Fig. 17 Close-up view of the VIN plate

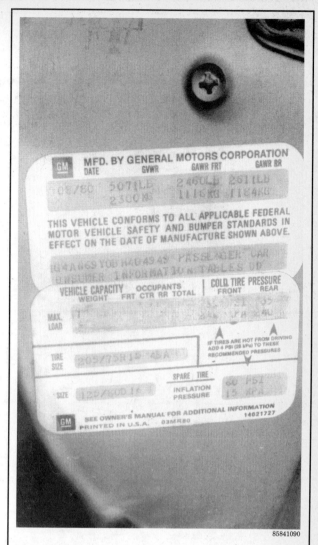

Fig. 18 These labels are located on the inside of the drivers door and provide the date of manufacture and other information

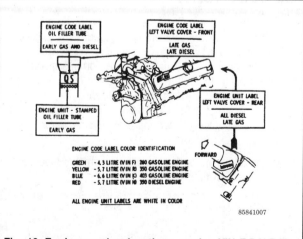

Fig. 19 Engine number locations, engine VIN F,P,N,R,Y and K. 1975-77 Olds and Pontiac number stamped on oil filler tube.

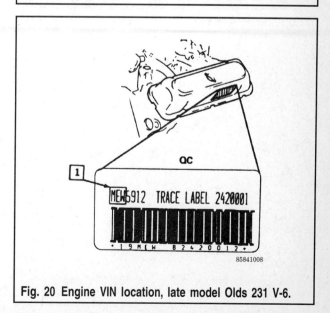

Fig. 20 Engine VIN location, late model Olds 231 V-6.

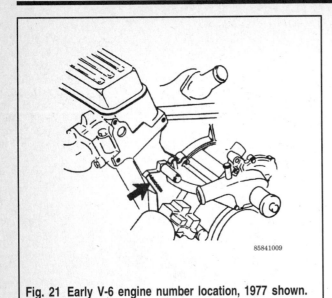

Fig. 21 Early V-6 engine number location, 1977 shown.

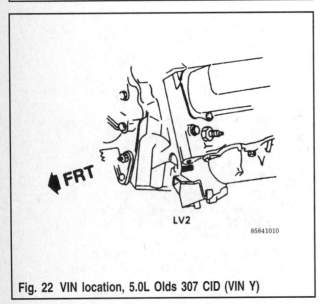

Fig. 22 VIN location, 5.0L Olds 307 CID (VIN Y)

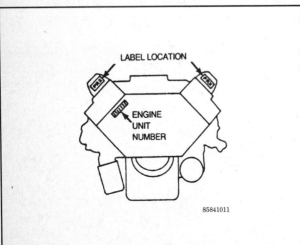

Fig. 23 Engine VIN locations, 265, 301, 305, and 350 (L-code) V-8s

Some models also have I.D. numbers stamped on the governor cover.

Buick models are equipped with the 200, 200C, 200-4R, 350, 375B and 400 transmissions. Oldsmobile uses the 200, 200C, 200-4R, 250, 350, 375B and 400 units, and Pontiacs are equipped with the 200, 200C, 200-4R, 350, and 400 transmissions. The 375B transmission was last used in 1976, while the 200-4R was introduced in 1981.

A quick way to visually identify the transmissions is to look at the shapes of the pans. The 250, 350 and 375B have a squarish pan with the right rear corner cut off. The 200 pan is similar but more rectangular. The pan of the 400 model transmission is irregularly shaped.

The 200, 250, 350 and 375B models are also identified by their kickdown linkage, which is actuated by a cable attached to the accelerator pedal linkage. The 400 model transmission has an electric kickdown connected to a switch on the accelerator linkage.

The 200 model transmission was first used in 1977 and is the first all metric unit built by GM in the U.S. This transmission sometimes has the word METRIC stamped on the pan. The 200-4R model is an automatic overdrive version of the 200 transmission. The 200C, 250C and 350C transmissions are similar to those given these number designations without the C except that they incorporate a lockup clutch in the torque converter.

There is little visual difference between the 350 and 375B transmissions, except that the latter has a longer output shaft and extension housing.

## Drive Axle Identification

▶ See Figure 26

The drive axle identification is stamped on the forward portion of the housing or on a tag bolted to the rear cover.

## Vehicle Emission Control Information Label

▶ See Figures 26 and 27

The Vehicle Emission Control Information (VECI) label is located in the engine compartment (fan shroud, radiator support, hood underside, etc.) of every vehicle produced by General Motors. The label contains important emission specifications and setting procedures, as well as a vacuum hose schematic with various emissions components identified.

When servicing your Buick, Oldsmobile or Pontiac, this label should always be checked for up-to-date information pertaining specifically to your vehicle.

➡Always follow the timing procedures on this label when adjusting ignition timing.

## ENGINE IDENTIFICATION CODES

| Engine | Eng. Mfg. | Bbl. | '75 | '76 | '77 | '78 | '79 | '80 | '81 | '82 | '83 | '84 | '85 | '86 | '87 | '88 | '89 | '90 |
|---|---|---|---|---|---|---|---|---|---|---|---|---|---|---|---|---|---|---|
| **BUICK** | | | | | | | | | | | | | | | | | | |
| 6-231 | Buick | 2 | | | C | A | A | A | A | A | A | A | A | A | A | | | |
| 6-231 | Buick | 2, 4-Turbo | | | | G,3 | 3 | 3 | | | | | | | | | | |
| 6-252 | Buick | 4 | | | | | | 4 | 4 | 4 | 4 | 4 | 4 | | | | | |
| 8-267 | Chev. | 2 | | | | | | | J | | | | | | | | | |
| 8-301 | Pont. | 2 | | | Y | Y | Y | | | | | | | | | | | |
| 8-301 | Pont. | 4 | | | | | | W | W | | | | | | | | | |
| 8-305 | Chev. | 2 | | | | U | | | | | | | | | | | | |
| 8-307 | Olds. | 4 | | | | | | | Y | Y | Y | Y | Y | Y | Y | Y | Y | Y |
| 8-350 | Olds. | 4 | | | R | R | R | R | | | | | | | | | | |
| 8-350 | Chev. | 4 | | | | L | | | | | | | | | | | | |
| 8-350 | Buick | 4 | J | J | J | X | X | X | | | | | | | | | | |
| 8-350 | Olds. | Diesel | | | | | | N | N | N | N | N | N | | | | | |
| 8-400 | Pont. | 4 | | | | Z | | | | | | | | | | | | |
| 8-403 | Olds. | 4 | | | K | K | K | | | | | | | | | | | |
| 8-455 | Buick | 4 | T | T | | | | | | | | | | | | | | |
| **OLDSMOBILE** | | | | | | | | | | | | | | | | | | |
| 6-231 | Buick | 2 | | | C | A | A | A | A | A | A | A | | | | | | |
| 6-252 | Buick | 4 | | | | | | | 4 | 4 | 4 | | | | | | | |
| 8-260 | Olds. | 2 | | | F | F | F | F | F | F | | | | | | | | |
| 8-301 | Pont. | 2 | | | | | Y | | | | | | | | | | | |
| 8-307 | Olds. | 4 | | | | | | Y | Y | Y | Y | Y | Y | Y | Y | Y | Y | Y |
| 8-350 | Buick | 4 | | | | X | | | | | | | | | | | | |
| 8-350 | Olds. | 4 | K | R | R | R | R | R | | | | | | | | | | |
| 8-350 | Chev. | 4 | | | L | | | | | | | | | | | | | |
| 8-350 | Olds. | Diesel | | | | N | N | N | N | N | N | N | N | | | | | |
| 8-400 | Olds. | 2 | R | | | | | | | | | | | | | | | |
| 8-400 | Olds. | 4 | S | | | | | | | | | | | | | | | |
| 8-403 | Olds. | 4 | | | K | K | K | | | | | | | | | | | |
| 8-455 | Olds. | 4 | T | T | | | | | | | | | | | | | | |
| **PONTIAC** | | | | | | | | | | | | | | | | | | |
| 6-231 | Buick | 2 | | | C | A | A | A | A | A | A | A | A | A | | | | |
| 6-252 | Buick | 4 | | | | | | | | 4 | | | | | | | | |
| 6-262 | Chev. | F.I. | | | | | | | | | | | Z | Z | | | | |
| 8-265 | Pont. | 2 | | | | | | S | S | | | | | | | | | |
| 8-301 | Pont. | 2 | | | Y | Y | Y | | | | | | | | | | | |
| 8-301 | Pont. | 4 | | | | W | W | W | | | | | | | | | | |
| 8-305 | Chev. | 2 | | | U | | | | H | H | H | H | H | H | | | | |
| 8-307 | Olds. | 4 | | | | | | | Y | | | | | | | Y | Y | Y |
| 8-350 | Olds. | 4 | | | R | R | R | R | | | | | | | | | | |
| 8-350 | Pont. | 4 | | | P | | | | | | | | | | | | | |
| 8-350 | Buick | 4 | | | | X | X | X | X | | | | | | | | | |
| 8-350 | Olds. | Diesel | | | | | | N | N | N | N | N | N | | | | | |
| 8-400 | Pont. | 2 | R | R | | | | | | | | | | | | | | |
| 8-400 | Pont. | 4 | S | S | Z | | | | | | | | | | | | | |
| 8-403 | Olds. | 4 | | | K | K | K | | | | | | | | | | | |
| 8-455 | Pont. | 4 | W | W | | | | | | | | | | | | | | |

858410C1

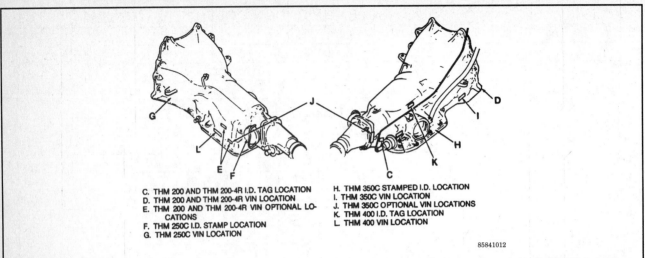

C. THM 200 AND THM 200-4R I.D. TAG LOCATION
D. THM 200 AND THM 200-4R VIN LOCATION
E. THM 200 AND THM 200-4R VIN OPTIONAL LO-
   CATIONS
F. THM 250C I.D. STAMP LOCATION
G. THM 250C VIN LOCATION

H. THM 350C STAMPED I.D. LOCATION
I. THM 350C VIN LOCATION
J. THM 350C OPTIONAL VIN LOCATIONS
K. THM 400 I.D. TAG LOCATION
L. THM 400 VIN LOCATION

85841012

**Fig. 24 Transmission I.D. location. The 375B unit is the same as the 350, except for a longer output shaft and extension housing.**

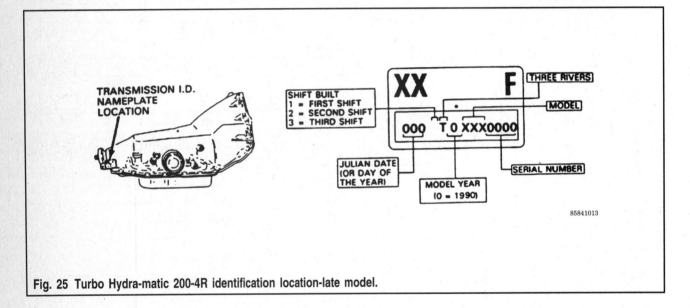

TRANSMISSION I.D. NAMEPLATE LOCATION

SHIFT BUILT
1 = FIRST SHIFT
2 = SECOND SHIFT
3 = THIRD SHIFT

XX    F

THREE RIVERS

MODEL

000   T 0 XXX0000

JULIAN DATE
(OR DAY OF
THE YEAR)

MODEL YEAR
(0 = 1990)

SERIAL NUMBER

85841013

**Fig. 25 Turbo Hydra-matic 200-4R identification location-late model.**

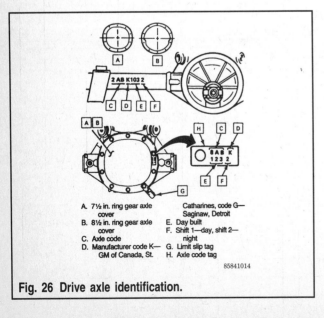

A. 7½ in. ring gear axle
   cover
B. 8½ in. ring gear axle
   cover
C. Axle code
D. Manufacturer code K—
   GM of Canada, St.

Catharines, code G—
Saginaw, Detroit
E. Day built
F. Shift 1—day, shift 2—
   night
G. Limit slip tag
H. Axle code tag

85841014

**Fig. 26 Drive axle identification.**

## ROUTINE MAINTENANCE

### Air Cleaner

All engines are equipped with dry type air cleaners that utilize replaceable air filter elements. The Positive Crankcase Ventilation (PCV) system air filter element on gasoline engines is also found in the air filter housing (usually mounted on the inside of the housing rim). Both of these filter elements should be replaced at 30,000 mile or 1½ year intervals (36 month intervals on 1983 and later models) on all models, except in extremely dusty or smoggy conditions where replacement should be much more frequent.

➡**Never remove the air cleaner from a diesel with the engine running. The intake vacuum is strong, and dirt or nearby objects (even the air cleaner wing nut!) may be sucked directly into the combustion chambers. This will almost always cause major engine damage.**

**Fig. 27 Emissions label location**

### Air Cleaner Element and PCV Filter

▶ **See Figures 28, 29 and 30**

#### REMOVAL & INSTALLATION

1. Remove the wing nut(s) from the top of the air cleaner assembly and lay it aside.
2. Remove the air cleaner cover and gently lift the air cleaner element out of the housing without knocking any dirt into the carburetor.
3. Pull the PCV filter out of the retainer.
4. Wipe the inside of the air cleaner housing with a paper towel or clean rag.
5. Clean the inside of the PCV filter retainer and install a new PCV filter element.
6. Install a new air cleaner element.
7. Replace the air cleaner cover and install the wing nut(s).

### Gasoline Fuel Filter

There are three types of fuel filters; internal (in the carburetor fitting), in-line (in the fuel line), and in-tank (the sock on the fuel pickup tube).

### ❊❊CAUTION

**Before removing any fuel system component, always relieve pressure from the system.**

#### FUEL PRESSURE RELEASE

**Carbureted**

To release the fuel pressure on the carbureted system, remove the fuel filler cap from the fuel tank in order to allow the

---

General Motors emissions decal, 1979 231 V6 shown.

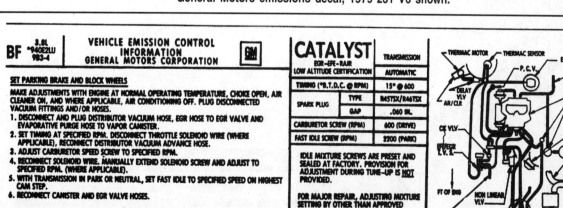

Fig. 28 Remove the wing nut and air cleaner cover

Fig. 29 Remove and replace the air cleaner element if it is dirty

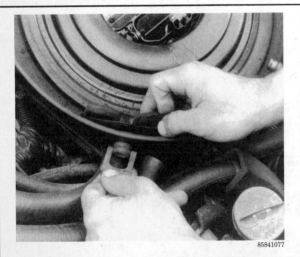

Fig. 30 On this model, the PCV filter can be removed by disconnecting the hose and pulling the retaining clip

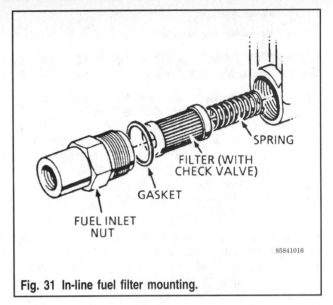

Fig. 31 In-line fuel filter mounting.

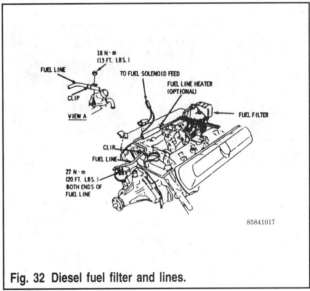

Fig. 32 Diesel fuel filter and lines.

expanded vapor to escape, then reinstall the cap. A rag should be placed around a fuel fitting to catch any remaining fuel which may escape.

### Throttle Body Injection (TBI)

When servicing TBI vehicles, the fuel filler cap should be removed in order to relieve tank pressure, then reinstalled. The TBI unit used on these engines contains a constant bleed feature in the pressure regulator that relieves pressure any time the engine is off. Therefore, no special relief procedure is required. However, a small amount of fuel may be released when the fuel line is disconnected.

### ❋❋CAUTION

**To reduce the chance of personal injury, cover the fuel line with cloth to collect escaping fuel and then place the cloth in an approved container.**

## REMOVAL & INSTALLATION

### Internal Filter

The carburetor inlet fuel filter should be replaced every year or 15,000 miles or more often if necessary. This paper element filter is located behind the large fuel line inlet nut on the carburetor. Some vehicles may also have an in-line fuel filter located between the fuel pump and carburetor. This filter should be changed at the same time as the inlet-type filter; in both cases filters should only be changed when the engine is cold for safety related reasons.

1. Disconnect the fuel line connection at the fuel inlet filter nut on the carburetor. A backup wrench should be used to prevent the fuel filter nut from loosening while trying to remove the line.
2. Carefully loosen and remove the fuel inlet filter nut from the carburetor.
3. Remove the filter and spring.

**To install:**

➡If a check valve is not present with the filter, one must be installed when the filter is replaced. The check valve is necessary in order to meet Motor Vehicle Safety Standards (MVSS) for roll-over.

4. Install the spring, filter and check valve making sure the valve end of the filter is facing the fuel line. Ribs on the fuel filter will prevent it from being installed incorrectly, unless it is forced into position.
5. Connect the fuel line to the filter inlet nut.
6. Start the engine and check for leaks.

### In-line Filter

▶ See Figure 31

To locate the in-line filter, follow the fuel line back from the carburetor or throttle body. In-line filters are often mounted to the frame rail underneath the vehicle. It may be necessary to raise and safely support the vehicle using jackstands in order to access the filter.

1. Disconnect the negative battery cable to prevent fuel spillage if the ignition is accidentally turned ON.
2. Using a backup wrench to prevent overtorquing the lines or fittings, loosen, and disconnect the fuel lines from the filter. Be sure to position a rag in order to catch any remaining fuel which may escape when the fittings are loosened.
3. Loosen the retaining bolt, then remove the retaining bracket and/or fuel filter from the vehicle.

**To install:**

4. Position the filter and retaining bracket with the directional arrow facing away from the fuel tank, towards the carburetor or throttle body.

➡The filter has an arrow (fuel flow direction) on the side of the case, be sure to install it correctly in the system, with the arrow facing away from the fuel tank.

5. Install and tighten the filter/bracket retainer.
6. Connect the fuel lines to the filter and tighten using a backup wrench to prevent damage.

7. Connect the negative battery cable, then start the engine and check for leaks.

### In-Tank Filter

To service the in-tank fuel filter, please refer to the electric fuel pump removal and installation procedure in Section 5 of this manual.

## Diesel Fuel Filter

The diesel fuel filter is mounted on the rear of the intake manifold, and is larger than that on a gasoline engine because diesel fuel generally is "dirtier" (has more suspended particles) than gasoline.

The diesel fuel filter should be changed every 30,000 miles or two years.

## REMOVAL & INSTALLATION

▶ See Figures 32, 33 and 34

1. Disconnect the negative battery cable.
2. With the engine cool, place absorbent rags underneath the fuel line fittings at the filter.
3. Disconnect the fuel lines from the filter. If possible, use a backup wrench to prevent overtorquing and damaging the fuel lines.
4. Loosen the fasteners and remove the filter from its bracket.

**To install:**

5. Position a new filter to the bracket and secure.
6. Connect the fuel lines to the fittings being careful not to overtorque or damage the lines.
7. Connect the negative battery cable, then start the engine and check for leaks. Run the engine for about two minutes, then shut off the engine for the same amount of time to allow any trapped air in the injection system to bleed off.

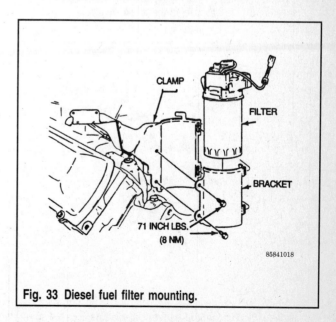

Fig. 33 Diesel fuel filter mounting.

GM diesel cars also have a fuel filter inside the fuel tank which is maintenance-free.

➡ If the filter element ever becomes clogged, the engine will stop. This stoppage is usually preceded by a hesitation or sluggish running. General Motors recommends that after changing the diesel fuel filter, the Housing Pressure Cold Advance be activated manually, if the engine temperature is above 125°F (52°C). Activating the H.P.C.A. will reduce engine cranking time. To activate the H.P.C.A. solenoid, disconnect the two lead connector at the engine temperature switch and bridge the connector with a jumper. After the engine is running, remove the jumper and reconnect the connector to the engine temperature switch. When the new filter element is installed, start the engine and check for leaks.

## Positive Crankcase Ventilation (PCV) Valve

▶ See Figures 35, 36 and 37

The PCV system must be operating properly in order to allow removal of fuel vapors and water from the crankcase. This system should be checked and serviced every year or 15,000 miles. The PCV valve should be replaced every two years or 30,000 miles. Normal service includes cleaning the passages of the systems hoses with solvent, inspecting them for cracks and breaks, and replacing them as necessary.

The PCV system is designed to prevent the emission of gases from the crankcase into the atmosphere. It does this by connecting a crankcase outlet (usually the valve cover) to the intake manifold with a hose. The crankcase gases travel through the hose to the intake manifold where they are returned to the combustion chambers to be burned. If maintained properly, this system reduces condensation in the crankcase and the resultant formation of harmful acids and oil dilution. A clogged PCV valve will often cause a slow or rough idle due to a richer fuel mixture. A car equipped with a PCV system has air going through a hose to the intake manifold from an outlet on the valve cover. To compensate for this extra air going to the manifold, carburetor specifications require a richer mixture at the carburetor. If the PCV valve or hose is clogged, this air doesn't go to the intake manifold which makes the mixture too rich and results in a slow, rough idle. The valve should be checked before making any carburetor adjustments. Disconnect the valve from the engine or clamp the hose shut. If the engine speed decreases less than 50 rpm, the valve is clogged and should be replaced. If the engine speed decreased much more than 50 rpm, then the valve is good. The PCV valve is an inexpensive item and it is suggested that it be replaced. If the new valve doesn't noticeably improve engine idle, the problem may be a restriction in the PCV hose. For further details on PCV operation refer to Section 4 of this manual.

### REMOVAL & INSTALLATION

1. Grasp the valve and withdraw it from the valve cover.

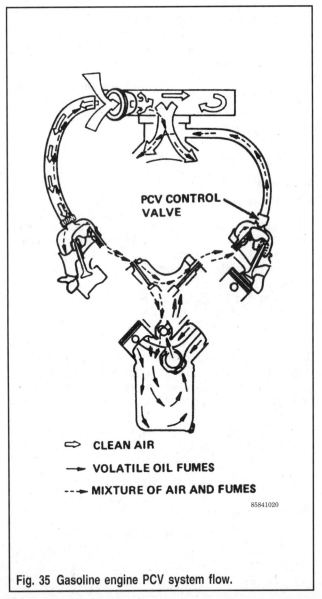

⇨ **CLEAN AIR**

➡ **VOLATILE OIL FUMES**

---➤ **MIXTURE OF AIR AND FUMES**

85841020

Fig. 35 Gasoline engine PCV system flow.

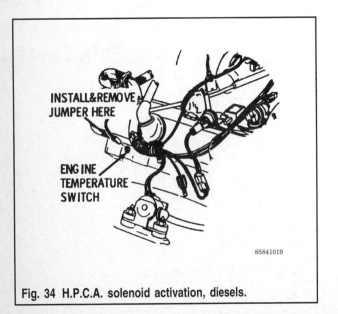

Fig. 34 H.P.C.A. solenoid activation, diesels.

2. Holding the valve in one hand and the hose in the other, carefully pull the valve from the hose and remove it from the vehicle.

➡Some PCV valve hoses will be retained to the valve using a clamp. If so, use a pair of pliers to slide the clamp back on the hose until it is clear of the bulged area on the end of the PCV valve nipple. With the clamp in this position, the hose should be free to slip from the valve.

3. Check the PCV valve for deposits or clogging. The valve should rattle when shaken. If the valve does not rattle, clean the valve with solvent until the plunger is free or replace the valve.
4. Install the PCV valve to the grommet in the valve cover.
5. Connect the PCV hose to the valve.

**Fig. 36 On some models, it may be necessary to remove a clamp on the PCV hose**

**Fig. 37 Once the clip has been slid back on the hose, the valve can be removed**

## Crankcase Depression Regulator and Flow Control Valve

◆ **See Figures 38 and 39**

The Crankcase Depression Regulator (CDR), found on 1981 and later diesels, and the flow control valve, used from 1978 to 1980, are designed to scavenge crankcase vapors in basically the same manner as the PCV valve on gasoline engines. The valves are located either on the left rear corner of the intake manifold (CDR), or on the rear of the intake crossover pipe (flow control valve). On each system there are two filters, one per valve cover. The filter assemblies should be cleaned every 15,000 miles by simply prying them carefully from the valve covers (without damaging the grommets underneath), and washing them in solvent. The ventilation pipes and tubes should also be cleaned. Both the CDR and flow control valves should also be cleaned every 30,000 miles (the cover can be removed from the CDR; the flow control valve can simply be flushed with solvent). Dry each valve, filter and hose with compressed air before installation.

➡Do not attempt to test the crankcase controls on these diesels. Instead, clean the valve cover filter assembly and vent pipes and check the vent pipes.

Replace the breather cap and assembly every 30,000 miles. Replace all rubber fittings as required every 15,000 miles.

## Evaporative Canister

◆ **See Figures 40 and 41**

The evaporative canister, sometimes referred to as a charcoal canister, is mounted inside the engine compartment. The canister and its filter are part of the evaporative emissions system (see Section 4) and work to eliminate the release of unburned fuel vapor into the atmosphere. The vapor is absorbed by the carbon in the canister and stored until manifold vacuum, when the engine is running, draws the vapors into the engine for burning.

The filter in the bottom of canisters with open bottoms must be changed every two years or 24,000 miles, or more often under extremely dusty or smoggy conditions.

### SERVICING

1. Tag and disconnect all hoses connected to the evaporative canister.
2. Loosen the retaining clamps and then lift out the canister.
3. Grasp the filter element in the bottom of the canister with your fingers and pull it out. Replace it with a new element.
4. Replace the canister in the clamps and reconnect all hoses. If any of the hoses are brittle or cracked, replace them only with fuel-resistant replacement hose marked EVAP.

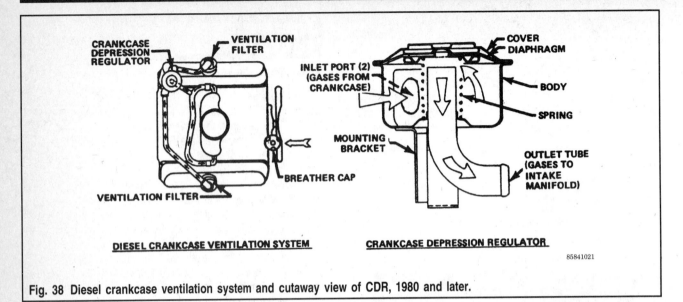

Fig. 38 Diesel crankcase ventilation system and cutaway view of CDR, 1980 and later.

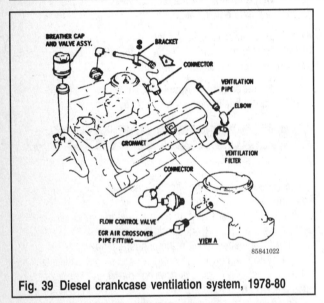

Fig. 39 Diesel crankcase ventilation system, 1978-80

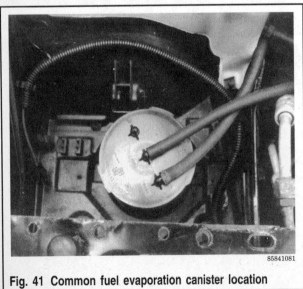

Fig. 41 Common fuel evaporation canister location

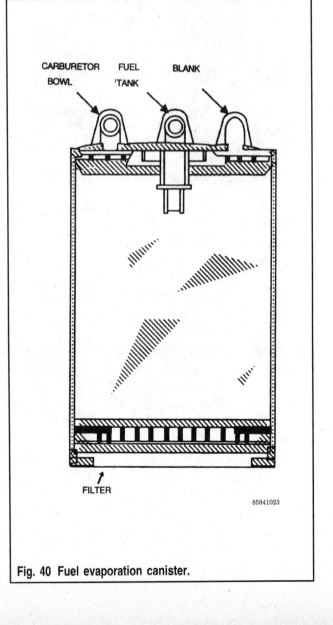

Fig. 40 Fuel evaporation canister.

## Battery

### GENERAL MAINTENANCE

All batteries, regardless of type, should be kept clean on the outside and should be kept tightly secured by a battery hold-down device. If this is not done, battery acid can leak out, shortening the life of the battery, make it discharge more quickly and the corrosive acid can eat away components under the hood. A battery that is not a maintenance-free type must be checked periodically for water level. A maintenance-free type battery cannot have water added to it, but it must also be checked for electrolyte level. This can be done by looking at the color of the 'eye'. If this battery is too low on electrolyte, it must be replaced.

### FLUID LEVEL

▶ See Figure 42

**Except Maintenance-Free Batteries**

### ✳✳CAUTION

**Batteries give off hydrogen gas which is explosive. Keep any spark or flame source away and DO NOT SMOKE around the battery! The battery electrolyte contains sulfuric acid; if you should splash any into your eyes or skin, flush with plenty of clear water and get immediate medical help.**

Fill each cell to about ⅜ in. (9.5mm) above the tops of the plates. Always use distilled water (available in supermarkets or auto parts stores), because most tap water contains chemicals and minerals that may slowly damage the plates of your battery.

**Maintenance-Free Batteries**

All later model cars are equipped with sealed maintenance-free batteries which do not require normal attention as far as fluid level checks are concerned. However, the terminals require periodic cleaning which should be performed at least once a year.

### CLEANING CABLES AND CLAMPS

▶ See Figures 43, 44, 45 and 46

Once a year, the battery terminal posts and the cable clamps should be cleaned. Loosen the clamp bolts (you may have to brush off any corrosion with a baking soda and water solution if they are really messy) and remove the cables, negative cable first. On batteries with posts on top, the use of a battery clamp puller is recommended. It is easy to break off a battery terminal if a clamp gets stuck without the puller. These pullers are inexpensive and available in most auto parts stores or auto departments. Side terminal battery cables are secured with a bolt.

The best tool for battery clamp and terminal maintenance is a battery terminal brush. This inexpensive tool has a female ended wire brush for cleaning terminals, and a male ended wire brush inside for cleaning the insides of battery clamps. When using this tool, make sure you get both the terminal posts and the insides of the clamps nice and shiny. Any oxidation, corrosion or foreign material will prevent a sound electrical connection and inhibit either starting or charging. If your battery has side terminals, there is also a cleaning tool available for these.

Before installing the cables, remove the battery hold-down clamp or strap and remove the battery. Inspect the battery casing for leaks or cracks (which unfortunately can only be fixed by buying a new battery). Check the battery tray, wash it off with warm soapy water, rinse and dry. Any rust on the tray should be sanded away, and the tray given at least two coats of a quality anti-rust paint. Replace the battery, and install the hold-down clamp or strap, but do not overtighten.

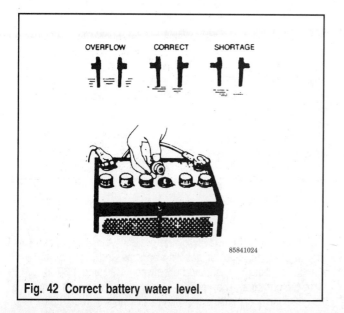

Fig. 42 Correct battery water level.

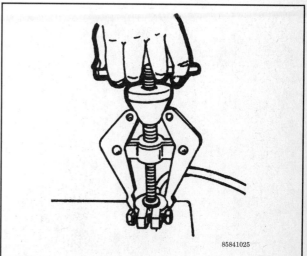

Fig. 43 Top terminal battery clamps may be removed with this inexpensive tool.

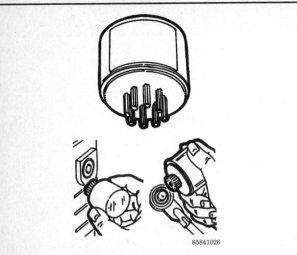

Fig. 44 Side terminal batteries require a small stiff wire brush.

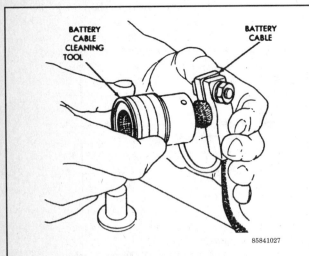

Fig. 45 Make sure both the clamps and terminal posts are cleaned until shiny.

Fig. 46 An example of a battery cable in need of cleaning

Fig. 47 An inexpensive hydrometer will test the battery state of charge.

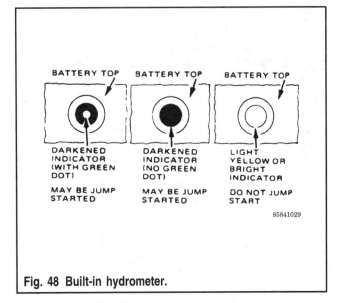

Fig. 48 Built-in hydrometer.

Reinstall your clean battery cables, negative cable last. Tighten the cables on the terminal posts snugly; do not over-tighten. Wipe a thin coat of petroleum jelly or grease all over the outside of the clamps. This will help to inhibit corrosion.

Finally, check the battery cables themselves. If the insulation of the cables is cracked or broken, or if the ends are frayed, replace the cable with a new cable of the same length and gauge.

## TESTING

**Specific Gravity**

▶ See Figures 47 and 48

Check the specific gravity of the battery (your diesel has two) at every tune-up for gasoline engines and at every oil change for diesels. It should be between 1.20 and 1.30 at room temperature. The specific gravity is checked with a hydrometer, an inexpensive instrument available in most auto parts stores, auto departments and many hardware stores. The hydrometer looks like a turkey baster, having a rubber squeeze bulb on one end and a nozzle at the other. Insert the nozzle end into each battery cell and suck enough electrolyte (battery water) into the hydrometer to just lift the float. The specific gravity is then read by the graduations on the float. Some hydrometers are color coded, with each color signifying a certain range of specific gravity.

All cells of your battery should produce nearly equal specific gravity readings. Do not be extremely alarmed if all of your battery's cells are equally low (but check to see if your alternator belt is tight); however, a big difference between two or more cells should be a concern. Generally, if after charging, the specific gravity between any two cells varies more than 50 points (0.050), the battery is bad and should be replaced.

Batteries should be checked for proper electrolyte level at least once a month or more frequently. Keep a close eye on any cell or cells that are unusually low or seem to constantly need water. This may indicate a battery on its last legs, a leak, or a problem with the charging system.

The maintenance-free battery cannot be checked for charge by checking the specific gravity using a hand-held hydrometer. Instead, the built-in hydrometer must be used in order to determine the current state of charge. If the eye on top of the battery is dark, the battery electrolyte level is all right. If the eye is light, the electrolyte level is too low and the battery must be replaced.

### Load Testing

▶ See Figures 49 and 50

1. Connect a battery load tester and a voltmeter across the battery terminals (the battery cables should be disconnected from the battery). Apply a 300 amp load to the battery for 15 seconds to remove the surface charge. Remove the load.
2. Wait 15 seconds to allow the battery to recover.
3. Apply the appropriate test load for 15 seconds, as specified in the accompanying charts, while reading the voltage. Disconnect the load.
4. Check the results against the appropriate chart. If the battery voltage was at or above the specified voltage for the temperature listed, the battery is good. If the voltage falls below what's listed, the battery should be replaced.

### Cars Up to 1983

| Battery | Test Load |
|---|---|
| Y85-4 | 130 amps |
| R85-5 | 170 amsp |
| R87-5 | 210 amps |
| R89-5 | 230 amps |

### 1984–85 Cars

| Battery | Test Load |
|---|---|
| 1981099 | 150 |
| 1981103 | 200 |
| 1981104 | 250 |
| 1981106 | 270 |
| 1981107 | 380 |
| 1981110 | 190 |
| 1981140 | 550 |
| 1981157 | 230 |
| 1981296 | 310 |

### 1986 Cars

| Battery | Test Load |
|---|---|
| 1981101 | 160 |
| 1981102 | 200 |
| 1981103 | 200 |
| 1981104 | 250 |
| 1981296 | 315 |
| 1981577 | 260 |
| 1981607 | 280 |

### 1987–90 Cars

| Battery | Test Load |
|---|---|
| 1981730 | 260 |
| 1981601 | 310 |
| 1981600 | 260 |
| 1981731 | 280 |
| 1981735 | 360 |

85841030

Fig. 49 Appropriate test loads.

## CHARGING

Generally, a battery should be charged at a slow rate to keep the plates inside from getting too hot. However, if some batteries are allowed to discharge until they are almost 'dead', they may have to be charged at a high rate to bring them back to life. On maintenance-free batteries it may be necessary to tip the battery from side to side to get the green dot to appear after charging.

Charge the battery at the proper charging rate (amps) and time span.

- 75 amps - 40 min.
- 50 amps - 1 hr.
- 25 amps - 2hr.
- 10 amps - 5hr.

| Temperature (°F) | Minimum Voltage |
|---|---|
| 70 or above | 9.6 |
| 60 | 9.5 |
| 50 | 9.4 |
| 40 | 9.3 |
| 30 | 9.1 |
| 20 | 8.9 |
| 10 | 8.7 |
| 0 | 8.5 |

85841031

**Fig. 50 Minimum test voltages during load test.**

Always connect the battery charger according to manufacturers instructions.

**✳✳CAUTION**

Batteries naturally give off a certain amount of explosive hydrogen gas, more so when they are being charged. Keep any flame or spark source away from batteries at all times. Do not charge the battery for more than 50 amp/hours (to figure this, multiply the amps of the charging rate by the number of hours). If the green dot appears, or if electrolyte squirts out of the vent hole, stop the charge.

## REPLACEMENT

When battery replacement becomes necessary, select a battery with a rating equal to or greater than the one which was originally installed. Deterioration and aging of the battery cables, starter motor, and associated wires makes the battery's job harder in successive years. The slow increase in electrical resistance over time makes it prudent to install a battery with greater capacity than the old one. Details on the role the battery plays in the vehicle's electrical systems are covered in Section 3 of this manual.

1. Carefully disconnect the negative cable from the battery terminal.

**✳✳CAUTION**

Always use caution when working on or near the battery. Never allow a tool to bridge the gap between the negative and positive battery terminals. Also, do not wear metal watches or jewelry and be careful not to allow a tool to provide a ground between the positive cable and any metal component on the vehicle. Either of these conditions will cause a short leading to sparks and possibly, personal injury.

2. With the negative battery cable disconnected and out of the way, carefully disconnect the positive cable from the battery terminal.

3. Loosen the nut and/or bolt retaining the battery strap or clamp. Remove the battery retainer.

4. Wearing an old pair of work gloves or using a battery lifting tool, carefully lift the battery out of the vehicle and place it in a safe location. Be sure to keep the battery from open flame and to protect surrounding areas from acid.

**To install:**

5. Inspect the battery tray and cables for damage and corrosion. As necessary, clean or repair the tray and cables.

6. Carefully lower the battery and position it in the tray, making sure not to allow the terminals to short on any bare metal during installation.

7. Position and secure the battery retainer strap or clamp.

8. Connect the positive cable to the positive battery terminal.

9. Connect the negative cable to the negative battery terminal.

## Early Fuel Evaporation System (Heat Riser)

▶ See Figures 51 and 52

The EFE system uses a throttling type valve in the exhaust manifold on one side of V6 and V8 engines. The valve is actuated by a vacuum diaphragm and will quickly develop operating problems if it binds due to corrosion. The shafts should be thoroughly soaked with a solvent designed to remove rust from heat risers every 30,000 miles. There is also an electrically heated EFE system used. For details on the EFE system refer to Section 4 in this manual.

## SERVICING

Every 30,000 miles, apply 10 in. of vacuum to the valve from an external source, or start the engine from an overnight cold condition. The valve should close all the way. If the valve

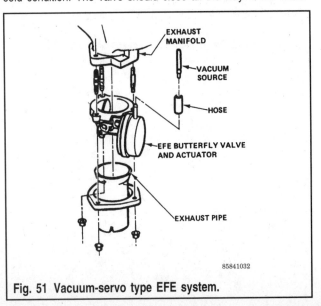

**Fig. 51 Vacuum-servo type EFE system.**

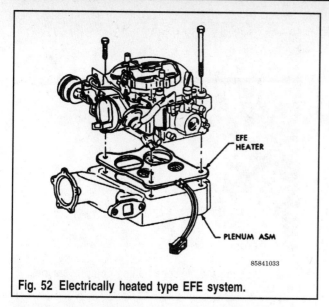

**Fig. 52 Electrically heated type EFE system.**

binds and cannot be unstuck through application of solvent, it should be replaced.

## Belts

### INSPECTION

Inspect your vehicle's drive belts every 7,500 miles or six months for evidence of wear such as cracking, fraying, and incorrect tension. Replace the belts at a maximum of 30,000 miles, even if they still look acceptable.

### ADJUSTING

▶ **See Figures 53, 54, 55, 56, 57, 58 and 59**

You can determine belt tension at a point halfway between the pulleys by pressing on the belt with moderate thumb pressure. The amount of deflection should be in proportion to the length of the belt between pulleys (measured from the center of each pulley). For example, a belt stretched 13-16 in. (330-406mm) between pulleys should deflect ½ in. (13mm) at the halfway point; a belt stretched 7-10 in. (178-254mm) should deflect ¼ in. (6.3mm), etc. If the deflection is found to be too little or too tight, an adjustment must be made.

Before adjusting any of your engine's drive belts, clean all mounting bolts on the component being adjusted and apply penetrating oil if necessary on those bolts which are hard to reach; which may be many if your vehicle has a V8 with lots of power options. Loosen the mounting and adjusting bolts of whichever component (alternator, air pump, air conditioner compressor, power steering pump, etc.) you are adjusting. Pull outward, away from the engine, on the component until the belt seems tight. Temporarily snug up on the adjusting bolt

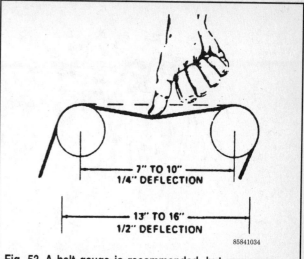

**Fig. 53 A belt gauge is recommended, but you can check tension with thumb pressure.**

and check belt deflection; if it is OK, tighten the mounting bolts and adjusting bolt.

➡ **Avoid using a metal pry bar when adjusting belt tension of any component; a sawed-off broom handle or large wooden dowel rod works fine. Excessive force on any of the component housings (which are usually aluminum) will damage the housings.**

### REMOVAL & INSTALLATION

When replacing a serpentine belt, insert a ½in. breaker bar into the slot provided on the self-adjusting belt tensioner and pry up enough to slip the belt out from under the pulley. During installation, DO NOT allow the tensioner to "snap" back. Be sure to release the tensioner pressure slowly onto the belt.

1. If you are working near a battery, disconnect the negative battery cable. This is also advisable in order to prevent

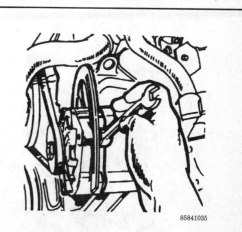

**Fig. 54 To adjust belt tension or to replace belts, first loosen the component's mounting and adjusting bolts slightly.**

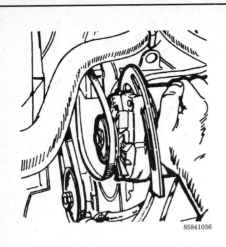

Fig. 55 Push the component towards the engine and slip off the belt.

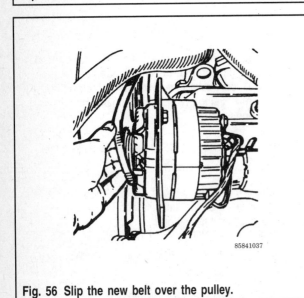

Fig. 56 Slip the new belt over the pulley.

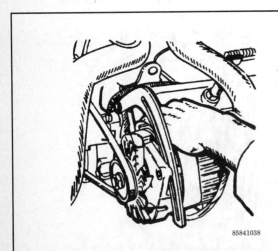

Fig. 57 Pull outward on the component and tighten the mounting bolts.

Fig. 58 Adjusting the air conditioning compressor belt, all models similar

Fig. 59 Adjusting the vacuum pump belt

personal injury should someone try to start the engine while your hands are near the radiator fan or on a drive belt.

2. Loosen the mounting and adjusting bolts on the component whose belt is going to be removed.

3. Pivot the component inward toward the engine and slip the belt off the component's pulley.

4. Remove the belt from the crankshaft pulley, then remove the belt from the vehicle.

**To install:**

5. Position the belt to the engine and over the pulleys.

6. Properly adjust the belt by pivoting the component outward until the proper tension is achieved, then tighten the mounting and adjusting bolts.

7. Reconnect the negative battery cable.

## Hoses

Hoses are frequently overlooked in normal maintenance. Both upper and lower radiator hoses and all heater hoses should be checked for deterioration, leaks and loose hose clamps at every tune-up. Check the hoses by feel; they should be pliable. Any hose that feels hard or brittle should be replaced as soon as possible; in any case, replace radiator hoses as necessary every two years or 30,000 miles.

## REMOVAL & INSTALLATION

1. Remove the radiator pressure cap.

### ❋❋CAUTION

**Never remove the pressure cap while the engine is running or personal injury from scalding hot coolant or steam may result. If possible, wait until the engine has cooled to remove the pressure cap. If this is not possible, wrap a thick cloth around the pressure cap and turn it slowly to the stop. Step back while the pressure is released from the cooling system. When you are sure all the pressure has been released, still using the cloth turn and remove the cap.**

2. Position a clean container under the radiator and/or engine drain cock or plug, then open the drain and allow the cooling system to drain to an appropriate level. For some upper hoses only a little coolant may need to be drained, to remove lower hoses the entire cooling system must be drained.

### ❋❋CAUTION

**When draining the coolant, keep in mind that cats and other animals are attracted by the ethylene glycol antifreeze, and are likely to drink any that is left on the ground or in an open container. This can prove to be fatal in sufficient quantity. Always drain coolant into a suitable container. Coolant may be reused unless it is contaminated or several years old.**

3. Loosen the hose clamps at each end of the hose requiring replacement. Pull clamps back on the hose away from the connection.

4. Twist, pull, and slide the hose off the fitting taking care not to damage the neck of the component.

➡**If the hose is stuck at the connection, do not try to insert a screwdriver or other sharp tool under the hose end to release it, as the connection may become damaged. If the hose is to be replaced, use a single-edged razor blade to make a cut perpendicular to the end of the hose. The hose can then be peeled off the connection and discarded.**

5. Clean both hose mounting connections. Inspect the condition of the hose clamps and replace them if necessary.

**To install:**

6. Dip the ends of the hose in coolant for ease of installation.

7. Slide the hose clamps over the hose and slide the hose ends onto the connections.

8. Position and secure the clamps at least 1/4 in. from the end of the hose. Make sure they are located inside the raised bead of the connector.

9. Close the radiator and engine drain plugs and properly refill the cooling system with the drained engine coolant or a suitable $^{50}/_{50}$ mix of ethylene glycol and water.

10. If available, install a pressure tester and check for leaks.

11. Leave the radiator cap off, then start and run the engine until it reaches normal operating temperature. When the engine is at operating temperature and the thermostat has opened, continue to fill the radiator until the level stabilizes just below the filler neck.

12. Install the pressure cap and check the system for leaks.

13. Shut the engine off and allow to cool. After the engine has cooled, recheck the coolant level and add as necessary.

## Air Conditioning

### SAFETY WARNINGS

Because of the the inherent dangers involved with working on air conditioning systems and R-12 refrigerant, the following safety precautions must be strictly adhered to in order to service the system safely.

1. Avoid contact with a charged refrigeration system, even when working on another part of the air conditioning system or vehicle. If a heavy tool comes into contact with a section of tubing, or a heat exchanger, it can cause the relatively soft material to rupture.

2. When it is necessary to apply force to a fitting which contains refrigerant, as when checking that all system couplings are securely tightened, use a wrench on both parts of the fitting involved, if possible. This will avoid putting torque on the refrigerant tubing. (It is advisable, when possible, to use line wrenches when tightening these flare nut fittings.)

➡**R-12 refrigerant is a chlorofluorocarbon which when released in the atmosphere can contribute to the depletion of the ozone layer in the upper atmosphere. Ozone filters out harmful radiation from the sun.**

3. Do not attempt to discharge the system by merely loosening a filter, or removing the service valve caps and opening these valves. Precise control is possible only when using a proper A/C refrigerant recovery station. Wear protective gloves when connecting or disconnecting service gauge hoses.

➡**Be sure to consult the laws in your area before servicing the air conditioning system. In some states it is illegal to preform repairs involving refrigerant unless the work is done by a certified technician.**

4. Never start a system without first verifying that both service valves are properly installed, and that all fittings throughout the system are snugly connected.

5. Avoid applying heat to any refrigerant line or storage vessel. Never allow a refrigerant storage container to sit out in the sun, or any other sources of heat, such as a radiator.

6. Always wear goggles to protect your eyes when working on a system. If refrigerant contacts the eyes, it is advisable in all cases to see a physician as soon as possible.

7. Frostbite from liquid refrigerant should be treated by first gradually warming the area with cool water, and then gently applying petroleum jelly. A physician should be consulted.

8. Always keep refrigerant drum fittings capped when not in use. If the container is equipped with a safety cap to protect the valve, make sure the cap is in place when the can is not being used. Avoid sudden shock to the drum, which might occur from dropping it, or from banging a heavy tool against it. Never carry a drum in the passenger compartment of a car.

9. Always completely discharge the system into a suitable recovery unit before painting the vehicle (if the paint is to be baked on), or before welding anywhere near refrigerant lines.

10. When servicing the system, minimize the time that any refrigerant line is open to the air, in order to prevent dirt and moisture entering the system. Always replace O-rings on lines or fittings which are disconnected. Prior to installation coat, but do not soak, replacement O-rings with suitable compressor oil.

## SYSTEM INSPECTION

➡ **R-12 refrigerant is a chlorofluorocarbon which when released in the atmosphere can contribute to the depletion of the ozone layer in the upper atmosphere. Ozone filters out harmful radiation from the sun.**

The easiest and often most important check for the air conditioning system consists of a visual inspection of the system components. Visually inspect the air conditioning system for refrigerant leaks, damaged compressor clutch, compressor drive belt tension and condition, plugged evaporator drain tube, blocked condenser fins, disconnected or broken wires, blown fuses, corroded connections and poor insulation.

A refrigerant leak will usually appear as an oily residue at the leakage point in the system. The oily residue soon picks up dust or dirt particulars from the surrounding air and appears greasy. Through time, this will build up and appear to be a heavy, dirt impregnated grease. Most leaks are caused by damaged or missing O-ring seals at the component connections, damaged charging valve cores or missing service gauge port caps.

For a thorough visual and operational inspection, check the following:

1. Check the surface of the radiator and condenser for dirt, leaves and other material which might block air flow.

2. Check for kinks in hoses and lines. Check the system for leaks.

3. Make sure the drive belt is under the proper tension. When the air conditioning is operating, make sure the drive belt is free of noise or slippage.

4. Make sure the blower motor operates at all appropriate positions, then check for distribution of the air from all outlets with the blower on.

➡ **Keep in mind that under conditions of high humidity, air discharged from the A/C vents may not feel as cold as expected, even if the system is operating properly. This is because the vaporized moisture in humid air retains heat more effectively than dry air, making humid air more difficult to cool.**

5. Make sure the air passage selection lever is operating correctly. Start the engine and warm it to normal operating temperature, then make sure the hot/cold selection lever is operating properly.

## REFRIGERANT LEVEL CHECKS

### ❈❈CAUTION

**Do not attempt to charge or discharge the refrigerant system unless you have access to a recovery station and are thoroughly familiar with the system's operation and the hazards involved. The compressed refrigerant used in the air conditioning system expands and evaporates (boils) into the atmosphere at a temperature of -21.7°F (-29.8°C) or less. This will freeze any surface that it comes in contact with, including your eyes. In addition, the gas can decompose into poisonous gas in the presence of a flame.**

There are two ways to check refrigerant level, depending on the model year of your vehicle.

➡ **If your vehicle is equipped with an aftermarket (non GM) air conditioner, the following checks may not apply. Contact the manufacturer for instructions on system checks.**

**With Sight Glass**

*1975-77*

◆ **See Figure 60**

The sight glass, for checking the refrigerant charge, is located on top of the VIR (valves in receiver). The VIR looks like a small fire extinguisher and is located on the front of the engine compartment, usually on the left side of the radiator or at the heater plenum at the firewall. This test is most effective if the outside temperature is warm; approximately 70°F (21°C) or above.

1. Place the transmission in **PARK**, and apply the parking brake.

2. Have a helper control the accelerator pedal and run the engine to 1500 rpm (fast idle).

3. Set the air conditioner controls on the instrument panel for maximum cold with the blower on HIGH.

4. Look at the sight glass on top of the VIR. (You'll probably have to wipe it clean first). If a steady stream of bubbles is

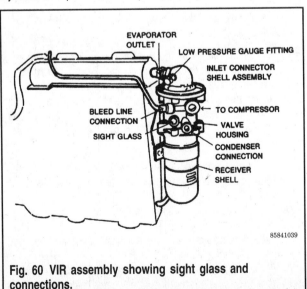

EVAPORATOR OUTLET

LOW PRESSURE GAUGE FITTING

INLET CONNECTOR SHELL ASSEMBLY

BLEED LINE CONNECTION

SIGHT GLASS

TO COMPRESSOR

VALVE HOUSING

CONDENSER CONNECTION

RECEIVER SHELL

85841039

**Fig. 60 VIR assembly showing sight glass and connections.**

present in the sight glass, the system is low on charge. There is a good chance the system has a leak.

5. If no bubbles are present, the system is either full charged or completely empty. Feel the high and low pressure lines at the compressor; if no appreciable temperature difference is felt, the system is empty or nearly so.

6. If one hose is warm (high pressure) and the other is cold (low pressure), the system may be OK. However, you are probably making these tests because there is something wrong with your air conditioner, so proceed to the next step.

7. Have your helper turn the fan control on and off to operate the compressor clutch. Watch the sight glass.

8. If bubbles appear when the clutch is disengaged and disappear when it is engaged, the system is properly charged.

9. If the refrigerant takes more than 45 seconds to bubble when the clutch is disengaged, the system is more than likely overcharged. This condition will usually result in poor air conditioner operation (poor cooling) at low speeds.

10. Finally, check for oil streaks in the sight glass, which are a sign of trouble. Most of the time, if you see oil in the sight glass it will appear as a series of streaks, although occasionally it may be a solid stream of oil. In either case, it means that part of the charge has been lost.

→ **If you are sure that the system has a leak, it should be repaired as soon as possible. Leaks may allow moisture into the system, causing internal rust. The system will have to be flushed, evacuated, leak tested and recharged.**

## Without Sight Glass

### 1978 and Later

▶ **See Figure 61**

The vehicles built in these years are not equipped with a sight glass in their Cycling Clutch Orifice Tube (CCOT) systems. On these vehicles it is necessary to feel the temperature difference in the inlet and outlet lines at the compressor to gauge the refrigerant level. Use the following procedure. A set of manifold gauges can be hooked up to read the refrigerant levels.

### ✳✳CAUTION

**Always wear safety goggles when working on a system to protect the eyes. If refrigerant contacts the eye, it is advisable in all cases to see a physician as soon as possible.**

1. Connect a gauge set (engine not running). The LOW side gauge hose to the suction line near the accumulator and the HIGH side gauge hose to the liquid line or muffler. The muffler is a round shaped can about three times larger than the liquid line.

2. Close (clockwise) both gauge set valves.

3. Park the vehicle in the shade, at least 5 feet from any walls. Start the engine, set the parking brake, place the transmission in NEUTRAL and establish an idle of 1,100-2,00 rpm.

4. Run the air conditioning system for full cooling, in the **MAX or COLD** mode.

5. The low pressure gauge should read 5-20 psi; the high pressure gauge should indicate 120-180 psi.

### ✳✳WARNING

**These pressures are the norm for an ambient temperature of 70-80°F (21-27°C). Higher air temperatures along with high humidity will cause higher system pressures. At idle speed and an ambient temperature of 110°F (43°C), the high pressure reading can exceed 300 psi. Under these extreme conditions, you can keep the pressures down by directing a large electric floor fan through the condenser.**

## TEST GAUGES

▶ **See Figure 62**

Most of the service work performed in air conditioning requires the use of a set of two gauges, one for the high (discharge) pressure side of the system, the other for the low (suction) side.

The low side gauge records both pressure and vacuum. Vacuum readings are calibrated from 0 to 30 inches Hg and the pressure graduations read from 0 to no less than 60 psi.

The high side gauge measures pressure from 0 to at least 600 psi.

Both gauges are threaded into a manifold that contains two hand shut-off valves. Proper manipulation of these valves and the use of the attached test hoses allow the user to perform the following services:

1. Test high and low side pressures.

2. Remove air, moisture, and contaminated refrigerant.

The manifold valves are designed so that they have no direct effect on gauge readings, but serve only to provide for, or cut off, flow of refrigerant through the manifold. During all testing and hook-up operations, the valves are kept in a close position to avoid disturbing the refrigeration system. **DO NOT USE THE GAUGES AS A MEANS FOR DISCHARGING THE SYSTEM!**

## DISCHARGING THE SYSTEM

→ **R-12 refrigerant is a chlorofluorocarbon which when released in the atmosphere can contribute to the depletion of the ozone layer in the upper atmosphere. Ozone filters out harmful radiation from the sun.**

Consult laws in your area before servicing the air conditioning system. In some states it is illegal to perform repairs involving refrigerant unless the work done by a certified technician

The use of refrigerant recovery systems and recycling stations makes possible the recovery and reuse of refrigerant after contaminants and moisture have been removed. If a recovery and recycling station is available, the following general procedures should be observed, in addition to the operating instructions provided by the equipment manufacturer.

1. Check the system for pressure using the manifold gauge set. Take note, if a recovery system is used to draw refrigerant from the system that is already ruptured and open to the atmosphere, only air may be pulled into the tank.

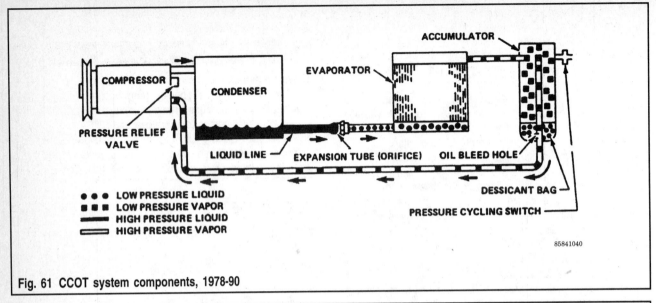

**Fig. 61 CCOT system components, 1978-90**

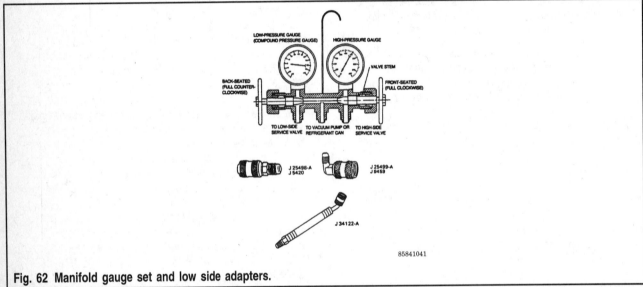

**Fig. 62 Manifold gauge set and low side adapters.**

2. Connect the recycling station hoses to the vehicle's air conditioning service ports and the recovery stations inlet fitting.

➡**Hoses should have shut-off devices or check valves within 12 in. (305mm) of the hose end to minimize the introduction of air into the recycling station and the amount of refrigerant released when the hoses are disconnected.**

3. Turn the power to the recycling station **ON** to start the recovery process. Allow the station to pump the refrigerant from the system until the station pressure goes into a vacuum. On some stations, the pump will be shut off automatically by a low pressure switch in it's electrical system. On other units it may be necessary to turn off the pump manually.

4. Once the recycling station has evacuated the system, close the station inlet valve. Then switch **OFF** the electrical power.

5. Allow the vehicle air conditioning system to remain closed for about 2 minutes. Observe the system vacuum level as shown on the gauge. If the pressure does not rise, disconnect the station's hoses.

6. If the system pressure rises, repeat steps 3, 4 and 5 until the vacuum level remains stable for 2 minutes.

7. If A/C oil is expelled during the discharge procedure, measure the amount discharged so the proper quantity of oil can be replaced when charging.

## EVACUATING/CHARGING THE SYSTEM

Evacuating and charging the air conditioning system is a combined procedure in which the lines are purged, then refrigerant is added to the system in proper quantity. Charging is always conducted through the low pressure fitting. NEVER attempt to charge the air conditioner through the high pressure side of the system.

Once again, evacuation and charging should not be attempted unless the proper equipment, such as a charging station and pump is available in order to properly service the system. If a charging station and pump is available, the following general procedures should be observed, in addition to the operating instructions provided by the manufacturer.

1. The proper amount of fresh compressor oil must be added to the system before charging. This can be accomplished by disconnecting the suction hose and pouring the fresh oil into the hose or pipe and then reconnecting the system.

2. Properly connect a manifold gauge set to the vehicle, then connect the center manifold gauge hose to a vacuum pump.

3. Turn the vacuum pump ON and slowly open the high and the low side valves to the pump. Allow the system to evacuate for 25-30 minutes, then note the gauge readings. If the system is unable to reach 28-29 in. of vacuum, the system and vacuum pump must be checked for leaks and repaired before proceeding further.

4. After the system has been evacuated for at least 25 minutes, close the gauge high and low side valves , then shut the pump OFF.

5. Watch the low side gauge for vacuum loss. If vacuum loss is in excess of 1 in. Hg (3.38 kPa), then leak test the system, repair the leaks and return to Step 1. Before leak testing, remember to disconnect the gauge high side connector from the service port.

6. If after 1-3 minutes, the loss is less than 1 in. Hg (3.38 kPa), then proceed with the system charging.

7. Disconnect the gauge high side connection from the service port and the hose from the vacuum pump.

8. Engage the center manifold connection to an R-12 source. If you are using a refrigerant drum instead of a charging station, place the drum on a scale to determine the amount of refrigerant being used.

9. Open the source and the low side gauge valve, then monitor the weight of the drum or the rate at which the charging system is introducing the R-12 into the system.

10. When 1 lb. of R-12 has been added to the system, start the engine and turn the air conditioning system ON. Set the temperature level to full cold, the blower speed on high and the selector lever to the dash outlets. Under this condition, slowly draw in the remainder of the R-12 charge. The proper amount can be found on a label either on the compressor or on the evaporator case on the firewall.

11. When the system is charged, turn the source valve OFF and continue to run the engine for 30 seconds in order to clear the gauges and the lines.

12. With the engine still running, carefully remove the gauge low side hose from the suction pipe service fitting. Unscrew the connection rapidly to avoid excess refrigerant loss.

## ✳✳CAUTION

If the hoses of the manifold gauge set can be disconnected from the gauge, NEVER remove a hose from the gauge while the other end of the hose is still connected to the service port. Since the service valve fitting check valve is depressed by the hose connection, this would cause a complete and uncontrolled discharge of the system. Serious personal injury could be caused by the escaping R-12.

13. Install the protective service fitting caps and hand tighten.

14. Turn the engine and air conditioning OFF.

15. If an electronic or halide leak tester is available, test the system for leaks.

16. If there are no leaks, perform the refrigerant level test to verify proper system charging.

## LEAK TESTING

Whenever a refrigerant leak is suspected, begin by checking for leaks at the fitting or valves. There are several methods of detecting leaks in the air conditioning system; among them the two most popular are (1) halide leak detection or the "open flame method", and (2) electronic leak-detection. Use of an electronic leak detector, if available, is preferable for ease and safety of operation.

The halide leak detector is a torch-like device which produces a yellow-green color when refrigerant is introduced into the flame at the burner. A purple or violet color indicates large amounts of refrigerant at the burner.

An electronic leak detector is a small portable electronic device with an extended probe. With the unit activated the probe is passed along those components of the system which contain refrigerant. If a leak is detected, the unit will sound an alarm signal or activate a display signal depending on the manufacturer's design. Follow the manufacturer's instructions carefully. Move the probe at approximately 1 in. (25.4mm) per second around the suspected leak area. When escaping refrigerant gas is located, the ticking or beeping signal from the detector will increase in beeps per second. If the gas is relatively concentrated, the signal will be a constant shrill.

## ✳✳CAUTION

Care should be taken to operate either type of detector in well ventilated areas, so as to reduce the chance of personal injury, which may result from coming in contact with the poisonous gases produced when R-12 is exposed to flame or electric spark.

If a tester is not available, perform a visual inspection and apply a soap and water solution to the questionable area or fitting. Bubbles will form to indicate a leak. Make sure to rinse the solution from the area before making repairs.

## Troubleshooting Basic Air Conditioning Problems

| Problem | Cause | Solution |
|---|---|---|
| There's little or no air coming from the vents (and you're sure it's on) | • The A/C fuse is blown<br>• Broken or loose wires or connections<br>• The on/off switch is defective | • Check and/or replace fuse<br>• Check and/or repair connections<br>• Replace switch |
| The air coming from the vents is not cool enough | • Windows and air vent wings open<br>• The compressor belt is slipping<br>• Heater is on<br>• Condenser is clogged with debris<br>• Refrigerant has escaped through a leak in the system<br>• Receiver/drier is plugged | • Close windows and vent wings<br>• Tighten or replace compressor belt<br>• Shut heater off<br>• Clean the condenser<br>• Check system<br><br>• Service system |
| The air has an odor | • Vacuum system is disrupted<br>• Odor producing substances on the evaporator case<br>• Condensation has collected in the bottom of the evaporator housing | • Have the system checked/repaired<br>• Clean the evaporator case<br><br>• Clean the evaporator housing drains |
| System is noisy or vibrating | • Compressor belt or mountings loose<br>• Air in the system | • Tighten or replace belt; tighten mounting bolts<br>• Have the system serviced |
| Sight glass condition<br>Constant bubbles, foam or oil streaks<br>Clear sight glass, but no cold air<br>Clear sight glass, but air is cold<br>Clouded with milky fluid | • Undercharged system<br><br>• No refrigerant at all<br>• System is OK<br>• Receiver drier is leaking dessicant | • Charge the system<br><br>• Check and charge the system<br><br>• Have system checked |
| Large difference in temperature of lines | • System undercharged | • Charge and leak test the system |
| Compressor noise | • Broken valves<br>• Overcharged<br><br>• Incorrect oil level<br><br><br>• Piston slap<br>• Broken rings<br>• Drive belt pulley bolts are loose | • Replace the valve plate<br>• Discharge, evacuate and install the correct charge<br>• Isolate the compressor and check the oil level. Correct as necessary.<br>• Replace the compressor<br>• Replace the compressor<br>• Tighten with the correct torque specification |
| Excessive vibration | • Incorrect belt tension<br>• Clutch loose<br>• Overcharged<br><br>• Pulley is misaligned | • Adjust the belt tension<br>• Tighten the clutch<br>• Discharge, evacuate and install the correct charge<br>• Align the pulley |
| Condensation dripping in the passenger compartment | • Drain hose plugged or improperly positioned<br>• Insulation removed or improperly installed | • Clean the drain hose and check for proper installation<br>• Replace the insulation on the expansion valve and hoses |
| Frozen evaporator coil | • Faulty thermostat<br>• Thermostat capillary tube improperly installed<br>• Thermostat not adjusted properly | • Replace the thermostat<br>• Install the capillary tube correctly<br>• Adjust the thermostat |
| Low side low—high side low | • System refrigerant is low<br><br>• Expansion valve is restricted | • Evacuate, leak test and charge the system<br>• Replace the expansion valve |
| Low side high—high side low | • Internal leak in the compressor—worn | • Remove the compressor cylinder head and inspect the compressor. Replace the valve plate assembly if necessary. If the compressor pistons, rings or |

85841071

## Windshield Wipers

▶ **See Figure 63**

Intense heat from the sun, snow and ice, road oils, and the chemicals used in windshield washer solvent combine to deteriorate the rubber wiper blades of your windshield wipers. If you live in a big city, smog will also deteriorate the rubber rapidly. The rubber refills should be replaced about twice a year or whenever the blades begin to streak or chatter.

Normally, if the wipers are not cleaning the windshield properly, only the refill has to be replaced. The blade and arm usually require replacement only in the event of damage. It is not necessary (except in new Tridon refills) to remove the arm or the blade to replace the refill, though you may have to position the arm higher on the glass. You can do this by turning the ignition switch on and operating the wipers, when they are positioned where they are accessible, turn the switch off.

There are three basic types of refills and your Buick, Olds or Pontiac could have any kind, since aftermarket blades and arms may not use exactly the same type refill as the original equipment.

Some types, such as Anco use a release button that is pushed down to allow the refill to slide out of the yoke jaws. The new refill slides in and locks in place. Some of these refills are removed by locating where the metal backing strip or the refill is wider. Insert a small prybar between the frame and metal backing strip. Press down to release the refill from the retaining tab.

Another type, such as Trico, is unlocked at one end by squeezing two metal tabs, and then sliding the refill out of the frame jaws. When the new refill is installed, the tabs will click into place, locking the refill.

The third, or polycarbonate type is held in place by a locking lever that is pushed downward and out of the groove in the arm to free the refill. When the new refill is installed, it will lock in place automatically.

Regardless of the type of refill used, make sure that all of the frame jaws are engaged as the refill is pushed into place and locked. The metal blade holder and frame will scratch the glass if allowed to touch it.

## Tires and Wheels

### TIRE ROTATION

▶ **See Figure 64**

Tire wear can be equalized by switching the position of the tires about every 6,000 miles. Including a conventional spare in the rotation pattern can give up to 20% more tire life.

### ✳✳CAUTION

**Do not include the new Space Saver® or temporary spare tires in the rotation pattern. These tires are designed ONLY to get you to the next service facility after a flat tire; they are NOT designed for high speed or extended driving.**

There are certain exceptions to tire rotation, however. Studded snow tires should not be rotated, and radials should be kept on the same side of the vehicle, maintaining the same direction of rotation. The belts on radial tires get set in a pattern after they accumulate mileage, and if the direction of rotation is reversed, it can cause a rough ride, vibration and possible ill handling.

### TIRE DESIGN

When buying new tires, give some thought to the following points about tire design, especially if you are considering a switch to larger tires or a different profile series:

1. All four tires must be of the same construction type. This rule cannot be violated. Radial, bias, and bias belted tires must not be mixed.
2. The wheels should be the correct width for the tire. Tire dealers have charts of tire and rim compatibility. A mismatch will cause sloppy handling and rapid tire wear. The tread width should match the rim width (inside bead to inside bead) within an inch. For radial tires, the rim width should be 80% or less of the tire (not tread) width.
3. The height (mounted diameter) of the new tires can change speedometer accuracy, engine speed at a given road speed, fuel mileage, acceleration, and ground clearance. Tire manufacturers furnish full measurement specifications.
4. The spare tire should be usable, at least for short distance and low speed operation, with the new tires.
5. There should not be any body interference when loaded, on bumps or in turns.

### TIRE STORAGE

Store tires at a proper inflation pressures if they are mounted on wheels. Mark radial and studded snow tires with an arrow showing direction of rotation so they can be mounted the same way. All tires should be kept in a cool, dry place. If tires are stored in the garage or basement, do not let them stand on a concrete floor; lay them down on strips of wood.

### TIRE INFLATION

▶ **See Figures 65, 66, 67 and 68**

Tire inflation is probably the most ignored area of auto maintenance. Gasoline mileage can drop as much as 0.8% for every 1 pound per square inch (psi) of under inflation. Proper tire inflation is also a very important factor in the handling and safety of the vehicle. Tire life is also affected by air pressure.

Tires should be checked weekly for proper air pressure. A chart, located either in the glove compartment or on the driver's or passenger's door, gives the recommended inflation pressures for your vehicle depending on type of tires used (radial or bias-ply) and whether the vehicle is loaded or unloaded.

Tire pressures should be checked before driving when the tires are still cool. Every 10°F rise (or drop) in tire temperature means a difference of 1 psi, which explains why your vehicle's tires look low on a cold morning. Two items should be a

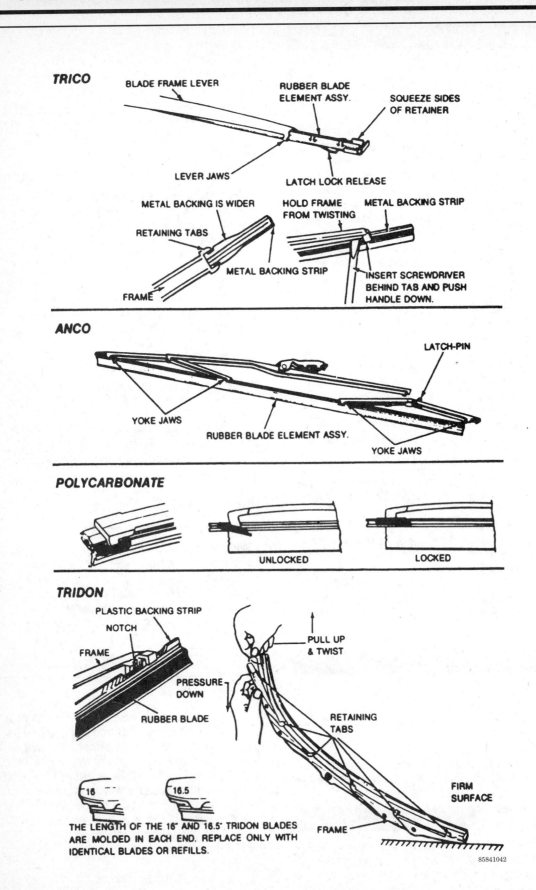

**TRICO**

BLADE FRAME LEVER

RUBBER BLADE ELEMENT ASSY.

SQUEEZE SIDES OF RETAINER

LEVER JAWS

LATCH LOCK RELEASE

METAL BACKING IS WIDER

HOLD FRAME FROM TWISTING

METAL BACKING STRIP

RETAINING TABS

METAL BACKING STRIP

FRAME

INSERT SCREWDRIVER BEHIND TAB AND PUSH HANDLE DOWN.

**ANCO**

LATCH-PIN

YOKE JAWS

RUBBER BLADE ELEMENT ASSY.

YOKE JAWS

**POLYCARBONATE**

UNLOCKED

LOCKED

**TRIDON**

PLASTIC BACKING STRIP

NOTCH

FRAME

PULL UP & TWIST

PRESSURE DOWN

RUBBER BLADE

RETAINING TABS

FIRM SURFACE

16   16.5

THE LENGTH OF THE 16" AND 16.5" TRIDON BLADES ARE MOLDED IN EACH END. REPLACE ONLY WITH IDENTICAL BLADES OR REFILLS.

FRAME

85841042

Fig. 63 Popular styles of wiper refills.

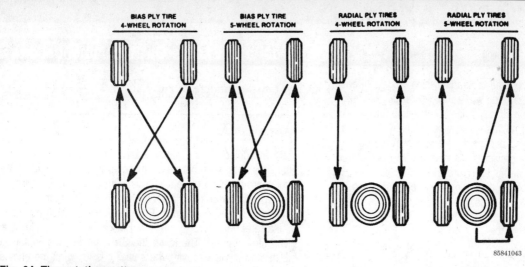

**Fig. 64 Tire rotation patterns.**

permanent fixture in every vehicle's glove compartment; a tire pressure gauge and a tread depth gauge. Never trust the gauge that is built into service station air pumps; they are notoriously inaccurate.

### ❄❄CAUTION

**Never counteract excessive pressure build-up in a hot tire by bleeding off air pressure (letting some air out). This will only further raise the tire operating temperature. It is best under these circumstances to let the tire cool the next time you stop, then bleed off the pressure.**

Before starting on a long trip with lots of luggage, add about 2 to 4 psi to the tires to make them run cooler, but never exceed the maximum inflation pressure marked on the side of the tire.

## Care For Special Wheels

Aluminum wheels should be cleaned and waxed regularly. Do not use abrasive cleaners because they may damage the protective coating.

**Fig. 65 Radials have a slight 'bulge' when properly inflated.**

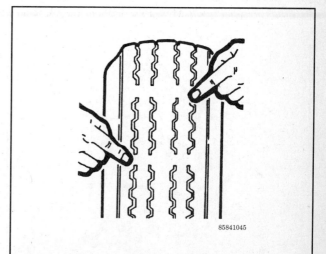

**Fig. 66 Tread wear indicators are built into the tire tread and appear as bands when the tire is worn.**

## FLUIDS AND LUBRICANTS

### Fluid Disposal

Used fluids such as engine oil, transmission fluid, antifreeze and brake fluid are hazardous wastes and must be disposed of properly. Before draining any fluids, check local laws concerning the disposal of hazardous wastes. In many areas, waste oils, etc. are being accepted as a part of recycling programs. A number of service stations and auto parts stores are also accepting waste fluids for recycling.

Be sure of the recycling center's policies before draining any fluids, as many will not accept different fluids that have been mixed together, such as oil and antifreeze.

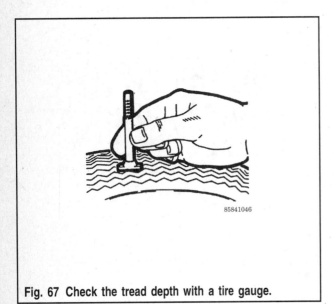

85841046

Fig. 67 Check the tread depth with a tire gauge.

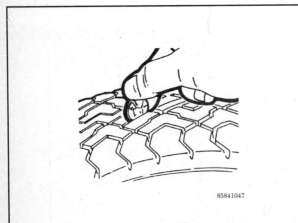

85841047

Fig. 68 A penny can also be used to approximate tread depth. If the top of Lincoln's head is visible in two adjacent grooves, replace the tire.

### Fuel and Engine Oil Recommendations

#### GASOLINE ENGINE OIL

▶ See Figure 69

When adding oil to the crankcase or changing the oil or filter, it is important that oil of an equal quality to original equipment be used in your vehicle. The use of inferior oils may void the warranty, damage your engine, or both.

The Society of Automotive Engineers (SAE) grade number of oil indicates the viscosity of the oil (its ability to lubricate at a given temperature). The lower the SAE number, the lighter the oil; the lower the viscosity, the easier it is to crank the engine in cold weather but the less the oil will lubricate and protect the engine at high temperatures. This number is marked on every oil container.

Oil viscosities should be chosen from those oils recommended for the lowest anticipated temperatures during the oil change interval. Multigrade oils have been developed because of the need for an oil that embodies both good lubrication at high temperatures and easy cranking in cold weather. All oils are thick at low temperatures and thin out as the temperature rises. Basically, a multigrade oil is thinner at lower temperatures and thicker at high temperatures relative to straight weight oils. For example, a 10W40 oil (the W stands for winter) exhibits the characteristics of a 10 weight (SAE 10) oil when the vehicle is first started and the oil is cold. Its lighter weight allows it to travel to the lubricating surfaces quicker and offer less resistance to starter motor cranking than say, a straight 30 weight (SAE 30) oil. But after the engine reaches operating temperature, the 10W40 oil begins acting like straight 40 weight (SAE 40) oil, its heavier weight providing greater lubrication with less chance of foaming than a straight 30 weight oil would at that temperature.

After extensive testing of 10W40 oils, General Motors recently concluded that they should be replaced by oils that offer less of a viscosity range. Note that 10W30 or 15W40 oils are preferred for use by GM on 1984 and later models, as shown in the viscosity chart that accompanies this section of this book.

➡Single grade (straight weight) oils such as SAE 30 are more satisfactory than multi-viscosity oils for highway driving in diesel engines.

The American Petroleum Institute (API) designation, also found on the oil container, indicates the classification of engine oil used under certain given operating conditions. Only oils designated for use Service **SE**, or **SF** heavy duty detergent should be used in your Buick, Olds or Pontiac. For 1984 and later models, only **SF** oils are approved by GM. Oils of the **SE** and **SF** type perform many functions inside the engine besides their basic function of lubrication. Through a balanced system of metallic detergents and polymeric dispersants, the oil prevents high and low temperature deposits and also keeps sludge and dirt particles in suspension. Acids, particularly sulfuric acid, as well as other by-products of engine combustion are neutralized by the oil. If these acids are allowed to concentrate, they can cause corrosion and rapid wear of the internal engine parts.

### ✳✳CAUTION

**Non-detergent or straight mineral oils should not be used in your GM engine.**

## DIESEL ENGINE OIL

▶ See Figure 70

Diesel engines require different engine oil from those used in gasoline engines. Besides performing the same functions as gasoline engine oil, a diesel engine oil must also deal with increased engine heat and the diesel blow-by gases, which create sulfuric acid, a highly corrosive compound.

Under the American Petroleum Institute (API) classifications, gasoline engine oil codes begin with an **S**, and diesel engine oil codes begin with a **C**. This first letter designation is followed by a second letter code which explains what type of service (heavy, moderate, light) the oil is meant for. For example, the top of a typical oil can will include: API SERVICES SC, SD, SE, CA, CB, CC. This means the oil in the can is a good, moderate duty engine oil when used in a diesel engine.

It should be noted here that the further down the alphabet the second letter of the API classification is, the greater the oil's protective qualities are (CD is the severest duty diesel engine oil, CA is the lightest duty oil, etc.) The same is true for gasoline engine oil classifications (SG is the severest duty gasoline engine oil, SA is the lightest duty oil, etc.).

Many diesel manufacturers recommend an oil with both gasoline and diesel engine API classifications. Consult the owner's manual for specifications.

The top of the oil can will also contain an SAE (Society of Automotive Engineers) designation, which gives the oil's viscosity. A typical designation will be: SAE 10W 30, which means the oil is a winter viscosity oil, meaning it will flow and give protection at low temperatures.

On the diesel engine, oil viscosity is critical, because the diesel is much harder to start (due to its higher compression) than a gasoline engine. Obviously, if you fill the crankcase with a very heavy oil during the winter (SAE 20W50, for example) the starter is going to require a lot of current from the battery to turn the engine. And, since batteries don't function well in cold weather in the first place, you may find yourself stranded some morning. Consult the owner's manual for recommended oil specifications for the climate you live in.

## SYNTHETIC OIL

There are excellent synthetic and fuel efficient oils available that, under the right circumstances, can help provide better fuel mileage and better engine protection. However, these advantages come at a price, which can be three or four times the price per quart of conventional motor oils.

Before pouring any synthetic oils into your vehicle's engine, you should consider the condition of the engine and the type of driving you do. Also, check the vehicle's warranty conditions regarding the use of synthetics.

Generally, it is best to avoid the use of synthetic oil in both brand new and older, high mileage engines. New engines require a proper break-in, and the synthetics are so slippery that they can prevent this; most manufacturers recommend that you wait at least 5,000 miles before switching to a synthetic oil. Conversely, older engines are looser and tend to use more oil; synthetics will slip past worn parts more readily than regular oil, and will be used up faster. If your vehicle already leaks and/or uses oil (due to worn parts and bad seals or gaskets), it will leak and use more with a slippery synthetic inside.

Consider your type of driving. If most of your accumulated mileage is on the highway at higher, steadier speeds, a synthetic oil will reduce friction and probably help delivery better fuel mileage. Under such ideal highway conditions, the oil change interval can be extended, as long as the oil filter will operate effectively for the extended life of the oil. If the filter can't do its job for this extended period, dirt and sludge will build up in your engine's crankcase, sump, oil pump and lines, no matter what type of oil is used. If using synthetic oil in this

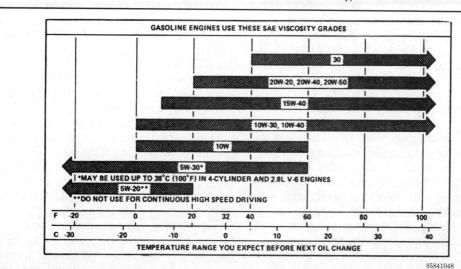

Fig. 69 Gasoline engine oil viscosity chart.

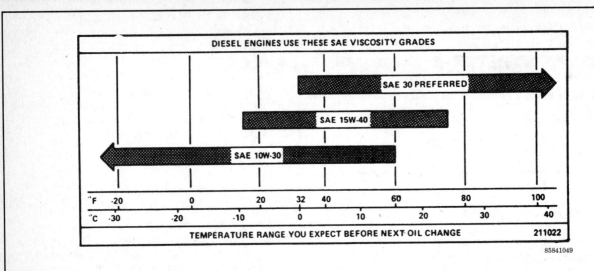

Fig. 70 Diesel oil viscosity chart.

manner, you should continue to change the oil filter at the recommended intervals.

Vehicles used under harder, stop-and-go, short hop circumstances should always be serviced more frequently and for these vehicles synthetic oil may not be a wise investment. Because of the necessary shorter change interval needed for this type of driving, you cannot take advantage of the long recommended change interval of most synthetic oils.

Finally, most synthetic oils are not compatible with conventional oils and cannot be added to them. This means you should always carry a couple of quarts of synthetic oil with you while on a long trip, as not all service stations carry this oil.

The latest development in synthetics, is a blend of conventional oil and synthetic oil. This provides the advantages of both oils at a cost significantly lower than a straight synthetic oil.

## FUEL

### Gasoline

It is important you use fuel of the proper octane rating in your vehicle. Octane rating is based on the quantity of anti-knock compounds added to the fuel and it determines the speed at which the gasoline will burn. The lower the octane, the faster the gas burns. The higher the octane, the slower the fuel burns and a greater percentage of compounds in the fuel prevent spark ping (knock), detonation and preignition, and post ignition (dieseling).

All 1975 and later models covered in this guide will perform happily on unleaded regular gasoline. Owners of turbocharged Buick vehicles may opt for unleaded premium fuel of at least 91 octane to protect against detonation. Since many factors such as altitude, terrain, air temperature, and humidity affect operating efficiency, knocking may result even though the recommended fuel grade is being used. If persistent knocking occurs, it may be necessary to switch to a higher grade of

fuel. Continuous or heavy knocking may result in engine damage.

➡ **Your engine's fuel requirement can change with time, mainly due to carbon buildup, which will in turn change the compression ratio. If your engine pings, knocks, or diesels (runs with the ignition off) switch to a higher grade of fuel. Sometimes just changing brands will cure the problem. If it becomes necessary to retard the timing from the specifications, don't change it more than a few degrees. Retarded timing will reduce power output and fuel mileage, in addition to making the engine run hotter.**

### Diesel Fuel

Fuel makers produce two grades of diesel fuel, No. 1 and No. 2, for use in automotive diesel engines. Generally speaking, No. 2 fuel is recommended over No. 1 for driving in temperatures above 20°F ( -7°C). In fact, in many areas, No. 2 diesel is the only fuel available. By comparison, No. 2 diesel fuel is less volatile than No. 1 fuel, and gives better fuel economy. No. 2 fuel is also a better injection pump lubricant.

Two important characteristics of diesel fuel are its cetane number and its viscosity. The cetane number of a diesel fuel refers to the ease with which a diesel fuel ignites. High cetane numbers mean that the fuel will ignite with relative ease so that it ignites well in an engine being cranked at low temperatures. Naturally, the lower the cetane number, the higher the temperature must be to ignite the fuel. Most commercial fuels have cetane numbers that range from 35 to 65. No. 1 diesel fuel generally has a higher cetane rating than No. 2 fuel.

Viscosity is the ability of a liquid, in this case diesel fuel, to flow. Using straight No. 2 diesel fuel below 20°F (-7°C) can cause problems, since this fuel tends to become cloudy at low temperatures, meaning wax crystals begin to form in the fuel. This is often called the cloud point for No. 2 fuel. In extreme cold weather, No. 2 fuel can stop flowing altogether. In either case, fuel flow is restricted, which can result in a no start condition or poor engine performance. Fuel manufacturers often winterize No. 2 diesel fuel by using various fuel additives and blends (No. 1 diesel fuel, kerosene, etc.) to lower its winter time viscosity. Generally speaking, though, No. 1 diesel fuel is more satisfactory in extremely cold weather.

➡No. 1 and No. 2 diesel fuels will mix and burn with no ill effects, although the engine manufacturer will undoubtedly recommend one or the other. Consult the owner's manual for information.

Depending on local climate, most fuel manufacturers make winterized No. 2 fuel available seasonally.

Many automobile manufacturers (Oldsmobile, for example) publish pamphlets giving the locations of diesel fuel stations nationwide. Contact the local dealer for information.

Do not substitute home heating oil for automotive diesel fuel. While basic characteristics of these oils are similar, the heating oil is not capable of meeting diesel cetane ratings. This means that using it might offer not only hard starting but engine knock; even under warm operating conditions. This could result in unnecessary engine wear or damage.

Further, furnace oil is not blended for operation at colder temperatures as most heating oil filters are located indoors. It could easily clog fuel filters with wax.

The equipment used in burning furnace oil does not contain the extremely fine machined surfaces or extremely tiny nozzle openings used in a diesel engine fuel system. Very small amounts of dirt and abrasives that will pass right through a heating oil fuel system could play havoc with your diesel's injection system. Finally, minimum standards regarding sulphur and ash that help keep deposits out of your diesel engine and minimize corrosion may not be met by furnace oil.

One more word on diesel fuels. Don't thin diesel fuel with gasoline. The result is the most highly explosive mixture possible in your fuel tank and unwarranted danger. Fuel thinned with gasoline may not adequately lubricate the injection system, leading to premature pump and nozzle failure and need for an expensive overhaul. Cetane rating will also be effected in an undesirable way.

It's best to buy No. 1 or blended No. 2 fuel for wintertime use. If you must use some means to keep No. 2 fuel from waxing, blend it with No. 1 or use a quality anti-waxing agent.

## Engine

### OIL LEVEL CHECK

▶ See Figures 71, 72 and 73

Every time you stop for fuel, check the engine oil as follows:
1. Make sure the vehicle is parked on level ground.
2. When checking the oil level it is best for the engine to be at normal operating temperature, although checking the oil immediately after stopping will lead to a false reading. Wait a few minutes after turning off the engine to allow the oil to drain back into the crankcase.
3. Open the hood and locate the dipstick which will be on either the right or left side depending upon your particular engine. Pull the dipstick from its tube, wipe it clean and then reinsert it.
4. Pull the dipstick out again and, holding it horizontally, read the oil level. The oil should be between the FULL and ADD marks on the dipstick. If the oil is below the ADD mark,

add oil of the proper viscosity through the capped opening in the top of the valve cover. See the Oil and Fuel Recommendations chart in this section for the proper viscosity and rating of oil to use.
5. Replace the dipstick and check the oil level again after adding any oil. Be careful not to overfill the crankcase. Approximately one quart of oil will raise the level from the ADD mark to the FULL mark. Excess oil will generally be consumed at a faster rate.

### OIL AND FILTER CHANGE

▶ See Figures 74, 75, 76, 77, 78, 79, 80, 81, 82, 83, 84 and 85

The oil in the engine of your Buick, Olds or Pontiac should be changed every six months or 7,500 miles, whichever comes first (except turbo V6 and diesels). If you live in an extremely dusty or smoggy area, or drive for moderately short distances

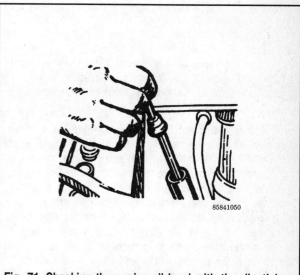

Fig. 71 Checking the engine oil level with the dipstick.

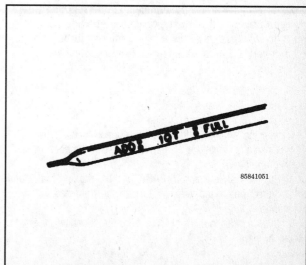

Fig. 72 The oil level should show between the 'ADD' and the 'FULL' marks.

Fig. 73 Add oil through the capped opening in the valve cover.

in cold weather (less than four miles with the temperature below freezing), change your vehicle's oil more frequently. The oil should be changed every 3,000 miles or four months under these conditions. A new filter should be installed with every oil change. The used oil should be placed into a suitable container and taken to a collection or reclamation point for recycling (many garages and gas stations have storage tanks for this purpose).

➡ GM recommends that the filter be changed every other oil change, unless the vehicle is driven under those conditions requiring more frequent changes or those in which the time limit expires before the mileage limit. Our recommendation is that, regardless of the interval, the filter should be changed at every oil change. This offers excellent protection against a situation in which the filter becomes clogged, bypassing dirty oil directly to the engine's wearing parts. It also permits a more complete removal of dirty oil from the engine's filter and oil galleries, which hold a quart or more of contaminated fluid. Change the oil in turbocharged vehicles every 3,000 miles; change the oil in diesel vehicles every 5,000 miles. On diesels, if you are towing a trailer, if it is dusty, or you are driving trips of four miles or less in below freezing temperatures, change the oil every 2,500 miles or three months, whichever comes first.

The oil should always be changed while hot, so the dirt and particles will still be suspended in the oil when it drains out of the engine. To change the oil and filter:

1. Run the engine until it reaches normal operating temperature. Once the engine is at normal operating temperature, turn the engine OFF.
2. Put the transmission in **PARK**, set the parking brake and jack up the front of the vehicle. Support the front end with jackstands.
3. Slide a drain pan of at least 6 quarts capacity under the engine oil pan.

4. Loosen the drain plug. Turn the plug out slowly by hand, keeping an inward pressure on the plug as you unscrew it so the hot oil will not escape until the plug is completely removed.

### ✳✳CAUTION

**When you are ready to release the plug, pull it away from the drain hole quickly, to avoid being burned by the hot oil.**

5. Allow the oil to drain completely and then install the drain plug. DO NOT OVERTIGHTEN the plug, or you will strip the threads in the drain hole and you'll have to buy a new pan or an over-sized replacement plug.
6. Using an oil filter strap wrench, remove the oil filter. Keep in mind that it's holding about a quart of dirty, hot oil.
7. As soon as you remove the oil filter, hold it upright until you can empty it into the drain pan. Dispose of the filter.

### ✳✳CAUTION

**The EPA warns that prolonged contact with used engine oil may cause a number of skin disorders, including cancer! You should take every effort to minimize your exposure to used engine oil. Protective gloves should be worn when changing the oil. Wash your hands and any other exposed skin areas as soon as possible after exposure to used engine oil. Soap and water, or waterless hand cleaner should be used.**

8. Using a clean rag, wipe off the filter mounting adaptor on the engine block. Be sure that the rag does not leave any lint which could clog an oil passage.
9. Wipe a coating of clean engine oil on the rubber gasket of the new filter. Spin it onto the engine by hand. DO NOT use the strap wrench. When the gasket starts to snug up against the adaptor surface, give it another $1/2$-$3/4$ turn by hand (check the instructions provided by the filter manufacturer). Don't turn it any more, or you'll squash the gasket and the filter will leak.
10. Refill the engine with the correct amount of fresh oil through the valve cover cap, or breather tube (diesels). See the Capacities Chart located in this section.
11. Check the oil level on the dipstick. It is normal for the oil level to be slightly above the full mark right after an oil change because the filter and engine oil passages are dry. Start the engine and allow it to idle for a few minutes to fill these passages and the filter.

### ✳✳CAUTION

**Do not run the engine above idle speed until the oil pressure light (usually red) goes out, indicating the engine has built up oil pressure.**

12. Shut off the engine and allow the oil to drain back down for a few minutes before checking the dipstick again. Add more oil, if necessary. Check for oil leaks around the filter and drain plug.

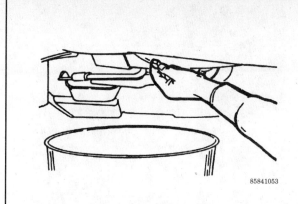

85841053

**Fig. 74** Keep an inward pressure on the plug as you unscrew it so the oil won't escape until you pull the plug away.

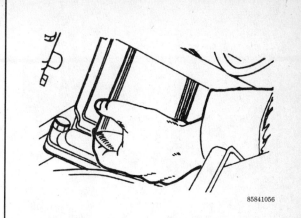

85841056

**Fig. 77** Install the new filter by hand. DO NOT use the strap wrench.

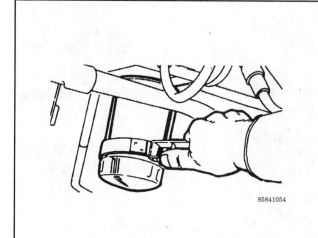

85841054

**Fig. 75** Use a strap wrench to remove the oil filter.

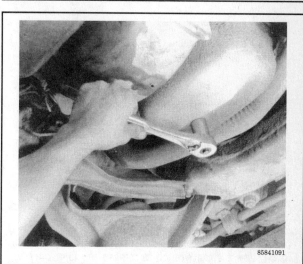

85841091

**Fig. 78** To drain the oil, start by loosening the drain plug on the oil pan with a wrench

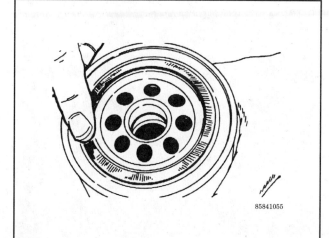

85841055

**Fig. 76** Apply a light coat of oil to the rubber gasket on the oil filter before installing it.

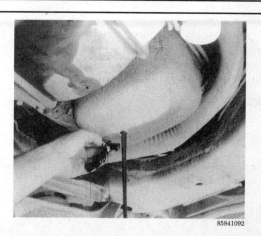

85841092

**Fig. 79** Remove the plug the rest of the way by hand while keeping an inward pressure as you unscrew it. Quickly pull the plug away to keep the oil from running over your hand

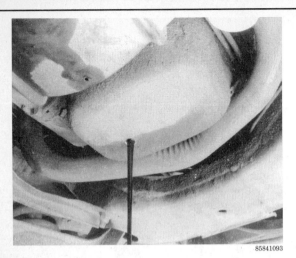

Fig. 80 Allow all the oil to drain into a pan for several minutes and reinstall the drain plug when done

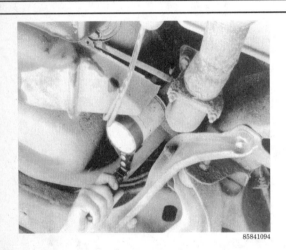

Fig. 81 Use a strap wrench to remove the filter only. Install the new filter by hand, be sure to coat the gasket with oil

Fig. 82 Remove the oil filler cap

Fig. 83 Place a funnel into the filler and add the correct amount of oil, be sure the drain plug has been reinstalled

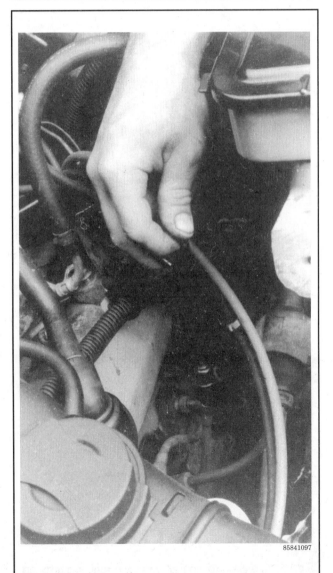

Fig. 84 Locate the oil level dipstick and pull it out

85841098

**Fig. 85 Wipe the dipstick and check the oil level, add if necessary**

## Automatic Transmission

### FLUID RECOMMENDATIONS

➡️**Always use DEXRON®II ATF. The use of ATF Type F or any other fluid will cause severe damage to the transmission.**

There are two basic types of automatic transmission fluid. They have radically different viscosities, meaning that they will behave quite differently as to both clutch operation and seal efficiency, which are critical aspects of automatic transmission operation. The Type F fluid is used only in certain transmissions used in Ford Motor Co. products. Using it in a General Motors Corp. automatic transmission will produce disastrous results, including leaks and rough shifting.

The fluid used in G.M. units, as well as many other products, was originally known as Type A. An additive package that met Type A viscosity requirements but also included appropriate resistance to breakdown at high temperatures and leakage was developed and named Dexron®. It incorporated a rare type of whale oil that became unavailable in 1973. A new designation, Dexron®II was developed to replace the original Dexron®, utilizing soybean oil rather than whale oil. Dexron®II meets all the basic standards for what had been Dexron® and Type A.

It is vitally important to understand that, while some older G.M. vehicles might have been able to use one of the earlier designations, all the models covered in this book should use only Dexron®II. In case you should run into remaining supplies of either Dexron® or Type A fluid, it is important to understand that:

1. Only Dexron®II should be used in the models covered by this book.

2. You must not allow yourself to be sold on the use of the wrong designation, merely because the fluid is of the same basic type. The wrong fluid could work for some time without producing problems, and then create them many miles later.

### LEVEL CHECK

▶ **See Figures 86 and 87**

Check the automatic transmission fluid level at least every 7,500 miles. The dipstick can be found in the rear of the engine compartment. The fluid level should be checked only when the transmission is hot (normal operating temperature). The transmission is considered hot after about 20 miles of highway driving.

1. Park the vehicle on a level surface with the engine idling. Shift the transmission into **NEUTRAL** and set the parking brake.

2. Remove the dipstick, wipe it clean and then reinsert it firmly. Be sure that it has been pushed all the way in. Remove the dipstick again and check the fluid level while holding it horizontally. With the engine running, the fluid level should be between the second notch and the FULL HOT line. If the fluid must be checked when it is cool, the level should be between the first and second notches.

3. If the fluid level is below the second notch (engine hot) or the first notch (engine cold), add DEXRON®II automatic transmission fluid through the dipstick tube. This is easily done with the aid of a funnel. Check the level often as you are filling the transmission. Be extremely careful not to overfill it. Overfilling will cause slippage, seal damage and overheating. Approximately one pint of ATF will raise the fluid level from one notch/line to the other.

The fluid on the dipstick should always be a bright red color. If it is discolored (brown or black), or smells burnt, serious transmission troubles, probably due to overheating, should be suspected. The transmission should be inspected by a qualified technician to locate the cause of the burnt fluid.

### DRAIN, REFILL, AND FILTER CHANGE

▶ **See Figures 88, 89, 90, 91, 92, 93 and 94**

The four types of pan gaskets on the automatic transmissions covered here are pictured for ready identification.

The fluid should be changed with the transmission warm. A 20 minute drive at highway speeds should accomplish this.

1. Raise and support the vehicle with jackstands, preferably in a level attitude.

2. The support crossmember may have to be removed on some models. Support the transmission with a transmission jack or equivalent before removing the crossmember.

3. Place a large pan under the transmission pan. Remove all the front and side pan bolts. Loosen the rear bolts about four turns.

4. Pry the pan loose and let it drain.

5. Remove the pan and gasket. Clean the pan thoroughly with solvent and air dry it. Be very careful not to get any lint from rags in the pan.

➡️**It is normal to find a SMALL amount of metal shavings in the pan. An excessive amount of metal shavings indicates transmission damage which must be handled by a professional automatic transmission mechanic.**

6. Remove the strainer-to-valve body screws, the strainer, and the gasket. Most 350 transmissions will have a throw-

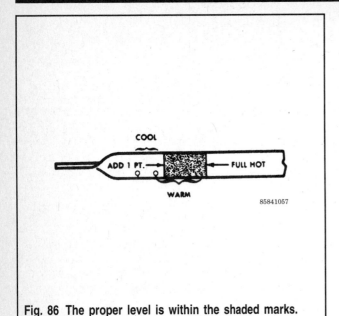

**Fig. 86 The proper level is within the shaded marks.**

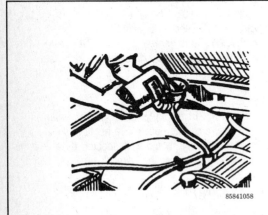

**Fig. 87 Add automatic transmission fluid through the transmission dipstick tube.**

away filter instead of a strainer. On the 400 and 200-4R transmission, remove the filter retaining bolt, filter, and intake pipe O-ring.

7. If there is a strainer, clean it in solvent and air dry.

8. Install the new filter or cleaned strainer with a new gasket. Tighten the screws to 12 ft. lbs. (16 Nm). On the 400, install a new intake pipe O-ring and a new filter, tightening the retaining bolt to 120 inch lbs. (14 Nm).

➡️**While the transmission pan is removed, you may want to install an after market oil pan drain plug kit, available at a local parts distributor or transmission repair shop. This will make future fluid changes easier.**

9. Install the pan with a new gasket. Tighten the bolts evenly to 97 inch. lbs. (11 Nm). Do NOT overtighten, gasket may break causing a leak.

10. Lower the vehicle enough to add the proper amount of DEXRON®II automatic transmission fluid through the dipstick tube.

11. Start the engine in Park and let it idle. Do not race the engine. Shift into each shift lever position, shift back into Park, and check the fluid level on the dipstick. The level should be ¼ in. (6.3mm) below ADD. Be very careful not to overfill. Recheck the level after the vehicle has been driven long enough to thoroughly warm up the transmission. Add fluid as necessary. The level should then be at FULL when the transmission is at normal operating temperature.

## Drive Axle

### FLUID RECOMMENDATIONS

Most gear oils come in a plastic squeeze bottle with a nozzle end, which makes adding lubricant simple. You can also

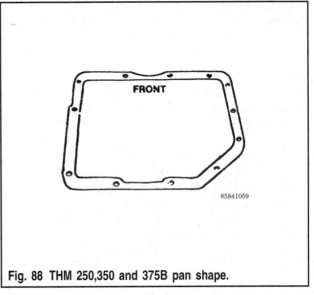

**Fig. 88 THM 250,350 and 375B pan shape.**

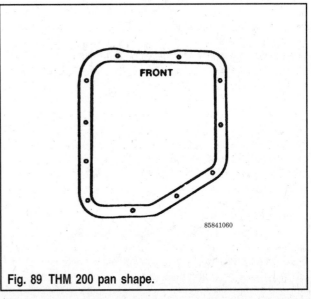

**Fig. 89 THM 200 pan shape.**

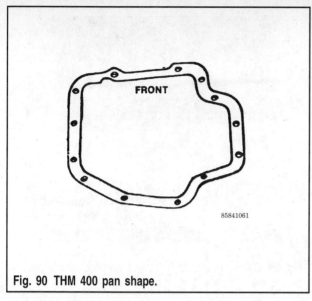

Fig. 90 THM 400 pan shape.

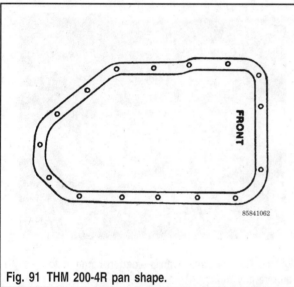

Fig. 91 THM 200-4R pan shape.

Fig. 92 To refill the transmission, locate and pull out the transmission fluid level dipstick

Fig. 93 Add the proper amount and type of fluid

Fig. 94 After the engine has been started and the transmission put through the gears, recheck the fluid level

use a common turkey baster for this job. Use only standard GL-5 hypoid-type gear oil--SAE 80W or SAE 80W/90.

➡️On all models equipped with a posi-traction/limited slip differential, GM recommends that you use only special GM lubricant available at your local Buick, Oldsmobile or Pontiac parts department. Also, the standard GL-5 fluid with a limited slip additive can be used.

## LEVEL CHECK

▶ See Figure 95

The oil in the differential should be checked at least every 7,500 miles.

1. Park the vehicle on a level surface and remove the filler plug from the front side of the differential.

2. If the oil begins to trickle out of the hole when the plug is removed, the differential is full. If no lubricant trickles out, carefully insert your finger (watch out for sharp threads) into

Fig. 95 Remove the filler plug to check the lubricant level in the rear axle.

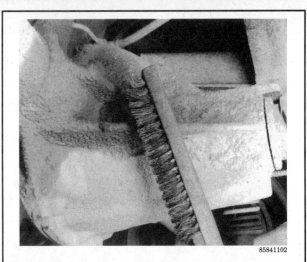

Fig. 96 Clean around the rear axle fill plug with a wire brush, then remove it

the hole and check that the oil is up to the bottom edge of the filler hole.

3. If not, add oil through the hole until the level is at the edge of the hole. Torque the fill plug to 29 ft. lbs. (39 Nm).

## DRAIN AND REFILL

▶ See Figures 96, 97, 98, 99 and 100

There is no recommended change interval for the rear axle lubricant, but it is always a good idea to change the lube if you have purchased the vehicle used or if it has been driven in water high enough to reach the axle.

1. Park the vehicle on a level surface and set the parking brake.
2. Remove the rear axle filler plug on the front side of the differential housing.
3. Place a large drain pan underneath the rear axle.
4. Unscrew the retaining bolts and remove the rear axle cover. The axle lubricant will now be able to drain into the container.
5. Clean all gasket mating surfaces. Using a new cover gasket and sealant, install the axle cover. Tighten the retaining bolts in a crisscross pattern to 22 ft. lbs. (30 Nm).
6. Refill the axle with the proper quantity of SAE 80W, SAE 80W-90 GL-5 or limited slip gear lubricant. Replace the filler plug and torque to 29 ft. lbs. (39 Nm). Take the vehicle for a short ride and check for any leaks around the plug or rear cover.

## Cooling System

The efficiency of the radiator can be seriously impaired by blockage of the radiator fins. Leaves, insects, road dirt and paper are common obstacles to fresh air entering your radiator and doing its job.

Large pieces of debris, leaves and large insects can be removed from the fins by hand. The smaller pieces can be washed out with water pressure from a garden hose. This is often a neglected area of auto maintenance, so do a thorough job.

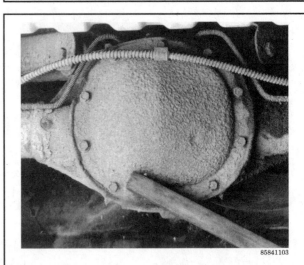

Fig. 97 Tap the cover with a wooden hammer to remove any loose dirt

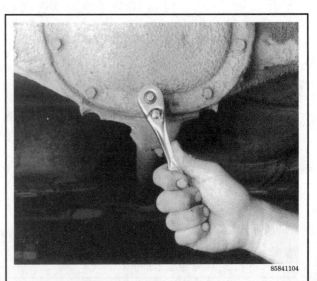

Fig. 98 Remove the rear axle cover bolts

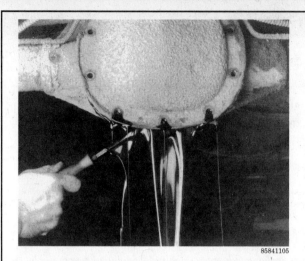

**Fig. 99 Gently pry the cover open and allow the fluid to drain into a pan**

**Fig. 100 Remove the cover. When installing the cover, be sure to clean the gasket surfaces**

Bent radiator fins can be straightened carefully with a pair of noodlenosed pliers. The fins are soft, so don't wiggle them; move them once.

Anytime you check the coolant level, check the radiator cap as well. A worn or cracked gasket can mean improper sealing, which can cause lost coolant, lost pressure, and engine overheating (the cooling system is pressurized and the radiator cap has a pressure rating above the pressure of the system).

A worn cap should be replaced with a new one. Make sure the new cap has the proper pressure rating for your vehicle's system; this is usually marked on the standard factory cap. Never buy a cap having a rating less than the pressure of your vehicle's system.

Check the protection level of your antifreeze mix with an antifreeze tester (a small, inexpensive syringe-type device available at any auto parts store). The tester has five or six small colored balls inside, each of which signify a certain temperature rating. Insert the tester in the recovery tank and suck just enough coolant into the syringe to float as many individual balls as you can (without sucking in too much coolant and floating all the balls at once). A table supplied with the tester will explain how many floating balls equal protection down to a certain temperature.

## FLUID RECOMMENDATIONS

A quality, ethylene glycol coolant containing corrosion inhibitors and compatible with aluminum engine parts, meeting GM Specification 1825-M should be used. Antifreeze concentration should be high enough to maintain freezing protection down to -34°F (-37°C).

## LEVEL CHECK

It is best to check the coolant level when the engine and radiator are cool. Buick, Oldsmobile and Pontiac vehicles covered in this guide are equipped with coolant recovery tanks connected by hoses to the radiator and mounted on the inner fender skirt. If the coolant level is at or near the FULL COLD (engine cold) or the FULL HOT (engine hot) lines on the tank, the level is satisfactory.

Check the freezing protection rating at least twice a year, preferably in mid-fall and mid-spring. This can be done with an antifreeze tester, the use of which is detailed under Cooling System in this section.

### ✳✳CAUTION

**Never add coolant to a hot engine. Stop the engine and allow it to cool. Then, start it to circulate coolant uniformly through the block and add coolant slowly as the engine idles. Otherwise you risk cracking the block. The coolant recovery tank is the only accurate place to check the coolant level; however, coolant can be added to either the tank or directly to the radiator. NEVER REMOVE THE RADIATOR CAP UNTIL THE ENGINE HAS HAD AMPLE TIME TO COOL TO BELOW OPERATING TEMPERATURE.**

If you find the coolant level low, add a 50/50 mixture of ethylene glycol based antifreeze and clean water. Do not add straight water unless you are out on the road and in emergency circumstances; if this is the case, drain the radiator and replenish the cooling system with an ethylene glycol mix at the next opportunity. Modern ethylene glycol antifreezes are special blends of anti-corrosive additives and lubricants that help keep the cooling system clean and help lubricate the water pump seal, which is why they are recommended by the manufacturers.

## DRAIN, FLUSH AND REFILL

▶ **See Figures 101, 102, 103, 104, 105 and 106**

The cooling system in your vehicle accumulates some internal rust and corrosion in its normal operation. A simple method of keeping the system clean is known as flushing the system. It is performed by circulating a can of radiator flush through the system, and then draining and refilling the system with the normal coolant. Radiator flush is marketed by several different manufacturers, and is available in cans at auto departments, parts stores, and many hardware stores. This operation should be performed every 30,000 miles or once every two years.

1. Drain the existing antifreeze and coolant. Open the radiator and engine drain petcocks (located near the bottom of the radiator and on the side of the engine block, down low, respectively), or disconnect the bottom radiator hose at the radiator outlet.

→Before opening the radiator petcock, spray it with some penetrating oil.

### ❊❊CAUTION

Be aware that if the engine has been run up to operating temperature, the coolant emptied will be HOT.

2. Close the petcock or reconnect the lower hose and fill the system with water; hot water, if possible, if the engine has been run. Fill slowly with the engine idling.

3. Add a can of quality radiator flush to the radiator, following any special instructions on the can.

4. Idle the engine as long as specified on the can of flush, or until the upper radiator hose gets hot.

5. Drain the system again. There should be quite a bit of scale and rust in the drained water.

6. Repeat the rinsing process until the drained water is almost completely clear.

7. Close all petcocks and connect all hoses.

8. Flush the coolant recovery reservoir with water and leave empty.

9. Determine the capacity of your vehicle's cooling system (see Capacities specifications in this guide). Add a 50/50 mix of ethylene glycol antifreeze and water to provide the desired protection.

10. Run the engine to operating temperature, then stop the engine and check for leaks. Check the coolant level and top up if necessary.

**Fig. 101 To drain the coolant, first locate the radiator drain cock**

## Brake Master Cylinder

### FLUID RECOMMENDATIONS

When making additions of brake fluid, use only fresh, uncontaminated brake fluid which meets or exceeds DOT 3 standards (as stated on the container).

### LEVEL CHECK

▶ See Figures 107, 108, 109 and 110

The brake master cylinder is located under the hood, in the left rear section of the engine compartment. It is divided into two sections (reservoirs) and the fluid must be kept within $1/4$ in. (6.3mm) of the top edge of both reservoirs or between the MAX. and MIN. level markers. The level should be checked at least every 7,500 miles.

→Any sudden decrease in the level of fluid indicates a possible leak in the system and should be checked out immediately.

To check the fluid level, simply pry off the retaining bail or lift the retaining tabs and then lift off the top cover of the master cylinder. Be careful not to spill any brake fluid on painted surfaces, as it eats paint. Do not allow the brake fluid container or the master cylinder reservoir to remain open any longer than necessary; brake fluid is hygroscopic (absorbs moisture from the air), reducing its effectiveness and causing corrosion in the lines.

→The reservoir cover on some later models may be without a retaining bail. If so, simply pry the cover off with your fingers.

## Power Steering Pump

### FLUID RECOMMENDATIONS

If the level is low, fill the pump reservoir with DEXRON®II Automatic Transmission Fluid on 1975-76 vehicles. 1977 and later models require GM Power Steering Fluid, part No. 1052271, 1050017 or 1052884, available at any Buick, Olds, Pontiac or Chevrolet dealer, or the equivalent.

### LEVEL CHECK

▶ See Figures 111 and 112

Power steering fluid level should be checked at least every 7,500 miles. The power steering pump is belt driven and has the dipstick built into the filler cap. To prevent possible overfilling, check the fluid level only when the fluid has warmed up to operating temperature and with the front wheels turned straight ahead. Fill the reservoir until the fluid level measures FULL on the reservoir dipstick. When the fluid level is low, there is usually a moaning sound coming from the pump as

Fig. 102 Loosen the drain cock to drain the coolant from the radiator

Fig. 105 Once the radiator has been filled, fill the coolant reservoir to the proper level

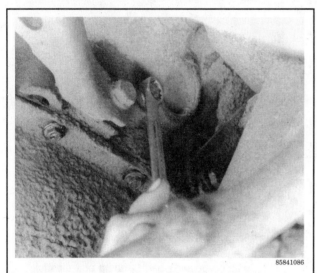

Fig. 103 Locate and remove the engine drain plug

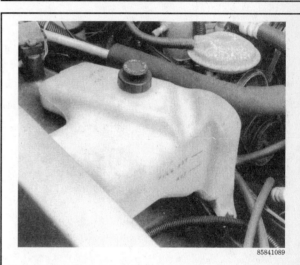

Fig. 106 Recheck the coolant level after the vehicle has reached operating temperature

Fig. 104 Before filling the cooling system, be sure the engine drain plug is reinstalled and the radiator drain cock is closed

Fig. 107 Late model fluid reservoir showing fluid level marks

Fig. 108 To fill the reservoir, first pry the cover open

Fig. 109 Remove the rubber gasket

Fig. 110 Add fluid to the proper level

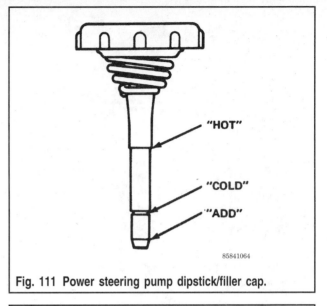

Fig. 111 Power steering pump dipstick/filler cap.

Fig. 112 Common power steering pump and dipstick location

the front wheels are turned, especially when standing still or parking. The steering wheel will also be difficult to turn when fluid level in the pump reservoir gets low.

## Battery

Check the battery fluid level (except in maintenance free batteries) in each cell at least once a month, more often during extreme weather (mid-summer and mid-winter) and extended periods of travel. The electrolyte (water) level should be about ⅜ in. (9.5mm) above the plates as you look down into each cell. Filling each cell to the bottom of the cell ring is satisfactory.

Some battery makes are equipped with an eye in the cap of one cell. If this eye glows or has an amber color, the level is low and only distilled water should be added. If the eye has a dark appearance, the battery electrolyte level is high enough. It is also wise to check each cell individually on these eye type batteries.

## FLUID RECOMMENDATIONS

Distilled water is the only fluid you should add to your vehicle's battery. It is widely available in supermarkets and auto stores. Tap water in most areas of the U.S. contains chemicals and minerals that are harmful in the long run to battery plates.

➡When adding water to a battery in freezing weather, the vehicle should be driven immediately for a few miles so that the water and electrolyte mix. Otherwise, the battery may freeze.

### Windshield Washer Reservoir

The windshield washer pump fluid reservoir is a plastic container usually found on the left or right side of the engine compartment.

## FLUID RECOMMENDATIONS

The reservoir should be filled to the top of the container using a wiper fluid solution which can be found in most automotive stores. Do not further dilute the mixture (unless manufacturers instructions tell you to do so) as this will affect it's ability to keep from freezing in low temperatures. Never place other fluids in the reservoir, such as a water/antifreeze mix, as other fluids could damage the pump seals.

### Chassis Greasing

## FRONT SUSPENSION

▶ See Figure 113

Every year or 7,500 miles the front suspension ball joints, both upper and lower on each side of the vehicle, must be greased. Most vehicles covered in this guide should be equipped with grease nipples on the ball joints, although some may have plugs which must be removed and nipples installed.

Raise the front end of the vehicle and safely support it with jackstands. Block the rear wheels and firmly apply the parking brake. If the vehicle has been parked in temperatures below 20°F (-7°C) for any length of time, park it in a heated garage for an hour or so until the ball joints loosen up enough to accept the grease.

Depending on which front wheel you work on first, turn the wheel and tire outward, either full lock right or full lock left. You now have the ends of the upper and lower suspension control arms in front of you; the grease nipples are visible pointing up (top ball joint) and down (lower ball joint) through the end of each control arm. If the nipples are not accessible enough, remove the wheel and tire. Wipe all dirt and crud from the nipples or from around the plugs (if installed). If plugs are on the vehicle, remove them and install grease nipples in the holes (nipples are available in various thread sizes at most auto parts stores). Using a hand operated, low pressure

grease gun loaded with a quality chassis grease, grease the ball joint only until the rubber joint boot begins to swell out.

➡Do not pump so much grease into the ball joint that excess grease squeezes out of the rubber boot. This destroys the watertight seal.

## STEERING LINKAGE

The steering linkage should be greased at the same interval as the ball joints. Grease nipples are installed on the steering tie rod ends on most models. Wipe all dirt and crud from around the nipples at each tie rod end. Using a hand operated, low pressure grease gun loaded with a suitable chassis grease, grease the linkage until the old grease begins to squeeze out around the tie rod ends. Wipe off the nipples and any excess grease. Also grease the nipples on the steering idler arms.

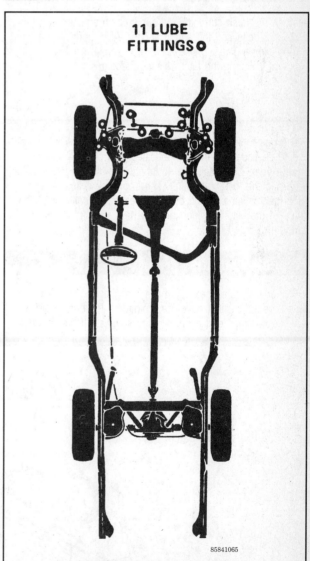

Fig. 113 Front suspension and steering linkage lubrication fitting locations.

## PARKING BRAKE LINKAGE

▶ **See Figure 114**

Use chassis grease on the parking brake cable where it contacts the cable guides, levers and linkage.

## AUTOMATIC TRANSMISSION LINKAGE

Apply a small amount of clean engine oil to the kickdown and shift linkage points at 7,500 mile intervals.

## Body Lubrication

### HOOD LATCH AND HINGES

Clean the latch surfaces and apply clean engine oil to the latch pilot bolts and the spring anchor. Also lubricate the hood hinges with engine oil. Use a chassis grease to lubricate all the pivot points in the latch release mechanism.

### DOOR HINGES

The gas tank filler door, vehicle doors, and trunk lid hinges should be wiped clean and lubricated with clean engine oil once a year. Use engine oil to lubricate the trunk lock mechanism and the lock bolt striker. The door lock cylinders and latch mechanisms should be lubricated periodically with a few drops of graphite lock lubricant or a few shots of silicone spray.

## Wheel Bearings

Properly adjusted bearings have a slightly loose feeling. Wheel bearings must never be preloaded. Preloading will damage the bearings and eventually the spindles. If the bearings are too loose, they should be cleaned, inspected, and then adjusted.

Hold the tire at the top and bottom and move the wheel in and out of the spindle. If the movement is greater than 0.005 in. (0.127mm), the bearings are too loose. Rear wheel bearings are covered in Section 7 of this manual.

### ADJUSTMENT

1. Raise and support the vehicle by the lower control arm with jackstands.
2. Remove the hub cap, then remove the dust cap from the hub.
3. Remove the cotter pin and loosen the spindle nut.
4. Spin the wheel forward by hand. Tighten the nut until snug (about 12 ft. lbs. (16 Nm) to fully seat the bearings.
5. Back off the nut 1/4-1/2 turn until it is just loose, then tighten it finger-tight.
6. Loosen the nut until either hole in the spindle lines up with a slot in the nut and then insert the cotter pin. This may appear to be too loose, but it is the correct adjustment. The spindle nut should be finger tight.
7. Proper adjustment creates 0.001-0.005 in. (0.025-0.127mm) of end-play.

### REMOVAL, PACKING AND INSTALLATION

## ✳✳CAUTION

**Some brake pads contain asbestos, which has been determined to be a cancer causing agent. Never clean the brake surfaces with compressed air! Avoid inhaling any dust from any brake surface! When cleaning brake surfaces, use a commercially available brake cleaning fluid.**

1. Raise the vehicle and support with jackstands.
2. Remove the wheel and brake caliper. Support the caliper using mechanics wire. Do not stretch the brake hose.
3. Remove the dust cap from the hub.

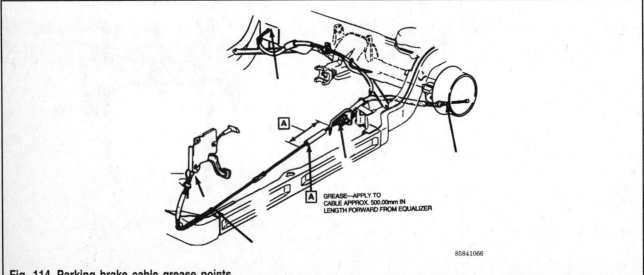

GREASE—APPLY TO CABLE APPROX. 500.00mm IN LENGTH FORWARD FROM EQUALIZER

85841066

**Fig. 114 Parking brake cable grease points.**

4. Remove the cotter pin and the spindle nut. Then remove the outer roller bearing assembly from the hub.

5. Remove the rotor/hub assembly from the spindle. The inner bearing assembly can be removed after prying out the inner seal. Discard the seal.

6. Wash all parts in solvent and check for excessive wear or damage.

### ✳✳CAUTION

**If using compressed air to dry the bearings, DO NOT allow the bearing to turn without lubrication.**

### To install:

7. To replace the outer or inner race, knock out the old race with a hammer and brass drift. Drive new races into hub assembly using the proper size drivers. Do not use a driver that will contact the inner bearing surface of the race, as damage to the bearing will result. New races must be installed squarely and evenly to avoid damage.

### ✳✳WARNING

**Never use old bearing parts with new parts. If the old bearing is damaged, the entire bearing assembly will have to be replaced including the outer race.**

8. Pack the bearings with a high melting point bearing lubricant. Apply a sizable dab of lubricant to the palm of one hand. Using your other hand, work the bearing into the lubricant so that the grease is pushed through the rollers and out the other side. Keep rotating the bearing while continuing to push the lubricant through it.

9. Lightly grease the spindle and the inside of the hub.

10. Place the inner bearing in the hub race and install a new grease seal.

11. Carefully install the hub and disc assembly.

12. Install the outer wheel bearing.

13. Install the washer and nut and adjust the bearings according to the procedure outlined above.

14. Install the caliper and torque the mounting bolts to 35 ft. lbs. (48 Nm).

15. Install the dust cap, wheel and tire assembly, then lower the vehicle to the ground.

16. Prior to moving the vehicle, pump the brakes until a firm pedal is felt.

## TRAILER TOWING

### General Recommendations

Your vehicle is designed and intended to be used mainly to carry people. Towing a trailer will affect handling, durability and economy. Your safety and satisfaction depend upon proper use of correct equipment. Also, you should avoid overloads and other abusive use.

Factory trailer towing packages are available on most vehicles. However, if you are installing a trailer hitch and wiring on your vehicle, there are a few thing that you ought to know.

Information on trailer towing, special equipment and optional equipment is available at your local dealership. You can write to Oldsmobile Customer Service Department, P.O. Box 30095, Lansing, MI 48909 or Pontiac Customer Service Department, One Pontiac Plaza, Pontiac, Michigan 48053. In Canada, General Motors of Canada Limited, Customer Service Department, Oshawa, Ontario L1J 5Z6.

### Trailer Weight

Trailer weight is the first, and most important, factor in determining whether or not your vehicle is suitable for towing the trailer you have in mind. The horsepower-to-weight ratio should be calculated. The basic standard is a ratio of 35:1. That is, 35 pounds of GVW (gross vehicle weight) for every horsepower.

To calculate this ratio, multiply you engine's rated horsepower by 35, then subtract the weight of the vehicle, including passengers and luggage. The resulting figure is the ideal maximum trailer weight that you can tow. One point to consider: a numerically higher axle ratio can offset what appears to be a low trailer weight. If the weight of the trailer that you have in mind is somewhat higher than the weight you just calculated, you might consider changing your rear axle ratio to compensate.

### Hitch Weight

There are three kinds of hitches: bumper mounted, frame mounted, and load equalizing.

Bumper mounted hitches are those which attach solely to the vehicle's bumper. Many states prohibit towing with this type of hitch, when it attaches to the vehicle's stock bumper, since it subjects the bumper to stresses for which it was not designed. Aftermarket rear step bumpers, designed for trailer towing, are acceptable for use with bumper mounted hitches.

### ✳✳CAUTION

**DO NOT attach any hitch to the bumper bar on the vehicle. A hitch attachment may be made through the bumper mounting locations, but only if an additional attachment is also made.**

Frame mounted hitches can be of the type which bolts to two or more points on the frame, plus the bumper, or just to several points on the frame. Frame mounted hitches can also be of the tongue type, for Class I towing, or, of the receiver type, for classes II and III.

Load equalizing hitches are usually used for large trailers. Most equalizing hitches are welded in place and use equalizing bars and chains to level the vehicle after the trailer is hooked up.

The bolt-on hitches are the most common, since they are relatively easy to install.

Check the gross weight rating of your trailer. Tongue weight is usually figured as 10% of gross trailer weight. Therefore, a trailer with a maximum gross weight of 2,000 lbs. will have a maximum tongue weight of 200 lbs. Class I trailers fall into this category. Class II trailers are those with a gross weight rating of 2,000-3,500 lbs., while Class III trailers fall into the 3,500-6,000 lbs. category. Class IV trailers are those over 6,000 lbs. and are for use with fifth wheel trucks, only.

When you have determined the hitch that you'll need, follow the manufacturer's installation instructions, exactly, especially when it comes to fastener torques. The hitch will subjected to a lot of stress and good hitches come with hardened bolts. Never substitute an inferior bolt for a hardened bolt.

More frequent service is required when using your vehicle to pull a trailer. The automatic transmission fluid, engine oil/filter and rear axle lubricant change requirements for change. Change the engine oil/filter every 3,000 miles (5,000 km), transmission and rear axle fluid every 15,000 miles (25,000 km).

## Wiring

Wiring the vehicle for towing is fairly easy. There are a number of good wiring kits available and these should be used, rather than trying to design your own. All trailers will need brake lights and turn signals as well as tail lights and side marker lights. Most states require extra marker lights for overly wide trailers. Also, most states have recently required back-up lights for trailers, and most trailer manufacturers have been building trailers with back-up lights for several years.

Additionally, some Class I, most Class II and just about all Class III trailers will have electric brakes.

Add to this number an accessories wire, to operate trailer internal equipment or to charge the trailer's battery, and you can have as many as seven wires in the harness.

Determine the equipment on your trailer and buy the wiring kit necessary. The kit will contain all the wires needed, plus a plug adapter set which includes the female plug, mounted on the bumper or hitch, and the male plug, wired into, or plugged into the trailer harness.

When installing the kit, follow the manufacturer's instructions. The color coding of the wires is standard throughout the industry.

One point to note, some domestic vehicles, and most imported vehicles, have separate turn signals. On most domestic vehicles, the brake lights and rear turn signals operate with the same bulb. For those vehicles with separate turn signals, you can purchase an isolation unit so that the brake lights won't blink whenever the turn signals are operated, or, you can go to your local electronics supply house and buy four diodes to wire in series with the brake and turn signal bulbs. Diodes will isolate the brake and turn signals. The choice is yours. The isolation units are simple and quick to install, but far more expensive than the diodes. The diodes, however, require more work to install properly, since they require the cutting of each bulb's wire and soldering in place of the diode.

One final point, the best kits are those with a spring loaded cover on the vehicle mounted socket. This cover prevents dirt and moisture from corroding the terminals. Never let the vehicle socket hang loosely. Always mount it securely to the bumper or hitch.

## PUSHING AND TOWING

All Buick, Oldsmobile and Pontiac models covered in this guide are equipped with automatic transmissions and thus cannot be push started. The vehicle can be towed, however, with the transmission in Neutral as long as the speed does not exceed 35 mph and the distance does not exceed 15 miles. If the above speeds and distances must be exceeded, the vehicle's driveshaft must be disconnected first, or the rear wheels raised. The tow truck operator typically has a special dolly for this purpose. Towing with the rear wheels raised also requires the steering wheels to be locked in the straight ahead position (do not rely on the steering column lock for this purpose).

## JACKING

▶ See Figure 115

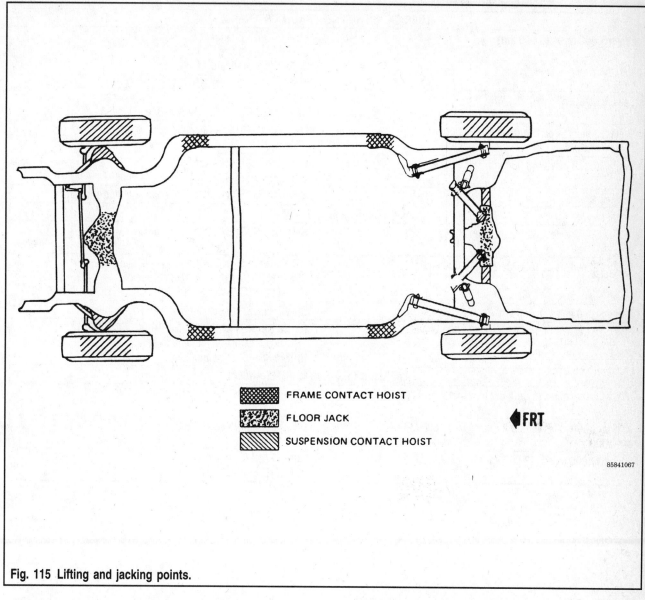

FRAME CONTACT HOIST

FLOOR JACK

SUSPENSION CONTACT HOIST

◀FRT

85841067

**Fig. 115 Lifting and jacking points.**

All models covered in this guide are equipped from the factory with a ratchet-type bumper jack. This jack was only designed to aid tire changing in emergency situations; it was NOT designed as a maintenance tool. Never get under the vehicle when it is supported by only a jack.

➡**A sturdy set of jackstands (at least two) and a hydraulic floor jack of at least 1½ ton capacity are two of the best investments you can make if you are serious about maintaining your own vehicle. The added safety and utility of a hydraulic floor jack makes this tool pay for itself many times over through the years.**

Drive-on ramps are also commercially available; they raise the front end of the vehicle up about 10-12 in. (254-305mm). Make sure yours are of all-welded construction and made from strong, square tubing. You must make sure the rear wheels are blocked when using ramps.

## ✳✳CAUTION

**NEVER Use concrete cinder blocks for supporting any type of vehicle. Their use can be extremely dangerous, as they easily break if the load is not perfectly distributed.**

Regardless of the method of jacking or hoisting the vehicle, there are only certain areas of the undercarriage and suspension you can safely use to support the vehicle. Some models are equipped with slots in the bumpers, into which the bumper jack engages for changing tires. See the accompanying illustration, and make sure that only the shaded areas are used. Also, be especially careful not to damage the catalytic converter when jacking or supporting the vehicle.

## DIESEL MAINTENANCE INTERVALS

| When to Perform Services (Months or Miles, Whichever Occurs First) | Services |
|---|---|
| **LUBRICATION AND GENERAL MAINTENANCE** ||
| Every 5,000 miles (8 000 km) | *ENGINE OIL—Change<br>*OIL FILTER—Change<br>•CHASSIS—Lubricate<br>•FLUID LEVELS—Check |
| See Explanation | TIRES—Rotation<br>REAR AXLE OR FINAL DRIVE—Check lube |
| Every 12 months or 15,000 miles (24 000 km) | *COOLING SYSTEM—Check<br>*CRANKCASE VENTILATION—Service |
| Every 30,000 miles (48 000 km) | WHEEL BEARINGS—Repack<br>FINAL DRIVE BOOTS AND SEALS—Check |
| See Explanation | AUTOMATIC TRANSMISSION—Change fluid and filter |
| **SAFETY MAINTENANCE** ||
| At first 5,000 miles (8 000 km) then at 15,000/30,000/45,000 miles | *EXHAUST SYSTEM—Check condition |
| Every 12 months or 10,000 miles (16 000 km) | TIRES, WHEEL AND DISC BRAKE—Check<br>SUSPENSION AND STEERING—Check<br>BRAKES AND POWER STEERING—Check |
| Every 5,000 miles (8 000 km) | *DRIVE BELTS—Check condition and adjustment |
| Every 12 months or 15,000 miles (24 000 km) | DRUM BRAKES AND PARKING BRAKE—Check<br>THROTTLE LINKAGE—Check operation<br>BUMPERS—Check condition |
| **EMISSION CONTROL MAINTENANCE** ||
| At first 5,000 miles (8 000 km) then at 15,000/30,000/45,000 miles | EXHAUST PRESSURE REGULATOR VALVE |
| At first 5,000 miles (8 000 km) then at 30,000 MILES (48 000 km) | ENGINE IDLE SPEED—Adjust |
| Every 30,000 miles (48 000 km) | AIR CLEANER—Replace<br>FUEL FILTER—Replace |

• Also a Safety Service
* Also an Emission Control Service

85841070

## GASOLINE-ENGINED CARS MAINTENANCE INTERVALS
### 1975-76

| Interval At Which Services Are To Be Performed | Service |
|---|---|
| **LUBRICATION AND GENERAL MAINTENANCE** | |
| Every 6 months or 7,500 miles | *CHASSIS—Lubricate<br>•*FLUID LEVELS—Check<br>*ENGINE OIL—Change |
| At first oil change—then every 2nd | *ENGINE OIL FILTER—Replace (V-6 Replace each oil change) |
| See Explanation of Maintenance Schedule | TIRES—Rotate<br>DIFFERENTIAL or TORONADO FINAL DRIVE |
| Every 12 months | AIR CONDITIONING SYSTEM—Check charge & hose condition<br>TEMPMATIC AIR FILTER—Replace every other year |
| Every 12 months or 15,000 miles | *COOLING SYSTEM—See Explanation of Maintenance Schedule |
| Every 30,000 miles | WHEEL BEARINGS—(Toronado rear)—Clean and replace<br>WHEEL BEARINGS—Clean & repack (except Toronado)<br>FINAL DRIVE AXLE BOOTS & OUTPUT SHAFT SEAL—<br>    Check Cond.<br>*AUTOMATIC TRANS.—Change fluid and service filter<br>MANUAL STEERING GEAR—Check seals<br>CLUTCH CROSS SHAFT—Lubricate |
| **SAFETY MAINTENANCE** | |
| Every 6 months or 7,500 miles | TIRES AND WHEELS—Check condition<br>*EXHAUST SYSTEM—Check condition of system<br>*DRIVE BELTS—Check condition & adjustment; replace every<br>    30,000 miles<br>FRONT AND REAR SUSPENSION & STEERING SYSTEM—<br>    Check condition<br>BRAKES AND POWER STEERING—Check all lines and hoses |
| **SAFETY MAINTENANCE** | |
| Every 12 months or 15,000 miles | DRUM BRAKES AND PARKING BRAKE—Check condition of<br>    linings; adjust parking brake<br>THROTTLE LINKAGE—Check operation and condition<br>UNDERBODY—Flush and check condition<br>BUMPERS—Check condition |
| **EMISSION CONTROL MAINTENANCE** | |
| At 1st 6 months or 7,500 miles—then at 18 month/22,500 mile intervals thereafter | THERMOSTATICALLY CONTROLLED AIR CLEANER—<br>    Check operation<br>CARBURETOR CHOKE—Check operation<br>ENGINE IDLE SPEED ADJUSTMENT<br>EFE VALVE—Check operation<br>CARBURETOR—Torque attaching bolts or nuts to manifold |
| Every 12 months or 15,000 miles | CARBURETOR FUEL INLET FILTER—Replace<br>VACUUM ADVANCE SYSTEM AND HOSES—Check operation<br>PCV SYSTEMS—See Explanation of Maintenance Schedule |
| Every 18 months or 22,500 miles | IDLE STOP SOLENOID OR DASHPOT—Check operation<br>SPARK PLUG AND IGNITION COIL WIRES—Inspect and clean |
| Every 22,500 miles | SPARK PLUGS—Replace<br>ENGINE TIMING ADJUSTMENT & DISTRIBUTOR CHECK |
| Every 24 months or 30,000 miles | ECS SYSTEM—See Explanation of Maintenance Schedule<br>FUEL CAP, TANK AND LINES—Check condition |
| Every 30,000 miles | AIR CLEANER ELEMENT—Replace |

\* Also Required Emission Control Maintenance
• Also a Safety Service

85841068

## GASOLINE-ENGINED CARS MAINTENANCE INTERVALS
### 1977 and Later

| When to Perform Services (Months or Miles, Whichever Occurs First) | Services |
|---|---|
| **LUBRICATION AND GENERAL MAINTENANCE** | |
| Every 12 months or 7,500 miles (12 000 km) | •CHASSIS—Lubricate<br>•FLUID LEVELS—Check<br>CLUTCH PEDAL FREE TRAVEL—Check/Adjust |
| See Explanation of Maintenance Schedule | *ENGINE OIL—Change<br>*ENGINE OIL FILTER—Replace<br>TIRES—Rotation (Radial Tires)<br>REAR AXLE OR FINAL DRIVE—Check lube |
| Every 12 months or 15,000 miles (24 000 km) | *COOLING SYSTEM—See Explanation of Maintenance Schedule |
| Every 30,000 miles (48 000 km) | WHEEL BEARINGS—Repack<br>FINAL DRIVE BOOTS AND SEALS (Toronado)—Check condition<br>CLUTCH CROSS SHAFT—Lubricate |
| See Explanation | AUTOMATIC TRANSMISSION—Change fluid and service filter |
| **SAFETY MAINTENANCE** | |
| Every 12 months or 7,500 miles (12 000 km) | TIRES, WHEELS AND DISC BRAKES—Check condition<br>*EXHAUST SYSTEM—Check condition<br>SUSPENSION & STEERING SYSTEM—Check condition<br>BRAKES AND POWER STEERING—Check all lines and hoses |
| Every 12 months or 15,000 miles (24 000 km) | *DRIVE BELTS—Check condition and adjustment ①<br>DRUM BRAKES AND PARKING BRAKE—Check condition of linings; adjust parking brake<br>THROTTLE LINKAGE—Check operation and condition<br>BUMPERS—Check condition<br>*FUEL CAP, TANK AND LINES—Check |
| **EMISSION CONTROL MAINTENANCE** | |
| At first 6 months or 7,500 miles (12 000 km)—then at 24-month/30,000 mile (48 000 km) intervals as indicated in Log, except choke which requires service at 45,000 miles (72 000 km) | CARBURETOR CHOKE & HOSES—Check ②<br>ENGINE IDLE SPEED—Check adjustment ②<br>EFE SYSTEM—Check operation (if so equipped)<br>CARBURETOR—Torque attaching bolts or nuts to manifold ② |
| Every 30,000 miles (48 000 km) | THERMOSTATICALLY CONTROLLED AIR CLEANER—Check operation<br>VACUUM ADVANCE SYSTEM AND HOSES—Check ③<br>SPARK PLUG WIRES—Check<br>IDLE STOP SOLENOID AND/OR DASHPOT OR ISC—Check operation<br>SPARK PLUGS—Replace ②<br>ENGINE TIMING ADJUSTMENT AND DISTRIBUTOR—Check<br>AIR CLEANER AND PCV FILTER ELEMENT—Replace ②<br>PCV VALVE—Replace<br>EGR VALVE—Service |

• Also a Safety Service
* Also an Emission Control Service
① In California, a separately driven air pump belt check is recommended but not required at 15,000 miles (24 000 km) and 45,000 miles (72 000 km).
② Only these emission control maintenance items are considered to be required maintenance as defined by the California Air Resources Board (ARB) regulation and are, according to such regulation, the minimum maintenance an owner in California must perform to fulfill the minimum requirements of the emission warranty. All other emission maintenance items are recommended maintenance as defined by such regulation. General Motors urges that all emission control maintenance items be performed.
③ Not applicable on vehicles equipped with electronic spark timing (EST).

85841069

## CAPACITIES

| Year | Engine No. Cyl. Displacement (Cu. In.) | Engine Crankcase Add 1 Qt. For New Filter* | Transmission (Pts. To Refill After Draining) Automatic | Drive Axle (pts.) | Fuel Tank (gals.) | Cooling System (qts.) With Heater | With A/C | Heavy Duty Cooling |
|------|----|---|---|---|---|---|---|---|
| | | | | **OLDSMOBILE 88, 98, WAGONS** | | | | |
| 1975 | 8-350 | 4 | 6 | 5.4① | 26② | 20 | 22.5 | 22.5 |
| | 8-400 | 5 | 6 | 5.4① | 26② | 21 | 21.5 | 23.5 |
| | 8-455 | 4 | 6 | 5.4① | 26② | 21 | 21.5 | 23.5 |
| 1976 | 8-350 | 4 | 6 | 5.4① | 26② | 20 | 22.5 | 22.5 |
| | 8-455 | 4 | 6 | 5.4① | 26② | 21 | 21.5 | 23.5 |
| 1977 | 6-231 | 4 | 6 | 4.25 | 21 | 12.7 | 12.8 | — |
| | 8-260 | 4 | 6 | 4.25 | 21 | 16.9 | 17.0 | — |
| | 8-350 Chev. | 4 | 6 | 4.25 | 21 | 16.0 | 16.7 | — |
| | 8-350 Olds. 88 | 4 | 6 | 4.25 | 21 | 14.6 | 15.3 | — |
| | 8-350 Olds. 98 | 4 | 6 | 4.25 | 24.5 | 14.6 | 15.3 | — |
| | 8-403 | 4 | 6 | 4.25 | 24.5 | 15.7 | 16.4 | — |
| 1978 | 6-231 | 4 | 6 | ㉔ | 25.25 | 12.25 | 12.25 | 12.25 |
| | 8-260 | 4 | 6 | ㉔ | 22.25④ | 16.25 | 16.25 | 16.75 |
| | 8-350 Olds. | 4 | 6 | ㉔ | 22.25④ | 14.5 | 14.5 | 15.5 |
| | 8-350 Buick | 5 | ⑩ | ㉔ | 22.25④ | 14.5 | 14.5 | 15.5 |
| | 8-350 Diesel | 7⑤ | 6 | ㉔ | 22.0 | 18.0 | 18.0 | 18.0 |
| | 8-403 | 4 | 6 | ㉔ | ⑥ | 15.75 | 16.5 | 16.5 |
| 1979 | 6-231 | 4 | 6 | 4.25 | 25.0⑦ | 13.3 | 13.3 | — |
| | 8-260 | 4 | 6 | 4.25 | 25.0⑦ | 16.25 | 16.25 | 16.25 |
| | 8-301 | 4⑧ | 6 | 4.25 | 25.0⑦ | 20 | 20 | 21 |
| | 8-350 | 4 | 6 | 4.25 | 25.0⑦ | 14.5 | 14.5 | 15.5 |
| | 8-350 Diesel | 7⑤ | 6 | 4.25 | 27 | 18.0 | 18 | — |
| | 8-403 | 4 | 6 | 4.25 | 25.0⑦ | 15.75 | 16.4 | 16.25 |
| 1980 | 6-231 | 4 | 6 | ㉔ | 20.75 | 13.0 | 13.0 | — |
| | 8-260 | 4 | 6 | ㉔ | 25⑦ | 19 | 19.75 | 19.75 |
| | 8-307 | 4 | 6 | ㉔ | 25⑦ | 15.5 | 15.25 | 16.25 |
| | 8-350 | 4 | 6 | ㉔ | 25 | 14.5 | 14.5 | 15.5 |
| | 8-350 Diesel | 7⑤ | 6 | ㉔ | 27④ | 18.0 | 18.0 | 18.0 |
| 1981 | 6-231 | 4 | 6 | 4 | 25 | 13 | 13 | — |
| | 6-252 | 4 | 6 | 4 | 25 | 12.8 | 12.8 | 12.8 |
| | 8-260 | 4 | 6 | 4 | 25④ | 15.9 | 15.5 | 16.5 |
| | 8-307 | 4 | 6 | 4 | 25④ | 15.6 | 15.3 | 16.2 |
| | 8-350 Diesel | 7⑤ | 6 | 4 | 27④ | 18.0 | 18.0 | 18.0 |
| 1982 | 6-231 | 4 | 6 | 4 | 25 | 13.0 | 13.0 | — |
| | 6-252 | 4 | 6 | 4 | 25 | 12.8 | 12.8 | 12.8 |
| | 8-260 | 4 | 6 | 4 | 25 | 16.5 | 16.2 | 17.2 |
| | 8-307 | 4 | 6 | 4 | 25 | 16.2 | 16.1 | 16.1 |
| | 8-350 Diesel | 7⑤ | 6 | 4 | 27④ | 18.0 | 18.0 | 18.0 |

85841c02

## CAPACITIES

| Year | Engine No. Cyl. Displacement (Cu. In.) | Engine Crankcase Add 1 Qt. For New Filter* | Transmission (Pts. To Refill After Draining) Automatic | Drive Axle (pts.) | Fuel Tank (gals.) | Cooling System (qts.) With Heater | With A/C | Heavy Duty Cooling |
|---|---|---|---|---|---|---|---|---|
| | OLDSMOBILE 88, 98, WAGONS (cont.) |
| 1983 | 6-231 | 4 | 6 | 4 | 25 | 13.7 | 13.7 | — |
| | 6-252 | 4 | 6 | 4 | 25 | 13.7 | 13.7 | 13.7 |
| | 8-307 | 4 | 6 | 4 | 25 | 16.2 | 16.2 | 16.1 |
| | 8-350 Diesel | 7⑤ | 6 | 4 | 27④ | 18.3 | 18.3 | 18.0 |
| 1984 | 6-231 | 4 | 7⑲ | 4.25⑳ | 25 | 13 | 13 | — |
| | 8-307 | 4 | 7㉑ | 4.25⑳ | 25 | 25.5 | 15.25 | 16 |
| | 8-350 Diesel | 6 | 7㉑ | 4.25⑳ | 27 | 18.25 | 18 | 18 |
| 1985 | 6-231 | 4 | 7⑲ | 4.25⑳ | 25 | 13 | 13 | — |
| | 8-307 | 4 | 7㉑ | 4.25⑳ | 25 | 25.5 | 15.25 | 16 |
| | 8-350 Diesel | 6 | 7㉑ | 4.25⑳ | 27 | 18.25 | 18 | 18 |
| 1986 | 8-307 | 4 | 7 | 4.25⑳ | 22 | — | 15.3 | — |
| 1987 | 8-307 | 4 | 7 | 4.25⑳ | 22 | — | 15.3 | — |
| 1988 | 8-307 Wagon | 4 | 7 | ㉔ | 22 | — | 15.3 | 16.0 |
| 1989 | 8-307 Wagon | 4 | 7 | ㉔ | 22 | 17.0 | 17.0 | 17.6 |
| 1990 | 8-307 Wagon | 4 | 7 | ㉔ | 22 | 15.9 | 15.9 | 16.4 |
| | BUICK LE SABRE, ELECTRA, WAGONS |
| 1975 | 8-350 | 4 | 6 | 4.25 | 18.5 | 12.7 | 12.7 | — |
| | 8-455 | 4 | 7 | 5.4 | 26.0 | 16.9 | 17.2 | — |
| 1976 | 8-350 | 4 | 6 | 4.25 | 26.0 | 16.9 | 17.2 | — |
| | 8-455 | 4 | 7 | 5.4 | 26.0 | 16.9 | 17.2 | — |
| 1977 | 6-231 | 4 | 6 | 4.25 | 26.0 | 16.9 | 17.2 | — |
| | 8-301 | 5.5 | 6 | 4.25 | 21.0 | 18.3 | 19.1 | — |
| | 8-350 Buick, Olds. | 4 | 6 | 4.25 | 21.0 | 14.6 | 15.4 | — |
| | 8-403 | 4 | 7 | 4.25 | 21.0⑨ | 15.7 | 16.6 | — |
| 1978 | 6-231 | 4 | ⑩ | ㉔ | 21.0 | 12.9 | 12.9 | 12.9 |
| | 8-301 | 5 | ⑩ | ㉔ | 21.0 | 20.9 | 20.9 | 21.6 |
| | 8-305 | 4 | ⑩ | ㉔ | 21.0 | 16.6 | 16.7 | 16.7 |
| | 8-350 Buick | 5 | ⑩ | ㉔ | 25.3② | 14.1 | 14.1 | 14.9 |
| | 8-350 Chev. | 4 | ⑩ | ㉔ | 21.0 | 16.6 | 16.7 | 18.0 |
| | 8-350 Olds. | 4 | ⑩ | ㉔ | 21.0②⑫ | 14.6 | 14.5 | 15.4 |
| | 8-400 Pont. | 5 | ⑩ | ㉔ | 25.3② | 15.7 | 16.6 | 16.6 |
| | 8-403 | 4 | ⑩ | ㉔ | 25.3② | 15.7 | 16.6 | 16.6 |
| 1979 | 6-231 | 4 | ⑩ | ㉔ | 21.0 | 12.9 | 12.9 | 12.9 |
| | 8-301 | 4 | ⑩ | ㉔ | 21.0 | 20.9 | 20.9 | 20.9 |
| | 8-350 Buick | 4 | ⑩ | ㉔ | 25.3 | 14.6 | 14.5 | 15.4 |
| | 8-350 Olds. | 4 | ⑩ | ㉔ | 21.0 | 14.6 | 14.5 | 15.4 |
| | 8-403 | 4 | ⑩ | ㉔ | 25.3 | 15.7 | 16.6 | 16.6 |

85841c03

## CAPACITIES

| Year | Engine No. Cyl. Displacement (Cu. In.) | Engine Crankcase Add 1 Qt. For New Filter* | Transmission (Pts. To Refill After Draining) Automatic | Drive Axle (pts.) | Fuel Tank (gals.) | Cooling System (qts.) With Heater | With A/C | Heavy Duty Cooling |
|---|---|---|---|---|---|---|---|---|
| | | | **BUICK LE SABRE, ELECTRA, WAGONS (cont.)** | | | | | |
| 1980 | 6-231 | 4 | ⑩ | ㉔ | 25.0 | 13.0 | 13.0 | 13.0 |
| | 6-252 | 4 | ⑩ | ㉔ | 25.0 | 13.0 | 13.0 | 13.0 |
| | 8-301 | 4 | ⑩ | ㉔ | 25.0 | 18.9 | 18.9 | 18.9 |
| | 8-350 Buick | 4 | ⑩ | ㉔ | 25.0 | 14.3 | 14.2 | 14.7 |
| | 8-350 Olds. | 4 | ⑩ | ㉔ | 25.0 | — | 14.5 | 15.2 |
| | 8-350 Diesel | 7⑤ | ⑩ | ㉔ | 23.0⑭ | 18.3 | 18.0 | 18.0 |
| 1981 | 6-231 | 4 | ⑩ | ㉔ | 25.0 | 13.0 | 13.0 | 13.0 |
| | 6-252 | 4 | ⑩ | ㉔ | 25.0 | 13.0 | 13.0 | 13.0 |
| | 8-267 | 4 | ⑩ | ㉔ | 25.0 | 21.0 | 21.0 | 21.0 |
| | 8-301 | 4 | ⑩ | ㉔ | 25.0⑭ | 18.9 | 18.9 | 18.9 |
| | 8-307 | 4 | ⑩ | ㉔ | 25.0 | 15.6 | 16.3 | 16.0 |
| | 8-350 Diesel | 7⑤ | ⑩ | ㉔ | 23.0 | 18.3 | 18.0 | 18.0 |
| 1982 | 6-231, 6-252 | 4 | ⑩ | ㉔ | 25.0 | 13.0 | 13.0 | 13.0 |
| | 8-307 | 4 | ⑩ | ㉔ | 25.0 | 15.4 | 16.2 | 16.2 |
| | 8-350 Diesel | 7⑤ | ⑩ | ㉔ | 23.0⑭ | 18.3 | 18.0 | 18.0 |
| 1983 | 6-231, 6-252 | 4 | ⑩ | ㉔ | 25.0 | 13.0 | 13.1 | 13.1 |
| | 8-307 | 4 | ⑩ | ㉔ | 25.0 | 15.4 | 16.2 | 16.2 |
| | 8-350 Diesel | 7⑤ | ⑩ | ㉔ | 23.0⑭ | 18.3 | 18.0 | 18.0 |
| 1984 | 6-231 | 4 | ㉓ | ㉔ | ㉕ | 13 | 13 | 13 |
| | 6-252 | 4 | ㉓ | ㉔ | ㉕ | 13 | 13 | 13 |
| | 8-307 | 4 | ㉓ | ㉔ | ㉕ | 15.4 | 16 | 16 |
| | 8-350 Diesel | 6.5 | ㉓ | ㉔ | ㉕ | 18.3 | 17.9 | 17.9 |
| 1985 | 6-231 | 4 | ㉓ | ㉔ | ㉕ | 13.0 | 13.0 | — |
| | 6-252 | 4 | ㉓ | ㉔ | ㉕ | 13.0 | 13.0 | 13.0 |
| | 8-307 | 4 | ㉓ | ㉔ | ㉖ | 15.4 | 16.0 | 16.0 |
| | 8-350 Diesel | 6.5 | ㉓ | ㉔ | ㉕ | 18.3 | 17.9 | 17.9 |
| 1986 | 6-231 | 4 | 7 | ㉔ | 18.1 | 12.9 | 13.0 | 13.5 |
| | 8-307 | 4 | 7 | ㉔ | 18.1 | 14.9 | 15.6 | 15.5 |
| | 8-307 Wagon | 4 | 7 | ㉔ | 22 | 15.4 | 16.0 | 16.0 |
| 1987 | 8-307 Wagon | 4 | 7 | ㉔ | 22 | 15.4 | 16.0 | 16.0 |
| 1988 | 8-307 Wagon | 4 | 10.1 | 4.25 | 22 | 15.0 | 15.0 | 16.0 |
| 1989 | 8-307 Wagon | 4 | 7 | ㉔ | 22 | 17.0 | 17.0 | 17.6 |
| 1990 | 8-307 Wagon | 4 | 7 | ㉔ | 22 | 15.9 | 15.9 | 16.4 |
| | | | **PONTIAC BONNEVILLE, CATALINA, WAGON** | | | | | |
| 1975 | 8-400 | 5 | 7.5 | 5.5 | 25.8② | 18.6 | 19.8 | 19.8 |
| | 8-455 | 5 | 7.5 | 5.5 | 25.8② | 18.0 | 18.4 | 18.4 |
| 1976 | 8-400 | 5 | 7.5 | 5.5 | 25.8② | 21.6 | 22.4 | — |
| | 8-455 | 5 | 7.5 | 5.5 | 25.8② | 18.0 | 18.4 | 18.4 |

## CAPACITIES

| Year | Engine No. Cyl. Displacement (Cu. In.) | Engine Crankcase Add 1 Qt. For New Filter* | Transmission (Pts. To Refill After Draining) Automatic | Drive Axle (pts.) | Fuel Tank (gals.) | Cooling System (qts.) With Heater | With A/C | Heavy Duty Cooling |
|---|---|---|---|---|---|---|---|---|
| | | | **PONTIAC BONNEVILLE, CATALINA, WAGON (cont.)** | | | | | |
| 1977 | 6-231 | 4 | ⑮ | ㉔ | 21 | 14.2 | 14.1 | 14.1 |
| | 8-301 | 5 | ⑮ | ㉔ | 21 | 20.2 | 20.1 | 20.8 |
| | 8-305 | 4 | ⑮ | ㉔ | 18.1 | 17.7 | 17.4 | 18.1 |
| | 8-350 Olds. | 4 | 6 | 3.5 | 20 | 15.1 | 15.1 | — |
| | 8-350 Pont. | 5 | 6 | 3.5 | 20 | 19.8 | 21.0 | — |
| | 8-400 | 5 | 7.5 | ㉔ | 21 | 26.3 | 20.3 | 20.3 |
| | 8-403 | 4 | 7.5 | 4.25 | 24.5 | 16.1 | 16.1 | 16.1 |
| 1978 | 6-231 | 4 | ⑮ | ㉔ | 21 | 14.2 | 14.1 | 14.1 |
| | 8-301 | 5 | ⑮ | ㉔ | 21 | 20.2 | 20.1 | 20.8 |
| | 8-350 Buick | 5 | 7.5 | ㉔ | 22 | 18.6 | 19.1 | 19.1 |
| | 8-350 Olds. | 4 | 7.5 | ㉔ | 21 | 16.5 | 16.5 | 16.4 |
| | 8-403 | 4 | 7.5 | ㉔ | 21 | 17.7 | 23.0 | 23.0 |
| 1979 | 6-231 | 4 | 6 | 3.5 | 21 | 13.9 | 13.9 | 13.9 |
| | 8-301 | 4 | 6 | 3.5 ⑯ | 21 | 20.2 | 20.1 | 20.9 |
| | 8-350 Olds. | 4 | 6 | 3.5 ⑯ | 21 | 16.5 | 16.4 | 17.1 |
| | 8-350 Buick | 4 | 6 | 3.5 ⑯ | 21 | 16.6 | 18.6 | 16.6 |
| | 8-403 | 4 | 6 | 3.5 ⑯ | 21 | 17.7 | 23.0 | 18.5 |
| 1980 | 6-231 | 4 | 8 | 3.5 | 21 | 12.6 | 12.6 | — |
| | 8-265 | 4 | 8 | 3.4 | 20.7 | 20 | 20 | 20 |
| | 8-301 | 4 | 6 | 3.4 | 20.7 | 20 | 20 | 20 |
| | 8-350 Olds. | 4 | 6 | 3.5 | 21 | 16.5 | 16.4 | 17.1 |
| | 8-350 Buick | 4 | 6 | 3.5 ⑯ | 21 | 16.6 | 18.6 | 16.6 |
| | 8-350 Diesel | 7 ⑤ | ⑩ | ㉔ | 23.0 | — | 17.0 | 17.0 |
| 1981 | 6-231 | 4 | 8 | 3.4 | 20.7 | — | 17.0 | 17.0 |
| | 8-265 | 4 | 8 | 3.4 | 25.0 | 20 | 20 | 20 |
| | 8-305 | 4 | ⑰ | ㉔ | 25 | 16.1 | 16.1 | — |
| | 8-307 | 4 | 8 | 3.4 | 25.0 | 14.9 | 15.6 | 15.6 |
| | 8-350 Buick | 4 | 6 | 3.5 ⑯ | 21 | 16.6 | 18.6 | 16.6 |
| | 8-350 Diesel | 7 ⑤ | ⑩ | 3.5 ⑦ | 23.0 | — | 17.0 | 17.0 |
| 1982 | 6-231 | 4 | 8 | 3.4 | 18.1 | — | 17.0 | 17.0 |
| | 8-305 | 4 | ⑰ | 3.5 | 18.1 | 15.0 | 15.1 | 15.1 |
| | 8-350 Diesel | 7 ⑤ | ⑰ | 3.5 | 19.8 ⑱ | 17.3 | 17.3 | 17.3 |
| 1983 | 6-231 | 4 | 8 | 3.4 | 18.1 | — | 17.0 | 17.0 |
| | 8-305 | 4 | ⑰ | 3.5 | 18.1 | 15.0 | 15.1 | 15.1 |
| | 8-350 Diesel | 7 ⑤ | ⑰ | 3.5 | 19.8 ⑱ | 17.3 | 17.3 | 17.3 |
| 1984 | 6-231 | 4 | 8.5 | ㉔ | 17.5 ⑪ | 12.9 | 12.9 | 12.9 |
| | 8-305 | 4 | 9.9 | ㉔ | 17.5 ⑪ | 15.3 | 16.1 | 16.1 |
| | 8-350 Diesel | 6.5 | ⑰ | ㉔ | 19.8 | 17.2 | 17.2 | 17.2 |

85841c05

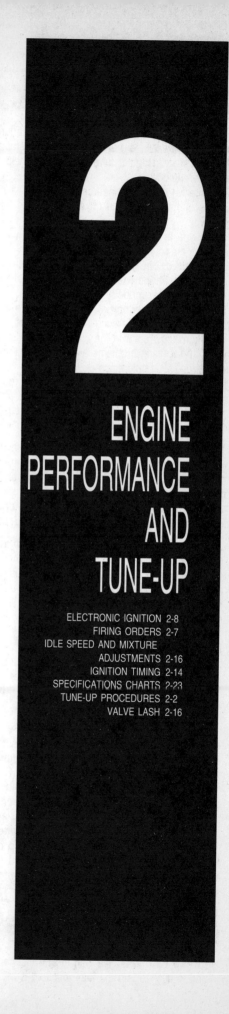

# 2

# ENGINE PERFORMANCE AND TUNE-UP

## TUNE-UP PROCEDURES

The tune-up is a routine maintenance procedure which is essential for the efficient and economical operation of your vehicle's engine. Regular tune-ups will also help prolong the life of the engine.

The interval between tune-ups is a variable factor which depends upon the way you drive your vehicle, the conditions under which you drive it (city versus highway, weather, etc.), and the type of engine installed. A complete tune-up should be performed on your Buick, Olds or Pontiac at least every 15,000 miles or one year, whichever comes first. 1981-83 vehicles have an increased tune-up interval of 25,000 miles. On 1984 and later models, it is 30,000 miles.

This interval should be halved if the vehicle is operated under severe conditions such as trailer towing, prolonged idling (a common occurrence in the city), start and stop driving, or if starting and running problems are noticed. It is assumed here that the routine maintenance described in Section 1 has been followed, as this goes hand-in-hand with the recommended tune-up procedures. The end result of a tune-up can only be the sum of all the various steps, so every step applicable to the tune-up should be followed.

➡**If the specifications on the underhood sticker in the engine compartment of your vehicle disagree with the Tune-Up Specifications chart in this chapter, the figures on the sticker must be used. The sticker often reflects changes made during the production run, or displays specifications that apply only to your particular engine.**

The replaceable parts involved in a tune-up include the spark plugs, air filter, distributor cap, rotor, and the spark plug wires. In addition to these parts and the adjustments involved in properly installing them, there are several adjustments of other parts involved in completing the job. These include carburetor idle speed and air/fuel mixture, ignition timing, and valve clearance adjustments.

This section gives specific procedures on how to tune-up your Buick, Pontiac or Oldsmobile, and is intended to be as complete and basic as possible.

### ✳✳CAUTION

**When working with a running engine, make sure that there is proper ventilation. Also make sure that the transmission is in Neutral (unless otherwise specified) and the parking brake is fully applied. Always keep hands, clothing and tools well clear of the hot exhaust manifolds and radiator and especially the belts and fan. Remove any wrist or long neck jewelry or ties before beginning any job, and tuck long hair under a cap. When the engine is running, do not grasp ignition wires, distributor cap or coil wires as a shock in excess of 50,000 volts could result. Whenever working around the distributor, make sure the ignition is OFF.**

### Diesel Engine Precautions

1. Never run the engine with the air cleaner removed; if anything is sucked into the inlet manifold it will go straight to the combustion chambers, or jam behind a valve and cause major engine damage.
2. Never wash a diesel engine: the reaction of a warm fuel injection pump to cold (or even warm) water can ruin the pump.
3. Never operate a diesel engine with one or more fuel injectors removed unless fully familiar with injector testing procedures: some diesel injection pumps spray fuel at up to 1400 psi; enough pressure to allow the fuel to penetrate your skin!
4. NEVER skip engine oil and filter changes.
5. Strictly follow the manufacturer's oil and fuel recommendations as given in the owner's manual.
6. Do not use home heating oil as fuel for your diesel unless it's a dire emergency.
7. Do not use starting fluids in the automotive diesel engine, as it can cause severe internal engine damage.
8. Do not run a diesel engine with the Water in Fuel warning light ON in the dashboard. See Section 5 for water purging procedure.
9. If removing water from the fuel tank yourself, use the same caution you would use when working around gasoline engine fuel components.
10. Do not allow diesel fuel to come in contact with rubber hoses or components on the engine, as it can damage them.

### Spark Plugs

▸ **See Figure 1**

A typical spark plug consists of a metal shell surrounding a ceramic insulator. A metal electrode extends downward through the center of the insulator and protrudes a short distance. Located at the end of the plug and attached to the side of the outer metal shell is the side electrode. This side electrode bends in at 90° so its tip is even with, and parallel to, the tip of the center electrode. This distance between these two electrodes (measured in thousandths of an inch) is called the spark plug gap. The spark plug in no way produces a spark but merely provides a gap across which the current can arc. The electronic ignition system produces approximately 50,000 volts, which travels to the distributor where it is distributed through the spark plug wires to the plugs. The current passes along the center electrode and jumps the gap to the side electrode and, in so doing, ignites the air/fuel mixture in the combustion chamber. All plugs used since 1969 have a resistor built into the center electrode to reduce interference to any nearby radio and television receivers. The resistor also reduces the rate of erosion of the plug electrodes caused by excessively long sparking. Resistor spark plug wiring is original equipment on all models.

Spark plug life and efficiency depend upon the condition of the engine and the temperatures to which the plug is exposed. Combustion chamber temperatures are affected by many factors such as compression ratio of the engine, fuel/air mixtures, exhaust emission equipment, and the type of driving you do. Spark plugs are designed and classified by number according to the heat range at which they will operate most efficiently. The amount of heat that the plug absorbs is determined by the length of the lower insulator. The longer the insulator (it extends farther into the engine), the hotter the plug will operate; the shorter it is, the cooler it will operate. A plug that has a short path for heat transfer and remains too cool will quickly accumulate deposits of oil and carbon since it is not hot enough to burn them off. This leads to plug fouling and consequently to misfiring. A plug that has a long path for heat transfer will have no deposits but, due to the excessive heat, the electrodes will burn away quickly and, in some instances, pre-ignition may result. Pre-ignition takes place when plug tips get so hot that they glow sufficiently to ignite the fuel/air mixture before the spark does. This early ignition will usually cause a pinging (sounding much like castanets) during low speeds and heavy loads. In severe cases, the heat may become great enough to start the fuel/air mixture burning throughout the combustion chamber rather than just to the front of the plug as in normal operation. At this time, the piston is rising in the cylinder making its compression stroke. The burning mass is compressed and explosion results, producing tremendous pressure. Something has to give, the pistons are often damaged. Obviously, this detonation (explosion) is a destructive condition that can be avoided by installing a spark plug designed and specified for your particular engine.

A set of spark plugs usually requires replacing after 15,000 miles depending on the type of driving you do; this interval has been increased to 25,000 miles for 1981 and 1982 models and 30,000 miles for 1983 and later models. The electrode on a new spark plug has a sharp edge but, with use, this edge becomes rounded by erosion causing the plug gap to increase. In normal operation, the plug gap can be expected to increase no more than 0.001 in. (0.025mm) for every 1,000-2,000 miles. As the gap increases, the plug's voltage requirement also increases. It requires a greater voltage to jump the wider gap and about two to three times as much voltage to fire a plug at acceleration than at idle.

The higher voltage produced by the High Energy Ignition (HEI) coil is one of the primary reasons for the prolonged replacement interval for spark plugs in the 1975 and later vehicles covered in this guide. A consistently hotter spark prevents the fouling of plugs for much longer than could normally be expected; this spark is also able to jump across a larger gap more efficiently than a spark from a conventional system. However, even plugs used with the HEI system wear after time in the engine.

Worn plugs become obvious during acceleration. Voltage requirement is greatest during acceleration and a plug with an enlarged gap may require more voltage than the coil is able to produce. As a result, the engine misses and sputters until acceleration is reduced. Reducing acceleration reduces the plug's voltage requirement and the engine runs smoother. Slow, city driving is hard on plugs. The long periods of idle experienced in traffic creates an overly rich gas mixture. The engine is not running fast enough to completely burn the gas and, consequently, the plugs are fouled with gas deposits and engine idle becomes rough. In many cases, driving under the right conditions can effectively clean these fouled plugs. Fouled spark plugs can also be caused by oil getting past the piston rings into the combustion chamber. A hotter plug may temporarily solve the problem, but in this case engine repair may be necessary.

➡Normal driving is assumed to be a mixture of idling, slow speed and high speed operation, with some of each making up the daily total driving. Occasional high speed driving is essential to good spark plug performance as the increased combustion heat burns away excess deposits of carbon and oxides that build up from frequent idling or stop-and-go driving.

The type of driving you do may require a change in spark plug heat range. If the majority of your driving is done in the city and rarely at high speeds, plug fouling may necessitate changing to a plug with a heat range one number higher than that specified by the vehicle manufacturer. For example, a 1980 Buick with 231 V6 engine requires an R45TS plug. Frequent city driving may foul these plugs making engine operation rough. An R46SX is the next hottest plug in the AC heat range (the higher the AC number, the hotter the plug) and its insulator is longer than the R45TS so that it can absorb and retain more heat than the shorter R45. On the other hand, if the aforementioned Buick were used almost exclusively for long distance high speed driving, the specified R45TS might be too hot resulting in rapid electrode wear. In this case, it might be wise to change to a colder R44. If the vehicle is used for abnormal driving (as in the examples above), or the engine has been modified for higher performance, then a change to a plug of a different heat range may be necessary. For a modified vehicle it is always wise to go to a colder plug as a protection against pre-ignition. It will require more frequent plug cleaning, but destructive detonation during acceleration will be avoided.

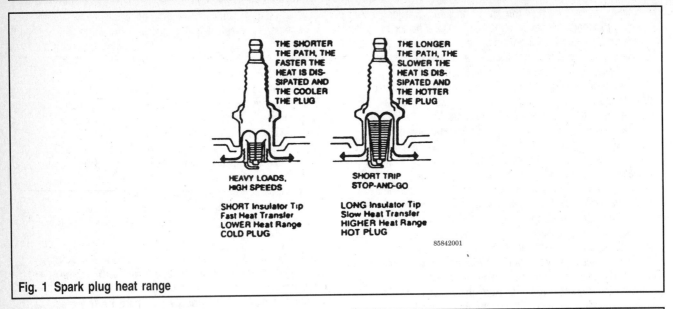

THE SHORTER THE PATH, THE FASTER THE HEAT IS DISSIPATED AND THE COOLER THE PLUG

THE LONGER THE PATH, THE SLOWER THE HEAT IS DISSIPATED AND THE HOTTER THE PLUG

HEAVY LOADS, HIGH SPEEDS

SHORT TRIP STOP-AND-GO

SHORT Insulator Tip
Fast Heat Transfer
LOWER Heat Range
COLD PLUG

LONG Insulator Tip
Slow Heat Transfer
HIGHER Heat Range
HOT PLUG

85842001

**Fig. 1 Spark plug heat range**

## REMOVAL & INSTALLATION

▶ See Figures 2, 3, 4, 5, 6 and 7

When you're removing spark plugs, you should work on them one at a time. Don't start by removing the plug wires all at once because unless you number them, they're going to get mixed up. On some models though, it will be more convenient for you to remove all the wires before you start to work on the plugs. If this is necessary, take a minute before you begin and number the wires with tape before you take them off. The time you spend here will pay off later on.

1. Twist the spark plug boot and remove the boot from the plug. You may also use a plug wire removal tool designed especially for this purpose. Do not pull on the wire itself as you will almost certainly destroy it. When the wire has been removed, take a wire brush and clean the area around the plug. Make sure that all the grime is removed so that none will enter the cylinder after the plug has been removed.

2. Remove the plug using the proper size socket, extensions, and universals as necessary. Most of the spark plugs

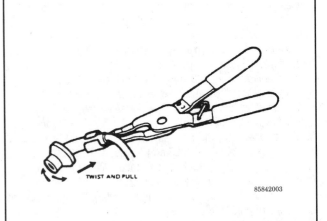

TWIST AND PULL

85842003

**Fig. 3 Special pliers used to remove the boots and wire from the plug**

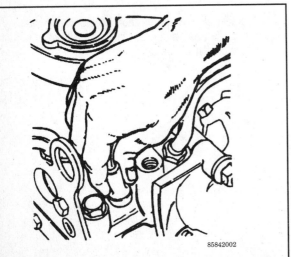

85842002

**Fig. 2 Twist and pull on the rubber boot; never pull on the wire itself**

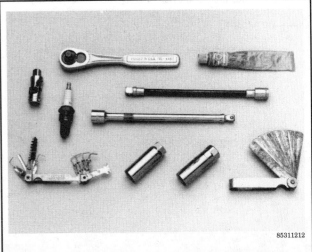

85311212

**Fig. 4 A variety of tools and gauges are needed for spark plug service**

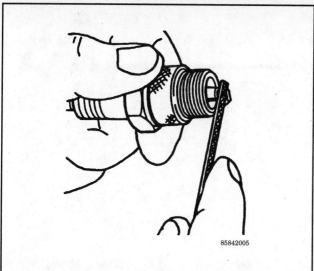

**Fig. 5 Plugs in good condition can be filed and reused**

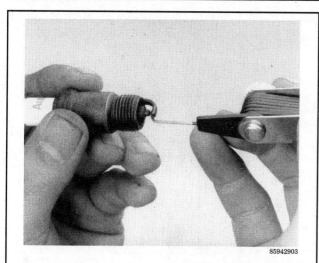

**Fig. 6 Always use a wire gauge to check the electrode gap**

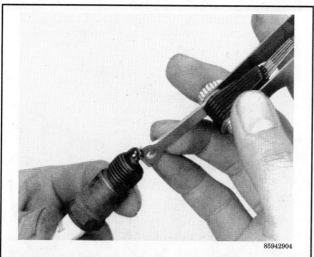

**Fig. 7 Adjust the electrode gap by bending the side electrode**

on the engines covered in this guide take a ⅝ in. plug socket, but some may take a ¹³⁄₁₆ in. socket.

➡**Allow the engine to cool completely before removing the spark plugs on engines with aluminum cylinder heads. Damage to the spark plug threads may result.**

3. If removing the plug is difficult, drip some penetrating oil on the plug threads, allow it to work, then remove the plug. Also, be sure that the socket is straight or square on the plug, especially on those hard to reach near the back of the engine.

Check the plugs for deposits and wear. If they are not going to be replaced, clean the plugs thoroughly. Remember that any kind of deposit will decrease the efficiency of the plug. Plugs can be cleaned on a spark plug cleaning machine, which can sometimes be found in service stations, or you can do an acceptable job of cleaning with a stiff brush. If the plugs are cleaned, the electrodes must be filed flat. Use an ignition points file, not an emery board or the like, which will leave deposits. The electrodes must be filled perfectly flat with sharp edges; rounded edges reduce the spark plug voltage by as much as 50%.

Check spark plug gap before installation. The ground electrode (the L-shaped one connected to the body of the plug) must be parallel to the center electrode and the specified size wire gauge (see Tune-Up Specifications) should pass through the gap with a slight drag. Always check the gap on new plugs; NEVER trust "pre-gapped" plugs. Use a spark plug gapping tool, which has wire gauges for gapping and a special bending tool for adjusting the side electrode. Do not use a flat feeler gauge when measuring the plug gap because it will give an inaccurate reading, and absolutely never bend the center electrode. Also, be careful not to bend the side electrode too far or too often; it may weaken and break off within the engine (causing engine damage and requiring removal of the cylinder head to retrieve it).

**To install:**

4. Lubricate the threads of the spark plugs with a drop of oil. Install the plugs and tighten them hand-tight. Take care not to cross-thread them.

5. Tighten the spark plugs with the socket. Do not apply the same amount of force you would use for a bolt; just snug them in. If a torque wrench is available, tighten to 11-15 ft. lbs. (14-20 Nm).

6. Install the wires on their respective plugs. Make sure the wires are firmly connected. You will be able to feel them click into place.

## Spark Plug Wires

### TESTING

◆ **See Figure 8**

Every 10,000 miles, inspect the spark plug wires for burns, cuts, or breaks in the insulation. One way to check for "leaking" wires is to lightly spray them with water, start the vehicle, and watch for tiny sparks around the wires (it is easiest to see them at night). If you see sparks, replace the wires as this can cause rough idle and misfire, especially in damp weather.

Check the boots and the nipples on the distributor cap. Replace any damaged wiring.

Every 30,000 miles or so, the resistance of the wires should be checked with an ohmmeter. Wires with excessive resistance will cause misfiring, and may make the engine difficult to start in damp weather. Generally, the useful life of the cables is between 45,000-60,000 miles.

To check resistance, remove the distributor cap, leaving the wires in place. Connect one lead of an ohmmeter to an electrode within the cap; connect the other lead to the corresponding spark plug terminal (remove it from the spark plug for this test). Replace any wire which shows a resistance over 30,000Ω. Generally speaking, however, resistance should not be over 25,000Ω and 30,000Ω must be considered the outer limit of acceptability.

Fig. 9 In most cases, it will be necessary to remove the retainer ring to replace the spark plug wires

### HEI Plug Wire Resistance Chart

| Wire Length | Minimum | Maximum |
|---|---|---|
| 0–15 inches | 3000 ohms | 10,000 ohms |
| 15–25 inches | 4000 ohms | 15,000 ohms |
| 25–35 inches | 6000 ohms | 20,000 ohms |
| Over 35 inches | | 25,000 ohms |

85842008

Fig. 8 Acceptable limits for plug wire resistance

It should be remembered that resistance is also a function of length; the longer the wire, the greater the resistance. Thus, if the wires on your vehicle are longer than the factory originals, the resistance will be higher, possibly outside these limits.

## REMOVAL & INSTALLATION

▶ See Figures 9, 10 and 11

➡To avoid confusion, replace spark plug wires one at a time.

To remove the wires, twist and pull the boot off of the spark plug and the distributor terminal.

When installing new wires, replace them one at a time to avoid mix-ups. Start by replacing the longest one first. Install the boot firmly over the spark plug. Route the wire over the same path as the original. Insert the nipple firmly onto the tower on the distributor cap, then install the cap cover and latches to secure the wires.

Fig. 10 Always label the terminal and wires to ease installation

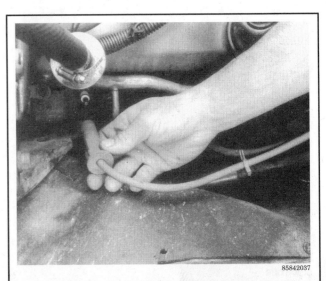

Fig. 11 Replace one wire at a time to avoid confusion

## FIRING ORDERS

▶ See Figures 12, 13, 14, 15 and 16

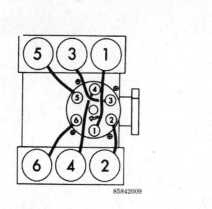

85842009

**Fig. 12 Buick-built 231, 252 V6**
**Engine firing order: 1-6-5-4-3-2**
**Distributor rotation: Clockwise**

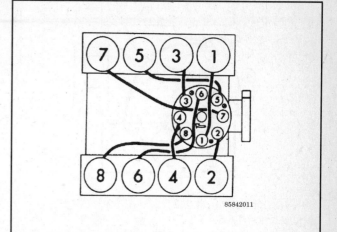

85842011

**Fig. 14 Buick-built 350 V8**
Firing order: 1-8-4-3-6-5-7-2
Distributor rotation: Clockwise

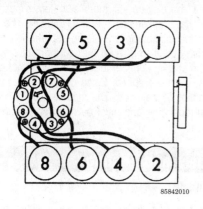

85842010

**Fig. 13 Olds-built 260, 307, 350, 400, 403, 455 V8**
**Pontiac-built 265, 301, 350, 400, 455 V8**
**Engine Firing Order: 1-8-4-3-6-5-7-2**
**Distributor rotation: Counter-clockwise**

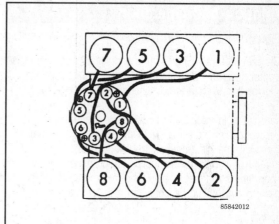

85842012

**Fig. 15 Chevrolet-built 267, 305, 350 V8**
Firing Order: 1-8-4-3-6-5-7-2
Distributor rotation: clockwise

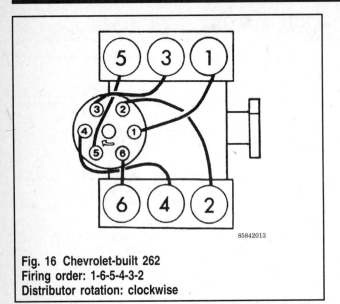

85842013

**Fig. 16 Chevrolet-built 262**
**Firing order: 1-6-5-4-3-2**
**Distributor rotation: clockwise**

## ELECTRONIC IGNITION

### Description and Operation

▶ See Figure 17

The General Motors HEI system is a pulse-triggered, transistor controlled, inductive discharge electronic ignition system. The entire ignition system is contained within the distributor cap.

The distributor, in addition to housing the mechanical and vacuum advance mechanisms (1975 through 1980), contains the ignition coil, the electronic control module, and the magnetic triggering device. The magnetic pick-up assembly contains a permanent magnet, a pole piece with internal teeth, and a pick-up coil (not to be confused with the ignition coil).

All spark timing changes in the 1981 and later distributors are done electronically by the Electronic Control Module (ECM), which monitors information from various engine sensors, computes the desired spark timing and then signals the distributor to change the timing accordingly. No vacuum or mechanical advance units are used.

In the HEI system, as in other electronic ignition systems, the breaker points have been replaced with an electronic switch (a transistor), which is located within the control module. This switching transistor performs the same function the points did in older conventional ignition systems; it simply turns coil primary current on and off at the correct time. So, electronic and conventional points-type ignition systems operate on the same basic principle.

The module which houses the switching transistor is controlled (turned on and off) by a magnetically generated impulse, induced in the pick-up coil. When the teeth of the rotating "timer" align with the teeth of the pole piece, the induced voltage in the pick-up coil signals the electronic module to allow current to flow to the coil primary circuit. As the rotating "timer" moves away from the pole piece, the electronic module is signaled to stop the current flow to the primary circuit, and

high voltage is induced in the ignition coil secondary windings which is then directed through the rotor and spark plug wires to fire the spark plugs.

In essence, the pick-up coil module system simply replaces the conventional breaker points and condenser. The condenser found within the distributor is for radio suppression purposes only and has nothing to do with the ignition process. The module automatically controls the dwell period, increasing it with increasing engine speed. Since dwell is automatically controlled, it cannot be adjusted. The module itself is non-adjustable and non-repairable and must be replaced if found defective.

### Diagnosis and Testing

▶ See Figure 18

The symptoms of a defective component within the HEI system are exactly the same as those you would encounter in a conventional system. Some of these symptoms are:
- Hard or No Starting
- Rough Idle
- Poor Fuel Economy
- Engine misses under load or while accelerating.

If you suspect a problem in your ignition system, there are certain preliminary checks which you should carry out before you begin to check the electronic portions of the system. First, it is extremely important to make sure the vehicle battery is in a good state of charge. A defective or poorly charged battery will cause the various components of the ignition system to read incorrectly when they are being tested. Second, make sure all wiring connections are clean and tight, not only at the battery, but also at the distributor cap, ignition coil, and at the electronic control module.

Instruments designed specifically for testing HEI systems are available from several tool manufacturers. Some of these will

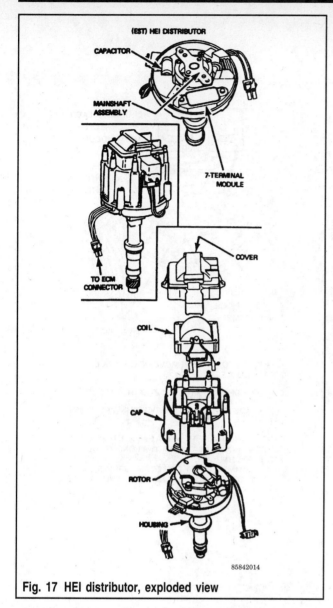

**Fig. 17 HEI distributor, exploded view**

even test the module itself. However, the tests given in this section will require only an ohmmeter and a voltmeter.

### ✳✳CAUTION

**The HEI ignition system can generate voltage of 30,000-50,000 volts. When testing the system, DO NOT hold a spark plug wire while the engine is running or cranking. Personal injury and or damage to the ignition system may result if this caution is not followed.**

Since the only change between electronic and conventional ignition systems is in the distributor component area, it is imperative to check the secondary ignition circuit first. If the secondary circuit checks out properly, then the engine condition is probably not the fault of the ignition system.

If the engine won't start, perform this test. This will narrow the problem area down considerably.

1. Remove one of the plug wires and insert a HEI spark tester tool in the plug socket.

2. Ground the spark tester to the block and crank the engine. DO NOT touch the spark plug wire while the engine is cranking.

3. The spark should be crisp and bright blue in color. If a normal spark occurs, try each spark plug wire until a no spark condition or a weak orange color spark is found. If all sparks are good, the problem is probably not in the ignition system. Check for fuel system problems, or fouled spark plugs.

If no spark occurs, check for the presence of normal battery voltage at the battery (BAT) terminal in the distributor cap. The ignition switch must be in the **ON** position for this test. Either a voltmeter or a test light may be used for this test. Connect the test light wire to ground and the probe end to the BAT terminal at the distributor. If the light comes on, you have voltage to the distributor. If the light fails to come on, this indicates an open circuit in the ignition primary wiring leading to the distributor. In this case, you will have to check wiring continuity back to the ignition switch using a test light. If there is battery voltage at the BAT terminal, but no spark at the plugs, then the problem lies within the distributor assembly. Go on to the distributor components test section.

If the engine runs, but runs roughly or cuts out, make sure the plug wires are in good shape first. There should be no obvious cracks or breaks. You can check the plug wires with an ohmmeter, but do not pierce the wires with a probe.

If the plug wires are OK, remove the cap assembly and check for moisture, cracks, chips, carbon tracks, or any other high voltage leaks or failures. Replace the cap if any defects are found. Make sure the timer wheel rotates when the engine is cranked. If everything is all right so far, go on to the distributor components test section.

## DISTRIBUTOR COMPONENTS TESTING

▶ **See Figures 19 and 20**

If the trouble has been narrowed down to the units within the distributor, the following tests can help pinpoint the defective component. An ohmmeter with both high and low ranges should be used. These tests are made with the cap assembly removed and the battery wire disconnected. If a tachometer is

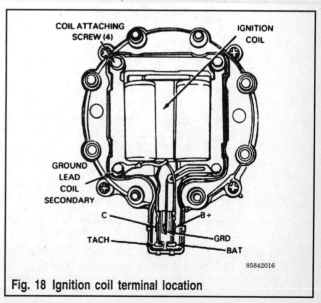

**Fig. 18 Ignition coil terminal location**

connected to the TACH terminal, disconnect it before making these tests.

1. Connect an ohmmeter between the TACH and BAT terminals in the distributor cap. The primary coil resistance should be 0Ω or nearly 0Ω. If not replace the coil.

2. To check the coil secondary resistance, connect an ohmmeter between the rotor button and the BAT terminal. Note the reading. Connect the ohmmeter between the rotor button and the TACH terminal. Note the reading. The resistance in both cases should be between 6,000 and 30,000Ω. Be sure to test between the rotor button and both the BAT and TACH terminals.

3. Replace the coil only if the readings in Step 1 and Step 2 are infinite resistance or out of specification.

➡These resistance checks will not disclose shorted coil windings. This condition can only be detected with scope analysis or a suitably designed coil tester. If these instruments are unavailable, replace the coil with a known good coil as a final coil test.

4. To test the pick-up coil, first disconnect the white and green module leads. Set the ohmmeter on the high scale and connect it between a ground and either the white or green lead. Any resistance measurement less than infinite requires replacement of the pick-up coil.

5. Pick-up coil continuity is tested by connecting the ohmmeter (on low range) between the white and green leads. Normal resistance is between 650 and 850Ω, or 500 and 1,500Ω on 1977 and later models. Move the vacuum advance arm while performing this test (early models). This will detect any break in coil continuity. Such a condition can cause intermittent misfiring. Replace the pick-up coil if the reading is outside the specified limits.

6. If no defects have been found at this time, and you still have a problem, then the module will have to be checked. If you do not have access to a module tester, the only possible alternative is a substitution test. If the module fails the substitution test, replace it.

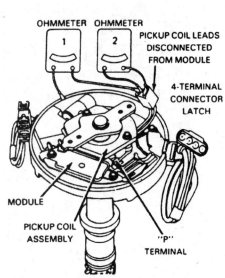

REMOVE ROTOR THEN REMOVE PICKUP COIL LEADS FROM MODULE.

CONNECT OHMMETER TEST 1 AND THEN TEST 2.

FLEX LEADS BY HAND TO CHECK FOR INTERMITTENT OPENS.

TEST 1 – SHOULD READ INFINITE AT ALL TIMES.
TEST 2 – SHOULD READ STEADY AT ONE VALUE WITHIN 500-1500 OHM RANGE.
NOTE: OHMMETER MAY DEFLECT IF TURNING SHAFT CAUSES TEETH TO ALIGN. THIS IS NOT A DEFECT.

85842018

**Fig. 20 Pick-up coil testing**

## Adjustments

All Buick, Olds and Pontiac models covered in this guide are equipped with electronic ignition systems using the HEI (High Energy Ignition) distributors. Dwell angle is permanently set on these units, requiring no adjustment or checking. There are no ignition points or other electro-mechanical parts to service.

## Component Replacement

### INTERNAL IGNITION COIL

▶ See Figures 21, 22 and 23

1. Disconnect the negative battery cable.
2. Disconnect the feed and module wire terminal connectors from the distributor cap.
3. Remove the ignition set retainer.

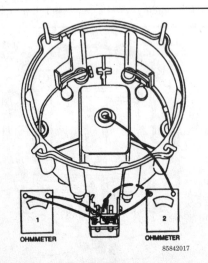

85842017

**Fig. 19 Checking coil resistance. Ohmmeter 1 shows primary test. Ohmmeter 2 shows secondary test.**

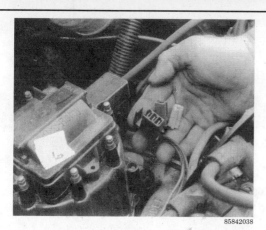

Fig. 21 To gain access to the internal coil, first disconnect the feed and module wires. Note: Spark plug wires were removed for illustration purposes only, this will be unnecessary during actual service

Fig. 22 Removing the coil attaching screws

Fig. 23 Remove the coil cover from the distributor cap

Fig. 24 Push down and twist the retainers to release the distributor cap, be sure to label the cap and wires to ease installation

Fig. 25 Once all four retainers have been released, the distributor cap can be removed

4. Remove the 4 coil cover-to-distributor cap screws and the coil cover.

5. Using a blunt drift, press the coil wire spade terminals up out of distributor cap.

6. Lift the coil up out of the distributor cap.

7. Remove and clean the coil spring, rubber seal washer and coil cavity of the distributor cap.

**To install:**

8. Coat the rubber seal with a dielectric lubricant furnished in the replacement ignition coil package.

9. Install the coil spring, coil assembly and press the coil terminals into the distributor cap. Refer to the coil terminal illustration for terminal location.

10. Install the coil cover and torque the attaching screws to 60 inch lbs. (6 Nm).

11. Position the spark plug wire and retainer over the correct cap terminals, then engage the retainer and plug wires to the cap. Attach the distributor feed wires and negative battery cable.

## DISTRIBUTOR CAP

▶ **See Figures 24 and 25**

1. Disconnect the negative battery cable.
2. Remove the air cleaner, feed and module wire terminal connectors from the distributor cap.
3. Remove the retainer and spark plug wires from the cap. Remember to label them first.
4. Depress and release the 4 distributor cap-to-housing retainers and lift off the cap assembly.
5. Remove the four coil cover screws and cover.
6. Using a finger or a blunt drift, push the coil spade terminals up out of the distributor cap.
7. Remove all four coil screws and lift the coil, coil spring and rubber seal washer out of the cap coil cavity.
8. Using a new distributor cap, reverse the above procedures to assemble being sure to clean and lubricate the rubber seal washer with dielectric lubricant. Torque the coil cover attaching screws to 60 inch lbs. (6 Nm). Make sure the spark plug wire retainer and the four cap-to-housing retainers are fully engaged. Connect the negative battery cable.

## ROTOR

▶ **See Figures 26 and 27**

1. Disconnect the negative battery cable and remove the air cleaner assembly.
2. Disconnect the feed and module wire connectors from the distributor.
3. Depress and release the 4 distributor cap-to-housing retainers and lift off the cap assembly.
4. Remove the two rotor attaching screws and rotor.
5. Install the rotor, make sure the square shaft tab is properly engaged with the rotor and torque the retaining screws to 60 inch lbs. (6 Nm). Reinstall the cap and connect the negative battery cable.

**Fig. 26 Removing the rotor attaching screws**

**Fig. 27 Lift the rotor straight up after removing the attaching screws**

## VACUUM ADVANCE UNIT

### 1975-80

1. Disconnect the negative battery cable and remove the air cleaner. Remove the distributor cap and rotor as previously described.
2. Disconnect the vacuum hose from the vacuum advance unit.
3. Remove the two vacuum advance retaining screws, pull the advance unit outward, rotate and disengage the operating rod from its tang.
4. Install the vacuum advance and engage the operating rod, torque the screws to 60 inch lbs. (6 Nm) and install the distributor cap.
5. Install the air cleaner and connect the negative battery cable.

## MODULE

▶ **See Figures 28 and 29**

1. Disconnect the negative battery cable. Remove the air cleaner.
2. Remove the distributor cap and rotor as previously described.
3. Disconnect the harness connector and pick-up coil spade connectors from the module. Be careful not to damage the wires when removing the connector.
4. Remove the two screws and module from the distributor housing.
5. Coat the bottom of the new module with dielectric silicone lubricant supplied with the new module.
  **To install:**

➡ **The silicone lubricant supplied with new modules MUST be applied, as it serves as a heat conductor and aids in module cooling. Running the engine and ignition system without the silicone lubricant is the equivalent of running the engine without antifreeze! That is, the module will cook itself without the lubricant!**

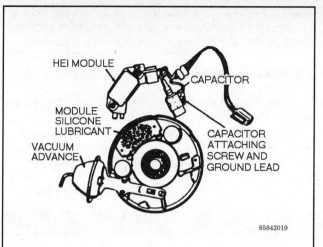

**Fig. 28 Be sure to coat the mating surfaces of the module**

6. Install the module and torque the retaining screws to 48 inch lbs. (5 Nm).

7. Connect the module wiring harnesses and install the distributor cap.

8. Connect the negative battery cable and install the air cleaner.

## PICK-UP COIL

▶ **See Figures 30, 31, 32 and 33**

1. Disconnect the negative battery cable.
2. Remove the air cleaner assembly.
3. Mark the base of the distributor and the position of the rotor-to-housing. Remove the distributor-to-engine block retainer and bolt. Make sure the distributor base is marked with a scribe or grease pen for proper timing after installation.
4. Remove the distributor cap and disconnect the cap harnesses.
5. Twist and pull upward to remove the distributor assembly from the block.

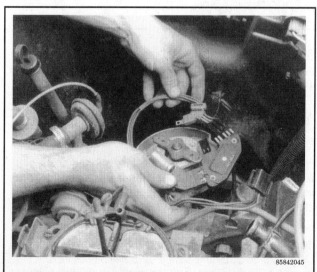

**Fig. 29 Disconnecting the module connector**

6. Mark the distributor shaft and gear so they can be reassembled in the position.

7. Drive out the roll pin with a flat punch or equivalent.

8. Remove the gear and pull the shaft out of the distributor housing.

9. Disconnect the pick-up harness.

10. Remove the three pick-up coil attaching screws and remove the magnetic shield, C washer, pick-up coil, magnet and pole piece.

**To install:**

11. Install the pick-up coil so wires go through the opening provided.

12. Install the magnet, pole piece and torque the three screws to 50 inch lbs. (5 Nm).

13. Clean the shaft with solvent to remove the varnish to ease installation.

14. Install the C washer, shaft, gear and tap in the roll pin. Make sure the marks are lined up. Connect the pick-up wiring harness.

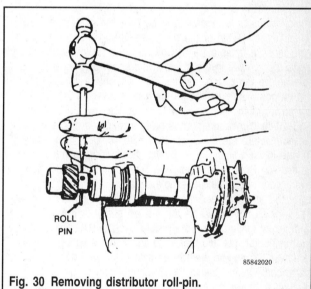

**Fig. 30 Removing distributor roll-pin.**

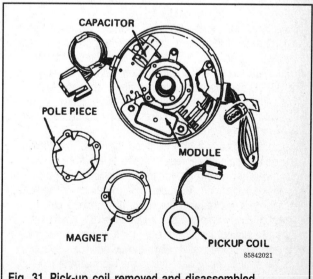

**Fig. 31 Pick-up coil removed and disassembled**

15. Install the distributor into the block at the original marked position.

**Make sure the distributor seats into the block fully. The base of the housing will stick up about ¼ of an inch until the distributor gear engages the oil pump drive. Damage to the oil pump, distributor and engine may result if the distributor is forced into position by tightening the distributor retainer bolt. If the distributor will not fully seat, grab the housing and shaft, twist and wiggle until the distributor drops into the oil pump drive. If this does not work,**

**install a socket wrench onto the large bolt on the front of the crankshaft pulley. Slowly turn the crankshaft in either direction until the distributor drops into the block fully.**

16. Install the distributor and retainer. Hand tighten the bolt at this time.
17. Install the distributor cap, connect the wiring harness and negative battery cable.
18. Plug all disconnected vacuum lines, install a inductive timing light and adjust the timing to specifications. Refer to the underhood sticker and timing procedures in this section for more information.
19. Install the air cleaner and connect the vacuum hoses.

## IGNITION TIMING

### Timing

▶ **See Figures 34 and 35**

Ignition timing is the measurement, in degrees of crankshaft rotation, of the point at which the spark plugs fire in each of the cylinders. It is measured in degrees before or after Top Dead Center (TDC) of the compression stroke.

Because it takes a fraction of a second for the spark plug to ignite the mixture in the cylinder, the spark plug must fire a little before the piston reaches TDC. Otherwise, the mixture will not be completely ignited as the piston passes TDC and the full power of the explosion will not be used by the engine.

The timing measurement is given in degrees of crankshaft rotation before the piston reaches TDC (BTDC). If the setting for the ignition timing is 5° BTDC, the spark plug must fire 5° before each piston reaches TDC. This only holds true, however, when the engine is at idle speed.

As the engine speed increases, the pistons go faster. The spark plugs have to ignite the fuel even sooner if it is to be completely ignited when the piston reaches TDC. To do this, the distributor has two means to advance the timing of the spark as the engine speed increases. This is accomplished by centrifugal weights within the distributor, and a vacuum diaphragm mounted on the side of the distributor (early models). The later model engines control the spark timing through the ECM (Electronic Control Module).

If the ignition is set too far advanced (BTDC), the ignition and expansion of the fuel in the cylinder will occur too soon and cause engine ping. If the ignition spark is set too far retarded, after TDC (ATDC), the piston will have already passed TDC and started on its way down when the fuel is ignited. This will cause the piston to be forced down for only a portion of its travel. This will result in poor engine performance and lack of power.

Timing marks consist of a notch on the rim of the crankshaft pulley and a scale of degrees attached to the front of the engine. The notch corresponds to the position of the piston in the number 1 cylinder. A stroboscopic (dynamic) timing light is used, which is hooked into the circuit of the No. 1 cylinder spark plug. Every time the spark plug fires, the timing light flashes. By aiming the timing light at the timing marks, the exact position of the piston within the cylinder can be read, since the stroboscopic flash makes the mark on the pulley

appear to be standing still. Proper timing is indicated when the notch is aligned with the correct number on the scale.

There are three basic types of timing lights available. The first is a simple neon bulb with two wire connections (one for the spark plug and one for the plug wire, connecting the light in series). This type of light is quite dim, and must be held closely to the marks to be seen, but it is inexpensive. The second type of light operates from the vehicle's battery. Two alligator clips connect to the battery terminals, while a third wire connects to the spark plug with an adapter. This type of light is more expensive, but the xenon bulb provides a nice bright flash which can even be seen in sunlight. The third type replaces the battery source with 110 volt house current. Some timing lights have other functions built into them, such as dwell meters, tachometers, or remote starting switches. These are convenient, in that they reduce the tangle of wires under the hood, but may duplicate the functions of the tools you already have.

If your vehicle has electronic ignition, you should use a timing light with an inductive pickup. This pickup simply clamps onto the No. 1 spark plug wire, eliminating the adapter. It is not susceptible to cross firing or false triggering, which may occur with a conventional light, due to the greater voltages produced by the electronic ignition.

## INSPECTION & ADJUSTMENT

**Non-ESC Models**

➡**The non-ESC (Electronic Spark Controlled) vehicles are equipped with a vacuum advance unit at the distributor.**

1. Warm the engine to normal operating temperature. Shut off the engine and connect the timing light to the No. 1 spark plug, located on the left (driver's side) front of the engine.

➡**DO NOT, under any circumstances, pierce a spark plug wire to hook up the light. Once the insulation is broken, voltage will jump to the nearest ground, and the spark plug will not fire properly.**

2. Clean off the timing marks and mark the pulley or damper notch and the timing scale with white chalk or paint. The timing notch on the damper or pulley can be elusive. Bump the engine around with the starter or turn the crankshaft

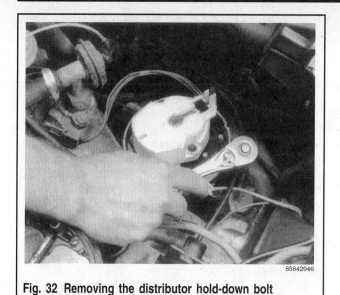

Fig. 32 Removing the distributor hold-down bolt

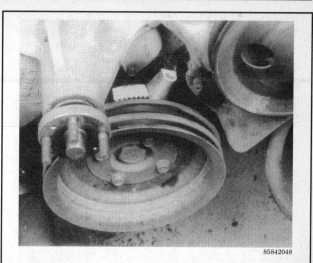

Fig. 35 Timing indicator on an Olds 307 (VIN Y); all models similar

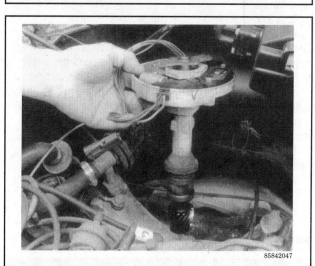

Fig. 33 After removing the distributor, be sure to mark the gear and distributor shaft

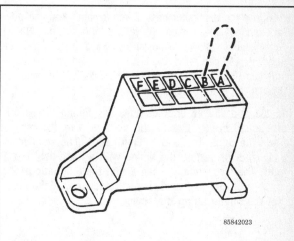

Fig. 36 For ESC equipped vehicles, ground the A and B terminals at the ALDL. This is usually located next to the fuse panel.

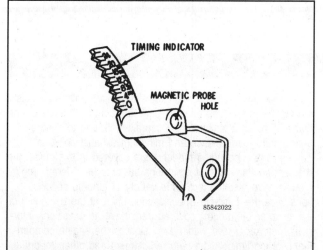

Fig. 34 Timing indicator, located just above the harmonic balancer

with a wrench on the front pulley bolt to get it to an accessible position.

3. Disconnect and plug the vacuum advance hose at the distributor, to prevent any distributor advance. The vacuum line is the rubber hose connected to the metal cone-shaped canister on the side of the distributor. A short screw, pencil, or a golf tee can be used to plug the hose.

4. Start the engine and adjust the idle speed to that specified in the Tune-Up Specifications chart. If the chart differs from the underhood emissions label, use the specs on the label. Some vehicles require that the timing be set with the transmission in Neutral. You can disconnect the idle solenoid, if any, to get the speed down. Otherwise, adjust the idle speed screw. This is to prevent any centrifugal advance of timing in the distributor.

On 1975-77 HEI systems, the tachometer connects to the TACH terminal on the distributor and to a ground. For 1978 and later models, all tachometer connections are to the TACH terminal. Some tachometers must connect to the TACH terminal and to the positive battery terminal. Some tachometers won't work at all with HEI. Consult the tachometer manufacturer if the instructions supplied with the unit do not give the proper connection.

### ✳✳CAUTION

**Never ground the HEI TACH terminal; serious system damage will result, including module burnout.**

5. Aim the timing light at the timing marks. Be careful not to touch the fan, which may appear to be standing still. Keep your clothes and hair, and the light's wires clear of the fan, belts, and pulleys. If the pulley or damper notch is not aligned with the proper timing mark (see the Tune-Up Specifications chart or Underhood Emissions Label), the timing will have to be adjusted.

➡**TDC or Top Dead Center corresponds to 0 degrees, Before Top Dead Center or BTDC may also be shown as BEFORE; A, ATDC, or After Top Dead Center, may be shown as AFTER.**

6. Loosen the distributor base clamp locknut. You can buy special wrenches which make this task a lot easier on V8s. Turn the distributor slowly to adjust the timing, holding it by the body and not the cap. Turn the distributor in the direction of rotor rotation (found in the Firing Order illustration) to retard, and against the direction to advance.

➡**The 231 and 252 V6 engines have two timing marks on the crankshaft pulley. One timing mark is ⅛ in. (3.1mm) wide and the other, is ¹/₁₆ in. (1.6mm) wide. The smaller mark is used for setting the timing with a hand-held timing light. The larger mark is used with the magnetic probe and is only of use to a professional mechanic. Make sure you set the timing using the smaller mark.**

7. Tighten the locknut. Check the timing, in case the distributor moved as you tightened it.
8. Replace the distributor vacuum hose, if removed. Correct the idle speed.
9. Shut off the engine and disconnect the light.

### ESC Models
▶ **See Figure 36**

➡**ESC (Electronic Spark Control) equipped models do not have a vacuum advance unit on the distributor. The spark is controlled by the ECM (Electronic Control Module). ESC distributors have a four wire connector instead of a vacuum advance unit.**

1. The timing marks are the same as the non-ESC vehicles. Refer to the underhood sticker for proper timing procedures and specifications. If there is no sticker, follow these procedures to adjust ignition timing.
2. Start the engine and allow it to reach normal operating temperature.
3. If equipped, make sure the air conditioner is turned OFF.
4. Ground the Diagnostic terminal of the ALDL (Assembly Line Diagnostic Link) located under the dash panel on the left (driver) side. Using a small piece of wire, ground the A to B terminal as in the ALDL terminal illustration in this section.
5. Using a timing light, set the timing at the specified rpm by loosening the distributor hold-down clamp and rotating the distributor until the specified timing is obtained at the timing marks on the crankshaft pulley.
6. Tighten the hold-down clamp and recheck the timing to ensure the distributor has not moved during this procedures.
7. With the engine RUNNING, remove the ground wire at the ALDL under the dash panel. The engine should be running so no trouble codes are stored in the ECM.
8. Make any necessary carburetor adjustments and reconnect any removed vacuum lines.

## Valve Lash

All engines covered in this guide are equipped with hydraulic valve lifters. Engines so equipped operate with zero clearance in the valve train; because of this the rocker arms are non-adjustable. The hydraulic lifters themselves do not require any adjustment as part of the normal tune-up, although they occasionally become noisy (especially on high mileage engines) and need to be replaced. Hydraulic lifter service is covered in Section 3.

## IDLE SPEED AND MIXTURE ADJUSTMENTS

To check idle speed, a tachometer is used. On 1975-77 HEI systems, the tachometer connects to the TACH terminal on the distributor and to a ground. For 1978 and later models, all tachometer connections are to the TACH terminal. Some tachometers must connect to the TACH terminal and to the positive battery terminal. Some tachometers won't work at all with HEI. Consult the tachometer manufacturer if the instructions supplied with the unit do not give the proper connection.

### ✳✳CAUTION

**Never ground the HEI TACH terminal; serious system damage will result, including module burnout.**

Idle mixture and idle speed adjustments are critical aspects of engine tune-up and exhaust emission control. It is important that all tune-up instructions be carefully followed to ensure good engine performance and minimum exhaust pollution. Through the succeeding model years covered in this guide, the different combinations of emissions systems on different engine models have resulted in a wide variety of tune-up specifications. See the Tune-Up Specifications chart at the beginning of this chapter. All models covered here have an emissions information sticker placed within easy sight in the engine compartment, giving timing, carburetor adjustment and other important tune-up information. If there is any difference between the specifications listed in this guide and those on your vehicle's emissions sticker, always follow the specs on the sticker.

The following carburetor adjustment procedures are listed by year, carburetor type, and engine displacement and code where necessary (consult the Engine Identification Code chart in this guide), as many of the carburetors covered are used simultaneously by all four GM divisions. Other carburetor adjustments and maintenance are found in Section 5.

➡ **Idle mixture screws have been preset and capped at the factory. The caps should be removed only in the case of major carburetor overhaul, or if all other possible causes of poor idle have been thoroughly checked. If you must adjust the idle mixture, have the carbon monoxide (CO) concentration checked at a professional shop equipped with a CO meter. Mixture adjustments are included only where it is possible for the owner/mechanic to perform them.**

## Curb Idle

## ADJUSTMENTS

◆ **See Figures 37, 38, 39, 40, 41, 42 and 43**

**Rochester 2GC, GE, GV**

1. With the engine at normal operating temperature, remove the air cleaner and disconnect the air cleaner vacuum hose at the intake manifold. Plug the fitting with a clean rag.
2. Make sure the choke plate is open and the air conditioning is off.
3. Set the parking brake and block the drive wheels.
4. Disconnect the evaporative emission hose from the air cleaner.
5. Disconnect the hose from the E.G.R. valve. Plug the hose to the carburetor with a golf tee or pencil.
6. Connect a tachometer to the engine.
7. Check, and if necessary, adjust the timing.
8. On cars without A/C, open the throttle momentarily to extend the solenoid plunger. Turn the solenoid screw to adjust the speed to the curb idle rpm listed on the underhood sticker. Turn the idle speed screw to the specified rpm.
9. On cars with A/C, turn the idle speed screw to obtain the specified rpm. Disconnect the A/C compressor wire and turn the A/C on. Open the throttle momentarily to extend the solenoid plunger. Turn the solenoid screw to adjust the speed to the curb idle rpm listed on the underhood sticker.
10. Reconnect all hoses and wires. Disconnect the tachometer.

### 1975-76 Rochester M4MC

1. Run the engine to normal operating temperature. Remove the air cleaner and disconnect the air cleaner vacuum hose at the intake manifold. Plug the fitting with a clean rag.
2. Make sure the choke plate is open and the air conditioning turned off.
3. Set the parking brake and block the rear wheels. Connect a tachometer to the engine.
4. Disconnect and plug the carburetor hoses from the vapor canister and the E.G.R. valve. Plug the hoses with golf tees or pencils.

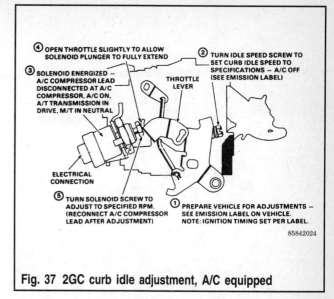

**Fig. 37 2GC curb idle adjustment, A/C equipped**

5. With the timing adjusted properly, set the slow idle screw to obtain 550 rpm (non-California 350 and 455 cu. in. V8s) or 600 rpm (Calif.) in **DRIVE**. Adjust 400 V8s to 650 rpm in **DRIVE**. If the sticker specs vary from these, adjust to sticker specifications.

## ✳✳CAUTION

**When adjusting idle speeds with the vehicle in DRIVE, always have a helper in the vehicle with his or her foot on the brake and the parking brake fully applied.**

6. Adjust the idle speed-up solenoid on 350 and 455 V8s with air conditioning off to 650 rpm. The air conditioning compressor wires must be disconnected at the air conditioning compressor, and the transmission must be in **DRIVE**.
7. Reconnect the compressor wires and reconnect all hoses.

**All Other Models To 1982**

*WITHOUT A/C*

1. On non-air conditioned vehicles equipped with the idle solenoid, open the throttle (with solenoid energized) to allow the plunger to extend.
2. Adjust the solenoid screw to obtain the specified solenoid energized idle rpm.
3. Disconnect the electrical lead attached to the solenoid. With the solenoid de-energized, adjust the idle speed screw to obtain the specified curb idle rpm.

*WITH A/C*

1. Adjust the idle speed screw until the engine is turning the specified curb idle rpm.
2. Disconnect the air conditioning compressor clutch lead at the compressor.
3. Turn on the air conditioning to energize the idle solenoid. Place the transmission in **DRIVE**, making sure the parking brake is firmly applied and that a helper is in the vehicle

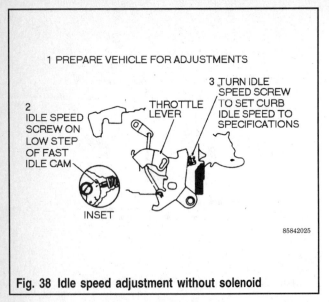

1 PREPARE VEHICLE FOR ADJUSTMENTS

2 IDLE SPEED SCREW ON LOW STEP OF FAST IDLE CAM

THROTTLE LEVER

3 TURN IDLE SPEED SCREW TO SET CURB IDLE SPEED TO SPECIFICATIONS

INSET

85842025

**Fig. 38 Idle speed adjustment without solenoid**

with his or her foot on the brake. Open the throttle slightly to allow the solenoid plunger to fully extend.

### ❊❊CAUTION

**When adjusting idle speeds with the vehicle in DRIVE, always have a helper in the vehicle with his or her foot on the brake and the parking brake fully applied.**

4. Adjust the idle solenoid screw to obtain the specified solenoid energized rpm.

5. Reconnect the air conditioning compressor clutch lead and disconnect the tachometer.

### Idle Load Compensator Adjustment

➡**To accomplish this adjustment, you'll need not only a tachometer, but a special adjusting tool J-29607, BT-8022 or equivalent, a ³⁄₃₂ in. hex key, and a spare rubber cap, drilled to accept this key.**

1. Prepare the vehicle for adjustment by following instructions on the engine compartment sticker.

2. Connect a tachometer to the distributor side of the TACH filter or other connector. Remove the air cleaner. Disconnect and plug vacuum hoses going to: the Thermal Vacuum Valve, EGR valve, the canister purge port, and the ILC (Idle Load Compensator).

3. Back out the idle stop screw on the carburetor three turns. Make sure air conditioning is OFF. Set the parking brake, put the transmission in **PARK**, and block the drive wheels.

4. Start the engine. If it is not hot already, idle it until it is warm (water flowing through the radiator). Hold the jam nut with a wrench while you turn the plunger as necessary to obtain 725 rpm. Make sure to hold the nut securely as, if it turns, it could damage guide tabs.

5. Now, remove the plug and reconnect the ILC vacuum hose to the ILC port. Read the idle speed on the tach. It should be 500 rpm in **DRIVE**. Have someone apply the brake pedal and put the transmission in Drive before taking your reading. If the reading meets specification, proceed to Step 11. Otherwise, proceed with the steps below.

### ❊❊CAUTION

**When adjusting idle speeds with the vehicle in DRIVE, always have a helper in the vehicle with his or her foot on the brake and the parking brake fully applied.**

6. Stop the engine, remove the ILC, and then plug the vacuum hose leading to it with a rubber plug.

7. Remove the rubber cap from the center outlet tube of the ILC and, if there is one, remove the metal plug from the tube. Install the ILC back onto the carburetor and re-attach any items that were detached, such as the throttle return spring. Remove the plug from the vacuum hose and reconnect the hose to the ILC.

8. Install the rubber cap through which you have drilled a hole with the hex wrench passing through the hole in the cap. Engage the wrench with the adjusting screw inside the ILC.

9. Have a helper start the engine with the brake applied and put the transmission in **DRIVE**. Then, adjust the wrench until the rpm is 500. Turn the screw counterclockwise to increase speed and clockwise to decrease it. One turn equals

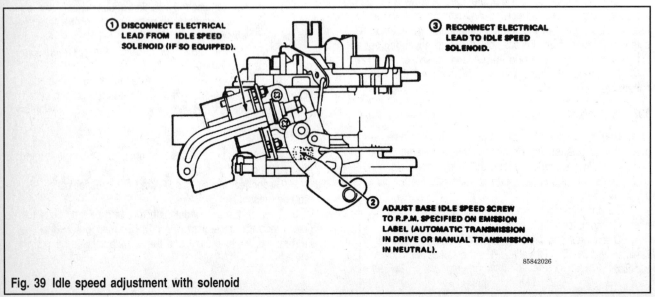

① DISCONNECT ELECTRICAL LEAD FROM IDLE SPEED SOLENOID (IF SO EQUIPPED).

③ RECONNECT ELECTRICAL LEAD TO IDLE SPEED SOLENOID.

② ADJUST BASE IDLE SPEED SCREW TO R.P.M. SPECIFIED ON EMISSION LABEL (AUTOMATIC TRANSMISSION IN DRIVE OR MANUAL TRANSMISSION IN NEUTRAL).

85842026

**Fig. 39 Idle speed adjustment with solenoid**

about 75-100 rpm. When 500 rpm is attained, remove the wrench and drilled cap. Replace the complete rubber cap.

10. If the rpm is not correct, you'll have to repeat the adjustment, allowing for the amount and direction of the discrepancy. For example, if the rpm is 450, turn the screw one half turn counterclockwise. The adjustment is not correct until the engine runs at 500 rpm with the complete rubber cap installed.

11. With the engine running and transmission in **DRIVE**, as before, measure the distance from the jam nut to the tip of the plunger (Dimension A). It must not exceed 1 in. (25.4mm).

12. Disconnect and plug the vacuum hose again. Apply a vacuum source such as a vacuum pump to the port to fully retract the plunger. Now, adjust the idle stop screw on the carburetor float bowl to give 500 rpm in **DRIVE**. Then, put the transmission in **PARK**, and turn the engine off.

13. Remove vacuum hose plugs and reconnect all hoses. Reinstall the air cleaner.

### I.S.C. Adjustment

**➡Used on the E4ME and E2ME carburetors, this device controls idle speed electronically via the Electronic Control Module. It is factory adjusted and does not require adjustment as a matter of routine maintenance. If diagnostic work on the vehicle indicates that idle speed is not to specification, it may be adjusted. A special tool J-29607, BT-8022 or equivalent is required to make the adjustment. The plunger has an unusual head to discourage tampering. You'll also need separate tach and dwell meters.**

1. Look at the unthreaded portion of the adjustable plunger, just below the head, for a letter code. If there is a letter, note what it is for later use, and then go on to the next step. Except on the 3.8L V6 in 1986-87, if there is no letter, use the special wrench to remove the plunger by unscrewing it. Then, measure the length (Dimension A) from the threaded end to the inner surface of the head. Note and record this dimension for later use. On the 3.8L V6 in 1986-87, use the second line of the chart, showing dimensions of $^{41}/_{64}$ in. (16mm) and $^{5}/_{16}$ in. (8mm).

2. Prepare the engine for adjustments as detailed on the engine compartment sticker. Connect a tachometer, using the distributor side of the tach filter, if one is used.

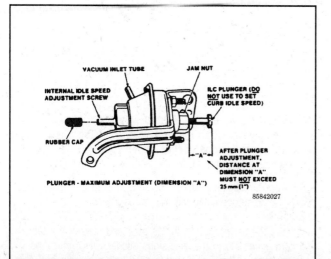

**Fig. 40 Adjusting Idle Load Compensator on 1983-1990 models**

### Idle Speed Control Adjustment Chart

| Identification Letter | Plunger Length (in.) | Dimension "B" (in.) |
|---|---|---|
| NONE | $^{9}/_{16}$ | $^{7}/_{32}$ |
| NONE | $4^{1}/_{64}$ | $^{5}/_{16}$ |
| X | $47/_{64}$ | $25/_{64}$ |
| A | $49/_{64}$ | $27/_{64}$ |
| Y | $51/_{64}$ | $15/_{32}$ |
| S | $27/_{32}$ | $^{1}/_{2}$ |
| Z | $^{7}/_{8}$ | $35/_{63}$ |
| G | $29/_{32}$ | $37/_{64}$ |
| E | 1 | $43/_{64}$ |
| L | $13/_{32}$ | $^{3}/_{4}$ |
| J | $13/_{16}$ | $27/_{32}$ |
| N | $1^{17}/_{64}$ | $59/_{64}$ |
| T | $1^{11}/_{32}$ | 1 |

85842028

**Fig. 41 ISC plunger identification**

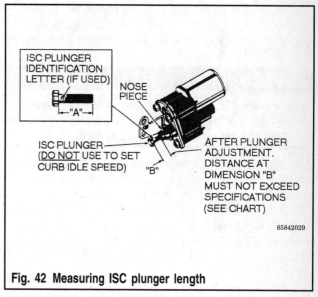

**Fig. 42 Measuring ISC plunger length**

3. Connect a dwell meter to the mixture control solenoid (M/C) dwell lead. Set the dwell meter (or read the meter) on the six cylinder scale regardless of the type of engine.

4. Turn the A/C off.

5. Start the engine and run it until the ECM system enters closed loop operation. At this point the dwell meter reading will begin to vary, indicating that the oxygen sensor is regulating fuel flow through a solenoid in the carburetor.

6. Now, turn the ignition switch off and unplug the connector going to the ISC motor.

7. Ground the **D** terminal of the motor connection (see illustration) with a jumper wire. Then, connect another jumper wire from the battery positive terminal to the **C** connection while simultaneously applying pressure with your finger to the plunger to help it retract. If the plunger is not assisted in this way, the internals of the ISC may be damaged. Also, as soon as the plunger is retracted, remove the 12 volt jumper to prevent damage to the ISC. Make sure you make the right connections. If you were to connect across terminals **A** and **B**, this also would cause ISC damage.

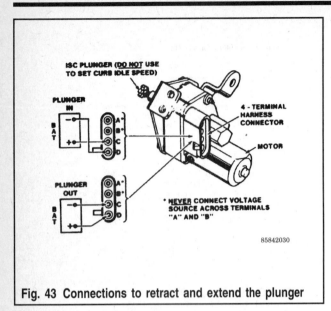

**Fig. 43 Connections to retract and extend the plunger**

8. Block drive wheels and apply the parking brake. Start the engine and run it until the dwell meter reading varies. Then, put the transmission in **DRIVE**. Make sure the carburetor is not on the fast idle cam.

## ✳✳CAUTION

**When adjusting idle speeds with the vehicle in DRIVE, always have a helper in the vehicle with his or her foot on the brake and the parking brake fully applied.**

9. Now, note the rpm on the tach and adjust the carburetor slow idle stop screw (minimum authority) to the lower figure shown in the tune-up chart. Then put it back in **PARK**.

10. Now, ground terminal **C** again, and jumper the 12 volt source to terminal **D** to fully extend the plunger. Leave the power connected only long enough to extend the plunger, or the ISC may be damaged. Again, make sure you are making the right connection.

With the transmission in **PARK**, use the special tool to preset the plunger for 1,500 rpm. Then, set the parking brake and block the drive wheels and put the transmission in **DRIVE**, have a helper in the car with the parking brake applied and his or her foot on the brake. Then, use the special tool to turn the plunger to get the higher figure (Maximum Authority) shown in the tune-up chart.

Now reapply power as described in Step 10 to make sure the plunger is fully extended. Recheck the Maximum Authority rpm to make sure it is still correct. Readjust if necessary.

11. Now measure dimension **B**, as shown in the illustration. This is the distance from the back side of the plunger head to the front surface of the nose piece-the portion of the assembly the plunger fits into. This is the dimension you determined in Step 1. If the dimension should be too great, adjust the plunger with the special tool until it is within the specified limit.

12. Fully retract the plunger by jumping to connections as described in Step 7. Put the transmission in **PARK**. Turn the ignition switch off. Remove all instruments and jumper wires and reconnect the ISC motor connector. On engines using the E2ME 2-barrel carburetor, an INTERMITTENT trouble code will be sent. To clear this, you must remove battery voltage from the ECM (Electronic Control Module). With the ignition off, pull the fuse in the fuse box which is labeled ECM. The power must be interrupted for 10 seconds and **MUST ONLY** be interrupted with the ignition switch **OFF**.

### Throttle Body Fuel Injection

This is a simple procedure, but it is never performed in routine maintenance. It is required after throttle body replacement, only. See Section 5 for applicable procedures.

## Fast Idle

➡Refer to the underhood sticker for all carburetor adjustments. If there is no sticker present, refer to the procedures and illustrations that closely resemble your fuel system. Read all procedures carefully and understand them before performing any adjustments to your vehicle.

## ADJUSTMENTS

### 1975-76 2GC, GE, GV

➡The fast idle is present on some Oldsmobile 400 V8 engines when the slow idle is adjusted.

1. Place the fast idle cam follower on the low step of the fast idle cam, against the shoulder of the next higher step.
2. Adjust the fast idle screw to obtain the following specified idle speeds (with transmission in **PARK**):
   - 900 rpm, 350 V8 (non-Calif.)
   - 1000 rpm, 350 V8 (Calif.)
   - 1800 rpm, 400 V8 (where adjustable)

### 1975-76 M4MC

1. On 350 and 455 V8s, place the fast idle cam follower on the lowest step of the fast idle cam against the shoulder of the next highest step. Adjust the fast idle screw to 900 rpm in **PARK**.
2. On 400 cu. in. V8s, place the cam follower on the highest step of the fast idle cam. Adjust the fast idle screw until the engine is turning 800 rpm in **PARK**.
3. Reconnect all hoses and install the air cleaner. Disconnect the tach.

### 1977 Models

No fast idle adjustment is necessary, as the fast idle is automatically adjusted when the curb idle is set.

### 1978-80 Models

➡The fast idle on all 231 V6 and some 305 V8 engines is automatically set when the curb idle adjustment is made. Refer to the emissions sticker under your vehicle's hood for this specific application.

Prepare the engine and vehicle according to the emissions sticker before proceeding with the steps below.
   **Buick V8**
1. Set the cam follower on the specified step of the fast idle cam according to the emissions sticker. Disconnect the vacuum hose at the E.G.R. valve on 2-barrel models and plug this.

2. Turn the fast idle screw out until the butterfly valves in the primary throttle boxes are closed. You can see this by looking down into the carburetor; the butterfly valves are at the bottom of the bores.

3. Turn the fast idle screw in to adjust the idle speed to specifications. On 4-barrel models, turn the fast idle screw in until it just contacts the lever, then turn it in an additional three turns. Adjust to specified rpm.

**Pontiac V8**

1. After making all adjustment preparations according to the emissions sticker, place the transmission in **Neutral**.
2. Place the cam follower on the specified step of the fast idle cam.
3. Disconnect and plug the E.G.R. vacuum hose, using a golf tee or pencil, at the E.G.R. valve.
4. Adjust the fast idle speed screw to obtain the specified rpm using a tachometer.

**Oldsmobile V8**

Since the carburetor tuning procedures vary by model and component application, the procedure given on the emissions sticker in the engine compartment should be followed.

**1981-90 Models**

Carburetor adjustment procedures for 1981-90 models vary by model and component application. Follow the procedure on the underhood emissions sticker.

## Idle Mixture

### ADJUSTMENTS

**2GC, GE, GV Models**

1. Adjust the slow idle as outlined above. Keep all hoses disconnected, and keep the tachometer connected. Make sure the parking brake is set and the drive wheels blocked.
2. Break off the mixture tabs, using care not to damage the mixture adjusting screws.
3. Turn out the mixture screws equally until the maximum idle speed is achieved. Turning the screws in richens the mixture. Reset the speed if necessary with the solenoid screw to 80 rpm above specified rpm. If the mixture screws were out of balance, lightly seat both screws then back both out 5 full turns to attain an equal adjustment point.
4. Equally lean (turn in) the mixture screws until the specified idle speed is reached. The carburetor solenoid must be energized for this procedure. Reset the slow idle speed if necessary with the air cleaner in place.

**All Other 2 Barrel Models To 1977**

On models with the air conditioning idle solenoid, energize the solenoid (by opening the throttle slightly so the plunger extends) until the engine is turning the specified solenoid energized rpm. Turn off the A/C and adjust the carburetor idle speed screw to the specified curb idle rpm.

1. Run the engine to normal operating temperature and turn the A/C off. Set the parking brake and block the wheels.

2. Remove the air cleaner for access to the carburetor, but leave the hoses connected. Follow instructions on the emission sticker in disconnecting other hoses.
3. Connect a tachometer to the engine. Disconnect the vacuum advance hose and plug it.
4. Make sure the timing is set correctly, then reconnect the hose.
5. Break off the mixture tabs from the caps.
6. Turn the screws in until they lightly seat themselves, then back both screws out until the engines just idles.
7. Place the transmission in DRIVE.

### **❊❊CAUTION**

**When making adjustments with the vehicle in DRIVE, always have a helper in the car with his or her foot on the brake and the parking brake fully applied .**

8. Back mixture screws out a little at a time equally, until the highest possible idle speed is obtained.
9. Adjust the idle speed to obtain the specified curb idle.
10. Reconnect all hoses and install the air cleaner.

**4 Barrel Models To 1977**

*EXCEPT CALIFORNIA*

1. Run the engine to normal operating temperature. Remove the air cleaner, disconnect the vacuum hose at the intake manifold, and plug the fitting.
2. Make sure the choke plate is open and the air conditioning is off.
3. Block the rear wheels and firmly set the parking brake.
4. Disconnect the carburetor hoses from the vapor (charcoal) canister and E.G.R. valve and plug the hoses with golf tees or pencils. Leave the distributor vacuum hose connected.
5. Break off the mixture tabs from the caps, using care not to damage the screws. Connect a tachometer and an accurate vacuum gauge to the engine.
6. If the mixture screws appear out of balance or the carburetor is being overhauled, turn the screws in until they both lightly seat themselves, then back both screws out equally 3 full turns.
7. Equally richen (turn out) the mixture screws until maximum idle speed is achieved. Note the manifold vacuum reading.
8. With the transmission in DRIVE, adjust the idle speed screw until the engine is turning 580 rpm. Observe the cautions in above sections on tuning an engine while the transmission is in DRIVE.
9. Equally lean (turn in) the mixture screws until the idle speed is 550 rpm. Manifold vacuum should not be reduced more than 2 in. Hg from the reading obtained in Step 7. If the reading is reduced more than 2 in. Hg, repeat the procedure.
10. Reconnect the canister and E.G.R. hoses, and install the air cleaner and air cleaner vacuum hoses. Disconnect the tach.

*CALIFORNIA MODELS*

1. Follow Steps 1 through 5 of the above procedure.
2. Turn in the idle mixture screws until they seat themselves lightly. Equally richen (turn out) the screws 4 full turns. Note the manifold vacuum reading.

3. With the transmission in **DRIVE** (and observing the above Cautions), adjust the idle speed screw so the engine is turning 625 rpm.

4. Equally lean (turn in) the mixture screws until the idle speed is 600 rpm. Manifold vacuum should not be reduced by more than 2 in. Hg from the reading obtained in Step 2. If the reading is less than this, repeat the procedure.

5. Reconnect the distributor, canister, and E.G.R. hoses. Disconnect the vacuum gauge and tachometer.

6. Install the air cleaner and air cleaner vacuum hoses.

### 1978-90 All V6 and V8

These models require extensive carburetor modifications to gain access to mixture adjustments and, in many cases, a number of special tools. Idle mixture on these models is constantly monitored and controlled by computer and only extreme carburetor misadjustment at the factory will necessitate service adjustment.

If your engine does not idle properly, and you have ruled out vacuum leaks and ordinary maintenance problems such as improperly adjusted ignition timing or worn spark plugs, we suggest you have idle mixture checked and adjusted by a competent professional who has the specialized tools and equipment required to do the job.

## Diesel Fuel Injection

## IDLE SPEED ADJUSTMENT

▶ **See Figure 44**

### All 350 V8 Diesels

A special tachometer with an rpm counter suitable for the 350 V8 diesel is necessary for this adjustment; a standard tach suitable for gasoline engines will not work.

1. Place the transmission in **PARK**, block the rear wheels and firmly set the parking brake.

2. If necessary, adjust the throttle linkage as described in Section 7.

3. Start the engine and allow it to warm up for 10-15 minutes.

4. Shut off the engine and remove the air cleaner.

5. Clean off any grime from the timing probe holder on the front cover; also clean off the crankshaft balancer rim.

6. Install the magnetic probe end of the tachometer fully into the timing probe holder. Complete the remaining tachometer connections according to the tach manufacturer's instructions.

7. Disconnect the two-lead connector from the generator.

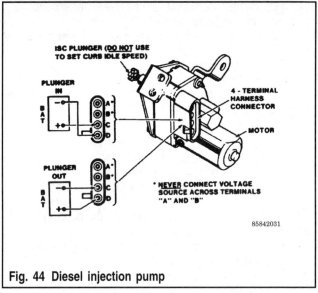

**Fig. 44 Diesel injection pump**

8. Make sure all electrical accessories are OFF.

➡**At no time should either the steering wheel or the brake pedal be touched.**

9. Start the engine and place the transmission in **DRIVE**.

### ✳✳CAUTION

**When adjusting idle speeds with the vehicle in DRIVE, always have the parking brake fully applied.**

10. Check the slow idle speed reading against the one printed on the underhood emissions sticker. Reset if necessary.

11. Unplug the connector from the fast idle cold advance (engine temperature) switch, and install a jumper wire between the connector terminals.

➡**DO NOT allow the jumper to ground.**

12. Check the fast idle speed and reset if necessary according to the specification printed on the underhood emissions sticker.

13. Remove the jumper wire and reconnect it to the temperature switch.

14. Recheck the slow idle speed and reset if necessary.

15. Shut off the engine.

16. Reconnect the leads at the generator and air conditioning compressor.

17. Disconnect and remove the tachometer.

18. If the vehicle is equipped with cruise control, adjust the servo throttle rod to minimum slack, then put the clip in the first free hole closest to the bellcrank or throttle lever.

19. Install the air cleaner.

## GASOLINE ENGINE TUNE-UP SPECIFICATIONS

(When analyzing compression test results, look for uniformity among cylinders rather than specific pressures)

| Year | Engine V.I.N. Code | Engine Type (No. of cyl- C.I.D.) | Engine Manufac- turer | Spark Plugs Orig. Type | Gap (in.) | Distributor Point Dwell (deg.) | Point Gap (in.) | Ignition Timing (deg. B.T.D.C) Automatic Transmission | Intake Valve Opens (°B.T.D.C.) | Fuel Pump Pressure (psi) | Idle Speed (rpm) Automatic Transmission |
|------|------|------|------|------|------|------|------|------|------|------|------|
| **OLDSMOBILE 88, 98, WAGONS** | | | | | | | | | | | |
| **1975** | K | 8-350 | Olds. | R46SX | 0.080 | Electronic | | 20B @ 1100 | 16 | 5.5–6.5 | 650/550 |
| | R, S | 8-400 | Olds. | R45TSX | 0.060 | Electronic | | 16B | 20 | 5.5–6.5 | 650 |
| | T | 8-455 | Olds. | R46SX | 0.080 | Electronic | | 16B @ 1100 | 20 | 5.5–6.5 | 650/550 |
| **1976** | R | 8-350 | Olds. | R45SX | 0.080 | Electronic | | 20B | 16 | 5.5–6.5 | 650① /550 (600) |
| | T | 8-455 | Olds. | R46SX | 0.080 | Electronic | | 16B② | 20 | 5.5–6.5 | 650① /550 (600) |
| **1977** | C | 6-231 | Buick | R46TSX | 0.060③ | Electronic | | 12B | 17 | 5.5–6.5 | 670/600 |
| | F | 8-260 | Olds. | R46SZ | 0.060 | Electronic | | 16B @ 1100 | 14 | 5.5–6.5 | 650/550 |
| | L | 8-350 | Chev. | R45TS | 0.045 | Electronic | | 8B | 28 | 5.5–6.5 | 650/500 |
| | R | 8-350 | Olds. | R46SZ | 0.060 | Electronic | | 20B② @ 1100 | 16 | 5.5–6.5 | 650/550 [700/600] |
| | K | 8-403 | Olds. | R46SZ | 0.060 | Electronic | | 20B @ 1100 | 16 | 5.5–6.5 | 650/550 [700/600] |
| **1978** | A | 6-231 | Buick | R46TSX | 0.060 | Electronic | | 15B | 17 | 5.5–6.5 | 600 |
| | F | 8-260 | Olds. | R46SZ | 0.060 | Electronic | | 18B @ 1100 | 14 | 5.5–6.5 | 550 |
| | R | 8-350 | Olds. | R46SZ | 0.060 | Electronic | | 20B @ 1100 | 16 | 5.5–6.5 | 650 [700] |
| | X | 8-350 | Buick | R46TSX | 0.060 | Electronic | | 15B @ 600 | 16 | 5.5–6.5 | 550 |
| | K | 8-403 | Olds. | R46SZ | 0.060 | Electronic | | 18B④ @ 1100 | 16 | 5.5–6.5 | 550 [600] |
| **1979** | A | 6-231 | Buick | R46TSX | 0.060 | Electronic | | 12B | 16 | 5.5–6.5 | 550 |
| | F | 8-260 | Olds. | R46SZ | 0.060 | Electronic | | 18B @ 1100 | 14 | 5.5–6.5 | 550 |
| | Y | 8-301 | Pont. | R46TSX | 0.060 | Electronic | | 12B | 16 | 5.5–6.5 | 650 (500) |
| | R | 8-350 | Olds. | R46SZ | 0.060 | Electronic | | 20B @ 1100 | 16 | 5.5–6.5 | 550 |
| | K | 8-403 | Olds. | R46SZ | 0.060 | Electronic | | 24B (20B) @ 1100 | 16 | 5.5–6.5 | 550 |
| **1980** | A | 6-231 | Buick | R45TS⑤ | 0.040⑥ | Electronic | | 15B | 16 | 5.5–6.5 | 670/550⑦ |
| | F | 8-260 | Olds. | R46SX | 0.080 | Electronic | | 18B | 14 | 5.5–6.5 | 650/550 |
| | Y | 8-307 | Olds. | R46SX | 0.080 | Electronic | | 20B | 20 | 5.5–6.5 | 600/500 |
| | R | 8-350 | Olds. | R46SX | 0.080 | Electronic | | 18B | 15 | 5.5–6.5 | 600 (650)/ 600 (550) |
| **1981** | A | 6-231 | Buick | R45TSX | 0.080 | Electronic | | ⑧ | 16 | 5.5–6.5 | ⑧ |
| | 4 | 6-252 | Buick | R45TSX | 0.080 | Electronic | | ⑧ | 16 | 5.5–6.5 | ⑧ |
| | F | 8-260 | Olds. | R46SX | 0.080 | Electronic | | 18B | 14 | 5.5–6.5 | ⑧ |
| | Y | 8-307 | Olds. | R46SX | 0.080 | Electronic | | 15B | 20 | 5.5–6.5 | ⑧ |
| **1982** | A | 6-231 | Buick | R45TS | 0.040 | Electronic | | ⑧ | 16 | 5.5–6.5 | ⑧ |
| | 4 | 6-252 | Buick | R45TS8 | 0.080 | Electronic | | ⑧ | 16 | 5.5–6.5 | ⑧ |
| | F | 8-260 | Olds. | R46SX | 0.080 | Electronic | | ⑧ | 14 | 5.5–6.5 | ⑧ |
| | Y | 8-307 | Olds. | R46SX | 0.080 | Electronic | | ⑧ | — | 5.5–6.5 | ⑧ |
| **1983** | A | 6-231 | Buick | R45TS | 0.040 | Electronic | | ⑧ | 16 | 5.5–6.5 | ⑧ |
| | 4 | 6-252 | Buick | R45TS8 | 0.080 | Electronic | | ⑧ | 16 | 5.5–6.5 | ⑧ |
| | Y | 8-307 | Olds. | R46SX | 0.080 | Electronic | | ⑧ | — | 5.5–6.5 | ⑧ |
| **1984** | A | 6-231 | Buick | R45TSX | 0.060 | Electronic | | 15B | NA | 5.5–6.5 | 450/1000⑱ |
| | Y | 8-307 | Olds. | R46SX | 0.080 | Electronic | | 20B @ 1100 | NA | 5.5–6.5 | 500/575⑱ |

85842c01

## GASOLINE ENGINE TUNE-UP SPECIFICATIONS

(When analyzing compression test results, look for uniformity among cylinders rather than specific pressures)

| Year | Engine V.I.N. Code | Engine Type (No. of cyl- C.I.D.) | Engine Manufac- turer | Spark Plugs Orig. Type | Spark Plugs Gap (in.) | Distributor Point Dwell (deg.) | Distributor Point Gap (in.) | Ignition Timing (deg. B.T.D.C) Automatic Transmission | Intake Valve Opens (°B.T.D.C.) | Fuel Pump Pressure (psi) | Idle Speed (rpm) Automatic Transmission |
|------|------|------|------|------|------|------|------|------|------|------|------|
| **OLDSMOBILE 88, 98, WAGONS** |||||||||||| 
| 1985 | Y | 8-307 | Olds. | FR3LS6 | 0.060 | Electronic | | 20B @ 1100 | NA | 5.5–6.5 | 450/700 ⑱ |
| 1986 | Y | 8-307 | Olds. | FR3LS6 | 0.060 | Electronic | | 20B | NA | 5.5–6.5 | ⑧ |
| 1987 | Y | 8-307 | Olds. | FR3LS6 | 0.060 | Electronic | | 20B | NA | 5.5–6.5 | ⑧ |
| 1988 | Y | 8-307 | Olds. | FR3LS6 | 0.060 | Electronic | | ⑧ | NA | 5.5–6.5 | ⑧ |
| 1989 | Y | 8-307 | Olds. | FR3LS6 | 0.060 | Electronic | | ⑧ | NA | 5.5–6.5 | 450/475 ⑱ |
| 1990 | Y | 8-307 | Olds. | FR3LS6 | 0.060 | Electronic | | ⑧ | NA | 5.5–6.5 | 450/475 ⑱ |
| **BUICK LE SABRE, ELECTRA, WAGONS** |||||||||||| 
| 1975 | J | 8-350 | Buick | R45TSX | 0.060 | Electronic | | 12B | 19 | 5.5–6.5 | 600 |
| | T | 8-455 | Buick | R45TSX | 0.060 | Electronic | | 12B | 10 | 5.5–6.5 | 600 |
| 1976 | J | 8-350 | Buick | R45TSX | 0.060 | Electronic | | 12B | 13.5 | 5.5–6.5 | 600 |
| | T | 8-455 | Buick | R45TSX | 0.060 | Electronic | | 12B | 10 | 5.5–6.5 | 600 |
| 1977 | C | 6-231 | Buick | R46TS or R46TSX | 0.040 0.060 | Electronic | | 12B | 17 | 5.5–6.5 | 600 |
| | Y | 8-301 | Pont. | R46TSX | 0.060 | Electronic | | 12B | 27 | 5.5–6.5 | 650/550 |
| | R | 8-350 | Olds. | R46SZ | 0.060 | Electronic | | 20B @ 1100 ⑨ | 16 | 5.5–6.5 | 650/550 [650/600] |
| | J | 8-350 | Buick | R45TS or R46TSX | 0.040 | Electronic | | 12B | 13.5 | 5.5–6.5 | 600 |
| | K | 8-403 | Olds. | R46SX | 0.060 | Electronic | | 24B (20B) [20B] @ 110 | 16 | 5.5–6.5 | 650/550 [650/600] |
| 1978 | A | 6-231 | Buick | R46TSX | 0.060 | Electronic | | 15B | 17 | 5.5–6.5 | 670/600 |
| | G | 6-231 Turbo | Buick | R44TSX | 0.060 | Electronic | | 15B @ 600 | 17 | 5.5–6.5 | 650 |
| | 3 | 6-231 Turbo | Buick | R44TSX | 0.060 | Electronic | | 15B @ 600 | 17 | 5.5–6.5 | 650 |
| | Y | 8-301 | Pont. | R46TSX | 0.060 | Electronic | | 12B @ 550 | 27 | 5.5–6.5 | 650/550 |
| | U | 8-305 | Chev. | R45TS | 0.045 | Electronic | | 48 @ 500 (6B @ 500) [8B @ 600] | 28 | 5.5–6.5 | 600/500 (650/500) [700/600] |
| | R | 8-350 | Olds. | R46SZ | 0.060 | Electronic | | 20B @ 1100 | 16 | 5.5–6.5 | 650/550 [700/600] |
| | L | 8-350 | Chev. | R45TS | 0.045 | Electronic | | 8B @ 500 [8B @ 600] | 28 | 5.5–6.5 | 600/500 [650/600] |
| | X | 8-350 | Buick | R46TSX | 0.060 | Electronic | | 15B @ 600 | 16 | 5.5–6.5 | 550 |
| | Z | 8-400 | Pont. | R45TSX | 0.060 | Electronic | | 16B | 29 | 5.5–6.5 | 575 |
| | K | 8-403 | Olds. | R46SZ | 0.060 | Electronic | | 20B @ 1100 | 16 | 5.5–6.5 | 650/550 [700/600] |

85842c02

## GASOLINE ENGINE TUNE-UP SPECIFICATIONS

(When analyzing compression test results, look for uniformity among cylinders rather than specific pressures)

| Year | Engine V.I.N. Code | Engine Type (No. of cyl-C.I.D.) | Engine Manufac-turer | Spark Plugs Orig. Type | Gap (in.) | Distributor Point Dwell (deg.) | Point Gap (in.) | Ignition Timing (deg. B.T.D.C) Automatic Transmission | Intake Valve Opens (°B.T.D.C.) | Fuel Pump Pressure (psi) | Idle Speed (rpm) Automatic Transmission |
|---|---|---|---|---|---|---|---|---|---|---|---|
| | | | | | BUICK LE SABRE, ELECTRA, WAGONS | | | | | | |
| 1979 | A | 6-231 | Buick | R45TSX or R46TSX | 0.060 0.060 | Electronic | | 15B @ 800 | 16 | 5.5–6.5 | 670/550 (600) [600] |
| | 3 | 6-231 Turbo | Buick | R44TSX | 0.060 | Electronic | | 15B | 16 | 5.5–6.5 | 650 |
| | Y | 8-301 | Pont. | R46TSX | 0.060 | Electronic | | 12B @ 550 | 27 | 5.5–6.5 | 650/550 |
| | R | 8-350 | Olds. | R46SZ | 0.060 | Electronic | | 20B @ 1100 | 16 | 5.5–6.5 | 650/550 (600/500) [700/600] |
| | X | 8-350 | Buick | R45TSX or R46TSX | 0.060 0.060 | Electronic | | 15B | 13.5 | 5.5–6.5 | 550 |
| | K | 8-403 | Olds. | R46SZ | 0.060 | Electronic | | 20B @ 1100 | 16 | 5.5–6.5 | 650/550 (600/500) [700/600] |
| 1980 | A | 6-231 | Buick | R45TSX | 0.060 | Electronic | | 15B @ 550 | 16 | 5.5–6.5 | 670/550 ⑪ (620/650) ⑫ 550 ⑬ |
| | 3 | 6-231 | Buick | R45TS | 0.040 | Electronic | | 15B @ 650 | 16 | 5.5–6.5 | 650 |
| | 4 | 6-252 | Buick | R45TSX | 0.060 | Electronic | | 15B @ 550 | 16 | 5.5–6.5 | 680/550 ⑭ 550 ⑬ |
| | W | 8-301 | Pont. | R45TSX | 0.060 | Electronic | | 12B @ 500 | 27 | | 650/550 ⑭ 550 ⑬ |
| | R | 8-350 | Olds. | R46SX or R47SX | 0.080 0.080 | Electronic | | 18B @ 1100 | 16 | 5.5–6.5 | 650/550 |
| | X | 8-350 | Buick | R45TSX | 0.060 | Electronic | | 15B @ 550 | 13.5 | | 550 |
| 1981 | A | 6-231 | Buick | R45TS8 | 0.080 | Electronic | | ⑮ | 16 | 5.5–6.5 | ⑮ |
| | 4 | 6-252 | Buick | R45TS8 | 0.080 | Electronic | | ⑮ | 16 | 5.5–6.5 | ⑮ |
| | J | 8-267 | Chev. | R45TS | 0.045 | Electronic | | 12B | NA | 5.5–6.5 | ⑮ |
| | W | 8-301 | Pont. | R45TSX | 0.060 | Electronic | | 12B @ 500 | 27 | 5.5–6.5 | ⑮ |
| | Y | 8-307 | Olds. | R45TS4 | 0.060 | Electronic | | ⑮ | 20 | 5.5–6.5 | ⑮ |
| 1982 | A | 6-231 | Buick | R45TS8 | 0.080 | Electronic | | ⑮ | 16 | 5.5–6.5 | ⑮ |
| | 4 | 6-252 | Buick | R45TS8 | 0.080 | Electronic | | ⑮ | 16 | 5.5–6.5 | ⑮ |
| | Y | 8-307 | Olds. | R46SX | 0.080 | Electronic | | ⑮ | 20 | 5.5–6.5 | ⑮ |
| 1983 | A | 6-231 | Buick | R45TS8 | 0.080 | Electronic | | ⑮ | 16 | 5.5–6.5 | ⑮ |
| | 4 | 6-252 | Buick | R45TS8 | 0.080 | Electronic | | ⑮ | 16 | 5.5–6.5 | ⑮ |
| | Y | 8-307 | Olds. | R46SX | 0.080 | Electronic | | ⑮ | 20 | 5.5–6.5 | ⑮ |
| 1984 | A | 6-231 | Buick | R45TS8 | ⑧ | Electronic | | ⑧ | NA | 5.5–6.5 | 450/1000 ⑱ |
| | 4 | 6-252 | Buick | R45TS8 | ⑧ | Electronic | | ⑧ | NA | 5.5–6.5 | 450/900 ⑱ |
| | Y | 8-307 | Olds. | R46SX | ⑧ | Electronic | | ⑧ | NA | 5.5–6.5 | 500/725 ⑱ |

85842c03

## GASOLINE ENGINE TUNE-UP SPECIFICATIONS

(When analyzing compression test results, look for uniformity among cylinders rather than specific pressures)

| Year | Engine V.I.N. Code | Engine Type (No. of cyl- C.I.D.) | Engine Manufac- turer | Spark Plugs Orig. Type | Gap (in.) | Distributor Point Dwell (deg.) | Point Gap (in.) | Ignition Timing (deg. B.T.D.C) Automatic Transmission | Intake Valve Opens (°B.T.D.C.) | Fuel Pump Pressure (psi) | Idle Speed (rpm) Automatic Transmission |
|---|---|---|---|---|---|---|---|---|---|---|---|
| BUICK LE SABRE, ELECTRA, WAGONS |||||||||||| 
| 1985 | A | 6-231 | Buick | R45TS8 | ⑧ | Electronic | | ⑧ | NA | 5.5–6.5 | 450/1000 ⑱ |
| | 4 | 6-252 | Buick | R45TS8 | ⑧ | Electronic | | ⑧ | NA | 5.5–6.5 | 450/900 ⑱ |
| | Y | 8-307 | Olds. | R46SX | ⑧ | Electronic | | ⑧ | NA | 5.5–6.5 | 500/725 ⑱ |
| 1986 | A | 6-231 | Buick | R45TSX | ⑧ | Electronic | | ⑧ | ⑧ | 5.5–6.5 | ⑧ |
| | Y | 8-307 | Olds. | FR3LS6 | 0.060 | Electronic | | ⑧ | ⑧ | 5.5–6.5 | ⑧ |
| 1987 | A | 6-231 | Buick | R45TSX | ⑧ | Electronic | | ⑧ | ⑧ | 5.5–6.5 | ⑧ |
| | Y | 8-307 | Olds. | FR3LS6 | 0.060 | Electronic | | ⑧ | ⑧ | 5.5–6.5 | ⑧ |
| 1988 | Y | 8-307 | Olds. | FR3LS6 | 0.060 | Electronic | | ⑧ | NA | 5.5–6.5 | ⑧ |
| 1989 | Y | 8-307 | Olds. | FR3LS6 | 0.060 | Electronic | | ⑧ | NA | 5.5–6.5 | 450/475 ⑱ |
| 1990 | Y | 8-307 | Olds. | FR3LS6 | 0.060 | Electronic | | ⑧ | NA | 5.5–6.5 | 450/475 ⑱ |
| PONTIAC BONNEVILLE, CATALINA, WAGONS |||||||||||| 
| 1975 | R | 8-400 | Pont. | R46TSX | 0.060 | Electronic | | 16B | 22 | 5.5–6.5 | 650 |
| | S | 8-400 | Pont. | R45TSX | 0.060 | Electronic | | 16B (12B) | 30 | 5.5–6.5 | 650 |
| | W | 8-455 | Pont. | R45TSX | 0.060 | Electronic | | 16B (12B) | 23 | 5.5–6.5 | 650 (625) |
| 1976 | R | 8-400 | Pont. | R46TSX | 0.060 | Electronic | | 16B | 22 | 5.5–6.5 | 650 |
| | S | 8-400 | Pont. | R45TSX | 0.060 | Electronic | | 16B (12B) | 30 | 5.5–6.5 | 650 |
| | W | 8-455 | Pont. | R45TSX | 0.060 | Electronic | | 16B (10B) | 23 | 5.5–6.5 | 650 (625) |
| 1975 | C | 6-231 | Buick | R46TSX | 0.040 | Electronic | | 12B | 19 | 5.5–6.5 | 600 |
| | Y | 8-301 | Pont. | R46TSX | 0.060 | Electronic | | 12B | 27 | 5.5–6.5 | 550 |
| | U | 8-305 | Chev. | R45TS | 0.045 | Electronic | | 8B | 28 | 5.5–6.5 | 600 |
| | R | 8-350 | Olds. | R46SX R46SZ | 0.080 | Electronic | | 20B @ 1100 | 16 | 5.5–6.5 | 600,500 ⑧ |
| | P | 8-350 | Pont. | R45TSX | 0.060 | Electronic | | 16B | 29 | 5.5–6.5 | 575,600 ⑧ |
| | Z | 8-400 | Pont. | R45TSX | 0.060 | Electronic | | 16B | 29 | 5.5–6.5 | 575 |
| | K | 8-403 | Olds. | R46SX or R46SZ | 0.080 | Electronic | | 20B @ 1100 | 16 | 5.5–6.5 | 600,500 ⑧ |
| 1978 | A | 6-231 | Buick | R46TSX | 0.060 | Electronic | | 15B | 17 | 5.5–6.5 | 600 |
| | Y | 8-301 | Pont. | R46TSX | 0.060 | Electronic | | 12B | 27 | 5.5–6.5 | 550 |
| | W | 8-301 | Pont. | R46TSX | 0.060 | Electronic | | 12B | 27 | 5.5–6.5 | 550 |
| | R | 8-350 | Olds. | R46SZ | 0.060 | Electronic | | 20B @ 1100 | 17 | 5.5–6.5 | 550 |
| | X | 8-350 | Buick | R46TSX | 0.060 | Electronic | | 15B | 16 | 5.5–6.5 | 550 |
| | K | 8-403 | Olds. | R46SX | 0.060 | Electronic | | 20B @ 1100 | 16 | 5.5–6.5 | 600(550) |
| 1979 | A | 6-231 | Buick | R45TSX | 0.060 | Electronic | | 15B | 16 | 5.5–6.5 | 600 |
| | Y | 8-301 | Pont. | R46TSX | 0.060 | Electronic | | 12B | 16 | 5.5–6.5 | 650 |
| | W | 8-301 | Pont. | R45TSX | 0.060 | Electronic | | 12B | 16 ⑯ | 5.5–6.5 | 500(650) |
| | R | 8-350 | Olds. | R46SZ | 0.060 | Electronic | | 20B @ 1100 | 16 | 5.5–6.5 | 550 |
| | X | 8-350 | Buick | R46TSX | 0.060 | Electronic | | 15B | 16 | 5.5–6.5 | 550 |
| | K | 8-403 | Olds. | R46SX | 0.060 | Electronic | | 18B(20B) @ 1100 | 16 | 5.5–6.5 | 500(500) |

85842c04

## GASOLINE ENGINE TUNE-UP SPECIFICATIONS

(When analyzing compression test results, look for uniformity among cylinders rather than specific pressures)

| Year | Engine V.I.N. Code | Engine Type (No. of cyl- C.I.D.) | Engine Manufac- turer | Spark Plugs Orig. Type | Gap (in.) | Distributor Point Dwell (deg.) | Point Gap (in.) | Ignition Timing (deg. B.T.D.C.) Automatic Transmission | Intake Valve Opens (°B.T.D.C.) | Fuel Pump Pressure (psi) | Idle Speed (rpm) Automatic Transmission |
|---|---|---|---|---|---|---|---|---|---|---|---|
| PONTIAC BONNEVILLE, CATALINA, PARISIENNE, WAGONS | | | | | | | | | | | |
| 1980 | A | 6-231 | Buick | R45TSX ⑰ | 0.060 ⑰ | Electronic | | 15B | 16 | 5.5–6.5 | 620/550 |
|  | S | 8-265 | Pont. | R45TSX | 0.060 | Electronic | | 10B | 27 | 5.5–6.5 | 650/550 |
|  | W | 8-301 | Pont. | R45TSX | 0.060 | Electronic | | 12B | 16 | 5.5–6.5 | 650/500 |
|  | R | 8-350 | Olds. | R46SZ | 0.060 | Electronic | | 6B | 28 | 5.5–6.5 | 650/550 |
|  | X | 8-350 | Buick | R45TSX | 0.060 | Electronic | | 15B | 16 | 5.5–6.5 | 550 |
| 1981 | A | 6-231 | Buick | R45TS8 | 0.080 | Electronic | | ⑧ | 16 | 5.5–6.5 | ⑧ |
|  | S | 8-265 | Pont. | R45TSX | 0.060 | Electronic | | 12B | 16 | 5.5–6.5 | ⑧ |
|  | H | 8-305 | Chev. | R45TS | 0.045 | Electronic | | ⑧ | NA | 5.5–6.5 | ⑧ |
|  | Y | 8-307 | Olds. | R46SX | 0.080 | Electronic | | 15B | 14 | 5.5–6.5 | ⑧ |
|  | X | 8-350 | Buick | R45TSX | 0.060 | Electronic | | 15B | 16 | 5.5–6.5 | 550 |
| 1982 | A | 6-231 | Buick | R45TS8 | 0.080 | Electronic | | 15B | 16 | 5.5–6.5 | ⑧ |
|  | H | 8-305 | Chev. | R45TS | 0.045 | Electronic | | ⑧ | NA | 5.5–6.5 | ⑧ |
| 1983 | A | 6-231 | Buick | R45TS8 | 0.080 | Electronic | | 15B | 16 | 5.5–6.5 | ⑧ |
|  | H | 8-305 | Chev. | R45TS | 0.045 | Electronic | | ⑧ | NA | 5.5–6.5 | ⑧ |
| 1984 | A | 6-231 | Buick | R45TSX | 0.060 | Electronic | | ⑧ | NA | 5.5–6.5 | 450/900 ⑱ |
|  | H | 8-305 | Chev. | R45TS | 0.045 | Electronic | | ⑧ | NA | 5.5–6.5 | ⑧ |
| 1985 | A | 6-231 | Buick | R45TSX | 0.060 | Electronic | | ⑧ | NA | 5.5–6.5 | 450/900 ⑱ |
|  | Z | 6-262 | Chev. | R43TS | 0.035 | Electronic | | ⑧ | NA | 9–13 | 400 |
|  | H | 8-305 | Chev. | R45TS | 0.045 | Electronic | | ⑧ | NA | 5.5–6.5 | ⑧ |
| 1986 | A | 6-231 | Buick | R45TSX | 0.045 | Electronic | | ⑧ | NA | 5.5–6.5 | 450/900 ⑱ |
|  | Z | 6-262 | Chev. | R43TS | 0.035 | Electronic | | ⑧ | NA | 9–13 | 400 |
|  | H | 8-305 | Chev. | R45TS | 0.045 | Electronic | | ⑧ | NA | 5.5–6.5 | 450/700 ⑱ |
| 1987 | Y | 8-307 | Olds. | FR3LS6 | 0.060 | Electronic | | 20B | NA | 5.5–6.5 | ⑧ |
| 1988 | Y | 8-307 | Olds. | FR3LS6 | 0.060 | Electronic | | ⑧ | NA | 5.5–6.5 | ⑧ |
| 1989 | Y | 8-307 | Olds. | FR3LS6 | 0.060 | Electronic | | ⑧ | NA | 5.5–6.5 | 450/475 ⑱ |

**NOTE:** The underhood specifications sticker often reflects tune-up specification changes made in production. Sticker figures must be used if they disagree with those in this chart.

Part numbers in this chart are not recommendations by Chilton for any product or brand name.

Figures in parenthesis ( ) indicates a special figure for California models; figure in brackets [ ] indicates a special figure for high-altitude models.

Where two idle speed figures appear separated by a slash, the first is idle speed with solenoid energized, the second is idle speed with solenoid disconnected.

① A/C on and A/C compressor clutch wires disconnected
② 18B with 2.4:1 axle ratio in 98
③ 0.040 with R46TS
④ 88 station wagon: 20B @ 1100
⑤ With C-4 ignition: R45TSX
⑥ With C-4 ignition: 0.060
⑦ With C-4 ignition: 620/550
⑧ See underhood sticker
⑨ Except Calif. Le Sabre coupes and sedans, which should be set at 18B @ 1100
⑩ With solenoid energized, set solenoid screw to 600 rpm; with solenoid de-energized, set the carburetor screw to 550 rpm for models with A/C, 500 for models without A/C
⑪ With A/C, 49 states only
⑫ With A/C, Calif. models only

⑬ All models without A/C
⑭ All models with A/C
⑮ On vehicles equipped with computerized emissions systems (which have no distributor vacuum advance unit) with idle speed and ignition timing are controlled by the emissions computer. These adjustments should be performed professionally on models so equipped.
⑯ High performance—27
⑰ Low altitude without C-4 ignition: R45TS, gap 0.040
⑱ Refers to minimum authority and maximum authority adjustments; see text

85842c05

## DIESEL TUNE-UP SPECIFICATIONS

| Year | Engine V.I.N. Code | Engine No. Cyl. Displacement (Cu. In.) | Engine Mfg. | Fuel Pump Pressure (psi) | Compression (lbs)▲ | Injection/ Ignition Timing (deg.) Auto. Trans. | Intake Valve Opens (deg.) | Idle Speed● (rpm) |
|---|---|---|---|---|---|---|---|---|
| 1978 | N | 8-350 | Olds. | 5.8–8.7 | 275 min. | ① | 16 | 650/575 |
| 1979 | N | 8-350 | Olds. | 5.8–8.7 | 275 min. | ① | 16 | 650/575 |
| 1980 | N | 8-350 | Olds. | 5.8–8.7 | 275 min. | 5B②① | 16 | 750/600 |
| 1981 | N | 8-350 | Olds. | 5.8–8.7 | 275 min. | ① | 16 | ① |
| 1982 | N | 8-350 | Olds. | 5.8–8.7 | 275 min. | ① | 16 | ① |
| 1983 | N | 8-350 | Olds. | 5.8–8.7 | 275 min. | ① | 16 | ① |
| 1984 | N | 8-350 | Olds. | 5.8–8.7 | 300 min. | 4A③① | 16 | 750/600 |
| 1985 | N | 8-350 | Olds. | 5.8–8.7 | 300 min. | 4A③① | 16 | 750/600 |

**NOTE:** The underhood specifications sticker often reflects changes made in production. Sticker figures must be used if they disagree with those in this chart.
● Where two idle speed figures appear separated by a slash, the first is idle speed with solenoid energized; the second is with solenoid disconnected
▲ The lowest cylinder reading should not be less than 70% of the highest cylinder reading on models to 1983. On 1984 and later models, the lowest cylinder reading should be 80% of the highest
① See underhood specifications sticker
② Static
③ Injection timing @ 1250 rpm in Park

85842c06

# 3

# ENGINE AND ENGINE REBUILDING

## Understanding The Engine Electrical System

The engine electrical system can be broken down into three separate and distinct systems:

1. The starting system
2. The charging system
3. The ignition system

The battery is the first link in the chain of mechanisms which work together to provide cranking of the automobile engine. In most modern vehicles, the battery is a lead-acid electrochemical device consisting of six two-volt (2V) subsections connected in series so the unit is capable of producing approximately 12V of electrical pressure. Each subsection, or cell, consists of a series of positive and negative plates held a short distance apart in a solution of sulfuric acid and water. The two types of plates are of dissimilar metals. This causes a chemical reaction to be set up, and it is this reaction which produces current flow from the battery when its positive and negative terminals are connected to an electrical appliance such as a lamp or motor. The continued transfer of electrons would eventually convert the sulfuric acid in the electrolyte to water, and make the two plates identical in chemical composition. As electrical energy is removed from the battery, its voltage output tends to drop. Thus, measuring battery voltage and battery electrolyte composition are two ways of checking the ability of the unit to supply power. During the starting of the engine, electrical energy is removed from the battery. However, if the charging circuit is in good condition and the operating conditions are normal, the power removed from the battery will be replaced by the generator (or alternator) which will force electrons back through the battery, reversing the normal flow, and restoring the battery to its original chemical state.

The battery and starting motor are linked by very heavy electrical cables designed to minimize resistance to the flow of current. Generally, the major power supply cable that leaves the battery goes directly to the starter, while other electrical system needs are supplied by a smaller cable. During the starter operation, power flows from the battery to the starter and is grounded through the vehicle's frame and the battery's negative ground strap.

The starting motor is a specially designed, direct current electric motor capable of producing a very great amount of power for its size. One thing that allows the motor to produce a great deal of power is its tremendous rotating speed. It drives the engine through a tiny pinion gear (attached to the starter's armature), which drives the very large flywheel ring gear at a greatly reduced speed. Another factor allowing it to produce so much power is that only intermittent operation is required of it. Thus, little allowance for air circulation is required, and the windings can be built into a very small space.

The starter solenoid is a magnetic device which employs the small current supplied by the starting switch circuit of the ignition switch. This magnetic action moves a plunger which mechanically engages the starter and electrically closes the heavy switch which connects it to the battery. The starting switch circuit consists of the starting switch contained within the ignition switch, a transmission neutral safety switch or clutch pedal switch, and the wiring necessary to connect these with the starter solenoid or relay.

A pinion gear is mounted to a one-way drive clutch. This clutch is splined to the starter armature shaft. When the ignition switch is moved to the START position, the solenoid plunger slides the pinion toward the flywheel ring gear via collar and spring. If the teeth on the pinion and flywheel match properly, the pinion will engage the flywheel immediately. If the gear teeth butt one another, the spring will be compressed and will force the gears to mesh as soon as the starter turns far enough to allow them to do so. As the solenoid plunger reaches the end of its travel, it closes the contacts that connect the battery and starter, then the engine is cranked.

As soon as the engines starts, the flywheel ring gear begins turning fast enough to drive the pinion at an extremely high rate of speed. At this point, the one-way clutch begins allowing the pinion to spin faster than the starter shaft so that the starter will not operate at excessive speed. When the ignition switch is released from the starter position, the solenoid is de-energized, and a spring contained within the solenoid assembly pulls the gear out of mesh and interrupts the current flow to the starter.

Some starters employ a separate relay, mounted away from the starter, to switch the motor and solenoid current on and off. The relay thus replaces the solenoid electrical switch, but does not eliminate the need for a solenoid mounted on the starter used to mechanically engage the starter drive gears. The relay is used to reduce the amount of current the starting switch must carry.

The automobile charging system provides electrical power for operation of the vehicle's ignition and starting systems, as well as for all electrical accessories. The battery serves as an electrical surge or storage tank, storing (in chemical form) the energy originally produced by the engine driven generator (alternator). The system also provides a means of regulating generator output to protect the battery from being overcharged and to avoid excessive voltage to the accessories.

As stated earlier, the storage battery is a chemical device incorporating parallel lead plates in a tank containing a sulfuric acid-water solution. Adjacent plates are slightly dissimilar, and the chemical reaction of the two dissimilar plates produces electrical energy when the battery is connected to a load such as the starter motor. The chemical reaction is reversible, so that when the generator is producing a voltage (electrical pressure) greater than that produced by the battery, electricity is forced into the battery, which is then returned to its fully charged state.

The vehicle's generator is driven mechanically, through V-belts, by the engine crankshaft. It consists of two coils of fine wire, one stationary (the stator) and one movable (the rotor). The rotor may also be known as the armature, and consists of fine wire wrapped around an iron core which is mounted on a shaft. The electricity which flows through the two coils of wire (provided initially by the battery in some cases) creates an intense magnetic field around both rotor and stator. The interaction between the two fields creates voltage, allowing the generator to power the accessories and charge the battery.

Newer automobiles use alternating current generators or alternators because they are more efficient, can be rotated at higher speeds, and have fewer brush problems. In an alternator, the field rotates while all the current produced passes only through the stator windings. The brushes bear against continuous slip rings rather than a commutator. This causes the current produced to periodically reverse the direction of its flow. Diodes (electrical one-way switches) block the flow of current from traveling in the wrong direction. A series of diodes is wired together to permit the alternating flow of the stator to be converted to a pulsating, but unidirectional flow at the alternator output. The alternator's field is wired in series with the voltage regulator.

## Safety Precautions

Observing these precautions will ensure safe handling of the electrical system components, and will avoid damage to the vehicle's electrical system:

• Be absolutely sure of the polarity of a booster battery before making connections. Connect the cables positive-to-positive, and negative-to-negative. Connect positive cables first and then make the last connection to a ground on the body of the booster vehicle so that arcing cannot ignite hydrogen gas that may have accumulated near the battery. Even momentary connection of a booster battery with the polarity reserved will damage alternator diodes.

• Disconnect both vehicle battery cables before attempting to charge a battery.

• Never ground the alternator output or battery terminal. Be cautious when using metal tools around a battery to avoid creating a short circuit between the terminals.

• Never ground the field circuit between the alternator and regulator.

• Never run an alternator or generator without load unless the field circuit is disconnected.

• Never attempt to polarize an alternator.

• Never wear metal jewelry when working on any electrical system. This includes watches!

## Ignition Coil

### TESTING

▶ See Figure 1

#### Coil-in-Cap

1. Remove the distributor cap from the housing assembly. For details, please refer to Section 2 of this manual.

2. Connect an ohmmeter across the primary connections, as shown by the ohmmeter and wiring on the left side (#1) of the illustration. The resistance should be zero or very close to zero. High resistance or infinite resistance indicates a partial or complete open circuit, and the need to replace the coil.

3. Connect the ohmmeter between the primary ground and the coil secondary connector. Set the resistance to the higher scale. Test resistance as shown by the solid wire connections and then repeat the test with the wire connected as shown by

the dotted line. If both readings are infinite, the coil is bad. If both or either show continuity, the coil is okay.

#### Separately Mounted Coil

▶ See Figure 2

1. Disconnect the secondary lead and unplug the primary leads. Remove the mounting bolts and remove the coil from the engine.

2. First connect an ohmmeter, set to the high scale, as shown on the left (#1) in the illustration. The resistance should be nearly infinite. If it is not, replace the coil.

3. Connect the ohmmeter as shown in the center picture. Use the low resistance scale. The reading should be very low, nearly zero. Otherwise, replace the coil.

4. Reset the ohmmeter to the high resistance scale and connect it as shown on the right. There should be obvious continuity; the ohmmeter should not read infinite. If it does replace the coil. If all three tests are passed, the coil is satisfactory.

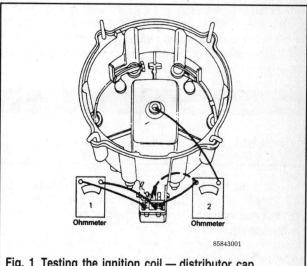

**Fig. 1 Testing the ignition coil — distributor cap mounted coil assemblies**

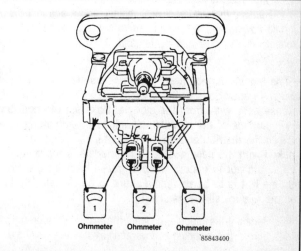

**Fig. 2 Testing the ignition coil — separately (external) mounted coil**

## REMOVAL & INSTALLATION

1. Mark the high tension wires. Then, carefully disconnect each from the distributor cap. Squeeze the latches together and then disconnect the connector that runs from the cap to the distributor base.

2. Use a large, flat bladed prybar to first depress and then rotate the wire type latch away from the underside of the distributor on either side. Remove the cap.

3. Turn the cap upside down. Remove the four bolts from the four corners of the coil, noting the location of the secondary ground lead. Then, remove the primary wiring from the connector in the cap, noting the routing of positive and negative leads.

4. Remove the coil and wiring. Then, remove the arc seal from underneath.

5. Wipe the mounting area for the coil clean with a soft cloth. Inspect the cap for defects, especially heat or carbon tracks, and replace it if necessary.

6. Install a new coil into position, and carefully route the primary wiring positive and negative leads properly.

7. Position the coil ground wire as it was at removal and then install and snug up the four coil mounting bolts. Install the cap and wiring in reverse order.

## Ignition Module

### REMOVAL & INSTALLATION

1. Mark the high tension wires. Then, carefully disconnect each from the distributor cap. Squeeze the latches together and then disconnect the connector that runs from the cap to the distributor base.

2. Use a large, flat bladed prybar to first depress and then rotate the wire type latch away from the underside of the distributor on either side. Remove the cap.

3. Carefully note the colors of the two leads. Mark them, if necessary. Then disconnect them.

4. Remove the two module attaching screws and pull the module upward and out, being careful not to disturb the grease, if the module may be re-used.

**To install:**

➡**The module is mounted via a thick layer of grease. This grease is analogous to the coolant in an engine. It carries intense heat away from the module. Make sure to coat the lower surface of the module, as well as the mounting surface in the distributor with the grease included in the packed with the new module if the module is replaced. Make sure not to disturb the old grease layer on the old module if it is to be re-used. Failure to do this will cause the module to fail prematurely!**

5. Remount the module, connect the leads in the proper order, tighten the retaining screws and reinstall the distributor cap.

## High Energy Ignition (HEI) Distributor

The Delco-Remy High Energy Ignition (HEI) system is a breakerless (has no ignition points), pulse triggered, transistor controlled, inductive discharge ignition system that is standard on the Buick, Olds and Pontiac vehicles covered in this guide.

There are only nine electrical connections in the system; the ignition switch feed wire and the eight spark plug leads (early models). After 1980, the EST wiring harness has to be disconnected. On most models, the coil is located in the distributor cap, connecting directly to the rotor.

The magnetic pick up assembly located inside the distributor contains a permanent magnet, a pole piece with internal teeth, and a pick up coil. When the teeth of the rotating timer core and pole piece align, an induced voltage in the pick-up coil signals the electronic module to open the coil primary circuit. As the primary current decreases, a high voltage is induced in the secondary windings of the ignition coil directing a spark through the rotor and high voltage leads to fire the spark plugs. The dwell period is automatically controlled by the electronic module and is increased with increasing engine rpm. The HEI system features, as do most electronic ignition systems, a longer spark duration which is instrumental in firing today's lean and EGR-diluted fuel/air mixtures (a lean mixture requires a much hotter, longer duration spark to ignite it than does a rich mixture). A capacitor, which looks like the condenser in the old points-type ignition systems, is located within the HEI distributor and is used for noise (static) suppression in conjunction with the vehicle's radio. The capacitor is not a regularly replaced component.

As noted in Section 2, 1981 and later models continue to use the HEI distributor, although it now incorporates an Electronic Spark Timing system. With the EST system, all spark timing changes are performed electronically by the Electronic Control Module (ECM) which monitors information from various engine sensors, computes the desired spark timing and then signals the distributor to change the timing accordingly. Because all timing changes are controlled electronically, no vacuum or mechanical advance systems are used.

### REMOVAL & INSTALLATION

#### Engine Not Disturbed

➡**Do not rotate the engine while the distributor is removed in order to make installing it simpler and easier. If the engine is inadvertently disturbed while the distributor is out, please refer to the appropriate procedure.**

1. Disconnect the ground cable from the battery. On 1984 and later models, disconnect the ignition switch battery feed wire and, if the vehicle is equipped with a tach, the tachometer lead from the cap.

2. Tag and disconnect the feed and module terminal connectors from the distributor cap. DO NOT use a screwdriver to release the terminal connectors.

3. On 1975-80 models, disconnect the hose at the vacuum advance unit.

4. Depress and release the 4 distributor cap-to-housing retainers and lift off the cap assembly.

5. Using a magic marker, matchmark the rotor-to-housing and housing-to-engine block positions so they can be matched during installation.

➡ **The distributor must be installed with the rotor and housing in the correct position.**

6. Loosen and remove the distributor clamp and bolt. Carefully lift the distributor just until the point where the rotor stops turning. Be careful not to disturb the position of the rotor. Now, again mark the relative positions of the rotor-to-distributor housing. The rotor must be aligned with this position before you engage distributor and camshaft drive gears during installation.

**To install:**

7. With a new O-ring on the distributor housing and the rotor aligned with the second mark, install the distributor, taking care to align the mark on the housing with the one on the engine. It may be necessary to lift the distributor and turn the rotor slightly to align the gears and the oil pump driveshaft.

### ✳✳WARNING

**Make sure the distributor seats into the block fully. The base of the housing will stick up about ¼ in. until the distributor gear engages the oil pump drive. Damage to the oil pump, distributor and engine may result if the distributor is forced into position by tightening the distributor clamp bolt. If the distributor will not fully seat, grab the housing and shaft, twist and wiggle until the distributor drops into the oil pump drive. If this does not work, install a socket wrench onto the large bolt on the front of the crankshaft pulley. Slowly turn the crankshaft in either direction until the distributor drops into the block fully.**

8. With the respective marks aligned, install the clamp and the bolt finger-tight.

9. Install and secure the distributor cap.

10. Connect the feed and module connectors to the distributor cap. Reconnect the ignition switch battery feed wire and tach connector where necessary.

11. Connect a timing light to the engine and plug the vacuum hose, if so equipped.

12. Connect the ground cable to the battery.

13. Start the engine and set the timing to specifications.

14. Turn the engine off and torque the distributor clamp bolt to 15 ft. lbs. (20 Nm). Disconnect the timing light and unplug and disconnect the hose to the vacuum advance.

**Engine Disturbed**

### ✳✳CAUTION

**The engine MUST be completely cooled down before performing this procedure. A hot engine may cause burns and personal injury.**

1. Disconnect the negative battery cable.

2. Remove the No. 1 cylinder spark plug. Turn the engine using a socket wrench on the large bolt on the front of the crankshaft pulley. Place a finger near the No. 1 spark plug hole and turn the crankshaft until the piston reaches Top Dead Center (TDC). As the engine approaches TDC, you will feel air being expelled by the No. 1 cylinder. If the crankshaft timing

indicator says TDC has been reached but the other condition is not being met, turn the engine another full turn (360 degree). Once the engine's position is correct, replace the spark plug. Line the mark on the crankshaft damper with the 0 degree mark on the timing indicator.

➡ **When the timing marks are lined up at 0 degree, the No. 1 piston can be either on the exhaust stroke or the compression stroke. But only on the compression stroke will air be forced from the hole (on the exhaust stroke, then exhaust valve is open allowing air to escape through the manifold. Therefore, when air is felt being forced out of the spark plug hole, you can be sure the cylinder is on its compression stroke. The timing will be incorrect if the distributor is installed while aligning the rotor to fire that spark plug on the exhaust stroke.**

3. Using the firing order illustration if necessary, find No. 1 cylinder on the distributor cap. Turn the rotor until the rotor contact is approximately aligned with the wire going to No. 1 cylinder, as if the distributor had just fired No. 1 cylinder. Install the distributor as described above, turning the rotor slightly to mesh the gear teeth and oil pump driveshaft so that the rotor comes out in the proper position. Make sure the distributor is fully seated in the block before tightening the hold-down clamp.

## Alternator

The alternating current generator (alternator) supplies a continuous output of electrical energy at all engine speeds. The belt-driven alternator generates electrical energy and recharges the battery by supplying it with electrical current. The alternator consists of four main assemblies; two end frame assemblies, a stator assembly, and a rotor assembly. The rotor assembly is supported in the drive end frame by a ball bearing and at the other end by a roller bearing. These bearings are permanently lubricated and require no maintenance. There are six diodes in the end frame assembly. These diodes are electrical check valves that also change the alternating current developed within the stator windings to direct current (DC) at the output (BAT) terminal. Three of these diodes are negative and are mounted flush with the end frame while the other three are positive and are mounted into a component called a heat sink (which serves as a reservoir for excess heat, thus protecting the alternator). The positive diodes are easily identified as the ones within small cavities or depressions.

No periodic adjustments or maintenance of any kind, except for regular belt adjustments, are required on the entire alternator assembly. Alternator output in amps, is sometimes stamped on the case of each unit, near the mounting hole. Regulator voltages range between 13.6 and 16 volts at 75°F.

## ALTERNATOR PRECAUTIONS

### ✳✳WARNING

**To prevent serious damage to the alternator and the rest of the charging system, the following precautions must be observed:**

1. When installing a battery, make sure that the positive cable is connected to the positive terminal and the negative to the negative.

2. When jump-starting the vehicle with another battery, make sure that like terminals are connected. This also applies when using a battery charger.

3. Never operate the alternator with the battery disconnected or otherwise on an uncontrolled open circuit. Double-check to see that all connections are tight.

4. Do not short across or ground any alternator or regulator terminals.

5. Do not try to polarize the alternator.

6. Do not apply full battery voltage to the field (brown) connector.

7. Always disconnect the battery ground cable before disconnecting the alternator lead.

## TESTING

◆ See Figures 3 and 4

If you suspect a defect in your charging system, first perform these general checks before going on to more specific tests.

1. Check the condition of the alternator belt and tighten if necessary.

2. Clean the battery cable connections at the battery. Make sure the connections between the battery wires and the battery clamps are good. Reconnect the negative terminal only and proceed to the next step.

3. With the key off, insert a test light between the positive terminal on the battery terminal clamp. If the test light comes on, there is a short in the electrical system of the vehicle. The short must be repaired before proceeding. If the light does not come on, then proceed to the next step.

➡ If the vehicle is equipped with an electric clock, the clock must be disconnected.

4. Check the charging system wiring for any obvious breaks or shorts.

5. Check the battery to make sure it is fully charged and in good condition.

### Operational Test

➡ You will need a current indicator to perform this test. If the current indicator is to give an accurate reading, the battery cables must be the same gauge and length as the original equipment.

1. With the engine running and all electrical systems turned off, place a current indicator over the positive battery cable.

2. If a charge of roughly five amps is recorded, the charging system is working. If a draw of about five amps is recorded, the system is not working. The needle moves toward the battery when a charge condition is indicated, and away from the battery when a draw condition is indicated.

3. If a draw is indicated, proceed with further testing. If an excessive charge (10-15 amps) is indicated, the regulator may be at fault.

### Output Test

#### 1975 TO 1987 SI SERIES

1. You will need an ammeter for this test.

2. Disconnect the battery ground cable.

3. Disconnect the wire from the battery terminal on the alternator.

4. Connect the ammeter negative lead to the battery terminal wire removed in step three, and connect the ammeter positive lead to the battery terminal on the alternator.

5. Reconnect the battery ground cable and turn on all electrical accessories. If the battery is fully charged, disconnect the coil wire and bump the starter a few times to partially discharge it.

6. Start the engine and run it until you obtain a maximum current reading on the ammeter.

7. If the current is within ten amps of the rated output of the alternator, the alternator is working properly. If the current is not within ten amps, insert a probe into the test hole in the end frame of the alternator and ground the tab in the test hole against the side of the hole.

➡ The 1975-87 SI series alternator is equipped with the test hole, where the 1987 to present CS series alternator is not equipped with a test hole.

8. If the current is now within ten amps of the rated output, remove the alternator and have the voltage regulator replaced. If it is still below ten amps of rated output, have the alternator repaired. See the alternator and regulator output chart in this section.

#### 1987 TO 1990 CS SERIES

The CS series alternator comes in a variety of sizes as does the SI series. The most used sizes are the 130 and 144. These numbers represent the outside diameter of the stator laminations in millimeters. The main difference between the CS and SI series is the newly designed voltage regulator and the absence of a diode trio. The remaining components are basic to the earlier SI models. The CS series may have a combination of a four terminal connector at the alternator. All or only two connections may be used depending on the vehicle. The

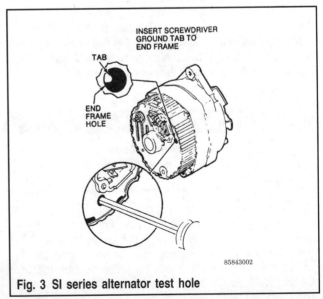

85843002

Fig. 3 SI series alternator test hole

terminals are labeled S, F, L, P. The P terminal is connected to the stator and a diesel tachometer, if so equipped. The L terminal is connected to the charge indicator bulb. The F terminal is connected internally to the field positive and may be used as a fault indicator. The S terminal may be connected to a external voltage source, such as battery voltage. The P, F and S terminals are optional.

1. Check all preliminary charging system tests before continuing.

2. With the ignition switch ON and the engine NOT running, the alternator lamp should be ON. If not, check for an open circuit between the grounding lead and ignition switch. Check for a burned out bulb.

3. With the engine RUNNING at moderate speed, the lamp should be OFF. If not, turn OFF the engine and disconnect the harness connector at the alternator. Start the engine and check the lamp. If the lamp goes OFF, repair or replace the alternator. If the lamp stays ON, check for a grounded L terminal wire in the harness.

4. Is the battery undercharged or overcharged?

a. Disconnect the wiring harness connector from the alternator.

b. With ignition switch ON, engine NOT running, connect a voltmeter from ground to the **L** terminal. A zero reading indicates an open circuit between the terminal and battery.

c. Reconnect the harness connector and run the engine at moderate speed. Measure the voltage across the battery. If it is above 16V, repair or replace the alternator.

d. Turn on all accessories, load the battery with a carbon pile to obtain maximum amperage. Maintain voltage at 13V or greater. If the amperage is within 15 amps of rated output, the alternator is OK. If NOT within 15 amps, replace or repair the alternator.

## REMOVAL & INSTALLATION

▶ **See Figures 5, 6, 7, 8 and 9**

1. Disconnect the battery ground cable to prevent diode damage.

2. Tag and disconnect the alternator wiring.

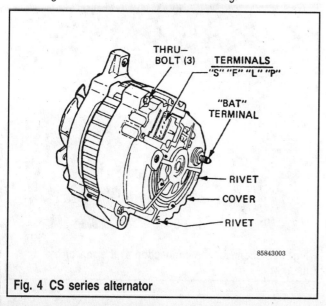

THRU-
BOLT (3)

TERMINALS
"S" "F" "L" "P"

"BAT"
TERMINAL

RIVET

COVER

RIVET

85843003

**Fig. 4 CS series alternator**

3. Remove the alternator brace bolt. If the vehicle is equipped with power steering, loosen the pump brace and mount nuts. Detach the drive belt(s).

4. Support the alternator and remove the mount bolt(s). Remove the unit from the vehicle.

**To install:**

5. To install, position the alternator into the mounting brackets and hand tighten the mounting bolts. Alternator belt tension is quite critical. A belt that is too tight may cause alternator bearing failure; one that is too loose will cause a gradual battery discharge as well as belt wear. For details on correct belt adjustment, see Drive Belts in Section 1.

➡**When adjusting alternator belt tension, apply pressure at the center of the alternator unit, NEVER against either end frame.**

## Regulator

The voltage regulator works with the battery and alternator to comprise the charging system. As the voltage regulator's name e implies, it regulates the voltage output of the alternator to a safe level (so the alternator does not overcharge the battery). A properly working regulator also prevents excessive voltage from burning out wiring, bulbs and other electrical components. All Buick, Olds and Pontiac models covered in this guide are equipped with integral regulators, which are built into the alternator case. The regulators are solid state and require no maintenance or adjustment.

### REMOVAL & INSTALLATION

▶ **See Figures 10, 11 and 12**

#### 1975-1987 SI Series

1. Remove the alternator from the vehicle. Position the assembly in a suitable holding fixture.

2. Make scribe marks on the case end frames to aid in reassembly.

3. Remove the through bolts. Separate the drive end frame assembly from the rectifier end frame assembly.

4. Remove the rectifier attaching nuts and the regulator attaching screws from the end frame assembly. Note the position of the screws with the insulated washers for reassembly.

5. Remove the voltage regulator from the end frame assembly.

**To install:**

6. Position the brushes in the brush holder and retain them in place using a brush retainer wire or equivalent.

7. Assemble the brush holder, regulator, resistor, diode trio and rectifier bridge to the end frame. Be sure to assemble the screws with the insulated washers in the correct locations.

8. Assemble the end frames together with the through bolts. **Remove the brush retainer wire.**

#### 1987-1990 CS Series

##### TYPE 130

1. Remove the alternator from the vehicle. Scribe marks on the end frames to facilitate assembly. Remove the through bolts and separate the end frames.

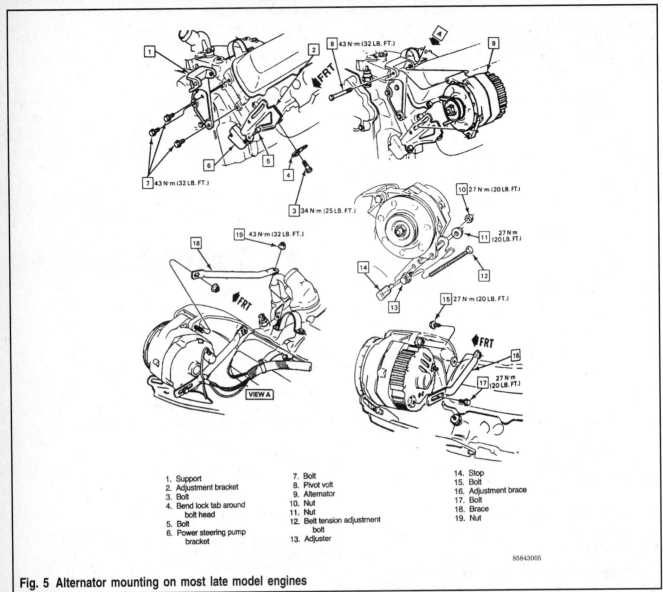

1. Support
2. Adjustment bracket
3. Bolt
4. Bend lock tab around bolt head
5. Bolt
6. Power steering pump bracket
7. Bolt
8. Pivot volt
9. Alternator
10. Nut
11. Nut
12. Belt tension adjustment bolt
13. Adjuster
14. Stop
15. Bolt
16. Adjustment brace
17. Bolt
18. Brace
19. Nut

85843005

**Fig. 5 Alternator mounting on most late model engines**

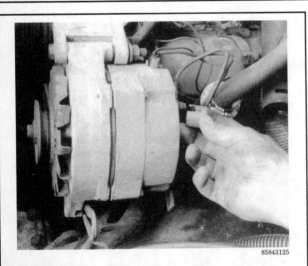

85843125

**Fig. 6 Disconnect the electrical connectors from the back of the alternator**

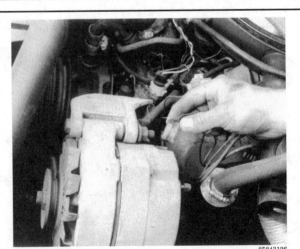

85843126

**Fig. 7 Disconnect the connection at the top of the alternator**

Fig. 8 Remove the alternator attaching bolts

Fig. 9 Once the belt is slipped off and all bolts/wiring removed, the alternator can be removed from the vehicle

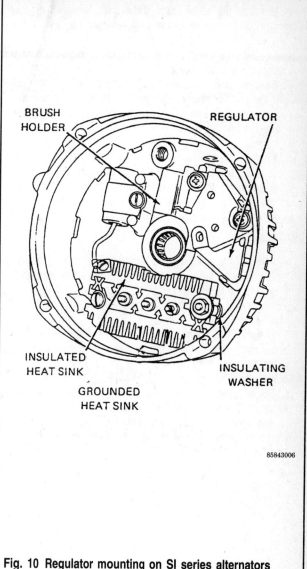

Fig. 10 Regulator mounting on SI series alternators

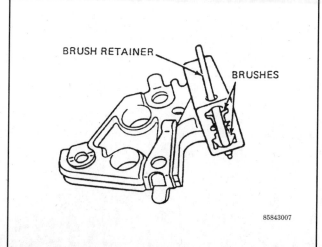

Fig. 11 On all alternator models, the brushes can be retained with a wire in the holder

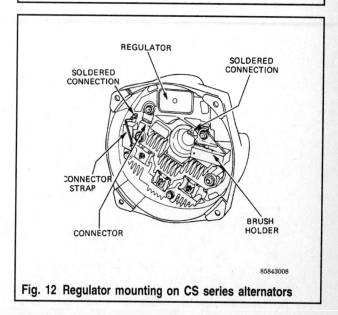

Fig. 12 Regulator mounting on CS series alternators

2. Remove the cover rivets or pins and remove the cover.

3. Unsolder the stator leads at the three terminals on the rectifier bridge. Avoid excessive heat, as damage to the assembly will occur. Remove the stator.

4. Remove the brush holder screw. Disconnect the terminal and remove the brush holder assembly.

5. Unsolder and pry open the terminal between the regulator and the rectifier bridge. Remove the terminal and the retaining screws. Remove the regulator and the rectifier bridge from the end frame.

**To install:**

6. Position the brushes in the brush holder and retain them in place using a brush retainer wire or equivalent.

7. Assembly is the reverse of disassembly. Be sure to remove the brush retainer wire when the alternator has been reassembled.

### TYPE 144

1. Remove the alternator from the vehicle. Scribe marks on the end frames to facilitate assembly. Remove the through bolts and separate the end frames.

2. Remove the stator attaching nuts and the stator from the end frame.

3. Unsolder the connections, remove the retaining screws and connector from the end frame. Separate the regulator and brush holder from the end frame.

**To install:**

4. Position the brushes in the brush holder and retain them in place using a brush retainer wire or equivalent.

5. Assembly is the reverse of disassembly. Be sure to remove the brush retainer wire when the alternator has been reassembled.

## Battery

### REMOVAL & INSTALLATION

### ✳✳CAUTION

**When working on the battery, be careful at all times to keep metal wrenches from connecting across the battery terminal posts. DO NOT wear any type of metal jewelry, this includes watches!**

1. Use a wrench to loosen the through-bolt for the terminal. If necessary, use a prybar to carefully spread the terminal halves apart. Disconnect the negative terminal. Then, repeat the process to disconnect the positive terminal.

2. Remove the retainer screw from the retaining block located behind the battery. Remove the retainer.

3. Carefully lift the battery out of the engine compartment using a battery lifting strap or equivalent.

4. Thoroughly clean the entire battery box area. Use a mild solution of baking soda and water to cut through the corrosion. This is done because the battery retains its charge better in a clean environment.

5. Replace the battery with one having an equal or higher rating in amp/hours. Note that the older a vehicle is, the more likely it is to benefit from an increase in battery capacity due to increased resistance in the wiring.

6. Replace the battery in exact reverse order, making sure it is securely mounted before starting to connect the wiring. Make sure the battery terminals are clean, using a special brush designed for that purpose, if necessary.

7. Connect the positive terminal first, and then the negative, tightening them securely. Coat the terminals with petroleum jelly to protect them from corrosion.

## ALTERNATOR OUTPUT SPECIFICATIONS

| Year | Alternator Part No. | Field Current @ 12V | Output (amps) | Regulator Volts @ 75°F |
|------|---------------------|---------------------|---------------|------------------------|
| | | | BUICK | |
| **1975** | 1102389 | 4–4.5 | 42 | 13.6–14.2 |
| | 1102391 | 4–4.5 | 61 | 13.6–14.2 |
| | 1102939 | 4–4.5 | 63 | 13.6–14.2 |
| **1976** | 1102389 | 4–4.5 | 42 | 13.6–14.2 |
| | 1102391 | 4–4.5 | 61 | 13.6–14.2 |
| | 1102939 | 4–4.5 | 63 | 13.6–14.2 |
| **1977** | 1102485 | 4–4.5 | 42 | 13.6–14.2 |
| | 1102486 | 4–4.5 | 61 | 13.6–14.2 |
| | 1102854 | 4–4.5 | 63 | 13.6–14.2 |
| **1978** | 1102841 | 4–4.5 | 42 | 13.6–14.2 |
| | 1102391 | 4–4.5 | 61 | 13.6–14.2 |
| **1979** | 1102389 | 4–4.5 | 42 | 13.9–14.5 |
| | 1102392 | 4–4.5 | 63 | 13.9–14.5 |
| | 1102842 | 4–4.5 | 63 | 13.9–14.5 |
| **1980** | 1103043 | 4–4.5 | 42 | 13.9–14.5 |
| | 1103085 | 4–4.5 | 55 | 13.9–14.5 |
| | 1103111 | 4–4.5 | 63 | 13.9–14.5 |
| | 1103121 | 4–4.5 | 63 | 13.9–14.5 |
| | 1101066 | 4–4.5 | 70 | 13.9–14.5 |
| **1981** | 1100164 | 4–4.5 | 55 | 13.9–14.5 |
| | 1100156 | 4–4.5 | 55 | 13.9–14.5 |
| | 1100121 | 4–4.5 | 63 | 13.9–14.5 |
| | 1101037 | 4–4.5 | 70 | 13.9–14.5 |
| **1982** | 1101037 | 4–4.5 | 70 | 13.6–14.5 |
| | 1100121 | 4–4.5 | 60 | 13.6–14.5 |
| | 1100121 | 4–4.5 | 63 | 13.6–14.5 |
| **1983** | 1101037 | 4–4.5 | 70 | 13.6–14.5 |
| | 1100121 | 4–4.5 | 60 | 13.6–14.5 |
| | 1100121 | 4–4.5 | 63 | 13.6–14.5 |
| **1984** | 1100239 | 4–4.5 | 56 | 13.6–14.5 |
| | 1105564 | 4–4.5 | 66 | 13.6–14.5 |
| | 1105566 | 4–4.5 | 66 | 13.6–14.5 |

| Year | Alternator Part No. | Field Current @ 12V | Output (amps) | Regulator Volts @ 75°F |
|------|---------------------|---------------------|---------------|------------------------|
| | | | BUICK | |
| | 1105250 | 4–4.5 | 66 | 13.6–14.5 |
| | 1100200 | 4–4.5 | 78 | 13.6–14.5 |
| | 1100260 | 4–4.5 | 78 | 13.6–14.5 |
| | 1105567 | 4–4.5 | 78 | 13.6–14.5 |
| | 1105565 | 4–4.5 | 78 | 13.6–14.5 |
| | 1105443 | 4–4.5 | 94 | 13.6–14.5 |
| | 1105493 | 4–4.5 | 94 | 13.6–14.5 |
| **1985** | 1100239 | 4–4.5 | 56 | 13.6–14.5 |
| | 1105564 | 4–4.5 | 66 | 13.6–14.5 |
| | 1105521 ③ | 4–4.5 | 78 | 13.6–14.5 |
| | 1105544 ④ | 4–4.5 | 94 | 13.6–14.5 |
| **1986** | 1100239 | 4–4.5 | 55 | 13.6–14.5 |
| | 1105197 | 4–4.5 | 70 | 13.6–14.5 |
| | 1100200 | 4–4.5 | 78 | 13.6–14.5 |
| | 1105565 | 4–4.5 | 78 | 13.6–14.5 |
| **1987** | 1100239 | 4–4.5 | 55 | 13.6–14.5 |
| | 1105197 | 4–4.5 | 70 | 13.6–14.5 |
| | 1100200 | 4–4.5 | 78 | 13.6–14.5 |
| | 1105565 | 4–4.5 | 78 | 13.6–14.5 |
| **1988** | 1101229 | 4–4.5 | 85 | 13.5–16.0 |
| | 1101253 | 4–4.5 | 85 | 13.5–16.0 |
| | 1101254 | 4–4.5 | 120 | 13.6–14.5 |
| | 1101454 | 4–4.5 | 120 | 13.6–14.5 |
| **1989** | 1101229 | 4–4.5 | 85 | 13.5–16.0 |
| | 1101253 | 4–4.5 | 85 | 13.5–16.0 |
| | 1101254 | 4–4.5 | 120 | 13.6–14.5 |
| | 1101454 | 4–4.5 | 120 | 13.6–14.5 |
| **1990** | 1101229 | 4–4.5 | 85 | 13.5–16.0 |
| | 1101253 | 4–4.5 | 85 | 13.5–16.0 |
| | 1101254 | 4–4.5 | 120 | 13.6–14.5 |
| | 1101454 | 4–4.5 | 120 | 13.6–14.5 |

85843A01

## ALTERNATOR OUTPUT SPECIFICATIONS (CONT.)

| Year | Part No. | Field Current @ 12V | Output (amps) | Regulator Volts @ 75°F | Year | Part No. | Field Current @ 12V | Output (amps) | Regulator Volts @ 75°F |
|------|----------|---------------------|---------------|------------------------|------|----------|---------------------|---------------|------------------------|
| | | OLDSMOBILE | | | | | OLDSMOBILE | | |
| 1975 | 1102483 | 4–4.5 | 37 | 13.6–14.2 | | 1100121-HT | 4–4.5 | 63 | 13.5–14.5 |
| | 1102488 | 4–4.5 | 57 | 13.6–14.2 | | 1100156-AY | 4–4.5 | 55 | 13.5–14.5 |
| | 1102550 | 4–4.5 | 63 | 13.6–14.2 | 1983 | 1100230 | 4–4.5 | 42 | 13.5–14.5 |
| 1976 | 1102841 | 4–4.5 | 42 | 13.6–14.2 | | 1100239 | 4–4.5 | 55 | 13.5–14.5 |
| | 1102843 | 4–4.5 | 61 | 13.6–14.2 | | 1100100 | 4–4.5 | 78 | 13.5–14.5 |
| | 1102842 | 4–4.5 | 63 | 13.6–14.2 | | 1100260 | 4–4.5 | 78 | 13.5–14.5 |
| | 1102844 | 4–4.5 | 63 | 13.6–14.2 | | 1105343 | 4–4.5 | 85 | 13.5–14.5 |
| 1977 | 1102841 | 4–4.5 | 42 | 13.6–14.2 | | 1105198 | 4–4.5 | 85 | 13.5–14.5 |
| | 1102843 | 4–4.5 | 61 | 13.6–14.2 | | 1100300 | 4–4.5 | 63 | 13.5–14.5 |
| | 1102844 | 4–4.5 | 63 | 13.6–14.2 | | 1105022 | 4–4.5 | 78 | 13.5–14.5 |
| | 1102842 | 4–4.5 | 63 | 13.6–14.2 | | 1100247 | 4–4.5 | 63 | 13.5–14.5 |
| 1978 | 1102841 | 4–4.5 | 42 | 13.6–14.5 | 1984 | 1100239 | 4–4.5 | 55 | 13.5–14.5 |
| | 1102479 | 4–4.5 | 55 | 13.6–14.5 | | 1100260 | 4–4.5 | 78 | 13.5–14.5 |
| | 1102843 | 4–4.5 | 61 | 13.6–14.5 | | 1105564 | 4–4.5 | 66 | 13.5–14.5 |
| | 1102844 | 4–4.5 | 63 | 13.6–14.5 | | 1105565 | 4–4.5 | 78 | 13.5–14.5 |
| | 1102842 | 4–4.5 | 63 | 13.6–14.5 | | 1105566 | 4–4.5 | 66 | 13.5–14.5 |
| | 1101016 | 4–4.5 | 80 | 13.6–14.5 | | 1105567 | 4–4.5 | 78 | 13.5–14.5 |
| 1979 | 1102841 | 4–4.5 | 42 | 13.6–14.5 | 1985 | 1100239 | 4–4.5 | 55 | 13.5–14.5 |
| | 1102479 | 4–4.5 | 55 | 13.6–14.5 | | 1100260 | 4–4.5 | 78 | 13.5–14.5 |
| | 1102843 | 4–4.5 | 61 | 13.6–14.5 | | 1105564 | 4–4.5 | 66 | 13.5–14.5 |
| | 1102844 | 4–4.5 | 63 | 13.6–14.5 | | 1105565 | 4–4.5 | 78 | 13.5–14.5 |
| | 1102842 | 4–4.5 | 63 | 13.6–14.5 | | 1105566 | 4–4.5 | 66 | 13.5–14.5 |
| | 1101016 | 4–4.5 | 80 | 13.6–14.5 | | 1105567 | 4–4.5 | 78 | 13.5–14.5 |
| 1980 | 1103043 | 4–4.5 | 42 | 13.9–14.5 | 1986 | 1105565 | 4–4.5 | 78 | 13.5–14.5 |
| | 1103085 | 4–4.5 | 55 | 13.9–14.5 | 1987 | 1105565 | 4–4.5 | 78 | 13.5–14.5 |
| | 1103111 | 4–4.5 | 63 | 13.9–14.5 | 1988 | 1101229 | 4–4.5 | 85 | 13.5–16.0 |
| | 1103121 | 4–4.5 | 63 | 13.9–14.5 | | 1101253 | 4–4.5 | 85 | 13.5–16.0 |
| | 1101066 | 4–4.5 | 70 | 13.9–14.5 | | 1101254 | 4–4.5 | 100 | 13.5–14.5 |
| 1981 | 1100164 | 4–4.5 | 55 | 13.9–14.5 | | 1101454 | 4–4.5 | 120 | 13.5–14.5 |
| | 1100156 | 4–4.5 | 55 | 13.9–14.5 | 1989 | 1101229 | 4–4.5 | 85 | 13.5–16.0 |
| | 1100121 | 4–4.5 | 63 | 13.9–14.5 | | 1101253 | 4–4.5 | 85 | 13.5–16.0 |
| | 1101037 | 4–4.5 | 70 | 13.0–14.5 | | 1101254 | 4–4.5 | 100 | 13.5–14.5 |
| 1982 | 1100110-NL | 4–4.5 | 42 | 13.5–14.5 | | 1101454 | 4–4.5 | 120 | 13.5–14.5 |
| | 1101037-ZU | 4–4.5 | 70 | 13.5–14.5 | 1990 | 1101229 | 4–4.5 | 85 | 13.5–16.0 |
| | 1101088-AX | 4–4.5 | 70 | 13.5–14.5 | | 1101253 | 4–4.5 | 85 | 13.5–16.0 |
| | 1101045-FZ | 4–4.5 | 85 | 13.5–14.5 | | 1101254 | 4–4.5 | 100 | 13.5–14.5 |
| | 1101084-NU | 4–4.5 | 85 | 13.5–14.5 | | 1101454 | 4–4.5 | 120 | 13.5–14.5 |
| | 1101064-FM | 4–4.5 | 55 | 13.5–14.5 | | | | | |

85843A02

## ALTERNATOR OUTPUT SPECIFICATIONS (CONT.)

| Year | Alternator Part No. | Field Current @ 12V | Output (amps) | Regulator Volts @ 75°F |
|------|---------------------|---------------------|---------------|------------------------|
| | | PONTIAC | | |
| 1975 | 1102481 | 4–4.5 | 37 | 13.6–14.2 |
| | 1102482 | 4–4.5 | 55 | 13.6–14.2 |
| | 1101027 | 4–4.5 | 80 | 13.6–14.2 |
| 1976 | 1102481 | 4–4.5 | 37 | 13.6–14.2 |
| | 1102482 | 4–4.5 | 55 | 13.6–14.2 |
| | 1102486 | 4–4.5 | 61 | 13.6–14.2 |
| | 1102384 | 4–4.5 | 37 | 13.6–14.2 |
| | 1102385 | 4–4.5 | 55 | 13.6–14.2 |
| | 1101027 | 4–4.5 | 80 | 13.6–14.2 |
| 1977 | 1102841 | 4–4.5 | 42 | 13.6–14.2 |
| | 1102906 | 4–4.5 | 61 | 13.6–14.2 |
| | 1102882 | 4–4.5 | 63 | 13.6–14.2 |
| | 1102485 | 4–4.5 | 42 | 13.6–14.2 |
| | 1102486 | 4–4.5 | 61 | 13.6–14.2 |
| | 1102854 | 4–4.5 | 63 | 13.6–14.2 |
| | 1102843 | 4–4.5 | 61 | 13.6–14.2 |
| | 1101016 | 4–4.5 | 80 | 13.6–14.2 |
| 1978 | 1102485 | 4–4.5 | 42 | 13.6–14.2 |
| | 1102841 | 4–4.5 | 42 | 13.6–14.2 |
| | 1102389 | 4–4.5 | 42 | 13.6–14.2 |
| | 1102906 | 4–4.5 | 61 | 13.6–14.2 |
| | 1102391 | 4–4.5 | 61 | 13.6–14.2 |
| | 1102843 | 4–4.5 | 61 | 13.6–14.2 |
| | 1102892 | 4–4.5 | 63 | 13.6–14.2 |
| | 1102844 | 4–4.5 | 63 | 13.6–14.2 |
| | 1101016 | 4–4.5 | 80 | 13.6–14.2 |
| 1979 | 1103033 | 4–4.5 | 42 | 13.9–14.5 |
| | 1103055 | 4–4.5 | 42 | 13.9–14.5 |
| | 1102389 | 4–4.5 | 42 | 13.9–14.5 |
| | 1103056 | 4–4.5 | 63 | 13.9–14.5 |
| | 1103058 | 4–4.5 | 63 | 13.9–14.5 |
| | 1102392 | 4–4.5 | 63 | 13.9–14.5 |
| | 1103076 | 4–4.5 | 63 | 13.9–14.5 |
| | 1102842 | 4–4.5 | 63 | 13.9–14.5 |
| | 1101016 | 4–4.5 | 80 | 13.9–14.5 |
| 1980 | 1103043 | 4–4.5 | 42 | 13.5–16.0 |
| | ② | 4–4.5 | 63 | 13.5–16.0 |
| | ② | 4–4.5 | 70 | 13.5–16.0 |
| 1981 | 1103088 | 4–4.5 | 55 | 13.5–14.5 |
| | 1103091 | 4–4.5 | 63 | 13.5–14.5 |
| | 1101037 | 4–4.5 | 70 | 13.5–14.5 |
| | 1101038 | 4–4.5 | 70 | 13.5–14.5 |

| Year | Alternator Part No. | Field Current @ 12V | Output (amps) | Regulator Volts @ 75°F |
|------|---------------------|---------------------|---------------|------------------------|
| | | PONTIAC | | |
| 1982 | 1100230 | 4–4.5 | 42 | 13.5–14.5 |
| | 1105523 | 4–4.5 | 56 | 13.5–14.5 |
| | 1100247 | 4–4.5 | 66 | 13.5–14.5 |
| | 1105197 | 4–4.5 | 70 | 13.5–14.5 |
| | 1105343 | 4–4.5 | 85 | 13.5–14.5 |
| 1983 | 1100230 | 4–4.5 | 42 | 13.5–14.5 |
| | 1105523 | 4–4.5 | 56 | 13.5–14.5 |
| | 1100247 | 4–4.5 | 66 | 13.5–14.5 |
| | 1105197 | 4–4.5 | 70 | 13.5–14.5 |
| | 1105343 | 4–4.5 | 85 | 13.5–14.5 |
| 1984 | 1100230 | 4–4.5 | 42 | 13.5–14.5 |
| | 1100237 ⑤ | 4–4.5 | 56 | 13.5–14.5 |
| | 1100555 ⑥ | 4–4.5 | 66 | 13.5–14.5 |
| | 1100200 ⑦ | 4–4.5 | 78 | 13.5–14.5 |
| | 1105444 | 4–4.5 | 85 | 13.0–14.5 |
| | 1105651 | 4–4.5 | 94 | 13.5–14.5 |
| 1985 | 1100230 | 4–4.5 | 42 | 13.5–14.5 |
| | 1100237 ⑤ | 4–4.5 | 56 | 13.5–14.5 |
| | 1100555 ⑥ | 4–4.5 | 66 | 13.5–14.5 |
| | 1100200 ⑦ | 4–4.5 | 78 | 13.5–14.5 |
| | 1105444 | 4–4.5 | 85 | 13.5–14.5 |
| | 1105651 | 4–4.5 | 94 | 13.5–14.5 |
| 1986 | 1100239 | 4–4.5 | 55 | 13.5–14.5 |
| | 1105197 | 4–4.5 | 70 | 13.5–14.5 |
| | 1100200 | 4–4.5 | 78 | 13.5–14.5 |
| | 1105565 | 4–4.5 | 78 | 13.5–14.5 |
| 1987 | 1100239 | 4–4.5 | 55 | 13.5–14.5 |
| | 1105197 | 4–4.5 | 70 | 13.5–14.5 |
| | 1100200 | 4–4.5 | 78 | 13.5–14.5 |
| | 1105565 | 4–4.5 | 78 | 13.5–14.5 |
| 1988 | 1101229 | 4–4.5 | 85 | 13.5–16.0 |
| | 1101253 | 4–4.5 | 85 | 13.5–16.0 |
| | 1101254 | 4–4.5 | 100 | 13.5–14.5 |
| | 1101454 | 4–4.5 | 120 | 13.5–14.5 |
| 1989 | 1101229 | 4–4.5 | 85 | 13.5–16.0 |
| | 1101253 | 4–4.5 | 85 | 13.5–16.0 |
| | 1101254 | 4–4.5 | 100 | 13.5–14.5 |
| | 1101454 | 4–4.5 | 120 | 13.5–14.5 |

**NOTE:** All alternators made by Delco-Remy Regulators aer integral with alternator unit
① 1978: 13.6–14.2
② Not available
③ Diesel—1105569
④ 307 (Y)—1105493
   Diesel—1105617
⑤ 231 (A)—1100239
   305 (H)—11005523
⑥ Diesel—1100566
⑦ 305 (H)—11005521
   Diesel—11005568

85843A03

## Starter

### REMOVAL & INSTALLATION

▶ See Figures 13, 14, 15, 16 and 17

**Gasoline Engines**

➡The starters on some engines require the addition of shims to provide proper clearance between the starter pinion gear and the flywheel. These shims are available in 0.015 in. (0.4mm) sizes from Buick, Oldsmobile and Pontiac dealers. Flat washers can be used if shims are unavailable.

1. **Important:** disconnect the negative battery cable before proceeding.
2. Raise the vehicle to a convenient working height and safely support it with jackstands.
3. Remove the exhaust crossover pipe.
4. Disconnect all wiring from the starter solenoid. Replace each nut as the connector is removed, as thread sizes differ from connector to connector. Tag the wires for later connection.
5. Remove the flywheel housing cover and disconnect the oil cooler lines at the transmission, if necessary.
6. Starter removal on certain models may necessitate the removal of the frame support. This support runs from the corner of the frame to the front crossmember. To remove:
   a. Loosen the mounting bolt that attaches the support to the corner of the frame.
   b. Loosen and remove the mounting bolt that attaches the support to the front crossmember and then swing the support out of the way.
   c. Install the crossmember and mounting bolts. Torque the bolts to 80 ft. lbs. (109 Nm).
7. Remove the front bracket from the starter and the two mounting bolts. On engines with a starter solenoid heat shield, remove the front bracket upper bolt and detach the bracket from the starter.
8. Remove the front bracket bolt or nut. Lower the starter front end first, then remove the unit from the vehicle.
9. Installation is the reverse of removal. Make sure that any shims removed are replaced (please refer to the shimming procedure). Torque the two mounting bolts to 25-35 ft. lbs. (34-48 Nm). Connect the starter wires and install heat shields if removed.

**Diesel Engines**

1. Disconnect both batteries. Raise the vehicle and support it securely with jackstands.
2. Remove the flywheel cover.
3. Remove the starter heat shield upper bolt and side nut and then remove the shield.
4. Label the wires and then disconnect them, keeping attaching nuts in order. On the Olds 88 and 98 models, it may be necessary to work on the wiring from the front of the engine.
5. Support the starter from underneath. Remove the two mounting bolts that can be reached from underneath the

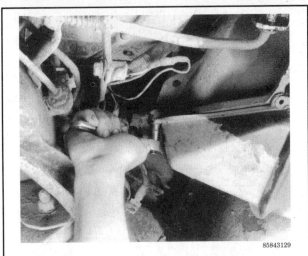

Fig. 13 It may be necessary to remove the flywheel cover on some models to remove the starter

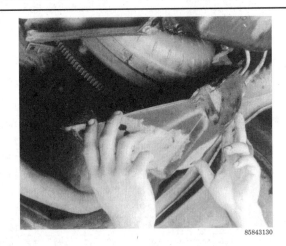

Fig. 14 On some models it may be helpful to disconnect the cooler lines at the transmission before removing the flywheel cover

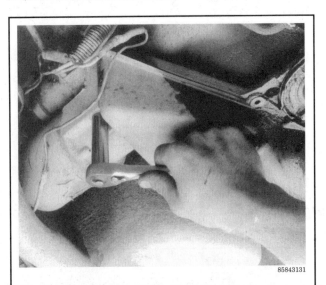

Fig. 15 Removing the starter attaching bolts

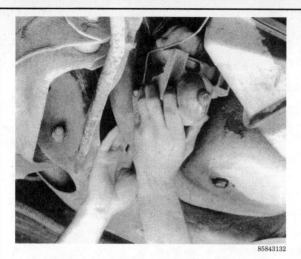

**Fig. 16 To remove the starter from the vehicle, first pull it straight out then lower it away from the vehicle**

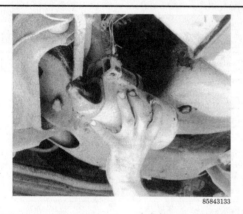

**Fig. 17 On some models the connections at the starter solenoid are not accessible when it is installed. Do not let the starter hang by it's wires once it has been lowered from it's mount. Have a helper hold it, then disconnect the wires**

starter, and remove it by pulling it out between the flywheel and exhaust crossover.

**To install:**

6. Support the starter and connect the wiring harness as previously marked.

7. Position the starter into the mounting area and install the shims (if used) and mounting bolts. Torque the mounting bolts to 35 ft. lbs. (47 Nm).

8. Install the flywheel cover and heat shield, if so equipped.

9. Connect the battery cables and start the engine to check for proper operation.

## SHIMMING

▶ See Figures 18 and 19

Starter noise during cranking and after the engine fires is often a result of too much or too little distance between the starter pinion gear and the flywheel. A high pitched whine

during cranking (before the engine fires) can be caused by the pinion and flywheel being too far apart. Likewise, a whine after the engine starts (as the key is released) is often a result of the pinion-flywheel relationship being too close. In both cases flywheel damage can occur. Shims are available in 0.015 in. (0.4mm) sizes to properly adjust the starter on its mount. You will also need a flywheel turning tool, available at most auto parts stores or from any auto tool store or salesperson.

If your vehicle's starter emits the above noises, follow the shimming procedure:

1. Disconnect the negative battery cable.

2. Remove the flywheel inspection cover on the bottom of the bellhousing.

3. Using the flywheel turning tool, turn the flywheel and examine the flywheel teeth. If damage is evident, the flywheel should be replaced.

4. Insert a suitable prybar into the small hole in the bottom of the starter and move the starter pinion and clutch assembly so the pinion and flywheel teeth mesh. If necessary, rotate the flywheel so that a pinion tooth is directly in the center of the two flywheel teeth and on the centerline of the two gears, as shown in the accompanying illustration.

5. Check the pinion-to-flywheel clearance by using a 0.020 in. (0.5mm) wire gauge (a spark plug wire gauge may work here, or you can make your own). Make sure you center the pinion tooth between the flywheel teeth and the gauge, NOT in the corners, as you may get a false reading. If the clearance is under this minimum, shim the starter away from the flywheel by adding shim(s) one at a time to the starter mount. Check clearance after adding each shim.

6. If the clearance is a good deal over 0.020 in. (0.5mm), in the vicinity of 0.050 in. (1.27mm) plus, shim the starter toward the flywheel. Broken or severely mangled flywheel teeth are also a good indicator that the clearance here is too great. Shimming the starter toward the flywheel is done by adding shims to the outboard starter mounting pad only. Check the clearance after each shim is added. A shim of 0.015 in. (0.4mm) at this location will decrease the clearance about 0.010 in. (0.25mm).

## SOLENOID REPLACEMENT

▶ See Figure 20

1. Disconnect the negative battery cable.

2. Remove the starter motor from the vehicle as previously outlined.

3. Remove the screw and washer from the field strap terminal.

4. Remove the two solenoid-to-housing retaining screws and the motor terminal bolt.

5. Remove the solenoid by twisting the unit 90 degrees.

**To install:**

6. Install the solenoid and twist 90 degrees. Make sure the return spring is on the plunger, and rotate the solenoid unit into place on the starter.

7. Install the retaining screws and torque to 100 inch lbs. (11 Nm).

8. Connect the field strap terminal, install the starter, connect the negative battery cable and start the engine to check for proper operation.

## BATTERY AND STARTER SPECIFICATIONS

| Year | Engine No. Cyl. Displacement (cu. in.) | Engine VIN Code | Battery Ampere Hour Capacity② | Volts | Terminal Grounded | Starter Lock Test Amps | Volts | Torque (ft. lbs.) | No-Load Test Amps | Volts | RPM | Brush String Tension (oz.)① |
|------|------|------|------|------|------|------|------|------|------|------|------|------|
| 1975 | 8-350 | K | 350 | 12 | Neg | Not Recommended | | | 45–80 | 9 | 3500–6000 | 35 |
| | 8-350 | J | 310 | 12 | Neg | Not Recommended | | | 55–80 | 9 | 3500–6000 | 35 |
| | 8-400 | R③ | 430 | 12 | Neg | Not Recommended | | | 55–80 | 9 | 3500–6000 | 35 |
| | 8-400 | S③ | 450 | 12 | Neg | Not Recommended | | | 55–80 | 9 | 3500–6000 | 35 |
| | 8-400 | R④ | 430 | 12 | Neg | Not Recommended | | | 55–80 | 9 | 3500–6000 | 35 |
| | 8-400 | S④ | 450 | 12 | Neg | Not Recommended | | | 55–80 | 9 | 3500–6000 | 35 |
| | 8-455 | T③ | 450 | 12 | Neg | Not Recommended | | | 45–80 | 9 | 4000–6000 | 35 |
| | 8-455 | T⑤ | 420 | 12 | Neg | Not Recommended | | | 45–80 | 9 | 4000–6500 | 35 |
| | 8-455 | W④ | 420 | 12 | Neg | Not Recommended | | | 45–80 | 9 | 4000–6500 | 35 |
| 1976 | 8-350 | R | 350 | 12 | Neg | Not Recommended | | | 55–80 | 9 | 3500–6000 | 35 |
| | 8-350 | J | 350 | 12 | Neg | Not Recommended | | | 55–80 | 9 | 3500–6000 | 35 |
| | 8-400 | R | 450 | 12 | Neg | Not Recommended | | | 55–80 | 9 | 3500–6000 | 35 |
| | 8-400 | S | 430 | 12 | Neg | Not Recommended | | | 55–80 | 9 | 3500–6000 | 35 |
| | 8-455 | T③ | 420 | 12 | Neg | Not Recommended | | | 45–80 | 9 | 4000–6500 | 35 |
| | 8-455 | W④ | 420 | 12 | Neg | Not Recommended | | | 45–80 | 9 | 4000–6500 | 35 |
| | 8-455 | Y⑤ | 420 | 12 | Neg | Not Recommended | | | 45–80 | 9 | 4000–6500 | 35 |
| 1977 | 6-231 | C | 275 | 12 | Neg | Not Recommended | | | 50–80 | 9 | 5500–10,000 | 35 |
| | 8-260 | F | 310 | 12 | Neg | Not Recommended | | | 55–80 | 9 | 7000–11,900 | 35 |
| | 8-301 | Y | 350 | 12 | Neg | Not Recommended | | | 55–80 | 9 | 3500–6000 | 35 |
| | 8-305 | U | 310 | 12 | Neg | Not Recommended | | | 60–85 | 9 | 6800–10,300 | 35 |
| | 8-350 | R③ | 350 | 12 | Neg | Not Recommended | | | 55–80 | 9 | 3500–6000 | 35 |
| | 8-350 | L⑥ | 350 | 12 | Neg | Not Recommended | | | 60–95 | 9 | 7500–10,500 | 35 |
| | 8-400 | Z | 380 | 12 | Neg | Not Recommended | | | 65–95 | 9 | 7500–10,500 | 35 |
| | 8-350 | P④ | 350 | 12 | Neg | Not Recommended | | | 65–95 | 9 | 7500–10,500 | 35 |
| | 8-350 | J⑤ | 350 | 12 | Neg | Not Recommended | | | 55–80 | 9 | 3500–6000 | 35 |
| | 8-403 | K | 430 | 12 | Neg | Not Recommended | | | 55–80 | 9 | 3500–6000 | 35 |
| 1978 | 6-231 | A,G,3 | 275 | 12 | Neg | Not Recommended | | | 60–85 | 9 | 6800–10,300 | 35 |
| | 8-260 | F | 310 | 12 | Neg | Not Recommended | | | 45–70 | 9 | 7000–11,900 | 35 |
| | 8-301 | Y,W | 310 | 12 | Neg | Not Recommended | | | 45–70 | 9 | 7000–11,900 | 35 |
| | 8-305 | U | 310 | 12 | Neg | Not Recommended | | | 60–85 | 9 | 6800–10,300 | 35 |
| | 8-350 | R | 310 | 12 | Neg | Not Recommended | | | 65–95 | 9 | 7500–10,500 | 35 |
| | 8-350 | N | 550 | 12 | Neg | Not Recommended | | | 40–140 | 9 | 8000–13,000 | 35 |
| | 8-350 | L | 310 | 12 | Neg | Not Recommended | | | 60–95 | 9 | 7500–10,500 | 35 |
| | 8-350 | X | 310 | 12 | Neg | Not Recommended | | | 60–85 | 9 | 6800–10,300 | 35 |
| | 8-400 | Z | 380 | 12 | Neg | Not Recommended | | | 65–95 | 9 | 7500–10,500 | 35 |
| | 8-403 | K | 430 | 12 | Neg | Not Recommended | | | 65–95 | 9 | 7500–10,500 | 35 |

85843B04

## BATTERY AND STARTER SPECIFICATIONS

| Year | Engine No. Cyl. Displacement (cu. in.) | Engine VIN Code | Battery Ampere Hour Capacity ② | Volts | Terminal Grounded | Starter Lock Test Amps | Volts | Torque (ft. lbs.) | No-Load Test Amps | Volts | RPM | Brush String Tension (oz.) ① |
|------|------|------|------|------|------|------|------|------|------|------|------|------|
| 1979 | 6-231 | A,3 | 275 | 12 | Neg | Not Recommended | | | 60–85 | 9 | 6800–10,300 | 35 |
| | 8-260 | F | 310 | 12 | Neg | Not Recommended | | | 45–70 | 9 | 7000–11,900 | 35 |
| | 8-301 | Y,W | 310 | 12 | Neg | Not Recommended | | | 45–70 | 9 | 7000–11,900 | 35 |
| | 8-350 | R | 310 | 12 | Neg | Not Recommended | | | 65–95 | 9 | 7500–10,500 | 35 |
| | 8-350 | X | 310 | 12 | Neg | Not Recommended | | | 65–95 | 9 | 7500–10,500 | 35 |
| | 8-350 | N | 500 | 12 | Neg | Not Recommended | | | 40–140 | 9 | 8000–13,000 | 35 |
| | 8-403 | K | 430 | 12 | Neg | Not Recommended | | | 65–95 | 9 | 7500–10,500 | 35 |
| 1980 | 6-231 | A,3 | 275 | 12 | Neg | Not Recommended | | | 60–85 | 9 | 6800–10,300 | 35 |
| | 6-252 | 4 | 350 | 12 | Neg | Not Recommended | | | 65–95 | 9 | 7500–10,500 | 35 |
| | 8-260 | F | 350 | 12 | Neg | Not Recommended | | | 45–70 | 9 | 7000–11,900 | 35 |
| | 8-265 | S | 350 | 12 | Neg | Not Recommended | | | 45–70 | 9 | 7000–11,900 | 35 |
| | 8-301 | W | 350 | 12 | Neg | Not Recommended | | | 45–70 | 9 | 7000–11,900 | 35 |
| | 8-307 | Y | 350 | 12 | Neg | Not Recommended | | | 45–70 | 9 | 7000–11,900 | 35 |
| | 8-350 | R | 350 | 12 | Neg | Not Recommended | | | 65–95 | 9 | 7500–10,500 | 35 |
| | 8-350 | X | 350 | 12 | Neg | Not Recommended | | | 65–95 | 9 | 7500–10,500 | 35 |
| | 8-350 | N | 550 | 12 | Neg | Not Recommended | | | 40–140 | 9 | 8000–13,000 | 35 |
| 1981 | 6-231 | A | 350 | 12 | Neg | Not Recommended | | | 60–85 | 9 | 6800–10,300 | 35 |
| | 6-252 | 4 | 350 | 12 | Neg | Not Recommended | | | 65–95 | 9 | 7500–10,500 | 35 |
| | 8-260 | F | 350 | 12 | Neg | Not Recommended | | | 45–70 | 9 | 7000–11,900 | 35 |
| | 8-265 | S | 370 | 12 | Neg | Not Recommended | | | 45–70 | 9 | 7000–11,900 | 35 |
| | 8-267 | J | 370 | 12 | Neg | Not Recommended | | | 45–70 | 9 | 7000–11,900 | 35 |
| | 8-301 | W | 350 | 12 | Neg | Not Recommended | | | 45–70 | 9 | 7000–11,900 | 35 |
| | 8-305 | H | 350 | 12 | Neg | Not Recommended | | | 45–70 | 9 | 7000–11,900 | 35 |
| | 8-307 | Y | 350 | 12 | Neg | Not Recommended | | | 45–70 | 9 | 7000–11,900 | 35 |
| | 8-350 | X | 350 | 12 | Neg | Not Recommended | | | 65–95 | 9 | 7500–10,500 | 35 |
| | 8-350 | N | 550 | 12 | Neg | Not Recommended | | | 100–230 | 9 | 8000–14,000 | 35 |
| 1982 | 6-231 | A | 350 | 12 | Neg | Not Recommended | | | 60–85 | 9 | 6800–10,300 | 35 |
| | 8-252 | 4 | 370 | 12 | Neg | Not Recommended | | | 65–95 | 9 | 7500–10,500 | 35 |
| | 8-260 | F | 350 | 12 | Neg | Not Recommended | | | 45–70 | 9 | 7000–11,900 | 35 |
| | 8-305 | H | 350 | 12 | Neg | Not Recommended | | | 45–70 | 9 | 7000–11,900 | 35 |
| | 8-307 | Y | 350 | 12 | Neg | Not Recommended | | | 45–70 | 9 | 7000–11,900 | 35 |
| | 8-350 | N | 550 | 12 | Neg | Not Recommended | | | 160–220 | 9 | 4000–5500 | 35 |
| 1983 | 6-231 | A | 350 | 12 | Neg | Not Recommended | | | 60–85 | 9 | 6800–10,300 | 35 |
| | 6-252 | 4 | 370 | 12 | Neg | Not Recommended | | | 65–95 | 9 | 7500–10,500 | 35 |
| | 8-305 | H | 350 | 12 | Neg | Not Recommended | | | 45–70 | 9 | 7000–11,900 | 35 |
| | 8-307 | Y | 350 | 12 | Neg | Not Recommended | | | 45–70 | 9 | 7000–11,900 | 35 |
| | 8-350 | N | 550 | 12 | Neg | Not Recommended | | | 160–220 | 9 | 4000–5500 | 35 |

## BATTERY AND STARTER SPECIFICATIONS

| Year | Engine No. Cyl. Displacement (cu. in.) | Engine VIN Code | Battery Ampere Hour Capacity② | Volts | Terminal Grounded | Starter Lock Test Amps | Volts | Torque (ft. lbs.) | No-Load Test Amps | Volts | RPM | Brush String Tension (oz.)① |
|------|------|------|------|------|------|------|------|------|------|------|------|------|
| **1984** | 6-231 | A | 315⑧ | 12 | Neg | Not Recommended | | | 70–110 | 10 | 6500–10,700 | — |
| | 6-252 | 4 | 390⑨ | 12 | Neg | Not Recommended | | | 70–110 | 10 | 6500–10,700 | — |
| | 8-305 | H | 500 | 12 | Neg | Not Recommended | | | 50–75 | 10 | 6000–11,900 | — |
| | 8-307 | Y | 390⑩ | 12 | Neg | Not Recommended | | | 50–75 | 10 | 6000–11,900 | — |
| | 8-350 | N | 405⑪ | 12 | Neg | Not Recommended | | | 160–240⑦ | 9 | 4400–6300 | — |
| **1985** | 6-231 | A | 315⑧ | 12 | Neg | Not Recommended | | | 70–110 | 10 | 6500–10,700 | — |
| | 6-252 | 4 | 390⑨ | 12 | Neg | Not Recommended | | | 70–110 | 10 | 6500–10,700 | — |
| | 6-262 | Z | 630 | 12 | Neg | Not Recommended | | | 70–110 | 10 | 6500–10,700 | — |
| | 8-305 | H | 500 | 12 | Neg | Not Recommended | | | 50–75 | 10 | 6000–11,900 | — |
| | 8-307 | Y | 390⑩ | 12 | Neg | Not Recommended | | | 50–75 | 10 | 6000–11,900 | — |
| | 8-350 | N | 405⑪ | 12 | Neg | Not Recommended | | | 160–240⑦ | 9 | 4400–6300 | — |
| **1986** | 6-231 | A | 500⑫ | 12 | Neg | Not Recommended | | | 70–110 | 10 | 6500–10,700 | — |
| | 6-262 | Z | 630 | 12 | Neg | Not Recommended | | | 70–110 | 10 | 6500–10,700 | — |
| | 8-305 | H | 500 | 12 | Neg | Not Recommended | | | 50–75 | 10 | 6000–11,900 | — |
| | 8-307 | Y | 525⑫ | 12 | Neg | Not Recommended | | | 70–110 | 10 | 6500–10,700 | — |
| **1987** | 6-231 | A | 430 | 12 | Neg | Not Recommended | | | 60–90 | 10 | 6500–10,500 | — |
| | 8-307 | Y | 525 | 12 | Neg | Not Recommended | | | 50–75 | 10 | 6000–11,900 | — |
| **1988** | 8-307 | Y | 525 | 12 | Neg | Not Recommended | | | 50–75 | 10 | 6000–11,900 | — |
| **1989** | 8-307 | Y | 430 | 12 | Neg | Not Recommended | | | 50–75 | 10 | 6000–11,900 | — |
| **1990** | 8-307 | Y | 570⑫ | 12 | Neg | Not Recommended | | | 50–75 | 10 | 6000–11,900 | — |

**NOTE:** All 350 V8 diesels use two (2) 12 volt batteries
① Minimum Tension
② Cold Cranking Power in amps @ 0°F
③ Olds
④ Pontiac
⑤ Buick
⑥ Chevrolet
⑦ Figures apply to 15MT. Some engines use the ALU/GR. Test figures are: 125–170 amps at 10 volts, 3200—4100 pinion rpm
⑧ Heavy Duty—500
　 Olds 88—390
⑨ Heavy Duty—550
⑩ Heavy Duty—500
⑪ Heavy Duty—550
⑫ Heavy Duty—570
　 All diesels use two batteries

85843B06

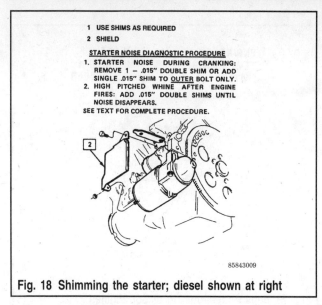

1 USE SHIMS AS REQUIRED

2 SHIELD

**STARTER NOISE DIAGNOSTIC PROCEDURE**

1. STARTER NOISE DURING CRANKING: REMOVE 1 — .015" DOUBLE SHIM OR ADD SINGLE .015" SHIM TO UNDER BOLT ONLY.

2. HIGH PITCHED WHINE AFTER ENGINE FIRES: ADD .015" DOUBLE SHIMS UNTIL NOISE DISAPPEARS.

SEE TEXT FOR COMPLETE PROCEDURE.

85843009

**Fig. 18 Shimming the starter; diesel shown at right**

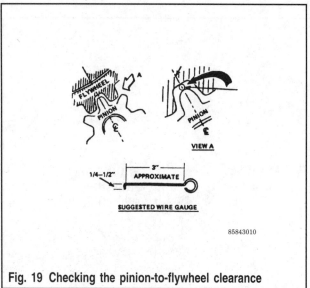

85843010

**Fig. 19 Checking the pinion-to-flywheel clearance**

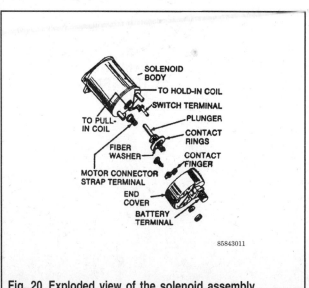

85843011

**Fig. 20 Exploded view of the solenoid assembly**

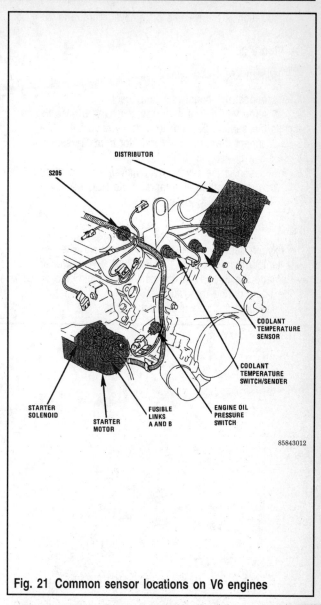

85843012

**Fig. 21 Common sensor locations on V6 engines**

## Sending Units and Sensors

### REMOVAL & INSTALLATION

▶ See Figures 21 and 23

**Coolant Temperature**

1. Disconnect the negative battery cable.
2. Drain the coolant to a level below the coolant temperature sensor or sending unit.
3. Disconnect the electrical connection.
4. Remove the sensor or sending unit from the engine.
5. Installation is the reverse of removal. Torque to 23 ft. lbs (32 Nm).

**Oil Pressure**

1. Disconnect the negative battery cable.
2. Disconnect the electrical connector.
3. Remove the sending unit from the engine.

4. Installation is the reverse of removal. Torque to 23 ft. lbs (32 Nm).

▶ **See Figure 22**

### Knock Sensor

1. Disconnect the negative battery cable.
2. On some vehicles, it may be necessary to raise the car to access the sensor. Be sure to properly secure it.
3. Disconnect the electrical connector from the sensor.
4. Remove the sensor from the engine.
5. Installation is the reverse of removal. Apply a thread sealer, such as a soft sealing tape, to the ESC sensor threads. Torque to 23 ft. lbs (32 Nm).

### Oxygen Sensor

The oxygen sensor may be difficult to remove when the engine temperature is below 120°F (48°C). Excessive force may damage the threads in the exhaust manifold or pipe. Care must be taken during removal.

1. Disconnect the negative battery cable.

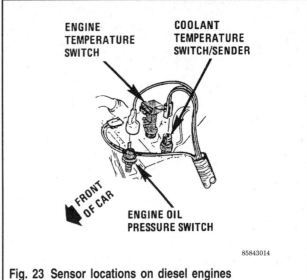

Fig. 23 Sensor locations on diesel engines

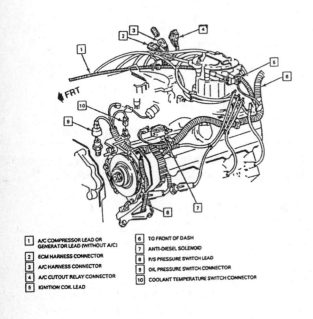

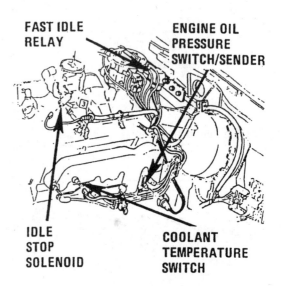

Fig. 22 Common sensor locations on V8 gasoline engines

2. Disconnect the electrical connector.

3. Carefully remove the oxygen sensor using a special sensor removal tool.

**To install:**

4. Coat the threads of the sensor with a special oxygen sensor anti-seize compound. Do not use a anti-seize compound not made for oxygen sensors.

5. Install the sensor and torque to 30 Ft. lbs (41 Nm).

6. Connect the electrical connector and negative battery cable.

## ENGINE MECHANICAL

### Design

All Buick, Olds and Pontiac engines covered in this guide, whether V6 or V8, are watercooled powerplants with pushrod valve actuation. All engines use cast iron cylinder blocks and heads.

The gasoline V8s are all very similar in construction and share common design features such as chain-driven camshafts, hydraulic valve lifters and pressed-steel rocker arms. The Oldsmobile 307 cu. in. (VIN Y) engine uses roller valve lifters after 1985. The Buick engines, including V6s, differ in that they have their rockers mounted on shafts. Because of this similarity between the engines, many removal and installation procedures given here will simultaneously cover all three manufacturers' engines. Likewise, the 231 and 252 V6 engines are nearly identical to each other and to the Buick V8s.

The 350 diesel is derived from the 350 cu. in. gasoline engine, but virtually all major engine parts were strengthened to withstand the higher compression ratio and combustion pressures. Fairly early in the production run the standard valve lifters were replaced with roller type hydraulic lifters because the particles generated in diesel combustion were causing camshaft and lifter wear problems. The diesel engine cylinder head design is different from the gasoline engine design, in that the diesel incorporates a special steel insert that forms a precombustion chamber and must be properly fitted to ensure proper operation.

One especially important difference in the diesel relates to the high compression ratio. The area between the piston top surface and the lower surface of the cylinder head is very small and there is minimal clearance between the piston and valves. For this reason, any engine work related to the valves, lifters and intake manifold requires particular attention to special diesel service procedures. Failure to follow these procedures will often result in bent valves or valve gear.

The diesel fuel system is considerably more complex than the typical gasoline engine carburetor. Particular attention must be paid to fuel cleanliness and maintenance of various fuel filters and water separators. Service on this system usually requires extensive specialized tooling and training. It should never be tampered with, as this can result in personal injury. Make sure you are properly equipped and fully aware of proper service procedures before you begin work on it.

### Engine Overhaul Tips

Most engine overhaul procedures are fairly standard. In addition to specific parts replacement procedures and complete specifications for your individual engine, this section. also is a guide to accept rebuilding procedures. Examples of standard rebuilding practice are shown and should be used along with specific details concerning your particular engine.

Competent and accurate machine shop services will ensure maximum performance, reliability and engine life. In most instances it is more profitable for the do-it-yourself mechanic to remove, clean and inspect the component, buy the necessary parts and deliver these to a shop for actual machine work.

## TOOLS

The tools required for an engine overhaul or parts replacement will depend on the depth of your involvement. With a few exceptions, they will be the tools found in a mechanic's tool kit. More in-depth work will require any or all of the following:

- a dial indicator (reading in thousandths) mounted on a universal base
- micrometers and telescope gauges
- jaw and screw-type pullers
- scraper
- valve spring compressor
- ring groove cleaner
- piston ring expander and compressor
- ridge reamer
- cylinder hone or glaze breaker
- Plastigage®
- engine lift and stand

Most of these tools can be rented for a one-time use from a local parts jobber or tool supply house specializing in automotive work. Occasionally, the use of special tools will be recommended or necessary.

## INSPECTION TECHNIQUES

Procedures and specifications are given in this section for inspecting, cleaning and assessing the wear limits of most major components. Other procedures such as Magnaflux® and Zyglo® can be used to locate material flaws and stress cracks. Magnaflux® is a magnetic process applicable only to ferrous materials (not aluminum). The Zyglo® process coats the material with a fluorescent dye penetrant and can be used on any material. Checking for suspected surface cracks can be more readily made using spot check dye. The dye is sprayed onto the suspected area, wiped off and the area sprayed with a developer. Cracks will show up brightly.

## OVERHAUL TIPS

Aluminum has become extremely popular for use in engines, due to its low weight. Observe the following precautions when handling aluminum parts:
• Never hot tank aluminum parts (the caustic hot tank solution will eat the aluminum.
• Remove all aluminum parts (identification tag, etc.) from engine parts prior to the tanking.
• Always coat threads lightly with engine oil or anti-seize compounds before installation, to prevent seizure.
• Never over-torque bolts or spark plugs especially in aluminum threads.

Stripped threads in any component can be repaired using any of several commercial repair kits (Heli-Coil®, Microdot®, Keenserts®, etc.).

When assembling the engine, any parts that will be subject to frictional contact must be prelubed to provide lubrication at initial start-up. Any product specifically formulated for this purpose can be used, but engine oil is not recommended as a prelube.

When semi-permanent (locked, but removable) installation of bolts or nuts is desired, threads should be cleaned and coated with Loctite® or other similar, commercial non-hardening sealant.

## REPAIRING DAMAGED THREADS

▶ **See Figures 24, 25, 26, 27 and 28**

Several methods of repairing damaged threads are available. Heli-Coil® , Keenserts® and Microdot® are among the most widely used. All involve basically the same principle; drilling out stripped threads, tapping the hole and installing a prewound insert making welding, plugging and oversize fasteners unnecessary.

Two types of thread repair inserts are usually supplied. A standard type for most Inch Coarse, Inch Fine, Metric Course and Metric Fine thread sizes and a spark lug type to fit most spark plug port sizes. Consult the individual manufacturer's catalog to determine exact applications. Typical thread repair kits will contain a selection of prewound threaded inserts, a tap (corresponding to the outside diameter threads of the insert) and an installation tool. Spark plug inserts usually differ because they require a tap equipped with pilot threads and a combined reamer/tap section. Most manufacturers also supply blister-packed thread repair inserts separately in addition to a master kit containing a variety of taps and inserts plus installation tools.

Before effecting a repair to a threaded hole, remove any snapped, broken or damaged bolts or studs. Penetrating oil can be used to free frozen threads; the offending item can be removed with locking pliers or with a screw or stud extractor. After the hole is clear, the thread can be repaired.

## Checking Engine Compression

A noticeable lack of engine power, excessive oil consumption and/or poor fuel mileage measured over an extended period are all indicators of internal engine wear. Worn piston

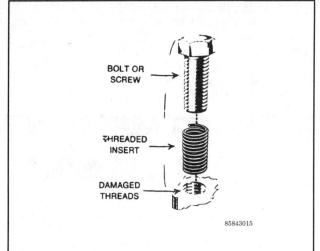

**Fig. 24 Damaged bolt holes can be repaired with thread repair inserts**

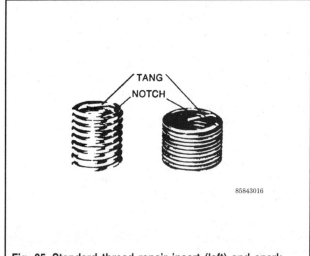

**Fig. 25 Standard thread repair insert (left) and spark plug thread insert (right)**

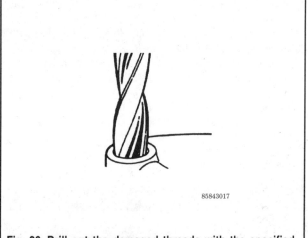

**Fig. 26 Drill out the damaged threads with the specified drill. Drill out completely through the hole or to the bottom of a blind hole**

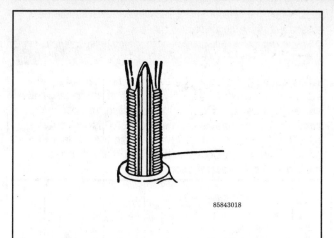

**Fig. 27 With the tap supplied, tap the hole to receive the thread insert. Keep the tap well oiled and back it out frequently to avoid clogging the threads**

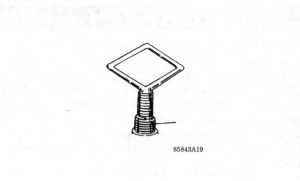

**Fig. 28 Screw the threaded insert onto the installation tool until the tang engages the slot. Screw the insert into the tapped hole until it is ¼ to ½ turn below the top surface. After installation, break the tang off**

rings, scored or worn cylinder bores, blown head gaskets, sticking or burnt valves and worn valve seats are all possible culprits here. A check of each cylinder's compression will help you locate the problems.

As mentioned in Tools and Equipment of Section 1, a screw-in type compression gauge is more accurate than the type you simply hold against the spark plug hole, although it takes slightly longer to use. It's worth it to obtain a more accurate reading.

## GASOLINE ENGINES

▶ **See Figure 29**

1. Warm up the engine to normal operating temperature. Turn the engine OFF.
2. Remove all spark plugs.

3. Disable the ignition system by disconnecting the battery feed to the coil.
4. Fully open the throttle either by operating the carburetor throttle linkage by hand or by having an assistant floor the accelerator pedal.
5. Apply engine oil to the gauge fitting and screw the compression gauge into the No.1 spark plug hole until the fitting is snug.

➡**Be careful not to crossthread the plug hole. On aluminum cylinder heads use extra care, as the threads in these heads are easily crossthreaded.**

6. Ask an assistant to depress the accelerator pedal fully on both carbureted and fuel injected vehicles. Then, while you read the compression gauge, ask the assistant to crank the engine two or three times in short bursts using the ignition switch.
7. Read the compression gauge at the end of each series of cranks, and record the highest of these readings. Repeat this procedure for each of the engine's cylinders. Compare the highest reading of each cylinder.

A cylinder's compression pressure is usually acceptable if it is not less than 80% of maximum. The difference between each cylinder should be no more than 12-14 pounds.

8. If a cylinder is unusually low, pour a tablespoon of clean engine oil into the cylinder through the spark plug hole and repeat the compression test. If the compression comes up after adding the oil, it appears that the cylinder's piston rings or bore are damaged or worn. If the pressure remains low, the valves may not be seating properly (a valve job is needed), or the head gasket may be blown near that cylinder. If compression in any two adjacent cylinders is low, and if the addition of oil does not help the compression, there is leakage past the head gasket. Oil and coolant water in the combustion chamber can result from this problem. There may be evidence of water droplets on the engine dipstick when a head gasket has blown. Another sign of a blown head gasket is white smoke coming from the exhaust pipe when the engine is at normal operating temperature.

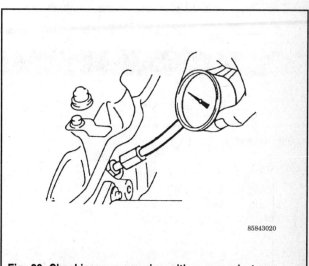

**Fig. 29 Checking compression with a screw-in type compression gauge**

## DIESEL ENGINES

▶ **See Figure 30**

Checking cylinder compression on diesel engines is basically the same procedure as on gasoline engines except for the following:

1. A special compression gauge adaptor suitable for diesel engines (because these engines have much greater compression pressures) must be used.
2. Remove the injector tubes and remove the injectors from each cylinder.

➡**Do not forget to remove the washer underneath each injector; otherwise, it may get lost when the engine is cranked.**

3. When fitting the compression gauge adaptor to the cylinder head, make sure the bleeder of the gauge (if equipped) is closed.
4. When reinstalling the injector assemblies, install new washers underneath each injector.

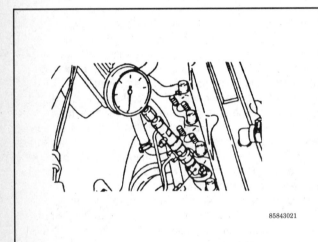

85843021

**Fig. 30 Diesel engines require a special compression gauge adaptor**

## Engine

### REMOVAL & INSTALLATION

▶ **See Figures 31, 32, 33, 34, 35, 36, 37, 38 and 39**

**Buick Built V6**

1. Scribe marks around the hood hinges and hinge bracket, so the hood can be installed easily. Remove the hood.
2. Disconnect both battery cables.

3. Drain the coolant into a suitable container; it can be reused if in fresh condition.

**❋❋CAUTION**

**When draining the coolant, keep in mind that cats and dogs are attracted by the ethylene glycol antifreeze, and are quite likely to drink any that is left in an uncovered container or in puddles on the ground. This will prove fatal in sufficient quantity. Always drain the coolant into a sealable container. Coolant should be reused unless it is contaminated or several years old.**

4. Remove the air cleaner.
5. Disconnect the radiator and heater hoses and position them out of the way.
6. On air conditioned vehicles, disconnect the A/C compressor ground wire from the mounting bracket. Remove the electrical connector from the compressor clutch, remove the compressor-to-mounting bracket attaching bolts and position the compressor out of the way. DO NOT disconnect the refrigerant hoses.

**❋❋CAUTION**

**If the compressor refrigerant lines do not have enough slack to position the compressor out of the way without discharging the refrigerant lines, the air conditioning system will have to be discharged by a trained air conditioning specialist with a recovery/recycling station. Under no circumstances should an untrained person attempt to disconnect the air conditioning refrigerant lines. These lines contain pressurized R-12 refrigerant, which can be extremely dangerous.**

7. Remove the fan blade, pulleys and belts.
8. Remove the fan shroud assembly.
9. Remove the power steering pump-to-mounting bracket bolts and position the pump out of the way.
10. Tag, remove and plug the fuel pump hoses.
11. Tag and disconnect the vacuum lines from the engine to parts not attached to the engine. Disconnect the engine wiring harness.
12. Disconnect and tag the throttle cable, downshift cable and/or throttle valve cable at the carburetor.
13. Disconnect the transmission oil cooler lines at the transmission. Disconnect the oil and coolant sending unit switch connections at the engine.
14. Disconnect the engine-to-body ground strap at the engine.
15. Raise and support the front end of the vehicle with jackstands. Disconnect the starter cables and the cable shield from the engine.
16. Disconnect the exhaust pipes from the exhaust manifolds and support the exhaust system.
17. Remove the flywheel cover pan. Remove the flywheel-to-torque converter bolts. Using a scribe or felt tip marker, matchmark the flywheel-to-torque converter relationship for later assembly.
18. Remove the transmission-to-engine attaching bolts from the transmission bell housing.
19. Remove the cruise control bracket, if so equipped.

20. Remove the motor mount bolts.

21. Lower the vehicle and support the transmission with a floor jack.

22. Check to make sure that all wiring and hoses have been disconnected. Attach a lifting device to the engine and raise the engine just enough so that the engine mount through-bolts can be removed.

23. Raise the engine and transmission alternately until the engine can be disengaged and removed.

**To install:**

24. It may be necessary to alternately raise and lower the transmission to fit the motor mount through-bolts into position. Torque the through-bolt nuts to 35 ft. lbs. (48 Nm). Torque the automatic transmission-to-engine bolts to 35 ft. lbs. (48 Nm).

25. Raise the vehicle and support the transmission with a floor jack.

26. Install the motor mount bolts and torque to 55 ft. lbs. (75 Nm).

27. Install the cruise control bracket, if so equipped.

28. Install the transmission-to-engine attaching bolts to the transmission bell housing.

29. Install the flywheel cover pan. Install the flywheel-to-torque converter bolts at the matchmark of the flywheel-to-torque converter relationship.

30. Connect the exhaust pipes to the exhaust manifolds.

31. Lower the front end of the vehicle. Connect the starter cables and the cable shield to the engine.

32. Connect the engine-to-body ground strap at the engine.

33. Connect the transmission oil cooler lines at the transmission. Connect the oil and coolant sending unit switch connections at the engine.

34. Connect the throttle cable, downshift cable and/or throttle valve cable at the carburetor.

35. Connect the vacuum lines attached to the engine. Connect the engine wiring harness.

36. Connect the fuel pump hoses.

37. Install the power steering pump-to-mounting bracket bolts.

38. Install the fan shroud assembly.

39. Install the fan blade, pulleys and belts.

40. On air conditioned vehicles, connect the A/C compressor ground wire to the mounting bracket. Install the electrical connector to the compressor clutch, install the compressor and bracket attaching bolts.

41. Connect the radiator and heater hoses.

42. Install the air cleaner.

43. Refill the coolant into the radiator and reservoir. DON'T FORGET to refill the engine with the specified engine oil.

44. Connect both battery cables.

45. Install the hood around the marks on the hood hinges and hinge bracket.

46. Start the engine and check for vacuum, coolant, oil, fuel and refrigerant leaks. Adjust timing and idle speed to specification.

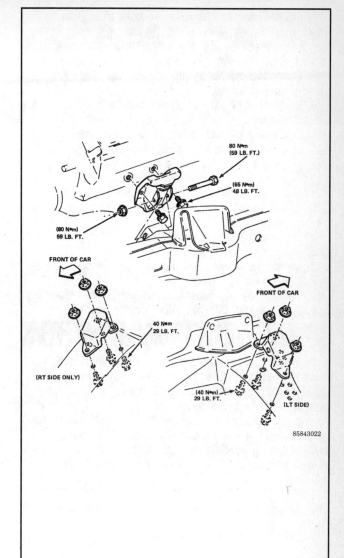

**Fig. 31 Exploded view of a common engine mount assembly**

**V8 Including Diesel**

1. Drain the cooling system.

**✳✳CAUTION**

When draining the coolant, keep in mind that cats and dogs are attracted by the ethylene glycol antifreeze, and are quite likely to drink any that is left in an uncovered container or in puddles on the ground. This will prove fatal in sufficient quantity. Always drain the coolant into a sealable container. Coolant should be reused unless it is contaminated or several years old.

2. Scribe the hinge outline on the underside of the hood. Remove the hood attaching bolts and remove the hood.

3. Disconnect the battery cables.

4. Remove the radiator and heater hoses and remove the air cleaner.

5. Remove the V-belts to avoid damaging them as the engine is pulled out of the engine compartment.

6. Disconnect the transmission oil cooler lines. Remove the fan shroud, fan belts, and pulleys. On diesels, disconnect the engine oil cooler lines at the radiator. Remove the upper radiator support and remove the radiator.

7. Disconnect the battery ground cable from the engine. Remove the radiator.

8. Disconnect the exhaust pipe or pipes or crossover at the exhaust manifolds.

9. Disconnect the vacuum line to the power brake unit.

10. Disconnect the accelerator to carburetor linkage. On diesels, disconnect the hairpin clip at the bellcrank.

11. Disconnect and label all the engine component wiring that would interfere with the engine removal, such as alternator wires, gauge sending unit wires, primary ignition wires, engine-to-body ground strap, etc.

12. Disconnect and plug the fuel line at the fuel pump. On diesels, also disconnect fuel pump wiring.

13. Detach the power steering pump and position to the left. Do not disconnect the hoses.

14. Detach the air conditioner compressor at the bracket and position to the right. DO NOT disconnect the hoses.

## ✳✳CAUTION

**If the compressor refrigerant lines do not have enough slack to position the compressor out of the way without disconnecting the refrigerant lines, the air conditioning system will have to be discharged by a trained air conditioning specialist with a recovery/recycling station. Under no conditions should an untrained person attempt to disconnect the air conditioning refrigerant lines. These lines contain pressurized R-12 gas which can be extremely dangerous.**

15. Disconnect the starter cable and remove the cable shield.

16. Disconnect the AIR pipe-to-catalytic converter, if there is one.

17. Remove the flywheel cover pan. Remove the flywheel-to-torque converter bolts. Matchmark the flywheel and torque converter for reassembly.

18. Separate the engine from the transmission at the bell housing. On 1987 models, remove 5 of the bolts and leave the lower/left bolt in place.

19. Remove the cruise control bracket, if so equipped.

20. Support the transmission with a floor jack.

21. Attach a lifting device to the engine and raise the engine slightly so the engine mount through-bolts can be removed.

22. Check to make sure all of the wiring and hoses have been disconnected. Raise the engine enough to clear the motor mounts.

23. Raise the engine and transmission alternately until the engine can be disengaged and removed. Once both are raised slightly, remove the remaining transmission-to-engine bolt on the 1987 models.

24. Install by reversing the procedure. When installing an engine, the front mounting pad to frame bolts should be the last mounting bolts to be tightened. Note that there are dowel pins in the block that have matching holes in the bellhousing. These pins must be in almost perfect alignment before the engine will go together with the transmission. Torque the through-bolt nuts to 35 ft. lbs. (48 Nm). Torque the automatic

transmission-to-engine bolts to 35 ft. lbs. (48 Nm). When tightening the three converter-to-drive plate bolts, first tighten all three finger tight, and then torque to 46 ft. lbs. (63 Nm), all three. Make sure to retighten and torque the first bolt tightened.

**To install:**

25. When installing an engine, the front mounting pad to frame bolts should be the last mounting bolts to be tightened.

➡**There are dowel pins in the block that have matching holes in the bellhousing. These pins must be in almost perfect alignment before the engine will go together with the transmission.**

26. Torque the through-bolt nuts to 35 ft.lbs. (48 Nm). Torque the automatic transmission-to-engine bolts to 35 ft.lbs. (48 Nm). When tightening the three converter-to-drive plate bolts, first tighten all three finger tight, and then torque (46 ft.lbs. 63 Nm), all three. Make sure to retighten and torque the first bolt tightened.

27. Lower the engine and transmission alternately until the engine can be engaged. Once both are lowered slightly, install the remaining transmission-to-engine bolts.

28. Check to make sure all of the wiring and hoses have not gotten pinched between the engine and transmission. Lower the engine enough to engage the motor mounts.

29. Using the lifting device, raise the engine slightly so the engine mount through-bolts can be installed.

30. Support the transmission with a floor jack.

31. Install the cruise control bracket, if so equipped.

32. Install and tighten the flywheel-to-torque converter bolts to 50 ft. lbs. (68 Nm). Install the flywheel cover. Matchmark the flywheel and torque converter.

33. Connect the AIR pipe-to-catalytic converter, if there is one.

34. Connect the starter cable and install the cable shield.

35. Reposition the air conditioner compressor to the bracket.

36. Connect the power steering pump. Do not disconnect the hoses.

37. Connect the fuel line at the fuel pump. On diesels, also connect the fuel pump wiring.

38. Connect all the engine component wiring that would interfere with the engine installation, such as alternator wires, gauge sending unit wires, primary ignition wires, engine-to-body ground strap, etc.

39. Connect the accelerator to carburetor linkage. On diesels, connect the hairpin clip at the bellcrank.

40. Connect the vacuum line to the power brake unit.

41. Connect the exhaust pipe or pipes or crossover at the exhaust manifolds.

42. Connect the battery ground cable to the engine. Install the radiator.

43. Connect the transmission oil cooler lines. Install the fan shroud, fan belts, and pulleys. On diesels, connect the engine oil cooler lines at the radiator. Install the upper radiator support.

44. Install the V-belts.

45. Install the radiator, heater hoses and install the air cleaner.

46. Connect the battery cables.

47. Install the hood and attaching bolts at the scribes on the hinge outline on the underside of the hood.

48. Refill the engine cooling system. DON'T FORGET to refill the engine with the specified engine oil.

49. Start the engine and check for vacuum, coolant, oil, fuel and refrigerant leaks. Adjust timing and idle speed to specification.

## Rocker Arm (Valve) Cover

### REMOVAL & INSTALLATION

♦ See Figures 40, 41, 42 and 43

1. Remove air cleaner and negative battery cable.
2. Disconnect, label and reposition as necessary any vacuum or PCV hoses that obstruct the valve covers.
3. Disconnect and label electrical wire(s) (spark plug, etc.) from the valve cover clips.
4. Unbolt and remove the valve covers.

➡Do not pry the covers off if they seem stuck. Instead, use a seal breaker tool J-34144 or gently tap around each cover with a rubber mallet until the old gasket or sealer breaks loose.

To install:

5. Use a new valve cover gasket and/or RTV (or any equivalent) sealer. If using sealer, follow directions on the tube. Install valve cover and tighten cover bolts to 36 inch lbs. (4 Nm).

6. Install all wires and hoses in the same location as removed.

7. Connect and reposition all vacuum and PCV hoses, and reconnect electrical and/or spark plug wires at the cover clips. Install the air cleaner.

Fig. 33 Mark the hood around the hinges to make installation easier later

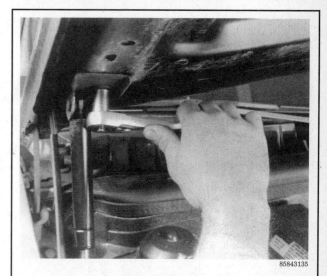

Fig. 34 Removing the hood attaching bolts

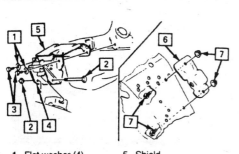

1. Flat washer (4)
2. 55 ft. lbs. (73 Nm)
3. 75 ft. lbs. (100 Nm)
4. Mount assembly
5. Shield
6. Bracket
7. 35 ft. lbs. (48 Nm)

Fig. 32 Oldsmobile 307 (Y) engine mount assembly

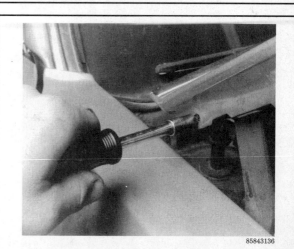

Fig. 35 Some models may utilize a small attaching bolt on the side. Be sure an assistant holds the hood during removal

Fig. 36 Labeling hoses and wiring before disconnection will make installation much easier

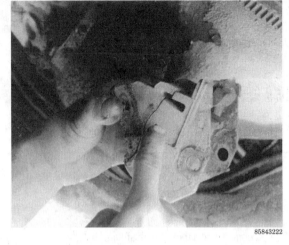

Fig. 39 Inspect the motor mounts for cracks and other types of damage

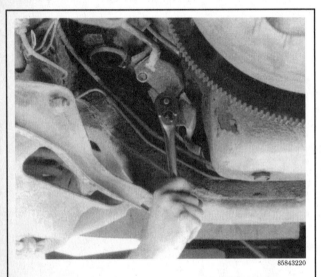

Fig. 37 Removing the motor mount attaching bolts

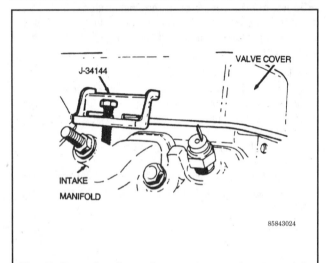

Fig. 40 Removing the rocker arm cover using a special seal breaker tool

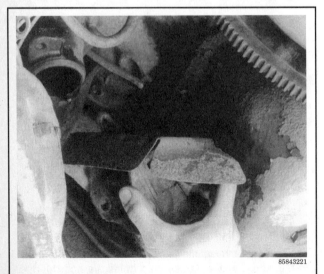

Fig. 38 Removing the motor mount from the vehicle

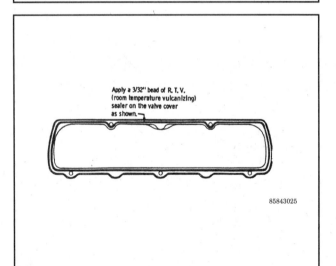

Fig. 41 Applying sealer to the valve cover before assembling

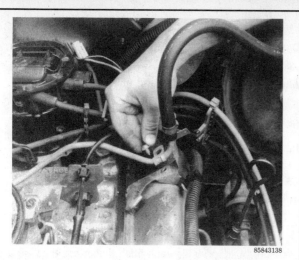

**Fig. 42 Remove any brackets mounted on the valve cover**

**Fig. 43 If the valve cover cannot be easily lifted off, a special seal breaker tool can be used**

## Rocker Arms and Shafts

### REMOVAL & INSTALLATION

♦ See Figures 44, 45 and 46

#### Buick Built Engines

1. Disconnect the negative battery cable and remove the valve covers as previously outlined.
2. Remove the rocker arm shaft assembly bolts.
3. Remove the rocker arm shaft assembly and place it on a clean surface.
4. To remove the rocker arms from the shaft, you must first remove the nylon arm retainers. These can be removed with locking jaw pliers, by prying them out, or by breaking them by hitting them below the head with a chisel.
5. Remove the rocker arms from the shaft. Make sure you keep them in order. Also note that the external rib on each

arm points away from the rocker arm shaft bolt located between each pair of rocker arms.
6. If you are installing new rocker arms, note that the replacement rocker arms are marked **R** and **L** for right and left side installation. Do not interchange them.

**To install:**

7. Install the rocker arms on the shaft and lubricate them with oil.

➡Install the rocker arms for each cylinder only when the lifters are off the cam lobe and both valves are closed.

8. Center each arm on the ¼ in. (6.3mm) hole in the shaft. Install new nylon rocker arm retainers in the holes using a ½ in. (12.7mm) drift.
9. Locate the pushrods in the rocker arm cups and insert the shaft bolts. Tighten the bolts a little at a time to 30 ft. lbs. (41 Nm).
10. Install the valve covers using sealer or new gaskets as previously outlined in this section.
11. Start the engine and check for oil leaks.

#### Chevrolet Built Engines

1. Remove the rocker arm covers as previously outlined.
2. Remove the rocker arm nuts, rocker arm balls, rocker arms and push rods. Place the rocker arms, balls and push rods in a rack so they may be installed in the same locations.

**To install:**

➡Whenever new rocker arms or rocker arm balls are being installed, coat the bearing surfaces of the rocker arms and rocker arm balls with Molykote® or it's equivalent.

3. Install the push rods making sure they seat in the lifter socket.
4. Install the rocker arms, rocker arm balls and nuts. Tighten the rocker arm nuts until all lash is eliminated.
   Adjust the valves as follows:
5. Crank engine until the mark on the harmonic balancer lines up with the center or "0" mark on the timing tab fastened to the crankcase front cover and the engine is in the No. 1 cylinder firing position. You can determine this by placing your fingers on the No. 1 valves as the mark on the harmonic

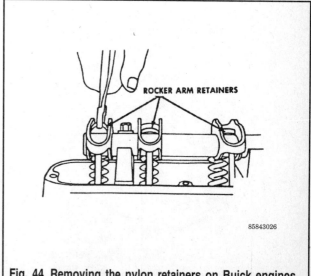

**Fig. 44 Removing the nylon retainers on Buick engines**

balancer comes near the "0" mark on the timing tab. If the valves are not moving, the engine is in the No. 1 firing position. If the valves do move, the engine is on the No. 6 firing position (No. 4 on V6) and should be turned over one more time to reach the No. 1 position.

The following valves may now be adjusted:
- V8-Exhaust - 1, 3, 4, 8
- V8-Intake - 1, 2, 5, 7
- V6-Exhaust - 1, 5, 6
- V6-Intake - 1, 2, 3

6. Back out the adjusting nut until lash is felt at the push rod then turn in the adjusting nut until all lash is removed. This can be determined by rotating the push rod while turning the adjusting nut. Once the play has been removed, turn the adjusting nut one full turn to center the lifter plunger.

7. Crank engine one revolution until the mark on the harmonic balancer lines up with the center or "0" mark on the timing tab once again. The engine is now in the No. 6 (No. 4 on V6) cylinder firing position.

The following valves may now be adjusted:
- V8-Exhaust - 2, 5, 6, 7
- V8-Intake - 3, 4, 6, 8
- V6-Exhaust - 2, 3, 4
- V6-Intake - 4, 5, 6

8. Adjust these valves using the same procedure as the first set of valves.

9. Install the rocker arm covers and adjust the idle speed, if necessary.

### Oldsmobile and Pontiac Built Engines

#### EXCEPT DIESEL

1. Disconnect the negative battery cable.
2. Remove the valve cover.
3. Remove the rocker arm flanged bolts, and remove the rocker pivots.
4. Remove the rocker arms.

➡**Remove each set of rocker arms (one set per cylinder) as a unit.**

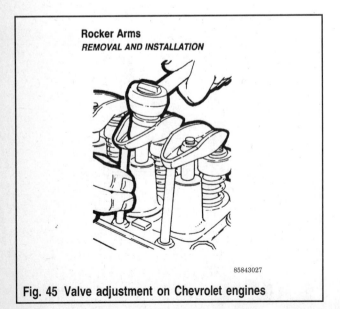

**Rocker Arms**
*REMOVAL AND INSTALLATION*

85843027

**Fig. 45 Valve adjustment on Chevrolet engines**

**To install:**

5. Position a set of rocker arms (for one cylinder) in the proper location.

➡**Install the rocker arms for each cylinder only when the lifters are off the cam lobe and both valves are closed.**

6. Coat the replacement rocker arm and pivot with SAE 90 gear oil and install the pivots.

7. Install the flanged bolts and tighten alternately. Torque the bolts to 25 ft. lbs. (34 Nm).

8. Install the valve cover, connect the negative battery cable, start the engine and check for oil leaks.

#### DIESEL

➡**When the diesel engine rocker arms are removed or loosened, the lifters must be bled down to prevent oil pressure buildup inside each lifter, which could cause it to raise up higher than normal and bring the valves within striking distance of the pistons.**

1. Disconnect the negative battery cable.
2. Remove the valve cover.
3. Remove the rocker arm pivot bolts, the bridged pivot and rocker arms.
4. Remove each rocker set as a unit.

**To install:**

5. Lubricate the pivot wear points and position each set of rocker arms in its proper location. Do not tighten the pivot bolts for fear of bending the valves when the engine is turned.

6. On 1980 and earlier models: The lifters can be bled down for six cylinders at once with the crankshaft in either of the following two positions:

  a. For cylinders numbered 3, 5, 7, 2, 4 and 8, turn the crankshaft so the saw slot on the harmonic balancer is at 0 degrees on the timing indicator.

  b. For cylinders 1, 3, 7, 2, 4 and 6, turn the crankshaft so the saw slot on the harmonic balancer is at 4 o'clock.

7. On these models only, tighten the rocker arm bolts on the numbered cylinders for the position the engine is in only. Torque to 28 ft. lbs. (35 Nm). It will take 45 minutes to completely bleed down the lifters. If additional lifters must be bled, wait till the 45 minutes has passed, and then turn the engine to the other position. Then tighten the remaining rocker arm pivot bolts and torque them to 28 ft. lbs. (35 Nm). Make sure you again wait 45 minutes before turning the crankshaft.

8. On 1981 and later models: Before installing any rockers, turn the crankshaft so No. 1 cylinder is at 32 degrees before Top Dead Center on the compression stroke. 32 degrees BTC is 50mm or 2 in. counterclockwise from the 0 degrees pointer. If only the right valve cover was removed for the work you did so that No. 1 cylinder's valves have not been disturbed you can determine that you're on the compression stroke for No. 1 by removing the glow plug for that cylinder and feeling for expulsion of air through that hole as you turn the engine (in the direction of normal rotation) up to the required position. If you have disturbed the rockers for No. 1, the left side valve cover will be off and you can rotate the crankshaft until the No. 5 cylinder intake valve pushrod ball is 7mm or 0.28 in. above the No. 5 cylinder exhaust pushrod ball. If this cover is off even if you did not disturb No. 1 cylinder, you may wish to use the pushrod measurement method to save time. Once the engine is in proper position, install the No. 5 cylinder rockers

and rocker nuts, but DO NOT TIGHTEN THEM FULLY. Instead, turn them down by hand cautiously, alternating between intake and exhaust valves and turning both nuts an equal amount just until the intake valve nut begins to be harder to turn, indicating that the intake valve has just begun to crack open. Proceed cautiously so you don't turn too far. You'll see the valve begin to be depressed by the rocker, too.

9. At this point, torque all the remaining rocker nuts except those for cylinder No. 3. For cylinders No. 3 and 5, you'll have to turn the rocker bolts down very cautiously. On these cylinders, the cams are in such a position that installing the rocker nuts fully would open the valves all the way and then bend the pushrods. You'll have to feel very carefully for increased resistance as the valve reaches fully open position. Continue to turn the rocker nuts down on these three valves, always proceeding cautiously and stopping just as increased resistance is felt. Alternate, giving some time between tightening operations for the lifters to bleed down somewhat, until you can torque the nuts smoothly (without a sudden increase in resistance) to the required 28 ft. lbs. (35 Nm). Now, wait a full 45 minutes before the crankshaft is turned for any reason to permit all the lifters to bleed down fully.

10. Assemble the remaining components in reverse of disassembly. The rocker covers do not use gaskets, but are sealed with a bead of Room Temperature Vulcanizing (RTV) silicone sealer.

11. Connect the negative battery cable, start the engine and check for oil leaks.

## Thermostat

## REMOVAL & INSTALLATION

▶ See Figures 47, 48, 49 and 50

1. Disconnect the negative battery cable.

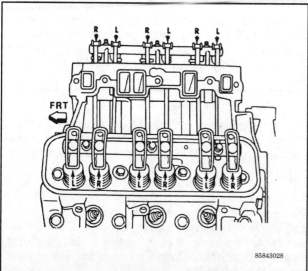

**Fig. 46 Rocker arm positioning; Buick shown**

2. Drain the radiator until the level is below the thermostat level (below the level of the intake manifold).

### ✳✳CAUTION

**When draining the coolant, keep in mind that cats and dogs are attracted by the ethylene glycol antifreeze, and are quite likely to drink any that is left in an uncovered container or in puddles on the ground. This will prove fatal in sufficient quantity. Always drain the coolant into a sealable container. Coolant should be reused unless it is contaminated or several years old.**

3. Remove the attaching bolts and the water outlet elbow assembly from the engine. Remove the thermostat from inside the elbow.

4. Install new thermostat in the reverse order of removal, making sure the spring side is inserted into the elbow. Clean the gasket surfaces on the water outlet elbow and the intake manifold. Use a new gasket and RTV sealer when installing the elbow to the manifold. Refill the radiator to approximately 2½ inches below the filler neck or, if there is a coolant recovery system, fill it up all the way.

## Intake Manifold

## REMOVAL & INSTALLATION

▶ See Figures 51, 52, 53, 54, 55, 56, 57, 58, 59, 60 and 61

**Buick Built V6**

1. Disconnect the battery, remove the air cleaner and drain the radiator.

### ✳✳CAUTION

**When draining the coolant, keep in mind that cats and dogs are attracted by the ethylene glycol antifreeze, and are quite likely to drink any that is left in an uncovered container or in puddles on the ground. This will prove fatal in sufficient quantity. Always drain the coolant into a sealable container. Coolant should be reused unless it is contaminated or several years old.**

2. Disconnect the following:
   a. The upper radiator hose and coolant bypass hose at the manifold. If the dipstick tube connects to the alternator adjusting brace, remove it, also, at this time.
   b. The alternator upper bracket, on 1986-87 models.
   c. Accelerator downshift and/or throttle valve cable(s) and bracket at the manifold.
   d. Booster vacuum pipe at the manifold.
   e. The EFE valve vacuum line at the manifold, if so equipped.
   f. Carburetor fuel line and choke pipes.
   g. Automatic transmission vacuum modulator line.
   h. Idle stop solenoid wire or idle Speed Control wiring.
   i. Distributor primary wires and the temperature sending unit wires.
   j. Any remaining vacuum hoses. On 1983 Olds, remove the A/C top bracket, if so equipped. On 1986-90 models,

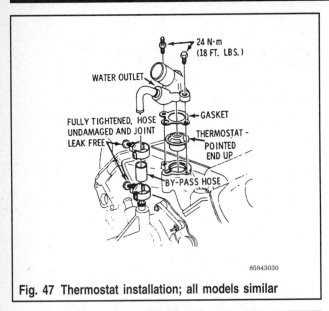

Fig. 47 Thermostat installation; all models similar

Fig. 48 Once the water outlet elbow has been removed, the thermostat can be removed as well

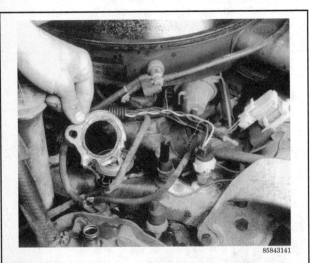

Fig. 49 Always discard the old gasket and clean the mating surfaces

Fig. 50 Be sure to install the thermostat in the proper direction

remove the air conditioner compressor brace and disconnect the bracket at the manifold.

3. Remove the distributor cap and rotor for access to the left side manifold head bolt that is a Torx® type bolt on engines built before 1986. On 1986-87 models, remove the distributor and, if there is a separate coil, the coil as well.

4. Remove the plug wires and accelerator linkage springs.

5. Remove the manifold bolts. The Torx® bolt may be removed with a No. 45 Torx® socket. Remove the manifold.

**To install:**

6. Clean all gasket surfaces with a gasket scraper and solvent.

7. Place a new gasket and rubber seals in position at the front and rear rail of the block. Make sure the pointed end of the seal fits snugly against both the block and head. Coat both ends of these seals with Room Temperature Vulcanizing (RTV) sealant.

8. With an assistant, carefully position the manifold over the seals and gasket so that the seals and gasket remain in proper position.

### ✳✳WARNING

DO NOT slide the manifold into position if the bolts will not line up. This may cause the gasket to become dislodged. With an assistant, remove the manifold, reposition the gasket and try again until the manifold bolts will thread.

9. Start the manifold bolts.

10. Using the proper tightening sequence, tighten the No. 1 and No. 2 bolts first until snug. Then, continue with the rest of the bolts in sequence until all are just snug. Finally, torque in sequence to 45 ft. lbs. (61 Nm).

11. Install the plug wires and accelerator linkage springs.

12. Install the distributor, cap and rotor, if removed. Adjust the timing after all components have been installed.

13. Install any remaining vacuum hoses. On 1983 Olds, install the A/C top bracket, if so equipped. On 1986-87 models, install the air conditioner compressor brace and connect the bracket at the manifold.

14. Install the distributor primary wires and the temperature sending unit wires.

15. Connect the idle stop solenoid wire or idle Speed Control wiring.

16. Connect the automatic transmission vacuum modulator line.

17. Connect the carburetor fuel line and choke pipes.

18. Connect the EFE valve vacuum line at the manifold, if so equipped.

19. Connect the booster vacuum pipe at the manifold.

20. Install the accelerator downshift and/or throttle valve cable(s) and bracket at the manifold.

21. Install the alternator upper bracket, on 1986-87 models.

22. Install the upper radiator hose and coolant bypass hose at the manifold. If the dipstick tube connects to the alternator adjusting brace, install it, also, at this time.

23. Connect the battery, install the air cleaner and refill the radiator with engine coolant.

24. Start the engine and check for leaks. Adjust the timing at this time.

**All Other Engines Except Diesel**

1. Disconnect the negative battery cable and drain the cooling system.

### ✳✳CAUTION

When draining the coolant, keep in mind that cats and dogs are attracted by the ethylene glycol antifreeze, and are quite likely to drink any that is left in an uncovered container or in puddles on the ground. This will prove fatal in sufficient quantity. Always drain the coolant into a sealable container. Coolant should be reused unless it is contaminated or several years old.

2. Remove the air cleaner assembly.

3. Remove the thermostat housing and the bypass hose. It is not necessary to disconnect the top radiator hose at the thermostat housing.

4. Disconnect the heater hose at the rear of the manifold.

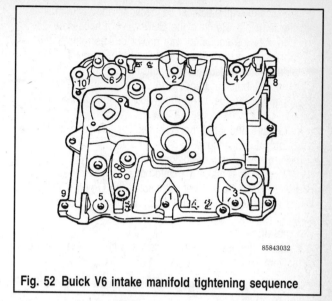
Fig. 52 Buick V6 intake manifold tightening sequence

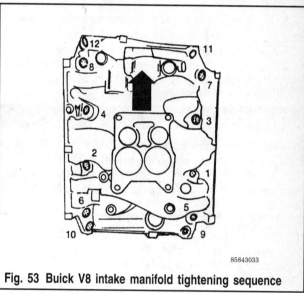
Fig. 53 Buick V8 intake manifold tightening sequence

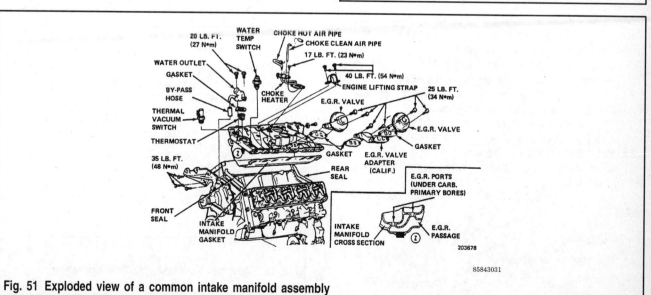
Fig. 51 Exploded view of a common intake manifold assembly

5. Disconnect all electrical connections and vacuum lines from the manifold. Remove the EGR valve if necessary.

6. On vehicles equipped with power brakes remove the vacuum line from the vacuum booster to the manifold.

7. Mark rotor and distributor housing-to-block locations. Remove the distributor (if necessary).

8. Remove the fuel line(s) to the carburetor or the throttle body.

9. Remove and label the carburetor or throttle body linkage and electrical connections.

10. Remove the carburetor or throttle body.

11. Remove the intake manifold bolts. Remove the manifold and the gaskets. Remember to reinstall the O-ring seal between the intake manifold and timing chain cover during assembly, if so equipped.

**To install:**

12. Clean all gasket mating surfaces with a gasket scraper and solvent.

➡ **Use care not to damage aluminum engine parts during gasket removal.**

Use plastic gasket retainers to prevent the manifold gasket from slipping out of place, if so equipped.

13. Install the intake manifold gaskets. Remember to reinstall the O-ring seal between the intake manifold and timing chain cover during assembly, if so equipped. With an assistant, carefully position the manifold onto the engine.

### ❊❊WARNING

**DO NOT slide the manifold into position if the bolts will not line up. This may cause the gasket to become dislodged. With an assistant, remove the manifold, reposition the gasket and try again until the manifold bolts will thread.**

14. Torque the intake manifold in the proper tightening sequence and to the proper torque.

15. Install the carburetor or throttle body.

16. Install the carburetor or throttle body linkage and reconnect the electrical connections.

17. Install the fuel line(s) to the carburetor or throttle body.

18. Install the distributor at the housing-to-block and rotor locations. Install the distributor (if removed).

19. On vehicles equipped with power brakes install the vacuum line from the vacuum booster to the manifold.

20. Connect all electrical connections and vacuum lines to the manifold. Install the EGR valve if necessary.

21. Connect the heater hose at the rear of the manifold.

22. Install the thermostat housing and the bypass hose.

23. Install the air cleaner assembly.

24. Connect the negative battery cable and refill the cooling system.

25. Start the engine and check for oil, vacuum, coolant and fuel leaks.

### Diesel Engines

1. Remove the air cleaner.

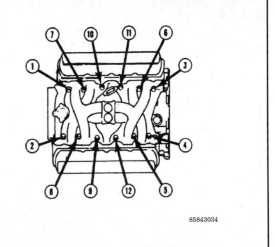

Fig. 54 Oldsmobile V8 intake manifold tightening sequence; gasoline shown

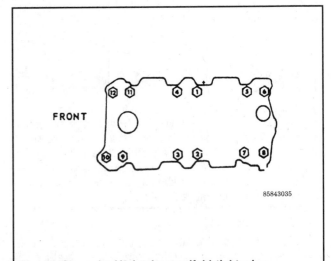

Fig. 55 Chevrolet V8 intake manifold tightening sequence

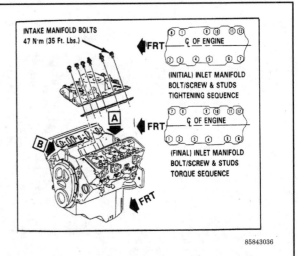

Fig. 56 Chevrolet V6 intake manifold tightening sequence

2. Drain the radiator. Loosen the upper bypass hose clamp, remove the thermostat housing bolts, and remove the housing and the thermostat from the intake manifold.

## **✷✷CAUTION**

**When draining the coolant, keep in mind that cats and dogs are attracted by the ethylene glycol antifreeze, and are quite likely to drink any that is left in an uncovered container or in puddles on the ground. This will prove fatal in sufficient quantity. Always drain the coolant into a sealable container. Coolant should be reused unless it is contaminated or several years old.**

3. Remove the breather pipes from the rocker covers and the air crossover. Remove the air crossover.

4. Disconnect the throttle rod and the return spring. If equipped with cruise control, remove the servo.

5. Remove the hairpin clip at the bellcrank and disconnect the cables. Remove the throttle cable from the bracket on the manifold; position the cable away from the engine. Disconnect and label any wiring as necessary.

6. Remove the alternator bracket if necessary. If equipped with air conditioning, remove the compressor mounting bolts and move the compressor aside, without disconnecting any of the hoses. Remove the compressor mounting bracket from the intake manifold.

7. Disconnect the fuel line from the pump and the fuel filter. Remove the fuel filter and bracket.

8. Remove the fuel injection pump and lines.

9. Disconnect and remove the vacuum pump or oil pump drive assembly from the rear of the engine.

10. Remove the intake manifold drain tube.

11. Remove the intake manifold bolts and remove the manifold. Remove the adapter seal. Remove the injection pump adapter.

**To install:**

12. Clean the mating surfaces of the cylinder heads and the intake manifold using a gasket scraper and solvent.

13. Coat both sides of the gasket surface that seal the intake manifold to the cylinder heads with G.M. sealer #1050026 or the equivalent.

## **✷✷WARNING**

**DO NOT slide the manifold into position if the bolts will not line up. This may cause the gasket to become dislodged. With an assistant, remove the manifold, reposition the gasket and try again until the manifold bolts will thread.**

14. With an assistant, position the intake manifold gaskets on the cylinder heads. Install the end seals, making sure that the ends are positioned under the cylinder heads.

15. Carefully lower the intake manifold into place on the engine.

16. Clean the intake manifold bolts thoroughly, then dip them in clean engine oil. Install the bolts and torque to 15 ft. lbs. (20 Nm) in the proper sequence. Next, torque all the bolts to 30 ft. lbs. (41 Nm), in sequence, and finally tighten to 40 ft. lbs. (54 Nm) in sequence.

17. Install the intake manifold drain tube and clamp.

18. Install injection pump adapter. Make sure not to run the engine without the vacuum pump in place as this drives the oil pump.

19. Install the fuel injection pump and lines.

20. Connect the fuel line to the pump and the fuel filter. Install the fuel filter and bracket.

21. Install the alternator bracket if removed. If equipped with air conditioning, install the compressor bracket and compressor. Install the compressor mounting bracket bolts to the intake manifold.

22. Install the hairpin clip to the bellcrank and connect the cables. Install the throttle cable to the bracket on the manifold.

23. Connect any wiring as necessary.

24. Connect the throttle rod and the return spring. If equipped with cruise control, install the servo.

25. Install the air crossover and connect the breather pipes to the rocker covers and the air crossover.

26. Install the thermostat, gasket and housing bolts to the intake manifold.

27. Refill the radiator with engine coolant.

28. Connect the negative battery cable and install the air cleaner.

29. Start the engine and check for leaks and proper engine operation.

## Exhaust Manifold

### REMOVAL & INSTALLATION

▶ **See Figures 62, 63, 64 and 65**

Tab locks are used on the front and rear pairs of bolts on each exhaust manifold. When removing the bolts, straighten the tabs from beneath the vehicle using a suitable tool. When installing the tab locks, bend the tabs against the flats on the sides of the bolt, not over the top of the bolt.

1. Disconnect the negative battery cable.

2. Remove the air cleaner. Number and then disconnect the spark plug wires.

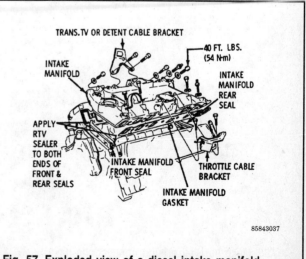

**Fig. 57 Exploded view of a diesel intake manifold assembly**

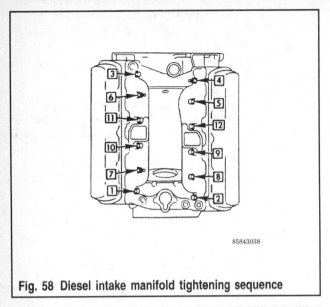

Fig. 58 Diesel intake manifold tightening sequence

Fig. 61 Removing the intake manifold from the engine

Fig. 59 Removing the intake manifold bolts

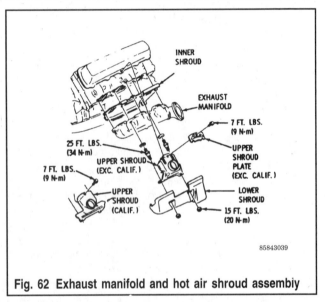

Fig. 62 Exhaust manifold and hot air shroud assembiy

3. Remove the hot air shroud (if so equipped). If the vehicle has Early Fuel Evaporation (EFE), disconnect the vacuum hose, if it is in the way.

4. Loosen the alternator and remove its lower bracket. Disconnect the pipe for the Air Injection Reactor (AIR) system.

5. Raise the vehicle and support it with jackstands.

6. Disconnect the crossover pipe from both manifolds.

7. On models with air conditioning, especially on V8 engines when removing the left side manifold, it may be necessary to remove the compressor and tie it out of the way. On V8 engines, to remove the left manifold, loosen the compressor mounting bracket at the front of the head, remove the rear bracket, and then hang the compressor so you don't put strain on the refrigerant lines.

**✳✳CAUTION**

Do not disconnect the compressor lines! This should only be done after the system is discharged by a trained technician with a recovery/recycling station.

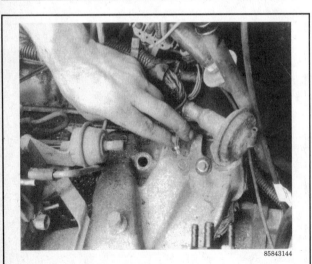

Fig. 60 Make sure all ground connections have been removed from the intake manifold

8. Remove the manifold bolts and remove the exhaust manifold(s). Some models have lock tabs on the front and rear manifold bolts which must be removed before removing the bolts. These tabs can be bent with a drift pin.

**To install:**

9. Install the manifold and bolts. Some models have lock tabs on the front and rear manifold bolts which must be bent over the flats of the bolts to prevent loosening. These tabs can be bent with a drift pin. Torque the bolts to specifications found in the Torque specifications chart in the beginning of this section.

10. On models with air conditioning, especially on V8 engines when installing the left side manifold, reinstall the compressor, tighten the belt and mounting bolts. DO NOT put strain on the refrigerant lines.

11. Raise the vehicle and support it with jackstands.

12. Connect the crossover pipe to both manifolds. Lower the vehicle.

13. Tighten the alternator and install its lower bracket. Connect the pipe for the Air Injection Reactor (AIR) system.

14. Install the hot air shroud (if so equipped). If the vehicle has Early Fuel Evaporation (EFE), connect the vacuum hose, if it was disconnected.

15. Install the air cleaner. Connect the spark plug wires.

16. Connect the negative battery cable, start the engine and check for exhaust leaks.

## Turbocharger

### REMOVAL & INSTALLATION

▶ See Figures 66, 67, 68 and 69

### ✳✳CAUTION

If the turbocharger unit has to be removed, first clean around the unit thoroughly with a non-caustic solution. When removing the turbocharger, take great care to avoid bending, nicking or in ANY WAY damaging the compressor or turbine blades. Any damage to the blades will re-

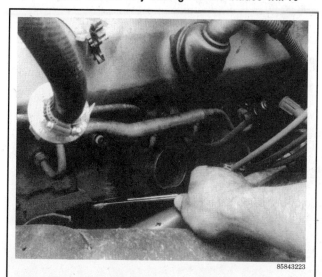
Fig. 63 Removing the exhaust manifold attaching bolts

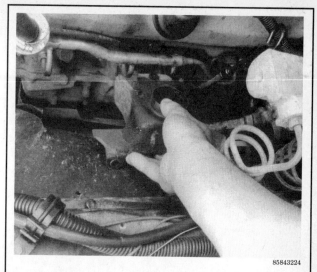
Fig. 64 Removing the hot air shroud

Fig. 65 Removing the exhaust manifold from the engine

sult in imbalance, failure of the center housing bearing, damage to the unit and possible personal injury or damage to the other engine parts.

#### Wastegate Actuator

1. Disconnect the negative battery cable and two hoses from the actuator.

2. Remove the wastegate linkage-to-actuator rod clip.

3. Remove the two bolts attaching the actuator to the compressor housing.

4. Installation is the reverse of removal. Torque the bolts to 100 inch lbs. (11 Nm). Connect the negative battery cable and check for proper operation.

#### Turbocharger and Actuator

1. Disconnect the negative battery cable and remove the air cleaner.

2. Disconnect the exhaust inlet and outlet pipes from the turbocharger.

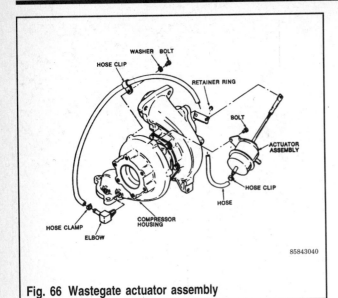

**Fig. 66 Wastegate actuator assembly**

3. Disconnect the oil feed pipe from the center housing.

4. Remove the nut attaching the air intake elbow to the carburetor and remove the elbow and flex tube from the carburetor.

5. Disconnect and tag the accelerator, cruise control and detent linkages from the carburetor. Disconnect the plenum linkage bracket.

6. Remove the two bolts attaching the plenum to the side bracket.

7. Disconnect and tag the fuel line and all vacuum lines from the carburetor.

8. Drain the cooling system and save the coolant if it is in good condition.

### ✳✳CAUTION

**When draining the coolant, keep in mind that cats and dogs are attracted by the ethylene glycol antifreeze, and are quite likely to drink any that is left in an uncovered container or in puddles on the ground. This will prove fatal in sufficient quantity. Always drain the coolant into a sealable container. Coolant should be reused unless it is contaminated or several years old.**

9. Disconnect the coolant lines from the front and rear of the plenum.

10. Disconnect and tag the power brake vacuum line from the plenum.

11. Remove the two bolts attaching the turbine housing to the intake manifold bracket.

12. Remove the two bolts attaching the EGR valve manifold to the plenum. Loosen the two bolts attaching the EGR valve to the intake manifold.

13. Remove the AIR bypass hose from the check valve.

14. Remove the three bolts attaching the compressor housing to the intake manifold.

15. Remove the turbocharger, actuator, carburetor and plenum from the engine.

16. Remove the six bolts attaching the carburetor and plenum to the turbocharger and actuator.

17. Remove the oil drain from the center housing.

**To install:**

18. Install the oil drain on the center housing. Torque to 15 ft. lbs. (20 Nm).

19. Install the six turbocharger/actuator-to-carburetor/plenum bolts.

20. Place the assembly on the engine and connect all vacuum hoses.

21. Install the three bolts attaching the compressor housing to the intake manifold. Torque to 35 ft. lbs. (48 Nm).

22. Install the AIR bypass hose.

23. Loosely install the two bolts attaching the EGR valve manifold to the plenum. Tighten the two bolts attaching the EGR valve to 15 ft. lbs. (20 Nm). Tighten the EGR manifold-to-plenum bolts to 15 ft. lbs. (20 Nm).

24. Install the two bolts attaching the turbine housing to the intake manifold bracket. Torque to 20 ft. lbs. (27 Nm).

25. Connect the power brake vacuum line at the plenum. Torque to 10 ft. lbs. (14 Nm).

26. Connect the plenum front bracket and install one bolt attaching the bracket to the manifold. Torque to 20 ft. lbs. (27 Nm).

27. Connect the coolant hoses to the plenum.

28. Refill the cooling system.

29. Connect the carburetor fuel line and remaining vacuum hoses.

30. Install the two bolts attaching the plenum to the side bracket. Torque to 20 ft. lbs. (27 Nm).

31. Connect the linkage bracket to the plenum. Torque to 20 ft. lbs. (27 Nm).

32. Connect the accelerator, detent and cruise linkages to the carburetor.

33. Install the nut attaching the air intake elbow to the carburetor. Torque to 15 ft. lbs. (20 Nm).

34. Connect the oil feed pipe to the center housing. Torque to 7 ft. lbs. (10 Nm).

35. Connect the inlet and outlet pipes to the turbocharger. Torque to 14 ft. lbs. (19 Nm).

36. Connect the negative battery cable, start the engine and check for exhaust, coolant and vacuum leaks.

### Plenum

1. Disconnect the negative battery cable.

2. Remove the turbocharger and actuator assembly as previously described.

3. Remove the four bolts attaching the carburetor to the plenum.

4. Installation is the reverse of removal. Torque the bolts to 20 ft. lbs. (27 Nm).

5. Connect the negative battery cable and start the engine to check for normal operation.

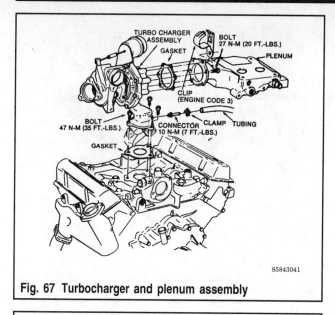

Fig. 67 Turbocharger and plenum assembly

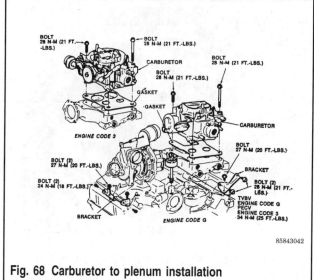

Fig. 68 Carburetor to plenum installation

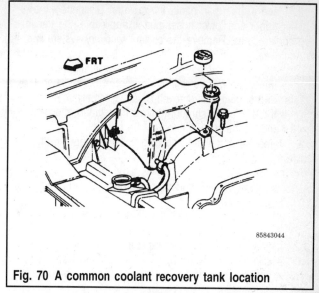

Fig. 70 A common coolant recovery tank location

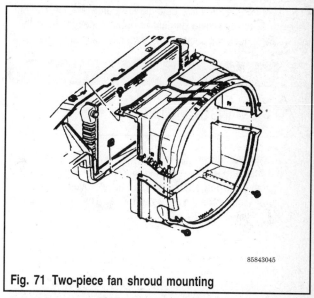

Fig. 71 Two-piece fan shroud mounting

## Radiator

### REMOVAL & INSTALLATION

▶ See Figures 70, 71, 72, 73, 74, 75, 76, 77, 78, 79 and 80

1. Disconnect the negative battery cable and drain the cooling system.

### ✳✳CAUTION

When draining the coolant, keep in mind that cats and dogs are attracted by the ethylene glycol antifreeze, and are quite likely to drink any that is left in an uncovered container or in puddles on the ground. This will prove fatal in sufficient quantity. Always drain the coolant into a sealable container. Coolant should be reused unless it is contaminated or several years old.

Fig. 69 Turbocharger exhaust pipe connection

2. Place a drain pan under the radiator. Disconnect the radiator upper and lower hoses and, if applicable, the transmission coolant lines. Remove the coolant recovery system line, if so equipped.

3. Remove the radiator upper panel if so equipped.

4. If there is a radiator shroud in front of the radiator, the radiator and shroud are removed as an assembly.

5. If there is a fan shroud, remove the shroud attaching screws and let the shroud hang on the fan.

6. Remove the radiator attaching bolts and remove the radiator.

**To install:**

7. Install the radiator and attaching bolts. Torque the bolts to 15 ft. lbs. (20 Nm).

8. If there is a fan shroud, install the shroud and attaching screws.

9. Install the radiator upper panel if so equipped.

10. Connect the radiator upper and lower hoses and, if applicable, the transmission coolant lines. Connect the coolant recovery system line, if so equipped.

11. Connect the negative battery cable and refill the cooling system with the specified amount of engine coolant. Start the engine and check for coolant and transmission fluid leaks.

## Engine Fan

### REMOVAL & INSTALLATION

1. Disconnect the negative battery cable.
2. If necessary, remove the fan shroud.
3. Remove the fan attaching nuts and remove the fan.
4. Installation is the reverse of removal. Torque the nuts to 20 ft. lbs (27 Nm).

Fig. 73 To remove the radiator from the vehicle, the fan shroud must first be removed

Fig. 74 Two piece fan shrouds also have attaching bolts here

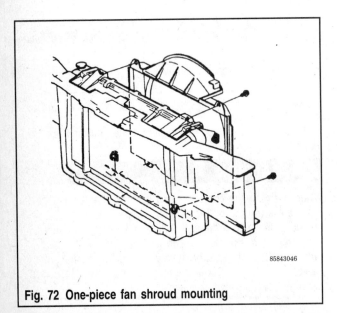

Fig. 72 One-piece fan shroud mounting

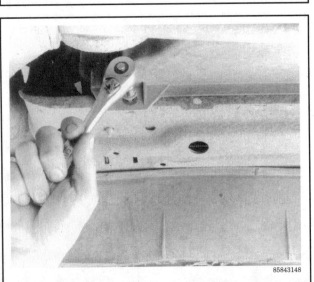

Fig. 75 Removing the lower shroud attaching bolts

Fig. 76 Removing the upper half of a two piece shroud from the vehicle

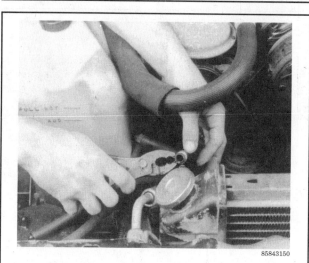

Fig. 77 Remove the coolant recovery tank hose by sliding the clamp down the hose

Fig. 78 Be careful not to damage the radiator neck when removing the hose

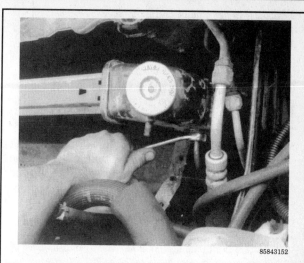

Fig. 79 Transmission and oil cooler lines must be disconnected before removing the radiator

Fig. 80 Removing the radiator from the vehicle

## Water Pump

### REMOVAL & INSTALLATION

▶ See Figures 81, 82, 83, 84, 85, 86 and 87

1. Disconnect the negative battery cable.
2. Drain the radiator.

### ✳✳CAUTION

When draining the coolant, keep in mind that cats and dogs are attracted by the ethylene glycol antifreeze, and are quite likely to drink any that is left in an uncovered container or in puddles on the ground. This will prove fatal in sufficient quantity. Always drain the coolant into a sealable container. Coolant should be reused unless it is contaminated or several years old.

3. Loosen the alternator and other accessories at their adjusting points, and remove the fan belts from the fan pulley.

4. Remove the fan and pulley.

5. Remove any accessory brackets that might interfere with water pump removal.

6. Disconnect the hose from the water pump inlet and the heater hose from the nipple on the pump. Remove the bolts, pump assembly and old gasket from the timing chain cover.

7. Check the pump shaft bearings for end play or roughness in operation. Water pump bearings usually emit a squealing sound with the engine running when the bearings need to be replaced. Replace the pump if the bearings are not in good shape or have been leaking.

**To install:**

8. Make sure the gasket surfaces on the pump and timing chain cover are clean. Install the pump assembly with a new gasket. Torque the pump-to-front cover bolts to 10 ft. lbs. (14 Nm) and the pump-to-block bolts to 22 ft. lbs. (30 Nm), uniformly.

9. Connect the hose to the water pump inlet and the heater hose to the nipple on the pump.

10. Install any accessory brackets that were removed.

11. Install the fan and pulley.

12. Tighten the alternator and other accessories at their adjusting points.

13. Refill the radiator with engine coolant.

14. Connect the negative battery cable.

## Cylinder Head

### REMOVAL & INSTALLATION

◗ See Figures 88, 89, 90, 91, 92,     93, 95, 96, 97, 98, 99, 100, 101 and 102

**Gasoline Engines**

1. Disconnect the negative battery cable.

Fig. 82 Remove the fan attaching bolts and remove the fan

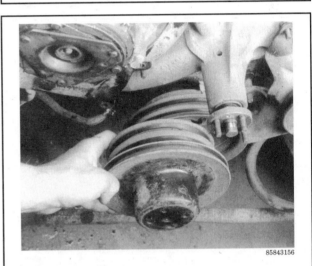

Fig. 83 Once the fan has been removed, the pulley can be removed as well

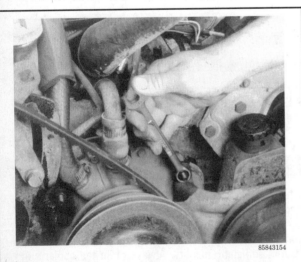

Fig. 81 Remove any accessory brackets which may interfere with water pump removal

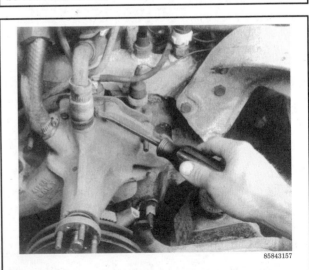

Fig. 84 Remove all the hoses attached to the water pump

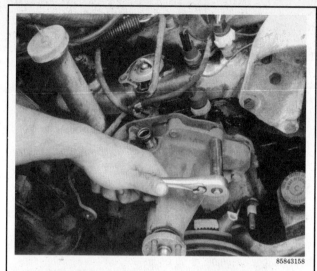

Fig. 85 Removing the water pump attaching bolts

Fig. 86 Removing the water pump from the vehicle

Fig. 87 Always clean the gasket surfaces before installing the new water pump

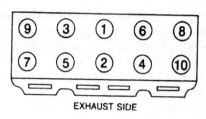

EXHAUST SIDE

Fig. 88 Buick built 350 and 455 cylinder head bolt torque sequence

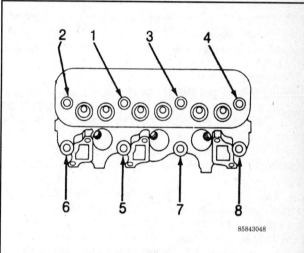

Fig. 89 Buick built V6 cylinder head bolt torque sequence; except 1985-1987 231

2. Drain the coolant and save it if still fresh.

### ✳✳CAUTION

When draining the coolant, keep in mind that cats and dogs are attracted by the ethylene glycol antifreeze, and are quite likely to drink any that is left in an uncovered container or in puddles on the ground. This will prove fatal in sufficient quantity. Always drain the coolant into a sealable container. Coolant should be reused unless it is contaminated or several years old.

3. Remove the air cleaner.
4. Remove the air conditioning compressor, but do not disconnect any A/C lines. Secure the compressor to one side.
5. Disconnect the AIR hose at the check valve. Remove the turbocharger assembly, if so equipped.
6. Remove the intake manifold.
7. When removing the right cylinder head, loosen the alternator belt, disconnect the wiring and remove the alternator.

8. When removing the left cylinder head, remove the dipstick, power steering pump and air pump if so equipped.

9. Label the spark plug wires and disconnect them.

10. Disconnect the exhaust manifold from the head being removed.

11. Remove the valve cover. Scribe the rocker arms with an identifying mark for reassembly; it is important that the rocker assembly is reinstalled in the same position as it was removed. Remove the rocker arm bolts, rocker arms and pivots.

12. Take a piece of heavy cardboard and cut 16 or 12 holes (depending on whether the engine is a V6 or a V8 or 8 or 6 holes if you are only removing one head) in it the same diameter as the pushrod stems. Number the holes in relation to the pushrods being removed. This cardboard holder will keep the pushrods in order (and hopefully out of harm's way) while they are out of the engine. Remove the pushrods.

➡Pushrods MUST be returned to their original locations.

13. On models equipped with power brakes, it is necessary to disconnect the brake booster and turn it sideways to remove the No. 7 pushrod.

14. Remove the cylinder head bolts, and remove the cylinder head and gasket. If the head seems stuck to the block, gently tap around the edge of the head with a rubber mallet until the joint breaks.

**To install:**

15. NEW head gasket(s) should always be used. Match the old gasket with the new one to make sure they are exactly the same. Gaskets on the 260 V8 must be installed with the stripe facing up: 307 V8 gaskets do not have a stripe. If the gasket has a bead, install it so the bead is upward. If there are dowel pins, locate the holes in the gasket over them. On the 285 and 301 engines, coat all rocker stud lower threads, the cylinder head bolt threads, and the underside of the bolt head with thread sealer. On 1986-87 3.8L V6 engines, coat the bolt threads with a heavy body thread sealer. On all engines, the head bolts should be dipped in clean oil before installing. Except on the 1986-87 3.8L V6 and 1988-90 5.0L V8, tighten all head bolts in sequence and in small stages to the specified torque.

16. **On the 1986-87 3.8L V6:**

a. First follow the sequence, torquing the bolts to 25 ft. lbs. (34 Nm).

b. Watching the torque reading, turn the bolts, in the same sequence, 90 degrees tighter. If the torque reading reaches 60 ft. lbs. (81 Nm), stop turning that bolt and proceed to the next one.

c. Repeat the step above, turning the bolts another 90 degrees in sequence, but, again, stopping if a bolt reaches 60 ft. lbs. (81 Nm).

17. **On the 1988-90 5.0L V8:**

a. First follow the sequence, torquing the bolts to 40 ft. lbs. (54 Nm).

b. After torquing, turn the bolts, in the same sequence, the specified number of degrees.

- Bolts 1 through 7 and 9 - 120 degrees
- Bolts 8 and 10 - 95 degrees

➡When installing the intake manifold remember to use new gaskets and new O-ring seals, if the manifold has them. Pushrods MUST be returned to their original locations.

18. Install the pushrods into their original location as removed.

19. Install the rocker arm assemblies into their original location. It is important that the rocker assembly is reinstalled in the same position as it was removed. Torque the bolts to specifications. Also, refer to the Rocker Arm section in this section.

20. Install the valve cover with a new gasket.

21. Connect the exhaust manifold to the head that was removed.

22. Reconnect the spark plug wires.

23. When installing the left cylinder head, install the dipstick, power steering pump and air pump if so equipped.

24. When installing the right cylinder head, install the alternator, connect the wiring and tighten the belt.

25. Install the intake manifold using a new gasket.

26. Connect the AIR hose at the check valve. Install the turbocharger assembly, if so equipped.

27. Install the air conditioning compressor if so equipped.

28. Install the air cleaner.

29. Refill the radiator with coolant.

30. Connect the negative battery cable.

### Diesel Engines

1. Disconnect the negative battery cable. Remove the intake manifold, using the procedure outlined in the Intake Manifold section in this section.

2. Remove the rocker arm cover(s), after removing any accessory brackets which interfere with cover removal.

3. Disconnect and label the glow plug wiring.

4. If the right cylinder head is being removed, remove the ground strap from the head.

5. Remove the rocker arm bolts, the bridged pivots, the rocker arms, and the pushrods, keeping all the parts in order so that they can be returned to their original positions. It is a good practice to number or mark the parts to avoid interchanging them.

6. Remove the fuel return lines from the nozzles.

7. Remove the exhaust manifold(s), using the procedure outlined above.

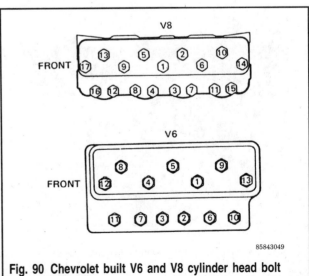

Fig. 90 Chevrolet built V6 and V8 cylinder head bolt torque sequence

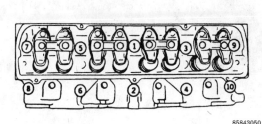

Fig. 91 Oldsmobile built V8 cylinder head bolt torque sequence; except diesel

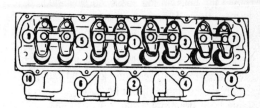

Fig. 94 Oldsmobile built V8 350 diesel cylinder head bolt torque sequence

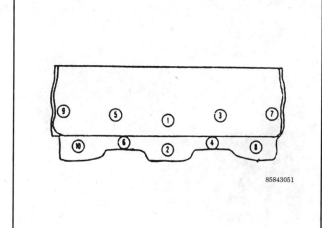

Fig. 92 Pontiac built V8 cylinder head bolt torque sequence

Fig. 95 Disconnect the hose from the AIR pipe, if equipped

8. Remove the engine block drain plug on the side of the engine from which the cylinder head is being removed.

### ✷✷CAUTION

When draining the coolant, keep in mind that cats and dogs are attracted by the ethylene glycol antifreeze, and are quite likely to drink any that is left in an uncovered container or in puddles on the ground. This will prove fatal in sufficient quantity. Always drain the coolant into a sealable container. Coolant should be reused unless it is contaminated or several years old.

9. Remove the head bolts. Remove the cylinder head.
**To install:**
10. Clean the mating surfaces thoroughly with a gasket scraper and solvent. Install new head gaskets on the engine block. Make sure the new gasket matches the old gasket exactly. DO NOT coat the gaskets with any sealer. The gaskets have a special coating that eliminates the need for sealer. The use of sealer will interfere with this coating and cause leaks.

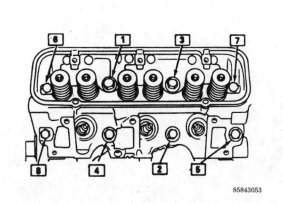

Fig. 93 Torque sequence for the 1985-1987 Buick V6 231

11. Install the cylinder head onto the block.

12. Clean the head bolts thoroughly. Dip the bolts in clean engine oil and install into the cylinder block until the heads of the bolts lightly contact the cylinder head.

13. Torque the bolts, in the sequence illustrated, to 100 ft. lbs. (136 Nm). When all bolts have been tightened to this figure, begin the torquing sequence again, and torque all bolts to 130 ft. lbs. (176 Nm).

14. Install the engine block drain plugs, the exhaust manifolds, the fuel return lines, the glow plug wiring, and the ground strap for the right cylinder head.

15. **Valve lifter draining:** Install the valve train assembly. You'll have to remove, disassemble, and drain oil from all eight lifters associated with the removal of one cylinder head or, if both heads have been removed, all 16 lifters. Remove the valve lifter guide retaining bolts, and then remove the lifter guide. Then, remove each lifter from its bore, keeping it in order for replacement in the same bore. This is especially important since some lifters are 0.010 in. (0.254mm) oversize (these bores are marked with an oval). To disassemble each lifter, remove the retainer ring with a small prybar. Then, remove the pushrod seat and oil metering valve. Remove the plunger and plunger spring (the plunger, valve disc, spring, and check retainer may remain fully assembled). Now, turn the lifter upside down and drain the oil from the lifter body completely.

Don't wipe any of the parts dry, however, as there must be some lubrication at startup. Then, reassemble each lifter by first installing the plunger spring over the check retainer. Hold the plunger upside down so that the spring will not cock and insert it into the lifter bore. Then, install the oil metering valve and pushrod seat into the bore and install the retaining ring.

Install the lifters (in original bores) and the lifter guide and retaining bolts. Install the pushrods in their original positions with the wing at the top. Install the rockers and pivots and bolts, torquing the bolts alternately to 28 ft. lbs. (37 Nm).

16. Install the intake manifold. Refer to the procedure in the Intake Manifold procedure in this section.

17. Install the valve covers. These are sealed with Room Temperature Vulcanizing (RTV) silicone sealer instead of a gasket. Use GM #1052434 or an equivalent. Install the cover to the head within 10 minutes, while the sealer is still wet.

## CLEANING & INSPECTION

▶ See Figures 103, 104 and 105

➡ **Any diesel cylinder head work should be handled by a reputable machine shop familiar with diesel engines. Disassembly, valve lapping, and assembly can be completed by following the gasoline engine procedures.**

Once the cylinder head has been removed, it can be inspected, cleaned and machined (if necessary). Set the head(s) on a clean work space, so the combustion chambers are facing up. Begin cleaning the chambers and ports with a hardwood chisel or other non-metallic tool (to avoid nicking or gouging the chamber, ports and especially the valve seats).

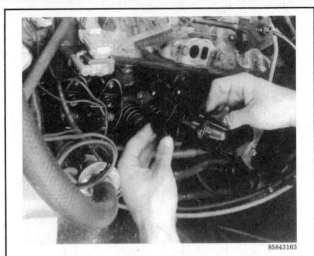

**Fig. 97 When removing the rocker arms, label them to be sure they will be returned to their original position**

**Fig. 98 Removing the pushrods from the engine; return these to their original position when installing as well**

**Fig. 96 Removing the rocker arm bolts**

Fig. 99 Removing the cylinder head bolts

Fig. 101 A view with the cylinder head removed from the engine

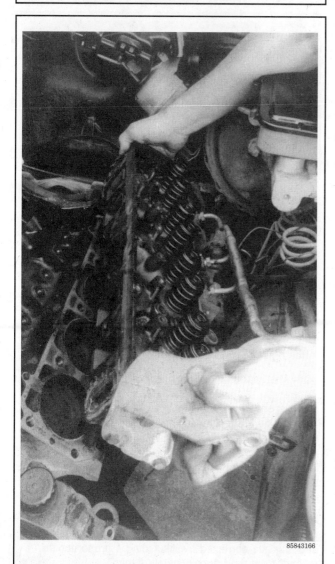

Fig. 100 Be careful when removing the cylinder head form the engine; it's heavy!

Fig. 102 Be sure to torque all the bolts to specification when installing the cylinder head

Chip away the major carbon deposits, then remove the remainder of carbon with a wire brush fitted to an electric drill.

➡Be sure that the carbon is actually removed, rather than just burnished.

After decarbonizing is completed, remove the valve train and take the head(s) to a machine shop and have the head hot tanked (cast iron only). In this process, the head is lowered into a hot chemical bath that very effectively cleans all grease, corrosion, and scale from all internal and external head surfaces. Also have the machinist check the valve seats and re-cut them if necessary. When you bring the clean head(s) home, place them on a clean surface. Completely clean the entire valve train with solvent.

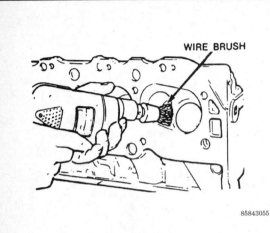

**Fig. 103 Using a wire brush and drill to remove carbon from the cylinder head**

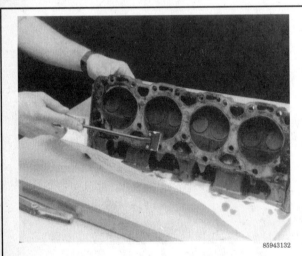

**Fig. 104 A gasket scraper can be used to remove the bulk of the old head gasket from the mating surface**

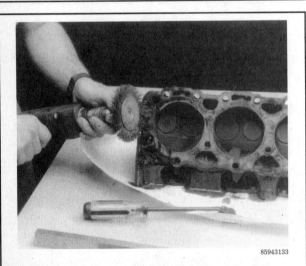

**Fig. 105 A wire wheel will expedite complete gasket removal**

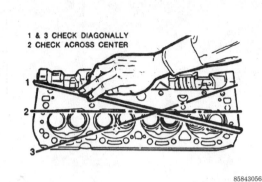

**Fig. 106 Angles for checking warpage of the cylinder head**

**Fig. 107 Checking the cylinder head for warpage along the center using a straightedge and a feeler gauge**

## RESURFACING

▶ **See Figures 106, 107 and 108**

Lay the head down with the combustion chambers facing up. Place a straightedge across the gasket surface of the head, both diagonally and straight across the center. Using a flat feeler gauge, determine the clearance at the center of the straightedge. If warpage exceeds 0.003 in. (0.076mm) in a 6 in. (152mm) span, or 0.006 in. (0.152mm) over the total length, the cylinder head must be resurfaced (which is similar to planing a piece of wood). Resurfacing can be performed at most machine shops.

➡ When resurfacing the cylinder head(s) of V6 or V8 engines, the intake manifold mounting position is altered, and must be corrected by machining a proportionate amount from the intake manifold flange.

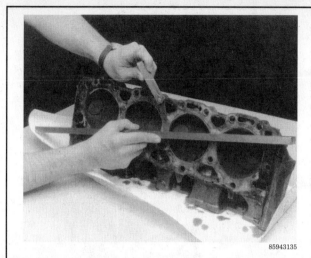

Fig. 108 Checking for warpage across the head at a diagonal

## Valves

### REMOVAL & INSTALLATION

▶ See Figures 109, 110, 111, 112, 113 and 114

1. Remove the head(s), and place on a clean work surface.
2. Using a suitable spring compressor (for pushrod-type overhead valve engines), compress the valve spring and remove the valve spring cap keys. Release the spring compressor and remove the valve spring and cap (and valve rotator on some engines). If the keys will not release, tap on the valve cap with a brass hammer with the compressor removed.

➡Use care in removing the keys; they are easily lost.

3. Remove the valve seals from the intake valve guides. Throw these old seals away, as you'll be installing new seals during reassembly.
4. Slide the valves out of the head from the combustion chamber side.
5. Make a holder for the valves out of a piece of wood or cardboard, as outlined for the pushrods in Cylinder Head Removal. Make sure you number each hole in the cardboard to keep the valves in proper order. Slide the valves out of the head from the combustion chamber side; they MUST be installed as they were removed.

### INSPECTION

▶ See Figures 115, 116, 117, 118, 119, 120, 121 and 122

Inspect the valve faces and seats (in the head) for pits, burned spots and other evidence of poor seating. If a valve face is in such bad shape that the head of the valve must be ground in order to true up the face, discard the valve because the sharp edge will run too hot. Check the Valve Specification chart for the correct angle for the valve faces. We recommend the refacing be done at a reputable machine shop.

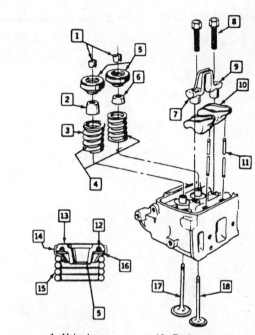

1. Valve keys
2. Intake valve seal
3. Spring
4. Dampener Spring
5. Valve rotator
6. Exhaust valve seal
7. Identification pad
8. 22 ft. lbs. (28 Nm)
9. Rocker arm pivot
10. Rocker arms
11. Pushrods
12. Coil spring
13. Body
14. Collar
15. Valve spring
16. Flat washer
17. Intake valve
18. Exhaust valve

Fig. 109 Exploded view of valve train components; all models similar except Buick

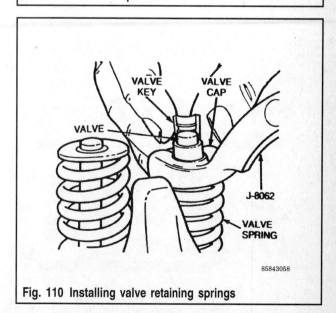

Fig. 110 Installing valve retaining springs

Fig. 111 Use a valve spring compressor to relieve spring tension from the valve caps

Fig. 112 A small magnet will help in removal of the valve keys

Fig. 113 Be careful not to lose the valve keys

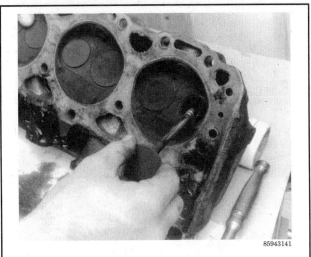

Fig. 114 Invert the cylinder head and withdraw the valve from the guide

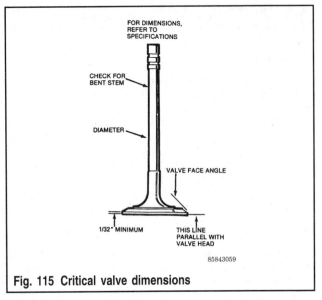

Fig. 115 Critical valve dimensions

Check the valve stem for scoring and burned spots. If not noticeably scored or damaged, clean the valve stem with solvent to remove all gum and varnish. Clean the valve guides using solvent and an expanding wire-type valve guide cleaner. If you have access to a dial indicator for measuring valve stem-to-guide clearance, mount it so that the stem of the indicator is at 90 degrees to the valve stem, and as close to the valve guide as possible. Move the valve off its seat, and measure the valve guide-to-stem clearance by rocking the stem back and forth to actuate the dial indicator. Measure the valve stems using a micrometer, and compare to specifications to determine whether stem or guide wear is responsible for the excess clearance. If a dial indicator and micrometer are not available to you, take your cylinder head and valves to a reputable machine shop for inspection.

Some of the engines covered in this guide are equipped with valve rotators, which double as valve spring caps. In normal operation the rotators put a certain degree of wear on the tip of the valve stem; this wear appears as concentric rings on the stem tip. However, if the rotator is not working properly, the wear may appear as straight notches or **X** patterns across the valve stem tip. Whenever the valves are removed from the cylinder head, the tips should be inspected for improper pattern, which could indicate valve rotator problems. Valve stem tips will have to be ground flat if rotator patterns are severe.

## REFACING

▶ See Figures 123 and 124

If inspection reveals that the valve is usable, then it can be refaced by a machine shop. After the valve faces and seats have been refaced and recut, or if they are determined to be in good condition, the valves must be lapped in to ensure efficient sealing when the valve closes against the seat. Do not lap new valves, however, as a protective coating will be destroyed.

1. Invert the cylinder head so that the combustion chambers are facing up.

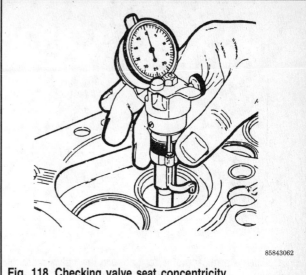

Fig. 118 Checking valve seat concentricity

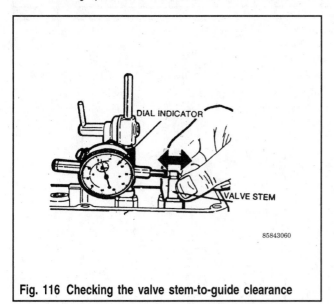

Fig. 116 Checking the valve stem-to-guide clearance

Fig. 119 Once the valve has been removed the valve seats can be inspected for damage and wear

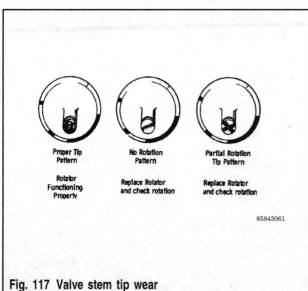

Fig. 117 Valve stem tip wear

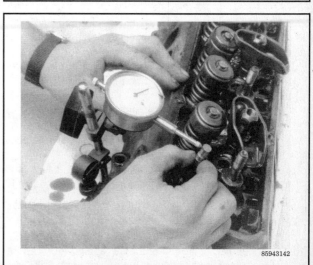

Fig. 120 A dial indicator can be used to check valve stem-to-guide clearance

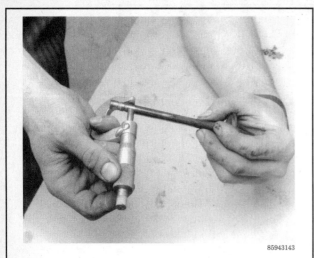

Fig. 121 Use a micrometer to measure the valve stem diameter

Fig. 123 Lapping the valves by hand

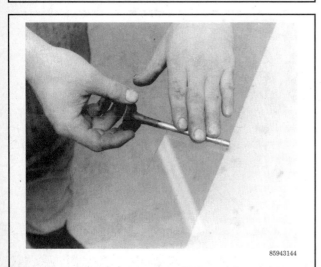

Fig. 122 Valve stems may be rolled on a flat surface to check for bends

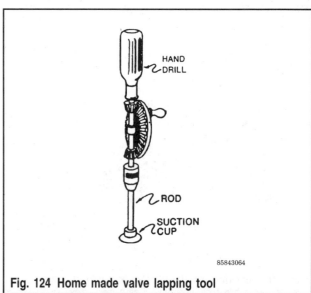

Fig. 124 Home made valve lapping tool

2. Lightly lubricate the valve stems with clean oil, and coat the valve seats with valve grinding compound. Install the valves in the head as numbered.

3. Attach the suction cup of a valve lapping tool to a valve head. You'll probably have to moisten the cup to securely attach the tool to the valve.

4. Rotate the tool between the palms, changing position and lifting the tool often to prevent grooving. Lap the valve until a smooth, polished seat is evident (you may have to add a bit more compound after some lapping is done).

5. Remove the valve and tool, and remove ALL traces of grinding compound with solvent-soaked rag, or rinse the head with solvent.

➡Valve lapping can also be done by fastening a suction cup to a piece of drill rod in a hand eggbeater type drill. Proceed as above, using the drill as a lapping tool. Due to the higher speeds involved when using the hand drill, care must be exercised to avoid grooving the seat. Lift the tool and change direction of rotation often.

## Valve Stem Seals

New valve seals must be installed when the valve train is put back together. Umbrella seals slip over the valve stem and guide boss, while others require that the boss be machined. In some applications Teflon guide seals are available. Check with a machinist and/or automotive parts store for a suggestion on the proper seals to use.

## REPLACEMENT

▶ See Figures 125, 122 and 127

### Cylinder Head Installed

1. Remove the rocker arm cover.

2. Be sure both valves are closed on the cylinder to be serviced.

3. Remove the spark plug, rocker arms and push rods on the cylinder to be serviced.

4. Install air line adaptor tool J-23590 or equivalent to the spark plug port and apply compressed air to hold the valves in place.

5. Compress the valve spring and remove the valve locks, rotator, and spring.

6. Remove the valve stem seal or head oil seal, if present.

**To install:**

7. Install the head oil seal over the valve stem and seat it against the head, if used.

8. Set the valve spring and rotator in place. Compress the spring and install the valve stem seal in the lower groove of the stem, making sure the seal is flat and not twisted. A light coat of oil on the seal will help prevent twisting.

9. Install the valve locks and release the compressor making sure the locks seat properly in the upper groove of the valve stem. Grease may be used to help retain the locks in place while releasing the compressor.

10. Install the spark plug and install the push rods and rocker arms.

11. Adjust the valves (Chevrolet built engines only), and install the rocker arm cover.

**Cylinder Head Removed**

1. Remove the cylinder head from the engine.
2. Remove the rocker assembly.
3. Remove the valve springs and remove the old oil seals.
4. Lubricate the valve stems with clean engine oil.
5. Lubricate and position the seals and valve springs, again one valve at a time.
6. Install the spring retainers, and compress the springs.
7. With the valve key groove exposed above the compressed valve spring, wipe some wheel bearing grease around the groove. This will retain the keys as you release the spring compressor.
8. Using needlenose pliers (or your fingers), place the keys in the key grooves. The grease should hold the keys in place. Slowly release the spring compressor; the valve cap or rotator will raise up as the compressor is released, retaining the keys.
9. Install the rocker assembly, and install the cylinder head(s).

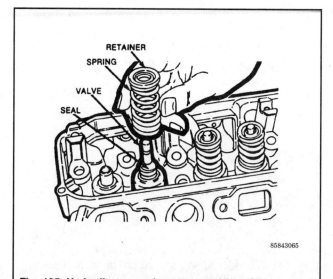

85843065

**Fig. 125 Umbrella type valve stem seal location**

## Valve Springs

### REMOVAL & INSTALLATION

Valve spring removal and installation is part of the Valves removal and installation procedure covered in this section.

### INSPECTION

◆ **See Figures 128, 129, 130 and 131**

1. Place the valve spring on a flat, clean surface next to a square.

2. Measure the height of the spring, and rotate it against the edge of the square to measure distortion (out-of-roundness). If spring height varies between springs by more than $\frac{1}{16}$ in. (1.6mm) or if the distortion exceeds $\frac{1}{16}$ in. (1.6mm), replace the spring.

A valve spring tester is needed to test spring test pressure, so the valve springs must usually be taken to a professional machine shop for this test. Spring pressure at the installed and compressed heights is checked, and a tolerance of plus or minus 5 lbs. (plus or minus 1 lb. on the 231 V6 is permissible on the springs covered in this guide.

## Valve Seats

### REMOVAL & INSTALLATION

Replacement of the valve seat inserts which are worn beyond resurfacing or broken, must be done by a machine shop.

## Valve Guides

### REMOVAL & INSTALLATION

The V6 and V8 engines covered in this guide use integral valve guides; that is, they are a part of the cylinder head and cannot be replaced. The guides can, however, be reamed oversize if they are found to be worn past an acceptable limit. Occasionally, a valve guide bore will be oversize as manufactured. These are marked on the inboard side of the cylinder heads on the machined surface just above the intake manifold.

If the guides must be reamed (this service is available at most machine shops), then valves with oversize stems must be fitted. Valves are usually available in 0.001 in. (0.025mm), 0.003 in. (0.076mm) and 0.005 in. (0.127mm) stem oversizes. Valve guides which are not excessively worn or distorted may, in some cases, be knurled rather than reamed. Knurling is a process in which the metal on the valve guide bore is displaced and raised, thereby reducing clearance. Knurling also provides excellent oil control. The option of knurling rather than reaming valve guides should be discussed with a reputable machinist or engine specialist.

Fig. 126 Removing the O-ring type oil seal

Fig. 127 Removing the umbrella type oil seal

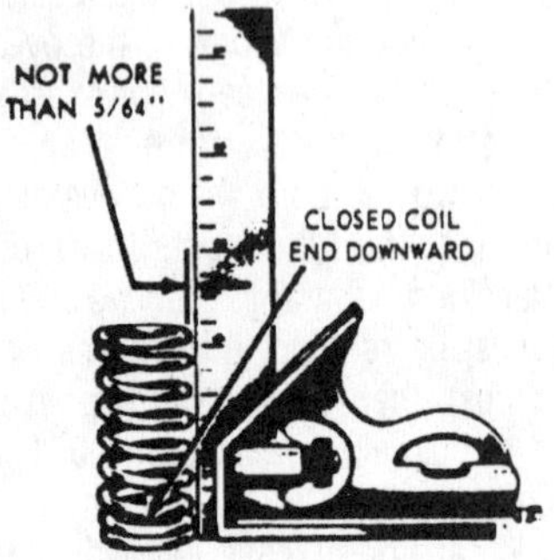

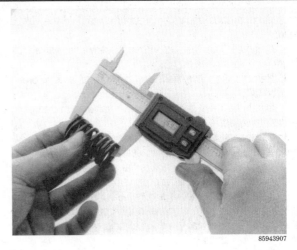

Fig. 129 A caliper gauge can be used to check valve spring free-length

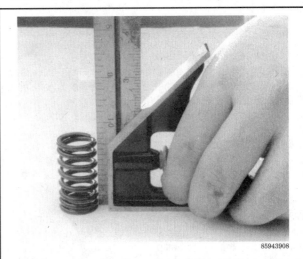

Fig. 130 A carpenters square can be used to check free-length and squareness

NOT MORE
THAN 5/64"

CLOSED COIL
END DOWNWARD

Fig. 128 Be sure the closed coil end is facing downward when checking squareness

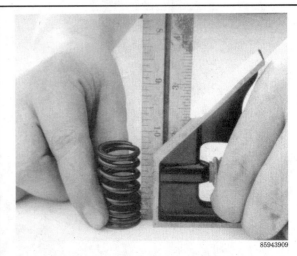

Fig. 131 The valve spring should not be more than 1/16 in. (1.6 mm) out of square

## Valve Lifters

### REMOVAL & INSTALLATION

▶ See Figure 130

**Gasoline and Diesel**

➡Valve lifters and pushrods should be kept in order so they can be reinstalled in their original position. Some engines will have both standard size and oversize 0.010 in. (0.254mm) valve lifters as original equipment. The oversize lifters are etched with an O on their sides; the cylinder block will also be marked with an O if the oversize lifter is used.

1. Remove the intake manifold and gasket.
2. Remove the valve covers, rocker arm assemblies and pushrods.
3. If the lifters are coated with varnish, apply carburetor cleaning solvent to the lifter body. The solvent should dissolve the varnish in about 10 minutes.
4. Remove the lifters. On engines equipped with roller lifters, remove the lifter retainer guide bolts, and remove the guides. A special tool for removing lifters is available, and is helpful for this procedure.
5. New lifters must be primed before installation, as dry lifters will seize when the engine is started. Submerge the lifters in clean engine oil and work the lifter plunger up and down. On Olds diesels, the lifters must be internally and externally lubricated before assembly, but they must be virtually empty of oil. New lifters should be disassembled and thoroughly lubricated on all wear surfaces, but accumulated oil should be drained out prior to reassembly. Re-useable lifters should be disassembled and drained of oil but left damp with oil. Do not attempt to wipe them dry! If they have been cleaned, use the procedure for new lifters. See the procedure for cylinder head removal for lifter disassembly procedures.
6. Install the lifters and pushrods into the cylinder block in their original order. On roller lifter engines, install the lifter retainer guide.
7. Install the intake manifold gaskets and manifold.
8. Position the rocker arms, pivots and bolts on the cylinder head.
9. Install the valve covers, connect the spark plug wires and install the air cleaner.

### OVERHAUL

▶ See Figure 133

1. While holding down the plunger, use a small screwdriver to remove the retainer ring.
2. Remove the seat and oil metering valve.
3. Remove the plunger and the plunger spring.
4. Remove the check ball retainer, check ball spring, and check ball. Pry the check ball retainer loose from the plunger with the blade of a small screwdriver.
5. Inspect all parts carefully. If any parts are damaged or worn, replace the entire lifter assembly.

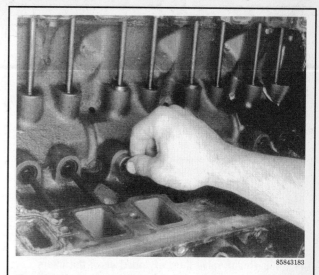

Fig. 132 Removing a lifter from its bore

**To install:**
6. Install the check ball on the small hole in the bottom of the plunger.
7. Install the check ball on the seat and place it over the check ball so the spring rests on the ball.
8. Install the retainer ring into position in the plunger with the blade of a small screwdriver.
9. Place the plunger spring over the ball retainer and slide the lifter body over the spring and plunger being careful to line up the oil feed holes in the lifter body and plunger. Fill the assembly with SAE 10 oil.

➡Do not attempt to force or pump the plunger.

10. Insert the end of a 1/8 in. drift pin into the plunger and press down until it bottoms. At this point the oil holes in the lifter body and plunger assembly will be aligned.
11. Insert a 1/16 in. drift pin through both oil holes to holder the plunger down against the lifter spring tension.
12. Remove the 1/8 in. drift pin.
13. Refill the assembly with SAE 10 oil.
14. Install the metering valve, pushrod seat and retainer.
15. Push down on the seat and remove the 1/16 in. drift pin from the oil holes.

## Oil Pan

### REMOVAL & INSTALLATION

▶ See Figures 134, 135, 131, 137, 138, 139, 140, 141, 142 and 143

**Gasoline Engines**

➡Pan removal may be easier if the engine is turned to No. 1 cylinder firing position. This positions the crankshaft in a position which provides the least interference with pan removal.

1. Disconnect the negative battery terminal.
2. Remove the fan shroud-to-radiator tie bar screws.

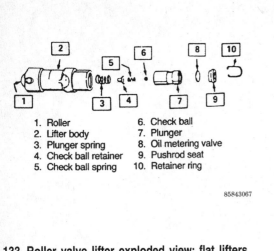

**Fig. 133 Roller valve lifter exploded view; flat lifters similar**

1. Roller
2. Lifter body
3. Plunger spring
4. Check ball retainer
5. Check ball spring
6. Check ball
7. Plunger
8. Oil metering valve
9. Pushrod seat
10. Retainer ring

85843067

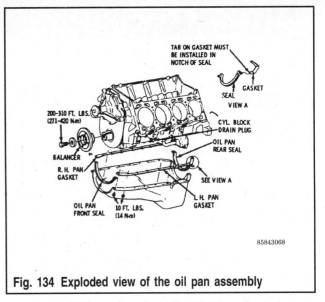

**Fig. 134 Exploded view of the oil pan assembly**

85843068

3. Remove the air cleaner and disconnect the throttle linkage.

4. Raise the vehicle and support it on jackstands.

5. Drain the oil.

6. Remove the lower flywheel housing, remove the shift linkage attaching bolt and swing it out of the way, and disconnect the exhaust crossover pipe at the engine.

7. Remove the front engine mounting bolts.

8. Raise the engine by placing a jack under the crankshaft pulley mounting.

### ✳✳CAUTION

**On air conditioned vehicles, place a support under the right side of the transmission before raising the engine. If you don't do this, the engine and transmission will cock to the right due to the weight of the air conditioning equipment.**

9. Remove the oil pan bolts and remove the pan.

**To install:**

10. Use gasket sealer and new gaskets (if gaskets are used). Torque the pan bolts to 14 ft. lbs. (18 Nm).

11. Lower the engine with a jack under the crankshaft pulley mounting.

12. Install the front engine mounting bolts.

13. Install the lower flywheel housing, shift linkage attaching bolt, and connect the exhaust crossover pipe at the engine.

14. Refill the engine with oil.

15. Lower the vehicle.

16. Install the air cleaner and connect the throttle linkage.

17. Install the fan shroud-to-radiator tie bar screws.

18. Connect the negative battery terminal.

### Diesel Engines

1. Remove the vacuum pump and drive (with A/C or the oil pump drive without A/C).

2. Disconnect the batteries and remove the dipstick.

3. Remove the upper radiator support and fan shroud.

4. Raise and support the vehicle. Drain the oil.

5. Remove the flywheel cover.

6. Disconnect the exhaust and crossover pipes.

7. Remove the oil cooler lines at the filter base.

8. Remove the starter assembly. Support the engine with a jack.

9. Remove the engine mounts from the block.

10. Raise the front of the engine and remove the oil pan.

**To install:**

11. Install the oil pan, torque the retaining bolts 12 ft. lbs. (16 Nm).

12. Install the engine mounts to the block.

13. Install the starter assembly.

14. Install the oil cooler lines at the filter base.

15. Connect the exhaust and crossover pipes.

16. Install the flywheel cover.

17. Lower the vehicle.

18. Refill the engine with the proper amount of high quality engine oil suitable for diesel engines.

19. Install the upper radiator support and fan shroud.

20. Connect the batteries and install the dipstick.

21. Install the vacuum pump and drive.

22. Start the engine and check for oil leaks.

### Oil Pump

## REMOVAL & INSTALLATION

▶ **See Figure 144**

### Buick Built V6

The oil pump is located in the timing chain cover and is connected by a drilled passage to the oil screen housing and pipe assembly in the oil pan. All oil is discharged from the pump to the oil pump cover assembly, on which the oil filter is mounted.

1. To remove the oil pump cover and gears, first remove the oil filter.

2. Remove the screws which attach the oil pump cover assembly to the timing chain cover.

3. Remove the cover assembly and slide out the oil pump gears.

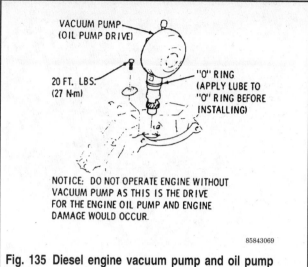

VACUUM PUMP
(OIL PUMP DRIVE)

20 FT. LBS.
(27 N·m)

"O" RING
(APPLY LUBE TO
"O" RING BEFORE
INSTALLING)

NOTICE: DO NOT OPERATE ENGINE WITHOUT
VACUUM PUMP AS THIS IS THE DRIVE
FOR THE ENGINE OIL PUMP AND ENGINE
DAMAGE WOULD OCCUR.

85843069

Fig. 135 Diesel engine vacuum pump and oil pump
drive

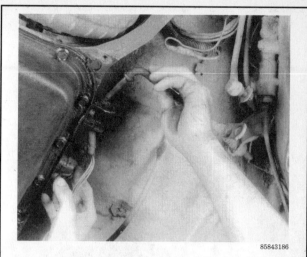

85843186

Fig. 138 Disconnecting the shift linkage from the
transmission

85843184

Fig. 136 Disconnecting the throttle linkage

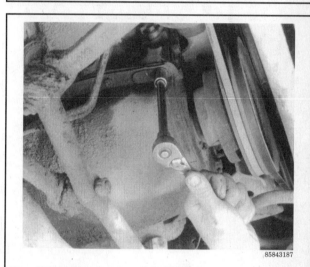

85843187

Fig. 139 Make sure the oil is drained before removing
the oil pan bolts

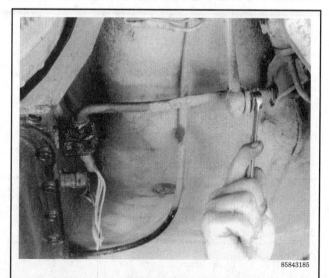

85843185

Fig. 137 Removing the shift linkage attaching bolt

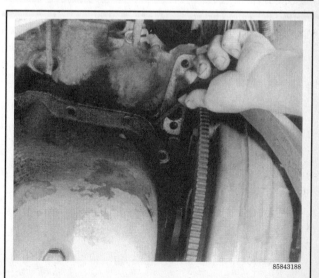

85843188

Fig. 140 Carefully pry the oil pan away from the engine

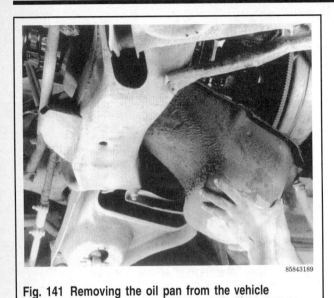

Fig. 141 Removing the oil pan from the vehicle

Fig. 142 The gasket mating surfaces can be cleaned by using a gasket scraper

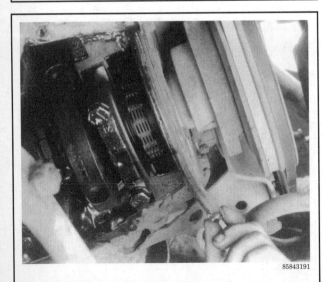

Fig. 143 Removing the oil pan front seal

Fig. 144 A common oil pump location

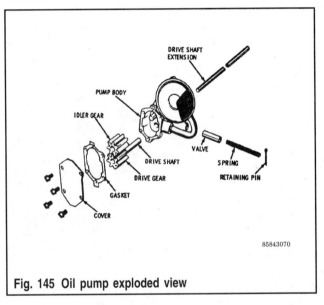

Fig. 145 Oil pump exploded view

4. Remove the oil pressure relief valve cap, spring and valve.

**To install:**

5. Lubricate the pressure relief valve and spring and place them in the cover. Install the cap and the gasket. Torque the cap to 35 ft. lbs. (48 Nm).

6. Pack the oil pump gear cavity full of petroleum jelly. Do not use gear lube. Reinstall the oil pump gears so that the petroleum jelly is forced into every cavity of the gear pocket, and between the gear teeth. There must be no air spaces. This step is very important.

**✳✳CAUTION**

**Unless the pump is primed this way, it won't produce any oil pressure when the engine is started.**

7. Install the cover assembly using a new gasket and sealer. Tighten the screws to 10 ft. lbs. (14 Nm).

8. Install the oil filter.

### All Other Engines

The oil pump is mounted to the bottom of the block and is accessible only by removing the oil pan.

1. Remove the oil pan,
2. Remove the pump attaching bolts.
3. Remove the pump and driveshaft extension.

**To install:**

4. Pack the inside of the pump completely with petroleum jelly. DO NOT use engine oil. The pump MUST be primed this way or it won't produce any oil pressure when the engine is started.
5. Install the cover screws and tighten alternately and evenly to 8 ft. lbs. (11 Nm).
6. Position the pressure regulator valve into the pump cover, closed end first, then install the spring and retaining pin.

➡**When assembling the driveshaft extension to the driveshaft, the end of the extension nearest the washers must be inserted into the driveshaft.**

7. Insert the driveshaft extension through the opening in the main bearing cap and block until the shaft mates into the distributor drive gear.
8. Install the pump onto the rear main bearing cap and install the attaching bolts. Torque the bolts to 35 ft. lbs. (48 Nm).
9. Install the oil pan.
10. Start the engine and check for oil leaks.

## OVERHAUL

◆ **See Figures 145, 146, 147 and 148**

### Buick Built V6

1. Clean the oil pump gears and inspect them for any obvious defects such as chipping or scoring.
2. Clean the oil pressure relief valve cap, spring and valve and inspect them for wear or scoring. Check the relief valve spring to see that it is not worn on its side or collapsed, Replace the spring if it seems questionable.
3. Check the relief valve for a correct fit in its bore. It should be an easy slip fit and no more. If any perceptible shake can be felt, the valve and/or the cover should be replaced.
4. Install the oil pump gears (if removed) and the shaft in the oil pump body section of the timing chain cover to check the gear end clearance and gear side clearance. Check gear end clearance by placing a straight edge over the gears and measure the clearance between the straight edge and the gasket surface. Clearance should be 0.002-0.006 in. (0.050
5. Check the pump cover flatness by placing a straight edge across the cover face, with a feeler gauge between the straight edge and the cover. If clearance is 0.001 in. (0.025mm) or more, replace the cover.

### All Other Engines

1. Remove the cotter pin, spring and the pressure regulator valve.

2. Remove the oil pump cover attaching screws and remove the oil pump cover and gasket. Clean the pump in solvent or kerosene, and wash out the pick-up screen.
3. Remove the drive gear and idler gear from the pump body.
4. Check the gears for scoring and other damage. Install the gears if in good condition, or replace them if damaged. Check gear end clearance by placing a straight edge over the gears and measure the clearance between the straight edge and the gasket surface with a feeler gauge. End clearance for the diesel is 0.0005-0.0075 in. (0.0127-0.1905mm); 350 (R) and 403 (K) is 0.0015-0.0085 in. 0.0381-0.2159mm); and other V8s is 0.002-0.0065 in. (0.0508-0.1651mm). If end clearance is excessive, check for scores in the cover that would bring the total clearance over the specs.
5. Check gear side clearance by inserting the feeler gauge between the gear teeth and the side wall of the pump body. Clearance should be 0.002-0.005 in. (0.0508-0.1270mm).

## Crankshaft Damper

### REMOVAL & INSTALLATION

◆ **See Figures 149, 150, 151, 151 and 152**

1. Disconnect the negative battery cable.
2. Remove the belts from the crankshaft pulley.
3. Remove the crankshaft damper attaching bolt.

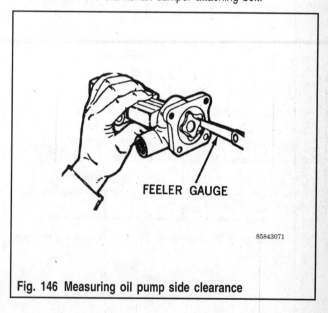

FEELER GAUGE

85843071

**Fig. 146 Measuring oil pump side clearance**

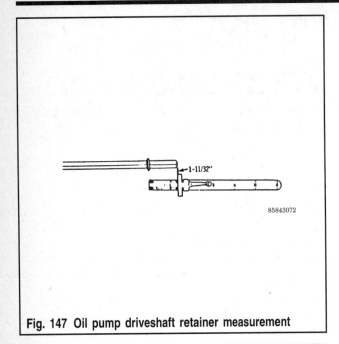

Fig. 147 Oil pump driveshaft retainer measurement

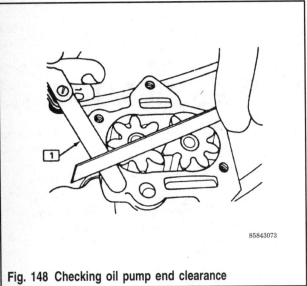

Fig. 148 Checking oil pump end clearance

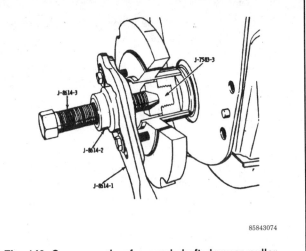

Fig. 149 One example of a crankshaft damper puller tool

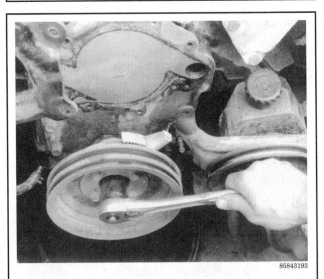

Fig. 150 Removing the crankshaft damper bolt

Fig. 151 Do not attempt to pry on the damper to remove it from the crankshaft, use a puller only

4. Attach a suitable puller to the damper and remove the damper from the crankshaft.

➡On certain models, removal of the cooling fan, fan shroud or radiator may be necessary for clearance.

### ✳✳WARNING

DO NOT pry on the damper assembly to remove it from the vehicle or component damage will result. Remove the damper using a puller only.

5. Installation is the reverse of removal. Torque the damper bolt to specification.

Fig. 152 Removing the damper from the crankshaft

Fig. 153 When installing the damper, thread the bolt by hand first to prevent cross-threading

## Timing Chain Cover and Seal

### REMOVAL & INSTALLATION

▶ See Figures 154, 155, 156, 157, 158, 159, 160, 161 and 162

**Buick Built Engines**

1. Disconnect the negative battery cable. Drain the cooling system.

### ✲✲CAUTION

When draining the coolant, keep in mind that cats and dogs are attracted by the ethylene glycol antifreeze, and are quite likely to drink any that is left in an uncovered

container or in puddles on the ground. This will prove fatal in sufficient quantity. Always drain the coolant into a sealable container. Coolant should be reused unless it is contaminated or several years old.

2. Remove the radiator, fan, pulley and belt.
3. Remove the fuel pump and alternator, if necessary to remove cover.
4. Remove the distributor. If the timing chain and sprockets will not be disturbed, note the position of the distributor for installation in the same position.
5. Remove the thermostat bypass hose.
6. Remove the harmonic balancer.
7. Remove the timing chain-to-crankcase bolts.
8. Remove the oil pan-to-timing chain cover bolts and remove the timing chain cover.
9. Using a punch, drive out the old seal and the shedder toward the rear of the seal.

**To install:**

10. Coil the new packing around the opening so the ends are at the top. Drive in the shedder using a punch. Stake it in place at three locations. Properly size the packing by rotating a hammer handle around the packing until the balancer hub can be inserted through the opening. Before beginning reassembly, remove the oil pump cover and pack the entire oil pump cavity tightly with petroleum grease. If this is not done, the oil pump cannot prime itself and the engine will be damaged. Coat the cover bolts with sealer.
11. Install the oil pan-to-timing chain cover and bolts.
12. Install the timing chain-to-crankcase bolts and torque to 35 ft. lbs. (48 Nm).
13. Install the harmonic balancer using balancer installer tool.
14. Install the thermostat bypass hose.
15. Install the distributor to the same position as removed.
16. Install the fuel pump and alternator.
17. Install the radiator, fan, pulley and belt.
18. Connect the negative battery cable. Refill the cooling system.

**Pontiac Built Engines**

1. Disconnect the negative battery cable. Drain the radiator and the cylinder block.

### ✲✲CAUTION

When draining the coolant, keep in mind that cats and dogs are attracted by the ethylene glycol antifreeze, and are quite likely to drink any that is left in an uncovered container or in puddles on the ground. This will prove fatal in sufficient quantity. Always drain the coolant into a sealable container. Coolant should be reused unless it is contaminated or several years old.

2. Loosen the alternator adjusting bolts.
3. Remove the fan, fan pulley, accessory drive belts, and water pump.
4. Disconnect the radiator hoses.
5. Remove the fuel pump.
6. Remove the harmonic balancer bolt and washer.

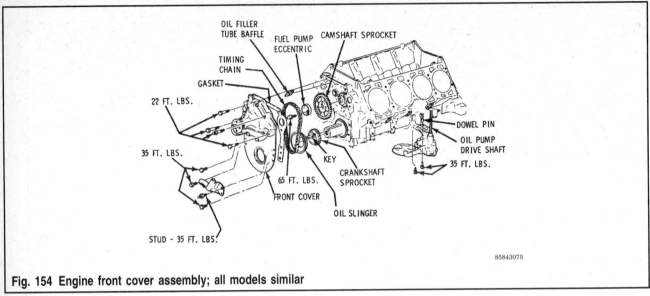

Fig. 154 Engine front cover assembly; all models similar

7. Remove harmonic balancer.

➡ **Do not pry on rubber mounted balancers. If only the seal is to be replaced, proceed to Step 12.**

8. Remove the front four oil pan to timing cover bolts.
9. Remove the timing cover bolts and nuts and cover to intake manifold bolt.
10. Pull the cover forward and remove.
11. Remove the O-ring from the recess in the intake manifold.

**To install:**

12. Clean all the gasket surfaces.
13. To replace the seal, pry it out of the cover using a prybar. Install the new seal with the lip inward.

➡ **The seal can be replaced with the cover installed.**

14. Making sure all gaskets are replaced. Torque the four oil pan bolts to 12 ft. lbs. (16 Nm), and the fan pulley bolts to 20 ft. lbs. (27 Nm).
15. Install harmonic balancer and torque the bolt to specifications.
16. Install the fuel pump.
17. Connect the radiator hoses.
18. Install the water pump, fan, pulley, accessory drive belts.
19. Tighten the alternator adjusting bolts.
20. Connect the negative battery cable. Refill the radiator and the cylinder block.

**Oldsmobile Built Gasoline Engines**

1. Disconnect the negative battery cable. Drain the coolant. Disconnect the radiator hose and the bypass hose. Remove the fan, belts and pulley.

### ✳✳CAUTION

When draining the coolant, keep in mind that cats and dogs are attracted by the ethylene glycol antifreeze, and are quite likely to drink any that is left in an uncovered container or in puddles on the ground. This will prove

fatal in sufficient quantity. Always drain the coolant into a sealable container. Coolant should be reused unless it is contaminated or several years old.

2. Remove the vibration damper and crankshaft pulley.
3. On 1975-76 models only (which have no dowel pins), remove the oil pan.
4. Remove the front cover attaching bolts and remove the cover, timing indicator and water pump from the front of the engine. This requires removing all the bolts (four) that hold the cover on at the bottom, and four larger water pump mounting bolts that go right through the cover into the block. The two top center water pump mounting bolts and the two bottom such bolts remain in place and retain the water pump and gasket to the front of the cover. The other four water pump mounting bolts are removed. On 1977 and later models, remove the two dowel pins from the block. You may have to grind a flat on each pin to get a good grip.
5. On 1977 and later models, grind a chamfer on the end of each dowel pin as illustrated. When installing the dowel pins, they must be inserted chamfered end first. Trim about ⅛ in. (3.1mm) from each end of the new front pan seal and trim any excess material from the front edge of the oil pan gasket. Be sure all mating surfaces are clean.
6. On 1975-76 models apply a sealer around water holes on the new cover gasket before applying it to the block.
7. On 1977 and later models:
   a. Clean all seal mating surfaces with solvent.
   b. When installing the new front cover gasket, first apply sealer to the water pump bolt hole areas of the seal and then position the gasket to the block.
   c. Apply RTV sealer to the junction of block, pan, and front cover.
   d. In positioning the front cover onto the block and gasket, press it downward to compress the seal. Then, rotate the cover left and right while you guide the pan seal into the cavity with a small prybar, as shown. Now, apply oil to the threads and install two of the bolts finger tight to hold the cover in place. Install the two dowel pins, chamfered end first.

8. To install, note these points:

a. When installing cover bolts, first coat them with engine oil. Tighten evenly, torquing the four lower bolts to 35 ft. lbs. (48 Nm) and the four bolts passing through the water pump to 22 ft. lbs. (30 Nm).

b. Apply a high quality lubricant (an example is GM 1050169) to the sealing surface of the balancer.

c. When installing the balancer bolt, torque to proper specifications. Crankshaft pulley attaching bolts are torqued to 10 ft. lbs. (14 Nm); fan pulley attaching bolts are torqued to 20 ft. lbs. (27 Nm).

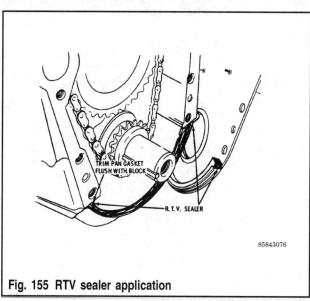

Fig. 155 RTV sealer application

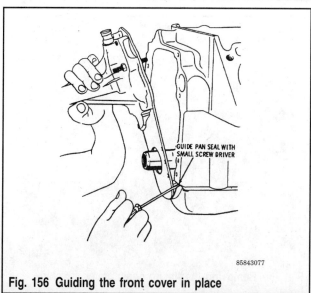

Fig. 156 Guiding the front cover in place

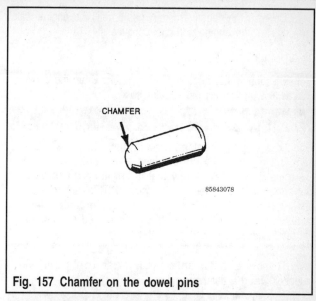

Fig. 157 Chamfer on the dowel pins

**Chevrolet Built Engines**

1. Disconnect the negative battery cable. Drain the cooling system.

### ✳✳CAUTION

When draining the coolant, keep in mind that cats and dogs are attracted by the ethylene glycol antifreeze, and are quite likely to drink any that is left in an uncovered container or in puddles on the ground. This will prove fatal in sufficient quantity. Always drain the coolant into a sealable container. Coolant should be reused unless it is contaminated or several years old.

2. Remove the crankshaft pulley with a puller. Remove the water pump. Remove the screws holding the timing case cover to the block and remove the cover and gaskets.

3. Use a suitable tool to pry the old seal out of the front face of the cover.

**To install:**

4. Install the new seal so that open end is toward the inside of the cover.

➡Coat the lip of the new seal with oil prior to installation.

5. Check that the timing chain oil slinger is in place against the crankshaft sprocket.

6. Apply a ⅛ in. (3.1mm) bead of RTV sealer to the joint formed by the oil pan and cylinder block.

7. Coat the cover gasket with sealer and position it on the block. Coat the bottom of the crankshaft seal with engine oil and carefully position the cover over the crankshaft and onto the locating dowels. Make sure you don't force the cover over the dowels, or it will be distorted. Now, loosely install the cover-to-block upper attaching screws.

8. Tighten the screws alternately in several stages, while you hold the cover downward and in position so that the dowels do not bind in the cover holes. Install the remaining screws and tighten alternately and in several stages to 6-8 ft. lbs. (8-11 Nm).

9. Install the vibration damper and water pump. Torque the vibration damper bolt to specification.

10. Connect the negative battery cable, refill the engine with coolant, start the engine and check for leaks.

### Diesel Engine

1. Disconnect the negative battery cable. Drain the cooling system and disconnect the radiator hoses.

### ✳✳CAUTION

When draining the coolant, keep in mind that cats and dogs are attracted by the ethylene glycol antifreeze, and are quite likely to drink any that is left in an uncovered container or in puddles on the ground. This will prove fatal in sufficient quantity. Always drain the coolant into a sealable container. Coolant should be reused unless it is contaminated or several years old.

2. Remove all belts, fan and pulley, crankshaft pulley and balancer, using a balancer puller.

### ✳✳CAUTION

The use of any other type of puller, such as a universal claw type which pulls on the outside of the hub, can destroy the balancer. The outside ring of the balancer is bonded in rubber to the hub. Pulling on the outside will break the bond. The timing mark is on the outside ring. If it is suspected that the bond is broken, check that the center of the keyway is 16 degrees from the center of the timing slot. In addition, there are chiseled aligning marks between the weight and the hub.

3. Unbolt and remove the cover, timing indicator and water pump.

4. Remove the two dowel pins from the block. It may be necessary to grind a flat on each pin to get a grip on it.

**To install:**

5. Grind a chamfer on one end of each dowel pin.

6. Cut the excess material from the front end of the oil pan gasket on each side of the block.

7. Clean the block, oil pan and front cover mating surfaces with solvent and a gasket scraper.

8. Trim about ⅛ in. (3.1mm) off each end of a new front pan seal.

9. Install a new front cover gasket on the block and a new seal in the front cover.

10. Apply sealer to the gasket around the coolant holes.

11. Apply sealer to the block at the junction of the pan and front cover.

12. Place the cover on the block and press down to compress the seal. Rotate the cover left and right and guide the pan seal into the cavity using a small prybar. Oil the bolt threads and install two bolts to hold the cover in place. Install both dowel pins (chamfered end first), then install the remaining front cover bolts.

13. Apply a lubricant, compatible with rubber, on the balancer seal surface.

14. Install the balancer and bolt. Torque the bolt to specification.

15. Install the belts, connect the negative battery cable, refill the engine with coolant, start the engine and check for leaks.

## Timing Chain

### REMOVAL & INSTALLATION

▶ See Figures 163, 164, 165, 166, 168 and 179

#### Buick Built V6 and V8

1. Disconnect the negative battery cable. Remove the front cover as previously outlined.

2. Align the timing marks on the sprockets.

3. Remove the camshaft sprocket bolt without changing the position of the sprocket. On the V6 and 455, remove the oil pan.

4. Remove the front crankshaft oil slinger.

5. On the 350, remove the crankshaft distributor drive gear retaining bolt and washer. Remove the drive gear and the fuel pump eccentric. On the V6 and the 455, remove the camshaft sprocket bolts.

**Fig. 158 Front cover seal installation; Chevrolet built engine shown**

**Fig. 159 Removing the timing chain cover attaching bolts**

Fig. 160 Removing the cover from the engine

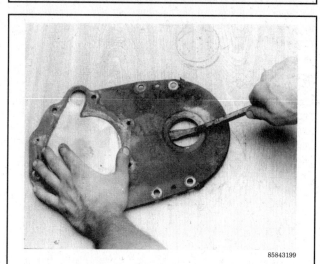

Fig. 161 Prying the old seal from the timing chain cover

Fig. 162 A seal driver or large socket can be used to install the front seal

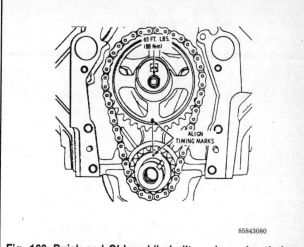

Fig. 163 Buick and Oldsmobile built engine valve timing marks; except Olds 400 V8

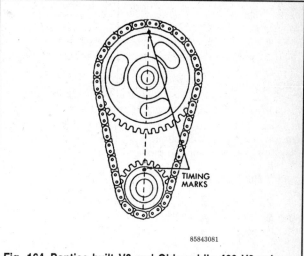

Fig. 164 Pontiac built V8 and Oldsmobile 400 V8 valve timing marks

6. Using two large prybars, carefully pry the camshaft sprocket and the crankshaft sprocket forward until they are free. Remove the sprockets and the chain.

7. Remove the crankshaft sprocket using a jaw puller or equivalent tool.

**To install:**

8. Make sure, with sprockets temporarily installed, that No. 1 piston is at top dead center and the camshaft sprocket O-mark is straight down and on the centerline of both shafts.

9. Remove the camshaft sprocket and assemble the timing chain on both sprockets. Then slide the sprockets-and-chain assembly on the shafts with the O-marks in their closest together position and on a centerline with the sprocket hubs.

10. Assemble the slinger on the crankshaft with I.D. against the sprocket, (concave side toward the front of engine). Install the oil pan, if removed.

11. On the 350, slide the fuel pump eccentric on the camshaft and the Woodruff key with the oil groove forward. On the six cylinder and the 455, install the camshaft sprocket bolts.

12. Install the distributor drive gear.

13. Install the drive gear and eccentric bolt and retaining washer Torque to 40-55 ft. lbs. (54-75 Nm). Turn the crankshaft over twice to see if the timing marks align. If they do not align, the chain is not in the right position and will have to be realigned.

14. Install the timing case cover. Install a new seal by lightly tapping it in place. The lip of the seal faces inward. Pay particular attention to the following points.

   a. Remove the oil pump cover and pack the space around the oil pump gears completely full of petroleum jelly. There must be no air space left inside the pump. Reinstall the pump cover using a new gasket.

   b. The gasket surface of the block and timing chain cover must be clean and smooth. Use a new gasket correctly positioned.

   c. Install the chain cover being certain the dowel pins engage the dowel pin holes before starting the attaching bolts.

   d. Lube the bolt threads before installation and install them.

   e. If the vehicle has power steering the front pump bracket should be installed at this time.

   f. Lube the O.D. of the harmonic balancer hub before installation to prevent damage to the seal when starting the engine.

➡The V6 engine has two timing marks on the harmonic balancer. A 1 in. (25.4mm) long, thin scribe mark is used for strobe light timing. Another mark, 4 in. (102mm) back, has a wider slot and is about ½ in. (12.7mm) long. This mark is used for magnetic pick-up timing.

### Pontiac Built Engines

1. Disconnect the negative battery cable. Remove the timing chain cover as previously outlined in this section.

2. Remove the camshaft bolt, fuel pump eccentric and bushing.

3. Align the timing marks to simplify proper positioning of the sprockets during reassembly.

4. Slide the timing chain and camshaft gear off at the same time.

➡If you intend to remove the gear on the crankshaft you will need a puller to do so.

**To install:**

5. Install the new timing chain and or sprockets, making sure the marks on both sprockets are exactly on a straight line passing through the shaft centers. The camshaft should extend through the sprocket so that the hole in the fuel pump eccentric will locate on the shaft.

6. Install the fuel pump eccentric and bushing. Install the retainer bolt and tighten it to 40 ft. lbs. (54 Nm).

7. Reinstall the timing gear cover, water pump, and harmonic balancer. Remember to install a new O-ring in the water

passage. Connect the negative batter cable and check for proper operation.

➡When reassembling the timing case cover, extra care should be taken to make sure that the oil seal between the bottom of the timing case cover and the front of the oil pan is still good. Gasket cement should be used at the joint to prevent oil leaks.

### Oldsmobile Built Engines

1. Disconnect the negative battery cable.

2. Remove the timing case cover and take off the camshaft gear.

➡The fuel pump operating cam is bolted to the front of the camshaft sprocket and the sprocket is located on the camshaft by means of a dowel.

3. Remove the oil slinger, timing chain, and the camshaft sprocket. If the crankshaft sprocket is to be replaced, remove it also at this time. Remove the crankshaft key before using the puller. If the key can not be removed, align the puller so it does not overlap the end of the key, as the keyway is only machined part of the way into the crankshaft gear.

**To install:**

4. Reinstall the crankshaft sprocket being careful to start it with the keyway in perfect alignment since it is rather difficult to correct for misalignment after the gear has been started on the shaft. Turn the timing mark on the crankshaft gear until it points directly toward the center of the camshaft. Mount the timing chain over the camshaft gear and start the camshaft gear up on to its shaft with the timing marks as close as possible to each other and in line between the shaft centers. Rotate the camshaft to align the shaft with the new gear.

5. Install the fuel pump eccentric with the flat side toward the rear.

6. Drive the key in with a hammer until it bottoms.

7. Install the oil slinger.

8. Install the timing cover, vibration damper, belts, fan, connect the negative battery cable. Start the engine and check for normal operation.

➡Any time the timing chain and gears are replaced on the diesel engine it will be necessary to retime the engine.

### Chevrolet Built Engines

To replace the chain, remove the radiator, water pump, the harmonic balancer and the crankcase front cover. This will allow access to the timing chain. Crank the engine until the timing marks on both sprockets are nearest each other and in line between the shaft centers. Then take out the three bolts that hold the camshaft gear to the camshaft. This gear is a light press fit on the camshaft and will come off easily. It is located by a dowel.

The chain comes off with the camshaft gear.

A gear puller will be required to remove the crankshaft gear.

Without disturbing the position of the engine, mount the new crankshaft gear on the shaft, and mount the chain over the camshaft gear. Arrange the camshaft gear in such a way that the timing marks will line up between the shaft centers and the camshaft locating dowel will enter the dowel hole in the cam sprocket.

Place the cam sprocket, with its chain mounted over it, in position on the front of the vehicle and pull up with the three bolts that hold it to the camshaft.

After the gears are in place, turn the engine two full revolutions to make certain that the timing marks are in correct alignment between the shaft centers.

End play of the camshaft is zero.

## Camshaft and Bearings

### REMOVAL & INSTALLATION

▶ See Figures 169, 170 and 171

**Gasoline Engines**

1. Disconnect the negative battery cable. Drain and remove the radiator.

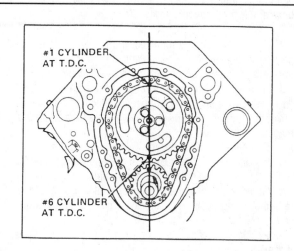

Fig. 165 Chevrolet built engine valve timing marks

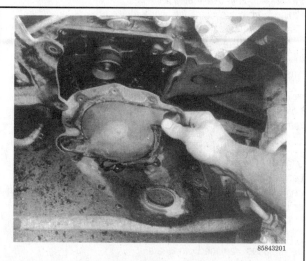

Fig. 166 The timing chain can be accessed after removing the timing chain cover

Fig. 167 Before removing the timing chain, make sure the valve timing marks are properly aligned

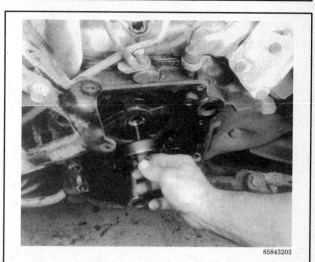

Fig. 168 Removing the camshaft sprocket attaching bolt and fuel pump eccentric

2. Have a trained technician discharge the A/C system with a recovery/recycling station. Remove the air conditioning condenser. If disconnected, immediately cap condenser openings. Remove the A/C condenser.

3. Remove any accessories which may interfere with camshaft removal.

4. Remove the intake manifold.

5. Remove valve covers.

6. Remove rocker arm and shaft assemblies, pushrods and valve lifters. Mark parts as necessary and keep pushrods in order for later assembly.

7. Remove timing chain cover, timing chain and sprocket. Refer to the appropriate procedure in this section.

8. Install long bolts into the camshaft sprocket bolt holes to help support the camshaft. Carefully slide camshaft forward, out of the bearing bores, working slowly to avoid marring the bearing surfaces. Remove camshaft.

**To install:**

9. Liberally coat the entire cam with assembly lube or equivalent. Slowly slide the camshaft into the engine block, exercising extreme care not to damage the cam bearings.

10. Install the timing chain and sprockets and timing chain cover. Refer to the appropriate procedure in this section.

11. Install the rocker arm and shaft assemblies, pushrods and valve lifters into their original locations as removed.

12. Install valve covers.

13. Install the intake manifold.

14. Install any accessories which were removed.

15. Install the air conditioning condenser. Evacuate and recharge the A/C system as outlined in Section 1.

16. Install and refill the radiator. Reconnect the negative battery cable.

17. Start the engine and check for proper operation and leaks.

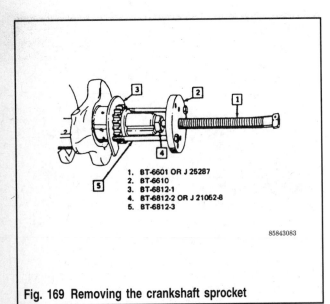

1. BT-6601 OR J 25287
2. BT-6610
3. BT-6812-1
4. BT-6812-2 OR J 21062-8
5. BT-6812-3

85843083

**Fig. 169 Removing the crankshaft sprocket**

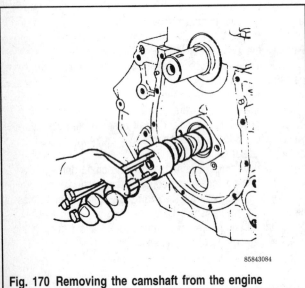

85843084

**Fig. 170 Removing the camshaft from the engine**

**Diesel Engine**

➡**If equipped with air conditioning, the system must be discharged before the camshaft can be removed. The condenser must also be removed from the vehicle.**

Removal of the camshaft also requires removal of the injection pump drive and driven gears, removal of the intake manifold, disassembly of the valve lifters, and re-timing of the injection pump.

1. Disconnect the negative battery cables. Drain the coolant. Remove the radiator.

**✳✳CAUTION**

**When draining the coolant, keep in mind that cats and dogs are attracted by the ethylene glycol antifreeze, and are quite likely to drink any that is left in an uncovered container or in puddles on the ground. This will prove fatal in sufficient quantity. Always drain the coolant into a sealable container. Coolant should be reused unless it is contaminated or several years old.**

2. Remove the intake manifold and gasket and the front and rear intake manifold seals. Refer to the Intake Manifold removal and installation procedure in this section.

3. Remove the balancer pulley and the balancer. See Caution under diesel engine front cover removal and installation, above. Remove the engine front cover using the appropriate procedure.

4. Remove the valve covers. Remove the rocker arms, pushrods and valve lifters. Be sure to keep the parts in order so that they may be returned to their original positions.

5. Remove the camshaft sprocket retaining bolt, and remove the timing chain and sprockets, using the procedure outlined earlier.

6. Position the camshaft dowel pin at the 3 o'clock position on the V8.

7. On V8s, push the camshaft rearward and hold it there, being careful not to dislodge the oil gallery plug at the rear of the engine. Remove the fuel injection pump drive gear by sliding it from the camshaft while rocking the pump driven gear.

8. To remove the fuel injection pump driven gear, remove the pump adapter, the snapring, and remove the selective washer. Remove the driven gear and spring.

➡**Thread long bolts into the camshaft-to-sprocket bolt holes. The bolts are used to support the camshaft during removal.**

9. Remove the camshaft by sliding it out the front of the engine. Be extremely careful not to allow the cam lobes to contact any of the bearings, or the journals to dislodge the bearings during camshaft removal. Do not force the camshaft, or bearing damage will result.

**To install:**

10. If either the injection pump drive or driven gears are to be replaced, replace both gears.

11. Coat the camshaft and the cam bearings with a high quality assembly lube, GM lubricant #1052365 or the equivalent.

12. Carefully slide the camshaft into position in the engine.

13. Fit the crankshaft and camshaft sprockets, aligning the timing marks as shown in the timing chain removal and installation procedure, above. Remove the sprockets without disturbing the timing.

14. Install the injection pump driven gear, spring, shim, and snapring. Check the gear end play. If the end play is not within 0.002-0.006 in. (0.0508-0.1524mm) on V8s through 1979, and 0.002-0.015 in. (0.0508-0.3810mm) on 1980 and later, replace the shim to obtain the specified clearance. Shims are available in 0.003 in. (0.0762mm) increments, from 0.080-0.115 in. (0.2032-2.9210mm).

15. Position the camshaft dowel pin at the 3 o'clock position. Align the zero marks on the pump drive gear and pump driven gear. Hold the camshaft in the rearward position and slide the pump drive gear onto the camshaft. Install the camshaft bearing retainer.

16. Install the timing chain and sprockets, making sure the timing marks are aligned.

17. Install the lifters, pushrods and rocker arms. See the procedure for cylinder head removal for diesel engines for lifter disassembly and draining procedures. If the lifters are not disassembled and drained, valves could be bent or pushrods damaged at start-up.

18. Install the injection pump adapter and injection pump. See the appropriate sections under Fuel System above for procedures.

19. Install the valve covers after the rocker arms have been adjusted. Be sure to install all valve parts into their original positions.

20. Install the front cover, balancer and pulley. Torque the balancer bolt to 200-310 ft. lbs. (270-420 Nm). See Caution under diesel engine front cover removal and installation, above.

21. Install the intake manifold and gaskets. Refer to the Intake Manifold removal and installation procedure in this section.

22. Connect the negative battery cables. Install the radiator and refill the engine coolant.

## INSPECTION

▶ See Figure 172

Completely clean the camshaft with solvent, paying special attention to cleaning the oil holes. Visually inspect the cam lobes and bearing journals for excessive wear. If a lobe is questionable, have the cam checked at a reputable machine ship; if a journal or lobe is worn, the camshaft must be reground or replaced. Also have the camshaft checked for straightness on a dial indicator.

➡ **If a cam journal is worn, there is a good chance that the bearings are worn.**

## CAMSHAFT BEARINGS

▶ See Figures 173 and 174

If excessive camshaft wear is found, or if the engine is being completely rebuilt, the camshaft bearings should be replaced.

➡ **The front and rear bearings should be removed last, and installed first. Those bearings act as guides for the other bearings and pilot.**

1. Drive the camshaft rear plug from the block.
2. Assemble the removal puller with its shoulder on the bearing to be removed. Gradually tighten the puller nut until the bearing is removed.
3. Remove the remaining bearings, leaving the front and rear for last. To remove these, reverse the position of the puller, so as to pull the bearings toward the center of the block. Leave the tool in this position, pilot the new front and rear bearings on the installer, and pull them into position.
4. Return the puller to its original position and pull the remaining bearings into position.

➡ **Ensure that the oil holes align when installing the bearings. This is very important!**

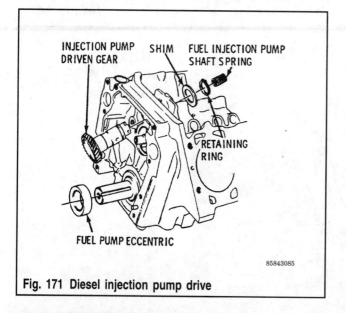

**Fig. 171 Diesel injection pump drive**

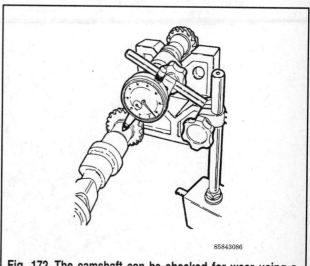

**Fig. 172 The camshaft can be checked for wear using a dial indicator**

5. Replace the camshaft rear plug, and stake it into position.

6. Coat the bearings and camshaft with high quality assembly lube before installing the camshaft. Use long bolts threaded into the camshaft-to-sprocket bolt holes to ease installation and help prevent bearing damage.

## Pistons And Connecting Rods

### REMOVAL

▶ **See Figures 175, 176, 177, 178 and 179**

Before removing the pistons, the top of the cylinder bore must be examined for a ridge. A ridge at the top of the bore is the result of normal cylinder wear, caused by the piston rings only traveling so far up the bore in the course of the piston stroke. The ridge can be felt by hand; it must be removed before the pistons are removed.

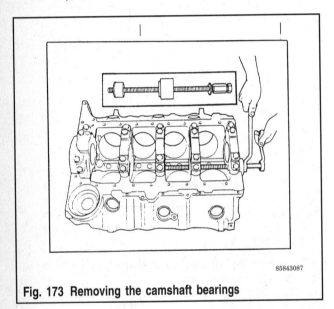

Fig. 173 Removing the camshaft bearings

A ridge reamer is necessary for this operation. Place the piston at the bottom of its stroke, and cover it with a rag. Cut the ridge away with the ridge reamer, using extreme care to avoid cutting too deeply. Remove the rag, and remove the cuttings that remain on the piston with a magnet and a rag soaked in clean oil. Make sure the piston top and cylinder bore are absolutely clean before removing the piston.

1. Remove intake manifold and cylinder head or heads.
2. Remove oil pan.
3. Remove oil pump assembly if necessary.
4. Matchmark the connecting rod cap to the connecting rod with a scribe; each cap must be reinstalled on its proper rod in the proper direction. Remove the connecting rod bearing cap and the rod bearing. Number the top of each piston with silver paint or a felt tip pen for later assembly.
5. Cut lengths of ⅜ in. (9.5mm) diameter hose to use as rod bolt guides. Install the hose over the threads of the rod bolts, to prevent the bolt threads from damaging the crankshaft journals and cylinder walls when the piston is removed.
6. Squirt some clean engine oil onto the cylinder wall from above, until the wall is coated. Carefully push the piston and rod assembly up and out of the cylinder by tapping on the bottom of the connecting rod with a wooden hammer handle.
7. Place the rod bearing and cap back on the connecting rod, and install the nuts temporarily. Using a number stamp or punch, stamp the cylinder number on the side of the connecting rod and cap; this will help keep the proper piston and rod assembly on the proper cylinder.

➡**On V6 engines, starting at the front the cylinders are numbered 2-4-6 on the right bank and 1-3-5 on the left. On all V8s, starting at the front the right bank cylinders are 2-4-6-8 and the left bank 1-3-5-7.**

8. Remove remaining pistons in a similar manner.

On all engines, the notch on the piston will face the front of the engine for assembly. The chamfered corners of the bearing caps should face toward the front of the engine for the right bank and to the rear of the engine on the left bank. On some Pontiac built engines, the rods have three dimples on one side of the rod and a single dimple on the rod cap. The dimples must face to the rear on the right bank and forward on the

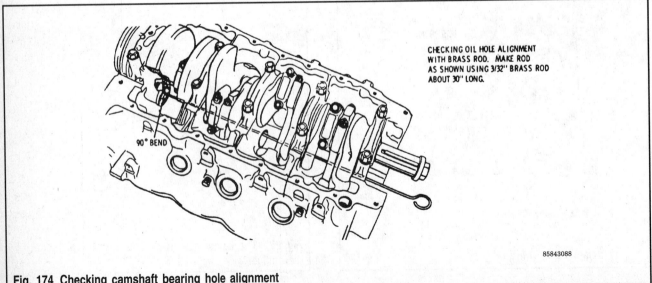

CHECKING OIL HOLE ALIGNMENT WITH BRASS ROD. MAKE ROD AS SHOWN USING 3/32" BRASS ROD ABOUT 30" LONG.

90° BEND

Fig. 174 Checking camshaft bearing hole alignment

left. Where there are numbers on the pistons and rods, the numbers must be on the same side when the two are assembled.

On various engines, the piston compression rings are marked with a dimple, a letter **T**, a letter **O**, **GM** or the word **TOP** to identify the side of the ring which must face toward the top of the piston.

## CLEANING AND INSPECTION

▶ **See Figures 180, 181, 182, 183 and 184**

A piston ring expander is necessary for removing piston rings without damaging them; any other method (screwdriver blades, pliers, etc.) usually results in the rings being bent, scratched or distorted, or the piston itself being damaged. When the rings are removed, clean the ring grooves using an appropriate ring groove cleaning tool, using care not to cut too

Fig. 177 Push the piston and rod out with a hammer handle

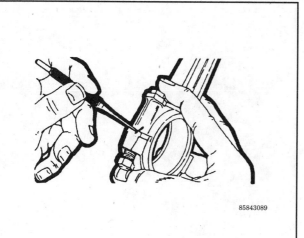
Fig. 175 Match the connecting rods to their caps with a scribe mark

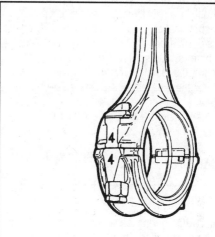
Fig. 178 Match the connecting rods to their cylinders with a number stamp

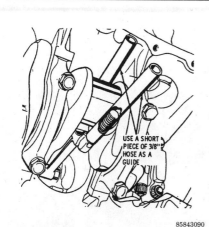
Fig. 176 Cover the connecting rod bolts with small pieces of hose to prevent damage to the crank journals and cylinder walls during removal

Fig. 179 Removing the rod bearing cap from the connecting rod

deeply. Thoroughly clean all carbon and varnish from the piston with a non-caustic solvent.

**❊❊CAUTION**

**Do not use a wire brush or caustic solvent (acids, etc.) on pistons.**

Inspect the pistons for scuffing, scoring, cracks, pitting, or excessive ring groove wear. If these are evident, the piston must be replaced.

The piston should also be checked in relation to the cylinder diameter. Using a telescoping gauge and micrometer, or a dial gauge, measure the cylinder bore diameter perpendicular to the piston pin, 2½ in. (63.5mm) below the cylinder block deck (surface where the block mates with the heads). Then, with the micrometer, measure the piston perpendicular to its wrist pin on the skirt. The difference between the two measurements is the piston clearance. If the clearance is within specifications or slightly below (after the cylinders have been bored or honed), finish honing is all that is necessary. If the clearance is excessive, try to obtain a slightly larger piston to bring clearance to within specifications. If this is not possible, obtain the first oversize piston and bore the cylinder to size. Generally, if the cylinder bore is tapered 0.005 in. (0.127mm) or more or is out-of-round 0.003 in. (0.0762mm) or more, it is advisable to rebore for the smallest possible oversize piston and rings.

After measuring, mark pistons with a felt-tip for reference and for assembly.

## RIDGE REMOVAL AND HONING

▶ See Figures 185, 186, 187 and 188

➡Cylinder honing and/or boring should be performed by a reputable, professional machine shop with the proper equipment. In some cases, clean-up honing can be done with the cylinder block in the vehicle, but most excessive honing and all cylinder boring must be done with the block stripped and removed from the vehicle.

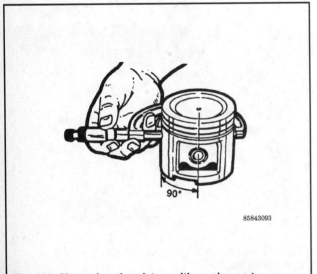

Fig. 180 Measuring the piston with a micrometer

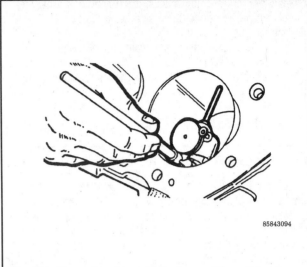

Fig. 181 Measuring the cylinder bore with a dial gauge

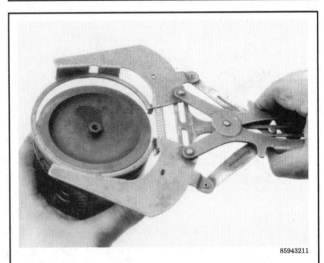

Fig. 182 A ring expander tool should be used to remove the piston rings

Fig. 183 Clean the piston grooves using a ring groove cleaner

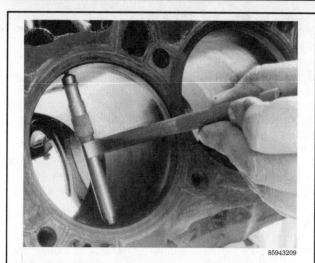

Fig. 184 A telescoping gage and micrometer may be used to measure the cylinder bore diameter

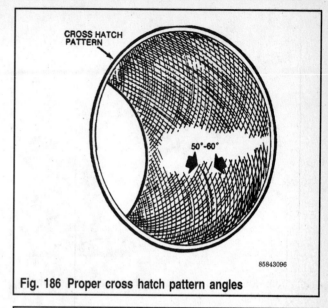

Fig. 186 Proper cross hatch pattern angles

As the cylinder bore wears, a ridge is formed at the top of the cylinder where the rings never scrape. Removing this ridge makes piston removal easier and prevents damage to the rings. A ridge reamer is installed into the cylinder, tightened, then the cutters of the reamer are moved upward as the threaded portion of the reamer is rotated.

When new piston rings are installed in an engine, the cylinder bore must have a cross-hatch pattern finish. This allows the rings and bore wear together and provide better oil control and compression. This cross-hatch pattern is achieved by honing. No more than 0.0008 in (0.02 mm) should be removed during this process, since the finished roundness of the cylinder will be destroyed.

## PISTON PIN REPLACEMENT

▶ See Figure 189

Most of the engines covered in this guide utilize pistons with pressed-in wrist pins; these must be removed by a special press designed for this purpose and should only be performed

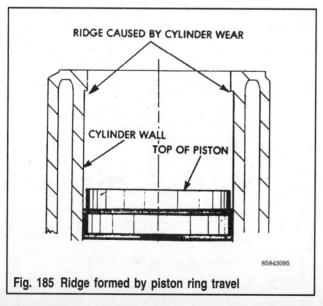

Fig. 185 Ridge formed by piston ring travel

Fig. 187 Remove the ridge from the cylinder bore using a ridge cutter

Fig. 188 Honing the cylinder bore with a flexible hone

by a machine shop. Other pistons have their wrist pins secured by snaprings, which are easily removed with snapring pliers. Separate the piston from the connecting rod once the snaprings have been removed.

**✳✳CAUTION**

DO NOT try to press out the piston wrist pin without using the specified tools (unless retained by snaprings). Severe damage may occur to the piston and connecting rod, causing internal engine damage and failure.

## PISTON RING REPLACEMENT

▶ See Figures 190, 191, 192, 193, 194, 195 and 196

Piston ring end gap should be checked while the rings are removed from the pistons. Incorrect end gap indicates that the wrong size rings are being used; ring breakage could occur.

Compress the piston rings to be used in a cylinder, one at a time, into that cylinder. Squirt clean oil into the cylinder, so that the rings and the top 2 in. (51mm) of cylinder wall are coated. Using an inverted piston, press the rings approximately 1 in. (25mm) below the deck of the block (on diesels, measure ring gap clearance with the ring positioned at the bottom of ring travel in the bore). Measure the ring end gap with a feeler gauge, and compare to the Ring Gap chart in this section. Carefully pull the ring out of the cylinder and file the ends squarely with a fine file to obtain the proper clearance.

Check the pistons to see that the ring grooves and oil return holes have been properly cleaned. Slide a piston ring into its groove, and check the side clearance with a feeler gauge. On gasoline engines, make sure you insert the gauge between the ring and its lower land (lower edge of the groove), because any wear that occurs forms a step at the inner portion of the lower land. On diesels, insert the gauge between the ring and the upper land. If the piston grooves have worn to the extent that relatively high steps exist on the lower land, the piston should be replaced, because these will interfere with the operation of the new rings and ring clearances will be excessive. Piston rings are not furnished in oversize widths to compensate for ring groove wear.

Install the rings on the piston, lowest ring first, using a piston ring expander. There is a high risk of breaking or distorting the rings, or scratching the piston, if the rings are installed by hand or other means.

Position the rings on the piston as illustrated; spacing of the various piston ring gaps is crucial to proper oil retention and even cylinder wear. When installing new rings, refer to the installation diagram furnished with the new parts.

## ROD BEARING REPLACEMENT

▶ See Figures 197, 198 and 199

Connecting rod bearings for the engines covered in this guide consist of two halves or shells which are interchangeable in the rod and cap. When the shells are placed in position, the ends extend slightly beyond the rod and cap surfaces so that when the rod bolts are torqued the shells will be clamped

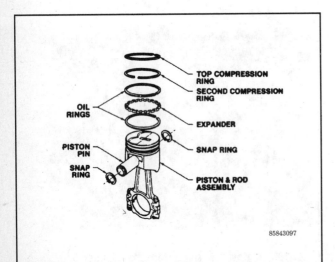
Fig. 189 Exploded view of a piston assembly; note that the piston pin is secured with snap rings

TOP COMPRESSION RING
SECOND COMPRESSION RING
OIL RINGS
EXPANDER
PISTON PIN
SNAP RING
SNAP RING
PISTON & ROD ASSEMBLY

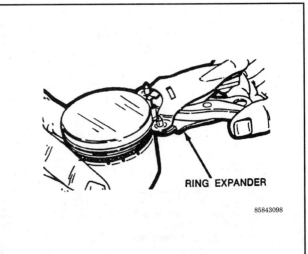
Fig. 190 Removing the piston rings with a ring expander

RING EXPANDER

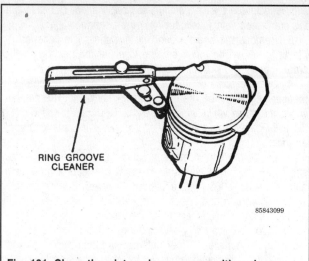

Fig. 191 Clean the piston ring grooves with a ring groove cleaner

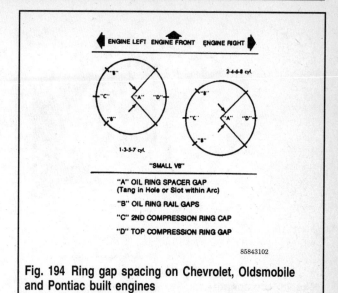

Fig. 194 Ring gap spacing on Chevrolet, Oldsmobile and Pontiac built engines

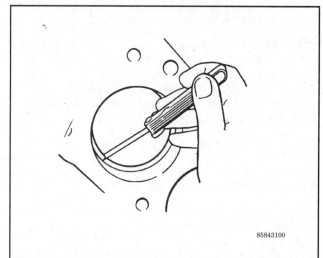

Fig. 192 Checking the piston ring end gap with a feeler gauge

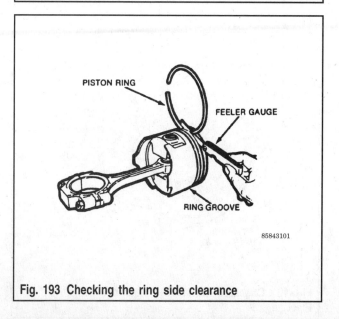

Fig. 193 Checking the ring side clearance

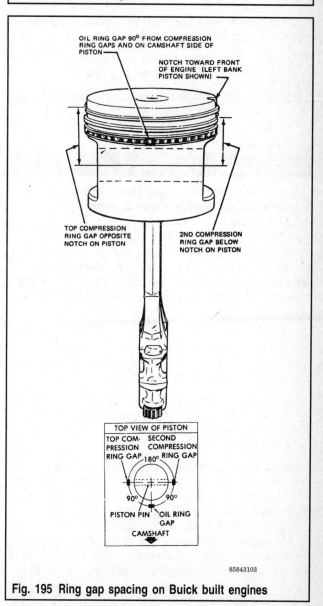

Fig. 195 Ring gap spacing on Buick built engines

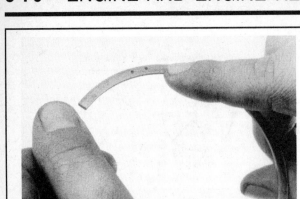

Fig. 196 Most rings are marked to show which side should face upward

tightly in place to insure positive seating and to prevent turning. A tang holds the shells in place.

➡ The ends of the bearing shells must never be filed flush with the mating surface of the rod and cap.

If a rod bearing becomes noisy or is worn so that its clearance on the crank journal is sloppy, a new bearing of the correct undersize must be selected and installed since there is no provision for adjustment.

## ✳✳CAUTION

**Under no circumstances should the rod end or cap be filed to adjust the bearing clearance, nor should shims of any kind be used.**

Inspect the rod bearings while the rod assemblies are out of the engine. If the shells are scored or show flaking, they should be replaced. If they are in good shape check for proper clearance on the crank journal. Any scoring or ridges on the crank journal means the crankshaft must be replaced, or reground and fitted with undersized bearings.

➡ If turbo V6 crank journals are scored or ridged the crankshaft must be replaced, as regrinding will reduce the durability and strength of the crankshaft.

➡ Make sure connecting rods and their caps are kept together, and that the caps are installed in the proper direction. On some engines like the Buick built 350 V8, the caps can only be installed one way.

Replacement bearings are available in standard size, and in undersizes for reground crankshafts. Connecting rod-to-crankshaft bearing clearance is checked using Plastigage® at either the top or bottom of each crank journal. The Plastigage® has a range of 0.001-0.003 in. (0.0254-0.0762mm).

1. Remove the rod cap with the bearing shell. Completely clean the bearing shell and the crank journal, and blow any oil from the oil hole in the crankshaft; Plastigage® is soluble in oil.

2. Place a piece of Plastigage® lengthwise along the bottom center of the lower bearing shell, then install the cap with

shell and torque the bolt or nuts to specification. DO NOT turn the crankshaft with Plastigage® in the bearing.

3. Remove the bearing cap with the shell. The flattened Plastigage® will be found sticking to either the bearing shell or crank journal. Do not remove it yet.

4. Use the scale printed on the Plastigage® envelope to measure the flattened material at its widest point. The number within the scale which most closely corresponds to the width of the Plastigage® indicates bearing clearance in thousandths of an inch.

5. Check the specifications chart in this section for the desired clearance. It is advisable to install a new bearing if clearance exceeds 0.003 in. (0.0762mm); however, if the bearing is in good condition and is not being checked because of bearing noise, bearing replacement is not necessary.

6. If you are installing new bearings, try a standard size, then each undersize in order until one is found that is within the specified limits when checked for clearance with Plastigage®. Each undersize shell has its size stamped on it.

7. When the proper size shell is found, clean off the Plastigage®, oil the bearing thoroughly, reinstall the cap with its shell and torque the rod bolt nuts to specification.

➡ With the proper bearing selected and the nuts torqued, it should be possible to move the connecting rod back and forth freely on the crank journal as allowed by the specified connecting rod and clearance. If the rod cannot be moved, either the rod bearing is too far undersize or the rod is misaligned.

## INSTALLATION

◆ See Figures 200, 201, 202, 203 and 204

Install the connecting rod to the piston, making sure piston installation notches and any marks on the rod are in proper relation to one another. Lubricate the wrist pin with clean engine oil, and install the pin into the rod and piston assembly, either by hand or by using a wrist pin press as required. Install snaprings if equipped, and rotate them in their grooves to

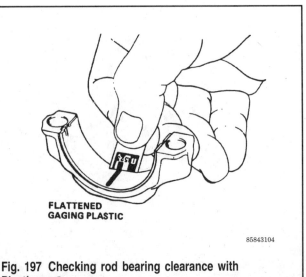

FLATTENED GAGING PLASTIC

Fig. 197 Checking rod bearing clearance with Plastigage®

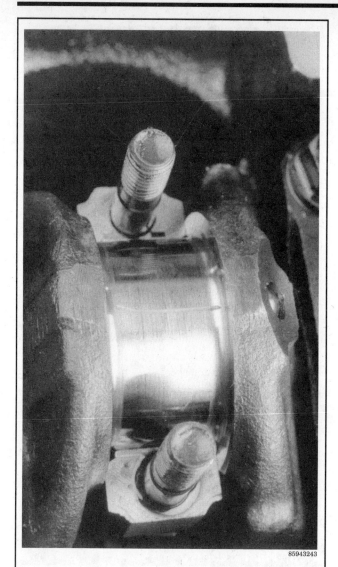

Fig. 198 Apply a strip of gauging material to the bearing, then install the cap and torque the cap

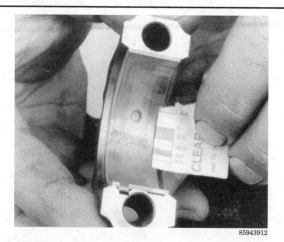

Fig. 199 After the bearing cap has been removed, use the gauge supplied with the gauge material to check bearing clearances

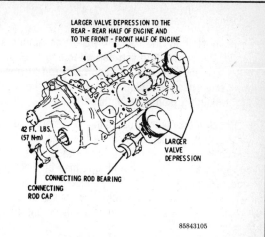

Fig. 200 Piston positioning in block, diesels up to 1981. On 1982 and later models face the notches on the pistons towards the front

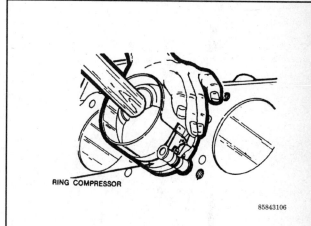

Fig. 201 Using a wooden hammer handle, gently tap the piston down through the ring compressor and into the cylinder

make sure they are seated. To install the piston and connecting rod assembly:

1. Make sure connecting rod big end bearings (including end cap) are of the correct size and properly installed.

2. Fit rubber hoses over the connecting rod bolts to protect the crankshaft journals, as in the Piston Removal procedure. Coat the rod bearings with high quality assembly lube (not engine oil).

3. Using the proper ring compressor, insert the piston assembly into the cylinder so that the notch in the top of the piston faces the front of the engine. This assumes that the dimple(s) or other markings on the connecting rods are in correct relation to the piston notch(es).

4. From beneath the engine, coat each crank journal with assembly lube. Pull the connecting rod, with the bearing shell in place, into position against the crank journal.

5. Remove the rubber hoses. Install the bearing cap and cap nuts and torque to specification. On the 1988-1990 5.0 L

V8, torque the nuts to 18 ft. lbs (24 Nm), then turn the nuts an additional 70 degrees.

➡When more than one rod and piston assembly is being installed, the connecting rod cap attaching nuts should only be tightened enough to keep each rod in position until all have been installed. This will ease the installation of the remaining piston assemblies.

6. Check the clearance between the sides of the connecting rods and the crankshaft using a feeler gauge. Spread the rods slightly with a prybar to insert the gauge. If clearance is below the minimum tolerance, the rod may be machined to provide adequate clearance. If clearance is excessive, substitute an unworn rod, and recheck. If clearance is still outside specifications, the crankshaft must be welded and reground or replaced.

7. Install the oil pump and oil pan.
8. Install the cylinder head(s) and intake manifold.

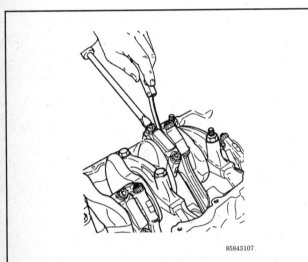

**Fig. 202 Checking the connecting rod side clearance with a feeler gauge**

**Fig. 203 Match the tang on the bearing insert with the tang on the bearing cap**

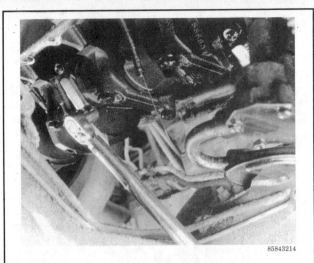

**Fig. 204 Be sure to torque the bearing caps to specification**

## Freeze Plugs

### REMOVAL & INSTALLATION

▶ See Figures 205 and 206

1. Drill a small hole in the middle of the freeze plug.
2. Thread a large sheet metal screw into the hole and remove the plug with a slide hammer.
**To install:**
3. Coat the freeze plugs with sealer and tap into position using a piece of pipe, slightly smaller than the plug, as a driver. To ensure retention, stake the edges of the plugs.

## Rear Main Seal

### REMOVAL & INSTALLATION

▶ See Figures 207, 208, 209 and 210

**Except One Piece Seal**

1. Remove the oil pan. Remove the oil pump where required. Remove the main bearing cap.
2. Pry the lower seal out of the bearing cap with a suitable tool, being careful not to gouge the cap surface.
3. Remove the upper seal by lightly tapping on the one end with a brass pin punch until the other end can be grasped and pulled out.
4. Clean the bearing cap, cylinder block and crankshaft mating surfaces with solvent. Inspect these surfaces for gouges, nicks and burrs.
5. Apply a light coat of engine oil on the seal lips and bead, but keep the seal ends clean.
6. Insert the tip of the installation tool between the crankshaft and the seal in the cylinder block. Place the seal between the crankshaft and the seal of the cylinder block. Place

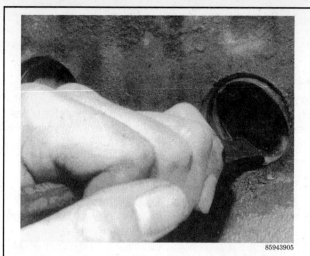

Fig. 205 The freeze plug can also be loosened using a punch and a hammer

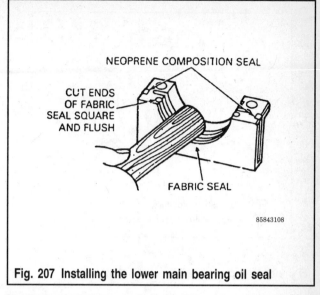

Fig. 207 Installing the lower main bearing oil seal

Fig. 206 Once the freeze plug has been loosened, it can be removed from the block

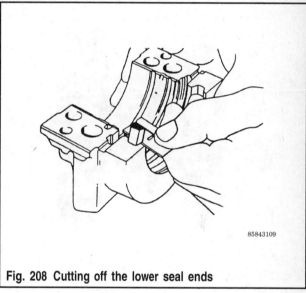

Fig. 208 Cutting off the lower seal ends

the seal between the tip of the tool and the crankshaft, so that the bead contacts the tip of the tool.

➡ Do not remove the tool until the opposite end of the seal is flush with the cylinder block surface.

7. Remove the installation tool, being careful not to pull the seal out at the same time.

8. Using the same procedure, install the lower seal into the bearing cap. Use your finger and thumb or a wooden hammer handle to level the seal into the cap.

9. Apply sealer to the cylinder block only where the cap mates to the surface. Do not apply sealer to the seal ends.

10. Install the rear cap and torque to specification.

11. Install the oil pump and oil pan.

### One Piece Seal

1. Remove the transmission from the vehicle.

2. Using the notches provided in the rear seal retainer, pry out the seal using the proper tool.

➡ Care should be taken when removing the seal so as not to nick the crankshaft sealing surface.

3. Before installation lubricate the inside and outside diameter of the new seal with clean engine oil.

4. Install the seal on tool J-3561 or equivalent. Thread the tool into the rear of the crankshaft. Tighten the screws snugly, this is to insure that the seal will be installed squarely over the crankshaft. Tighten the tool wing nut until it bottoms.

5. Remove the tool from the crankshaft.

6. Install the transmission.

### One Piece Seal Retainer and Gasket

1. Remove the transmission from the vehicle.

2. Remove the oil pan.

3. Remove the retainer and seal assembly.

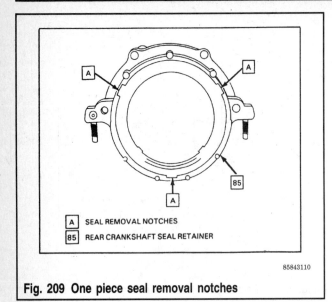

A — SEAL REMOVAL NOTCHES
85 — REAR CRANKSHAFT SEAL RETAINER

85843110

**Fig. 209 One piece seal removal notches**

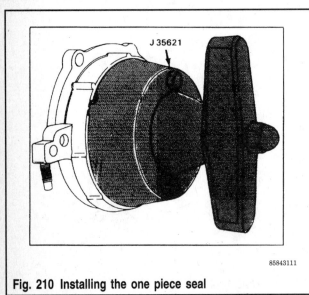

J 35621

85843111

**Fig. 210 Installing the one piece seal**

4. Remove the gasket.

➡Whenever the retainer is removed a new retainer gasket and rear main seal must be installed.

5. Installation is the reverse of removal. Once the oil pan has been installed, the rear main seal may be installed.

## Crankshaft and Main Bearings

### REMOVAL & INSTALLATION

▶ **See Figures 211, 212 and 213**

1. Disconnect the negative battery cable. Drain the engine oil and remove the engine from the vehicle. Mount the engine on a work stand in a suitable working area. Invert the engine, so the oil pan is facing up.

2. Remove the engine front (timing) cover.
3. Remove the timing chain and gears.
4. Remove the oil pan.
5. Remove the oil pump.
6. Stamp the cylinder number on the machined surfaces of the bolt bosses of the connecting rods and caps for identification when reinstalling. If the pistons are to be removed eventually from the connecting rod, mark the cylinder number on the pistons with silver paint or felt-tip pen for proper cylinder identification and cap-to-rod location.
7. Remove the connecting rod caps. Install lengths of rubber hose on each of the connecting rod bolts, to protect the crank journals when the crank is removed.
8. Mark the main bearing caps with a number punch or punch so that they can be reinstalled in their original positions.
9. Remove all main bearing caps.
10. Note the position of the keyway in the crankshaft so it can be installed in the same position.
11. Install rubber bands between a bolt on each connecting rod and oil pan bolts that have been reinstalled in the block. This will keep the rods from banging on the block when the crank is removed.
12. Carefully lift the crankshaft out of the block. The rods will pivot to the center of the engine when the crank is removed.

**To install:**

13. When main bearing clearance has been checked, bearings examined and/or replaced, the crankshaft can be installed. Thoroughly clean the upper and lower bearing surfaces, and lube them with clean engine oil. Install the crankshaft and main bearing caps.
14. Dip all main bearing cap bolts in clean oil, and torque all main bearing caps, excluding the thrust bearing cap, to specifications. Tighten the thrust bearing bolts finger tight. To align the thrust bearing, pry the crankshaft the extent of its axial travel several times, holding the last movement toward the front of the engine. Add thrust washers if required for proper alignment. Torque the thrust bearing cap to specifications.
15. To check crankshaft end play, pry the crankshaft to the extreme rear of its axial travel, then to the extreme front of its travel. Using a feeler gauge, measure the end play at the front of the rear main bearing. End play may also be measured at the thrust bearing. Install a new rear main bearing oil seal in the cylinder block and main bearing cap. Continue to reassemble the engine.

On the 1986 and 1987 231 and 307 cu. in. engines, it is necessary to line up the rear main bearing and crankshaft thrust surfaces. Torque all main caps to specification except the one at the rear. Torque the rear main cap to 10-12 ft. lbs. (14-16 Nm). Using a lead hammer, tap the end of the crankshaft first backward and then forward. Now, retorque all caps to specification.

### INSPECTION

Like connecting rod bearings, the crankshaft main bearings are shell type inserts that do not utilize shims and cannot be adjusted. The bearings are available in various standard and undersizes; if main bearing clearance is found to be out of

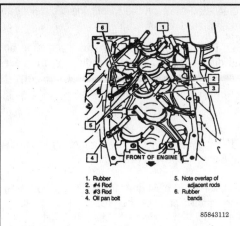

1. Rubber
2. #4 Rod
3. #3 Rod
4. Oil pan bolt
5. Note overlap of adjacent rods
6. Rubber bands

FRONT OF ENGINE

85843112

Fig. 211 To keep the rods from banging on the block, install rubber bands between a bolt on each connecting rod and oil pan bolts that have been reinstalled in the block

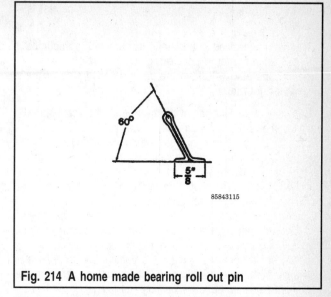

60°

5"/8

85843115

Fig. 214 A home made bearing roll out pin

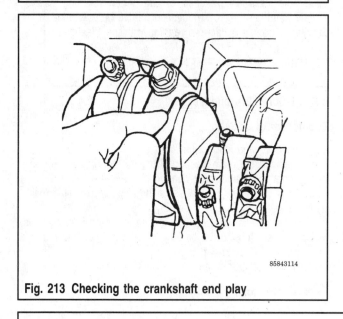

85843114

Fig. 213 Checking the crankshaft end play

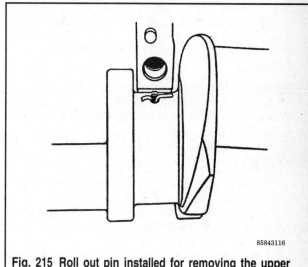

85843116

Fig. 215 Roll out pin installed for removing the upper half of the main bearing

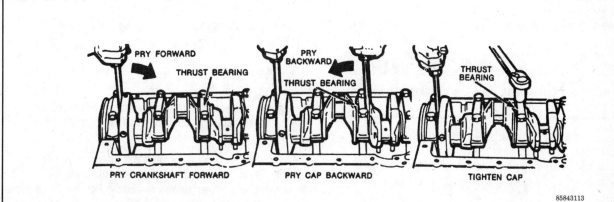

PRY FORWARD
THRUST BEARING
PRY CRANKSHAFT FORWARD

PRY BACKWARD
THRUST BEARING
PRY CAP BACKWARD

THRUST BEARING
TIGHTEN CAP

85843113

Fig. 212 Aligning the thrust bearing

specification, a new bearing (both upper and lower halves) is required.

➡**Factory undersized crankshafts are marked, sometimes with a 9 and/or a large spot of light green paint; the bearing caps also will have the paint on each side of the undersized journal.**

Generally, the lower half of the bearing shell (except No. 1 bearing) shows greater wear and fatigue. If the lower half only shows the effects of normal wear (no heavy scoring or discoloration), it can usually be assumed that the upper half is also in good shape; conversely, if the lower half is heavily worn or damaged, both halves should be replaced. Never replace one bearing half without replacing the other.

Main bearing clearance can be checked with the crankshaft in the vehicle and with the engine out of the vehicle. If the engine block is still in the vehicle, the crankshaft should be supported both front and rear (by the damper and to remove clearance from the upper bearing. Total clearance can then be measured between the lower bearing and journal. If the block has been removed from the vehicle, and is inverted, the crank will rest on the upper bearings and the total clearance can be measured between the lower bearing and journal. Clearance is checked in the same manner as the connecting rod bearings, with Plastigage®.

➡**Crankshaft bearing caps and bearing shells should NEVER be filed flush with the cap-to-block mating surface to adjust for wear in the old bearings. Always install new bearings. The low cost of new bearings outweighs the aggravation of having to do the job twice because of failed bearings.**

1. If the crankshaft has been removed, install it (block removed from vehicle). If the block is still in the vehicle, remove the oil pan and oil pump. Starting with the rear bearing cap, remove the cap and wipe all oil from the crank journal and bearing cap.

2. In order to check bearing clearance, the crankshaft must rest against the upper bearings. If the engine is out of the vehicle, turning the block upside down will take care of this requirement. If the engine is in the vehicle, the crankshaft must be supported at either end so that it rests against the upper bearings and all clearance is present at the lower bearing. Place a strip of Plastigage® the full width of the bearing, (parallel to the crankshaft), on the journal.

### ✳✳CAUTION

**Do not rotate the crankshaft while the gauging material is between the bearing and the journal.**

3. Install the bearing cap and evenly torque the cap bolts to specification.

4. Remove the bearing cap. The flattened Plastigage® will be sticking to either the bearing shell or the crank journal.

5. Use the graduated scale on the Plastigage® envelope to measure the material at its widest point.

➡**If the flattened Plastigage® tapers toward the middle or ends, there is a difference in clearance indicating the bearing or journal has a taper, low spot or other irregularity. If this is indicated, measure the crank journal with a micrometer.**

6. If bearing clearance is within specifications, the bearing insert is in good shape. Replace the insert if the clearance is not within specifications. Always replace both upper and lower inserts as a unit.

7. Standard, 0.001 in. (0.0254mm) or 0.002 in. (0.0508mm) undersize bearings should produce the proper clearance. If these sizes still produce too sloppy a fit, the crankshaft must be reground for use with the next undersize bearing. Recheck all clearances after installing new bearings.

8. Replace the rest of the bearings in the same manner. After all bearings have been checked, rotate the crankshaft to make sure there is no excessive drag. When checking the No. 1 main bearing, loosen the accessory drive belts (engine in vehicle) to prevent a tapered reading with the Plastigage®.

## BEARING REPLACEMENT

▶ **See Figures 214 and 215**

### Engine Out of vehicle

1. Remove and inspect the crankshaft.

2. Remove the main bearings from the bearing saddles in the cylinder block and main bearing caps.

3. Coat the bearing surfaces of the new, correct size main bearings with high quality assembly lube and install them in the bearing saddles in the block and in the main bearing caps. Make sure the tabs in the bearing insert align with the notch in the block and bearing cap.

4. Install the crankshaft.

### Engine in vehicle

1. With the oil pan, oil pump and spark plugs removed, remove the cap from the main bearing needing replacement and remove the bearing from the cap.

2. Make a bearing roll-out pin, using a bent cotter pin. Install the end of the pin in the oil hole in the crankshaft journal.

3. Rotate the crankshaft clockwise as viewed from the front of the engine. This will roll the upper bearing out of the block.

➡**Turn the crankshaft in the opposite direction of the bearing insert tab. The bearing insert will only turn on way.**

4. Lube the new upper bearing with clean engine oil and insert the plain (unnotched) end between the crankshaft and the indented or notched side of the block. Roll the bearing into place, making sure that the oil holes are aligned. Remove the roll pin from the oil hole.

5. Lube the new lower bearing and install the main bearing cap. Install the main bearing cap, making sure it is positioned in proper direction with the matchmarks in alignment.

6. Torque the main bearing cap bolts to specification.

➡️**See crankshaft removal and installation for thrust bearing alignment.**

## Flywheel and Ring Gear

### REMOVAL & INSTALLATION

The ring gear is an integral part of the flywheel and is not replaceable.

1. Remove the transmission. Refer to the removal procedure in Section 7.

2. Remove the six bolts attaching the flywheel to the crankshaft flange. Remove the flywheel.

3. Inspect the flywheel for cracks, and inspect the ring gear for burrs or worn teeth. Replace the flywheel if any damage is apparent. Remove burrs with a mill file.

4. Install the flywheel. The flywheel will only attach to the crankshaft in one position, as the bolt holes are unevenly spaced. Install the bolts and torque to specification.

## EXHAUST SYSTEM

### Safety Precautions

For a number of reasons, exhaust system work can be the most dangerous type of work you can do on your vehicle. Always observe the following precautions:

• Support the vehicle extra securely. Not only will you often be working directly under it, but you'll frequently be using a lot of force to dislodge rusted parts. This can cause a vehicle that's improperly supported to shift and possibly fall.

• Wear goggles. Exhaust system parts are always rusty. Metal chips can be dislodged, even when you're only turning rusted bolts. Attempting to pry pipes apart with a chisel makes the chips fly even more frequently.

• If you're using a cutting torch, keep it a great distance from either the fuel tank or lines. Stop what you're doing and feel the temperature of the fuel bearing pipes on the tank frequently. Even slight heat can expand and/or vaporize fuel, resulting in accumulated vapor, or even a liquid leak, near your torch.

• Watch where your hammer blows fall and make sure you hit squarely. You could easily tap a brake or fuel line when you hit an exhaust system part with a glancing blow. Inspect all lines and hoses in the area where you have been working.

### Special Tools

A number of special exhaust system tools can be rented from auto supply houses or local stores that rent special equipment. A common one is a tail pipe expander, designed to enable you to join pipes of identical diameter.

It may also be quite helpful to use solvents designed to loosen rusted bolts or flanges. Soaking rusted parts the night before you do the job can speed the work of freeing those parts considerably. Remember that these solvents are are often flammable. Apply only to parts after they are cool!

## Crossover Pipe

### REMOVAL & INSTALLATION

▶ **See Figures 216, 217, 218 and 219**

Place safety glasses over your eyes. The crossover pipe is typically connected to the manifolds by flanged connections or collars. In some cases, bolts that are unthreaded for part of their length are used in conjunction with springs. Make sure you install the springs and that they are in good mechanical condition (no broken coils) when installing the new pipe. Replace ring type seals, also.

## Headpipe

### REMOVAL & INSTALLATION

▶ **See Figure 220**

Place safety glasses over your eyes. The headpipe is typically attached to the rear of one exhaust manifold with a flange or collar type connector and flagged to the front of the catalytic converter. Remove nuts and bolts and if springs are used to maintain the seal. The pipe may then be separated from the rest of the system at both flanges.

Replace ring seals; inspect springs and replace them if any coils are broken.

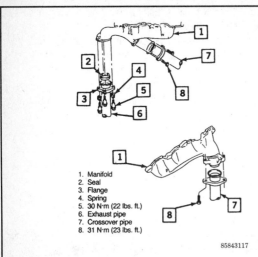

Fig. 216 Crossover pipe connections at the exhaust manifolds; all models similar

1. Manifold
2. Seal
3. Flange
4. Spring
5. 30 N·m (22 lbs. ft.)
6. Exhaust pipe
7. Crossover pipe
8. 31 N·m (23 lbs. ft.)

85843117

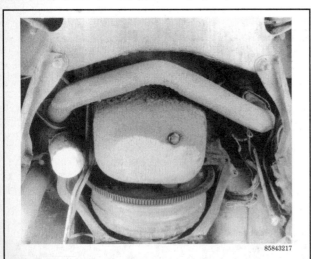

Fig. 217 A common crossover pipe used on V6 and V8 engines

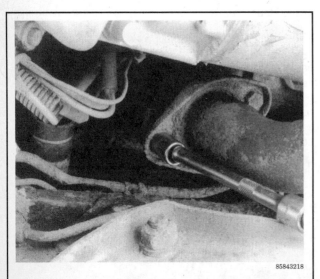

Fig. 218 Removing the crossover pipe attaching bolts

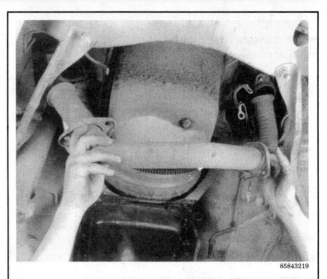

Fig. 219 Removing the crossover pipe from the vehicle

## Catalytic Converter

### REMOVAL & INSTALLATION

▶ See Figure 221

### ❊❊CAUTION

**The catalytic converter maintains a high temperature for an extended time after the engine is turned off. Allow the vehicle to cool for at least two hours before servicing the exhaust system or personal injury may occur.**

Place safety glasses over your eyes. Remove bolts at the flange at the rear end. Then, loosen nuts and remove U-clamp to remove the catalyst. Slide the catalyst out of the outlet pipe. Replace all ring seals. In some cases, you'll have to disconnect an air line coming from the engine compartment before catalyst removal. In some cases, a hanger supports the converter via one of the flange bolts. Make sure the hanger gets properly reconnected. Also, be careful to retain all parts used to heat shield the converter and reinstall them.

Make sure the converter is replaced for proper direction of flow and air supply connections.

## Mufflers and Tailpipes

### REMOVAL & INSTALLATION

Place safety glasses over your eyes. These units are typically connected by flanges at the rear of the converter and at either end of mufflers either by an original weld or by U-clamps working over a pipe connection in which one side of the connection is slightly larger than the other. You may have to cut the original connection and use the pipe expander to allow the original equipment exhaust pipe to be fitted over the new muffler. In this case, you'll have to purchase new U-clamps to fasten the joints. GM recommends that whenever

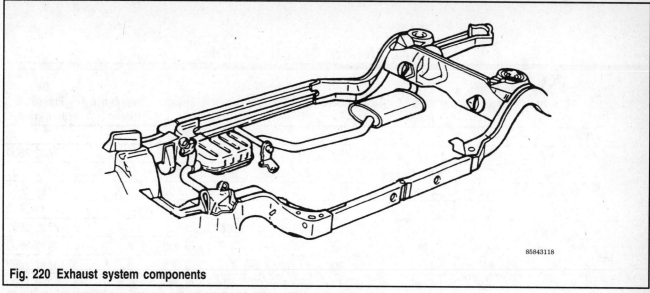

**Fig. 220 Exhaust system components**

you replace a muffler, all parts to the rear of the muffler in the exhaust system must be replaced. Also, all slip joints rearward of the converter should be coated with sealer before they are assembled.

Place safety glasses over your eyes. Be careful to connect all U-clamps or other hanger arrangements so the exhaust system will not flex. Assemble all parts loosely and rotate parts inside one another or clamps on the pipes to ensure proper routing of all exhaust system parts to avoid excessive heating of the floorpan, fuel lines and tank, etc. Also, make sure there is clearance to prevent the system from rattling against spring shackles, the differential, etc. You may be able to bend long pipes slightly by hand to help get enough clearance, if necessary.

While disassembling the system, keep your eye open for any leaks or for excessively close clearance to any brake system parts. Inspect the brake system for any sort of heat damage and repair as necessary.

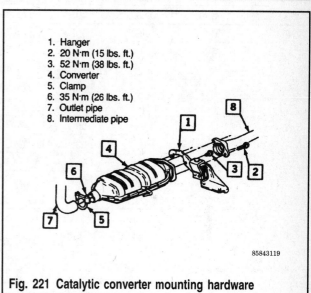

1. Hanger
2. 20 N·m (15 lbs. ft.)
3. 52 N·m (38 lbs. ft.)
4. Converter
5. Clamp
6. 35 N·m (26 lbs. ft.)
7. Outlet pipe
8. Intermediate pipe

**Fig. 221 Catalytic converter mounting hardware**

## GENERAL ENGINE SPECIFICATIONS

| Year | Engine V.I.N. Code | Engine Type (No. of cyl-C.I.D.) | Engine Manufacturer | Carb Type | Horsepower @ rpm ① | Torque @ rpm (ft. lbs.) ① | Bore × Stroke (in.) | Compression Ratio | Oil Pressure (psi @ rpm) |
|------|------|------|------|------|------|------|------|------|------|
| | | | | | **BUICK** | | | | |
| 1975 | J | 8-350 | Buick | 4 bbl | 165 @ 3800 | 260 @ 2200 | 3.800 × 3.850 | 8.0:1 | 37 @ 2600 |
| | T | 8-455 | Buick | 4 bbl | 205 @ 3800 | 345 @ 2000 | 4.312 × 3.900 | 7.9:1 | 40 @ 2400 |
| 1976 | J | 8-350 | Buick | 4 bbl | 155 @ 3400 | 280 @ 1800 | 3.800 × 3.850 | 8.0:1 | 37 @ 2600 |
| | T | 8-455 | Buick | 4 bbl | 205 @ 3800 | 345 @ 2000 | 4.312 × 3.900 | 7.9:1 | 40 @ 2400 |
| 1977 | C | 6-231 | Buick | 2 bbl | 105 @ 3200 | 185 @ 2000 | 3.800 × 3.400 | 8.0:1 | 37 @ 2600 |
| | Y | 8-301 | Pont. | 2 bbl | 135 @ 4000 | 250 @ 1600 | 4.000 × 3.000 | 8.2:1 | 40 @ 2600 |
| | J | 8-350 | Buick | 4 bbl | 155 @ 3400 | 275 @ 1800 | 4.057 × 3.385 | 8.0:1 | 37 @ 2600 |
| | R | 8-350 | Olds. | 4 bbl | 170 @ 3800 | 275 @ 2400 | 4.057 × 3.385 | 8.0:1 | 40 @ 1500 |
| | K | 8-403 | Olds. | 4 bbl | 185 @ 3600 | 315 @ 2400 | 4.351 × 3.385 | 7.9:1 | 40 @ 1500 |
| 1978 | A | 6-231 | Buick | 2 bbl | 105 @ 3400 | 285 @ 2000 | 3.800 × 3.400 | 8.0:1 | 37 @ 2600 |
| | G | 6-231 | Buick | 2 bbl-Turbo | 150 @ 3800 | 245 @ 2400 | 3.800 × 3.400 | 8.0:1 | 37 @ 2600 |
| | 3 | 6-231 | Buick | 4 bbl-Turbo | 165 @ 4000 | 285 @ 2800 | 3.800 × 3.400 | 8.0:1 | 37 @ 2600 |
| | Y | 8-301 | Pont. | 2 bbl | 140 @ 3600 | 235 @ 2000 | 4.000 × 3.000 | 8.2:1 | 37 @ 2600 |
| | U | 8-305 | Chev. | 4 bbl | 160 @ 4000 | 285 @ 2400 | 3.736 × 3.480 | 8.5:1 | 35–40 @ 2400 |
| | L | 8-350 | Chev. | 4 bbl | 170 @ 3800 | 275 @ 2000 | 4.000 × 3.480 | 8.5:1 | 35–40 @ 2400 |
| | R | 8-350 | Olds. | 4 bbl | 170 @ 3600 | 265 @ 2000 | 4.057 × 3.385 | 8.0:1 | 40 @ 1500 |
| | X | 8-350 | Buick | 4 bbl | 155 @ 3400 | 280 @ 1800 | 3.800 × 3.850 | 8.0:1 | 37 @ 2600 |
| | Z | 8-400 | Pont. | 4 bbl | 180 @ 3600 | 325 @ 1600 | 4.121 × 3.750 | 7.7:1 | 55–60 @ 2600 |
| | K | 8-403 | Olds. | 4 bbl | 185 @ 3600 | 320 @ 2000 | 4.351 × 3.385 | 8.0:1 | 40 @ 1500 |
| 1979 | A | 6-231 | Buick | 2 bbl | 115 @ 3800 | 190 @ 2000 | 3.800 × 3.400 | 8.0:1 | 37 @ 2600 |
| | 3 | 6-231 | Buick | 4 bbl-Turbo | 165 @ 4000 | 285 @ 2800 | 3.800 × 3.400 | 8.0:1 | 37 @ 2600 |
| | Y | 8-301 | Pont. | 2 bbl | 140 @ 3600 | 235 @ 2000 | 4.000 × 3.000 | 8.2:1 | 40 @ 2000 |
| | R | 8-350 | Olds. | 4 bbl | 170 @ 3800 | 275 @ 2000 | 4.057 × 3.385 | 8.0:1 | 40 @ 1500 |
| | X | 8-350 | Buick | 4 bbl | 155 @ 3400 | 280 @ 1800 | 3.800 × 3.850 | 8.0:1 | 37 @ 2400 |
| | K | 8-403 | Pont. | 4 bbl | 185 @ 3600 | 320 @ 2000 | 4.351 × 3.385 | 8.0:1 | 40 @ 1500 |
| 1980 | A | 6-231 | Buick | 2 bbl | 115 @ 3800 | 190 @ 2000 | 3.800 × 3.400 | 8.0:1 | 37 @ 2400 |
| | 3 | 6-231 | Buick | 4 bbl-Turbo | 165 @ 4000 | 265 @ 2800 | 3.800 × 3.400 | 8.0:1 | 37 @ 2400 |
| | 4 | 6-252 | Buick | 4 bbl | 125 @ 4000 | 205 @ 2000 | 3.965 × 3.400 | 8.0:1 | 37 @ 2400 |
| | W | 8-301 | Pont. | 4 bbl | 150 @ 4000 | 240 @ 2000 | 4.000 × 3.000 | 8.2:1 | 40 @ 2600 |
| | N | 8-350 | Olds. | Diesel | 120 @ 3600 | 220 @ 2200 | 4.057 × 3.385 | 22.5:1 | 37 @ 1500 |
| | R | 8-350 | Olds. | 4 bbl | 170 @ 3800 | 275 @ 2000 | 4.057 × 3.385 | 8.5:1 | 37 @ 1500 |
| | X | 8-350 | Buick | 4 bbl | 155 @ 3400 | 280 @ 1800 | 3.800 × 3.850 | 8.0:1 | 37 @ 2400 |
| 1981 | A | 6-231 | Buick | 2 bbl | 110 @ 3800 | 190 @ 1600 | 3.800 × 3.400 | 8.0:1 | 37 @ 2400 |
| | 4 | 6-252 | Buick | 4 bbl | 125 @ 4000 | 205 @ 2000 | 3.965 × 3.400 | 8.0:1 | 37 @ 2400 |
| | J | 8-267 | Chev. | 2 bbl | 115 @ 4000 | 200 @ 2400 | 3.500 × 3.480 | 8.3:1 | 45 @ 2000 |
| | W | 8-301 | Pont. | 4 bbl | 155 @ 4000 | 240 @ 2000 | 4.000 × 3.000 | 8.2:1 | 40 @ 2600 |
| | Y | 8-307 | Olds. | 4 bbl | 148 @ 3800 | 250 @ 2400 | 3.800 × 3.385 | 8.0:1 | 40 @ 1500 |
| | N | 8-350 | Olds. | Diesel | 125 @ 3600 | 225 @ 1600 | 4.057 × 3.385 | 22.5:1 | 40 @ 1500 |

85843A07

## GENERAL ENGINE SPECIFICATIONS

| Year | Engine V.I.N. Code | Engine Type (No. of cyl- C.I.D.) | Engine Manufac- turer | Carb Type | Horsepower @ rpm [1] | Torque @ rpm (ft. lbs.) [1] | Bore × Stroke (in.) | Compression Ratio | Oil Pressure (psi @ rpm) |
|---|---|---|---|---|---|---|---|---|---|
| 1982 | A | 6-231 | Buick | 2 bbl | 110 @ 3800 | 190 @ 1600 | 3.800 × 3.400 | 8.0:1 | 37 @ 2400 |
| | 4 | 6-252 | Buick | 4 bbl | 125 @ 4000 | 205 @ 2000 | 3.965 × 3.400 | 8.0:1 | 37 @ 2400 |
| | Y | 8-307 | Olds. | 4 bbl | 150 @ 3800 | 260 @ 2400 | 3.800 × 3.385 | 8.5:1 | 30–45 @ 1500 |
| | N | 8-350 | Olds. | Diesel | 105 @ 3200 | 200 @ 1600 | 4.057 × 3.385 | 21.6:1 | 30–45 @ 1500 |
| 1983 | A | 6-231 | Buick | 2 bbl | 110 @ 3800 | 190 @ 1600 | 3.800 × 3.400 | 8.0:1 | 37 @ 2400 |
| | 4 | 6-252 | Buick | 4 bbl | 125 @ 4000 | 205 @ 2000 | 3.965 × 3.400 | 8.0:1 | 37 @ 2400 |
| | Y | 8-307 | Olds. | 4 bbl | 150 @ 3800 | 260 @ 2400 | 3.800 × 3.385 | 8.5:1 | 30–45 @ 1500 |
| | N | 8-350 | Olds. | Diesel | 105 @ 3200 | 200 @ 1600 | 4.057 × 3.385 | 21.6:1 | 30–45 @ 1500 |
| 1984 | A | 6-231 | Buick | 2 bbl | 110 @ 3800 | 190 @ 1600 | 3.800 × 3.400 | 8.0:1 | 37 @ 2400 |
| | 4 | 6-252 | Buick | 4 bbl | 125 @ 4000 | 205 @ 2000 | 3.965 × 3.400 | 8.0:1 | 37 @ 2400 |
| | Y | 8-307 | Olds. | 4 bbl | 140 @ 3600 | 240 @ 1600 | 3.800 × 3.385 | 8.5:1 | 30 @ 1500 |
| | N | 8-350 | Olds. | Diesel | 105 @ 3200 | 200 @ 1600 | 4.057 × 3.385 | 22.5:1 | 30–45 @ 1500 |
| 1985 | A | 6-231 | Buick | 2 bbl | 110 @ 3800 | 190 @ 1600 | 3.800 × 3.400 | 8.0:1 | 37 @ 2400 |
| | 4 | 6-252 | Buick | 4 bbl | 125 @ 4000 | 205 @ 2000 | 3.965 × 3.400 | 8.0:1 | 37 @ 2400 |
| | Y | 8-307 | Olds. | 4 bbl | 140 @ 3600 | 240 @ 1600 | 3.800 × 3.385 | 8.5:1 | 30 @ 1500 |
| | N | 8-350 | Olds. | Diesel | 105 @ 3200 | 200 @ 1600 | 4.057 × 3.385 | 22.5:1 | 30–45 @ 1500 |
| 1986 | A | 6-231 | Buick | 2 bbl | 110 @ 3800 | 190 @ 1600 | 3.800 × 3.400 | 8.0:1 | 37 @ 2400 |
| | Y | 8-307 | Olds. | 4 bbl | 140 @ 3200 | 255 @ 2000 | 3.800 × 3.385 | 8.5:1 | 30–45 @ 1500 |
| 1987 | A | 6-231 | Buick | 2 bbl | 110 @ 3800 | 190 @ 1600 | 3.800 × 3.400 | 8.0:1 | 37 @ 2400 |
| | Y | 8-307 | Olds. | 4 bbl | 140 @ 3200 | 255 @ 2000 | 3.800 × 3.385 | 8.5:1 | 30–45 @ 1500 |
| 1988 | Y | 8-307 | Olds. | 4 bbl | 140 @ 3200 | 255 @ 2000 | 3.800 × 3.385 | 8.0:1 | 30 @ 1500 |
| 1989 | Y | 8-307 | Olds. | 4 bbl | 140 @ 3200 | 255 @ 2000 | 3.800 × 3.385 | 8.0:1 | 30 @ 1500 |
| 1990 | Y | 8-307 | Olds. | 4 bbl | 140 @ 3200 | 255 @ 2000 | 3.800 × 3.385 | 8.0:1 | 30 @ 1500 |
| **OLDSMOBILE** | | | | | | | | | |
| 1975 | K | 8-350 | Olds. | 4 bbl | 160 @ 3800 | 275 @ 2400 | 4.057 × 3.385 | 8.5:1 | 30–45 |
| | R | 8-400 | Olds. | 2 bbl | 180 @ 3600 | 290 @ 2200 | 4.121 × 3.750 | 8.5:1 | 30–45 |
| | S | 8-400 | Olds. | 4 bbl | 185 @ 3600 | 300 @ 2200 | 4.121 × 3.750 | 8.5:1 | 30–45 |
| | T | 8-455 | Olds. | 4 bbl | 190 @ 3400 | 350 @ 2000 | 4.126 × 4.250 | 8.5:1 | 30–45 @ 1500 |
| 1976 | R | 8-350 | Olds. | 4 bbl | 170 @ 3800 | 275 @ 2400 | 4.057 × 3.385 | 8.5:1 | 30–45 |
| | T | 8-455 | Olds. | 4 bbl | 190 @ 3400 | 350 @ 2000 | 4.126 × 4.250 | 8.5:1 | 30–45 @ 1500 |
| 1977 | C | 6-231 | Buick | 2 bbl | 105 @ 3400 | 185 @ 2000 | 3.800 × 3.400 | 8.0:1 | 37 |
| | F | 8-260 | Olds. | 2 bbl | 110 @ 3400 | 205 @ 1800 | 3.500 × 3.385 | 7.5:1 | 40 |
| | L | 8-350 | Chev. | 4 bbl | 170 @ 3800 | 275 @ 2000 | 4.057 × 3.385 | 22.5:1 | 30–45 |
| | R | 8-350 | Olds. | 4 bbl | 170 @ 3800 | 270 @ 2400 | 4.057 × 3.385 | 8.0:1 | 40 |
| | K | 8-403 | Olds. | 4 bbl | 185 @ 3600 | 320 @ 2200 | 4.351 × 3.385 | 8.0:1 | 40 |
| 1978 | A | 6-231 | Buick | 2 bbl | 105 @ 3400 | 185 @ 2000 | 3.800 × 3.400 | 8.0:1 | 37 |
| | F | 8-260 | Olds. | 2 bbl | 110 @ 3400 | 205 @ 1800 | 3.500 × 3.385 | 7.5:1 | 40 |
| | R | 8-350 | Olds. | 4 bbl | 170 @ 3800 | 275 @ 2000 | 4.057 × 3.385 | 8.0:1 | 40 |
| | X | 8-350 | Buick | 4 bbl | 165 @ 4000 | 290 @ 1600 | 3.800 × 3.850 | 8.0:1 | 37 [2] |
| | N | 8-350 | Olds. | Diesel | 120 @ 3600 | 220 @ 1800 | 4.057 × 3.385 | 22.0:1 | 40 |
| | K | 8-403 | Olds. | 4 bbl | 185 @ 3600 | 320 @ 2200 | 4.351 × 3.385 | 8.0:1 | 40 |

85843A08

## GENERAL ENGINE SPECIFICATIONS

| Year | Engine V.I.N. Code | Engine Type (No. of cyl- C.I.D.) | Engine Manufac- turer | Carb Type | Horsepower @ rpm ① | Torque @ rpm (ft. lbs.) ① | Bore × Stroke (in.) | Compression Ratio | Oil Pressure (psi @ rpm) |
|---|---|---|---|---|---|---|---|---|---|
| | | | | | OLDSMOBILE | | | | |
| 1979 | A | 6-231 | Buick | 2 bbl | 115 @ 3800 | 190 @ 2000 | 3.800 × 3.400 | 8.0:1 | 37 @ 2000 |
| | F | 8-260 | Olds. | 2 bbl | 105 @ 3600 | 205 @ 1800 | 3.500 × 3.385 | 7.5:1 | 40 @ 2000 |
| | Y | 8-301 | Pont. | 2 bbl | 135 @ 3800 | 240 @ 1600 | 4.000 × 3.000 | 8.2:1 | 35 @ 2000 |
| | N | 8-350 | Olds. | Diesel | 125 @ 3600 | 225 @ 1600 | 4.057 × 3.385 | 22.5:1 | 40 @ 2000 |
| | R | 8-350 | Olds. | 4 bbl | 170 @ 3800 | 275 @ 2000 | 4.057 × 3.385 | 8.0:1 | 40 @ 2000 |
| | K | 8-403 | Olds. | 4 bbl | 175 @ 3600 | 310 @ 2000 | 4.351 × 3.385 | 7.8:1 | 40 @ 2000 |
| 1980 | A | 6-231 | Buick | 2 bbl | 110 @ 3800 | 190 @ 1600 | 3.800 × 3.400 | 8.0:1 | 37 @ 2000 |
| | F | 8-260 | Olds. | 2 bbl | 105 @ 3600 | 205 @ 1800 | 3.500 × 3.385 | 7.5:1 | 40 @ 2000 |
| | S | 8-265 | Pont. | 2 bbl | 110 @ 3400 | 207 @ 1800 | 3.74 × 3.00 | 8.2:1 | 40 @ 2000 |
| | Y | 8-307 | Olds. | 4 bbl | 148 @ 3800 | 250 @ 2400 | 3.800 × 3.385 | 7.9:1 | 40 @ 2000 |
| | R | 8-350 | Olds. | 4 bbl | 170 @ 3800 | 275 @ 2000 | 4.057 × 3.385 | 8.0:1 | 40 @ 2000 |
| | N | 8-350 | Olds. | Diesel | 125 @ 3600 | 225 @ 1600 | 4.057 × 3.385 | 22.5:1 | 40 @ 2000 |
| 1981 | A | 6-231 | Buick | 2 bbl | 110 @ 3800 | 190 @ 1600 | 3.800 × 3.400 | 8.0:1 | 37 @ 2000 |
| | 4 | 6-252 | Buick | 4 bbl | 125 @ 4000 | 205 @ 2000 | 3.965 × 3.400 | 8.0:1 | 37 @ 2400 |
| | F | 8-260 | Olds. | 2 bbl | 105 @ 3600 | 205 @ 1800 | 3.500 × 3.385 | 7.5:1 | 40 @ 1500 |
| | Y | 8-307 | Olds. | 4 bbl | 148 @ 3800 | 250 @ 2400 | 3.800 × 3.385 | 8.0:1 | 40 @ 1500 |
| | N | 8-350 | Olds. | Diesel | 125 @ 3600 | 225 @ 1600 | 4.057 × 3.385 | 22.5:1 | 40 @ 1500 |
| 1982 | A | 6-231 | Buick | 2 bbl | 110 @ 3800 | 190 @ 1600 | 3.800 × 3.400 | 8.0:1 | 37 @ 2000 |
| | 4 | 6-252 | Buick | 4 bbl | 125 @ 4000 | 205 @ 2000 | 3.965 × 3.400 | 8.0:1 | 37 @ 2400 |
| | F | 8-260 | Olds. | 2 bbl | 105 @ 3600 | 205 @ 1800 | 3.500 × 3.385 | 7.5:1 | 40 @ 1500 |
| | Y | 8-307 | Olds. | 4 bbl | 148 @ 3800 | 250 @ 2400 | 3.800 × 3.385 | 8.0:1 | 40 @ 1500 |
| | N | 8-350 | Olds. | Diesel | 125 @ 3600 | 225 @ 1600 | 4.057 × 3.385 | 22.5:1 | 40 @ 1500 |
| 1983 | A | 6-231 | Buick | 2 bbl | 110 @ 3800 | 190 @ 1600 | 3.800 × 3.400 | 8.0:1 | 37 @ 2000 |
| | 4 | 6-252 | Buick | 4 bbl | 125 @ 4000 | 205 @ 2000 | 3.965 × 3.400 | 8.0:1 | 37 @ 2400 |
| | Y | 8-307 | Olds. | 4 bbl | 148 @ 3800 | 250 @ 2400 | 3.800 × 3.385 | 8.0:1 | 40 @ 1500 |
| | N | 8-350 | Olds. | Diesel | 125 @ 3600 | 225 @ 1600 | 4.057 × 3.385 | 22.5:1 | 40 @ 1500 |
| 1984 | A | 6-231 | Buick | 2 bbl | 110 @ 3800 | 190 @ 1600 | 3.800 × 3.400 | 8.0:1 | 37 @ 2000 |
| | Y | 8-307 | Olds. | 4 bbl | 140 @ 3600 | 240 @ 1600 | 3.800 × 3.385 | 8.5:1 | 30 @ 1500 |
| | N | 8-350 | Olds. | Diesel | 105 @ 3200 | 200 @ 1600 | 4.06 × 3.39 | 22.5:1 | 30–45 @ 1500 |
| 1985 | Y | 8-307 | Olds. | 4 bbl | 140 @ 3600 | 240 @ 1600 | 3.800 × 3.385 | 8.5:1 | 30 @ 1500 |
| | N | 8-350 | Olds. | Diesel | 105 @ 3200 | 200 @ 1600 | 4.06 × 3.39 | 22.5:1 | 30–45 @ 1500 |
| 1986 | Y | 8-307 | Olds. | 4 bbl | 140 @ 3600 | 240 @ 1600 | 3.800 × 3.385 | 8.5:1 | 30 @ 1500 |
| 1987 | Y | 8-307 | Olds. | 4 bbl | 140 @ 3600 | 240 @ 1600 | 3.800 × 3.385 | 8.5:1 | 30 @ 1500 |
| 1988 | Y | 8-307 | Olds. | 4 bbl | 140 @ 3600 | 225 @ 2000 | 3.800 × 3.385 | 8.0:1 | 30 @ 1500 |
| 1989 | Y | 8-307 | Olds. | 4 bbl | 140 @ 3600 | 225 @ 2000 | 3.800 × 3.385 | 8.0:1 | 30 @ 1500 |
| 1990 | Y | 8-307 | Olds. | 4 bbl | 140 @ 3600 | 225 @ 2000 | 3.800 × 3.385 | 8.0:1 | 30 @ 1500 |

85843A09

## GENERAL ENGINE SPECIFICATIONS

| Year | Engine V.I.N. Code | Engine Type (No. of cyl- C.I.D.) | Engine Manufac- turer | Carb Type | Horsepower @ rpm ① | Torque @ rpm (ft. lbs.) ① | Bore × Stroke (in.) | Compression Ratio | Oil Pressure (psi @ rpm) |
|------|------|------|------|------|------|------|------|------|------|
| | | | | | **PONTIAC** | | | | |
| 1975 | R | 8-400 | Pont. | 2 bbl | 170 @ 3600 | 315 @ 2000 | 4.12 × 3.75 | 8.0:1 | 55–60 @ 2600 |
| | S | 8-400 | Pont. | 4 bbl | 185 @ 4000 | 320 @ 2400 | 4.12 × 3.75 | 8.0:1 | 55–60 @ 2600 |
| | W | 8-455 | Pont. | 4 bbl | 200 @ 3600 | 355 @ 2400 | 4.15 × 4.21 | 8.0:1 | 55–60 @ 2600 |
| 1976 | R | 8-400 | Pont. | 2 bbl | 170 @ 4000 | 305 @ 2000 | 4.121 × 3.750 | 7.6:1 | 55–60 @ 2600 |
| | S | 8-400 | Pont. | 4 bbl | 185 @ 3600 | 310 @ 1600 | 4.121 × 3.750 | 7.6:1 | 55–60 @ 2600 |
| | W | 8-455 | Pont. | 4 bbl | 200 @ 3500 | 330 @ 2000 | 4.152 × 4.210 | 7.6:1 | 55–60 @ 2600 |
| 1977 | C | 6-231 | Buick | 2 bbl | 105 @ 3200 | 185 @ 2000 | 3.800 × 3.400 | 8.0:1 | 37 @ 2600 |
| | Y | 8-301 | Pont. | 2 bbl | 135 @ 4000 | 250 @ 1600 | 4.000 × 3.000 | 8.2:1 | 40 @ 2600 |
| | U | 8-305 | Chev. | 4 bbl | 160 @ 4000 | 285 @ 2499 | 3.736 × 3.480 | 8.5:1 | 35–40 @ 2400 |
| | R | 8-350 | Olds. | 4 bbl | 170 @ 3800 | 275 @ 2000 | 4.057 × 3.385 | 8.0:1 | 32–40 |
| | P | 8-350 | Pont. | 4 bbl | 170 @ 4000 | 275 @ 1800 | 3.876 × 3.750 | 7.6:1 | 30–45 @ 2400 |
| | Z | 8-400 | Pont. | 4 bbl | 180 @ 3600 | 325 @ 1600 | 4.120 × 3.750 | 7.7:1 | 35–40 @ 2600 |
| | K | 8-403 | Olds. | 4 bbl | 185 @ 3600 | 320 @ 2200 | 4.351 × 3.385 | 8.0:1 | 35–40 @ 2400 |
| 1978 | A | 6-231 | Buick | 2 bbl | 105 @ 3200 | 185 @ 2000 | 3.800 × 3.400 | 8.0:1 | 37 @ 2600 |
| | Y | 8-301 | Pont. | 2 bbl | 135 @ 4000 | 250 @ 1600 | 4.000 × 3.000 | 8.2:1 | 35–40 @ 2600 |
| | W | 8-301 | Pont. | 4 bbl | 150 @ 4000 | 265 @ 1600 | 4.000 × 3.000 | 8.2:1 | 35–40 @ 2600 |
| | X | 8-350 | Buick | 4 bbl | 165 @ 1600 | 290 @ 4000 | 3.800 × 3.850 | 8.0:1 | 37 ② |
| | R | 8-350 | Olds. | 4 bbl | 160 @ 1600 | 280 @ 4000 | 4.057 × 3.385 | 7.9:1 | 30–45 @ 1500 |
| | K | 8-403 | Olds. | 4 bbl | 180 @ 3400 | 315 @ 2200 | 4.351 × 3.385 | 7.9:1 | 30–45 @ 1500 |
| 1979 | A | 6-231 | Buick | 2 bbl | 115 @ 3800 | 190 @ 2000 | 3.800 × 3.400 | 8.2:1 | 34 |
| | Y | 8-301 | Pont. | 2 bbl | 140 @ 3600 | 235 @ 2000 | 4.000 × 3.000 | 8.1:1 | 35–40 |
| | W | 8-301 | Pont. | 4 bbl | 150 @ 4000 | 240 @ 2000 | 4.000 × 3.000 | 8.1:1 | 35–40 |
| | X | 8-350 | Buick | 4 bbl | 155 @ 3400 | 280 @ 1800 | 3.800 × 3.850 | 8.0:1 | 35 |
| | R | 8-350 | Olds. | 4 bbl | 170 @ 3800 | 275 @ 2000 | 4.057 × 3.385 | 8.0:1 | 35 |
| | K | 8-403 | Olds. | 4 bbl | 185 @ 3600 | 320 @ 2200 | 4.351 × 3.385 | 8.0:1 | 40 |
| 1980 | A | 6-231 | Buick | 2 bbl | 115 @ 3800 | 188 @ 2000 | 3.800 × 3.400 | 8.0:1 | 37 |
| | S | 8-265 | Pont. | 2 bbl | 120 @ 3600 | 210 @ 1600 | 3.750 × 3.000 | 8.0:1 | 40 @ 2600 |
| | W | 8-301 | Pont. | 4 bbl | 150 @ 4000 | 240 @ 2000 | 4.000 × 3.000 | 8.2:1 | 40 @ 2600 |
| | R | 8-350 | Olds. | 4 bbl | 160 @ 3800 | 260 @ 2400 | 4.000 × 3.480 | 8.5:1 | 40 |
| | X | 8-350 | Buick | 4 bbl | 155 @ 3400 | 280 @ 1800 | 3.800 × 3.850 | 8.0:1 | 35 |
| | N | 8-350 | Olds. | Diesel | 125 @ 3600 | 225 @ 1600 | 4.057 × 3.385 | 22.5:1 | 40 @ 1500 |

85843A10

## GENERAL ENGINE SPECIFICATIONS

| Year | Engine V.I.N. Code | Engine Type (No. of cyl- C.I.D.) | Engine Manufac- turer | Carb Type | Horsepower @ rpm ① | Torque @ rpm (ft. lbs.) ① | Bore × Stroke (in.) | Compression Ratio | Oil Pressure (psi @ rpm) |
|------|------|------|------|------|------|------|------|------|------|
| | | | | | **PONTIAC** | | | | |
| 1981 | A | 6-231 | Buick | 2 bbl | 115 @ 3800 | 188 @ 2000 | 3.800 × 3.400 | 8.0:1 | 37 |
| | S | 8-265 | Pont. | 2 bbl | 120 @ 3600 | 210 @ 1600 | 3.750 × 3.000 | 8.0:1 | 40② |
| | H | 8-305 | Chev. | 4 bbl | 150 @ 3800 | 240 @ 2400 | 3.735 × 3.480 | 8.6:1 | 45 |
| | Y | 8-307 | Olds. | 4 bbl | 148 @ 3800 | 250 @ 2400 | 3.800 × 3.385 | 8.0:1 | 40 @ 1500 |
| | X | 8-350 | Buick | 4 bbl | 155 @ 3400 | 280 @ 1800 | 3.800 × 3.850 | 8.0:1 | 35 |
| | N | 8-350 | Olds. | Diesel | 105 @ 3200 | 205 @ 1600 | 4.057 × 3.385 | 22.5:1 | 40 @ 1500 |
| 1982 | A | 6-231 | Buick | 2 bbl | 110 @ 3800 | 190 @ 1600 | 3.800 × 3.400 | 8.0:1 | 37 |
| | 4 | 6-252 | Buick | 4 bbl | 125 @ 4000 | 205 @ 2000 | 3.965 × 3.400 | 8.0:1 | 37 |
| | H | 8-305 | Chev. | 4 bbl | 150 @ 3800 | 240 @ 2400 | 3.735 × 3.480 | 8.6:1 | 45 |
| | N | 8-350 | Olds. | Diesel | 105 @ 3200 | 200 @ 1600 | 4.057 × 3.385 | 21.6:1 | 40 |
| 1983 | A | 6-231 | Buick | 2 bbl | 110 @ 3800 | 190 @ 1600 | 3.800 × 3.400 | 8.0:1 | 37 |
| | H | 8-305 | Chev. | 4 bbl | 150 @ 3800 | 240 @ 2400 | 3.735 × 3.480 | 8.6:1 | 45 |
| | N | 8-350 | Olds. | Diesel | 105 @ 3200 | 200 @ 1600 | 4.057 × 3.385 | 21.6:1 | 40 @ 1500 |
| 1984 | A | 6-231 | Buick | 2 bbl | 110 @ 3800 | 190 @ 1600 | 3.800 × 3.400 | 8.0:1 | 37 @ 2400 |
| | H | 8-305 | Chev. | 4 bbl | 150 @ 4000 | 240 @ 2400 | 3.74 × 3.48 | 8.6:1 | 32–40 @ 2000 |
| | N | 8-350 | Olds. | Diesel | 105 @ 3200 | 200 @ 1600 | 4.06 × 3.39 | 22.5:1 | 30–45 @ 1500 |
| 1985 | A | 6-231 | Buick | 2 bbl | 110 @ 3800 | 190 @ 1600 | 3.800 × 3.400 | 8.0:1 | 37 @ 2400 |
| | Z | 6-262 | Chev. | EFI | 140 @ 3800 | 225 @ 2200 | 4.000 × 3.480 | 9.3:1 | 45 @ 2000 |
| | H | 8-305 | Chev. | 4 bbl | 150 @ 4000 | 240 @ 2400 | 3.74 × 3.48 | 8.6:1 | 32–40 @ 2000 |
| | N | 8-350 | Olds. | Diesel | 105 @ 3200 | 200 @ 1600 | 4.06 × 3.39 | 22.5:1 | 30–45 @ 1500 |
| 1986 | A | 6-231 | Buick | 2 bbl | 110 @ 3800 | 190 @ 1600 | 3.800 × 3.400 | 8.0:1 | 37 @ 2400 |
| | Z | 6-262 | Chev. | EFI | 140 @ 3800 | 225 @ 2200 | 4.000 × 3.480 | 9.3:1 | 45 @ 2000 |
| | H | 8-305 | Chev. | 4 bbl | 150 @ 4000 | 240 @ 2400 | 3.74 × 3.48 | 8.6:1 | 32–40 @ 2000 |
| 1987 | Y | 8-307 | Olds. | 4 bbl | 140 @ 3600 | 240 @ 1600 | 3.800 × 3.385 | 8.5:1 | 30 @ 1500 |
| 1988 | Y | 8-307 | Olds. | 4 bbl | 140 @ 3600 | 225 @ 2000 | 3.800 × 3.385 | 8.0:1 | 30 @ 1500 |
| 1989 | Y | 8-307 | Olds. | 4 bbl | 140 @ 3600 | 225 @ 2000 | 3.800 × 3.385 | 8.0:1 | 30 @ 1500 |

C.I.D. – Cubic Inch Displacement
① Horsepower and torque are SAE net figures. They are measured at the rear of the transmission with all accessories installed and operating. Since the figures vary when a given engine is installed in different models, some are representative rather than exact.
② Above 2600 rpm

85843A11

## VALVE SPECIFICATIONS

| Year | Engine No. Cyl. Displacement (cu. in.) | Seat Angle (deg.) | Face Angle (deg.) | Spring Test Pressure ▲ (lbs. @ in.) | Spring Installed Height (in.) | Stem to Guide Clearance (in.) Intake | Exhaust | Stem Diameter (in.) Intake | Exhaust |
|---|---|---|---|---|---|---|---|---|---|
| | | | | **BUICK** | | | | | |
| 1975 | 8-350 Buick | 45 | 45 | 164 @ 1.34 | 1 47/64 | 0.0015–0.0035 | 0.0015–0.0032 | 0.3407 | 0.3409 |
| | 8-455 Buick | 45 | 45 | 177 @ 1.45 | 1 57/64 | 0.0015–0.0035 | 0.0015–0.0032 | 0.3725 | 0.3727 |
| 1976 | 8-350 Buick | 45 | 45 | 164 @ 1.34 | 1 47/64 | 0.0015–0.0035 | 0.0015–0.0032 | 0.3407 | 0.3409 |
| | 8-455 Buick | 45 | 45 | 177 @ 1.45 | 1 57/64 | 0.0015–0.0035 | 0.0015–0.0032 | 0.3725 | 0.3727 |
| 1977 | 6-231 Buick | 45 | 45 | 164 @ 1.34 | 1 47/64 | 0.0015–0.0035 | 0.0015–0.0035 | 0.3400 | 0.3400 |
| | 8-301 Pont. | 46 | 45 | 170 @ 1.26 | 1 47/64 | 0.0017–0.0020 | 0.0015–0.0020 | 0.3400 | 0.3400 |
| | 8-350 Olds. | 45[2] | 44[2] | 180 @ 1.34 | 1 47/64 | 0.0010–0.0027 | 0.0015–0.0032 | 0.3425 | 0.3420 |
| | 8-350 Buick | 45 | 45 | 180 @ 1.34 | 1 47/64 | 0.0015–0.0032 | 0.0015–0.0032 | 0.3730 | 0.3727 |
| | 8-403 Olds. | 45[2] | 44[2] | 180 @ 1.27 | 1 47/64 | 0.0010–0.0027 | 0.0015–0.0032 | 0.3425 | 0.3420 |
| 1978 | 6-231 Buick | 45 | 45 | 168 @ 1.327 | 1 47/64 | 0.0015–0.0032 | 0.0015–0.0032 | 0.3405–0.3412 | 0.3405–0.3412 |
| | 8-301 Pont. | 46 | 45 | 170 @ 1.260 | 1 47/64 | 0.0017–0.0020 | 0.0017–0.0020 | 0.3400–0.3405 | 0.3400–0.3405 |
| | 8-305 Chev. | 46 | 45 | 200 @ 1.160 | [4] | 0.0010–0.0037 | 0.0010–0.0037 | 0.3410–0.3417 | 0.3410–0.3417 |
| | 8-350 Buick | 45 | 45 | [3] | 1 47/64 | 0.0015–0.0035 | 0.0015–0.0032 | 0.3720–0.3730 | 0.3723–0.3730 |
| | 8-350 Chev. | 46 | 45 | 200 @ 1.160 | [4] | 0.0010–0.0037 | 0.0010–0.0037 | 0.3410–0.3417 | 0.3410–0.3417 |
| | 8-350 Olds. | 45[2] | 44[2] | 187 @ 1.270 | 1 47/64 | 0.0010–0.0027 | 0.0015–0.0032 | 0.3425–0.3432 | 0.3420–0.3427 |
| | 8-400 Pont. | 30 | 29 | 135 @ 1.18 | 1 27/50 | 0.0016–0.0033 | 0.0021–0.0038 | 0.3425 | 0.3425 |
| | 8-403 Olds. | 45[2] | 44[2] | 187 @ 1.270 | 1 47/64 | 0.0010–0.0027 | 0.0015–0.0032 | 0.3425–0.3432 | 0.3420–0.3427 |
| 1979 | 6-231 Buick | 45 | 45 | 164 @ 1.34[5] | 1 47/64 | 0.0015–0.0035 | 0.0015–0.0032 | 0.3401–0.3412 | 0.3405–0.3412 |
| | 8-301 Pont. | 46 | 45 | 170 @ 1.27 | 1 47/64 | 0.0017–0.0020 | 0.0017–0.0020 | 0.3400 | 0.3400 |
| | 8-350 Buick | 45 | 45 | [3] | 1 47/64 | 0.0015–0.0035 | 0.0015–0.0032 | 0.3720–0.3730 | 0.3723–0.3730 |
| | 8-350 Olds. | 45[2] | 44[2] | 187 @ 1.27 | 1 47/64 | 0.0010–0.0027 | 0.0015–0.0032 | 0.3425–0.3432 | 0.3420–0.3427 |
| | 8-403 Olds. | 45[2] | 44[2] | 187 @ 1.27 | 1 47/64 | 0.0010–0.0027 | 0.0015–0.0032 | 0.3425–0.3432 | 0.3420–0.3427 |
| 1980 | 6-231 Buick | 45 | 45 | 164 @ 1.34[5] | 1 47/64 | 0.0015–0.0035 | 0.0015–0.0032 | 0.3401–0.3412 | 0.3405–0.3412 |
| | 6-252 Buick | 45 | 45 | 164 @ 1.34[5] | 1 47/64 | 0.0015–0.0035 | 0.0015–0.0032 | 0.3401–0.3412 | 0.3405–0.3412 |
| | 8-301 Pont. | 46 | 45 | 170 @ 1.27 | 1 47/64 | 0.0017–0.0020 | 0.0017–0.0020 | 0.3400 | 0.3400 |
| | 8-350 Buick | 45 | 45 | [3] | 1 47/64 | 0.0015–0.0035 | 0.0015–0.0032 | 0.3720–0.3730 | 0.3723–0.3730 |
| | 8-350 Olds. | 45[2] | 44[2] | 187 @ 1.27 | 1 47/64 | 0.0010–0.0027 | 0.0015–0.0032 | 0.3425–0.3432 | 0.3420–0.3427 |
| | 8-350 Olds. Diesel | 45[2][9] | 44[2][9] | 151 @ 1.30[6] | 1 47/64 | 0.0010–0.0027 | 0.0015–0.0032 | 0.3425–0.3432 | 0.3420–0.3427 |
| 1981 | 6-231 Buick | 45 | 45 | 164 @ 1.34[5] | 1 47/64 | 0.0015–0.0035 | 0.0015–0.0032 | 0.3401–0.3412 | 0.3405–0.3412 |
| | 6-252 Buick | 45 | 45 | 164 @ 1.34[5] | 1 47/64 | 0.0015–0.0035 | 0.0015–0.0032 | 0.3401–0.3412 | 0.3405–0.3412 |
| | 8-267 Chev. | 46 | 45 | 180 @ 1.25 | 1 23/32 | 0.0010–0.0027 | 0.0010–0.0027 | 0.3414 | 0.3414 |
| | 8-301 Pont. | 46 | 45 | 170 @ 1.27 | 1 47/64 | 0.0017–0.0020 | 0.0017–0.0020 | 0.3400 | 0.3400 |
| | 8-307 Olds. | [7] | [8] | 187 @ 1.27 | 1 47/64 | 0.0010–0.0027 | 0.0015–0.0032 | 0.3428 | 0.3424 |
| | 8-350 Olds. Diesel | 45[2][9] | 44[2][9] | 151 @ 1.30[6] | 1 47/64 | 0.0010–0.0027 | 0.0015–0.0032 | 0.3425–0.3432 | 0.3420–0.3427 |
| 1982 | 6-231 Buick | 45 | 45 | 164 @ 1.34[5] | 1 47/64 | 0.0015–0.0035 | 0.0015–0.0032 | 0.3401–0.3412 | 0.3405–0.3412 |
| | 6-252 Buick | 45 | 45 | 164 @ 1.34[5] | 1 47/64 | 0.0015–0.0035 | 0.0015–0.0032 | 0.3401–0.3412 | 0.3405–0.3412 |
| | 8-307 Olds. | 46[2] | 45[2] | 187 @ 1.27 | 1 47/64 | 0.0010–0.0027 | 0.0015–0.0032 | 0.3425–0.3432 | 0.3400–0.3427 |
| | 8-350 Diesel | 45[2] | 44[2] | 210 @ 1.23 | 1 47/64 | 0.0010–0.0027 | 0.0015–0.0032 | 0.3425–0.3432 | 0.3400–0.3427 |

85843A12

## VALVE SPECIFICATIONS

| Year | Engine No. Cyl. Displacement (cu. in.) | Seat Angle (deg.) | Face Angle (deg.) | Spring Text Pressure ▲ (lbs. @ in.) | Spring Installed Height (in.) | Stem to Guide Clearance (in.) Intake | Exhaust | Stem Diameter (in.) Intake | Exhaust |
|---|---|---|---|---|---|---|---|---|---|
| 1983 | 6-231 Buick | 45 | 45 | 164 @ 1.34 [5] | 1 47/64 | 0.0015–0.0035 | 0.0015–0.0032 | 0.3401–0.3412 | 0.3405–0.3412 |
| | 6-252 Buick | 45 | 45 | 164 @ 1.34 [5] | 1 47/64 | 0.0015–0.0035 | 0.0015–0.0032 | 0.3401–0.3412 | 0.3405–0.3412 |
| | 8-307 Olds. | 44 [2] | 45 [2] | 187 @ 1.27 | 1 47/64 | 0.0010–0.0027 | 0.0015–0.0032 | 0.3425–0.3432 | 0.3400–0.3427 |
| | 8-350 Diesel | 45 [2] | 44 [2] | 210 @ 1.23 | 1 47/64 | 0.0010–0.0027 | 0.0015–0.0032 | 0.3425–0.3432 | 0.3420–0.3427 |
| **BUICK** | | | | | | | | | |
| 1984 | 6-231 Buick | 46 | 45 | 164 @ 1.34 | 1 47/64 | 0.0015–0.0035 | 0.0015–0.0032 | 0.3401–0.3412 | 0.3405–0.3412 |
| | 6-252 Buick | 46 | 45 | 164 @ 1.34 | 1 47/64 | 0.0015–0.0035 | 0.0015–0.0032 | 0.3401–0.3412 | 0.3405–0.3412 |
| | 8-307 Olds. | 45 [2] | 44 [2] | 187 @ 1.27 | 1 43/64 | 0.0010–0.0027 | 0.0015–0.0032 | 0.3425–0.3432 | 0.3420–0.3427 |
| | 8-350 Diesel | 45 [2] | 44 [2] | 210 @ 1.23 | 1 43/64 | 0.0010–0.0027 | 0.0015–0.0032 | 0.3424–0.3432 | 0.3420–0.3428 |
| 1985 | 6-231 Buick | 46 | 45 | 164 @ 1.34 | 1 47/64 | 0.0015–0.0035 | 0.0015–0.0032 | 0.3401–0.3412 | 0.3405–0.3412 |
| | 6-252 Buick | 46 | 45 | 164 @ 1.34 | 1 47/64 | 0.0015–0.0035 | 0.0015–0.0032 | 0.3401–0.3412 | 0.3405–0.3412 |
| | 8-307 Olds. | 45 [2] | 44 [2] | 187 @ 1.27 | 1 43/64 | 0.0010–0.0027 | 0.0015–0.0032 | 0.3425–0.3432 | 0.3420–0.3427 |
| | 8-350 Diesel | 45 [2] | 44 [2] | 210 @ 1.23 | 1 43/64 | 0.0010–0.0027 | 0.0015–0.0032 | 0.3424–0.3432 | 0.3420–0.3428 |
| 1986 | 6-231 Buick | 45 | 45 | 164 @ 1.34 | 1 47/64 | 0.0010–0.0027 | 0.0015–0.0032 | 0.3425–0.3432 | 0.3420–0.3412 |
| | 8-307 Olds. | 45 [2] | 44 [2] | 187 @ 1.27 | 1 43/64 | 0.0010–0.0027 | 0.0015–0.0032 | 0.3425–0.3432 | 0.3420–0.3427 |
| 1987 | 6-231 Buick | 45 | 45 | 164 @ 1.34 | 1 47/64 | 0.0010–0.0027 | 0.0015–0.0032 | 0.3425–0.3432 | 0.3420–0.3412 |
| | 8-307 Olds. | 45 [2] | 44 [2] | 187 @ 1.27 | 1 43/64 | 0.0010–0.0027 | 0.0015–0.0032 | 0.3425–0.3432 | 0.3420–0.3427 |
| 1988 | 8-307 Olds. | 45 [2] | 44 [2] | 187 @ 1.27 | 1 43/64 | 0.0010–0.0027 | 0.0015–0.0032 | 0.3425–0.3432 | 0.3420–0.3427 |
| 1989 | 8-307 Olds. | 45 [2] | 44 [2] | 187 @ 1.27 | 1 43/64 | 0.0010–0.0027 | 0.0015–0.0032 | 0.3425–0.3432 | 0.3420–0.3427 |
| 1990 | 8-307 Olds. | 45 [2] | 44 [2] | 187 @ 1.27 | 1 43/64 | 0.0010–0.0027 | 0.0015–0.0032 | 0.3425–0.3432 | 0.3420–0.3427 |
| **OLDSMOBILE** | | | | | | | | | |
| 1975 | 8-350 Olds. | [11] | [12] | 187 @ 1.27 | 1 21/32 | 0.0010–0.0027 | 0.0015–0.0032 | 0.3429 | 0.3424 |
| | 8-400 Olds. | [13] | [14] | NA | 1 21/32 | 0.0016–0.0033 | 0.0021–0.0038 | 0.3419–0.3412 | 0.3414–0.3407 |
| | 8-455 Olds. | [11] | [12] | 187 @ 1.27 | 1 21/32 | 0.0010–0.0027 | 0.0015–0.0032 | 0.3429 | 0.3424 |
| 1976 | 8-350 | [11] | [12] | 187 @ 1.27 | 1 21/32 | 0.0010–0.0027 | 0.0015–0.0032 | 0.3429 | 0.3424 |
| | 8-455 | [11] | [12] | 187 @ 1.27 | 1 21/32 | 0.0010–0.0027 | 0.0015–0.0032 | 0.3429 | 0.3424 |
| 1977 | 6-231 Buick | 45 | 45 | 168 @ 1.327 | 1 46/64 | 0.0015–0.0032 | 0.0015–0.0032 | 0.3409 | 0.3409 |
| | 8-260 Olds. | [11] | [12] | 187 @ 1.270 | 1 43/64 | 0.0010–0.0027 | 0.0015–0.0032 | 0.3429 | 0.3427 |
| | 8-350 Chev. | 46 | 45 | 200 @ 1.250 | 1 45/64 | 0.0010–0.0037 | 0.0010–0.0037 | 0.3414 | 0.3414 |
| | 8-350 Olds. | [11] | [12] | 187 @ 1.270 | 1 43/64 | 0.0010–0.0027 | 0.0015–0.0032 | 0.3429 | 0.3427 |
| | 8-403 Olds. | [11] | [12] | 187 @ 1.270 | 1 43/64 | 0.0010–0.0027 | 0.0015–0.0032 | 0.3429 | 0.3427 |
| 1978 | 6-231 Buick | 45 | 45 | 168 @ 1.327 | 1 47/64 | 0.0015–0.0032 | 0.0015–0.0032 | 0.3405–0.3412 | 0.3405–0.3412 |
| | 8-260 Olds. | [11] | [12] | 187 @ 1.270 | 1 47/64 | 0.0010–0.0027 | 0.0015–0.0032 | 0.3425–0.3432 | 0.3420–0.3427 |
| | 8-350 Olds. | [11] | [12] | 187 @ 1.270 | 1 47/64 | 0.0010–0.0027 | 0.0015–0.0032 | 0.3425–0.3432 | 0.3420–0.3427 |
| | 8-350 Buick | 45 | 45 | [3] | 1 47/64 | 0.0015–0.0035 | 0.0015–0.0032 | 0.3720–0.3730 | 0.3723–0.3730 |
| | 8-350 Diesel | [11] | [12] | 151 @ 1.300 | 1 47/64 | 0.0010–0.0027 | 0.0015–0.0032 | 0.3425–0.3432 | 0.3420–0.3427 |
| | 8-403 Olds. | [11] | [12] | 187 @ 1.270 | 1 47/64 | 0.0010–0.0027 | 0.0015–0.0032 | 0.3425–0.3432 | 0.3420–0.3427 |

85843A13

## VALVE SPECIFICATIONS

| Year | Engine No. Cyl. Displacement (cu. in.) | Seat Angle (deg.) | Face Angle (deg.) | Spring Text Pressure ▲ (lbs. @ in.) | Spring Installed Height (in.) | Stem to Guide Clearance (in.) Intake | Exhaust | Stem Diameter (in.) Intake | Exhaust |
|---|---|---|---|---|---|---|---|---|---|
| 1979 | 6-231 Buick | 45 | 45 | 168 @ 1.340 | $1\frac{47}{64}$ | 0.0015–0.0035 | 0.0015–0.0032 | 0.3402–0.3412 | 0.3405–0.3412 |
| | 8-260 Olds. | [11] | [12] | 187 @ 1.270 | $1\frac{43}{64}$ | 0.0010–0.0027 | 0.0015–0.0032 | 0.3425–0.3432 | 0.3420–0.3427 |
| | 8-301 Pont. | 46 | 45 | 170 @ 1.290 | $1\frac{43}{64}$ | 0.0010–0.0027 | 0.0010–0.0027 | 0.3425 | 0.3425 |
| | 8-350 Olds. | [11] | [12] | 187 @ 1.270 | $1\frac{43}{64}$ | 0.0010–0.0027 | 0.0015–0.0032 | 0.3425–0.3432 | 0.3420–0.3427 |
| | 8-350 Diesel | [11] | [12] | 151 @ 1.300 | $1\frac{47}{64}$ | 0.0010–0.0027 | 0.0015–0.0032 | 0.3425–0.3432 | 0.3420–0.3427 |
| | 8-403 Olds. | [11] | [12] | 187 @ 1.270 | $1\frac{43}{64}$ | 0.0010–0.0027 | 0.0015–0.0032 | 0.3425–0.3432 | 0.3420–0.3427 |
| 1980 | 6-231 Buick | 45 | 45 | 168 @ 1.340 | $1\frac{47}{64}$ | 0.0015–0.0035 | 0.0015–0.0032 | 0.3402–0.3412 | 0.3405–0.3412 |
| | 8-260 Olds. | [11] | [12] | 187 @ 1.270 | $1\frac{43}{64}$ | 0.0010–0.0027 | 0.0015–0.0032 | 0.3425–0.3432 | 0.3420–0.3427 |
| | 8-265 Pont. | 46 | 45 | 170 @ 1.290 | $1\frac{43}{64}$ | 0.0010–0.0027 | 0.0010–0.0027 | 0.3425 | 0.3425 |
| | 8-307 Olds. | [11] | [12] | 187 @ 1.270 | $1\frac{43}{64}$ | 0.0010–0.0027 | 0.0015–0.0032 | 0.3429 | 0.3424 |
| | 8-350 Olds. | [11] | [12] | 187 @ 1.270 | $1\frac{43}{64}$ | 0.0010–0.0027 | 0.0015–0.0032 | 0.3425–0.3432 | 0.3420–0.3427 |
| | 8-350 Diesel | [11] | [12] | 151 @ 1.300 | $1\frac{47}{64}$ | 0.0010–0.0027 | 0.0015–0.0032 | 0.3425–0.3432 | 0.3420–0.3427 |
| **OLDSMOBILE** | | | | | | | | | |
| 1981 | 6-231 Buick | 45 | 45 | 182 @ 1.340 | $1\frac{47}{64}$ | 0.0015–0.0035 | 0.0015–0.0032 | 0.3407 | 0.3409 |
| | 6-252 Buick | 45 | 45 | 182 @ 1.340 | $1\frac{47}{64}$ | 0.0015–0.0035 | 0.0015–0.0032 | 0.3407 | 0.3409 |
| | 8-260 Olds. | [11] | [12] | 187 @ 1.270 | $1\frac{43}{64}$ | 0.0010–0.0027 | 0.0015–0.0032 | 0.3429 | 0.3424 |
| | 8-307 Olds. | [11] | [12] | 187 @ 1.270 | $1\frac{43}{64}$ | 0.0010–0.0027 | 0.0015–0.0032 | 0.3429 | 0.3424 |
| | 8-350 Diesel | [11] | [12] | 210 @ 1.220 | $1\frac{43}{64}$ | 0.0010–0.0027 | 0.0015–0.0032 | 0.3429 | 0.3424 |
| 1982 | 6-231 Buick | 45 | 45 | 182 @ 1.340 | $1\frac{47}{64}$ | 0.0015–0.0035 | 0.0015–0.0032 | 0.3407 | 0.3409 |
| | 6-252 Buick | 45 | 45 | 182 @ 1.340 | $1\frac{47}{64}$ | 0.0015–0.0035 | 0.0015–0.0032 | 0.3407 | 0.3409 |
| | 8-260 Olds. | [11] | [12] | 187 @ 1.270 | $1\frac{43}{64}$ | 0.0010–0.0027 | 0.0015–0.0032 | 0.3429 | 0.3424 |
| | 8-307 Olds. | [11] | [12] | 187 @ 1.270 | $1\frac{43}{64}$ | 0.0010–0.0027 | 0.0010–0.0032 | 0.3429 | 0.3429 |
| | 8-350 Diesel | [11] | [12] | 210 @ 1.22 | $1\frac{43}{64}$ | 0.0010–0.0027 | 0.0015–0.0032 | 0.3429 | 0.3429 |
| 1983 | 6-231 Buick | 45 | 45 | 182 @ 1.340 | $1\frac{47}{64}$ | 0.0015–0.0035 | 0.0015–0.0032 | 0.3407 | 0.3409 |
| | 6-252 Buick | 45 | 45 | 182 @ 1.340 | $1\frac{47}{64}$ | 0.0015–0.0035 | 0.0015–0.0032 | 0.3407 | 0.3409 |
| | 8-307 Olds. | [11] | [12] | 187 @ 1.270 | $1\frac{43}{64}$ | 0.0010–0.0027 | 0.0010–0.0032 | 0.3429 | 0.3429 |
| | 8-350 Diesel | [11] | [12] | 210 @ 1.22 | $1\frac{43}{64}$ | 0.0010–0.0027 | 0.0015–0.0032 | 0.3429 | 0.3429 |
| 1984 | 6-231 Buick | 46 | 45 | 164 @ 1.34 | $1\frac{47}{64}$ | 0.0015–0.0035 | 0.0015–0.0032 | 0.3401–0.3412 | 0.3405–0.3412 |
| | 8-307 Olds. | 45[2] | 45[2] | 187 @ 1.27 | $1\frac{43}{64}$ | 0.0010–0.0027 | 0.0015–0.0032 | 0.3425–0.3432 | 0.3420–0.3427 |
| | 8-350 Diesel | 45[2] | 45[2] | 210 @ 1.23 | $1\frac{43}{64}$ | 0.0010–0.0027 | 0.0015–0.0032 | 0.3424–0.3432 | 0.3420–0.3428 |
| 1985 | 8-307 Olds. | 45[2] | 45[2] | 187 @ 1.27 | $1\frac{43}{64}$ | 0.0010–0.0027 | 0.0015–0.0032 | 0.3425–0.3432 | 0.3420–0.3427 |
| | 8-350 Diesel | 45[2] | 45[2] | 210 @ 1.23 | $1\frac{43}{64}$ | 0.0010–0.0027 | 0.0015–0.0032 | 0.3424–0.3432 | 0.3420–0.3428 |
| 1986 | 8-307 Olds. | 45[2] | 44[2] | 187 @ 1.27 | $1\frac{43}{64}$ | 0.0010–0.0027 | 0.0015–0.0032 | 0.3425–0.3432 | 0.3420–0.3427 |
| 1987 | 8-307 Olds. | 46[2] | 45[2] | 187 @ 1.27 | $1\frac{43}{64}$ | 0.0010–0.0027 | 0.0015–0.0032 | 0.3425–0.3432 | 0.3420–0.3427 |
| 1988 | 8-307 Olds. | 45[2] | 44[2] | 187 @ 1.27 | $1\frac{43}{64}$ | 0.0010–0.0027 | 0.0015–0.0032 | 0.3425–0.3432 | 0.3420–0.3427 |
| 1989 | 8-307 Olds. | 45[2] | 44[2] | 187 @ 1.27 | $1\frac{43}{64}$ | 0.0010–0.0027 | 0.0015–0.0032 | 0.3425–0.3432 | 0.3420–0.3427 |
| 1990 | 8-307 Olds. | 45[2] | 44[2] | 187 @ 1.27 | $1\frac{43}{64}$ | 0.0010–0.0027 | 0.0015–0.0032 | 0.3425–0.3432 | 0.3420–0.3427 |
| **PONTIAC** | | | | | | | | | |
| 1975 | 8-400 2 bbl | 45 | 44 | 139 @ 1.17 | $1\frac{9}{16}$ | 0.0016–0.0033 | 0.0021–0.0038 | 0.3416 | 0.3411 |
| | 8-400 4 bbl | 45 | 44 | 143 @ 1.15 | $1\frac{19}{32}$ | 0.0016–0.0033 | 0.0021–0.0038 | 0.3416 | 0.3411 |
| | 8-455 4 bbl | 45 | 44 | 143 @ 1.15 | $1\frac{9}{16}$ | 0.0016–0.0033 | 0.0021–0.0038 | 0.3416 | 0.3411 |

85843A14

## VALVE SPECIFICATIONS

| Year | Engine No. Cyl. Displacement (cu. in.) | Seat Angle (deg.) | Face Angle (deg.) | Spring Text Pressure ▲ (lbs. @ in.) | Spring Installed Height (in.) | Stem to Guide Clearance (in.) Intake | Exhaust | Stem Diameter (in.) Intake | Exhaust |
|---|---|---|---|---|---|---|---|---|---|
| 1976 | 8-400 2 bbl | 30 | 29 | 134 @ 1.16 ⑨ | 1$^{19}$/$_{32}$ | 0.0016–0.0033 | 0.0021–0.0038 | 0.3416 | 0.3411 |
| | 8-400 4 bbl | 30 | 29 | 135 @ 1.13 ⑩ | 1$^9$/$_{16}$ | 0.0016–0.0033 | 0.0021–0.0038 | 0.3416 | 0.3411 |
| | 8-455 Pont. | 30 | 29 | 135 @ 1.16 | 1$^9$/$_{16}$ | 0.0016–0.0033 | 0.0021–0.0038 | 0.3416 | 0.3411 |
| 1977 | 6-231 Buick | 45 | 45 | 164 @ 1.34 | 1$^{47}$/$_{64}$ | 0.0015–0.0035 | 0.0015–0.0035 | 0.3400 | 0.3400 |
| | 8-301 Pont. | 46 | 45 | 170 @ 1.26 | 1$^{47}$/$_{64}$ | 0.0017–0.0020 | 0.0015–0.0020 | 0.3400 | 0.3400 |
| | 8-305 Chev. | 46 | 45 | 200 @ 1.160 | ④ | 0.0010–0.0037 | 0.0010–0.0037 | 0.3410–0.3417 | 0.3410–0.3417 |
| | 8-350 Olds. | 45 ⑪ | 44 ⑫ | 180 @ 1.34 | 1$^{47}$/$_{64}$ | 0.0010–0.0027 | 0.0015–0.0032 | 0.3425 | 0.3420 |
| | 8-350 Pont. | 30 | 29 | 131 @ 1.19 | 1$^{19}$/$_{32}$ | 0.0016–0.0033 | 0.0021–0.0038 | 0.3416 | 0.3411 |
| | 8-400 Pont. | 30 | 29 | 135 @ 1.18 | 1$^{27}$/$_{50}$ | 0.0016–0.0033 | 0.0021–0.0038 | 0.3425 | 0.3425 |
| | 8-403 Olds. | 45 ⑪ | 44 ⑫ | 180 @ 1.34 | 1$^{47}$/$_{64}$ | 0.0010–0.0027 | 0.0015–0.0032 | 0.3425 | 0.3420 |
| 1978 | 6-231 Buick | 45 | 45 | 182 @ 1.34 | 1$^{47}$/$_{64}$ | 0.0015–0.0032 | 0.0015–0.0032 | 0.3402–0.3412 | 0.3405–0.3412 |
| | 8-301 Pont. | 46 | 45 | 165 @ 1.29 | 1$^2$/$_3$ | 0.0010–0.0027 | 0.0010–0.0027 | 0.3425 | 0.3425 |
| | 8-350 Buick | 45 | 45 | 180 @ 1.34 | 1$^{47}$/$_{64}$ | 0.0015–0.0032 | 0.0015–0.0035 | 0.3720–0.3730 | 0.3723–0.3730 |
| | 8-350 Olds. | 45 ⑪ | 44 ⑫ | 190 @ 1.27 | 1$^{47}$/$_{64}$ | 0.0010–0.0027 | 0.0015–0.0032 | 0.3425–0.3432 | 0.3420–0.3427 |
| | 8-403 Olds. | 45 ⑪ | 46 ⑫ | 190 @ 1.27 | 1$^{47}$/$_{64}$ | 0.0010–0.0027 | 0.0015–0.0032 | 0.3425–0.3432 | 0.3420–0.3427 |
| **PONTIAC** | | | | | | | | | |
| 1979 | 6-231 Buick | 45 | 45 | 182 @ 1.340 | 1$^{23}$/$_{32}$ | 0.0015–0.0032 | 0.0015–0.0032 | 0.3402–0.3412 | 0.3405–0.3412 |
| | 8-301 Pont. | 46 | 45 | 170 @ 1.290 | 1$^{43}$/$_{64}$ | 0.0010–0.0027 | 0.0010–0.0027 | 0.3425 | 0.3425 |
| | 8-350 Olds. | 45 ② | 44 ② | 187 @ 1.270 | 1$^{47}$/$_{64}$ | 0.0010–0.0027 | 0.0015–0.0032 | 0.3425–0.3432 | 0.3420–0.3427 |
| | 8-350 Buick | 45 | 45 | ③ | 1$^{47}$/$_{64}$ | 0.0015–0.0035 | 0.0015–0.0032 | 0.3720–0.3730 | 0.3723–0.3730 |
| | 8-403 Olds. | 45 ② | 44 ② | 187 @ 1.27 | 1$^{47}$/$_{64}$ | 0.0010–0.0027 | 0.0015–0.0032 | 0.3425–0.3432 | 0.3420–0.3427 |
| 1980 | 6-231 Buick | 45 | 45 | 182 @ 1.340 | 1$^{23}$/$_{32}$ | 0.0015–0.0032 | 0.0015–0.0032 | 0.3402–0.3412 | 0.3405–0.3412 |
| | 8-265 Pont. | 46 | 45 | 170 @ 1.290 | 1$^{43}$/$_{64}$ | 0.0010–0.0027 | 0.0010–0.0027 | 0.3425 | 0.3425 |
| | 8-301 Pont. | 46 | 45 | 170 @ 1.290 | 1$^{43}$/$_{64}$ | 0.0010–0.0027 | 0.0010–0.0027 | 0.3425 | 0.3425 |
| | 8-350 Olds. | 45 ② | 44 ② | 187 @ 1.270 | 1$^{47}$/$_{64}$ | 0.0010–0.0027 | 0.0015–0.0032 | 0.3425–0.3432 | 0.3420–0.3427 |
| | 8-350 Buick | 45 | 45 | ③ | 1$^{47}$/$_{64}$ | 0.0015–0.0035 | 0.0015–0.0032 | 0.3720–0.3730 | 0.3723–0.3730 |
| | 8-350 Diesel | 45 ②⑨ | 44 ②⑨ | 151 @ 1.30 ⑥ | 1$^{47}$/$_{64}$ | 0.0010–0.0027 | 0.0015–0.0032 | 0.3425–0.3432 | 0.3420–0.3427 |
| 1981 | 6-231 Buick | 45 | 45 | 182 @ 1.340 ⑮ | 1$^{47}$/$_{64}$ | 0.0015–0.0035 | 0.0015–0.0032 | 0.3401–0.3412 | 0.3405–0.3412 |
| | 8-265 Pont. | 46 | 45 | 175 @ 1.290 | 1$^{43}$/$_{64}$ | 0.0010–0.0027 | 0.0010–0.0027 | 0.3418–0.3425 | 0.3418–0.3425 |
| | 8-307 Olds. | ⑪ | ⑨ | 187 @ 1.270 | 1$^{43}$/$_{64}$ | 0.0010–0.0027 | 0.0015–0.0032 | 0.3429 | 0.3424 |
| | 8-305 Chev. | 46 | 45 | 200 @ 1.25 | 1.70 | 0.0010–0.0027 | 0.0010–0.0027 | 0.3414 | 0.3414 |
| | 8-350 Buick | 45 | 45 | ③ | 1$^{47}$/$_{64}$ | 0.0015–0.0035 | 0.0015–0.0032 | 0.3720–0.3730 | 0.3723–0.3730 |
| | 8-350 Olds. Diesel | 45 ②⑨ | 44 ②⑨ | 210 @ 1.300 | 1$^{43}$/$_{64}$ | 0.0010–0.0027 | 0.0015–0.0032 | 0.3429 | 0.3424 |
| 1982 | 6-231 Buick | 45 | 45 | 182 @ 1.340 | 1$^{23}$/$_{32}$ | 0.0015–0.0032 | 0.0015–0.0032 | 0.3402–0.3412 | 0.3405–0.3412 |
| | 6-252 Buick | 45 | 45 | 182 @ 1.340 | 1$^{47}$/$_{64}$ | 0.0015–0.0032 | 0.0015–0.0032 | 0.3407 | 0.3407 |
| | 8-305 Chev. | 46 | 45 | 200 @ 1.25 | 1.70 | 0.0010–0.0027 | 0.0010–0.0027 | 0.3414 | 0.3414 |
| | 8-350 Diesel | 45 ②⑨ | 44 ②⑨ | 210 @ 1.300 | 1$^{43}$/$_{64}$ | 0.0010–0.0027 | 0.0015–0.0032 | 0.3429 | 0.3424 |
| 1983 | 6-231 Buick | 45 | 45 | 182 @ 1.340 | 1.72 | 0.0015–0.0032 | 0.0015–0.0032 | 0.3402–0.3412 | 0.3405–0.3412 |
| | 8-305 Chev. | 46 | 45 | 200 @ 1.25 | 1.70 | 0.0010–0.0027 | 0.0010–0.0027 | 0.3414 | 0.3414 |
| | 8-350 Diesel | 45 ②⑨ | 44 ②⑨ | 210 @ 1.22 | 1$^{43}$/$_{64}$ | 0.0010–0.0027 | 0.0015–0.0032 | 0.3429 | 0.3429 |

85843A15

## VALVE SPECIFICATIONS

| Year | Engine No. Cyl. Displacement (cu. in.) | Seat Angle (deg.) | Face Angle (deg.) | Spring Text Pressure ▲ (lbs. @ in.) | Spring Installed Height (in.) | Stem to Guide Clearance (in.) | | Stem Diameter (in.) | |
|---|---|---|---|---|---|---|---|---|---|
| | | | | | | Intake | Exhaust | Intake | Exhaust |
| **1984** | 6-231 Buick | 46 | 45 | 182 @ 1.340 | 1⁴⁷/₆₄ | 0.0015–0.0035 | 0.0015–0.0032 | 0.3401–0.3412 | 0.3405–0.3412 |
| | 8-305 Chev. | 46 | 45 | 200 @ 1.25 | 1⁴⁵/₆₄ | 0.0010–0.0027 | 0.0010–0.0027 | — | — |
| | 8-350 Diesel | 45② | 44② | 210 @ 1.22 | 1⁴³/₆₄ | 0.0010–0.0027 | 0.0015–0.0032 | 0.3424–0.3432 | 0.3420–0.3428 |
| **1985** | 6-231 Buick | 46 | 45 | 182 @ 1.340 | 1⁴⁷/₆₄ | 0.0015–0.0035 | 0.0015–0.0032 | 0.3401–0.3412 | 0.3405–0.3412 |
| | 6-262 Chev. | 46 | 45 | 200 @ 1.25 | 1.70 | 0.0010–0.0027 | 0.0010–0.0027 | 0.3414 | 0.3414 |
| | 8-305 Chev. | 46 | 45 | 200 @ 1.25 | 1⁴⁵/₆₄ | 0.0010–0.0027 | 0.0010–0.0027 | — | — |
| | 8-350 Diesel | 45② | 44② | 210 @ 1.22 | 1⁴³/₆₄ | 0.0010–0.0027 | 0.0015–0.0032 | 0.3424–0.3432 | 0.3420–0.3428 |
| **1986** | 6-231 Buick | 46 | 45 | 182 @ 1.340 | 1⁴⁶/₆₄ | 0.0010–0.0027 | 0.0010–0.0027 | 0.3462–0.3412 | 0.3405–0.3412 |
| | 6-262 Chev. | 46 | 45 | 200 @ 1.25 | 1.70 | 0.0010–0.0027 | 0.0010–0.0027 | 0.3414 | 0.3414 |
| **1987** | 8-307 Olds. | ② | 44② | 187 @ 1.27 | 1⁴³/₆₄ | 0.0010–0.0027 | 0.0015–0.0032 | 0.3425–0.3432 | 0.3420–0.3426 |
| **1988** | 8-307 Olds. | 45② | 44② | 187 @ 1.27 | 1⁴³/₆₄ | 0.0010–0.0027 | 0.0015–0.0032 | 0.3425–0.3432 | 0.3420–0.3426 |
| **1989** | 8-307 Olds. | 45② | 44② | 76–84 @ 1.670 | 1⁴³/₆₄ | 0.0010–0.0027 | 0.0015–0.0032 | 0.3425–0.3432 | 0.3420–0.3426 |

▲ Spring test pressure with valve open
NA—Not available
① Exhaust—175 @ 1.34
② Exhaust valve seat angle—31, exhaust valve face angle—30

③ Intake: 180 @ 1.340
   Exhaust: 177 @ 1.450
④ Intake: 1²³/₃₂
   Exhaust: 1¹⁹/₃₂
⑤ Exhaust: 182 @ 1.34
⑥ 1981 210 @ 1.23

⑦ Intake—45°, exhaust—59°
⑧ Intake—56°, exhaust—60°
⑨ 1981 Seat: Intake—45°, exhaust—59°
   Face: Intake—46°, exhaust—60°
⑩ Exhaust: 140 @ 1.12
⑪ Intake—45°, exhaust 31°

⑫ Intake—44°, exhaust 30°
⑬ Intake—30°, exhaust 45°
⑭ Intake—29°, exhaust 44°
⑮ Intake—: 164 @ 1.34
⑯ Exhaust—59°, 60°
⑰ Exhaust—31°, 30°

8584301a

## CAMSHAFT SPECIFICATIONS

All measurements given in inches.

| Year | VIN | No. Cylinder Displacement cu. in. (liters) | Journal Diameter | | | | | Lobe Lift | | Bearing Clearance | Camshaft End Play |
|---|---|---|---|---|---|---|---|---|---|---|---|
| | | | 1 | 2 | 3 | 4 | 5 | In. | Ex. | | |
| 1981 | A | 6-231 (3.8) | 1.785–1.786 | 1.785–1.786 | 1.785–1.786 | 1.785–1.786 | 1.785–1.786 | NA | NA | ① | NA |
| | 4 | 6-252 (4.1) | 1.785–1.786 | 1.785–1.786 | 1.785–1.786 | 1.785–1.786 | 1.785–1.786 | NA | NA | ① | NA |
| | F | 8-260 (4.3) | 2.036 | 2.016 | 1.9961 | 1.9761 | 1.9561 | 0.396 | 0.400 | 0.0039 | 0.011–0.077 |
| | S | 6-265 (4.3) | NA | NA | NA | NA | NA | NA | NA | NA | NA |
| | J | 8-267 (4.3) | 1.868–1.869 | 1.868–1.869 | 1.868–1.869 | 1.868–1.869 | 1.868–1.869 | 0.357 | 0.340 | NA | 0.004–0.012 |
| | W | 8-301 (4.8) | NA | NA | NA | NA | NA | NA | NA | NA | NA |
| | H | 8-305 (5.0) | 1.868–1.869 | 1.868–1.869 | 1.868–1.869 | 1.868–1.869 | 1.868–1.869 | 0.2484 | 0.2667 | NA | 0.004–0.012 |
| | Y | 8-307 (5.0) | 2.035–2.036 | 2.015–2.016 | 1.995–1.996 | 1.975–1.976 | 1.955–1.956 | 0.400 | 0.400 | 0.0020–0.0058 | 0.011–0.077 |
| | X | 8-350 (5.7) | NA | NA | NA | NA | NA | NA | NA | NA | NA |
| | N | 8-350 (5.7) | 2.035–2.036 | 2.015–2.016 | 1.995–1.996 | 1.975–1.976 | 1.955–1.956 | NA | NA | NA | 0.011–0.077 |
| 1982 | A | 6-231 (3.8) | 1.785 | 1.785 | 1.785 | 1.785 | — | NA | NA | 0.0005–0.0035 ① | NA |
| | 4 | 6-252 (4.1) | 1.785 | 1.785 | 1.785 | 1.785 | — | NA | NA | 0.0005–0.0035 ① | NA |
| | F | 8-260 (4.3) | 2.0361 | 2.0161 | 1.9961 | 1.9761 | 1.9561 | 0.396 | 0.400 | 0.0039 | 0.011–0.077 |
| | H | 8-305 (5.0) | 1.8682–1.8692 | 1.8682–1.8692 | 1.8682–1.8692 | 1.8682–1.8692 | 1.8682–1.8692 | 0.234 | 0.257 | NA | 0.004–0.012 |
| | Y | 8-307 (5.0) | 2.0365 | 2.0166 | 1.9965 | 1.9765 | 1.9565 | 0.400 | 0.400 | 0.0020–0.0058 | 0.011–0.077 |
| | N | 8-350 (5.7) | 2.0361 | 2.0161 | 1.9961 | 1.9761 | 1.9561 | NA | NA | 0.0039 | 0.011–0.077 |
| 1983 | A | 6-231 (3.8) | 1.785 | 1.785 | 1.785 | 1.785 | — | NA | NA | 0.0005–0.0035 ① | NA |
| | H | 8-305 (5.0) | 1.8682–1.8692 | 1.8682–1.8692 | 1.8682–1.8692 | 1.8682–1.8692 | 1.8682–1.8692 | 0.234 | 0.257 | NA | 0.004–0.012 |
| | Y | 8-307 (5.0) | 2.0365 | 2.0166 | 1.9965 | 1.9765 | 1.9565 | 0.400 | 0.400 | 0.0020–0.0058 | 0.011–0.077 |
| | N | 8-350 (5.7) | 2.0361 | 2.0161 | 1.9961 | 1.9761 | 1.9561 | NA | NA | 0.0039 | 0.011–0.077 |

85843A16

## CAMSHAFT SPECIFICATIONS

All measurements given in inches.

| Year | VIN | No. Cylinder Displacement cu. in. (liters) | Journal Diameter | | | | | Lobe Lift | | Bearing Clearance | Camshaft End Play |
|---|---|---|---|---|---|---|---|---|---|---|---|
| | | | 1 | 2 | 3 | 4 | 5 | In. | Ex. | | |
| 1984 | A | 6-231 (3.8) | 1.785 | 1.785 | 1.785 | 1.785 | — | NA | NA | 0.0005–0.0035 ① | NA |
| | 4 | 6-252 (4.1) | 1.785 | 1.785 | 1.785 | 1.785 | — | NA | NA | 0.0005–0.0035 ① | NA |
| | H | 8-305 (5.0) | 1.8682–1.8692 | 1.8682–1.8692 | 1.8682–1.8692 | 1.8682–1.8692 | 1.8682–1.8692 | 0.234 | 0.257 | NA | 0.004–0.012 |
| | Y | 8-307 (5.0) | 2.0361 | 2.0161 | 1.9961 | 1.9761 | 1.9561 | 0.400 | 0.400 | 0.0020–0.0058 | 0.011–0.077 |
| | N | 8-350 (5.7) | 2.0361 | 2.0161 | 1.9961 | 1.9761 | 1.9561 | NA | NA | 0.0039 | 0.011–0.077 |
| 1985 | A | 6-231 (3.8) | 1.785 | 1.785 | 1.785 | 1.785 | — | NA | NA | 0.0005–0.0035 ① | NA |
| | Z | 6-262 (4.3) | 1.8682–1.8692 | 1.8682–1.8692 | 1.8682–1.8692 | 1.8682–1.8692 | 1.8682–1.8692 | 0.234 | 0.257 | NA | 0.004–0.012 |
| | H | 8-305 (5.0) | 1.8682–1.8692 | 1.8682–1.8692 | 1.8682–1.8692 | 1.8682–1.8692 | 1.8682–1.8692 | 0.234 | 0.257 | NA | 0.004–0.012 |
| 1985 | Y | 8-307 (5.7) | 2.0365 | 2.0166 | 1.9965 | 1.9765 | 1.9565 | 0.247 | 0.251 | 0.0020–0.0058 | 0.006–0.022 |
| | 4 | 6-252 (4.1) | 1.785 | 1.785 | 1.785 | 1.785 | — | NA | NA | 0.0005–0.0035 ① | NA |
| | N | 8-350 (5.7) | 2.0361 | 2.0161 | 1.9961 | 1.9761 | 1.9561 | NA | NA | 0.0039 | 0.011–0.077 |
| 1986 | A | 6-231 (3.8) | 1.785 | 1.785 | 1.785 | 1.785 | — | NA | NA | 0.0005–0.0035 | NA |
| | Z | 6-262 (4.3) | 1.8682–1.8692 | 1.8682–1.8692 | 1.8682–1.8692 | 1.8682–1.8692 | 1.8682–1.8692 | 0.234 | 0.257 | NA | 0.004–0.012 |
| | H | 8-305 (5.0) | 1.8682–1.8692 | 1.8682–1.8692 | 1.8682–1.8692 | 1.8682–1.8692 | 1.8682–1.8692 | 0.234 | 0.257 | NA | 0.004–0.012 |
| | Y | 8-307 (5.0) | 2.0365 | 2.0166 | 1.9965 | 1.9765 | 1.9565 | 0.247 | 0.251 | 0.0020–0.0058 | 0.006–0.022 |
| 1987 | A | 6-231 (3.8) | 1.785 | 1.785 | 1.785 | 1.785 | — | NA | NA | 0.0005–0.0035 ① | NA |
| | Y | 8-307 (5.0) | 2.0365 | 2.0166 | 1.9965 | 1.9765 | 1.9565 | 0.247 | 0.251 | 0.0020–0.0058 | 0.006–0.022 |
| 1988 | Y | 8-307 (5.0) | 2.0365 | 2.0166 | 1.9965 | 1.9765 | 1.9565 | 0.247 | 0.251 | 0.0020–0.0058 | 0.006–0.022 |
| 1989 | Y | 8-307 (5.0) | 2.0365 | 2.0166 | 1.9965 | 1.9765 | 1.9565 | 0.247 | 0.251 | 0.0020–0.0058 | 0.006–0.022 |
| 1990 | Y | 8-307 (5.0) | 2.0365 | 2.0166 | 1.9965 | 1.9765 | 1.9565 | 0.247 | 0.251 | 0.0020–0.0058 | 0.006–0.022 |

NA—Not available at time of publication
① No. 1: 0.0005–0.0025
  No. 2, 3, 4: 0.0005–0.0035

85843A17

## CRANKSHAFT AND CONNECTING ROD SPECIFICATIONS

| Year | Engine Displacement (cu in.) | Crankshaft | | | | Connecting Rod | | |
|---|---|---|---|---|---|---|---|---|
| | | Main Brg. Journal Dia. | Main Brg. Oil Clearance | Shaft End-Play | Thrust on No. | Journal Diameter | Oil Clearance | Side Clearance |
| | | | | BUICK | | | | |
| 1975 | 8-350 | 2.9995 | 0.0004–0.0015 | 0.002–0.006 | 3 | 1.9995 | 0.0005–0.0026 | 0.006–0.026 |
| | 8-455 | 3.2500 | 0.0007–0.0018 | 0.003–0.009 | 3 | 2.2491 | 0.0005–0.0026 | 0.005–0.025 |
| 1976 | 8-350 | 2.9995 | 0.0004–0.0015 | 0.002–0.006 | 3 | 1.9995 | 0.0005–0.0026 | 0.006–0.026 |
| | 8-455 | 3.2500 | 0.0007–0.0018 | 0.003–0.009 | 3 | 2.2491 | 0.0005–0.0026 | 0.005–0.025 |
| 1977 | 6-231 Buick | 2.4995 | 0.0004–0.0015 | 0.004–0.008 | 2 | 2.000 | 0.0005–0.0026 | 0.006–0.027 |
| | 8-301 Pont. | 3.0000 | 0.0004–0.0020 | 0.003–0.009 | 4 | 2.000 | 0.0005–0.0025 | 0.006–0.027 |
| | 8-350 Buick | 2.9995 | 0.0004–0.0015 | 0.002–0.006 | 3 | 1.9995 | 0.0005–0.0026 | 0.006–0.026 |
| | 8-350 Olds. | 2.4990 | 0.0005–0.0021 ① | 0.004–0.014 | 3 | 2.1243 | 0.0004–0.0015 | 0.006–0.027 |
| | 8-403 Olds. | 2.4990 | 0.0005–0.0021 ① | 0.004–0.014 | 3 | 2.1243 | 0.0005–0.0026 | 0.006–0.020 |
| 1978 | 6-231 Buick | 2.4995 | 0.0003–0.0017 | 0.004–0.008 | 2 | 2.2487–2.2495 | 0.0005–0.0026 | 0.006–0.027 |
| | 8-301 Pont. | 3.0000 | 0.0004–0.0020 | 0.006–0.022 | 4 | 2.2500 | 0.0005–0.0025 | 0.006–0.022 |
| | 8-305 Chev. | ③ | 0.0010–0.0035 ⑤ | 0.002–0.006 | 5 | 2.0990–2.1000 | 0.0010–0.0035 | 0.008–0.014 |
| | 8-350 Buick | 3.0000 | 0.0004–0.0015 | 0.003–0.009 | 3 | 1.9910–2.0000 | 0.0005–0.0026 | 0.006–0.027 |
| | 8-350 Chev. | ③ | 0.0010–0.0035 ⑤ | 0.002–0.006 | 5 | 2.0990–2.1000 | 0.0010–0.0035 | 0.008–0.014 |
| | 8-350 Olds. | 2.4985–2.4995 ② | 0.0005–0.0021 ① | 0.0035–0.0135 | 3 | 2.1238–2.1248 | 0.0004–0.0033 | 0.006–0.020 |
| | 8-400 Pont. | 3.0000 | 0.0002–0.0020 | 0.003–0.009 | 4 | 2.2500 | 0.0005–0.0025 | 0.006–0.022 |
| | 8-403 Olds. | 2.4985–2.4995 ② | 0.0005–0.0021 ① | 0.0035–0.0135 | 3 | 2.1238–2.1248 | 0.0004–0.0033 | 0.006–0.020 |
| 1979 | 6-231 Buick | 2.4995 | 0.0003–0.0018 | 0.003–0.009 | 2 | 2.2487–2.2498 | 0.0005–0.0026 | 0.006–0.023 |
| | 8-301 Pont. | 3.000 | 0.0004–0.0020 | 0.006–0.022 | 4 | 2.2500 | 0.0005–0.0025 | 0.006–0.022 |
| | 8-350 Buick | 3.0000 | 0.0004–0.0015 | 0.003–0.009 | 3 | 1.9910–2.0000 | 0.0005–0.0026 | 0.006–0.023 |
| | 8-350 Olds. | 2.4985–2.4995 ② | 0.0005–0.0021 ① | 0.0035–0.0135 | 3 | 2.1238–2.1248 | 0.0004–0.0033 | 0.006–0.020 |
| | 8-403 Olds. | 2.4985–2.4995 | 0.0005–0.0021 ① | 0.0035–0.0135 | 3 | 2.1238–2.1248 | 0.0005–0.0033 | 0.006–0.020 |
| 1980 | 6-231 Buick | 2.4995 | 0.0003–0.0018 | 0.003–0.009 | 2 | 2.2487–2.2498 | 0.0005–0.0026 | 0.006–0.023 |
| | 6-252 Buick | 2.4995 | 0.0003–0.0018 | 0.003–0.009 | 2 | 2.2487–2.2495 | 0.0005–0.0026 | 0.006–0.023 |
| | 8-301 Pont. | 3.0000 | 0.0004–0.0020 | 0.006–0.022 | 4 | 2.2500 | 0.0005–0.0025 | 0.006–0.022 |
| | 8-350 Buick | 3.0000 | 0.0004–0.0015 | 0.003–0.009 | 3 | 1.9910–2.0000 | 0.0005–0.0026 | 0.006–0.023 |
| | 8-350 Olds. | 2.4985–2.4995 ② | 0.0005–0.0021 ① | 0.0035–0.0135 | 3 | 2.1238–2.1248 | 0.0004–0.0033 | 0.006–0.020 |
| | 8-350 Olds. Diesel | 2.9993–3.003 | 0.0005–0.0021 ① | 0.0035–0.0135 | 3 | 2.2495–2.2500 | 0.0005–0.0026 | 0.006–0.020 |
| 1981 | 6-231 Buick | 2.4995 | 0.0003–0.0018 | 0.003–0.009 | 2 | 2.2487–2.2498 | 0.0005–0.0026 | 0.006–0.023 |
| | 6-252 Buick | 2.4995 | 0.0003–0.0018 | 0.003–0.009 | 2 | 2.2487–2.2495 | 0.0005–0.0026 | 0.006–0.023 |
| | 8-267 Chev. | 2.4484–2.4493 ⑰ | 0.0008–0.0020 ⑱ | 0.002–0.006 | 5 | 2.0986–2.0998 | 0.0013–0.0035 | 0.006–0.014 |
| | 8-301 Pont. | 3.0000 | 0.0004–0.0020 | 0.006–0.022 | 4 | 2.2500 | 0.0005–0.0025 | 0.006–0.022 |
| | 8-307 Olds. | 2.4973–2.4998 ⑥ | 0.0005–0.0021 ① | 0.0035–0.0135 | 3 | 2.1238–2.1248 | 0.0004–0.0033 | 0.006–0.020 |
| | 8-350 Olds. Diesel | 2.9993–3.003 | 0.0005–0.0021 ① | 0.0035–0.0135 | 3 | 2.2495–2.2500 | 0.0005–0.0026 | 0.006–0.020 |
| 1982 | 6-231 Buick | 2.4995 | 0.0003–0.0018 | 0.003–0.009 | 2 | 2.2487–2.2495 | 0.0005–0.0026 | 0.006–0.023 |
| | 6-252 Buick | 2.4995 | 0.0003–0.0018 | 0.003–0.009 | 2 | 2.2487–2.2495 | 0.0005–0.0026 | 0.006–0.023 |
| | 8-307 Olds. | 2.4973–2.4998 ⑥ | 0.0005–0.0021 ① | 0.0035–0.0135 | 3 | 2.1238–2.1248 | 0.0004–0.0033 | 0.006–0.020 |
| | 8-350 Olds. Diesel | 2.9993–3.003 | 0.0005–0.0021 ① | 0.0035–0.0135 | 3 | 2.2495–2.2500 | 0.0005–0.0026 | 0.006–0.020 |

85843C18

## CRANKSHAFT AND CONNECTING ROD SPECIFICATIONS

| Year | Engine Displacement (cu in.) | Crankshaft Main Brg. Journal Dia. | Main Brg. Oil Clearance | Shaft End-Play | Thrust on No. | Connecting Rod Journal Diameter | Oil Clearance | Side Clearance |
|---|---|---|---|---|---|---|---|---|
| 1983 | 6-231 Buick | 2.4995 | 0.0003–0.0018 | 0.003–0.009 | 2 | 2.2487–2.2495 | 0.0005–0.0026 | 0.006–0.023 |
| | 6-252 Buick | 2.4995 | 0.0003–0.0018 | 0.003–0.009 | 2 | 2.2487–2.2495 | 0.0005–0.0026 | 0.006–0.023 |
| | 8-307 Olds. | 2.4973–2.4998 ⑥ | 0.0005–0.0021 ① | 0.0035–0.0135 | 3 | 2.1238–2.1248 | 0.0004–0.0033 | 0.006–0.020 |
| | 8-350 Olds. Diesel | 2.9993–3.003 | 0.0005–0.0021 ① | 0.0035–0.0135 | 3 | 2.2495–2.2500 | 0.0005–0.0026 | 0.006–0.020 |
| 1984 | 6-231 Buick | 2.4995 | 0.0003–0.0018 | 0.003–0.009 | 2 | 2.2487–2.2495 | 0.0005–0.0026 | 0.006–0.020 |
| | 6-252 Buick | 2.4995 | 0.0003–0.0018 | 0.003–0.009 | 2 | 2.2487–2.2495 | 0.0005–0.0026 | 0.005–0.026 |
| | 8-307 Olds. | 2.4990–2.4995 ⑫ | 0.0015–0.0021 ⑧ | 0.0035–0.0135 | 3 | 2.1238–2.1248 | 0.0004–0.0033 | 0.006–0.020 |
| | 8-350 Olds. Diesel | 2.9993–3.0003 | 0.0021–0.005 ① | 0.0035–0.0135 | 3 | 2.1238–2.1248 | 0.0005–0.0025 | 0.006–0.020 |
| 1985 | 6-231 Buick | 2.4995–2.5000 | 0.0003–0.0018 | 0.003–0.009 | 2 | 2.2487–2.2495 | 0.0005–0.0026 | 0.006–0.023 |
| | 6-252 Buick | 2.4955 | 0.0003–0.0018 | 0.003–0.009 | 2 | 2.2487–2.2495 | 0.0005–0.0026 | 0.006–0.023 |
| | 8-307 Olds | 2.4985–2.4995 ⑬ | 0.0005–0.0021 ⑧ | 0.0035–0.0135 | 3 | 2.1238–2.1248 | 0.0004–0.0033 | 0.006–0.020 |
| | 8-350 Diesel | 2.9993–3.0003 | 0.0005–0.0021 ⑧ | 0.0035–0.0135 | 3 | 2.1238–2.1248 | 0.0005–0.0026 | 0.006–0.020 |
| 1986 | 6-231 Buick | 2.4995 | 0.0003–0.0018 | 0.003–0.009 | 2 | 2.2487–2.2495 | 0.0005–0.0026 | 0.004–0.015 |
| | 8-307 Olds. | 2.4985–2.4995 ⑬ | 0.0005–0.0021 ⑧ | 0.035–0.0135 | 3 | 2.1238–2.1248 | 0.0004–0.0033 | 0.006–0.020 |
| 1987 | 6-231 Buick | 2.4995 | 0.0003–0.0018 | 0.003–0.009 | 2 | 2.2487–2.2495 | 0.0005–0.0026 | 0.004–0.015 |
| | 8-307 Olds. | 2.4985–2.4995 ⑬ | 0.0005–0.0021 ⑧ | 0.0035–0.0135 | 3 | 2.1238–2.1248 | 0.0004–0.0033 | 0.006–0.020 |
| 1988 | 8-307 Olds. | 2.4985–2.4995 ⑬ | 0.0005–0.0021 ⑧ | 0.0035–0.0135 | 3 | 2.1238–2.1248 | 0.0004–0.0033 | 0.006–0.020 |
| 1989 | 8-307 Olds. | 2.4985–2.4995 ⑬ | 0.0005–0.0021 ⑧ | 0.0035–0.0135 | 3 | 2.1238–2.1248 | 0.0004–0.0033 | 0.006–0.020 |
| 1990 | 8-307 Olds. | 2.4985–2.4995 ⑬ | 0.0005–0.0021 ⑧ | 0.0035–0.0135 | 3 | 2.1238–2.1248 | 0.0004–0.0033 | 0.006–0.020 |
| | | | **OLDSMOBILE** | | | | | |
| 1975 | 8-350 Olds. | 2.4990 ⑦ | 0.0005–0.0021 ⑧ | 0.004–0.008 | 3 | 2.1238–2.1248 | 0.0004–0.0033 | 0.006–0.020 |
| | 8-400 Olds. | 3.000 | 0.0002–0.0017 | 0.0035–0.0085 | 4 | 2.250 | 0.0005–0.0026 | 0.012–0.017 |
| | 8-455 Olds. | 2.9998 | 0.0005–0.0021 ⑨ | 0.004–0.008 | 3 | 2.4988–2.4998 | 0.0004–0.0033 | 0.006–0.020 |
| 1976 | 8-350 Olds. | 2.4990 ⑦ | 0.0005–0.0021 ⑧ | 0.004–0.008 | 3 | 2.1238–2.1248 | 0.0004–0.0033 | 0.006–0.020 |
| | 8 455 Olds. | 2.9998 | 0.0005–0.0021 ⑦ | 0.004–0.008 | 3 | 2.4988–2.4998 | 0.0004–0.0033 | 0.006–0.020 |
| 1977 | 6-231 Buick | 2.4998 | 0.0004–0.0015 | 0.004–0.008 | 2 | 1.9960 | 0.0005 | 0.006–0.027 |
| | 8-260 Olds. | 2.4990 ⑦ | 0.0005–0.0021 | 0.004–0.014 | 3 | 2.21243 | 0.0004–0.0033 | 0.006–0.020 |
| | 8-350 Chev. | ⑥ | 0.0035 max ⑤ | 0.002–0.006 | 3 | 2.1995 | 0.0035 max | 0.008–0.014 |
| | 8-350 Olds. | 2.4990 ⑦ | 0.0005–0.0021 | 0.004–0.014 | 3 | 2.21243 | 0.0004–0.0033 | 0.006–0.020 |
| | 8-403O Olds | 2.4985–2.4995 ② | 0.0005–0.0021 ⑧ | 0.0035–0.0135 | 3 | 2.1238–2.1248 | 0.0004–0.0033 | 0.006–0.020 |
| 1978 | 6-231 Buick | 2.4995 | 0.0003–0.0017 | 0.004–0.008 | 2 | 2.487–2.495 | 0.0005–0.0026 | 0.006–0.027 |
| | 8-260 Olds. | 2.4985–2.4995 ② | 0.0005–0.0021 ⑧ | 0.0035–0.0135 | 3 | 2.1238–2.1248 | 0.0004–0.0033 | 0.006–0.020 |
| | 8-350 Olds. | 2.4985–2.4995 ② | 0.0005–0.0021 ⑧ | 0.0035–0.0135 | 3 | 2.1238–2.1248 | 0.0004–0.0033 | 0.006–0.020 |
| | 8-350 Buick | 3.0000 | 0.0004–0.0015 | 0.003–0.009 | 3 | 1.9910–2.0000 | 0.0005–0.0026 | 0.006–0.027 |
| | 8-350 Diesel | 2.9993–3.0003 | 0.0005–0.0021 ⑧ | 0.0035–0.0135 | 3 | 2.1238–2.1248 | 0.0005–0.0026 | 0.006–0.020 |
| | 8-403 Olds. | 2.4985–2.4995 ② | 0.0005–0.0021 ⑧ | 0.0035–0.0135 | 3 | 2.1238–2.1248 | 0.0004–0.0033 | 0.006–0.020 |

85843019

## CRANKSHAFT AND CONNECTING ROD SPECIFICATIONS

| Year | Engine Displacement (cu in.) | Crankshaft Main Brg. Journal Dia. | Crankshaft Main Brg. Oil Clearance | Crankshaft Shaft End-Play | Thrust on No. | Connecting Rod Journal Diameter | Connecting Rod Oil Clearance | Connecting Rod Side Clearance |
|---|---|---|---|---|---|---|---|---|
| 1979 | 6-231 Buick | 2.4995 | 0.0003–0.0018 | 0.004–0.008 | 2 | 2.487–2.2495 | 0.0005–0.0026 | 0.006–0.027 |
| | 8-260 Olds. | 2.4985–2.4995② | 0.0005–0.0021⑧ | 0.0035–0.0135 | 3 | 2.1238–2.1248 | 0.0004–0.0033 | 0.006–0.020 |
| | 8-301 Pont. | 3.000 | 0.0002–0.0020 | 0.003–0.009 | 4 | 2.250⑩ | 0.0005–0.0025 | 0.006–0.022 |
| | 8-350 Olds. | 2.4985–2.4995② | 0.0005–0.0021⑧ | 0.0035–0.0135 | 3 | 2.1238–2.1248 | 0.0004–0.0033 | 0.006–0.020 |
| | 8-350 Diesel | 2.9993–3.0003 | 0.0005–0.0021⑧ | 0.0035–0.0135 | 3 | 2.1238–2.1248 | 0.0005–0.0026 | 0.006–0.020 |
| | 8-403 Olds. | 2.4985–2.4995② | 0.0005–0.0021⑧ | 0.0035–0.0135 | 3 | 2.1238–2.1248 | 0.0004–0.0033 | 0.006–0.020 |
| 1980 | 6-231 Buick | 2.4995 | 0.0003–0.0018 | 0.004–0.008 | 2 | 2.2487–2.2495 | 0.0005–0.0026 | 0.006–0.027 |
| | 8-260 Olds. | 2.4985–2.4995② | 0.0005–0.0021⑧ | 0.0035–0.0135 | 3 | 2.1238–2.1248 | 0.0004–0.0033 | 0.006–0.020 |
| | 8-265 Pont. | 3.000 | 0.0004–0.0020 | 0.006–0.022 | 4 | 2.000 | 0.0005–0.0025 | 0.006–0.022 |
| | 8-307 Olds. | 2.4985–2.4995② | 0.0005–0.0021⑧ | 0.0035–0.0135 | 3 | 2.1238–2.1248 | 0.0004–0.0033 | 0.006–0.020 |
| | 8-350 Olds. | 2.4985–2.4995② | 0.0005–0.0021⑧ | 0.0035–0.0135 | 3 | 2.1238–2.1248 | 0.0004–0.0033 | 0.006–0.020 |
| | 8-350 Diesel | 2.9993–3.0003 | 0.0005–0.0021⑧ | 0.0035–0.0135 | 3 | 2.1238–2.1248 | 0.0005–0.0026 | 0.006–0.020 |
| 1981 | 6-231 Buick | 2.4995 | 0.0003–0.0018 | 0.011–0.003 | 2 | 2.487–2.2495 | 0.0005–0.0026 | 0.006–0.023 |
| | 6-252 Buick | 2.4955 | 0.0003–0.0018 | 0.011–0.003 | 2 | 2.487–2.2495 | 0.0005–0.0026 | 0.006–0.023 |
| | 8-260 Olds. | 2.5000 | 0.0005–0.0021⑧ | 0.0035–0.0135 | 3 | 2.1238–2.1248 | 0.0004–0.0033 | 0.006–0.020 |
| | 8-307 Olds. | 2.4990–2.4995 | 0.0005–0.0021⑧ | 0.0035–0.0135 | 3 | 2.1238–2.1248 | 0.0004–0.0033 | 0.006–0.020 |
| | 8-350 Diesel | 2.9993–3.0003 | 0.0005–0.0021⑧ | 0.0035–0.0135 | 3 | 2.24995–2.500 | 0.0005–0.0026 | 0.006–0.020 |
| 1982 | 6-231 Buick | 2.4995 | 0.0003–0.0018 | 0.011–0.003 | 2 | 2.2487–2.2495 | 0.0005–0.0026 | 0.006–0.023 |
| | 6-252 Buick | 2.4955 | 0.0003–0.0018 | 0.011–0.003 | 2 | 2.2487–2.2495 | 0.0005–0.0026 | 0.006–0.023 |
| | 8-260 Olds. | 2.5000 | 0.0005–0.0021⑧ | 0.0035–0.0135 | 3 | 2.1238–2.1248 | 0.0003–0.0033 | 0.006–0.020 |
| | 8-307 Olds. | 2.4990–2.4995 | 0.0005–0.0021⑧ | 0.0035–0.0135 | 3 | 2.2138–2.1248 | 0.0003–0.0033 | 0.006–0.020 |
| | 8-350 Diesel | 2.9993–3.0003 | 0.0005–0.0021⑧ | 0.0035–0.0135 | 3 | 2.24995–2.500 | 0.0005–0.0026 | 0.006–0.020 |
| 1983 | 6-231 Buick | 2.4995 | 0.0003–0.0018 | 0.011–0.003 | 2 | 2.2487–2.2495 | 0.0005–0.0026 | 0.006–0.023 |
| | 6-252 Buick | 2.4955 | 0.0003–0.0018 | 0.011–0.003 | 2 | 2.2487–2.2495 | 0.0005–0.0026 | 0.006–0.023 |
| | 8-307 Olds. | 2.4990–2.4995 | 0.0005–0.0021⑧ | 0.0035–0.0135 | 3 | 2.1238–2.1248 | 0.0004–0.0033 | 0.006–0.020 |
| | 8-350 Diesel | 2.9993–3.0003 | 0.0005–0.0021⑧ | 0.0035–0.0135 | 3 | 2.2495–2.5000 | 0.0005–0.0026 | 0.006–0.020 |
| 1984 | 6-231 Buick | 2.4995 | 0.0003–0.0018 | 0.003–0.009 | 2 | 2.2487–2.2495 | 0.0005–0.0026 | 0.005–0.026 |
| | 8-307 Olds. | 2.4990–2.4995⑫ | 0.0015–0.0021⑧ | 0.0035–0.0135 | 3 | 2.1238–2.1248 | 0.0004–0.0033 | 0.006–0.020 |
| | 8-350 Diesel | 2.9993–3.0003 | 0.0009–0.0021⑨ | 0.0035–0.0135 | 3 | 2.1238–2.1248 | 0.0005–0.0025 | 0.006–0.020 |
| 1985 | 8-307 Olds. | 2.4990–2.4995⑫ | 0.0015–0.0021⑧ | 0.0035–0.0135 | 3 | 2.1238–2.1248 | 0.0004–0.0033 | 0.006–0.020 |
| | 8-350 Diesel | 2.9993–3.0003 | 0.0009–0.0021⑨ | 0.0035–0.0135 | 3 | 2.1238–2.1248 | 0.0005–0.0025 | 0.006–0.020 |
| 1986 | 8-307 Olds. | 2.4985–2.4995⑬ | 0.0005–0.0021⑧ | 0.0035–0.0135 | 3 | 2.1238–2.1248 | 0.0004–0.0033 | 0.006–0.020 |
| 1987 | 8-307 Olds. | 2.4985–2.4995⑬ | 0.0005–0.0021⑧ | 0.0035–0.0135 | 3 | 2.1238–2.1248 | 0.0004–0.0033 | 0.006–0.020 |
| 1988 | 8-307 Olds. | 2.4985–2.4995⑬ | 0.0005–0.0021⑧ | 0.0035–0.0135 | 3 | 2.1238–2.1248 | 0.0004–0.0033 | 0.006–0.020 |
| 1989 | 8-307 Olds. | 2.4985–2.4995⑬ | 0.0005–0.0021⑧ | 0.0035–0.0135 | 3 | 2.1238–2.1248 | 0.0004–0.0033 | 0.006–0.020 |
| 1990 | 8-307 Olds. | 2.4985–2.4995⑬ | 0.0005–0.0021⑧ | 0.0035–0.0135 | 3 | 2.1238–2.1248 | 0.0004–0.0033 | 0.006–0.020 |
| **PONTIAC** | | | | | | | | |
| 1975 | 8-400 | 3.000 | 0.0002–0.0017 | 0.0030–0.0090 | 4 | 2.250 | 0.0005–0.0025 | 0.012–0.017 |
| | 8-455 | 3.250 | 0.0005–0.0021 | 0.0030–0.0090 | 4 | 2.250 | 0.0010–0.0031 | 0.012–0.017 |
| 1976 | 8-400 | 3.000 | 0.0002–0.0017 | 0.0030–0.0090 | 4 | 2.250 | 0.0005–0.0025 | 0.012–0.017 |
| | 8-455 | 3.250 | 0.0005–0.0021 | 0.0030–0.0090 | 4 | 2.250 | 0.0010–0.0031 | 0.012–0.017 |

85843C20

## CRANKSHAFT AND CONNECTING ROD SPECIFICATIONS

| Year | Engine Displacement (cu in.) | Crankshaft | | | | Connecting Rod | | |
|---|---|---|---|---|---|---|---|---|
| | | Main Brg. Journal Dia. | Main Brg. Oil Clearance | Shaft End-Play | Thrust on No. | Journal Diameter | Oil Clearance | Side Clearance |
| 1977 | 6-231 Buick | 2.4995 | 0.0004–0.0015 | 0.004–0.008 | 2 | 2.000 | 0.0005–0.0026 | 0.006–0.027 |
| | 8-301 Pont. | 3.0000 | 0.0004–0.0020 | 0.003–0.009 | 4 | 2.000 | 0.0005–0.0025 | 0.006–0.027 |
| | 8-305 Chev. | ③ | ④ | 0.002–0.006 | 5 | 2.099–2.100 | 0.0035 max | 0.006–0.014 |
| | 8-350 Pont. | 3.000 | 0.0002–0.0017 | 0.0035–0.0085 | 4 | 2.250 | 0.0005–0.0026 | 0.002–0.017 |
| | 8-350 Olds. | 2.4990 | 0.0005–0.0021 ① | 0.004–0.014 | 3 | 2.1243 | 0.0004–0.0015 | 0.006–0.027 |
| | 8-400 Pont. | 3.0000 | 0.0002–0.0020 | 0.003–0.009 | 4 | 2.2500 | 0.0005–0.0025 | 0.006–0.022 |
| | 8-403 Olds. | 2.4990 | 0.0005–0.0021 ① | 0.004–0.014 | 3 | 2.1243 | 0.0005–0.0026 | 0.006–0.020 |
| 1978 | 6-231 Buick | 2.4995–2.5000 | 0.0003–0.0017 | 0.003–0.009 | 2 | 2.2487–2.2495 | 0.0005–0.0026 | 0.006–0.020 |
| | 8-301 Pont. | 3.0000 | 0.0004–0.0020 | 0.003–0.009 | 4 | 2.2500 | 0.0005–0.0025 | 0.006–0.022 |
| | 8-350 Olds. | 2.4985–2.4995 ⑬ | 0.0005–0.0021 ⑧ | 0.0035–0.0135 | 3 | 2.1238–2.1248 | 0.0004–0.0033 | 0.006–0.020 |
| | 8-350 Buick | 3.0000–3.0005 | 0.0004–0.0015 | 0.003–0.009 | 3 | 1.9910–2.0000 | 0.0005–0.0026 | 0.006–0.027 ⑮ |
| | 8-403 Olds. | 2.4985–2.4995 | 0.0005–0.0021 ⑧ | 0.0035–0.0135 | 5 | 2.1238–2.1248 | 0.0009–0.0026 | 0.006–0.020 |
| 1979 | 6-231 Buick | 2.4995–2.5000 | 0.0003–0.0017 | 0.003–0.009 | 2 | 2.2487–2.2495 | 0.0005–0.0026 | 0.006–0.020 |
| | 8-301 Pont. | 3.0000 | 0.0004–0.0020 | 0.003–0.009 | 4 | 2.2500 | 0.0005–0.0025 | 0.006–0.022 |
| | 8-350 Olds. | 2.4985–2.4995 ⑬ | 0.0005–0.0021 ⑧ | 0.0035–0.0135 | 3 | 2.1238–2.1248 | 0.0004–0.0033 | 0.006–0.020 |
| | 8-350 Buick | 3.0000–3.0005 | 0.0004–0.0015 | 0.003–0.009 | 3 | 1.9910–2.0000 | 0.0005–0.0026 | 0.006–0.027 ⑮ |
| | 8-403 Olds. | 2.4985–2.4995 | 0.0005–0.0021 ⑧ | 0.0035–0.0135 | 5 | 2.1238–2.1248 | 0.0009–0.0026 | 0.006–0.020 |
| 1980 | 6-231 Buick | 2.4995–2.5000 | 0.0003–0.0017 | 0.003–0.009 | 2 | 2.2487–2.2495 | 0.0005–0.0026 | 0.006–0.020 |
| | 8-265 Pont. | 3.00 | 0.0002–0.0018 | 0.003–0.009 | 4 | 2.000 | 0.0005–0.0025 | 0.006–0.022 |
| | 8-301 Pont. | 3.0000 | 0.0004–0.0020 | 0.003–0.009 | 4 | 2.2500 | 0.0005–0.0025 | 0.006–0.022 |
| | 8-350 Olds. | 2.4985–2.4995 ⑬ | 0.0005–0.0021 ⑧ | 0.0035–0.0135 | 3 | 2.1238–2.1248 | 0.0004–0.0033 | 0.006–0.020 |
| | 8-350 Buick | 3.0000–3.0005 | 0.0004–0.0015 | 0.003–0.009 | 3 | 1.9910–2.0000 | 0.0005–0.0026 | 0.006–0.027 ⑮ |
| | 8-350 Diesel | 2.9993–3.0003 | 0.0005–0.0021 ⑧ | 0.0035–0.0135 | 3 | 2.1238–2.1248 | 0.0005–0.0026 | 0.006–0.020 |
| 1981 | 6-231 Buick | 2.4995–2.5000 | 0.0003–0.0018 | 0.003–0.009 | 2 | 2.2487–2.2495 | 0.0005–0.0026 | 0.006–0.023 |
| | 8-265 Pont. | 3.0000 | 0.0002–0.0018 | 0.0035–0.0085 | 4 | 2.0000 | 0.0005–0.0026 | 0.006–0.022 |
| | 8-307 Olds. | 2.4985–2.4995 ⑬ | 0.0005–0.0021 ⑧ | 0.0035–0.0135 | 3 | 2.1238–2.1248 | 0.0004–0.0033 | 0.006–0.020 |
| | 8-305 Chev. | ③ | ⑯ | 0.002–0.006 | 5 | 2.0995 | 0.0013–0.0035 | 0.006–0.016 |
| | 8-350 Buick | 3.000–3.0005 | 0.0004–0.0015 | 0.003–0.009 | 3 | 1.9910–2.0000 | 0.0005–0.0026 | 0.006–0.027 ⑮ |
| | 8-350 Diesel | 2.9993–3.0003 | 0.0005–0.0021 ⑧ | 0.0035–0.0135 | 3 | 2.1238–2.1248 | 0.0005–0.0026 | 0.006–0.020 |
| 1982 | 6-231 Buick | 3.4955 | 0.0003–0.0018 | 0.003–0.011 | 2 | 2.2491 | 0.0005–0.0026 | 0.006–0.023 |
| | 6-252 Buick | 2.4955 | 0.0003–0.0018 | 0.003–0.009 | 2 | 2.2487–2.2495 | 0.0005–0.0026 | 0.006–0.023 |
| | 8-305 Chev. | ⑤ | ⑯ | 0.002–0.006 | 5 | 2.0955 | 0.0013–0.0035 | 0.006–0.016 |
| | 8-350 Diesel | 3.000 | 0.0005–0.0021 ⑧ | 0.0035–0.0135 | 3 | 2.1243 | 0.0005–0.0026 | 0.006–0.020 |
| 1983 | 6-231 Buick | 3.4955 | 0.0003–0.0018 | 0.003–0.011 | 2 | 2.2491 | 0.0005–0.0026 | 0.006–0.020 |
| | 8-305 Chev. | ③ | ⑯ | 0.002–0.006 | 5 | 2.0995 | 0.0013–0.0035 | 0.006–0.016 |
| | 8-350 Diesel | 2.9998 | 0.0005–0.0021 | 0.0035–0.0135 | 3 | 2.1243 | 0.0005–0.0026 | 0.006–0.020 |
| 1984 | 6-231 Buick | 3.4995 | 0.0003–0.0018 | 0.003–0.011 | 2 | 2.1243 | 0.0005–0.0026 | 0.006–0.020 |
| | 8-305 Chev. | ③ | ⑯ | 0.002–0.006 | 5 | 2.0995 | 0.0013–0.0035 | 0.006–0.016 |
| | 8-350 Diesel | 2.9998 | 0.0005–0.0021 | 0.0035–0.0135 | 3 | 2.1243 | 0.0005–0.0026 | 0.006–0.020 |

85843C21

## CRANKSHAFT AND CONNECTING ROD SPECIFICATIONS

| Year | Engine Displacement (cu in.) | Crankshaft | | | | Connecting Rod | | |
| | | Main Brg. Journal Dia. | Main Brg. Oil Clearance | Shaft End-Play | Thrust on No. | Journal Diameter | Oil Clearance | Side Clearance |
|---|---|---|---|---|---|---|---|---|
| 1985 | 6.231 Buick | 3.4995 | 0.0003–0.0018 | 0.003–0.011 | 2 | 2.1243 | 0.0005–0.0026 | 0.006–0.020 |
| | 6-262 Chev. | 2.4484–2.4493 ⑰ | 0.0008–0.0020 ⑲ | 0.002–0.006 | 4 | 2.2487–2.2498 | 0.0013–0.0035 | 0.006–0.014 |
| | 8-305 Chev. | ③ | ⑯ | 0.002–0.006 | 5 | 2.0995 | 0.0013–0.0035 | 0.006–0.016 |
| | 8-350 Diesel | 2.9998 | 0.0005–0.0021 | 0.0035–0.0135 | 3 | 2.1243 | 0.0005–0.0026 | 0.006–0.020 |
| 1986 | 6.231 Buick | 2.4988–2.4998 | 0.0003–0.0018 | 0.003–0.011 | 2 | 2.487–2.2495 | 0.0005–0.0026 | 0.004–0.015 |
| | 6-262 Chev. | 2.4484–2.4493 ⑰ | 0.0008–0.0020 ⑲ | 0.002–0.006 | 4 | 2.2487–2.2498 | 0.0013–0.0035 | 0.006–0.014 |
| 1987 | 8-307 Olds. | 2.4985–2.4995 ⑬ | 0.0005–0.0021 ⑧ | 0.0035–0.0135 | 3 | 2.1238–2.1248 | 0.0004–0.0033 | 0.006–0.020 |
| 1988 | 8-307 Olds. | 2.4985–2.4995 ⑬ | 0.0005–0.0021 ⑧ | 0.0035–0.0135 | 3 | 2.1238–2.1248 | 0.0004–0.0033 | 0.006–0.020 |
| 1989 | 8-307 Olds. | 2.4985–2.4995 ⑬ | 0.0005–0.0021 ⑧ | 0.0035–0.0135 | 3 | 2.1238–2.1248 | 0.0004–0.0033 | 0.006–0.020 |

**NOTE:** Side clearance is total for 2 rods
① Number five main bearing clearance—
  .0015–0.0031
② —1:2.4988–2.4988
③ #1:2.4484–2.4493 2,3,4:2.4481–2.4490
  #5:2.4479–2.4488
④ 1979 #1:.0020, all others .0035. 1980:
  #1:.0015, #2,3,4:.0025, #5:.0035
⑤ #1:.0020 max.
⑥ 2.4990–2.4995 (#2,3,4,5)
⑦ #1:2.4993 in.
⑧ #5:.0015–0.0031 in.
⑨ #5:.0020–0.0034 in.
⑩ Front—.001–0.0015
  Intermediate—.001–0.0025
  Rear—.0025–0.0035
⑪ Diameter may also be 2.240
⑫ #1:2.4973–2.4998
⑬ #1:2.4988–2.4998
⑭ #1:.001–0.0015 #2,3,4:.001–0.0025
  #5:.0025–0.0035
⑮ 1979 and later:.006–0.023
⑯ #1:.0008–0.0020
  #2:.0011–0.0023
  #3:.0017–0.0033
⑰ Intermediate—2.4481–2.4490
  Rear—2.4479–2.4488
⑱ Intermediate—.0011–0.0020
  Rear—.0017–0.0032
⑲ Intermediate—.0011–0.0034
  Rear—.0015–0.0031

8584321a

## PISTON AND RING SPECIFICATIONS

| Year | Engine | Piston-Bore Clearance | Ring Side Clearance | | | Ring Gap | | |
| --- | --- | --- | --- | --- | --- | --- | --- | --- |
| | | | Top Compression | Bottom Compression | Oil Control | Top Compression | Bottom Compression | Oil Control |
| | | | | BUICK | | | | |
| 1975 | 8-350 Buick | 0.0008–0.0014 | 0.003–0.005 | 0.003–0.005 | 0.0035 Max. | 0.013–0.023 | 0.015–0.035 | 0.015–0.035 |
| | 8-455 Buick | 0.0010–0.0016 | 0.003–0.005 | 0.003–0.005 | 0.0035 Max. | 0.013–0.023 | 0.013–0.023 | 0.015–0.035 |
| 1976 | 8-350 Buick | 0.0008–0.0014 | 0.003–0.005 | 0.003–0.005 | 0.0035 Max. | 0.013–0.023 | 0.015–0.035 | 0.015–0.035 |
| | 8-455 Buick | 0.0010–0.0016 | 0.003–0.005 | 0.003–0.005 | 0.0035 Max. | 0.013–0.023 | 0.013–0.023 | 0.015–0.035 |
| 1977 | 6-231 Buick | 0.0008–0.0020 | 0.003–0.005 | 0.003–0.005 | 0.0035 Max. | 0.013–0.023 | 0.015–0.035 | 0.015–0.035 |
| | 8-301 Pont. | 0.0025–0.0033 | 0.0015–0.0035 | 0.0015–0.0035 | 0.0015–0.0035 | 0.010–0.020 | 0.010–0.020 | 0.035 |
| | 8-350 Olds. | 0.0010–0.0020 | 0.0020–0.0040 | 0.0020–0.0040 | 0.0015–0.0035 | 0.010–0.023 | 0.010–0.023 | 0.015–0.055 |
| | 8-350 Buick | 0.0008–0.0014 | 0.003–0.005 | 0.003–0.005 | 0.0035 Max. | 0.013–0.023 | 0.013–0.023 | 0.015–0.055 |
| | 8-403 Olds. | 0.0010–0.0020 | 0.002–0.004 | 0.002–0.004 | 0.0015–0.0035 | 0.010–0.023 | 0.010–0.023 | 0.015–0.055 |
| 1978 | 6-231 Buick | 0.0008–0.0020 ① | 0.003–0.005 | 0.003–0.005 | 0.0035 | 0.010–0.020 | 0.010–0.020 | 0.015–0.035 |
| | 8-301 Pont. | 0.0025–0.0033 | 0.0015–0.0035 | 0.0015–0.0035 | 0.0015–0.0035 | 0.010–0.020 | 0.010–0.020 | 0.015–0.055 |
| | 8-305 Chev. | 0.0027 Max. | 0.0012–0.0042 | 0.0012–0.0042 | 0.0020–0.0080 | 0.010–0.030 | 0.010–0.035 | 0.010–0.035 |
| | 8-350 Olds. | 0.0010–0.0020 | 0.0020–0.0040 | 0.0020–0.0040 | 0.0015–0.0035 | 0.010–0.023 | 0.010–0.023 | 0.015–0.055 |
| | 8-350 Chev. | 0.0027 Max. | 0.0012–0.0042 | 0.0012–0.0042 | 0.0020–0.0080 | 0.010–0.030 | 0.010–0.035 | 0.015–0.056 |
| | 8-350 Buick | 0.0008–0.0020 ① | 0.003–0.005 | 0.003–0.005 | 0.0035 | 0.010–0.020 | 0.010–0.020 | 0.015–0.035 |
| | 8-400 Pont. | 0.0025–0.0033 ⑭ | 0.0015–0.0035 | 0.0015–0.0035 | 0.0015–0.0035 | 0.009–0.019 | 0.005–0.015 | 0.015–0.035 |
| | 8-403 Olds. | 0.0010–0.0020 | 0.0020–0.0040 | 0.0020–0.0040 | 0.0015–0.0035 | 0.010–0.023 | 0.010–0.023 | 0.015–0.035 |
| 1979 | 6-231 Buick | 0.0008–0.0020 ① | 0.003–0.005 | 0.003–0.005 | 0.0035 | 0.013–0.023 | 0.013–0.023 | 0.015–0.035 |
| | 8-301 Pont. | 0.0025–0.0023 | 0.0015–0.0035 | 0.0015–0.0035 | 0.0015–0.0035 | 0.010–0.020 | 0.010–0.020 | 0.035 Max. |
| | 8-350 Buick | 0.0008–0.0020 ① | 0.0030–0.0050 | 0.0030–0.0050 | 0.0035 | 0.010–0.020 ③ | 0.010–0.020 ③ | 0.015–0.055 |
| | 8-350 Olds. | 0.0010–0.0027 | 0.0020–0.0040 | 0.0020–0.0040 | 0.001–0.005 | 0.010–0.023 ② | 0.010–0.023 ② | 0.015–0.055 |
| | 8-403 Olds. | 0.0010–0.0020 | 0.0020–0.0040 | 0.0020–0.0040 | 0.001–0.005 | 0.010–0.023 ② | 0.010–0.023 ② | 0.015–0.055 |
| 1980 | 6-231 Buick | 0.0008–0.0020 ① | 0.003–0.005 | 0.003–0.005 | 0.0035 | 0.013–0.023 | 0.013–0.023 | 0.015–0.035 |
| | 6-252 Buick | 0.0008–0.0020 ① | 0.003–0.005 | 0.003–0.005 | 0.0035 | 0.013–0.023 | 0.013–0.023 | 0.015–0.035 |
| | 8-301 Pont. | 0.0025–0.0023 | 0.0015–0.0035 | 0.0015–0.0035 | 0.0015–0.0035 | 0.010–0.020 | 0.010–0.020 | 0.035 Max. |
| | 8-350 Olds. | 0.0010–0.0027 | 0.0020–0.0040 | 0.0020–0.0040 | 0.001–0.005 | 0.010–0.023 ② | 0.010–0.023 ② | 0.015–0.055 |
| | 8-350 Buick | 0.0008–0.0020 ① | 0.0030–0.0050 | 0.0030–0.0050 | 0.0035 | 0.010–0.020 ③ | 0.010–0.020 ③ | 0.015–0.055 |
| | 8-350 Olds. Diesel | 0.005–0.006 | 0.004–0.006 | 0.0018–0.0038 | 0.001–0.005 | 0.015–0.025 | 0.015–0.025 | 0.015–0.055 |
| 1981 | 6-231 Buick | 0.0008–0.0020 ① | 0.003–0.005 | 0.003–0.005 | 0.0035 | 0.013–0.023 | 0.013–0.023 | 0.015–0.035 |
| | 6-252 Buick | 0.0008–0.0020 ① | 0.003–0.005 | 0.003–0.005 | 0.0035 | 0.013–0.023 | 0.013–0.023 | 0.015–0.035 |
| | 8-267 Chev. | 0.0027 Max. | 0.0012–0.0032 | 0.0012–0.0032 | 0.0020–0.0080 | 0.010–0.030 | 0.010–0.035 | 0.015–0.065 |
| | 8-301 Pont. | 0.0025–0.0033 | 0.0015–0.0035 | 0.0015–0.0035 | 0.0015–0.0035 | 0.010–0.020 | 0.010–0.020 | 0.035 |
| | 8-307 Olds. | 0.0075–0.00175 | 0.0020–0.0040 | 0.0020–0.0040 | 0.0010–0.0050 | 0.019–0.019 ④ | 0.009–0.019 ④ | 0.015–0.055 ⑤ |
| | 8-350 Olds. Diesel | 0.005–0.006 | 0.004–0.006 | 0.0018–0.0038 | 0.001–0.005 | 0.015–0.025 | 0.015–0.025 | 0.015–0.055 |
| 1982 | 6-231 Buick | 0.0008–0.0020 ① | 0.003–0.005 | 0.003–0.005 | 0.0035 | 0.013–0.023 | 0.013–0.023 | 0.015–0.035 |
| | 6-252 Buick | 0.0008–0.0020 ① | 0.003–0.005 | 0.003–0.005 | 0.0035 | 0.013–0.023 | 0.013–0.023 | 0.015–0.035 |
| | 8-307 Olds. | 0.0075–0.00175 | 0.0020–0.0040 | 0.0020–0.0040 | 0.0010–0.0050 | 0.019–0.019 ④ | 0.009–0.019 ④ | 0.015–0.055 ⑤ |
| | 8-350 Diesel | 0.005–0.006 | 0.004–0.006 | 0.0018–0.0038 | 0.001–0.005 | 0.015–0.025 | 0.015–0.025 | 0.015–0.055 |

85843C22

## PISTON AND RING SPECIFICATIONS

| Year | Engine | Piston-Bore Clearance | Ring Side Clearance | | | Ring Gap | | |
|------|--------|----------------------|---------------------|---|---|----------|---|---|
| | | | Top Compression | Bottom Compression | Oil Control | Top Compression | Bottom Compression | Oil Control |
| **BUICK** | | | | | | | | |
| **1983** | 6-231 Buick | 0.0008–0.0020 ① | 0.003–0.005 | 0.003–0.005 | 0.0035 | 0.010–0.020 | 0.010–0.020 | 0.015–0.035 |
| | 6-252 Buick | 0.0008–0.0020 ① | 0.003–0.005 | 0.003–0.005 | 0.0035 | 0.013–0.023 | 0.013–0.023 | 0.015–0.035 |
| | 8-307 Olds. | 0.0075–0.00175 | 0.0020–0.0040 | 0.0020–0.0040 | 0.0010–0.0050 | 0.019–0.019 ④ | 0.009–0.019 ④ | 0.015–0.055 ⑤ |
| | 8-350 Diesel | 0.005–0.006 | 0.004–0.006 | 0.0018–0.0038 | 0.001–0.005 | 0.015–0.025 | 0.015–0.025 | 0.015–0.055 |
| **1984** | 6-231 Buick | 0.0008–0.0020 ⑥ | 0.003–0.005 | 0.003–0.005 | 0.0035 | 0.013–0.023 | 0.013–0.023 | 0.015–0.035 |
| | 6-252 Buick | 0.0008–0.0020 ⑥ | 0.003–0.005 | 0.003–0.005 | 0.0035 | 0.013–0.023 | 0.013–0.023 | 0.015–0.035 |
| | 8-307 Olds. | 0.00075–0.00175 ⑥ | 0.002–0.004 | 0.002–0.004 | 0.001–0.005 | 0.009–0.020 | 0.009–0.019 | 0.010–0.025 |
| | 8-350 Diesel | 0.0035–0.0045 ⑥ | 0.005–0.007 | 0.003–0.005 | 0.001–0.005 | 0.019–0.027 | 0.013–0.021 | 0.015–0.035 |
| **1985** | 6-231 Buick | 0.0008–0.0020 ⑥ | 0.003–0.005 | 0.003–0.005 | 0.0035 | 0.013–0.023 | 0.013–0.023 | 0.015–0.035 |
| | 6-252 Buick | 0.0008–0.0020 ⑥ | 0.003–0.005 | 0.003–0.005 | 0.0035 | 0.013–0.023 | 0.013–0.023 | 0.015–0.035 |
| | 8-307 Olds. | 0.00075–0.00175 ⑥ | 0.002–0.004 | 0.002–0.004 | 0.001–0.005 | 0.009–0.020 | 0.009–0.019 | 0.010–0.025 |
| | 8-350 Diesel | 0.0035–0.0045 ⑥ | 0.005–0.007 | 0.003–0.005 | 0.001–0.005 | 0.019–0.027 | 0.013–0.021 | 0.015–0.035 |
| **1986** | 6-231 Buick | 0.0013–0.0035 | 0.003–0.005 | 0.003–0.005 | 0.0035 | 0.010–0.020 | 0.010–0.020 | 0.015–0.035 |
| | 8-307 Olds. | 0.00075–0.00175 | 0.0018–0.0038 | 0.0018–0.0038 | 0.001–0.005 | 0.009–0.019 | 0.009–0.019 | 0.015–0.055 |
| **1987** | 6-231 Buick | 0.0013–0.0035 | 0.003–0.005 | 0.003–0.005 | 0.0035 | 0.010–0.020 | 0.010–0.020 | 0.015–0.035 |
| | 8-307 Olds. | 0.00075–0.00175 | 0.0018–0.0038 | 0.0018–0.0038 | 0.001–0.005 | 0.009–0.019 | 0.009–0.019 | 0.015–0.055 |
| **1988** | 8-307 Olds. | 0.00075–0.00175 | 0.0018–0.0038 | 0.0018–0.0038 | 0.001–0.005 | 0.009–0.019 | 0.009–0.019 | 0.015–0.055 |
| **1989** | 8-307 Olds. | 0.00075–0.00175 | 0.0018–0.0038 | 0.0018–0.0038 | 0.001–0.005 | 0.009–0.019 | 0.009–0.019 | 0.015–0.055 |
| **1990** | 8-307 Olds. | 0.00075–0.00175 | 0.0018–0.0038 | 0.0018–0.0038 | 0.001–0.005 | 0.009–0.019 | 0.009–0.019 | 0.015–0.055 |
| **OLDSMOBILE** | | | | | | | | |
| **1975** | 8-350 Olds. | 0.0010–0.0020 | 0.0020–0.0040 | 0.0020–0.0040 | 0.001–0.005 | 0.010–0.023 | 0.010–0.023 | 0.015–0.055 |
| | 8-400 Olds. | 0.0010–0.0020 | 0.0020–0.0040 | 0.0020–0.0040 | 0.001–0.005 | 0.010–0.023 | 0.010–0.023 | 0.015–0.055 |
| | 8-455 Olds. | 0.0010–0.0020 | 0.0020–0.0040 | 0.0020–0.0040 | 0.002–0.008 | 0.010–0.023 | 0.010–0.023 | 0.015–0.055 |
| **1976** | 8-350 | 0.0010–0.0020 | 0.0020–0.0040 | 0.0020–0.0040 | 0.001–0.005 | 0.010–0.023 | 0.010–0.023 | 0.015–0.055 |
| | 8-455 | 0.0010–0.0020 | 0.0020–0.0040 | 0.0020–0.0040 | 0.002–0.008 | 0.010–0.023 | 0.010–0.023 | 0.015–0.055 |
| **1977** | 6-231 Buick | 0.0013–0.0035 ⑥ | 0.0030–0.0050 | 0.0030–0.0050 | 0.0035 | 0.013–0.023 | 0.015–0.035 | 0.015–0.035 |
| | 8-260 Olds. | 0.0010–0.0020 | 0.0020–0.0040 | 0.0020–0.0040 | 0.005–0.011 | 0.010–0.023 | 0.010–0.023 | 0.015–0.055 |
| | 8-350 Chev. | 0.0010–0.0020 | 0.0020–0.0040 | 0.0020–0.0040 | 0.001–0.005 | 0.010–0.023 | 0.010–0.023 | 0.015–0.055 |
| | 8-350 Olds. | 0.0027 Max. | 0.0012–0.0032 | 0.0012–0.0032 | 0.001–0.005 | 0.010–0.030 | 0.010–0.035 | 0.015–0.065 |
| | 8-403 Olds. | 0.0010–0.0020 | 0.0020–0.0040 | 0.0020–0.0040 | 0.001–0.005 | 0.010–0.023 | 0.010–0.035 | 0.015–0.055 |
| **1978** | 6-231 Buick | 0.0013–0.0035 ⑥ | 0.0030–0.0050 | 0.0030–0.0050 | 0.0035 | 0.013–0.023 | 0.015–0.035 | 0.015–0.035 |
| | 8-260 Olds. | 0.0010–0.0020 | 0.0020–0.0040 | 0.0020–0.0040 | 0.005–0.011 | 0.010–0.023 | 0.010–0.023 | 0.015–0.055 |
| | 8-350 Olds. | 0.0010–0.0020 | 0.0020–0.0040 | 0.0020–0.0040 | 0.001–0.005 | 0.010–0.023 | 0.010–0.023 | 0.015–0.055 |
| | 8-350 Buick | 0.0013–0.0035 ⑥ | 0.0030–0.0050 | 0.0030–0.0050 | 0.0035 Max. | 0.010–0.020 | 0.010–0.020 | 0.015–0.055 |
| | 8-350 Diesel | 0.005–0.006 ⑥ | 0.005–0.007 | 0.0018–0.0038 | 0.0010–0.0050 | 0.015–0.025 | 0.015–0.025 | 0.015–0.055 |
| | 8-403 Olds. | 0.0010–0.0020 | 0.0020–0.0040 | 0.0020–0.0040 | 0.001–0.005 | 0.010–0.023 | 0.010–0.035 | 0.015–0.055 |
| **1979** | 6-231 Buick | 0.0013–0.0035 ⑥ | 0.0030–0.0050 | 0.0030–0.0050 | 0.0035 | 0.010–0.020 ⑦ | 0.010–0.020 | 0.015–0.035 |
| | 8-260 Olds. | 0.0008–0.0018 ⑥⑧ | 0.0020–0.0040 | 0.0020–0.0040 | 0.005–0.011 | 0.010–0.020 ⑫ | 0.010–0.020 ⑫ | 0.015–0.055 ⑨ |
| | 8-301 Pont. | 0.0025–0.0033 | 0.0015–0.0035 | 0.0015–0.0035 | 0.0015–0.0035 | 0.010–0.020 | 0.010–0.020 | 0.0035 |
| | 8-350 Olds. | 0.0008–0.0018 ⑧ | 0.0020–0.0040 | 0.0020–0.0040 | 0.001–0.005 | 0.013–0.023 ⑭② | 0.013–0.023 ⑩② | 0.015–0.055 |
| | 8-350 Diesel | 0.005–0.006 ⑥ | 0.005–0.007 | 0.0018–0.0038 | 0.0010–0.0050 | 0.015–0.025 | 0.015–0.025 | 0.015–0.055 |
| | 8-403 Olds. | 0.0005–0.0015 ⑪ | 0.0020–0.0040 | 0.0020–0.0040 | 0.001–0.005 | 0.010–0.020 ⑫ | 0.010–0.020 ⑫ | 0.015–0.055 |

85843C23

## PISTON AND RING SPECIFICATIONS

| Year | Engine | Piston-Bore Clearance | Ring Side Clearance | | | Ring Gap | | |
|------|--------|----------------------|---------------------|---|---|----------|---|---|
| | | | Top Compression | Bottom Compression | Oil Control | Top Compression | Bottom Compression | Oil Control |
| | | | **OLDSMOBILE** | | | | | |
| 1980 | 6-231 Buick | 0.0013-0.0035 ⑥ | 0.0030-0.0050 | 0.0030-0.0050 | 0.0035 | 0.010-0.020 ⑦ | 0.010-0.020 | 0.015-0.035 |
| | 8-260 Olds. | 0.0008-0.0018 ⑥ ⑧ | 0.0020-0.0040 | 0.0020-0.0040 | 0.005-0.011 | 0.010-0.020 ⑫ | 0.010-0.020 ⑫ | 0.015-0.055 ⑨ |
| | 8-265 Pont. | 0.0017-0.0041 ⑥ | 0.0015-0.0035 | 0.0015-0.0035 | 0.0015-0.0035 | 0.010-0.022 | 0.010-0.028 | 0.010-0.055 |
| | 8-307 Olds. | 0.0005-0.0015 | 0.0020-0.0040 | 0.0020-0.0040 | 0.001-0.005 | 0.009-0.019 | 0.009-0.019 | 0.015-0.055 |
| | 8-350 Olds. | 0.0008-0.0018 ⑧ | 0.0020-0.0040 | 0.0020-0.0040 | 0.001-0.005 | 0.013-0.023 ⑭② | 0.013-0.023 ⑭② | 0.015-0.055 |
| | 8-350 Diesel | 0.005-0.006 ⑥ | 0.005-0.007 | 0.0018-0.0038 | 0.0010-0.0050 | 0.015-0.025 | 0.015-0.025 | 0.015-0.055 |
| 1981 | 6-231 Buick | 0.0016-0.0038 ⑥ | 0.0030-0.0050 | 0.0030-0.0050 | 0.0035 | 0.013-0.023 | 0.013-0.023 | 0.015-0.055 |
| | 6-252 Buick | 0.0016-0.0038 ⑥ | 0.0030-0.0050 | 0.0030-0.0050 | 0.0035 | 0.013-0.023 | 0.013-0.023 | 0.015-0.055 |
| | 8-260 Olds. | 0.0008-0.0018 ⑥ | 0.0020-0.0040 | 0.0020-0.0040 | 0.005-0.011 | 0.010-0.020 ⑫ | 0.010-0.020 ⑫ | 0.015-0.055 ⑨ |
| | 8-307 Olds. | 0.0008-0.0018 | 0.0020-0.0040 | 0.0020-0.0040 | 0.001-0.005 | 0.009-0.019 | 0.009-0.019 | 0.015-0.055 |
| | 8-350 Diesel | 0.005-0.006 ⑥ | 0.005-0.007 | 0.0018-0.0038 | 0.0010-0.0050 | 0.015-0.025 | 0.015-0.025 | 0.015-0.055 |
| 1982 | 6-231 Buick | 0.0016-0.0038 ⑥ | 0.0030-0.0050 | 0.0030-0.0050 | 0.0035 | 0.013-0.023 | 0.013-0.023 | 0.015-0.055 |
| | 6-252 Buick | 0.0016-0.0038 ⑥ | 0.0030-0.0050 | 0.0030-0.0050 | 0.0035 | 0.013-0.023 | 0.013-0.023 | 0.015-0.055 |
| | 8-260 Olds. | 0.0008-0.0018 ⑥ | 0.0020-0.0040 | 0.0020-0.0040 | 0.005-0.011 | 0.010-0.020 ⑫ | 0.010-0.020 ⑫ | 0.015-0.055 ⑨ |
| | 8-307 Olds. | 0.0008-0.0018 | 0.0020-0.0040 | 0.0020-0.0040 | 0.001-0.005 | 0.009-0.019 | 0.009-0.019 | 0.015-0.055 |
| | 8-350 Diesel | 0.005-0.006 ⑥ | 0.005-0.007 | 0.0018-0.0038 | 0.0010-0.0050 | 0.015-0.025 | 0.015-0.025 | 0.015-0.055 |
| 1983 | 6-231 Buick | 0.0016-0.0038 ⑥ | 0.0030-0.0050 | 0.0030-0.0050 | 0.0035 | 0.013-0.023 | 0.013-0.023 | 0.015-0.055 |
| | 6-252 Buick | 0.0016-0.0038 ⑥ | 0.0030-0.0050 | 0.0030-0.0050 | 0.0035 | 0.013-0.023 | 0.013-0.023 | 0.015-0.055 |
| | 8-307 Olds. | 0.00075-0.00175 | 0.002-0.004 | 0.002-0.004 | 0.001-0.005 | 0.009-0.019 ④ | 0.009-0.019 ④ | 0.015-0.055 ⑤ |
| | 8-350 Diesel | 0.005-0.006 ⑥ | 0.005-0.007 | 0.0018-0.0038 | 0.0010-0.0050 | 0.015-0.025 | 0.015-0.025 | 0.015-0.055 |
| 1984 | 6-231 Buick | 0.008-0.020 | 0.003-0.005 | 0.003-0.005 | 0.0035 | 0.013-0.023 | 0.013-0.023 | 0.015-0.035 |
| | 8-307 Olds. | 0.00075-0.00175 | 0.002-0.004 | 0.002-0.004 | 0.001-0.005 | 0.009-0.019 ④ | 0.009-0.019 ④ | 0.015-0.055 ⑤ |
| | 8-350 Diesel | 0.0035-0.0045 ① | 0.005-0.007 | 0.003-0.005 | 0.001-0.005 | 0.019-0.027 | 0.013-0.021 | 0.010-0.022 |
| 1985 | 8-307 Olds. | 0.0008-0.0018 | 0.0020-0.0040 | 0.0020-0.0040 | 0.001-0.005 | 0.009-0.019 | 0.009-0.019 | 0.015-0.055 |
| | 8-350 Diesel | 0.005-0.006 ⑥ | 0.005-0.007 | 0.0010-0.0038 | 0.0010-0.0050 | 0.015-0.025 | 0.015-0.025 | 0.015-0.055 |
| 1986 | 8-307 Olds. | 0.00075-0.00175 | 0.0018-0.0038 | 0.0018-0.0038 | 0.001-0.005 | 0.009-0.019 | 0.009-0.019 | 0.015-0.055 |
| 1987 | 8-307 Olds. | 0.00075-0.00175 | 0.0018-0.0038 | 0.0018-0.0038 | 0.001-0.005 | 0.009-0.019 | 0.009-0.019 | 0.015-0.055 |
| 1988 | 8-307 Olds. | 0.00075-0.00175 | 0.0018-0.0038 | 0.0018-0.0038 | 0.001-0.005 | 0.009-0.019 | 0.009-0.019 | 0.015-0.055 |
| 1989 | 8-307 Olds. | 0.00075-0.00175 | 0.0018-0.0038 | 0.0018-0.0038 | 0.001-0.005 | 0.009-0.019 | 0.009-0.019 | 0.015-0.055 |
| 1990 | 8-307 Olds. | 0.00075-0.00175 | 0.0018-0.0038 | 0.0018-0.0038 | 0.001-0.005 | 0.009-0.019 | 0.009-0.019 | 0.015-0.055 |
| | | | **PONTIAC** | | | | | |
| 1975 | 8-400 2 bbl | 0.0029-0.0037 ① | 0.0015-0.005 | 0.0015-0.005 | 0.0015-0.005 | 0.010-0.030 | 0.010-0.030 | 0.015-0.055 |
| | 8-400 4 bbl | 0.0029-0.0037 ① | 0.0015-0.005 | 0.0015-0.005 | 0.0015-0.005 | 0.010-0.030 | 0.010-0.030 | 0.015-0.055 |
| | 8-455 4 bbl | 0.0021-0.0029 | 0.0020-0.0040 | 0.0020-0.0040 | 0.0021-0.0031 | 0.010-0.023 | 0.010-0.023 | 0.015-0.055 |
| 1976 | 8-400 2 bbl | 0.0029-0.0037 ① | 0.0015-0.005 | 0.0015-0.005 | 0.0015-0.005 | 0.010-0.030 | 0.010-0.030 | 0.015-0.055 |
| | 8-400 4 bbl | 0.0029-0.0037 ① | 0.0015-0.005 | 0.0015-0.005 | 0.0015-0.005 | 0.010-0.030 | 0.010-0.030 | 0.015-0.055 |
| | 8-455 Pont. | 0.0021-0.0029 | 0.0020-0.0040 | 0.0020-0.0040 | 0.0021-0.0031 | 0.010-0.023 | 0.010-0.023 | 0.015-0.055 |

85843C24

## PISTON AND RING SPECIFICATIONS

| Year | Engine | Piston-Bore Clearance | Ring Side Clearance | | | Ring Gap | | |
|------|--------|----------------------|---------------------|---|---|----------|---|---|
| | | | Top Compression | Bottom Compression | Oil Control | Top Compression | Bottom Compression | Oil Control |
| | | | **PONTIAC** | | | | | |
| 1977 | 6-231 Buick | 0.0025–0.0033 ⑭ | 0.0015–0.0035 | 0.0015–0.0035 | 0.0015–0.0035 | 0.010–0.020 | 0.010–0.020 | 0.0035 |
| | 8-301 Pont. | 0.0025–0.0033 ⑭ | 0.0015–0.0035 | 0.0015–0.0035 | 0.0015–0.0035 | 0.010–0.020 | 0.010–0.020 | 0.0035 |
| | 8-305 Chev. | 0.0027 Max. | 0.0012–0.0032 | 0.0012–0.0032 | 0.0020–0.0080 | 0.010–0.030 | 0.010–0.035 | 0.015–0.065 |
| | 8-350 Olds. | 0.0008–0.0018 ⑮ | 0.0020–0.0040 | 0.0020–0.0040 | 0.001–0.005 | 0.013–0.023 ⑩ ② | 0.013–0.023 ⑩ ② | 0.015–0.055 |
| | 8-350 Pont. | 0.0013–0.0035 | 0.0030–0.0050 | 0.0030–0.0050 | 0.0035 Max. | 0.010–0.020 | 0.010–0.020 | 0.015–0.055 |
| | 8-400 Pont. | 0.0025–0.0033 ⑭ | 0.0015–0.0035 | 0.0015–0.0035 | 0.0015–0.0035 | 0.009–0.019 | 0.005–0.015 | 0.015–0.035 |
| | 8-403 Olds. | 0.0008–0.0018 ⑮ | 0.0020–0.0040 | 0.0020–0.0040 | 0.001–0.005 | 0.010–0.020 | 0.010–0.020 | 0.015–0.055 |
| 1978 | 6-231 Buick | 0.0025–0.0033 ⑭ | 0.0015–0.0035 | 0.0015–0.0035 | 0.0015–0.0035 | 0.010–0.020 | 0.010–0.020 | 0.0035 |
| | 8-301 Pont. | 0.0025–0.0033 ⑭ | 0.0015–0.0035 | 0.0015–0.0035 | 0.0015–0.0035 | 0.010–0.020 | 0.010–0.020 | 0.0035 |
| | 8-350 Buick | 0.0013–0.0035 ⑥ | 0.0020–0.0050 | 0.0030–0.0050 | 0.0035 Max. | 0.010–0.020 | 0.010–0.020 | 0.015–0.055 |
| | 8-350 Olds. | 0.0008–0.0018 ⑮ | 0.0020–0.0040 | 0.0020–0.0040 | 0.001–0.005 | 0.013–0.023 ⑩ ② | 0.013–0.023 ⑩ ② | 0.015–0.055 |
| | 8-403 Olds. | 0.0008–0.0018 ⑮ | 0.0020–0.0040 | 0.0020–0.0040 | 0.001–0.005 | 0.010–0.020 | 0.010–0.020 | 0.015–0.055 |
| 1979 | 6-231 Buick | 0.0013–0.0035 ⑥ | 0.0030–0.0050 | 0.0030–0.0050 | 0.0035 | 0.010–0.020 ⑦ | 0.010–0.020 | 0.015–0.035 |
| | 8-301 Pont. | 0.0025–0.0033 | 0.0015–0.0035 | 0.0015–0.0035 | 0.0015–0.0035 | 0.010–0.020 | 0.010–0.020 | 0.0035 |
| | 8-350 Olds. | 0.0008–0.0018 ⑮ | 0.0020–0.0040 | 0.0020–0.0040 | 0.001–0.005 | 0.013–0.023 ⑩ ② | 0.013–0.023 ⑩ ② | 0.015–0.055 |
| | 8-350 Buick | 0.0008–0.0020 ① | 0.0030–0.0050 | 0.0030–0.0050 | 0.0035 | 0.010–0.020 ③ | 0.010–0.020 ③ | 0.015–0.055 |
| | 8-403 Olds. | 0.0008–0.0018 ⑮ | 0.0020–0.0040 | 0.0020–0.0040 | 0.001–0.005 | 0.010–0.020 | 0.010–0.020 | 0.015–0.055 |
| 1980 | 6-231 Buick | 0.0013–0.0035 | 0.003–0.005 | 0.003–0.005 | 0.0035 | 0.010–0.020 | 0.010–0.020 | 0.015–0.055 |
| | 8-265 Pont. | 0.0017–0.0041 ⑥ | 0.0015–0.0035 | 0.0015–0.0035 | 0.0015–0.0035 | 0.010–0.022 | 0.010–0.028 | 0.010–0.050 |
| | 8-301 Pont. | 0.0025–0.0033 ⑭ | 0.0015–0.0035 | 0.0015–0.0035 | 0.0015–0.0035 | 0.010–0.020 | 0.010–0.020 | 0.0035 |
| | 8-350 Olds. | 0.0008–0.0018 ⑮ | 0.0020–0.0040 | 0.0020–0.0040 | 0.001–0.005 | 0.013–0.023 ⑩ ② | 0.013–0.023 ⑩ ② | 0.015–0.055 |
| | 8-350 Buick | 0.0013–0.0035 ⑥ | 0.0030–0.0050 | 0.0030–0.0050 | 0.0035 Max. | 0.010–0.020 | 0.010–0.020 | 0.015–0.055 |
| | 8-350 Diesel | 0.005–0.006 | 0.005–0.007 | 0.005–0.007 | 0.001–0.005 | 0.015–0.025 | 0.015–0.025 | 0.015–0.055 |
| 1981 | 6-231 Buick | 0.0016–0.0038 ⑥ | 0.0030–0.0050 | 0.0030–0.0050 | 0.0035 Max. | 0.013–0.023 | 0.013–0.023 | 0.015–0.035 |
| | 8-265 Pont. | 0.0017–0.0041 ⑥ | 0.0015–0.0035 | 0.0015–0.0035 | 0.0015–0.0035 | 0.010–0.022 | 0.010–0.028 | 0.010–0.050 |
| | 8-305 | 0.0012 Max. | 0.0012–0.0032 | 0.0012–0.0032 | 0.002–0.007 | 0.010–0.020 | 0.010–0.025 | 0.015–0.055 |
| | 8-307 | 0.0006–0.0018 | 0.0020–0.0040 | 0.0020–0.0040 | 0.001–0.005 | 0.009–0.019 | 0.009–0.019 | 0.015–0.055 |
| | 8-350 Buick | 0.0013–0.0035 ⑥ | 0.0030–0.0050 | 0.0030–0.0050 | 0.0035 Max. | 0.010–0.020 | 0.010–0.020 | 0.015–0.055 |
| | 8-350 Olds. Diesel | 0.005–0.006 | 0.005–0.007 | 0.005–0.007 | 0.001–0.005 | 0.015–0.025 | 0.015–0.025 | 0.015–0.055 |
| 1982 | 6-231 Buick | 0.0016–0.0038 ⑥ | 0.0030–0.0050 | 0.0030–0.0050 | 0.0035 Max. | 0.013–0.023 | 0.013–0.023 | 0.015–0.035 |
| | 6-252 Buick | 0.0016–0.0038 ⑥ | 0.0030–0.0050 | 0.0030–0.0050 | 0.0035 Max. | 0.010–0.020 | 0.010–0.020 | 0.015–0.055 |
| | 8-305 Chev. | 0.0012 Max. | 0.0012–0.0032 | 0.0012–0.0032 | 0.002–0.007 | 0.010–0.020 | 0.010–0.025 | 0.015–0.055 |
| | 8-350 Diesel | 0.005–0.006 ⑥ | 0.005–0.007 | 0.0018–0.0038 | 0.0010–0.0050 | 0.015–0.025 | 0.015–0.025 | 0.015–0.055 |
| 1983 | 6-231 Buick | 0.001–0.002 ① | 0.003–0.005 | 0.003–0.005 | 0.0035 | 0.01–0.02 | 0.01–0.02 | 0.015–0.035 |
| | 8-305 Chev. | 0.00075–0.00175 ① | 0.012–0.0032 | 0.012–0.0032 | 0.002–0.007 | 0.01–0.02 | 0.01–0.02 | 0.01–0.055 |
| | 8-350 Diesel | 0.0035–0.0045 ① | 0.005–0.007 | 0.003–0.005 | 0.001–0.005 | 0.019–0.027 | 0.013–0.021 | 0.015–0.055 |
| 1984 | 6-231 Buick | 0.001–0.002 ① | 0.003–0.005 | 0.003–0.005 | 0.0035 | 0.01–0.02 | 0.01–0.02 | 0.015–0.035 |
| | 8-305 Chev. | 0.00075–0.00175 ① | 0.012–0.0032 | 0.012–0.0032 | 0.002–0.007 | 0.01–0.02 | 0.01–0.02 | 0.01–0.055 |
| | 8-350 Diesel | 0.0035–0.0045 ① | 0.005–0.007 | 0.003–0.005 | 0.001–0.005 | 0.019–0.027 | 0.013–0.021 | 0.015–0.055 |

85843C25

## PISTON AND RING SPECIFICATIONS

| Year | Engine | Piston-Bore Clearance | Ring Side Clearance | | | Ring Gap | | |
|------|--------|----------------------|---------------------|---|---|----------|---|---|
| | | | Top Compression | Bottom Compression | Oil Control | Top Compression | Bottom Compression | Oil Control |
| **PONTIAC** | | | | | | | | |
| **1985** | 6-231 Buick | 0.001–0.002 ① | 0.003–0.005 | 0.003–0.005 | 0.0035 | 0.01–0.02 | 0.01–0.02 | 0.015–0.035 |
| | 6-262 Chev. | 0.0007–0.0017 | 0.010–0.020 | 0.010–0.023 | 0.015–0.055 | 0.0012–0.0032 | 0.0012–0.0032 | 0.0020–0.0070 |
| | 8-305 Chev. | 0.00075–0.00175 ① | 0.012–0.0032 | 0.012–0.0032 | 0.002–0.007 | 0.01–0.02 | 0.01–0.02 | 0.01–0.055 |
| | 8-350 Diesel | 0.0035–0.0045 ① | 0.005–0.007 | 0.003–0.005 | 0.001–0.005 | 0.019–0.027 | 0.013–0.021 | 0.015–0.055 |
| **1986** | 6-231 Buick | 0.0013–0.0035 | 0.003–0.005 | 0.003–0.005 | 0.0035 | 0.010–0.020 | 0.010–0.020 | 0.015–0.055 |
| | 6-262 Chev. | 0.0007–0.0017 | 0.010–0.020 | 0.010–0.023 | 0.015–0.055 | 0.0012–0.0032 | 0.0012–0.0032 | 0.0020–0.0070 |
| **1987** | 8-307 Olds. | 0.00075–0.00175 | 0.0018–0.0038 | 0.0018–0.0038 | 0.001–0.005 | 0.009–0.019 | 0.009–0.019 | 0.015–0.055 |
| **1988** | 8-307 Olds. | 0.00075–0.00175 | 0.0018–0.0038 | 0.0018–0.0038 | 0.001–0.005 | 0.009–0.019 | 0.009–0.019 | 0.015–0.055 |
| **1989** | 8-307 Olds. | 0.00075–0.00175 | 0.0018–0.0038 | 0.0018–0.0038 | 0.001–0.005 | 0.009–0.019 | 0.009–0.019 | 0.015–0.055 |

① Measured at skirt top
② w/Sealed Power rings—0.010–0.020 in.
③ 1980—0.013–0.023 in.
④ w/TRW rings 0.010–0.020 in.
⑤ w/TRW rings 0.010–0.025
⑥ Measured at bottom of skirt
⑦ 1980—0.013–0.023 in. in both rings
⑧ 1978—0.0010–0.0020 in.
⑨ 1979—81 260 w/Muskegon rings—0.010–0.035 in.
⑩ 1978—0.010–0.023 in.
⑪ 1978—0.0010–0.0022 in.
⑫ w/Sealed Power rings—0.009–0.019 in.
⑭ Measured 1.1 in. from the top of piston
⑮ Measured ¾ in. below piston pin centerline
⑯ 1978 0.0012–0.0027 in.
⑰ 1978 0.0050 Max.

8584325a

## TORQUE SPECIFICATIONS
(All readings in ft. lbs.)

| Year | Engine | Cylinder Head Bolts | Rod Bearing Bolts | Main Bearing Bolts | Crankshaft Damper or Pulley Bolt | Flywheel to Crankshaft Bolts | Manifold Intake | Exhaust |
|------|--------|---------------------|-------------------|--------------------|-----------------------------------|------------------------------|-----------------|---------|
| | | | | **BUICK** | | | | |
| 1975 | 8-350 Buick | 80 | 40 | 115 | 140 | 60 | 45 | 28 |
| | 8-455 Buick | 100 | 45 | 115 | 200 | 60 | 45 | 28 |
| 1976 | 8-350 Buick | 80 | 40 | 115 | 140 | 60 | 45 | 28 |
| | 8-455 Buick | 100 | 45 | 115 | 200 | 60 | 45 | 28 |
| 1977 | 6-231 Buick | 85 | 42 | 80③ | 310 | 60 | 40 | 25 |
| | 8-301 Pont. | 90 | 35 | 60① | 160 | 95 | 40 | 35 |
| | 8-350 Buick | 80 | 40 | 115 | 175 | 60 | 45 | 25 |
| | 8-350, 8-403 Olds. | 130⑤ | 42 | 80③ | 200–310 | 60 | 40⑤ | 25 |
| 1978 | 6-231 Buick | 80 | 40 | 100 | 225② | 60 | 45 | 25 |
| | 6-252 Buick | 80 | 40 | 100 | 225② | 60 | 45 | 25 |
| | 8-301 Pont. | 90 | 35 | 60① | 160 | 95 | 40 | 35 |
| | 8-305 Chev. | 65 | 45 | 70 | 60 | 60 | 30 | 20 |
| | 8-350 Buick | 80 | 40 | 100 | 225② | 60 | 45 | 25 |
| | 8-350 Chev. | 65 | 45 | 70 | 60 | 60 | 30 | 20 |
| | 8-307, 8-350, 8-403 Olds. | 130⑤ | 42 | 80③ | 255② | 60 | 40⑤ | 25 |
| | 8-350 Olds. Diesel | 130⑤ | 42 | 120 | 200–310② | 60 | 40⑤ | 25 |
| | 8-400 Pont. | 95 | 40 | 100③ | 160 | 95 | 35 | 40 |
| 1979 | 6-231 Buick | 80 | 40 | 100 | 225② | 60 | 45 | 25 |
| | 6-252 Buick | 80 | 40 | 100 | 225② | 60 | 45 | 25 |
| | 8-301 Pont. | 90 | 35 | 60① | 160 | 95 | 40 | 35 |
| | 8-305 Chev. | 65 | 45 | 70 | 60 | 60 | 30 | 20 |
| | 8-350 Buick | 80 | 40 | 100 | 225② | 60 | 45 | 25 |
| | 8-350 Chev. | 65 | 45 | 70 | 60 | 60 | 30 | 20 |
| | 8-307, 8-350, 8-403 Olds. | 130⑤ | 42 | 80③ | 255② | 60 | 40⑤ | 25 |
| | 8-350 Olds. Diesel | 130⑤ | 42 | 120 | 200–310② | 60 | 40⑤ | 25 |
| 1980 | 6-231 Buick | 80 | 40 | 100 | 225② | 60 | 45 | 25 |
| | 6-252 Buick | 80 | 40 | 100 | 225② | 60 | 45 | 25 |
| | 8-301 Pont. | 90 | 35 | 60① | 160 | 95 | 40 | 35 |
| | 8-305 Chev. | 65 | 45 | 70 | 60 | 60 | 30 | 20 |
| | 8-350 Buick | 80 | 40 | 100 | 225② | 60 | 45 | 25 |
| | 8-350 Chev. | 65 | 45 | 70 | 60 | 60 | 30 | 20 |
| | 8-307, 8-350, 8-403 Olds. | 130⑤ | 42 | 80③ | 255② | 60 | 40⑤ | 25 |
| | 8-350 Olds. Diesel | 130⑤ | 42 | 120 | 200–310② | 60 | 40⑤ | 25 |

85843C26

## TORQUE SPECIFICATIONS

(All readings in ft. lbs.)

| Year | Engine | Cylinder Head Bolts | Rod Bearing Bolts | Main Bearing Bolts | Crankshaft Damper or Pulley Bolt | Flywheel to Crankshaft Bolts | Manifold Intake | Manifold Exhaust |
|------|--------|--------------------|-------------------|--------------------|----------------------------------|------------------------------|--------|---------|
| | | | | **BUICK** | | | | |
| 1981 | 6-231 Buick | 80 | 40 | 100 | 225② | 60 | 45 | 25 |
| | 6-252 Buick | 80 | 40 | 100 | 225② | 60 | 45 | 25 |
| | 8-267 Chev. | 65 | 45 | 70 | 60 | 60 | 30 | 20 |
| | 8-301 Pont. | 90 | 35 | 60① | 160 | 95 | 40 | 35 |
| | 8-305 Chev. | 65 | 45 | 70 | 60 | 60 | 30 | 20 |
| | 8-350 Buick | 80 | 40 | 100 | 225② | 60 | 45 | 25 |
| | 8-350 Chev. | 65 | 45 | 70 | 60 | 60 | 30 | 20 |
| | 8-307, 8-350, 8-403 Olds. | 130⑤ | 42 | 80③ | 255② | 60 | 40⑤ | 25 |
| | 8-350 Olds. Diesel | 130⑤ | 42 | 120 | 200–310② | 60 | 40⑤ | 25 |
| 1982 | 6-231 Buick | 80 | 40 | 100 | 225 | 60 | 45 | 25 |
| | 6-252 Buick | 80 | 40 | 100 | 225 | 60 | 45 | 25 |
| | 8-307 Olds. | 125 | 42 | 80③ | 200–310 | 60 | 45 | 25 |
| | 8-350 Diesel | 130 | 42 | 120 | 200–310 | 60 | 45 | 25 |
| | 8-350 Buick | 80 | 40 | 115 | 175 | 60 | 45 | 25 |
| | 8-350, 8-403 Olds. | 130⑤ | 42 | 80③ | 200–310 | 60 | 40⑤ | 25 |
| 1983 | 6-231 Buick | 80 | 40 | 100 | 225 | 60 | 45 | 25 |
| | 6-252 Buick | 80 | 40 | 100 | 225 | 60 | 45 | 25 |
| | 8-307 Olds. | 125 | 42 | 80③ | 200–310 | 60 | 45 | 25 |
| | 8-350 Diesel | 130 | 42 | 120 | 200–310 | 60 | 45 | 25 |
| 1984 | 6-231 Buick | 80 | 40 | 100 | 225 | 60 | 45 | 25 |
| | 6-252 Buick | 80 | 40 | 100 | 225 | 60 | 45 | 25 |
| | 8-307 Olds. | 125 | 42 | 80③ | 200–310 | 60 | 45 | 25 |
| | 8-350 Diesel | 130 | 42 | 120 | 200–310 | 60 | 45 | 25 |
| 1985 | 6-231 Buick | 25⑨ | 40 | 135 | 135 | 60 | 45 | 20 |
| | 8-307 Olds. | 125 | 42 | ④ | 200–310 | 60 | 40⑤ | 25 |
| 1986 | 6-231 Buick | 25⑨ | 40 | 135 | 135 | 60 | 45 | 20 |
| | 8-307 Olds. | 125 | 42 | ④ | 200–310 | 60 | 40⑤ | 25 |
| 1987 | 8-307 Olds. | 40⑤ | 18 | ④ | 200–310 | 60 | 40⑤ | 25 |
| 1988 | 8-307 Olds. | 40⑤ | 18 | ④ | 200–310 | 60 | 40⑤ | 25 |
| 1989 | 8-307 Olds. | 40⑤ | 18 | ④ | 200–310 | 60 | 40⑤ | 25 |
| 1990 | 8-307 Olds. | 40⑤ | 18 | ④ | 200–310 | 60 | 40⑤ | 25 |
| | | | | **OLDSMOBILE** | | | | |
| 1975 | 8-350 Olds. | 85 | 42 | 120④ | 200–310 | 60 | 40 | 25 |
| | 8-400 Olds. | 95 | 43 | 100③ | 160 | 95 | 40 | 30 |
| | 8-455 Olds. | 85③ | 42 | 120 | 200–310 | 60 | 40 | 25 |
| 1976 | 8-350, 8-403, 8-455 | 85⑤ | 42 | 120④ | 200–310 | 60 | 40 | 25 |
| 1977 | 6-231 Buick | 80 | 40 | 115 | 175 | 60 | 45 | 25 |
| | 8-260 Olds. | 85 | 42 | ④ | 200–300 | 60 | 40 | 25 |
| | 8-350 Chev. | 65 | 45 | 70 | 60 | 60 | 30 | 20 |
| | 8-350 Olds. Diesel | 130⑤ | 42 | 120 | 200–300 | 60 | 40⑤ | 25 |
| | 8-350, 8-403 Olds. | 130⑤ | 42 | ④ | 200–310 | 60 | 40⑤ | 25 |

85843C27

## TORQUE SPECIFICATIONS

(All readings in ft. lbs.)

| Year | Engine | Cylinder Head Bolts | Rod Bearing Bolts | Main Bearing Bolts | Crankshaft Damper or Pulley Bolt | Flywheel to Crankshaft Bolts | Manifold Intake | Manifold Exhaust |
|------|--------|---------------------|-------------------|--------------------|----------------------------------|------------------------------|-----------------|------------------|
| | | | | OLDSMOBILE | | | | |
| 1978 | 6-231 Buick | 80 | 40 | 100 | 225 | 60 | 45 | 25 |
| | 6-252 Buick | 80 | 40 | 100 | 225 | 60 | 45 | 25 |
| | 8-260 Olds. | 85 ⑤ | 42 | ④ | 200–310 | 60 | 40 ⑤ | 25 |
| | 8-301 Pont. | 95 | 35 | ⑧ | 160 | 95 | 40 | 25 |
| | 8-307 Olds. | 130 ⑤ | 42 | ④ | 200–310 | 60 | 40 ⑤ | 25 |
| | 8-350 Olds. | 130 ⑤ | 42 | ④ | 200–310 | 60 | 40 ⑤ | 25 |
| | 8-350 Diesel | 130 ⑤ | 42 | 120 | 200–310 | 60 | 40 ⑤ | 25 |
| | 8-350 Buick | 80 | 40 | 100 | 225 ② | 60 | 45 | 25 |
| | 8-403 Olds. | 130 ⑤ | 42 | ④ | 200–310 | 60 | 40 ⑤ | 25 |
| 1979 | 6-231 Buick | 80 | 40 | 100 | 225 | 60 | 45 | 25 |
| | 6-252 Buick | 80 | 40 | 100 | 225 | 60 | 45 | 25 |
| | 8-260 Olds. | 85 ⑤ | 42 | ④ | 200–310 | 60 | 40 ⑤ | 25 |
| | 8-301 Pont. | 95 | 35 | ⑧ | 160 | 95 | 40 | 25 |
| | 8-307 Olds. | 130 ⑤ | 42 | ④ | 200–310 | 60 | 40 ⑤ | 25 |
| | 8-350 Olds. | 130 ⑤ | 42 | ④ | 200–310 | 60 | 40 ⑤ | 25 |
| | 8-350 Diesel | 130 ⑤ | 42 | 120 | 200–310 | 60 | 40 ⑤ | 25 |
| | 8-403 Olds. | 130 ⑤ | 42 | ④ | 200–310 | 60 | 40 ⑤ | 25 |
| 1980 | 6-231 Buick | 80 | 40 | 100 | 225 | 60 | 45 | 25 |
| | 6-252 Buick | 80 | 40 | 100 | 225 | 60 | 45 | 25 |
| | 8-260 Olds. | 85 ⑤ | 42 | ④ | 200–310 | 60 | 40 ⑤ | 25 |
| | 8-301 Pont. | 95 | 35 | ⑧ | 160 | 95 | 40 | 25 |
| | 8-307 Olds. | 130 ⑤ | 42 | ④ | 200–310 | 60 | 40 ⑤ | 25 |
| | 8-350 Olds. | 130 ⑤ | 42 | ④ | 200–310 | 60 | 40 ⑤ | 25 |
| | 8-350 Diesel | 130 ⑤ | 42 | 120 | 200–310 | 60 | 40 ⑤ | 25 |
| 1981 | 6-231 Buick | 80 | 40 | 100 | 225 | 60 | 45 | 25 |
| | 6-252 Buick | 80 | 40 | 100 | 225 | 60 | 45 | 25 |
| | 8-260 Olds. | 85 ⑤ | 42 | ④ | 200–310 | 60 | 40 ⑤ | 25 |
| | 8-301 Pont. | 95 | 35 | ⑧ | 160 | 95 | 40 | 25 |
| | 8-307 Olds. | 130 ⑤ | 42 | ④ | 200–310 | 60 | 40 ⑤ | 25 |
| | 8-350 Olds. | 130 ⑤ | 42 | ④ | 200–310 | 60 | 40 ⑤ | 25 |
| | 8-350 Diesel | 130 ⑤ | 42 | 120 | 200–310 | 60 | 40 ⑤ | 25 |
| 1982 | 6-231 Buick | 80 | 40 | 100 | 225 | 60 | 45 | 25 |
| | 6-252 Buick | 80 | 40 | 100 | 225 | 60 ⑥ | 45 | 25 |
| | 8-260 Olds. | 85 ⑤ | 42 | ④ | 200–310 | 60 | 40 ⑤ | 25 |
| | 8-307 Olds. | 130 ⑤ | 42 | ④ | 200–310 | 60 | 40 ⑤ | 25 |
| | 8-350 Diesel | 130 ⑤ | 42 | 120 | 200–310 | 60 | 40 ⑤ | 25 |
| 1983 | 6-231 Buick | 80 | 40 | 100 | 225 | 60 ⑥ | 45 | 25 |
| | 6-252 Buick | 80 | 40 | 100 | 225 | 60 | 45 | 25 |
| | 8-260 Olds. | 85 ⑤ | 42 | ④ | 200–310 | 60 | 40 ⑤ | 25 |
| | 8-307 Olds. | 130 ⑤ | 42 | ④ | 200–310 | 60 | 40 ⑤ | 25 |
| | 8-350 Diesel | 130 ⑤ | 42 | 120 | 200–310 | 60 | 40 ⑤ | 25 |

85843C28

## TORQUE SPECIFICATIONS
(All readings in ft. lbs.)

| Year | Engine | Cylinder Head Bolts | Rod Bearing Bolts | Main Bearing Bolts | Crankshaft Damper or Pulley Bolt | Flywheel to Crankshaft Bolts | Manifold Intake | Exhaust |
|---|---|---|---|---|---|---|---|---|
| | | | | **OLDSMOBILE** | | | | |
| 1984 | 6-231 Buick | 80 | 40 | 100 | 225 | 60 | 45 | 25 |
| | 8-307 Olds. | 130 ⑤ | 42 | ④ | 200–310 | 60 | 40 ⑤ | 25 |
| | 8-350 Diesel | 130 ⑤ | 42 | 120 | 200–310 | 60 | 40 ⑤ | 25 |
| 1985 | 6-231 Buick | 80 | 40 | 100 | 225 | 60 | 45 | 25 |
| | 8-307 Olds. | 130 ⑤ | 42 | ④ | 200–310 | 60 | 40 ⑤ | 25 |
| | 8-350 Diesel | 130 ⑤ | 42 | 120 | 200–310 | 60 | 40 ⑤ | 25 |
| 1986 | 8-307 Olds. | 125 ⑤ | 42 | ④ | 200–310 | 60 | 40 ⑤ | 25 |
| 1987 | 8-307 Olds. | 125 ⑤ | 42 | ④ | 200–310 | 60 | 40 ⑤ | 25 |
| 1988 | 8-307 Olds. | 40 ⑤ | 18 | ④ | 200–310 | 60 | 40 ⑤ | 25 |
| 1989 | 8-307 Olds. | 40 ⑤ | 18 | ④ | 200–310 | 60 | 40 ⑤ | 25 |
| 1990 | 8-307 Olds. | 40 ⑤ | 18 | ④ | 200–310 | 60 | 40 ⑤ | 25 |
| | | | | **PONTIAC** | | | | |
| 1975 | 8-400 Pont. | 95 | 43 | 100 ③ | 160 | 95 | 40 | 30 |
| | 8-455 Pont. | 95 | 43 ⑦ | 100 ③ | 160 | 95 | 40 | 30 |
| 1976 | 8-400 Pont. | 95 | 43 | 100 ③ | 160 | 95 | 40 | 30 |
| | 8-455 Pont. | 95 | 43 ⑦ | 100 ③ | 160 | 95 | 40 | 30 |
| 1977 | 6-231 Buick | 80 | 40 | 100 | 225 | 60 | 45 | 25 |
| | 8-301 Pont. | 95 | 30 | 70 ⑧ | 160 | 95 | 35 | 40 |
| | 8-305 Chev. | 65 | 45 | 70 | 60 | 60 | 30 | 20 |
| | 8-350 Chev. | 65 | 45 | 70 | 60 | 60 | 30 | 20 |
| | 8-350 Buick | 80 | 40 | 100 | 225 | 60 | 45 | 25 |
| | 8-350 Olds. | 130 | 42 | 80 ③ | 220 | 60 | 40 | 25 |
| | 8-400 Pont. | 95 | 40 | 100 ③ | 160 | 95 | 35 | 40 |
| | 8-403 Olds. | 130 | 42 | 80 ③ | 220 | 60 | 40 | 25 |
| 1978 | 6-231 Buick | 80 | 40 | 100 | 225 | 60 | 45 | 25 |
| | 8-301 Pont. | 95 | 30 | 70 ⑧ | 160 | 95 | 35 | 40 |
| | 8-350 Chev. | 65 | 45 | 70 | 60 | 60 | 30 | 20 |
| | 8-350 Buick | 80 | 40 | 100 | 225 | 60 | 45 | 25 |
| | 8-350 Olds. | 130 | 42 | 80 ③ | 220 | 60 | 40 | 25 |
| | 8-400 Pont. | 95 | 40 | 100 ③ | 160 | 95 | 35 | 40 |
| | 8-403 Olds. | 130 | 42 | 80 ③ | 220 | 60 | 40 | 25 |
| 1979 | 6-231 Buick | 80 | 40 | 100 | 225 | 60 | 45 | 25 |
| | 8-301 Pont. | 95 | 30 | 70 ⑧ | 160 | 95 | 35 | 40 |
| | 8-350 Chev. | 65 | 45 | 70 | 60 | 60 | 30 | 20 |
| | 8-350 Buick | 80 | 40 | 100 | 225 | 60 | 45 | 25 |
| | 8-350 Olds. | 130 | 42 | 80 ③ | 220 | 60 | 40 | 25 |
| | 8-400 Pont. | 95 | 40 | 100 ③ | 160 | 95 | 35 | 40 |
| | 8-403 Olds. | 130 | 42 | 80 ③ | 220 | 60 | 40 | 25 |

85843C29

## TORQUE SPECIFICATIONS

(All readings in ft. lbs.)

| Year | Engine | Cylinder Head Bolts | Rod Bearing Bolts | Main Bearing Bolts | Crankshaft Damper or Pulley Bolt | Flywheel to Crankshaft Bolts | Manifold Intake | Manifold Exhaust |
|------|--------|---------------------|-------------------|--------------------|---------------------------------|------------------------------|-----------------|------------------|
| | | | | **PONTIAC** | | | | |
| 1980 | 6-231 Buick | 80 | 40 | 100 | 225 | 60 | 45 | 25 |
| | 8-265, 8-301 Pont. | 95 | 30 | ⑧ | 160 | 95 | 35 | 40 |
| | 8-307 Olds. | 130 ⑤ | 45 | 70 ③ | 200–310 | 60 | 40 ⑤ | 25 |
| | 8-350 Olds. | 130 ⑤ | 45 | 70 | 200–310 | 60 | 45 ⑤ | 25 |
| | 8-350 Diesel | 130 ⑥ | 42 | ④ | 200–310 | 60 | 40 ⑤ | 25 |
| | 8-350 Buick | 80 | 40 | 100 | 225 ② | 60 | 45 | 25 |
| 1981 | 6-231 Buick | 80 | 40 | 100 | 225 | 60 | 45 | 25 |
| | 8-265, 8-301 Pont. | 95 | 30 | ⑧ | 160 | 95 | 35 | 40 |
| | 8-305 Chev. | 65 | 45 | 70 | 60 | 60 | 30 | 20 |
| | 8-307 Olds. | 130 ⑤ | 45 | 70 ③ | 200–310 | 60 | 40 ⑤ | 25 |
| | 8-350 Olds. | 130 ⑤ | 45 | 70 | 200–310 | 60 | 45 ⑤ | 25 |
| | 8-350 Diesel | 130 ⑥ | 42 | ④ | 200–310 | 60 | 40 ⑥ | 25 |
| | 8-350 Buick | 80 | 40 | 100 | 225 ② | 60 | 45 | 25 |
| 1982 | 6-231 Buick | 80 | 40 | 100 | 225 | 60 | 40 | 25 |
| | 6-252 Buick | 80 | 40 | 100 | 225 | 60 | 40 | 25 |
| | 8-305 Chev. | 65 | 45 | 70 | 60 | 60 | 30 | 20 |
| | 8-350 Diesel | 130 ⑤ | 42 | ④ | 200–310 | 60 | 40 ⑤ | 25 |
| 1983 | 6-231 Buick | 80 | 40 | 100 | 225 | 60 | 40 | 25 |
| | 6-252 Buick | 80 | 40 | 100 | 225 | 60 | 40 | 25 |
| | 8-305 Chev. | 65 | 45 | 70 | 60 | 60 | 30 | 20 |
| | 8-350 Diesel | 130 ⑤ | 42 | ④ | 200–310 | 60 | 40 ⑤ | 25 |
| 1984 | 6-231 Buick | 80 | 40 | 100 | 225 | 60 | 45 | 25 |
| | 8-305 Chev. | 65 | 45 | 70 | 60 | 60 | 30 | 20 |
| | 8-350 Diesel | 130 ⑤ | 42 | 120 | 200–310 | 60 | 40 ③ | 25 |
| 1985 | 6-231 Buick | 80 | 40 | 100 | 225 | 60 | 45 | 25 |
| | 6-262 Chev. | 60–75 | 60–85 | 42–47 | 70 | 70 | 25–45 | 20 |
| | 8-305 Chev. | 65 | 45 | 70 | 60 | 60 | 30 | 20 |
| | 8-350 Diesel | 130 ⑤ | 42 | 120 | 200–310 | 60 | 40 ③ | 25 |
| 1986 | 6-231 Buick | 25 ⑨ | 45 | 100 | 200 | 60 | 45 | 20 |
| | 6-262 Chev. | 60–75 | 70–85 | 42–47 | 70 | 70 | 25–45 | 20 |
| | 8-307 Olds. | 125 ⑤ | 42 | 80 ④ | 200–310 | 60 | 40 | 25 |

8584329A

## TORQUE SPECIFICATIONS
### (All readings in ft. lbs.)

| Year | Engine | Cylinder Head Bolts | Rod Bearing Bolts | Main Bearing Bolts | Crankshaft Damper or Pulley Bolt | Flywheel to Crankshaft Bolts | Manifold Intake | Exhaust |
|------|--------|--------------------|-------------------|--------------------|-----------------------------------|------------------------------|-----------------|---------|
| | | | | **PONTIAC** | | | | |
| **1987** | 6-231 Buick | 25 ⑨ | 45 | 100 | 200 | 60 | 45 | 20 |
| | 8-307 Olds. | 125 ⑤ | 42 | 80 ④ | 200–310 | 60 | 40 | 25 |
| **1988** | 6-307 Olds. | 40 ⑤ | 18 | ④ | 200–310 | 60 | 40 ⑤ | 25 |
| **1989** | 6-307 Olds. | 40 ⑤ | 18 | ④ | 200–310 | 60 | 40 ⑤ | 25 |

① Rear main—100 ft. lbs.
② Fan pulley to balancer—20 ft. lbs.
③ Rear main—120 ft. lbs.
④ 80 ft. lbs. on No. 1-4, 120 ft. lbs. on No. 5
⑤ Dip bolt in oil before torquing
⑥ 1983—48 ft. lbs.
⑦ 63 ft. lbs. on 455 S.D. engines
⑧ 7/16 in. bolt—70; 1/2 in. bolt—100;
   rear main—100
⑨ See text for the complete procedure, as bolts
   are final-torqued using angle torquing

8584329B

## TORQUE SPECIFICATIONS

| Component | U.S. | Metric |
|---|---|---|
| Damper bolt | | |
| Oldsmobile engines | | |
|   1979 403 VIN K | 225 ft. lbs. | 306 Nm |
|   All others | 200–310 ft. lbs. | 272–422 Nm |
| Pontiac engines | 160 ft. lbs. | 218 Nm |
| Buick engines | | |
|   1975–76 350 VIN J | 140 ft. lbs. | 190 Nm |
|   1975–76 455 VIN T | 210 ft. lbs. | 285 Nm |
|   1977 350 VIN J | 175 ft. lbs. | 238 Nm |
|   All others | 225 ft. lbs. | 306 Nm |
| Chevrolet engines | | |
|   1981 267 VIN J | 60 ft. lbs. | 82 Nm |
|   1981–86 305 VIN H | 160 ft. lbs. | 218 Nm |
|   1985–86 262 VIN Z | 70 ft. lbs. | 95 Nm |
|   All others | 60 ft. lbs. | 82 Nm |
| Main bearing bolts | | |
| Buick engines | | |
|   1977 231 VIN C | 80 ft. lbs. ③ | 109 Nm③ |
|   1975–77 | 115 ft. lbs. | 157 Nm |
|   1978–85 | 100 ft. lbs. | 137 Nm |
|   1986–87 | 135 ft. lbs. | 184 Nm |
| Oldsmobile engines | | |
|   1975–76 350 VIN R, K | 120 ft. lbs. ④ | 163 Nm④ |
|   1978–85 350 VIN N | 120 ft. lbs. | 163 Nm |
|   1980–83 307 VIN Y | 70 ft. lbs. ③ | 95 Nm③ |
|   All others | 80 ft. lbs. ③ | 109 Nm③ |
| Pontiac engines | | |
|   1977 301 VIN Y | 60 ft. lbs. | 82 Nm |
|   1978–81 265 VIN S | ⑧ | ⑧ |
|   1978–81 301 VIN Y | ⑧ | ⑧ |
|   All others | 100 ft. lbs. ③ | 137 Nm③ |
| Chevrolet engines | | |
|   1977–78 | 70 ft. lbs. | 95 Nm |
|   1982–85 305 VIN H | ⑧ | ⑧ |
|   1985–86 262 VIN Z | 70 ft. lbs. | 95 Nm |

85843C35

## TORQUE SPECIFICATIONS

| Component | U.S. | Metric |
|---|---|---|
| Rod bearing bolts | | |
|   Buick engines | | |
|     1977 231 VIN C | 42 ft. lbs. | 57 Nm |
|     All others | 40 ft. lbs. | 54 Nm |
|   Oldsmobile engines | | |
|     1981–83 307 VIN Y | 45 ft. lbs. | 61 Nm |
|     1983–87 307 VIN Y | 42 ft. lbs. | 57 Nm |
|     1988–90 307 VIN Y | 18 ft. lbs. [9] | 24 Nm [9] |
|     All others | 43 ft. lbs. | 58 Nm |
|   Pontiac engines | | |
|     301 VIN Y, W | 35 ft. lbs. | 48 Nm |
|     265 VIN S | 30 ft. lbs. | 41 Nm |
|     400 VIN R, S, Z | 43 ft. lbs. | 58 Nm |
|     455 VIN W | 43 ft. lbs. | 58 Nm |
|   Chevrolet engines | 45 ft. lbs. | 61 Nm |
| Water pump | | |
|   Pump cover | 10 ft. lbs. | 14 Nm |
|   Through bolts | 25–35 ft. lbs. | 33–47 Nm |
| Water outlet | | |
|   All engines | 18–23 ft. lbs. | 24–31 Nm |
| Rocker arm cover | | |
|   All engines | 50–65 inch lbs. | 5–7 Nm |
| Rocker arms | | |
|   Buick engines | | |
|     V6 | 25 ft. lbs. | 35 Nm |
|     V8 | 30 ft. lbs. | 41 Nm |
|   Pontiac engines | 25 ft. lbs. | 34 Nm |
|   Oldsmobile engines | | |
|     307 VIN Y | 22 ft. lbs. | 28 Nm |
|     All others | 28 ft. lbs. | 35 Nm |

85843C36

## TORQUE SPECIFICATIONS

| Component | U.S. | Metric |
|---|---|---|
| Intake manifold | | |
|   Buick engines | 45 ft. lbs. | 61 Nm |
|   Oldsmobile engines | 40 ft. lbs. | 54 Nm |
|   Pontiac engines | 40 ft. lbs. | 54 Nm |
|   Chevrolet engines | 30 ft. lbs. | 41 Nm |
| Exhaust manifold | | |
|   Buick engines | | |
|     350 VIN J | 28 ft. lbs. | 35 Nm |
|     1986–87 231 VIN A | 25 ft. lbs. | 34 Nm |
|     All others | 20 ft. lbs. | 27 Nm |
|   Pontiac engines | | |
|     1975–76 | 30 ft. lbs. | 41 Nm |
|     1977 and up | 40 ft. lbs. | 54 Nm |
|   Oldsmobile engines | 25 ft. lbs. | 34 Nm |
|   Chevrolet engines | 20 ft. lbs. | 27 Nm |
| Cylinder head bolts | | |
|   Buick engines | | |
|     1977 231 VIN C | 85 ft. lbs. | 115 Nm |
|     All others 1975–85 | 80 ft. lbs. | 109 Nm |
|     1986–87 | 25 ft. lbs. ⑨ | 34 Nm ⑨ |
|   Oldsmobile engines | | |
|     1984–87 307 VIN Y | 125 ft. lbs. | 170 Nm |
|     1988–90 307 VIN Y | 40 ft. lbs. ⑤⑨ | 54 Nm ⑤⑨ |
|     1975 350 VIN K | 85 ft. lbs. ⑤ | 115 Nm ⑤ |
|     1977–82 260 VIN F | 85 ft. lbs. ⑤ | 115 Nm ⑤ |
|     All others | 130 ft. lbs. | 177 Nm |
|   Pontiac engines | | |
|     1977 301 VIN Y | 90 ft. lbs. | 122 Nm |
|     1977 350 VIN P | 100 ft. lbs. | 137 Nm |
|     All others | 95 ft. lbs. | 129 Nm |
|   Chevrolet engines | 65 ft. lbs. | 88 Nm |
| Drive plate | | |
|   Buick engines | 60 ft. lbs. | 82 Nm |
|   Oldsmobile engines | 60 ft. lbs. | 82 Nm |
|   Chevrolet engines | | |
|     1985–86 262 VIN Z | 70 ft. lbs. | 95 Nm |
|     All others | 60 ft. lbs. | 82 Nm |
|   Pontiac engines | 95 ft. lbs. | 129 Nm |

85843C37

## TORQUE SPECIFICATIONS

| Component | U.S. | Metric |
| --- | --- | --- |
| Converter-to-drive plate | | |
| All engines | 46 ft. lbs. | 63 Nm |
| Motor mounts | | |
| All engines | 55 ft. lbs. | 75 Nm |
| Transmission-to-engine | | |
| All engines | 25–40 ft. lbs. | 33–54 Nm |
| Oil pan | | |
| All engines | 14 ft. lbs. | 18 Nm |
| Oil pump | | |
| Cover | 10 ft. lbs. | 14 Nm |
| Pump | 35 ft. lbs. | 48 Nm |
| Timing chain cover | | |
| All engines | 69–130 inch lbs. | 7–14 Nm |
| Camshaft sprocket | | |
| All engines | 13–23 ft. lbs. | 17–31 Nm |
| Distributor clamp bolt | | |
| All engines | 15 ft. lbs. | 20 Nm |
| Starter | | |
| Cross-member | 80 ft. lbs. | 109 Nm |
| Mount bolts | 25–35 ft. lbs. | 34–48 Nm |
| Solenoid | 100 inch lbs. | 11 Nm |
| Radiator | | |
| Mount bolts | 15 ft. lbs. | 20 Nm |

85843C38

## TORQUE SPECIFICATIONS

| Component | U.S. | Metric |
|---|---|---|
| Turbocharger | | |
|   Oil drain clamp | 15 ft. lbs. | 20 Nm |
|   Compressor housing | 35 ft. lbs. | 48 Nm |
|   EGR valve and plenum bolts | 15 ft. lbs. | 20 Nm |
|   Brackets | 20 ft. lbs. | 27 Nm |
| Spark plugs | | |
|   All engines | 15 ft. lbs. | 21 Nm |
| Balancer pulley | 20 ft. lbs. | 27 Nm |
| Fan pulley | 20 ft. lbs. | 27 Nm |
| Alternator bracket | 35 ft. lbs. | 48 Nm |
|   Adjusting bolt | 20 ft. lbs. | 27 Nm |
| Flywheel housing cover | 4 ft. lbs. | 6 Nm |
| Oil pan drain plug | 14 ft. lbs. | 20 Nm |
| Engine block coolant drain plug | 16 ft. lbs. | 22 Nm |

① Rear main: 100 ft. lbs. (136 Nm)
② Fan pulley to balancer: 20 ft. lbs. (27 Nm)
③ Rear main: 120 ft. lbs. (163 Nm)
④ 80 ft. lbs. (109 Nm) on No. 1–4; 120 ft. lbs. (163 Nm) on No. 5
⑤ Dip bolt in oil before torquing
⑥ 1983: 48 ft. lbs. (65 Nm)
⑦ 63 ft. lbs. (85 Nm) on 455 S.D. engines
⑧ 7/16 in. bolt: 70 ft.lbs. (95 Nm); 1/2 in. bolt: 100 ft. lbs. (136 Nm); rear main: 100 ft. lbs. (136 Nm)
⑨ See text for complete procedure; bolts are final-torqued using angle torquing

85843C39

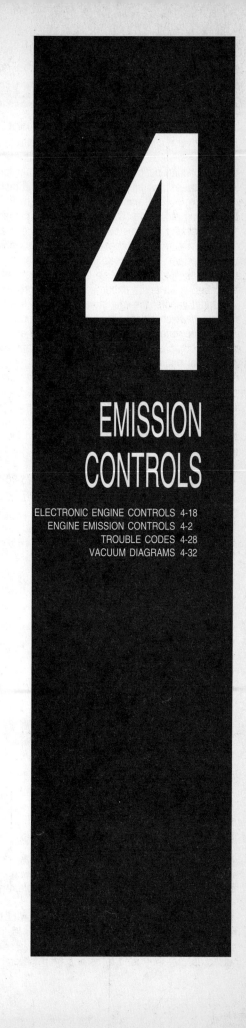

# 4

# EMISSION CONTROLS

## ENGINE EMISSION CONTROLS

In its normal operation, the internal combustion engine releases several compounds into the atmosphere. Since most of these compounds are harmful to our health if inhaled or ingested for long periods (and in sufficient quantity), the Federal Government has placed a limit on the quantities of the three main groups of compounds: unburned hydrocarbons (HC); carbon monoxide (CO); and oxides of nitrogen (NOx).

The emissions systems covered in this section are designed to regulate the output of these fumes by your vehicle's engine and fuel system. Three areas of the automobile are covered, each with its own anti-pollution system or systems; the engine crankcase, which emits unburned hydrocarbons in the form of oil and fuel vapors; the fuel storage system (fuel tank and carburetor), which also emits unburned hydrocarbons in the form of evaporated gasoline; and the engine exhaust. Exhaust emissions comprise the greatest quantity of auto emissions, in the forms of unburned hydrocarbons, carbon monoxide, and oxides of nitrogen. Because of this, there are more pollution devices on your vehicle dealing with exhaust emissions than there are dealing with the other two emission types.

Exhaust emission controls comprise the largest body of emission controls installed on your vehicle. Included in this category are:
- Thermostatic Air Cleaner (THERMAC)
- Air Injection Reactor System (A.I.R., 1975-80)
- Air Management System (1981 and later)
- Early Fuel Evaporation system (EFE)
- Exhaust Gas Recirculation
- Controlled Combustion System (CCS)
- Computer Controlled Catalytic Converter system (C-4)
- Computer Command Control (CCC)
- Mixture Control Solenoid (M/C)
- Throttle Position Sensor (TPS)
- Idle Speed Control (ISC)
- Electronic Spark Timing (EST)
- Electronic Spark Control (ESC)
- Transmission Converter Clutch (TCC)
- Catalytic Converter and the Oxygen Sensor system

A brief description of each system and any applicable service procedures follows.

## Crankcase Ventilation Systems

### OPERATION

#### Gasoline Engines
▶ See Figures 1 and 2

All Buick, Oldsmobile, Chevrolet and Pontiac gasoline engines covered in this guide are equipped with a positive crankcase ventilation (PCV) system to control crankcase blow-by vapors. The system functions as follows:

When the engine is running, a small portion of the gases which are formed in the combustion chamber leak by the piston rings and enter the crankcase. Since these gases are under pressure, they tend to escape from the crankcase and enter the atmosphere. If these gases are allowed to remain in the crankcase for any period of time, they contaminate the engine oil and cause sludge to build up in the crankcase. If the gases are allowed to escape into the atmosphere, they pollute the air with unburned hydrocarbons. The job of the crankcase emission control equipment is to recycle these gases back into the engine combustion chamber where they are reburned.

The crankcase (blow-by) gases are recycled in the following way: as the engine is running, clean, filtered air is drawn through the air filter and into the crankcase. As the air passes through the crankcase, it picks up the combustion gases and carries them out of the crankcase, through the oil separator, through the PCV valve, and into the induction system. As they enter the intake manifold, they are drawn into the combustion chamber where they are reburned.

The most critical component in the system is the PCV valve. Located in the valve cover or intake manifold, this valve controls the amount of gases which are recycled into the combustion chamber. At low engine speeds, the valve is partially closed, limiting the flow of the gases into the intake manifold. As engine speed increases, the valve opens to admit greater quantities of the gases into the intake manifold. As engine speed increases, the valve opens to admit greater quantities of the gases into the intake manifold. If the valve should become blocked or plugged, the gases will be prevented from escaping from the crankcase by the normal route. Since these gases are under pressure, they will find their own way out of the crankcase. This alternate route is usually a weak oil seal or gasket in the engine. As the gas escapes by the gasket, it also creates an oil leak. Besides causing oil leaks, a clogged PCV valve also allows these gases to remain in the crankcase for an extended period of time, promoting the formation of sludge in the engine. See Section 1 for PCV valve replacement intervals.

#### Diesel Engines
▶ See Figure 3

A Crankcase Depression Regulator Valve (CDRV) or flow control valve is used to regulate (meter) the flow of crankcase gases back into the engine to be burned. The CDRV is designed to limit vacuum in the crankcase as the gases are drawn from the valve covers through the CDRV and into the intake manifold (air crossover).

Fresh air enters the engine through the combination filter, check valve and oil fill cap. The fresh air mixes with blow-by gases and enters both valve covers. The gases pass through a filter installed on the valve covers and are drawn into connecting tubing.

Intake manifold vacuum acts against a spring loaded diaphragm to control the flow of crankcase gases. Higher intake vacuum levels pull the diaphragm closer to the top of the outlet tube. This reduces the amount of gases being drawn from the crankcase and decreases the vacuum level in the crankcase. As the intake vacuum decreases, the spring pushes the diaphragm away from the top of the outlet tube allowing more gases to flow to the intake manifold.

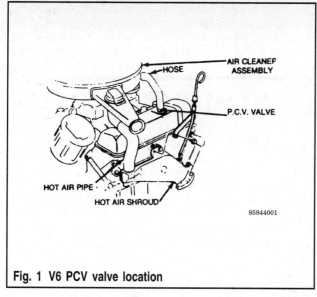

Fig. 1 V6 PCV valve location

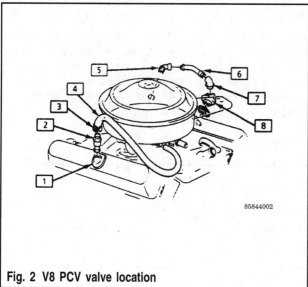

Fig. 2 V8 PCV valve location

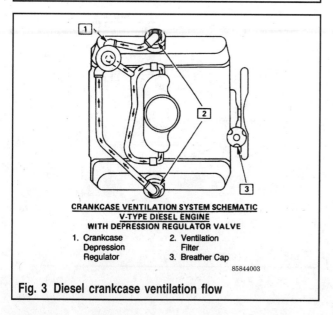

CRANKCASE VENTILATION SYSTEM SCHEMATIC
V-TYPE DIESEL ENGINE
WITH DEPRESSION REGULATOR VALVE

1. Crankcase Depression Regulator
2. Ventilation Filter
3. Breather Cap

Fig. 3 Diesel crankcase ventilation flow

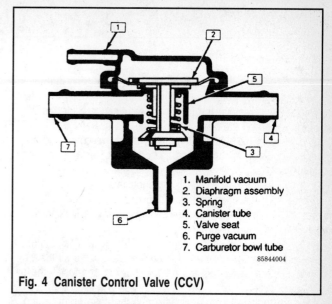

1. Manifold vacuum
2. Diaphragm assembly
3. Spring
4. Canister tube
5. Valve seat
6. Purge vacuum
7. Carburetor bowl tube

Fig. 4 Canister Control Valve (CCV)

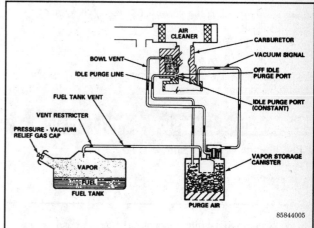

Fig. 5 Open canister evaporative emission control system (EECS). This system is more common than the closed system

## SERVICE

### Gasoline Engines

Slow, unstable idling, frequent stalling, oil leaks and oil in the air cleaner are all signs that the PCV valve may be clogged or faulty. Follow the PCV valve testing procedure in Section 1 and replace the valve if necessary. Check the valve at every tune-up.

### Diesel Engines

Do not attempt to test these valves. Instead, follow the cleaning procedures in Section 1 if you are experiencing problems with the system.

## REMOVAL & INSTALLATION

### Gasoline Engines

1. To replace the filter, slide the rubber coupling that joins the tube coming from the valve cover to the filter off the filter nipple. Then, remove the top of the air cleaner. Slide the spring clamp off the filter, and remove the filter.

2. Inspect the rubber grommet in the valve cover and the rubber coupling for brittleness and cracking. Replace parts as necessary.

3. Insert the new PCV filter through the hole in the air cleaner with the open portion of the filter upward. Make sure that the square portion of filter behind the nipple fits into the (square) hole in the air cleaner.

4. Install a new spring clamp onto the nipple. Make sure the clamp goes under the ridge on the filter nipple all the way around. Then, reconnect the rubber coupling and install the air cleaner cover.

5. To replace the valve, gently pull the hose from the top of the valve, then pull the valve out of the cover grommet.

6. Installation is the reverse of removal.

### Diesel Engines

The filter assemblies can be removed by carefully prying them from the valve covers.

## Evaporative Emission Control System

▶ **See Figures 4, 5, 6, 7 and 8**

## OPERATION

This system reduces the amount of escaping gasoline vapors. Float bowl emissions are controlled by internal carburetor modifications. Redesigned bowl vents, reduced bowl capacity, heat shields, and improved intake manifold-to-carburetor insulation reduce vapor loss into the atmosphere. The venting of fuel tank vapors into the air has been stopped by means of the carbon canister storage method. This method transfers fuel vapors to an activated carbon storage device which absorbs and stores the vapor that is emitted from the engine's induction system while the engine is not running. When the engine is running, the stored vapor is purged from the carbon storage device by the intake air flow and then consumed in the normal combustion process. As the manifold vacuum reaches a certain point, it opens a purge control valve atop the charcoal storage canister. This allows air to be drawn into the canister, thus forcing the existing fuel vapors back into the engine to be burned normally.

On 1981 and later V6s, the purge function is electronically controlled by a purge solenoid in the line which is itself controlled by the Electronic Control Module (ECM). When the system is in the Open Loop mode, the solenoid valve is energized, blocking all vacuum to the purge valve. When the system is in the Closed Loop mode, the solenoid is de-ener-

gized, thus allowing existing vacuum to operate the purge valve. This releases the trapped fuel vapor and it is forced into the induction system.

Some canister systems (those without a vapor vent valve) starting in 1981 have a Canister Control Valve (C.C.V.). This is mounted near the carburetor and has four hoses connected to it. When the engine is off, manifold vacuum is non-existent at the C.C.V. and a spring loaded valve in the C.C.V. interconnects the carburetor vent hose to the canister via a Thermostatic Vacuum Valve which opens at 170°F (77°C). Vapors generated in the carburetor float bowl thus pass into the canister. When the engine is restarted, this valve closes as manifold vacuum is applied to it. When the TVS is open, the canister is purged as fuel vapors are drawn out of the canister and into the carburetor throttle body.

Most carbon canisters used are of the open design, which means that the incoming air is drawn directly from the air cleaner.

## SERVICE

The only service required for the evaporative emissions system is the periodic replacement of the charcoal canister filter. Closed canisters do not require that this operation be performed. If the fuel tank cap on your vehicle ever requires replacement, make sure that it is of the same type as the original.

## REMOVAL & INSTALLATION

1. Tag and disconnect all hoses.
2. Loosen the retainer clamps and lift out the canister.
3. Grasp the filter element and pull it out.
4. Replace the filter, then place the canister in the clamps and reconnect all hoses.

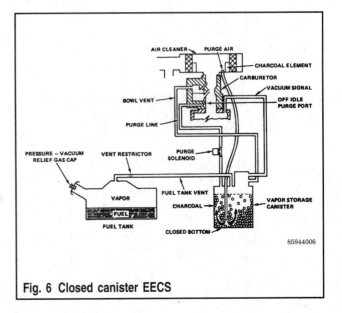

**Fig. 6 Closed canister EECS**

**Fig. 7 Common EECS canister**

**Fig. 8 This model has a TVS located on the air cleaner**

## Exhaust Gas Recirculation (EGR) System

### OPERATION

#### Gasoline Engines
▶ See Figures 9, 10 and 11

All engines covered in this guide are equipped with exhaust gas recirculation (EGR). This system consists of a metering valve, a vacuum line to the carburetor, and cast-in exhaust gas passages in the intake manifold. The EGR valve is controlled by carburetor vacuum, and accordingly opens and closes to admit exhaust gases into the fuel/air mixture. The exhaust gases lower the combustion temperature, and reduce the amount of oxides of nitrogen (NOx) produced. The valve is closed at idle between the two extreme throttle positions.

In most installations, vacuum to the EGR valve is controlled by a thermal vacuum switch (TVS); the switch, which is in-

stalled into the engine block, shuts off vacuum to the EGR valve until the engine is hot. This prevents the stalling and rough idle which would result if EGR occurred when the engine was cold.

As the vehicle accelerates, the carburetor throttle plate uncovers the vacuum port for the EGR valve. At 3-5 in. Hg, the EGR valve opens and then some of the exhaust gases are allowed to flow into the air/fuel mixture to lower the combustion temperature. At full throttle the valve closes again. Some California engines are equipped with a dual diaphragm EGR valve. This valve further limits the exhaust gas opening (compared to the single diaphragm EGR valve) during high intake manifold vacuum periods, such as high speed cruising, and provides more exhaust gas recirculation during acceleration when manifold vacuum is low. In addition to the hose running to the thermal vacuum switch, a second hose is connected directly to the intake manifold.

For 1977, all California models and vehicles delivered in areas above 4000 feet are equipped with back pressure EGR valves. This valve is also used on all 1978-81 models. The EGR valve receives exhaust back pressure through its hollow shaft. This exerts a force on the bottom of the control valve diaphragm, opposed by a light spring. Under low exhaust pressure (low engine load and partial throttle), the EGR signal is reduced by an air bleed. Under conditions of high exhaust pressure (high engine load and large throttle opening), the air bleed is closed and the EGR valve responds to an unmodified vacuum signal. At wide open throttle, the EGR flow is reduced in proportion to the amount of vacuum signal available.

1979 and later models have a ported signal vacuum EGR valve. The valve opening is controlled by the amount of vacuum obtained from a ported vacuum source on the carburetor and the amount of backpressure in the exhaust system.

Some late model vehicles with V6 and V8 engines use EGR Vacuum Control. This system uses a solenoid controlled by the Electronic Control Module to control vacuum going to the EGR valve. The ECM evaluates a number of engine parameters to determine EGR requirements, and then opens and closes the solenoid many times a second to produce the required vacuum. The length of each open cycle is increased to transmit increased vacuum.

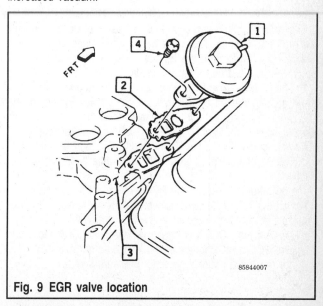

**Fig. 9 EGR valve location**

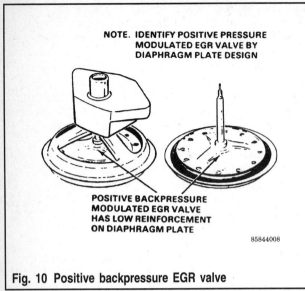

NOTE. IDENTIFY POSITIVE PRESSURE MODULATED EGR VALVE BY DIAPHRAGM PLATE DESIGN

POSITIVE BACKPRESSURE MODULATED EGR VALVE HAS LOW REINFORCEMENT ON DIAPHRAGM PLATE

85844008

Fig. 10 Positive backpressure EGR valve

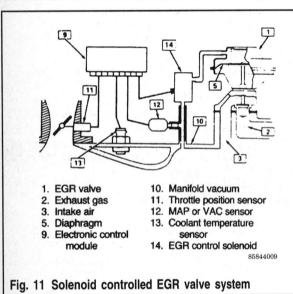

| 1. EGR valve | 10. Manifold vacuum |
|---|---|
| 2. Exhaust gas | 11. Throttle position sensor |
| 3. Intake air | 12. MAP or VAC sensor |
| 5. Diaphragm | 13. Coolant temperature |
| 9. Electronic control | sensor |
| module | 14. EGR control solenoid |

85844009

Fig. 11 Solenoid controlled EGR valve system

## Diesel Engines

The diesel EGR systems work in the same basic manner as the gasoline engines. There are two systems used on the V8 diesels. One is used on the B-body station wagons and the other type is used on all other models.

On the B-body type EGR, vacuum from a vacuum pump is modulated by the Vacuum Regulator Valve (VRV) mounted on the injection pump. Vacuum is highest at idle and decreases to zero at wide open throttle. A Response Vacuum Reducer Valve is used between the VRV and the EGR valve to allow the EGR to change position quickly as throttle position is changed.

On all other V8 diesels, the EGR system is the same as used on the B-body system, except a solenoid is added to the system that shuts off vacuum to the EGR valve when the Torque Converter Clutch is engaged. This solenoid is fed 12V from the TCC switch portion of the VRV and is grounded through the transmission's governor pressure switch.

## COMPONENT TESTING

### Gasoline Engines

To check the EGR valve operation, check with a mirror under the valve to see if the valve moves when the throttle is opened. If the diaphragm does not move, there is either a problem with vacuum or the valve is stuck. With the valve stuck open, the engine will run very rough at idle or may not even start. If it is stuck closed, you would likely experience severe pinging when the engine is under load or on acceleration. With a vacuum gauge hooked up at the EGR vacuum line, you should see vacuum on the gauge when the throttle is opened. To find out if the exhaust gas is actually recirculating, use a hand vacuum pump to open the EGR valve with the engine idling. If the engine runs rough or stalls, the exhaust gas is recirculating. If it does not, remove the EGR valve and clean it as well as the EGR ports in the intake manifold. When testing with a hand vacuum pump, EGR valves should hold a steady vacuum and not leak. If they do leak, they must be replaced.

The newer back-pressure type EGR valves cannot be tested with a vacuum pump. The only practical way to test these valves is by substitution of a known good valve.

### Diesel Engines

#### VACUUM REGULATOR VALVE (VRV)

▶ See Figure 12

The Vacuum Regulator Valve is attached to the side of the injection pump and regulates vacuum in proportion to throttle angle. Vacuum from the vacuum pump is supplied to port A and vacuum at port B is reduced as the throttle is opened. At closed throttle, the vacuum is 15 in. Hg; at half throttle, 6 in. Hg; at wide open throttle there is zero vacuum.

#### EXHAUST GAS RECIRCULATION (EGR) VALVE

▶ See Figure 13

Apply vacuum to vacuum port. The valve should be fully open at 10.5 in. Hg and closed below 6 in. Hg on 1984 and

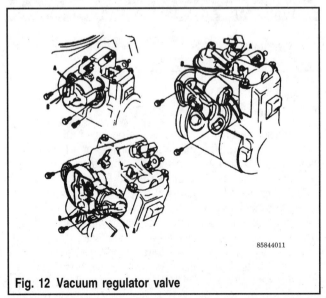

85844011

Fig. 12 Vacuum regulator valve

earlier models. On 1985 models, the valve should be wide open at 21 in. Hg and closed below 6 in. Hg.

### RESPONSE VACUUM REDUCER (RVR)

▶ See Figure 14

Connect a vacuum gauge to the port marked **To EGR valve** or **T.C.C. solenoid.** Connect a hand operated vacuum pump to the VRV port. Draw a 50.66 kPa (15 in. Hg) vacuum on the pump and the reading on the vacuum gauge should be lower than the vacuum pump reading. Models up to 1983: 0.75 in. Hg Except High Altitude; 2.5 in. Hg High Altitude. 1984 Models: 2 in. Hg.

### TORQUE CONVERTER CLUTCH OPERATED SOLENOID

When the torque converter clutch is engaged, an electrical signal energizes the solenoid allowing ports 1 and 2 to be interconnected. When the solenoid is not energized, port 1 is closed and ports 2 and 3 are interconnected. Specific operation is listed below.

**Models up to 1983:**
Solenoid Energized — Ports 1 and 3 are connected
Solenoid De-energized — Ports 2 and 3 are connected
**1984 Models:**
Solenoid Energized — Ports 1 and 2 are connected
Solenoid De-energized — Ports 2 and 3 are connected

### QUICK VACUUM RESPONSE VALVE

▶ See Figure 15

Tee a vacuum gauge into the line running from this valve to the Exhaust Pressure Regulator (EPR) valve, which is located on the bottom of the exhaust manifold. Disconnect the hose that runs from the inlet port S and connect a hand vacuum pump to the open end of the hose. Draw a vacuum of 22 in. Hg at the pump. The gauge located at the outlet side should read 20.7 in. Hg within two seconds. Reduce the vacuum coming from the pump to 0.9 in. Hg. The vacuum gauge should read the same within half a second.

### EGR-TVS (1984-85 MODELS)

▶ See Figure 16

1. Drain coolant from the engine until the level is below the EGR-TVS. Then, remove the valve from the engine by disconnecting all vacuum lines and electrical leads and unscrewing it with a wrench on the flats.

### ✳✳CAUTION

**When draining the coolant, keep in mind that cats and dogs are attracted by the ethylene glycol antifreeze, and are quite likely to drink any that is left in an uncovered container or in puddles on the ground. This will prove fatal in sufficient quantity. Always drain the coolant into a sealable container.**

2. Inspect the valve for any visible defects and replace it if any are visible. Allow the valve to cool to room temperature.

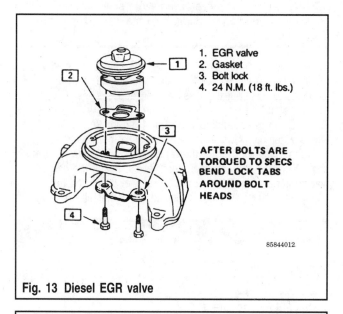

1. EGR valve
2. Gasket
3. Bolt lock
4. 24 N.M. (18 ft. lbs.)

AFTER BOLTS ARE TORQUED TO SPECS BEND LOCK TABS AROUND BOLT HEADS

85844012

**Fig. 13  Diesel EGR valve**

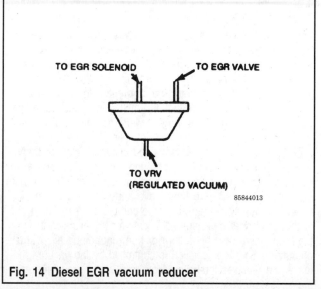

TO EGR SOLENOID      TO EGR VALVE

TO VRV (REGULATED VACUUM)

85844013

**Fig. 14  Diesel EGR vacuum reducer**

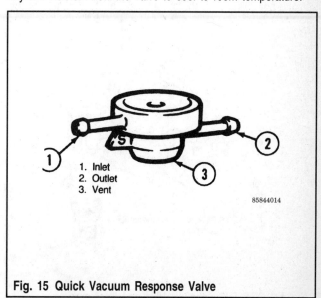

1. Inlet
2. Outlet
3. Vent

85844014

**Fig. 15  Quick Vacuum Response Valve**

3. Connect a vacuum gauge to port 2 and hand operated vacuum pump to port 4.

4. Connect a self-powered test lamp across the switch terminals.

5. Immerse just the bottom (threaded portion) of the valve in a pan of cool water. Put a thermometer in the water and then heat the water slowly as you pull vacuum and watch the vacuum gauge and also watch the test lamp. The two functions of the switch should respond as specified below:

Vacuum: Port 2 and 3 should become connected and Port 1 should become blocked as the temperature passes 100°F ± 3.6° (38°C).

Electrical: The contacts should open at 107°F ± 3.6° (42°C).

6. Now remove the water from heat, watch the temperature, and check for an appropriate response as the temperature falls:

Vacuum: Port 2 and 1 should be connected and port 3 blocked as the temperature falls below 89°F ± 3.6° (32°C).

Electrical: The contacts should close at 89°F ± 3.6° (32°C).

7. If any of the tests are failed, the valve must be replaced. Coat the threads of the old or replacement valve with sealer and install it. Make all vacuum and electrical connections, replace water/antifreeze mix, operate the engine until hot and check for leaks.

## REMOVAL & INSTALLATION

### Gasoline and Diesel Engines

◆ **See Figures 17, 18 and 19**

1. Detach the vacuum lines from the EGR valve.

2. Unfasten the two bolts or bolt and clamp which attach the valve to the manifold. Withdraw the valve.

**To install:**

3. Clean the valve and intake manifold. For valves that protrude from the mounting face, hold the valve assembly in hand, tap the valve lightly with a small plastic hammer to remove exhaust deposits from the valve seat. Shake out any loose particles. DO NOT put the valve in a vise. Carefully remove any exhaust deposits from the mounting surface of the

valve with a wire wheel or putty knife. Do not damage the mounting surface. Depress the valve diaphragm and inspect the valve seating area through the valve outlet for cleanliness. If the valve and/or seat are not completely clean, repeat procedure. Look for exhaust deposits in the valve outlet, and remove any deposits with a suitable cleaning tool. For valves that do not protrude, clean the base of the valve with a wire brush or wheel to remove exhaust deposits from the mounting surface. Clean the valve seat and valve in an abrasive-type spark plug cleaning machine or sandblaster. Most machine shops provide this service. Make sure the valve portion is cleaned (blasted) for about 30 seconds, and that the valve is also cleaned with the diaphragm spring fully compressed (valve unseated). The cleaning should be repeated until all deposits are removed. The valve must be blown out with compressed air thoroughly to ensure all abrasive material is removed from the valve.

### ✳✳WARNING

**DO NOT wash the valve assembly in solvents or degreasers; permanent damage to the valve diaphragm may result.**

4. Clean the mounting surface of the intake manifold.

5. With the valve removed, start the engine for two seconds to blow out the loose carbon deposits.

**To install:**

6. Clean the mounting surfaces of the intake manifold and valve assembly. Always use a new gasket between the valve and the manifold. Torque the retaining bolts or nuts to 15 ft. lbs. (20 Nm). On dual diaphragm valves, attach the carburetor vacuum line to the tube at the top of the valve, and the manifold vacuum line to the tube at the center of the valve.

## Thermostatic Air Cleaner (THERMAC)

### OPERATION

◆ **See Figures 20 and 21**

All engines covered in this guide utilize the THERMAC system (in 1978 it was called TAC, but was the same). This system is designed to warm the air entering the carburetor when underhood temperatures are low, and to maintain a controlled air temperature into the carburetor at all times. By allowing preheated air to enter the carburetor, the amount of time the choke is on is reduced, resulting in better fuel economy and lower emissions. Engine warm-up time is also reduced.

The Thermac system is composed of the air cleaner body, a filter, sensor unit, vacuum diaphragm, damper door, and associated hoses and connections. Heat radiating from the exhaust manifold is trapped by a heat stove and is ducted to the air cleaner to supply heated air to the carburetor. A movable door in the air cleaner case snorkel allows air to be drawn in from the heat stove (cold operation) or from underhood air (warm operation). The door position is controlled by the vacuum motor, which receives intake manifold vacuum as modulated by the temperature sensor.

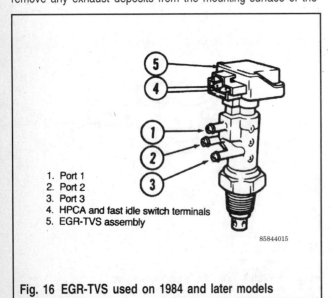

1. Port 1
2. Port 2
3. Port 3
4. HPCA and fast idle switch terminals
5. EGR-TVS assembly

85844015

**Fig. 16 EGR-TVS used on 1984 and later models**

**Fig. 17 After you disconnect the vacuum hose, be sure to label it**

**Fig. 18 On some EGR valves you must pry the lock-tab away from the bolt**

**Fig. 19 Removing the EGR valve from the engine**

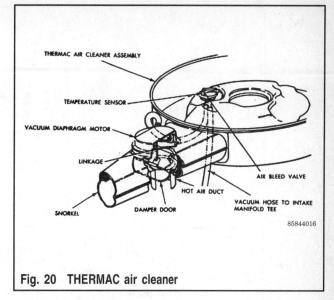

**Fig. 20  THERMAC air cleaner**

## COMPONENT TESTING

1. Check the vacuum hoses for leaks, kinks, breaks, or improper connections and correct any defects.
2. With the engine off, check the position of the damper door within the snorkel. A mirror can be used to make this job easier. The damper door should be open to admit outside air.
3. Apply at least 7 in. Hg of vacuum to the damper diaphragm unit. The door should close. If it does not, check the diaphragm linkage for binding and correct hookup.
4. With vacuum still applied and the door closed, clamp the tube to trap the vacuum. If the door does not remain closed, there is a leak in the diaphragm assembly.
5. If the diaphragm is holding vacuum and the system has source vacuum, the last choose is the air bleed valve located in the air cleaner assembly.
6. The air bleed may be holding the damper door closed even after the vehicle has warmed up. Or the valve may not close the door at all. In any case, if the damper diaphragm and vacuum source are OK, replace the air bleed valve.

## REMOVAL & INSTALLATION

▶ **See Figures 22, 23, 24, 25 and 26**

**Vacuum Motor**

1. Remove the air cleaner and the vacuum hose from the motor.
2. Drill out the two spot welds and remove the retaining strap.
3. Lift up motor, cocking it to one side to unhook the motor linkage at the control damper assembly.
4. Install the vacuum motor linkage into the control damper assembly.
5. Use a sheet metal screw to resecure the motor retaining strap.
6. Reinstall the vacuum hose and the air cleaner.

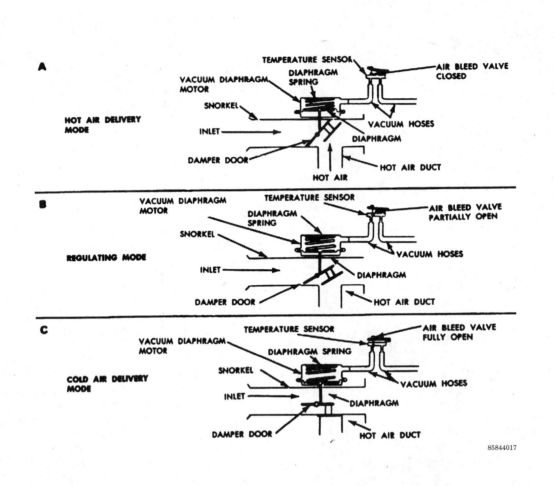

**A**
HOT AIR DELIVERY MODE

TEMPERATURE SENSOR
DIAPHRAGM SPRING
VACUUM DIAPHRAGM MOTOR
SNORKEL
INLET
DAMPER DOOR
HOT AIR
AIR BLEED VALVE CLOSED
VACUUM HOSES
DIAPHRAGM
HOT AIR DUCT

**B**
REGULATING MODE

VACUUM DIAPHRAGM MOTOR
TEMPERATURE SENSOR
DIAPHRAGM SPRING
SNORKEL
INLET
DAMPER DOOR
AIR BLEED VALVE PARTIALLY OPEN
VACUUM HOSES
DIAPHRAGM
HOT AIR DUCT

**C**
COLD AIR DELIVERY MODE

VACUUM DIAPHRAGM MOTOR
TEMPERATURE SENSOR
DIAPHRAGM SPRING
SNORKEL
INLET
DAMPER DOOR
AIR BLEED VALVE FULLY OPEN
VACUUM HOSES
DIAPHRAGM
HOT AIR DUCT

85844017

**Fig. 21 Vacuum motor positions**

### Sensor

1. Remove the air cleaner and vacuum hoses.
2. Pry up the tabs on the sensor retaining clip. Remove the clip and the sensor from the air cleaner. Note the position of sensor for installation.
3. Install the sensor and gasket in original position.
4. Install vacuum hoses and air cleaner.

## Air Injection Reactor System (A.I.R.)

### OPERATION

▶ See Figure 27

The AIR system injects compressed air into the exhaust system, near enough to the exhaust valves to continue burning the normally unburned segment of the exhaust gases. To do this it employs an air injection pump and a system of hoses, valves, tubes, etc., necessary to carry the compressed air from

85844109

**Fig. 22 Remove the air cleaner cover and element**

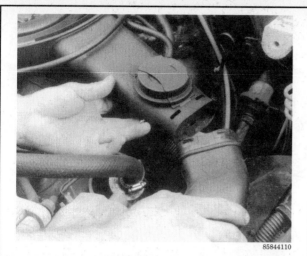

Fig. 23 On some models, the air intake hose is retained by small lock tabs

Fig. 24 Be sure to label all vacuum hoses when disconnecting them

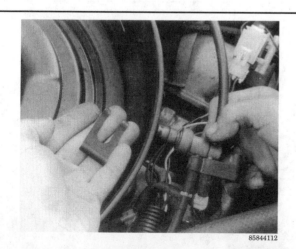

Fig. 25 To remove any other sensors or switches from the side of the air cleaner, simply pull the retaining clip out

Fig. 26 The Thermac sensor is located on the bottom of the air cleaner. Pry the retaining off to remove the sensor

the pump to the exhaust manifolds. Carburetors and distributors for AIR engines have specific modifications to adapt them to the air injection system; those components should not be interchanged with those intended for use on engines that do not have the system.

A diverter valve is used to prevent backfiring. The valve senses sudden increases in manifold vacuum and ceases the injection of air during fuel rich periods. During coasting, this valve diverts the entire air flow through the pump muffler and during high engine speeds, expels it through a relief valve. Check valves in the system prevent exhaust gases from entering the pump.

➡The AIR system on the V6 engines is slightly different, but its purpose remains the same.

## SERVICE

The AIR system's effectiveness depends on correct engine idle speed and ignition timing. These settings should be strictly adhered to and checked frequently. All hoses and fittings should be inspected for condition and tightness of connections. Check the drive belt for wear and tension every 12 months or 12,000 miles.

## REMOVAL & INSTALLATION

▶ See Figures 28, 29 and 30

Air Pump

### ✳✳CAUTION

Do not pry on the pump housing or clamp the pump in a vise; the housing is soft aluminum and may become distorted.

1. Disconnect the negative (-) battery cable and the air hoses at the pump.
2. Hold the pump pulley from turning and loosen the pulley bolts.

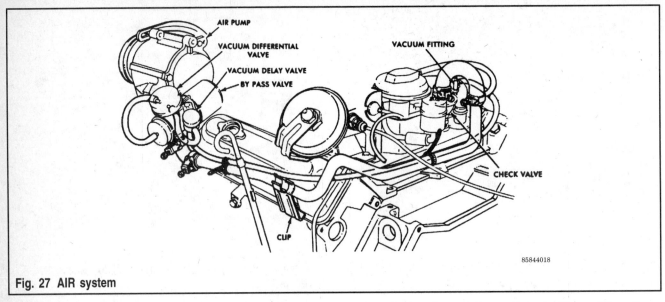

**Fig. 27 AIR system**

3. Loosen the pump mounting bolt and adjustment bracket bolt. Remove the drive belt.

4. Remove the mounting bolts, and then remove the pump.

**To install:**

5. Position the pump into the mounting brackets and loosely install the bolts.

6. Install the drive belt and adjust the tension to 146 ft. lbs. for a new belt and 90 ft. lbs. for an old belt. Torque the mounting bolts to 25 ft. lbs. (34 Nm).

7. Install and reconnect the pump hoses and electrical connections.

**Pump Filter**

1. Remove the drive belt and pump pulley.

2. Using needlenose pliers, pull the fan/filter unit from the pump hub.

➡**Use care to prevent any dirt or fragments from entering the air intake hole. DO NOT insert a screwdriver between the pump and the filter, and do not attempt to remove the metal hub. It is seldom possible to remove the filter without destroying it.**

3. To install a new filter, draw it on with the pulley and pulley bolts. Do not hammer or press the filter onto the pump.

4. Draw the filter down evenly by torquing the bolts alternately. Make sure the outer edge of the filter slips into the housing. A slight amount of interference with the housing bore is normal.

➡**The new filter may squeal initially until the sealing lip on the pump outer diameter has worn in.**

**Diverter (Anti-Afterburn) Valve**

1. Detach the vacuum sensing line and electrical connections from the valve.

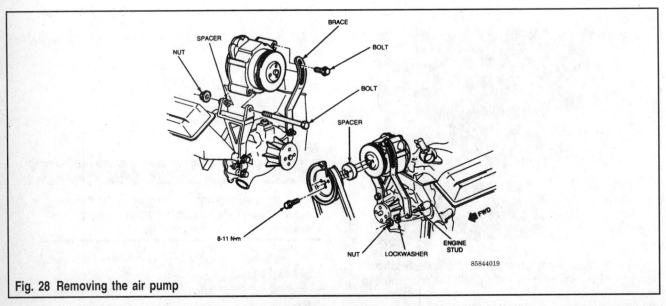

**Fig. 28 Removing the air pump**

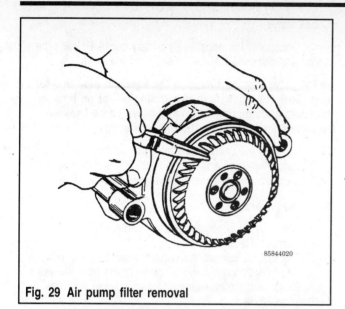

**Fig. 29 Air pump filter removal**

**Fig. 30 Common air pump mounting and location**

2. Remove the other hose(s) from the valve.

3. Unfasten the diverter valve from the elbow or the pump body.

**To install:**

4. Always use a new gasket. Tighten the valve securing bolts to 85 inch lbs. (10 Nm).

## Air Management System

▶ See Figures 31 and 32

## OPERATION

The Air Management system is used on 1981 and later vehicles to provide additional oxygen to continue the combustion process after the exhaust gases leave the combustion chamber; it works in much the same way as the AIR system described earlier in this section. Air is injected into either the exhaust port(s), the exhaust manifold(s) or the catalytic con-

verter by an engine driven air pump. The system is in operation at all times and will bypass air only momentarily during deceleration and at high speeds. The bypass function is performed by the air management valve, while the check valve protects the air pump by preventing any backflow of exhaust gases.

The AIR system helps to reduce HC and CO contents in the exhaust gases by injecting air into the exhaust ports during cold engine operation. This air injection also helps the catalytic converter to reach the proper temperature quicker during warm-up. When the engine is warm (closed loop), the AIR system injects air into the beds of a three-way converter to lower the HC and CO content in the exhaust. The air management system utilizes the following components:

1. An engine driven air pump
2. Air management valves (Air Control and Air Switching)
3. Air flow and control hoses
4. Check valves
5. A dual-bed, three-way catalytic converter

The belt driven, vane type air pump is located at the front of the engine and supplies clean air to the system for purposes already stated. When the engine is cold, the Electronic Control Module (ECM) energizes an air control solenoid. This allows air to blow to the air switching valve. The air switching valve is then energized to direct air into the exhaust ports.

When the engine is warm, the ECM de-energizes the air switching valve, thus directing the air between the beds of the catalytic converter. This then provides additional oxygen for the oxidizing catalyst in the second bed to decrease HC and CO levels, while at the same time keeping oxygen levels low in the first bed, enabling the reducing catalyst to effectively decrease the levels of NOx.

If the air control valve detects a rapid increase in manifold vacuum (deceleration), certain operating modes (wide open throttle, etc.) or if the ECM self-diagnostic system detects any problems in the system, air is diverted to the air cleaner or directly into the atmosphere.

The primary purpose of the ECM's divert mode is to prevent backfiring. Throttle closure at the beginning of deceleration will temporarily create air/fuel mixtures which are too rich to burn completely. These mixtures will become burnable when they

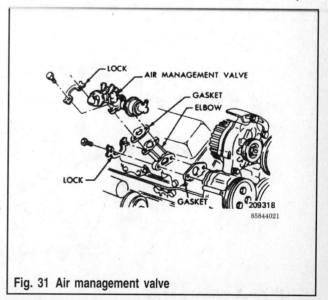

**Fig. 31 Air management valve**

reach the exhaust if they are combined with injection air. The next firing of the engine will ignite the mixture causing an exhaust backfire. Momentary diverting of the injection air from the exhaust prevents this.

The air management system check valves and hoses should be checked periodically for any leaks, cracks or deterioration.

## SERVICE

This effectiveness depends on correct engine idle speed and ignition timing. These settings should be strictly adhered to and checked frequently. All hoses and fittings should be inspected for condition and tightness of connections. Check the drive belt for wear and tension every 12 months or 12,000 miles.

## REMOVAL & INSTALLATION

### Air Pump

1. Disconnect the negative (-) battery cable. Remove the valves and/or adapter at the air pump.
2. Loosen the air pump adjustment bolt and remove the drive belt.
3. Unscrew the three mounting bolts and then remove the pump pulley.
4. Unscrew the pump mounting bolts and then remove the pump.
   **To install:**
5. Be sure to adjust the drive belt tension after installing the pump.
6. Install the three mounting bolts and adjust the belt to 146 ft. lbs. for a new belt and 90 ft. lbs. for an old belt.
7. Torque the air pump adjustment bolt to 25 ft. lbs. (34 Nm).
8. Connect the negative (-) battery cable. Install the valves and/or adapter at the air pump.

### Check Valve

1. Disconnect the negative (-) battery cable. Release the clamp and disconnect the air hoses from the valve.

➡**The valve may be seized to the injection pipe due to rust. Soak the fitting with penetrating oil for an hour or two before attempting removal. Always use a backup wrench when attempting to remove the valve.**

2. Unscrew the check valve from the air injection pipe.
3. Install the valve and torque to 30 ft. lbs. (41 Nm). Connect all disconnected hoses and negative battery cable.

### Air Management Valve

1. Disconnect the negative battery cable.
2. Remove the air cleaner.
3. Tag and disconnect the vacuum hose from the valve.
4. Tag and disconnect the air outlet hoses from the valve
5. Bend back the lock tabs and then remove the bolts holding the elbow to the valve.
6. Tag and disconnect any electrical connections at the valve and then remove the valve from the elbow.
   **To install:**
7. Install the valve and connect any electrical connections at the valve.
8. Torque the valve bolts to 10 ft. lbs. (14 Nm) and bend back the lock tabs.
9. Connect the air outlet hoses to the valve
10. Connect the vacuum hose to the valve.
11. Install the air cleaner.
12. Connect the negative battery cable.

### Pump Filter

1. Remove the drive belt and pump pulley.
2. Using needlenose pliers, pull the fan/filter unit from the pump hub.

➡**Use care to prevent any dirt or fragments from entering the air intake hole. DO NOT insert a screwdriver between the pump and the filter, and do not attempt to remove the metal hub. It is seldom possible to remove the filter without destroying it.**

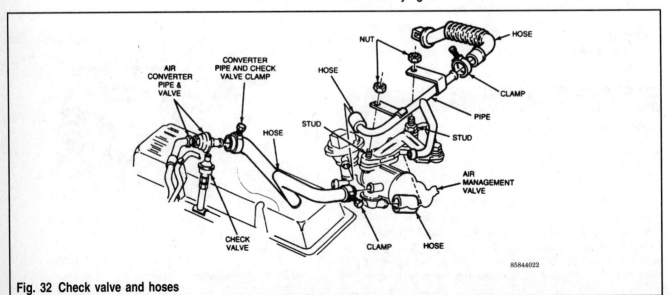

Fig. 32 Check valve and hoses

3. To install a new filter, draw it on with the pulley and pulley bolts. Do not hammer or press the filter onto the pump.

4. Draw the filter down evenly by torquing the bolts alternately. Make sure the outer edge of the filter slips into the housing. A slight amount of interference with the housing bore is normal.

➥**The new filter may squeal initially until the sealing lip on the pump outer diameter has worn in.**

## Early Fuel Evaporation (EFE) System

▶ **See Figures 33, 34 and 35**

## OPERATION

Two types of EFE have been used on the engines covered in this guide. Both provide quick heat to the induction system. This helps evaporate fuel (allowing the choke to close faster and thus reducing emissions) when the engine is cold. It also aids cold driveability. The vacuum servo EFE system uses a valve between the exhaust manifold and exhaust pipe, operated by vacuum and controlled by either a thermal vacuum valve or electric solenoid. The valve causes hot exhaust gas to enter the intake manifold heat riser passages, heating the incoming fuel mixture. The electrically heated type EFE uses a ceramic heater plate located under the carburetor, controlled through the ECM. The vacuum type EFE should be checked for proper operation at every tune-up.

➥**On 1981 and later V6 engines, the EFE system is controlled by the ECM.**

## COMPONENT TESTING

### Vacuum type

1. Locate the EFE valve on the exhaust manifold and not the position of the actuator arm. On some vehicles, the valve and arm are covered by a two-piece cover which must be removed for access. Make sure the engine is overnight cold.

2. Watch the actuator arm when the engine is started. The valve should close when the engine is started cold; the actuator link will be pulled into the diaphragm housing.

3. If the valve does not close, stop the engine. Remove the hose from the EFE valve and apply 10 in. Hg of vacuum by hand pump. The valve should close and stay closed for at least 20 seconds (you will hear it close). If the valve opens in less than 20 seconds, replace it. The valve could also be seized if it does not close; lubricate it with spray type manifold heat valve lube. If the valve does not close when vacuum is applied and when it is lubricated, replace the valve.

4. If the valve closes, the problem is not with the valve. Check for loose, cracked, pinched or plugged hoses, and replace as necessary. Test the EFE solenoid (located on the valve cover bracket); if it is working, the solenoid plunger will emit a noise when the current is applied.

5. Warm up the engine to operating temperature.

6. Watch the EFE valve to see if it has opened. It should now be open. If the valve is still closed, replace the solenoid if

faulty, and/or check the engine thermostat; the engine coolant may not be reaching normal operating temperature.

### Electric type

1. To test the EFE heater, turn the ignition OFF and disconnect the electrical connector.

2. Using an ohmmeter, check the resistance between the two terminals of the heater connector.

3. If resistance is under two ohms, the heater is good. If not, replace the heater.

## REMOVAL & INSTALLATION

### Vacuum type EFE valve

➥**If the vehicle is equipped with an oxygen sensor, it is located near the EFE valve. Use care when removing the EFE valve as not to damage the oxygen sensor.**

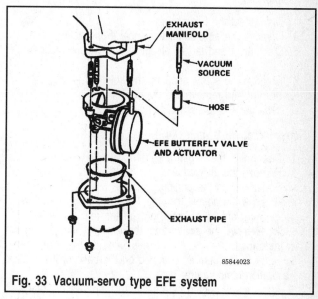

**Fig. 33 Vacuum-servo type EFE system**

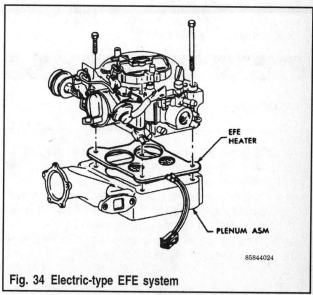

**Fig. 34 Electric-type EFE system**

1. Disconnect the negative (-) battery cable and vacuum hose at the EFE valve.

2. Remove the exhaust pipe-to-manifold nuts, and the washers and tension springs if used.

3. Lower the exhaust cross-over pipe. On some models, complete removal of the pipe is not necessary.

4. Remove the EFE valve.

**To install:** Always install new seals and gaskets. Torque the exhaust nuts to 22 ft. lbs. (30 Nm). Connect the negative battery cable and vacuum hose to the valve.

### Electric type EFE

1. Remove the air cleaner.
2. Disconnect all vacuum, electrical and fuel connections from the carburetor.
3. Disconnect the EFE heater electrical connector.
4. Remove the carburetor.
5. Remove the EFE heater insulator (plate) assembly.
6. Installation is the reverse of removal.

### EFE Solenoid

1. Disconnect the battery ground.
2. Remove the air cleaner assembly if necessary.
3. Disconnect and tag all electrical and vacuum hoses as required.
4. Remove the screw securing the solenoid to the valve cover bracket and remove the solenoid.
5. Installation is reverse of removal.

### Thermal Vacuum Switch (TVS)

1. Disconnect the negative (-) battery cable.
2. Remove the air cleaner.
3. Partially drain the engine coolant.
4. Remove the hoses from the TVS assembly located in the engine coolant outlet housing or at the rear of the intake manifold. Remove the switch from the engine.

**To install:**

5. Refer to the number stamped on the base of the TVS for calibration temperature.
6. Apply a soft setting pipe sealant to the switch threads.
7. Install the switch and torque to 120 inch lbs. (14 Nm). Reconnect the vacuum hoses and negative battery cable.
8. Install the air cleaner assembly.

## Controlled Combustion System

### OPERATION

The CCS system relies upon leaner air/fuel mixtures and altered ignition timing to improve combustion efficiency. A special air cleaner with a thermostatically controlled opening is used on most CCS equipped models to ensure that air entering the carburetor is kept at 100°F (38°C). This allows leaner carburetor settings and improves engine warm-up. A 15°F higher temperature thermostat is employed on CCS vehicles to further improve emission control.

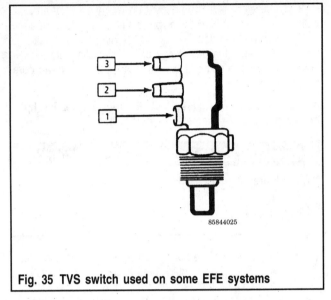

85844025

**Fig. 35 TVS switch used on some EFE systems**

### SERVICE

Since the only extra component added with a CCS system is the thermostatically controlled air cleaner, there is no additional maintenance required; however, tune-up adjustments such as idle speed, ignition timing, and dwell become much more critical. Care must be taken to ensure that these settings are correct, both for trouble free operation and a low emission level.

## Catalytic Converter

▶ See Figures 36, 37 and 38

### OPERATION

The catalytic converter is a muffler-like container built into the exhaust system to aid in the reduction of exhaust emissions. The catalyst element consists of individual pellets or a honeycomb monolithic substrate coated with a metal such as platinum, palladium, rhodium or a combination of these. When the exhaust gases come into contact with the catalyst, a chemical reaction occurs which will reduce the pollutants into harmless substances like water and carbon dioxide.

There are essentially two types of catalytic converters: an oxidizing type is used on all 1975-80 models with the exception of those 1980 models built for California. It requires the addition of oxygen to spur the catalyst into reducing the engine's HC and CO emissions into $H_2O$ and $CO_2$. Because of this need for oxygen, the AIR system is used with all these models.

The oxidizing catalytic converter, while effectively reducing HC and CO emissions, does nothing in the way of reducing NOx emissions. Thus, the three-way catalytic converter was developed to reduce the NOx emissions.

The three-way converter, unlike the oxidizing type, is capable of reducing HC, CO and NOx, emissions, all at the same time. In theory, it seems impossible to reduce all three pollutants in one system since the reduction of HC and CO requires the

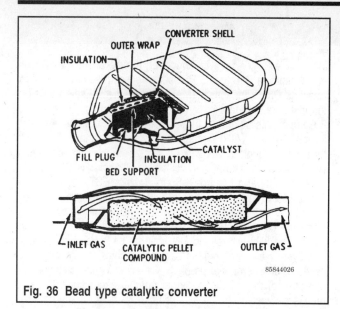

**Fig. 36 Bead type catalytic converter**

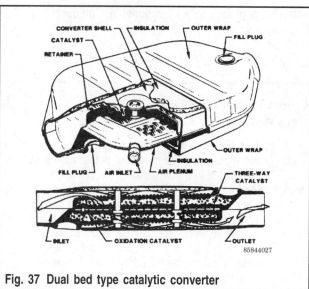

**Fig. 37 Dual bed type catalytic converter**

addition of oxygen, while the reduction of NOx calls for the removal of oxygen. In actuality, the three-way system really can reduce all three pollutants, but only if the amount of oxygen in the exhaust system is precisely controlled. Due to this precise oxygen control requirement, the three-way converter system is used only in vehicles equipped with an oxygen sensor system (1980 Calif. vehicles and all 1981 and later models).

## SERVICE

There are no service procedures required for the catalytic converter, although the converter body should be inspected occasionally for damage. Some models with the V6 engine require a catalyst change at 30,000 mile intervals (consult your Owner's Manual).

## REMOVAL & INSTALLATION

Refer to Section 3 for Removal and Installation procedures.

## Service Flags

### RESETTING

Vehicles equipped with the C-4 system have an emission indicator flag which will appear in the odometer window when service is necessary. The flags are marked SENSOR, EMISSION, and CATALYST, depending on the device that is scheduled for regular maintenance.

To reset the flag, first remove the instrument panel trim plate and cluster cover lens. There are reset notches on the drivers side of the indicator flag. Insert a long, pointed probe diagonally into the detents on the upper left side and rotate the flag downward until an alignment mark becomes visible in the left side of the odometer window. Once the flag has been reset, replace the cluster lens and trim plate.

C-4 and CCC vehicles are equipped with a **Service Engine Soon or Check Engine** light. This light is on the instrument panel below the fuel gauge. The light will come ON during engine start-up to let you know the bulb is working. Have the system checked by your dealer if the light does not come on during start-up or if the light illuminates intermittently or continuously while driving. These conditions may indicate that the Computer Command Control system is in need of service. In most cases, the vehicle will not have to be towed, but the vehicle should be serviced as soon as possible.

For more information about the service light, refer to Computer Command Control section in this section.

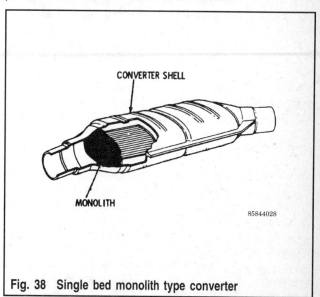

**Fig. 38 Single bed monolith type converter**

## ELECTRONIC ENGINE CONTROLS

## Computerized Engine Systems

### OPERATION

▶ **See Figures 39 and 40**

There are two types of computerized engine systems used on the vehicles covered in this manual. The Computer Controlled Catalytic Converter System (C-4), installed on certain 1979 and all 1980 vehicles sold in California, is an electronically controlled exhaust emissions system. The Computer Command Control System (CCC), installed on all 1981 and later vehicles, is basically a modified version of the C-4 system.

The purpose of the C-4 system is to maintain the ideal air/fuel ratio at which the catalytic converter is most effective. Major components of the system include an Electronic Control Module (ECM), coolant temperature sensor, vacuum control switches, an oxygen sensor, an electronically controlled carburetor and a three-way oxidation reduction \catalytic converter. The system also includes a maintenance reminder flag connected to the odometer which becomes visible in the instrument cluster at regular intervals.

The ECM receives input signals from all sensors. It processes these signals and generates a control signal sent to the carburetor. The control signal cycles between on (lean command) and off (rich command). The amount of on and off time is a function of the input voltage sent to the ECM by the oxygen sensor.

A Check Engine Light is included in the C-4 System installation. When a fault develops, the light comes on, and a trouble code is set into the ECM memory. However, if the fault is intermittent, the light will go out, but the trouble code will remain in the ECM memory as long as the engine is running. The trouble codes are used as a diagnostic aid, and are pre-programmed.

Unless the required tools are available, troubleshooting the C-4 System should be confined to mechanical checks of electrical connectors, vacuum hoses and the like. All diagnosis and repair should be performed by a qualified mechanic with the proper diagnostic equipment.

The CCC system's main advantage over its predecessor is that it can monitor and control a larger number of interrelated emission control systems.

This new system can monitor up to 15 engine/vehicle operating conditions and then use this information to control as many as 9 engine related systems. The system is thereby making constant adjustments to maintain good vehicle performance under all normal driving conditions while at the same time allowing the catalytic converter to effectively control the emissions of NOx, HC and CO.

The CCC system has some components in common with the C-4 system, although they are not interchangeable. These components include the Electronic Control Module (ECM), which, as previously stated, controls many more functions than does its predecessor, an oxygen sensor system, an electronically controlled variable mixture carburetor or throttle body fuel injection, a 3-way catalytic converter, throttle position and coolant sensors, a Barometric Pressure Sensor (BARO), a Manifold Absolute Pressure Sensor (MAP) and a Check Engine light in the instrument panel.

Components unique to the CCC system include the Air Injection Reaction (AIR) management system, a charcoal canister purge solenoid, EGR valve controls, a vehicle speed sensor (VSS), a transmission converter clutch solenoid (TCC), idle speed control and Electronic Spark Timing (EST).

In addition, the system has a built in diagnostic system that recognizes and identifies possible operational problems and alerts the driver through a Check Engine light in the instrument panel. The light will remain ON until the problem is corrected. The system also has built in back-up systems that in most cases of an operational problem, will allow for the continued operation of the vehicle in a near normal manner until the repairs can be made.

➡**Not all engines use all components. Component applications may differ.**

### COMPONENT TESTING

#### Coolant Temperature Sensor
▶ **See Figure 41**

The coolant sensor is a thermistor (a resistor which changes values based on temperature) mounted in the coolant stream. The ECM supplies a five volt signal to the coolant sensor through a resistor in the ECM and measures the voltage. The voltage will be high when the engine is cold and low when the engine is hot. By measuring the voltage, the ECM knows the coolant temperature which affects most systems the ECM controls. A failure in this circuit should set a trouble code 14 or 15. The sensor itself can be tested by removing the sensor (as outlined in Section 3), then subjecting the sensor to changes in temperature and measuring the resistance at the terminals. This may be done with a water bath and a thermometer. Heat the water, watch the thermometer and measure the resistance across the terminals. Compare the readings to the chart. If the resistance values are out of range, replace the sensor.

#### Manifold Air Pressure (MAP) Sensor
▶ **See Figures 42, 43 and 44**

The MAP sensor measures changes in the intake manifold pressure which result from engine load and speed changes, and converts this to a voltage output. MAP is the opposite of what you would read with a vacuum gauge. When manifold pressure is high, vacuum is low. The ECM uses the MAP sensor to control fuel delivery and ignition timing. A failure in this circuit should set a trouble code 34. To test the MAP sensor, have the ignition ON with the engine not running. Check voltage from sensor terminal B to A. It should be within the value specified in the chart. Apply 10 inches of vacuum to the sensor with a vacuum pump. There should be a 1.2-2.3 voltage change. If the sensor did not meet either of these requirements, have the system diagnosed and repaired by a qualified technician.

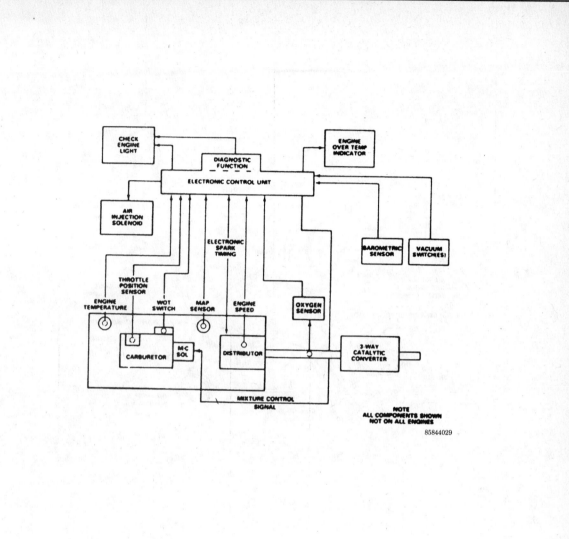

**Fig. 39 C-4 system schematic**

## VAC Sensor

▶ See Figure 45

The differential pressure sensor is similar in appearance to the MAP and BARO sensors. However, it operates just the opposite of the MAP sensor in that it measures the difference between the manifold pressure and atmospheric pressure. The output of the sensor increases as the vacuum increases. A failure in this circuit should set a trouble code 34. To test this sensor, check vacuum at the sensor with a vacuum gauge. It should read at least 10 inches of vacuum. If it is not, repair before continuing. With the ignition ON and engine not running, check voltage from terminals B to A. It should be 0.50-0.64 volts. Connect a vacuum pump to the vacuum port on the sensor and apply 10 inches of vacuum. Voltage should be 2.25-2.95 volts and respond quickly. If the sensor did not meet either of these requirements, have the system diagnosed and repaired by a qualified technician.

## Barometric (BARO) Pressure Sensor

▶ See Figures 46 and 47

The BARO sensor works like the MAP sensor, except that instead of measuring engine manifold pressure, it is open to the outside air, so it can measure barometric pressure. This allows the ECM to adjust for improved driveability at high altitudes. This sensor looks like the MAP sensor but it has a red insert in the harness connector cavity. A failure in the BARO circuit should set a trouble code 32. To test the BARO sensor, have the ignition ON with the engine not running. Check voltage from sensor terminal B to A. It should be within the value specified in the chart. Apply 10 inches of vacuum to the sensor with a vacuum pump. There should be a 1.2-2.3 voltage change. If the sensor did not meet either of these requirements, have the system diagnosed and repaired by a qualified technician.

85844030

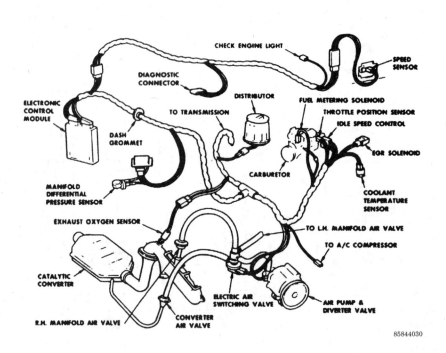

Fig. 40 Common CCC system schematic

| COOLANT SENSOR | | |
|---|---|---|
| TEMPERATURE TO RESISTANCE VALUES (APPROXIMATE) | | |
| °F | °C | OHMS |
| 210 | 100 | 185 |
| 160 | 70 | 450 |
| 100 | 38 | 1,600 |
| 70 | -20 | 3,400 |
| 40 | -4 | 7,500 |
| 20 | -7 | 13,500 |
| 0 | -18 | 25,000 |
| -40 | -40 | 100,700 |

85844031

Fig. 41 Temperature to resistance values

85844032

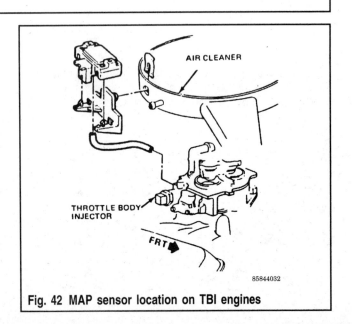

Fig. 42 MAP sensor location on TBI engines

| **Altitude | Voltage Range | |
|---|---|---|
| Below 1,000' | 3.8 — | 5.5V |
| 1,000—2,000' | 3.6 — | 5.3V |
| 2,000—3,000' | 3.5 — | 5.1V |
| 3,000—4,000' | 3.3 — | 5.0V |
| 4,000—5,000' | 3.2 — | 4.8V |
| 5,000—6,000' | 3.0 — | 4.6V |
| 6,000—7,000' | 2.9 — | 4.5V |
| 7,000—8,000' | 2.8 — | 4.3V |
| 8,000—9,000' | 2.6 — | 4.2V |
| 9,000—10,000' | 2.5 — | 4.0V |

85844033

Fig. 43 MAP sensor values (Non-Turbo)

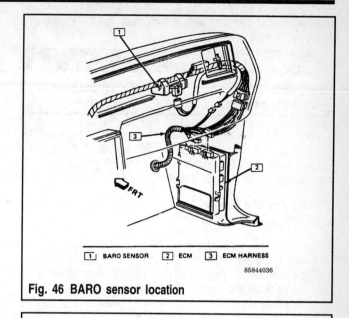

| 1 | BARO SENSOR | 2 | ECM | 3 | ECM HARNESS |

85844036

Fig. 46 BARO sensor location

| **Altitude | Voltage Range | |
|---|---|---|
| Below 1,000' | 1.7 — | 3.2V |
| 1,000—2,000' | 1.6 — | 3.0V |
| 2,000—3,000' | 1.5 — | 2.8V |
| 3,000—4,000' | 1.4 — | 2.7V |
| 4,000—5,000' | 1.3 — | 2.6V |
| 5,000—6,000' | 1.3 — | 2.5V |
| 6,000—7,000' | 1.2 — | 2.5V |
| 7,000—8,000' | 1.1 — | 2.4V |
| 8,000—9,000' | 1.1 — | 2.3V |
| 9,000—10,000' | 1.0 — | 2.2V |

85844034

Fig. 44 MAP sensor values (Turbo)

| **Altitude | Voltage Range | |
|---|---|---|
| Below 1,000' | 3.8 — | 5.5V |
| 1,000—2,000' | 3.6 — | 5.3V |
| 2,000—3,000' | 3.5 — | 5.1V |
| 3,000—4,000' | 3.3 — | 5.0V |
| 4,000—5,000' | 3.2 — | 4.8V |
| 5,000—6,000' | 3.0 — | 4.6V |
| 6,000—7,000' | 2.9 — | 4.5V |
| 7,000—8,000' | 2.8 — | 4.3V |
| 8,000—9,000' | 2.6 — | 4.2V |
| 9,000—10,000' | 2.5 — | 4.0V |

85844037

Fig. 47 BARO sensor values

### Oxygen Sensor

▶ **See Figure 48**

An oxygen sensor is used on all 1980 models built for California and on all 1981 and later models for all 50 states. The sensor protrudes into the exhaust stream and monitors the oxygen content of the exhaust gases. The difference between the oxygen content of the exhaust gases and that of the outside air generates a voltage signal to the ECM. The ECM monitors this voltage and, depending upon the value of the signal received, issues a command to adjust for a rich or a lean condition. A failure in the oxygen sensor circuit can cause trouble codes 13, 44 or 45. To test the oxygen sensor, connect a dwell meter on the 6 cylinder scale to the mixture control solenoid dwell terminal. Start and run the engine until it

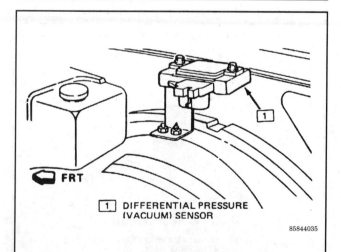

| 1 | DIFFERENTIAL PRESSURE (VACUUM) SENSOR |

85844035

Fig. 45 VAC or MAP sensor location on carbureted engines

reaches normal operating temperature, then run the engine at fast idle for 1 minute.

**⁕⁕CAUTION**

**Keep hands, hair, clothing, wires or any objects clear of moving engine parts.**

Return the engine at idle and note dwell readings. It should be varying between 10 degrees and 50 degrees. If the sensor did not meet these requirements, have the system diagnosed and repaired by a qualified technician.

### Throttle Position Sensor
▶ **See Figures 49 and 50**

On carbureted engines, the throttle position sensor is mounted in the carburetor body and is used to supply throttle position information in the ECM. The ECM memory stores an average of operating conditions with the ideal air/fuel ratios for each of those conditions. When the ECM receives a signal that indicates throttle position change, it immediately shifts to the last remembered set of operating conditions that resulted in an ideal air/fuel ratio control. The memory is continually being updated during normal operations. The TPS is used to regulate the mixture control solenoid, idle speed, EST and TCC lockup. To test the TPS on carbureted engines, first clear any stored codes as outlined in Trouble Codes later in this section. With the engine running at specified idle speed, have an assistant put the car in Drive while applying both the service and parking brakes. Stand to the side of the car and fully depress the TPS plunger for 15 seconds. Ground the diagnostic terminal and check for a trouble code 21. If this test did not set the code, have the system diagnosed and repaired by a qualified technician.

**⁕⁕CAUTION**

**Keep hands, hair, clothing, wires or any objects clear of moving engine parts.**

On throttle body injection engines, the TPS is connected to the throttle shaft on the TBI unit. It is a potentiometer with one end connected to 5 volts from the ECM and the other to ground. A third wire is connected to the ECM to measure the voltage from the TPS. As throttle valve angle changes, so does the output of the TPS. On these engines, a failure in the TPS circuit should cause a trouble code 21 or 22. To test the TPS on TBI engines, have the ignition ON with the engine not running. Check voltage from sensor terminal B to A. It should be approximately 0.5 volts at idle and increase smoothly to about 5 volts at wide open throttle. If the sensor did not meet these requirements, have the system diagnosed and repaired by a qualified technician.

### Idle Speed Control (ISC)

The idle speed control on carbureted engines does just what its name implies; it controls the idle. The ISC is used to maintain low engine speeds while at the same time preventing stalling due to engine load changes. The system consists of a motor assembly mounted on the carburetor which moves the throttle lever so as to open or close the throttle blades.

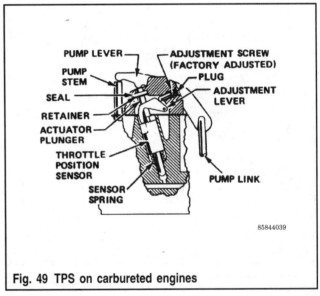

Fig. 49 TPS on carbureted engines

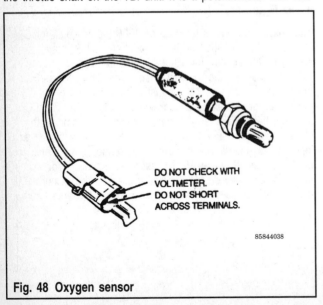

Fig. 48 Oxygen sensor

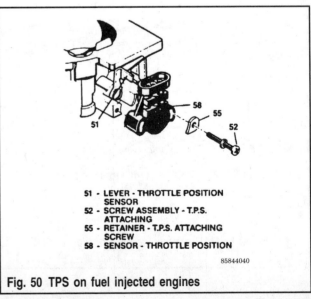

51 - LEVER - THROTTLE POSITION SENSOR
52 - SCREW ASSEMBLY - T.P.S. ATTACHING
55 - RETAINER - T.P.S. ATTACHING SCREW
58 - SENSOR - THROTTLE POSITION

Fig. 50 TPS on fuel injected engines

The whole operation is controlled by the ECM. The ECM monitors engine load to determine the proper idle speed. To prevent stalling, it monitors the air conditioning compressor switch, the transmission, the park/neutral switch and the ISC throttle switch. The ECM processes all this information and then uses it to control the ISC motor which in turn will vary the idle speed as necessary. To test the ISC motor operation, ground the diagnostic connector with the ignition ON, engine not running. The ISC should pulse smoothly in and out. If it did not meet these requirements, have the system diagnosed and repaired by a qualified technician.

## Idle Air Control (IAC)

The purpose of the IAC valve on TBI engines, is to control idle speed, while preventing stalls due to engine engine load. The IAC valve mounted on the throttle body, controls idle by bypassing air around the throttle plates. If idle is too low, more air is bypassed around the plates to increase rpm. If it is too high, less air is bypassed to decrease rpm.

During idle, the proper position of the IAC valve is calculated by the ECM based on battery voltage, coolant temperature, engine load and engine rpm. To test IAC valve operation, have the engine idling at normal operating temperature in Park. Record idle speed.

### ❊❊CAUTION

**Keep hands, hair, clothing, wires or any objects clear of moving engine parts.**

Stop engine and disconnect the IAC valve, then restart the engine and recheck rpm. There should be an idle rpm increase. Stop the engine and reconnect the IAC valve, then restart the engine and recheck rpm once again. The idle should return to the original reading. If it did not meet these requirements, have the system diagnosed and repaired by a qualified technician.

## Electronic Spark Timing (EST)
▶ **See Figure 51**

All 1980 models with the 231 V6 engine and all 1981 and later models use EST. The EST distributor, as described in an earlier section, contains no vacuum or centrifugal advance mechanism and uses a seven terminal HEI module. It has four wires going to a four terminal connector in addition to the connectors normally found on HEI distributors. A reference pulse, indicating engine rpm is sent to the ECM. The ECM determines the proper spark advance for the engine operating conditions and then sends an EST pulse back to the distributor.

Under most normal operating conditions, the ECM will control the spark advance. However, under certain operating conditions such as cranking or when setting base timing, the distributor is capable of operating without ECM control. This condition is called BYPASS and is determined by the BYPASS lead which runs from the ECM to the distributor. When the BYPASS lead is at the proper voltage (5), the ECM will control the spark. If the lead is grounded or open circuited, the HEI module itself will control the spark. Disconnecting the 4-terminal EST connector will also cause the engine to operate in the BYPASS mode. To check EST performance, with the transmis-

sion in Park run the engine at fast idle and note timing change with a timing light as diagnostic lead is grounded.

### ❊❊CAUTION

**Keep hands, hair, clothing, wires or any objects clear of moving engine parts.**

If there is no change, stand to the side of the car and have an assistant in the car apply both the parking and service brakes. Perform the same test with the engine at idle in Drive as not all engines have EST operating when in Park. If there was no timing change in at least one of these tests, have the system diagnosed and repaired by a qualified technician.

## Electronic Spark Control (ESC)
▶ **See Figures 52, 53 and 54**

The Electronic Spark Control (ESC) system is a closed loop system that controls engine detonation by adjusting the spark timing. There are two basic components in this system, the module and the detonation sensor.

The module processes the sensor signal and modifies the EST signal to the distributor to adjust the spark timing. The process is continuous so that the presence of detonation is monitored and controlled. The module is not capable of memory storage.

The sensor is a magneto-restrictive device (meaning that is magnetically controls the flow of electricity), mounted in the engine block that detects the presence, or absence, and intensity of detonation according to the vibration characteristics of the engine. The output is an electrical signal which is sent to the controller. To test the ESC system, run the engine at fast idle and note RPM. Use a steel rod (eg. socket wrench breaker bar) to tap the front area of the intake manifold.

### ❊❊CAUTION

**Keep hands, hair, clothing, wires or any objects clear of moving engine parts.**

Tap the manifold rapidly with medium to heavy taps. Observe engine speed drop of 200 or more rpm. The engine should return to original rpm within 20 seconds after tapping stops. If the ESC system did not meet this requirement, have the system diagnosed and repaired by a qualified technician.

## Transmission Converter Clutch (TCC)
▶ **See Figure 55**

All 1981 and later models with an automatic transmission use TCC. The ECM controls the converter by means of a solenoid mounted in the transmission. When the vehicle speed reaches a certain level, the ECM energizes the solenoid and allows the torque converter to mechanically couple the transmission to the engine. When the operating conditions indicate that the transmission should operate as a normal fluid coupled transmission, the ECM will de-energize the solenoid. Depressing the brake will also return the transmission to normal automatic operation.

The TCC may lock up early and give a feeling of engine lugging or vibration if you install over-size tires on your vehicle. This is because the clutch engages at a certain vehicle speed,

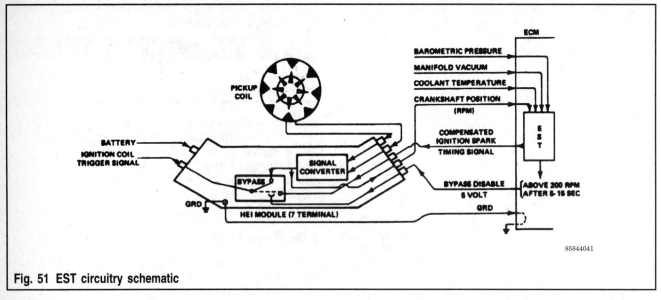

**Fig. 51 EST circuitry schematic**

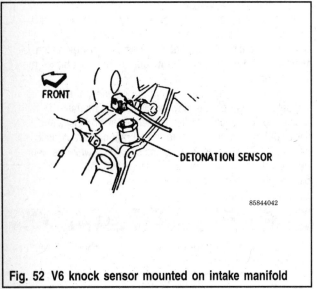

**Fig. 52 V6 knock sensor mounted on intake manifold**

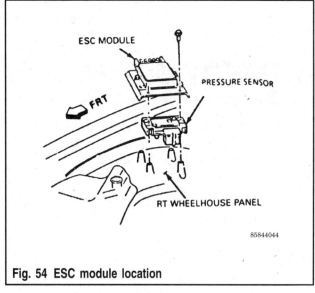

**Fig. 54 ESC module location**

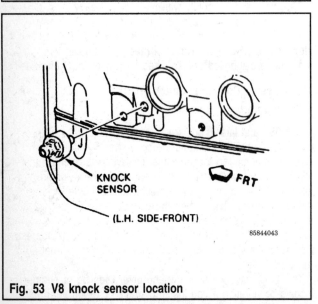

**Fig. 53 V8 knock sensor location**

not at a certain engine rpm. You can usually install tires one size larger than the original equipment tires, but if they are two sizes or more larger than original equipment, you may experience this form of engine roughness. Testing of the TCC should be left to a qualified technician.

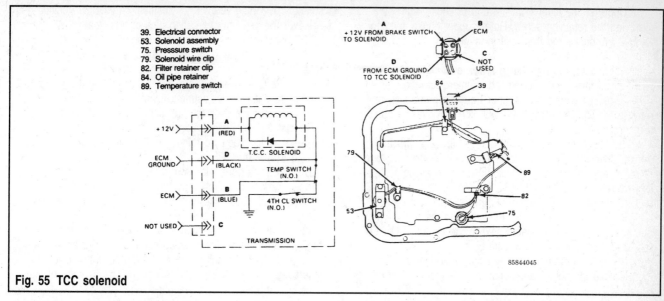

39. Electrical connector
53. Solenoid assembly
75. Presssure switch
79. Solenoid wire clip
82. Filter retainer clip
84. Oil pipe retainer
89. Temperature switch

**Fig. 55 TCC solenoid**

## REMOVAL & INSTALLATION

### Electronic Control Module (ECM)

1. Disconnect the negative battery cable.

#### ✳✳WARNING

**To prevent ECM damage, the ignition must always be OFF, BEFORE disconnecting the negative battery cable. The cable should be left disconnected when installing or removing the ECM. Before handling any electronic components, be sure to eliminate any possibility of electrostatic discharge by wearing a grounding strap attached to your wrist. Also, when replacing the PROM, it is possible to install it backwards. If it is installed backwards when the ignition key is turned ON, the PROM will be destroyed. Always note position of the PROM before removing it.**

2. Remove the right hand hush panel.
3. Disconnect the connectors to the ECM.
4. Remove the ECM.
5. If you are replacing the ECM, remove the PROM from the ECM and place it in the new ECM. Read the warning above.
6. Installation is the reverse of removal.

### Coolant Temperature Sensor

1. Disconnect the negative battery cable.
2. Disconnect the senor electrical sensor.

➡On most vehicles it will be necessary to drain the engine cooling system to a level just below the sensor, or the system will drain itself as the sensor is removed.

3. Carefully back out the coolant sensor.
4. Installation is the reverse of removal.

### MAP, BARO, VAC Sensors

1. Disconnect the negative battery cable.
2. Disconnect the electrical harness connection.
3. Disconnect the vacuum hose.

4. Remove the sensor from it's mounting bracket.
5. Installation is the reverse of removal.

### Oxygen Sensor

➡Take care when handling the oxygen sensor. The in-line connector and louvered end must be kept free of grease and other contaminants. Also, avoid using cleaning solvents of any type. Do not drop or roughly handle the oxygen sensor.

1. Disconnect the negative battery cable.
2. Disconnect the sensor's electrical connection.
3. Carefully back out the oxygen sensor. The sensor may be hard to remove when the engine temperature is below 128°F (48°C). Excessive force may damage threads in the exhaust manifold or exhaust pipe. If removing sensor while the engine is warm, wear protection such as heavy gloves and long sleeves to prevent injury and burns.

To install:
4. Coat the threads of the oxygen sensor with anti-seize compound. Use only the special compound made for oxygen sensors.
5. Install sensor and torque to 30 ft. lbs. (41 Nm).
6. Connect the electrical connector.
7. Connect the negative battery cable.

### Throttle Position Sensor

#### CARBURETED ENGINES

▶ See Figures 56, 57 and 58

➡Adjustment of the throttle position sensor is required after it's replacement. This requires the use expensive special tools. Review the procedures below before attempting replacement of the sensor.

1. Disconnect the negative battery cable.
2. Remove the air cleaner and vacuum hose.
3. Disconnect the idle speed control or idle speed solenoid electrical connections.
4. Remove the air horn:
    a. Attaching screws and remove the idle speed control, idle speed solenoid or idle load compensator.

b. Upper choke lever from the end of choke shaft by removing the retaining screw. Rotate upper choke lever to remove the choke rod from slot in lever.

c. Choke rod from the lower lever inside the float bowl casting. Remove rod by holding lower lever outward with a small screwdriver and twisting rod counterclockwise.

d. (E4ME) Remove the retainer from the pump link, and remove the link from the lever. DO NOT remove the pump lever from the air horn.

e. (E2ME) With tool J-25322 or a $^3/_{32}$ in. (2.4mm) drift punch, drive roll pin (pump lever pivot pin) inward until end of pin is against air cleaner locating boss on air horn casting. Remove pump lever and lever from pump rod.

f. Front vacuum break hose from tube on float bowl.

g. Air horn-to-bowl screws; then remove the two countersunk attaching screws located next to the venturi. DO NOT drop the screws down the throttle bores.

h. Air horn from float bowl by lifting it straight up.

5. Remove the solenoid-metering rod plunger by lifting it straight up.

6. Remove the air horn gasket by lifting it from the dowel locating pins on the float bowl. DISCARD GASKET.

7. Remove the staking holding the TPS in bowl as follows:

a. Lay a flat tool or metal piece across the bowl casting to protect the gasket sealing surface.

b. Use a small screwdriver to depress TPS sensor lightly and hold against spring tension.

c. Carefully pry upward with a small chisel or equivalent to remove bowl staking, make sure prying force is exerted against the metal piece and not against the bowl casting.

d. Push up from bottom on electrical connector and remove TPS and connector assembly from bowl.

**To install:**

8. Align and install TPS and connector assembly with aligning groove in bowl casting. Push down on connector and sensor assembly so that connector and wires are located below the bowl surface. Be sure the green TPS actuator is in place in the air horn.

9. Install air horn, holding down on pump plunger assembly against return spring tension, and aligning holes in gasket over TPS plunger, solenoid plunger return spring, metering rods,

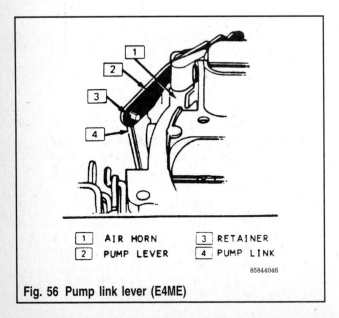

| 1 | AIR HORN | 3 | RETAINER |
| 2 | PUMP LEVER | 4 | PUMP LINK |

85844046

**Fig. 56 Pump link lever (E4ME)**

solenoid attaching screw and electrical connector. Position gasket over the two dowel locating pins on the float bowl.

10. Install solenoid-metering rod plunger, holding down on air horn gasket and pump plunger assembly, and aligning slot in end of plunger with solenoid attaching screw.

11. Carefully lower air horn assembly onto float bowl while positioning the TPS adjustment lever over the TPS, and guiding pump plunger stem through seal in air horn casting. To ease installation, insert a thin screwdriver between air horn gasket and float bowl to raise the TPS adjustment lever positioning it over the TPS.

12. Install air horn attaching screws. Tighten all screws evenly and securely, following the air horn tightening sequence. Don't forget the countersunk screws in the venturi area.

13. Install the front vacuum break and bracket assembly on the air horn, using two attaching screws and tighten securely.

14. (E4ME) Re-install pump rod into hole in pump lever and insert retainer pin. (E2ME) Hook upper end of pump rod into hole in pump lever and place lever between raised bosses on air horn casting, making sure lever engages TPS actuator plunger and the pump plunger stem. Align hole in pump lever in holes in air horn casting bosses. Using a small drift or rod to diameter of the pump lever roll pin will aid alignment. Using sidecutting pliers on the end of the roll pin, pry the roll pin only enough to insert a thin blade screwdriver between the end of the pump lever roll pin and the air cleaner locating boss on the air horn casting. Use screwdriver to push pump lever roll pin back through the casting until the end of the pin is flush with the casting bosses in the air horn.

➡**Use care installing the roll pin to prevent damage to the pump lever bearing surface and casting bosses.**

15. Install the choke rod into the lower choke lever inside the bowl cavity. Install choke rod in slot in upper choke lever, and position lever on end of choke shaft, making sure the flats on the end of the shaft align with the flats in the lever. Install attaching screw and tighten securely. When properly installed, the lever will point to the rear of the carburetor and the number on the lever will face outward.

16. Install idle speed control motor.

17. Reconnect all electrical connections

18. Reconnect negative battery cable.

**To adjust:**

To adjust the TPS it is necessary to remove the plug covering the TPS adjusting screw first.

19. Using a $^5/_{16}$ in. (2mm) drill, drill a $^1/_8$ in. deep hole in the aluminum plug covering the TPS adjustment screw. Use care in drilling to prevent damage to the adjustment screw head.

20. Start a No. 8 $^1/_2$ in. long self-tapping screw in the drilled hole turning screw in only enough to ensure good thread engagement in hole.

21. Placing a wide-blade screwdriver between screw head and air horn casting, pry against screw heads and remove plug. DISCARD PLUG.

22. Adjustment is required if voltage reads different than 0.31 volts on the E2ME or 0.40 volts on the E4ME, by more than ±0.05 volts. If it is within these specifications, no adjustment is needed.

23. Using Tool J-28696, remove TPS adjustment screw.

24. Connect a digital voltmeter from TPS center terminal "B" to bottom terminal "C".

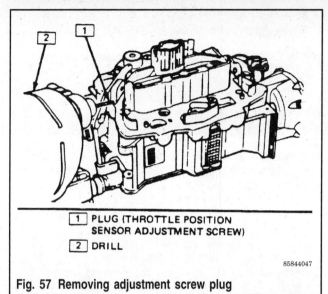

[1] PLUG (THROTTLE POSITION
SENSOR ADJUSTMENT SCREW)
[2] DRILL

85844047

**Fig. 57 Removing adjustment screw plug**

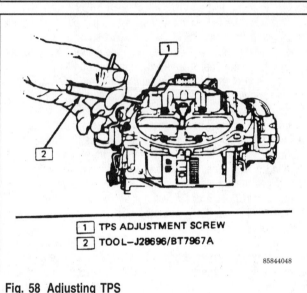

[1] TPS ADJUSTMENT SCREW
[2] TOOL–J28696/BT7967A

85844048

**Fig. 58 Adjusting TPS**

25. With ignition ON, engine not running, reinstall TPS adjustment screw and with Tool J-28696, BT-7967A quickly adjust screw to obtain 0.48 volts with the A/C off and throttle in curb idle position.

26. After adjustment, install new plug in air horn, driving plug into place until flush with raised boss on casting.

### TBI ENGINES

To remove the TPS on these engines, disconnect the electrical connector and remove the two attaching screws. Make sure throttle is in normal closed idle position then install the TPS on the TBI assembly. With the TPS lever located ABOVE the tang on the actuator lever, install the attaching screws using a thread locking compound. Reconnect electrical connector. No adjustment is necessary.

### ISC Motor

1. Disconnect the electrical connector with the ignition OFF.
2. Remove the ISC motor and bracket.

3. Installation is the reverse of removal. Refer to Section 2 for adjustment.

### IAC Valve

#### ♦ See Figure 59

1. Remove the air cleaner.
2. Disconnect the electrical connector.
3. Remove the valve using a 1¼ (32mm) wrench on the hex surface only.

### ✱✱WARNING

**Before installing a new IAC valve, measure the distance that the valve is extended. If the cone is extended too far, damage may occur to the valve when installed.**

#### To install:

4. Measure from motor housing to end of cone. Distance should be no more than 1⅛ in (28mm).

5. If necessary distance can be reduced as follows. Identify valve as being Type 1 or Type 2. For Type 1 valves, exert firm pressure on valve to retract it (a slight side-to-side movement may be helpful). For Type 2 valves, compress the retainer spring while turning valve in with a clockwise motion. Return spring to original position with straight portion of the spring end aligned with the flat surface of the valve.

6. Install the new valve and gasket to the throttle body. Tighten the valve to 13 ft. lbs. (18 Nm).

7. Reconnect the electrical connector and reinstall the air cleaner.

8. Start the engine and allow it to reach operating temperature.

9. The ECM will reset idle speed when vehicle is driven above 35 mph (56 kph).

### Electronic Spark Timing System

Refer to Section 2 for module removal and installation.

### Electronic Spark Control System

1. To remove the ESC Knock Sensor, disconnect the negative battery cable and the sensor connector.

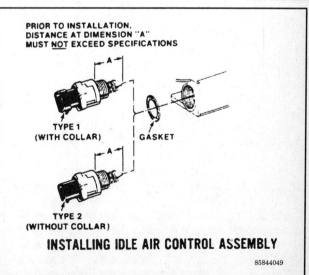

PRIOR TO INSTALLATION.
DISTANCE AT DIMENSION "A"
MUST **NOT** EXCEED SPECIFICATIONS

TYPE 1
(WITH COLLAR)

GASKET

TYPE 2
(WITHOUT COLLAR)

**INSTALLING IDLE AIR CONTROL ASSEMBLY**

85844049

**Fig. 59 Identifying Type 1 or 2 IAC valve**

2. Remove the sensor from the engine block

3. To install the sensor, first apply a sealer such as soft tape to the threads then install sensor.

4. Reconnect the sensor connector and battery cable.

5. To remove the ESC Module, disconnect the electrical connector and the attaching screws.

6. Remove the ESC Module.

7. Installation is the reverse of removal.

**Torque Converter Clutch**

For TCC removal procedures refer to Section 7.

# TROUBLE CODES

## Self-Diagnostics

▶ **See Figures 60, 61, 62 and 63**

The following explains how to activate and erase the trouble codes using the Check Engine light in the instrument cluster. This is not a full fledged C-4 or CCC system troubleshooting and isolation procedure.

Before suspecting the C-4 or CCC system, or any of its components as being faulty, check the ignition system (distributor, timing, spark plugs and wires). Check the engine compression, the air cleaner and any of the emission control components that are not controlled by the ECM. Also check the intake manifold for any leaks. Check the carburetor mounting bolts for tightness. Inspect all vacuum hoses for correct routing, pinching by a harness tie or any object in the engine compartment, cuts, cracks, or loose connections. Make sure to follow them under the air cleaner, generator, or other object to make sure they are in good condition and not pinched along their entire length. Inspect all wiring in a similar manner, checking for chafing of the insulation, burned spots, pinching (which could ground a wire), contact with any sharp edge, or routing too near any hot portion of the engine. Also check that all connections are clean and tight. This visual inspection is extremely important as many operating problems can be cleared up only by repair of bad wiring or vacuum hoses.

Trouble codes tell you there is a problem somewhere in a certain circuit. Because of this, the exact diagnosis of a problem is a very complex procedure involving expensive equipment and should be left to a qualified technician. Once you retrieve a code, you should never just simply replace a sensor in a circuit, as most trouble codes are incurred due to poor connections or bad wiring. Instead, perform a visual inspection of the connectors and wiring of that circuit. If the problem is not found, leave further diagnosis to an experienced technician.

## READING CODES

▶ **See Figures 64 and 65**

As a bulb and system check, the Check Engine light will come on when the ignition switch is turned to the ON position but the engine is not started.

The Check Engine light will also produce the trouble code/codes by a series of flashes which translate as follows: When the diagnostic test lead (C-4) or terminal (CCC) under the instrument panel is grounded, with the ignition in the ON position and the engine not running, the Check Engine light will flash once, pause, and then flash twice in rapid succession. This is a Code 12, which indicates that the diagnostic system is working. After a long pause, the Code 12 will repeat itself two more times. This whole cycle will then repeat itself with any other codes stored in memory until the engine is started or the ignition switch is turned OFF. If it only flashes a Code 12, there are no stored trouble codes.

When the engine is started, the Check Engine light will remain on for a few seconds and then turn off. If the Check Engine light remains on, the self-diagnostic system has detected a problem. If the test lead (C-4) or test terminal (CCC) is then grounded (stop the engine but leave the ignition ON), the trouble code will flash (3) three times. If more than one problem is found to be in existence, each trouble code will flash (3) three times and then change to the next one. Trouble codes will flash in numerical order (lowest code number to highest). The trouble code series will repeat themselves for as long as the test leads or terminal remains grounded.

In the case of an intermittent fault in the system, the Check Engine light will go out when the fault goes away, but the trouble code will remain in the memory of the ECM. Therefore, if a trouble code can be obtained even though the Check Engine light is not on, it must still be evaluated. It must be determined if the fault is intermittent or if the engine must be operating under certain conditions (acceleration, deceleration, etc.) before the Check Engine light will come on. In some cases, certain trouble codes will not be recorded in the ECM until the engine has been operated at part throttle for at least 5-18 minutes.

On the C-4 system, the ECM erases all trouble codes every time that the ignition is turned off. In the case of intermittent faults, a long term memory is desirable. This can be produced by connecting the orange connector/lead from terminal **S** of the ECM directly to the battery (or to a "hot" fuse panel terminal). This terminal must always be disconnected immediately after diagnosis as it puts an unnecessary drain on the battery.

On the C-4 system, activate the trouble code by grounding the trouble code test lead. Use the illustrations to help you locate the test lead under the instrument panel (usually a white and black wire with a green connector). Run a jumper wire from the lead to a suitable ground.

On the CCC system, locate the test terminal under the instrument panel (see illustration). Use a jumper wire and ground only the leads. Jumper **B** to **A** on all models where letters run from **F** to **A** going from right to left.

## CLEARING CODES

# ✱✱WARNING

**The ignition must ALWAYS be in the OFF position when connecting or disconnecting power from the ECM. The module could be destroyed if this is not followed.**

## Trouble Code Identification

| Trouble Code | Possible Problem Area |
|---|---|
| 12 | No reference pulses to the ECM. This is not stored in the memory and will only flash when the fault is present (not to be confused with the Code 12 discussed earlier). |
| 13 | Oxygen sensor circuit. The engine must run for at least 5 min. (18 min. on the C-4 equipped 231 V6) at part throttle before this code will show. |
| 13 & 14 (at same time) | See code 43. |
| 13 & 43 (at same time) | See code 43. |
| 14 | Shorted coolant sensor circuit. The engine must run 2–5 min. before this code will show. |
| 15 | Open coolant sensor circuit. The engine must run for at least 5 min. (18 min. on the C-4 equipped 231 V6) before this code will show. |
| 21 | Shorted wide open throttle switch and/or open closed-throttle switch circuit (when used).<br>Throttle position sensor circuit. The engine must run for at least 10 sec. below 800 rpm before this code will show. |
| 21 & 22 (at same time) | Grounded wide open throttle switch circuit (231 V6). |
| 22 | Grounded closed throttle or wide open throttle switch circuit (231 V6). |
| 23 | Open or grounded carburetor mixture control (M/C) solenoid circuit. |
| 24 | Vehicle speed sensor circuit. The engine must run for at least 5 min. at normal speed before this code will show. |
| 32 | Barometric pressure sensor (BARO) circuit output is low. |
| 32 & 55 (at same time) | Grounded +8V terminal or V(REF) terminal for BARO sensor, or a faulty ECM. |
| 34 | Manifold absolute pressure sensor (MAP) output is high. The engine must run for at least 10 sec. below 800 rpm before this code will show. |
| 35 | Idle speed control circuit shorted. The engine must run for at least 2 sec. above ½ throttle before this code will show. |
| 42 | Electronic spark timing (EST) bypass circuit grounded. |
| 43 | Throttle position sensor adjustment. The engine must run for at least 10 sec. before this code will show. |
| 44 | Lean oxygen sensor indication. The engine must run for at least 5 min. in closed loop (oxygen sensor adjusting carburetor mixture) at part throttle under load (drive car) before this code will show. |
| 44 & 55 (at same time) | Faulty oxygen sensor circuit. |
| 45 | Rich oxygen sensor indication. The engine must run for at least 5 min. before this code will show (see 44 for conditions). |
| 51 | Faulty calibration unit (PROM) or improper PROM installation in the ECM. It will take at least 30 sec. before this code will show. |
| 52 & 53 | "Check Engine" light off: intermittant ECM problem. "Check Engine" light on: faulty ECM—replace. |
| 52 | Faulty ECM. |
| 54 | Faulty mixture control solenoid circuit and/or faulty ECM. |
| 55 | Faulty throttle position sensor or ECM (all but 231 V6).<br>Faulty oxygen sensor, open MAP sensor or faulty ECM (231 V6 only). |

NOTE: *Not all codes will apply to every model.*

85844050

**Fig. 60 C-4 trouble code identification chart**

**TROUBLE CODE IDENTIFICATION**

The trouble codes indicate problems as follows:

TROUBLE CODE 12   No distributor reference signal to the ECM. This code is not stored in memory and will only flash while the fault is present. Normal code with ignition "on," engine not running.

TROUBLE CODE 13   Oxygen Sensor Circuit - The engine must run up to four minutes at part throttle, under road load, before this code will set.

TROUBLE CODE 14   Shorted coolant sensor circuit - The engine must run two minutes before this code will set.

TROUBLE CODE 15   Open coolant sensor circuit - The engine must run five minutes before this code will set.

TROUBLE CODE 21   Throttle Position Sensor (TPS) circuit voltage high (open circuit or misadjusted TPS). The engine must run 10 seconds, at specified curb idle speed, before this code will set.

TROUBLE CODE 22   Throttle Position Sensor (TPS) circuit voltage low (grounded circuit or misadjusted TPS). Engine must run 20 seconds at specified curb idle speed, to set code.

TROUBLE CODE 23   M/C solenoid circuit open or grounded.

TROUBLE CODE 24   Vehicle speed sensor (VSS) circuit - The vehicle must operate up to two minutes, at road speed, before this code will set.

TROUBLE CODE 32   Barometric pressure sensor (BARO) circuit low.

TROUBLE CODE 34   Vacuum sensor or Manifold Absolute Pressure (MAP) circuit - The engine must run up to two minutes, at specified curb idle, before this code will set.

TROUBLE CODE 35   Idle speed control (ISC) switch circuit shorted. (Up to 70% TPS for over 5 seconds.)

TROUBLE CODE 41   No distributor reference signal to the ECM at specified engine vacuum. This code will store in memory.

TROUBLE CODE 42   Electronic spark timing (EST) bypass circuit or EST circuit grounded or open.

TROUBLE CODE 43   Electronic Spark Control (ESC) retard signal for too long a time; causes retard in EST signal.

TROUBLE CODE 44   Lean exhaust indication - The engine must run two minutes, in closed loop and at part throttle, before this code will set.

TROUBLE CODE 45   Rich exhaust indication - The engine must run two minutes, in closed loop and at part throttle, before this code will set.

TROUBLE CODE 51   Faulty or improperly installed calibration unit (PROM). It takes up to 30 seconds before this code will set.

TROUBLE CODE 53   Exhaust Gas Recirculation (EGR) valve vacuum sensor has seen improper EGR vacuum.

TROUBLE CODE 54   M/C solenoid voltage high at ECM as a result of a shorted M/C solenoid circuit and/or faulty ECM.

85844051

**Fig. 61 CCC trouble code identification chart (Carbureted)**

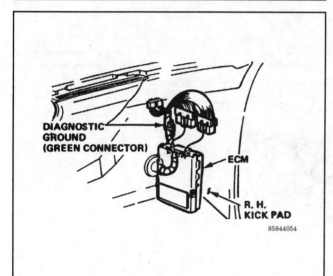

TROUBLE CODE IDENTIFICATION

The trouble codes indicate problems as follows:

Code 13 - Oxygen Sensor Circuit
Code 14 - Coolant Sensor (Low)
Code 15 - Coolant Sensor (High)
Code 21 - TPS (High)
Code 22 - TPS (Low)
Code 24 - Vehicle Speed Sensor
Code 32 - EGR System Failure
Code 33 - MAP Sensor (High)
Code 34 - MAP Sensor (Low)
Code 42 - EST
Code 43 - ESC
Code 44 - Lean Exhaust
Code 45 - Rich Exhaust
Code 51 - PROM
Code 52 - CALPAC
Code 55 - ECM

85844052

**Fig. 62 CCC trouble code identification chart (Fuel Injected)**

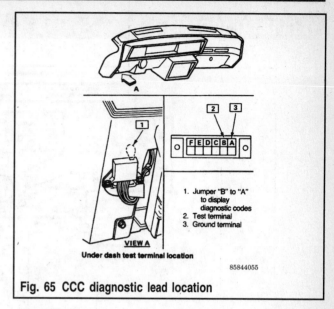

1. Jumper "B" to "A" to display diagnostic codes
2. Test terminal
3. Ground terminal

VIEW A
Under dash test terminal location

85844055

**Fig. 65 CCC diagnostic lead location**

Codes can be cleared by using any of the three following procedures:

1. Removing the ECM fuse from the fuse panel for 30 seconds.

2. Disconnecting the ECM pigtail near the battery.

3. The codes can also be cleared by disconnecting the negative battery cable, however, it will clear other memory systems such as the clock and radio as well.

If the codes reappear after clearing, it indicates the trouble area has not been repaired.

DIAGNOSTIC GROUND (GREEN CONNECTOR)

ECM

R. H. KICK PAD

85844054

**Fig. 64 C-4 diagnostic lead location**

TROUBLE CODE IDENTIFICATION

THE TROUBLE CODES INDICATE PROBLEMS AS FOLLOWS:

| | |
|---|---|
| CODE 12 | No engine RPM signal pulses to ECM term. "H" with vehicle standing. This code is not stored in memory and will only flash while the fault is present. Normal code with ignition "on," engine not running. (Verifies that ECM can detect a failure) |
| CODE 14 | Coolant Sensor Circuit - Signal voltage LOW on ECM terminal "W" |
| CODE 15 | Coolant Sensor Circuit - Signal voltage HIGH on ECM terminal "W" |
| CODE 21 | Metering Valve Sensor (MVS) Signal voltage LOW on ECM terminal "R" (grounded circuit or misadjusted MVS). |
| CODE 22 | Metering Valve Sensor (MVS) Signal voltage HIGH on ECM terminal "R" (open circuit or misadjusted MVS) |
| CODE 24 | Vehicle Speed Sensor (VSS) Signal - RPM and MVS signals indicate vehicle should be in motion with inadequate VSS signal. Disregard Code 24 set without drive wheels turning. |
| CODE 41 | No engine RPM signal pulses to ECM term. "H" with vehicle in motion This code will store in memory. |
| CODE 51 | Faulty or improperly installed calibration unit (PROM). |
| CODE 53 | Exhaust Gas Recirculation (EGR) valve MAP sensor has seen mproper EGR vacuum. |
| CODE 55 | Grounded 5V reference circuit and/or faulty ECM. Incorrect voltage on ECM term. "C" |

85844053

**Fig. 63 Diesel trouble code identification chart**

## VACUUM DIAGRAMS

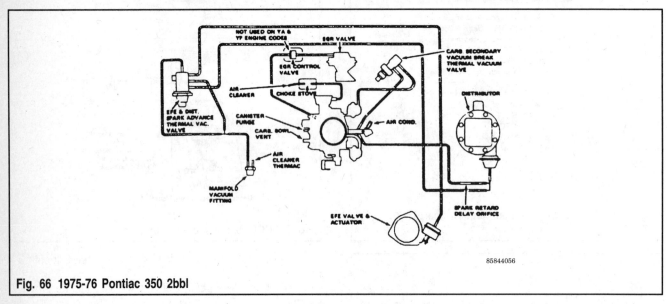

**Fig. 66 1975-76 Pontiac 350 2bbl**

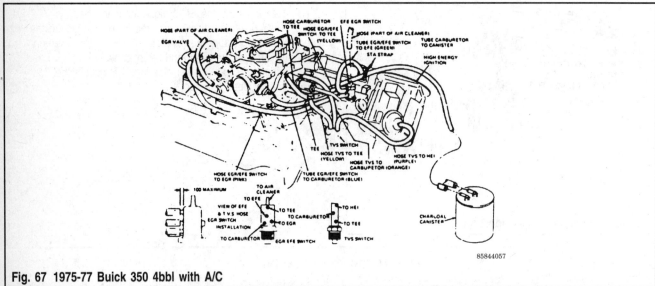

**Fig. 67 1975-77 Buick 350 4bbl with A/C**

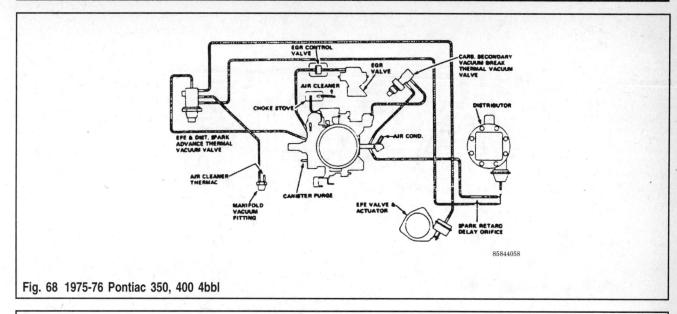

Fig. 68  1975-76 Pontiac 350, 400 4bbl

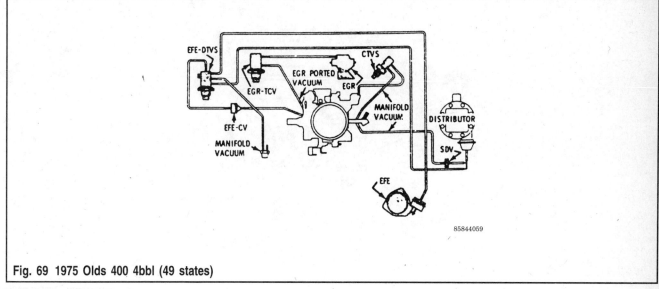

Fig. 69  1975 Olds 400 4bbl (49 states)

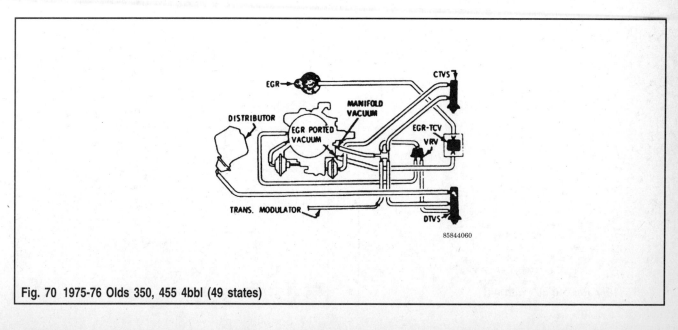

Fig. 70  1975-76 Olds 350, 455 4bbl (49 states)

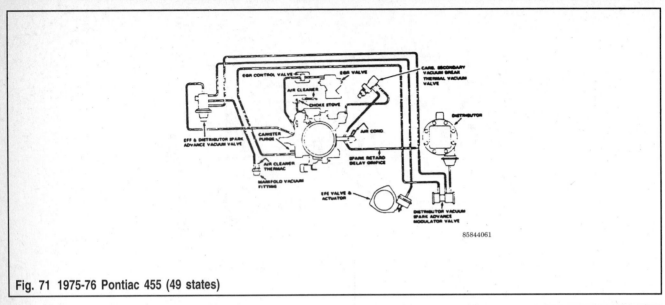

**Fig. 71 1975-76 Pontiac 455 (49 states)**

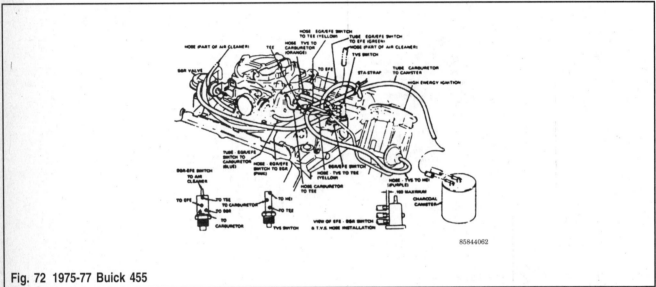

**Fig. 72 1975-77 Buick 455**

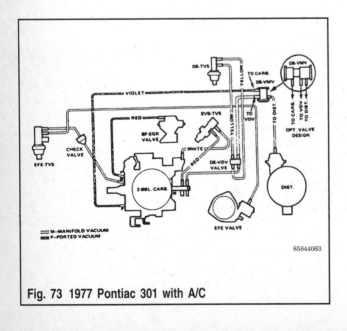

**Fig. 73 1977 Pontiac 301 with A/C**

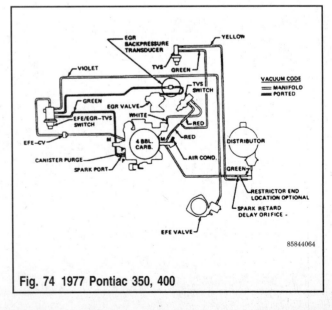

**Fig. 74 1977 Pontiac 350, 400**

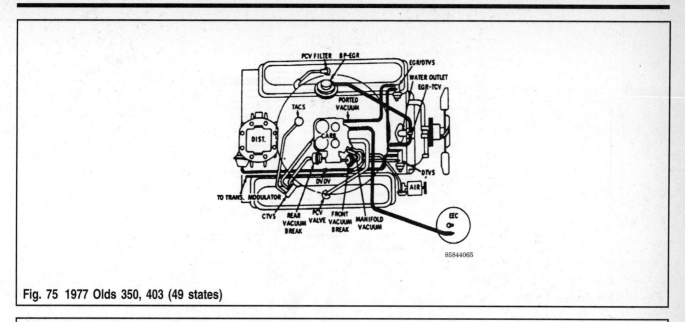

**Fig. 75  1977 Olds 350, 403 (49 states)**

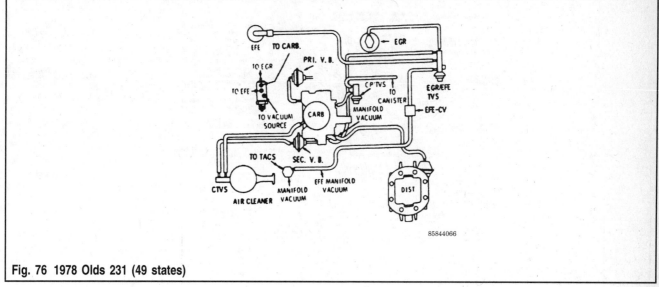

**Fig. 76  1978 Olds 231 (49 states)**

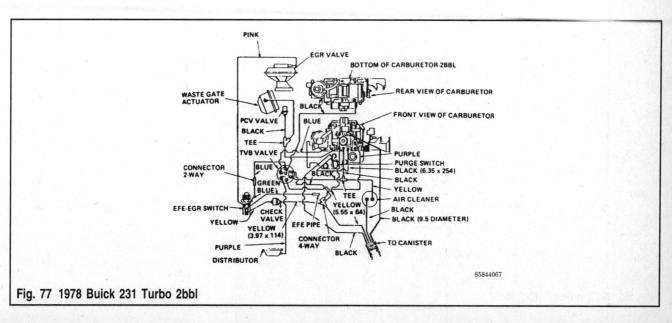

**Fig. 77  1978 Buick 231 Turbo 2bbl**

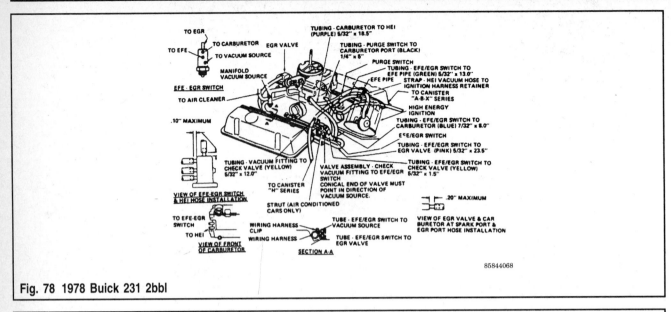

Fig. 78 1978 Buick 231 2bbl

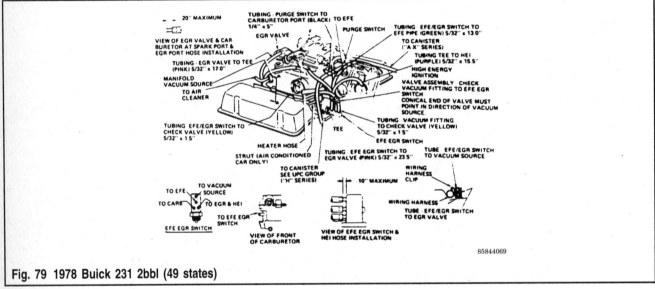

Fig. 79 1978 Buick 231 2bbl (49 states)

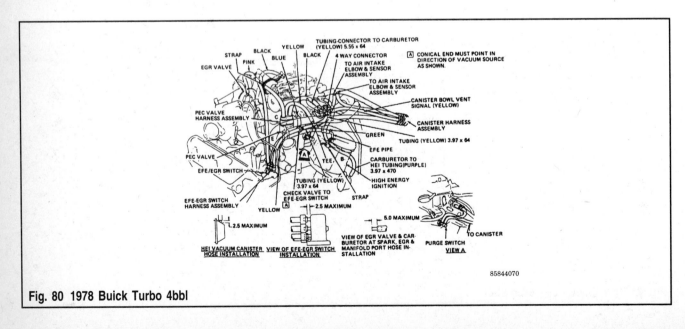

Fig. 80 1978 Buick Turbo 4bbl

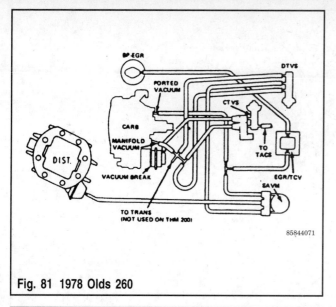

**Fig. 81  1978 Olds 260**

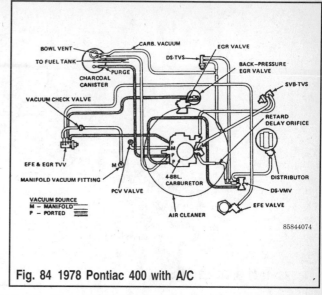

**Fig. 84  1978 Pontiac 400 with A/C**

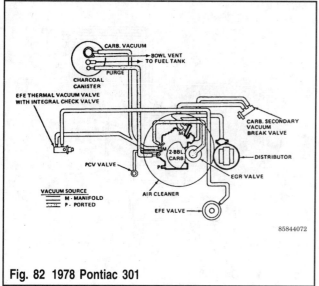

**Fig. 82  1978 Pontiac 301**

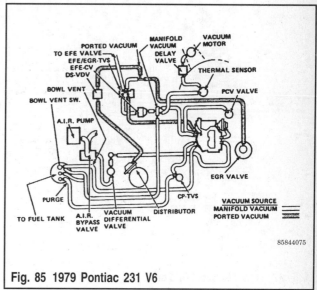

**Fig. 85  1979 Pontiac 231 V6**

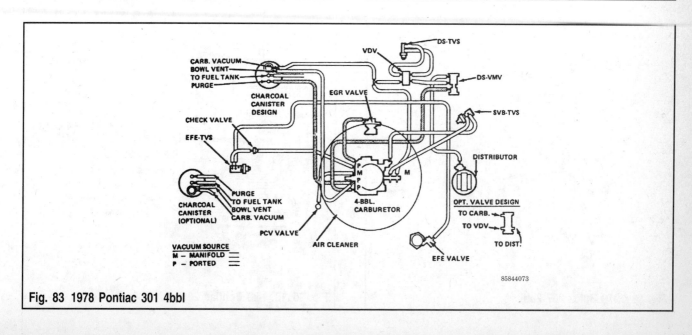

**Fig. 83  1978 Pontiac 301 4bbl**

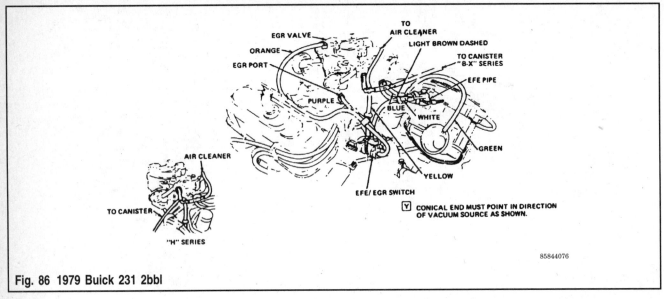

85844076

**Fig. 86 1979 Buick 231 2bbl**

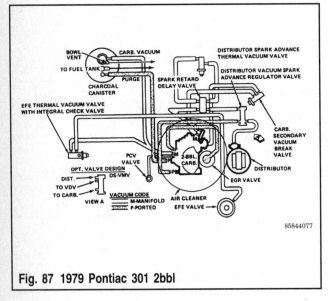

85844077

**Fig. 87 1979 Pontiac 301 2bbl**

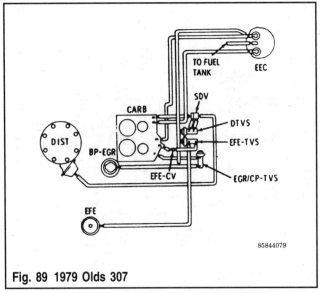

85844079

**Fig. 89 1979 Olds 307**

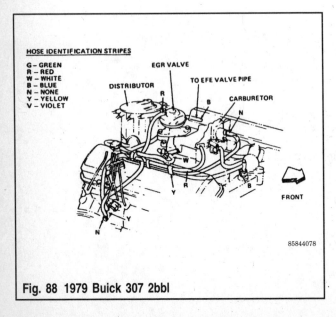

85844078

**Fig. 88 1979 Buick 307 2bbl**

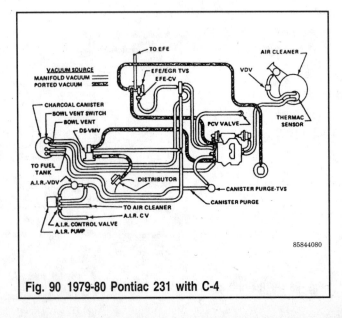

85844080

**Fig. 90 1979-80 Pontiac 231 with C-4**

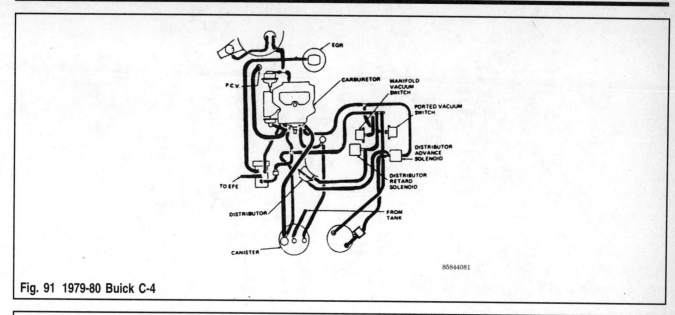

**Fig. 91  1979-80 Buick C-4**

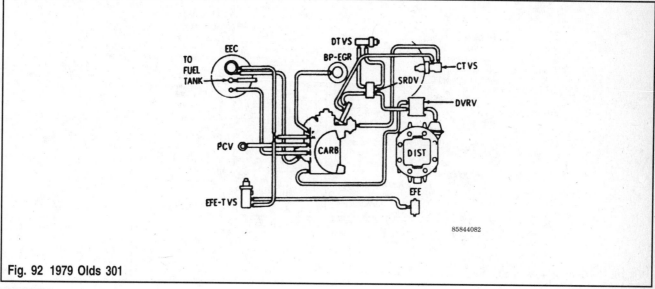

**Fig. 92  1979 Olds 301**

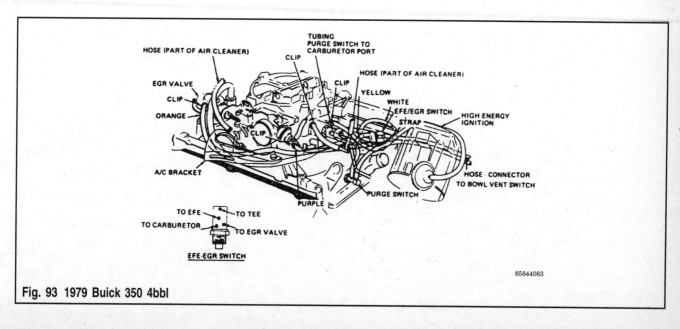

**Fig. 93  1979 Buick 350 4bbl**

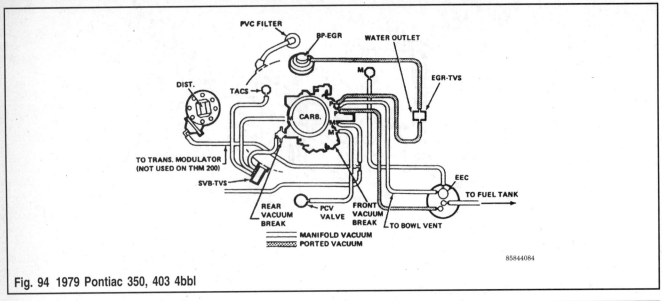

Fig. 94 1979 Pontiac 350, 403 4bbl

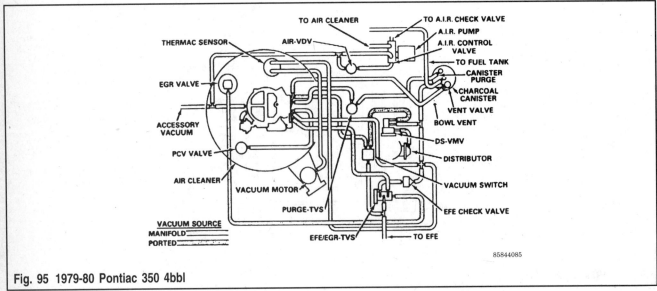

Fig. 95 1979-80 Pontiac 350 4bbl

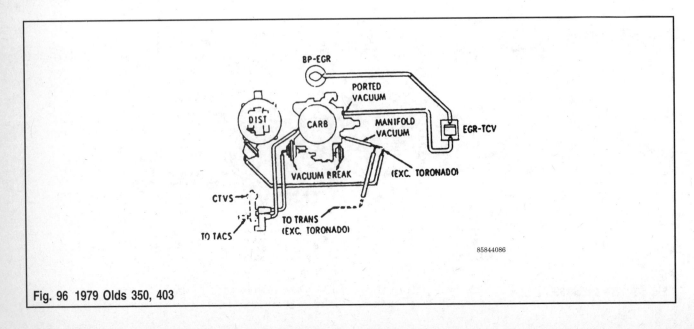

Fig. 96 1979 Olds 350, 403

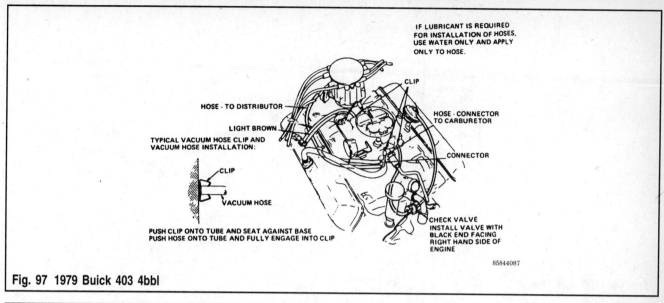

Fig. 97 1979 Buick 403 4bbl

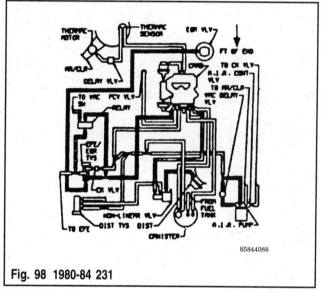

Fig. 98 1980-84 231

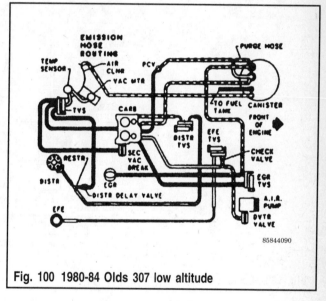

Fig. 100 1980-84 Olds 307 low altitude

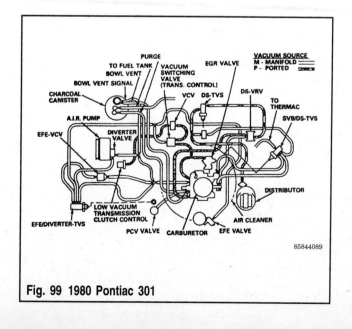

Fig. 99 1980 Pontiac 301

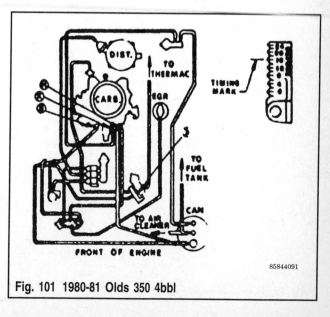

Fig. 101 1980-81 Olds 350 4bbl

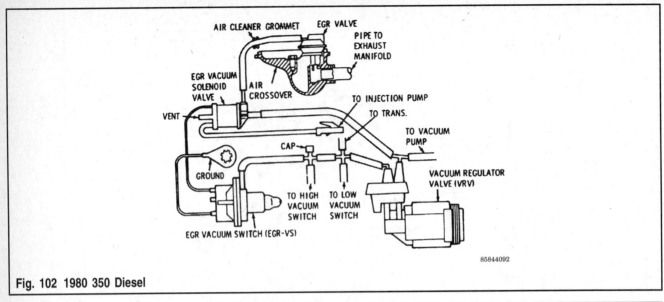

Fig. 102 1980 350 Diesel

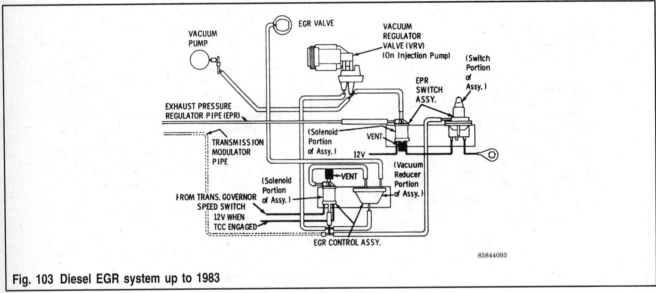

Fig. 103 Diesel EGR system up to 1983

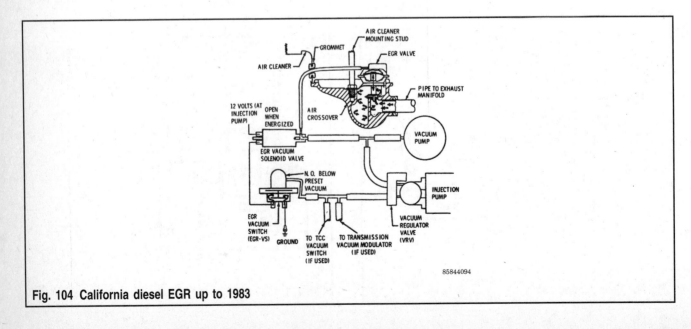

Fig. 104 California diesel EGR up to 1983

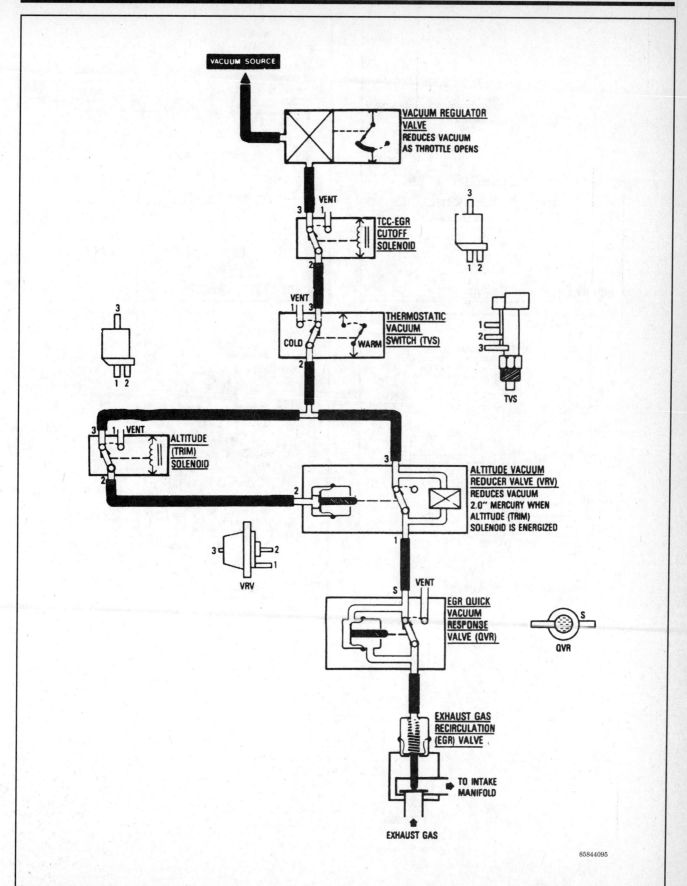

Fig. 105 Low altitude diesel EGR 1984 and up (high altitude similar BUT, VRV reduces vacuum when altitude solenoid is DE-ENGERGIZED)

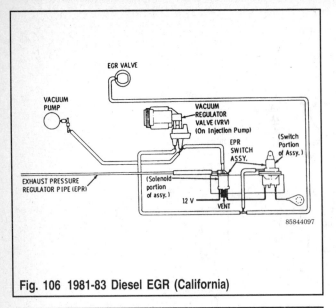

Fig. 106 1981-83 Diesel EGR (California)

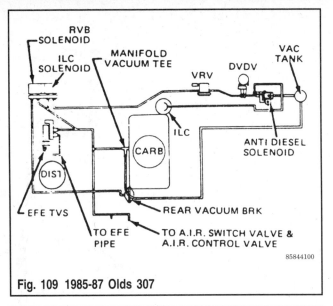

Fig. 109 1985-87 Olds 307

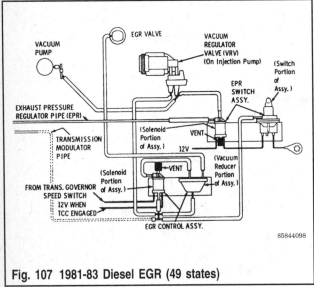

Fig. 107 1981-83 Diesel EGR (49 states)

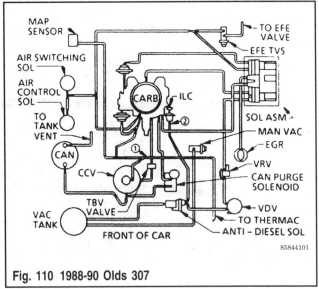

Fig. 110 1988-90 Olds 307

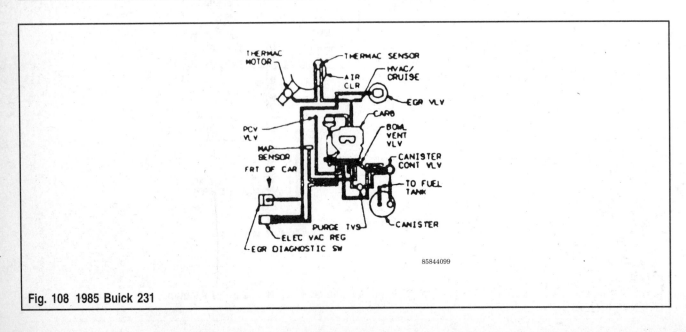

Fig. 108 1985 Buick 231

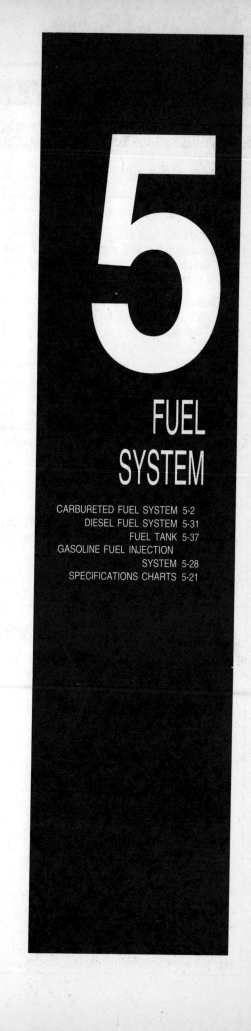

# 5

## FUEL SYSTEM

## CARBURETED FUEL SYSTEM

### Mechanical Fuel Pump

#### REMOVAL & INSTALLATION

▶ **See Figures 1, 2, 3 and 4**

➡**To remove the fuel pump on some engines, the alternator and/or the A/C compressor may have to be moved out of the way. DO NOT disconnect the A/C hoses from the compressor.**

1. Disconnect the negative (-) battery cable.
2. Locate the fuel pump on the side of the cylinder block, open the fuel filler cap and disconnect the fuel lines. Be careful of the fuel leakage.
3. Remove the two pump mounting bolts.

➡**On 305 and 350 Chevrolet built engines: if the pushrod is to be removed, take out the two adaptor bolts and lockwashers, then remove the adaptor and gasket. For installation use heavy grease to hold the pushrod in place. Coat the pipe plug threads or adaptor gasket with sealer if pushrod was removed.**

4. Remove the pump and the gasket.
5. Use a new gasket when installing the pump. Torque the mounting bolts to 22 ft. lbs. (30 Nm).
6. Install the fuel lines and tighten the fuel filler cap. Connect the negative battery cable, then start the engine and check for leaks.

#### TESTING

Fuel pumps used on all carbureted engines are of the single-action mechanical type. The fuel pump rocker arm is held in constant engagement with the eccentric on the camshaft by the rocker arm spring. As the end of the rocker arm which is

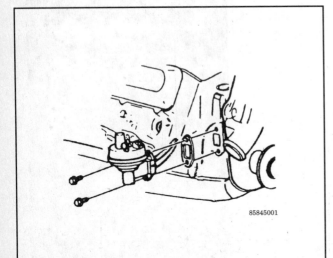

Fig. 1 Mechanical fuel pump; carbureted engines

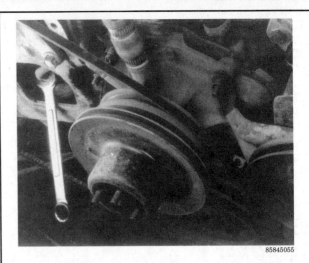

Fig. 2 Fuel pump and fuel line fitting location; all models similar

Fig. 3 Fuel pump upper attaching bolt location

in contact with the eccentric moves upward, the fuel link pulls the fuel diaphragm downward. The action of the diaphragm enlarges the fuel chamber, drawing fuel from the tank. Fuel flows to the carburetor only when the pressure in the outlet line is less than the pressure maintained by the diaphragm spring. The fuel pumps on these engines are not serviceable and must be replaced if defective.

The fuel line from the tank to the pump is the suction side of the system and the line from the pump to the carburetor is the pressure side of the system. A leak on the pressure side, therefore, would be made apparent by dripping fuel, but a leak on the suction side would not be apparent except for the reduction of the volume of fuel on the pressure side.

1. Tighten any loose line connections and look for bends or kinks.
2. Disconnect the fuel pipe at the carburetor. Disconnect the distributor-to-coil primary wire so that the engine can be

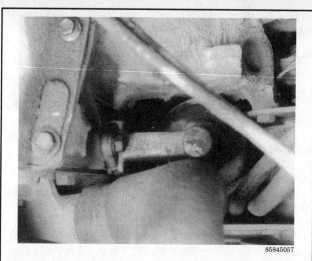

**Fig. 4 Under-car view of the fuel pump; lower attaching bolt shown**

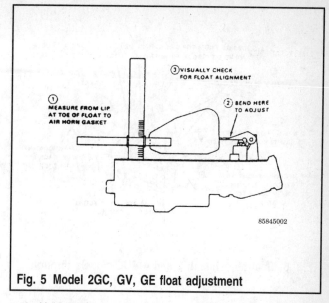

**Fig. 5 Model 2GC, GV, GE float adjustment**

cranked without firing. Place a container at the end of the pipe and crank the engine a few revolutions. If little or no gasoline flows from the open end of the pipe, the fuel pipe is clogged or the pump is defective.

3. If fuel flows from the pump in good volume from the pipe at the carburetor, check fuel pressure to be certain that the pump is operating within specified limits as follows:

    a. Attach a fuel pump pressure test gauge to the disconnected end of the pipe.

    b. Run the engine at approximately 450-1000 rpm on the gasoline still remaining in the carburetor bowl. Note the reading on the pressure gauge.

    c. If the pump is operating properly the pressure will be within the specifications listed in the Tune-Up Specifications chart found in Section 2. The pressure will remain constant between speeds of 450-1000 rpm. If the pressure is too low or too high at different speeds, the pump should be replaced.

➡There are no adjustments that can be made on these fuel pumps.

## Carburetor

## ADJUSTMENTS

**Float Level**

▶ See Figures 5, 6 and 7

### MODELS 2GC, GE, GV

1. Remove the air horn assembly from the carburetor.
2. Hold the air horn assembly upside down and measure the distance from the air horn gasket to the lip at the toe of the float. See the chart for the proper measurement.
3. Bend the float arm to adjust the float level to the proper specifications.

### ALL OTHER 2 & 4 BBL MODELS, EXCEPT 1985-90

1. Remove the air horn.

2. Hold the float retainer in place and lightly push down on the float against the needle.

3. Measure the gap between the casting surface and the top of the float at a point ³⁄₁₆ in. (4.7mm) back from the float toe.

4. To adjust, remove the float and bend the float arm.

5. On CCC and C-4 carburetors, if the float level varies more than ¹⁄₁₆ in. (1.6mm) either way, adjust as follows:

    a. Level too high. Hold the float retainer firmly in place and push down on the center of the float body until the correct gap is attained.

    b. Level too low: Lift out the metering rods. Remove the solenoid connector screw. Turn the lean mixture solenoid screw clockwise counting the number of turns until the screw is lightly seated. Then, remove the screw. Lift the solenoid and connector from the float bowl. Remove the float and bend the arm to adjust. Install the float and check the adjustment. Install the mixture screw to the exact number of turns noted earlier. Install all other parts.

### 1985-90 2 & 4 BBL MODELS

➡To make this adjustment, you will need a number of special tools. They are: GM Part No. J-34817-1, J-34817-3, J-9789-90, and J-34817-15 or equivalent.

1. The solenoid plunger, metering rods, and float bowl insert must be removed. Then attach J-34817-1 to the float bowl and place J-34817-3 into it with the contact pin resting on the outer edge of the float lever.

2. Use J-9789-90 to measure the distance from the top of the casting to the top of the float at a point ³⁄₁₆ in. (4.7mm) from the large end of the float.

3. If the reading is more than ¹⁄₁₆ in. (1.6mm) either above or below the specification, use J-34817-15 to bend the lever up or down. Specifications are:

- 1985 E2ME carburetor numbers 17085192 and 17085194 — ¹¹⁄₃₂ in. (8.7mm)
- All other 1985 E2ME and 1986-87 E2ME — ⁵⁄₁₆ in. (7.9mm)
- 1985-90 E4MC — ¹¹⁄₃₂ in. (8.7mm).

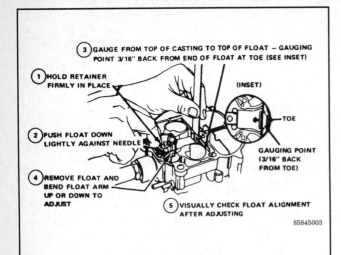

**Fig. 6 Float adjustment; 2 and 4 BBL models through 1984**

Remove this tool and remeasure. Repeat the procedure until the specification is met within the tolerance above or in the carburetor specification chart.

**Vacuum Breaks**
♦ See Figures 8, 9, 10, 11, 12, 13 and 14

### MODELS 2GV, GE, GC

1. Remove the air cleaner. Vehicles equipped with TAC air cleaners should have the sensor's vacuum take-off port plugged.
2. Using an external vacuum source, apply vacuum to the vacuum break diaphragm until the plunger is fully seated. Or, fully seat the plunger and place a piece of tape over the hose fitting.
3. When the plunger is seated, push the choke plate toward the closed position. Place the idle speed screw on the high step of the fast idle cam.
4. Holding the choke plate in the closed position, place the specified size gauge between the upper edge of the choke plate and the air horn wall.

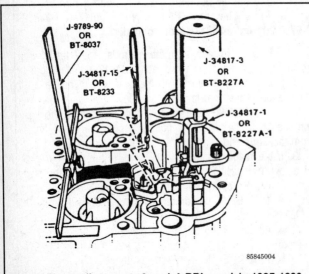

**Fig. 7 Float adjustment; 2 and 4 BBL models 1985-1990**

5. If the measurement is not correct, bend the vacuum break rod.

### ALL OTHER 2 BBL MODELS TO 1980

1. Place the cam follower on the highest step of the fast idle cam.
2. Seat the vacuum break diaphragm by using an outside vacuum source.
3. Remove the choke cover and coil, then push up on the coil lever until the tang on the vacuum break lever contacts the tang on the vacuum break plunger stem. Compress the backing spring for rich adjustment only.
4. With the choke rod in the bottom of the choke lever slot, measure the distance between the upper edge of the choke plate and the inside wall of the air horn.
5. Bend the link rod at the vacuum break plunger stem to adjust the lean setting. Bend the link rod at the opposite from the diaphragm to adjust the rich setting.

### 4 BBL MODELS TO 1980

1. Place the cam follower lever on the highest step of the fast idle cam.
2. Remove the choke cover and coil assembly from the choke housing.
3. Seat the front vacuum diaphragm using an outside vacuum source.
4. Push up on the inside choke coil lever until the tang on the vacuum break lever contacts the tang on the vacuum break plunger.
5. Place the proper size gauge between the upper edge of the choke plate and the inside of the air horn wall.
6. To adjust, turn the adjustment screw on the vacuum break plunger lever.
7. To adjust the secondary vacuum break, with the choke cover and coil removed, the cam follower on the highest step of the fast idle cam, tape over the bleed hole in the rear vacuum break diaphragm.
8. Seat the rear diaphragm using an outside vacuum source.
9. Close the choke by pushing up on the choke coil lever inside the choke housing. Make sure the choke rod is in the bottom of the slot in the choke lever.
10. Measure between the upper edge of the choke plate and the air horn wall with a wire type gauge.
11. To adjust, bend the vacuum break rod at the first bend near the diaphragm.

### 2 & 4 BBL MODELS 1981 AND LATER

1. To adjust the front vacuum break, attach a rubber band to the vacuum break lever of the intermediate choke shaft.
2. Open the throttle to allow the choke valve to close.
3. Set an angle gauge such as J-26701-A, BT-7704 or equivalent and set to specifications.
4. Plug the vacuum break plunger. Apply 15 in. Hg (51 k Pa) of vacuum to seat the vacuum break plunger. On some models, seat the bucking spring.
5. Adjust if the bubble is not recentered, by turning the screw.
6. To adjust the rear vacuum break, attach a rubber band to the vacuum break lever of the intermediate choke shaft.
7. Open the throttle to allow the choke valve to close.

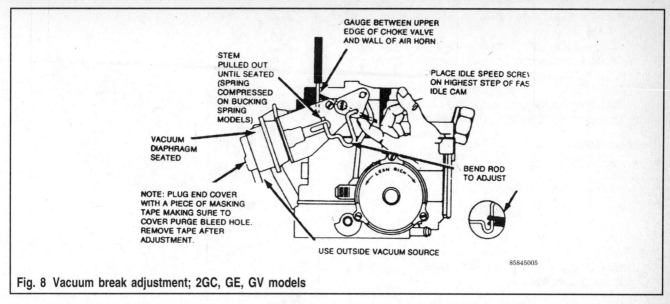

Fig. 8 Vacuum break adjustment; 2GC, GE, GV models

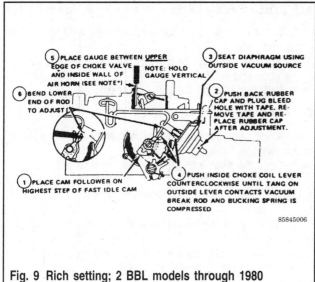

Fig. 9 Rich setting; 2 BBL models through 1980

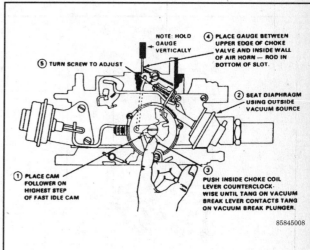

Fig. 11 Front vacuum break adjustment; 4 BBL models through 1980

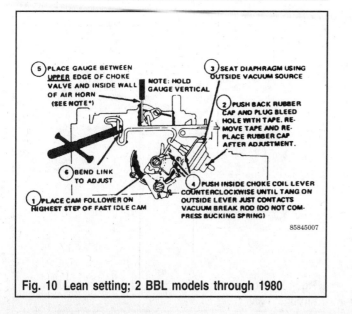

Fig. 10 Lean setting; 2 BBL models through 1980

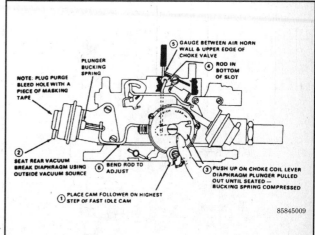

Fig. 12 Rear vacuum break adjustment; 4 BBL models through 1980

8. Set up the angle gauge J-26701-A, BT-7704 (or equivalent) and set to specifications.

9. Plug the vacuum break plunger. Apply 15 in. Hg (51 k Pa) of vacuum to seat the vacuum break plunger. Compress the plunger bucking spring, if so equipped.

10. Adjust if the bubble is not recentered, by either:

a. Supporting the "S" and bending the vacuum break link.

b. Or, turning the screw with a ⅛ in. hex wrench.

### Choke Unloader

▶ **See Figures 15, 16 and 17**

#### *MODELS 2GC, GE, GV*

1. Hold the throttle valves wide open.

2. Hold the choke valve towards the closed position with a rubber band.

3. Bend the unloader tang on the throttle lever to obtain the specified clearance between the upper edge of the choke plate and the air horn wall.

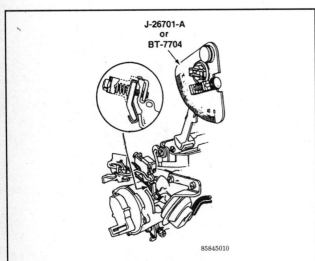

Fig. 13 Front vacuum break adjustment; 2 and 4 BBL models 1981-1990

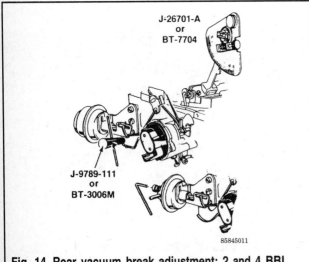

Fig. 14 Rear vacuum break adjustment; 2 and 4 BBL models 1981-1990

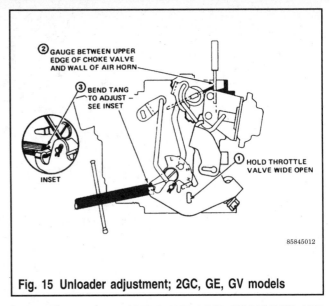

Fig. 15 Unloader adjustment; 2GC, GE, GV models

### *ALL OTHER 2 BBL MODELS AND 4 BBL MODELS TO 1980*

1. With the choke plate completely closed, hold the throttle plates wide open.

2. Measure the distance between the upper edge of the choke plate and the airhorn wall.

3. Bend the tang on the fast idle lever to adjust.

### *2 & 4 BBL MODELS 1981 AND LATER*

1. Attach a rubber band to the vacuum break intermediate choke shaft.

2. Open the throttle to allow the choke valve to close.

3. Set an angle gauge such as J-26701-A, BT-7704 or equivalent, to the angle specification in the specification chart in this chapter.

4. Hold the secondary throttle lockout lever away from the pin.

5. Hold the throttle lever in the wide open position.

6. Adjust, if the bubble is not recentered, by bending the fast idle lever using a bending tool such as J-9789 or B-3006M.

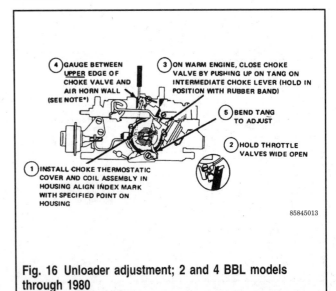

Fig. 16 Unloader adjustment; 2 and 4 BBL models through 1980

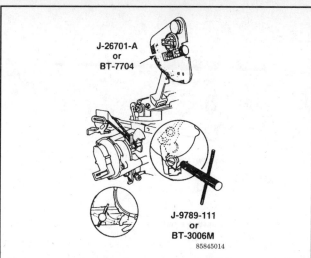

**Fig. 17 Unloader adjustment; 2 and 4 BBL models 1981 and later**

## Fast Idle Cam

▶ See Figures 18, 19 and 20

### MODELS 2GC, GE, GV

1. Place the idle speed screw on the second step of the fast idle cam against the shoulder of the high step for 2GV models, and on the highest step for the GC and GE models.
2. Push the choke plate closed.
3. On 2GV models, measure the distance between the upper edge of the choke plate and the air horn wall. To adjust, bend tang. On GE and GC models, insert the specified gauge into the choke housing slot. Choke coil lever should just contact gauge in the end of the slot. Adjust by bending "U" bend of the rod.

### ALL OTHER 2 BBL MODELS AND 4 BBL MODELS TO 1980

1. Place the cam follower on the second step of the fast idle cam.
2. Close the choke plate by pushing counterclockwise on the external choke lever. On 1975-80 models, remove the coil

assembly from the choke housing and push on the choke coil lever.
3. Measure between the upper edge of the choke plate and the air horn wall.
4. To adjust, bend the tang on the fast idle cam. Be sure that the tang rests against the cam after bending.

### 2 & 4 BBL MODELS 1981 AND LATER

1. Attach a rubber band to the vacuum break lever of the intermediate choke shaft.
2. Open the throttle to allow the choke valve to close.
3. Set up an angle gauge such as J-26701-A or BT-7704 and set to specifications.
4. Place the fast idle cam on the second step with the lever contacting the rise of the high step.
5. Adjust if the bubble is not centered, by bending the tang on the fast idle cam.

## Air Valve Link (Dashpot)

▶ See Figure 21

### ALL 4 BBL MODELS

1. Seat the front vacuum break diaphragm by using an outside vacuum source.
2. The air valves must be closed completely.
3. Measure the clearance between the air valve dashpot and the end of the slot in the air valve lever. The clearance should be 0.050 in. (1.27mm) on models through 1981. Later models use a clearance of 0.025 in. (0.635mm).
4. Bend the air valve link (dashpot) rod, if necessary, to adjust.

## Choke Coil Lever

▶ See Figures 22 and 23

### MODELS 2GV, GC, GE

1. Remove the choke coil lever.
2. Place the idle speed screw on the highest step of the fast idle cam.
3. Close the choke valve.

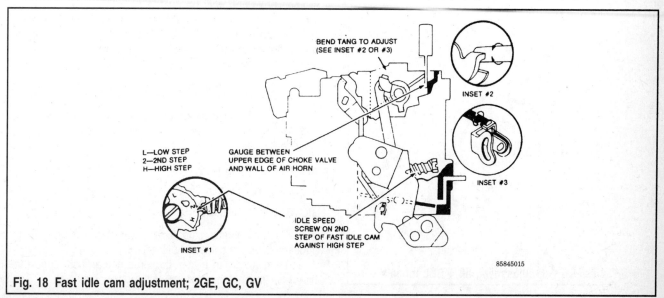

**Fig. 18 Fast idle cam adjustment; 2GE, GC, GV**

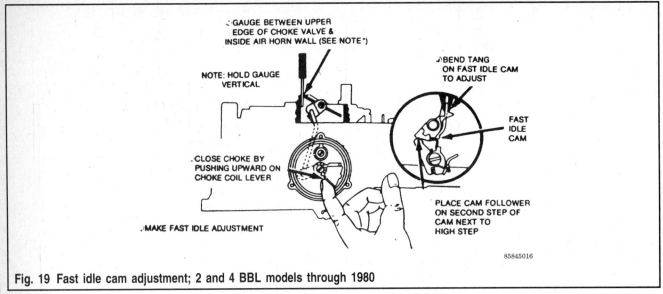

Fig. 19 Fast idle cam adjustment; 2 and 4 BBL models through 1980

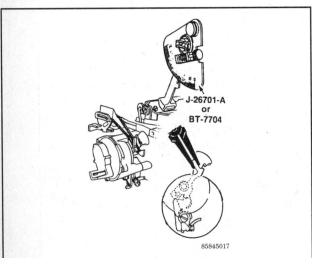

Fig. 20 Fast idle cam adjustment; 2 and 4 BBL models 1981-1990

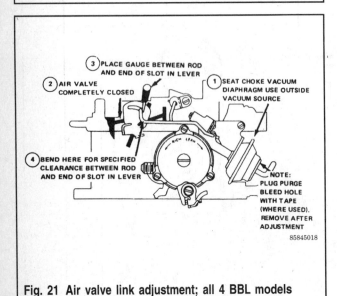

Fig. 21 Air valve link adjustment; all 4 BBL models

4. The edge of the coil lever must line up with the edge of a 0.120 in. plug gauge in the hole inside the choke housing.

5. Bend lever rod to adjust.

### ALL EXCEPT 2GV, GC, GE MODELS

1. Remove the choke cover and thermostatic coil from the choke housing.

2. Push the coil tang counterclockwise until the choke plate is fully closed.

3. Insert a 0.120 in. (3mm) gauge into the hole in the choke housing. The lower edge of the choke coil lever should just contact the side of the gauge.

4. Bend the choke rod to adjust, if necessary.

### Automatic Choke Coil

### ALL EXCEPT 2GC, GE, GV MODELS

1. Place the idle speed screw or follower on the highest step of the fast idle cam.

2. Loosen the choke coil cover retaining screws.

➡The choke coil may be riveted onto the carburetor housing on most later model vehicles. Drill and remove the rivet head by using a 5/16 in. (0.159) drill bit. Punch the remainder of the rivet out of the choke housing. Use the same size rivet for installation.

3. Rotate the choke cover counterclockwise until the choke plate just closes.

4. Align the index mark on the choke cover with the specified point on the choke housing. Tighten the cover screws or install new rivets.

### Accelerator Pump Rod

▸ See Figures 24 and 25

### MODELS 2GC, GE, GV

1. Back out throttle stop screw and fast idle screw so that throttle valves are completely closed.

2. Measure distance from the top of the air horn ring to the top of the pump connector rod at the pump lever.

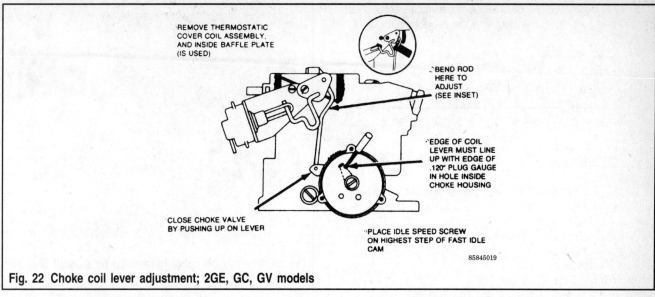

Fig. 22 Choke coil lever adjustment; 2GE, GC, GV models

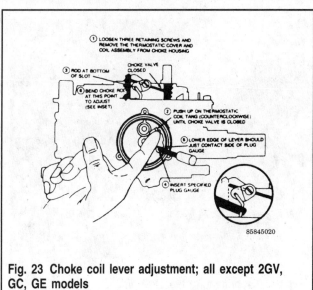

Fig. 23 Choke coil lever adjustment; all except 2GV, GC, GE models

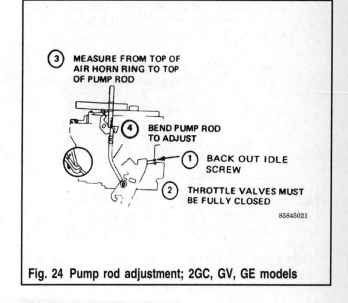

Fig. 24 Pump rod adjustment; 2GC, GV, GE models

3. If distance is incorrect, adjust by bending pump connector rod at the existing bend.

### ALL OTHER MODELS

➡This adjustment is not required on C-4 and CCC carburetors.

1. With the throttle valves completely closed, make sure fast idle cam follower is off the steps on the fast idle cam.
2. Make sure the pump rod is in the specified hole.
3. Gauge from top of choke valve wall, next to the vent stack, to the top of the pump stem.
4. Bend pump lever to adjust.

### Air Valve Spring
▶ See Figure 26

### ALL 4 BBL MODELS

1. Loosen lock screw using special hex wrench.
2. Turn tension adjusting screw counterclockwise until air valve opens part way.

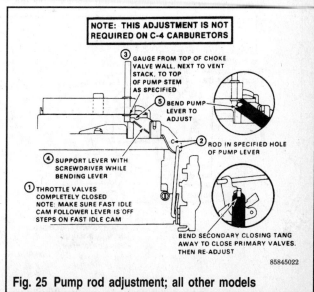

Fig. 25 Pump rod adjustment; all other models

3. Turn tension adjusting screw clockwise until air valve just closes, then turn the screw clockwise the specified number of turns.

4. Tighten lock screw.

## REMOVAL & INSTALLATION

▶ **See Figures 27, 28, 29, 30, 31, 32, 33, 34, 35, 36, 37 and 38**

1. Disconnect the negative (-) battery cable. Remove the air cleaner assembly.

2. Tag and disconnect all vacuum lines, electric wires and fuel lines from the carburetor. Tag and disconnect the throttle linkage and cruise control (if so equipped).

3. Disconnect the automatic transmission downshift linkage.

4. Remove the carburetor attaching nuts or bolts and remove the carburetor.

**To install:**

5. Use a new gasket and fill the float bowl with fuel to ease starting. On late model vehicles with bolts of two different lengths, torque the long bolts to 7 ft. lbs. (10 Nm) and the short bolts to 11 ft. lbs. (14 Nm). Use a cross pattern to torque.

6. Reconnect throttle and transmission linkages.

7. Reconnect the fuel line, all vacuum lines and electrical connections.

8. Reinstall the air cleaner and reconnect the negative battery cable.

## OVERHAUL

Efficient carburetion depends greatly on careful cleaning and inspection during overhaul, since dirt, gum, water, or varnish in or on the carburetor parts are often responsible for poor performance.

Overhaul your carburetor in a clean, dust free area. Carefully disassemble the carburetor, referring often to the exploded views and directions packaged with the rebuilding kit. Keep all similar and look-alike parts segregated during disassembly and

**Fig. 27 The throttle cable is retained by a small clip; all models similar**

**Fig. 28 Disconnecting the TPS sensor**

**Fig. 29 Disconnecting the mixture control solenoid**

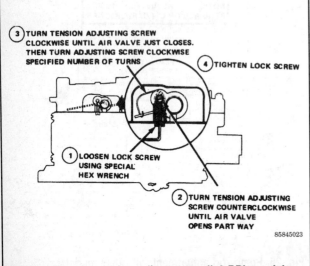
**Fig. 26 Air valve spring adjustment, all 4 BBL models**

Fig. 30 Be sure to label the vacumm hoses when disconnecting them

Fig. 31 Removing the fuel line from the carburetor

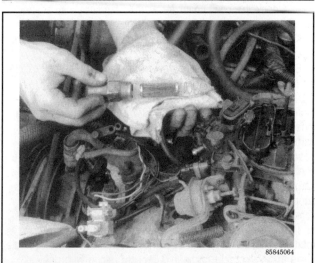

Fig. 32 Place a rag under the fuel fitting to catch any dripping fuel

Fig. 33 Carburetor inlet fuel filter assembly

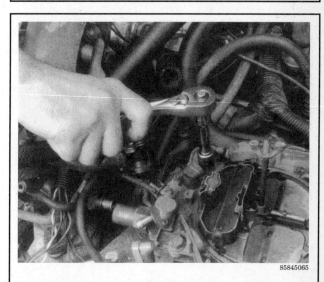

Fig. 34 Removing the carburetor attaching bolts

Fig. 35 Note the length of the bolts; be sure to install them in the correct location during reinstallation

Fig. 36 Removing the carburetor base attaching bolts

Fig. 37 Removing the carburetor from the vehicle

Fig. 38 Be sure to discard the old gasket; always use a new gasket during reassembly

cleaning to avoid accidental interchange during assembly. Make a note of all jet sizes.

When the carburetor is disassembled, wash all parts (except diaphragms, electric choke units, pump plunger, and any other plastic, leather, fiber, or rubber parts) in clean carburetor solvent. Do not leave parts in the solvent any longer than is necessary to sufficiently loosen the deposits. Excessive cleaning may remove the special finish from the float bowl and choke valve bodies, leaving these parts unfit for service. Rinse all parts in clean solvent and blow them dry with compressed air or allow them to air dry. Wipe clean all cork, plastic, leather, and fiber parts with a clean, lint-free cloth.

Blow out all passages and jets with compressed air and be sure that there are no restrictions or blockages. Never use wire or similar tools to clean jets, fuel passages, or air bleeds. **Clean all jets and valves separately to avoid accidental interchange.**

Check all parts for wear or damage. If wear or damage is found, replace the defective parts. Especially check the following:

1. Check the float needle and seat for wear. If wear is found, replace the complete assembly.

2. Check the float hinge pin for wear and the float(s) for dents or distortion. Replace the float if fuel has leaked into it.

3. Check the throttle and choke shaft bores for wear or an out-of-round condition. Damage or wear to the throttle arm, shaft, or shaft bore will often require replacement of the throttle body. These parts require a close tolerance of fit; wear may allow air leakage, which could affect starting and idling.

➡️**Throttle shafts and bushings are not included in overhaul kits. They can be purchased separately.**

4. Inspect the idle mixture adjusting needle for burrs or grooves. Any such condition requires replacement of the needle, since you will not be able to obtain a satisfactory idle.

5. Test the accelerator pump check valves. They should pass air one way but not the other. Test for proper seating by blowing and sucking on the valve. Replace the valve as necessary. If the valve is satisfactory, wash the valve again to remove breath moisture.

6. Check the bowl cover for warped surfaces with a straight edge.

7. Closely inspect the valves and seats for wear and damage, replacing as necessary.

8. After the carburetor is assembled, check the choke valve for freedom of operation.

Carburetor overhaul kits are recommended for each overhaul. These kits contain all gaskets and new parts to replace those which deteriorate most rapidly. Failure to replace all parts supplied with the kit (especially gaskets) can result in poor performance later.

After cleaning and checking all components, reassemble the carburetor, using new parts and referring to the exploded view supplied in the kit. When reassembling, make sure that all screws and jets are tight in their seats, but do not overtighten, as the tips will be distorted. Tighten all screws gradually, in rotation. DO NOT tighten needle valves into their seats; needle valve and valve seat damage will occur, along with uneven jetting. Always use new gaskets. Be sure to adjust the float level when reassembling.

➡C-4 and CCC carburetors incorporate a mixture solenoid. There are several adjustments that must be performed on this device when the carburetor receives a major rebuild. The adjustments are highly complex and require expensive special tools. Review the overhaul procedures before disassembling the carburetor.

Complete major rebuild and adjustment of late model carburetors is best performed by a properly trained and equipped mechanic.

### 2GV, GC, GE Models
▶ See Figures 39 and 40

1. Remove the fuel inlet fitting, gasket, fuel filter and spring. Remove the pump rod by removing the lower retaining clip and rotating the pump rod until lug on the upper end of the rod passes through the upper pump lever. Remove the fast idle cam attaching screw, then remove the fast idle cam and rod assembly by rotating until lug on upper end of the choke rod passes through slot in the upper choke lever and collar assembly.

2. Remove the vacuum break hose. Remove the vacuum break by removing the two attaching screws. Remove the break rod from the lever by rotating the rod until the end slides out of the slot in the lever, and the lug on the other end of the rod out of the slot of the vacuum diaphragm plunger shaft.

3. Remove the air horn attaching screws and guide the air horn gently upward from the bowl. Invert the air horn and remove the float hinge pin and float assembly. Remove the float needle from the arm then remove the float needle seat and gasket. Remove the power piston by depressing the stem and allowing it to snap free. Remove the pump plunger assembly from the inner pump arm by rotating the assembly until the end of the shaft will slide out of the hole in the inner pump lever. Loosen the set screw on the inner arm and remove the outer lever and shaft assembly.

➡A plastic washer is used between the outer pump lever and the air horn casting, do not immerse it in carburetor cleaner.

4. Remove the choke valve retaining screws and the choke valve from the shaft. Remove the shaft, then remove the lever and collar assembly from the shaft while noting the position of the choke lever in relation to the to the trip lever on the choke shaft.

5. Remove the pump plunger return spring from the well, then remove the check ball by inverting the bowl and shaking it into your hand. Remove the pump inlet screen, main jets, power valve and gasket. Remove the three venturi attaching screws, cluster and gasket.

➡The center cluster has a smooth shank and fiber gasket to seal accelerator pump by-pass.

6. Remove the plastic main well inserts, then using needle-nose pliers, remove the pump discharge ball spring "T" retainer, then remove discharge spring and ball. Invert the carburetor and remove the throttle body to bowl attaching screws,

throttle body and body-to-bowl gasket. On 2GC carburetors, remove the choke cover attaching screws, retainer, cover and coil assembly, and the gasket. Also on the 2GC, remove the baffle plate from the inside of the choke housing, then remove the choke housing attaching screws, choke housing and gasket. Then, remove the screw from the end of the intermediate choke shaft and remove the intermediate choke lever, choke coil lever, shaft assembly and dust seal from the choke housing.

**Reassembly:**
Reassemble the carburetor by reversing disassembly. Use all new seals and gaskets. Note the following:

7. After installing the mixture screws and springs, back out screws 2 turns as a preliminary idle adjustment.

8. Install the choke valve with identifying mark "RP" upward. Center choke valve before tightening screws. Valve can be centered by installing the fast idle lever and the choke trip lever on the end of the shaft and maintaining a 0.020 in. clearance between the fast idle lever and the air horn casting. Stake the choke valve screws lightly after tightening. The choke valve should move freely in the housing.

9. Lubricate the accelerator pump shaft with a suitable lubricant (light grease) when installing it in the bowl cover. Make certain that the pump check balls are not interchanged. Inlet check ball is aluminum, the discharge check ball is steel. Some models may have a two-piece pump plunger assembly in place of the inlet check ball.

### All Other 2 BBL Models
▶ See Figures 41, 42 and 43

#### EXCEPT C-4 AND CCC

1. Remove the air cleaner stud, idle speed solenoid and wide open throttle switch, if equipped.

2. Remove the upper choke lever from the end of the choke shaft by removing the retaining screw. Then rotate the upper choke lever to remove the choke rod from the slot in the lever.

3. Using a drift punch, drive the pump lever roll pin inward until pump lever can be removed from the air horn. Note position of the pump rod for later reassembly.

4. Remove the vacuum break "T" tube, if equipped.

5. Remove the seven air horn-to-bowl attaching screws; two countersunk screws are located next to the venturi.

6. Remove the air horn from the float bowl by lifting straight up. The air horn should remain on the float bowl for removal later.

7. Remove the front vacuum break hose. Then, remove the two attaching screws and remove the vacuum break and bracket assembly. Remove the pump plunger stem seal retainer by inverting the air horn and use a small screwdriver to remove the staking holding the seal retainer in place.

8. Remove the air horn gasket by lifting out of dowel locating pins and lifting tab of gasket from beneath the power piston hanger, being careful not to distort the springs holding the metering rods.

9. Remove the pump plunger and return spring from the pump well.

10. Remove the power piston and metering rods by depressing the piston and releasing it with a snap. This will cause the power piston to snap the piston up against the retainer. This

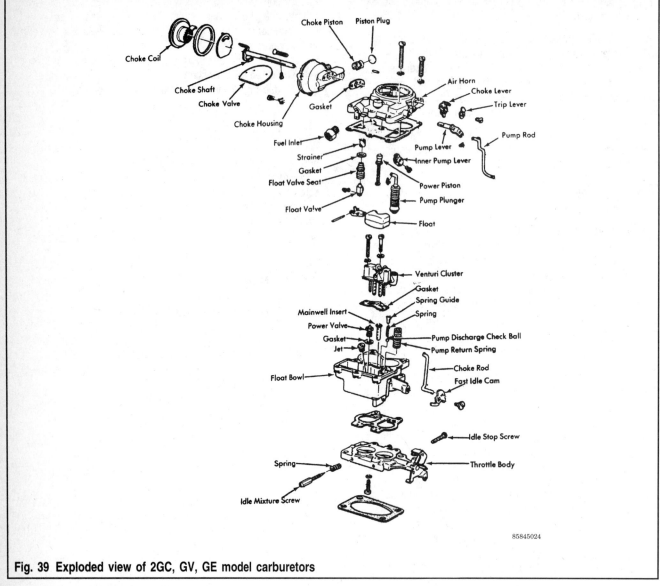

**Fig. 39 Exploded view of 2GC, GV, GE model carburetors**

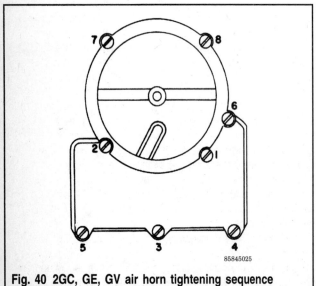

**Fig. 40 2GC, GE, GV air horn tightening sequence**

procedure may have to be repeated several times. Do not remove the power piston by using pliers.

➡**Use special care not to distort the metering rods.**

11. Remove the plastic filler block over the float valve.

12. Remove the float assembly and float needle by pulling up on the retaining pin. Remove the seat and gasket using a seat remover.

13. Remove the aneroid cavity insert from the float bowl.

14. Remove the pump discharge check ball retainer and check ball.

15. Remove the pump well fill slot baffle.

16. Where used, remove the rear vacuum break hose. Remove the two attaching screws and rotate the assembly to remove the vacuum break rod from the slot in the plunger head.

17. Remove the vacuum break rod by holding down on the fast idle cam; move end of vacuum break rod away from the float bowl. Disengage the rod from the hole in the intermediate choke lever.

18. Support the float bowl and throttle body as an assembly on a suitable holding fixture. Carefully align a number 21 drill (0.159 in.) on the pop-type rivet head and drill enough to remove only the head. Then, use an drift and a small hammer to drive the remainder of the rivet out of the choke housing.

19. Remove the retainers, choke cover and gasket from the housing.

20. Remove the choke housing from the float bowl by removing the retaining screw from inside the housing. The complete choke hosing can then be pulled from the bowl. Remove the cup seal and plastic tube seal.

21. Remove the lower choke lever from inside the float bowl by inverting the bowl.

22. Remove the fuel inlet nut, gasket, check valve filter assembly and spring.

23. Remove the throttle body and gasket by removing the attaching screws.

**Reassembly:**

Reassemble the carburetor by reversing disassembly. Use all new seals and gaskets. Note the following:

24. If the idle mixture needles were removed, back them out 3½ turns as a preliminary adjustment. Final adjustments should be performed by a qualified technician.

25. Using a holding tool, install the lower choke rod inner lever into the cavity in the float bowl and slide the intermediate choke shaft and housing into the lower choke rod inner lever. The intermediate choke shaft lever and fast idle cam are in the correct position when the tang on the lever is beneath the fast idle cam. Do not install the choke cover until the inside coil lever is adjusted.

26. Do not install the float needle pull clip into the holes in the float arm.

27. Do not force the air horn assembly onto the bowl; lower it carefully in place.

28. Install the air horn screws using the proper tightening sequence.

29. Perform all applicable adjustments.

### C-4 AND CCC

1. Remove the air cleaner stud, idle speed solenoid and wide open throttle switch, if equipped.

2. Remove the upper choke lever from the end of the choke shaft by removing the retaining screw. Then rotate the upper choke lever to remove the choke rod from the slot in the lever.

3. Using a drift punch, drive the pump lever roll pin inward until pump lever can be removed from the air horn. Note position of the pump rod for later reassembly.

4. Remove the vacuum break "T" tube, if equipped.

5. Remove the nine air horn-to-bowl attaching screws; two countersunk screws are located next to the venturi.

6. Remove the air horn from the float bowl by lifting straight up. The air horn should remain on the float bowl for removal later.

7. Remove the front vacuum break hose. Then, remove the two attaching screws and remove the vacuum break and bracket assembly. Remove the pump plunger stem and TPS seal retainers by inverting the air horn and use a small screwdriver to remove the staking holding the seal retainer in place.

8. Holding down on pump plunger stem, raise the corner of air horn gasket and remove the pump plunger from the well.

9. Remove the solenoid-metering rod plunger by lifting it straight up.

10. Remove the rubber seal from around the mixture control solenoid plunger.

11. Remove the air horn gasket by lifting it off of the dowel locating pins on the float bowl.

12. Remove the pump return spring from the pump well.

13. Remove the TPS by pushing up on the bottom of the connector.

14. Remove the plastic filler block over the float valve.

15. Carefully lift each metering rod out of the guided metering jet, checking to make sure the return spring is removed with each metering rod.

➡**Use special care not to distort the metering rods.**

16. Remove the solenoid connector attaching screw.

17. Using a suitable tool on the upper end of the mixture control solenoid screw, turn the screw counterclockwise and remove it from the float bowl. Then, carefully lift the mixture control solenoid and connector assembly from the float bowl.

18. Remove the plastic insert from the cavity in the float bowl.

19. Remove the solenoid screw tension spring.

20. Remove the float assembly, then the seat and gasket using a seat remover.

21. Remove the large mixture control solenoid tension spring from the boss on the bottom of the float bowl.

22. Remove the pump discharge check ball retainer and check ball.

23. Remove the pump well fill slot baffle.

24. Where used, remove the rear vacuum break hose. Remove the two attaching screws and rotate the assembly to remove the vacuum break rod from the slot in the plunger head.

25. Remove the vacuum break rod by holding down on the fast idle cam; move end of vacuum break rod away from the float bowl. Disengage the rod from the hole in the intermediate choke lever.

26. Support the float bowl and throttle body as an assembly on a suitable holding fixture. Carefully align a number 21 drill (0.159 in.) on the pop-type rivet head and drill enough to remove only the head. Then, use an drift and a small hammer to drive the remainder of the rivet out of the choke housing.

27. Remove the retainers, choke cover and gasket from the housing.

28. Remove the choke housing from the float bowl by removing the retaining screw from inside the housing. The complete choke hosing can then be pulled from the bowl. Remove the cup seal and plastic tube seal.

29. Remove the lower choke lever from inside the float bowl by inverting the bowl.

30. Remove the fuel inlet nut, gasket, check valve filter assembly and spring.

31. Remove the throttle body and gasket by removing the attaching screws.

**Reassembly:**

Reassemble the carburetor by reversing disassembly. Use all new seals and gaskets. Note the following:

32. If the idle mixture needles were removed, back them out 5½ turns as a preliminary adjustment. Final adjustments should be performed by a qualified technician.

| | | | | | | |
|---|---|---|---|---|---|---|
| 1 | Gasket - Air Cleaner | 42 | Pin - Pump Lever Hinge | 67 | Retainer - Pump Stem Seal |
| 5 | Gasket - Flange | 46 | Screw Assembly - Air Horn to Float Bowl | 68 | Seal - Pump Stem |
| 10 | Air Horn Assembly | 47 | Screw - Air Horn to Float Bowl (countersunk) | 70 | Plug - Solenoid Adjusting Screw |
| 11 | Rivet - Cover Attaching | 55 | Vacuum Break Assembly - Primary Side (Front) | 71 | Plug - Solenoid Stop Screw |
| 12 | Cover - Air Bleed Valve | 56 | Screw - Primary Side (Front) Vacuum Break Assembly Attaching | 72 | Screw - Solenoid Stop (Rich Mixture) |
| 15 | Air Bleed Valve Assembly | | | 200 | Float Bowl Assembly |
| 16 | O-ring - Air Bleed Valve - Lower | 57 | Hose - Primary Side (Front) Vacuum Break | 201 | Gasket - Air Horn to Float Bowl |
| 17 | O-ring - Air Bleed Valve - Upper | 60 | Plunger - Sensor Actuator | 205 | Pump Assembly |
| 35 | Lever - Choke | 61 | Plug - TPS Adjusting Screw | 206 | Spring - Pump Return |
| 36 | Screw - Choke Lever Attaching | 62 | Screw - TPS Adjusting | 210 | Sensor - Throttle Position (TPS) |
| 41 | Lever - Pump | 65 | Retainer - TPS Seal | 211 | Spring - Sensor Adjusting |
| | | 66 | Seal - TPS Plunger | 213 | Rod - Primary Metering |
| | | | | 215 | Plunger - Solenoid |
| | | | | 217 | Spring - Primary Metering Rod (E2M, E4M only) |
| | | | | 221 | Screw - Solenoid Connector Attaching |
| | | | | 222 | Gasket - Solenoid Connector to Air Horn |
| | | | | 225 | Mixture Control Solenoid Assembly |
| | | | | 226 | Screw - Solenoid Adjusting (Lean Mixture) |
| | | | | 227 | Stop - Rich Limit |
| | | | | 228 | Spring - Solenoid Adjusting Screw |
| | | | | 229 | Spring - Solenoid Return |
| | | | | 234 | Insert - Aneroid Cavity |
| | | | | 235 | Insert - Float Bowl |
| | | | | 236 | Hinge Pin - Float Description - E4ME |
| | | | | 237 | Float |
| | | | | 238 | Pull Clip - Float Needle |
| | | | | 239 | Needle - Float |
| | | | | 240 | Seat - Float Needle |
| | | | | 241 | Gasket - Float Needle Seat |
| | | | | 250 | Plug - Pump Discharge (Retainer) |
| | | | | 251 | Ball - Pump Discharge |
| | | | | 252 | Baffle - Pump Well |
| | | | | 255 | Primary Metering Jet Assembly |
| | | | | 315 | Hose - Secondary Side (Rear) Vacuum Break |
| | | | | 320 | Vacuum Break Assembly - Secondary Side (Rear) |
| | | | | 321 | Screw - Secondary Side (Rear) Vacuum Break Assembly Attaching |
| | | | | 322 | Link - Secondary Side (Rear) Vacuum Break to Choke |
| | | | | 330 | Rivet - Choke Cover Attaching |
| | | | | 331 | Retainer - Choke Cover |
| | | | | 335 | Electric Choke Cover and Stat Assembly |
| | | | | 340 | Choke Housing Assembly |
| | | | | 341 | Screw and Washer Assembly - Choke Housing to Float Bowl |
| | | | | 345 | Screw - Choke Stat Lever Attaching |
| | | | | 348 | Lever - Choke Stat |
| | | | | 350 | Intermediate Choke Shaft, Lever and Link Assembly |
| | | | | 352 | Fast Idle Cam Assembly |
| | | | | 354 | Lever - Intermediate Choke |
| | | | | 356 | Link - Choke |
| | | | | 364 | Seal - Intermediate Choke Shaft |
| | | | | 370 | Nut - Fuel Inlet |
| | | | | 372 | Gasket - Fuel Inlet Nut |
| | | | | 375 | Filter - Fuel Inlet |
| | | | | 377 | Spring - Fuel Filter |
| | | | | 380 | Screw - Throttle Stop |
| | | | | 381 | Spring - Throttle Stop Screw |
| | | | | 400 | Throttle Body Assembly |
| | | | | 401 | Gasket - Float Bowl to Throttle Body |
| | | | | 405 | Screw Assembly - Float Bowl to Throttle Body |
| | | | | 410 | Link - Pump |
| | | | | 420 | Needle - Idle Mixture |
| | | | | 421 | Spring - Idle Mixture Needle |
| | | | | 422 | Plug - Idle Mixture Needle |
| | | | | 425 | Screw - Fast Idle Adjusting |
| | | | | 426 | Spring - Fast Idle Adjusting Screw |
| | | | | 500 | Solenoid and Bracket Assembly |
| | | | | 501 | Screw - Bracket Attaching |
| | | | | 515 | Idle Speed Control Assembly |

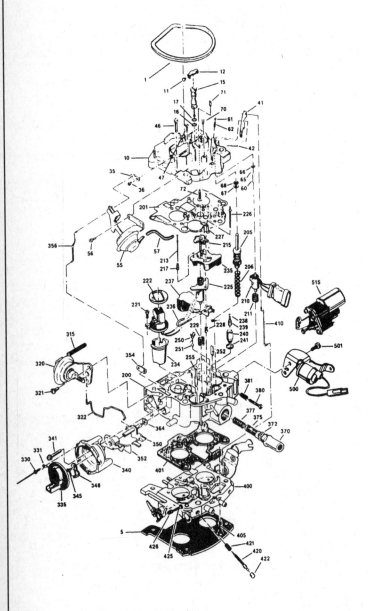

85845026

Fig. 41 Exploded view of all 2 BBL models; except 2GC, GV, GE

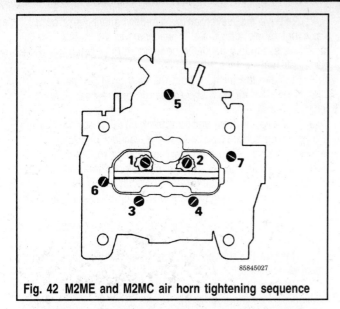

Fig. 42 M2ME and M2MC air horn tightening sequence

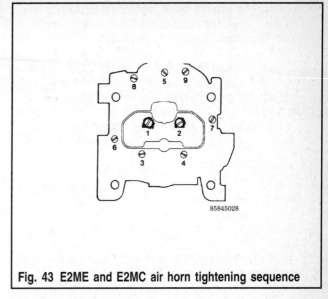

Fig. 43 E2ME and E2MC air horn tightening sequence

33. Using a holding tool, install the lower choke rod inner lever into the cavity in the float bowl and slide the intermediate choke shaft and housing into the lower choke rod inner lever. The intermediate choke shaft lever and fast idle cam are in the correct position when the tang on the lever is beneath the fast idle cam. Do not install the choke cover until the inside coil lever is adjusted.

34. Do not install the float needle pull clip into the holes in the float arm.

35. Turn the mixture control screw clockwise until it is bottomed lightly in the bowl. Turn the screw counterclockwise exactly 3½ turns. Final adjustments should be performed by a qualified technician.

36. Do not force the air horn assembly onto the bowl; lower it carefully in place while holding down on pump plunger assembly. Also take care not to pinch the TPS connector wires between the air horn and the float bowl.

37. Install the air horn screws using the proper tightening sequence.

38. Perform all applicable adjustments.

**All 4 BBL Models**
▶ **See Figures 44, 45 and 46**

*EXCEPT C-4 AND CCC*

1. Remove the idle speed solenoid and wide open throttle switch, if equipped.

2. Remove the upper choke lever from the end of the choke shaft by removing the retaining screw. Then rotate the upper choke lever to remove the choke rod from the slot in the lever.

3. Remove the choke rod from the lower lever inside the float bowl casting. Remove rod by holding lower lever outward with a small screwdriver and twisting the rod counterclockwise.

4. Remove the secondary metering rods by removing the small screw in the top of the metering rod hanger. Lift upward on the metering rod hanger until the secondary metering rods are completely out of the air horn.

5. Using a drift punch, drive the pump lever roll pin inward until pump lever can be removed from the air horn. Note position of the pump rod for later reassembly.

6. Remove the vacuum break "T" tube, if equipped.

7. Remove the nine air horn-to-bowl attaching screws; two countersunk screws are located next to the venturi. Remove the secondary air baffle deflector from beneath the two center air horn screws, where used.

8. Remove the air horn from the float bowl by lifting straight up. The air horn should remain on the float bowl for removal later.

9. Remove the front vacuum break hose. Then, remove the two attaching screws and remove the vacuum break and bracket assembly from the air valve dashpot rod and the dashpot rod from the air valve lever. Remove the pump plunger stem seal retainer by inverting the air horn and use a small screwdriver to remove the staking holding the seal retainer in place.

10. Remove the air horn gasket by lifting out of dowel locating pins and lifting tab of gasket from beneath the power piston hanger, being careful not to distort the springs holding the metering rods.

11. Remove the pump plunger and return spring from the pump well.

12. Remove the power piston and metering rods by depressing the piston and releasing it with a snap. This will cause the power piston to snap the piston up against the retainer. This procedure may have to be repeated several times. Do not remove the power piston by using pliers.

➡**Use special care not to distort the metering rods.**

13. Remove the plastic filler block over the float valve.

14. Remove the float assembly and float needle by pulling up on the retaining pin. Remove the seat and gasket using a seat remover.

15. Remove the aneroid cavity insert from the float bowl.

16. Remove the pump discharge check ball retainer and check ball.

17. Remove the pump well fill slot baffle.

18. Where used, remove the rear vacuum break hose. Remove the two attaching screws and rotate the assembly to remove the vacuum break rod from the slot in the plunger head.

19. Remove the vacuum break rod by holding down on the fast idle cam; move end of vacuum break rod away from the float bowl. Disengage the rod from the hole in the intermediate choke lever.

20. Support the float bowl and throttle body as an assembly on a suitable holding fixture. Carefully align a number 21 drill (0.159 in.) on the pop-type rivet head and drill enough to remove only the head. Then, use an drift and a small hammer to drive the remainder of the rivet out of the choke housing.

21. Remove the retainers, choke cover and gasket from the housing.

22. Remove the choke housing from the float bowl by removing the retaining screw from inside the housing. The complete choke hosing can then be pulled from the bowl. Remove the cup seal and plastic tube seal.

23. Remove the secondary throttle lock-out lever from the float bowl.

24. Remove the lower choke lever from inside the float bowl by inverting the bowl.

25. Remove the fuel inlet nut, gasket, check valve filter assembly and spring.

26. Remove the throttle body and gasket by removing the attaching screws.

**Reassembly:**

Reassemble the carburetor by reversing disassembly. Use all new seals and gaskets. Note the following:

27. If the idle mixture needles were removed, back them out 4 turns as a preliminary adjustment. Final adjustments should be performed by a qualified technician.

28. Using a holding tool, install the lower choke rod inner lever into the cavity in the float bowl and slide the intermediate choke shaft and housing into the lower choke rod inner lever. The intermediate choke shaft lever and fast idle cam are in the correct position when the tang on the lever is beneath the fast idle cam. Do not install the choke cover until the inside coil lever is adjusted.

29. Do not install the float needle pull clip into the holes in the float arm.

30. Do not force the air horn assembly onto the bowl; lower it carefully in place.

31. Install the air horn screws using the proper tightening sequence.

32. Perform all applicable adjustments.

## C-4 AND CCC

1. Remove the idle speed solenoid and wide open throttle switch, if equipped.

2. Remove the upper choke lever from the end of the choke shaft by removing the retaining screw. Then rotate the upper choke lever to remove the choke rod from the slot in the lever.

3. Remove the choke rod from the lower lever inside the float bowl casting. Remove rod by holding lower lever outward with a small screwdriver and twisting the rod counterclockwise.

4. Remove the secondary metering rods by removing the small screw in the top of the metering rod hanger. Lift upward on the metering rod hanger until the secondary metering rods are completely out of the air horn.

5. Using a drift punch, drive the pump lever roll pin inward until pump lever can be removed from the air horn. Note position of the pump rod for later reassembly.

6. Remove the vacuum break "T" tube, if equipped.

7. Remove the eleven air horn-to-bowl attaching screws; two countersunk screws are located next to the venturi. Remove the secondary air baffle deflector from beneath the two center air horn screws, where used.

8. Remove the air horn from the float bowl by lifting straight up. The air horn should remain on the float bowl for removal later.

9. Remove the front vacuum break hose. Then, remove the two attaching screws and remove the vacuum break and bracket assembly from the air valve dashpot rod and the dashpot rod from the air valve lever. Remove the pump plunger stem and TPS seal retainers by inverting the air horn and use a small screwdriver to remove the staking holding the seal retainer in place.

10. Remove the solenoid-metering rod plunger by lifting it straight up.

11. Remove the rubber seal from around the mixture control solenoid plunger.

12. Remove the air horn gasket by lifting it off of the dowel locating pins on the float bowl.

13. Remove the pump plunger and return spring from the pump well.

14. Remove the TPS by pushing up on the bottom of the connector.

15. Remove the plastic filler block over the float valve.

16. Carefully lift each metering rod out of the guided metering jet, checking to make sure the return spring is removed with each metering rod.

➡ **Use special care not to distort the metering rods.**

17. Remove the solenoid connector attaching screw.

18. Using a suitable tool on the upper end of the mixture control solenoid screw, turn the screw counterclockwise and remove it from the float bowl. Then, carefully lift the mixture control solenoid and connector assembly from the float bowl.

19. Remove the plastic insert from the cavity in the float bowl.

20. Remove the solenoid screw tension spring.

21. Remove the float assembly, then the seat and gasket using a seat remover.

22. Remove the large mixture control solenoid tension spring from the boss on the bottom of the float bowl.

23. Remove the pump discharge check ball retainer and check ball.

24. Remove the pump well fill slot baffle.

25. Where used, remove the rear vacuum break hose. Remove the two attaching screws and rotate the assembly to remove the vacuum break rod from the slot in the plunger head.

26. Remove the vacuum break rod by holding down on the fast idle cam; move end of vacuum break rod away from the float bowl. Disengage the rod from the hole in the intermediate choke lever.

27. Support the float bowl and throttle body as an assembly on a suitable holding fixture. Carefully align a number 21 drill (0.159 in.) on the pop-type rivet head and drill enough to remove only the head. Then, use an drift and a small hammer to drive the remainder of the rivet out of the choke housing.

28. Remove the retainers, choke cover and gasket from the housing.

29. Remove the choke housing from the float bowl by removing the retaining screw from inside the housing. The com-

| | | | | | |
|---|---|---|---|---|---|
| 1 | Gasket - Air Cleaner | 341 | Screw and Washer Assembly - Choke Housing to Float Bow | 405 | Screw Assembly - Float Bowl to Throttle Body |
| 5 | Gasket - Flange | 345 | Screw - Choke Stat Lever Attaching | 410 | Link - Pump |
| 10 | Air Horn Assembly | 348 | Lever - Choke Stat | 420 | Needle - Idle Mixture |
| 11 | Rivet - Cover Attaching | 350 | Intermediate Choke Shaft, Lever and Link Assembly | 421 | Spring - Idle Mixture Needle |
| 12 | Cover - Air Bleed Valve | 352 | Fast Idle Cam Assembly | 422 | Plug - Idle Mixture Needle |
| 15 | Air Bleed Valve Assembly | 354 | Lever - Intermediate Choke | 425 | Screw - Fast Idle Adjusting |
| 16 | O-ring - Air Bleed Valve - Lower | 356 | Link - Choke | 426 | Spring - Fast Idle Adjusting Screw |
| 17 | O-ring - Air Bleed Valve - Upper | 360 | Lever - Secondary Throttle Lockout | 500 | Solenoid and Bracket Assembly |
| 30 | Screw - Secondary Metering Rod Holder Attaching | 364 | Seal - Intermediate Choke Shaft | 501 | Screw - Bracket Attaching |
| 31 | Holder - Secondary Metering Rod | 370 | Nut - Fuel Inlet | 505 | Bracket - Solenoid |
| 32 | Rod - Secondary Metering | 372 | Gasket - Fuel Inlet Nut | 510 | Throttle Kicker Assembly |
| 35 | Lever - Choke | 375 | Filter - Fuel Inlet | 511 | Bracket - Throttle Kicker |
| 36 | Screw - Choke Lever Attaching | 377 | Spring - Fuel Filter | 512 | Nut - Throttle Kicker Assembly Attaching |
| 40 | Retainer - Pump Link | 380 | Screw - Throttle Stop | 513 | Washer - Tab Locking |
| 41 | Lever - Pump | 381 | Spring - Throttle Stop Screw | 515 | Idle Speed Control Assembly |
| 42 | Pin - Pump Lever Hinge | 400 | Throttle Body Assembly | | |
| 45 | Screw Assembly - Air Horn to Throttle Body | 401 | Gasket - Float Bowl to Throttle Body | | |
| 46 | Screw Assembly - Air Horn to Float Bowl | | | | |
| 47 | Screw - Air Horn to Float Bowl (countersunk) | | | | |
| 50 | Baffle - Air Horn | | | | |
| 55 | Vacuum Break Assembly - Primary Side (Front) | | | | |
| 56 | Screw - Primary Side (Front) Vacuum Break Assembly Attaching | | | | |
| 57 | Hose - Primary Side (Front) Vacuum Break | | | | |
| 58 | Link - Primary Side Vacuum Break - Air Valve Lever | | | | |
| 60 | Plunger - Sensor Actuator | | | | |
| 61 | Plug - TPS Adjusting Screw | | | | |
| 62 | Screw - TPS Adjusting | | | | |
| 65 | Retainer - TPS Seal | | | | |
| 66 | Seal - TPS Plunger | | | | |
| 67 | Retainer - Pump Stem Seal | | | | |
| 68 | Seal - Pump Stem | | | | |
| 70 | Plug - Solenoid Adjusting Screw | | | | |
| 71 | Plug - Solenoid Stop Screw | | | | |
| 72 | Screw - Solenoid Stop (Rich Mixture) | | | | |
| 73 | Spring - Rich Authority Adjusting | | | | |
| 201 | Gasket - Air Horn to Float Bowl | | | | |
| 205 | Pump Assembly | | | | |
| 206 | Spring - Pump Return | | | | |
| 210 | Sensor - Throttle Position (TPS) | | | | |
| 211 | Spring - Sensor Adjusting | | | | |
| 213 | Rod - Primary Metering | | | | |
| 215 | Plunger - Solenoid | | | | |
| 217 | Spring - Primary Metering Rod (E2M, E4M only) | | | | |
| 221 | Screw - Solenoid Connector Attaching | | | | |
| 222 | Gasket - Solenoid Connector to Air Horn | | | | |
| 225 | Mixture Control Solenoid Assembly | | | | |
| 226 | Screw - Solenoid Adjusting (Lean Mixture) | | | | |
| 227 | Stop - Rich Limit | | | | |
| 228 | Spring - Solenoid Adjusting Screw | | | | |
| 229 | Spring - Solenoid Return | | | | |
| 234 | Insert - Aneroid Cavity | | | | |
| 235 | Insert - Float Bowl | | | | |
| 236 | Hinge Pin - Float | | | | |
| 237 | Float | | | | |
| 238 | Pull Clip - Float Needle | | | | |
| 239 | Needle - Float | | | | |
| 240 | Seat - Float Needle | | | | |
| 241 | Gasket - Float Needle Seat | | | | |
| 250 | Plug - Pump Discharge (Retainer) | | | | |
| 251 | Ball - Pump Discharge | | | | |
| 252 | Baffle - Pump Well | | | | |
| 255 | Primary Metering Jet Assembly | | | | |
| 315 | Hose - Secondary Side (Rear) Vacuum Break | | | | |
| 316 | Tee - Secondary Side (Rear) Vacuum Break | | | | |
| 320 | Vacuum Break Assembly - Secondary Side (Rear) | | | | |
| 321 | Screw - Secondary Side (Rear) Vacuum Break Assembly Attaching | | | | |
| 322 | Link - Secondary Side (Rear) Vacuum Break to Choke | | | | |
| 330 | Rivet - Choke Cover Attaching | | | | |
| 331 | Retainer - Choke Cover | | | | |
| 335 | Electric Choke Cover and Stat Assembly | | | | |
| 340 | Choke Housing Assembly | | | | |

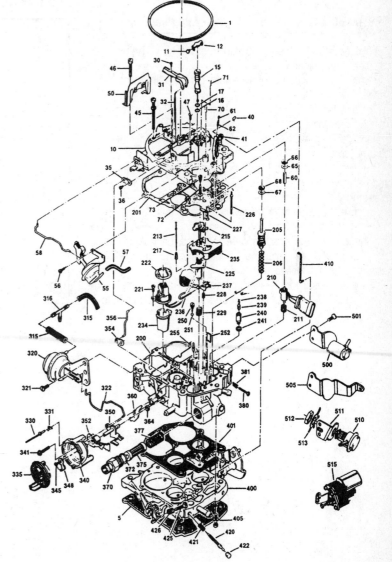

**Fig. 44 Exploded view of all 4 BBL models**

85845029

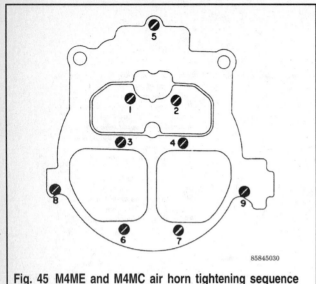

**Fig. 45 M4ME and M4MC air horn tightening sequence**

plete choke hosing can then be pulled from the bowl. Remove the cup seal and plastic tube seal.

30. Remove the secondary throttle lock-out lever from the float bowl.

31. Remove the lower choke lever from inside the float bowl by inverting the bowl.

32. Remove the fuel inlet nut, gasket, check valve filter assembly and spring.

33. Remove the throttle body and gasket by removing the attaching screws.

**Reassembly:**

Reassemble the carburetor by reversing disassembly. Use all new seals and gaskets. Note the following:

34. If the idle mixture needles were removed, back them out 3 turns as a preliminary adjustment. Final adjustments should be performed by a qualified technician.

35. Using a holding tool, install the lower choke rod inner lever into the cavity in the float bowl and slide the intermediate choke shaft and housing into the lower choke rod inner lever. The intermediate choke shaft lever and fast idle cam are in the correct position when the tang on the lever is beneath the fast idle cam. Do not install the choke cover until the inside coil lever is adjusted.

36. Do not install the float needle pull clip into the holes in the float arm.

37. Turn the mixture control screw clockwise until it is bottomed lightly in the bowl. Turn the screw counterclockwise 4 turns. Final adjustments should be performed by a qualified technician.

38. Do not force the air horn assembly onto the bowl; lower it carefully in place while holding down on pump plunger assembly. Also take care not to pinch the TPS connector wires between the air horn and the float bowl.

39. Install the air horn screws using the proper tightening sequence.

40. Perform all applicable adjustments.

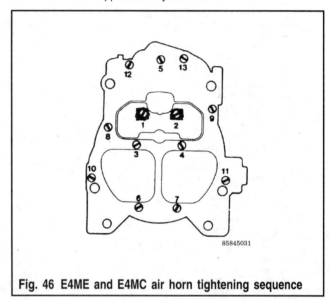

**Fig. 46 E4ME and E4MC air horn tightening sequence**

## 2GC, GE, GV 2-BARREL CARBURETOR SPECIFICATIONS

| Year | Carburetor Identification ① | Float Level (In.) | Air Valve Spring (turn) | Pump Rod (In.) | Primary Vacuum Break (In. or deg.) | Secondary Vacuum Break (In.) | Secondary Opening (In.) | Fast Idle Cam (Choke Rod) (In. or deg.) | Choke Unloader (In.) | Fast Idle Speed (rpm) |
|---|---|---|---|---|---|---|---|---|---|---|
| 1975 | 7045160 | $9/16$ | $1^7/32$ | $1^{11}/32$ | 0.145 | 0.265 | 1 Rich | 0.085 | 0.180 | Preset |
|  | 7045161 | $9/16$ | $1^7/32$ | $1^{11}/32$ | 0.145 | 0.265 | 1 Rich | 0.085 | 0.180 | Preset |
| 1976 |  | $9/16$ | $1^9/32$ | $1^{11}/32$ | 0.165 | 0.285 | 1 Rich | 0.085 | 0.180 | — |
| 1977 | 17057140 | $15/32$ | — | $1^9/16$ | 0.140 | 0.100 | — | 0.080 | 0.325 | ② |
|  | 17057141 | $7/16$ | — | $1^1/2$ | 0.110 | 0.110 | — | 0.080 | 0.140 | ② |
|  | 17057144 | $7/16$ | — | $1^{17}/32$ | 0.130 | 0.130 | — | 0.080 | 0.140 | ② |
|  | 17057145 | $7/16$ | — | $1^1/2$ | 0.110 | 0.110 | — | 0.080 | 0.140 | ② |
|  | 17057146 | $7/16$ | — | $1^{17}/32$ | 0.110 | 0.110 | — | 0.080 | 0.140 | ② |
|  | 17057147 | $7/16$ | — | $1^1/2$ | 0.110 | 0.110 | — | 0.080 | 0.140 | ② |
|  | 17057148 | $7/16$ | — | $1^{17}/32$ | 0.110 | 0.110 | — | 0.080 | 0.140 | ② |
|  | 17057445 | $7/16$ | — | $1^1/2$ | 0.140 | 0.140 | — | 0.080 | 0.140 | ② |
|  | 17057446 | $7/16$ | — | $1^1/2$ | 0.130 | 0.130 | — | 0.080 | 0.140 | ② |
|  | 17057447 | $7/16$ | — | $1^1/2$ | 0.130 | 0.130 | — | 0.080 | 0.140 | ② |
|  | 17057448 | $7/16$ | — | $1^1/2$ | 0.130 | 0.130 | — | 0.080 | 0.140 | ② |
|  | 17057112 | $19/32$ | — | $1^{21}/32$ | — | 0.130 | — | 0.260 | 0.325 | ② |
|  | 17057113 | $19/32$ | — | $2^{21}/32$ | — | 0.130 | — | 0.260 | 0.325 | ② |
|  | 17057114 | $19/32$ | — | $1^{21}/32$ | — | 0.130 | — | 0.260 | 0.325 | ② |
| 1978 | 17058145 | $7/16$ | — | $1^{19}/32$ | 0.110 | 0.060 | — | 0.080 | 0.160 | ② |
|  | 17058182 | $7/16$ | — | $1^{19}/32$ | 0.110 | 0.080 | — | 0.080 | 0.140 | ② |
|  | 17058183 | $7/16$ | — | $1^{19}/32$ | 0.110 | 0.080 | — | 0.080 | 0.140 | ② |
|  | 17058185 | $7/16$ | — | $1^{19}/32$ | 0.110 | 0.050 | — | 0.080 | 0.140 | ② |
|  | 17058187 | $7/16$ | — | $1^{19}/32$ | 0.110 | 0.080 | — | 0.080 | 0.140 | ② |
|  | 17058189 | $7/16$ | — | $1^{19}/32$ | 0.110 | 0.080 | — | 0.080 | 0.140 | ② |
|  | 17058147 | $7/16$ | — | $1^{19}/32$ | 0.140 | 0.100 | — | 0.080 | 0.140 | ② |
|  | 17058444 | $7/16$ | — | $1^{19}/32$ | 0.140 | 0.100 | — | 0.080 | 0.140 | ② |
|  | 17058448 | $7/16$ | — | $1^{19}/32$ | 0.140 | 0.100 | — | 0.080 | 0.140 | ② |
|  | 17058440 | $7/16$ | — | $1^{19}/32$ | 0.140 | 0.100 | — | 0.080 | 0.140 | ② |
|  | 17058446 | $7/16$ | — | $1^5/8$ | 0.140 | 0.140 | — | 0.080 | 0.140 | ② |

① Carburetor identification number is stamped on the float bowl next to the fuel inlet nut
② See underhood decal

85845c01

### 2MC, M2MC, M2ME, E2MC, E2ME 2-BARREL CARBURETOR SPECIFICATIONS

| Year | Carburetor Identification ① | Float Level (In.) | Fast Idle Cam (Choke Rod) (deg./In.) | Choke Unloader (deg./In.) | Vacuum Break Lean or Front (deg./In.) | Vacuum Break Rich or Rear (deg./In.) | Pump Roc (In.) | Choke Coil Lever (In.) | Automatic Choke (notches) |
|---|---|---|---|---|---|---|---|---|---|
| 1977 | 17057150 | 1/8 | 0.085 | 0.190 | 0.160 | 0.090 | 11/32 ③ | 0.120 | 2 Rich |
| | 17057152 | 1/8 | 0.085 | 0.190 | 0.160 | 0.090 | 11/32 ③ | 0.120 | 2 Rich |
| | 17057156 | 1/8 | 0.085 | 0.190 | 0.160 | 0.090 | 11/32 ③ | 0.120 | 1 Rich |
| | 17057158 | 1/8 | 0.085 | 0.190 | 0.160 | 0.090 | 11/32 ③ | 0.120 | 1 Rich |
| | 17057172 | 11/32 | 0.075 | 0.240 | 0.135 | 0.240 | 3/8 ③ | 0.120 | 2 Rich |
| 1978 | 17058150 | 3/8 | 0.065 | 0.203 | 0.203 | 0.133 | 1/4 ② | 0.120 | 2 Rich |
| | 17058151 | 3/8 | 0.065 | 0.203 | 0.229 | 0.133 | 11/32 ③ | 0.120 | 2 Rich |
| | 17058152 | 3/8 | 0.065 | 0.203 | 0.203 | 0.133 | 1/4 ② | 0.120 | 2 Rich |
| | 17058154 | 3/8 | 0.065 | 0.203 | 0.146 | 0.245 | 11/32 ③ | 0.120 | 2 Rich |
| | 17058155 | 3/8 | 0.065 | 0.203 | 0.146 | 0.245 | 11/32 ③ | 0.120 | 2 Rich |
| | 17058156 | 3/8 | 0.065 | 0.230 | 0.229 | 0.133 | 11/32 ③ | 0.120 | 2 Rich |
| | 17058158 | 3/8 | 0.065 | 0.203 | 0.229 | 0.133 | 11/32 ③ | 0.120 | 2 Rich |
| | 17058450 | 3/8 | 0.065 | 0.203 | 0.146 | 0.289 | 11/32 ③ | 0.120 | 2 Rich |
| 1979 | 17059160 | 11/32 | 0.110 | 0.195 | 0.129 | 0.187 | 1/4 ② | 0.120 | 2 Rich |
| | 17059150 | 3/8 | 0.071 | 0.220 | 0.195 | 0.129 | 1/4 ② | 0.120 | 2 Rich |
| | 17059151 | 3/8 | 0.071 | 0.220 | 0.243 | 0.142 | 11/32 ③ | 0.120 | 2 Rich |
| | 17059152 | 3/8 | 0.071 | 0.220 | 0.195 | 0.129 | 1/4 ② | 0.120 | 2 Rich |
| | 17059180 | 11/32 | 0.039 | 0.243 | 0.103 | 0.090 | 1/4 ② | 0.120 | 2 Rich |
| | 17059190 | 11/32 | 0.039 | 0.243 | 0.103 | 0.090 | 1/4 ② | 0.120 | 2 Rich |
| | 17059492 | 11/32 | 0.039 | 0.277 | 0.129 | 0.117 | 9/32 ② | 0.120 | 1 Rich |
| | 17059134 | 15/32 | 38 | 38 | 27 | — | 1/4 | 0.120 | 1 Lean |
| | 17059136 | 15/32 | 38 | 38 | 27 | — | 1/4 | 0.120 | 1 Lean |
| | 17059193 | 13/32 | 24.5 | 35 | 19 | 17 | 1/4 ② | 0.120 | 2 Rich |
| | 17059194 | 11/32 | 24.5 | 35 | 19 | 17 | 1/4 ② | 0.120 | 2 Rich |
| | 17059491 | 11/32 | 24.5 | 38 | 23 | 21 | 9/32 ② | 0.120 | 1 Lean |
| 1980 | 17080195 | 9/32 | 24.5 | 38 | 19 | 38 | — | 0.120 | — |
| | 17080197 | 9/32 | 24.5 | 38 | 19 | 38 | — | 0.120 | — |
| | 17080495 | 5/16 | 24.5 | 38 | 21 | 30 | — | 0.120 | — |
| | 17080493 | 5/16 | 24.5 | 38 | 21 | 30 | — | 0.120 | — |
| | 17080150 | 3/8 | 14 | 35 | 38 | 27 | 11/32 ③ | 0.120 | — |
| | 17080153 | 3/8 | 14 | 35 | 38 | 27 | 11/32 ③ | 0.120 | — |
| | 17080152 | 3/8 | 14 | 35 | 38 | 27 | 11/32 ③ | 0.120 | — |
| | 17080496 | 5/16 | 24.5 | 38 | 21 | 21 | 3/8 | 0.120 | ④ |
| | 17080498 | 5/16 | 24.5 | 38 | 21 | 21 | 3/8 | 0.120 | ④ |
| | 17080490 | 5/16 | 24.5 | 38 | 21 | 21 | 3/8 | 0.120 | ④ |
| | 17080492 | 5/16 | 24.5 | 38 | 21 | 21 | 3/8 | 0.120 | ④ |
| | 17080491 | 5/16 | 24.5 | 38 | 21 | 21 | 3/8 | 0.120 | ④ |
| | 17080190 | 9/32 | 24.5 | 38 | 22 | 20 | 1/4 | 0.120 | ④ |
| | 17080191 | 11/32 | 24.5 | 38 | 18 | 18 | 1/4 | 0.120 | ④ |
| | 17080195 | 9/32 | 24.5 | 38 | 19 | 14 | 1/4 | 0.120 | ④ |

85845c02

## 2MC, M2MC, M2ME, E2MC, E2ME 2-BARREL CARBURETOR SPECIFICATIONS (CONT.)

| Year | Carburetor Identification ① | Float Level (In.) | Fast Idle Cam (Choke Rod) (deg./In.) | Choke Unloader (deg./In.) | Vacuum Break Lean or Front (deg./In.) | Vacuum Break Rich or Rear (deg./In.) | Pump Roc (In.) | Choke Coil Lever (In.) | Automatic Choke (notches) |
|---|---|---|---|---|---|---|---|---|---|
| 1980 | 17080197 | 9/32 | 24.5 | 38 | 19 | 14 | 1/4 | 0.120 | ④ |
| | 17080192 | 9/32 | 24.5 | 38 | 22 | 20 | 1/4 | 0.120 | ④ |
| | 17080160 | 5/16 | 14.5 | 37.5 | 28.5 | 33.5 | 1/4 | 0.120 | ④ |
| 1981 | 17081191 | 5/16 | 24.5° | 38° | 28° | 24° | — | 0.120 | ④ |
| | 17081192 | 3/8 | 18° | 38° | 28° | 24° | — | 0.120 | ④ |
| | 17081994 | 3/8 | 18° | 38° | 28° | 24° | — | 0.120 | ④ |
| | 17081196 | 5/16 | 24.5° | 38° | 28° | 24° | — | 0.120 | ④ |
| | 17081197 | 3/8 | 18° | 38° | 28° | 24° | — | 0.120 | ④ |
| | 17081198 | 3/8 | 18° | 38° | 28° | 24° | — | 0.120 | ④ |
| | 17081199 | 3/8 | 18° | 38° | 28° | 24° | — | 0.120 | ④ |
| | 17081150 | 13/32 | 14° | 35° | 24° | 36° | — | 0.120 | ④ |
| | 17081152 | 13/32 | 14° | 35° | 24° | 36° | — | 0.120 | ④ |
| | 17080191 | 11/32 | 24.5° | 38° | 18° | 18° | 1/4 | 0.120 | ④ |
| | 17081492 | 9/32 | 24.5° | 38° | 17° | 19° | 1/4 | 0.120 | ④ |
| | 17081493 | 9/32 | 24.5° | 38° | 17° | 19° | 1/4 | 0.120 | ④ |
| | 17081170 | 13/32 | 20° | 38° | 25° | — | 1/4 | 0.120 | ④ |
| | 17081171 | 13/32 | 20° | 38° | 25° | — | 1/4 | 0.120 | ④ |
| | 17081174 | 9/32 | 20° | 38° | 25° | — | 1/4 | 0.120 | ④ |
| | 17081175 | 9/32 | 20° | 38° | 25° | — | 1/4 | 0.120 | ④ |
| 1982 | 17082130 | 3/8 | 20° | 38° | 27° | — | — | — | — |
| | 17082132 | 3/8 | 20° | 38° | 27° | — | — | — | — |
| | 17082138 | 3/8 | 20° | 38° | 27° | — | — | — | — |
| | 17082140 | 3/8 | 20° | 38° | 27° | — | — | — | — |
| | 17082150 | 13/32 | 14° | 35° | 24° | 38° | — | — | — |
| | 17082150 | 13/32 | 14° | 35° | 24° | 40° | — | — | — |
| | 17082182 | 5/16 | 18° | 32° | 28° | 24° | — | — | — |
| | 17082184 | 5/16 | 18° | 32° | 28° | 24° | — | — | — |
| | 17082186 | 5/16 | 18° | 27° | 21° | 19° | — | — | — |
| | 17082192 | 5/16 | 18° | 32° | 28° | 24° | — | — | — |
| | 17082194 | 5/16 | 18° | 32° | 28° | 24° | — | — | — |
| | 17082196 | 5/16 | 18° | 27° | 21° | 19° | — | — | — |
| 1983 | 17083190 | 5/16 | 18° | 32 | 28° | 24° | — | 0.1206 ⑤ | — |
| | 17083192 | 5/16 | 18° | 32 | 28° | 24° | — | 0.1206 ⑤ | — |
| | 17083193 | 5/16 | 18° | 27 | 24° | 28° | — | 0.1206 ⑤ | — |
| | 17083194 | 5/16 | 17° | 35 | 27° | 25° | — | 0.1206 ⑤ | — |
| 1984 | 17083191 | 5/16 | 18° | 32° | 28° | 24° | — | 0.120 ⑤ | — |
| 1985 | 17085190 | 10/32 | 18° | 32° | 28° | 24° | — | 0.120 | — |
| | 17085192 | 11/32 | 17° | 35° | 27° | 25° | — | 0.120 | — |
| | 17085194 | 11/32 | 17° | 35° | 27° | 25° | — | 0.120 | — |
| 1986 | 17086190 | 10/32 | 18° | 32° | 28° | 24° | — | 0.120 | — |
| 1987 | 17086190 | 10/32 | 18° | 32° | 28° | 24° | — | 0.120 | — |

① The carburetor identifications number is stamped on the float bowl, next to the fuel inlet nut.
② Inner hole
③ Outer hole
④ Tamper resistant choke
⑤ Use a gauge of required dimension

85845c03

## M4MC, M4ME, E4MC, E4ME 4-BARREL CARBURETOR SPECIFICATIONS

| Year | Carburetor Identification ① | Float Level (in.) | Air Valve Spring (turn) | Pump Rod (in.) | Primary Vacuum Break (in. or deg.) | Secondary Vacuum Break (in. or deg.) | Secondary Opening (in. or deg.) | Fast Idle Cam (Choke Rod) (in. or deg.) | Choke Unloader (in. or deg.) | Fast Idle Speed (rpm) |
|---|---|---|---|---|---|---|---|---|---|---|
| 1975 | 7045183 | 3/8 | 1/8 | 9/32 | 0.190 | 0.140 | — | 0.135 | 0.235 | ② |
| | 7045250 | 3/8 | 1/2 | 9/32 | 0.250 | 0.180 | — | 0.170 | 0.300 | ② |
| | 7045483 | 3/8 | 1/2 | 9/32 | 0.275 | 0.180 | — | 0.135 | 0.235 | ② |
| | 7045550 | 3/8 | 1/2 | 9/32 | 0.275 | 0.180 | — | 0.135 | 0.235 | ② |
| | 7045264 | 17/32 | 1/2 | 9/32 | 0.150 | 0.260 | — | 0.130 | 0.235 | ② |
| | 7045184 | 3/8 | 3/4 | 9/32 | 0.190 | 0.140 | — | 0.135 | 0.235 | ② |
| | 7045185 | 3/8 | 3/4 | 9/32 | 0.275 | 0.140 | — | 0.135 | 0.235 | ② |
| | 7045251 | 3/8 | 3/4 | 9/32 | 0.190 | 0.140 | — | 0.135 | 0.235 | ② |
| | 7045244 | 5/16 | 3/4 | 15/32 | 0.130 | 0.115 | Index | 0.095 | 0.240 | 1800 ③ |
| | 7045544 | 5/16 | 3/4 | 15/32 | 0.145 | 0.130 | Index | 0.095 | 0.240 | 1800 ③ |
| | 7045240 | 7/16 | 7/16 | 9/32 | 0.135 | 0.120 | Index | 0.095 | 0.240 | 1800 ③ |
| | 7045548 | 7/16 | 7/16 | 9/32 | 0.135 | 0.120 | Index | 0.095 | 0.240 | 1800 ③ |
| | 7045541 | 7/16 | 7/16 | 9/32 | 0.135 | 0.120 | Index | 0.095 | 0.240 | 1800 ③ |
| | 7045274 | 1/2 | — | 9/32 | 0.150 | 0.260 | — | 0.230 | 0.230 | 1800 |
| | 7045260 | 1/2 | — | 9/32 | 0.150 | 0.260 | — | 0.130 | 0.230 | 1800 |
| | 7045262 | 1/2 | — | 9/32 | 0.150 | 0.260 | — | 0.130 | 0.230 | 1800 |
| | 7045266 | 1/2 | — | 9/32 | 0.150 | 0.260 | — | 0.130 | 0.230 | 1800 |
| | 7045562 | 1/2 | — | 9/32 | 0.150 | 0.260 | — | 0.130 | 0.230 | 1800 |
| 1976 | 17056544 | 5/16 | 3/4 | 3/8 | 0.130 | 0.130 | Index | 0.095 | 0.250 | — |
| | 17056244 | 5/16 | 3/4 | 3/8 | 0.130 | 0.120 | Index | 0.095 | 0.250 | — |
| | 17056240 | 15/32 | 7/16 | 9/32 | 0.135 | 0.120 | Index | 0.095 | 0.250 | — |
| | 17056540 | 15/32 | 7/16 | 3/8 | 0.135 | 0.120 | Index | 0.095 | 0.250 | — |
| | 17056250 | 13/32 | 1/2 | 9/32 | 0.190 | 0.140 | — | 0.130 | 0.230 | 900 ④ |
| | 17056251 | 13/32 | 3/4 | 9/32 | 0.190 | 0.140 | — | 0.130 | 0.230 | 900 |
| | 17056253 | 13/32 | 1/2 | 9/32 | 0.190 | 0.140 | — | 0.130 | 0.230 | 900 ④ |
| | 17056255 | 13/32 | 3/4 | 9/32 | 0.190 | 0.140 | — | 0.130 | 0.230 | 900 |
| | 17056256 | 13/32 | 3/4 | 9/32 | 0.190 | 0.140 | — | 0.130 | 0.230 | 900 |
| | 17056257 | 13/32 | 3/4 | 9/32 | 0.190 | 0.140 | — | 0.130 | 0.230 | 900 |
| | 17056550 | 13/32 | 1/2 | 9/32 | 0.190 | 0.140 | — | 0.130 | 0.230 | 1000 |
| | 17056551 | 13/32 | 3/4 | 9/32 | 0.190 | 0.140 | — | 0.130 | 0.230 | 800 |
| | 17056553 | 13/32 | 1/2 | 9/32 | 0.190 | 0.140 | — | 0.130 | 0.230 | 1000 |
| 1977 | 17057202 | 15/32 | 7/8 | 9/32 | 0.160 | — | — | 0.325 | 0.280 | 1600 ⑤ |
| | 17057204 | 15/32 | 7/8 | 9/32 | 0.160 | — | — | 0.325 | 0.280 | 1600 ⑤ |
| | 1707250 | 13/32 | 1/2 | 9/32 | 0.135 | 0.180 | — | 0.100 | 0.220 | ⑦ |
| | 1707253 | 13/32 | 1/2 | 9/32 | 0.135 | 0.180 | — | 0.100 | 0.220 | ⑦ |
| | 1707255 | 13/32 | 1/2 | 9/32 | 0.135 | 0.180 | — | 0.100 | 0.220 | ⑦ |
| | 1707256 | 13/32 | 1/2 | 9/32 | 0.135 | 0.180 | — | 0.100 | 0.220 | ⑦ |
| | 1707258 | 13/32 | 1/2 | 9/32 | 0.135 | 0.225 | — | 0.100 | 0.220 | ⑦ |
| | 1707550 | 13/32 | 1/2 | 9/32 | 0.135 | 0.225 | — | 0.100 | 0.220 | ⑦ |

85845c04

## M4MC, M4ME, E4MC, E4ME 4-BARREL CARBURETOR SPECIFICATIONS (CONT.)

| Year | Carburetor Identification ① | Float Level (in.) | Air Valve Spring (turn) | Pump Rod (in.) | Primary Vacuum Break (in. or deg.) | Secondary Vacuum Break (in. or deg.) | Secondary Opening (in. or deg.) | Fast Idle Cam (Choke Rod) (in. or deg.) | Choke Unloader (in. or deg.) | Fast Idle Speed (rpm) |
|---|---|---|---|---|---|---|---|---|---|---|
| 1977 | 1707553 | 13/32 | 1/2 | 9/32 | 0.135 | 0.225 | — | 0.100 | 0.220 | ⑦ |
| | 17057262 | 17/32 | 1/2 | 3/8 | 0.150 | 0.240 | — | 0.130 | 0.220 | ⑦ |
| 1978 | 17058253 | 13/32 | 1/2 | 9/32 | 0.129 | 0.183 | — | 0.096 | 0.220 | ⑦ |
| | 17058250 | 13/32 | 1/2 | 9/32 | 0.129 | 0.183 | — | 0.096 | 0.220 | ⑦ |
| | 17058258 | 13/32 | 1/2 | 9/32 | 0.136 | 0.230 | — | 0.103 | 0.220 | ⑦ |
| | 17058553 | 13/32 | 1/2 | 9/32 | 0.136 | 0.230 | — | 0.103 | 0.220 | ⑦ |
| | 17058272 | 15/32 | 5/8 | 3/8 | 0.126 | 0.195 | — | 0.071 | 0.227 | ⑦ |
| | 17058241 | 5/16 | 3/4 | 3/8 | 0.117 | 0.103 | — | 0.096 | 0.243 | ⑦ |
| | 17058274 | 17/32 | 1/2 | 3/8 | 0.149 | 0.260 | — | 0.129 | 0.220 | ⑦ |
| | 17058264 | 17/32 | 1/2 | 3/8 | 0.149 | 0.260 | — | 0.129 | 0.220 | ⑦ |
| 1979 | 17059253 | 13/32 | 1/2 | 9/32 | 23 | 30.5 | — | 18 | 35 | ⑦ |
| | 17059250 | 13/32 | 1/2 | 9/32 | 23 | 30.5 | — | 18 | 35 | ⑦ |
| | 17059251 | 13/32 | 1/2 | 9/32 | 23 | 30.5 | — | — | 35 | ⑦ |
| | 17059258 | 13/32 | 1/2 | 9/32 | 24 | 32 | — | — | 35 | ⑦ |
| | 17059256 | 13/32 | 1/2 | 9/32 | 24 | 32 | — | — | 35 | ⑦ |
| | 17059553 | 13/32 | 1/2 | 9/32 | 24 | 36.5 | — | 19 | 35 | ⑦ |
| | 1709240 | 7/32 | 3/4 | 9/32 | 21 | 21 | — | 14.5 | 30 | ⑦ |
| | 1709243 | 7/32 | 3/4 | 9/32 | 21 | 21 | — | 14.5 | 30 | ⑦ |
| | 1709540 | 7/32 | 3/4 | 9/32 | 21 | 23 | — | 14.5 | 38 | ⑦ |
| | 1709543 | 7/32 | 3/4 | 9/32 | 21 | 23 | — | 14.5 | 38 | ⑦ |
| | 1709542 | 7/32 | 3/4 | 9/32 | 13 | 13 | — | 14.5 | 30 | ⑦ |
| 1980 | 17080253 | 13/32 | 1/2 | 9/32 | 26 | 34 | — | 17 | 35 | ⑦ |
| | 17080250 | 13/32 | 1/2 | 9/32 | 26 | 34 | — | 17 | 35 | ⑦ |
| | 17080252 | 13/32 | 1/2 | 9/32 | 26 | 34 | — | 17 | 35 | ⑦ |
| | 17080251 | 13/32 | 1/2 | 9/32 | 26 | 34 | — | 17 | 35 | ⑦ |
| | 17080259 | 13/32 | 1/2 | 9/32 | 26 | 34 | — | 17 | 35 | ⑦ |
| | 17080260 | 13/32 | 1/2 | 9/32 | 26 | 34 | — | 17 | 35 | ⑦ |
| | 17080553 | 15/32 | 1/2 | 9/32 | 25 | 35 | — | 17 | 35 | ⑦ |
| | 17080554 | 15/32 | 1/2 | 9/32 | 25 | 34 | — | 17 | 35 | ⑦ |
| | 17080272 | 15/32 | 5/8 | 3/8 | 23 | 29.5 | — | 14.5 | 33 | ⑦ |
| | 17080249 | 7/16 | 3/4 | 9/32 | 23 | 20.5 | — | 18 | 38 | ⑦ |
| | 17080270 | 15/32 | 5/8 | 3/8 | 26 | 34 | — | 14.5 | 35 | ⑦ |
| | 17080241 | 7/16 | 3/4 | 9/32 | 23 | 20.5 | — | 18 | 38 | ⑦ |
| | 17080249 | 7/16 | 3/4 | 9/32 | 23 | 20.5 | — | 18 | 38 | ⑦ |
| | 17080244 | 5/16 | 5/8 | 9/32 | 18 | 14 | — | 24.5 | 38 | ⑦ |
| | 17080242 | 13/32 | 9/16 | 9/32 | 15 | 18 | — | 14.5 | 35 | ⑦ |
| | 17080243 | 3/16 | 9/16 | 9/32 | 16 | 16 | — | 14.5 | 30 | ⑦ |
| 1981 | 17081248 | 3/8 | 5/8 | ⑥ | 28 | 24 | — | 24.5 | 38 | ⑦ |
| | 17081289 | 13/32 | 5/8 | ⑥ | 28 | 24 | — | 24.5 | 38 | ⑦ |

85845c05

## M4MC, M4ME, E4MC, E4ME 4-BARREL CARBURETOR SPECIFICATIONS (CONT.)

| Year | Carburetor Identification ① | Float Level (in.) | Air Valve Spring (turn) | Pump Rod (in.) | Primary Vacuum Break (in. or deg.) | Secondary Vacuum Break (in. or deg.) | Secondary Opening (in. or deg.) | Fast Idle Cam (Choke Rod) (in. or deg.) | Choke Unloader (in. or deg.) | Fast Idle Speed (rpm) |
|---|---|---|---|---|---|---|---|---|---|---|
| 1981 | 17081253 | 15/32 | 1/2 | ⑥ | 25 | 36 | — | 14 | 35 | ⑦ |
|  | 17081254 | 15/32 | 1/2 | ⑥ | 25 | 36 | — | 14 | 35 | ⑦ |
| 1982 | 17082202 | 11/32 | — | ⑥ | 20 | 20 | — | — | — | ⑦ |
|  | 17082204 | 11/32 | — | ⑥ | 20 | 20 | — | — | — | ⑦ |
|  | 17082244 | 7/16 | — | ⑥ | 32 | 21 | 16 | — | — | ⑦ |
|  | 17082245 | 3/8 | — | ⑥ | 32 | 26 | 26 | — | — | ⑦ |
|  | 17082246 | 3/8 | — | ⑥ | 32 | 26 | 26 | — | — | ⑦ |
|  | 17082247 | 13/32 | — | ⑥ | 38 | 28 | 24 | — | — | ⑦ |
|  | 17082248 | 13/32 | — | ⑥ | 38 | 28 | 24 | — | — | ⑦ |
|  | 17082251 | 15/32 | — | ⑥ | 35 | 25 | 45 | — | — | ⑦ |
|  | 17082253 | 15/32 | — | ⑥ | 35 | 25 | 36 | — | — | ⑦ |
|  | 17082264 | 7/16 | — | ⑥ | 32 | 21 | 16 | — | — | ⑦ |
|  | 17082265 | 3/8 | — | ⑥ | 32 | 26 | 26 | — | — | ⑦ |
|  | 17082266 | 3/8 | — | ⑥ | 32 | 26 | 26 | — | — | ⑦ |
| 1983 | 17083250 | 7/16 | 1/2 | ⑥ | 27° | 42° | — | 14° | 35 | ⑦ |
|  | 17083253 | 7/16 | 1/2 | ⑥ | 27° | 41° | — | 14° | 35 | ⑦ |
| 1984 | 17084205 | 11/32 | 7/8 | ⑥ | 27° | — | 0.015 | 38° | 38° | ⑦ |
|  | 17084208 | 11/32 | 7/8 | ⑥ | 27° | — | 0.015 | 20° | 38° | ⑦ |
|  | 17084209 | 11/32 | 7/8 | ⑥ | 27° | — | 0.015 | 38° | 38° | ⑦ |
|  | 17084210 | 11/32 | 7/8 | ⑥ | 27° | — | 0.015 | 20° | 38° | ⑦ |
|  | 17084240 | 5/16 | 1 | ⑥ | 24° | — | 0.015 | 24.5° | 32° | ⑦ |
|  | 17084244 | 5/16 | 1 | ⑥ | 24° | — | 0.015 | 24.5° | 32° | ⑦ |
|  | 17084246 | 5/16 | 1 | ⑥ | 22° | — | 0.015 | 24.5° | 32° | ⑦ |
|  | 17084248 | 5/16 | 1 | ⑥ | 24° | — | 0.015 | 24.5° | 32° | ⑦ |
|  | 17084252 | 7/16 | 1/2 | ⑥ | 27° | — | 0.015 | 14° | 35° | ⑦ |
|  | 17084254 | 7/16 | 1/2 | ⑥ | 27° | — | 0.015 | 14° | 35° | ⑦ |
|  | 17084256 | 11/32 | 1/2 | ⑥ | 27° | 41° | 0.015 | 14° | 35° | ⑦ |
|  | 17084258 | 11/32 | 1/2 | ⑥ | 27° | 41° | 0.015 | 14° | 35° | ⑦ |
| 1985 | 17084282 | 11/32 | 1/2 | ⑥ | 25° | 43° | 0.025 | 14° | 35° | ⑦ |
|  | 17085554 | 14/32 | 1/2 | ⑥ | 27° | 41° | 0.025 | 14° | 35° | ⑦ |
|  | 17085202 | 11/32 | 7/8 | ⑥ | 27° | — | 0.025 | 20° | 38° | ⑦ |
|  | 17085203 | 11/32 | 7/8 | ⑥ | 27° | — | 0.025 | 20° | 38° | ⑦ |
|  | 17085204 | 11/32 | 7/8 | ⑥ | 27° | — | 0.025 | 20° | 38° | ⑦ |
|  | 17085207 | 11/32 | 7/8 | ⑥ | 27° | — | 0.025 | 38° | 38° | ⑦ |
|  | 17085218 | 11/32 | 7/8 | ⑥ | 27° | — | 0.025 | 20° | 38° | ⑦ |
|  | 17085502 | 7/16 | 7/8 | ⑥ | 26° | 36° | 0.025 | 20° | 39° | ⑦ |
|  | 17085503 | 7/16 | 7/8 | ⑥ | 26° | 36° | 0.025 | 20° | 39° | ⑦ |
|  | 17085506 | 7/16 | 1 | ⑥ | 27° | 36° | 0.025 | 20° | 36° | ⑦ |
|  | 17085508 | 7/16 | 1 | ⑥ | 27° | 36° | 0.025 | 20° | 36° | ⑦ |

85845c06

## M4MC, M4ME, E4MC, E4ME 4-BARREL CARBURETOR SPECIFICATIONS (CONT.)

| Year | Carburetor Identification ① | Float Level (in.) | Air Valve Spring (turn) | Pump Rod (in.) | Primary Vacuum Break (in. or deg.) | Secondary Vacuum Break (in. or deg.) | Secondary Opening (in. or deg.) | Fast Idle Cam (Choke Rod) (in. or deg.) | Choke Unloader (in. or deg.) | Fast Idle Speed (rpm) |
|---|---|---|---|---|---|---|---|---|---|---|
| 1985 | 17085524 | 7/16 | 1 | ⑥ | 25° | 36° | 0.025 | 20° | 36° | ⑦ |
| | 17085526 | 7/16 | 1 | ⑥ | 25° | 36° | 0.025 | 20° | 36° | ⑦ |
| 1986 | 17086008 | 11/32 | 1/2 | ⑥ | 25° | 43° | 0.025 | 14° | 35° | ⑦ |
| | 17086077 | 11/32 | 1/2 | ⑥ | 25° | 43° | 0.025 | 14° | 35° | ⑦ |
| 1987 | 17086009 | 14/32 | 1/2 | ⑥ | 25° | 43° | 0.025 | 14° | 35° | ⑦ |
| | 17087130 | 11/32 | 7/8 | ⑥ | 27° | — | 0.025 | 20° | 38° | ⑦ |
| | 17087131 | 11/32 | 7/8 | ⑥ | 27° | — | 0.025 | 38° | 38° | ⑦ |
| | 17087133 | 11/32 | 7/8 | ⑥ | 27° | — | 0.025 | 38° | 38° | ⑦ |
| 1988 | 17086008 | 11/32 | 1/2 | ⑥ | 25° | 43° | 0.025 | 14° | 35° | ⑦ |
| | 17088115 | 11/32 | 1/2 | ⑥ | 25° | 43° | 0.025 | 14° | 35° | ⑦ |
| 1989 | 17086008 | 11/32 | 1/2 | ⑥ | 25° | 43° | 0.025 | 14° | 35° | ⑦ |
| | 17088115 | 11/32 | 1/2 | ⑥ | 25° | 43° | 0.025 | 14° | 35° | ⑦ |
| 1990 | 17086008 | 11/32 | 1/2 | ⑥ | 25° | 43° | 0.025 | 14° | 35° | ⑦ |
| | 17088115 | 11/32 | 1/2 | ⑥ | 25° | 43° | 0.025 | 14° | 35° | ⑦ |

① Carburetor identification number is stamped on the float bowl next to the fuel inlet nut
② 900 rpm with fast idle cam follower on lowest step of fast idle cam
③ Trans. in Park with fast idle cam follower on highest step of fast idle cam
④ In Park; 1000 rpm (Park) in California
⑤ In Park
⑥ No pump rod adjustment required on carburetors used with the CCC system
⑦ See underhood decal

85845c07

# GASOLINE FUEL INJECTION SYSTEM

## Description of System

▶ **See Figure 47**

This is a throttle body fuel injection system with two fuel injectors mounted at the top of the throttle body, which spray fuel down through the throttle valves and into the intake manifold. The throttle body resembles a carburetor in appearance but does away with much of the complexity (choke system, power valves, accelerator pump, fuel circuits, etc.), replacing them with an electronically operated fuel injector.

The injector is actually a solenoid which when activated, lifts a pintle off it's seat, allowing the pressurized fuel behind the valve to spray out. The nozzle of the injector is designed to atomize the fuel for a complete air/fuel mixture.

The activating signal for the injector originates with the Electronic Control Module (ECM), which monitors engine temperature, throttle position, vehicle speed and several other engine-related conditions. The ECM continuously updates the injector opening times in relation to the information given by these sensors.

Fuel pressure for the system is provided by an in-tank fuel pump. The pump is designed to provide fuel at about 18 psi (125 kPa). A fuel pressure regulator in the TBI unit keeps fuel available to the injectors at a constant pressure between 9-13 psi (62-90 kPa). Fuel in excess of injector needs is returned to the fuel tank by a separate line.

## Relieving Fuel System Pressure

This system incorporates a bleed in the pressure regulator which automatically relieves pressure any time the engine is turned off, but a small amount of fuel may be released when the fuel line is disconnected. To reduce the chance of personal injury, cover the fuel line with a shop cloth to collect the fuel, and then place the cloth in an approved container.

## Electric Fuel Pump

▶ **See Figure 48**

### REMOVAL & INSTALLATION

1. Allow the fuel pressure to bleed off.
2. Disconnect the negative battery cable.
3. Raise the rear of the car and support it with jackstands. Make sure to block the front wheels.
4. Remove the fuel tank. Pleaser refer to the Fuel Tank procedure found later in this section.
5. Remove the fuel lever sending unit and pump assembly by turning the cam lock ring counterclockwise. Lift the assembly from the fuel tank and remove the fuel pump from the fuel lever sending unit
6. Pull the pump up into the attaching hose while pulling outward away from the bottom support. Take care to prevent damage to the rubber insulator and strainer during removal.

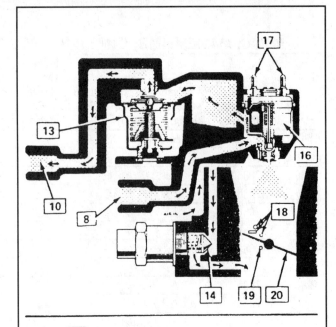

| 8 | FUEL SUPPLY |
| 10 | FUEL RETURN |
| 13 | PRESSURE REGULATOR (PART OF FUEL METER COVER) |
| 14 | IDLE AIR CONTROL (IAC) VALVE (SHOWN OPEN) |
| 16 | FUEL INJECTOR |
| 17 | FUEL INJECTOR TERMINALS |
| 18 | PORTED VACUUM SOURCES* |
| 19 | MANIFOLD VACUUM SOURCE* |
| 20 | THROTTLE VALVE |

*May Be Different on some Models.

85845032

**Fig. 47 TBI operation**

After pump assembly is clear of the bottom support, pull pump assembly out of the rubber connector for removal.

**To install:**
7. Inspect the pump attaching hose for any signs of deterioration. Replace as necessary. Also check the rubber sound insulator at the bottom of the pump; replace if required.
8. Push fuel pump assembly into the attaching hose.
9. Install the fuel lever sending unit and pump assembly into the tank assembly. Use new O-ring during reassembly.

➡**Care should be taken not to fold over or twist the strainer when installing the sending unit as this will restrict fuel flow.**

10. Install the cam lock over the assembly and lock by turning clockwise.
11. Reverse fuel tank removal procedure to finish installing.

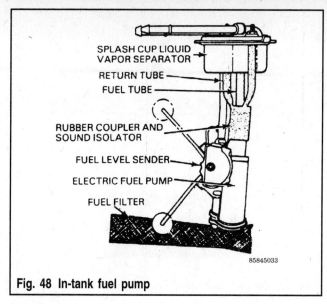

**Fig. 48 In-tank fuel pump**

## TESTING

### Flow Test

1. Allow the fuel pressure to bleed off.
2. Disconnect the fuel feed line and install a hose on the line.
3. Apply battery voltage (using a fused jumper wire) to terminal "G" of the Assembly Line Date Link (ALDL) connector located under the dash. Terminal "G" is the first terminal on the left of the bottom row.
4. The fuel pump should supply ½ pint or more in 15 seconds.

### Pressure Test

1. Allow the fuel pressure to bleed off.
2. Obtain two sections ⅜ in. steel tubing. Each should be about 10 in. (254mm) long. Double-flare one end of each section.
3. Install a flare nut on each section. Connect each of the above sections of tubing into the "flare nut-to-flare nut adapters" that are included in the J-29658-82 Gage Adapters.
4. Attach the pipe and adapter assemblies to the J-29658 gage.
5. Using proper procedures, raise and support the front of the car.
6. Disconnect the front fuel feed hose from the fuel pipe on the body.
7. Install the 10 in. (254 mm) length of ⅜ in. fuel hose onto the fuel feed pipe on the body. Attach the other end of the hose onto one of the sections of pipe mentioned earlier. Secure the hose connections with clamps.
8. Attach the front fuel feed hose onto the other section of tubing. Secure the hose connection with a clamp.
9. Start the engine and check for leaks.
10. Observe the fuel pressure reading. It should be 9-13 psi (62-90 kPa).

## Throttle Body

▶ See Figures 49, 50, 51, 52 and 53

### REMOVAL & INSTALLATION

1. Allow the fuel pressure to bleed off.
2. Disconnect the negative battery cable.
3. Remove the air cleaner assembly, noting and labeling the vacuum and electrical connections.
4. Disconnect and label the electrical connectors at the TBI unit.
5. Disconnect the throttle cable at the TBI unit.
6. Disconnect the fuel feed and return lines.
7. Unbolt and remove the TBI unit.
8. Installation is the reverse of removal.

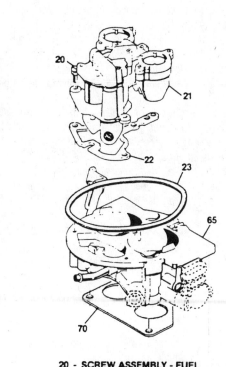

20 - SCREW ASSEMBLY - FUEL
   METER BODY - THROTTLE
   BODY ATTACHING
21 - FUEL METER BODY ASSEMBLY
22 - GASKET - THROTTLE BODY
   TO FUEL METER BODY
23 - GASKET - AIR FILTER
65 - THROTTLE BODY ASSEMBLY
70 - GASKET - FLANGE

85845034

**Fig. 49 TBI unit**

## INJECTOR REPLACEMENT

1. Allow the fuel pressure to bleed off and disconnect the negative battery cable.

2. Remove the air cleaner assembly.

3. Squeeze the two tabs of the injector connector and pull straight up.

4. Remove the fuel meter cover.

5. With the fuel meter cover gasket in place to prevent damage to the casting, use a screwdriver to lift the injector carefully until it is free from the fuel meter body.

6. Remove the small O-ring from the nozzle end of the injector. Carefully rotate the injector back and forth and remove the filter from the base of the injector.

7. Remove and discard the fuel meter cover gasket.

8. Remove the large O-ring and steel back-up washer from the top of the counterbore of the fuel meter body injector cavity.

**To install:**

9. Install the fuel injector nozzle filter on the nozzle end of the fuel injector. Use a twisting motion to position the filter against the base of the injector.

10. Lubricate a new small O-ring with automatic transmission fluid. Push the O-ring on the nozzle end of the injector until it presses against the injector fuel filter.

11. Install the steel backup washer in the top counterbore of the fuel meter body injector cavity.

12. Lubricate a new large O-ring with automatic transmission fluid and install it directly over the backup washer. Be sure the O-ring is seated properly in the cavity and is flush with the top of the fuel meter casting surface.

13. Install the injector in the cavity, aligning the raised lug on the injector base with the cast-in notch in the fuel meter body cavity. Push down on the injector until it is fully seated in the cavity.

14. Install the fuel meter cover. Thread locking compound must be used on the threads.

15. Install the injector electrical connector.

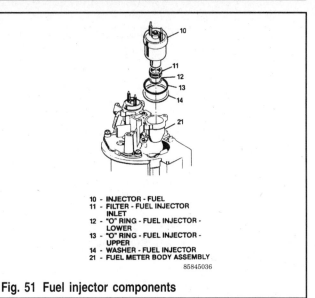

10 - INJECTOR - FUEL
11 - FILTER - FUEL INJECTOR INLET
12 - "O" RING - FUEL INJECTOR - LOWER
13 - "O" RING - FUEL INJECTOR - UPPER
14 - WASHER - FUEL INJECTOR
21 - FUEL METER BODY ASSEMBLY

85845036

**Fig. 51 Fuel injector components**

16. Install the air cleaner and reconnect the negative battery cable.

## Fuel Pressure Regulator

▸ See Figure 52

### REMOVAL & INSTALLATION

The fuel meter cover contains the pressure regulator and is only serviced as a complete preset assembly.

### ✳✳CAUTION

**DO NOT remove the four screws securing the pressure regulator to the fuel meter cover. The pressure regulator includes a large spring under heavy compression which could cause injury if released.**

## Throttle Position Sensor

### REMOVAL & INSTALLATION

1. Remove the air cleaner and disconnect the TPS electrical connector.

2. Remove the two attaching screws, washers and retainers.

3. Remove the sensor.

**To install:**

4. With the throttle valve in the normal closed idle position, install the TPS on the throttle body assembly. Make sure the TPS pickup lever is located ABOVE the tang on the throttle actuator lever.

5. Install the two attaching screws, washers and retainers. Use a thread locking compound on the threads.

6. Reconnect the electrical connector and install the air cleaner.

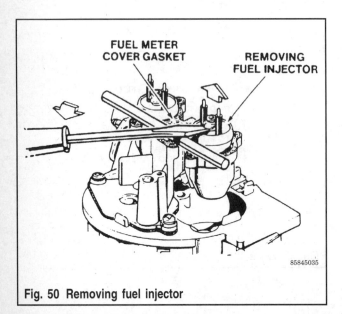

FUEL METER
COVER GASKET

REMOVING
FUEL INJECTOR

85845035

**Fig. 50 Removing fuel injector**

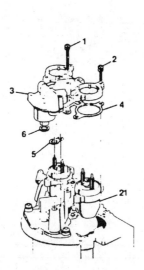

1 - SCREW ASSEMBLY - FUEL
    METER COVER ATTACHING -
    LONG
2 - SCREW ASSEMBLY - FUEL
    METER COVER ATTACHING -
    SHORT
3 - FUEL METER COVER
    ASSEMBLY
4 - GASKET - FUEL METER
    COVER
5 - GASKET - FUEL METER
    OUTLET
6 - SEAL - PRESSURE
    REGULATOR
21 - FUEL METER BODY
    ASSEMBLY

85845037

**Fig. 52 Fuel meter cover and pressure regulator assembly**

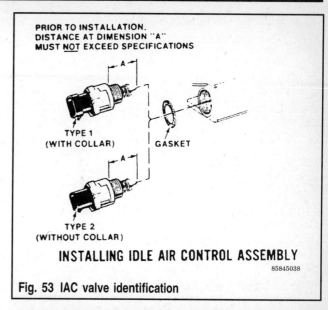

PRIOR TO INSTALLATION.
DISTANCE AT DIMENSION "A"
MUST **NOT** EXCEED SPECIFICATIONS

TYPE 1
(WITH COLLAR)     GASKET

TYPE 2
(WITHOUT COLLAR)

**INSTALLING IDLE AIR CONTROL ASSEMBLY**

85845038

**Fig. 53 IAC valve identification**

## Idle Air Control Valve

▶ See Figure 53

### REMOVAL & INSTALLATION

1. Remove the air cleaner and disconnect the IAC valve electrical connection.
2. Remove the valve using a 1¼ in. (32mm) wrench on the hex surface only.
   **To install:**
3. Before installing the new valve, measure from motor housing to the end of the cone. Distance should be no greater than 1⅛ in. (28 mm). If necessary, reduce the distance. On Type 1 valves exert firm pressure on the valve to retract it. On Type 2 valves, compress the retaining spring while turning valve in with a clockwise motion.
4. Install the new idle air control valve to the throttle body; use a new gasket.
5. Reconnect the electrical connector and install the air cleaner.
6. Start engine and allow it to reach operating temperature. The ECM will reset idle speed when the vehicle is driven above 35 mph (56 kph).

## DIESEL FUEL SYSTEM

## Injection Lines

▶ See Figure 54

### REMOVAL & INSTALLATION

➡ To perform this procedure, you will need screens to cover the intake manifold air inlets and plastic caps to fit the fuel line, nozzle, and pump openings.

1. Disconnect the negative (-) battery cable.

2. Remove the air cleaner. Remove the oil separator/filters and lines from the valve covers.
3. Remove the air crossover and gaskets from the intake manifold. Install the screen covers onto the manifold to prevent any foreign object from entering it.
4. Remove the line clamps. Note the routing of pump wiring. **With a backup wrench on each nozzle body upper (small) hex,** loosen the injection line connections at each nozzle. Loosen the connections at the injection pump (you don't need a backup wrench on these connections).
5. Cap off all the openings and remove the lines.

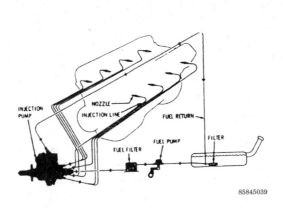

85845039

**Fig. 54 Diesel fuel system circuit**

**To install:**

6. Locate the injection lines in position. Route wiring between the #2 and #3 injection lines. Thread all caps loosely.

7. Torque each connection to 25 ft. lbs. (34 Nm), using a backup wrench on the nozzles as in loosening the connections.

8. Install the line clamps.

9. Remove the screened covers from the manifold, and install the crossover with new gaskets, torquing bolts to 22 ft. lbs. (30 Nm).

10. Reconnect the crankcase ventilation system piping and air cleaner.

11. Connect the negative battery cable and start the engine, then check for leaks or proper operation.

## Injectors

▶ **See Figures 55, 56 and 57**

### REMOVAL & INSTALLATION

#### 1978-79

1. Disconnect the negative (-) battery cable. Remove the fuel return line from the nozzle as previously outlined under injection lines.

2. Remove the nozzle hold-down clamp and spacer. Then, pull the nozzle out of the cylinder head with tool J-26952 or equivalent.

3. Cap the high pressure line and nozzle tip.

### ✳✳WARNING

The nozzle tip is highly susceptible to damage and must be protected at all times.

**To install:**

4. If an old nozzle is to be reinstalled, a new compression seal and carbon stop seal must be installed after removal of the used seals.

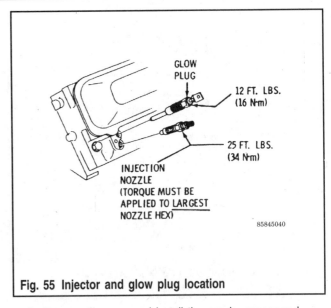

**Fig. 55 Injector and glow plug location**

5. Remove the caps and install the nozzle, spacer and clamp. Torque to 25 ft. lbs. (34 Nm).

6. Install return line.

7. Connect the negative battery cable, start the engine and check for leaks.

#### 1980 and Later Models

➡ **You will need a means to securely cap off fuel nozzles and lines before disconnecting fuel-containing parts.**

1. Disconnect the negative (-) battery cable.

2. Using a back-up wrench on the upper injection nozzle hex, disconnect the fuel line from the nozzle. Then, cap off both openings to prevent fuel contamination.

3. Using a wrench on the lower, larger nozzle hex, unscrew and remove the nozzle. Look to see if the copper gasket installed under the nozzle remained on the cylinder head. If so, remove it. Failure to do so will cause engine operating problems!

4. Nozzle testing requires specialized equipment, fluids, and training. However, it will be cost-effective for you to remove your own nozzles and have them tested and/or repaired at a diesel specialist. If you replace nozzles, make sure they are color coded with a blue band, meaning they are intended for use with the V8.

**To install:**

5. If the sealing washer remained on the nozzle tip, use diagonal cutters to force it off. Be careful not to squeeze the cutters to the point where they scratch the nozzle tip. Use them only to pry the washer loose. Clean the nozzle tip thoroughly with a safe solvent. Install a new copper washer and, if it will not stay on the tip, crimp it slightly so it will stay in place as you install the nozzle.

6. Remove protective caps. Install the nozzle by screwing it in, and then, using the largest hex, torque it to 25 ft. lbs. (34 Nm).

7. Connect the high pressure line and, using a back-up wrench on the upper nozzle hex, tighten the high pressure line fitting to 25 ft. lbs. (34 Nm).

8. Connect the negative battery cable, start the engine and check for leaks.

## Fuel Supply Pump

♦ **See Figure 58**

### REMOVAL & INSTALLATION

1. Remove the air cleaner and disconnect the negative battery cable.
2. Unplug the electrical leads from the pump.
3. Use a ¾ in. wrench to support the inlet fitting firmly and with a ⅝ in. wrench, unscrew the inlet tube.
4. Place a rag under the pump outlet side to collect fuel since the line is slightly pressurized.
5. Remove the pump mounting bracket nut and the pump.

**To install:**

6. Install the pump and bracket assembly on the engine, torque the lines to 19 ft. lbs. (26 Nm).

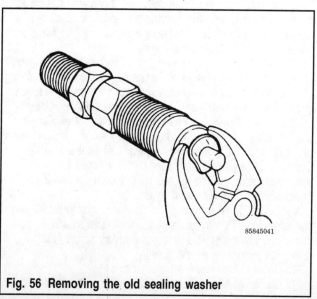

**Fig. 56 Removing the old sealing washer**

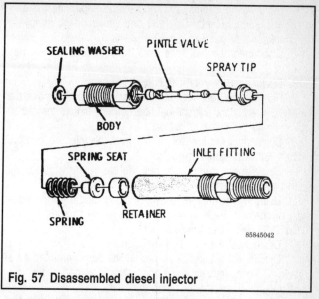

**Fig. 57 Disassembled diesel injector**

7. After the pump has been installed, disconnect the fuel line at the fuel filter in order to prime and bleed the lines. Use a basin to collect the fuel. When no air bubbles show up in the fuel, or the click-like sound stops, reconnect the fuel line.

## Injection Pump

### REMOVAL & INSTALLATION

♦ **See Figure 59**

1. Disconnect the negative (-) battery cable. Remove the air cleaner.
2. Remove the filters and pipes from the valve covers and air crossover.
3. Remove the air crossover and cap intake manifold with screened covers (tool J-26996-10).
4. Disconnect the throttle rod and return spring.
5. Remove the bellcrank.

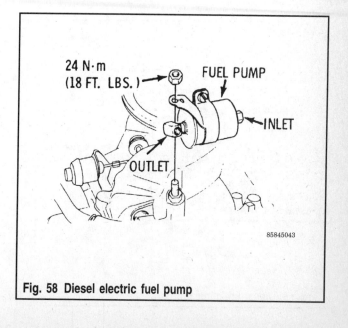

**Fig. 58 Diesel electric fuel pump**

6. Remove the throttle and transmission cables from the intake manifold brackets. On 1983 and later models, remove the crankcase depression regulator valve.

7. Disconnect the fuel lines from the filter and remove the filter.

8. Disconnect the fuel inlet line at the pump.

9. Remove the rear A/C compressor brace and remove the fuel line. If equipped with a fuel line heater, remove the fasteners retaining the line and heater.

10. Disconnect the fuel return line from the injection pump.

**On 1982 and earlier models:**

11. Remove the clamps and pull the fuel return lines from each injection nozzle.

12. Using two wrenches to avoid putting torque on the nozzles, disconnect the high pressure lines at the nozzles.

**On 1983 and later models:**

13. Disconnect the injection line clamps.

14. Disconnect the injection lines at the pump and cap all openings. Then, reposition the lines slightly as necessary to gain enough clearance for pump removal.

15. Remove the three injection pump retaining nuts with tool J-26987 or its equivalent.

16. Remove the pump. Immediately cap all lines and nozzles. Discard the pump-to-adapter O-ring.

**To install:**

17. Remove the protective caps.

18. Line up the offset tang on the pump driveshaft with the pump driven gar and install the pump.

19. Install, but do not tighten the pump retaining nuts.

20. On 1982 and earlier models, connect the high pressure lines at the nozzles.

21. Using two wrenches, torque the high pressure line nuts to 25 ft. lbs. (34 Nm) on 1982 and earlier models.

22. Connect the fuel return lines to the nozzles and pump on 1982 and earlier models.

23. Align the timing mark on the injection pump with the line on the timing mark adaptor and torque the mounting nuts to 35 ft. lbs. (47 Nm) on models up to 1979 and 18 ft. lbs. (25 Nm) on models built in 1980 and later years.

➡ **A ¾ in. (19mm) open end wrench on the boss at the front of the injection pump will aid in rotating the pump to align the marks.**

On 1983 and later models, remove the protective caps and connect the injection lines to the pump, torquing to 25 ft. lbs. (34 Nm). Then connect the injection lines to the pump, torquing to 25 ft. lbs. (34 Nm). Connect injection line clamps on these models. Also on these models only, install the fuel filter and bracket, tighten fuel line fittings, and install the fuel line heater clamps (where equipped). Install the crankcase depression regulator.

24. Adjust the throttle rod:

a. Remove the clip from the cruise control rod and remove the rod from the bellcrank.

b. Loosen the locknut on the throttle rod a few turns, then shorten the rod several turns.

c. Rotate the bellcrank to the full throttle stop, then lengthen the throttle rod until the injection pump lever contacts the injection pump full throttle stop, then release the bellcrank.

d. Tighten the throttle rod locknut.

25. Install the fuel inlet line between the transfer pump and the filter.

26. Install the rear A/C compressor brace.

27. Install the bellcrank and clip.

28. Connect the throttle rod and return spring.

29. Adjust the transmission cable:

a. Push the snap-lock to the disengaged position.

b. Rotate the injection pump lever to the full throttle stop and hold it there.

c. Push in the snap-lock until it is flush.

d. Release the injection pump lever.

30. Start the engine and check for fuel leaks.

31. Remove the screened covers and install the air crossover.

32. Install the tubes in the air flow control valve in the air crossover and install the ventilation filters in the valve covers.

33. Install the air cleaner.

34. On 1982 and earlier models, use this method to bleed air out of the injection pump: Start the engine and allow it to run for two minutes; stop the engine and allow it to stand for two minutes; then restart the engine.

35. On 1983 and later models, an extremely precise timing meter is used by professional mechanics to set injection timing by replacing the glow plug of No. 3 cylinder with an electronic probe. Since the probe sets timing by measuring crankshaft position when the injected fuel actually ignites, it eliminates a great number of possible kinds of error. Proper injection timing maximizes fuel economy and minimizes all engine stresses. Even though a precise alignment of the injection pump ensures reasonably accurate timing, you should have your timing set professionally to ensure best results.

Also, if you have disturbed the vacuum regulator valve position or replaced the injection pump, this valve should be adjusted professionally. The procedure is very simple, but requires an expensive special tool.

36. Connect the negative battery cable.

37. On all models, adjust the idle speed as described later in this section.

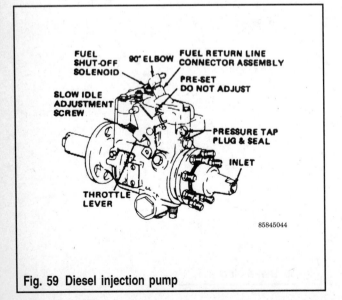

**Fig. 59 Diesel injection pump**

38. Start the engine and check for fuel leaks and proper operation.

## ADJUSTMENTS

### Slow Idle Speed

1. Apply the parking brake, put the transmission in Park and block the drive wheels. Check the throttle linkage adjustment and adjust it if necessary.
2. Start the engine and allow it to run until it is warm (about 15 minutes). Then, shut the engine off and remove the air cleaner.
3. Clean off the front cover rpm counter (the probe holder) and the rim of the crankshaft balancer. Install the magnetic pickup probe of the magnetic pickup tachometer fully into the rpm counter. Connect the battery leads (red to positive, black to negative).
4. Disconnect the two lead connector at the generator.
5. Turn off all electrical accessories.

#### ✳✳CAUTION

**Block all wheels and apply the emergency brake before placing the transmission in DRIVE. Personal injury may result if this procedure is not followed!**

6. Start the engine and place the transmission in Drive. Read the slow idle speed, making sure the steering wheel and brake pedal are not touched. Reset the idle speed by turning the screw if it does not agree with the figure on the engine compartment sticker. **If the sticker is not present, adjust the idle speed to 600 rpm in DRIVE.** Be sure to put the transmission back in Park, reconnect the generator lead, and reinstall the air cleaner when you have finished.

### Fast Idle Solenoid

#### MODELS TO 1981

#### ✳✳CAUTION

**Block all wheels and apply the emergency brake before placing the transmission in DRIVE. Personal injury may result if this procedure is not followed!**

1. Set the parking brake and block the drive wheels.
2. Run the engine to normal operating temperature.
3. Place the transmission in **DRIVE**, disconnect the compressor clutch wire and turn the A/C On. On vehicles without A/C, disconnect the solenoid wire, and connect jumper wires to the solenoid terminals. Ground one of the wires and connect the other to a 12 volt power source to activate the solenoid.
4. Adjust the fast idle solenoid plunger to obtain 650 rpm.

#### MODELS 1982 AND LATER

1. Unplug the connector from the EGR-TVS and install a jumper between the connector terminals WITHOUT ALLOWING THE JUMPER TO TOUCH GROUND!

2. Apply the parking brake, put the transmission in Park and block the drive wheels. Check the throttle linkage adjustment and adjust it if necessary.
3. Start the engine and allow it to run until it is warm (about 15 minutes). Then, shut the engine off and remove the air cleaner.
4. Clean off the front cover rpm counter (the probe holder) and the rim of the crankshaft balancer. Install the magnetic pickup probe of the magnetic pickup tachometer fully into the rpm counter. Connect the battery leads (red to positive, black to negative).
5. Disconnect the two lead connector at the generator.
6. Turn off all electrical accessories.

#### ✳✳CAUTION

**Block all wheels and apply the emergency brake before placing the transmission in DRIVE. Personal injury may result if this procedure is not followed!**

7. Place the transmission in Drive. Check the fast idle speed by reading the magnetic pickup tachometer and compare the reading to the fast idle solenoid speed specified on the engine compartment sticker. **If the sticker is not present, adjust the fast idle to 750 rpm in DRIVE.** Change the setting by turning the solenoid plunger at the flats.
8. Remove the jumper and reconnect the connector. Stop the engine, and then reconnect the generator connector.
9. Remove the tachometer. If the vehicle has cruise control, adjust the servo throttle rod to minimize the slack. Then, install the clip in the first free hole closest to the bellcrank or throttle lever but still within the bail on the servo. Install the air cleaner (make sure to reconnect the EGR hose).

### Cruise Control Servo Relay Rod

1. Turn the ignition switch to Off.
2. Adjust the rod to minimum slack then put the clip in the first free hole closest to the bellcrank, but within the servo bail.

## INJECTION TIMING

▶ **See Figure 60**

For the engine to be properly timed, the lines on the top of the injection pump adapter and the flange of the injection pump must be aligned.

1. The engine must be off for resetting the timing.
2. Loosen the three pump retaining nuts with tool J-26987, an injection pump intake manifold wrench, or its equivalent.
3. Align the timing marks and torque the pump retaining nuts to 35 ft. lbs. (47 Nm) on 1979 and earlier models and 18 ft. lbs. (25 Nm) on 1980 and later models. On 1982 and later models, timing should be precisely adjusted using the special timing meter discussed in the procedure for injection pump removal and installation.

➡ **The use of a ¾ in. (19mm) open end wrench on the boss at the front of the pump will aid in rotating the pump to align the marks.**

4. Adjust the throttle rod.

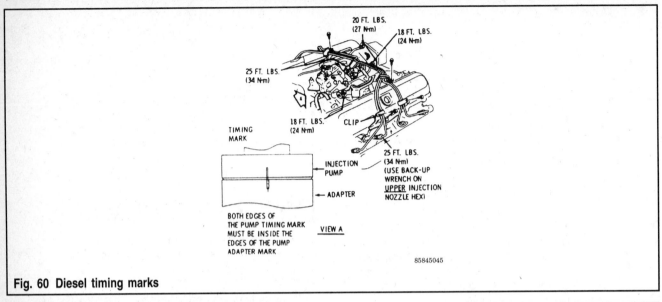

**Fig. 60 Diesel timing marks**

## Injection Pump Adapter

▶ **See Figures 61, 62 and 63**

### REMOVAL & INSTALLATION

1. Remove injection pump and lines as described earlier.
2. Remove the injection pump adapter.
3. Remove the seal from the adapter.
4. File the timing mark from the adapter. Do not file the mark off the pump.
5. Position the engine at TDC of No. 1 cylinder. Align the mark on the balancer with the zero mark on the indicator. The index is offset to the right when No. 1 is at TDC.
6. Apply a chassis lube to the seal areas. Install, but do not tighten the injection pump.
7. Install the new seal on the adapter using tool J-28425, or its equivalent.
8. Torque the adapter bolts to 25 ft. lbs. (34 Nm).

➡The following procedure involving the special timing tool, applies for models built through 1981. For 1982 and later models, set the injection pump at the center of the slots in the pump mounting flange, and then have the pump timed with the special timing device described in the Injection Pump Removal & Installation procedure.

9. Install timing tool J-26896 into the injection pump adapter. Torque the tool, toward No. 1 cylinder to 50 ft. lbs. (68 Nm). Mark the injection pump adapter. Remove the tool.
10. Install the injection pump.

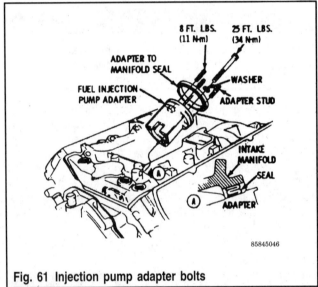

**Fig. 61 Injection pump adapter bolts**

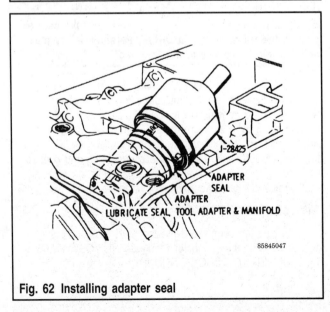

**Fig. 62 Installing adapter seal**

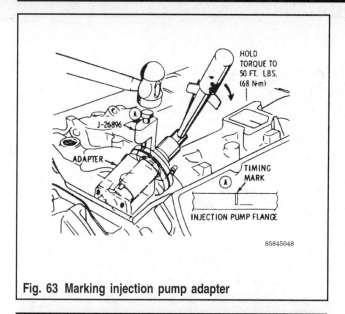

Fig. 63 Marking injection pump adapter

## Glow Plugs

▶ See Figure 64

### REMOVAL & INSTALLATION

➡A burned out glow plug tip may bulge and then break off and drop into the pre-chamber when the glow plug is removed. If this occurs, the cylinder head must be removed, remove the pre-chamber and remove the broken tip.

## FUEL TANK

### Tank Assembly

▶ See Figures 65, 66 and 67

➡If the vehicle is to be stored for any extended length of time, the fuel should be completely drained from the system, including carburetor or throttle body, fuel pump, all fuel lines, and the fuel tank in order to prevent gum formations and poor engine performance.

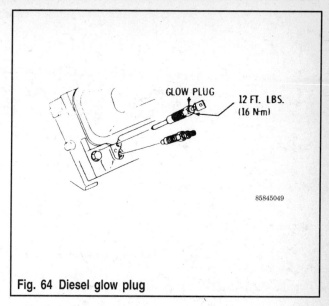

Fig. 64 Diesel glow plug

1. Disconnect the negative (-) battery cable and glow plug electrical connector.
2. Turn the plug out of the cylinder head slowly.
3. Coat the new plug with anti-seize compound for electrical components.
4. Torque the plug to 12 ft. lbs. (16 Nm) and connect the electrical connector.

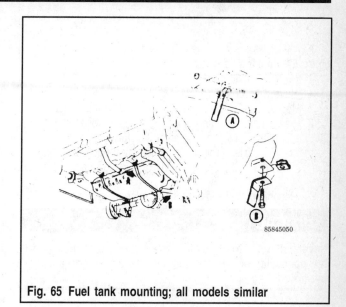

Fig. 65 Fuel tank mounting; all models similar

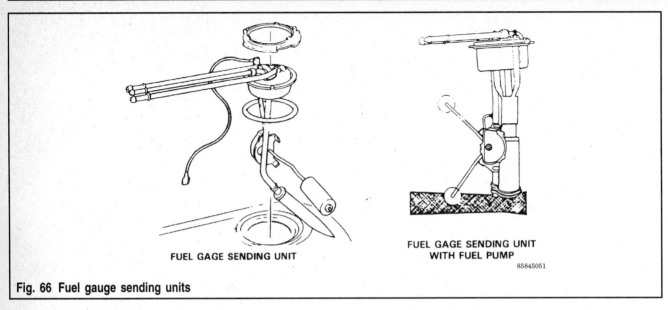

FUEL GAGE SENDING UNIT

FUEL GAGE SENDING UNIT
WITH FUEL PUMP

85845051

**Fig. 66 Fuel gauge sending units**

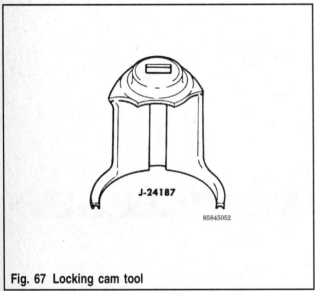

J-24187

85845052

**Fig. 67 Locking cam tool**

1. Have a carbon dioxide fire extinguisher near the work area. Remove the negative battery cable from the battery.

2. Use a hand-operated siphon pump, and follow the manufacturer's instructions for its use. As the fuel tank has a restrictor in the filler neck, connect the drain hose to the main fuel pipe at the fuel pump or at the tank gauge unit. Drain the fuel.

3. Reconnect any removed hoses, lines and cap.

### ✳✳CAUTION

**Never drain or store gasoline in an open container due to the possibility of fire or explosion. Never siphon gasoline by mouth!**

## REMOVAL & INSTALLATION

1. Disconnect the negative (-) battery cable.
2. Drain tank.
3. Disconnect tank unit wire from connector in rear compartment.
4. Remove the ground wire retaining screw from the underbody.
5. Disconnect the hoses from the tank unit.
6. Support the fuel tank with a suitable jack and disconnect the two fuel tank retaining straps.
7. Remove the tank from the vehicle.

**To install:**

8. On California emissions equipped vehicles, center the fuel filler pipe in the opening as required. Always replace the O-ring when the tank unit has been removed.
9. Support the tank with a suitable jack and position the tank into the vehicle.
10. Connect the fuel hoses and electrical connectors before installing the tank straps.
11. Install the tank strap bolt and nut to 96 inch lbs. (11 Nm) and the bolt-to-body to 26 ft. lbs. (35 Nm).
12. Connect the negative battery cable, refill the tank, start the engine and check for leaks.

## SENDING UNIT REPLACEMENT

1. Remove the tank as described above.
2. Remove the fuel gauge retaining cam, and remove the sending unit from the tank.
3. Installation is the reverse of removal.

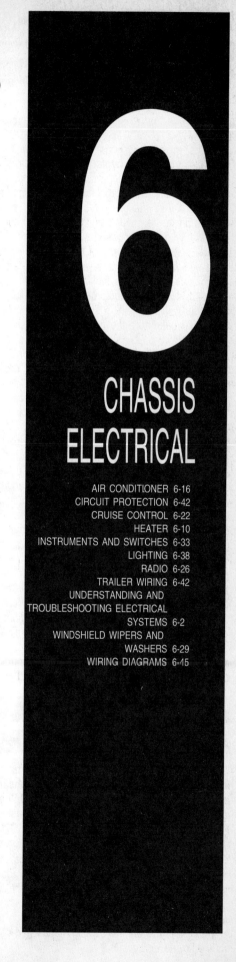

# 6

# CHASSIS
# ELECTRICAL

## UNDERSTANDING AND TROUBLESHOOTING ELECTRICAL SYSTEMS

With the rate at which both import and domestic manufacturers are incorporating electronic control systems into their production lines, it won't be long before every new vehicle is equipped with one or more on-board computer. These electronic components (with no moving parts) should theoretically last the life of the vehicle, provided nothing external happens to damage the circuits or memory chips.

While it is true that electronic components should never wear out, in the real world malfunctions do occur. It is also true that any computer-based system is extremely sensitive to electrical voltages and can not tolerate careless or haphazard testing or service procedures. An inexperienced individual can literally do major damage looking for a minor problem by using the wrong kind of test equipment or connecting test leads or connectors with the ignition switch ON. When selecting test equipment, make sure the manufacturers instructions state that the tester is compatible with whatever type of electronic control system is being serviced. Read all instructions carefully and double check all test points before installing probes or making any test connections.

The following section outlines basic diagnosis techniques for dealing with computerized automotive control systems. Along with a general explanation of the various types of test equipment available to aid in servicing modern electronic automotive systems, basic repair techniques for wiring harnesses and connectors is given. Read the basic information before attempting any repairs or testing on any computerized system, to provide the background of information necessary to avoid the most common and obvious mistakes that can cost both time and money. Although the replacement and testing procedures are simple in themselves, the systems are not, and unless one has a thorough understanding of all components and their function within a particular computerized control system, the logical test sequence these systems demand can not be followed. Minor malfunctions can make a big difference, so it is important to know how each component affects the operation of the overall electronic system to find the ultimate cause of a problem without replacing good components unnecessarily. It is not enough to use the correct test equipment; the test equipment must be used correctly.

### Safety Precautions

#### ✳✳CAUTION

**Whenever working on or around any computer based microprocessor control system, always observe these general precautions to prevent the possibility of personal injury or damage to electronic components.**

• Never install or remove battery cables with the key ON or the engine running. Jumper cables should be connected with the key OFF to avoid power surges that can damage electronic control units. Engines equipped with computer controlled systems should avoid both giving and getting jump starts due to the possibility of serious damage to components from arcing in the engine compartment when connections are made with the ignition ON.

• Always remove the battery cables before charging the battery. Never use a high output charger on an installed battery or attempt to use any type of "hot shot" (24 volt) starting aid.

• Exercise care when inserting test probes into connectors to insure good connections without damaging the connector or spreading the pins. Always probe connectors from the rear (wire) side, NOT the pin side, to avoid accidental shorting of terminals during test procedures.

• Never remove or attach wiring harness connectors with the ignition switch ON, especially to an electronic control module.

• Do not drop any components during service procedures and never apply 12 volts directly to any component (like a solenoid or relay) unless instructed specifically to do so. Some component electrical windings are designed to safely handle only 4 or 5 volts and can be destroyed in seconds if 12 volts are applied directly to the connector.

• Remove the electronic control module if the vehicle is to be placed in an environment where temperatures exceed approximately 176°F (80°C), such as a paint spray booth or when arc or gas welding near the control unit location in the vehicle.

### Organized Troubleshooting

When diagnosing a specific problem, organized troubleshooting is a must. The complexity of a modern automobile demands that you approach any problem in a logical, organized manner. There are certain troubleshooting techniques that are standard:

1. Establish when the problem occurs. Does the problem appear only under certain conditions? Were there any noises, odors, or other unusual symptoms?

2. Isolate the problem area. To do this, make some simple tests and observations; then eliminate the systems that are working properly. Check for obvious problems such as broken wires, dirty connections or split or disconnected vacuum hoses. Always check the obvious before assuming something complicated is the cause.

3. Test for problems systematically to determine the cause once the problem area is isolated. Are all the components functioning properly? Is there power going to electrical switches and motors? Is there vacuum at vacuum switches and/or actuators? Is there a mechanical problem such as bent linkage or loose mounting screws? Doing careful, systematic checks will often turn up most causes on the first inspection without wasting time checking components that have little or no relationship to the problem.

4. Test all repairs after the work is done to make sure that the problem is fixed. Some causes can be traced to more than one component, so a careful verification of repair work is important to pick up additional malfunctions that may cause a problem to reappear or a different problem to arise. A blown fuse, for example, is a simple problem that may require more than another fuse to repair. If you don't look for a problem that caused a fuse to blow, for example, a shorted wire may go undetected.

Experience has shown that most problems tend to be the result of a fairly simple and obvious cause, such as loose or corroded connectors or air leaks in the intake system; making careful inspection of components during testing essential to quick and accurate troubleshooting. Special, hand held computerized testers designed specifically for diagnosing the HEI-EST system are available from a variety of aftermarket sources, as well as from the vehicle manufacturer, but care should be taken that any test equipment being used is designed to diagnose that particular computer controlled system accurately without damaging the control module (ECM) or components being tested.

➡Pinpointing the exact cause of trouble in an electrical system can sometimes only be accomplished by the use of special test equipment. The following describes commonly used test equipment and explains how to put it to best use in diagnosis. In addition to the information covered below, the manufacturer's instructions booklet provided with the tester should be read and clearly understood before attempting any test procedures.

## TEST EQUIPMENT

### Jumper Wires

Jumper wires are simple, yet extremely valuable, pieces of test equipment. Jumper wires are merely wires that are used to bypass sections of a circuit. The simplest type of jumper wire is merely a length of multistrand wire with an alligator clip at each end. Jumper wires are usually fabricated from lengths of standard automotive wire and whatever type of connector (alligator clip, spade connector or pin connector) that is required for the particular vehicle being tested. The well equipped tool box will have several different styles of jumper wires in several different lengths. Some jumper wires are made with three or more terminals coming from a common splice for special purpose testing. In cramped, hard-to-reach areas it is advisable to have insulated boots over the jumper wire terminals in order to prevent accidental grounding, sparks, and possible fire, especially when testing fuel system components.

Jumper wires are used primarily to locate open electrical circuits, on either the ground side of the circuit or on the hot (+) side. If an electrical component fails to operate, connect the jumper wire between the component and a good ground. If the component operates only with the jumper installed, the ground circuit is open. If the ground circuit is good, but the component does not operate, the circuit between the power feed and component is open. You can sometimes connect the jumper wire directly from the battery to the hot terminal of the component, but first make sure the component uses 12 volts in operation. Some electrical components, such as fuel injectors, are designed to operate on about 4 volts and running 12 volts directly to the injector terminals can burn out the wiring. By inserting an inline fuseholder between a set of test leads, a fused jumper wire can be used for bypassing open circuits. Use a 5 amp fuse to provide protection against voltage spikes. When in doubt, use a voltmeter to check the voltage input to the component and measure how much voltage is being applied normally. By moving the jumper wire

successively back from the lamp toward the power source, you can isolate the area of the circuit where the open is located. When the component stops functioning, or the power is cut off, the open is in the segment of wire between the jumper and the point previously tested.

### ✳✳CAUTION

**Never use jumpers made from wire that is of lighter gauge than used in the circuit under test. If the jumper wire is of too small gauge, it may overheat and possibly melt. Never use jumpers to bypass high resistance loads (such as motors) in a circuit. Bypassing resistances, in effect, creates a short circuit which may, in turn, cause damage and fire. Never use a jumper for anything other than temporary bypassing of components in a circuit.**

### 12 Volt Test Light

The 12 volt test light is used to check circuits and components while electrical current is flowing through them. It is used for voltage and ground tests. Twelve volt test lights come in different styles but all have three main parts; a ground clip, a probe, and a light. The most commonly used 12 volt test lights have pick-type probes. To use a 12 volt test light, connect the ground clip to a good ground and probe wherever necessary with the pick. The pick should be sharp so that it can penetrate wire insulation to make contact with the wire, without making a large hole in the insulation. The wrap-around light is handy in hard to reach areas or where it is difficult to support a wire to push a probe pick into it. To use the wrap around light, hook the wire to probed with the hook and pull the trigger. A small pick will be forced through the wire insulation into the wire core.

### ✳✳CAUTION

**Do not use a test light to probe electronic ignition spark plug or coil wires. Never use a pick-type test light to probe wiring on computer controlled systems unless specifically instructed to do so. Any wire insulation that is pierced by the test light probe should be taped and sealed with silicone after testing.**

Like the jumper wire, the 12 volt test light is used to isolate opens in circuits. But, whereas the jumper wire is used to bypass the open to operate the load, the 12 volt test light is used to locate the presence of voltage in a circuit. If the test light glows, you know that there is power up to that point; if the 12 volt test light does not glow when its probe is inserted into the wire or connector, you know that there is an open circuit (no power). Move the test light in successive steps back toward the power source until the light in the handle does glow. When it does glow, the open is between the probe and point previously probed.

➡The test light does not detect that 12 volts (or any particular amount of voltage) is present; it only detects that some voltage is present. It is advisable before using the test light to touch its terminals across the battery posts to make sure the light is operating properly.

## Self-Powered Test Light

The self-powered test light usually contains a 1.5 volt penlight battery. One type of self-powered test light is similar in design to the 12 volt test light. This type has both the battery and the light in the handle and pick-type probe tip. The second type has the light toward the open tip, so that the light illuminates the contact point. The self-powered test light is dual purpose piece of test equipment. It can be used to test for either open or short circuits when power is isolated from the circuit (continuity test). A powered test light should not be used on any computer controlled system or component unless specifically instructed to do so. Many engine sensors can be destroyed by even this small amount of voltage applied directly to the terminals.

## Voltmeter

A voltmeter is used to measure voltage at any point in a circuit, or to measure the voltage drop across any part of a circuit. It can also be used to check continuity in a wire or circuit by indicating current flow from one end to the other. Voltmeters usually have various scales on the meter dial and a selector switch to allow the selection of different voltages. The voltmeter has a positive and a negative lead. To avoid damage to the meter, always connect the negative lead to the negative side of circuit (to ground or nearest the ground side of the circuit) and connect the positive lead to the positive (+) side of the circuit (to the power source or the nearest power source). Note that the negative voltmeter lead will always be black and that the positive voltmeter will always be some color other than black (usually red). Depending on how the voltmeter is connected into the circuit, it has several uses.

A voltmeter can be connected either in parallel or in series with a circuit and it has a very high resistance to current flow. When connected in parallel, only a small amount of current will flow through the voltmeter current path; the rest will flow through the normal circuit current path and the circuit will work normally. When the voltmeter is connected in series with a circuit, only a small amount of current can flow through the circuit. The circuit will not work properly, but the voltmeter reading will show if the circuit is complete or not.

## Ohmmeter

The ohmmeter is designed to read resistance (ohms) in a circuit or component. Although there are several different styles of ohmmeters, all will usually have a selector switch which permits the measurement of different ranges of resistance (usually the selector switch allows the multiplication of the meter reading by 10, 100, 1000, and 10,000). A calibration knob allows the meter to be set at zero for accurate measurement. Since all ohmmeters are powered by an internal battery (usually 9 volts), the ohmmeter can be used as a self-powered test light. When the ohmmeter is connected, current from the ohmmeter flows through the circuit or component being tested. Since the ohmmeter's internal resistance and voltage are known values, the amount of current flow through the meter depends on the resistance of the circuit or component being tested.

The ohmmeter can be used to perform continuity test for opens or shorts (either by observation of the meter needle or as a self-powered test light), and to read actual resistance in a circuit. It should be noted that the ohmmeter is used to check the resistance of a component or wire while there is no voltage applied to the circuit. Current flow from an outside voltage source (such as the vehicle battery) can damage the ohmmeter, so the circuit or component should be isolated from the vehicle electrical system before any testing is done. Since the ohmmeter uses its own voltage source, either lead can be connected to any test point.

➡**When checking diodes or other solid state components, the ohmmeter leads can only be connected one way in order to measure current flow in a single direction. Make sure the positive (+) and negative (-) terminal connections are as described in the test procedures to verify the one-way diode operation.**

In using the meter for making continuity checks, do not be concerned with the actual resistance readings. Zero resistance, or any resistance readings, indicate continuity in the circuit. Infinite resistance indicates an open in the circuit. A high resistance reading where there should be none indicates a problem in the circuit. Checks for short circuits are made in the same manner as checks for open circuits except that the circuit must be isolated from both power and normal ground. Infinite resistance indicates no continuity to ground, while zero resistance indicates a dead short to ground.

## Ammeters

An ammeter measures the amount of current flowing through a circuit in units called amperes or amps. Amperes are units of electron flow which indicate how fast the electrons are flowing through the circuit. Since Ohms Law dictates that current flow in a circuit is equal to the circuit voltage divided by the total circuit resistance, increasing voltage also increases the current level (amps). Likewise, any decrease in resistance will increase the amount of amps in a circuit. At normal operating voltage, most circuits have a characteristic amount of amperes, called "current draw" which can be measured using an ammeter. By referring to a specified current draw rating, measuring the amperes, and comparing the two values, one can determine what is happening within the circuit to aid in diagnosis. An open circuit, for example, will not allow any current to flow so the ammeter reading will be zero. More current flows through a heavily loaded circuit or when the charging system is operating.

An ammeter is always connected in series with the circuit being tested. All of the current that normally flows through the circuit must also flow through the ammeter; if there is any other path for the current to follow, the ammeter reading will not be accurate. The ammeter itself has very little resistance to current flow and therefore will not affect the circuit, but it will measure current draw only when the circuit is closed and electricity is flowing. Excessive current draw can blow fuses and drain the battery, while a reduced current draw can cause motors to run slowly, lights to dim and other components to not operate properly. The ammeter can help diagnose these conditions by locating the cause of the high or low reading.

## Multimeters

Different combinations of test meters can be built into a single unit designed for specific tests. Some of the more common combination test devices are known as Volt/Amp testers, Tach/Dwell meters, or Digital Multimeters. The

Volt/Amp tester is used for charging system, starting system or battery tests and consists of a voltmeter, an ammeter and a variable resistance carbon pile. The voltmeter will usually have at least two ranges for use with 6, 12 and 24 volt systems. The ammeter also has more than one range for testing various levels of battery loads and starter current draw and the carbon pile can be adjusted to offer different amounts of resistance. The Volt/Amp tester has heavy leads to carry large amounts of current and many later models have an inductive ammeter pickup that clamps around the wire to simplify test connections. On some models, the ammeter also has a zero-center scale to allow testing of charging and starting systems without switching leads or polarity. A digital multimeter is a voltmeter, ammeter and ohmmeter combined in an instrument which gives a digital readout. These are often used when testing solid state circuits because of their high input impedance (usually 10 megohms or more).

The tach/dwell meter combines a tachometer and a dwell (cam angle) meter and is a specialized kind of voltmeter. The tachometer scale is marked to show engine speed in rpm and the dwell scale is marked to show degrees of distributor shaft rotation. In most electronic ignition systems, dwell is determined by the control unit, but the dwell meter can also be used to check the duty cycle (operation) of some electronic engine control systems. Some tach/dwell meters are powered by an internal battery, while others take their power from the vehicle battery in use. The battery powered testers usually require calibration much like an ohmmeter before testing.

### Special Test Equipment

A variety of diagnostic tools are available to help troubleshoot and repair computerized engine control systems. The most sophisticated of these devices are the console type engine analyzers that usually occupy a garage service bay, but there are several types of aftermarket electronic testers available that will allow quick circuit tests of the engine control system by plugging directly into a special connector located in the engine compartment or under the dashboard. Several tool and equipment manufacturers offer simple, hand held testers that measure various circuit voltage levels on command to check all system components for proper operation. Although these testers usually cost about $500 to $1,500, consider that the average computer control unit (or ECM) can cost just as much and the money saved by not replacing perfectly good sensors or components in an attempt to correct a problem could justify the purchase price of a special diagnostic tester the first time it's used.

These computerized testers can allow quick and easy test measurements while the engine is operating or while the vehicle is being driven. In addition, the on-board computer memory can be read to access any stored trouble codes; in effect allowing the computer to tell you where it hurts and aid trouble diagnosis by pinpointing exactly which circuit or component is malfunctioning. In the same manner, repairs can be tested to make sure the problem has been corrected. The biggest advantage these special testers have is their relatively easy hookups that minimize or eliminate the chances of making the wrong connections and getting false voltage readings or damaging the computer accidentally.

➡ **It should be remembered that these testers check voltage levels in circuits; they don't detect mechanical problems or failed components if the circuit voltage falls within the preprogrammed limits stored in the tester PROM unit. Also, most of the hand held testers are designed to work only on one or two systems made by a specific manufacturer.**

A variety of aftermarket testers are available to help diagnose different computerized control systems. Kent-Moore Tool Company 29784 Little Mack Roseville, MI 48066 2298, markets a device which plugs directly into the assembly line diagnostic link (ALDL). The tester makes diagnosis a simple matter of pressing the correct buttons and, by changing the internal PROM or inserting a different diagnosis cartridge, it will work on any model from full size to subcompact, over a wide range of years. An adapter is supplied with the tester to allow connection to all types of ALDL links, regardless of the number of pin terminals used. By inserting an updated PROM into the tester, it can be easily updated to diagnose any new modifications of computerized control systems.

## TEST PROCEDURES

### Open Circuit Testing

To use the self-powered test light to check for open circuits, first isolate the circuit from the vehicle's 12 volt power source by disconnecting the battery or wiring harness connector. Connect the test light ground clip to a good ground and probe sections of the circuit sequentially with the test light. (start from either end of the circuit). If the light is out, the open is between the probe and the circuit ground. If the light is on, the open is between the probe and end of the circuit toward the power source.

### Short Circuit Testing

By isolating the circuit both from power and from ground, and using a self-powered test light, you can check for shorts to ground in the circuit. Isolate the circuit from power and ground. Connect the test light ground clip to a good ground and probe any easy-to-reach test point in the circuit. If the light comes on, there is a short somewhere in the circuit. To isolate the short, probe a test point at either end of the isolated circuit (the light should be on). Leave the test light probe connected and open connectors, switches, remove parts, etc., sequentially, until the light goes out. When the light goes out, the short is between the last circuit component opened and the previous circuit opened.

➡The 1.5 volt battery in the test light does not provide much current. A weak battery may not provide enough power to illuminate the test light even when a complete circuit is made (especially if there are high resistances in the circuit). Always make sure that the test battery is strong. To check the battery, briefly touch the ground clip to the probe; if the light glows brightly the battery is strong enough for testing. Never use a self-powered test light to perform checks for opens or shorts when power is applied to the electrical system under test. The 12 volt vehicle power will quickly burn out the 1.5 volt light bulb in the test light.

### Available Voltage Measurement

Set the voltmeter selector switch to the 20V position and connect the meter negative lead to the negative post of the battery. Connect the positive meter lead to the positive post of the battery and turn the ignition switch ON to provide a load. Read the voltage on the meter or digital display. A well charged battery should register over 12 volts. If the meter reads below 11.5 volts, the battery power may be insufficient to operate the electrical system properly. This test determines voltage available from the battery and should be the first step in any electrical trouble diagnosis procedure. Many electrical problems, especially on computer controlled systems, can be caused by a low state of charge in the battery. Excessive corrosion at the battery cable terminals can cause a poor contact that will prevent proper charging and full battery current flow.

Normal battery voltage is 12 volts when fully charged. When the battery is supplying current to one or more circuits it is said to be "under load". When everything is off the electrical system is under a "no-load" condition. A fully charged battery may show about 12.5 volts at no load; will drop to 12 volts under medium load; and will drop even lower under heavy load. If the battery is partially discharged the voltage decrease under heavy load may be excessive, even though the battery shows 12 volts or more at no load. When allowed to discharge further, the battery's available voltage under load will decrease more severely. For this reason, it is important that the battery be fully charged during all testing procedures to avoid errors in diagnosis and incorrect test results.

### Voltage Drop

When current flows through a resistance, the voltage beyond the resistance is reduced (the larger the current, the greater the reduction in voltage). When no current is flowing, there is no voltage drop because there is no current flow. All points in the circuit which are connected to the power source are at the same voltage as the power source. The total voltage drop always equals the total source voltage. In a long circuit with many connectors, a series of small, unwanted voltage drops due to corrosion at the connectors can add up to a total loss

of voltage which impairs the operation of the normal loads in the circuit.

### INDIRECT COMPUTATION OF VOLTAGE DROPS

1. Set the voltmeter selector switch to the 20 volt position.
2. Connect the meter negative lead to a good ground.
3. Probe all resistances in the circuit with the positive meter lead.
4. Operate the circuit in all modes and observe the voltage readings.

### DIRECT MEASUREMENT OF VOLTAGE DROPS

1. Set the voltmeter switch to the 20 volt position.
2. Connect the voltmeter negative lead to the ground side of the resistance load to be measured.
3. Connect the positive lead to the positive side of the resistance or load to be measured.
4. Read the voltage drop directly on the 20 volt scale.

Too high a voltage indicates too high a resistance. If, for example, a blower motor runs too slowly, you can determine if there is too high a resistance in the resistor pack. By taking voltage drop readings in all parts of the circuit, you can isolate the problem. Too low a voltage drop indicates too low a resistance. If, for example, a blower motor runs too fast in the MED and/or LOW position, the problem can be isolated in the resistor pack by taking voltage drop readings in all parts of the circuit to locate a possibly shorted resistor. The maximum allowable voltage drop under load is critical, especially if there is more than one high resistance problem in a circuit because all voltage drops are cumulative. A small drop is normal due to the resistance of the conductors.

### HIGH RESISTANCE TESTING

1. Set the voltmeter selector switch to the 4 volt position.
2. Connect the voltmeter positive lead to the positive post of the battery.
3. Turn on the headlights and heater blower to provide a load.
4. Probe various points in the circuit with the negative voltmeter lead.
5. Read the voltage drop on the 4 volt scale. Some average maximum allowable voltage drops are:
   - FUSE PANEL   7 volts
   - IGNITION SWITCH   5 volts
   - HEADLIGHT SWITCH   7 volts
   - IGNITION COIL (+)   5 volts
   - ANY OTHER LOAD   1.3 volts

➡Voltage drops are all measured while a load is operating; without current flow, there will be no voltage drop.

### Resistance Measurement

The batteries in an ohmmeter will weaken with age and temperature, so the ohmmeter must be calibrated or "zeroed" before taking measurements. To zero the meter, place the selector switch in its lowest range and touch the two ohmmeter leads together. Turn the calibration knob until the meter needle is exactly on zero.

➡All analog (needle) type ohmmeters must be zeroed before use, but some digital ohmmeter models are automatically calibrated when the switch is turned on. Self-calibrating digital ohmmeters do not have an adjusting knob, but its a good idea to check for a zero readout before use by touching the leads together. All computer controlled systems require the use of a digital ohmmeter with at least 10 mega-ohms impedance for testing. Before any test procedures are attempted, make sure the ohmmeter used is compatible with the electrical system or damage to the on-board computer could result.

To measure resistance, first isolate the circuit from the vehicle power source by disconnecting the battery cables or the harness connector. Make sure the key is OFF when disconnecting any components or the battery. Where necessary, also isolate at least one side of the circuit to be checked to avoid reading parallel resistances. Parallel circuit resistances will always give a lower reading than the actual resistance of either of the branches. When measuring the resistance of parallel circuits, the total resistance will always be lower than the smallest resistance in the circuit. Connect the meter leads to both sides of the circuit (wire or component) and read the actual measured ohms on the meter scale. Make sure the selector switch is set to the proper ohm scale for the circuit being tested to avoid misreading the ohmmeter test value.

### ✳✳CAUTION

Never use an ohmmeter with power applied to the circuit. Like the self-powered test light, the ohmmeter is designed to operate on its own power supply. The normal 12 volt automotive electrical system current could damage the meter.

## Wiring Harnesses

The average automobile contains about a½ mile of wiring, with hundreds of individual connections. To protect the many wires from damage and to keep them from becoming a confusing tangle, they are organized into bundles, enclosed in plastic or taped together and called wire harnesses. Different wiring harnesses serve different parts of the vehicle. Individual wires are color coded to help trace them through a harness where sections are hidden from view.

A loose or corroded connection or a replacement wire that is too small for the circuit will add extra resistance and an additional voltage drop to the circuit. A ten percent voltage drop can result in slow or erratic motor operation, for example, even though the circuit is complete. Automotive wiring or circuit conductors can be in any one of three forms:
1. Single strand wire
2. Multistrand wire
3. Printed circuitry
Single strand wire has a solid metal core and is usually used inside such components as alternators, motors, relays and other devices. Multistrand wire has a core made of many small strands of wire twisted together into a single conductor.

Most of the wiring in an automotive electrical system is made up of multistrand wire, either as a single conductor or grouped together in a harness. All wiring is color coded on the insulator, either as a solid color or as a colored wire with an identification stripe. A printed circuit is a thin film of copper or other conductor that is printed on an insulator backing. Occasionally, a printed circuit is sandwiched between two sheets of plastic for more protection and flexibility. A complete printed circuit, consisting of conductors, insulating material and connectors for lamps or other components is called a printed circuit board. Printed circuitry is used in place of individual wires or harnesses in places where space is limited, such as behind instrument panels.

## WIRE GAUGE

Since computer controlled automotive electrical systems are very sensitive to changes in resistance, the selection of properly sized wires is critical when systems are repaired. The wire gauge number is an expression of the cross section area of the conductor. The most common system for expressing wire size is the American Wire Gauge (AWG) system.

Wire cross section area is measured in circular mils. A mil is 0.001 in.; a circular mil is the area of a circle one mil in diameter. For example, a conductor ¼ in. in diameter is 0.250 in. or 250 mils. The circular mil cross section area of the wire is 250 squared or 62,500 circular mils. Imported vehicle models usually use metric wire gauge designations, which is simply the cross section area of the conductor in square millimeters.

Gauge numbers are assigned to conductors of various cross section areas. As gauge number increases, area decreases and the conductor becomes smaller. A 5 gauge conductor is smaller than a 1 gauge conductor and a 10 gauge is smaller than a 5 gauge. As the cross section area of a conductor decreases, resistance increases and so does the gauge number. A conductor with a higher gauge number will carry less current than a conductor with a lower gauge number.

➡Gauge wire size refers to the size of the conductor, not the size of the complete wire. It is possible to have two wires of the same gauge with different diameters because one may have thicker insulation than the other.

12 volt automotive electrical systems generally use 10, 12, 14, 16 and 18 gauge wire. Main power distribution circuits and larger accessories usually use 10 and 12 gauge wire. Battery cables are usually 4 or 6 gauge, although 1 and 2 gauge wires are occasionally used. Wire length must also be considered when making repairs to a circuit. As conductor length increases, so does resistance. An 18 gauge wire, for example, can carry a 10 amp load for 10 feet without excessive voltage drop; however if a 15 foot wire is required for the same 10 amp load, it must be a 16 gauge wire.

An electrical schematic shows the electrical current paths when a circuit is operating properly. It is essential to understand how a circuit works before trying to figure out why it does not. Schematics break the entire electrical system down into individual circuits and show only one particular circuit. In a schematic, no attempt is made to represent wiring and components as they physically appear on the vehicle; switches and other components are shown as simply as possible. Face views of harness connectors show the cavity or terminal locations in all multi-pin connectors to help locate test points.

If you need to backprobe a connector while it is on the component, the order of the terminals must be mentally reversed. The wire color code can help in this situation, as well as a keyway, lock tab or other reference mark.

➡**Wiring diagrams are not included in this book. As vehicles have become more complex and available with longer option lists, wiring diagrams have grown in size and complexity. It has become almost impossible to provide a readable reproduction of a wiring diagram in a book this size. Information on ordering wiring diagrams from the vehicle manufacturer can be found in the owner's manual.**

## WIRING REPAIR

Soldering is a quick, efficient method of joining metals permanently. Everyone who has the occasion to make wiring repairs should know how to solder. Electrical connections that are soldered are far less likely to come apart and will conduct electricity much better than connections that are only "pig-tailed" together. The most popular (and preferred) method of soldering is with an electrical soldering gun. Soldering irons are available in many sizes and wattage ratings. Irons with higher wattage ratings deliver higher temperatures and recover lost heat faster. A small soldering iron rated for no more than 50 watts is recommended, especially on electrical systems where excess heat can damage the components being soldered.

There are three ingredients necessary for successful soldering; proper flux, good solder and sufficient heat. A soldering flux is necessary to clean the metal of tarnish, prepare it for soldering and to enable the solder to spread into tiny crevices. When soldering, always use a resin flux or resin core solder which is non-corrosive and will not attract moisture once the job is finished. Other types of flux (acid core) will leave a residue that will attract moisture and cause the wires to corrode. Tin is a unique metal with a low melting point. In a molten state, it dissolves and alloys easily with many metals. Solder is made by mixing tin with lead. The most common proportions are 40/60, 50/50 and 60/40, with the percentage of tin listed first. Low priced solders usually contain less tin, making them very difficult for a beginner to use because more heat is required to melt the solder. A common solder is 40/60 which is well suited for all-around general use, but 60/40 melts easier, has more tin for a better joint and is preferred for electrical work.

### Soldering Techniques

Successful soldering requires that the metals to be joined be heated to a temperature that will melt the solder; usually 360-460°F (182-238°C). Contrary to popular belief, the purpose of the soldering iron is not to melt the solder itself, but to heat the parts being soldered to a temperature high enough to melt the solder when it is touched to the work. Melting flux-cored

solder on the soldering iron will usually destroy the effectiveness of the flux.

➡**Soldering tips are made of copper for good heat conductivity, but must be "tinned" regularly for quick transference of heat to the project and to prevent the solder from sticking to the iron. To "tin" the iron, simply heat it and touch the flux-cored solder to the tip; the solder will flow over the hot tip. Wipe the excess off with a clean rag, but be careful as the iron will be hot.**

After some use, the tip may become pitted. If so, simply dress the tip smooth with a smooth file and "tin" the tip again. An old saying holds that "metals well cleaned are already half soldered." Flux-cored solder will remove oxides but rust, bits of insulation and oil or grease must be removed with a wire brush or emery cloth. For maximum strength in soldered parts, the joint must start off clean and tight. Weak joints will result in gaps too wide for the solder to bridge.

If a separate soldering flux is used, it should be brushed or swabbed on only those areas that are to be soldered. Most solders contain a core of flux and separate fluxing is unnecessary. Hold the work to be soldered firmly. It is best to solder on a wooden board, because a metal vise will only rob the piece to be soldered of heat and make it difficult to melt the solder. Hold the soldering tip with the broadest face against the work to be soldered. Apply solder under the tip close to the work, using enough solder to give a heavy film between the iron and the piece being soldered, while moving slowly and making sure the solder melts properly. Keep the work level or the solder will run to the lowest part and favor the thicker parts, because these require more heat to melt the solder. If the soldering tip overheats (the solder coating on the face of the tip burns up), it should be retinned. Once the soldering is completed, let the soldered joint stand until cool. Tape and seal all soldered wire splices after the repair has cooled.

### Wire Harness and Connectors

The on-board computer (ECM) wire harness electrically connects the control unit to the various solenoids, switches and sensors used by the control system. Most connectors in the engine compartment or otherwise exposed to the elements are protected against moisture and dirt which could create oxidation and deposits on the terminals. This protection is important because of the very low voltage and current levels used by the computer and sensors. All connectors have a lock which secures the male and female terminals together, with a secondary lock holding the seal and terminal into the connector. Both terminal locks must be released when disconnecting ECM connectors.

These special connectors are weather-proof and all repairs require the use of a special terminal and the tool required to service it. This tool is used to remove the pin and sleeve terminals. If removal is attempted with an ordinary pick, there is a good chance that the terminal will be bent or deformed. Unlike standard blade type terminals, these terminals cannot be straightened once they are bent. Make certain that the connectors are properly seated and all of the sealing rings in place when connecting leads. On some models, a hinge-type flap provides a backup or secondary locking feature for the terminals. Most secondary locks are used to improve the connector reliability by retaining the terminals if the small terminal lock tangs are not positioned properly.

Molded-on connectors require complete replacement of the connection. This means splicing a new connector assembly into the harness. All splices in on-board computer systems should be soldered to insure proper contact. Use care when probing the connections or replacing terminals in them as it is possible to short between opposite terminals. If this happens to the wrong terminal pair, it is possible to damage certain components. Always use jumper wires between connectors for circuit checking and never probe through weatherproof seals.

Open circuits are often difficult to locate by sight because corrosion or terminal misalignment are hidden by the connectors. Merely wiggling a connector on a sensor or in the wiring harness may correct the open circuit condition. This should always be considered when an open circuit or a failed sensor is indicated. Intermittent problems may also be caused by oxidized or loose connections. When using a circuit tester for diagnosis, always probe connections from the wire side. Be careful not to damage sealed connectors with test probes.

All wiring harnesses should be replaced with identical parts, using the same gauge wire and connectors. When signal wires are spliced into a harness, use wire with high temperature insulation only. With the low voltage and current levels found in the system, it is important that the best possible connection at all wire splices be made by soldering the splices together. It is seldom necessary to replace a complete harness. If replacement is necessary, pay close attention to insure proper harness routing. Secure the harness with suitable plastic wire clamps to prevent vibrations from causing the harness to wear in spots or contact any hot components.

➡**Weatherproof connectors cannot be replaced with standard connectors. Instructions are provided with replacement connector and terminal packages. Some wire harnesses have mounting indicators (usually pieces of colored tape) to mark where the harness is to be secured.**

In making wiring repairs, it's important that you always replace damaged wires with wires that are the same gauge as the wire being replaced. The heavier the wire, the smaller the gauge number. Wires are color-coded to aid in identification and whenever possible the same color coded wire should be used for replacement. A wire stripping and crimping tool is necessary to install solderless terminal connectors. Test all crimps by pulling on the wires; it should not be possible to pull the wires out of a good crimp.

Wires which are open, exposed or otherwise damaged are repaired by simple splicing. Where possible, if the wiring harness is accessible and the damaged place in the wire can be located, it is best to open the harness and check for all possible damage. In an inaccessible harness, the wire must be bypassed with a new insert, usually taped to the outside of the old harness.

When replacing fusible links, be sure to use fusible link wire, NOT ordinary automotive wire. Make sure the fusible segment is of the same gauge and construction as the one being replaced and double the stripped end when crimping the terminal connector for a good contact. The melted (open) fusible link segment of the wiring harness should be cut off as close to the harness as possible, then a new segment spliced in as described. In the case of a damaged fusible link that feeds two harness wires, the harness connections should be

replaced with two fusible link wires so that each circuit will have its own separate protection.

➡**Most of the problems caused in the wiring harness are due to bad ground connections. Always check all vehicle ground connections for corrosion or looseness before performing any power feed checks to eliminate the chance of a bad ground affecting the circuit.**

### Repairing Hard Shell Connectors

Unlike molded connectors, the terminal contacts in hard shell connectors can be replaced. Weatherproof hard-shell connectors with the leads molded into the shell have non-replaceable terminal ends. Replacement usually involves the use of a special terminal removal tool that depress the locking tangs (barbs) on the connector terminal and allow the connector to be removed from the rear of the shell. The connector shell should be replaced if it shows any evidence of burning, melting, cracks, or breaks. Replace individual terminals that are burnt, corroded, distorted or loose.

➡**The insulation crimp must be tight to prevent the insulation from sliding back on the wire when the wire is pulled. The insulation must be visibly compressed under the crimp tabs, and the ends of the crimp should be turned in for a firm grip on the insulation.**

The wire crimp must be made with all wire strands inside the crimp. The terminal must be fully compressed on the wire strands with the ends of the crimp tabs turned in to make a firm grip on the wire. Check all connections with an ohmmeter to insure a good contact. There should be no measurable resistance between the wire and the terminal when connected.

## Mechanical Test Equipment

### VACUUM GAUGE

Most gauges are graduated in inches of mercury (in. Hg), although a device called a manometer reads vacuum in inches of water (in. $H_2O$). The normal vacuum reading usually varies between 18 and 22 in. Hg at sea level. To test engine vacuum, the vacuum gauge must be connected to a source of manifold vacuum. Many engines have a plug in the intake manifold which can be removed and replaced with an adapter fitting. Connect the vacuum gauge to the fitting with a suitable rubber hose or, if no manifold plug is available, connect the vacuum gauge to any device using manifold vacuum, such as EGR valves, etc. The vacuum gauge can be used to determine if enough vacuum is reaching a component to allow its actuation.

### HAND VACUUM PUMP

Small, hand-held vacuum pumps come in a variety of designs. Most have a built-in vacuum gauge and allow the component to be tested without removing it from the vehicle. Operate the pump lever or plunger to apply the correct amount of vacuum required for the test specified in the diagnosis routines. The level of vacuum in inches of Mercury (in. Hg) is indicated on the pump gauge. For some testing, an additional vacuum gauge may be necessary.

Intake manifold vacuum is used to operate various systems and devices on late model vehicles. To correctly diagnose and solve problems in vacuum control systems, a vacuum source is necessary for testing. In some cases, vacuum can be taken from the intake manifold when the engine is running, but vacuum is normally provided by a hand vacuum pump. These hand vacuum pumps have a built-in vacuum gauge that allow testing while the device is still attached to the component. For some tests, an additional vacuum gauge may be used.

# HEATER

## Blower Motor

◗ See Figures 1, 2, 3 and 4

### REMOVAL & INSTALLATION

#### Buick

##### 1975 AND 1976

1. Disconnect the negative battery cable. Support the hood and loosen the hood hinge from the extension and plate assembly.
2. Remove the extension and plate assembly.
3. Disconnect the blower motor wire.
4. Remove the blower motor attaching screws and motor.

#### Oldsmobile and Pontiac

##### 1975 AND 1976

1. Raise the front of the vehicle, support with jackstands and remove the right front wheel.
2. Cut an access hole along the stamped outline on the right fender skirt, using an air chisel or electric hand sabre saw.
3. Disconnect the blower power wire.
4. Remove the blower.
   **To install:**
5. Install the blower with the fan, tighten the mounting screws, connect the motor wiring and covering the access hole with a metal plate secured with sealer and sheet metal screws if a hole was cut.
6. Connect the negative battery cable and check for proper operation.

#### All Models

##### 1977 TO 1990

1. Disconnect the negative battery cable, the blower motor feed wire and the ground wire.
2. Remove the blower motor retaining screws and remove the motor.
   **To install:**
3. Use sealer as needed to make a watertight seal, position the motor/fan into the heater module, tighten the mounting screws, connect the motor wiring and negative battery cable and check for proper operation.

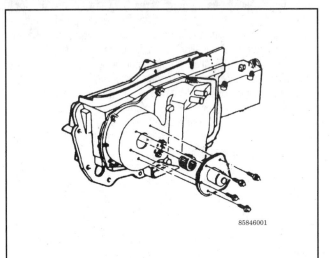

85846001

**Fig. 1 Blower motor and heater module without A/C; all models similar**

## Heater Core

### REMOVAL & INSTALLATION

◗ See Figures 5, 6, 7, 8, 9, 10, 11, 12, 13 and 14

#### Models Without A/C

##### 1975 AND 1976

1. Disconnect the negative battery cable. Drain the radiator and disconnect the heater inlet and outlet hoses at the dash. Be careful not to damage the heater core if the hoses are stuck onto the core.
2. Disconnect the control wires from the defroster door and vacuum hose diverter door actuator, and the control cable from the temperature door lever.
3. Remove the 4 nuts securing the heater assembly to the firewall.
4. Remove the screw securing the defroster outlet tab to the heater assembly.
5. Remove the heater from the vehicle.
   **To install:**
6. Make sure the heater assembly seal is in good condition.
7. Position the assembly onto the dash and tighten the retaining screws.
8. Reconnect the heater hoses, electrical connectors and negative battery cable. Refill the engine with coolant, start the vehicle and check for coolant leaks.

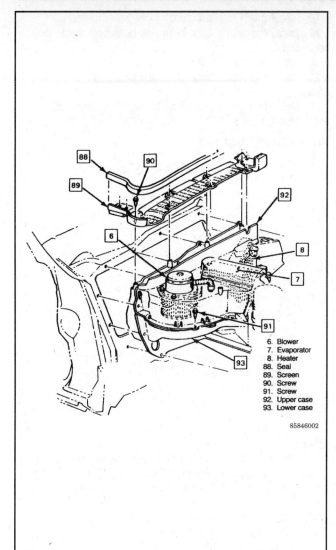

6. Blower
7. Evaporator
8. Heater
88. Seal
89. Screen
90. Screw
91. Screw
92. Upper case
93. Lower case

85846002

**Fig. 2 Blower motor and heater module with A/C; all models similar**

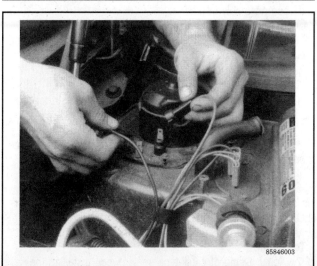

85846003

**Fig. 3 Disconnecting the electrical connections for blower motor removal**

85846004

**Fig. 4 Removing the blower motor from the heater module**

### 1977 TO 1981

1. Disconnect the negative battery cable and drain the cooling system.
2. Remove the heater hoses from the core tubes.
3. Disconnect the electrical connections.
4. Remove the front module cover screws, and remove the module assembly.
5. Remove the heater core from the module.
**To install:**
6. Make sure the heater assembly seal is in good condition.
7. Position the assembly onto the dash and tighten the retaining screws.
8. Reconnect the heater hoses, electrical connectors and negative battery cable. Refill the engine with coolant, start the vehicle and check for coolant leaks.

### 1982 AND 1983

1. Disconnect the negative battery cable and the Hoses from the core tubes. Plug them to avoid coolant loss.
2. On the engine side of the firewall, remove the heater core cover from the case.
3. Remove the core bracket and ground screw.
4. Lift out the core.
**To install:**
5. Make sure the heater assembly seal is in good condition.
6. Position the assembly onto the dash and tighten the retaining screws.
7. Reconnect the heater hoses, electrical connectors and negative battery cable. Refill the engine with coolant, start the vehicle and check for coolant leaks.

### 1984 AND LATER

1. Disconnect the negative battery cable, heater blower resistor wires and blower wires. Disconnect the heater core ground strap at the dash panel.
2. Drain the cooling system and then disconnect both heater hoses at the heater.
3. Remove the seven screws attaching the heater/blower case to the plenum and remove the heater/blower base.

4. Remove the four screws from the heater core shroud, and then remove the shroud and core assembly.

5. Separate the core from the shroud by removing the three screws and core mounting clamps and then separating the two.

**To install:**

6. Using sealer as necessary to prevent leaks at all joints and flanges.

7. Position the assembly onto the dash and tighten the retaining screws.

8. Reconnect the heater hoses, electrical connectors and negative battery cable. Refill the engine with coolant, start the vehicle and check for coolant leaks.

### Models with A/C

#### BUICK-1975 AND 1976

1. Disconnect the negative battery cable, drain the radiator and disconnect the hoses from the core.

2. Disconnect the wires from the defroster door, diverter door and temperature door.

3. Remove the four nuts securing the core assembly to the dash.

4. Remove the screw securing the defroster outlet tab to the heater assembly.

5. Remove the core assembly.

**To install:**

6. Using sealer as necessary to prevent leaks at all joints and flanges.

7. Position the assembly onto the dash and tighten the retaining screws.

8. Reconnect the heater hoses, electrical connectors and negative battery cable. Refill the engine with coolant, start the vehicle and check for coolant leaks.

#### OLDSMOBILE-1975 AND 1976

1. Disconnect the negative battery cable and drain the radiator.

2. Remove the heater case securing nuts. Disconnect the heater hoses.

3. Remove the instrument panel trim pad.

4. Remove the heater case-to-firewall bolts from inside the vehicle.

5. Remove the bottom air duct.

6. Remove the instrument panel crash pad. Unfasten the leads from the clock and glovebox light.

7. Remove the upper right hand trim panel.

8. Separate the air distribution manifold and defroster duct from the heater case.

9. Remove the lower dash trim panel.

10. Lift out the heater case and disconnect the hoses and cables from it.

11. Remove the core from the case.

**To install:**

12. Install the core into the case.

13. Connect the hoses and cables to the case.

14. Install the lower dash trim panel.

15. Connect the air distribution manifold and defroster duct to the heater case.

16. Install the upper right hand trim panel.

17. Install the instrument panel crash pad. Connect the leads from the clock and glovebox light.

18. Install the bottom air duct.

19. Install the heater case-to-firewall bolts from inside the vehicle.

20. Install the instrument panel trim pad.

21. Install the heater case securing nuts. Connect the heater hoses.

22. Refill the radiator, connect the negative battery cable and check for leaks.

#### PONTIAC-1975 AND 1976

1. Disconnect the negative battery cable and drain the coolant.

2. Disconnect the hoses from the heater core. Plug the tubes to prevent damage to the carpeting on removal.

3. Remove the three nuts and one screw holding the core and case assembly in place.

4. Remove the glove box and upper and lower instrument panel trim plates.

5. Remove the radio.

6. Remove the cold air duct.

7. Remove the heater outlet duct.

8. Remove the screw holding the defroster duct to the heater case.

9. Disconnect the vacuum hoses from the diaphragm, and the air conditioner temperature cable at the heater case.

10. Remove the core from the case, after removing the 3 retaining screws.

**To install:**

11. Install the core into the case and tighten the 3 retaining screws.

12. Connect the vacuum hoses to the diaphragm, and the air conditioner temperature cable to the heater case.

13. Install the screw holding the defroster duct to the heater case.

14. Install the heater outlet duct.

15. Install the cold air duct.

16. Install the radio.

17. Install the glove box and upper and lower instrument panel trim plates.

18. Install the three nuts and one screw holding the core and case assembly in place.

19. Connect the hoses to the heater core.

20. Connect the negative battery cable and refill the coolant.

21. Start the engine and check for leaks.

#### ALL MODELS-1977 AND LATER

1. Disconnect the negative battery cable and drain the cooling system.

2. Disconnect the heater hoses.

3. Remove the retaining bracket and the ground strap. Disconnect the module rubber seal and module screen.

4. Remove the right windshield wiper arm.

5. Remove the diaphragm connections, the hi/blower relay, the thermal switch mounting screws, and all the electrical connections from the module top.

6. Remove the module top cover and remove the core.

**To install:**

7. Apply a strip of caulk-type sealer when installing the module top.

8. Install the core and module top cover.

9. Install the diaphragm connections, the hi/blower relay, the thermal switch mounting screws, and all the electrical connections to the module top.

10. Install the right windshield wiper arm.

11. Install the retaining bracket and the ground strap. Connect the module rubber seal and module screen.

12. Connect the heater hoses.

13. Connect the negative battery cable and refill the cooling system.

14. Start the engine and check for coolant and vacuum leaks.

## Control Panel

### REMOVAL & INSTALLATION

▶ See Figure 15

1. Disconnect the negative battery cable.

Fig. 5 To remove the heater core, first remove the rubber seal

Fig. 6 Remove the windshield washer nozzle attaching screw

Fig. 7 Remove the washer nozzle from the heater module

Fig. 8 Lift the wiper arm and remove the module screen

Fig. 9 Remove the module top attaching screws

Fig. 10 Be sure to remove the module screws in the well

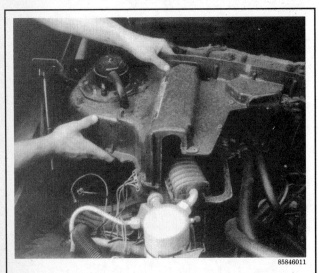

Fig. 11 Remove the module cover

Fig. 12 Remove the heater core hoses; be sure the cooling system is drained first

Fig. 13 Remove the heater core retainer

Fig. 14 Remove the heater core

2. Remove the center instrument panel trim. On some models, screws for this panel are covered by the left and right panel trims. If screws are hidden, first remove those panels on either side of the center panel; then remove the center panel.

3. Slide all controls all the way to the left.

➡Mark the routing of each cable to each damper lever. Then, unscrew the cable clip attaching screws from the heater case until the cable housing can be freed and the cable can be unhooked from the damper lever; then, free the cable and unhook the damper.

4. Remove the screws from the control face. Then, pull the face outward until you can gain access to the electrical and/or vacuum connectors. Disconnect all electrical and vacuum connections. Remove the control head, pulling the cables out through the hole in the dash.

**To install:**

5. Feed the cables through the hole in the dash and locate the head so the vacuum and electrical connections can be made. Connect vacuum and/or electrical connectors.

6. Install the mounting screws for the head. Then, connect the cables. Adjust each so that its damper is forced all the way closed or open, depending on its position.

7. Install the trim panels and moldings in reverse order of their removal.

## CABLE ADJUSTMENT

▶ See Figure 16

To adjust the vent cable, adjust the turnbuckle at the heater end of the cable so the shut-off valve is firmly seated with the selector lever in the heater position. This adjusts the shut-off valve for both the heater and vent modes. The center, left and right vent valve cables are not adjustable.

To adjust the defrost or temperature cables:

1. Slide the clip at the heater end of the cable away from the end of the cable.

2. Move the levers at the control to full "HOT" or "DEFROST" position. This adjusts the cables for proper operation of the valves.

## Blower Switch

### REMOVAL & INSTALLATION

1. Remove the control panel.
2. Disconnect the electrical connector.
3. Remove the switch screws and the switch.
4. Installation is the reverse of removal.

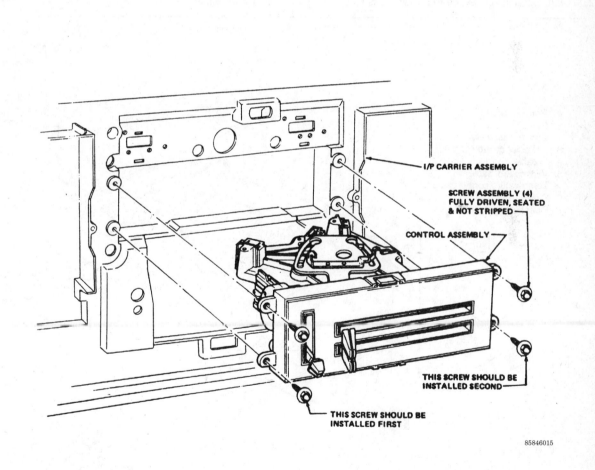

Fig. 15 Control panel installation; all models similar

## AIR CONDITIONER

Discharging the air conditioning system is required before the system is opened during service. Refer to Section 1 for discharging and charging information and proper procedures.

DO NOT service the air conditioning system unless you are equipped with the necessary tools and training. The refrigerant, R-12, is extremely cold when compressed, and when released into the air will instantly freeze any surface it contacts, including your eyes.

## Compressor

### REMOVAL & INSTALLATION

If possible, operate the compressor for 10 minutes at 1,500-2,000 rpm with the A/C set on maximum. This operation

is performed to effect return of oil to the compressor from other parts in the system.

1. Discharge the system as described in Section 1.
2. Disconnect the negative battery cable.
3. Slowly loosen the compressor fitting to the compressor. As the screw is being loosened, work the fitting assembly back and forth to break the seal.
4. Immediately cover all openings in the compressor and the hoses.
5. Disconnect the compressor wires. Remove the compressor bolts and remove the compressor from the car.

**To install:**

On R-4 compressor systems add 6 fluid ounces (180 ml) of 525 refrigerant oil. On DA-V5 and DA-6 compressor systems, add 8 fluid ounces (240 ml) of 525 refrigerant oil.

6. Installation is the reverse of removal, use new O-rings coated with refrigerant oil.

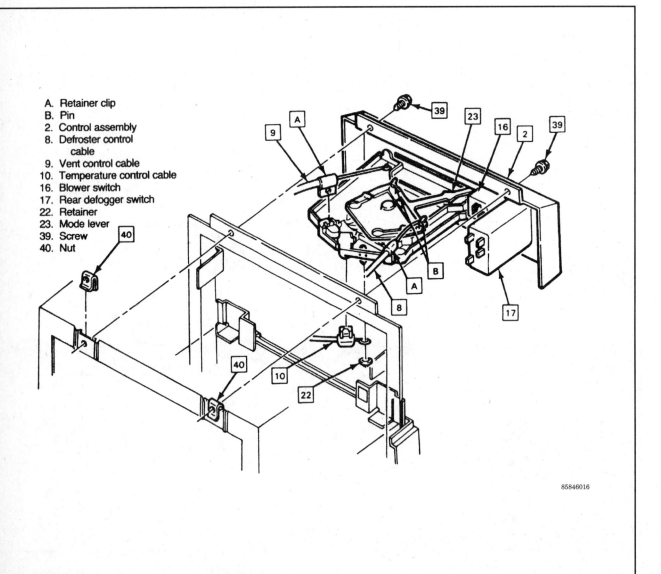

A. Retainer clip
B. Pin
2. Control assembly
8. Defroster control
   cable
9. Vent control cable
10. Temperature control cable
16. Blower switch
17. Rear defogger switch
22. Retainer
23. Mode lever
39. Screw
40. Nut

85846016

**Fig. 16 Control cable attachments at the control head**

7. Evacuate and recharge the system using the procedures in Section 1.

## Condenser

### REMOVAL & INSTALLATION

1. Discharge the system as described in Section 1.
2. Disconnect the negative battery cable.
3. Disconnect the refrigerant lines to the condenser.
4. Remove the air cleaner cold air duct from the core support.
5. Remove the fan shroud.
6. Remove the brackets and remove the compressor.
**To install:**
7. Add 1 fluid ounce (30 ml) of 525 refrigerant oil.
8. Installation is the reverse of removal.
9. Evacuate and recharge the system using the procedures in Section 1.

## Evaporator Core

### REMOVAL & INSTALLATION

▶ See Figure 17

1. Disconnect the negative battery cable.
2. Discharge the air conditioning system and recover the refrigerant as outlined in Section 1.
3. Disconnect the evaporator inlet and outlet pipe using a backup and a flare nut wrench. Seal the openings of the accumulator (large aluminum can) and evaporator to prevent moisture and contamination from entering the system.
4. Remove the air conditioner module upper case as outlined in this section.
5. Remove the evaporator clamp and evaporator by pulling the assembly straight up and out of the module lower case.
**To install:**
6. Add 3 fluid ounces (90 ml) of 525 refrigerant oil.
7. Install the evaporator and seals into the lower case. Make sure the seals and evaporator are properly positioned after the evaporator is in place.
8. Install the evaporator clamp.
9. Install the module upper case with a quality sealer.
10. Install new O-rings and torque the inlet and outlet fittings to the accumulator using a backup and flarenut wrench. Torque steel fittings to 32 ft. lbs. (44 Nm) and aluminum or copper fittings to 24 ft. lbs. (33 Nm).
11. Evacuate and recharge the air conditioning system as outlined in Section 1.
12. Connect the negative battery cable and test the system performance.

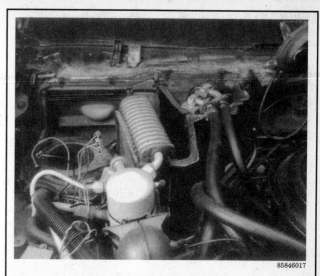

85846017

**Fig. 17 Evaporator core location; all models similar**

## Control Panel

### REMOVAL & INSTALLATION

1. Disconnect the negative battery cable.
2. Remove the center instrument panel trim. On some models, screws for this panel are covered by the left and right panel trims. If screws are hidden, first remove those panels on either side of the center panel; then remove the center panel.
3. Slide all controls all the way to the left.

➡**Mark the routing of each cable to each damper lever. Then, unscrew the cable clip attaching screws from the heater case until the cable housing can be freed and the cable can be unhooked from the damper lever; then, free the cable and unhook the damper.**

4. Remove the screws from the control face. Then, pull the face outward until you can gain access to the electrical and/or vacuum connectors. Disconnect all electrical and vacuum connections. Remove the control head, pulling the cables out through the hole in the dash.
**To install:**
5. Feed the cables through the hole in the dash and locate the head so the vacuum and electrical connections can be made. Connect vacuum and/or electrical connectors.
6. Install the mounting screws for the head. Then, connect the cables. Adjust each so that its damper is forced all the way closed or open, depending on its position.
7. Install the trim panels and moldings in reverse order of their removal.

### CABLE ADJUSTMENT

▶ See Figure 18

To adjust the vent cable, adjust the turnbuckle at the heater end of the cable so the shut-off valve is firmly seated with the selector lever in the heater position. This adjusts the shut-off valve for both the heater and vent modes. The center, left and right vent valve cables are not adjustable.

To adjust the defrost or temperature cables:

1. Slide the clip at the heater end of the cable away from the end of the cable.

2. Move the levers at the control to full "HOT" or "DEFROST" position. This adjusts the cables for proper operation of the valves.

To adjust the temperature cable on Tempmatic systems:

3. Remove the glove compartment.

4. Align the holes in the programmer lever and the programmer chassis with an awl or a nail.

5. Check the control panel temperature lever, it should be at 75°.

6. If not, adjust the turn buckle until the lever indicates 75°.

7. Remove the awl or nail and install the glove compartment.

## Blower Switch

### REMOVAL & INSTALLATION

1. Remove the control panel.
2. Disconnect the electrical connector.
3. Remove the switch screws and the switch.
4. Installation is the reverse of removal.

## Vacuum Selector Valve

### REMOVAL & INSTALLATION

1. Remove the control panel.
2. Disconnect the electrical and vacuum connector.
3. Remove the switch screws and the switch.
4. Installation is the reverse of removal.

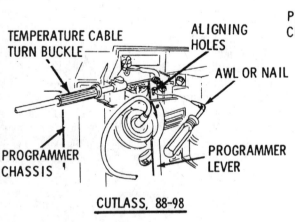
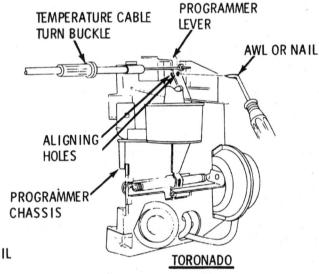

TEMPERATURE CONTROL CABLE ADJUSTMENT

1. REMOVE GLOVE COMPARTMENT.

2. ALIGN HOLES IN PROGRAMMER LEVER AND PROGRAMMER CHASSIS WITH AWL OR NAIL.

3. CHECK CONTROL PANEL TEMPERATURE LEVER.

4. IF NOT AT 75°. ADJUST TURN BUCKLE UNTIL LEVER INDICATES 75°.

5. REMOVE AWL OR PIN.

TEMPERATURE CABLE TURN BUCKLE

PROGRAMMER LEVER

AWL OR NAIL

ALIGNING HOLES

PROGRAMMER CHASSIS

TORONADO

TEMPERATURE CABLE TURN BUCKLE

ALIGNING HOLES

AWL OR NAIL

PROGRAMMER CHASSIS

PROGRAMMER LEVER

CUTLASS, 88-98

85846018

**Fig. 18 Temperature cable adjustment; Tempmatic systems**

## EEVIR and VIR Assembly

### REMOVAL & INSTALLATION

▶ **See Figure 19**

1. Discharge the system as described in Section 1.
2. Disconnect the negative battery cable.
3. Remove the suction line, liquid line and the liquid bleed line connections from the assembly.
4. Loosen the evaporator inlet and outlet connection nuts at the assembly.
5. Remove the mounting clamp from the receiver shell and carefully slide the assembly off the outlet tube first, then the inlet.

**To install:**

6. Installation is the reverse of removal, use new O-rings and lubricate with refrigerant oil.
7. Evacuate and recharge the system using the procedures in Section 1.

## Drier Desiccant Bag

### REMOVAL & INSTALLATION

The desiccant bag can be replaced on the EEVIR and VIR systems by removing the receiver shell. On CCOT systems, the entire accumulator must be replaced since it is a sealed unit.

1. Discharge the system as described in Section 1.
2. Clean dirt from the outside of the receiver shell.
3. Remove the receiver shell attaching screws.
4. Remove the mounting bracket clamp from the mounting bracket.
5. Hold the housing and push on the lower end of the receiver to break the seal.

**To install:**

6. Add one ounce of new refrigerant oil and a new desiccant bag. Use new O-ring seals and coat with refrigerant oil.
7. Installation is the reverse of removal, torque the mounting screws to 7 ft. lbs.
8. Evacuate and recharge the system using the procedures in Section 1.

## Accumulator

### REMOVAL & INSTALLATION

▶ **See Figure 20**

1. Discharge the system as described in Section 1.
2. Disconnect the electrical connection at the pressure cycling switch and remove the switch.
3. Disconnect the refrigerant lines at the accumulator inlet and outlet.
4. Remove the bracket screw and remove the accumulator from the vehicle.

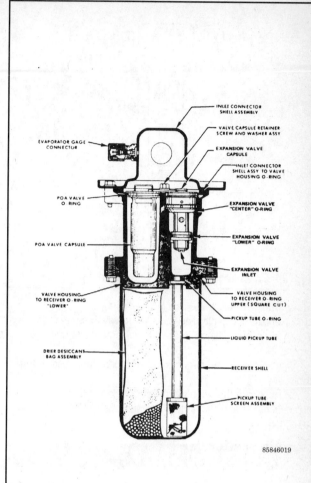

**Fig. 19 Cross-section of a EEVIR assembly; VIR assembly similar**

5. Immediately cap the refrigerant lines.

**To install:**

6. Check the amount of oil in the accumulator and add that amount of fresh 525 refrigerant oil plus 2 fluid ounces (60 ml).
7. Install the new accumulator. Use new O-ring seals and lubricate with refrigerant oil.
8. Evacuate and recharge the system using the procedures in Section 1.

## Refrigerant Lines

### DISCONNECT & CONNECT

▶ **See Figure 21**

1. Disconnect the negative battery cable.
2. Discharge the system as described in Section 1.
3. Remove the faulty line or hose. Always use line wrenches on both fittings to prevent twisting of the lines.

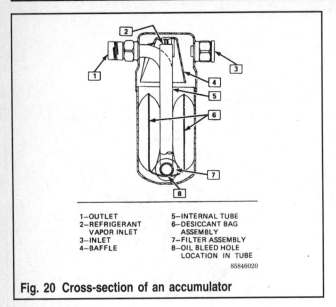

1—OUTLET
2—REFRIGERANT
   VAPOR INLET
3—INLET
4—BAFFLE
5—INTERNAL TUBE
6—DESICCANT BAG
   ASSEMBLY
7—FILTER ASSEMBLY
8—OIL BLEED HOLE
   LOCATION IN TUBE

85846020

**Fig. 20 Cross-section of an accumulator**

**To install:**

4. Replace the faulty line or hose. Always use line wrenches on both fittings to prevent twisting of the lines. Torque the fittings to specifications.

5. Always use new O-ring seals and coat them with refrigerant oil.

6. Reconnect the negative battery cable.

7. Evacuate and recharge the system using the procedures in Section 1.

## Pressure Cycling Switch

### REMOVAL & INSTALLATION

➡ **Do not discharge the system. The pressure cycling switch is mounted on a Schrader-type valve.**

| METAL TUBE OUTSIDE DIAMETER | THREAD AND FITTING SIZE | STEEL TUBING TORQUE | | ALUMINUM OR COPPER TUBING TORQUE | | NOMINAL TORQUE WRENCH SPAN |
|---|---|---|---|---|---|---|
| | | LB. FT. | N·m | LB. FT. | N·m | |
| 1/4 | 7/16 | 10-15 | 14-20 | 5-7 | 7-9 | 5/8 |
| 3/8 | 5/8 | 30-35 | 41-48 | 11-13 | 15-18 | 3/4 |
| 1/2 | 3/4 | 30-35 | 41-48 | 15-20 | 20-27 | 7/8 |
| 5/8 | 7/8 | 30-35 | 41-48 | 21-27 | 29-37 | 1 1/16 |
| 3/4 | 1 1/16 | 30-35 | 41-48 | 28-33 | 38-45 | 1 1/4 |

85846021

**Fig. 21 Refrigerant line torque chart**

1. Disconnect the negative battery cable.
2. Disconnect the electrical connector.
3. Remove the switch.
4. Installation is the reverse of removal. Install a new O-ring dipped in refrigerant oil. Torque switch to 7½ ft. lbs. (10 Nm).

## Orifice Tube

### REMOVAL & INSTALLATION

▶ **See Figure 22**

1. Disconnect the negative battery cable.
2. Discharge the system as described in Section 1.
3. Loosen the nut at the liquid line to the evaporator inlet pipe and remove the orifice tube carefully with Tool J-26549-C.

**To install:**

4. Install the new orifice tube with the shorter screen end in first.
5. Install the liquid line and torque to specification.
6. Reconnect the negative battery cable.
7. Evacuate and recharge the system using the procedures in Section 1.

## Water Control Valve

### REMOVAL & INSTALLATION

▶ **See Figures 23 and 24**

1. Partially drain the cooling system.
2. Disconnect the vacuum line and the hose connections on the water control valve.
3. Remove the valve.
4. Installation is the reverse of removal.

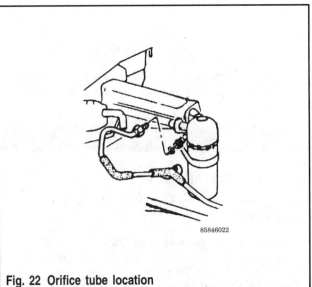

85846022

**Fig. 22 Orifice tube location**

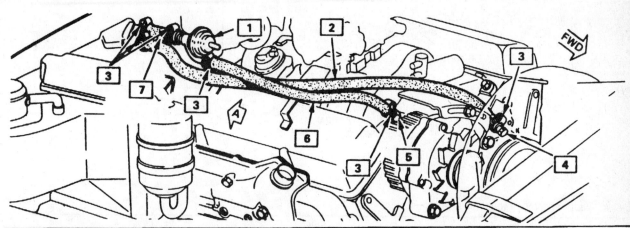

1—WATER VALVE ASSEMBLY

2—HOSE (OUTLET)

3—CLAMP

4—FITTING (ENGINE ASSEMBLY)

5—FITTING

6—HOSE (INLET)

7—HOSE

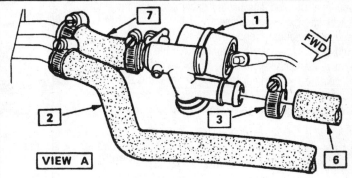

VIEW A

85846023

**Fig. 23 In-line mounted water control valve**

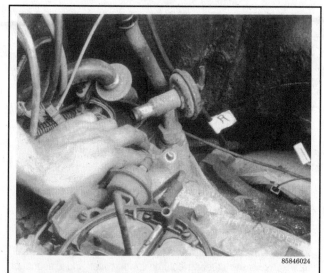

85846024

**Fig. 24 Intake manifold mounted water control valve**

## Vacuum Motors

### REMOVAL & INSTALLATION

▶ See Figure 25

1. Remove the heater outlet duct.
2. Disconnect the vacuum connection.
3. Remove the attaching screws and adjuster screw.
4. Installation is the reverse of removal.

## Programmer

### REMOVAL & INSTALLATION

▶ See Figure 26

➡This is used on Tempmatic systems only.

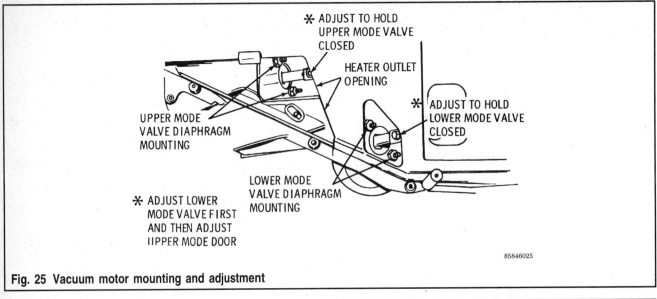

Fig. 25 Vacuum motor mounting and adjustment

1. Disconnect the negative battery cable and tape the end.
2. Remove the glove compartment.
3. Remove the aspirator and vacuum hoses.
4. Remove the temperature door rod from the crank.
5. Remove the temperature cable from the programmer.
6. Remove the programmer retaining screws and remove it from the case.
7. Installation is the reverse of removal.

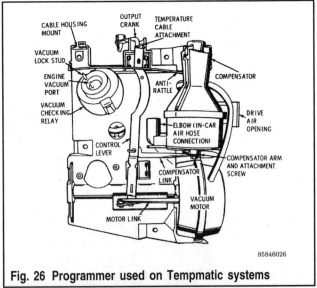

Fig. 26 Programmer used on Tempmatic systems

## CRUISE CONTROL

### ✳✳CAUTION

Do not attempt any service on the steering wheel, column or instrument panel on Buick and Oldsmobile models equipped with an air bag. Service on these models should only be performed by a professional technician.

## Control Switches

### REMOVAL & INSTALLATION

#### Engagement Switch
▶ See Figure 27

The engagement switch cannot be serviced. The complete turn signal lever must be replaced as an assembly.

*EXCEPT MULTI-FUNCTION LEVER*

1. Disconnect the negative battery cable.
2. Remove the steering column lower cover and disconnect the cruise control connector.
3. Remove the steering wheel and the lock plate.

4. Remove the turn signal retaining screw and remove the turn signal.

5. Installation is the reverse of removal.

### MULTI-FUNCTION LEVER

1. Disconnect the negative battery cable.

2. Remove the left-hand sound insulator panel.

3. Position the column with the shift lever in the low position and the turn signal in the right turn position. Keep tilt columns in the full up position.

4. Disconnect the cruise control connector and attach a long piece of mechanic's wire to the end of the harness connector.

5. Remove the multi-function switch by pulling out of the detented retaining clip inside the steering column.

6. Pull harness out gently. Removing the protective plastic sheathing for the cruise control wires may aid in removal and installation.

7. Installation is the reverse of removal. Make sure the wires are routed under the upper support bracket to prevent pinching the wires.

### Release Switch
▶ See Figures 28 and 29

#### VACUUM TYPE

1. Disconnect the vacuum hose and the retainer. Remove the switch.

**To install:**

2. Install the retainer. Reconnect the vacuum hose.

3. With the brake pedal depressed, insert switch into the retainer until it seats on the retainer.

4. Pull brake pedal fully rearward against pedal stop until no more clicks are heard.

#### ELECTRIC TYPE

1. Disconnect the negative battery cable and tape the end.

2. Disconnect the electrical connector.

3. Remove the switch.

**To install:**

4. Installation is the reverse of removal.

5. Turn the ignition switch to the ON position. Use a test light between the brown wire at the connector and ground.

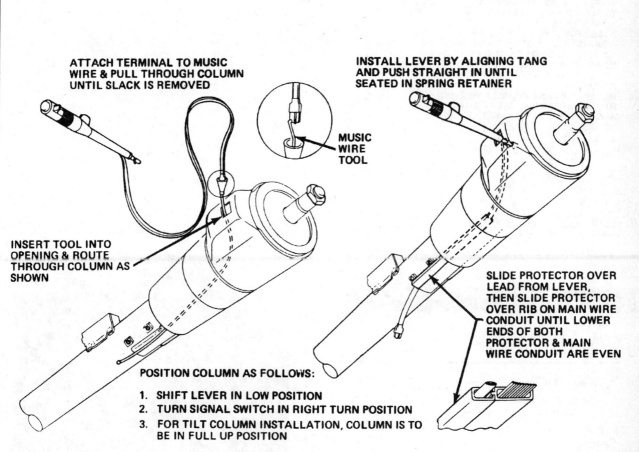

**Fig. 27 Engagement switch installation**

1. BRAKE PEDAL MOUNTING BRACKET
2. BRAKE PEDAL
3. SWITCH —STOP LAMP
4. HOSE —VACUUM RELEASE VALVE TO SERVO
5. VACUUM RELEASE VALVE

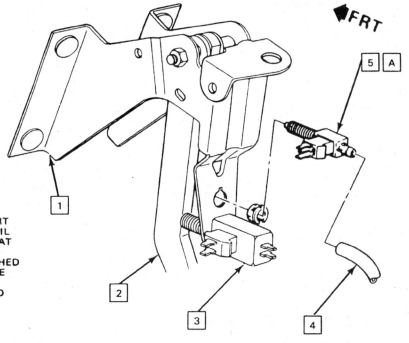

**A** **INSTALLATION OF SELF-ADJUSTING VACUUM RELEASE VALVE**

1. INSTALL RETAINER
2. WITH BRAKE PEDAL DEPRESSED, INSERT VALVE INTO TUBULAR RETAINER UNTIL VALVE SEATS ON RETAINER. NOTE THAT AUDIBLE "CLICKS" CAN BE HEARD AS THREADED PORTION OF VALVE IS PUSHED THROUGH THE RETAINER TOWARD THE BRAKE PEDAL.
3. PULL BRAKE PEDAL FULLY REARWARD AGAINST PEDAL STOP, UNTIL AUDIBLE "CLICKS" SOUNDS CAN NO LONGER BE HEARD. VALVE WILL BE MOVED IN TUBULAR RETAINER PROVIDING ADJUSTMENT.
4. RELEASE BRAKE PEDAL, AND THEN REPEAT STEP 3 TO ASSURE THAT NO AUDIBLE "CLICK" SOUNDS REMAIN.

85846027

**Fig. 28 Vacuum release switch**

Adjust switch so that the test light goes out within ½in. of brake pedal travel.

## Speed Sensor

### REMOVAL & INSTALLATION

1. Disconnect the negative battery cable.
2. Remove the instrument cluster.
3. Disconnect the electrical connector and remove the sensor attaching screw.
4. Remove the sensor.
5. Installation is the reverse of removal.

85846028

**Fig. 29 Combination electric release switch and stop lamp switch**

## Servo

▶ See Figure 30

### REMOVAL & INSTALLATION

1. Disconnect the electrical and vacuum connections.
2. Disconnect the linkage.
3. Remove the attaching screws.
4. Installation is the reverse of removal.

### LINKAGE ADJUSTMENT

With linkage at hot idle position (engine off), adjust the cable, chain, or rod to obtain minimum slack.

## Transducer

▶ See Figure 31

### REMOVAL & INSTALLATION

1. Disconnect the vacuum and electrical connections and the speedometer cables.

2. Remove the attaching screws and remove the transducer.
3. Installation is the reverse of removal.

### ADJUSTMENT

1. Drive the vehicle at 55 mph and engage the cruise control.
2. If the car cruises below the engagement speed, screw the orifice tube outward.
3. If the car cruises above the engagement speed, screw the orifice tube inward.

➡ **Each ¼ turn of the orifice tube will change cruise speed approximately 1 mph.**

## Control Module

### REMOVAL & INSTALLATION

▶ See Figure 32

1. Disconnect the electrical connector.
2. Remove the bracket attaching bolt and remove the module assembly.
3. Installation is the reverse of removal.

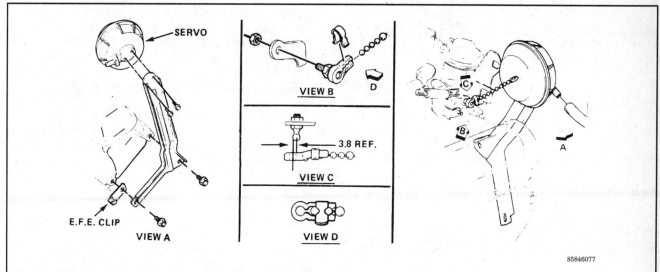

Fig. 30 Servo mounting and adjustment; all models similar

## RADIO

### Radio Receiver/Tape Player

The antenna trim must be adjusted on AM radios when major repair has been done to the unit or the antenna changed. The trimmer screw is located behind the right side knob. Raise the antenna to its full height. Tune to a weak station around 1400 on the dial, and turn the volume up to maximum. Turn the trimmer screw until the maximum volume is achieved.

### REMOVAL & INSTALLATION

▶ **See Figures 33, 34, 35, 36, 37, 38, 39 and 40**

**Buick**

*1975 AND 1976*

1. Disconnect the negative battery cable and tape the end.

### ✳✳CAUTION

**On models equipped with an air bag, you must tape the end of the battery cable to avoid accidental deployment and personal injury.**

2. Remove the lower trim panel.
3. Remove the knobs from the radio. If equipped with Trip-Set and/or Speed Alert, remove the cone shaped knobs.
4. Remove the face plate by pulling outward. Disconnect the terminal connector before completely removing the face plate, if equipped with Trip-Set/Speed-Alert.
5. Remove the two hex nuts from the control shafts.
6. Remove the ash tray and frame.
7. Disconnect the two connectors behind the dash and unplug the antenna.
8. Unscrew the support bracket nuts and remove the radio to the rear and downward.
   **To install:**
9. Install the radio part way.
10. Connect the two connectors behind the dash and connect the antenna.
11. Tighten the retaining nuts and install the ash tray and frame.
12. Install the two hex nuts to the control shafts.
13. Connect the terminal connector before completely installing the face plate, if equipped with Trip-Set/Speed-Alert. Install the face plate.
14. Install the knobs to the radio. If equipped with Trip-Set and/or Speed Alert, install the cone shaped knobs.

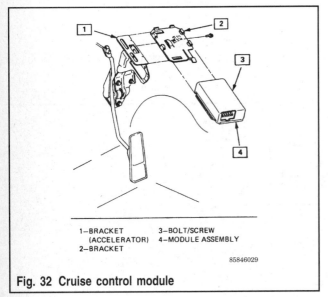

1—BRACKET          3—BOLT/SCREW
   (ACCELERATOR)   4—MODULE ASSEMBLY
2—BRACKET

85846029

**Fig. 32 Cruise control module**

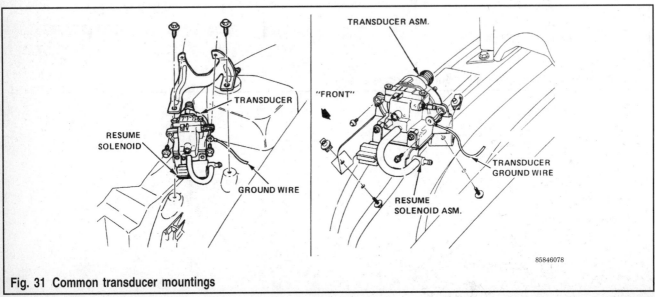

TRANSDUCER ASM.

TRANSDUCER

RESUME
SOLENOID

"FRONT"

GROUND WIRE

TRANSDUCER
GROUND WIRE

RESUME
SOLENOID ASM.

85846078

**Fig. 31 Common transducer mountings**

15. Connect the negative battery cable and check operation.

### 1977 TO 1990

1. Disconnect the negative battery cable. Remove the right side and center trim covers from the dash.

2. Remove the four screws that attach the front panel of the radio to the dash panel. Then, slide the radio out just far enough to gain access to all the connectors.

3. Disconnect the three electrical connectors. Unscrew and disconnect the antenna lead.

4. If the vehicle is equipped with a clock, unscrew and remove the glovebox and disconnect its lead through the glovebox opening.

5. Pull the radio out straight, to avoid snagging any protrusions on the dash panel.

**To install:**

6. Install the radio in straight, avoid snagging any protrusions on the dash panel.

7. If the vehicle is equipped with a clock, install and screw the glovebox and connect its lead through the glovebox opening.

8. Connect the three electrical connectors and antenna lead.

9. Install the four screws that attach the front panel of the radio to the dash panel.

10. Connect the negative battery cable. Install the center trim cover to the dash.

### Oldsmobile

### 1975 AND 1976

1. Disconnect the negative battery cable and tape the end.

### ❄❄CAUTION

**On models equipped with an air bag, you must tape the end of the battery cable to avoid accidental deployment and personal injury.**

2. Remove the lower trim pad.
3. Disconnect the wiring and the antenna lead.
4. Remove the support bracket-to-tie bar attaching screw.

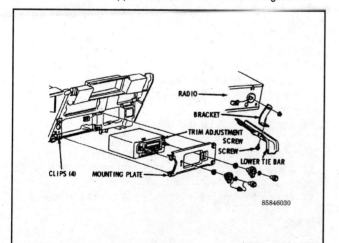

**Fig. 33 Exploded view of radio installation showing trim adjustment screw location**

**Fig. 34 To remove the radio, first remove the radio knobs**

**Fig. 35 Remove the left side trim panel**

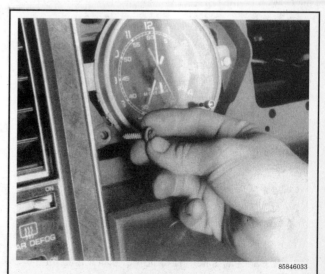

**Fig. 36 Remove the center trim panel attaching screws**

Fig. 37 Remove the center trim panel

Fig. 38 Remove the radio bracket attaching screws

Fig. 39 Carefully slide the radio out of it's mounting location

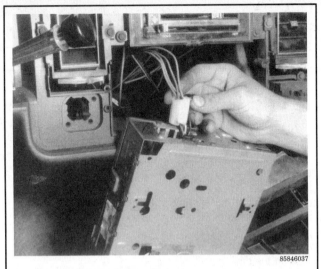
Fig. 40 Disconnect the radio electrical connections

5. Remove the knobs from the radio. Remove the two radio-to-instrument cluster attaching nuts.
6. Remove the radio from behind the instrument cluster.
**To install:**
7. Install the radio from behind the instrument cluster.
8. Install the two radio-to-instrument cluster attaching nuts and the knobs onto the radio.
9. Install the support bracket-to-tie bar attaching screw.
10. Connect the wiring and the antenna lead.
11. Install the lower trim pad.
12. Connect the negative battery cable and check operation.

### 1977 TO 1990

1. Disconnect the negative battery cable.
2. Remove the knobs from the radio and pull out the cigarette lighter.
3. Remove the two trim cover attaching screws and remove the cover.
4. Remove the radio bracket attaching screw from the lower tie bar.
5. Remove the four mounting plate screws and pull the radio out to obtain access to the electrical connections. Detach the wiring harness and the antenna lead.
6. Remove the mounting plate nuts and remove the radio.
**To install:**
7. Install the radio and mounting plate nuts.
8. Obtain access to the electrical connections and attach the wiring harness and the antenna lead. Install the four mounting plate screws.
9. Install the radio bracket attaching screw to the lower tie bar.
10. Install the trim cover and attaching screws.
11. Install the knobs onto the radio and push in the cigarette lighter.
12. Connect the negative battery cable and check operation.

### Pontiac

#### 1975 AND 1976

1. Disconnect the negative battery terminal, then remove the radio knobs and hex nuts.

2. Remove the upper and lower instrument panel trim plates and the lower front radio bracket.

3. Remove the glove box and disconnect the radio connections.

4. Loosen the side brace screw and slide the radio toward the front seat.

5. To install, reverse the removal procedure.

### 1977 TO 1981

1. Disconnect the negative battery terminal.

2. Remove the upper trimplate. Remove the radio trimplate by removing the two top screws, the ashtray assembly, disconnecting the lighter, and removing the ashtray bracket.

3. Remove the two radio screws.

4. Remove the radio through the instrument panel and detach all connectors.

5. Reverse the procedure for installation.

### 1982 TO 1984

1. Disconnect the battery.

2. Remove the radio knobs and bezels.

3. Remove the upper and lower instrument panel trim plates.

4. Remove the four front radio retaining screws.

5. Open the glove box door and lower by releasing the spring clip. Pull the radio out after loosening the rear right side nut. Disconnect all wiring and remove the radio.

6. To install, reverse the removal procedure. If the radio is to be replaced, remove the bushing from the rear of the radio and install it on the replacement radio.

### 1985 TO 1989

1. Disconnect the battery negative cable. Pull the control knobs off the radio shafts.

2. Remove its three mounting screws and then remove the radio trim plate. Remove the two screws and lower mounting nut securing the radio mounting bracket to the instrument panel.

3. Pull the unit out of the dash just far enough to gain access to all connectors. Then, disconnect the electrical connectors and unscrew and disconnect the antenna lead.

## WINDSHIELD WIPERS AND WASHERS

### Wiper Blade and Arm

▶ **See Figures 41, 42, 43 and 44**

## REMOVAL & INSTALLATION

1. On some models, it is necessary to raise the hood to gain access to the arm.

2. To remove the arm, pry underneath the arm with a suitable wiper arm removing tool. Be careful not to scratch the paint.

3. To install, position the arm over the shaft and press down. Make sure you install the arms in the same position on the windshield as they were when they were removed.

4. Remove the radio from the dash with the mounting bracket attached to it. If the radio is being replaced with a new unit, transfer the bracket to it.

**To install:**

5. Install the radio into the dash with the mounting bracket attached to it and connect the electrical connectors. If the radio is being replaced with a new unit, transfer the bracket to it.

6. Install the three mounting screws and the radio trim plate. Install the two screws and lower mounting nut securing the radio mounting bracket to the instrument panel.

7. Connect the battery negative cable. Push the control knobs onto the radio shafts and check operation.

## Speakers

### REMOVAL & INSTALLATION

#### Front Speakers

### ✳✳CAUTION

**On models equipped with an air bag, you must tape the end of the battery cable to avoid accidental deployment and personal injury.**

1. Disconnect the negative battery cable and tape the end.

2. Remove the instrument panel pad.

3. Remove the seal from the speaker and remove the attaching screws.

4. Remove the speaker and disconnect the electrical connector.

5. Installation is the reverse of removal.

#### Rear Speakers

1. Disconnect the negative battery cable.

2. From inside the trunk, remove the speaker insulator.

3. Disconnect the electrical connector.

4. Remove the attaching screw and remove the speaker.

5. Installation is the reverse of removal.

4. There are several different types of wiper blades. Most simply slide out of the arm assembly after the release is pressed. See Section 1 for wiper blade replacement.

### Wiper Motor

▶ **See Figures 45, 46, 47, 48 and 49**

## REMOVAL & INSTALLATION

The wiper motor is mounted on the driver's side of the cowl, accessible from the engine compartment. Once the hood is opened, you can gain access to the electrical connectors, washer hoses, and crank arm, on most models. On a few models, these items may be located under the cowl screen. If

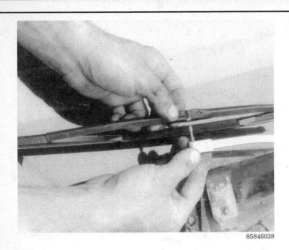

**Fig. 41 Depress the lock-tab and slide the blade from the arm. Be sure not to let the arm snap against the windshield**

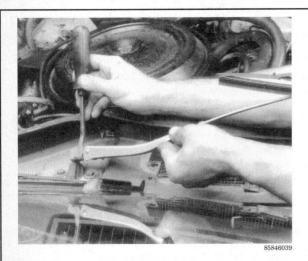

**Fig. 42 Use a small prybar to slide the lock-tab to it's stop**

**Fig. 43 Slide the wiper arm from the splined shaft**

necessary, you can remove this screen easily once the hood is opened.

1. Disconnect the negative battery cable.
2. Open the hood. If necessary, remove the cowl screen. Remove the driver's side wiper arm, as described above.
3. Snap the wiper drive link off the motor crank arm.
4. Disconnect the hoses and the electrical connector.
5. Remove the attaching bolts. Remove the motor, being careful that the rubber bushings remain in the slots of the motor base or are collected. Guide the crank arm out of the hole in the cowl and remove the motor.
   **To install:**
6. Install the motor, attaching bolts and torque to 15 ft. lbs. (20 Nm). Guide the crank arm into the hole in the cowl. Be careful that the rubber bushings remain in the slots of the motor base.
7. Connect the hoses and the electrical connector.
8. Snap the wiper drive link onto the motor crank arm.
9. If removed, install the cowl screen and driver's side wiper arm, as described above.
10. Connect the negative battery cable and check for proper operation.

## Wiper Linkage

### REMOVAL & INSTALLATION

▶ See Figure 50

1. Disconnect the negative battery cable. Raise the hood and remove the cowl screen.
2. Place a large screwdriver between the drive link and the crank arm and twist to remove the link retainer.
3. Remove the linkage to body attaching screws.
4. Remove the linkage while guiding it through the plenum chamber opening.
   **To install:**
5. Installation is the reverse of removal.

## Windshield Washer Fluid Resivoir

### REMOVAL & INSTALLATION

▶ See Figure 51

1. Remove the washer hose.
2. Remove the attaching screws and remove the resivoir from the vehicle.
3. Installation is the reverse of removal.

## Windshield Washer Motor

### REMOVAL & INSTALLATION

1. Remove the washer hoses from the pump.
2. Disconnect the wires from the pump relay.
3. Remove the plastic pump cover.

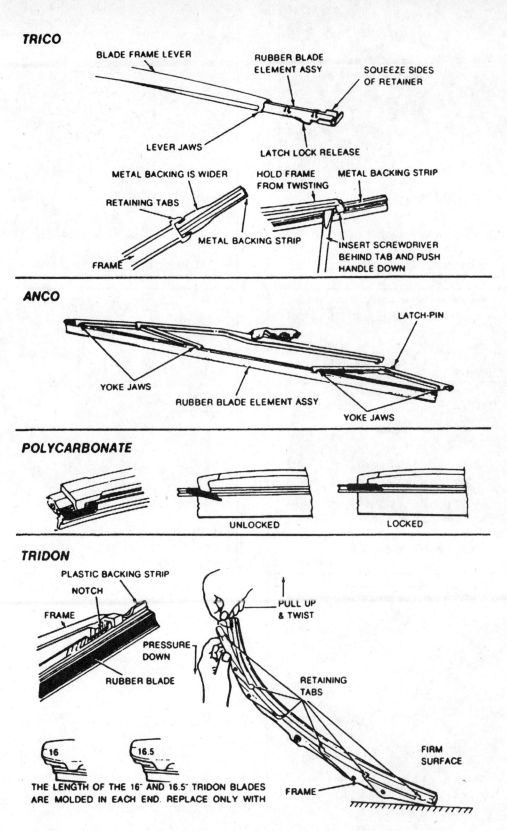

**Fig. 44 Wiper insert replacement**

Fig. 45 Label and disconnect the washer lines

Fig. 46 Disconnect the wiper motor electrical connection

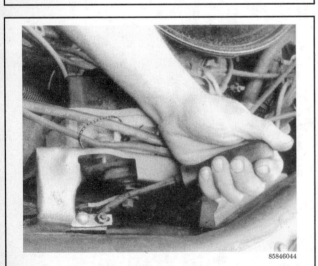

Fig. 47 Using a small prybar, snap the wiper drive link off the motor cranck arm

Fig. 48 Remove the wiper motor attaching bolts

Fig. 49 Guide the crank arm out of the hole and remove the motor. Take care not lose the rubber isolator bushings

4. Remove the attaching screws securing the pump frame and remove from the gearbox.

5. Installation is the reverse of removal.

## INSTRUMENTS AND SWITCHES

### Instrument Cluster

▶ See Figures 52, 53 and 54

REMOVAL & INSTALLATION

### ❊❊CAUTION

**Do not attempt any service on the steering wheel, column or instrument panel on Buick and Oldsmobile models equipped with an air bag. Service on these models should only be performed by a professional technician.**

#### Oldsmobile Models

1. Disconnect the negative battery cable. Slide the steering column collar up the column. Then, unsnap the steering column trim cover by pulling to the rear. Remove it.

2. Remove the screws attaching the gauge cluster to the carrier.

3. Pull the gauge cluster rearward just far enough to gain access behind it. Disconnect the gauge wiring connectors and two lamp sockets from the rear of the cluster. Remove the cluster.

4. Remove the screws attaching the gauge housing to the cluster. Then, remove the nuts attaching the back of the gauges to the gauge housing and remove the gauges.

   **To install:**

5. Connect the gauge wiring connectors and two lamp sockets at the rear of the cluster.

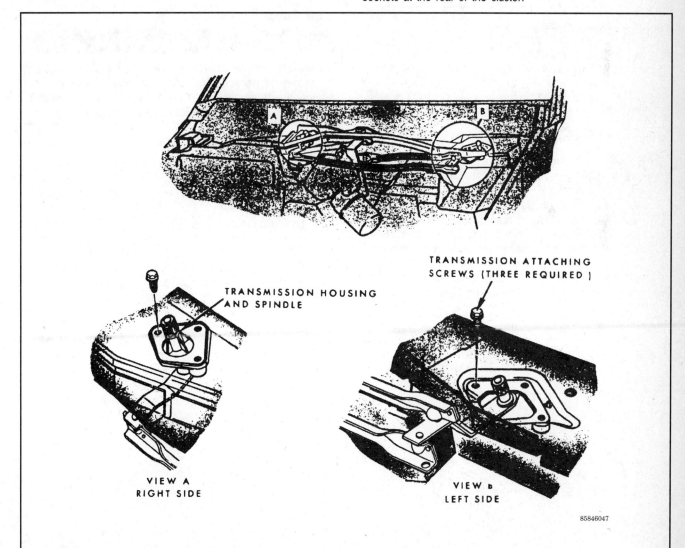

TRANSMISSION HOUSING AND SPINDLE

TRANSMISSION ATTACHING SCREWS (THREE REQUIRED)

VIEW A
RIGHT SIDE

VIEW b
LEFT SIDE

85846047

Fig. 50 Wiper linkage installation; all models similar

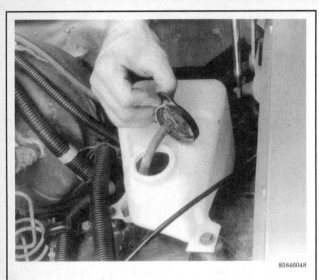

**Fig. 51 Washer fluid resivoir; all models similar**

6. Install the gauge cluster and nuts attaching the back of the gauges to the gauge housing. Install the screws attaching the gauge housing to the cluster.

7. Install the four screws attaching the gauge cluster to the left side trim cover.

8. Snap the steering column trim cover into place. Connect the negative battery cable and check operation.

### Pontiac Safari Wagons and Parisienne

1. Disconnect the negative battery cable. Remove the four screws securing the lower cover to the steering column and then remove the cover.

2. Remove the shift indicator cable from the column.

3. Remove the two mounting bolts attaching the column to the lower side of the dash panel from underneath. Then, lower the column carefully until the steering wheel rests on the seat.

4. Going around the perimeter of the plastic lens, remove the six screws and three snap-in plastic fasteners.

5. Remove the two screws from the upper surface of the gray sheet metal trim plate. Then remove the nuts from the two studs in the lower corner of the cluster.

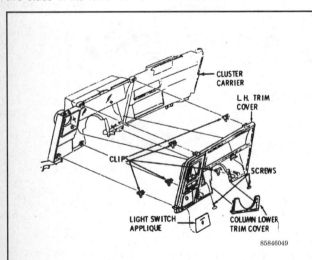

**Fig. 52 Oldsmobile left side trim cover; others similar**

6. Pull the cluster out just far enough for access to it from the rear. Reach behind the cluster and disconnect the speedometer cable by turning the collar until it unscrews. Then, pull it out of the dash panel.

**To install:**

7. Push the cluster in just far enough for access to it from the rear. Reach behind the cluster and connect the speedometer cable by turning the collar until it engages.

8. Install the two screws from the upper surface of the gray sheet metal trim plate. Then install the nuts from the two studs in the lower corner of the cluster.

9. Going around the perimeter of the plastic lens, install the six screws and three snap-in plastic fasteners.

10. Install the two mounting bolts attaching the column to the lower side of the dash panel from underneath.

11. Install the shift indicator cable to the column.

12. Remove the four screws securing the lower cover to the steering column and then remove the cover. Connect the negative battery cable and check operation.

### Buick Sedans

## ✳✳CAUTION

**Do not attempt any service on the steering wheel, column or instrument panel on Buick and Oldsmobile models equipped with an air bag. Service on these models should only be performed by a professional technician.**

### ANALOG CLUSTER

1. Disconnect the battery negative cable. Remove the left side trim cover.

2. Remove the four screws which fasten the cluster carrier to the instrument panel.

3. Look under the vehicle to see if the speedometer cable is of the two-piece design. If it is, disconnect the cable at the transmission end (this will give slack for later work).

4. Remove the steering column trim cover. Disconnect the clip which fastens the shift indicator in place.

5. Remove the two bolts that fasten the steering column to the dash panel and lower it onto the front seat.

6. Pull the cluster far enough out of the dash panel so that you can disconnect the speedometer cable and bulbs at the rear of the cluster.

7. Securely apply the parking brake or block the wheels. Pull the gear selector lever down into low gear. Pull the instrument cluster out far enough to remove the single screw which fastens the Speed Sensor optic head to the speedometer and then remove the cluster.

**To install:**

8. Securely apply the parking brake or block the wheels. Pull the gear selector lever down into low gear. Push the instrument cluster in far enough to install the single screw which fastens the Speed Sensor optic head to the speedometer.

9. Push the cluster far enough into the dash panel so that you can connect the speedometer cable and bulbs at the rear of the cluster.

10. Install the two bolts that fasten the steering column to the dash panel.

11. Install the steering column trim cover. Connect the clip which fastens the shift indicator in place.

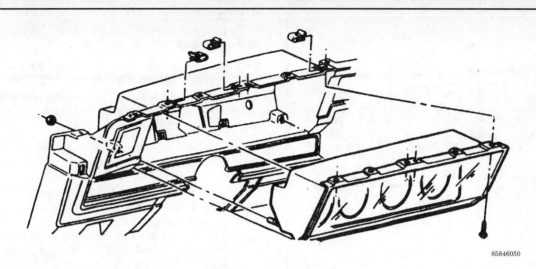

85846050

**Fig. 53 Instrument cluster removal; all models similar**

12. Connect the cable at the transmission end, if removed.

13. Install the four screws which fasten the cluster carrier to the instrument panel.

14. Connect the battery negative cable. Install the left side trim cover.

### Buick Sedans

#### DIGITAL CLUSTER

### ✳✳WARNING

**When handling electronic components, avoid touching the electrical terminals of these parts. Always touch a known good ground before handling the part and more frequently after sliding across the seat or sitting down from a standing or walking position. Failure to do so can result in component damage and failure.**

1. Disconnect the battery negative cable. Follow all the steps in the procedure above. Disconnect the harness connector and the ground strap at the back of the instrument carrier and then pull the entire unit out.

2. Unscrew the trip set lever knob. Remove the four screws from the corners of the clear cluster lens. Then, remove the lens and back filler.

3. Remove the spring and needle assembly from the shift indicator.

4. Remove the five screws fastening the tube and circuit board assembly to the cluster carrier. Then, lift the assembly out of the carrier, noting the position of the gasket which covers each of the indicator lights.

5. Hold the speedometer frame against the tube and circuit board face plate and remove the two standard head screws from the face plate. The mechanical odometer may now be removed, as necessary.

**To install:**

6. Hold the speedometer frame against the tube and circuit board face plate and install the two standard head screws to the face plate. The mechanical odometer may now be installed, as necessary.

7. Install the five screws fastening the tube and circuit board assembly to the cluster carrier.

8. Install the spring and needle assembly to the shift indicator.

9. Install the four screws into the corners of the clear cluster lens. Screw in the trip set lever knob.

10. Connect the battery negative cable and check operation.

### Buick Estate Wagons

Instead of an instrument cluster, this dash uses two separate gauge units; a speedometer on the left and a fuel gauge on the right. Removal is similar for the two units. Follow the parts of the procedure specified, depending upon which you need to service.

1. Disconnect the battery negative cable. Remove the left side trim cover.

2. Remove the four screws attaching the gauge unit you want to remove to the dash. If removing the speedometer, disconnect the cable at the transmission or cruise control transducer (under the hood).

3. Pull the unit out far enough to disconnect parts described below.

**Speedometer:**

• Two rear light bulb sockets by rotating to release and pulling them out.

• The speedometer cable by depressing the retaining clip while pulling the cable back.

• The VSS optic head by removing the single screw retaining it in place.

**Fuel gauge:**

• Two rear light bulb sockets by rotating to release and pulling them out.

• The electrical connector.

4. Slide the unit out of the dash.

### Speedometer, Tachometer, and Gauges

### REMOVAL & INSTALLATION

The gauges on all the models covered here can be replaced in the same basic manner. First, remove the instrument cluster

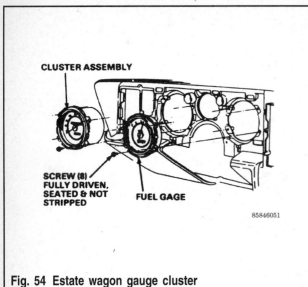

Fig. 54 Estate wagon gauge cluster

and the front lens. Then, remove the gauge's attaching screws on either the front or the back of the cluster.

When replacing a speedometer or odometer assembly, the law requires the odometer reading of the replacement unit to be set to register the same mileage as the prior odometer. If the mileage cannot be set, the law requires that the replacement be set at zero and a proper label be installed on the drivers door frame to show the previous odometer reading and date of replacement.

## Speedometer Cable

### REMOVAL & INSTALLATION

▶ **See Figures 55 and 56**

➡**Especially on late model vehicles, be careful to route the cable properly. Any bends in the cable must not have a radius of less than 6 in. (152mm) unless there is a pre-formed bend in the cable housing. Make sure the cable housing is not routed where it could be pinched or chafed by moving parts or overheated by an exhaust pipe or the catalytic converter.**

#### All Models

1. Disconnect the negative battery cable.
2. Remove the instrument cluster.
3. Disconnect the speedometer cable from the back of the speedometer. Push down on the spring tab to release.
4. Disconnect the other end of the speedometer cable (at rear side of transmission or the cruise control transducer) and remove the cable.
5. Remove any retaining clips that attach the cable to the body and carefully pull the cable out of the vehicle. If the cable will not pull out easily, it is still clipped to the vehicle at some point, or it is stuck on other wires or components.

**To install:**

6. Before installing, grease both ends of the cable with an approved speedometer cable lubricant.

➡**A new type speedometer cable is available as a replacement part for 1981 models only. The new cable is identified by the longer ferrule at the speedometer end. The old style (short ferrule) cable may be used on either the old or new style speedometer head.**

7. Install any retaining clips that attach the cable to the body. If the cable will not install easily, it is may be stuck on other wires or components.
8. Install the correct end of the speedometer cable at rear side of transmission or the cruise control transducer.
9. Connect the speedometer cable to the back of the speedometer. Push down on the spring tab to install.
10. Install the instrument cluster. Connect the negative battery cable.

## Printed Circuit Board

### REMOVAL & INSTALLATION

The printed circuit board on all models covered here are removed in the same basic manner. It is attached to the back of the instrument cluster, making it necessary to remove the cluster first. After the cluster has been removed, disconnect the bulb sockets and remove the attaching screws or clips. Handle the circuit board with care to prevent damage.

## Windshield Wiper Switch

### REMOVAL & INSTALLATION

The windshield wiper switches on all models covered here are removed in the same basic manner. All are mounted on the left side of the instrument panel, and are reached by

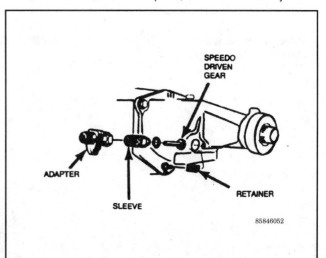

Fig. 55 Speedometer cable-to-drive attachment; all models similar

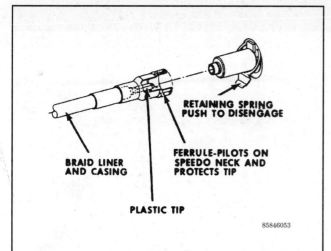

**Fig. 56 Speedometer cable attachment at the instument cluster**

removing the left side trim panel. Electrical connections must be disconnected at the rear of the switch before removing the switch unit from the dash. Be sure to note how the wires are connected before removing. The switch units are fixed to the instrument panel by two or four screws.

## Headlight Switch

### REMOVAL & INSTALLATION

The headlight switch is mounted on the left hand side of the instrument panel on all models covered here. To remove the switch, disconnect the negative battery cable and remove the left instrument panel trim plate. Remove the retaining nut securing the switch, and disconnect the electrical connector from the back of the switch. The switch can now be removed. Reverse the procedure for installation.

## Clock

▶ See Figure 57

### REMOVAL & INSTALLATION

1. Disconnect the negative battery cable.
2. On some models, it may be necessary to remove the trim plate cover and the instrument panel pad.
3. Disconnect the electrical connector and remove the lamp socket.
4. Remove the attaching screws. Some models are retained with clips. To remove these, push on the outer edges of the clock face to dislodge it.
5. Remove the clock from the vehicle.
6. Installation is the reverse of removal.

## Ignition Switch

### ✳✳CAUTION

Do not attempt any service on the steering wheel, column or instrument panel on Buick and Oldsmobile models equipped with an air bag. Service on these models should only be performed by a professional technician.

### REMOVAL & INSTALLATION

1. Turn the steering wheel so the vehicle's wheels are in the straight ahead position. Turn the key to the LOCK position.
2. Disconnect the negative battery cable.
3. Remove the column to instrument panel trim plates and attaching nuts.
4. Lower the column and disconnect the shift indicator cable.
5. Disconnect the ignition and dimmer switch connectors.
6. Remove the switch attaching screws and remove the switch.

**To install:**

7. Move the actuator rod hole in the switch to the lock position.
8. Install the switch with the rod in the hole. Adjust the switch as follows:

   a. Models to 1988- Move the switch slider to the extreme left ACC position, then move the slider 2 detents to the right to the OFF-UNLOCK position.

   b. 1989 and 1990- Place a $\frac{3}{32}$ in. drill bit in the hole on the switch to lock the switch into position. Move the switch slider to the extreme left position then move the slider 1 detent to the left LOCK position.

9. Position and reassemble the steering column in reverse of the disassembly procedure.

**Fig. 57 It may be necessary to remove the trim panel to acess the clock**

## LIGHTING

## Headlights

### REMOVAL & INSTALLATION

▶ See Figures 58, 59, 60, 61 and 62

**❄❄CAUTION**

**Halogen bulbs contain a gas under pressure. Handling a bulb improperly may cause the bulb to shatter into flying glass fragments. To help avoid personal injury, turn headlight switch OFF, allow the bulb to cool and wear eye protection.**

1. Remove the headlight bezel (outer trim around sealed beam).
2. Remove the sealed beam retainer ring screws and the retainer ring.
3. Lift the sealed beam out and disconnect it from the electrical connector. If the vehicle is equipped with monitor lights, remove the rubber sleeve from the bulb and retain it.
4. To install, connect the sealed beam to the electrical connector, and reinstall the monitor light sleeve if equipped. Hold the sealed beam in place and install the retaining ring and screws. Install the headlight bezel and adjust headlight aim.

### AIMING

▶ See Figures 63 and 64

The headlights must be properly aimed to provide the best, safest road illumination. The lights should be checked for proper aim, and adjusted if necessary, after installing a new sealed beam unit or if the front end sheet metal has been replaced. The headlamps should be aimed by a professional with a special alignment tool. Certain state and local authorities

Fig. 58 Remove the headlight bezel trim screws

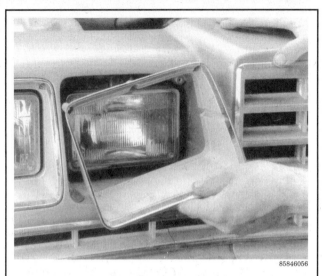

Fig. 59 Remove the bezel from the panel

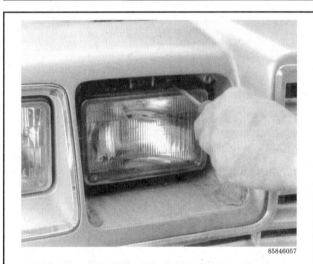

Fig. 60 Remove the retainer ring screws. It may be helpful to soak these with penetrating oil first

may vary this procedure, but use the procedure below for temporary adjustments.

➡**The vehicle's fuel tank should be about half full when adjusting the headlights. Tires should be properly inflated, and if a heavy load is carried in the trunk or in the cargo area of station wagons, it should remain there.**

Horizontal and vertical aiming of each sealed beam unit is provided by two adjusting screws, which move the mounting ring in the body against the tension of the coil spring.

1. Place the car on a level floor with headlamps 25 ft. from a light colored wall.
2. Tape three vertical lines on the wall, one for the vertical center of the car and two for the vertical center of the headlamps. Then, tape one horizontal line for the horizontal and vertical center of the headlamps.

Fig. 61 Remove the retainer ring; be careful not to damage it

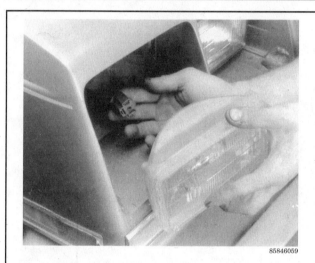

Fig. 62 Pull the headlight out only far enough to reach the connector, then disconnect it

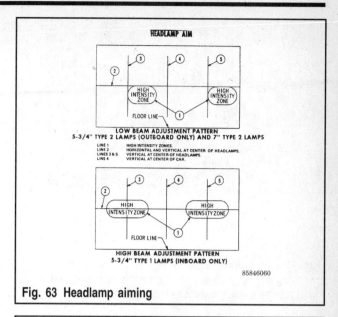

Fig. 63 Headlamp aiming

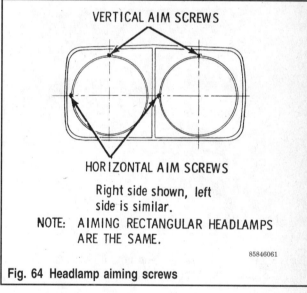

Fig. 64 Headlamp aiming screws

3. Adjust the low beams so the high intensity zone is just below the horizontal line and to the right of the outboard vertical lines.

4. Adjust the high beams so the high intensity zone is centered where the outboard lines intersect with the horizontal line.

## Signal and Marker Lights

### REMOVAL & INSTALLATION

#### Front Turn Signal and Parking Lights

♦ See Figures 65 and 66

1. To replace the bulbs, reach in and up behind the front bumper and twist the lamp socket counter-clockwise until it can be pulled backward and out.

2. Lightly depress the lamp and turn it counter-clockwise to release it. Install in reverse order.

If the entire housing must be replaced:

3. Remove the lamp sockets as described above. Remove the three screws securing the lamp housing to the bumper and remove it.

4. Remove the three J-nuts from the old housing and install them onto the new one. Install the new housing in reverse order.

#### Side Marker Lights

1. To replace the bulb, reach up behind the housing and twist the lamp socket counterclockwise until it can be pulled away from the housing and out.

2. Slightly depress the lamp and turn it counterclockwise to release it. Install in reverse order.

If the entire housing must be replaced:

3. Remove the headlight bezel. Remove the two screws that retain the marker light housing from inside the headlamp housing.

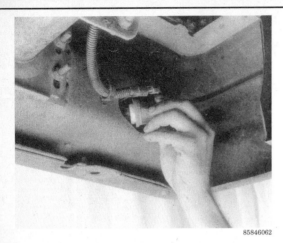

Fig. 65 The front turn signal lights can be removed by reaching in the access hole behind the bumper and twisting the socket counter-clockwise

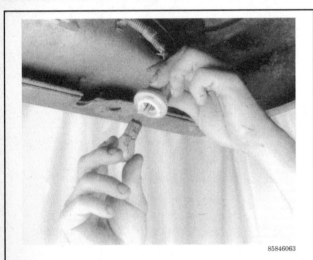

Fig. 66 Lightly depress the bulb until it bottoms and turn it counter-clockwise to release it

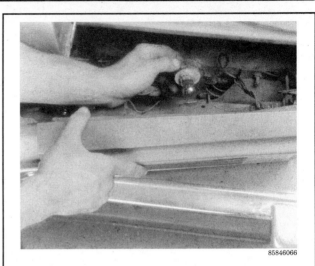

Fig. 69 Twist the socket and remove it from the lens assembly

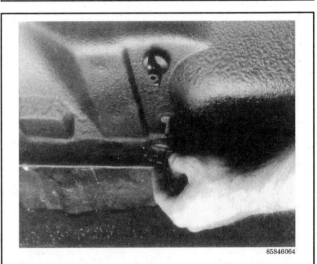

Fig. 67 The rear lens attaching nuts can be accessed from inside the luggage compartment

Fig. 68 Carefully slide the lens out only far enough to remove the bulb sockets

4. Remove the marker light housing. Disconnect and remove the bulb and socket as described just above. Unscrew and remove the lens.

5. Install the lens onto the new housing. Install the lamp into the new housing. Install the housing in reverse of removal.

### Rear Turn Signal, Brake and Parking Lights
▶ See Figures 67, 68, 69, 70 and 71

Most rear lenses are fastened in place from inside the luggage compartment. A stud is attached to the lens and passes through the sheet metal at the rear of the body. In some cases, the rear inner wheelhouse panel has to be removed. Remove the attaching nuts from inside the luggage compartment and pull this type of lens off. A few small lenses are attached with screws that are accessible from the rear. To remove these, simply remove the screws and remove the lens.

Once the lens is removed, the bulb can be replaced simply by depressing it, turning it counterclockwise, and removing it. Install in reverse order.

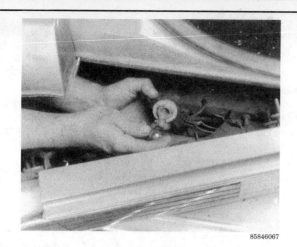

Fig. 70 This type of bulb can be removed by first depressing it lightly until it bottoms then twist and release it

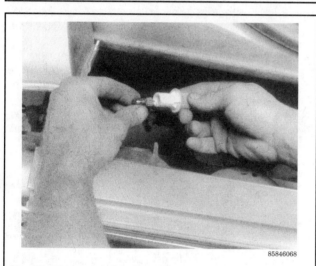

Fig. 71 This type of bulb can be removed by simply pulling it out of the socket

## High-mount Brake Light

### EXCEPT WAGON

1. Remove the two screws, one on each lamp base, and slide the assembly rearward.
2. Disconnect the electrical connector and remove the assembly.
3. Remove the two screws on the outside edges of the assembly.
4. Separate and remove the bulb.
5. Installation is the reverse of removal.

### WAGON

1. Remove the two screws in the lens.
2. Remove the lens and remove the bulb from the socket.
3. Installation is the reverse of removal.

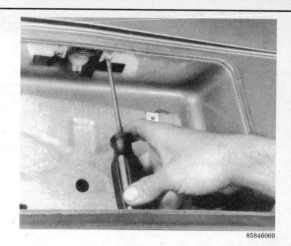

Fig. 72 Remove the attaching screws. Soaking the screws with penetrating oil first will make their removal easier

### Dome Light

1. Remove the dome light cover.
2. Remove the bulb.
3. Installation is the reverse of removal.

### Passenger Area Lamps

To replace the courtesy and glove box lamps, simply remove the bulb through the access hole. To replace the ashtray lamp, it is necessary to remove the ashtray and the ashtray retainer first.

### License Plate Lights

▶ See Figures 72, 73 and 74

1. Remove the lamp attaching bolts or screws.
2. Remove the lamp socket then remove the bulb.
3. Installation is the reverse of removal.

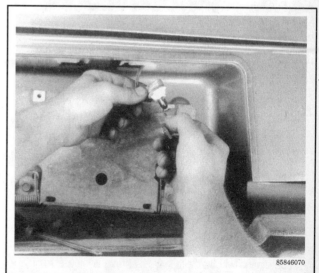

Fig. 73 Remove the socket from the lens

## TRAILER WIRING

Wiring the vehicle for towing is fairly easy. There are a number of good wiring kits available and these should be used, rather than trying to design your own. All trailers will need brake lights and turn signals as well as tail lights and side marker lights. Most states require extra marker lights for overly wide trailers. Also, most states have recently required back-up lights for trailers, and most trailer manufacturers have been building trailers with back-up lights for several years.

Additionally, some Class I, most Class II and just about all Class III trailers will have electric brakes.

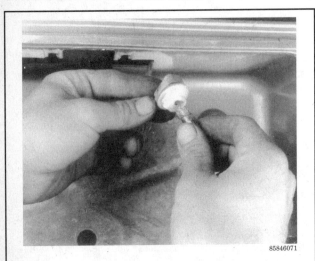

85846071

**Fig. 74 The bulb on this model can be removed by simply pulling it from it's socket**

Add to this number an accessories wire, to operate trailer internal equipment or to charge the trailer's battery, and you can have as many as seven wires in the harness.

Determine the equipment on your trailer and buy the wiring kit necessary. The kit will contain all the wires needed, plus a plug adapter set which included the female plug, mounted on the bumper or hitch, and the male plug, wired into, or plugged into the trailer harness.

When installing the kit, follow the manufacturer's instructions. The color coding of the wires is standard throughout the industry.

One point to note: some domestic vehicles, and most imported vehicles, have separate turn signals. On most domestic vehicles, the brake lights and rear turn signals operate with the same bulb. For those vehicles with separate turn signals, you can purchase an isolation unit so that the brake lights won't blink whenever the turn signals are operated, or, you can go to your local electronics supply house and buy four diodes to wire in series with the brake and turn signal bulbs. Diodes will isolate the brake and turn signals. The choice is yours. The isolation units are simple and quick to install, but far more expensive than the diodes. The diodes, however, require more work to install properly, since they require the cutting of each bulb's wire and soldering in place of the diode.

One final point, the best kits are those with a spring loaded cover on the vehicle mounted socket. This cover prevents dirt and moisture from corroding the terminals. Never let the vehicle socket hang loosely; always mount it securely to the bumper or hitch.

## CIRCUIT PROTECTION

### Fuses

REPLACEMENT

▶ **See Figures 75, 76, ? and 77**

The fuse block on most of the models covered in this guide is located underneath the far left side of the instrument panel, up towards the floor mat. On a few vehicles, it is located adjacent to the steering column and swings down. Two types of fuses have been used since 1975: the conventional type (cylindrical) fuse, found on 1975 through 1978 vehicles, and the new mini fuses, found on 1978 and later models. The conventional fuses are held in the fuse block by small tangs, and are best removed with a small prybar or awl. The mini fuses are simply pushed into their respective places in the block.

To determine whether either type of fuse is blown, remove the suspect fuse and examine the element in the fuse for a break. If the element (the strip of silver metal inside) is broken, replace the fuse with one of equal amperage. Some fuses have their amperage value molded into the fuse end, and

others (and all of the mini fuses) have a color coding system. Color codes are as follows:
- 3 amps Purple
- 5 amps Tan
- 7.5 amps Brown
- 10 amps Red
- 20 amps Yellow or Clear
- 25 amps White
- 30 amps Green

### Fusible Links

All Buick, Pontiac and Oldsmobile models covered in this guide are equipped with fusible links in their electrical systems. The link itself is a piece of wire that is several gauges smaller than the supply wires to which they are connected. The link functions like a fuse in that it will blow (in the case of the link, melt) in the event of an overloaded or short circuit, thus protecting the rest of the circuit.

An example of a burned-out fusible link would be headlights operating while the rest of the vehicle's electrical system is dead, or vice versa. When a melted fusible link is found, the cause of the link failure should also be found and repaired. Some causes include short circuits, component failures, loose or poor connections, or overloaded circuits (often caused by

Fig. 75 This fuse block location is common to most models

Fig. 76 Close-up view of a mini-fuse type block

improperly installed aftermarket accessories drawing too much current or overloading one circuit).

There are generally two fusible links on the vehicles covered here, up to 1983 models. Both on these models are connected to the lower ends of the main supply wires that connect the starter solenoid, and the links are usually black or red in color. On 1983 and later models, there are more links. Typically, V6 models will have two black links and one brown link at the starter, and one red link at the generator. V8 models, both gas and diesel, will have three at the starter; one brown and two black.

## REPLACEMENT

▶ See Figures 78 and 79

**All Models**

- Link A at starter, main power, black, wire size 1
- Link B at starter, main power, black, wire size 1
- Link C at starter, alternator, black, wire size 1
- Link K at alternator, electronic leveling control, rust, wire size 0.5

### ✳✳WARNING

**Replace the fusible link with only the specified wire size, color and approved fusible link wire. NOT following this procedure may cause severe electrical system damage.**

1. Disconnect the negative battery cable.
2. Cut the wire next to the fusible link splice and remove the damaged fusible link and splice.
3. Strip about ½ in. (13mm) of insulation from the end of the new link and from the harness wire so that each will project halfway through the soldering sleeve.
4. Crimp a soldering sleeve over the stripped wire ends and carefully solder the joint. Cover the new joint tightly with a double layer of electrical tape.
5. Install a new link connector eye on the solenoid terminal. Connect the negative battery terminal. To check the new link, simply feel and/or gently pull on each link. A good link will be intact and feel solid.

## Circuit Breakers

### RESETTING & REPLACEMENT

The are two circuit breakers located in the fuse block. A 30 amp power sunroof and window breaker is located in spot 4. A 30 amp power accessory breaker is located in the 14 position of the fuse block. The circuit breaker will automatically reset when the problem has been fixed. To replace the breaker, pull it out from the fuse block.

## Flashers

### REPLACEMENT

The turn signal flasher is located under the dash to the right of the steering column on most models, and is square in shape (as are most flashers). The hazard flasher is under the dash, to the left of the steering column. On 1980 and later models, both the turn signal flasher and the hazard flasher are located at the lower left hand and the upper right hand corners of the fuse block respectively. Remove these by pulling them from their connectors.

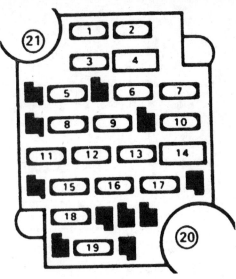

1. (5 amp) Instrument panel illumination
2. (20 amp) Choke heater
3. Spare
4. (30 amp) Circuit breaker
5. Spare
6. (25 amp) Heater and A/C
7. Spare
8. Spare
9. (25 amp) Windshield wiper
10. (20 amp) Stop and hazard lights
11. (10 amp) Instrument panel gauges
12. (20 amp) Tail lights
13. (10 amp) Radio
14. (30 amp) Circuit breaker for power accessory
15. (20 amp) Directional signal and backup lights
16. (20 amp) Clock and Cigar lighter
17. Spare
18. Spare
19. Spare
20. Turn signal flasher
21. Hazard flasher

85846080

Fig. 77 Mini type fuse application chart

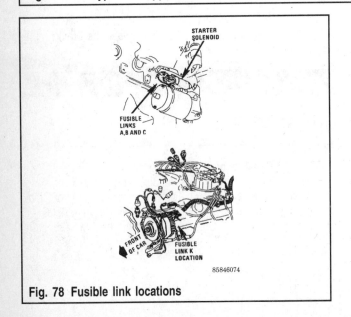

Fig. 78 Fusible link locations

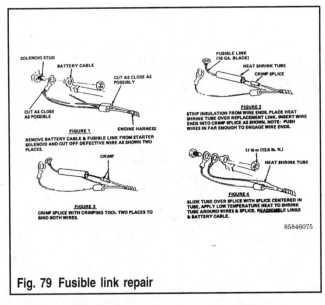

Fig. 79 Fusible link repair

## WIRING DIAGRAMS

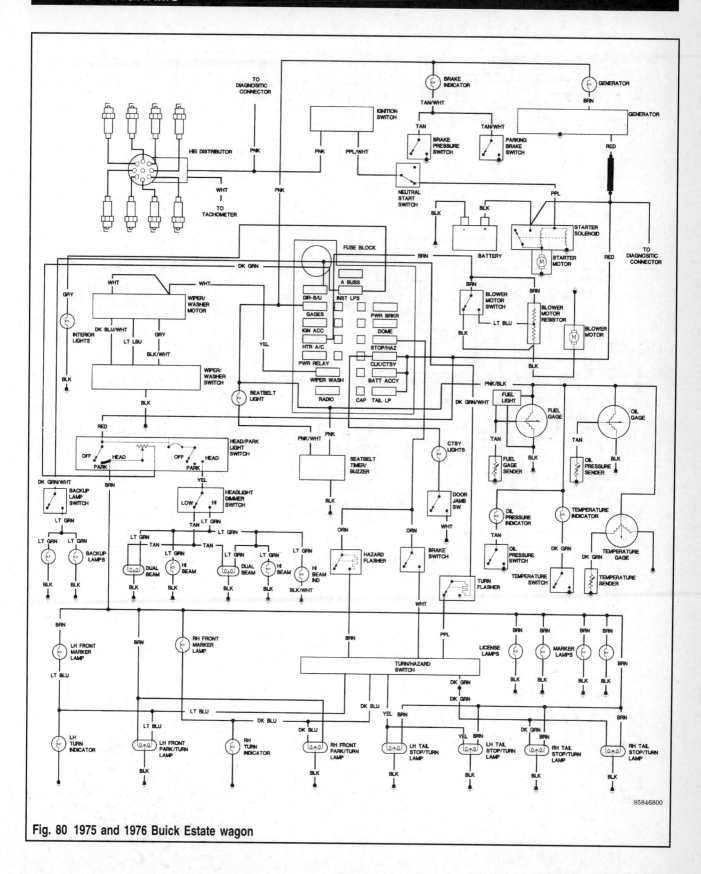

**Fig. 80 1975 and 1976 Buick Estate wagon**

85846800

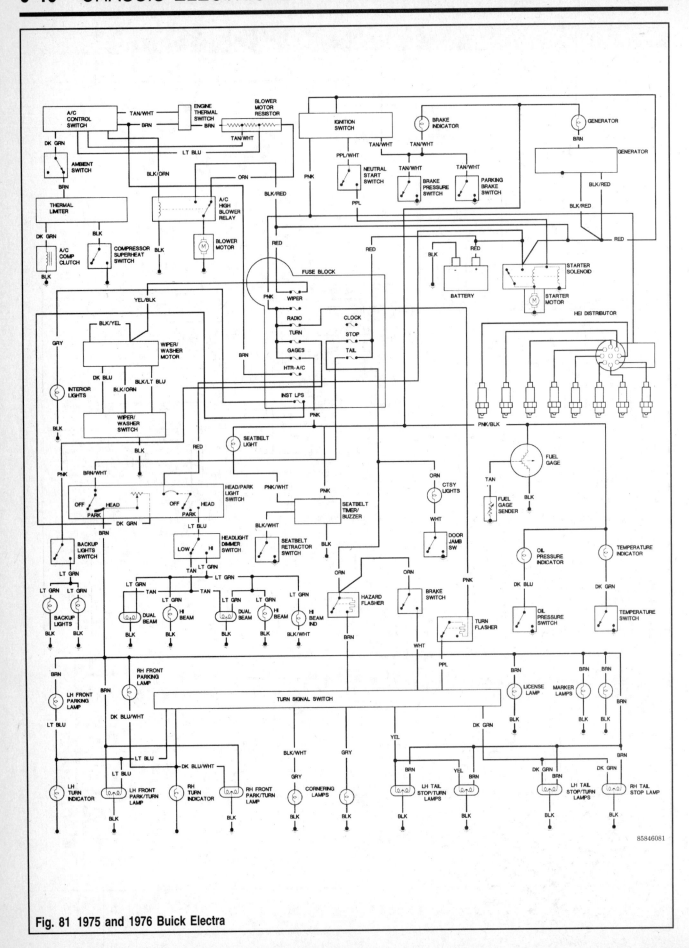

**Fig. 81** 1975 and 1976 Buick Electra

85846081

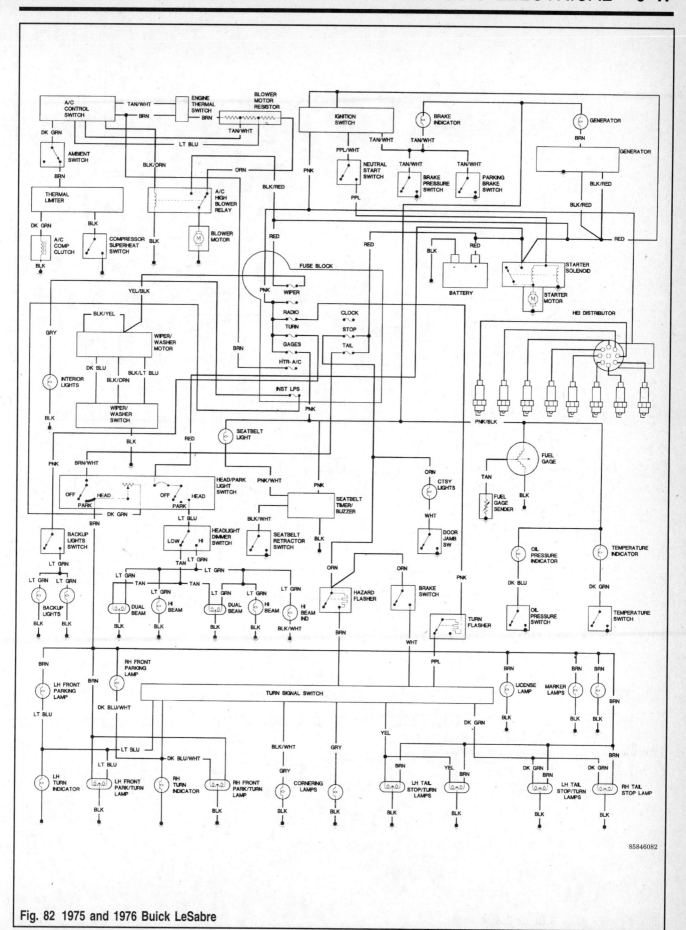

**Fig. 82 1975 and 1976 Buick LeSabre**

85846082

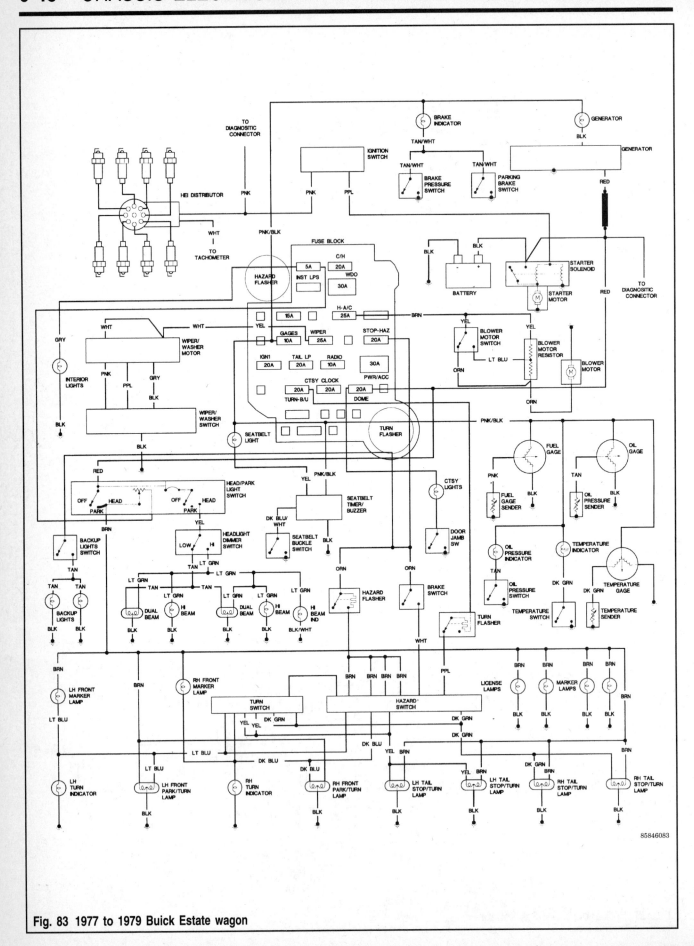

**Fig. 83  1977 to 1979 Buick Estate wagon**

85846083

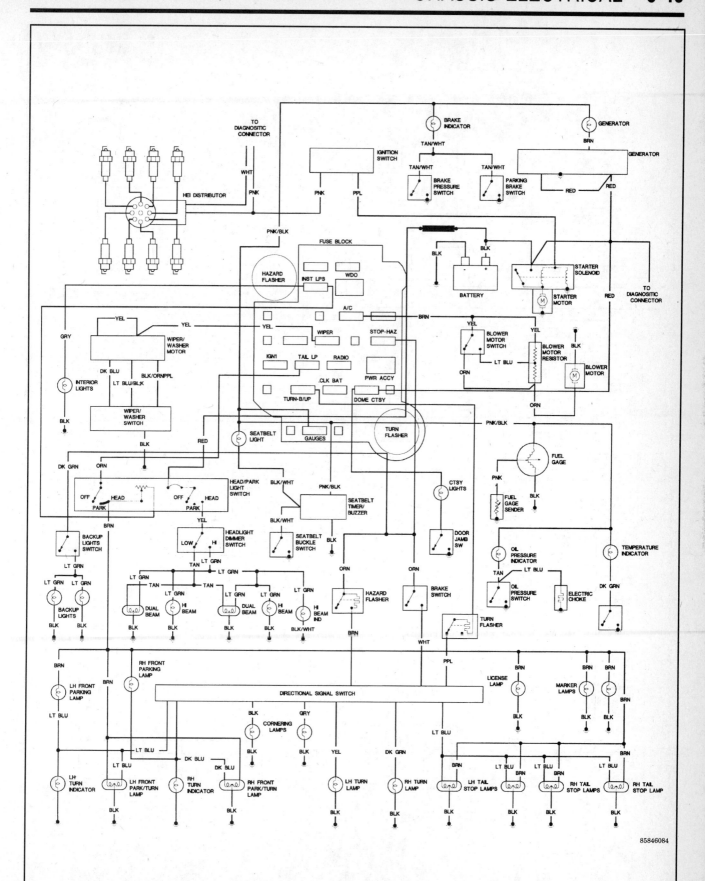

**Fig. 84 1977 Buick Electra**

85846084

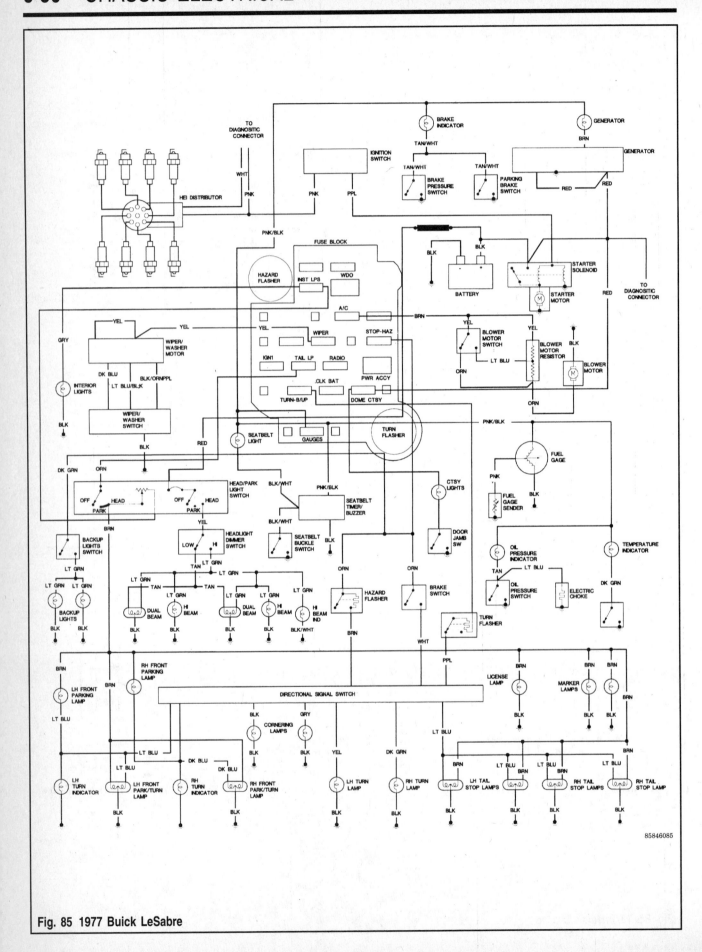

**Fig. 85 1977 Buick LeSabre**

85846085

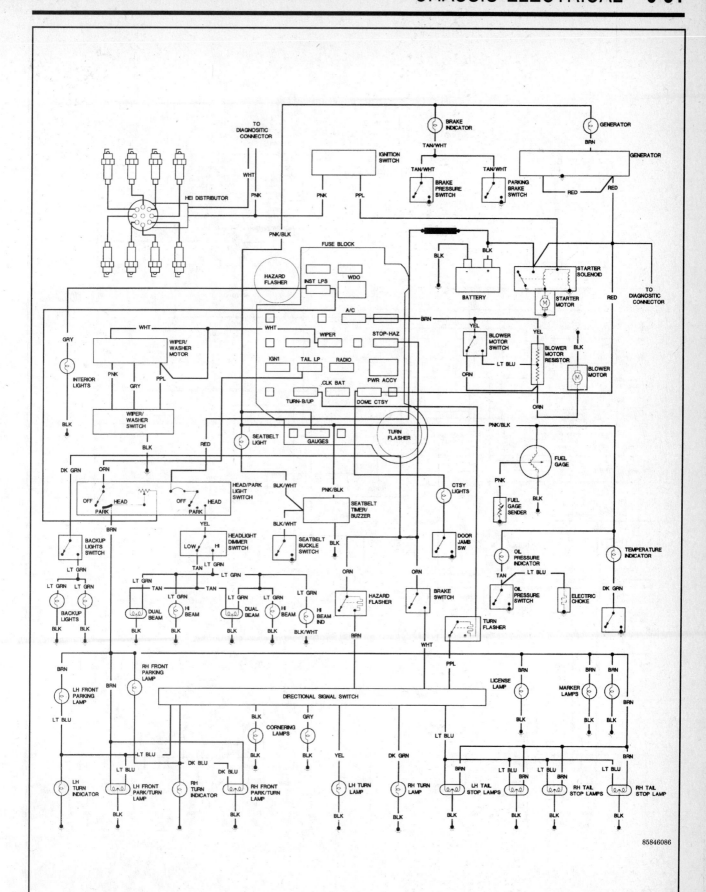

**Fig. 86 1978 Buick Electra**

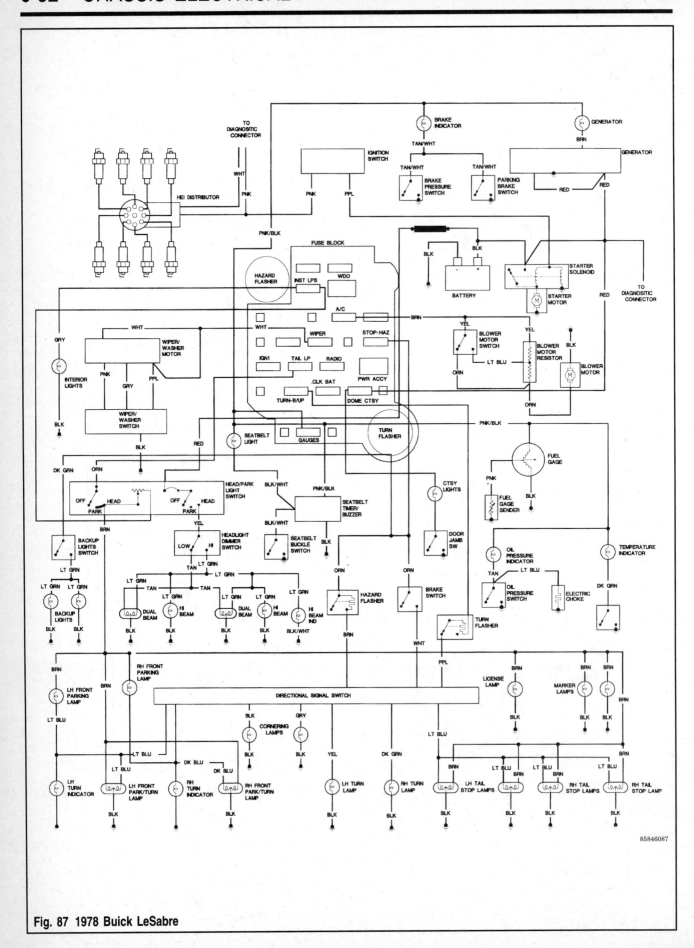

**Fig. 87** 1978 Buick LeSabre

85846087

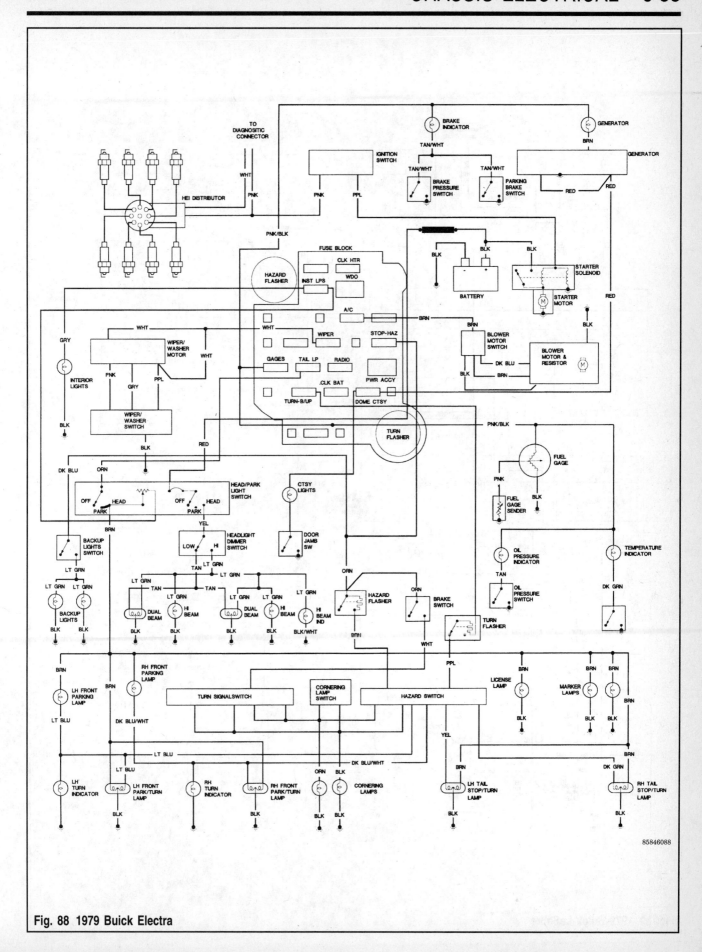

**Fig. 88 1979 Buick Electra**

85846088

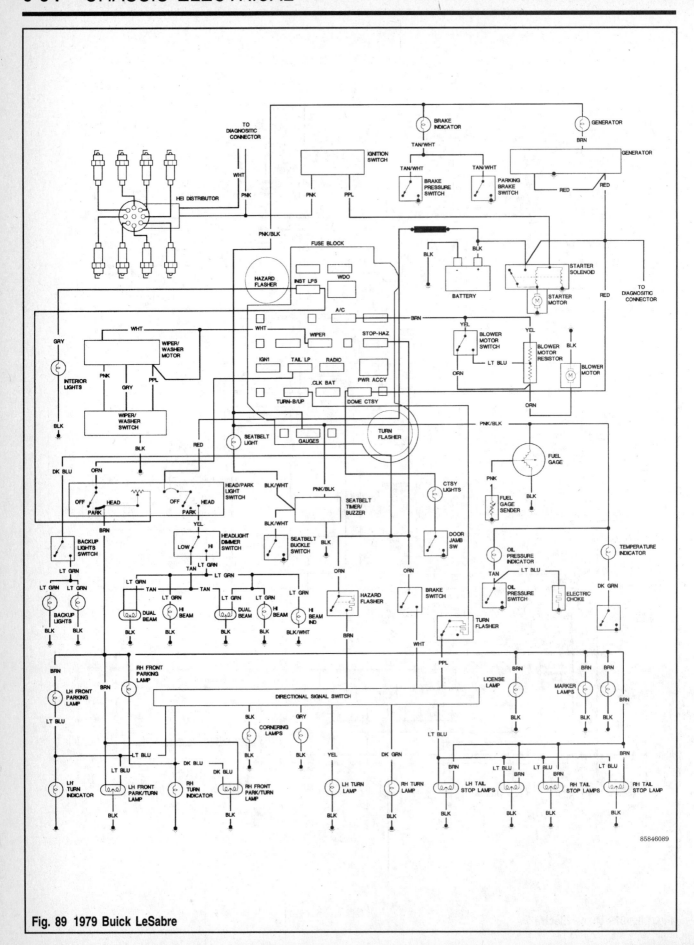

**Fig. 89  1979 Buick LeSabre**

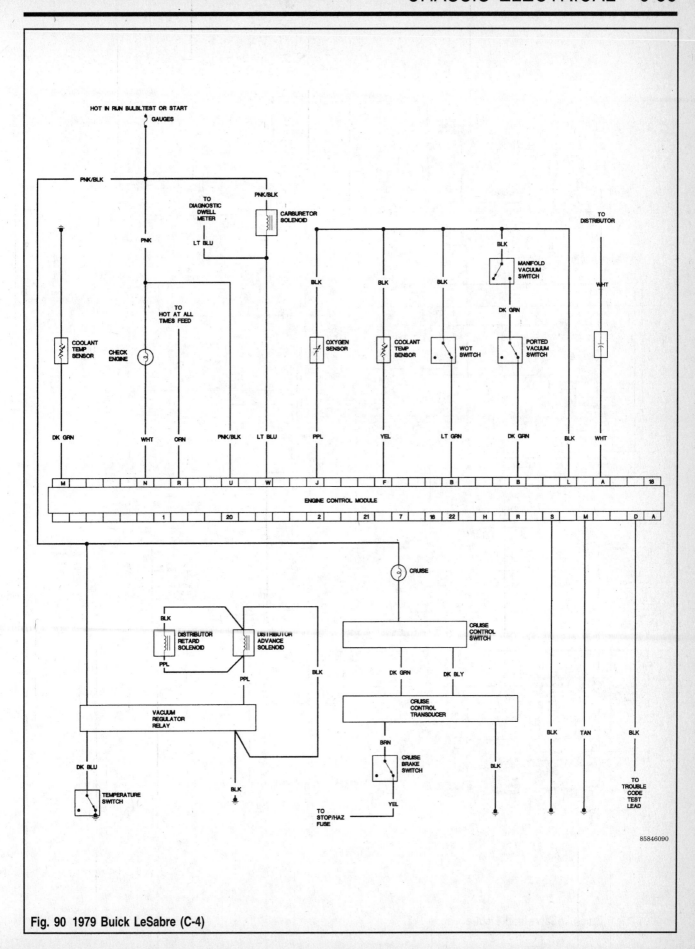

**Fig. 90  1979 Buick LeSabre (C-4)**

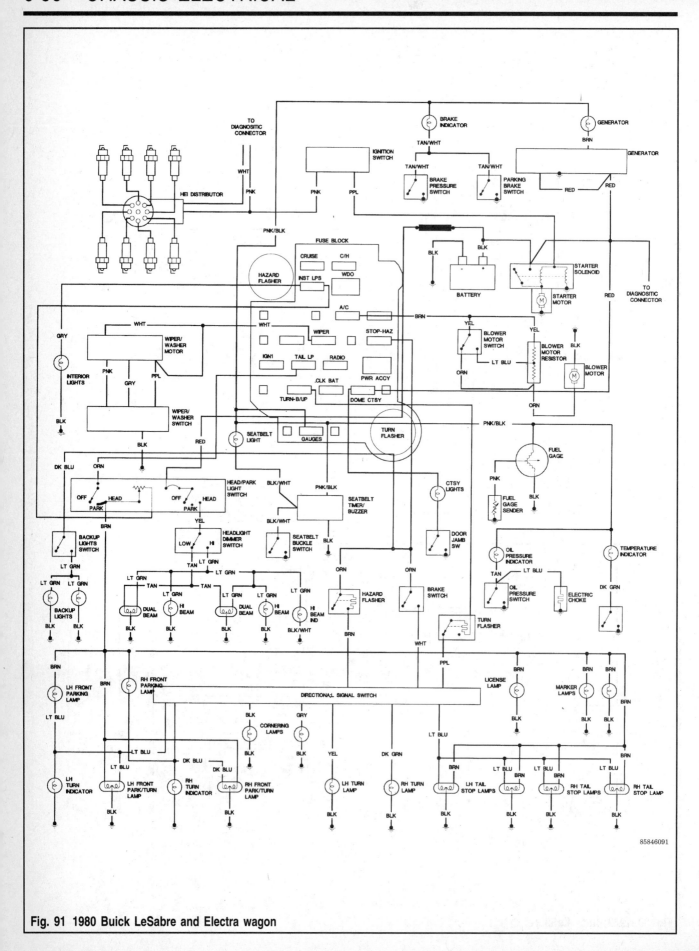

**Fig. 91 1980 Buick LeSabre and Electra wagon**

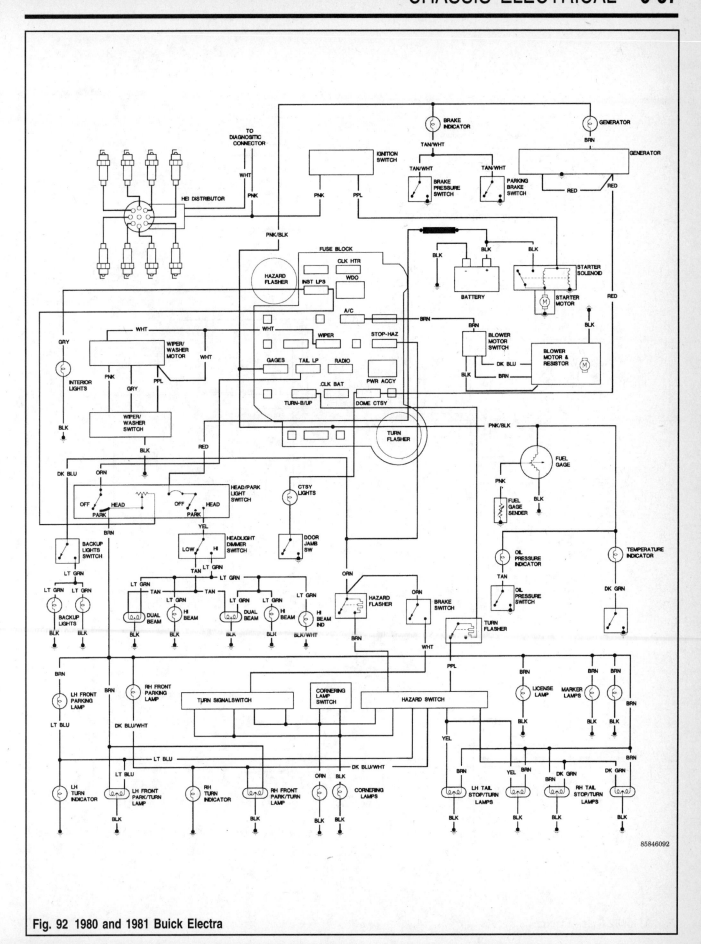

**Fig. 92 1980 and 1981 Buick Electra**

85846092

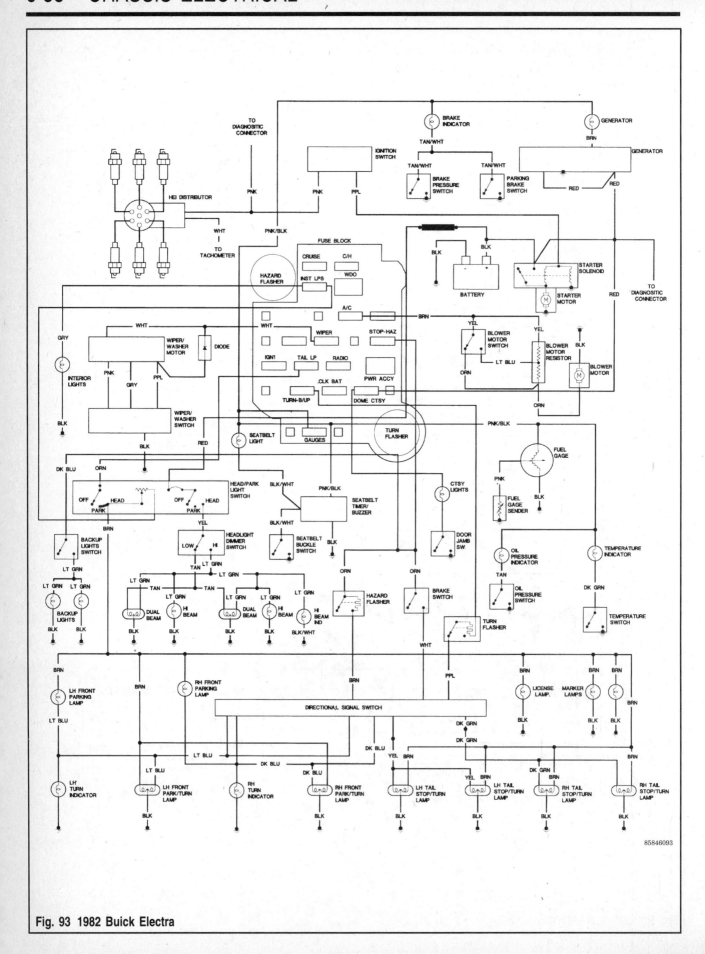

**Fig. 93  1982 Buick Electra**

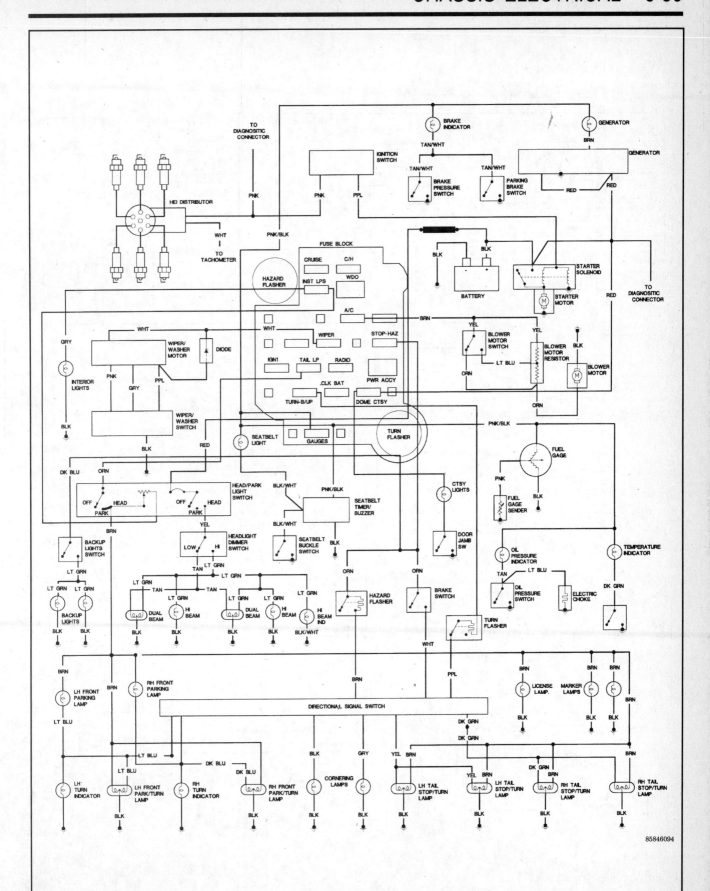

Fig. 94 1981 and 1982 Buick LeSabre and Electra wagon

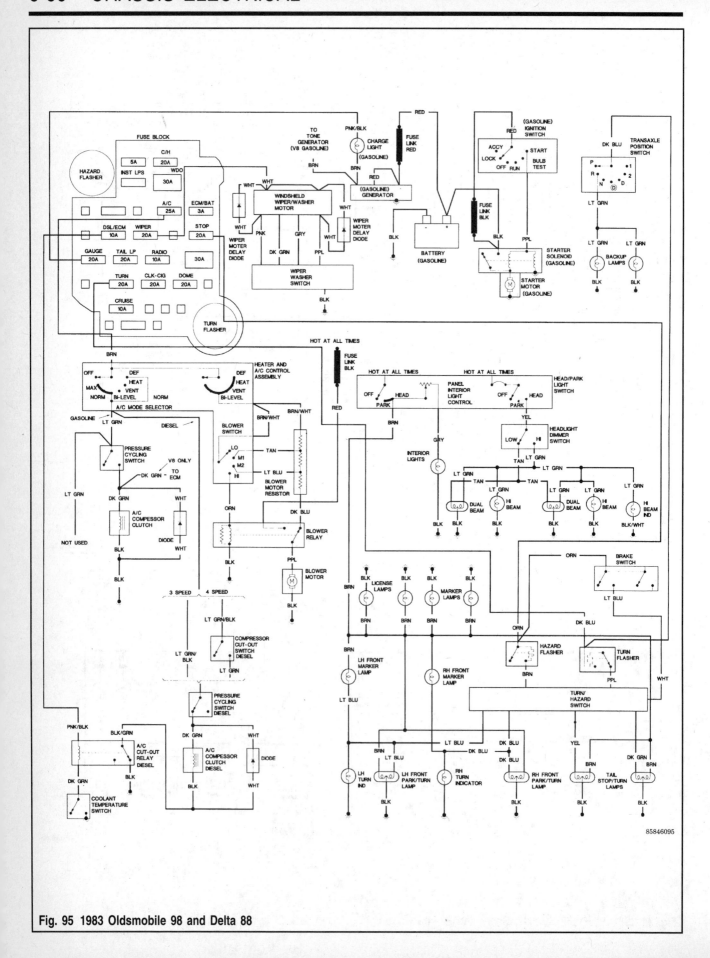

**Fig. 95 1983 Oldsmobile 98 and Delta 88**

85846095

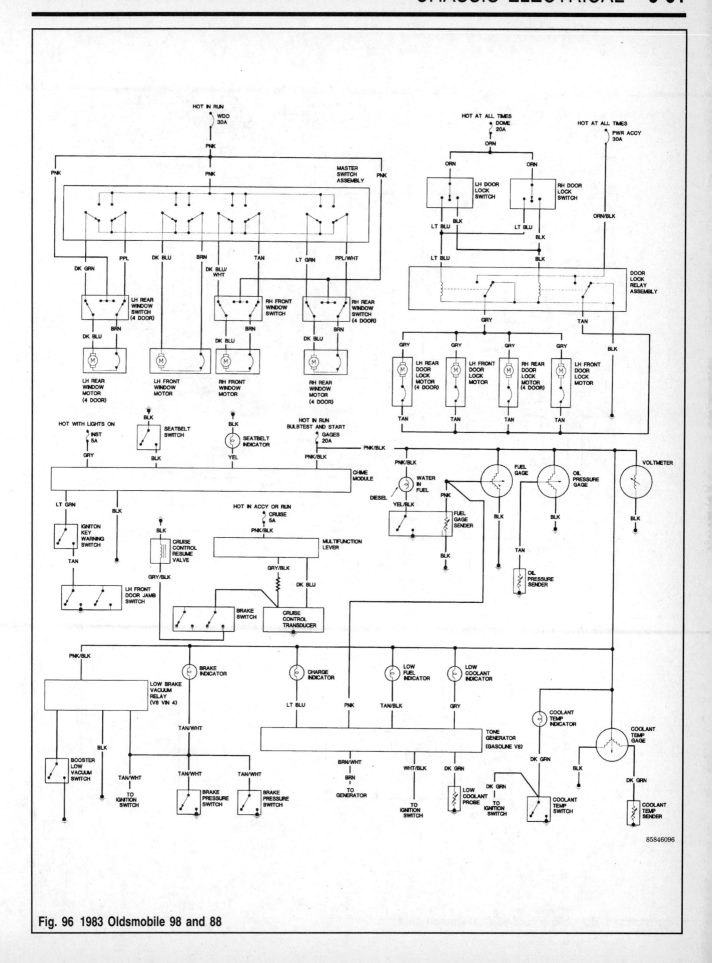

**Fig. 96  1983 Oldsmobile 98 and 88**

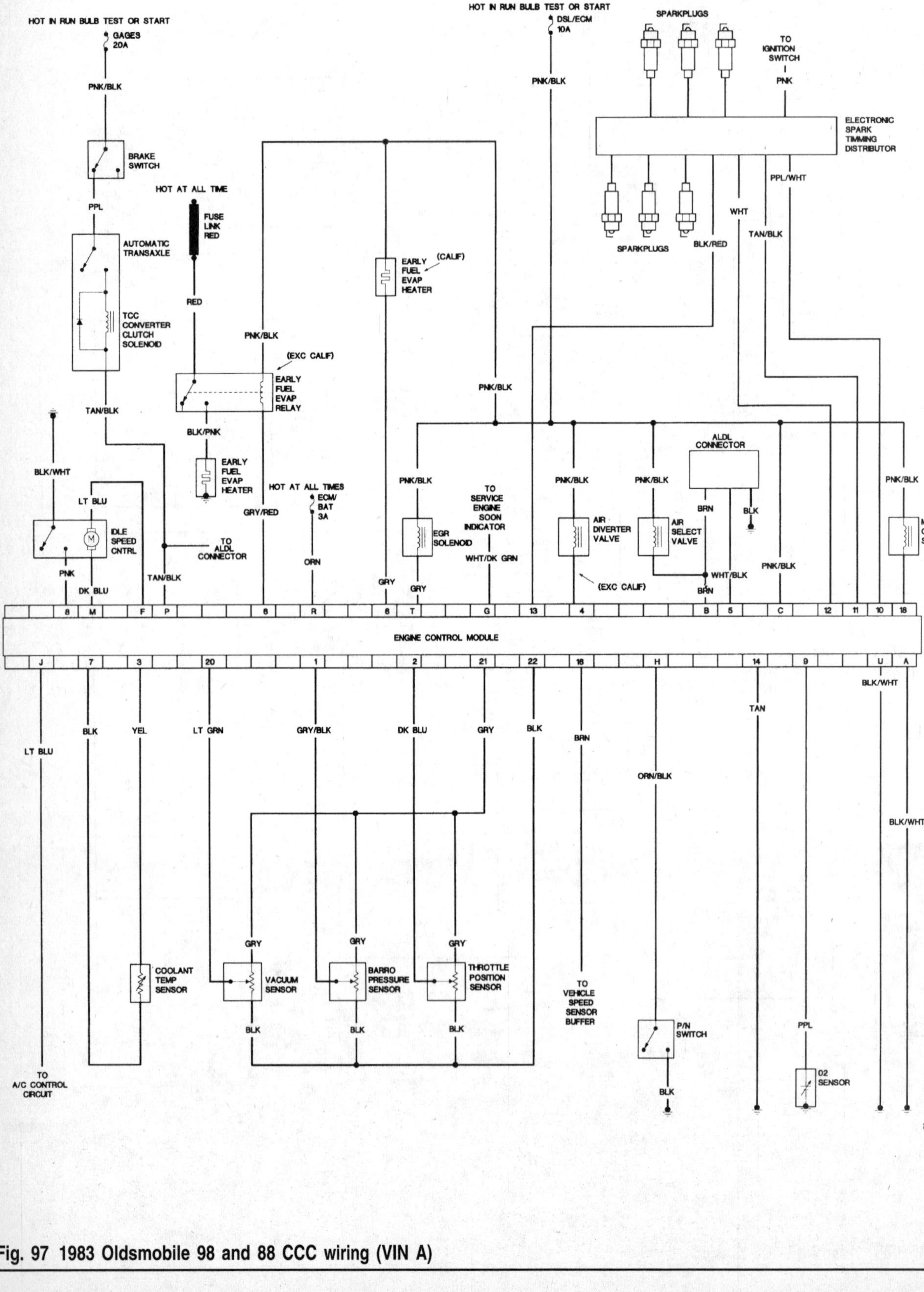

**Fig. 97  1983 Oldsmobile 98 and 88 CCC wiring (VIN A)**

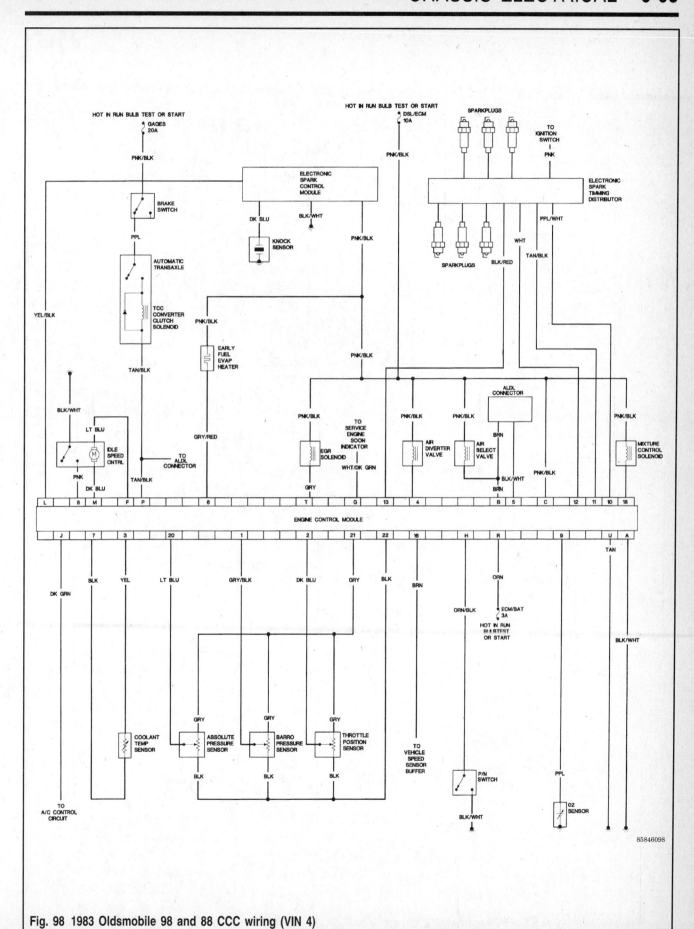

**Fig. 98 1983 Oldsmobile 98 and 88 CCC wiring (VIN 4)**

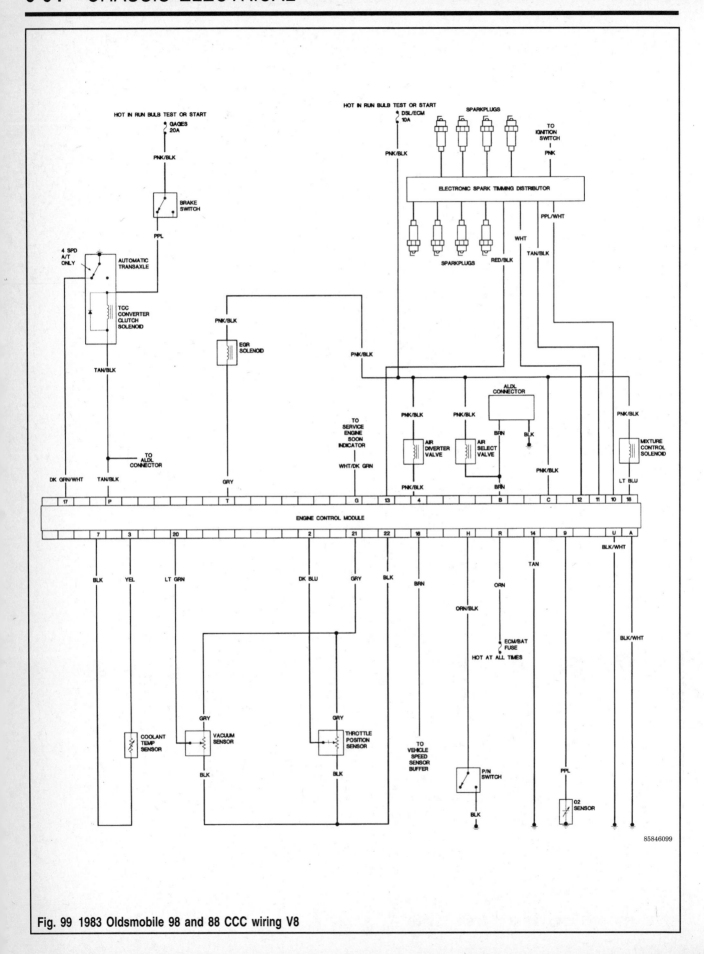

**Fig. 99 1983 Oldsmobile 98 and 88 CCC wiring V8**

85846099

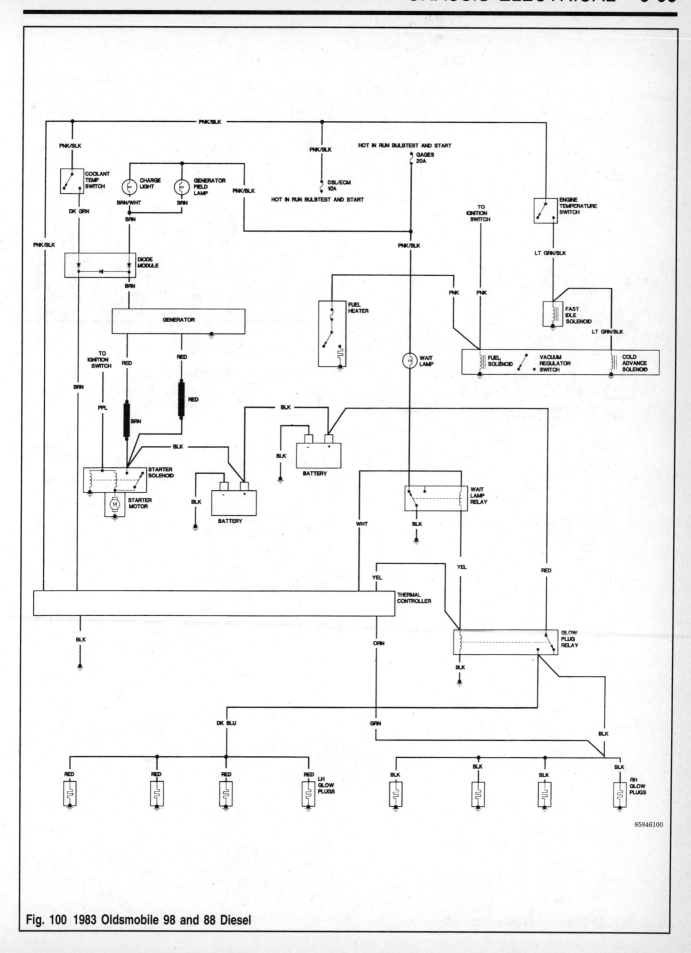

**Fig. 100 1983 Oldsmobile 98 and 88 Diesel**

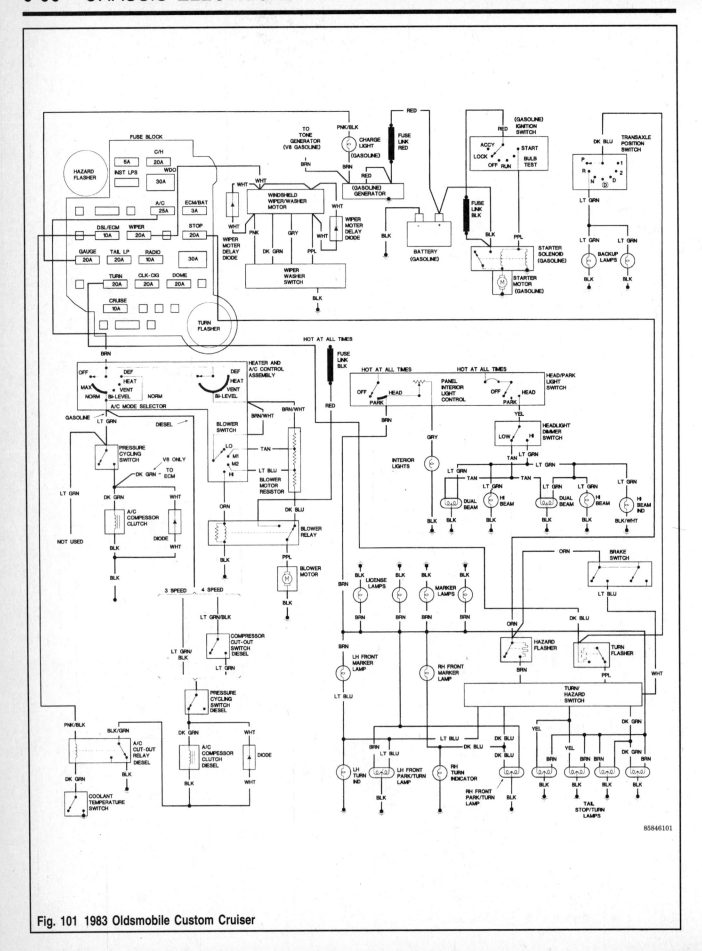

**Fig. 101** 1983 Oldsmobile Custom Cruiser

85846101

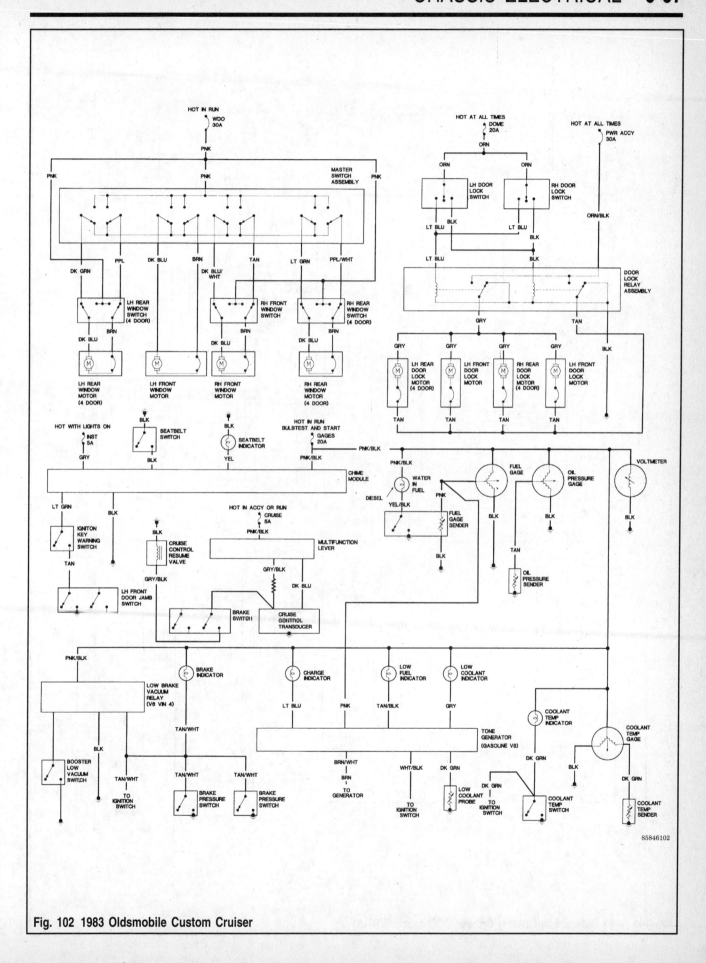

Fig. 102 1983 Oldsmobile Custom Cruiser

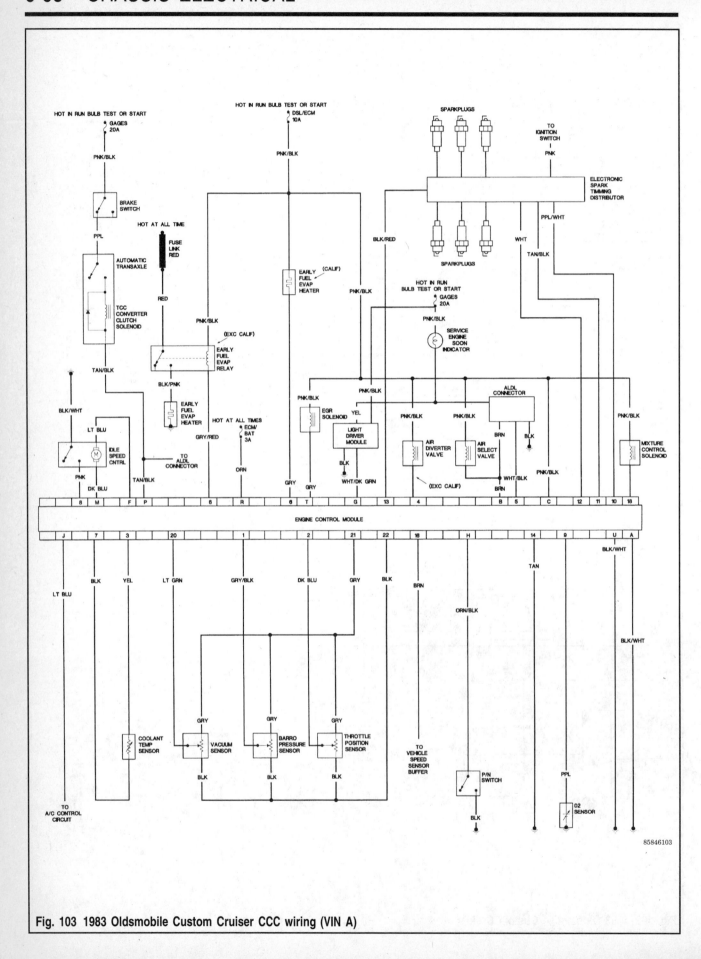

**Fig. 103** **1983 Oldsmobile Custom Cruiser CCC wiring (VIN A)**

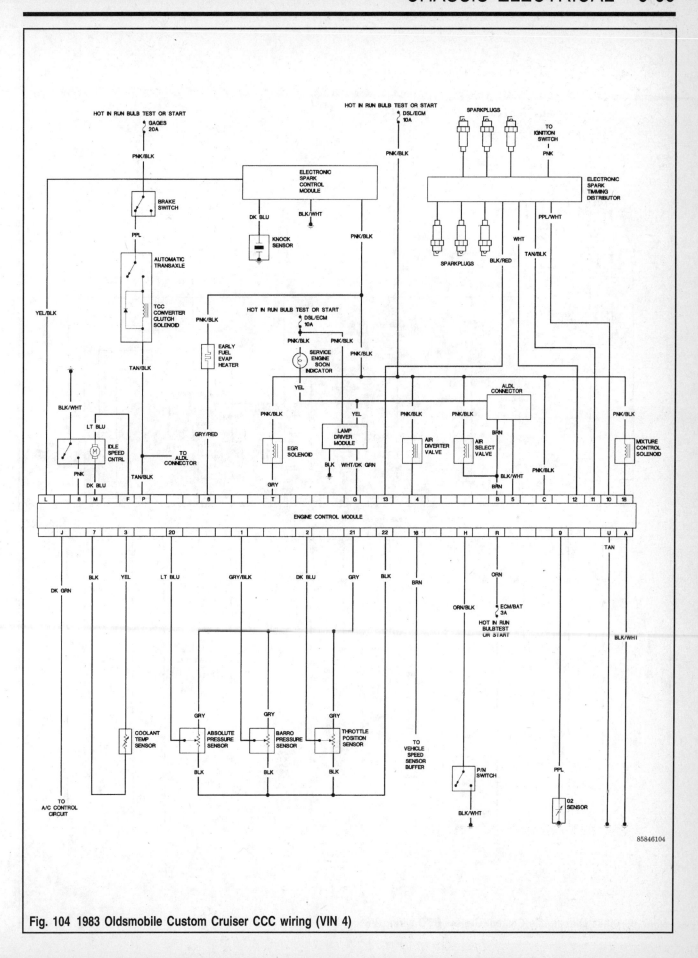

**Fig. 104  1983 Oldsmobile Custom Cruiser CCC wiring (VIN 4)**

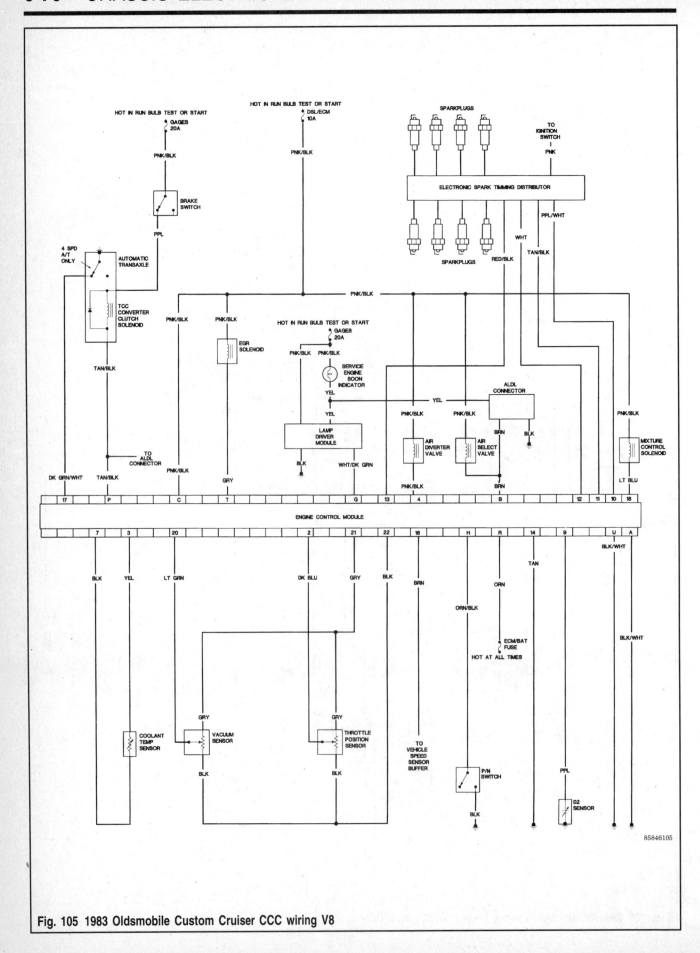

**Fig. 105** 1983 Oldsmobile Custom Cruiser CCC wiring V8

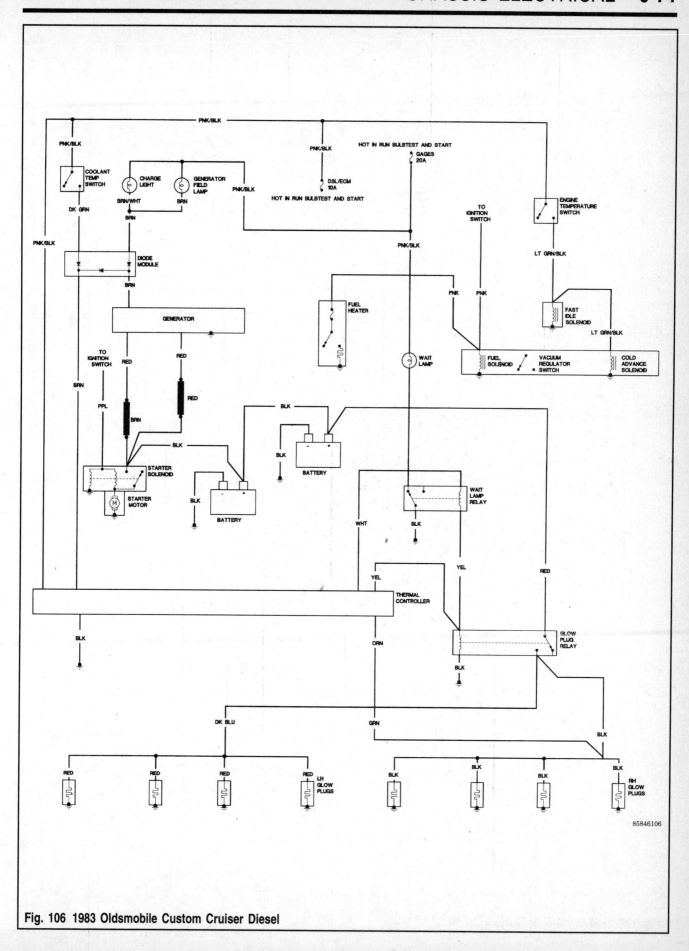

**Fig. 106  1983 Oldsmobile Custom Cruiser Diesel**

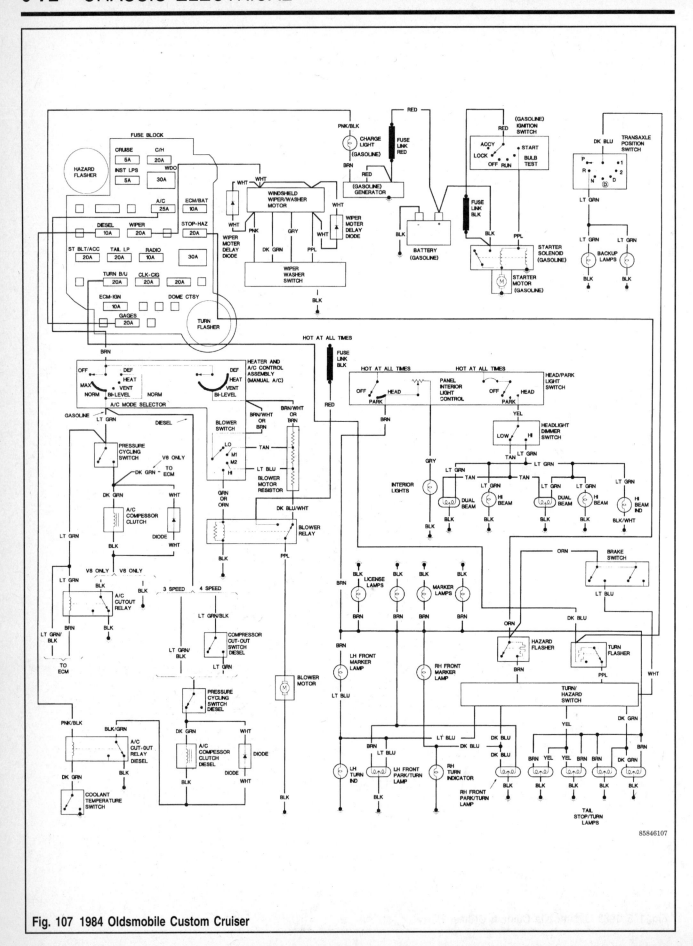

**Fig. 107  1984 Oldsmobile Custom Cruiser**

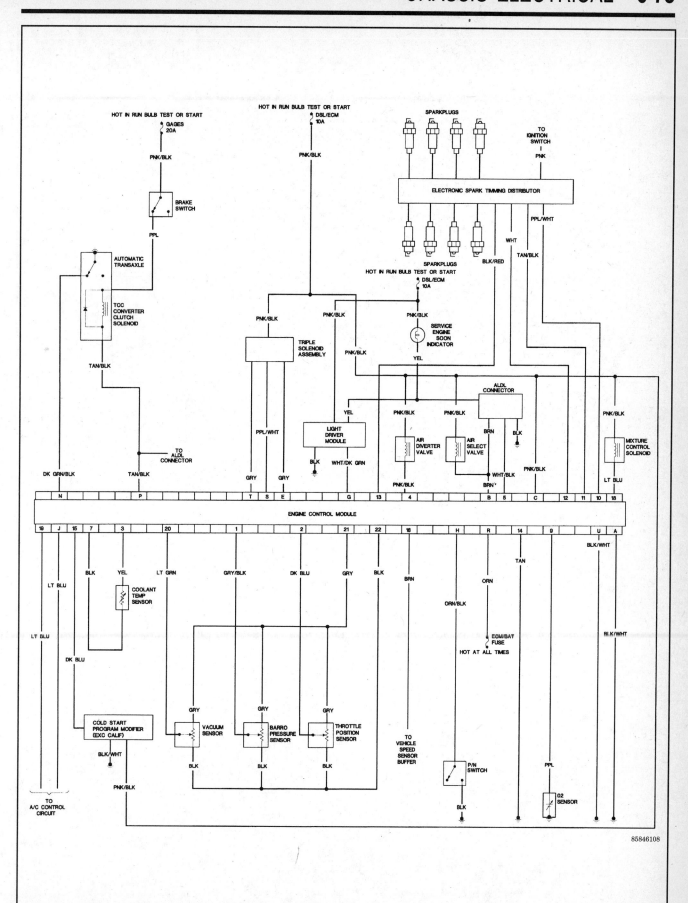

**Fig. 108 1984 Oldsmobile Custom Cruiser CCC wiring V8**

85846108

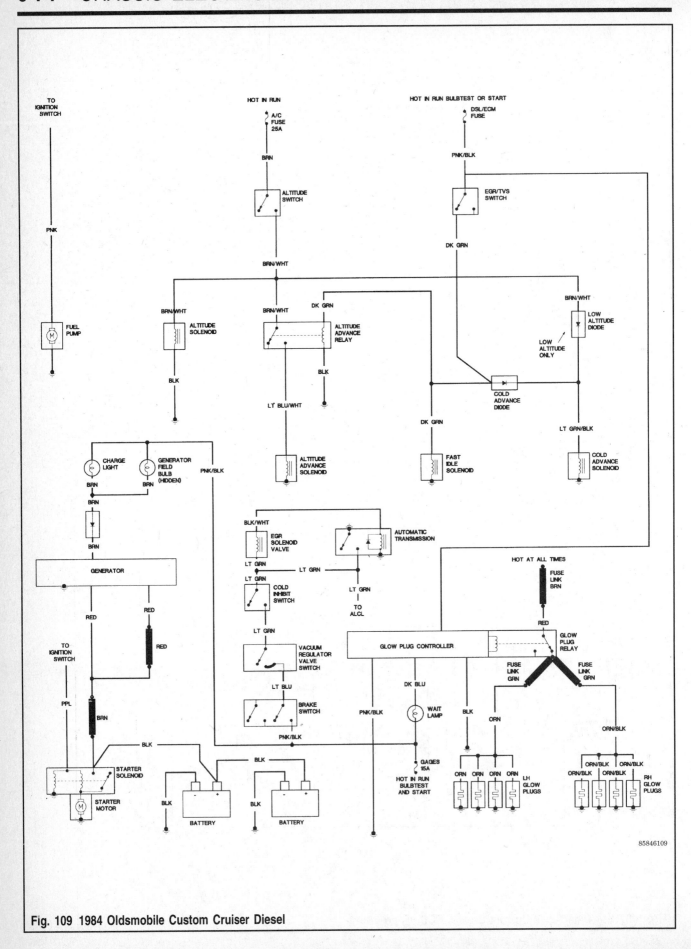

**Fig. 109  1984 Oldsmobile Custom Cruiser Diesel**

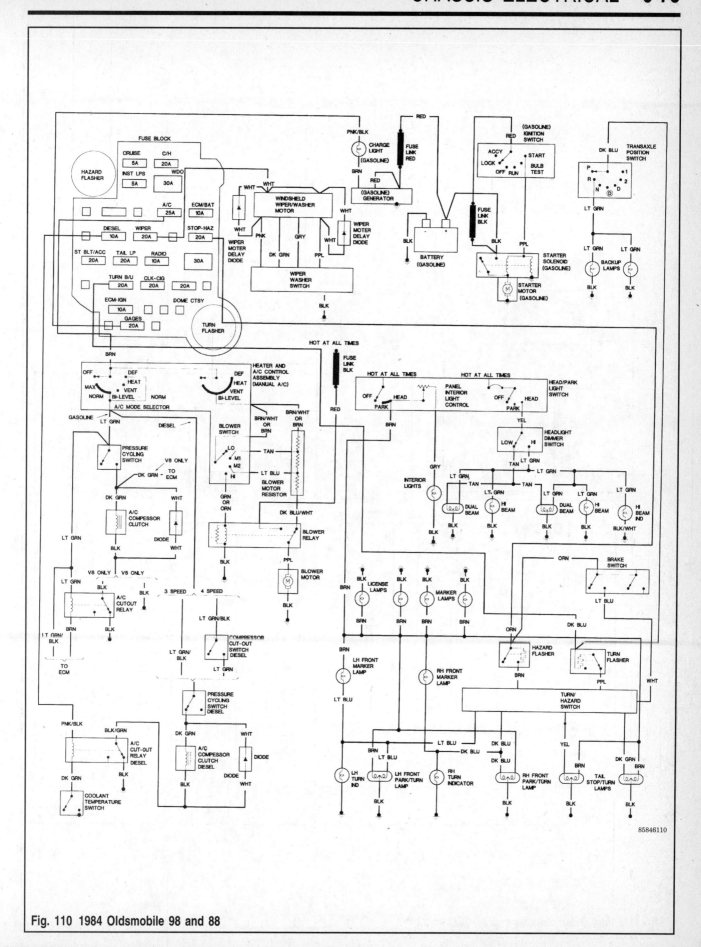

Fig. 110 1984 Oldsmobile 98 and 88

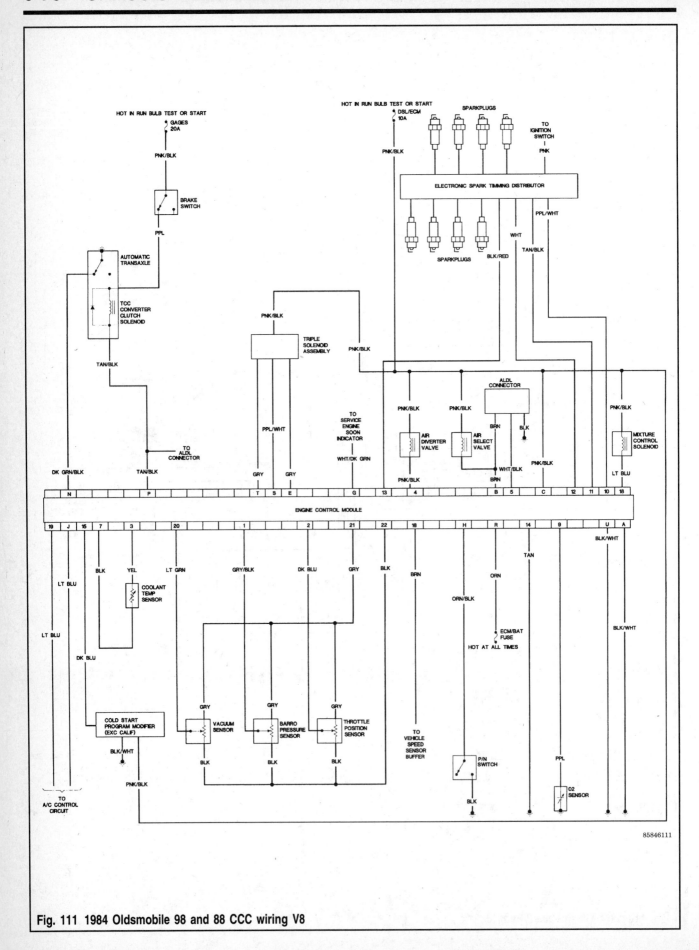

**Fig. 111** 1984 Oldsmobile 98 and 88 CCC wiring V8

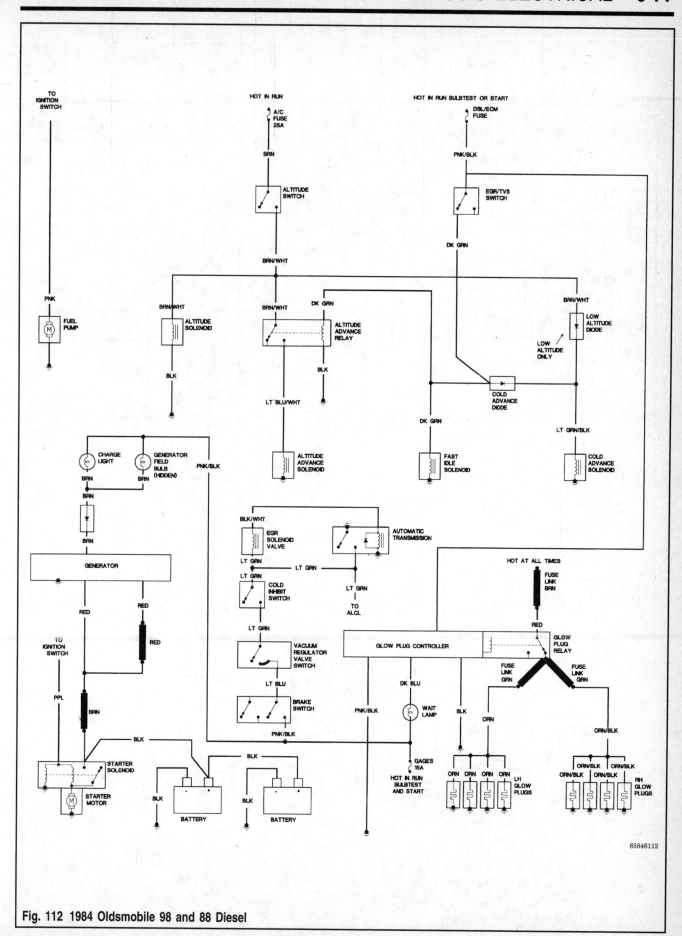

**Fig. 112 1984 Oldsmobile 98 and 88 Diesel**

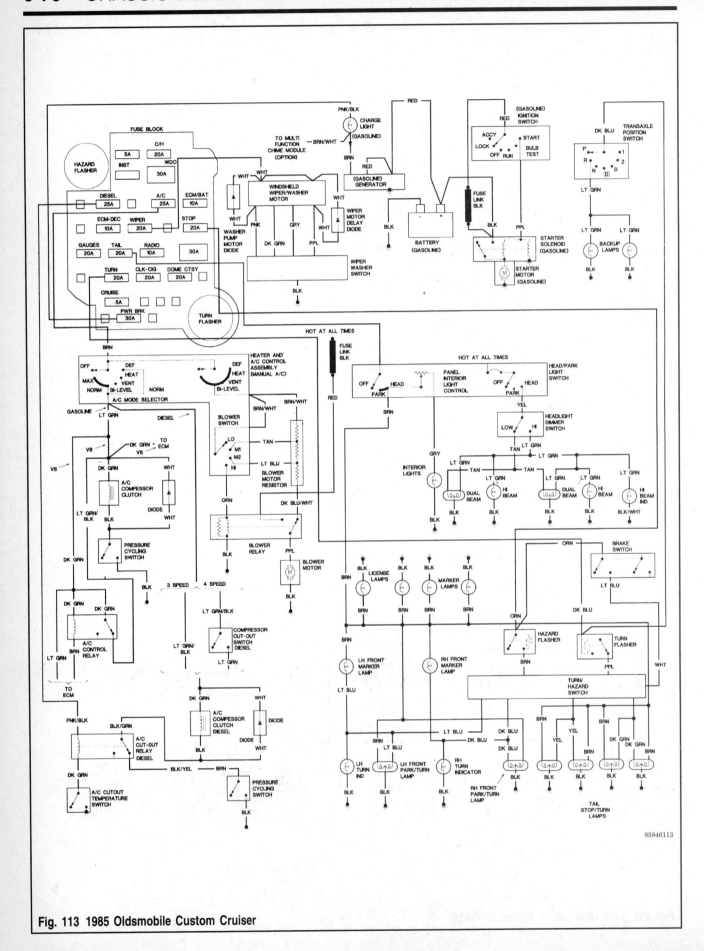

**Fig. 113** 1985 Oldsmobile Custom Cruiser

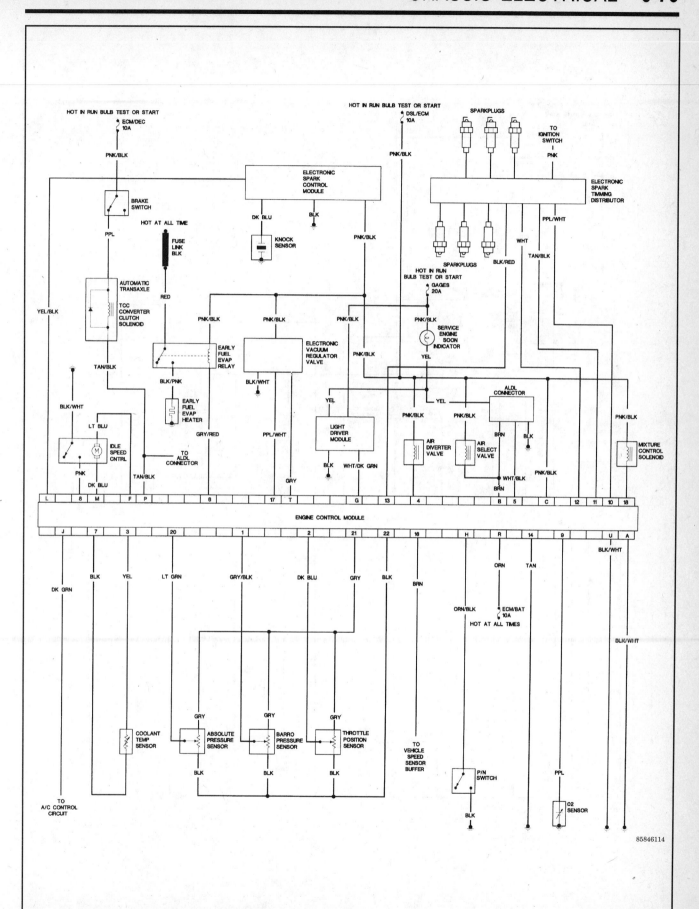

**Fig. 114 1985 Oldsmobile Custom Cruiser CCC wiring (VIN A)**

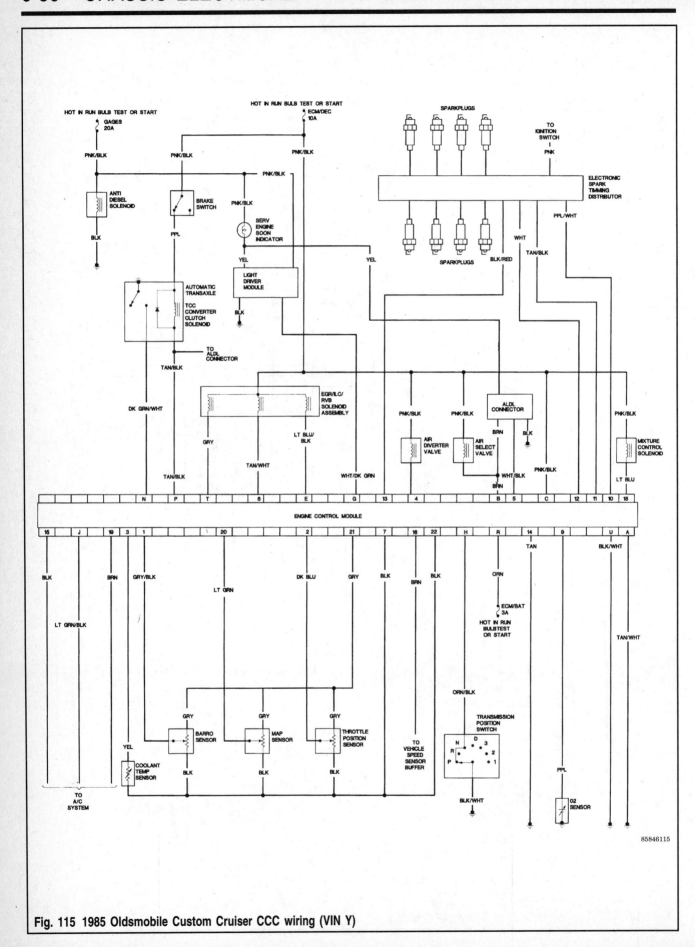

**Fig. 115 1985 Oldsmobile Custom Cruiser CCC wiring (VIN Y)**

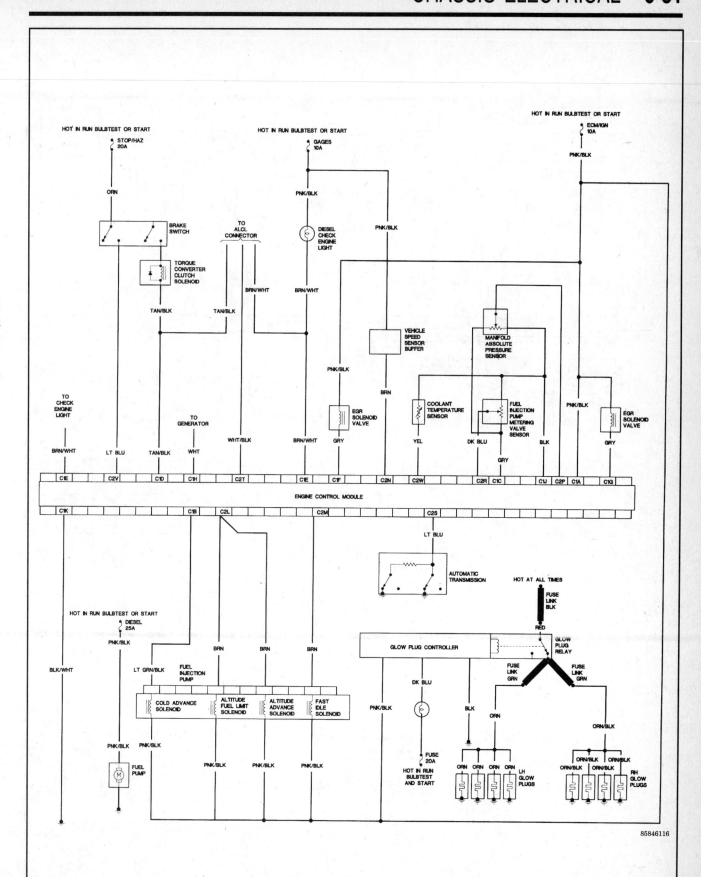

**Fig. 116 1985 Oldsmobile Custom Cruiser Diesel**

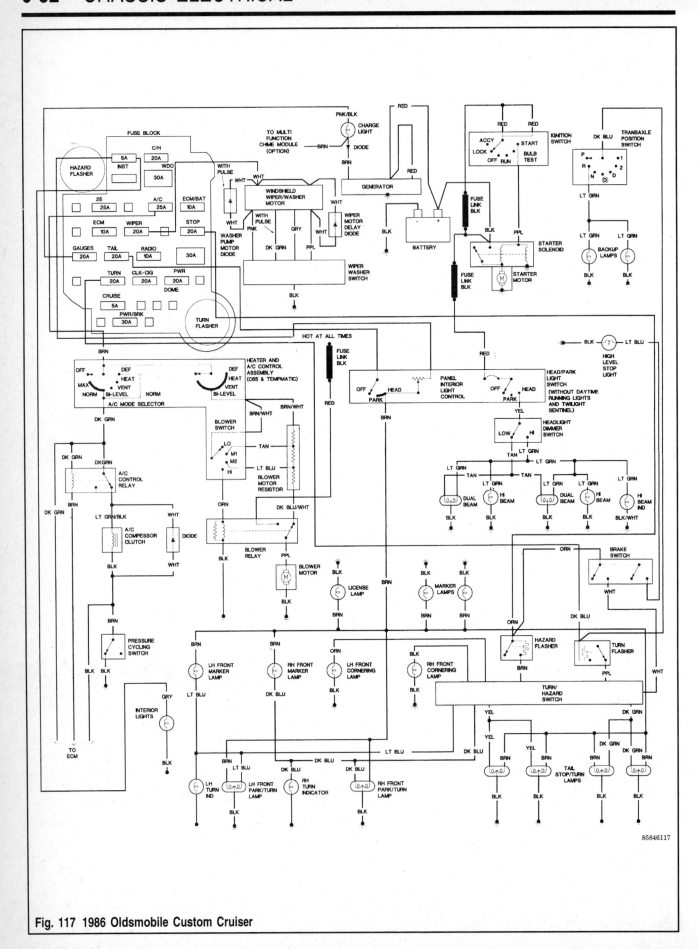

**Fig. 117 1986 Oldsmobile Custom Cruiser**

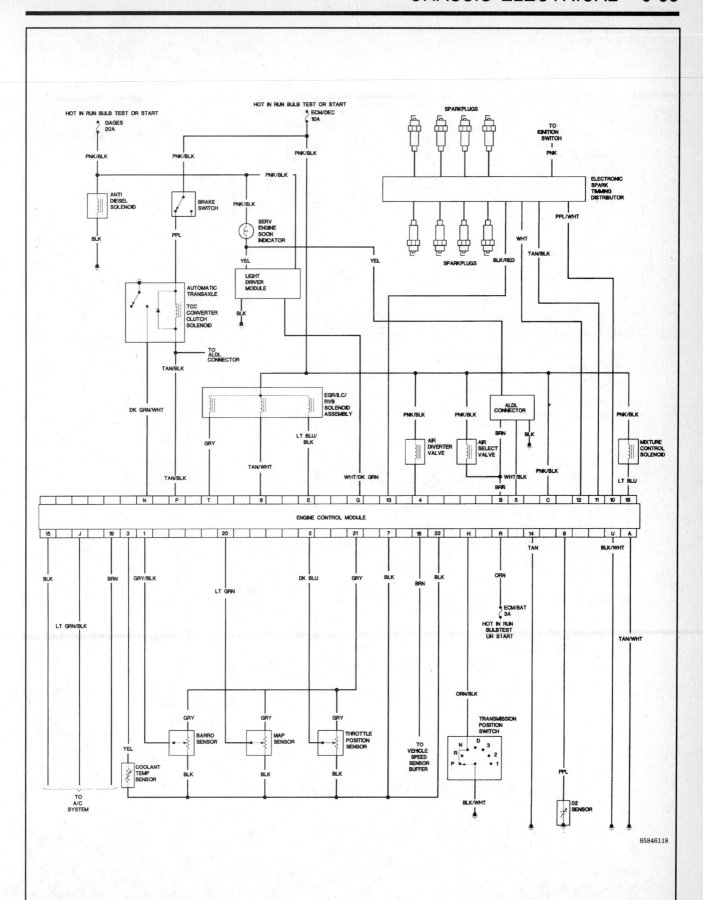

**Fig. 118 1986 Oldsmobile Custom Cruiser CCC wiring (VIN Y)**

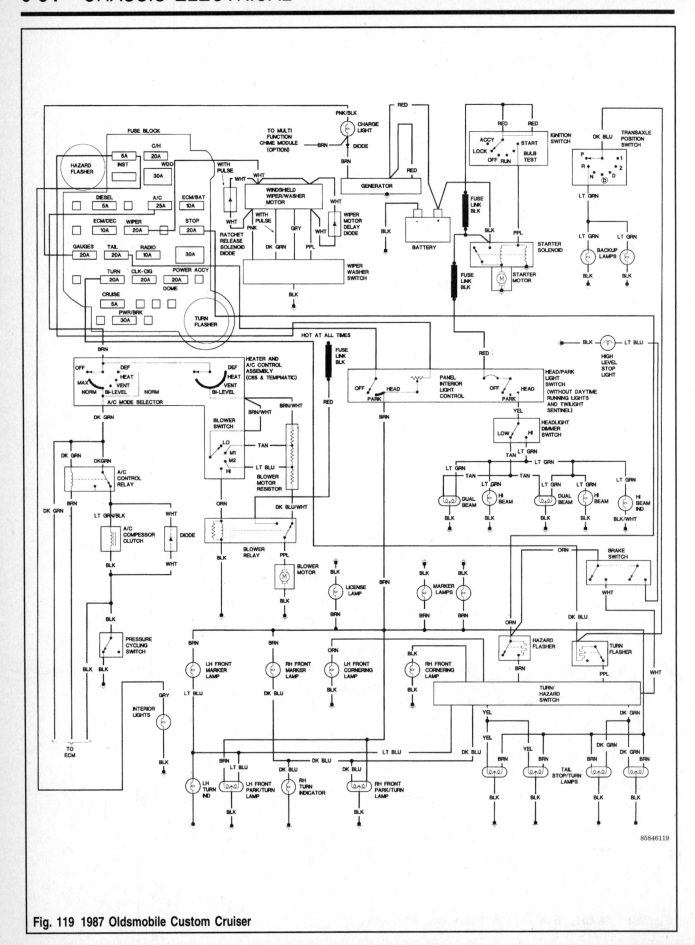

**Fig. 119  1987 Oldsmobile Custom Cruiser**

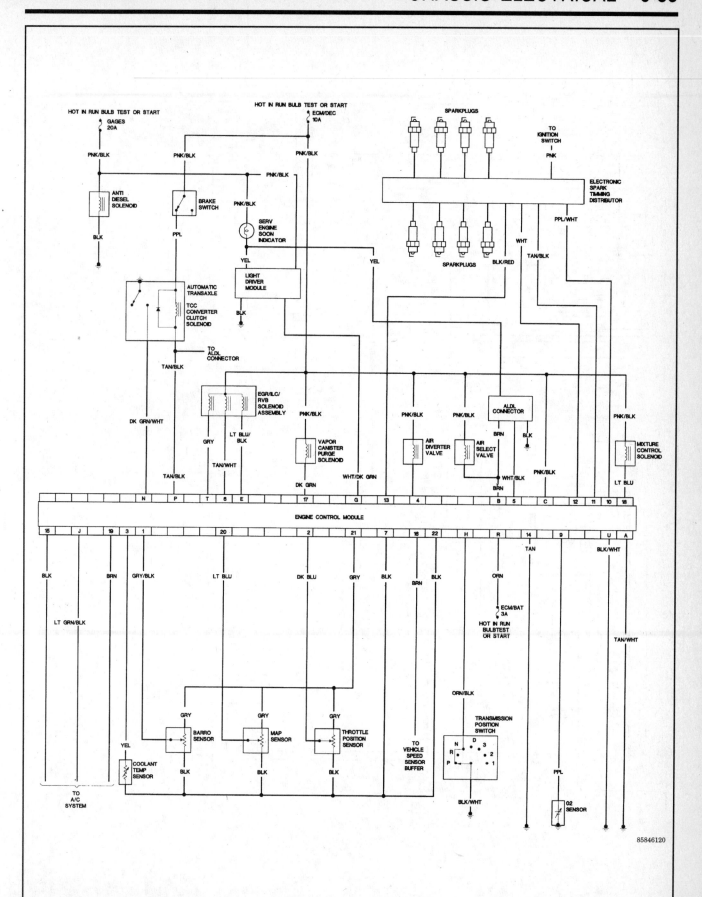

**Fig. 120 1987 Oldsmobile Custom Cruiser CCC wiring (VIN Y)**

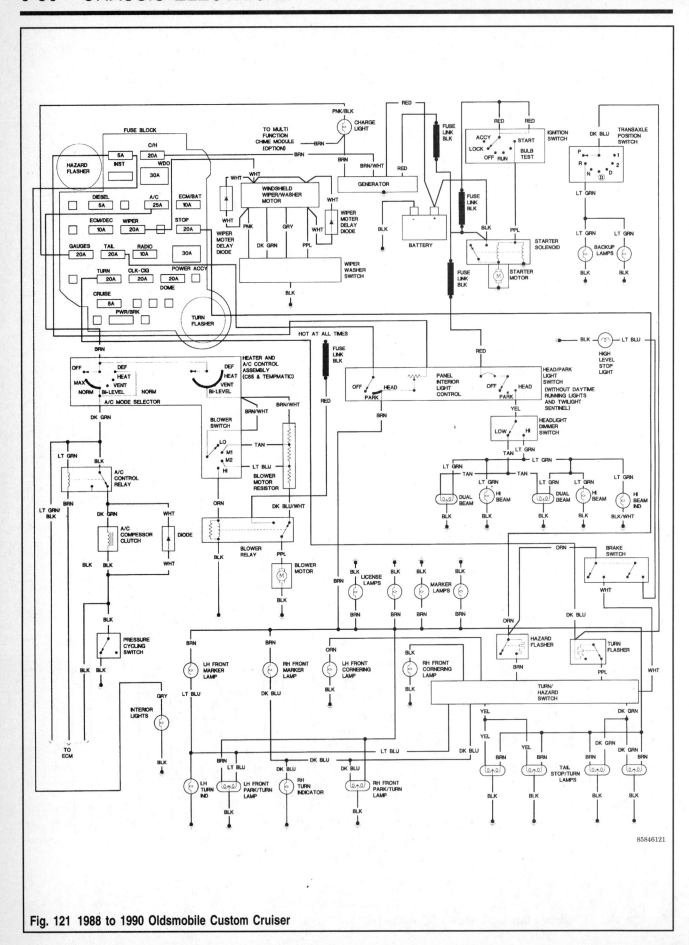

**Fig. 121 1988 to 1990 Oldsmobile Custom Cruiser**

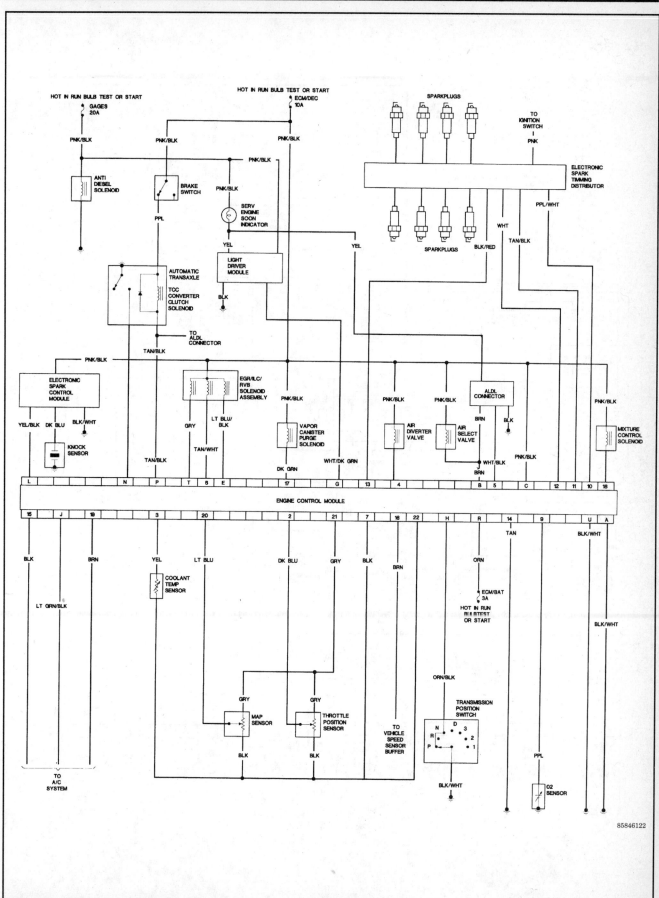

**Fig. 122 1988 to 1990 Oldsmobile Custom Cruiser CCC wiring (VIN Y)**

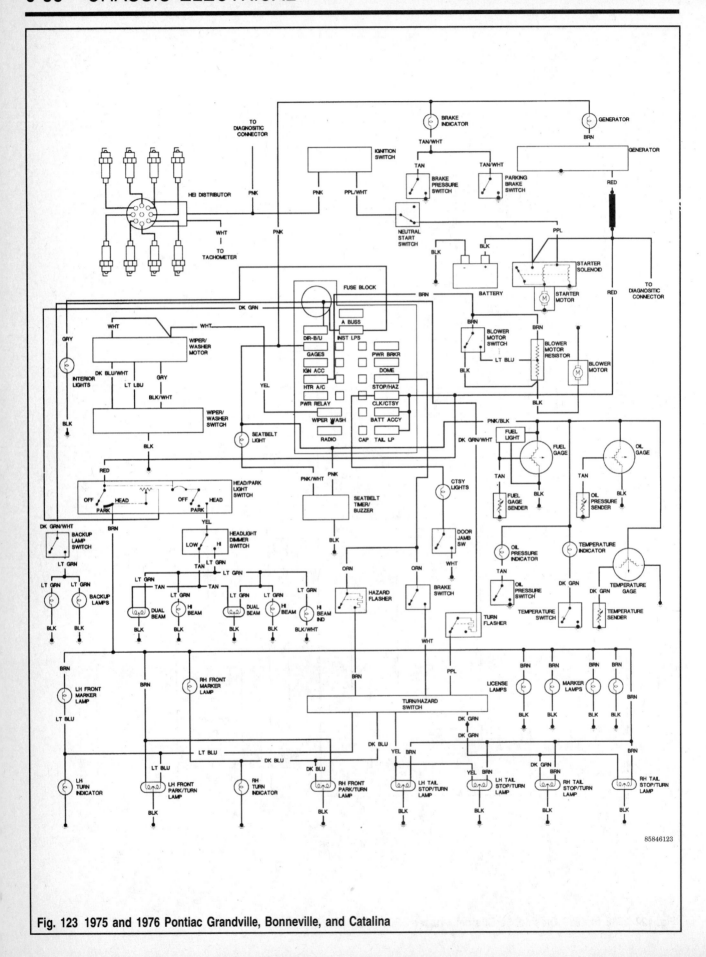

Fig. 123 1975 and 1976 Pontiac Grandville, Bonneville, and Catalina

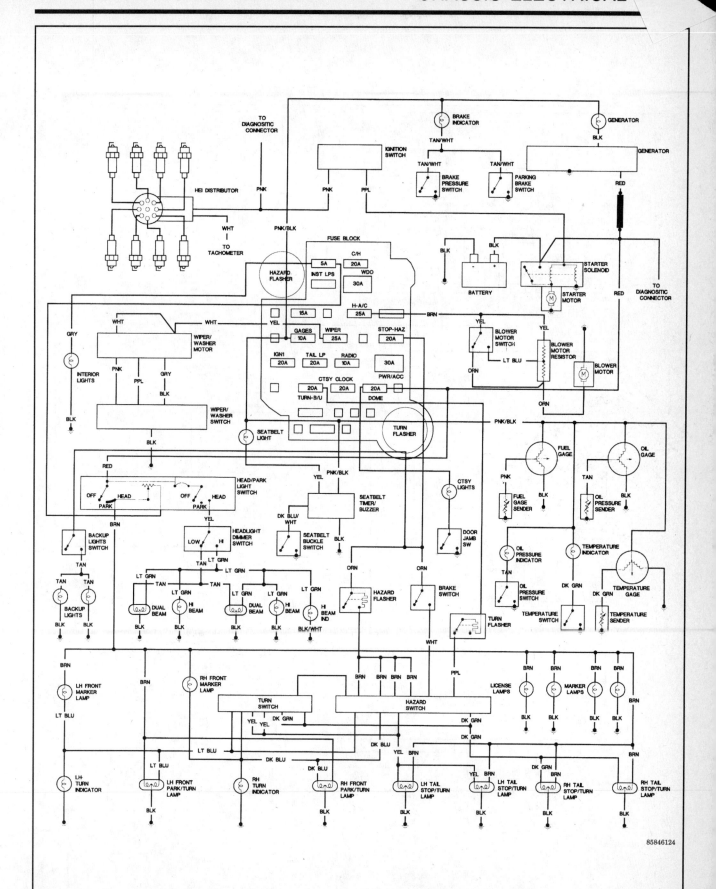

**Fig. 124 1977 to 1979 Pontiac Bonneville and Catalina**

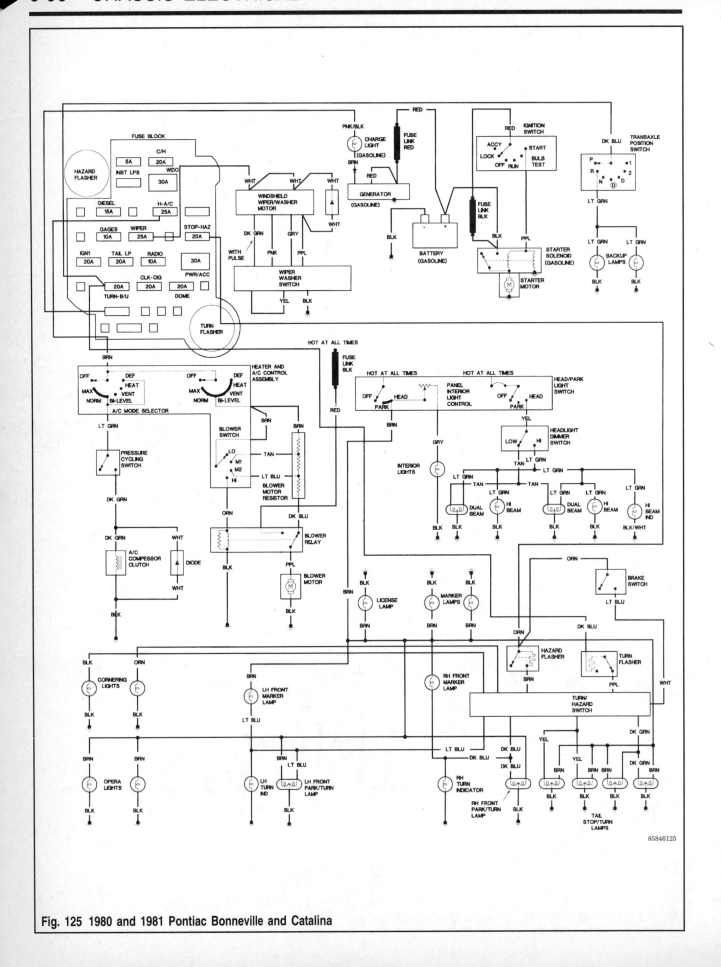

**Fig. 125** 1980 and 1981 Pontiac Bonneville and Catalina

85846125

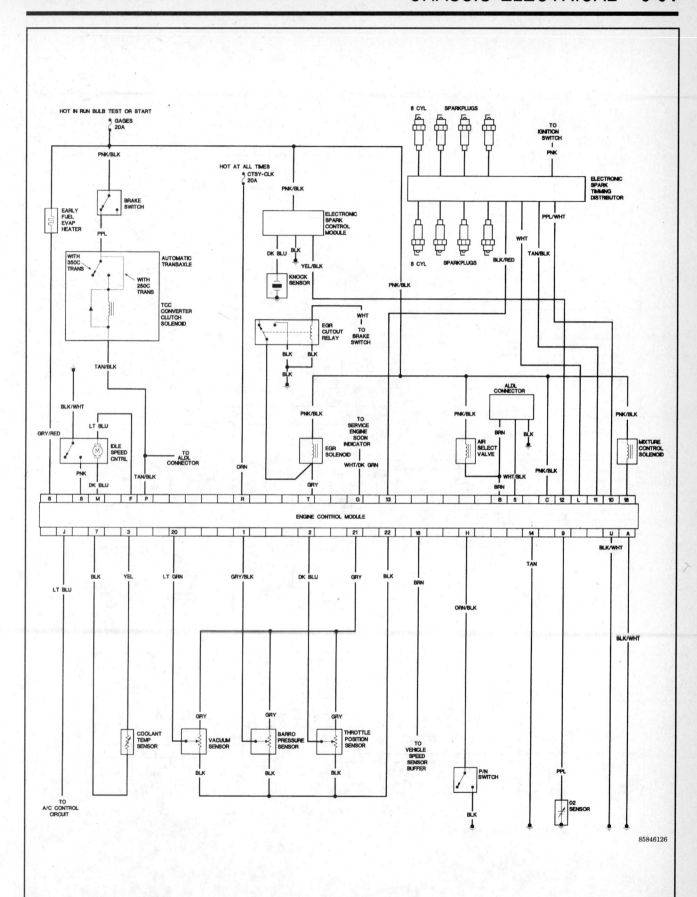

Fig. 126 1981 Pontiac Bonneville and Catalina CCC wiring

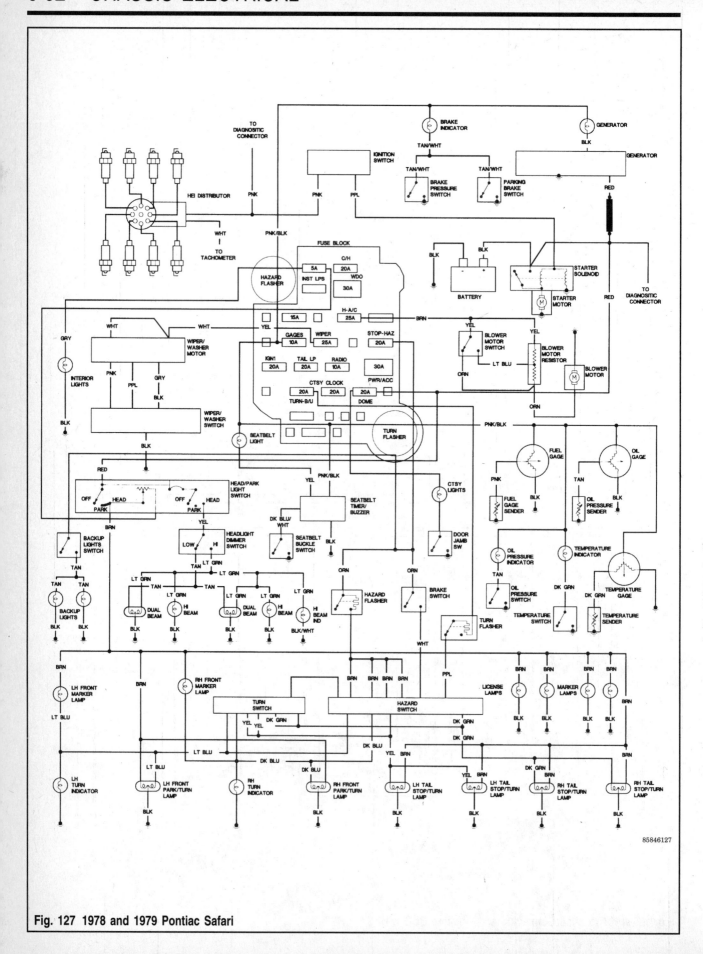

**Fig. 127** 1978 and 1979 Pontiac Safari

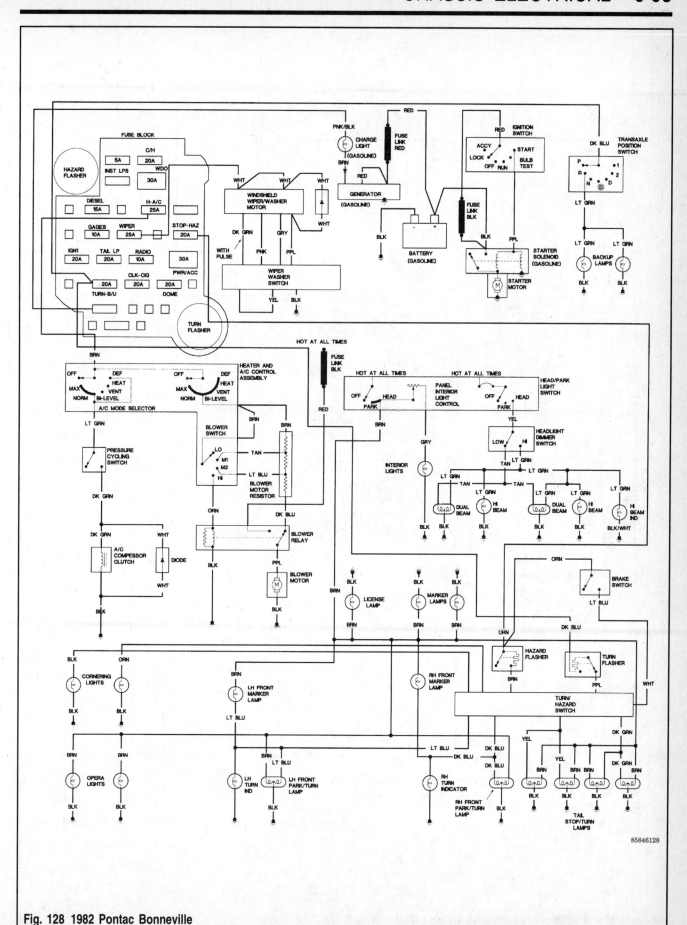

**Fig. 128 1982 Pontac Bonneville**

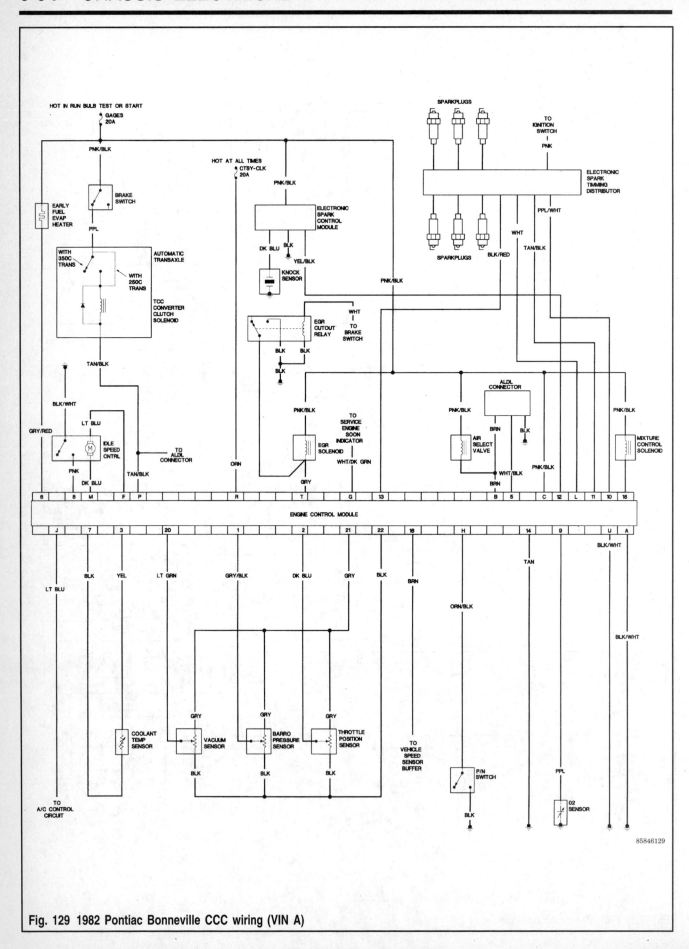

**Fig. 129 1982 Pontiac Bonneville CCC wiring (VIN A)**

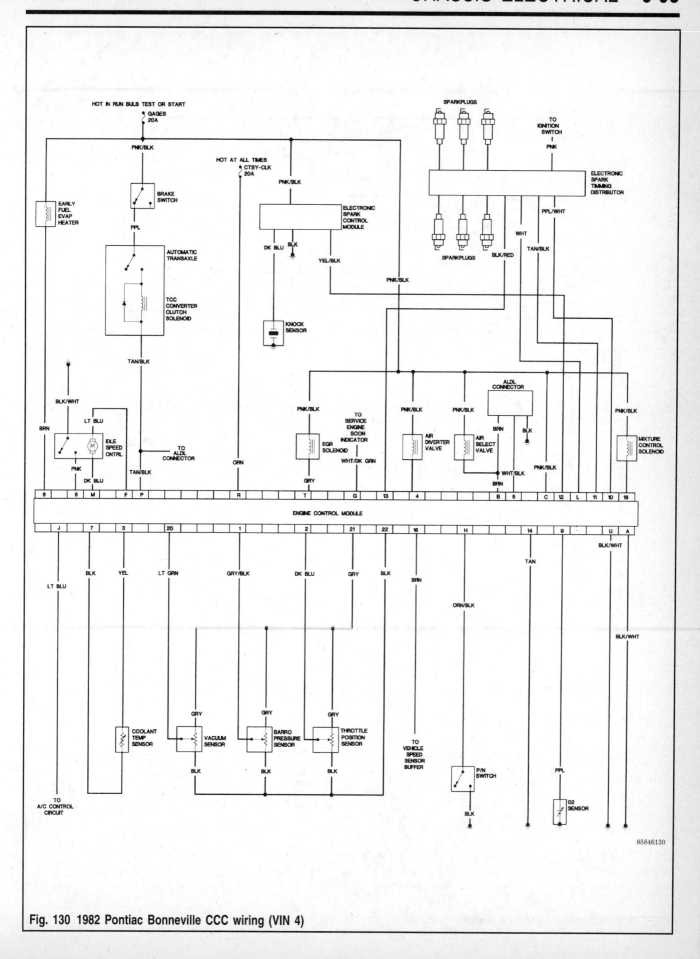

**Fig. 130 1982 Pontiac Bonneville CCC wiring (VIN 4)**

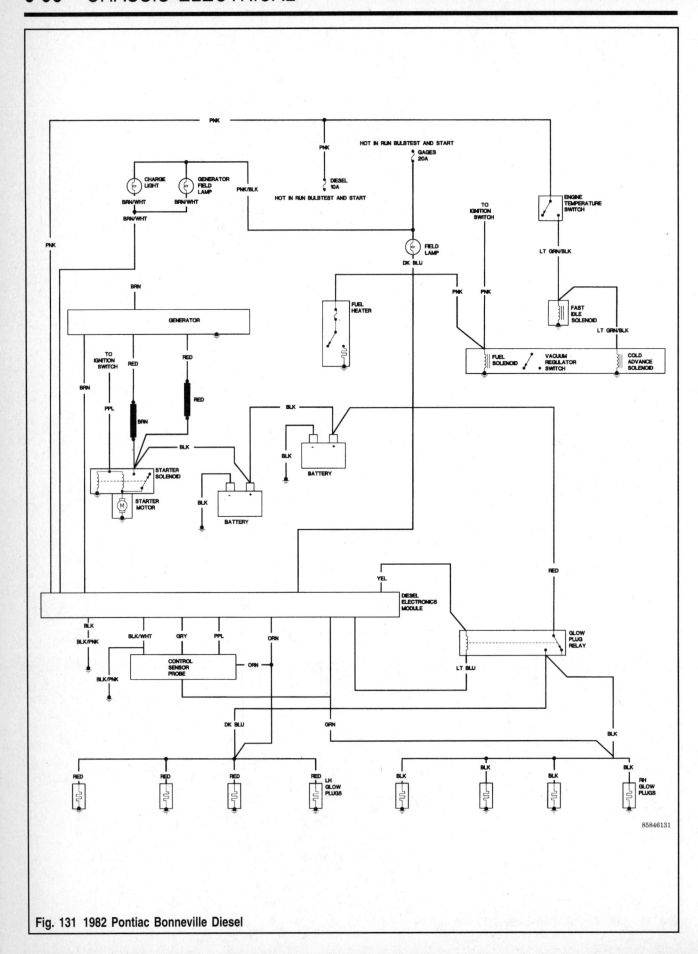

**Fig. 131 1982 Pontiac Bonneville Diesel**

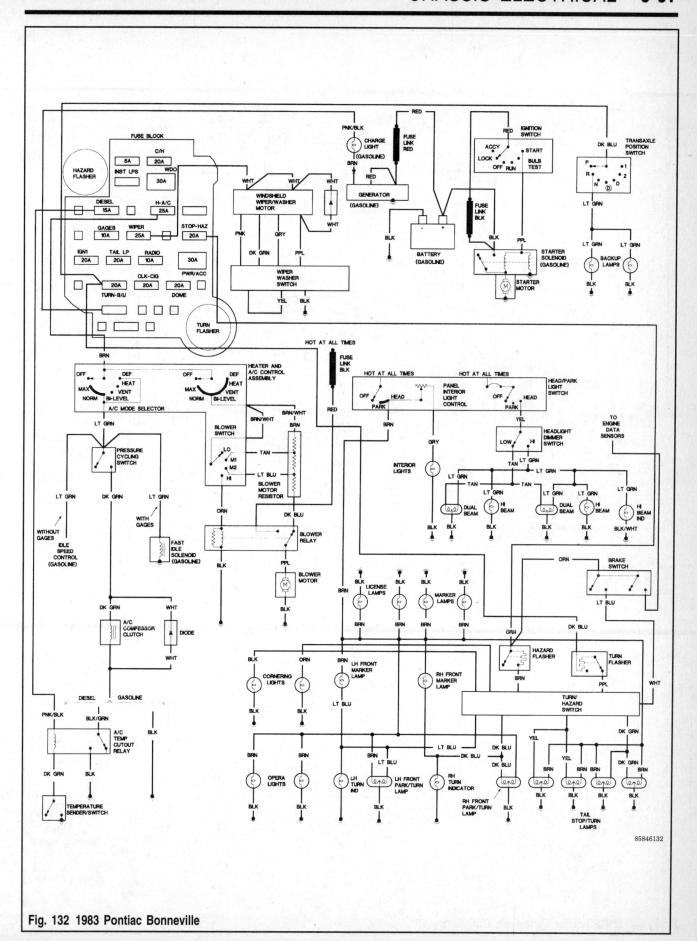

**Fig. 132 1983 Pontiac Bonneville**

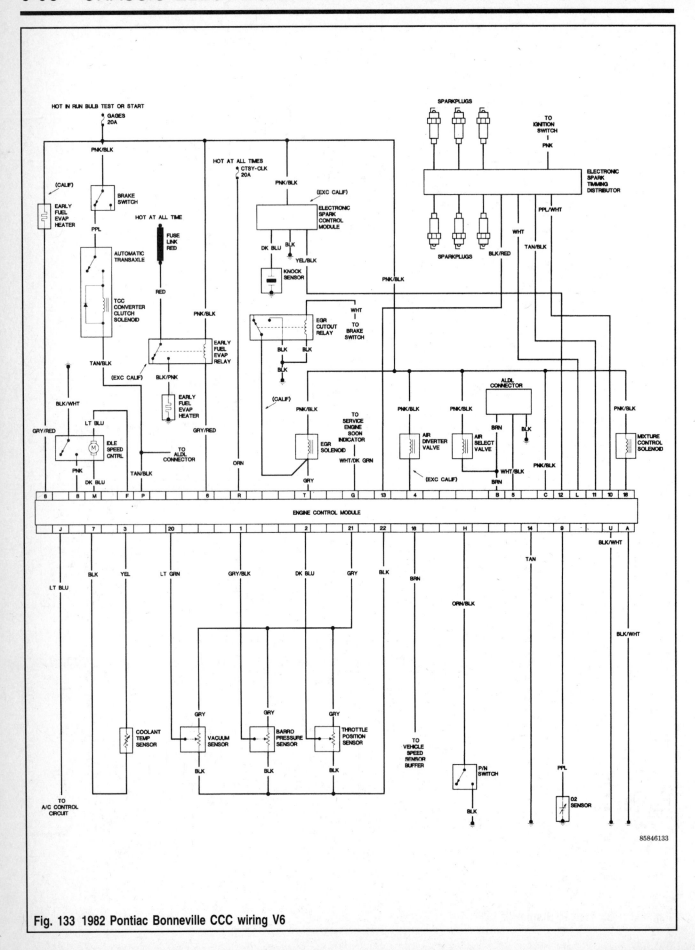

**Fig. 133 1982 Pontiac Bonneville CCC wiring V6**

85846133

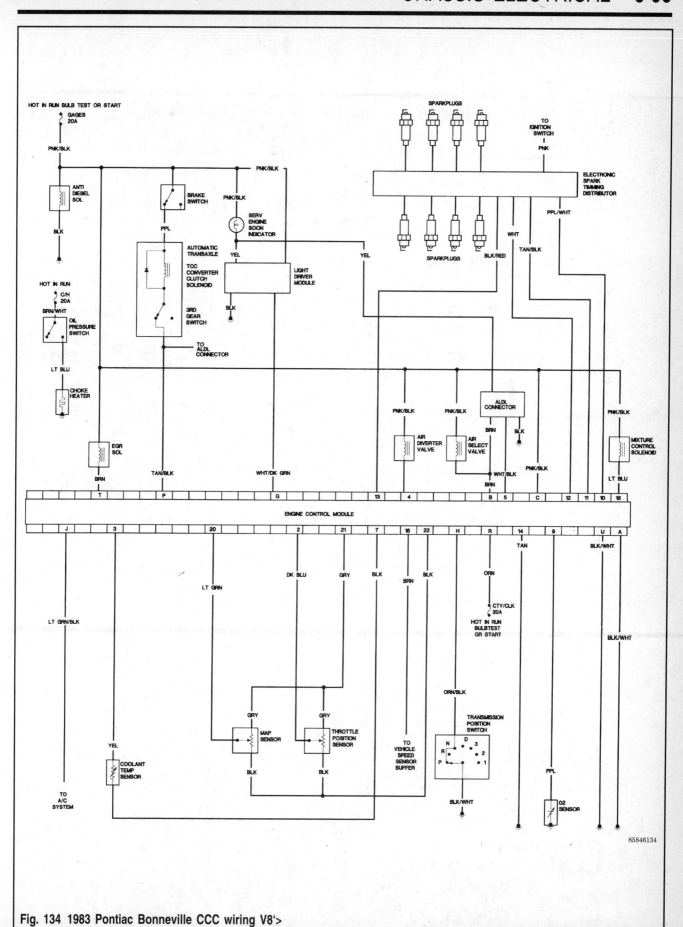

Fig. 134 1983 Pontiac Bonneville CCC wiring V8‹>

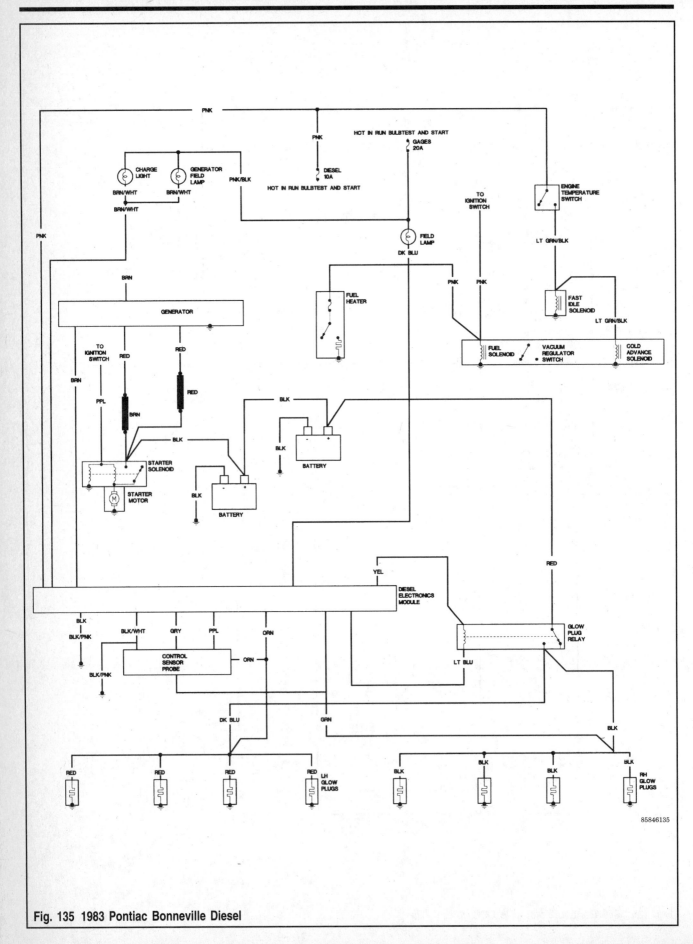

**Fig. 135 1983 Pontiac Bonneville Diesel**

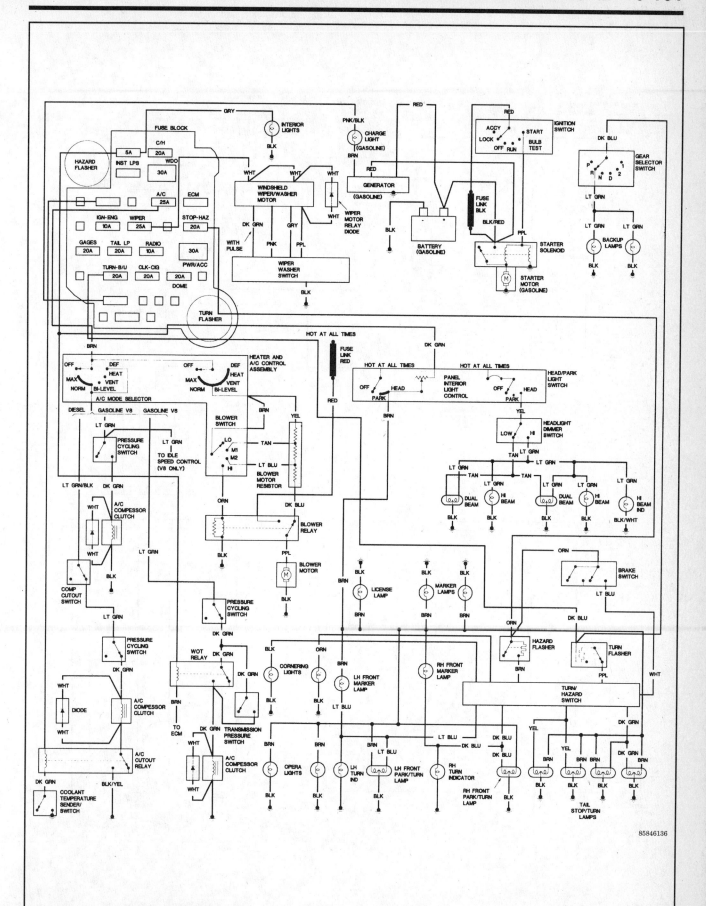

**Fig. 136 1983 Pontiac Parisienne**

85846136

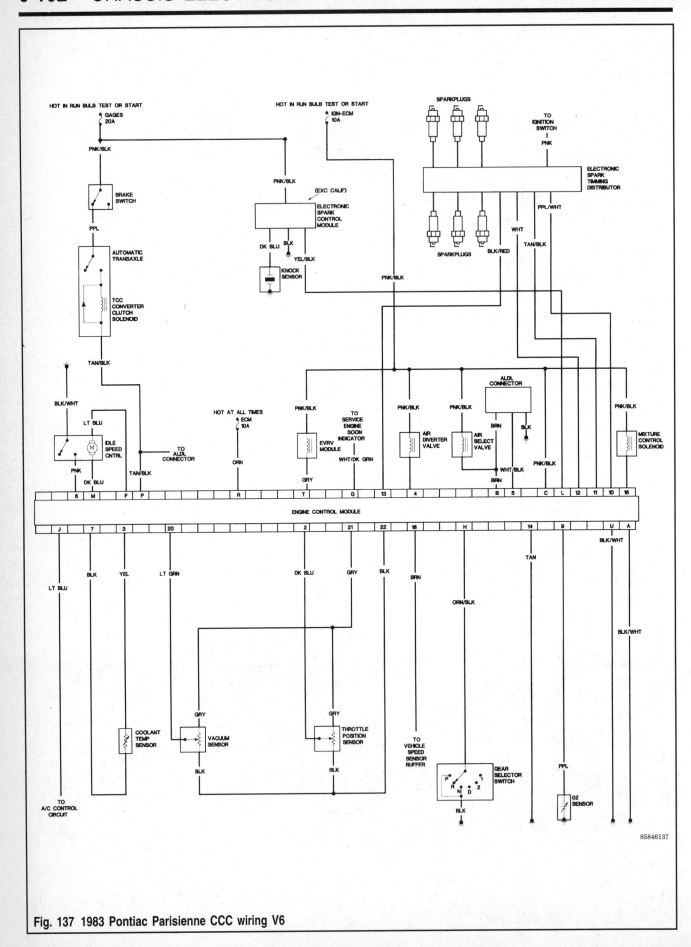

**Fig. 137 1983 Pontiac Parisienne CCC wiring V6**

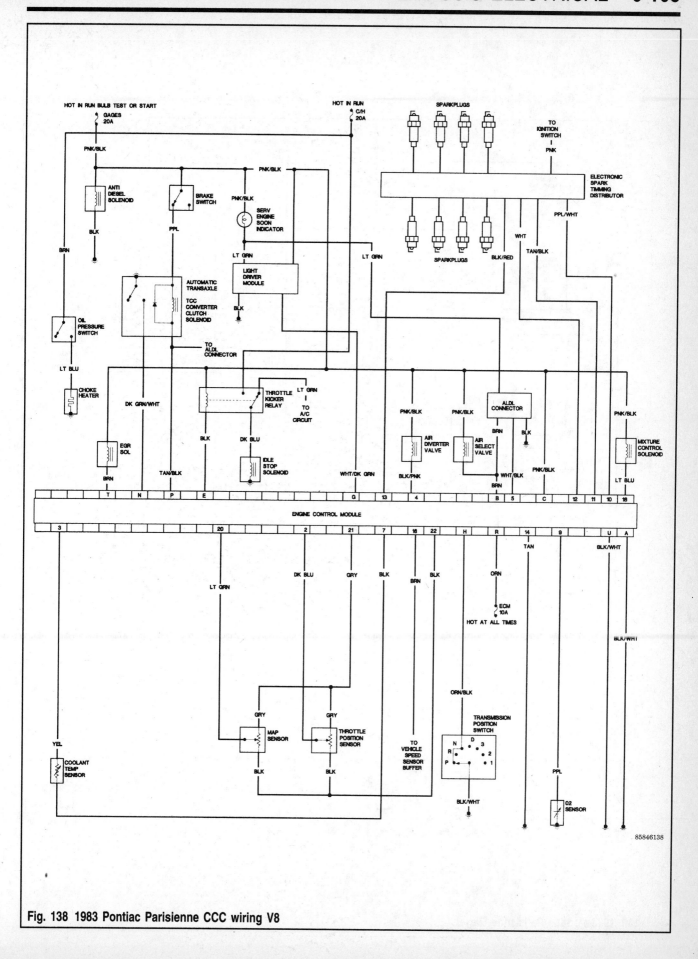

**Fig. 138 1983 Pontiac Parisienne CCC wiring V8**

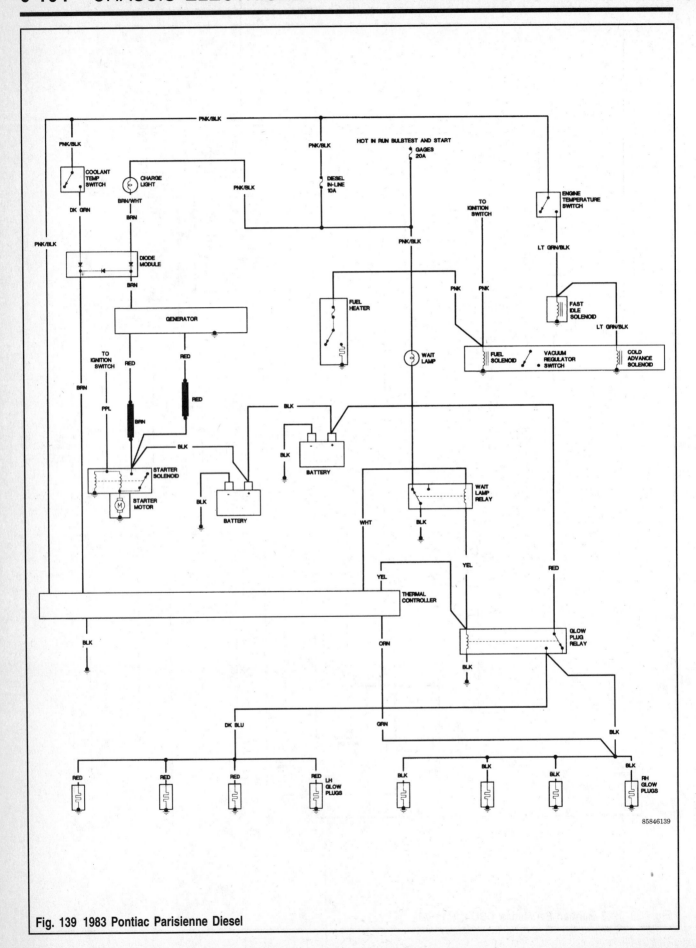

**Fig. 139  1983 Pontiac Parisienne Diesel**

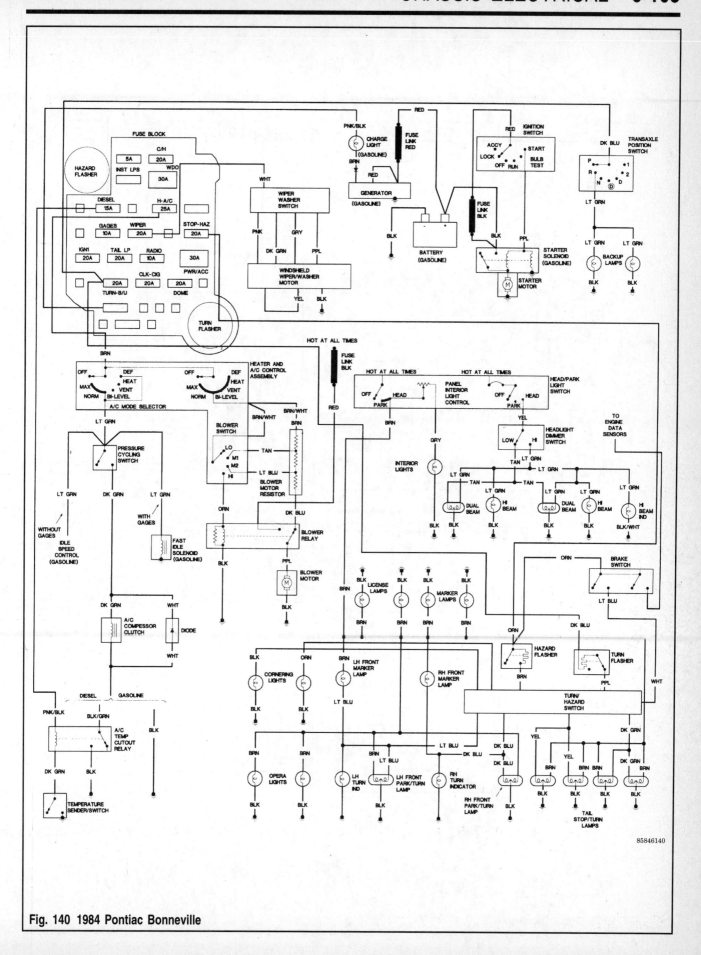

**Fig. 140 1984 Pontiac Bonneville**

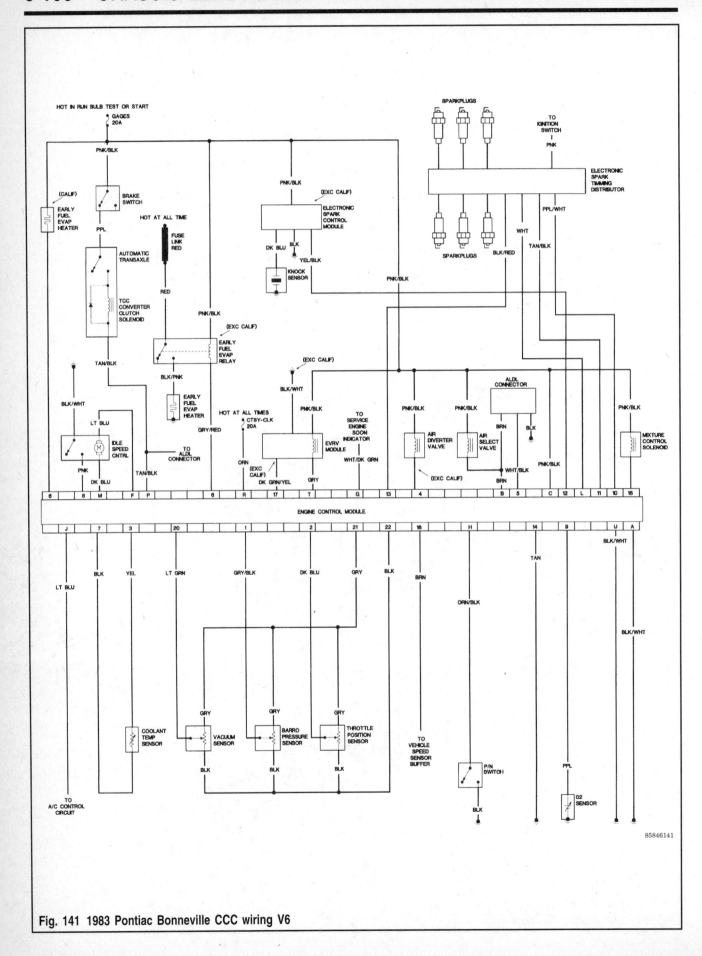

**Fig. 141 1983 Pontiac Bonneville CCC wiring V6**

85846141

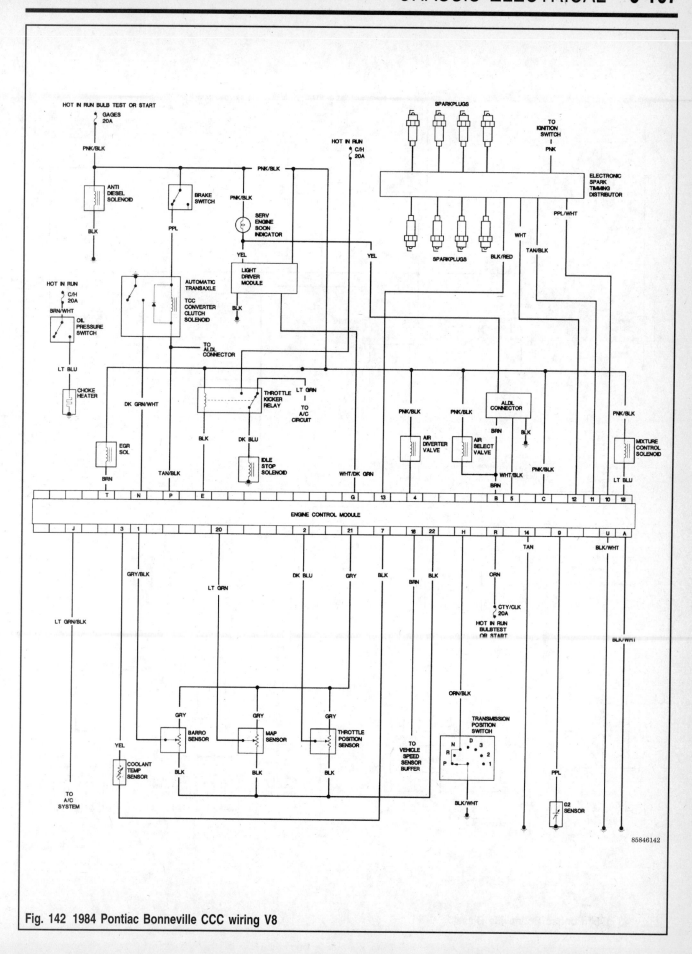

**Fig. 142 1984 Pontiac Bonneville CCC wiring V8**

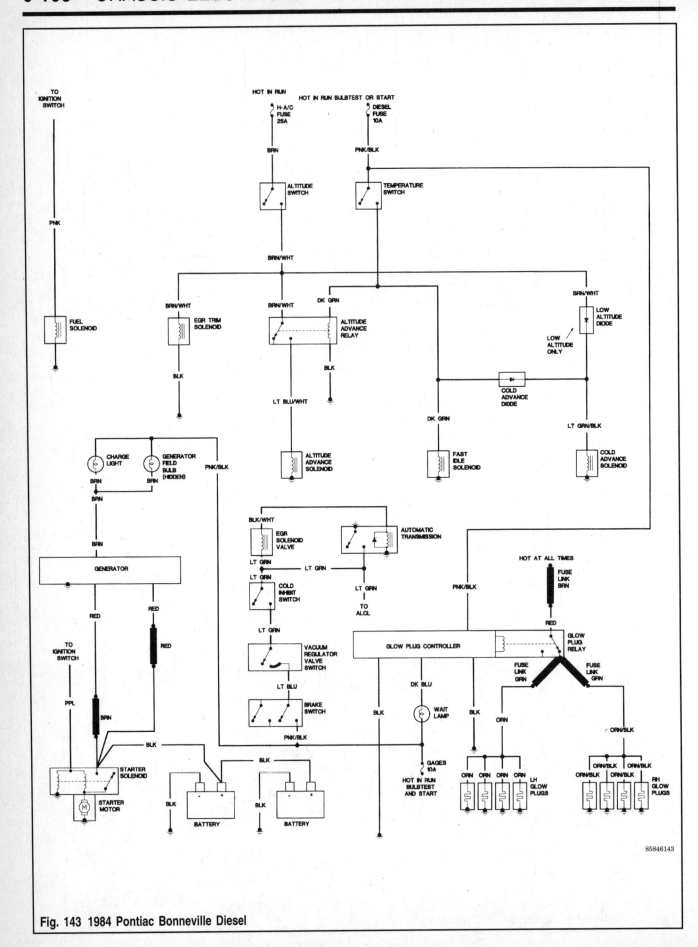

**Fig. 143** 1984 Pontiac Bonneville Diesel

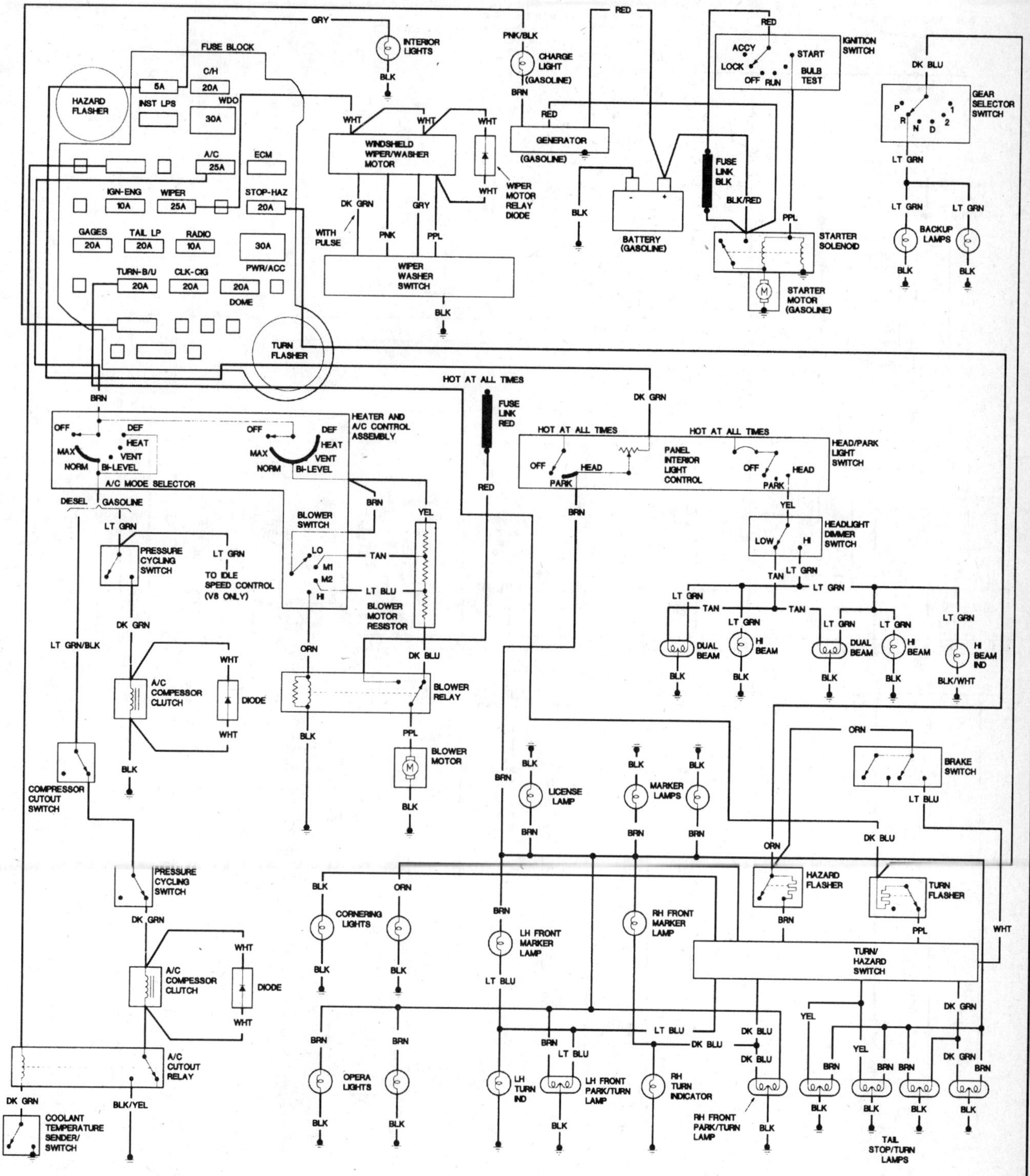

**Fig. 144  1984 Pontiac Parisienne**

85846144

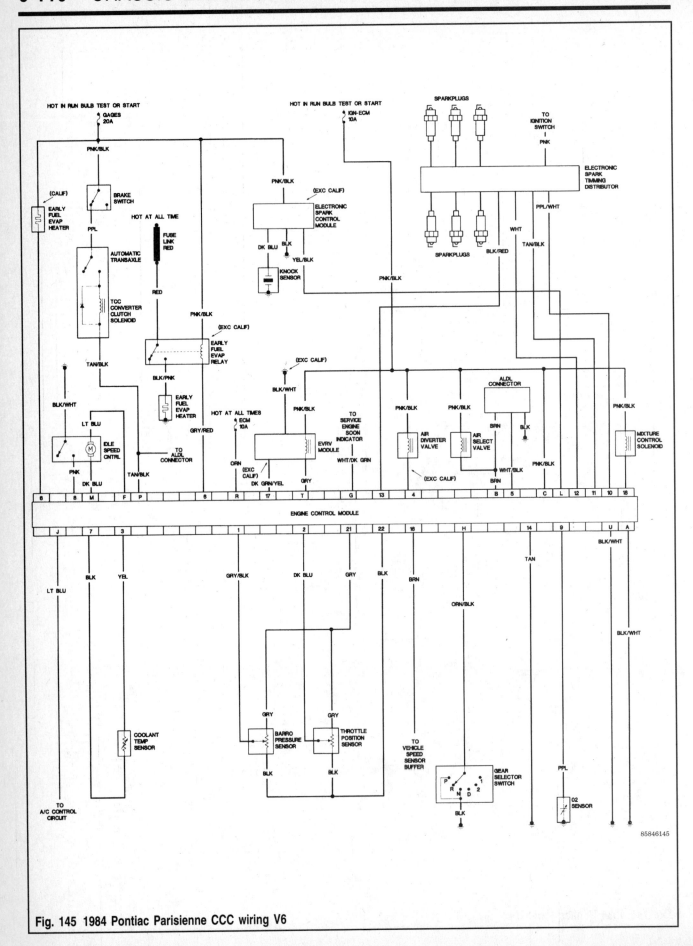

**Fig. 145 1984 Pontiac Parisienne CCC wiring V6**

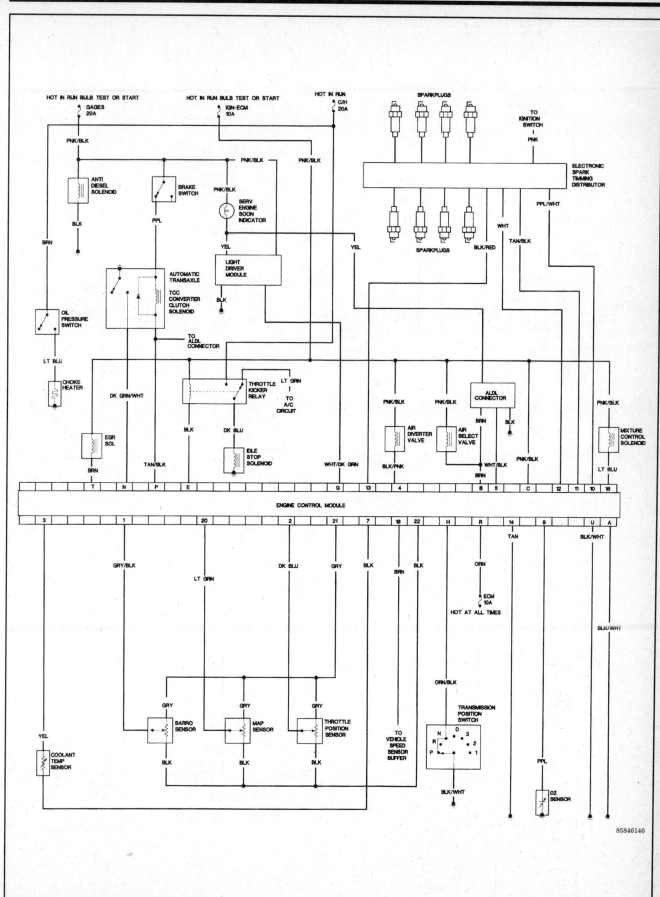

Fig. 146  1984 Pontiac Parisienne CCC wiring V8

85846146

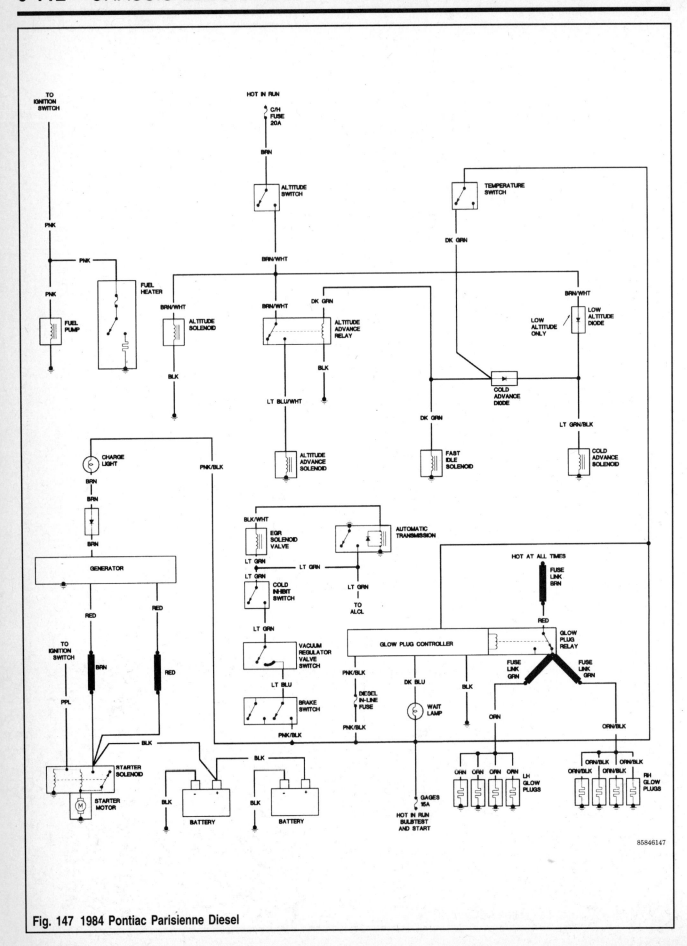

**Fig. 147 1984 Pontiac Parisienne Diesel**

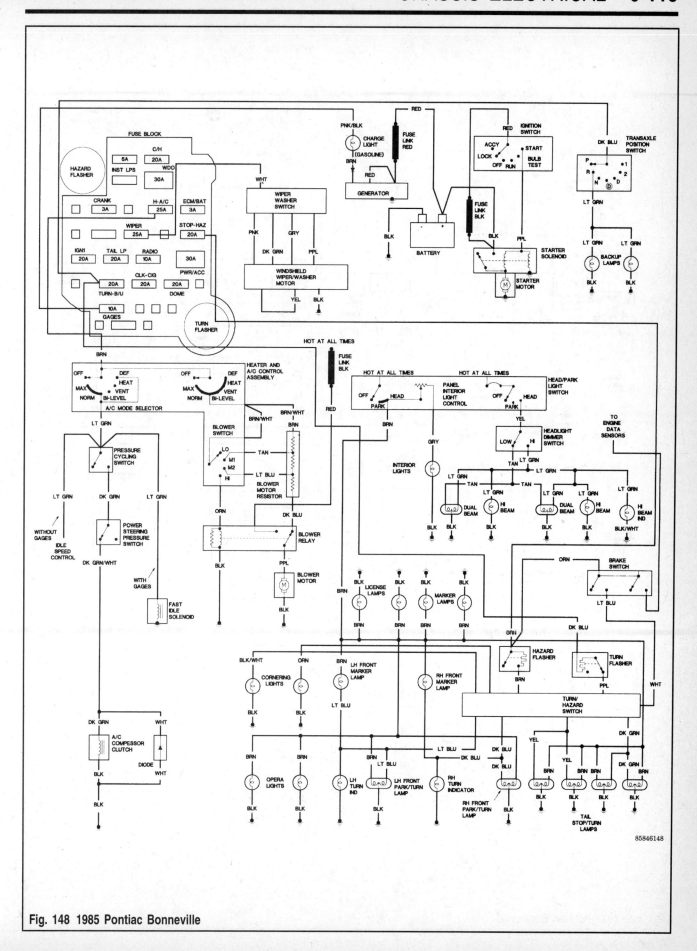

Fig. 148 1985 Pontiac Bonneville

85846148

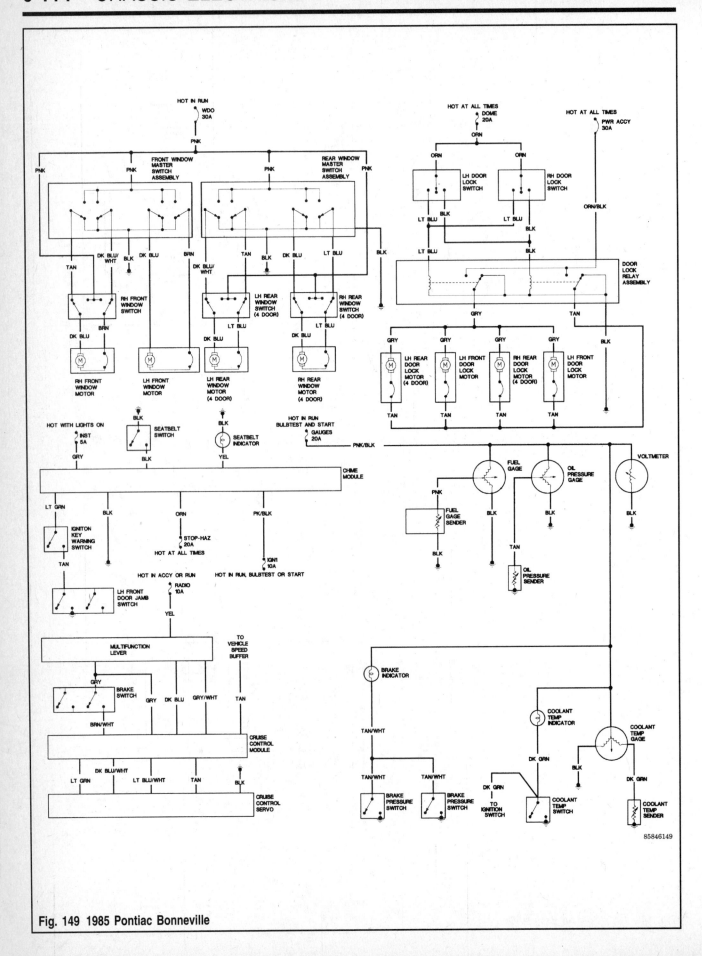

**Fig. 149 1985 Pontiac Bonneville**

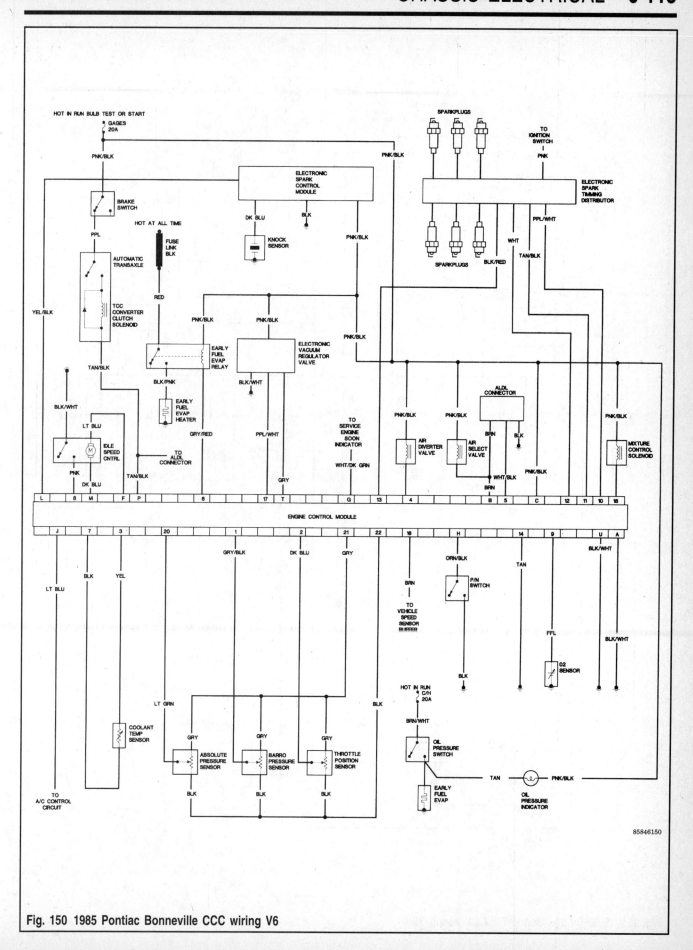

Fig. 150 1985 Pontiac Bonneville CCC wiring V6

85846150

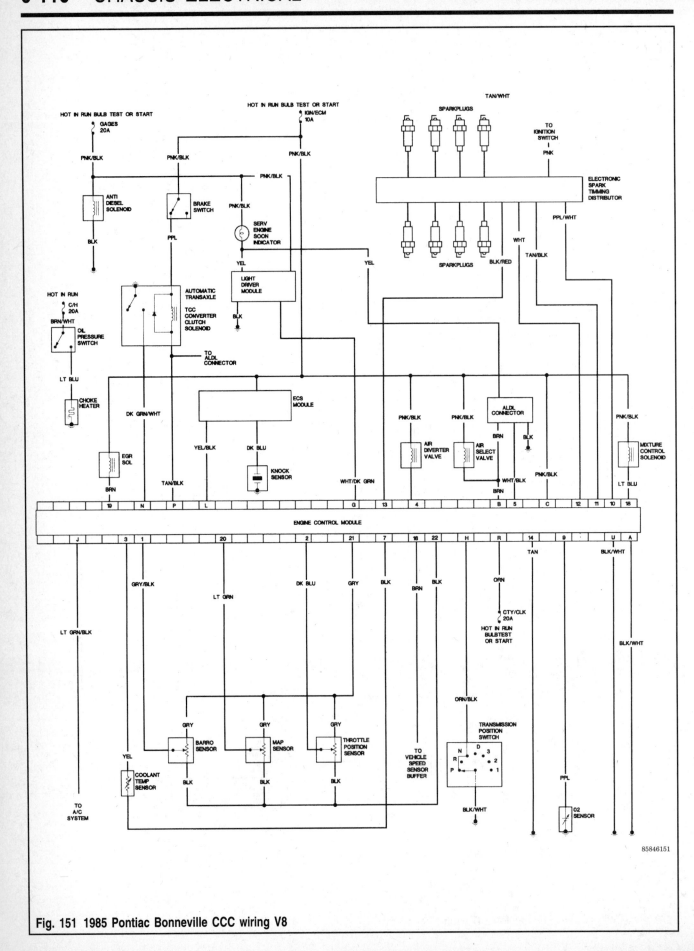

**Fig. 151 1985 Pontiac Bonneville CCC wiring V8**

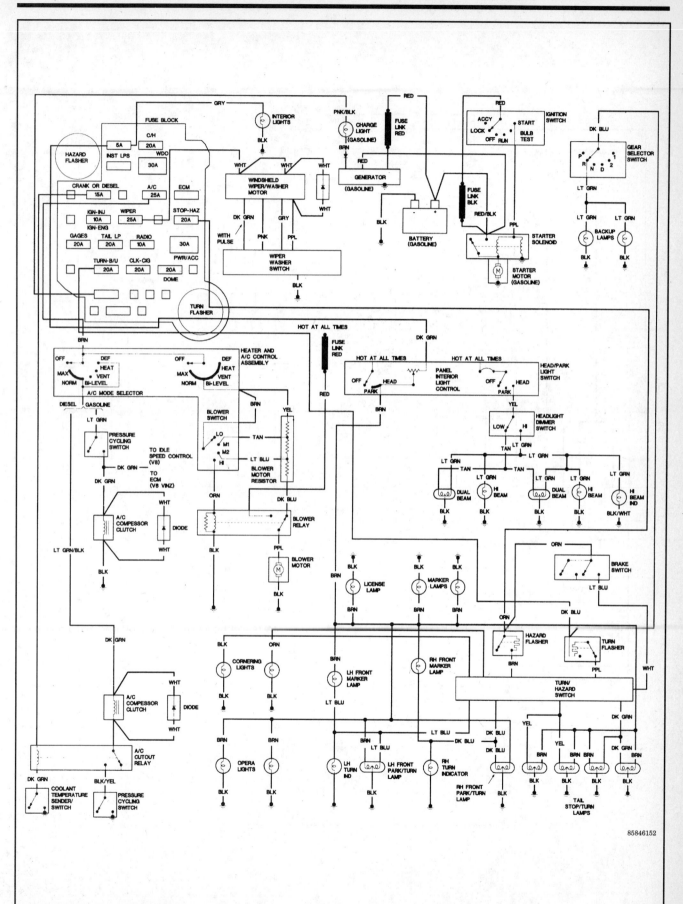

**Fig. 152 1985 Pontiac Parisienne**

85846152

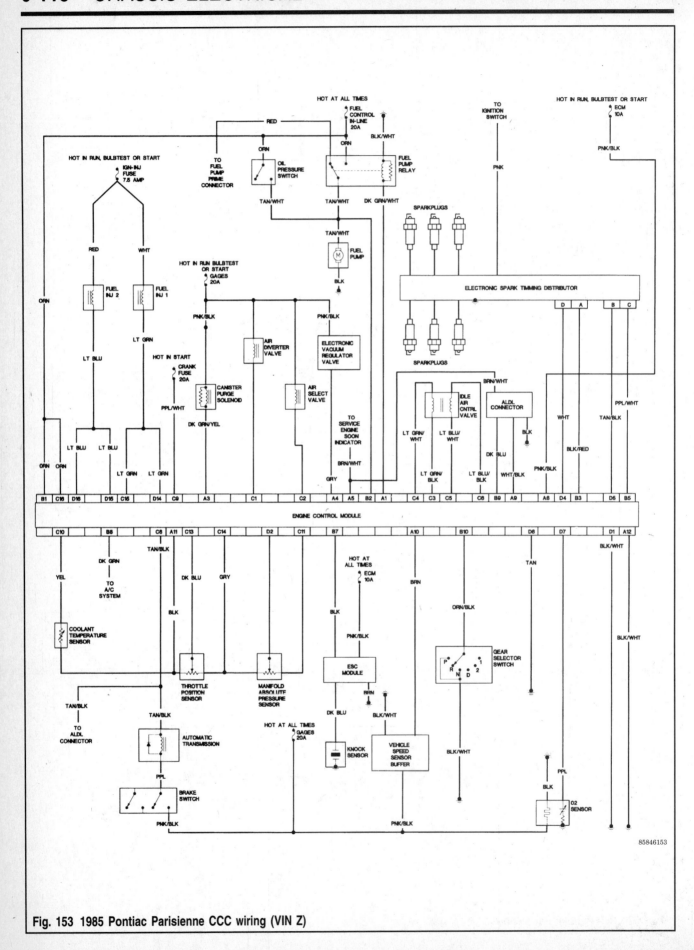

**Fig. 153** 1985 Pontiac Parisienne CCC wiring (VIN Z)

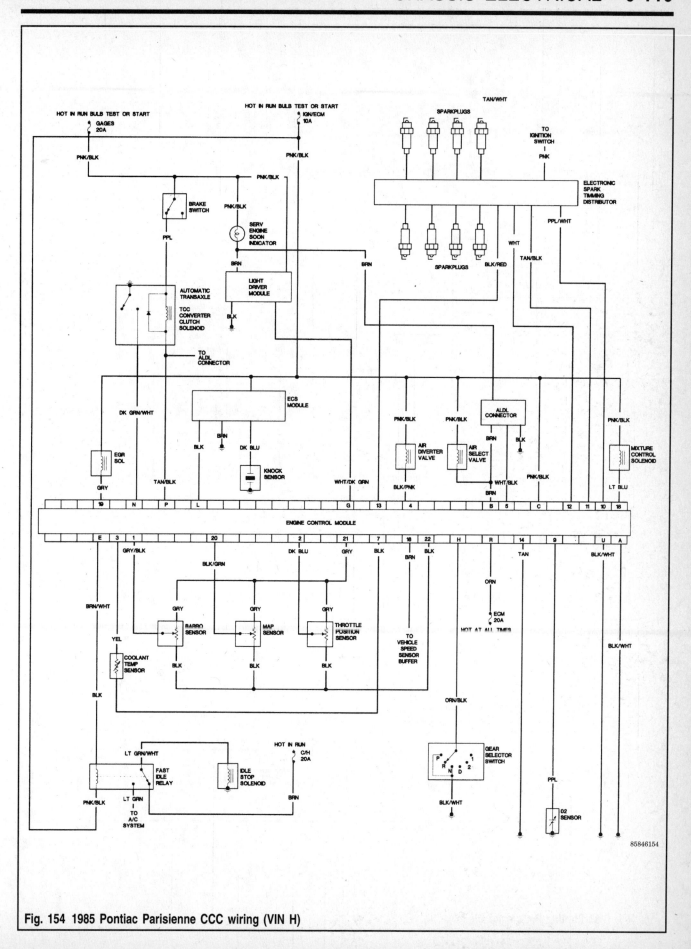

**Fig. 154 1985 Pontiac Parisienne CCC wiring (VIN H)**

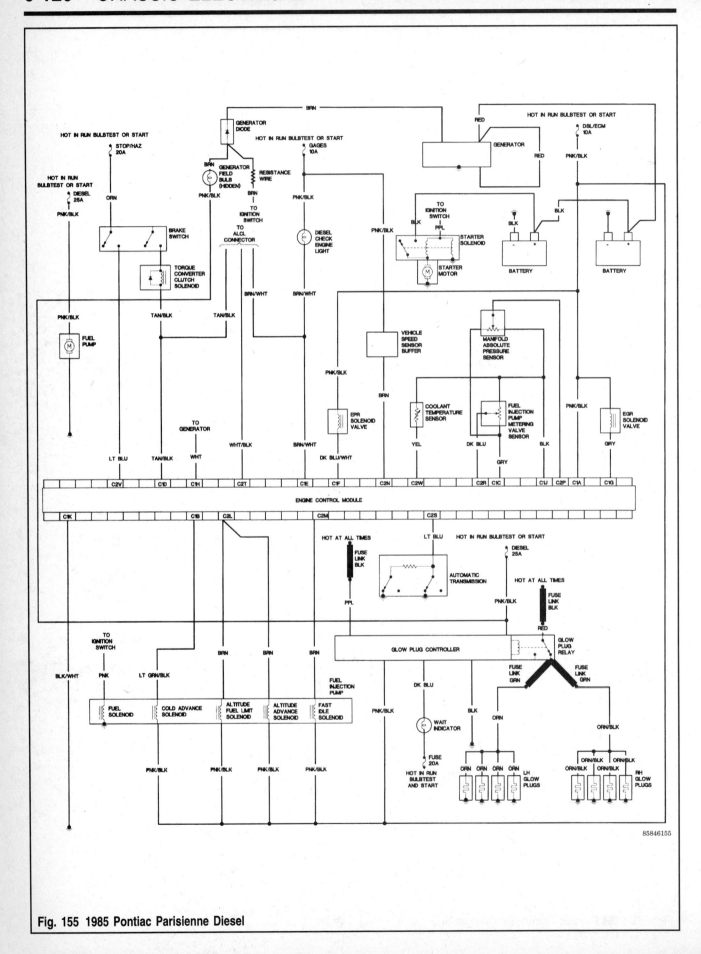

**Fig. 155** *1985 Pontiac Parisienne Diesel*

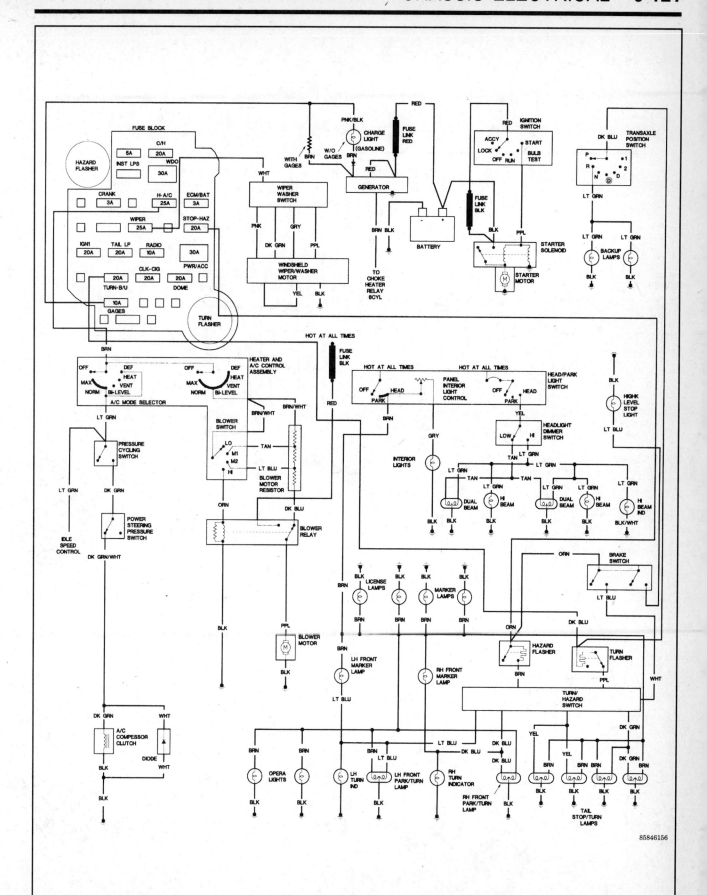

**Fig. 156 1986 Pontiac Bonneville**

85846156

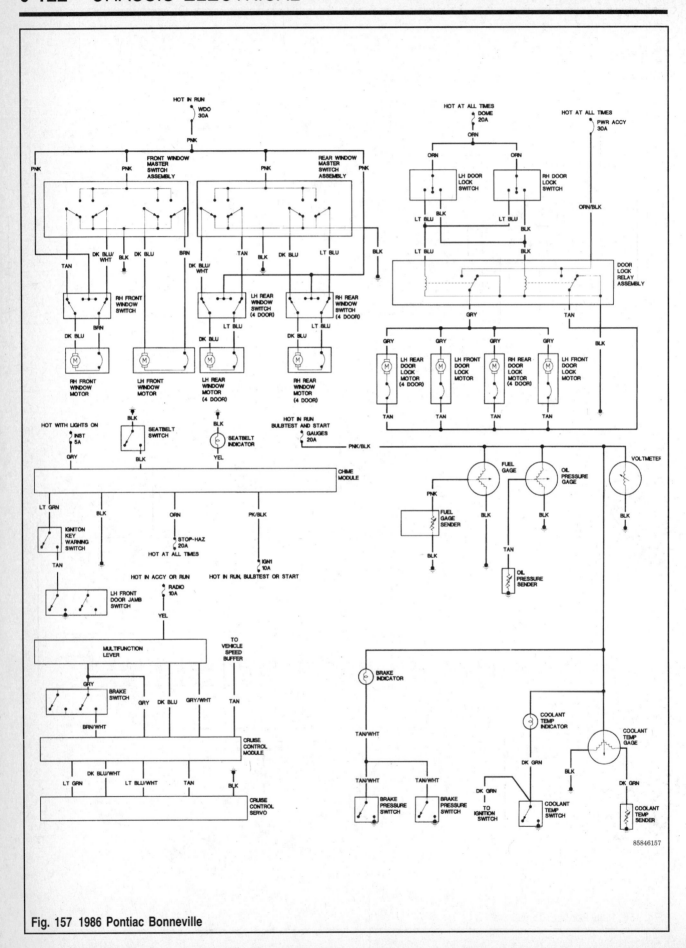

**Fig. 157 1986 Pontiac Bonneville**

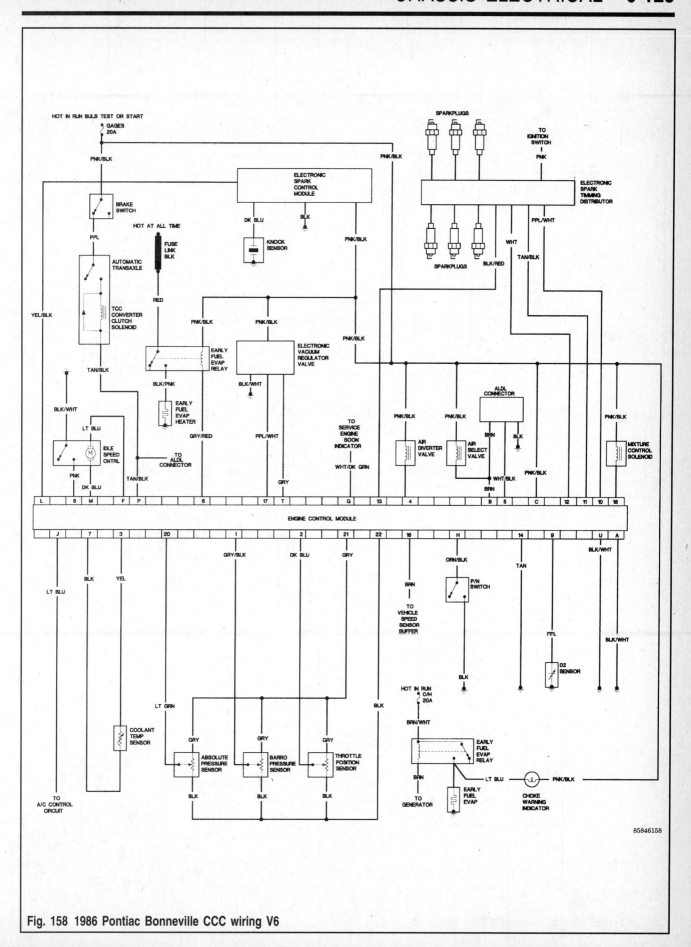

Fig. 158 1986 Pontiac Bonneville CCC wiring V6

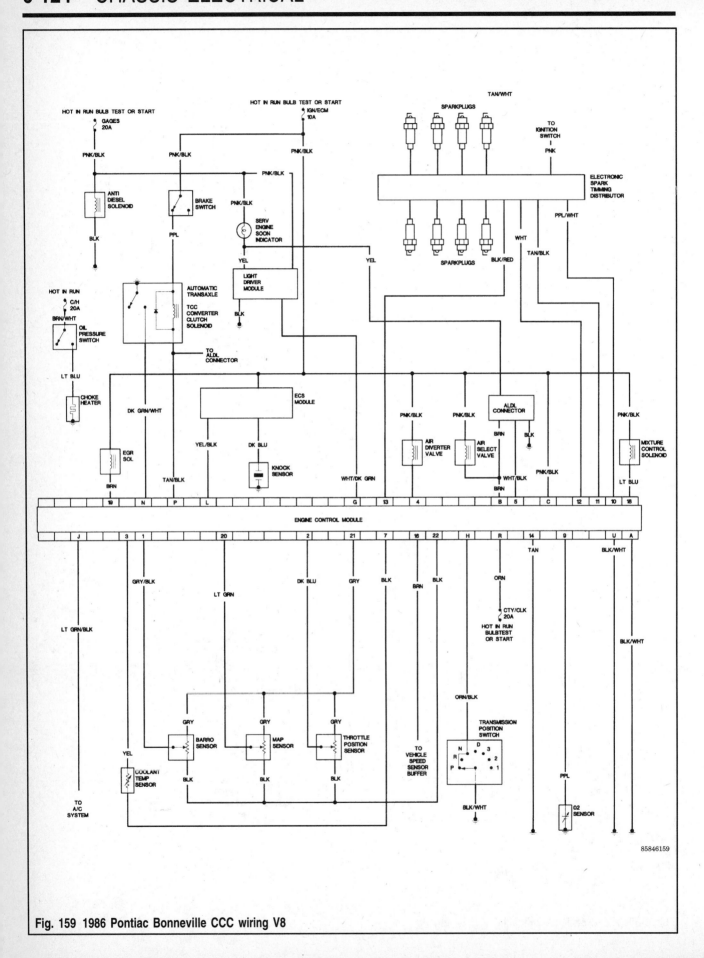

**Fig. 159** 1986 Pontiac Bonneville CCC wiring V8

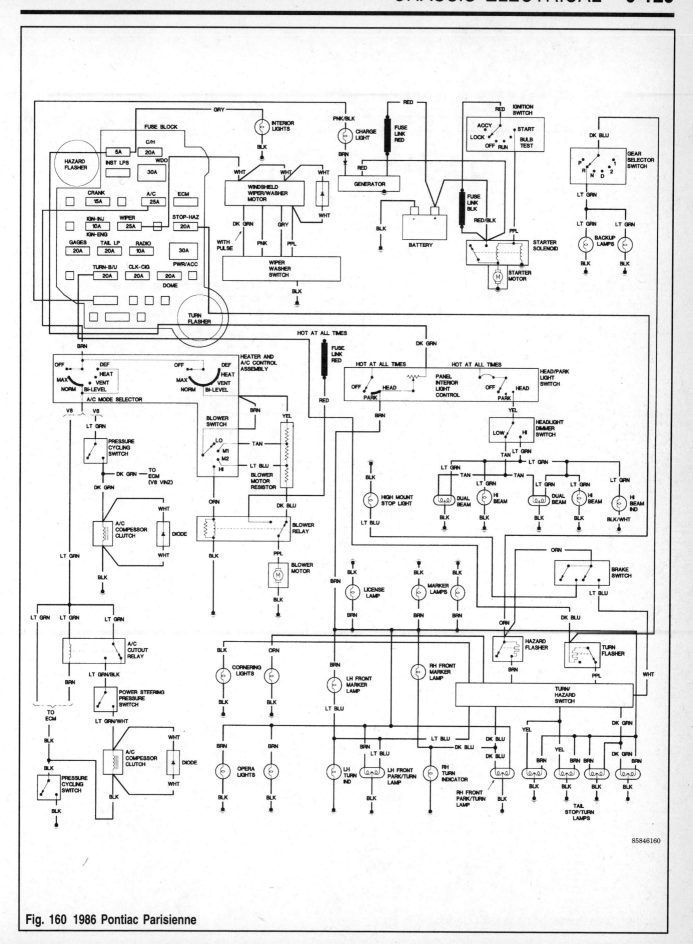

**Fig. 160 1986 Pontiac Parisienne**

85846160

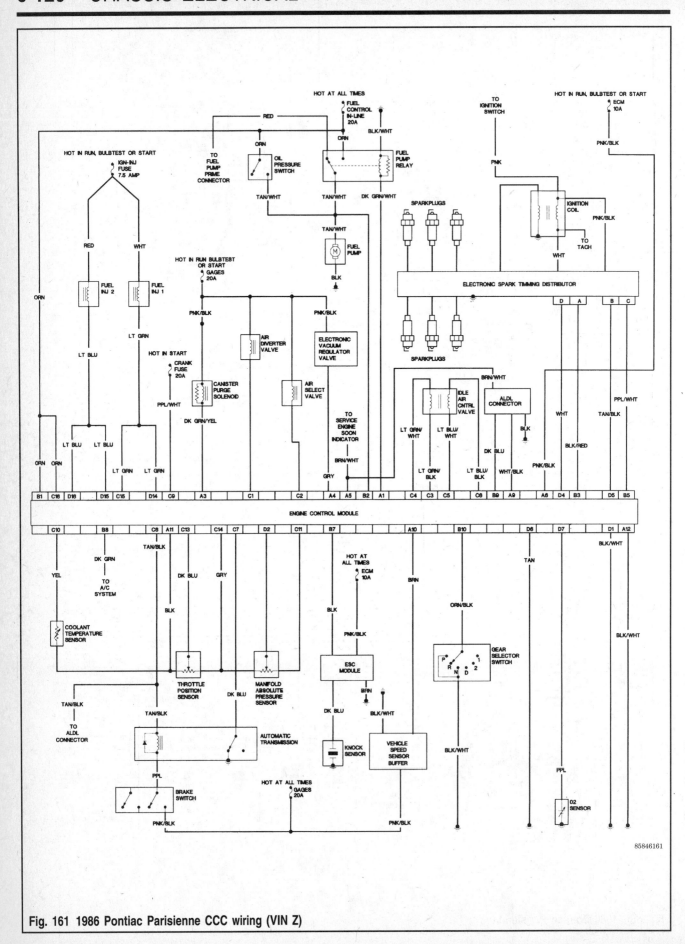

**Fig. 161 1986 Pontiac Parisienne CCC wiring (VIN Z)**

85846161

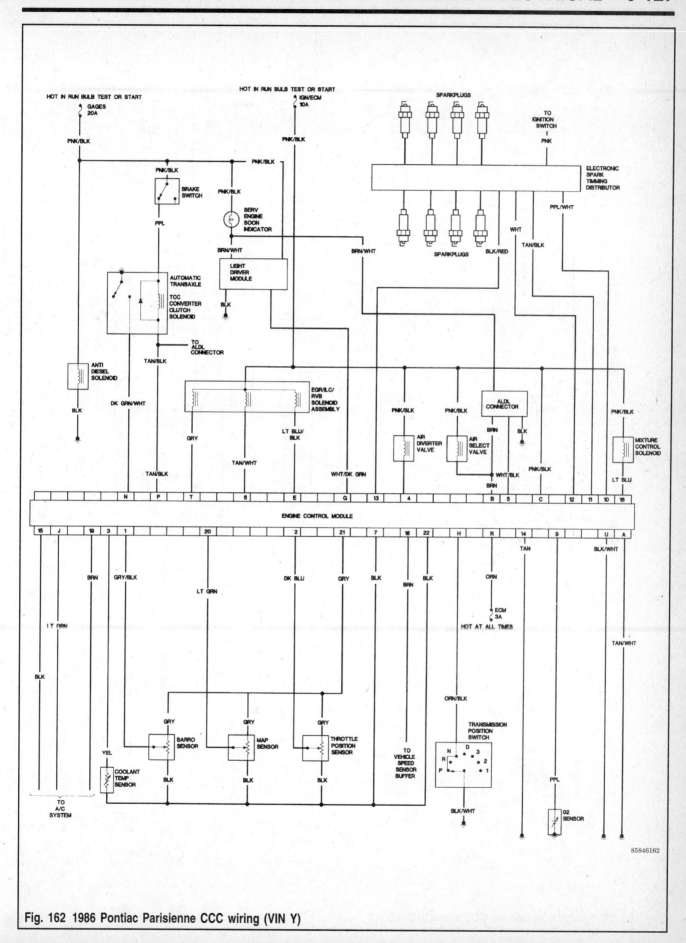

**Fig. 162  1986 Pontiac Parisienne CCC wiring (VIN Y)**

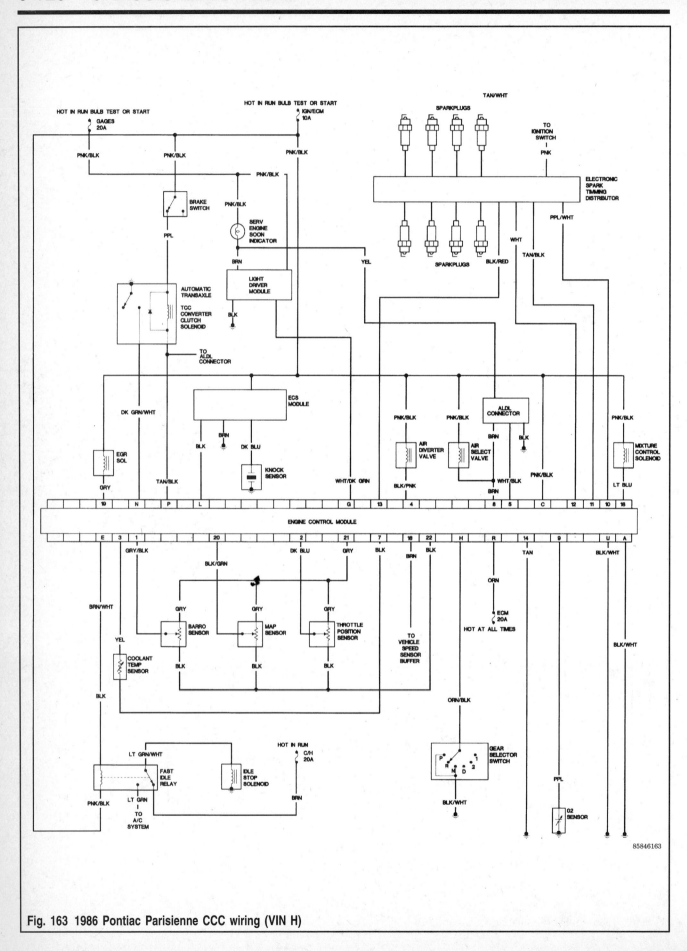

**Fig. 163 1986 Pontiac Parisienne CCC wiring (VIN H)**

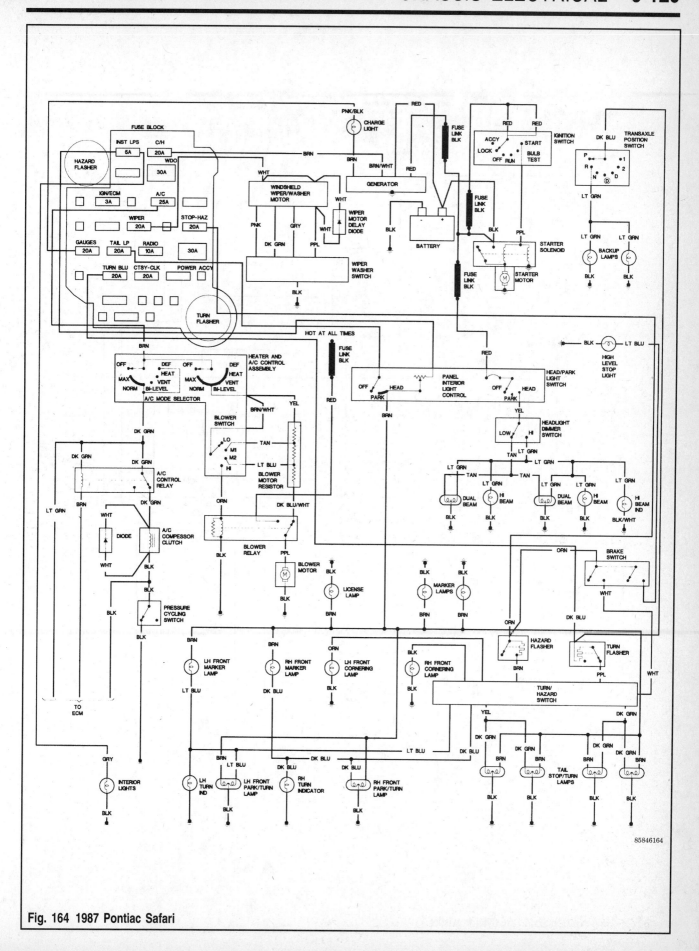

**Fig. 164 1987 Pontiac Safari**

85846164

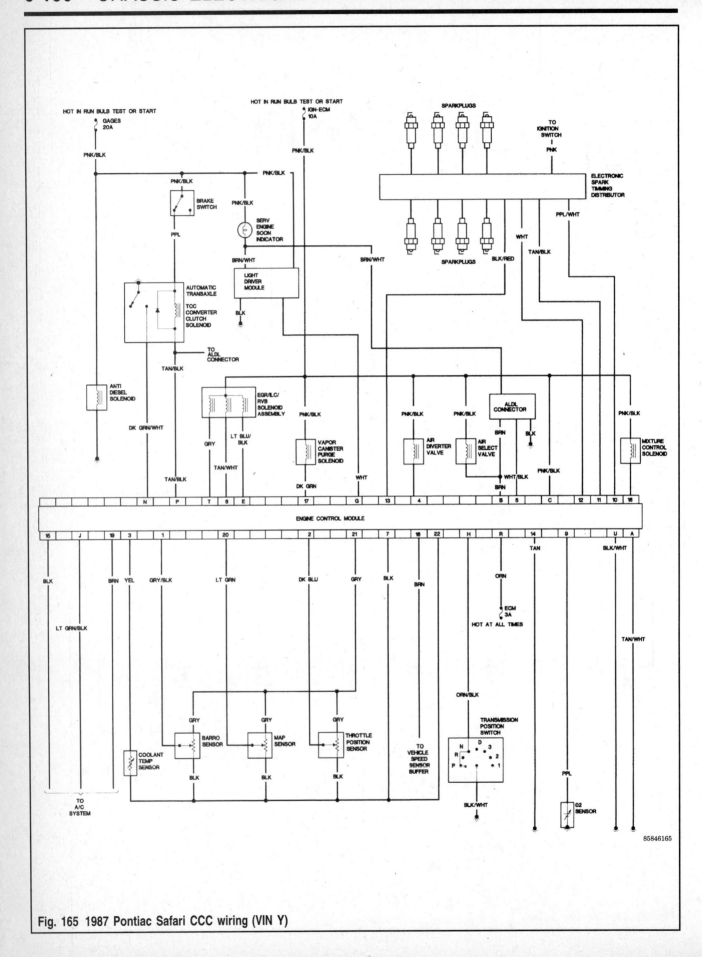

**Fig. 165  1987 Pontiac Safari CCC wiring (VIN Y)**

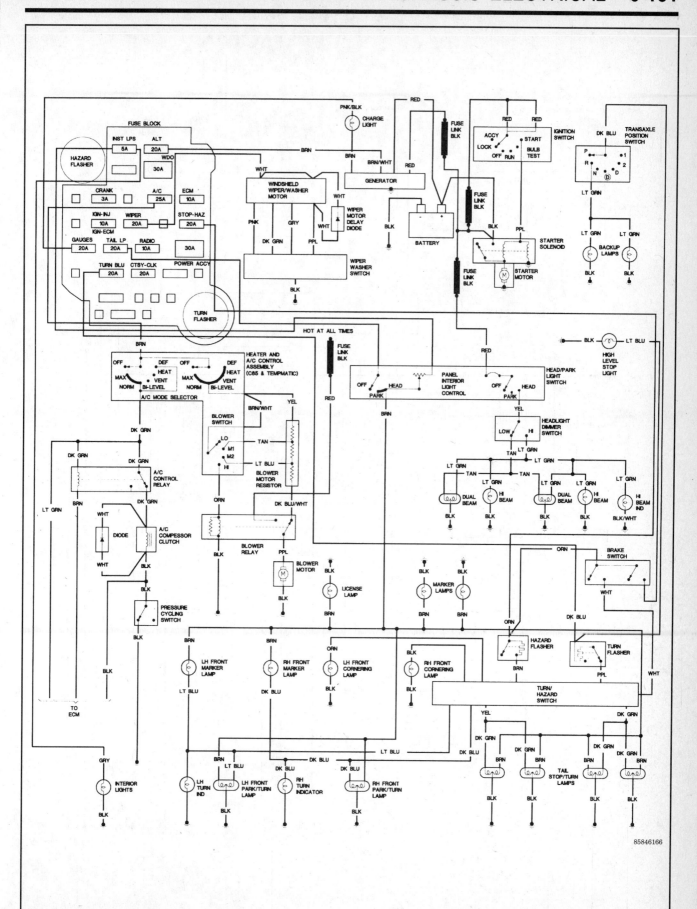

**Fig. 166 1988 Pontiac Safari**

85846166

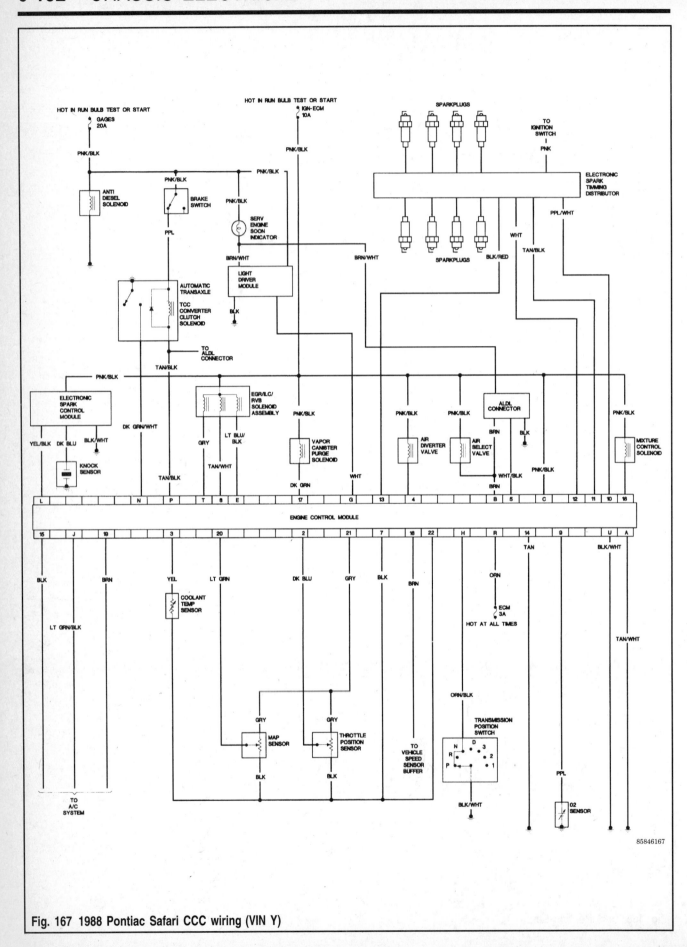

**Fig. 167** 1988 Pontiac Safari CCC wiring (VIN Y)

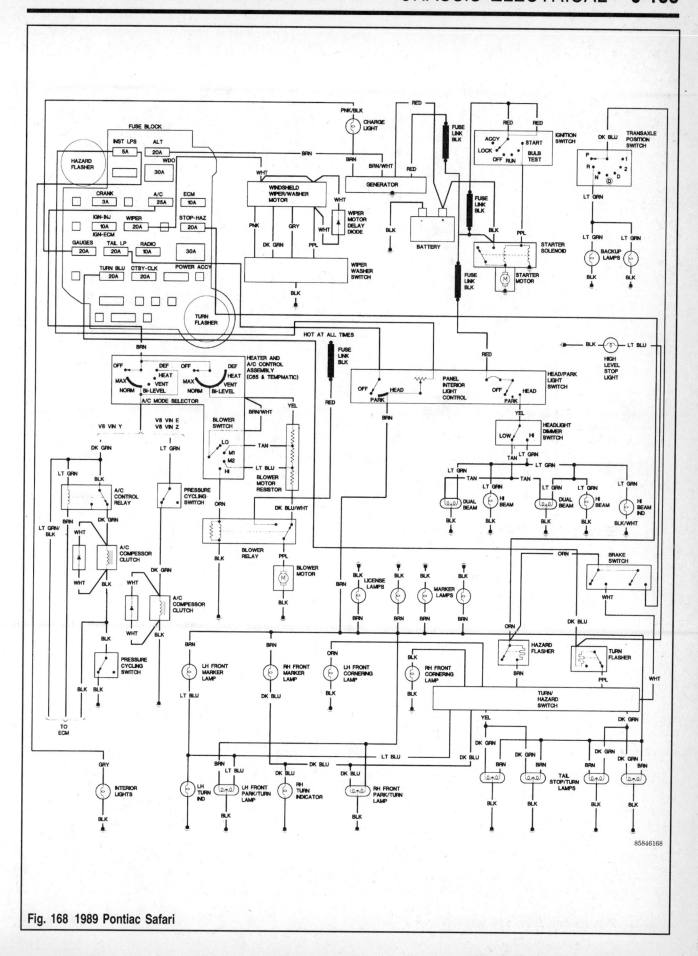

Fig. 168  1989 Pontiac Safari

85846168

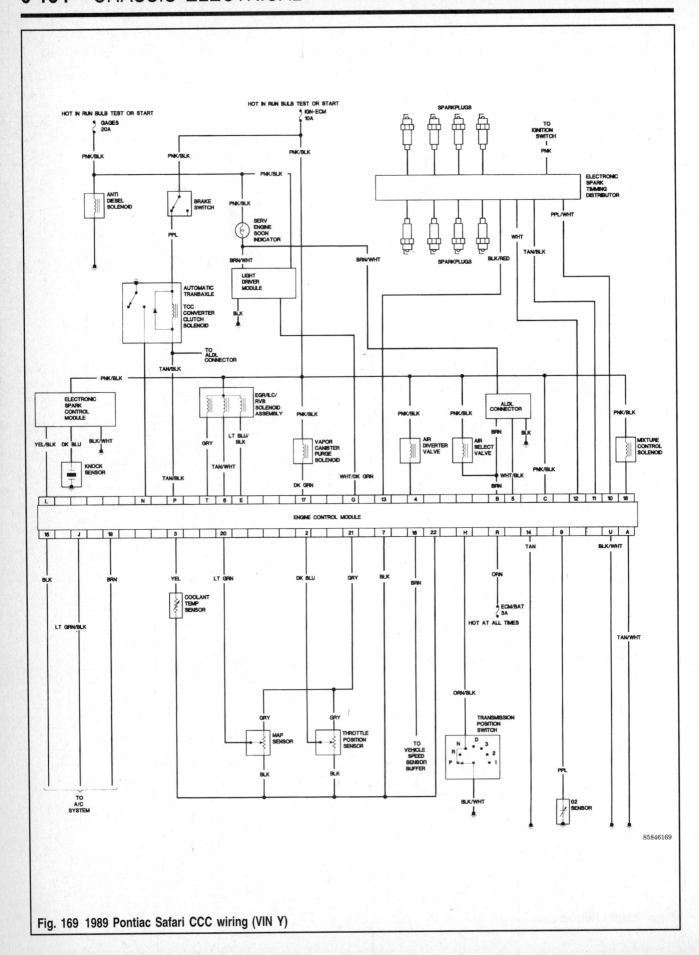

**Fig. 169** 1989 Pontiac Safari CCC wiring (VIN Y)

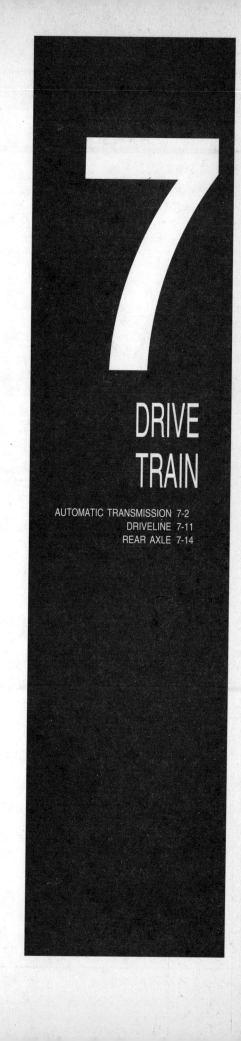

# 7

# DRIVE TRAIN

## AUTOMATIC TRANSMISSION

### Identification

▶ **See Figures 1, 2, 3, 4 and 5**

General Motors Turbo Hydra-Matic transmissions are used in all models covered in this guide. Through the years 1975-83, four basic transmission series have been used, covering four load capacities. The 200 series, which includes the 200C and 200-4R. The 250 series, which includes the 250C. The 350/375B series, including the 350C. And the 400.

Starting in 1984, most of the automatics used were in the 200 Series. The 200C offers a lockup clutch; the 2004R offers not only the lockup function, but a 4-speed, overdrive capability. These two transmissions are used through 1990. In addition, there is a 700 Series unit, known as the 700R4. This unit has four speeds with converter lockup.

### Fluid Pan

#### REMOVAL & INSTALLATION

The fluid should be changed with the transmission warm. A 20 minute drive at highway speeds should accomplish this.

1. Raise and support the vehicle, preferably in a level attitude.
2. On some models it may be necessary to remove the crossmember, make sure to support the transmission if this is necessary.
3. Place a large pan under the transmission pan. Remove all the front and side pan bolts. Loosen the rear bolts about four turns.
4. Pry the pan loose and let it drain.

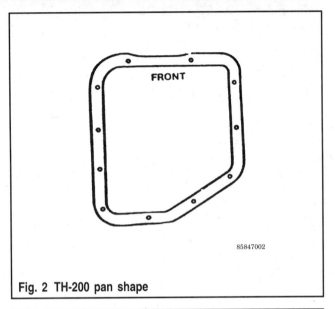

Fig. 2 TH-200 pan shape

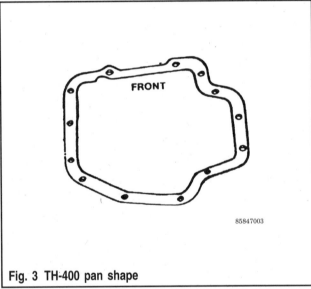

Fig. 3 TH-400 pan shape

5. Remove the pan and gasket. Clean the pan thoroughly with solvent and air dry it. Be very careful not to get any lint from rags in the pan.

➡ **It is normal to find a SMALL amount of metal shavings in the pan. An excessive amount of metal shavings indicates transmission damage which must be handled by a professional automatic transmission mechanic.**

6. Install the pan with a new gasket. Tighten the bolts evenly to 12 ft. lbs.
7. Lower the vehicle and add the proper amount of DEXRON®II automatic transmission fluid through the dipstick tube.
8. Start the engine in **PARK** and let it idle. Do not race the engine. Shift into each shift lever position, shift back into **PARK**, and check the fluid level on the dipstick. The level should be ¼ in. (6mm) below ADD. Be very careful not to

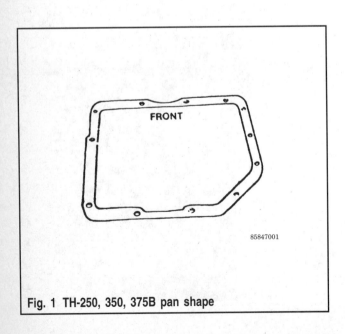

Fig. 1 TH-250, 350, 375B pan shape

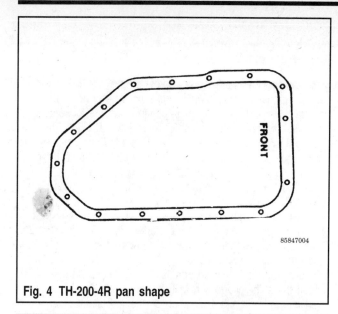

**Fig. 4 TH-200-4R pan shape**

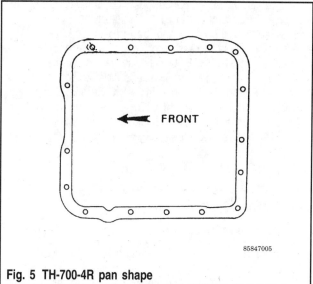

**Fig. 5 TH-700-4R pan shape**

overfill. Recheck the level after the vehicle has been driven long enough to thoroughly warm up the transmission. Add fluid as necessary. The level should then be at **FULL**.

## FILTER SERVICE

▶ **See Figures 6, 7, 8, 9 and 10**

1. Remove the fluid pan.
2. Remove the strainer-to-valve body screws, the strainer, and the gasket. Most transmissions will have a throw-away filter instead of a strainer. On the 400 transmission, remove the filter retaining bolt, filter, and intake pipe O-ring.
3. If there is a strainer, clean it in solvent and air dry.
4. Install the new filter or cleaned strainer with a new gasket. Tighten the screws to 12 ft. lbs. (16 Nm). On the 400, install a new intake pipe O-ring and a new filter, tightening the retaining bolt to 120 inch. lbs. (14 Nm).

5. Install the pan with a new gasket and add the proper amount of DEXRON®II automatic transmission fluid through the dipstick tube. Follow the procedure in removal and installation.

## Gasoline Engine Adjustments

### INTERMEDIATE BAND

**Turbo Hydra-Matic 250**

Only the 250 series has an externally adjustable band; the procedure is covered below.

The intermediate band must be adjusted with every required fluid change or whenever there is slippage.

1. Position the shift lever in **NEUTRAL**.
2. Loosen the locknut on the right side of the transmission. Tighten the adjusting screw to 30 inch lbs. (3 Nm).

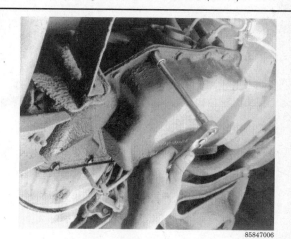

**Fig. 6 To replace the filter, start by removing the bolts on all but one side. These bolts will hold the pan while the fluid is draining**

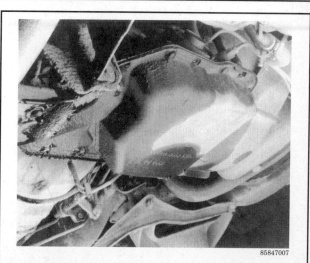

**Fig. 7 Loosen, but don't remove, the remaining bolts a few turns to allow the fluid in the pan to drain**

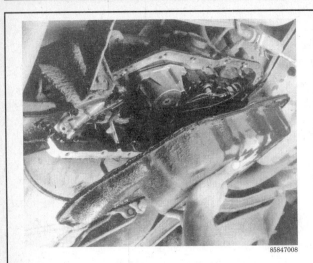

Fig. 8 After the fluid has drained, remove the remaining bolts and remove the pan

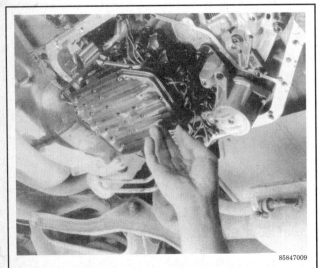

Fig. 9 On this model, the filter is retained by a clip

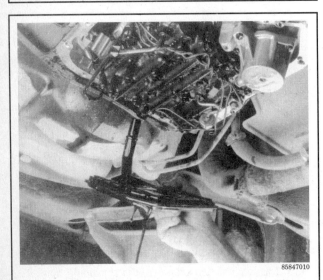

Fig. 10 Remove the filter from the valve body assembly

## SHIFT LINKAGE

▶ See Figure 11

1. Loosen the clamp spring screw on the shift linkage clamp. This is the screw which will slide up and down the rod coming down from the steering column once it is loosened.

2. Set the lever on the transmission into **NEUTRAL** by moving it counterclockwise to the L1 detent, then clockwise the correct number of detent positions to **NEUTRAL**. With three speed automatics, move the lever three positions to **NEUTRAL**; with four speed overdrive units, move it four positions to **NEUTRAL.**

3. Place the transmission selector lever (in the vehicle) in **NEUTRAL** as determined by the stop in the steering column. DO NOT Use the indicator pointer for reference.

4. Hold the clamp (into which the clamp spring screw is threaded) flush against the equalizer shaft lever and then tighten the shift linkage screw just finger tight. You must not exert any force in either direction on the rod or equalizer lever as you tighten the screw. Once the screw is hand tight and its position is fixed, torque it to 21 ft. lbs. (29 Nm).

5. Check that the key cannot be removed and that the steering wheel is not locked with the key in Run and the transmission in **REVERSE**. Check that the key can be removed and the transmission linkage is locked when the key is in Lock and the transmission is in **PARK**. Be sure the vehicle will start only in **PARK** and **NEUTRAL**. If it starts in any gear, the neutral start switch must be adjusted. Start the engine and check for proper shifting in all ranges.

## THROTTLE VALVE (TV) CABLE

▶ See Figures 12 and 13

### 200-4R and 700-4R Models

1. Make sure the ignition switch is off. Depress and hold the metal readjustment tab all the way down. This is located on the engine end of the Throttle Valve cable. Move the slider until it is located directly against the fitting, and then release the adjustment tab.

2. Rotate the throttle lever to give wide open throttle position. Watch the slider as you do this; it must move toward the lever as you rotate the throttle. If the slider works properly, this will complete the adjustment.

➡**After the adjustment, make sure the cable works freely after the engine has warmed to operating temperature.**

### All Other Models

1. With a small screwdriver, pry gently on the bottom of the snap lock to release the detent cable.

2. Push the throttle lever to the wide open throttle position (engine off) and hold. Push the snaplock tab downward until flush with the cable.

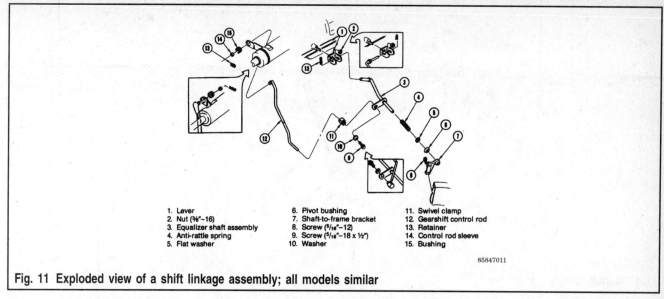

1. Lever
2. Nut (⅜"–16)
3. Equalizer shaft assembly
4. Anti-rattle spring
5. Flat washer
6. Pivot bushing
7. Shaft-to-frame bracket
8. Screw (⁵⁄₁₆"–12)
9. Screw (⁵⁄₁₆"–18 x ½")
10. Washer
11. Swivel clamp
12. Gearshift control rod
13. Retainer
14. Control rod sleeve
15. Bushing

85847011

Fig. 11 Exploded view of a shift linkage assembly; all models similar

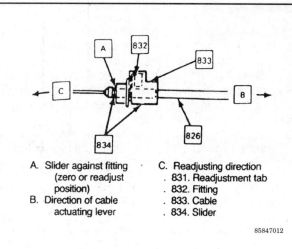

A. Slider against fitting (zero or readjust position)
B. Direction of cable actuating lever
C. Readjusting direction
. 831. Readjustment tab
. 832. Fitting
. 833. Cable
. 834. Slider

85847012

Fig. 12 Throttle valve cable adjustment; 200-4R and 700-4R models

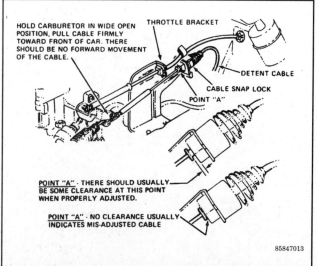

HOLD CARBURETOR IN WIDE OPEN POSITION, PULL CABLE FIRMLY TOWARD FRONT OF CAR. THERE SHOULD BE NO FORWARD MOVEMENT OF THE CABLE.

THROTTLE BRACKET

DETENT CABLE

CABLE SNAP LOCK

POINT "A"

POINT "A" - THERE SHOULD USUALLY BE SOME CLEARANCE AT THIS POINT WHEN PROPERLY ADJUSTED.

POINT "A" - NO CLEARANCE USUALLY INDICATES MIS-ADJUSTED CABLE

85847013

Fig. 13 Throttle valve cable adjustment; snap lock type

## DETENT (DOWNSHIFT) SWITCH ADJUSTMENT

▶ See Figure 14

### Turbo Hydra-Matic 400

All the General Motors divisions covered in this guide use the same detent switch on their THM 400 equipped models. The switch is mounted on the accelerator pedal bracket and is for all intents and purposes, self-adjusting. If a new switch is installed, a preliminary adjustment should be performed according to the accompanying illustration.

1. Perform the adjustment with the engine off.
2. Push the plunger of the downshift switch forward until it is flush with the switch housing.
3. Push the accelerator pedal to the wide open throttle position to set the switch.

## Diesel Engine Adjustments

➡ Before making any adjustments, check the injection timing, and adjust if necessary. Also note that these adjustments should be performed together. The vacuum valve adjustment (THM350's only) on 1979 and later models requires the use of several special tools. If you do not have these tools at your disposal, refer the adjustment to a qualified, professional technician.

## THROTTLE ROD

▶ See Figure 15

1. If equipped with cruise control, remove the clip from the control rod, then remove the rod from the bellcrank.
2. Remove the throttle valve cable (THM200) or detent cable (THM350) from the bellcrank.
3. Loosen the locknut on the throttle rod, then shorten the rod several turns.
4. Rotate the bellcrank to the full throttle stop, then lengthen the throttle rod until the injection pump lever contacts the injection pump full throttle stop. Release the bellcrank.

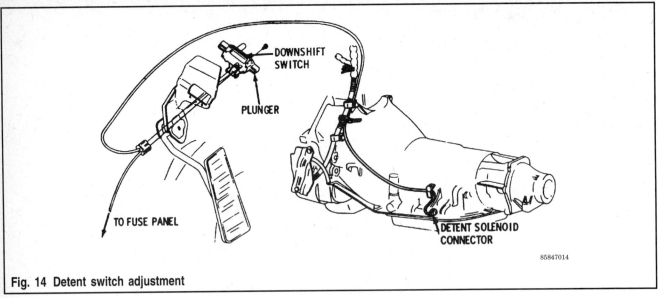

**Fig. 14 Detent switch adjustment**

5. Tighten the throttle rod locknut.

6. Connect the throttle valve or detent cable and cruise control rod to the bellcrank. Adjust if necessary.

## THROTTLE VALVE (TV) OR DETENT CABLE

▶ See Figure 16

**1979-82 Models**

1. Make sure the ignition switch is off. Depress and hold the metal readjustment tab all the way down. This is located on the engine end of the Throttle Valve cable. Move the slider until it is located directly against the fitting, and then release the adjustment tab.

2. Rotate the throttle lever to give wide open throttle position. Watch the slider as you do this; it must move toward the lever as you rotate the throttle. If the slider works properly, this will complete the adjustment.

➡ After the adjustment, make sure the cable works freely after the engine has warmed to operating temperature.

**1983-84 Models**

1. Disconnect the transmission detent cable from the throttle assembly. If the vehicle has cruise control, disconnect it from the cruise control servo rod as well.

2. Depress and hold the metal lock tab on the upper end of the cable. Move the slider through the fitting away from the bellcrank lever assembly until the slider stops against the metal fitting. Release the metal tab.

3. Install the cruise control serve rod if the vehicle has cruise control. Reconnect the cable. Then, rotate the bellcrank lever assembly until it reaches the full throttle stop and release it.

## VACUUM VALVE

**1978 Models**

▶ See Figure 17

1. Remove the throttle rod from the bellcrank.

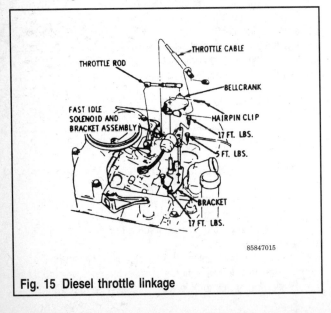

**Fig. 15 Diesel throttle linkage**

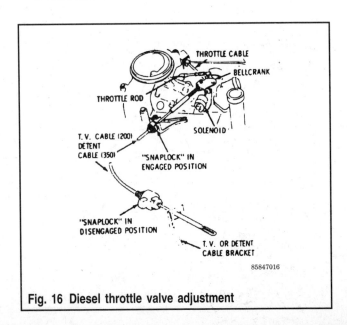

**Fig. 16 Diesel throttle valve adjustment**

2. Loosen the transmission vacuum valve attaching bolts just enough to disengage the valve from the injection pump shaft.

3. Hold the injection pump lever against the full throttle stop.

4. Rotate the valve to the full throttle position, then insert a 0.090 in. (2.28mm) pin to hold the valve in the full throttle position.

5. Rotate the assembly clockwise until the injection pump lever is contacted.

6. While holding the assembly in contact with the lever, tighten the two bolts holding the vacuum valve to the pump, remove the pin and release the lever, and reconnect the throttle rod to the bellcrank.

### 1979 and Later

▶ See Figures 18, 19, 20 and 21

1. Remove the air cleaner assembly.

2. Remove the air intake crossover from the intake manifold. Cover the intake manifold passages to prevent foreign material from entering the engine.

3. Disconnect the throttle rod from the injection pump throttle lever.

4. Loosen the transmission vacuum valve-to-injection pump bolts.

5. Mark and disconnect the vacuum lines from the vacuum valve.

6. Attach a carburetor angle gauge adapter (Kent-Moore tool J-26701-15 or its equivalent) to the injection pump throttle lever. Attach an angle gauge (J-26701 or its equivalent) to the gauge adapter.

7. Turn the throttle lever to the wide open throttle position. Set the angle gauge to 0.

8. Center the bubble in the gauge level.

9. Set the angle gauge to the correct setting according to the year and type of engine.

10. Attach a vacuum gauge to port 2 and a vacuum source (e.g. hand-held vacuum pump) to port 1 of the vacuum valve (as illustrated).

11. Apply 18-22 in. Hg of vacuum to the valve. Slowly rotate the valve until the vacuum reading drops to the correct value.

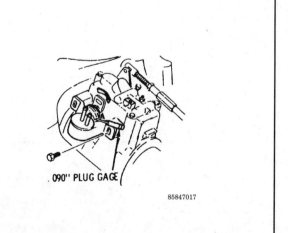

.090" PLUG GAGE

85847017

**Fig. 17 Vacuum valve adjustment; 1978 diesel models**

12. Tighten the vacuum valve retaining bolts.

13. Reconnect the original vacuum lines to the vacuum valve.

14. Remove the angle gauge and adapter.

15. Connect the throttle rod to the throttle lever.

16. Install the air intake crossover, using new gaskets.

17. Install the air cleaner assembly.

## Neutral Safety/Backup Switch

▶ See Figure 22

➡1977 and later full size Buick, Olds and Pontiac vehicles do not have a neutral safety switch. Instead, these vehicles have a mechanical interlock between the lock and the transmission selector, which is nonadjustable.

### REMOVAL & INSTALLATION

1. Remove any trim panels which may interfere with the switch removal.

2. Remove the switch attaching screws and disconnect the electrical connector.

3. Remove the switch.

**To install:**

4. Place the shift lever in **NEUTRAL**.

5. Mount the switch but do not tighten the screws. Reconnect the electrical connector.

6. Move the switch until you can insert a gauge pin, 0.092 in. (2.33mm), for 1975-76, into the hole in the switch and through to the alignment hole.

7. Tighten the screws and remove the pin.

8. Step on the brake pedal and check to see that the engine will only start in **NEUTRAL** or **PARK**.

## Vacuum Modulator

### REMOVAL & INSTALLATION

1. Raise and safely support the vehicle

2. Locate and remove the modulator retaining bolt. Disconnect the vacuum line.

3. Pull the modulator straight back from the case.

4. Installation is the reverse of removal. Lube the O-ring with petroleum jelly and torque the retaining bolt to 20 ft. lbs.

## Extension Housing Seal

### REMOVAL & INSTALLATION

1. Disconnect the negative battery cable.

2. Raise and properly support the vehicle

3. Mark the driveshaft and remove it from the vehicle.

4. Carefully distort the seal with a punch and remove it from the extension housing. Be careful not to damage the housing.

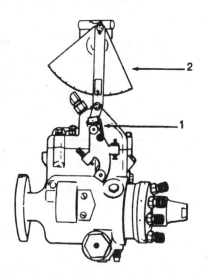
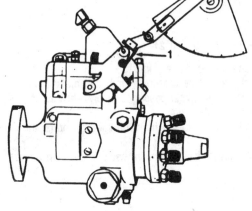

1. Adapter
2. Angle gauge

85847018

**Fig. 18 Angle gauge position for vacuum valve adjustment is dependent on the type of throttle lever used**

| Year | Engine | Setting |
|------|--------|---------|
| 1979 | V8 | 49° |
| 1980 | V8 | 49–50° |
| 1981 | V8—Calif. | 49–50° |
| 1981 | V8—non Calif. | 58° |
| 1982–84 | V8 | 58° |

85847019

**Fig. 19 Angle gauge settings**

| Year | In. Hg. |
|------|---------|
| 1979 | 8½–9 |
| 1980 | 7 |
| 1981 Calif. | 7–8 |
| 1981 non-Calif. | 8½–9 |
| 1982–84 | 10½ |

85847020

**Fig. 20 Vacuum setting values**

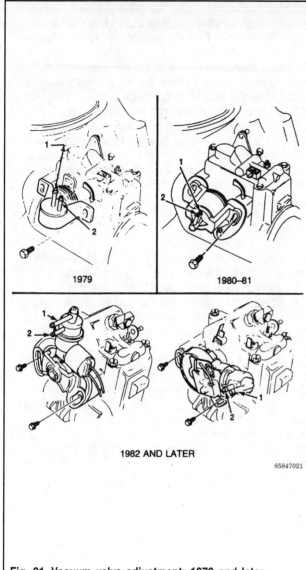

Fig. 21 Vacuum valve adjustment; 1979 and later

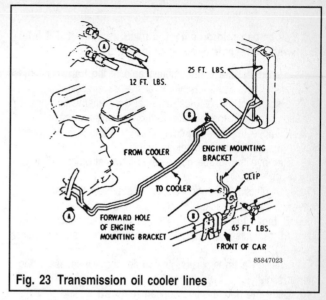

Fig. 23 Transmission oil cooler lines

## To install:

5. Apply a non-hardening sealer on the outside of the new seal and drive the new seal into the housing using the proper tool.

6. Install the driveshaft with the marks aligned.

7. Lower the car and reconnect the negative battery cable.

## Transmission

### REMOVAL & INSTALLATION

▶ See Figures 23 and 24

1. Disconnect the negative (-) battery cable. Open the hood and place protectors on the fenders. Remove the air cleaner assembly.

2. Disconnect the detent cable at its upper end.

3. Remove the transmission oil dipstick, and the bolt holding the dipstick tube if it is accessible.

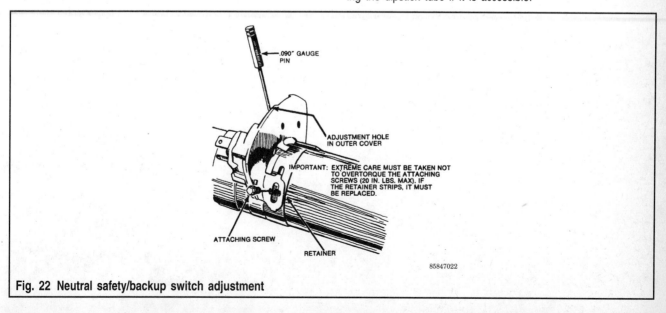

Fig. 22 Neutral safety/backup switch adjustment

4. Raise the vehicle and safety support it with jackstands.

➡**If a floor pan reinforcement is used, remove it if it interferes with driveshaft removal or installation.**

5. Disconnect the speedometer cable at the transmission.
6. Disconnect the shift linkage at the transmission.
7. Disconnect all electrical leads at the transmission and any clips that hold these leads to the transmission case.
8. Remove the flywheel cover and matchmark the flywheel and torque converter for later assembly.
9. Remove the torque converter-to-flywheel bolts and/or nuts.
10. On gasoline engined vehicles, disconnect the catalytic converter support bracket.
11. Remove the transmission support-to-transmission mount bolt and transmission support-to-frame bolts, and any insulators (if used).
12. Position a transmission jack under the transmission and raise it slightly.
13. Slide the transmission support rearward.
14. Loosen the transmission enough to gain access to the oil cooler lines and detent cable attachments.
15. Disconnect the oil cooler lines and detent cable. Plug all openings.
16. Support the engine and remove the engine-to-transmission bolts.
17. Disconnect the transmission assembly, being careful not to damage any cables, lines or linkage.
18. Install a C-clamp or torque converter holding tool onto the transmission housing to hold the converter in the housing. Remove the transmission assembly from the vehicle (a hydraulic floor jack is best for this).

**To install:**
19. Install the transmission assembly into the vehicle (a hydraulic floor jack is best for this). When installing the flex plate-to-converter bolts, make sure that the weld nuts on the converter are flush with the flex plate and that the converter rotates freely by hand. Coat the threads with thread locking compound, hand-start the three bolts, tighten them finger tight and torque them evenly to 35 ft. lbs. (48 Nm).
20. Support the engine and install the engine-to-transmission bolts. Torque the bolts to 40 ft. lbs. (54 Nm).
21. Connect the oil cooler lines and detent cable.
22. Slide the transmission support forward.
23. Position a transmission jack under the transmission and raise it slightly.
24. Install the transmission support-to-transmission mount bolt and transmission support-to-frame bolts, and any insulators (if used).
25. On gasoline engined vehicles, connect the catalytic converter support bracket.
26. Install the flywheel cover.
27. Connect all electrical leads to the transmission and any clips that hold these leads to the transmission case.
28. Connect the shift linkage at the transmission.
29. Connect the speedometer cable at the transmission.
30. Check to see if all under vehicle components and fasteners are properly installed and torqued.
31. Lower the vehicle safely.
32. Install the transmission oil dipstick, and the bolt holding the dipstick tube if it is accessible.
33. Connect the detent cable at its upper end.
34. Connect the negative (-) battery cable. Recheck all procedures for completion of repair. Close the hood and remove the protectors on the fenders.
35. Install the air cleaner assembly. Refill the transmission with fluid as outlined in the "Oil Pan" section in this chapter.
36. Start the vehicle and check operation.

## DRIVELINE

### Driveshaft and U-joints

Full-size Buick, Pontiac and Oldsmobile driveshafts are of the conventional, open type. Located at either end of the driveshaft is a U-joint or universal joint, which allows the driveshaft to move up and down to match the motion of the rear axle. The front U-joint connects the driveshaft to a slip-jointed yoke. This yoke is internally splined, and allows the driveshaft to move in and out on the transmission splines. The rear U-joint is clamped or bolted to a companion flange fastened to the rear axle drive pinion. The rear U-joint is secured in the yoke in one of two ways. Dana and Cleveland design driveshafts use a conventional type snapring to hold each bearing cup in the yoke. The snapring fits into a groove located in each yoke end, just on top of the bearing cup. A Saginaw design driveshaft secures the U-joints differently. Ny-lon material is injected through a small hole in the yoke during manufacture, and flows along a circular groove between the U-joint and the yoke creating a non-metallic snapring.

There are two methods of attaching the rear U-joint to the rear axle. One method employs a pair of straps, while the other method is a set of bolted flanges. Bad U-joints, requiring replacement, will produce a clunking sound when the vehicle is put into gear and when the transmission shifts from gear to gear. This is due to worn needle bearings or a scored trunnion end possibly caused by improper lubrication during assembly. U-joints require no periodic maintenance and therefore have no lubrication fittings, except replaced U-joints.

Some driveshafts, generally those in heavy duty applications, use a damper as part of the slip joint. This vibration damper cannot be serviced separately from the slip joint. If either component goes bad, the two must be replaced as a unit.

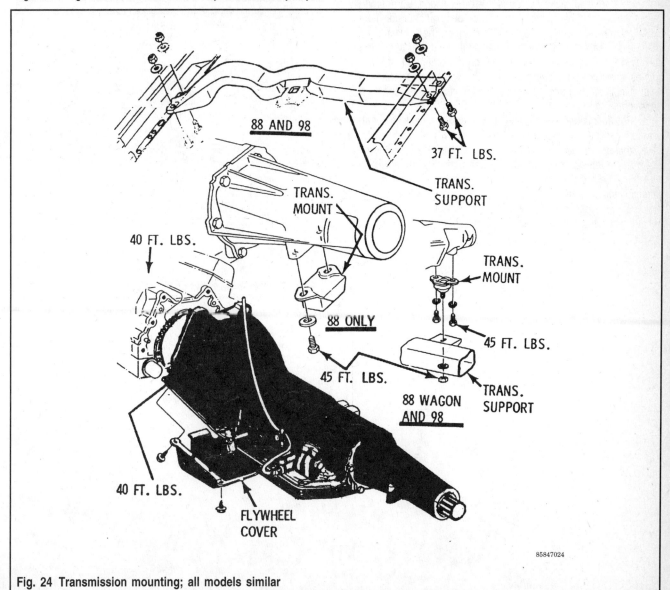

Fig. 24 Transmission mounting; all models similar

## REMOVAL & INSTALLATION

▶ **See Figures 25, 26 and 27**

1. Disconnect the negative (-) battery cable, raise the vehicle in the air and support it with jackstands.

2. Mark the relationship of the driveshaft to the differential flange so that they can be reassembled in the same position.

3. Disconnect the rear U-joint by removing the U-bolts or retaining straps.

4. To prevent the loss of the needle bearings, tape the bearing caps in place. If you are replacing the U-joint, this is not necessary.

5. Remove the driveshaft from the transmission by sliding it rearward. There will be some oil leakage from the rear of the transmission. It can be contained by placing a small plastic bag over the rear of the transmission and holding it in place with a rubber band.

6. To install the driveshaft, first inspect the outer diameter of the slip yoke to make sure it is not burred, or the transmission seal may be damaged. Apply automatic transmission fluid to all splined driveshaft yokes and then insert the driveshaft into the transmission. Don't force the shaft in. If you seem to be having trouble getting it to slip in, check alignment of the splines. If you're replacing the shaft, check for number and type of splines to make sure they are identical to the shaft you removed.

7. Before making the rear shaft connection, check the mating surfaces of the shaft and flange for nicks and burrs which could prevent proper seating of the shaft to the flange. Then, using the reference marks made earlier, align the driveshaft with the differential flange and secure it with the U-bolts or retaining straps. Make sure the bearings are aligned in the pinion flange yoke before installing bolts or bolts and straps. Torque bolt straps to 16 ft. lbs. (22 Nm).

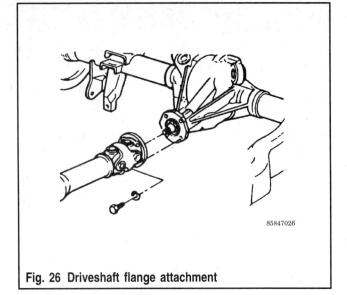

Fig. 26 Driveshaft flange attachment

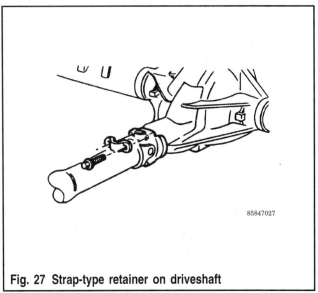

Fig. 27 Strap-type retainer on driveshaft

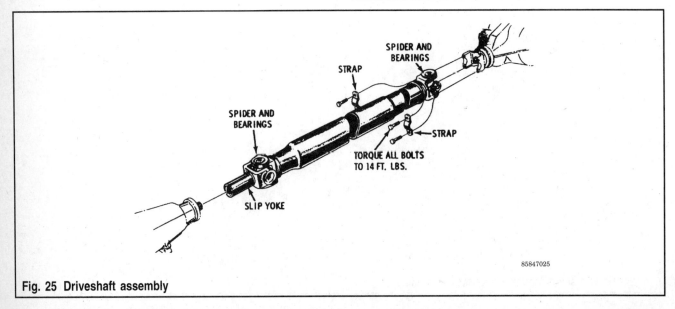

Fig. 25 Driveshaft assembly

## U-JOINT REPLACEMENT

◆ **See Figures 28, 29 and 30**

➡NEVER clamp a driveshaft in a vise, as the tube is easily dented. Always clamp on one of the yokes, and support the shaft horizontally.

1. Remove the driveshaft as explained above and remove the snaprings from the ends of the bearing cup.

### ✳✳WARNING

The driveshaft is easily damaged using improper service methods. Use care not the dent or bend the driveshaft when removing the U-joints. If the bearing caps will not come loose, have a machine shop press them out.

2. After removing the snaprings, place the driveshaft on the floor and place a large diameter socket under one of the bearing cups. Using a hammer and a drift, tap on the bearing opposite this one. This will push the trunnion through the yoke enough to force the bearing cup out of the yoke and into the socket. Repeat this procedure for the other bearing cups. If a hammer does not loosen the cups, they will have to be pressed out.

➡A Saginaw design driveshaft secures its U-joints in a different manner than the conventional snaprings of the Dana and Cleveland designs. Nylon material is injected through a small hole in the yoke and flows along a circular groove between the U-joint and the yoke thus creating a synthetic snapring. Disassembly of this Saginaw type U-joint requires that the joint be pressed from the yoke. If a press is not available, it may be carefully hammered out using the same procedure as the Dana design although it may require more force to break the nylon ring. Either method, press or hammer, will damage the bearing cups and destroy the nylon rings. Replacement kits include new bearing cups and conventional metal snaprings to replace the original nylon type rings.

3. Using solvent, thoroughly clean the entire U-joint assembly. Inspect for excessive wear in the yoke bores and on the four ends of the trunnion. The needle bearings should not be scored, broken, or loose in their cups. Bearing cups may suffer slight distortion during removal and should be replaced.

4. Pack the bearings with chassis lube (lithium base) and completely fill each trunnion end with the same lubricant.

5. Place new dust seals on trunnions with cavity of seal toward end of trunnion. Care must be taken to avoid distortion of the seal. A suitable size socket and a vise can be used to press on the seal.

6. Insert one bearing cup about ¼ of the way into the yoke and place the trunnion into yoke and bearing cup. Install another bearing cup and press both cups in and install the snaprings. Snaprings on the Dana and Cleveland shafts must go on the outside of the yoke while the Saginaw shaft requires that rings go on the inside of the yoke. The gap in the Saginaw ring must face in toward the yoke. Once installed, the trunnion must move freely in yoke.

➡The Saginaw shaft uses two different size bearing cups (the ones with the groove) fit into the driveshaft yoke.

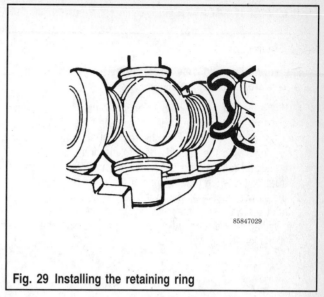
85847029

Fig. 29 Installing the retaining ring

85847030

Fig. 30 Tapping the yoke to seat the retaining ring

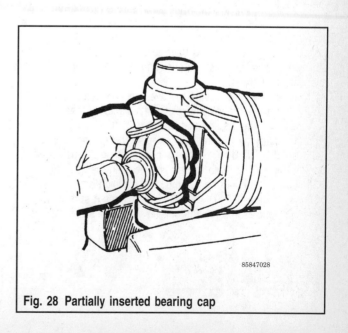
85847028

Fig. 28 Partially inserted bearing cap

## DRIVESHAFT BALANCING

▶ See Figure 31

➡This service should only be performed if you have access to a proper lift or hoist.

1. Place the car on a twin post hoist so that the rear of the car is supported on the rear axle housing and the rear wheels are free to rotate. Remove both the rear wheels and reinstall wheel lug nuts with the flat side next to the drum.
2. Mark and number the driveshaft at four points 90° apart at the rear of the shaft just forward of the balance weight.
3. Install two hose clamps on the rear of the shaft and slide them rearward until they stop at the nearest balance weight welded to the tube. Align both clamps to any one of the four marks and tighten them.

4. Run the car through the speed range of 50-55 mph (89 kph). Note the amount of imbalance.

### ❋❋CAUTION

Never run the car higher than 55 mph (89 kph). Also, everyone should stay clear of the area to avoid possible injury. Do not run the car for long periods of time on the lift due to danger of overheating the engine or transmission.

5. Loosen the clamps and rotate clamp heads 90° to the next mark on the shaft. Tighten the clamps and repeat Step 4.
6. Repeat Step 5 until the car has been run with clamps heads at all four marks on the shaft.
7. Position the clamps at the point of minimum imbalance. Rotate the clamp heads away from each other 45°. Run the car and note if imbalance has improved.
8. Continue to rotate the clamps apart at smaller angular increments until the balance is best.
9. Install the wheels and road test the car for a final check. Vibration felt on the lift may not show up on the road test. If the balance is not improved, replace the driveshaft.

## REAR AXLE

### Identification

▶ See Figure 32

The rear axle number is located in the right or left axle tube adjacent to the axle carrier (differential). Limit slip differentials are identified by a tag attached to the lower right section of the axle cover.

### Determining Axle Ratio

Determining the axle ratio of any given axle can be a very useful tool to the contemporary vehicle owner. Axle ratios are a major factor in a vehicle's fuel mileage, so the vehicle buyer of today should know both what he or she is looking for, and what the salesperson is talking about. Knowledge of axle ratios is also valuable to the owner/mechanic who is shopping through salvage yards for a used axle, who is repairing his or her own rear axle, or who is changing rear axle ratios by changing rear axles.

The rear axle ratio is said to have a certain ratio, say 4.11. It is called a 4.11 rear although the 4.11 actually means 4.11 to 1 (4.11:1). This means that the driveshaft will turn 4.11 times for every turn of the rear wheels. The number 4.11 is determined by dividing the number of teeth on the pinion gear into the number of teeth on the ring gear. In the case of a 4.11 rear, there could be 9 teeth on the pinion and 37 teeth on the ring gear (37/ 9 = 4.11). This provides a sure way, although troublesome, of determining your rear axle's ratio.

The axle must be drained and the rear cover removed to do this, and then the teeth counted.

A much easier method is to jack up the vehicle and safely support it with jackstands, so BOTH rear wheels are off the ground. Block the front wheels, set the parking brake and put the transmission in NEUTRAL. Make a chalk mark on the rear wheel and the driveshaft. Turn the rear wheel one complete revolution and count the number of turns that the driveshaft makes (having an assistant here to count one or the other is helpful). The number of turns the driveshaft makes in one complete revolution of the rear wheel is an approximation of the rear axle ratio.

### Axle Shaft, Bearing and Seal

Two types of axles are used on these models, the C-lock and the non C-lock type. Axle shafts in the C-lock type are retained by C-shaped locks, which fit grooves at the inner end of the shaft. Axle shafts in the non C-lock type are retained by the brake backing plate, which is bolted to the axle housing. Bearings in the C-lock type axle consist of an outer race, bearing rollers, and a roller cage retained by snaprings. The non C-lock type axle uses a unit roller bearing (inner race, rollers, and outer race), which is pressed onto the shaft up to a shoulder. When servicing C-lock or non C-lock type axles, it is imperative to determine the axle type before attempting any service. Before attempting any service to the drive axle or axle shafts, remove the axle carrier cover and visually determine if the axle shafts are retained by C-shaped locks at the inner end, or by the brake backing plate at the outer end.

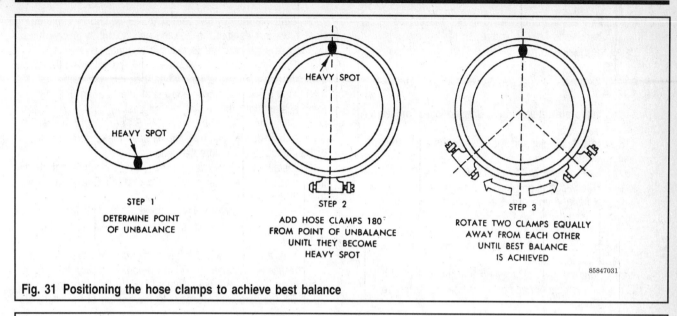

STEP 1
DETERMINE POINT
OF UNBALANCE

STEP 2
ADD HOSE CLAMPS 180°
FROM POINT OF UNBALANCE
UNITL THEY BECOME
HEAVY SPOT

STEP 3
ROTATE TWO CLAMPS EQUALLY
AWAY FROM EACH OTHER
UNTIL BEST BALANCE
IS ACHIEVED

85847031

Fig. 31 Positioning the hose clamps to achieve best balance

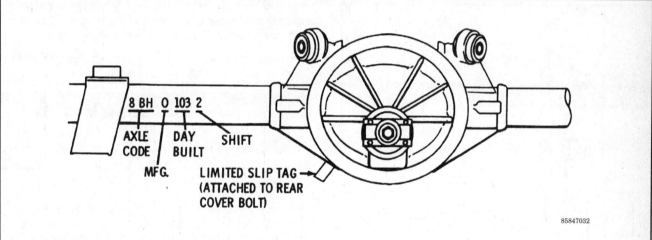

85847032

Fig. 32 Rear axle identification. Manufacturing codes are: P Pontiac; C Chevrolet-Buffalo; K GM Canada; G Chevrolet-Gear and Axle; O Oldsmobile

## REMOVAL & INSTALLATION

▶ See Figures 33, 34, 35, 36 and 37

### ✳✳CAUTION

**Since the brake shoes will be exposed as you perform this procedure, note that brake shoes contain asbestos, which has been determined to be a cancer causing agent. Never clean the brake surfaces with compressed air! Avoid inhaling any dust from any brake surface! If you have to clean in the area of the brake shoes, use a commercially available brake cleaning fluid to remove any brake dust first.**

### Non C-Lock Type

Design allows for maximum axle shaft endplay of 0.022 in. (0.558mm), which can be measured with a dial indicator. If endplay is found to be excessive, the bearing should be re-placed. Shimming the bearing is not recommended as this ignores endplay of the bearing itself and could result in improper seating of the bearing.

1. Remove the wheel, tire and brake drum.
2. Remove the nuts holding the retainer plate to the backing plate. Disconnect the brake line.
3. Remove the retainer and install nuts, finger tight, to prevent the brake backing plate from being dislodged.
4. Pull out the axle shaft and bearing assembly, using a slide hammer.
5. Using a chisel, nick the bearing retainer in three or four places. The retainer does not have to be cut, merely collapsed sufficiently, to allow the bearing retainer to be slid from the shaft.
6. Press off the bearing and install the new one by pressing it into position.
7. Press on the new retainer.

➡**Do not attempt to press the bearing and the retainer on at the same time.**

8. Assemble the shaft and bearing in the housing being sure that the bearing is seated properly in the housing.

9. Install the retainer, drum, wheel and tire. Bleed the brakes.

### C-Lock Type

If the axle shafts are retained by C-shaped locks, proceed as follows:

1. Raise the vehicle, support with jackstands and remove the wheels.

2. Remove the differential cover. Then, remove the differential pinion shaft lock-screw and the differential pinion shaft.

3. Push the flanged end of the axle shaft toward the center of the vehicle and remove the C-lock from the end of the shaft.

4. Remove the axle shaft from the housing, being careful not to damage the oil seal.

5. Remove the oil seal by inserting the button end of the axle shaft behind the steel case of the oil seal. Pry the seal loose from the bore.

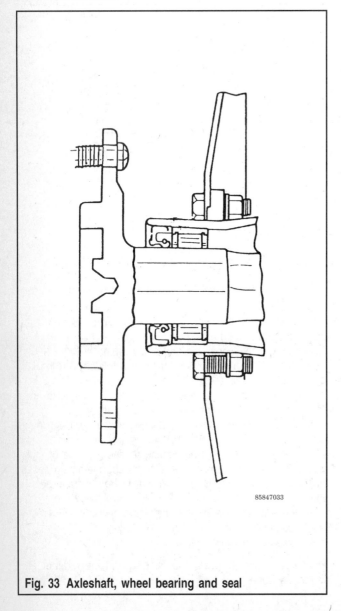

85847033

**Fig. 33 Axleshaft, wheel bearing and seal**

6. Seat the legs of the bearing puller behind the bearing. Seat a washer against the bearing and hold it in place with a nut. Use a slide hammer to pull the bearing.

7. Pack the cavity between the seal lips with wheel bearing lubricant and lubricate a new wheel bearing with same.

8. Use a suitable driver and install the bearing until it bottoms against the tube. Install the oil seal.

9. Slide the axle shaft into place. Be sure that the splines on the shaft do not damage the oil seal. Make sure that the splines engage the differential side gear.

10. Install the axle shaft C-lock on the inner end of the axle shaft and push the shaft outward so that the C-lock seats in the differential side gear counterbore.

11. Position the differential pinion shaft through the case and pinions, aligning the hole in the case with the hole for the lockscrew.

12. Use a new gasket and install the carrier cover. Be sure that the gasket surfaces are clean before installing the gasket and cover. Torque the cover bolts to 22 ft. lbs. (30 Nm).

13. Fill the axle with lubricant to the bottom of the filler hole.

➡ **Special limit slip differential fluid is needed to properly lubricate the limit slip carrier clutches or cones. Standard fluid may cause damage to the rear axle assembly.**

14. Install the brake drum and wheels and lower the vehicle. Check for leaks and road test the vehicle.

## Pinion Seal

### REMOVAL & INSTALLATION

▶ **See Figures 38 and 39**

1. Raise the vehicle and support with jackstands.

2. Mark the driveshaft and pinion yoke for reinstallation. Remove the driveshaft from the pinion yoke and wire it up to the frame. Tape the U-joint caps in place to prevent dirt from entering the U-joint.

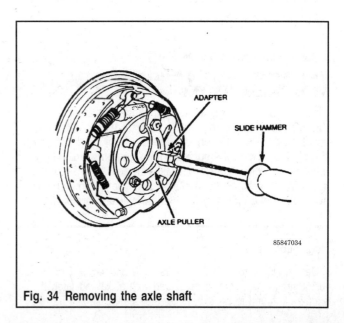

ADAPTER

SLIDE HAMMER

AXLE PULLER

85847034

**Fig. 34 Removing the axle shaft**

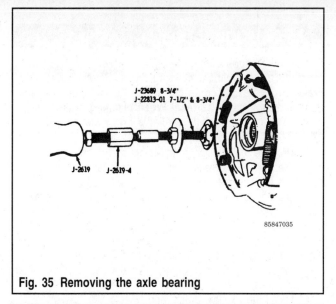

**Fig. 35 Removing the axle bearing**

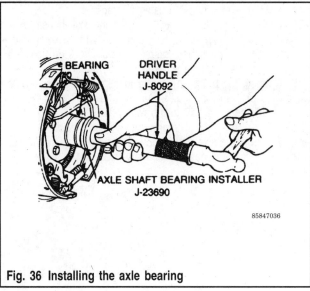

**Fig. 36 Installing the axle bearing**

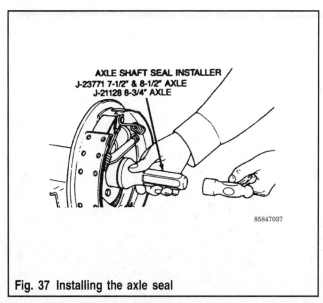

**Fig. 37 Installing the axle seal**

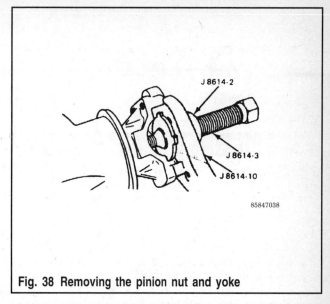

**Fig. 38 Removing the pinion nut and yoke**

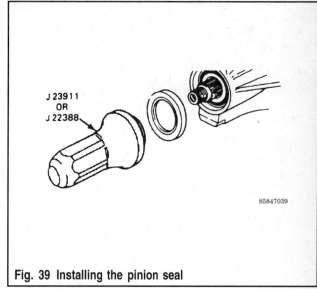

**Fig. 39 Installing the pinion seal**

3. Mark the position of the pinion yoke, pinion gear shaft and pinion yoke nut so the proper bearing preload can be maintained.

4. Place a drain pan under the pinion yoke. Remove the pinion nut and washer using a pinion yoke remover J-8614-10 or equivalent.

5. Remove the pinion yoke using removing tools J-8614-2, J-8614-3 and J-8614-10.

6. Remove the seal with a slide hammer or by driving it out of the carrier with a blunt chisel. Do NOT damage the carrier.

**To install:**

7. Clean all dirt, varnish, nicks and tool marks off of the yoke seal carrier with a small file or fine emery cloth.

8. Install a new pinion seal using a seal installer J-23911 or J-22388.

9. Lubricate the seal with differential fluid.

10. Install the pinion yoke, washer and nut.

11. Using the yoke holding tool, torque the nut to $1/16$ in. (1.6mm) past the alignment marks.

12. Install the driveshaft to the marks positions and lower the vehicle.

## Axle Housing

### REMOVAL & INSTALLATION

### ✳✳CAUTION

**The axle housing is a heavy component. Use care when supporting the housing to prevent personal injury.**

1. Disconnect the negative (-) battery cable.
2. Raise the vehicle and support the rear of the vehicle at the frame. A jack must remain under the rear axle housing.
3. Disconnect the shock absorbers from the axle housing.
4. Mark and remove the driveshaft from the rear yoke.
5. Disconnect and plug the brake line from the junction block. Disconnect the height sensor if equipped with Electronic Level Control (ELC).
6. Disconnect the upper control arms from the axle housing.

7. Lower the axle housing using the jack.

### ✳✳CAUTION

**Some brake shoes contain asbestos, which has been determined to be a cancer causing agent. Never clean the brake surfaces with compressed air! Avoid inhaling any dust from any brake surface! When cleaning brake surfaces, use a commercially available brake cleaning fluid.**

8. Remove the springs, rear wheels and drums.
9. Disconnect and remove the parking brake cables from the brake backing plates.
10. Disconnect the lower control arms and remove the axle housing.

**To install:**

11. Position the axle housing under the vehicle and connect the lower control arms. Only hand tight at this time.
12. Install and connect the parking brake cables to the brake backing plates.
13. Install the springs, drums and wheels.
14. Raise the axle housing using the jack.
15. Connect the upper control arms to the axle housing. Raise the axle housing until the frame starts to raise off of the supports. Torque the upper control arm bolts to 80 ft. lbs. (108 Nm) and the lower control arms to 122 ft. lbs. (165 Nm).
16. Connect the brake line to the junction block. Connect the height sensor if equipped with Electronic Level Control (ELC).
17. Install the driveshaft to the rear yoke.
18. Connect the shock absorbers to the axle housing.
19. Raise the vehicle and remove the support at the frame.
20. Connect the negative (-) battery cable and check operation.

# 8

# STEERING
# AND
# SUSPENSION

## WHEELS

### Wheel Assembly

#### REMOVAL & INSTALLATION

▶ See Figure 1

1. If using a lug wrench, loosen the lug nuts slightly before raising the vehicle.
2. Raise the vehicle and support it safely.
3. Remove the lug nuts and wheel from the vehicle.
**To install:**
4. Install the wheel and hand tighten the lug nuts until they are snug.
5. Lower the vehicle and torque the lug nuts evenly to 80 ft. lbs (110 Nm).

#### INSPECTION

1. Before putting on the wheels, check for any cracks on the wheels or enlarged bolt holes, remove any corrosion on the mounting surfaces with a wire brush. Installation of wheels without a good metal-tometal contact at the mounting surface can cause wheel nuts to loosen. Recheck the wheels after 1,000 miles of driving.

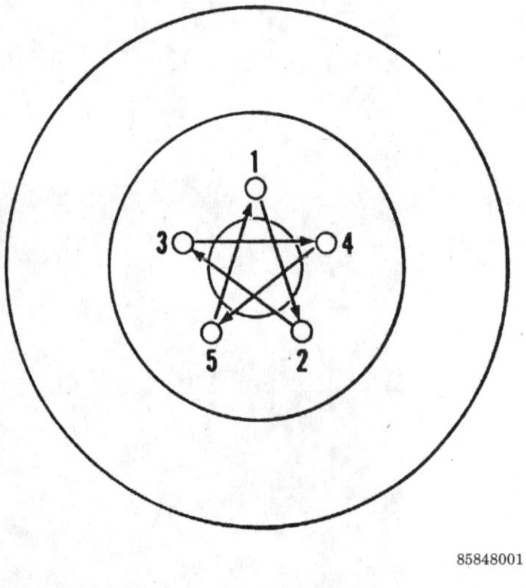

### Wheel Lug Studs

#### REPLACEMENT

▶ See Figures 2, 3 and 4

**Front Wheels**

1. Remove the rotor assembly from the car.
2. Remove the damaged bolt with a press. Do not damage the wheel mounting surface on the hub flange.
**To install:**
3. Install a new serrated bolt into the hole in the hub. Tap lightly with a hammer to start the bolt serrations in the hole, make sure the bolt is square with the hub flange.
The brake disc must be supported properly before pressing the wheel stud in or out.

**Rear Wheels**

1. Raise and support the car. Mark the relationship of the wheel assembly to the axle flange and remove the brake drum.
2. Using tool J-6627 press the wheel stud from the axle flange.
**To install:**
3. Insert a new wheel stud in the axle flange hole. Rotate the bolt slowly to assure the serrations are aligned with those made with the original bolt.
4. Place a flat washer over the outside end of the wheel stud and thread a standard wheel nut with the flatside against the washer. Tighten the wheel nut until the bolt head seats against the axle flange.

Fig. 1 Wheel nut tightening sequence

Fig. 2 Broken wheel studs should always be repaired

## FRONT SUSPENSION

▶ **See Figure 5**

The front suspension is designed to allow each wheel to compensate for changes in the road surface level without appreciably affecting the opposite wheel. Each wheel is independently connected to the frame by a steering knuckle, ball joint assemblies, and upper and lower control arms. The control arms are specifically designed and positioned to allow the steering knuckles to move in a prescribed three dimensional arc. The front wheels are held in proper relationship to each other by two tie rods which are connected to steering arms on the knuckles and to an intermediate rod.

Chassis coil springs are mounted between the spring housings on the frame or front end sheet metal and the lower control arms. Ride control is provided by double, direct acting, shock absorbers mounted inside the coil springs and attached to the lower control arms by bolts and nuts. The upper portion of each shock absorber extends through the upper control arm frame bracket and is secured with two grommets, two grommet retainers, and a nut.

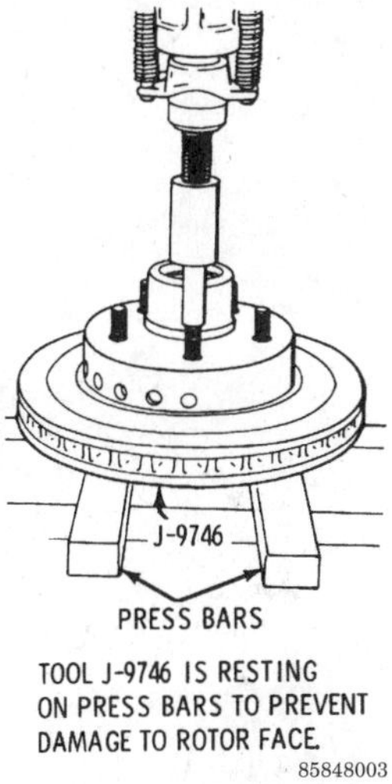

Side roll of the front suspension is controlled by a spring steel stabilizer shaft. It is mounted in rubber bushings which are held to the frame side rails by brackets. The ends of the stabilizer are connected to the lower control arms by link bolts isolated by rubber grommets.

The upper control arm is attached to a cross shaft through isolating rubber bushings. The cross shaft, in turn, is bolted to frame brackets.

A ball joint assembly is riveted to the outer end of the upper arm. It is pre-loaded by a rubber spring to insure proper seating of the ball in the socket. The upper ball joint is attached to the steering knuckle by a torque prevailing nut.

The inner ends of the lower control arm have pressed in bushings. Bolts, passing through the bushings, attach the arm to the frame. The lower ball joint assembly is a press fit in the arm and attaches to the steering knuckle with a torque prevailing nut.

Rubber grease seals are provided at ball socket assemblies to keep dirt and moisture from entering the joint and damaging bearing surfaces.

## Coil Springs

### REMOVAL & INSTALLATION

▶ **See Figures 6, 7 and 8**

### ✳✳CAUTION

**The coil springs are under a considerable amount of tension. Be extremely careful when removing or installing them; they can exert enough force to cause serious injury. Use only approved spring compressors for suspension servicing.**

1. Raise the front of the vehicle and support with jack-stands at the frame so the control arms hang free.
2. Remove the shock absorber. Disconnect the stabilizer bar at the steering knuckle.
3. Support the inner end of the control arm with a floor jack.
4. Raise the jack enough to take the tension off the lower control arm pivot bolts. Install the spring compressor through the spring and frame. Tighten the compressor until the lower control arm pivots bolts can be removed. Compress the spring far enough to remove the lower control arm and spring.
5. Remove the lower ball joint nut and separate from the knuckle using a ball joint separator tool J-23742 or equivalent.
6. Chain the spring to the lower control arm.
7. Remove first the rear, then the front pivot bolt.
8. Cautiously loosen the spring compressor until all spring tension is released.
9. Note the way in which the spring is installed in relation to the drain holes on the control arm and remove it.

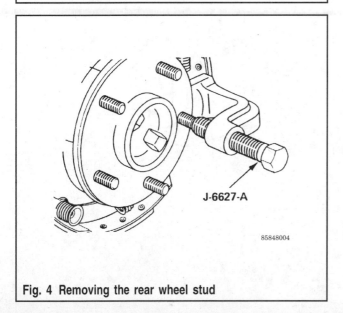

**Fig. 3 Pressing the front wheel studs out**

TOOL J-9746 IS RESTING ON PRESS BARS TO PREVENT DAMAGE TO ROTOR FACE.

J-9746

PRESS BARS

85848003

J-6627-A

85848004

**Fig. 4 Removing the rear wheel stud**

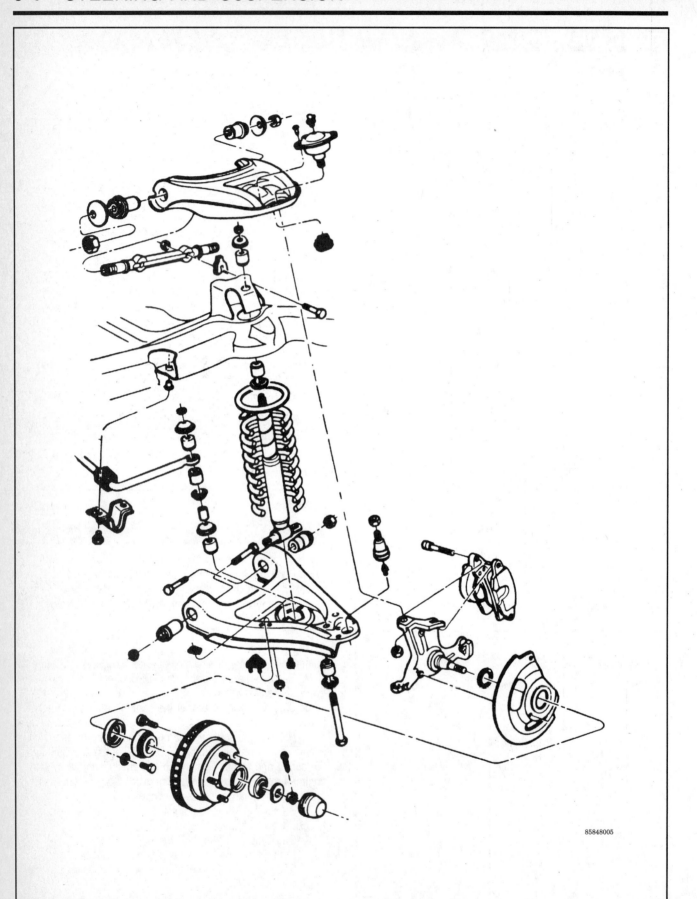

85848005

**Fig. 5 An exploded view of front suspension components**

**To install:**

10. On installation, position the spring to the control arm and raise it into place. On 1985 and later Oldsmobile models, note that the spring must be positioned so that the end of the coil covers all or part of one inspection/drain hole in the lower control arm, and the other hole must be only partly covered.

11. Compress the spring far enough to install the front and rear pivot bolts.

12. Install the pivot bolts and torque the nuts to 100 ft. lbs. (136 Nm) on models built through 1984. On 1985-90 models, torque the bolts to 90 ft. lbs. (122 Nm).

13. Install the lower ball joint to the knuckle, torque the nut to 85 ft. lbs. (112 Nm) and install a new cotter pin.

14. Replace the shock absorber and stabilizer bar.

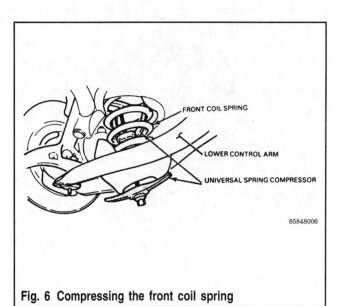

**Fig. 6 Compressing the front coil spring**

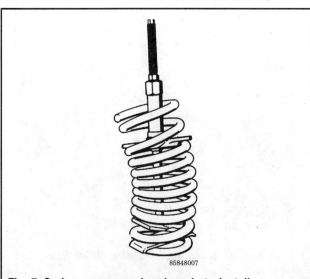

**Fig. 7 Spring compressed and ready to install**

## Shock Absorbers

### REMOVAL & INSTALLATION

▶ **See Figures 9, 10, 11 and 12**

1. Raise the vehicle, and with an open end wrench hold the upper stem of the shock absorber from turning. Remove the upper stem retaining nut, retainer and grommet.

2. Remove the two bolts retaining the lower shock absorber pivot to the lower control arm and then pull the shock out through the bottom of the control arm.

3. With the lower retainer and the rubber grommet in place over the upper stem, install the shock (fully extended) back through the lower control arm.

4. Install the upper grommet, retainer and nut onto the upper stem.

5. Hold the upper stem from turning with an open end wrench and then tighten the retaining nut.

6. Reinstall the retainers on the lower end of the shock.

### TESTING

Visually inspect the shock absorber. If there is evidence of leakage and the shock absorber is covered with oil, the shock has reached the end of its life and should be replaced.

If there is no sign of excessive leakage (a small amount of weeping is normal) bounce the vehicle at one corner by pressing down on the fender or bumper and releasing. When you have the vehicle bouncing as much as you can, release the fender or bumper. The vehicle should stop bouncing after the first rebound. If the bouncing continues past the center point of the bounce more than once, the shock absorbers are worn and should be replaced.

## Upper Ball Joints

▶ **See Figures 13, 14, 15 and 16**

### INSPECTION

➡**Before performing this inspection, make sure the wheel bearings are adjusted correctly and that the control arm bushings are in good condition. All models covered in this guide are equipped with wear indicators on the lower ball joint. As long as the indicator extends below the ball stud seat, replacement is unnecessary; if only the lower ball joint is bad, however, both upper and lower ball joints should be replaced.**

1. Raise the vehicle by placing the jack under the lower control arm at the spring seat.

2. Raise the vehicle until there is a 1-2 in. (25-51mm) clearance under the wheel.

3. Insert a bar under the wheel and pry upward. If the wheel raises more than 1/8 in. (3mm), the ball joints are worn. Determine whether the upper or lower ball joint is worn by visual inspection while prying on the wheel.

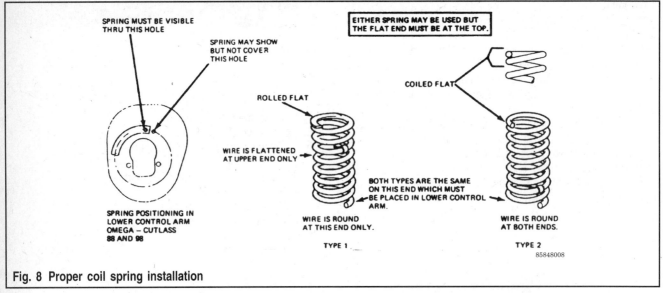

Fig. 8 Proper coil spring installation

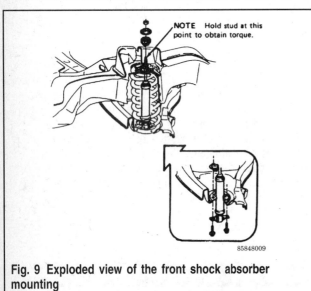

Fig. 9 Exploded view of the front shock absorber mounting

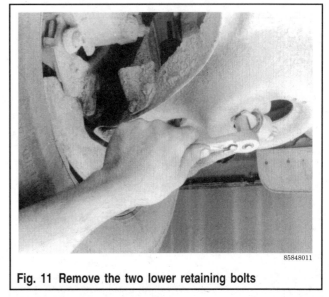

Fig. 11 Remove the two lower retaining bolts

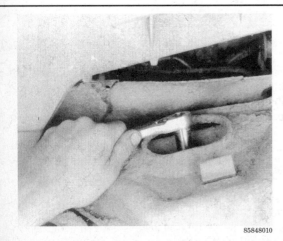
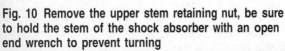

Fig. 10 Remove the upper stem retaining nut, be sure to hold the stem of the shock absorber with an open end wrench to prevent turning

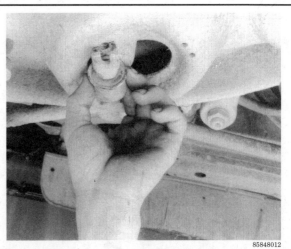

Fig. 12 Pull the shock absorber through the lower control arm

## REMOVAL & INSTALLATION

1. Raise the vehicle and support securely. Support the lower control arm securely with jackstands. Remove the tire and wheel.

2. Remove the upper ball stud cotter pin and loosen the ball stud nut just one turn.

3. Procure a special tool designed to press out ball joints. These tools are available at most automotive parts stores. Locate the tool between the upper and lower ball joints and press the joints out of the steering knuckle. Remove the tool.

4. Remove the ball joint stud nut, and separate the joint from the steering knuckle. Lift the upper arm up and place a block of wood between the frame and the arm to support it.

5. With the control arm in the raised position, drill a hole ¼ in. (6mm) deep hole into each rivet. Use a ⅛ in. (3mm) drill bit.

6. Use a ½ in. drill bit and drill off the heads of each rivet.

7. Punch out the rivets using a small punch and then remove the ball joint.

8. Install the new ball joint using fasteners that meet GM specifications. Bolts should come in from the bottom with the nuts going on top. Torque to specifications included in the ball joint kit.

9. Turn the ball stud cotter pin hole to the fore and aft position on models up to 1981. 1982 and later models use no cotter pin. Remove the block of wood from between the upper control arm and frame.

10. Clean and inspect the steering knuckle hole. Replace the steering knuckle if any out of roundness is noted.

11. Insert the ball stud into the steering knuckle, and install and torque the stud nut to 60 ft. lbs. (81 Nm). Install a new cotter pin. If the nut must be turned to align cotter pin holes, turn them further. Do not back off!

12. Install a lube fitting, and fill the joint with fresh grease.

13. Remove the lower control arm support (jack, etc.) and lower the vehicle.

## Lower Ball Joints

♦ **See Figures 17 and 18**

### INSPECTION

➡**Before performing this inspection, make sure the wheel bearings are adjusted correctly and that the control arm bushings are in good condition.**

All models covered in this guide are equipped with wear indicators on the lower ball joint. As long as the indicator extends below the ball stud seat, replacement is unnecessary; if only the lower ball joint is bad, however, both upper and lower ball joints should be replaced.

### REMOVAL & INSTALLATION

1. Raise the vehicle and support it securely. Support the lower control arm with a jack or jackstand. Remove the wheel.

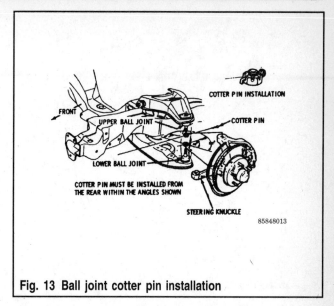

**Fig. 13 Ball joint cotter pin installation**

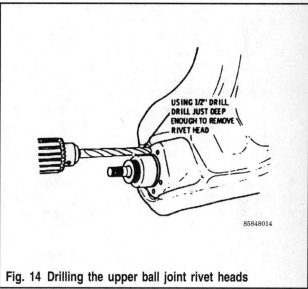

**Fig. 14 Drilling the upper ball joint rivet heads**

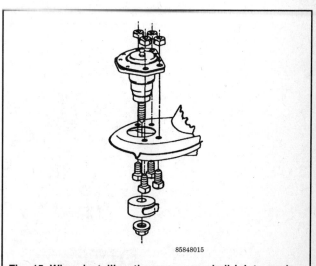

**Fig. 15 When installing the new upper ball joints, make sure the nuts are on top**

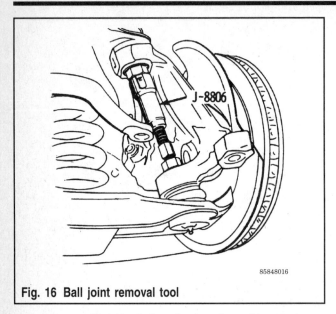

Fig. 16 Ball joint removal tool

2. Remove the lower ball stud cotter pin, and loosen the ball stud nut 2-3 turns.

3. Install a special tool designed for such work between the two ball studs, and press the stud downward in the steering knuckle to free it. Then, remove the stud nut.

4. Guide the lower control arm out of the opening in the splash shield with a putty knife or something similar. Lift up on the upper control arm and place a block of wood between it and the frame. Be careful not to put tension on the brake hose as you do this.

5. Remove the ball joint seal by prying off the retainer with a prybar or driving it off with a chisel.

6. Remove grease fittings and install a tool designed for this purpose and press the ball joint out of the lower control arm. On some models, you may have to disconnect the tie rod at the knuckle to do this.

**To install:**

7. Position the ball joint in the control arm so that the grease purge on the seal faces inboard. Press the joint in with a tool designed for this purpose until it bottoms on the control arm. Remove the block of wood and then insert the ballstud through the steering knuckle hole on the control arm.

8. Turn the ball stud cotter pin hole so it faces fore and aft. Install the nut on the ball stud and torque it to: 105 ft. lbs. (140 Nm) on 1975-77 vehicles; 83 ft. lbs. (112 Nm) on 1978-79 vehicles; 90 ft. lbs. (122 Nm) on 1980-81 vehicles; 70 ft. lbs. (95 Nm) on 1982-83 models; and 90 ft. lbs. (122 Nm) on 1984-90 models. Then, as necessary, turn the nut tighter to line up one of the castellations with the cotter pin hole. Finally, install the cotter pin and bend both prongs down and back against the nut. Lubricate the joint until grease appears at the seal. Remove supports and lower the vehicle.

## Sway Bar

▶ See Figures 19, 20 and 21

## REMOVAL & INSTALLATION

1. Raise the front end of the vehicle and safely support it with jackstands.

2. Disconnect each side of the sway bar linkage by removing the nut from the link bolt. Pull the bolt from the linkage and remove the retainers, grommets and spacer.

3. Remove the bracket-to-frame or body bolts on both sides of the vehicle and remove the sway bar, rubber bushings and brackets.

**To install:**

4. Make sure the rubber bushings are installed squarely in the bracket with the slit in the bushings facing the front of the vehicle. Torque the sway bar link nuts to 13 ft. lbs. (18 Nm).

## Upper Control Arm

▶ See Figures 22, 23, 24 and 25

## REMOVAL & INSTALLATION

1. Raise the vehicle and support safely with jackstands.

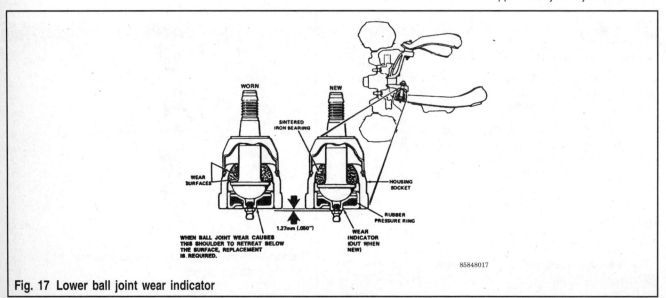

Fig. 17 Lower ball joint wear indicator

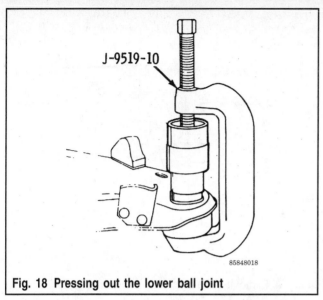

Fig. 18 Pressing out the lower ball joint

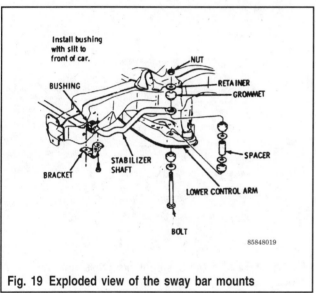

Fig. 19 Exploded view of the sway bar mounts

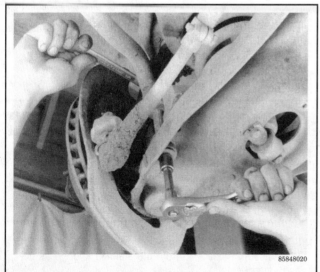

Fig. 20 Removing the sway bar link bolt

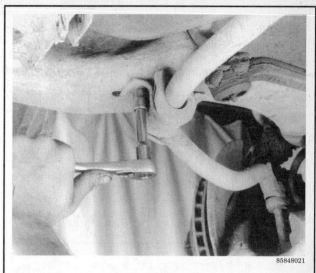

Fig. 21 Removing the bracket-to-frame bolts

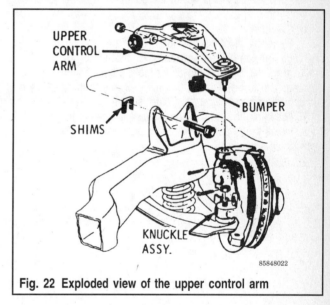

Fig. 22 Exploded view of the upper control arm

2. Support the outer end of the lower control arm with a jack.

**✳✳CAUTION**

Leave the jack in place during removal and installation, in order to keep the spring and control arm positioned.

3. Remove the wheel.
4. Separate the upper ball joint from the steering knuckle as described above under Upper Ball Joint Replacement.
5. Remove the control arm shaft-to-frame nuts.

➡Tape the shims together and identify them so that they can be installed in the positions from which they were removed.

6. Remove the bolts which attach the control arm shaft to the frame and remove the control arm. Note the positions of the bolts.

**To install:**

7. Make sure that the shaft-to-frame bolts are installed in the same position they were in before removal and that the shims are in their original positions.

8. Use free running nuts (not locknuts) to pull serrated bolts through the frame.

9. Install the locknuts. Tighten the thinner shim pack first.

10. After the vehicle has been lowered to the ground, bounce the front end to center the bushings and then tighten the bushing collar bolts to 45 ft. lbs. (61 Nm). Tighten the shaft-to-frame bolts to 90 ft. lbs. (122 Nm). The control arm shaft nuts are tightened to 75 ft. lbs. (102 Nm) on models through 1982. Use 85 ft. lbs. (115 Nm) on 1983-90 models.

## CONTROL ARM BUSHING REPLACEMENT

1. Remove the upper control arm assembly from the car.
2. Remove the nuts from the ends of the pivot shaft.
3. Push the bushings out of the control arm using suitable bushing removal tools.

**To install:**

4. Place the pivot shaft in the control arm and push new bushings into the control arm and over the end of the pivot shaft using suitable bushing driver tools. Upper control arm bushings are to be installed 0.5 in. (13.3 mm) from the face of the control arm to the bushing outer sleeve.

5. Assemble the nuts to the ends of the pivot shafts.

6. Install the upper control arm assembly following the procedures above.

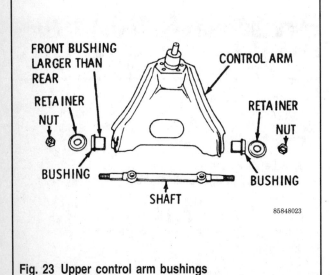

Fig. 23 Upper control arm bushings

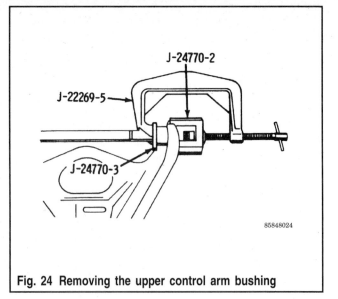

Fig. 24 Removing the upper control arm bushing

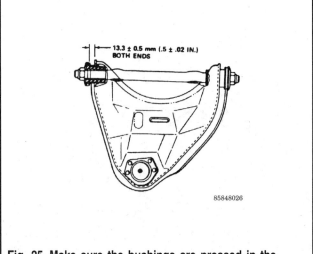

Fig. 25 Make sure the bushings are pressed in the proper distance

## Lower Control Arm

▶ See Figures 26, 27, 28, 29, 30 and 31

### REMOVAL & INSTALLATION

### ✳✳CAUTION

**The coil springs are under a considerable amount of tension. Be extremely careful when removing or installing them; they can exert enough force to cause serious injury. Use only approved spring compressors for suspension servicing.**

1. Remove the spring as described earlier.
2. Remove the ball stud from the steering knuckle as described earlier.
3. Remove the control arm pivot bolts and the control arm. On later models, you may have to guide the control arm out of

the splash shield, using a putty knife or similar tool to protect parts.

**To install:**

4. Position the control arm into spring and locate the bushing-to-frame brackets. If any bolts are to be replaced, do so with bolts of equal strength and quality.

5. Install the bolts and nuts loosely. Connect the control arm with the knuckle and torque the nut to 83 ft. lbs. (112 Nm). Install a **new** cotter pin.

6. With a jack supporting the lower control arm, torque the attaching bolts.

7. Install the shock absorber, sway bar and wheel. Lower the vehicle and check operation.

## CONTROL ARM BUSHING REPLACEMENT

**Front Bushing**

1. Remove the lower control arm.

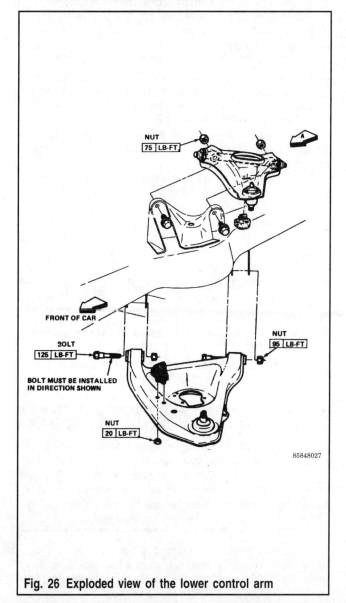

**Fig. 26 Exploded view of the lower control arm**

2. Using proper bushing removal tools remove the bushing from the control arm.

**To install:**

3. Using suitable bushing driver tools, install the bushing onto the control arm.

4. Remove the bushing driver tools and install a suitable bushing flaring tool.

5. Turn the nut until the bushing is flared.

**Rear Bushing**

1. Remove the bushing from the control arm using the proper bushing removal tools.

**To install:**

2. Install the bushings using the appropriate tools. When properly installed, the bushings should bottom against the control arm.

3. Install the control arm using the procedures above.

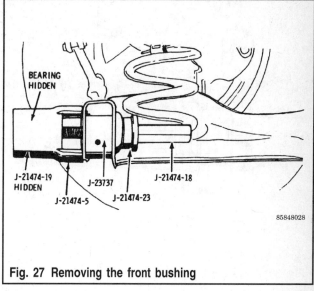

**Fig. 27 Removing the front bushing**

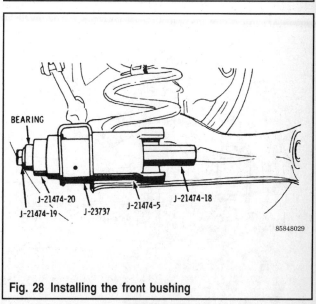

**Fig. 28 Installing the front bushing**

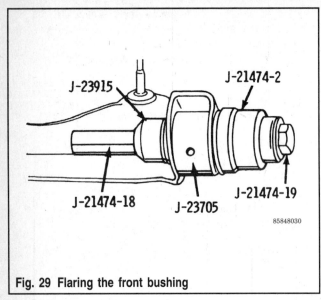

Fig. 29 Flaring the front bushing

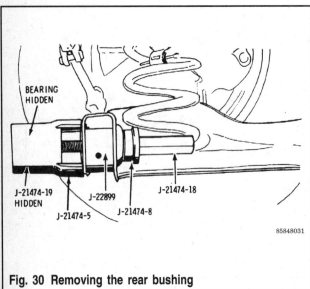

Fig. 30 Removing the rear bushing

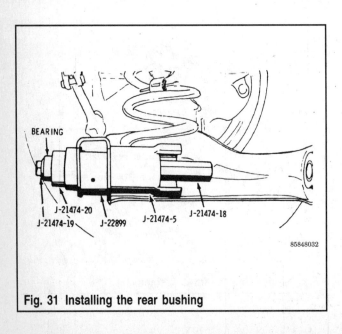

Fig. 31 Installing the rear bushing

## Knuckle and Spindle

### REMOVAL & INSTALLATION

➡️In order to perform this procedure, you will need a tool for forcing ball joint studs out of the control arms. It would also be helpful to have a tool that will permit you to press the tie rod end out of the steering knuckle. A special tool for seating the tie rod ends when installing them back into the knuckles, GM J-29193 or equivalent, will ensure proper seating.

1. Raise the vehicle and support it securely under the frame. Do not support the lower control arm yet.

### ✳✳CAUTION

Some brake pads contain asbestos, which has been determined to be a cancer causing agent. Never clean the brake surfaces with compressed air! Avoid inhaling any dust from any brake surface! When cleaning brake surfaces, use a commercially available brake cleaning fluid.

2. Refer to Section 9 and remove the brake caliper. Then, refer to the procedure for removing the brake disc in the same chapter and remove the disc and hub.
3. Remove the three bolts attaching the water shield to the steering knuckle. Remove the shield and its gasket. Disconnect the tie rod ends from the steering knuckle as described later in the 'Steering' section in this chapter.
4. Pry the knuckle seal off the knuckle carefully in order to avoid damaging the knuckle sealing surfaces and discard the old seal.
5. Remove the cotter pin and then loosen the ball joint stud retaining nut just a turn or two on both upper and lower ball joints. You want just enough clearance to break the ball joint studs loose in the control arms.

### ✳✳CAUTION

The nuts must remain on the studs with plenty of extra threads in order to prevent the release of spring tension.

Use an appropriate special tool to press the upper and lower ball joint studs out of the control arms until the nuts bottom out against the arms.

### ✳✳CAUTION

There is tremendous spring pressure forcing the lower control arm downward. You must assure yourself that you have a floor jack or other appropriate means to safely and securely support the lower control arm by the area under the spring in the next step; otherwise, remove the spring as described earlier to eliminate spring tension.

6. Securely support the lower control arm by the area directly under the spring. You can locate a floor jack directly under the control arm and raise it just until is contacts the control arm to do this. Then, remove the nuts from the ball studs.

7. Remove the tie rod end cotter pin, nut and rod end using a tie rod puller tool J-6627-A. Refer to the 'Steering' section in this chapter for assistance.

8. Raise the upper control arm for clearance and rock the knuckle outward so the ball stud clears the knuckle. Then, pull the knuckle upward and off the lower ball joint stud and remove it.

9. Inspect the tapered holes in the steering knuckle, cleaning out dirt and checking for any out-of-roundness, cracking, deformation, or other damage. Replace the knuckle if there are any such indications or dangerous front end problems could result.

**To install:**

10. Position the knuckle onto the lower ball joint stud and then raise the upper control arm, working the upper ball stud into the tapered hole in the top of the knuckle.

11. Install the ball joint stud nuts, torque them, and install the cotter pins as described under 'Ball Joint' removal and installation earlier in this chapter.

## ✳✳CAUTION

**It is vitally important that the tie rod end seat fully in the steering knuckle. You may want to use a tool such as GM J-29193 or equivalent to ensure complete seating. This tool is installed over the partly assembled knuckle and tie rod end and its nut is torqued to 15 ft. lbs. (20 Nm) to draw the tie rod end into the knuckle.**

12. Install the tie rod end into the steering knuckle. Install the nut and torque it to 40 ft. lbs. (54 Nm).

13. Install a new shield-to-knuckle splash shield and install the shield, torquing the three mounting bolts to 120 inch lbs. (14 Nm). Grease its lips with wheel bearing grease and carefully install a new grease seal.

14. Repack the wheel bearings, install the hub and rotor, and readjust the bearings.

15. Install the caliper and remaining parts in reverse order, referring to the 'Caliper' removal and installation procedure in Section 9.

## Front Wheel Bearings

▶ **See Figures 32, 33, 34, 35, 36, 37, 38, 39, 40 and 41**

## REPLACEMENT

1. Remove the front wheel and caliper assembly. Do not allow the caliper to hang by it's hose, secure it with a length of wire.

2. Remove the hub bearing cup and the cotter pin.

3. Remove the castellated nut and washer, then remove the outer bearing race and hub assembly.

4. Pry the seal from the hub, then remove the inner roller bearing assembly.

5. To replace the inner or outer bearing race, insert a brass drift into the hub, indexing the end of the drift with the notches in the hub and tap with a hammer.

**To install:**

6. Clean off any grease from the hub and spindle.

7. Drive the new inner and outer bearing races into the hub. Use tools J-8092 and J-8850 for the inner race and tools J-8092 and J-8457 for the outer race or their equivalent.

8. Use an approved high temperature front wheel bearing grease. Do not mix greases as this can change the properties and lead to poor performance.

9. Apply a thin film of grease to the spindle at the outer bearing seat and at the inner bearing seat, shoulder, and seal seat.

10. Put a small quantity of grease inboard of each bearing cup in the hub. This can be applied with your finger, forming a dam to provide extra grease availability to the bearing and to keep thinned grease from flowing out of the bearing.

11. Fill the bearing cone and roller assemblies full of grease. Work the grease thoroughly into the bearings between the rollers, cone and the cage. Failure to do so could result in premature bearing failure.

12. Place the inner bearing cone and roller assembly in the hub. Then, using your finger, put an additonal amount of grease outboard of the bearing.

13. Install a new seal using a large socket or flat plate until the seal is flush with the hub. Apply force only on the outer edge of the seal, not on the rubber portion. Lubricate the seal lip with a thin layer of grease.

14. Carefully install the rotor and hub assembly. Place the outer cone and roller assembly in the outer bearing cup. Install the washer and nut and intially tighten the nut to 12 ft. lbs (16 Nm) while turning the wheel assembly forward by hand. Put an additional quantity of grease outboard of the bearing. This provides extra grease availability to the bearing.

15. Adjust the wheel bearings according to the procedures in Section 1.

## Front End Alignment

▶ **See Figures 42 and 43**

➡**The procedure for checking and adjusting front wheel alignment requires specialized equipment and professional skills. The following descriptions and adjustment procedures are for general reference only.**

Front wheel alignment is the position of the front wheels relative to each other and to the vehicle. It is determined, and must be maintained to provide safe, accurate steering with minimum tire wear. Many factors are involved in wheel alignment and adjustments are provided to return those that might change due to normal wear to their original value. The factors which determine wheel alignment are dependent on one another; therefore, when one of the factors is adjusted, the others must be adjusted to compensate. Descriptions of these factors and their affects on the vehicle are provided below.

➡**Do not attempt to check and adjust the front wheel alignment without first making a thorough inspection of the front suspension components.**

## CASTER

Caster angle is the number of degrees that a line drawn through the steering knuckle pivots is inclined from the vertical, toward the front or rear of the vehicle. Caster improves direc-

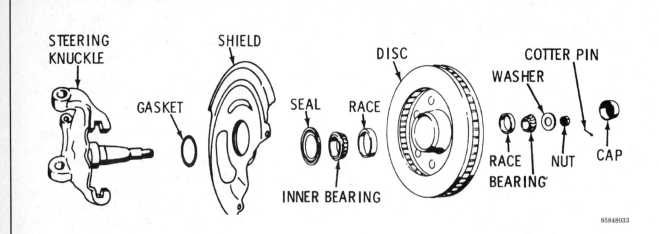

Fig. 32 An exploded view of the hub assembly

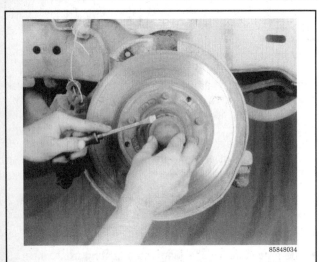

Fig. 33 Carefully pry the bearing cup out, be careful not to distort it

Fig. 35 Remove the castellated nut and the washer

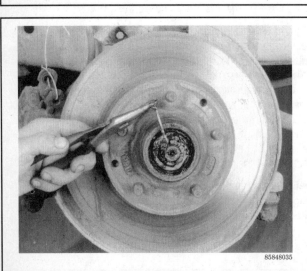

Fig. 34 Remove the cotter pin from the spindle; always use a new cotter pin during reassembly

Fig. 36 Once the above mentioned nut and washer is removed, the outer bearing can be removed from the hub

Fig. 37 Carefully pull the hub assembly off of the spindle

Fig. 38 Pry the seal from the hub; once the seal is removed the inner bearing can be removed

Fig. 39 When installing the new seal, be sure to apply force only on the outer edge of the seal. Don't forget the inner bearing must be installed first

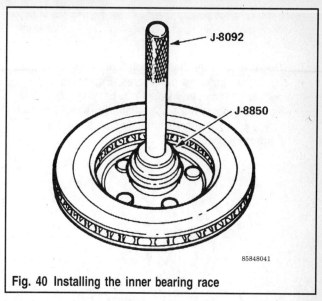

Fig. 40 Installing the inner bearing race

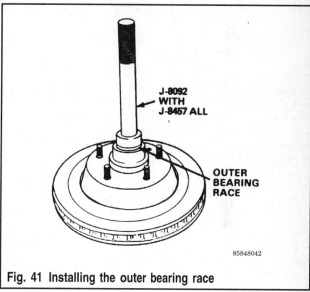

Fig. 41 Installing the outer bearing race

tional stability and decreases susceptibility to crosswinds or road surface deviations.

## CAMBER

Camber angle is the number of degrees that the centerline of the wheel is inclined from the vertical. Camber reduces loading of the outer wheel bearing and improves the tire contact patch while cornering.

## TOE-IN

Toe-in is the difference of the distance between the centers of the front and rear of the front wheels. It is most commonly measured in inches, but is occasionally referred to as an angle between the wheels. Toe-in is necessary to compensate for the tendency of the wheels to deflect rearward while in motion. Due to this tendency, the wheels of a vehicle, with properly adjusted toe-in, are traveling straight forward when the vehicle itself is traveling straight forward, resulting in directional stability and minimum tire wear.

➡The Do-it-Yourself mechanic should not attempt to perform any wheel alignment procedures. Expensive alignment tools are needed and would not be cost efficient to purchase these tools. The wheel alignment should be performed by a certified alignment technician using the proper alignment tools.

## STEERING AXIS INCLINATION

Steering axis inclination is the number of degrees that a line drawn through the steering knuckle pivots is inclined from the vertical, when viewed from the front of the vehicle. This, in combination with caster, is responsible for directional stability and self-centering of the steering. As the steering knuckle swings from lock to lock, the spindle generates an arc, the high point being the straight-ahead position of the wheel. Due to this arc, as the wheel turns, the front of the vehicle is raised. The weight of the vehicle acts against this lift and attempts to return the spindle to the high point of the arc, resulting in self-centering, when the steering wheel is released, and straight line stability.

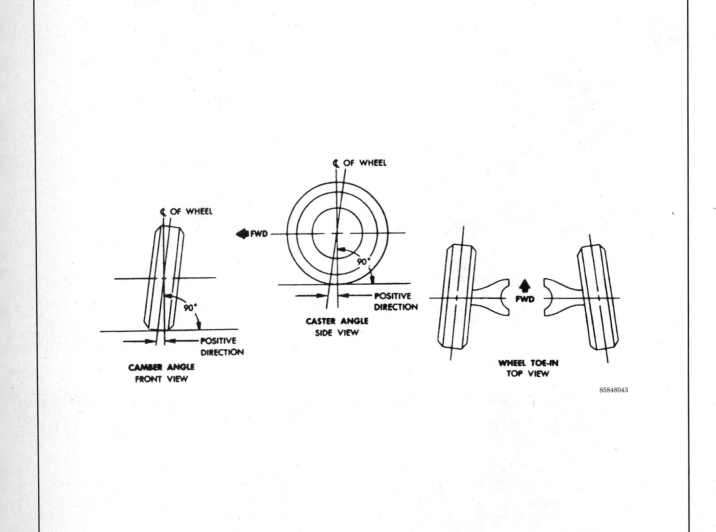

**Fig. 42 Caster, camber and toe-in**

## REAR SUSPENSION

▶ **See Figures 44 and 45**

A four link rear suspension is used on the large-body Buick, Oldsmobile and Pontiac models, except 1975-76 station wagons. The axle housing is connected to the frame by two upper and lower control arms with rubber bushings at each end of the arm. The control arms oppose torque reaction on acceleration and braking, and maintain the axle relationship to the frame.

Two coil springs support the weight of the vehicle in the rear. They are retained between seats in the frame and brackets welded to the axle housing. A rubber insulator is used on the upper side. Shock absorbers are mounted on brackets between the axle housing and the frame.

The rear suspension on 1975 and 1976 station wagons is by parallel leaf springs and shock absorbers.

A sway bar is optional equipment on coil spring models.

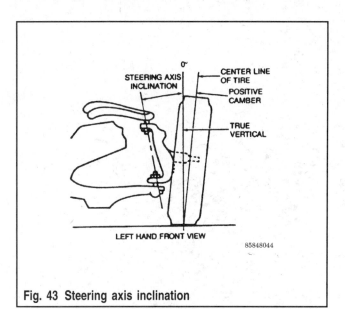

**Fig. 43 Steering axis inclination**

**Fig. 44 Under-car view of a coil spring suspension**

## Coil Springs

### REMOVAL & INSTALLATION

▶ **See Figure 46**

### ❊❊CAUTION

**When removing the rear coil springs without the aid of a spring compressor, be very careful the spring does not fly out and strike someone. If a spring compressor is available, use it. The following procedure does not use a spring compressor. However, if the axle housing is lowered slowly, the spring should come out without incident.**

1. Raise the rear of the vehicle on the axle housing and support it safely on the frame rails with jackstands. Do not lower the jack yet.
2. Disconnect the brake line at the axle housing.
3. Disconnect the upper control arms at the axle housing.
4. Remove the shock absorber at its lower mount.
5. Lower the jack slowly. Do not allow the rear brake hose to become kinked or stretched.
6. Remove the coil spring.

**To install:**

7. Mount the coil spring in place.
8. Jack up the rear axle until you are able to connect the shock at its lower mount.
9. Install the upper control arm bolts at the axle housing and torque to 95 ft. lbs. (128 Nm).
10. Connect the brake line at the axle housing. Bleed the brakes.
11. Remove the jackstands and lower the vehicle.

## Leaf Springs

### REMOVAL & INSTALLATION

▶ **See Figures 47 and 48**

1. Raise the rear axle housing and safely support the rear end of the vehicle with jackstands placed under the rear frame rails (ahead of the forward rear spring shackles). Do not lower the jack yet.

➡**If removing the right hand spring, loosen the tailpipe and resonator assembly.**

2. Remove the lower shock absorber nut and move the shock out of the bracket. Compress the shock out of the way.
3. Lower the jack until the springs are completely relaxed. The jack must remain underneath the axle housing for support until the spring is completely removed.

➡**Do not stretch the brake hose.**

4. Remove the bolts from the rear spring shackles.

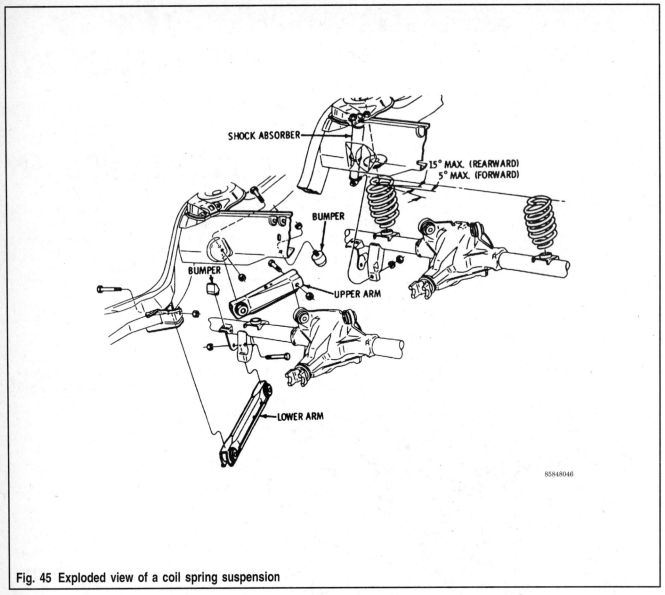

Fig. 45 Exploded view of a coil spring suspension

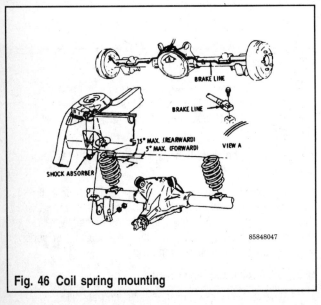

Fig. 46 Coil spring mounting

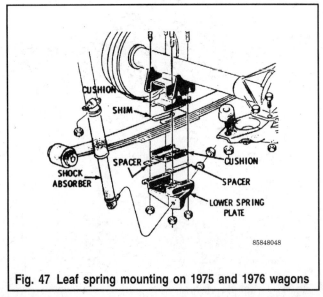

Fig. 47 Leaf spring mounting on 1975 and 1976 wagons

5. Remove the four U-bolt attaching nuts. Remove the spacers, which will be reused during installation.

6. Remove the NUT ONLY from the front shackle bolt, and while holding the spring up, remove the bolt from the shackle. Remove the spring from the vehicle.

**To install:**

➡Before installation, make sure that any parts, including bolts and nuts, that are replaced are replaced with parts of equal strength and quality. Rated nuts and bolts must be replaced with parts of equal rating.

7. Install the sleeves and bushing halves in the rear shackle (if removed) and loosely install the shackle bolt and nut.

## ✳✳CAUTION

**Do not tighten the shackle nuts until the weight of the vehicle is on the springs.**

8. Place the upper spring cushion pad on the spring so the cushion is indexed on the spring center locating bolt head.

9. Lower the axle housing onto the spring, keeping the jack underneath the housing.

10. Place the lower spring cushion pad on the spring and the shock absorber anchor plate with the dimple on the cushion indexed in the hole in the plate.

11. Position the spring and shock absorber anchor plate to the spring, with the nut of the spring center locating bolt indexed in the dimple of the lower spring cushion pad.

12. Install the lower spring plate, then loosely install the U-bolt nuts.

13. Raise the jack slightly, and install the shim spacers.

14. Lower the axle housing onto the spring, and torque the U-bolt nuts to 50 ft. lbs. (68 Nm). Install the shock absorber lower end stud into the spring plate, and tighten the shock lower end stud nut to 48 ft. lbs. (65 Nm). Make sure the shock stud does not rotate while the nut is tightened.

15. Raise the vehicle so the weight of the vehicle is on the springs. Torque the spring front bolt nut to 60 ft. lbs. (81 Nm), and the rear shackle nut to 105 ft. lbs. (140 Nm).

16. Remove the jack studs and lower the vehicle.

## Shock Absorbers

### REMOVAL & INSTALLATION

▶ See Figures 49, 50 and 51

➡Examine the shock absorbers following the Testing procedure given for front shocks in this chapter.

#### All Models

1. Raise the rear end of the vehicle and support it with jackstands. Support the rear axle with the hydraulic jack to prevent stretching the brake hose.

2. Remove the nut from the lower end stud of the shock. Tap the shock free from the bracket.

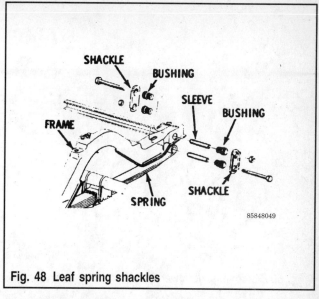

**Fig. 48 Leaf spring shackles**

3. Disconnect the shock at the top by removing the bolts, nuts and the lockwashers. Remove the shock from the vehicle.

4. Install the shock and torque the upper bolts to 20 ft. lbs. (27 Nm) and the lower nut to 48 ft. lbs. (65 Nm).

## Electronic Level Control (ELC)

▶ See Figures 50, 51 and 54

The ELC system is an option to the standard rear suspension on late model station wagons. The system adjusts the trim height with varying vehicle loads. The system is activated when weight is added or removed from the rear of the vehicle. A height sensor is mounted to the body and rear suspension to monitor suspension height. As weight is added to the rear of the vehicle the sensor signals the electric air compressor mounted on the right front inner fender to supply air to the rear shocks to raise the vehicle to the proper level. As the weight is removed, the sensor signals the exhaust solenoid to release air from the rear shocks to lower the vehicle.

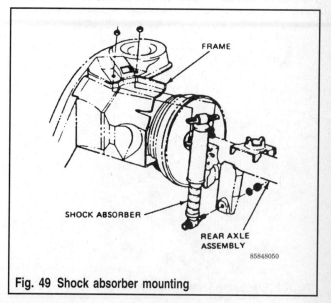

**Fig. 49 Shock absorber mounting**

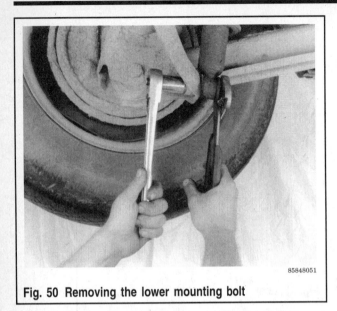
Fig. 50 Removing the lower mounting bolt

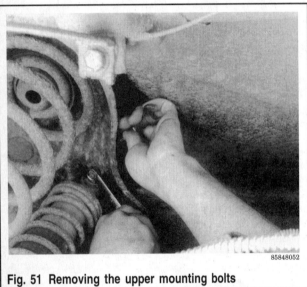
Fig. 51 Removing the upper mounting bolts

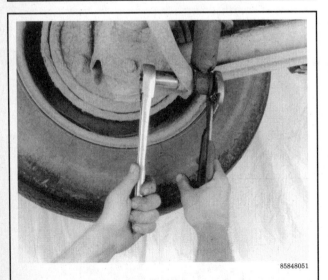
Fig. 52 Electronic level control pump and relay

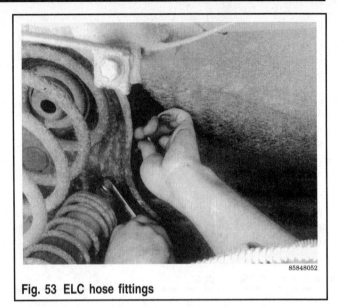
Fig. 53 ELC hose fittings

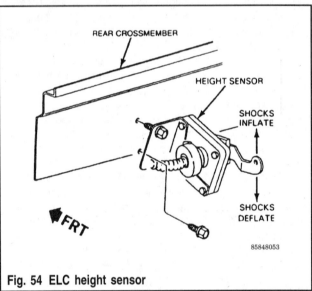
Fig. 54 ELC height sensor

## REMOVAL & INSTALLATION

### Shocks

The ELC shocks are removed the same way as the conventional shocks are removed. The only difference is the air hose has to be disconnected before shock removal

### Air Compressor

1. Disconnect the negative (-) battery cable.
2. Disconnect the high pressure hose at the air dryer by rotating the spring clip 90° while holding the connector end and removing the tube assembly.
3. Disconnect the solenoid and motor connections.
4. Remove the support bracket screws, bracket and compressor.
**To install:**
5. If replacing the compressor, install the dryer and bracket and torque the bolts to 34 inch lbs. (4 Nm). Install the

bracket/compressor assembly and torque the screws to 24 inch lbs. (3 Nm).

6. Make all electrical and air connections.

7. Connect the negative battery cable. Cycle the ignition switch and test for system operation and leaks at the dryer.

### Height Sensor

The sensor is mounted onto the rear frame crossmember and right control arm.

1. Disconnect the negative (-) battery cable and sensor connection.

2. Remove the link from the control arm, unbolt the sensor bracket and remove the sensor assembly from the vehicle.

**To install:**

Install the sensor and adjust trim height as follows:

3. Attach the link to the metal arm at the control arm.

4. To increase the vehicle trim height, move the plastic actuator arm upward and tighten the locknut.

5. To decrease the vehicle trim height, move the plastic actuator arm downward and tighten the locknut. **Height sensor adjustment of 1° = ¼ in. at the bumper. Adjustment of 5° total.**

## STEERING

### Steering Wheel

### ✳✳WARNING

**Do not atttempt to remove the steering wheel on cars equipped with an air bag. This service should be left to a professional service technician to avoid damage to the system and personal injury.**

## REMOVAL & INSTALLATION

◗ **See Figures 55, 56, 57, 58, 59, 60, 61, 62, 63 and 64**

**All Non-Tilt Wheels**

1. Disconnect the negative battery cable.

2. Remove the center pad assembly, either by removing the screws or by gently prying the pad off. Lift up on the pad and disconnect the horn wire by pushing in on the insulator and turning counterclockwise.

3. Remove the steering wheel nut retainer and attaching nut. Using a steering puller, remove the steering wheel.

4. To install, first align the marks on the wheel hub to the marks on the steering shaft.

5. Install the steering wheel, retainer and nut, and torque the nut to 30 ft. lbs. (41 Nm)

➡**When the mark on the steering wheel hub and the steering shaft are lined up, the wheel spokes should be horizontal as the vehicle is driven straight ahead. If they are not horizontal it may be necessary to adjust the tie rod ends until the steering wheel is properly aligned.**

6. Install the horn wire in the cam tower, push in and turn clockwise. Align the pad assembly into position and either press into place or install the screws. Connect the negative battery cable.

**Tilt and Telescope Wheels**

1. Disconnect the negative battery cable.

2. Remove the pad assembly by either removing the screws or prying the pad off. Disconnect the bayonet-type connector at the horn wire by pushing in and turning counterclockwise.

3. Push the locking lever counterclockwise until the full release position is obtained.

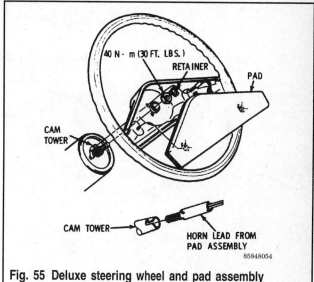

Fig. 55 Deluxe steering wheel and pad assembly

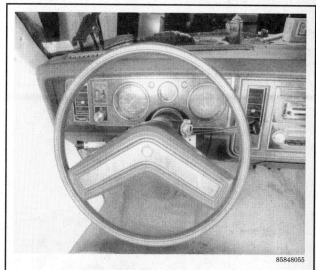

Fig. 56 A common non-tilt steering wheel and column

4. Scribe a mark on the plate assembly where the two attaching screws attach the plate assembly to the locking lever. Remove the two screws.

5. Unscrew the plate assembly and remove.

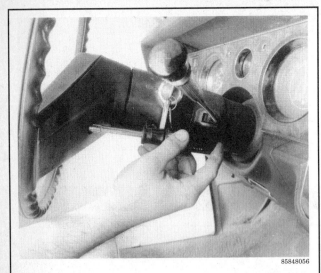

Fig. 57 Removing the horn pad attaching screws

Fig. 58 The horn pad can be removed from the steering wheel once the attaching screws have been removed

Fig. 59 Marking the steering wheel and shaft makes for easier installation

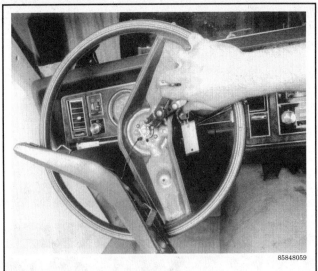

Fig. 60 Removing the steering wheel snap ring

Fig. 61 Removing the steering wheel attaching nut

Fig. 62 Always use a puller to remove the steering wheel

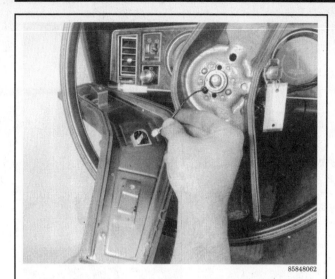

85848062

**Fig. 63 Disconnecting the horn pad electrical connector**

6. Remove the steering wheel nut retainer and nut. Using a puller, remove the wheel.

**To install:**

7. Install a 5/16 in. x 18 set screw into the upper shaft at the full extended position and lock.

8. Install the steering wheel, aligning the scribe mark on the hub with the slash mark on the end of the shaft. Make sure that the unattached end of the horn upper contact assembly is seated flush against the top of the horn contact assembly.

9. Install the nut on the upper steering shaft, along with the nut retainer. Torque to 30 ft. lbs. (41 Nm).

10. Remove the set screw installed in step 1.

11. Install the plate assembly and tighten finger tight.

12. Position the locking lever in the vertical position and move the lever counterclockwise until the holes in the plate align with the holes in the lever. Install the attaching screws.

13. Align the pad assembly with the holes in the steering wheel and install the retaining screws. Connect the negative battery cable. Check to see that the locking lever securely locks the wheel travel and that the wheel travel is free in the unlocked position.

## Turn Signal Switch

### ✳✳WARNING

Do not atttempt to remove the steering wheel on cars equipped with an air bag. This service should be left to a professional service technician to avoid damage to the system and personal injury.

## REMOVAL & INSTALLATION

▶ **See Figures 65 and 66**

**Models without Tilt and Telescopic Column**

1. Disconnect the negative battery cable.

2. Remove the steering wheel as described earlier.

3. Remove the covers from the steering column shaft. The plastic keepers under the cover are not necessary for installation.

4. Depress the lockplate and remove the snapring from the shaft. Remove the lock-plate and the canceling cam.

5. Remove the upper bearing preload spring.

6. Place the turn signal lever in the right turn position, then remove the turn signal lever attaching screw and the lever. On 1978 and later models with the dimmer switch in the turn signal lever, remove the actuator arm screw and the arm.

7. Push in on the hazard warning knob, then remove the screw and the hazard warning knob.

8. Remove the three turn signal switch attaching screws.

9. Remove the lower trim panel and then disconnect the turn signal connector from the wiring harness. Lift the connector from the mounting bracket on the right side of the jacket.

10. Remove the four bolts which attach the bracket assembly to the jacket.

11. Loosen the screw holding the shift indicator needle and disconnect the clip from the link.

12. Remove the two nuts from the column support bracket while holding the column in position. Remove the bracket assembly and wire protector from the wiring, then loosely install the bracket-to-support column.

13. Tape the turn signal wires at the connector, then carefully pull the turn signal switch and wiring from the top end of the column.

**To install:**

14. Use a new snapring. If the cover screws are to be replaced, make sure the replacement screws are the same size.

15. Untape the turn signal wires at the connector, then carefully push the turn signal switch and wiring into the top end of the column.

16. Install the two nuts from the column support bracket while holding the column in position. Install the bracket assembly and wire protector to the wiring.

17. Tighten the screw holding the shift indicator needle and connect the clip to the link.

18. Install the four bolts which attach the bracket assembly to the jacket.

19. Install the lower trim panel after connecting the turn signal connector to the wiring harness.

20. Install the three turn signal switch attaching screws.

21. Push in on the hazard warning knob, then install the screw and the hazard warning knob.

22. Place the turn signal lever in the right turn position, then install the turn signal lever attaching screw and the lever. On 1978 and later models with the dimmer switch in the turn signal lever, install the actuator arm screw and the arm.

23. Install the upper bearing preload spring.

24. Install the lock-plate and the canceling cam. Depress the lockplate and install the snapring to the shaft.

25. Install the covers to the steering column shaft. The plastic keepers under the cover are not necessary for installation.

26. Install the steering wheel and torque the nut to 30 ft. lbs. (41 Nm) as described earlier.

27. Connect the negative battery cable and check all functions.

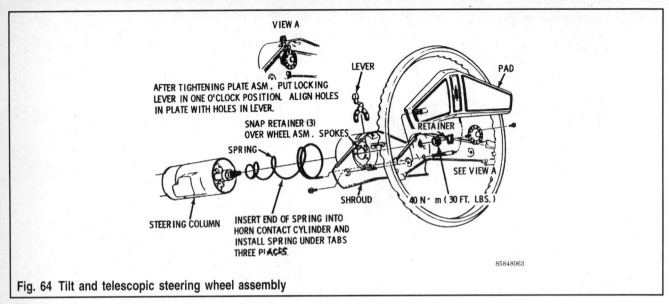

VIEW A

AFTER TIGHTENING PLATE ASM. PUT LOCKING
LEVER IN ONE O'CLOCK POSITION. ALIGN HOLES
IN PLATE WITH HOLES IN LEVER.

LEVER          PAD

SNAP RETAINER (3)
OVER WHEEL ASM. SPOKES          RETAINER

SPRING

SEE VIEW A

SHROUD          40 N·m ( 30 FT. LBS.)

STEERING COLUMN          INSERT END OF SPRING INTO
HORN CONTACT CYLINDER AND
INSTALL SPRING UNDER TABS
THREE PLACES.

85848063

**Fig. 64 Tilt and telescopic steering wheel assembly**

**Models with Tilt and Telescopic Column**

> ✳✳**CAUTION**
>
> All elements of energy-absorbing (telescopic) steering columns are very sensitive to damage. Do not strike any part of the column (nuts, bolts, etc.) as this could ruin the entire assembly.

1. Disconnect the negative battery cable.
2. Remove the steering wheel as outlined earlier.
3. Remove the cover from the steering column shaft.
4. Press down on the lockplate and pry the snapring from the shaft.
5. Remove the lockplate and the canceling cam.
6. Remove the upper bearing preload spring.
7. Remove the turn signal lever and the hazard flasher knob.
8. Lift up on the tilt lever and position the housing in its central position.
9. Remove the switch attaching screws.
10. Remove the lower trim cap from the instrument panel and disconnect the turn signal connector from the wiring harness.
11. Remove the four bolts which secure the bracket assembly to the jacket.
12. Loosen the screw that holds the shift indicator needle and disconnect the clip from the link.
13. Remove the two nuts from the column support bracket while holding the column in position. Remove the bracket assembly and wire protector from the wiring, then loosely install the support column bracket.
14. Tape the turn signal wires to the connector to keep them fit and parallel.
15. Carefully remove the turn signal switch and wiring from the column.

**To install:**

16. Carefully install the turn signal switch and wiring into the column.
17. Install the bracket assembly and wire protector to the wiring, then loosely install the support column bracket. Install the two nuts to the column support bracket while holding the column in position.
18. Tighten the screw that holds the shift indicator needle and connect the clip to the link.
19. Install the four bolts which secure the bracket assembly to the jacket.
20. Connect the turn signal connector to the wiring harness. Install the lower trim cap to the instrument panel.
21. Install the switch attaching screws.
22. Lift up on the tilt lever and position the housing in its central position.
23. Install the turn signal lever and the hazard flasher knob.
24. Install the upper bearing preload spring.
25. Install the lockplate and the canceling cam.
26. Press down on the lockplate and install the snapring to the shaft.
27. Install the cover to the steering column shaft.
28. Install the steering wheel as outlined earlier.
29. Connect the negative battery cable and check all functions.

## Ignition Switch

> ✳✳**WARNING**
>
> Do not atttempt this service on cars equipped with an air bag. This service should be left to a professional service technician to avoid damage to the system and personal injury.

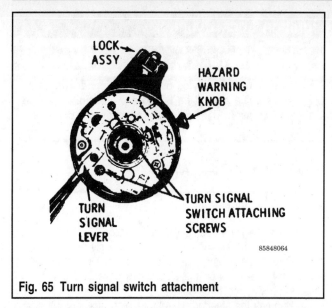

**Fig. 65 Turn signal switch attachment**

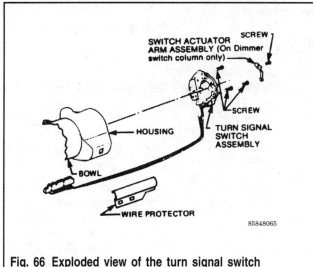

**Fig. 66 Exploded view of the turn signal switch assembly**

## REMOVAL & INSTALLATION

▶ **See Figure 67**

➡**This is an extremely difficult and lengthy procedure. You must remove the steering column from the vehicle and disassemble major portions of it. Because the column is collapsible in an accident, it is necessary that it be handled with care to avoid distortion of major parts. It must not be dropped, hammered on or even leaned on, or vitally important parts may deform. The procedure for replacing the ignition switch on tilt type columns is not included here because it involves substantial additional work and the use of several expensive special tools. Unless you are rather experienced, we recommend that the job be left to a competent professional mechanic.**

1. Disconnect the negative battery cable. Remove the clamp bolt from the steering coupling at the lower end of the steering column shaft (located near the steering box, under the hood).

2. Disconnect the shift linkage from the shift tube lever at the lower end of the column.

3. Remove the steering wheel with a puller, as described above.

4. Remove the left sound insulator and lower column cover.

5. Remove the trim cap or lower trim panel from the instrument panel, depending on equipment.

6. Remove the steering column cover and toe-pan attaching screws. Remove the shift indicator needle from the shift bowl.

7. Securely support the column in position and remove the two nuts attaching the column to the underside of the instrument panel.

8. Lower the column carefully, being careful to retain any spacers that may have been used in order. Disconnect the wiring. Then, carefully remove the column from the inside of the vehicle.

9. Begin disassembling the column, removing the lock plate, canceling cam, and turn signal switch. See the 'Turn Signal' Removal & Installation procedure above.

10. Remove the ignition lock and key warning switch as described below.

11. Remove the spring and bolt assembly, and the associated thrust washer. Then, remove the rack preload spring, switch rack, and actuator assembly.

12. Remove the upper shift lever spring. Then, remove the gear shift lever bowl.

13. Remove the shift bowl shroud and bowl lower bearing.

14. Unhook and remove the dimmer switch actuating rod. Remove the attaching nut and remove the dimmer switch.

15. Remove the attaching screw and stud and remove the ignition switch, disassembling the actuating rod from the hole in the sliding actuator.

**To install:**

16. Move the ignition switch sliding actuator all the way to the left (ACC) position. Then, move it two detents (OFF-UNLOCK) position to the right.

17. Then, position the actuating rod hole in the sliding actuator, and install the ignition switch, stud, and mounting screw.

18. Install the dimmer switch with its attaching nut tightened only loosely. Then, depress the switch slightly until you can insert a $\frac{3}{32}$ in. drill through the hole in the switch housing and slider. Force the switch upward to remove any lash and tighten the mounting screw with the switch in this position.

19. Put the shifter in **NEUTRAL** and install the shift lever.

20. Install the shift bowl shroud and bowl lower bearing.

21. Install the rack preload spring, switch rack, and actuator assembly. Install the spring and bolt assembly, and the associated thrust washer.

22. Install the ignition lock and key warning switch as described below.

23. Reinstall the column into the vehicle. Make sure when assembling the lower and upper dash covers that they can slide on the column. If the bracket which mounts the column to the dash has been removed, install the bolts in this order:

    a. Left rear

    b. Left front

    c. Right front

    d. Right rear

Tighten the bolts just snug to avoid distorting the column.

24. Install the switch connector to the ignition switch. Then, position the column in the body and support it there. Install the lockwashers and nuts for the coupling and tighten them. Then,

loosely assemble the nuts fastening the mounting bracket for the column to the lower side of the instrument panel.

25. Position the lower cover to the firewall and ensure that the cover is lined up by starting the left lower screw. Then, install and tighten the right lower screw. Then, tighten the left lower screw. Finally, install and tighten the two screws that fit into the top of the cover.

26. Tighten first the screw for the left side of the cover clamp; then tighten the screw for the right side of the cover clamp. Finally, install and tighten the remaining cover screws.

27. Finally, tighten the nuts fastening the column to the underside of the dash. Reinstall the bolt for the steering coupling clamp.

28. Install the lock plate, canceling cam, and turn signal switch. See the 'Turn Signal' Removal & Installation procedure in this chapter.

29. Connect the wiring.

30. Securely support the column in position and install the two nuts attaching the column to the underside of the instrument panel.

31. Install the shift indicator needle from the shift bowl. Install the steering column cover and toe-pan attaching screws.

32. Install the trim cap or lower trim panel to the instrument panel, depending on equipment.

33. Install the left sound insulator and lower column cover.

34. Install the steering wheel, as described above.

35. Connect the shift linkage to the shift tube lever at the lower end of the column.

36. Install the clamp bolt to the steering coupling at the lower end of the steering column shaft (located near the steering box, under the hood).

37. Connect the negative battery cable and check all column operations for free movement and smooth operation.

## Ignition Lock Cylinder

### ✳✳WARNING

Do not atttempt this service on cars equipped with an air bag. This service should be left to a professional service technician to avoid damage to the system and personal injury.

### REMOVAL & INSTALLATION

▶ **See Figures 68 and 69**

1. Disconnect the negative battery cable.
2. Remove the steering wheel as previously outlined.
3. On models equipped with a tilt and telescope column, pry up the three tabs on the plastic lock cover. On other models, remove the three screws.
4. Depress the steering wheel lock plate and pry the snapring from the shaft.
5. Remove the lock plat, canceling cam, and upper bearing spring.
6. Remove the turn signal lever. Push the hazard warning knob in and unscrew the knob.
7. Remove the turn signal switch screws and pull the switch up out of the way.
8. Turn the ignition key to the **RUN** position.
9. Insert a long thin prybar into the slot in the upper bearing housing and depress the release tab while pulling the cylinder from the column.

**To install:**

10. Insert a new lock cylinder into the column after aligning the key on the cylinder with the keyway in the column.
11. Press inward on the cylinder while turning it clockwise.
12. Install the turn signal switch and screws.
13. Install the turn signal lever. Push the hazard warning knob in and install the screw.
14. Install the upper bearing, canceling cam and lock plate.
15. Install the snapring to the shaft.

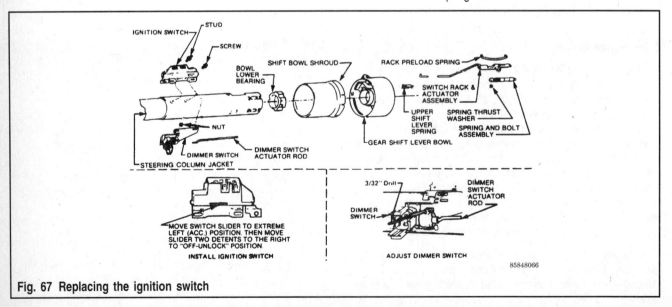

85848066

**Fig. 67 Replacing the ignition switch**

16. On models equipped with a tilt and telescope column, push down the three tabs on the plastic lock cover. On other models, install the three screws.

17. Install the steering wheel as previously outlined.

18. Connect the negative battery cable and check all column functions.

## Steering Column

### ✳✳WARNING

**Do not atttempt this service on cars equipped with an air bag. This service should be left to a professional service technician to avoid damage to the system and personal injury.**

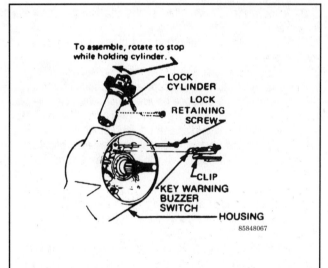

**Fig. 68 Ignition lock removal; standard columns**

## REMOVAL & INSTALLATION

➡**This is an extremely difficult and lengthy procedure. You must remove the steering column from the vehicle and disassemble major portions of it. Because the column is collapsible in an accident, it is necessary that it be handled with care to avoid distortion of major parts. It must not be dropped, hammered on or even leaned on, or vitally important parts may deform. Unless you are rather experienced, we recommend that the job be left to a competent professional mechanic.**

1. Disconnect the negative battery cable. Remove the clamp bolt from the steering coupling at the lower end of the steering column shaft (located near the steering box, under the hood).

2. Disconnect the shift linkage from the shift tube lever at the lower end of the column.

3. Remove the steering wheel with a puller, as described above.

4. Remove the left sound insulator and lower column cover.

5. Remove the trim cap or lower trim panel from the instrument panel, depending on equipment.

6. Remove the steering column cover and toe-pan attaching screws. Remove the shift indicator needle from the shift bowl.

7. Securely support the column in position and remove the two nuts attaching the column to the underside of the instrument panel.

8. Lower the column carefully, being careful to retain any spacers that may have been used in order. Disconnect the wiring. Then, carefully remove the column from the inside of the vehicle.

**To install:**

9. Position the column in the vehicle. Make sure when assembling the lower and upper dash covers that they can slide on the column. If the bracket which mounts the column to the dash has been removed, install the bolts in this order:

   a. Left rear

   b. Left front

   c. Right front

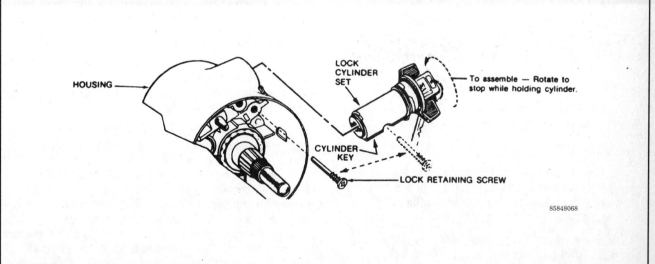

**Fig. 69 Ignition lock removal; tilt column**

d. Right rear

10. Install the switch connector to the ignition switch. Then, position the column in the body and support it there. Install the lockwashers and nuts for the coupling and tighten them. Then, loosely assemble the nuts fastening the mounting bracket for the column to the lower side of the instrument panel.

11. Position the lower cover to the firewall and ensure that the cover is lined up by starting the left lower screw. Then, install and tighten the right lower screw. Then, tighten the left lower screw. Finally, install and tighten the two screws that fit into the top of the cover.

12. Tighten first the screw for the left side of the cover clamp; then tighten the screw for the right side of the cover clamp. Finally, install and tighten the remaining cover screws.

13. Finally, tighten the nuts fastening the column to the underside of the dash. Reinstall the bolt for the steering coupling clamp.

14. Install the lock plate, canceling cam, and turn signal switch. See the 'Turn Signal' Removal & Installation procedure in this chapter.

15. Connect the wiring.

16. Securely support the column in position and install the two nuts attaching the column to the underside of the instrument panel.

17. Install the shift indicator needle from the shift bowl. Install the steering column cover and toe-pan attaching screws.

18. Install the trim cap or lower trim panel to the instrument panel, depending on equipment.

19. Install the left sound insulator and lower column cover.

20. Install the steering wheel, as described above.

21. Connect the shift linkage to the shift tube lever at the lower end of the column.

22. Install the clamp bolt to the steering coupling at the lower end of the steering column shaft (located near the steering box, under the hood).

23. Connect the negative battery cable and check all column operations for free movement and smooth operation.

## Steering Linkage

## REMOVAL & INSTALLATION

▶ **See Figures 70, 71, 72, 73 and 74**

### Pitman Arm

➡**To perform this procedure, you will need special pullers to pull the center link out of the pitman arm, and to pull the pitman arm off the steering box shaft without stressing the bearings in the steering box.**

1. Raise the vehicle and support it with jackstands by the frame rails. Remove the nut from the pitman arm ballstud.

2. Disconnect the center link at the pitman arm with a puller. Then, pull down on the intermediate rod to remove the stud.

3. Remove the pitman arm nut and lockwasher from the pitman shaft. Provide replacement parts and discard them.

4. Mark the relationship between the pitman arm and the steering box shaft. Then, pull the arm off the shaft. Mark the new arm at the same place as the old one was marked.

**To install:**

5. Install the new arm on the shaft, aligning the marks. Install the new nut and lockwasher, and torque the nut to 185 ft. lbs. (260 Nm).

6. Put the center link into position onto the pitman arm, install the attaching nut, and torque it to 40 ft. lbs. (54 Nm).

7. Lower the vehicle and check steering operation before driving.

### Idler Arm

➡**You will need a puller suitable for removing the tapered stud on the idler arm from the center link.**

1. Raise the vehicle and support it with jackstands by the frame rails. Remove the nuts, bolts, and washers that attach the idler arm to the frame.

2. Remove the nut that attaches the idler arm to the center link ballstud.

3. Pull the idler arm out of the center link with the puller and remove it.

4. Note that the idler arm has a threaded support. The threaded bushing must be loosened and the support turned in the arm to adjust the distance between the lower bolt hole and the top surface of the arm to $2^{11}/_{32}$ in. (59.5mm). This ensures that, when installed, the idler arm ball socket will be level with the Pitman arm ball socket. Retighten the threaded bushing. Make sure all idler supports will still be fully free to rotate at least 90°.

**To install:**

5. Position the idler arm support against the frame, lining up the two sets of holes. Install the bolts, washers and nuts, and torque to 60 ft. lbs. (81 Nm).

6. Install the center link to the idler arm by inserting the tapered section on the arm into the link. Make sure the seal is on the stud. Install the nut and torque it to 40 ft. lbs. (54 Nm). On some models, this nut uses a cotter pin. If so, tighten the nut just enough farther to line up holes and then install and secure a new cotter pin. Lower the vehicle.

### Center Link

➡**You will need pullers that are suitable for separating the tie rod ends, idler arm, and pitman arm from the center link. It is ideal to have a tool J-29193 or equivalent to seat the idler arm into the center link.**

1. Raise the vehicle and support it with jackstands by the frame rails. Remove the cotter pins, remove the nuts, and then disconnect the tie rod inner ends at the center link with pullers.

2. Remove the nut from the ballstud on the center link where it attaches to the pitman arm. Then, use a puller to remove the arm from the ballstud. Shift the linkage to eliminate torque and pull the link away from the pitman arm.

3. Remove the nut attaching the center link to the idler arm from the idler arm. Use a puller to separate the center link from the idler arm.

**To install:**

4. Inspect all seals and replace any that are damaged. Make sure all seals that are satisfactory are in place.

5. Install the center link onto the idler arm. If it is available, install the special tool, and torque its nut to 15 ft. lbs. (20 Nm). Remove the tool and install the attaching nut. Torque it to 40 ft. lbs. (54 Nm).

6. Raise the end of the center link and install it onto the pitman arm. Install the nut and torque it to 40 ft. lbs. (54 Nm).

7. Install the inner tie rod ends into the center link. Install the nuts and torque them to 30 ft. lbs. (41 Nm). Tighten them just enough farther to line up the holes and then install new cotter pins.

8. Have the toe-in set at an alignment shop.

**Tie Rod Ends**

1. Remove the cotter pins and nuts from the tie rod end studs.

2. Mark the tie rod adjustment sleeve at both ends with tape.

3. Using a tie rod end removing tool J-6627, remove the rod end from the steering knuckle.

4. Remove the inner stud in the same manner as the outer.

5. Loosen the clamp bolts and unscrew the ends if they are being replaced.

**To install:**

6. Lubricate the tie rod end threads with chassis grease if they were removed. Install each end assembly an equal distance from the sleeve.

7. Ensure that the tie rod end stud threads and nut are clean. Install new seals and install the studs into the steering arms and relay rod.

8. Install the stud nuts. Tighten the inner and outer end nuts to 35 ft. lbs. (41 Nm). Install new cotter pins.

9. Have a qualified alignment mechanic adjust the toe-in to specifications.

➡ Before tightening the sleeve clamps, ensure that the clamps are positioned so that adjusting sleeve slot is covered by the clamp. Never back the nut off to insert cotter pin, always tighten it until the pin can fit through the castellations.

## Power Steering Gearbox

### ADJUSTMENT

It is not recommended that the power steering gear be adjusted in the vehicle. It should be adjusted at time of major rebuild. It does not require adjustment as part of periodic maintenance.

### REMOVAL & INSTALLATION

▶ **See Figures 75 and 76**

1. Disconnect the negative (-) battery cable. Remove the coupling shield from the steering shaft.

2. Disconnect the hoses from the gearbox and cap or plug the hose fittings.

3. Raise the front end of the vehicle and support it with jackstands.

4. Remove the pitman shaft nut, then disconnect the pitman shaft using a special puller (it is a press-fit).

5. Remove the three bolts attaching the gearbox to the frame side rail and remove the gearbox.

**To install:**

➡ **If the mounting threads are stripped, do not repair; replace the housing.**

6. Before installing the gearbox, apply a sodium fiber grease to the gearbox mounting pads to prevent squeaks between the gar housing and the frame. Note that the flat on the gearbox lower shaft must index with the flat in the coupling flange and make sure there is a minimum of 0.040 in. (1mm) clearance between the coupling hub and the steering gearbox upper seal.

7. Before tightening the gearbox-to-frame bolts, shift the gearbox as necessary to place it in the same plane as the steering shaft so that the flexible coupling is not distorted. Torque the gearbox-to-frame bolts to 80 ft. lbs. (108 Nm) and the pitman shaft nut to 185 ft. lbs. (255 Nm).

8. After connecting the hoses to the pump add GM Power Steering Fluid or an equivalent to bring the fluid level to the full COLD mark. Bleed the system by running the engine at idle for 30 seconds then at a fast idle for one minute BEFORE turning the steering wheel. Then, with the engine still running, turn the steering wheel through its full travel two or three times. Recheck the oil level and top up if necessary.

## Power Steering Pump

### REMOVAL & INSTALLATION

▶ **See Figures 77 and 78**

1. Remove the hoses at the pump and tape the openings shut to prevent leakage.

2. Remove the pump drive belt.

3. Remove the retaining bolts, any braces and the pump.

4. If a new pump is being installed, and the pulley is being transferred, a puller is necessary to remove the pulley.

**To install:**

5. Torque hose fittings to 20 ft. lbs. (27 Nm). Fill the reservoir with approved power steering fluid and turn the pump backward (counterclockwise as viewed from in front) until bubbles no longer appear in the reservoir.

6. Any time the pump is removed, air must be bled from the system upon reinstallation. Bleed the system as described in the next procedure.

### BLEEDING

To bleed the system, proceed as follows:

1. Raise the vehicle in the air and support it with jackstands.

2. Start the engine and let it run at a fast idle.

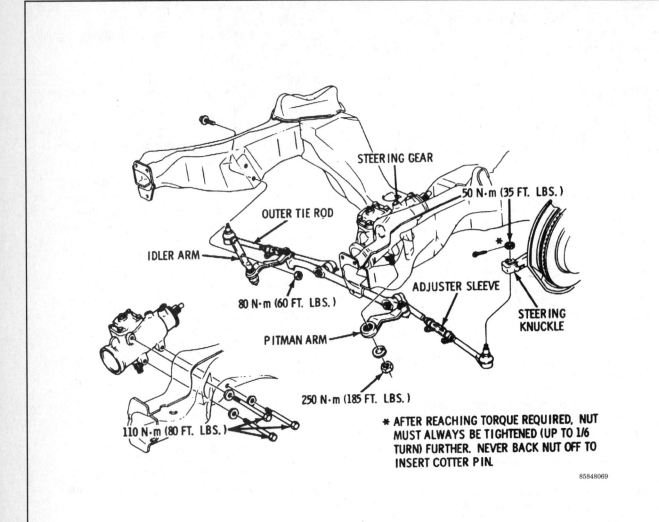

STEERING GEAR

OUTER TIE ROD

IDLER ARM

50 N·m (35 FT. LBS.)

ADJUSTER SLEEVE

STEERING KNUCKLE

80 N·m (60 FT. LBS.)

PITMAN ARM

250 N·m (185 FT. LBS.)

110 N·m (80 FT. LBS.)

* AFTER REACHING TORQUE REQUIRED, NUT MUST ALWAYS BE TIGHTENED (UP TO 1/6 TURN) FURTHER. NEVER BACK NUT OFF TO INSERT COTTER PIN.

85848069

Fig. 70 Steering linkage assembly; all models similar

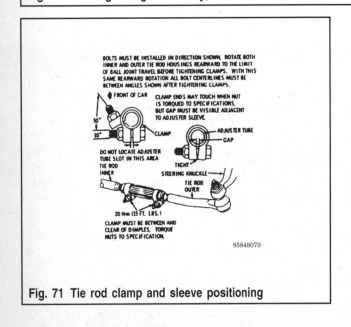

BOLTS MUST BE INSTALLED IN DIRECTION SHOWN. ROTATE BOTH INNER AND OUTER TIE ROD HOUSINGS REARWARD TO THE LIMIT OF BALL JOINT TRAVEL BEFORE TIGHTENING CLAMPS. WITH THIS SAME REARWARD ROTATION ALL BOLT CENTERLINES MUST BE BETWEEN ANGLES SHOWN AFTER TIGHTENING CLAMPS.

FRONT OF CAR

CLAMP ENDS MAY TOUCH WHEN NUT IS TORQUED TO SPECIFICATIONS, BUT GAP MUST BE VISIBLE ADJACENT TO ADJUSTER SLEEVE.

50°

10°

CLAMP

ADJUSTER TUBE

GAP

DO NOT LOCATE ADJUSTER TUBE SLOT IN THIS AREA

TIE ROD INNER

TIGHT

STEERING KNUCKLE

TIE ROD OUTER

20 N·m (15 FT. LBS.)

CLAMP MUST BE BETWEEN AND CLEAR OF DIMPLES. TORQUE NUTS TO SPECIFICATION.

85848070

Fig. 71 Tie rod clamp and sleeve positioning

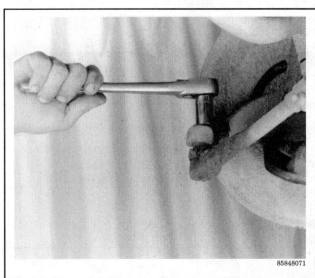

85848071

Fig. 72 Removing the outer tie rod attaching nut

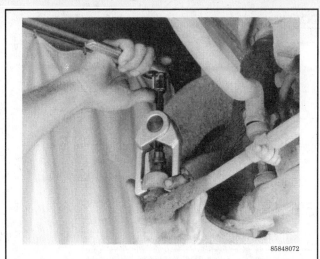

**Fig. 73 Use a suitable puller to disconnect the tie rod end**

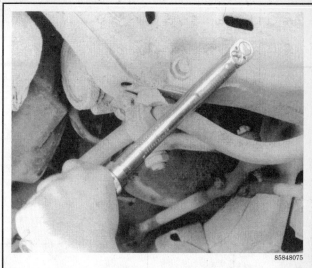

**Fig. 76 Torqueing the gearbox attaching bolts**

3. Having made sure the fluid level in the pump is correct, turn the wheels from side to side without hitting the stops.

4. After doing this several times, check the fluid. Fluid with air in it will have a light tan or red appearance.

5. Continue with this procedure until the air is bled from the system. Fill the pump with fluid and road-test the vehicle.

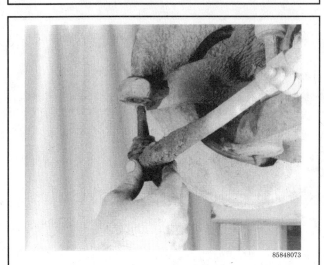

**Fig. 74 Removing the tie rod end from the steering knuckle**

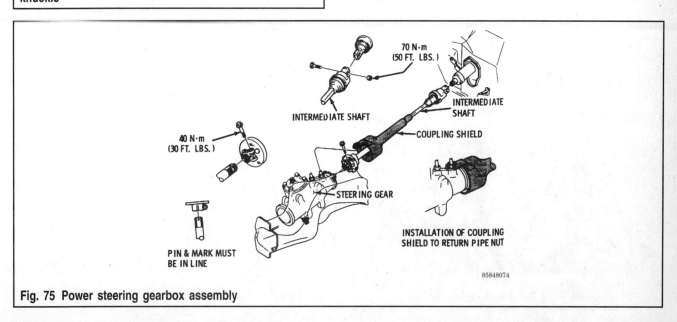

**Fig. 75 Power steering gearbox assembly**

### TORQUE SPECIFICATIONS

| Component | U.S. | Metric |
|---|---|---|
| Leaf springs | | |
|   U-bolt nuts | 50 ft. lbs. | 68 Nm |
|   Front bolt | 60 ft. lbs. | 81 Nm |
|   Rear bolt | 105 ft. lbs. | 140 Nm |
| Coil springs | | |
|   Rear axle upper control arm | 95 ft. lbs. | 128 Nm |
| Tie rod ends | | |
|   Stud nut | 40 ft. lbs. | 54 Nm |
| Pitman arm | | |
|   Shaft nut | 185 ft. lbs. | 260 Nm |
| Idler arm | 60 ft. lbs. | 81 Nm |
| Center link | | |
|   To Pitman arm | 40 ft. lbs. | 54 Nm |
|   To idler arm | 40 ft. lbs. | 54 Nm |
| Power steering | | |
|   Gear box-to-frame | 80 ft. lbs. | 108 Nm |
| Sway bar | | |
|   Link attaching nuts | 13 ft. lbs. | 18 Nm |

85848c04

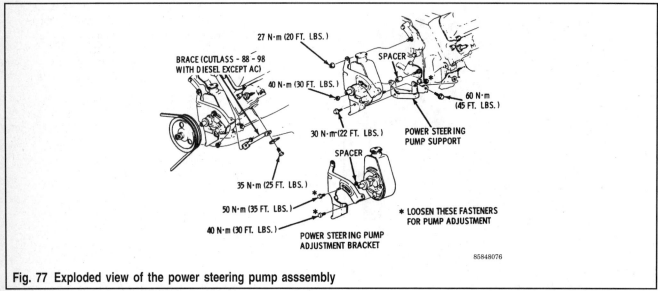

Fig. 77 Exploded view of the power steering pump asssembly

Fig. 78 A common power steering pump location

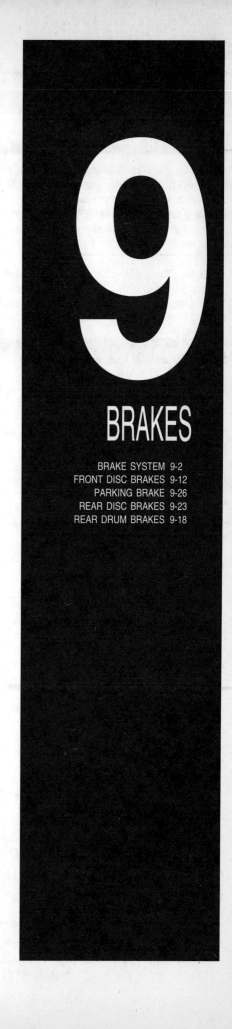

# 9

# BRAKES

# BRAKE SYSTEM

## ✳✳CAUTION

**Some brake pads contain asbestos, which has been determined to be a cancer causing agent. Never clean the brake surfaces with compressed air! Avoid inhaling any dust from any brake surface! When cleaning brake surfaces, use a commercially available brake cleaning fluid.**

All Buick, Oldsmobile and Pontiac models covered in this guide are equipped with front disc brakes and rear drum brakes as standard equipment. Four wheel disc brakes are optional on some models.

## Adjustments

### DISC BRAKES

There is no adjustment provision on hydraulic disc brakes; they are inherently self-adjusting.

### DRUM BRAKES

➥Drum brakes are self-adjusting, but provision is made for manual adjustment as follows:

1. Raise the rear of the vehicle and support it with jackstands.
2. The inner sides of the brake backing plates have a lanced area, oblong in shape. Knock this area out with a punch. You will have to remove the brake drum to clean out any metal pieces that will be deposited by the punch, and you will have to purchase rubber plugs at a parts distributor to plug the punched holes now in the backing plats. Many vehicles will already have the holes punched and plugs installed.
3. Adjustment to tighten:
    a.  Insert a brake adjusting spoon into the hole.
    b.  Turn the star-shaped adjusting screw inside the drum with the spoon, until the wheel has a slight drag. Do this to both wheels until there is equal drag on each wheel. DO NOT make the adjustment overtight!
4. Adjustment to loosen and remove the drum:
    a.  Insert a brake adjusting spoon and small prybar to hold the adjusting lever away from the sprocket.
    b.  Back off each adjusting screw until the drum turns freely. If the brake shoes drag with the adjusters backed off all the way, the parking brake cables could be excessively tight.

### BRAKE PEDAL

The pedal travel is measured as the distance which the pedal moves towards the floor from the fully released position. Inspection should be made with the pedal firmly depressed and the brake system cold. Pedal travel should be $2\frac{1}{4}$ in. on 1975 to 1984 models, $2\frac{3}{4}$ in. on 1985 to 1990 models and $3\frac{1}{3}$ in. on Hydro-boost systems.

➥If equipped with power brakes, pump the 3 times with the engine OFF to remove vacuum reserve before checking pedal travel.

1. Under the dash, remove the pushrod-to-pedal clevis pin.
2. Loosen the pushrod adjusting locknut and adjust the pushrod.
3. After the correct travel is established, tighten the locknut.
4. Engage the pushrod and secure using the clevis pin.

## Brake Light Switch

▶ See Figure 1

### REMOVAL & INSTALLATION

1. Disconnect the negative battery cable.
2. Disconnect the switch electrical connector.
3. Withdraw the switch from the pedal mounting bracket.
**To install:**
4. Make sure the clip is in the pedal mounting bracket.
5. Depress the brake pedal and insert the switch.
6. Pull the brake pedal rearward until it contacts the brake pedal stop. You should not hear any more clicks.
7. Check stop lamp switch operation by applying and releasing the brake, make certain the stop lamps go off when the brake pedal is in the released position.

## Master Cylinder

### REMOVAL & INSTALLATION

▶ See Figures 2, 3, 4, 5, 6 and 7

**Vacuum Power Brakes**

On vacuum power brake equipped models, the master cylinder can be removed without removing the power vacuum cylinder from the vehicle.

## ✳✳WARNING

**Only use flare nut wrenches when removing the brake lines from any component. Standard wrenches will damage the flare nut and line.**

1. Clean the area around the master cylinder.
2. Disconnect the hydraulic lines at the master cylinder using flare nut wrenches only. Plug or tape the ends of the lines to prevent dirt from entering and to prevent fluid from leaking out.
3. Remove the master cylinder attaching nuts and remove the master cylinder.

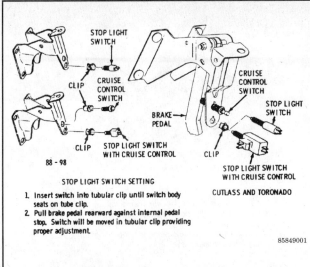

Fig. 1 Brake light switch installation and adjustment

4. Drain the master cylinder.

## ✳✳CAUTION

**Be careful to keep brake fluid away from all body paint. The fluid acts like paint remover, and a few drops will quickly bubble any paint with which it comes in contact.**

### Powermaster® Power Brakes

This system uses an electrically operated hydraulic pump and an accumulator (pressure storage system) to provide power braking assist.

## ✳✳CAUTION

**Because of the very high pressures used, always follow procedures very carefully, being especially sure to discharge the system prior to disconnecting anything.**

1. Disconnect the negative (-) battery cable. Turn the ignition switch off. Then, discharge all pressure from the system

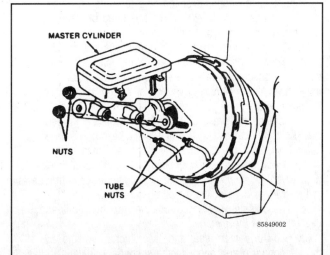

Fig. 2 Master cylinder mounting on cars equipped with vacuum power brakes

Fig. 3 Use a flare nut wrench when removing the brake lines

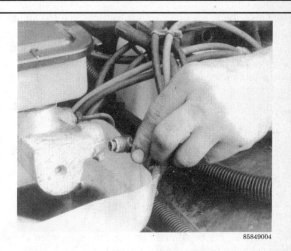

Fig. 4 Use a pan to catch any brake fluid; be sure to tape or plug the lines after removing them from the master cylinder

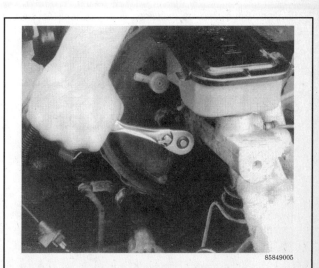

Fig. 5 The master cylinder attaching nuts can be removed after the lines have been disconnected

Fig. 6 Removing the master cylinder from the vehicle

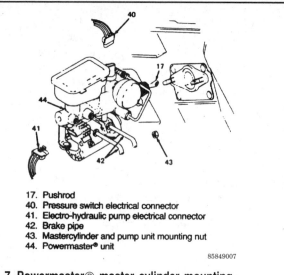

17. Pushrod
40. Pressure switch electrical connector
41. Electro-hydraulic pump electrical connector
42. Brake pipe
43. Mastercylinder and pump unit mounting nut
44. Powermaster® unit

Fig. 7 Powermaster® master cylinder mounting

by applying the brake pedal with maximum force (50 lbs. or more) at least 10 full strokes.

2. Disconnect the electrical connector from the pressure switch, located at the rear of the master cylinder on top.

3. Disconnect the electrical connector from the front of the pump, located under the master cylinder.

4. Disconnect the brake and hydraulic pressure pipes at the master cylinder and tape or cap the openings. Use a flare nut wrench only.

5. Remove the two attaching nuts. Pull the clevis pin out of the linkage to the brake pedal. Remove the unit.

**To install:**

6. Position the unit onto the firewall and torque the mounting nuts to 22-30 ft. lbs. (30-41 Nm) and the brake pipe nuts to 10-13 ft. lbs. (14-17 Nm).

7. Connect the brake and hydraulic pressure pipes at the master cylinder using a flare nut wrench.

8. Connect the electrical connector to the front of the pump, located under the master cylinder.

9. Connect the electrical connector to the pressure switch, located at the rear of the master cylinder on top.

10. Bleed the system as described in the System Bleeding procedures in this section.

## OVERHAUL

▶ See Figures 8, 9, 10, 11, 12, 13, 14 and 15

### Except Powermaster®

The models covered in this guide are equipped with either Moraine or Bendix master cylinders. The rebuilding kits may differ slightly, but the procedures are the same. Follow the instructions that come with each particular kit.

➡Overhaul procedures for power brake master cylinders and manual brake master cylinders is the same. Note the procedure below for Powermaster® units.

1. Remove the master cylinder from the vehicle.

2. Remove the mounting gasket and boot, and the main cover, and purge the unit of its fluid.

3. Secure the cylinder in a vise and remove the pushrod retainer and secondary piston stop bolt found inside the forward reservoir (Moraine iron cylinder only).

➡The plastic composite master cylinder reservoir can be removed by prying against the cylinder and reservoir. Work the reservoir from the rubber grommets using care not to damage either component.

4. Compress the retaining (lock) ring and extract it along with the primary piston assembly from the end of the bore.

5. Blow compressed air into the piston stop screw hole, if equipped, to force the secondary piston, spring, and retainer from the bore of the cylinder. An alternative method is to use hooked wire to snag and extract the secondary piston.

6. Check the bass tube fitting inserts and if they are damaged, remove them. Leave undamaged inserts in place.

7. If replacement is necessary, thread a $^3/_{16}$ in. · $^5/_8$ in. self-tapping screw into the insert. Hook the end of the screw with a claw hammer and pry the insert free.

8. An alternative way to remove the inserts is to first drill the outlet holes to $^{13}/_{64}$ in. and thread them with a $^1/_4$ in.-20 tap. Position a thick washer over the hole to serve as a spacer, and then thread a $^1/_4$ in.-20 · $^3/_4$ in. hex head bolt into the insert and tighten the bolt until the insert is freed.

9. Use denatured alcohol and compressed air to clean the parts. Slight rust may be removed with crocus cloth. Never use petroleum-based solvents to clean brake parts. Also, a brake hone is helpful in removing varnish and slight rust.

**To assemble:**

10. Replace the brass tube inserts by positioning them in their holes and threading a brake line tube nut into the outlet hole. Turn down the nut until the insert is seated.

11. Check the piston assemblies for correct identification and, when satisfied, position the replacement secondary seals in the twin grooves of the secondary piston.

12. The outside seal is correctly placed when its lips face the flat end of the piston.

13. Slip the primary seal and its protector over the end of the secondary piston opposite the secondary seals. The flat side of this seal should face the piston's compensating hole flange.

14. Replace the primary piston assembly with assembled pieces in the overhaul kit.

15. Moisten the cylinder bore and the secondary piston's inner and outer seals with clean brake fluid. Assemble the secondary piston spring to its retainer and position them over the end of the primary seal.

16. Insert the combined spring and piston assembly into the cylinder and use a small wooden dowel or pencil to seat the spring against the end of the bore.

17. Moisten the primary piston seals with brake fluid and push it, pushrod receptacle end out, into the cylinder.

18. Keep the piston pushed in and snap the retaining (lock) ring into place.

19. Relax the pressure on the pistons and allow them to seek their static positions.

20. Replace the secondary piston stop screw and torque it to 25-40 inch. lbs. (3-4 Nm), if so equipped.

21. Replace the reservoir diaphragm and cover.

22. Install the master cylinder and bleed the entire system.

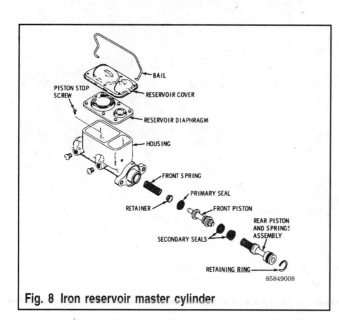

**Fig. 8 Iron reservoir master cylinder**

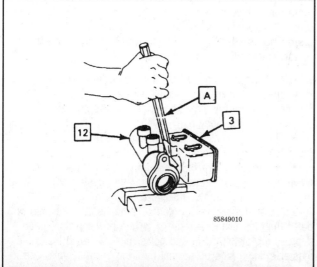

**Fig. 9 Removing the plastic master cylinder reservoir**

**Powermaster® Units**

**❋❋CAUTION**

**The Powermaster® master cylinder unit must be overhauled on a clean bench. Be especially careful that there are no traces of ordinary, mineral type lubricants, as these will ruin the seals.**

1. Remove the reservoir cover and diaphragm. Drain all brake fluid.

2. Remove:
   a. The pressure switch and O-ring.
   b. Accumulator and O-ring
   c. Electro-hydraulic pump and pressure hose assembly
   d. The sump hose clamps and the sump hose.
   e. The tube and nut assembly that runs from the sump hose to the master cylinder.
   f. Remove the two pump brackets from the master cylinder.

**❋❋CAUTION**

**Do not scratch or deform in any way the outside diameter and sealing surface at the pushrod end of the power piston assembly. Also avoid such damage to the bores of the Powermaster® body.**

3. Remove the retainer (it resembles a piston ring) from the groove in the rear of the unit. Then, pull the pushrod to remove the boot, retainer, pushrod and power piston group.

4. Remove the retainer, boot, pushrod, socket group, and piston guide from the power piston assembly.

5. Remove the O-ring from the piston guide. Then, remove the O-rings from the power piston assembly and piston guide.

6. Remove the reaction body group from the power piston assembly.

7. Remove the reaction piston and reaction disc from the reaction body group.

**❋❋CAUTION**

**Do not disassemble the reaction body group or power piston assembly any further! If either are damaged, they must be replaced only as complete assemblies.**

8. Use compressed air cautiously, building pressure slowly, to remove the primary and secondary piston assemblies. Direct the air pressure into the outlet port at the blind end of the master cylinder body. Block the port at the other end of the body.

9. Remove the secondary seal, spring retainer, and primary seal from the secondary piston.

10. Remove the spring from the master cylinder body bore.

11. Mount the master cylinder in a vise with the outboard side upward, **clamping the assembly by the mounting flange located at the rear, and not the body itself**. Then, carefully pry the reservoir off the body with a prybar.

12. Remove the reservoir grommets. Then, gently tap an Easy-Out® type threaded remover tool into the bore of the valve seat. Pull the tool straight out and remove the seat and seal. Discard the seat.

13. Remove the poppet and spring and discard the spring.

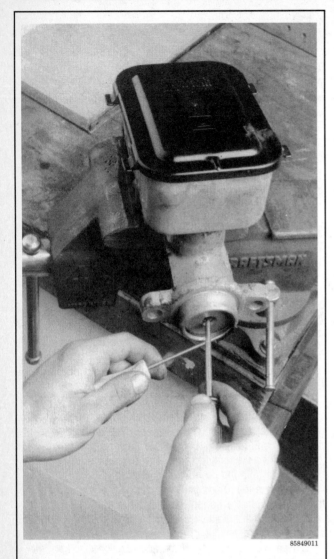

85849011

**Fig. 10 It may be helpful to slightly depress the piston when removing the lock ring**

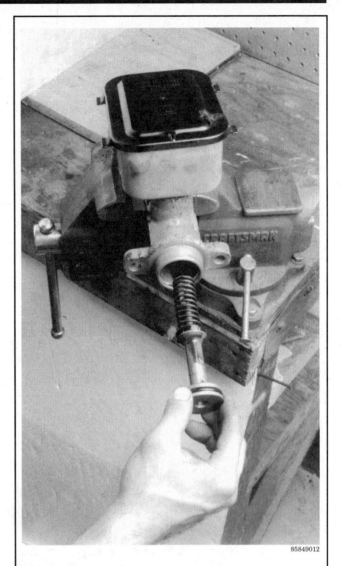

85849012

**Fig. 11 Removing the primary piston from the master cylinder**

**To assemble:**

14. Clean all parts **except the pressure switch and electro-hydraulic pump** in denatured alcohol. If necessary, wipe external surfaces of the pressure switch and electro-hydraulic pump clean with a cloth dampened slightly in denatured alcohol.

15. Inspect all metal parts for cracks, distortion or other damage. Inspect the primary piston sealing surfaces for scoring, deep scratches, or other damage where the damage could cause leaks. Replace the assembly if any of these defects are found.

16. Inspect the power piston and master cylinder bores for scoring or corrosion. Replace the assembly if either problem is noted.

### ✳✳CAUTION

Do not attempt to use an abrasive means to clean up these bores, or dangerous driving conditions could result!

➡Use clean, fresh brake fluid to lubricate all parts at sliding surfaces prior to assembly. Lubricate O-rings, grommets, and seals with the same fluid (all should be replaced). Lubricate both the master cylinder and power piston bores with the same fluid prior to installing the piston assemblies into these bores.

17. Install a new spring and poppet into the body of the Powermaster® unit. Then, install a new valve seat and seal. Bottom these out by threading the nut of the nut and tube assembly into the body port.

18. Remove the assembly from the vise. Install the three grommets (of two different sizes) into the top of the body **making sure they are fully seated**. Then, lay the reservoir down on its upper surface and install the master cylinder onto the reservoir from above, holding it upside down.

19. Install the remaining internal components in reverse order. When installing the retainer for the power piston group, depress the piston guide and power piston. Bench bleed the master cylinder side of the unit by filling the reservoirs and working the pistons back and forth.

85849013

Fig. 12 Removing the secondary piston

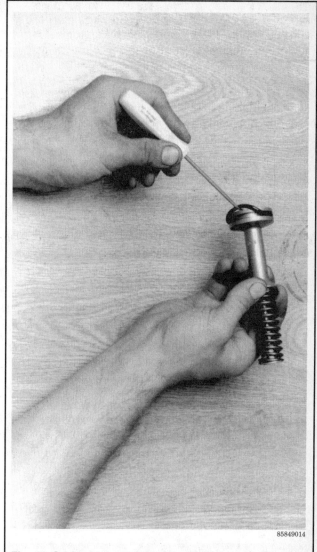

85849014

**Fig. 13 Seals can be removed from the piston with a small pick or awl**

20. Install the brackets with the mounting bolts. Install the sump hose, clamps, and hydraulic tube. Install the electro-hydraulic pump and pressure hose and clamp.

21. Install the accumulator and O-ring. Install the pressure switch and O-ring.

22. Install the master cylinder in the vehicle and make all connections as described above.

23. Fill both sides of the reservoir with clean, fresh brake fluid meeting the standards shown on the reservoir cover. Then, turn the ignition switch on. Time the running of the pump with your watch. It must not run more than 20 seconds. Have an assistant shut the ignition switch off after 20 seconds if the pump does not cycle off by itself. With the pump running, the fluid level in the booster side of the reservoir should drop. If necessary, add just enough brake fluid to keep the reservoir pump port covered and ensure an adequate supply of air-free fluid to the pump.

24. When the pump stops, check to make sure fluid does not flow back into the reservoir from the booster and check for leaks from the reservoir.

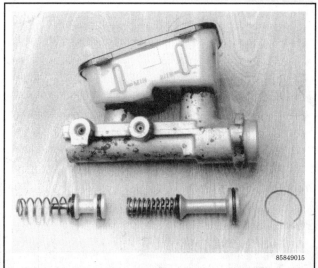

85849015

**Fig. 14 Internal components of a master cylinder**

25. Install the reservoir cover securely. Then, pump the brake pedal fully 10 times. Remove the reservoir cover and fill the reservoir to the full line. Again, turn the ignition switch on and time the operation of the pump. It should not run more than 20 seconds. Make sure fluid remains above the level of the reservoir pump port. Again, install the reservoir cover.

26. Turn the ignition switch on and then apply and release the brake pedal to cycle the pump on and off. Count the cycles and repeat the process until the total reaches 15. Make sure the pump does not run more than 20 seconds each cycle (turn the key off if necessary). Recheck the fluid levels and replenish. Check that the pump does not cycle on and off unless you apply the brakes.

27. Install the assembly onto the vehicle and bleed the entire system.

## Vacuum Power Booster

### REMOVAL & INSTALLATION

▶ See Figure 16

1. Disconnect the negative (-) battery cable. Disconnect the booster pushrod from the brake pedal arm by removing the retaining clip, and sliding the eyelet end of the pushrod off of the pin on the brake arm.
2. Disconnect the master cylinder from the booster.
3. Remove the attaching nuts and remove the booster from the firewall.

**To install:**

4. Install the booster to the firewall and torque the booster-to-firewall attaching nuts to 22-33 ft. lbs. (29-45 Nm). Reconnect the pushrod at the brake arm.
5. Install the master cylinder and bleed the system if the brake lines had to be disconnected.

## Hydraulic (Hydro-boost®) Power Booster

### REMOVAL & INSTALLATION

▶ See Figure 17

➡Power steering fluid and brake fluid cannot be mixed; also, power steering fluid damages seals designed for brake fluid, and brake fluid damages power steering type seals.

1. With the engine off, pump the brake pedal 5 times to deplete fluid stored in the accumulator.
2. Remove the two master cylinder mounting nuts and pull the master cylinder forward and away from the power booster with brake lines attached.
3. Disconnect the three hydraulic lines at the booster. Remove the retainer and washer at the brake pedal, inside the vehicle.
4. Remove the four nuts attaching the booster to the firewall from inside the vehicle and remove it. Remove the gasket.

**To install:**

5. Position the booster on the dash panel over the gasket and install the four mounting nuts onto the firewall from inside

the vehicle. Torque to 15 ft. lbs. (20 Nm). Install the pedal rod washer and retainer.

6. Position the master cylinder to the hydro-booster, install the mounting nuts, and torque to 20 ft. lbs. (27 Nm).
7. Install the three hydraulic lines, torquing the two high pressure lines (which are screwed in) to 20 ft. lbs. (27 Nm).
8. Install power steering fluid into the steering pump until fluid is at the base of the pump reservoir neck.
9. Disconnect the diesel injection pump 12V wire or the 12V wire to the distributor. THE ENGINE MUST NOT START.
10. Crank the engine for several seconds. Then, check the fluid level and replenish as necessary.
11. Connect wiring and start the engine. Turn the wheel from stop to stop two full times. Then, turn the engine off and depress the brake pedal five times to fully discharge the hydraulic accumulator. Check and if necessary replenish the hydraulic fluid.
12. Again start the engine and turn the wheel from lock to lock two full times. If there is visible foam in the power steering pump reservoir, wait an hour for it to dissipate (engine off). Then, replenish fluid.

## Combination Valve

▶ See Figures 18 and 19

The combination valve used on the large Buicks, Oldsmobiles and Pontiacs is a three-function valve. It serves as a metering valve, balance valve, and brake warning switch. There are two different valves, one manufactured by Bendix and one manufactured by Kelsey-Hayes. Both valves serve the same function and differ only in minor details. In any case, all combination valves are non-adjustable and must be replaced if they are found to be defective.

### REMOVAL & INSTALLATION

1. Disconnect all the brake lines at the valve. Plug the lines to prevent contamination and loss of fluid.
2. Disconnect the warning switch wiring connector from the valve switch terminal.
3. Remove the attaching bolts and remove the valve.
4. Install the valve and torque the brake lines to 20 ft. lbs. (27 Nm) using flare nut wrench only.
5. Bleed the entire brake system after valve installation.

## Brake Hoses and Pipes

### REMOVAL & INSTALLATION

**Brake Hose**

1. Raise the end of the vehicle with the hose to be replaced. Secure the vehicle properly with jackstands.
2. If necessary, remove the wheel.
3. Note the hose routing for ease of installation later.
4. Remove any attaching brackets and loosen the fittings using a flare nut wrench only.
5. Remove the hose any plug any open lines.

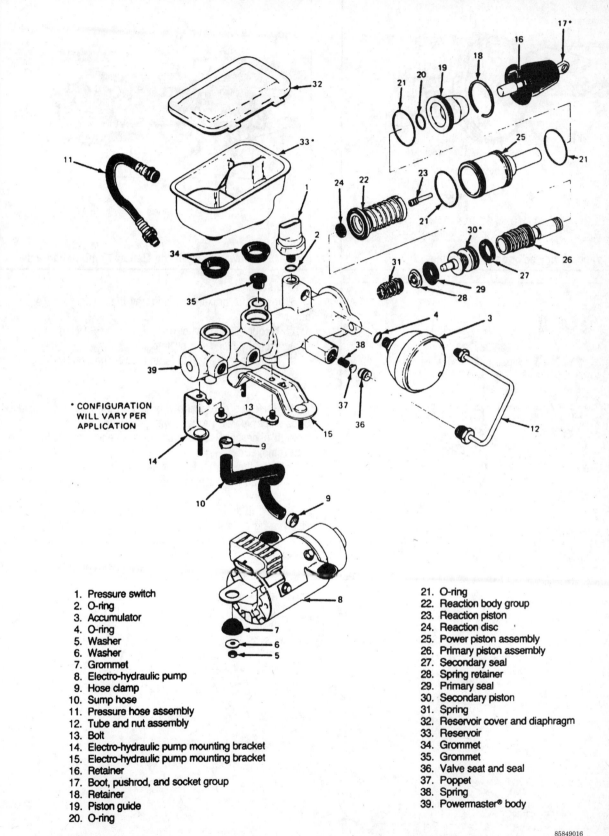

* CONFIGURATION
WILL VARY PER
APPLICATION

1. Pressure switch
2. O-ring
3. Accumulator
4. O-ring
5. Washer
6. Washer
7. Grommet
8. Electro-hydraulic pump
9. Hose clamp
10. Sump hose
11. Pressure hose assembly
12. Tube and nut assembly
13. Bolt
14. Electro-hydraulic pump mounting bracket
15. Electro-hydraulic pump mounting bracket
16. Retainer
17. Boot, pushrod, and socket group
18. Retainer
19. Piston guide
20. O-ring

21. O-ring
22. Reaction body group
23. Reaction piston
24. Reaction disc
25. Power piston assembly
26. Primary piston assembly
27. Secondary seal
28. Spring retainer
29. Primary seal
30. Secondary piston
31. Spring
32. Reservoir cover and diaphragm
33. Reservoir
34. Grommet
35. Grommet
36. Valve seat and seal
37. Poppet
38. Spring
39. Powermaster® body

85849016

Fig. 15 Exploded view of a Powermaster® master cylinder

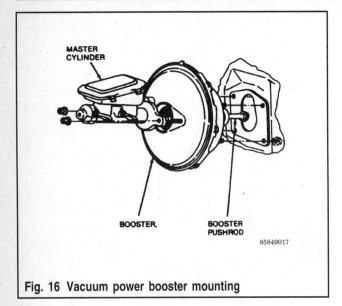

Fig. 16 Vacuum power booster mounting

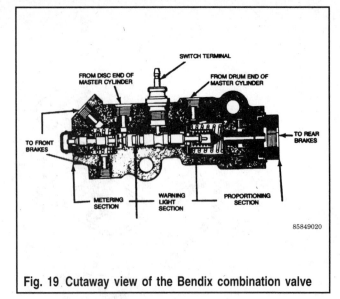

Fig. 19 Cutaway view of the Bendix combination valve

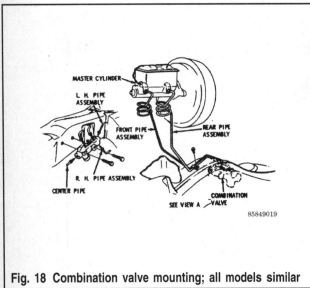

Fig. 18 Combination valve mounting; all models similar

**To install:**

6. Install the brake hose and any brackets which were removed.

7. Torque all fittings to 10-15 ft. lbs (14-20 Nm).

8. Properly bleed the system.

9. Remove the jackstands and lower the vehicle.

### Brake Pipe

1. Raise the end of the vehicle with the line to be replaced. Secure the vehicle properly with jackstands.

2. If necessary, remove any components which will interfere with removal.

3. Note the line routing for ease of installation later.

4. Loosen the fittings using a flare nut wrench only. Plug the open line.

5. Trace the line from one end to the other and loosen the fitting using a flare nut wrench only. Plug any open lines.

6. Remove any retaining clips and remove the line from the vehicle.

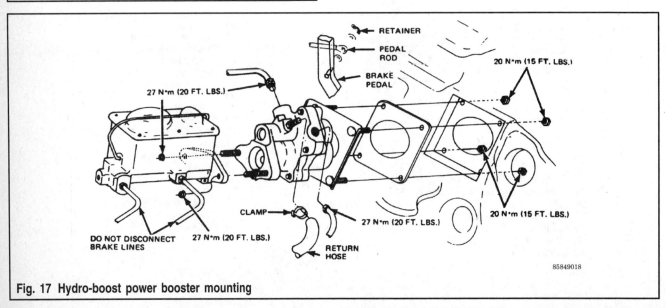

Fig. 17 Hydro-boost power booster mounting

**To install:**

7. Obtain a replacement line. If it is longer than the original, one end must be cut and flared.

8. If necessary, bend tubing using an approved tubing bender only.

➡**When bending, don't kink or crack the line. If it does kink or crack, the line must be replaced.**

9. Flush the line before installing.
10. Install the line and torque to 10-15 ft. lbs (14-20 Nm).
11. Bleed the system properly. Install any components removed earlier.

## BRAKE PIPE FLARING

Flaring steel lines is a skill which needs to be practiced before it should be done on a line to be used on a vehicle. A special flaring kit with double flaring adapters is required. It is essential that the flare be done uniformly to prevent any leaks when the brake system is under pressure. Only steel lines, not copper lines, should be used. It is also mandatory that the flare be a double flare. With the supply of parts available today, a pre-flared steel brake line should be available to fit your needs. Due to the high pressures in the brake system and the serious injuries that could occur if the flare should fail, it is strongly advised that pre-flared lines should be installed when repairing the braking system. If a line were to leak brake fluid due to a defective flare, and the leak were to go undetected, brake failure would result.

### ✳✳WARNING

**A double flaring tool must be used as single flaring tools cannot produce a flare strong enough to hold the necessary pressure.**

1. Determine the length of pipe needed. Allow ⅛ in. (3.2 mm) for each flare. Cut using an appropriate tool.
2. Square the end of the tube with a file and chamfer the edges. Remove any burrs.
3. Install the required fittings on the pipe.
4. Install the flaring tool into a vice and install the handle into the operating cam.
5. Loosen the die clamp screw and rotate the locking plate to expose the die carrier.
6. Select the required die set and install in the carrier.
7. Insert the prepared line through the rear of the die and push forward until the line end is flush with the die face.
8. Make sure the rear of both halves of the die are resting against the hexagon die stops. Then rotate the locking plate to the fully closed position and clamp the die firmly by tightening the clamp screw.
9. Rotate the punch turret until the appropriate size points towards the open end of the line to be flared.
10. Pull the operating handle against the line resistance in order to create the flare, then return the handle to the original position.
11. Release the clamp screw and rotate the locking plate to the open position.

12. Remove the die set and the line then separate by gently tapping both halves on the bench. Inspect the flare for proper size and shape.

### Brake Bleeding

The hydraulic brake system must be bled any time one of the lines is disconnected or any time air enters the system. If the brake pedal feels spongy upon application, and goes almost to the floor but regains height when pumped, air has entered the system. It must be bled out. Check for leaks that would have allowed the entry of air and repair them before bleeding the system. The correct bleeding sequence is: right rear wheel cylinder, left rear, right front, and left front. If the master cylinder is equipped with bleeder valves, bleed them first then go to the wheel cylinder nearest the master cylinder (left front) followed by the right front, left rear, and right rear.

## MANUAL BLEEDING

▶ **See Figures 20 and 21**

**Standard Systems**

This method of bleeding requires two people, one to depress the brake pedal and the other to open the bleeder screws.

1. Clean the top of the master cylinder, remove the cover and fill the reservoirs with clean fluid. To prevent squirting fluid, replace the cover.

### ✳✳CAUTION

**On vehicles with front disc brakes, it will be necessary to hold in the metering valve pin during the bleeding procedure. The metering valve is located beneath the master cylinder and the pin is situated under the rubber boot on the end of the combination valve housing. This may be taped in or held by an assistant. Never reuse brake fluid which has been bled from the system.**

2. Fill the master cylinder with brake fluid.
3. Install a box-end wrench on the bleeder screw on the right rear wheel.
4. Attach a length of small diameter, clear vinyl tubing to the bleeder screw. Submerge the other end of the rubber tubing in a glass jar partially filled with clean brake fluid. Make sure the rubber tube fits on the bleeder screw snugly or you may be squirted with brake fluid when the bleeder screw is opened.
5. Have your friend slowly depress the brake pedal. As this is done, open the bleeder screw half a turn and allow the fluid to run through the tube. Close the bleeder screw, then return the brake pedal to its fully released position.
6. Repeat this procedure until no bubbles appear in the jar. Refill the master cylinder.
7. Repeat this procedure on the left rear, right front, and left front wheels, in that order. Periodically refill the master cylinder so it does not run dry.
8. If the brake warning light is on, depress the brake pedal firmly. If there is no air in the system, the light will go out.

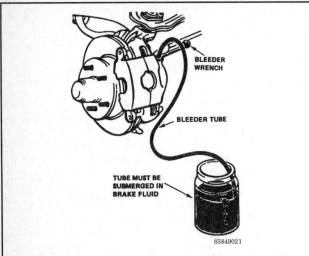

Fig. 20 Have an assistant pump the brake pedal while you bleed each wheel

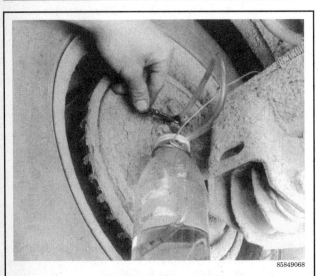

Fig. 21 Bleeder screw location on rear drum brakes

## Powermaster® System

1. Pump the brake pedal 10 times with the ignition switched off to remove all power boost effect from the system. Fill the reservoir to the indicated full mark with clean, fresh fluid meeting the specifications shown on the cover.

2. Disconnect the brake line connectors at the master cylinder outlet ports. Allow the fluid to bleed through the system by gravity until it flows out all four ports. Reconnect the brake lines to the ports. Refill the fluid reservoir, if necessary.

3. Tighten the connector closest to the cowl. Then, have an assistant slowly apply the brake pedal fully (50 lbs. pressure). As he holds this position, tighten the forward connector. Then, have the assistant release the pedal. Refill the fluid reservoir, if necessary.

4. Wait five seconds, and then have your assistant re-apply the brake pedal, and hold it down. Open the forward connector ½ turn to purge air. Before the pedal bottoms out, retighten the connector and have your assistant release the pedal again. Repeat the procedure in this step until all air is purged from this port. Refill the fluid reservoir, if necessary.

5. Repeat Steps 3 and 4 to bleed the remaining connectors (the connector closest to the cowl need not be bled). When the bleeding operation has been completed, operate the brakes with the ignition on and system pressure restored. Brake pedal travel should be normal and the brake warning indicator must not light when brakes are applied.

## FRONT DISC BRAKES

### Brake Pads

#### ✳✳CAUTION

Some brake pads contain asbestos, which has been determined to be a cancer causing agent. Never clean the brake surfaces with compressed air! Avoid inhaling any dust from any brake surface! When cleaning brake surfaces, use a commercially available brake cleaning fluid.

### REMOVAL & INSTALLATION

▶ See Figures 22, 23, 24, 25 and 26

1. Siphon off ⅔ of the brake fluid from the master cylinder.

➡The insertion of the thicker replacement pads will push the caliper piston back into its bore and will cause a full master cylinder to overflow.

2. Raise the vehicle and support it with jackstands. Remove the wheel(s).

3. Install a C-clamp on the caliper so that the solid side of the clamp rests against the back of the caliper and the screw end rests against the metal part of the outboard pad.

4. Tighten the clamp until the caliper moves enough to bottom the piston in its bore. Remove the clamp.

5. Remove the two allen head caliper mounting bolts enough to allow the caliper to be pulled off the disc.
6. Remove the inboard pad and dislodge the outboard pad. Place the caliper where it won't be supported by the brake hose (hang it by a wire hook from the frame).
7. Remove the pad support spring clip from the piston.
8. Remove the two bolt ear sleeves and the four rubber bushings from the ears.
9. Brake pads should be replaced when they are worn to within 1/32 in. of the rivet heads.

**To install:**

10. Check the inside of the caliper for leakage and the condition of the piston dust boot.
11. Lubricate the two new sleeves and four bushings with a silicone spray.
12. Install the bushings in each caliper ear. Install the two sleeves in the two inboard ears.
13. Install the pad support spring clip and the old pad into the center of the piston.

**➡On models with wear sensors, make sure the wear sensor is toward the rear of the caliper.**

14. Position the outboard shoe with the ears of the shoes over the caliper ears and the tab at the bottom engaged in the caliper cutout notch.
15. With the two shoes in position, place the caliper over the brake disc and align the holes in the caliper with those of the mounting bracket.

**✲✲CAUTION**

**Make certain that the brake hose is not twisted or kinked.**

16. Install the mounting bracket bolts through the sleeves in the inboard caliper ears and through the mounting bracket, making sure that the ends of the bolts pass under the retaining ears on the inboard shoe.
17. Tighten the bolts into the bracket and tighten to 35 ft. lbs. (48 Nm). Bend over the outer pad ears. On 1983 and 1984 vehicles, measure clearance between the caliper and bracket stops. It must be 0.005-0.012 in. (0.127-0.305mm).
18. Install the front wheel and lower the vehicle.
19. Add fluid to the master cylinder reservoirs so that they are 1/4 in. (6mm) from the top.
20. Test the brake pedal by pumping it to obtain a hard pedal is obtained. Bleed the brakes if necessary.

## INSPECTION

➧ See Figures 27 and 28

Brake pads should be inspected once a year or at 7,500 miles, whichever occurs first. Check both ends of the outboard shoe, looking in at each end of the caliper; then check the lining thickness on the inboard shoe, looking down through the inspection hole. Lining should be more than 0.020 in. (0.5mm) on 1975-82 vehicles; 0.030 in. (0.76mm) on 1983 and later vehicles, thick above the rivet (so that the lining is thicker than the metal backing.). Keep in mind that any applicable state

85849022

**Fig. 22 View of a common front wheel disc brake assembly**

85849023

**Fig. 23 Use a C-clamp to seat the piston in it's bore**

85849024

**Fig. 24 Removing the caliper mounting bolt**

Fig. 25 The caliper can be removed by pulling up after the mounting bolts have been removed

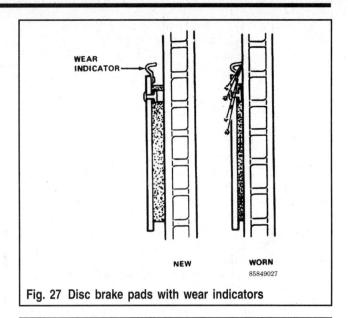
Fig. 27 Disc brake pads with wear indicators

Fig. 26 Support the caliper with a wire, not by it's hose

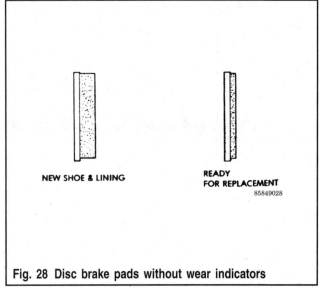
Fig. 28 Disc brake pads without wear indicators

inspection standards that are more stringent take precedence. All four pads must be replaced if one shows excessive wear.

➡All 1979 and later models have a wear indicator that makes a noise when the linings wear to a degree where replacement is necessary. The spring clip is an integral part of the inboard shoe and lining. When the brake pad reaches a certain degree of wear, the clip will contact the rotor and produce a warning noise.

## Brake Calipers

### REMOVAL & INSTALLATION

1. Perform the removal steps for pad replacement.
2. Disconnect the brake hose and plug the line.
3. Remove the U-shaped retainer from the fitting.

4. Pull the hose from the frame bracket and remove the caliper with the hose attached.
   **To install:**
5. Install the brake hose into the caliper using a new copper gasket.
6. Lubricate the new sleeves and rubber bushings. Install the bushings in the caliper ears. Install the sleeves so that the end toward the disc pad is flush with the machined surface.

➡Lubrication of the sleeves and bushings is essential to ensure the proper operation of the sliding caliper design.

7. Install the shoe support spring in the piston.
8. Install the disc pads in the caliper and remount the caliper on the hub. See Disc Brake Pad Removal and Installation.
9. Reconnect the brake hose to the steel brake line. Install the retainer clip. Bleed the brakes. See Brake Bleeding.
10. Replace the wheels, check the brake fluid level, check the brake pedal travel, and road-test the vehicle.

## OVERHAUL

▶ **See Figures 29, 30, 31, 32 and 33**

1. Clean the outside of the caliper with denatured alcohol.
2. Remove the brake hose and discard the copper gasket.
3. Remove the brake fluid from the caliper.
4. Place clean rags or a piece of wood inside the caliper opening to catch the piston when it is released.

### ✳✳CAUTION

**Do not place your fingers in front of the piston in an attempt to catch it while applying compressed air; serious injury could result.**

5. Apply compressed air to the caliper fluid inlet hole and force the piston out of its bore. Do not blow the piston out, but use just enough pressure to ease it out.
6. Use a prybar to pry the boot out of the caliper. Avoid scratching the bore.
7. Remove the piston seal from its groove in the caliper bore. Do not use a metal tool of any type for this operation.

**To install:**

8. Blow out all passages in the caliper and bleeder valve. Clean the piston and piston bore with fresh brake fluid.
9. Examine the piston for scoring, scratches or corrosion. If any of these conditions exist the piston must be replaced, as it is plated and cannot be refinished.
10. Examine the bore for the same defects. Light rough spots may be removed by rotating crocus cloth, using finger pressure, in the bore. Do not polish with an in and out motion or use any other abrasive.
11. Lubricate the piston bore and the new rubber parts with fresh brake fluid. Position the seal in the piston bore groove.
12. Lubricate the piston with brake fluid and assemble the boot into the piston groove so that the fold faces the open end of the piston.
13. Insert the piston into the bore, taking care not to unseat the seal.
14. Force the piston to the bottom of the bore. (This will require a force of 50-100 lbs.). Seat the boot lip around the caliper counterbore. Proper seating of the boot is very important for sealing out contaminants.

## Brake Disc (Rotor)

### REMOVAL & INSTALLATION

▶ **See Figure 34**

1. Raise the vehicle, support it with jackstands, and remove the wheel and tire assembly.
2. Remove the brake caliper as previously outlined.
3. Remove the dust cap and remove the wheel bearing nut after removing the cotter pin.
4. Remove the wheel bearing, hub, and disc assembly from the spindle.
5. Install the disc, bearing, washer and nut. Adjust the wheel bearing as follows:
   a. Spin the wheel forward by hand. Torque the nut to 12 ft. lbs. to fully seat the bearings.
   b. Back off the nut ¼-½ turn until it is just loose, the tighten the nut finger tight.
   c. Loosen the nut until either hole in the spindle lines up with a slot in the nut and then insert the cotter pin. This may appear to be too loose, but it is the correct adjustment.
   d. Proper adjustment creates a 0.001-0.005 in. (0.025-0.127mm) of end play.

### INSPECTION

▶ **See Figure 35**

1. Check the disc for any obvious defects such as excessive rust, chipping, or deep scoring. Light scoring is normal on disc brakes.
2. Make sure there is no wheel bearing play and then check the disc for runout as follows:
3. Install a dial indicator on the caliper so that its feeler will contact the disc about 1 in. below its outer edge.
4. Turn the disc and observe the runout reading. If the reading exceeds 0.002 in. (0.05mm), the disc should be replaced.

➡**All brake rotors (discs) have a minimum thickness dimension cast into them, on the hub between the lugs. This is the minimum wear dimension and not a refinish dimension. Do not reuse a brake rotor that will not meet specifications. Replace with a new rotor.**

Refinishing of brake rotors can be handled at machine shops equipped for brake work.

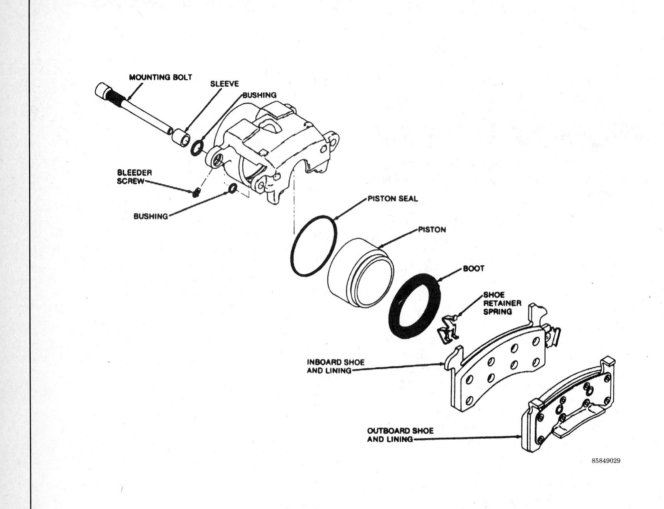

Fig. 29 Exploded view of the brake caliper

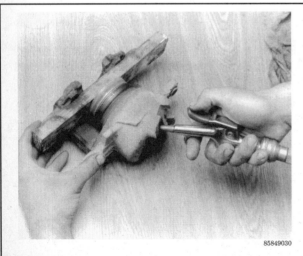

Fig. 30 Use a piece of wood to cushion the piston when blowing it out

Fig. 31 Removing the piston from the caliper

Fig. 32 Prying the dust boot from the caliper

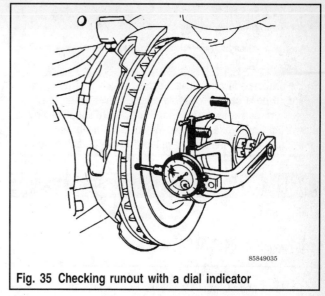

Fig. 35 Checking runout with a dial indicator

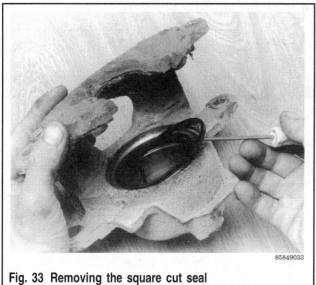

Fig. 33 Removing the square cut seal

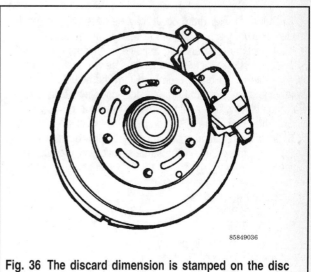

Fig. 36 The discard dimension is stamped on the disc hub

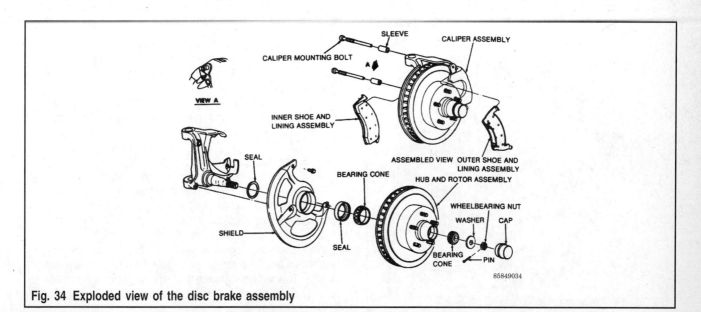

Fig. 34 Exploded view of the disc brake assembly

# REAR DRUM BRAKES

### ✳✳CAUTION

**Some brake pads contain asbestos, which has been determined to be a cancer causing agent. Never clean the brake surfaces with compressed air! Avoid inhaling any dust from any brake surface! When cleaning brake surfaces, use a commercially available brake cleaning fluid.**

## Brake Drum

▶ See Figure 37

### REMOVAL & INSTALLATION

1. Raise and support the vehicle with jackstands.
2. Remove the wheel or wheels.
3. Pull the brake drum off. It may be necessary to gently tap the rear edges of the drum to start it off the studs.
4. If extreme resistance to removal is encountered, it will be necessary to retract the adjusting screw. Knock out the access hole in the brake drum and turn the adjuster to retract the linings away from the drum. If this does not release the drum completely, use a rubber mallet to pound gently all around the outer edge of the drum to loosen it.
5. Install a replacement hole cover before reinstalling drum.
6. Install the drums in the same position on the hub as removed.

### INSPECTION

1. Check the drums for any cracks, scores, grooves, or an out-of-round condition. Replace if cracked. Slight scores can be removed with fine emery cloth while extensive scoring requires turning the drum on a lathe.
2. Never have a drum turned more than 0.060 in. (1.5mm).

85849037

**Fig. 37 View of a common brake drum**

## Brake Shoes

### INSPECTION

To inspect the brake shoes, first remove the drum as described above. Then, measure the thickness of the lining. To do this, you can lay a ruler next to the shoe, perpendicular to the surface, and measure the thickness of the lining alone. If the thickness does not meet or exceed the dimension shown in the specifications chart or state inspection standards in your state **whichever is thicker**, replace the lining. Remember, also, that there must be enough lining left so that the minimum thickness will still exist when you plan to perform your next inspection.

### REMOVAL & INSTALLATION

▶ See Figures 38, 39, 40, 41, 42, 43, 44, 45, 46, 47, 48, 49 and 52

### ✳✳CAUTION

**Some brake shoes contain asbestos, which has been determined to be a cancer causing agent. Never clean the brake surfaces with compressed air! Avoid inhaling any dust from any brake surface! When cleaning brake surfaces, use a commercially available brake cleaning fluid.**

1. Raise the vehicle and support it on jackstands.
2. Slacken the parking brake cable.
3. Remove the rear wheel and brake drum.
4. Free the brake shoe return springs, actuator pull-back spring, holddown pins and springs, and actuator assembly.

➡Special tools available from auto supply stores will ease removal of the spring and anchor pin, but the job may still be done with common hand tools.

5. On the rear wheels, disconnect the adjusting mechanism and spring, and remove the primary shoe. The primary shoe has a shorter lining than the secondary and is mounted at the front of the wheel.
6. Disconnect the parking brake lever from the secondary shoe and remove the shoe. Rear wheel shoes may be removed together.
   **To install:**
7. Clean and inspect all brake parts.
8. Check the wheel cylinders for seal condition and leaking.
9. Repack wheel bearings and replace the seals.
10. Inspect the replacement shoes for nicks or burrs, lubricate the backing plate contact points, brake cable and levers, and adjusting screws and then assemble.
11. Make sure that the right and left hand adjusting screws are not mixed. You can prevent this by working on one side at a time. This will also provide you with a reference for reassembly. The star wheel should be nearest to the secondary shoe when correctly installed.

12. When completed, make an initial adjustment as previously described.

➡️Maintenance procedures for the metallic lining option are the same as those for standard linings. Do not substitute these linings in standard drums, unless they have been honed to a 20 micro-inch finish and equipped with special heat resistant springs.

## Wheel Cylinders

### REMOVAL & INSTALLATION

▶ See Figures 50, 51, 53, 54, 55, 56, 57 and 58

1. Raise the vehicle and support with jackstands. Remove the wheels and brake drum as described above.
2. Clean all dirt away from around the brake line connection, and disconnect the brake line.
3. The wheel cylinders are retained by two types of fasteners. One type uses a round retainer with locking clips, which attaches to the wheel cylinder on the back side of the brake backing plate. Use two awls to release the two locking clips. The other type simply uses two bolts, which screw into the wheel cylinder from the back side of the backing plate. Remove the wheel cylinder from the backing plate.

**To install:**

4. Install the wheel cylinder onto the backing plate. Using a 1¹⁄₈ in. socket and extension, press the locking clip onto the wheel cylinder. Torque the retaining bolts to 15 ft. lbs. (20 Nm) for the other type.
5. Connect the brake pipe. Torque the connection to 100 inch lbs. (12 Nm).
6. Install brake shoes, drum, and wheel, and flush and bleed brakes.

Fig. 39 Removing the brake drum

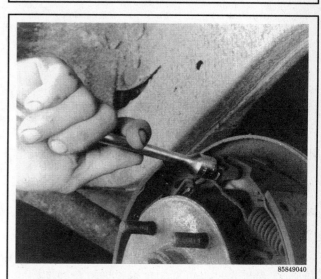
Fig. 40 This tool simplifies return spring removal

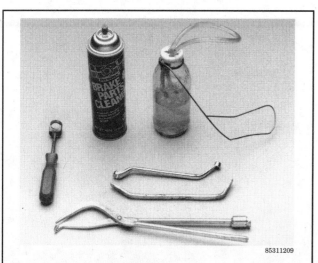
Fig. 38 Using specialized brake tools can save time and make the job easier

Fig. 41 Note the return spring position before removing it from the brake assembly

Fig. 42 Removing the actuating link

Fig. 45 Removing the hold down spring and pin

Fig. 43 After the return springs have been removed, the shoe guide can be removed from the anchor pin

Fig. 46 The rear wheel shoes can be removed together

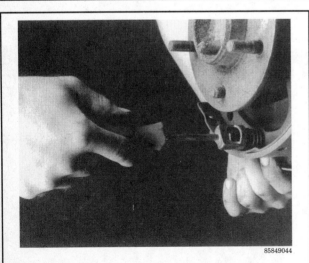

Fig. 44 Push and twist the hold down spring to disengage it from the hold down pin

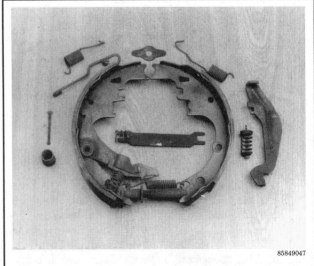

Fig. 47 A view of rear drum brake components

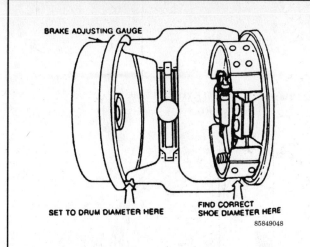

**Fig. 48 Measuring brake drum diameter for shoe adjustment**

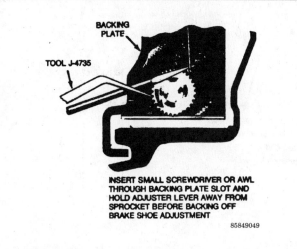

**Fig. 49 Adjusting rear drum brakes using a brake adjusting spoon**

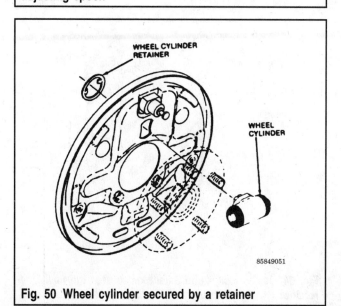

**Fig. 50 Wheel cylinder secured by a retainer**

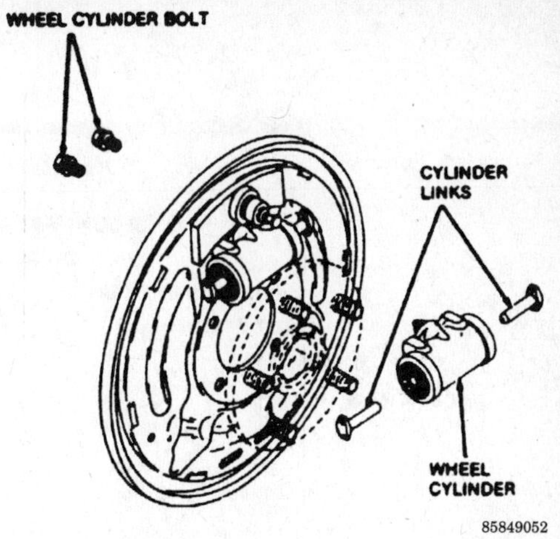

**Fig. 51 Wheel cylinder secured by bolts**

## Brake Backing Plate

### REMOVAL & INSTALLATION

1. Remove the wheel and brake drum.
2. Remove the brake hardware and linings.
3. Remove the axle shaft.
4. Remove the brake line from the wheel cylinder and the wheel cylinder from the backing plate.
5. Disconnect the parking brake cable from the backing plate.
6. Remove the backing plate attaching bolts and remove the backing plate.
7. Installation is the reverse of removal. Torque the backing plate attaching bolts to 40 ft. lbs. (54 Nm).

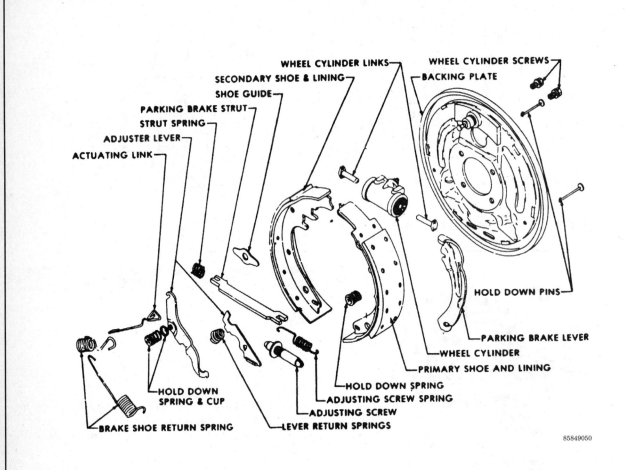

Fig. 52 Exploded view of a rear drum brake assembly

WHEEL CYLINDER LINKS
SECONDARY SHOE & LINING
SHOE GUIDE
PARKING BRAKE STRUT
STRUT SPRING
ADJUSTER LEVER
ACTUATING LINK
WHEEL CYLINDER SCREWS
BACKING PLATE
HOLD DOWN PINS
PARKING BRAKE LEVER
WHEEL CYLINDER
PRIMARY SHOE AND LINING
HOLD DOWN SPRING & CUP
HOLD DOWN SPRING
ADJUSTING SCREW SPRING
ADJUSTING SCREW
LEVER RETURN SPRINGS
BRAKE SHOE RETURN SPRING

85849050

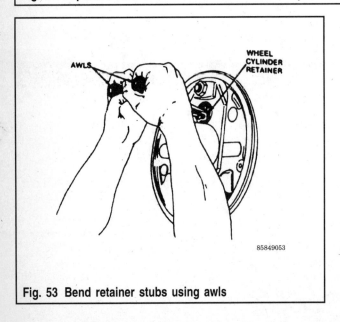

AWLS
WHEEL CYLINDER RETAINER

85849053

Fig. 53 Bend retainer stubs using awls

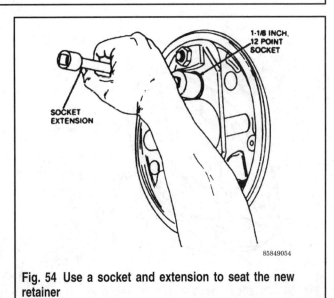

1-1/8 INCH, 12 POINT SOCKET
SOCKET EXTENSION

85849054

Fig. 54 Use a socket and extension to seat the new retainer

# REAR DISC BRAKES

**✳✳CAUTION**

Brake shoes contain asbestos, which has been determined to be a cancer causing agent. Never clean the brake surfaces with compressed air! Avoid inhaling any dust from any brake surface! When cleaning brake surfaces, use a commercially available brake cleaning fluid.

The brakes are almost identical in design and operation to the front disc brakes, with the exception of the parking brake mechanism that is built into the rear brake calipers. When the parking brake is applied, the lever turns the actuator screw which is threaded into a nut in the piston assembly. This causes the piston to move outward and the caliper to slide inward mechanically, forcing the linings against the brake disc. The piston assembly contains a self-adjusting mechanism for the parking brake.

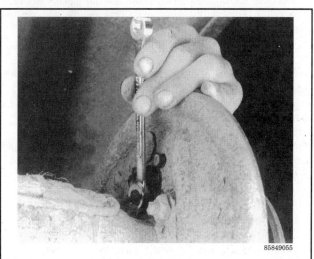

Fig. 55 Remove the brake line fittings with a flare nut wrench only

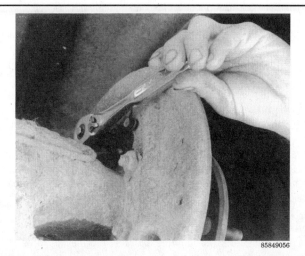

Fig. 56 The wheel cylinder on this vehicle is retained by bolts

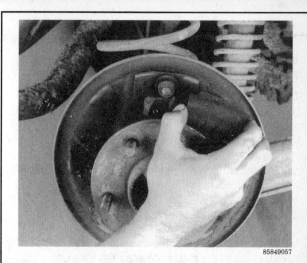

Fig. 57 Removing the wheel cylinder from the backing plate

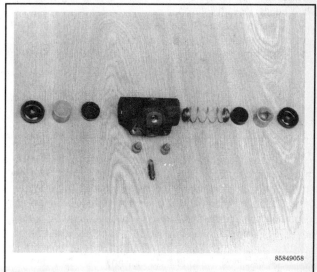

Fig. 58 Internal components of a wheel cylinder

## Brake Pads

### REMOVAL & INSTALLATION

1. Siphon off ⅔ of the brake fluid from the master cylinder.

➡The insertion of the thicker replacement pads will push the caliper piston back into its bore and will cause a full master cylinder to overflow.

2. Raise the rear of the vehicle and support it with safety stands. Remove the wheel and tire assembly.
3. Remove the caliper as detailed later in this section.
4. Remove the outboard brake shoe and lining by unsnapping the shoe springs from the caliper holes.

5. From the inside of the caliper, press on the edge of the inboard brake shoe and tilt it outward so that it is released from the shoe retainer.

6. Remove the flexible two way check valve from the end of the piston assembly with a small screwdriver.

➡**If new linings are to be installed, remove the parking brake lever and bottom the piston in the caliper bore.**

**To install:**

7. Lubricate a new two way check valve with silicone fluid and press it into the end of the piston.

8. Install the inboard brake shoe. Make sure that the shoe retainer and the piston are positioned as shown in the illustration. The tabs on the retainer are different; rotate the retainer into position if necessary. The buttons on the backing of the shoe must engage the larger, D-shaped notches in the piston. The piston will be properly aligned when the larger notches are aligned with the caliper mounting bolt holes as shown. Engage the inboard edge of the shoe with the straight tabs on the retainer, press downward and snap the shoe under the S-shaped tabs.

9. Install the outboard brake shoe. The shoe is properly installed when the wear sensor is at the trailing edge of the shoe during forward rotation.

10. Be sure to snap both shoe springs into the caliper holes so that the back of the shoe is flat against the caliper.

11. Install the caliper.

12. Bleed the brakes, install the wheels and lower the vehicle.

## INSPECTION

Brake pads should be inspected once a year or at 7,500 miles, whichever occurs first. Check both ends of the outboard shoe, looking in at each end of the caliper; then check the lining thickness on the inboard shoe, looking down through the inspection hole. Lining should be more than 0.020 in. (0.5mm) on 1975-82 vehicles; 0.030 in. (0.76mm) on 1983 and later vehicles, thick above the rivet (so that the lining is thicker than the metal backing.). Keep in mind that any applicable state inspection standards that are more stringent take precedence. All four pads must be replaced if one shows excessive wear.

➡**All 1979 and later models have a wear indicator that makes a noise when the linings wear to a degree where replacement is necessary. The spring clip is an integral part of the inboard shoe and lining. When the brake pad reaches a certain degree of wear, the clip will contact the rotor and produce a warning noise.**

## Brake Caliper

▶ **See Figure 59**

## REMOVAL & INSTALLATION

1. Siphon off ⅔ of the brake fluid from the master cylinder.

➡**The insertion of the thicker replacement pads will push the caliper piston back into its bore and will cause a full master cylinder to overflow.**

2. Raise the rear of the vehicle and support it with safety stands. Remove the wheel and tire assembly.

3. Reinstall two lug nuts to keep the rotor from turning.

4. Remove the retaining clip from the parking brake actuator lever.

5. Disconnect the parking brake cable and spring from the lever.

6. While holding the parking brake lever in place, remove the lock nut. Remove the lever, lever seal and the anti-friction washer.

7. If the caliper is to be overhauled or replaced, remove the bolt attaching the brake line inlet fitting.

8. Remove the caliper mounting bolts and then remove the caliper from the rotor and mounting bracket.

9. Check the lever seal and the anti-friction washer for wear and replace if worn.

10. Check the mounting bolts for any wear or damage, replace if necessary. Check the bolt boots, support bushings and caliper piston boot for any wear, cracking or other damage, replace as necessary.

11. Replace the insulators.

12. To install, coat the entire shaft of the caliper mounting bolts with a thin film of silicone grease.

13. Slide the caliper over the rotor and into the mounting bracket. Make sure that the new insulators are in position. Tighten the mounting bolts to 63 ft. lbs. (85 Nm).

14. If you disconnected the inlet fitting, install it and tighten to 32 ft. lbs. (44 Nm). Use two NEW copper washers.

15. Lubricate the parking brake lever seal with silicone grease and then install it and the anti-friction washer.

16. Install the lever onto the actuator screw hex so that it is pointing as shown in the illustration. Tighten the nut to 35 ft. lbs. (48 Nm) while holding the lever in position and then rotate the lever back against the stop on the caliper.

17. Install the spring with the damper and then connect the parking brake cable.

18. Install the retaining clip onto the lever so that it prevents the parking brake cable from sliding out of the slot in the lever.

19. Adjust the parking brake cable by tightening the cable at the adjuster until the lever begins to move off the stop on the caliper. Loosen the adjustment just enough so that the lever moves back against the stop. Apply and release the parking brake three times to verify proper adjustment.

20. Remove the two lug nuts and then replace the wheels. Lower the vehicle.

21. Bleed the brake system and recheck the fluid level.

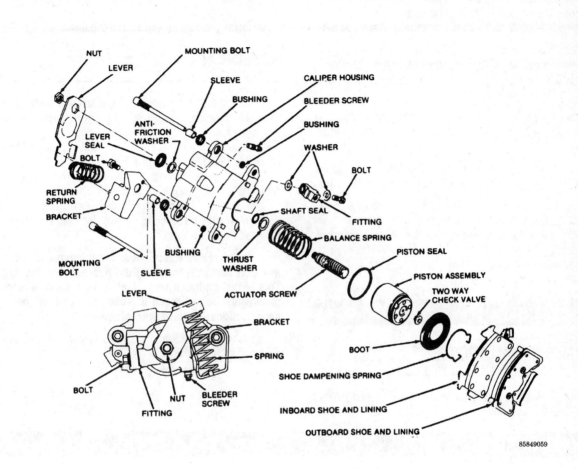

**Fig. 59 Exploded view of a rear disc caliper and parking brake assembly**

## OVERHAUL

1. Remove the caliper from the car.
2. Secure the caliper in a vise.
3. Remove the two mounting sleeves and four bushings from the caliper and discard.
4. Remove the brake shoes and lever return spring.

➡**Pad the caliper using shop towels to catch the piston and brake fluid when removing the piston.**

5. Rotate the lever back and forth to move the piston out of the caliper housing.

➡**If the piston will not move out of the housing by rotating the lever, it can be turned out using a wrench. Remove the lock nut, lever, lever seal, and anti-friction washer. Using a wrench, turn the screw hex in normal parking brake apply direction until the piston pops out of the housing.**

6. Remove the piston assembly and balance spring.

7. Remove the locknut, lever, lever seal, and anti-friction washer.
8. Push screw out of the housing. Clean the screw with denatured alcohol or clean brake fluid.
9. Remove the piston seal and boot.
10. Flush the caliper housing with clean denatured alcohol to remove all contaminants.
11. All passages should be blown out with filtered compressed air.

**To assemble:**

12. Install a new piston seal.
13. Install a new boot onto the new piston assembly. The lip of the boot fits in a groove provided in the piston.
14. Assemble a new thrust washer so that the gray teflon bearing surface is against the cast iron housing and the seal onto the actuator screw. Lubricate the seal with clean brake fluid.
15. Fit the actuator screw in the piston assembly. Piston assemblies are stamped by a letter on the end of the adjuster screw "L" and "R". These letters should match the letter on the caliper housing.

16. Coat the new piston seal with a thin film of clean brake fluid.

17. Fit the balance spring into the piston assembly spring retainer and start the assembly into the caliper housing.

18. Use tool J-23072 to install the piton until it seats in the housing.

➡**The piston must be pushed in straight or the actuator screw seal will be damaged as it passes through the hole in the rear of the piston bore.**

19. Before removing tool J-23072, install the anti-friction washer, lubricated with silicone; a new lever seal; lever and locknut.

➡**Install the lever away from the stop. Rotate in the apply direction and hold in position. Torque the nut to 25 ft. lbs. (34 Nm).**

20. Remove tool J-23072, rotate lever back to the stop.

21. Using tool J-28678, drive the boot until the seal bottoms in the housing.

22. Install the shoe and the linings.

23. Install the caliper.

## Brake Disc (Rotor)

### REMOVAL & INSTALLATION

1. Raise the vehicle, support it with jackstands, and remove the wheel and tire assembly.

## PARKING BRAKE

All models are equipped with a foot operated ratchet type parking brake. A cable assembly connects this pedal to an intermediate cable by means of an equalizer. Adjustment is made at the equalizer. The intermediate cable connects with two rear cables and each of these cables enters a rear wheel.

## Cables

### REMOVAL & INSTALLATION

▶ **See Figures 60, 61, 62 and 63**

#### Front cable

1. Raise the vehicle and support it securely by the frame. Loosen the adjusting nut and disconnect the front cable at the connector. Compress the fingers of the cable retainer and disconnect it at the frame.

2. Lower the vehicle to the ground. Then, remove the lower rear bolt from the wheelhouse panel and then pull the panel outward to gain access to the front cable. Disconnect the cable at the parking brake pedal assembly by compressing the fingers of the retainer and pulling it out.

3. Install a new cable in reverse order, checking carefully that it is properly routed and securely retained. Adjust the parking brake.

2. Remove the brake caliper as previously outlined.

3. Remove the brake disc.

**To install:**

4. Install the disc.

5. Install the caliper as described earlier.

### INSPECTION

1. Check the disc for any obvious defects such as excessive rust, chipping, or deep scoring. Light scoring is normal on disc brakes.

2. Make sure there is no wheel bearing play and then check the disc for runout as follows:

3. Install a dial indicator on the caliper so that its feeler will contact the disc about 1 in. below its outer edge.

4. Turn the disc and observe the runout reading. If the reading exceeds 0.002 in. (0.05mm), the disc should be replaced.

➡**All brake rotors (discs) have a minimum thickness dimension cast into them, on the hub between the lugs. This is the minimum wear dimension and not a refinish dimension. Do not reuse a brake rotor that will not meet specifications. Replace with a new rotor.**

Refinishing of brake rotors can be handled at machine shops equipped for brake work.

#### Left Rear Cable

##### DRUM BRAKES

1. Raise the vehicle and support it securely by the frame. Loosen the adjusting nut and compress the retainer fingers at the equalizer lever to loosen the cable.

2. Disconnect the cable at the connector and then remove it from the equalizer.

3. Mark the relationship between the wheel and axle flange and remove the wheel. Remove the brake drum as described above.

4. Using an appropriate tool, disconnect and remove the primary shoe return spring and parking brake strut.

5. Compress the retainer fingers and loosen the cable housing at the backing plate. Then, disconnect the cable from the parking brake lever and remove it.

6. Install a new cable in reverse order, checking carefully that it is properly routed and securely retained. Adjust the parking brake.

#### Right Rear Cable

##### DRUM BRAKES

1. Raise the vehicle and support it securely by the frame. Remove the adjusting nut at the equalizer lever. Compress the fingers of the retainers and then loosen the cable housing from

the retainers at the frame and at the axle housing retaining clip.

2. Mark the relationship between the wheel and axle flange and then remove the wheel. Remove the brake drum as described above.

3. Using an appropriate tool, disconnect and remove the primary shoe return spring and parking brake strut. Remove the secondary brake shoe holddown spring.

4. Compress the retainer fingers and loosen the cable housing at the backing plate. Then, disconnect the cable from the parking brake lever and remove it.

5. Install a new cable in reverse order, checking carefully that it is properly routed and securely retained. Adjust the parking brake.

## Rear Cables

### DISC BRAKES

1. Raise the vehicle and support it on safety stands.
2. Loosen the cable at the adjuster.
3. Disconnect all cables at the equalizer.
4. Disengage the cable housing retainer from the rear suspension crossmember assembly.
5. Remove the cable from the caliper assembly as detailed earlier in this section and then remove the cable.
6. To install, position the cables in the retainers.
7. Install the cable in the caliper assembly as described previously.
8. Reconnect all cables at the equalizer.
9. Adjust the parking brake.

## ADJUSTMENT

♦ **See Figures 64, 65, 66 and 67**

### Rear Drum Brakes

The need for parking brake adjustment is indicated if parking brake pedal travel is more than 15 clicks under heavy foot pressure.

1. Depress the parking brake pedal exactly two ratchet clicks.
2. Raise the vehicle and safely support it with jackstands.
3. Tighten the adjusting nut until the left rear wheel can just be turned rearward using two hands, but is locked when forward rotation is attempted.
4. With the mechanism totally disengaged, the rear wheels should turn freely in either direction with no brake drag.

➡ **It is very important that the parking brake cables are not adjusted too tightly causing brake drag.**

5. Remove the jackstands and lower the vehicle.

### Rear Disc Brakes

1. Lubricate the parking brake cables at the underbody rub points and at the equalizer hooks. Make sure there is free movement at all cables, and that the parking brake pedal is in the fully released position.
2. Raise the rear of the vehicle and support it with jackstands.
3. Hold the brake cable stud from turning and tighten the equalizer nut until all cable slack is removed.

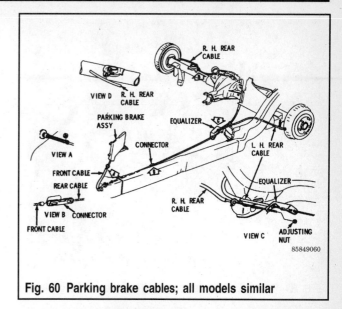
Fig. 60 Parking brake cables; all models similar

Fig. 61 Removing the rear cable from the parking brake lever

Fig. 62 A wrench can be used to compress the retaining fingers on the rear cable

Fig. 63 Removing the rear cable from the backing plate

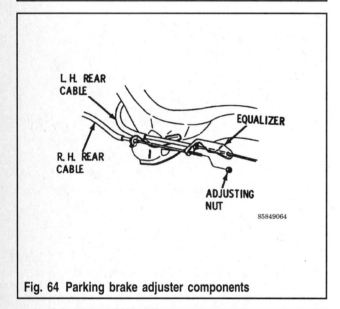

Fig. 64 Parking brake adjuster components

Fig. 65 Location for parking brake adjustment

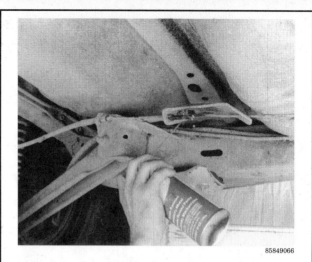

Fig. 66 It may be helpul to soak the adjuster with a penetrating fluid first

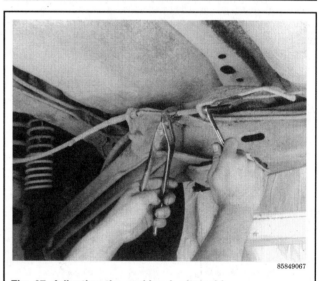

Fig. 67 Adjusting the parking brake cable

4. Make sure the caliper levers are against the stops on the caliper housings after tightening the equalizer nut.

5. If the levers are off the stops, loosen the cable until the levers return to the stops.

6. Operate the parking brake pedal several times to check the adjustment. When the cable is properly adjusted, the parking brake pedal should travel 4-5½ in. (102-140mm) with approximately 125 pounds of force on the pedal.

7. After the adjustment, the levers must be on the caliper stops. Back off the brake adjustment if necessary to keep the levers on the stops. Remove the jackstands and lower the vehicle.

# 10

## BODY AND TRIM

## EXTERIOR

### ✳✳WARNING

**If equipped with the air cushion restraint system, do not attempt any adjustment, repair or removal of any portion of the chassis sheet metal which would require removal or disconnecting of the bumper impulse detector until the ignition switch is turned to the LOCK position and the negative battery cable is disconnected and the end taped. This procedure must be followed to prevent accidental deployment of the system which could result in personal injury and/or damage to the systems components. In addition, care must be exercised to never bump or strike the bumper impulse detector in a manner which could cause inadvertent deployment or improper operation of the system.**

## Doors

### REMOVAL & INSTALLATION

▶ See Figure 1

### ✳✳CAUTION

**Removing a door is a simple operation, but it requires careful handling of a heavy object that is awkward to handle. You must have a helper who will hold the door and ensure that it does not get out of control, which could hurt someone or strip the threads of the mounting bolts. Put a floor jack or other adjustable means of holding the door underneath before starting, so that the helper must only keep the door from tipping as you remove the fasteners.**

The easiest and best way to remove the door is to remove the bolts that fasten the door assembly to the hinges, rather than attempting to remove the bolts fastening the hinges to the body. This is true because it is much easier to gain access to these bolts.

1. If the vehicle has power operated components in the doors (electric windows or motor operated mirrors), disconnect the negative battery cable, remove the trim panel (see the appropriate procedure later in this section), and lift the watershield out far enough to reach the electrical connectors. Then, disconnect these connectors. Detach the rubber wire conduit and pull the harness coming from the body out of the door.

2. Very precisely use a sharp scribe to mark the relationship between the door and the door hinges so that you can remount it without the need to adjust it.

3. Open the door all the way and, with the help of another person and using a floor jack or other means, support the door.

4. Remove both the upper and lower bolts attaching the door to the outer portions of the hinges. Remove the door.

**To install:**

5. Install the mounting bolts and turn them in until they are nearly ready to clamp the hinge to the door.

6. Position the door carefully so that the matchmarks line up.

7. Tighten the bolts alternately top and bottom until the door is tightly held in position. Torque the bolts to 15-21 ft. lbs. (20-28 Nm).

8. Install and connect all disconnected wiring and battery cable.

### ADJUSTMENT

Doors are adjustable by using floating plates inside both the doors and hinge pillars. Always mark locations of bolts before loosening them and beginning adjustment. It is best to remove the door lock striker to permit the door to hang free and then close the door so you can observe exactly how it fits onto the body.

**Front Doors**

1. If the door requires fore and aft or up or down adjustment, loosen the body hinge pillar adjustments. Shift the position of the door with the help of an assistant and a floor jack. Then, tighten the bolts. When the position fore and aft and up and down is correct, torque the bolts to 15-21 ft. lbs. (20-28 Nm). If you have to move the door to the rear, replace the door jamb light switch.

2. If the door must be adjusted in or out, loosen the bolts attaching the door at the hinge pillar attachments. Shift the position of the door with the help of an assistant and a floor jack. Then, tighten the bolts. When the position in or out is correct, torque the bolts to 15-21 ft. lbs. (20-28 Nm).

**Rear Doors**

1. If the door requires in or out or significant up or down adjustment, loosen the door side hinge attaching screws. Shift

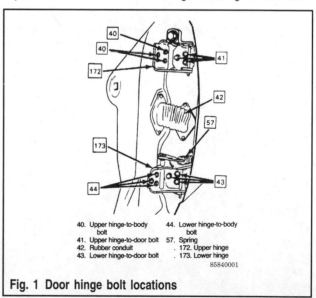

40. Upper hinge-to-body bolt
41. Upper hinge-to-door bolt
42. Rubber conduit
43. Lower hinge-to-door bolt
44. Lower hinge-to-body bolt
57. Spring
172. Upper hinge
173. Lower hinge

85840001

**Fig. 1 Door hinge bolt locations**

the position of the door with the help of an assistant and a floor jack. Then, tighten the bolts. When the position in or out and up and down is correct, torque the bolts to 15-21 ft. lbs. (20-28 Nm).

2. If the door requires fore or aft or a slight up or down adjustment, loosen the body side, center pillar hinge adjusting bolts. Shift the position of the door with the help of an assistant and a floor jack. Then, tighten the bolts. When the position is correct, torque the bolts to 15-21 ft. lbs. (20-28 Nm). If you have to move the door to the rear, replace the door jamb light switch.

## Hood

### REMOVAL & INSTALLATION

▶ See Figures 2 and 3

1. Raise the hood. Cover the fenders with protective pads. This is necessary to protect the paint because the hood will often contact these areas during removal or installation procedures. Place masking tape on the fender and hood covers and edges.
2. On models equipped with an underhood light disconnect the lamp wiring.
3. Very precisely use a sharp scribe to mark the relationship between the hood and the hood hinges so that you can remount it without the need to adjust it.
4. Support the hood, especially at the front, in a secure manner. Remove the bolts on either side that fasten the tops of the hinges to the underside of the hood. Remove the bolts starting at the front and moving toward the rear to help avoid placing stress on the assembly. Make sure the hood is securely supported to help prevent bending of it as you work.
5. When all the bolts are removed, lift the rear of the hood off the hinges and then lift the unit off the vehicle.

**To install:**
6. Carry the hood from either side and position it over the engine compartment in its normal position. Raise the front and position it at the right angle to the upper surfaces of the hinges. Pass all the bolts through the upper hinges and start them into the lower side of the hood. Do not tighten them, but leave plenty of clearance to adjust the position of the hood on the hinges.
7. Carefully shift the hood on both hinges simultaneously to align the matchmarks. Then, tighten the mounting bolts, torquing to 20 ft. lbs. (27 Nm). Close the hood and check its fit in the body and the alignment of the hood latch. If necessary, readjust the hood alignment as described below. Reconnect the underhood light wiring, if the vehicle is so equipped.

### ALIGNMENT

Close the hood and check its fit in the body and the alignment of the hood latch. If necessary, loosen all the mounting bolts just slightly and shift the adjustment in the correct direction. Repeat this procedure until the hood latches smoothly and securely and all gaps between the hood and body are of equal width. Torque the mounting bolts to 20 ft. lbs. (27 Nm).

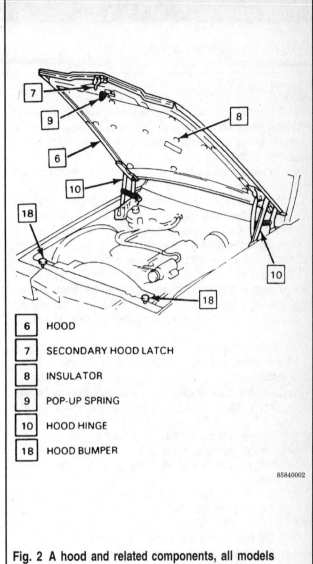

| 6 | HOOD |
| 7 | SECONDARY HOOD LATCH |
| 8 | INSULATOR |
| 9 | POP-UP SPRING |
| 10 | HOOD HINGE |
| 18 | HOOD BUMPER |

Fig. 2 A hood and related components, all models similar

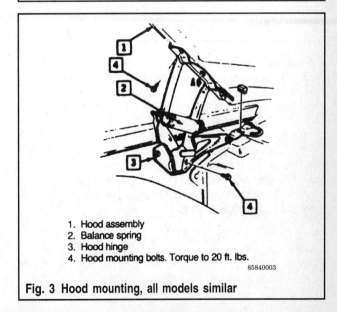

1. Hood assembly
2. Balance spring
3. Hood hinge
4. Hood mounting bolts. Torque to 20 ft. lbs.

Fig. 3 Hood mounting, all models similar

## Trunk Lid

### REMOVAL & INSTALLATION

▶ **See Figure 4**

1. Raise the trunk lid. Cover the fenders with some sort of protective pads. This is necessary to protect the paint because the trunk lid will often contact these areas during removal or installation procedures.

2. On models equipped with an underhood light disconnect the lamp wiring.

3. Very precisely use a sharp scribe to mark the relationship between the trunk lid and the hinges so that you can remount it without the need to adjust it.

4. Support the trunk lid, especially at the rear, in a secure manner. Remove the bolts on either side that fasten the sides of the hinges to the underside of the trunk lid. Remove the bolts starting at the rear and moving toward the front to help avoid placing stress on the assembly. Make sure the trunk lid is securely supported to help prevent bending of it as you work.

5. When all the bolts are removed, lift the rear of the trunk lid off the hinges and then lift the unit off the vehicle.

**To install:**

6. Carry the trunk lid from either side and position it over the luggage compartment in its normal position. Raise the rear and position it at the right angle to the upper surfaces of the hinges. Pass all the bolts through the trunk lid and start them into the side of the upper hinges. Do not tighten them, but leave plenty of clearance to adjust the position of the trunk lid on the hinges.

7. Carefully shift the trunk lid on both hinges simultaneously to align the matchmarks. Then, tighten the mounting bolts, torquing to 20 ft. lbs. (27 Nm). Close the trunk lid and check its fit in the body and the alignment of the trunk lid latch. If necessary, readjust the alignment. Reconnect the underhood light wiring, if the vehicle is so equipped.

### ADJUSTMENT

All adjustments (fore and aft and up and down) are made by loosening the hinge strap-to-lid attaching bolts. Loosen all the bolts before adjusting the position of the lid to avoid springing it and to make adjustment easier. Slide the hood back and forth, locating both sides as required; then tighten the bolts. No side-to-side adjustment is provided.

If the hood has adjustable rear bumpers and it does not sit level, loosen the locknuts and turn the bumper screws up or down as necessary. Retighten the locknuts. You may find it helpful to close the trunk lid and measure the gap between the hood and body with a finely calibrated ruler.

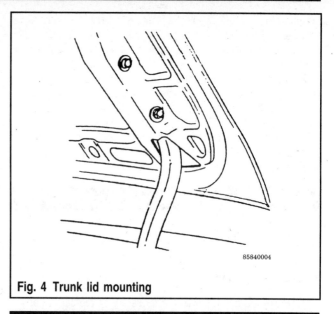

85840004

**Fig. 4 Trunk lid mounting**

## Station Wagon Tailgate

### REMOVAL & INSTALLATION

▶ **See Figure 5**

➡ **To perform this procedure, you will need a length of rod ³/₁₆ in. (5mm) in diameter and 12 in. (305mm) long. You will also need new, service hinge pins and retaining rings.**

1. First, rotate the tailgate up and down until the torque rod tension has been eliminated. This occurs at a point near the vertical position of the gate, when spring tension is not required to keep the gate under control. You should be able to feel the point at which there is no longer significant weight to be supported as you raise the gate, and stop there.

### ✳✳CAUTION

**Proceed carefully with the next step in case there is still some tension on the torque rod.**

2. Mark the position of the torque rod assist link on the rear body pillar, and then remove it.

3. Open the tailgate and support it in the horizontal position. When the gate is securely supported, disconnect the support cables at the sides of the gate.

4. Place the length of rod against the point of one of the hinge pins. Strike the rod hard with a hammer to force the pin out of the hinge. You have to shear the retaining ring tabs to do this. Repeat this on the hinge on the other side. Then, remove the tailgate.

**To install:**

5. Install new retaining rings in the grooves in the new hinge pins, positioning the rings so the tabs point toward the heads of the pins. To install, first align the gate to the body and so the hinge halves fit together properly. Then, tap the new hinge pins into position in the same direction in which the original pins were installed. Reverse the remaining procedures, installing the torque rod assist link in the same position, according to the markings made earlier.

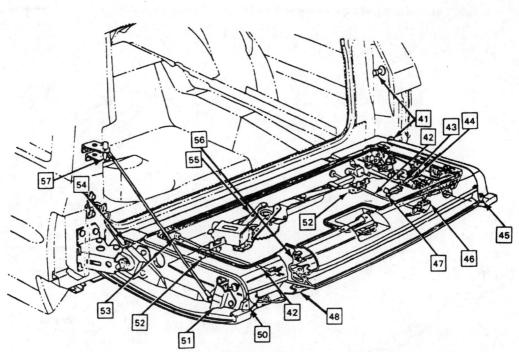

41. Upper right striker assembly
42. Window guide tube
43. Lock rod
44. Electric lock actuator rod
45. Right side weatherstrip
46. Outside handle
47. Lock cylinder
48. Sealing strip
50. Left side weatherstrip
51. Upper left hinge lock
52. Window sash plate
53. Window down bumper
54. Grommet
55. Regulator
56. Retainer
57. Upper left striker

85840005

**Fig. 5 Station wagon tailgate components**

## ALIGNMENT

Adjust the tailgate horizontally by loosening all the hinge-to-body bolts, repositioning the gate, and then retightening the bolts. Make sure to retain all the shims in position, unless the gate is too close to or too far from the body.

If it is necessary to move the tailgate bottom in or out, loosen the hinge bolts and add or subtract shims between the hinge and body.

## Bumpers

### REMOVAL & INSTALLATION

▶ **See Figures 6, 7, 8, 9, 10, 11 and 12**

**Front**

1. Raise the vehicle and support with jackstands.

2. Disconnect the parking lamp connectors.

3. With the aid of an assistant, remove the eight bumper reinforcement-to-energy absorber nuts and remove the bumper. Note the size and position of the shims if used.

**To install:**

4. With an assistant, install the bumper shims and nuts only hand tight.

5. Move the bumper from side to side to gain sideward adjustment. Add or subtract shims to gain in or out adjustment. Torque the retaining nuts to 18 ft. lbs. (24 Nm).

6. Connect the parking lamp wires and lower the vehicle.

**Rear**

1. Raise the vehicle and support with jackstands.

2. Disconnect the license plate lamp connectors.

3. With the aid of an assistant, remove the eight bumper reinforcement-to-energy absorber nuts and remove the bumper. Note the size and position of the shims if used.

**To install:**

4. With an assistant, install the bumper shims and nuts only hand tight.

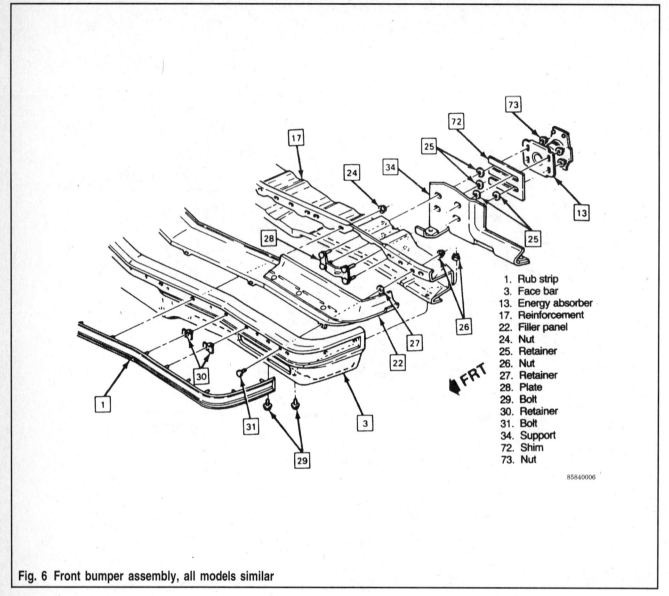

1. Rub strip
3. Face bar
13. Energy absorber
17. Reinforcement
22. Filler panel
24. Nut
25. Retainer
26. Nut
27. Retainer
28. Plate
29. Bolt
30. Retainer
31. Bolt
34. Support
72. Shim
73. Nut

85840006

**Fig. 6 Front bumper assembly, all models similar**

5. Move the bumper from side to side to gain sideward adjustment. Add or subtract shims to gain in or out adjustment. Torque the retaining nuts to 18 ft. lbs. (24 Nm).

6. Connect the license plate lamp wires and lower the vehicle.

## Grille

### REMOVAL & INSTALLATION

▶ **See Figures 13, 14 and 15**

**Buick**

1. Remove the two grille return springs, radiator grille nuts and grille.

2. Install the grille, torque the nuts to 97 inch lbs. (11 Nm) and install the return springs.

**Oldsmobile and Pontiac**

1. Remove the radiator grille bolts, grille and baffle if equipped.

2. Install the grille, baffle and bolts. Torque the bolts to 13 inch lbs. (1.5 Nm).

## Outside Mirrors

### REMOVAL & INSTALLATION

1. Disconnect the negative battery cable.

2. Remove the door trim panel, sound deflector and peel back the water shield as outlined in this chapter.

3. Remove the remote mirror control and cable from the instrument panel. If power mirrors, disconnect the electrical connector.

4. Disconnect the control cable guide clips from inside the door.

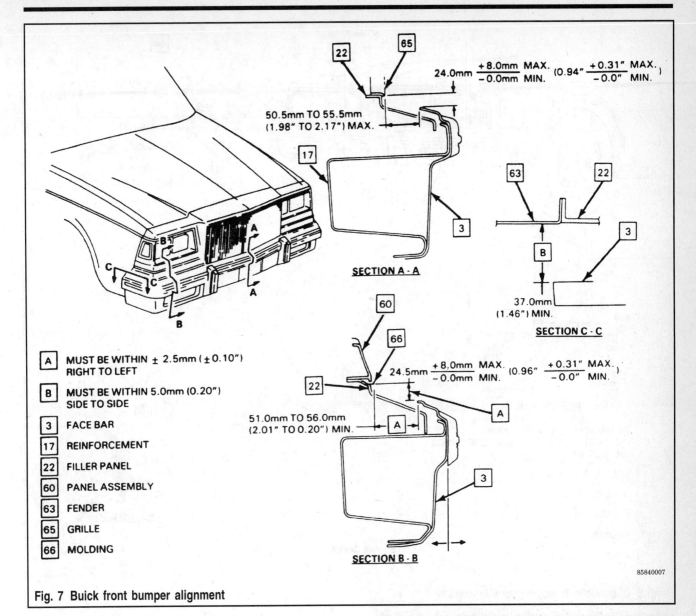

**Fig. 7 Buick front bumper alignment**

5. The window has to be down. Remove the two mirror-to-door retaining nuts and mirror.

**To install:**

6. Thread the control cable or wire through the access hole, install the mirror and insulator.

7. Reconnect the control cable or wiring to the retaining clips.

8. Install the water deflector, sound insulator and trim panel.

9. Install the remote control to the instrument panel.

## Antenna

### REPLACEMENT

▶ See Figure 16

**Fixed**

1. Remove the steel antenna out of the base and masking tape the front edge of the right door.

2. Using a antenna bezel socket, loosen the bezel nut at the top of the fender.

3. Remove the side mounting bolt and disconnect the antenna lead at the junction.

4. Raise the vehicle and support with jackstands.

5. Remove the lower fender-to-body bolt and rocker panel molding screws.

6. Remove the inner fender and block.

7. Remove the bezel and the antenna base assembly.

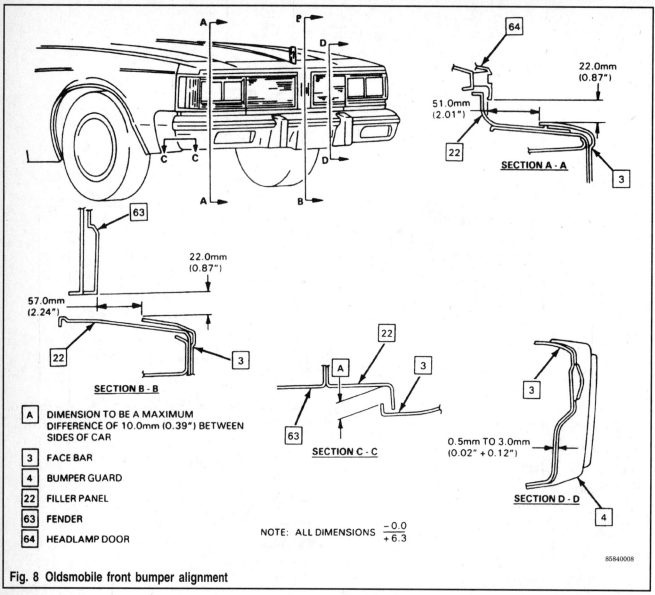

A | DIMENSION TO BE A MAXIMUM DIFFERENCE OF 10.0mm (0.39") BETWEEN SIDES OF CAR
3 | FACE BAR
4 | BUMPER GUARD
22 | FILLER PANEL
63 | FENDER
64 | HEADLAMP DOOR

NOTE: ALL DIMENSIONS $\frac{-0.0}{+6.3}$

85840008

**Fig. 8 Oldsmobile front bumper alignment**

**To install:**

8. Install the antenna assembly and loosely tighten the bezel nut.

9. Install the inner fender screws, rocker panel molding screws and lower fender-to-body bolt.

10. Lower the vehicle.

11. Connect the antenna leads and tighten the bezel nut using the bezel socket J 28641 or equivalent. Install the side mounting bolt.

### Power

1. Disconnect the negative battery cable.

2. Protect the door with masking tape and remove the five outer-to-inner fender panel screws.

3. Remove the lower fender-to-body bolt and rocker panel molding screws.

4. Remove the three fender-to-inner fender screws along the rear half of the wheel opening.

5. Remove the antenna bezel nut using a bezel nut socket tool J 28641 and disconnect the electrical wiring.

6. Block the lower edge of the fender out, remove the antenna bracket screw and remove the antenna assembly.

**To install:**

7. Install the antenna, gasket and bezel nut. Do NOT tighten at this time.

8. Install the mounting bolts. Do NOT tighten at this time.

9. Torque the bezel using the bezel socket and the lower mounting bolts.

10. Connect all antenna leads.

11. Install the fender bolts and screws.

12. Connect the negative battery cable and check operation.

## Fenders

Fenders are adjustable with shims. To add or remove shims, loosen the bolts at the shim locations and carefully apply force with a prybar to provide clearance for adding or removing shims.

➡**Tape fender and door edges with masking tape to prevent damage during replacement.**

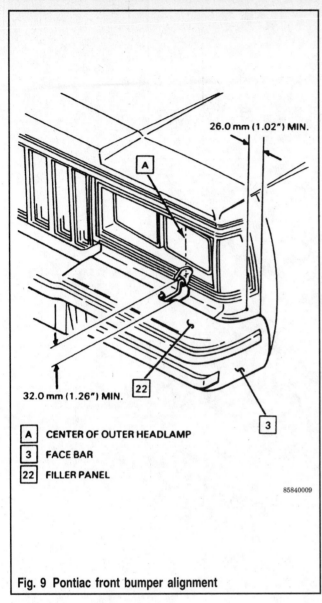

**Fig. 9 Pontiac front bumper alignment**

26.0 mm (1.02") MIN.

32.0 mm (1.26") MIN.

| A | CENTER OF OUTER HEADLAMP |
| 3 | FACE BAR |
| 22 | FILLER PANEL |

85840009

## REMOVAL & INSTALLATION

▶ See Figures 17, 18, 19, 20, 21, 22, 23 and 24

### 1975 and 1976

1. Disconnect the negative battery cable then the positive cable.
2. Tape the fender and the door edge.
3. Disconnect the side marker lamp wires.
4. Remove the tie bar to front end panel seal.
5. Disconnect the headlamp wires.
6. Remove the tie bar to fender brace.
7. Remove the cowl to fender brace.
8. Remove the dash to fender top bolt.
9. Remove the hood hinge from the fender and block the hood.
10. Remove the fender to support bolts.
11. Remove the fender to cowl bolts.

12. Remove the fender and filler plate.
13. Remove the fender from the filler plate.
14. Installation is the reverse of removal.

### 1977 to 1990

1. Disconnect the negative battery cable.
2. Remove the hood and hood hinges.
3. Remove the fender bolt from the battery ground strap, if applicable.
4. Remove the battery and battery tray if they are located on the side to be replaced.
5. Remove any components mounted on the wheel housing/fender assembly on the side to be replaced.
6. Remove the cowl to fender bolts and shims. Note the position and number of shims used.
7. Remove the body to fender bolts.
8. Remove the fender extension bolts.
9. Remove the bolt from the frame brace to fender, if equipped.
10. Remove the bumper filler attaching bolts.
11. Remove the wheelhousing to radiator support bolts.
12. Remove the front end panel to fender bolts.
13. Disconnect the side marker lamp electrical connections.
14. Remove the front fender and wheelhousing with the aid of a helper.
15. Installation is the reverse of removal.

## Power Sunroof

### REMOVAL & INSTALLATION

▶ See Figure 25

1. Disconnect the negative battery cable.
2. Place the sunshade in the stowed position.
3. Move the sliding panel rearward until the front rollers on the sliding panel contact the bottom of the cable guide ramp (forward down position).
4. Remove the garnish moldings, coat hooks, map lamp retainer, and dome lamp.
5. Remove the sunroof opening headlining close-out lace.
6. Remove the headlining material from the headlining retainer.
7. Disengage and lower the headlining.
8. Disconnect the wire harness from the switch and the dome lamp, remove the headlining.
9. Remove the dome lamp retaining studs.
10. Remove the hoses from the housing.
11. Remove the screws from each of the rearmost side supports.
12. Remove the screws holding the housing to the front header.
13. Support the sunroof housing and remove the nuts from the side front screws that retain the housing to the roof supports. Lower and remove the sun roof housing.
14. Installation is the reverse of removal. Torque nuts at the side front locations to 7-10 ft. lbs. (10-14 Nm).

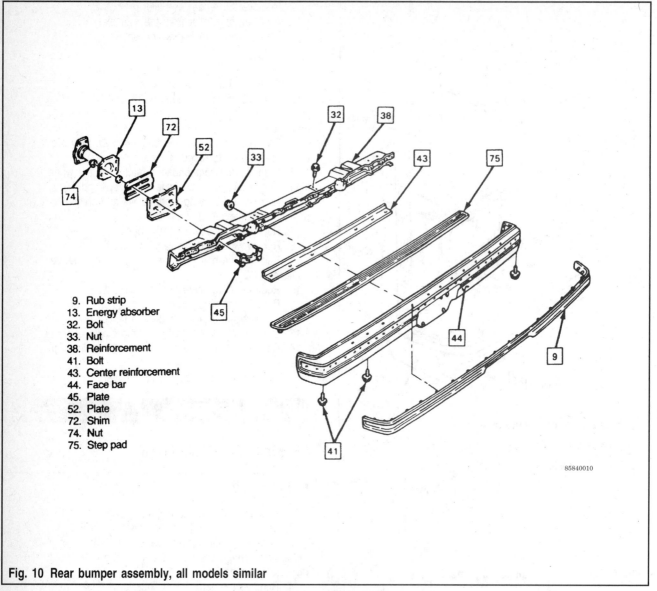

9. Rub strip
13. Energy absorber
32. Bolt
33. Nut
38. Reinforcement
41. Bolt
43. Center reinforcement
44. Face bar
45. Plate
52. Plate
72. Shim
74. Nut
75. Step pad

85840010

**Fig. 10 Rear bumper assembly, all models similar**

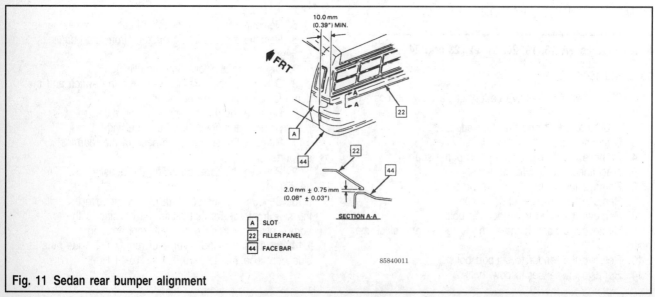

10.0 mm
(0.39") MIN.

FRT

2.0 mm ± 0.75 mm
(0.08" ± 0.03")

SECTION A-A

| A | SLOT |
| 22 | FILLER PANEL |
| 44 | FACE BAR |

85840011

**Fig. 11 Sedan rear bumper alignment**

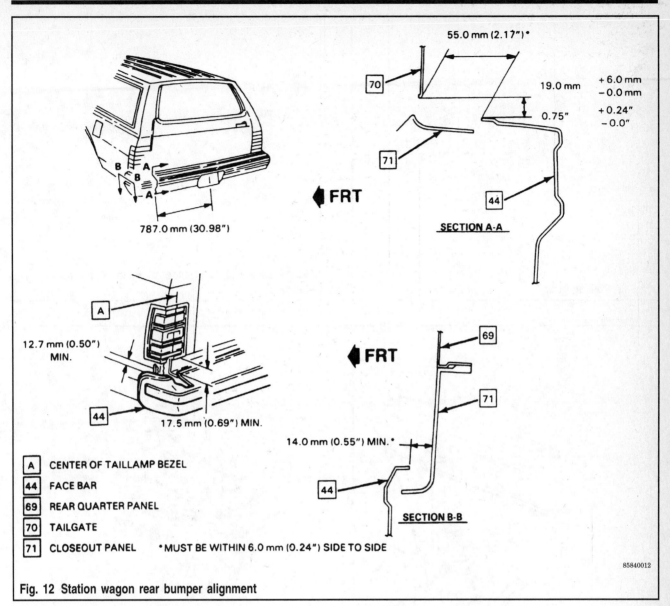

| | |
|---|---|
| A | CENTER OF TAILLAMP BEZEL |
| 44 | FACE BAR |
| 69 | REAR QUARTER PANEL |
| 70 | TAILGATE |
| 71 | CLOSEOUT PANEL    *MUST BE WITHIN 6.0 mm (0.24") SIDE TO SIDE |

85840012

Fig. 12 Station wagon rear bumper alignment

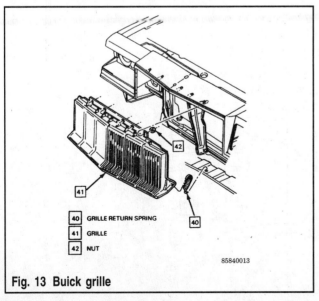

| | |
|---|---|
| 40 | GRILLE RETURN SPRING |
| 41 | GRILLE |
| 42 | NUT |

85840013

Fig. 13 Buick grille

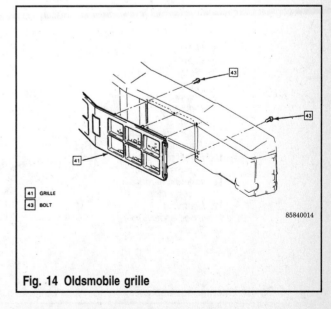

| | |
|---|---|
| 41 | GRILLE |
| 43 | BOLT |

85840014

Fig. 14 Oldsmobile grille

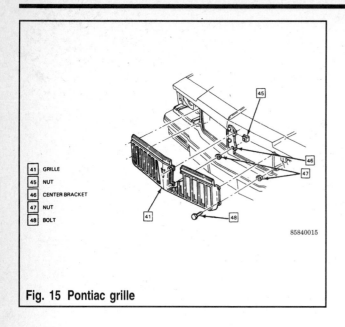

| 41 | GRILLE |
| 45 | NUT |
| 46 | CENTER BRACKET |
| 47 | NUT |
| 48 | BOLT |

85840015

**Fig. 15 Pontiac grille**

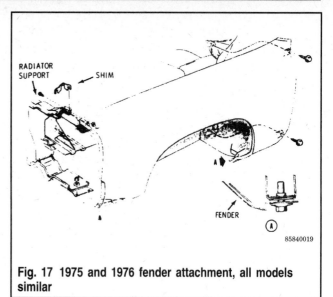

85840019

**Fig. 17 1975 and 1976 fender attachment, all models similar**

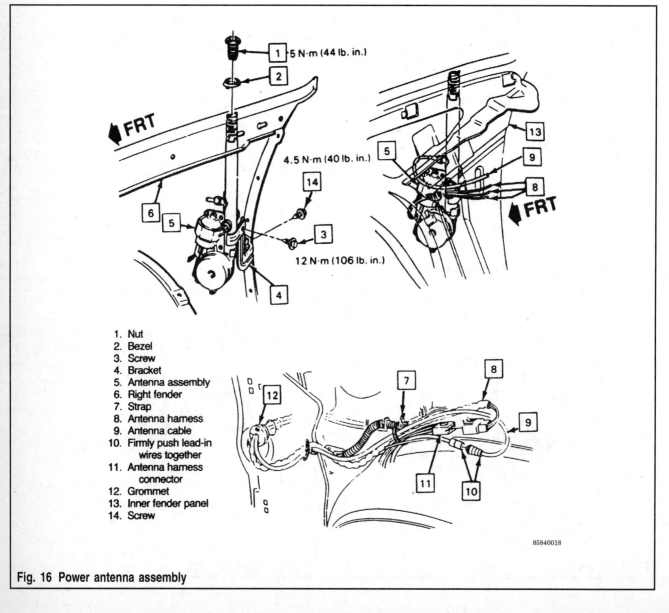

1 — 5 N·m (44 lb. in.)

4.5 N·m (40 lb. in.)

12 N·m (106 lb. in.)

1. Nut
2. Bezel
3. Screw
4. Bracket
5. Antenna assembly
6. Right fender
7. Strap
8. Antenna harness
9. Antenna cable
10. Firmly push lead-in wires together
11. Antenna harness connector
12. Grommet
13. Inner fender panel
14. Screw

85840018

**Fig. 16 Power antenna assembly**

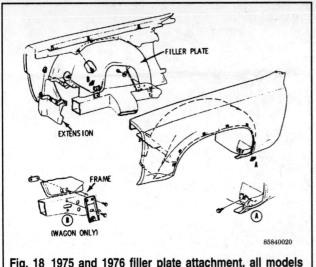

**Fig. 18  1975 and 1976 filler plate attachment, all models similar**

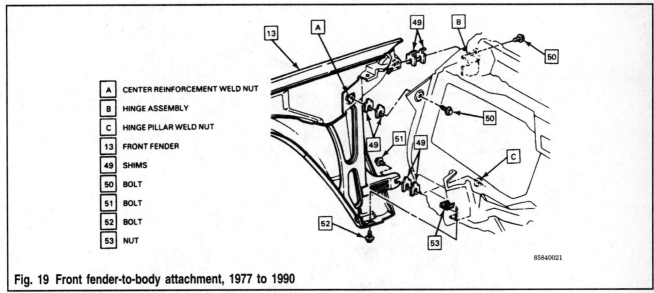

| A | CENTER REINFORCEMENT WELD NUT |
| B | HINGE ASSEMBLY |
| C | HINGE PILLAR WELD NUT |
| 13 | FRONT FENDER |
| 49 | SHIMS |
| 50 | BOLT |
| 51 | BOLT |
| 52 | BOLT |
| 53 | NUT |

**Fig. 19  Front fender-to-body attachment, 1977 to 1990**

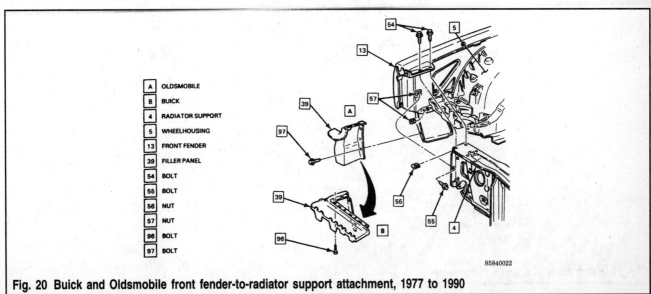

| A | OLDSMOBILE |
| B | BUICK |
| 4 | RADIATOR SUPPORT |
| 5 | WHEELHOUSING |
| 13 | FRONT FENDER |
| 39 | FILLER PANEL |
| 54 | BOLT |
| 55 | BOLT |
| 56 | NUT |
| 57 | NUT |
| 96 | BOLT |
| 97 | BOLT |

**Fig. 20  Buick and Oldsmobile front fender-to-radiator support attachment, 1977 to 1990**

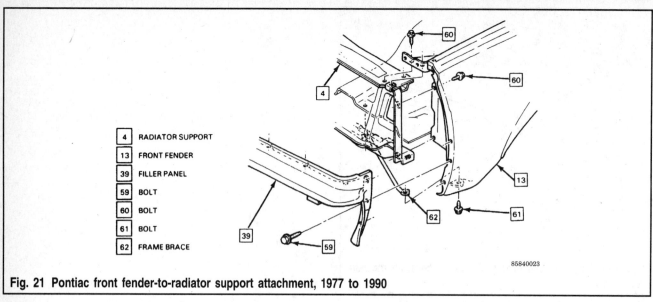

| | |
|---|---|
| 4 | RADIATOR SUPPORT |
| 13 | FRONT FENDER |
| 39 | FILLER PANEL |
| 59 | BOLT |
| 60 | BOLT |
| 61 | BOLT |
| 62 | FRAME BRACE |

85840023

**Fig. 21 Pontiac front fender-to-radiator support attachment, 1977 to 1990**

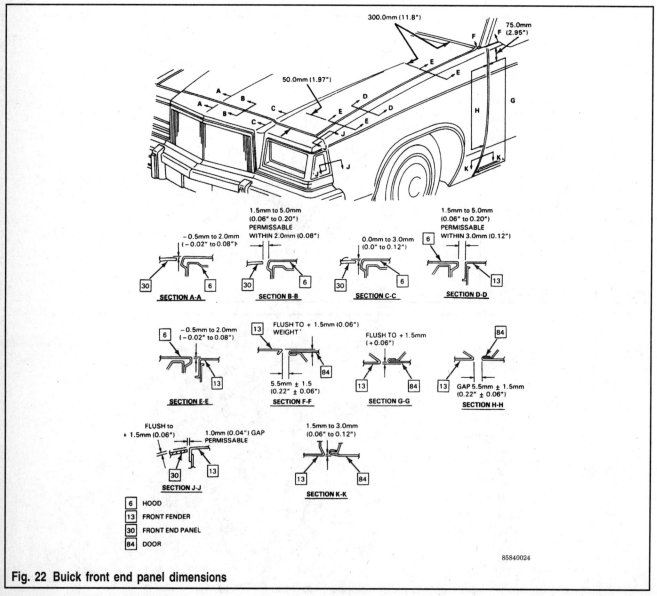

| | |
|---|---|
| 6 | HOOD |
| 13 | FRONT FENDER |
| 30 | FRONT END PANEL |
| 84 | DOOR |

85840024

**Fig. 22 Buick front end panel dimensions**

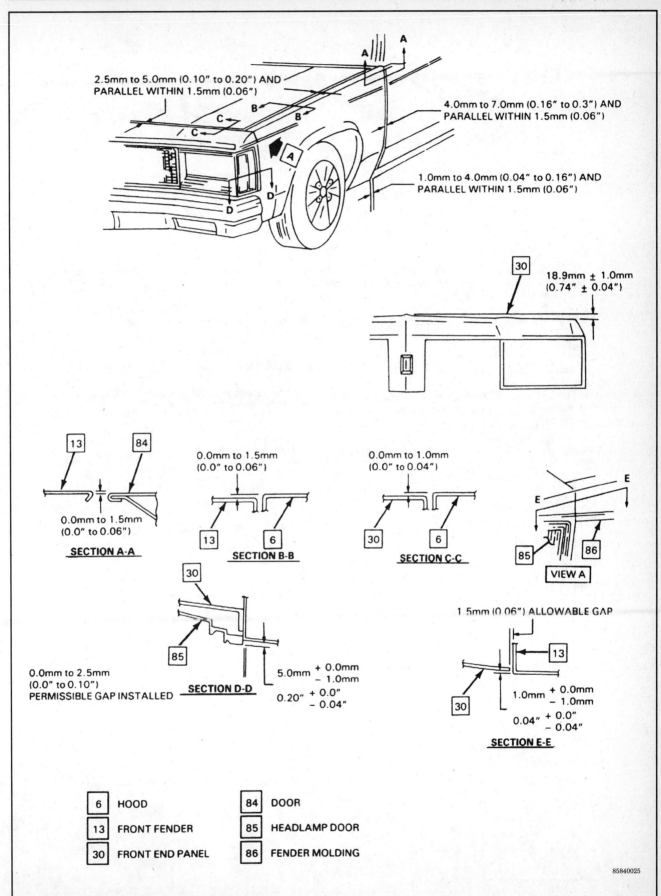

Fig. 23 Oldsmobile front end panel dimensions

85840025

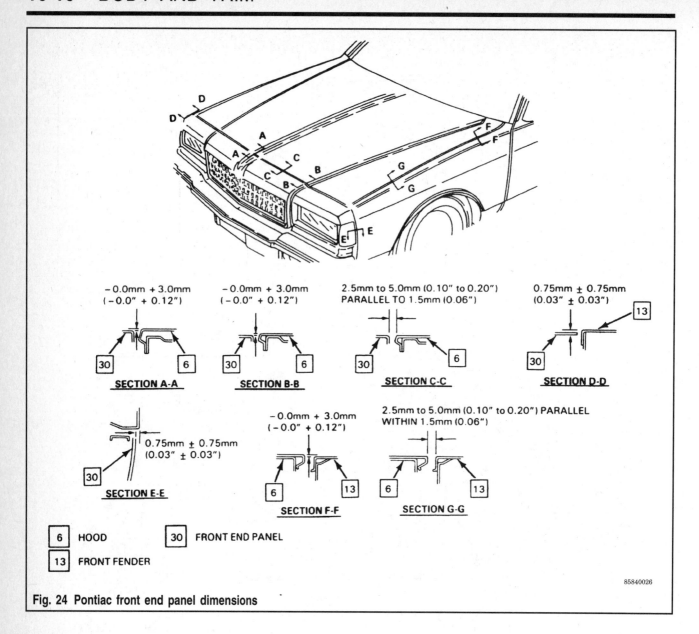

−0.0mm + 3.0mm
(−0.0″ + 0.12″)

30          6

**SECTION A-A**

−0.0mm + 3.0mm
(−0.0″ + 0.12″)

30          6

**SECTION B-B**

2.5mm to 5.0mm (0.10″ to 0.20″)
PARALLEL TO 1.5mm (0.06″)

30          6

**SECTION C-C**

0.75mm ± 0.75mm
(0.03″ ± 0.03″)

13

30

**SECTION D-D**

0.75mm ± 0.75mm
(0.03″ ± 0.03″)

30

**SECTION E-E**

−0.0mm + 3.0mm
(−0.0″ + 0.12″)

6          13

**SECTION F-F**

2.5mm to 5.0mm (0.10″ to 0.20″) PARALLEL
WITHIN 1.5mm (0.06″)

6          13

**SECTION G-G**

| 6 | HOOD | 30 | FRONT END PANEL |

| 13 | FRONT FENDER |

85840026

**Fig. 24 Pontiac front end panel dimensions**

## INTERIOR

### ✳✳WARNING

**If equipped with the air cushion restraint system, do not attempt any service which would require removal of the steering wheel, column, or dashboard. Any service procedures involving these components should only be performed by a professional. Do not attempt any other service until the ignition switch is turned to the LOCK position and the negative battery cable is disconnected and the end taped. This procedure must be followed to prevent accidental deployment of the system which could result in personal injury and/or damage to the systems components. In addition, care must be exercised to never bump or strike the bumper impulse detector in a manner which could cause inadvertent deployment or improper operation of the system.**

### Instrument Panel and Pad

#### REMOVAL & INSTALLATION

▶ **See Figures 26, 27, 28 and 29**

1. Disconnect the negative battery cable.
2. Remove the right and left sound insulators.
3. Remove the steering column trim plate.
4. Remove the instrument panel pad attaching screws. On some models it may be necessary to remove the speaker and defogger grilles to access some screws. Remove the pad.
5. Split the bulkhead connector by removing the bolt and screws on the inside on the fuse block and pull the harness free.

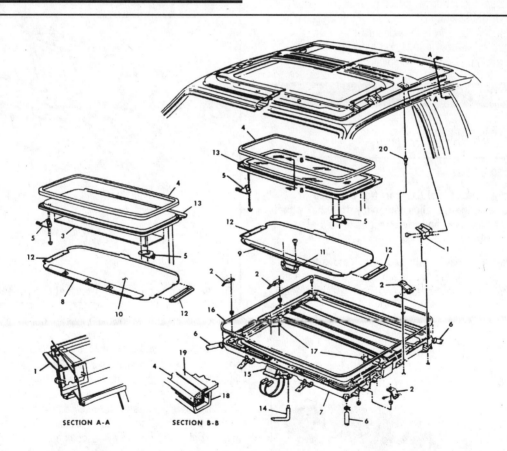

SECTION A-A          SECTION B-B

1. Roof Rail To Housing Support
2. Side Roof Rail Front and Center Support
3. Sliding Panel Insulator
4. Sliding Panel Weatherstrip
5. Sliding Panel Front Support
6. Sun Roof Housing Drain Tube
7. Sun Roof Housing
8. Sliding Panel Headlining (Metal)
9. Sliding Panel Sunshade (Glass)
10. Sliding Panel Sunshade Retainer (Metal)
11. Sliding Panel Sunshade Handle (Glass)
12. Sunshade and Headlining Panel Retainer
13. Sliding Panel
14. Manual Crank
15. Sliding Panel Actuator
16. Housing Weatherstrip
17. Sliding Panel Rear Support (Component Of Cable)
18. Sliding Glass Panel Finishing Cover
19. Sliding Glass Panel Frame
20. Roof To Housing Screw

85840027

**Fig. 25 Exploded view of the sunroof assembly**

6. Lower the steering column and disconnect all electrical connections that are connected to the instrument panel harness.

7. Disconnect the parking brake release cable.

8. Remove the A/C or heater control head.

9. If equipped, disconnect:
   a. Wire at switch for the rear compartment lid release.
   b. Antenna lead.
   c. Power antenna wire connector.
   d. Connector for rear window defogger.

10. Disconnect the speedometer cable at the transducer in the engine compartment, or the transmission for slack.

11. Remove the lower A/C duct by removing the screws and rotate the duct out.

12. Remove the instrument panel by removing:
   a. Nuts from the top left and right of the panel.
   b. Screws from the center support.
   c. Bolts from the steering column support bracket.
   d. The screws from the upper tie bar.
   e. Screws from the lower reinforcement.
   f. Bolts from the steering column opening, if present.
   g. Speedometer cable from the speedometer.
   h. Instrument panel from it's support brackets.

13. Installation is the reverse of removal.

## Door Panels

### REMOVAL & INSTALLATION

▶ **See Figures 30 and 31**

➡ **You can use a special tool GM Part No. BT 7323 or equivalent to disengage the clips fastening the inner panel to the door on front, rear, and lower edges. You'll also need a rubber mallet.**

1. Disconnect the negative battery cable. Remove the inside handles by removing the two attaching screws. These are usually Phillips® head screws and accessible from underneath via recesses.

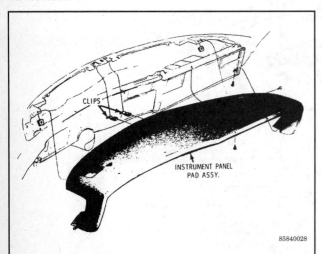

**Fig. 26 1975 and 1976 Oldsmobile instrument panel pad, other models similar**

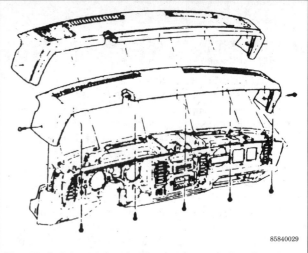

**Fig. 27 Buick and Pontiac instrument panel pad, 1977 to 1990**

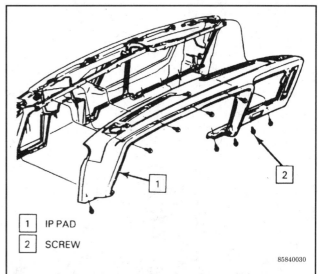

| 1 | IP PAD |
| 2 | SCREW |

**Fig. 28 Oldsmobile instrument panel pad, 1977 to 1990**

2. Unscrew and remove the inside door locking knob. If the vehicle is equipped with a strap type door pull handle, pull the escutcheons out of the centers of the strap mounts on either end to reveal the mounting screws. Since these screws pass through the door panel and into the metal shell of the door behind, remove them.

3. If the vehicle has a remote control mirror, remove the remote mirror escutcheon and then disengage the end of the mirror control cable from the escutcheon.

4. If the vehicle has a switch cover plate in the armrest, remove the screws securing the cover plate and disconnect the switch connectors and, if the vehicle has one, the cigar lighter connectors from the wiring harness.

5. If the vehicle has remote control cover plates, remove the attaching screws and remove the cover plates. Then, remove the screws (which were under the cover plate) which secure the cover plate to the inner panel.

6. If the vehicle has integral armrests, remove the screws inserted through the pull cup and into the armrest hanger support.

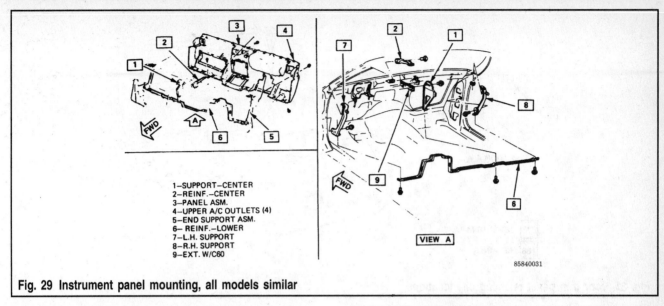

1—SUPPORT—CENTER
2—REINF.—CENTER
3—PANEL ASM.
4—UPPER A/C OUTLETS (4)
5—END SUPPORT ASM.
6— REINF.—LOWER
7—L.H. SUPPORT
8—R.H. SUPPORT
9—EXT. W/C60

85840031

Fig. 29 Instrument panel mounting, all models similar

7. If the vehicle has electric switches located in the door trim panel, disconnect the wiring harness at the switch. If the vehicle has courtesy or reading lamps in the panel, disconnect the wiring harness at the lamp.

8. Use a special tool or flat bladed prybar to carefully pry the panel out from the door, going around the periphery to release all the clips from the inner door.

9. To remove the panel, first push it slightly downward and then pull it outward to release it from the inner door at the beltline. Then, lift the panel upward to release it at the top of the door, where it hangs over.

**To install:**

10. First check that all trim retainers are securely installed and are undamaged. If any require replacement:

  a. Start the retainer with a ¼ in. (6mm) cutout into the attachment hole in the trim panel.

  b. Rotate the retainer until the flange that has the ¼ in. (6mm) cutout is inside the attachment hole.

11. Connect all electrical connectors.

12. Pull the inside door handle inward and position the inner panel near the door, passing the handle through the handle hole in the panel. Then, lift the panel slightly and install the retainers over the top of the inner door.

13. Position the inner panel so all retainers line up with the holes in the inner door. Start one into the retainer hole to ensure alignment and hold. Then, use a rubber mallet to tap all the retainers into the corresponding holes in the inner door.

14. Install all trim and handle screws, window crank and connect the negative battery cable.

## Interior Trim Panels

### REMOVAL & INSTALLATION

▶ See Figures 32, 33, 34, 35, 36, 37, 38, 39 and 40

#### Center Pillar Trim

1. Remove the door sill plate screws and the sill plate.

2. Remove the seat belt guide cover and remove the guide anchor bolt.

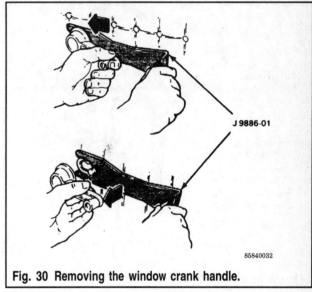

J 9886-01

85840032

Fig. 30 Removing the window crank handle.

3. Remove the upper and lower panel trim screws.

4. Remove the safety belt anchor bolt.

5. Remove the upper and lower trim panels.

6. Installation is the reverse of removal. Torque the anchor bolts to 31 ft. lbs. (42 Nm).

#### Body Lock Pillar Trim

1. Remove the seat cushion and rear seatback on sedans. Fold the second seat forward on wagons.

2. Remove the rear door sill plate and screws.

3. Remove the trim screws and remove the panel.

4. On wagons, disengage the plastic clips. Pull the body lock pillar panel from the wheelhouse trim panel or spare tire cover panel. Remove the lower panel.

5. Installation is the reverse of removal.

#### Quarter Upper Panel

1. Remove the rear seatback and cushion.

2. Remove the rear door sill plate and screws.

3. Remove the body lock pillar panel.

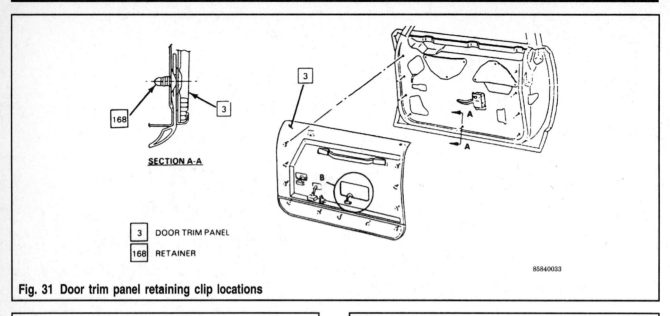

3     DOOR TRIM PANEL

168   RETAINER

85840033

**Fig. 31 Door trim panel retaining clip locations**

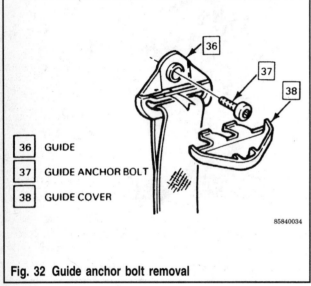

36   GUIDE

37   GUIDE ANCHOR BOLT

38   GUIDE COVER

85840034

**Fig. 32 Guide anchor bolt removal**

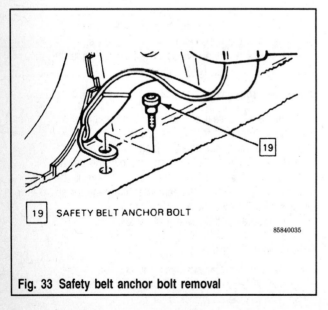

19   SAFETY BELT ANCHOR BOLT

85840035

**Fig. 33 Safety belt anchor bolt removal**

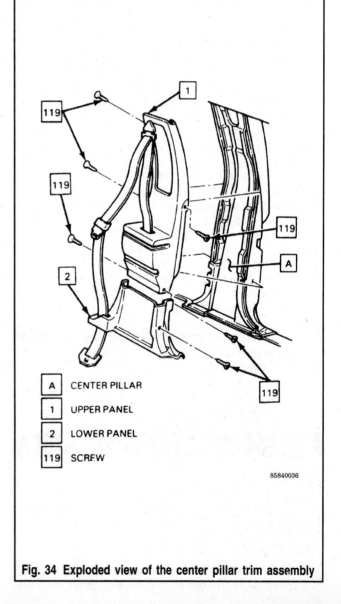

A     CENTER PILLAR

1     UPPER PANEL

2     LOWER PANEL

119   SCREW

85840036

**Fig. 34 Exploded view of the center pillar trim assembly**

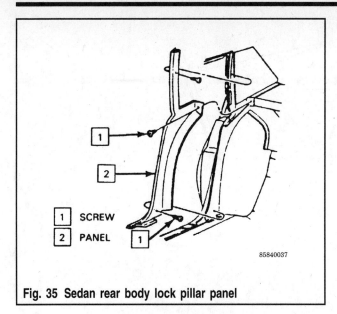

**Fig. 35 Sedan rear body lock pillar panel**

| 1 | SCREW |
| 2 | PANEL |

85840037

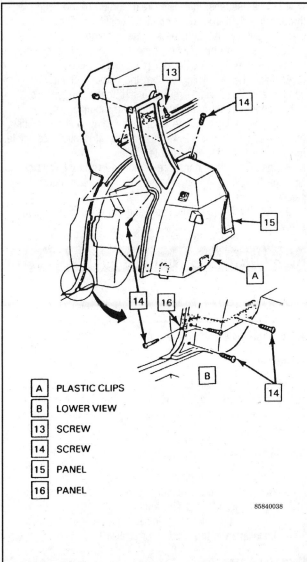

| A | PLASTIC CLIPS |
| B | LOWER VIEW |
| 13 | SCREW |
| 14 | SCREW |
| 15 | PANEL |
| 16 | PANEL |

85840038

**Fig. 36 Body lock pillar panel on wagons**

4. Remove the shelf-mounted stoplamp, if equipped.
5. Remove the back window garnish molding.
6. Remove the quarter upper panel using a retaining clip remover or tool J-24595-C. Make sure the tool engages around the fasteners, then pry in to remove the fasteners.
7. Installation is the reverse of removal.

### Spare Tire Cover Panel

1. To remove the spare tire cover on wagons, grasp the cover panel at the back body opening and pull in to disengage it from the rear tabs and retaining channels.
2. Installation is the reverse of removal.

### Trim Panel and Stowage Pocket Assembly

1. Remove the screws that secure the wheelhouse trim panel to the quarter belt rail. Open the stowage compartment door to reach these screws.
2. Pull the top of the trim panel inboard to separate it from the garnish molding. Lift the trim panel upward to disengage the bottom edge from the slot in the load floor. Pull the trim panel rearward to complete removal.
3. Installation is the reverse of removal.

### Back Body Pillar Panel

1. Remove the left wheelhouse trim panel or the spare tire cover panel.
2. Remove the panel attaching screws.
3. Remove the back body pillar panel by grasping the end of the back body molding and rotating it inboard to release it from the forward end of the back body pillar panel.
4. Installation is the reverse of removal.

## Headliner

Vehicles with deluxe trim use a formed type of headliner that, as a replacement part, comes in two pieces. The headliner cover must be glued to the foundation. This is an extremely difficult operation requiring the use of a number of special tools. It would best be left to a competent automotive upholstery shop. Only the procedure for the standard headliner, which is relatively straightforward, are included here.

### REMOVAL & INSTALLATION

➡On wagons, you will need a special tool J-2772 or equivalent to remove the headliner.

1. Remove the following items from the roof of the vehicle:
   a. Courtesy lamps.
   b. Sunshade supports.
   c. Coat hooks.
   d. Upper quarter trim finishing panels.
   e. Side roof rail moldings.
   f. Windshield and back window garnish moldings.
   g. Shoulder strap retainers.
   h. Windshield side garnish molding.
   i. Roof mounted assist straps.
   j. Sun roof trim finishing lace (if the vehicle has a sunroof).

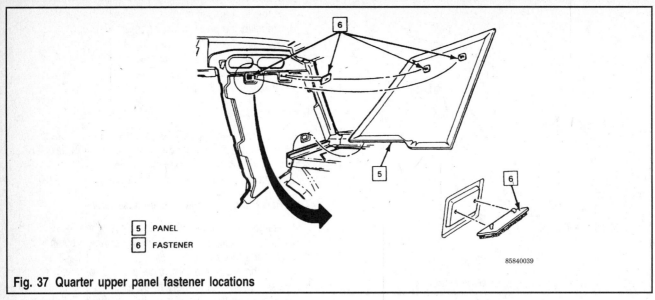

5 PANEL
6 FASTENER

85840039

**Fig. 37 Quarter upper panel fastener locations**

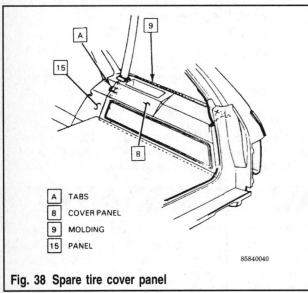

A TABS
8 COVER PANEL
9 MOLDING
15 PANEL

85840040

**Fig. 38 Spare tire cover panel**

k. Twin lift-off panel roof garnish moldings (if so-equipped).

2. Disengage tabs or clips on each side of the headlining from the attaching slots. On wagons, use the tool J 2772 at one end of the molding and pry the molding loose from the retainer.

3. Then, on sedans move the entire assembly far enough rearward to provide clearance for its front to be pulled out through the front door opening, and remove it. On wagons, remove the headlining through the body rear opening.

If the replacement lining does not have an insulator cemented to the upper surface, carefully remove the insulator from the original headlining. Then, spot cement the insulator to the replacement headlining to hold it in position during installation.

**✳✳CAUTION**

**Load the assembly into the vehicle very carefully and excessive flexing can cause permanent deformation.**

4. On all sedans, install the rear portion of the headlining through the right front door opening, holding it diagonally. On wagons, put it in through the tailgate opening.

5. Engage the headlining at the tabs to retain it temporarily to the roof. Install the side roof rail attaching clips.

6. Align the headlining so that the cutouts for the sunshades and dome lamp line up. Install these two types of accessories, but do not fully tighten the mounting screws.

7. On wagons, align the finishing molding at the centerline of the roof and engage it with its retainer. Install the complete molding on both the right and left sides.

8. Install all other hardware removed in Step 1. You can shift the headliner in that area slightly to fit each item into place.

9. Fully tighten the sunshade and dome lamp mounting screws.

## Heater/AC Ducts and Outlets

### REMOVAL & INSTALLATION

▶ **See Figures 41, 42, 43 and 44**

#### Heater Duct

The heater duct can be removed by removing the retaining screw at the top center of the duct and working it free of the cutout base in the heater module case. Installation is the reverse of removal.

#### Instrument Panel Outlet Duct

1. Remove the instrument panel.
2. Remove the duct attaching screws at the upper shroud mounting flange of the dash panel.
3. Remove the duct attaching screw at the heater module.
4. Installation is the reverse of removal.

#### Defroster Nozzle

1. Remove the instrument panel and the instrument panel outlet duct.

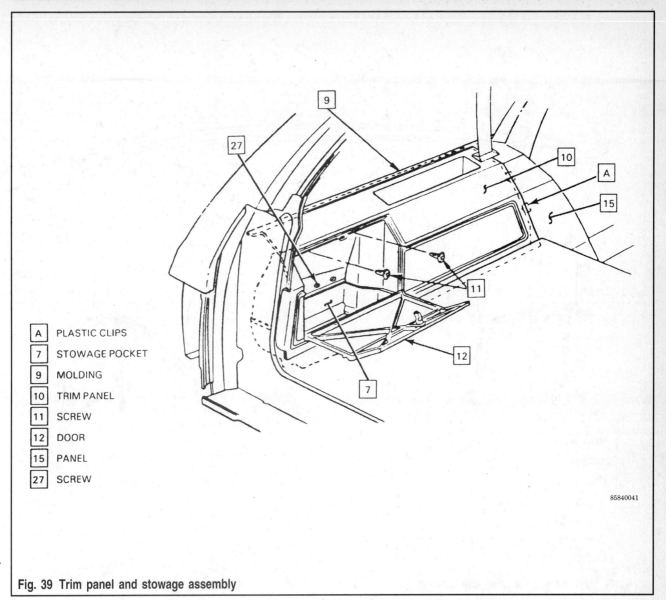

| A | PLASTIC CLIPS |
|---|---------------|
| 7 | STOWAGE POCKET |
| 9 | MOLDING |
| 10 | TRIM PANEL |
| 11 | SCREW |
| 12 | DOOR |
| 15 | PANEL |
| 27 | SCREW |

85840041

**Fig. 39 Trim panel and stowage assembly**

2. Remove the defroster attaching screws near the base of the windshield.

3. Remove the attaching screw at the top of the heater module.

4. Remove the defroster module.

5. Installation is the reverse of removal.

## Door Locks

### REMOVAL & INSTALLATION

▶ **See Figure 45**

1. Make sure the window is up all the way. Then, remove both the upper and lower portions of the trim panel as outlined in this chapter.

2. Going in through the largest access hole, disengage the rod connecting the remote control to the lock as follows:

a. Use a flat-bladed prybar to slide the spring clip out of engagement. The clip must be slid on the lock lever until the ends of the clip no longer engage with the grooved section of the end of the lock rod. You don't need to remove the clip from the lock lever. There is a slot in the rear side of the clip so it can shift on the lock lever even though the lockrod passes right through it.

b. Pull the lock rod out of the lock lever.

3. If the vehicle has electric locks, remove the solenoid.

4. Remove the three screws mounting the lock onto the door lock pillar section of the door and remove the lock. On some models, it may be necessary to remove the inside remote handle and then remove the lock and its connecting rod together. On four door models, it will be necessary to remove the lock, then separate the lockrod from the lock on a workbench, and install the rod onto the new lock.

5. Install in exact reverse order. Torque the lock mounting screws to 84-144 inch lbs. (10-15 Nm).

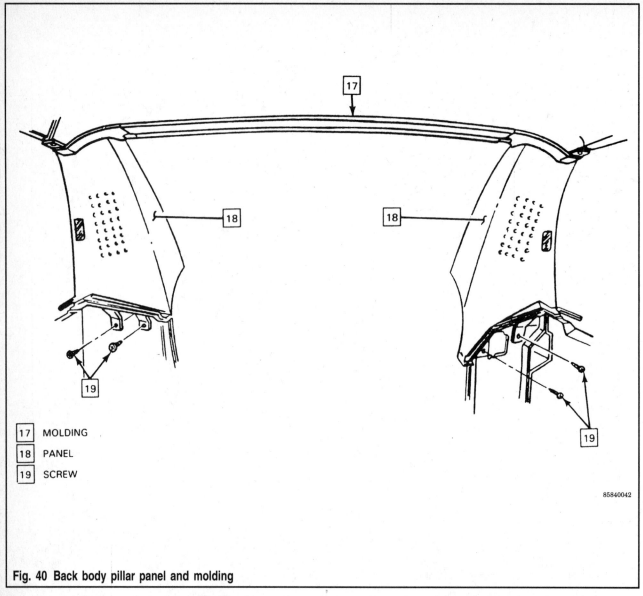

17 MOLDING
18 PANEL
19 SCREW

85840042

**Fig. 40 Back body pillar panel and molding**

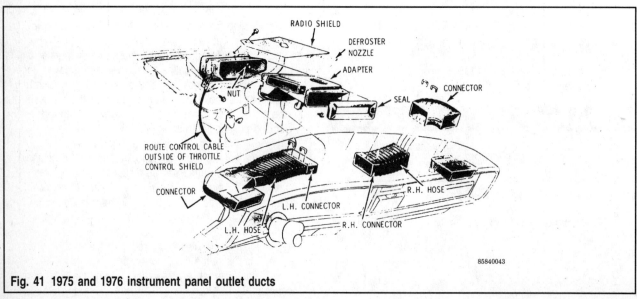

RADIO SHIELD

DEFROSTER NOZZLE

ADAPTER

NUT

SEAL

CONNECTOR

ROUTE CONTROL CABLE OUTSIDE OF THROTTLE CONTROL SHIELD

CONNECTOR

L.H. CONNECTOR

R.H. HOSE

L.H. HOSE

R.H. CONNECTOR

85840043

**Fig. 41 1975 and 1976 instrument panel outlet ducts**

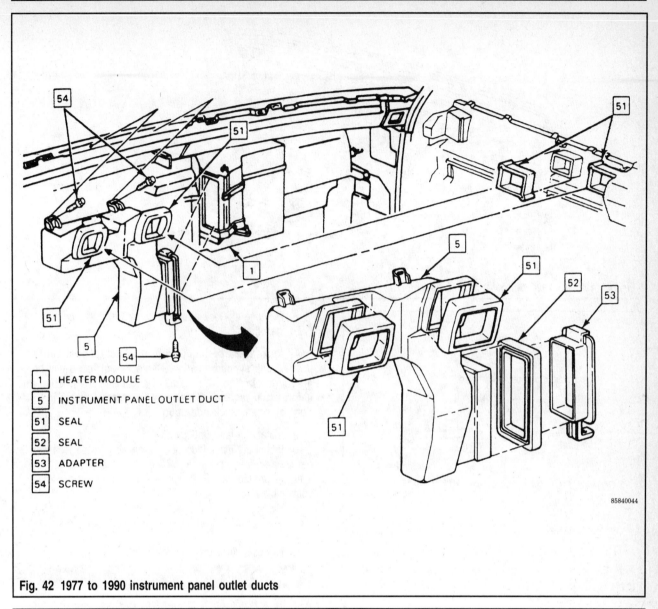

| 1 | HEATER MODULE |
| 5 | INSTRUMENT PANEL OUTLET DUCT |
| 51 | SEAL |
| 52 | SEAL |
| 53 | ADAPTER |
| 54 | SCREW |

85840044

**Fig. 42 1977 to 1990 instrument panel outlet ducts**

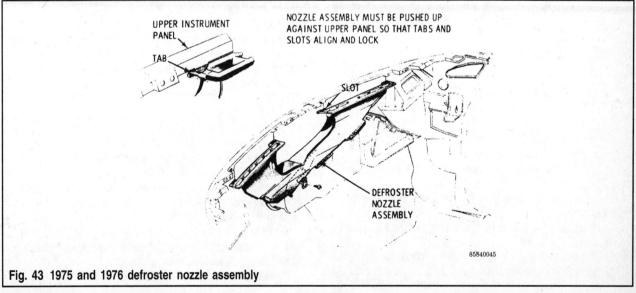

UPPER INSTRUMENT PANEL

TAB

NOZZLE ASSEMBLY MUST BE PUSHED UP AGAINST UPPER PANEL SO THAT TABS AND SLOTS ALIGN AND LOCK

SLOT

DEFROSTER NOZZLE ASSEMBLY

85840045

**Fig. 43 1975 and 1976 defroster nozzle assembly**

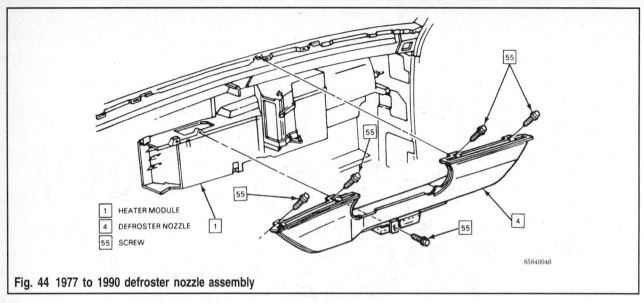

**Fig. 44 1977 to 1990 defroster nozzle assembly**

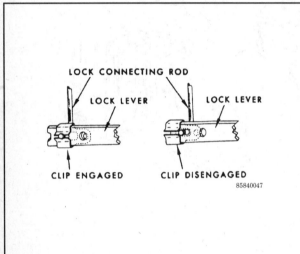

**Fig. 45 Removing the lock connecting rod from the lock lever**

## Tailgate Lock

### REMOVAL & INSTALLATION

▶ See Figures 46, 47, 48, 49 and 50

**Right Upper Lock**

1. Open the tailgate as a door with the glass up.
2. Remove the inside remote handle.
3. Remove the inside trim panel, water deflector and the right access hole cover.
4. Disconnect the upper right remote lock rod and the inside lock rod.
5. Disconnect the electric lock actuator rod and the glass blockout rod, if equipped.
6. Disconnect the electric lock electrical connector.
7. Remove the outside handle.

8. Remove the lock attaching screws and the lock.
**To install:**

➡ All locks must be installed in the latched position for proper lock synchronization. Replacement locks will have a synchronization wire installed and be in the latched position when received. This must be removed after installation for proper lock operation.

9. Install the right upper lock.
10. Install the glass blockout rod and the inside lock rod. Do not connect the upper to lower locking rod at this time.
11. Install the outside handle and reconnect the electrical connectors.
12. Disengage the left upper remote synchronization locking rod attaching swivel from the clip at the remote control assembly.
13. Manually latch the right lower lock assembly.

### ✷✷CAUTION

With the tailgate open in the door position and the right upper and lower locks engaged, the tailgate is in a vulnerable position and could drop from the left upper lock if the synchronization locking rod is pulled inboard. Do not pull on the left upper lock rod when making the swivel adjustment, as personal injury or damage to the tailgate could result.

14. Adjust the swivel on the left upper remote synchronization lock rod until it aligns with the hole in the remote control assembly. Insert the swivel end through the hole on the remote control assembly and engage the retaining clip.
15. Adjust the swivel on the right upper remote lock rod until it aligns with the hole in the remote control assembly. Insert the swivel end in the hole in the remote control assembly and engage the retaining clip.
16. Remove the synchronization wire from the right upper lock and unlatch the locks by actuating the tailgate outside handle. Perform synchronization checks.
17. Reinstall the inner trim panels and handle.

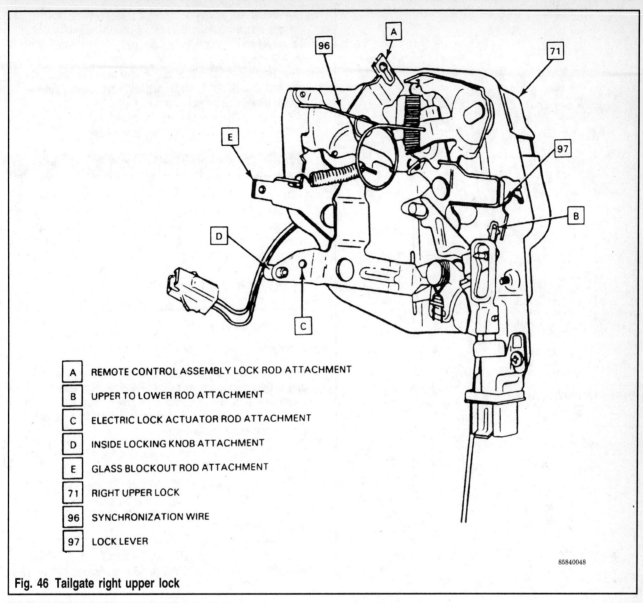

| A | REMOTE CONTROL ASSEMBLY LOCK ROD ATTACHMENT |
| B | UPPER TO LOWER ROD ATTACHMENT |
| C | ELECTRIC LOCK ACTUATOR ROD ATTACHMENT |
| D | INSIDE LOCKING KNOB ATTACHMENT |
| E | GLASS BLOCKOUT ROD ATTACHMENT |
| 71 | RIGHT UPPER LOCK |
| 96 | SYNCHRONIZATION WIRE |
| 97 | LOCK LEVER |

85840048

**Fig. 46 Tailgate right upper lock**

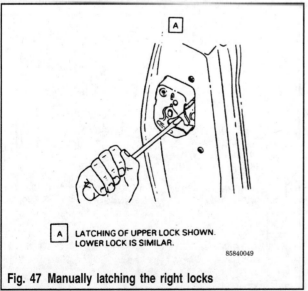

| A | LATCHING OF UPPER LOCK SHOWN. LOWER LOCK IS SIMILAR. |

85840049

**Fig. 47 Manually latching the right locks**

**Right Lower Lock**

1. Open the tailgate as a door with the glass up.
2. Remove the inside remote handle.
3. Remove the inside trim panel, water deflector and the right access hole cover.
4. Remove the electric lock actuator, if equipped.
5. Disconnect the right upper-to-lower synchronization locking rod swivel from the lock clip.
6. Disconnect the electrical connector from the tailgate ajar switch.
7. Remove the lock screws and remove the lock through the access hole.
8. Installation is the reverse of removal.
   **To install:**

➡ **All locks must be installed in the latched position for proper lock synchronization. Replacement locks will have a synchronization wire installed and be in the latched position when received. This must be removed after installation for proper lock operation.**

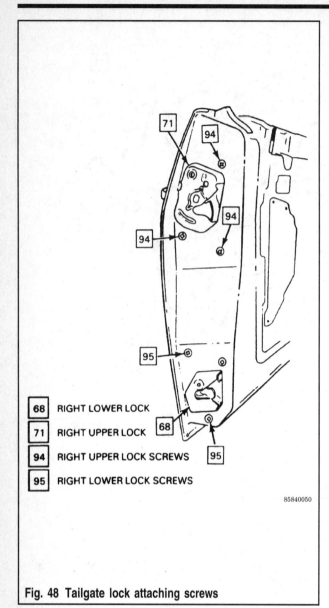

**Fig. 48 Tailgate lock attaching screws**

| 68 | RIGHT LOWER LOCK |
| 71 | RIGHT UPPER LOCK |
| 94 | RIGHT UPPER LOCK SCREWS |
| 95 | RIGHT LOWER LOCK SCREWS |

85840050

9. Install the right lower lock.
10. Reconnect the tailgate ajar switch harness.
11. Disengage the left upper remote synchronization locking rod attaching swivel from the clip at the remote control assembly.
12. Manually latch the right lower lock assembly.

### ✳✳CAUTION

With the tailgate open in the door position and the right upper and lower locks engaged, the tailgate is in a vulnerable position and could drop from the left upper lock if the synchronization locking rod is pulled inboard. Do not pull on the left upper lock rod when making the swivel adjustment, as personal injury or damage to the tailgate could result.

13. Adjust the swivel on the left upper remote synchronization lock rod until it aligns with the hole in the remote control assembly. Insert the swivel end through the hole on the remote control assembly and engage the retaining clip.

14. Adjust the swivel on the right upper remote lock rod until it aligns with the hole in the remote control assembly. Insert the swivel end in the hole in the remote control assembly and engage the retaining clip.
15. Remove the synchronization wire from the right upper lock and unlatch the locks by actuating the tailgate outside handle. Perform synchronization checks.
16. Reinstall the electric lock actuator.
17. Reinstall the inner trim panels and handle.

## Door Glass and Regulator

The glass and related regulator parts (the glass guide) are removed as an assembly and the glass is then separated from the regulator and rebonded on a bench. The regulator itself works through a metal tape, and is removed separately from the window and guide parts.

### REMOVAL & INSTALLATION

▶ **See Figures 51 and 52**

**Regulator**

➡**To perform this operation, you will need a ¼ in. drill and a rivet tool such as GM J 29022 or equivalent and aluminum ¼ in. x ½ in. peel type rivets. You will also need a soft adhesive to reseal the water deflector, a center punch and cloth-backed tape.**

1. Disconnect the negative battery cable. Remove the door inner panel as described above.
2. Remove the trim panel and peel the water deflector off the soft sealer.
3. With the glass up all the way, tape the glass to the upper door frame.
4. Remove the lower sash channel bolts.
5. Use the punch to drive out the centers of the regulator mounting rivets. Then, drill the remaining portions of the rivets out with the ¼ in. drill.

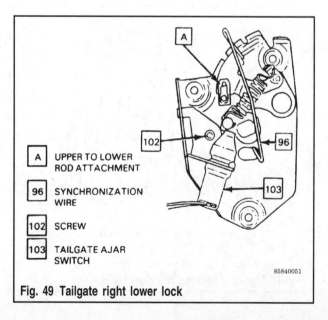

| A | UPPER TO LOWER ROD ATTACHMENT |
| 96 | SYNCHRONIZATION WIRE |
| 102 | SCREW |
| 103 | TAILGATE AJAR SWITCH |

85840051

**Fig. 49 Tailgate right lower lock**

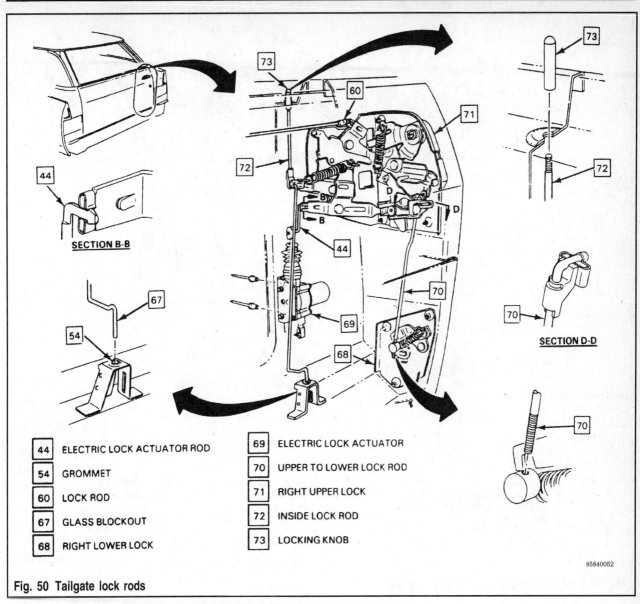

| | | | |
|---|---|---|---|
| **44** | ELECTRIC LOCK ACTUATOR ROD | **69** | ELECTRIC LOCK ACTUATOR |
| **54** | GROMMET | **70** | UPPER TO LOWER LOCK ROD |
| **60** | LOCK ROD | **71** | RIGHT UPPER LOCK |
| **67** | GLASS BLOCKOUT | **72** | INSIDE LOCK ROD |
| **68** | RIGHT LOWER LOCK | **73** | LOCKING KNOB |

85840052

**Fig. 50 Tailgate lock rods**

6. If the vehicle has electric windows, disconnect it from the wiring harness at the connector.

7. Pull the window regulator out through the access hole in the inner panel.

**To install:**

8. Position the new regulator in the door in reverse of the removal procedure.

9. Install the rivets with the rivet tool. Bolt and nut sets with thread locking compound may be used. Connect the negative battery cable.

### Window Glass

**✳✳CAUTION**

**If the glass is being removed because of breakage or a crack, wear gloves and eye protection as you handle it to protect yourself from cuts.**

1. Remove the door inner panel as described above.

2. Remove the door trim panel and peel the water deflector off the soft sealer.

3. With the glass up all the way, tape the glass to the upper door frame.

4. Remove the bolts that hold the lower sash channel to the regulator sash.

5. Reattach the regulator handle without fastening it and use it to run the regulator all the way down. Remove the regulator sash by rotating it 90° and pulling it out.

6. Support the glass in a secure manner and then remove the tape. When the glass is free, lower it carefully all the way.

7. Now, disengage the front edge of the glass from the front glass run channel. Slide the glass forward, tilt it slightly, and remove the guide from the retainer in the run channel located in the rear leg of the door frame.

8. Now, tilt the glass forward and remove it from the door.

**To install:**

9. On a workbench, unbolt the lower sash channel from the glass and bolt it onto the new glass.

10. Use the following method to install the guide retainer:

a. Install the glass and raise it about half way.

b. Supporting the glass with one hand on the lower edge, rotate it rearward to snap the guide into the retainer.

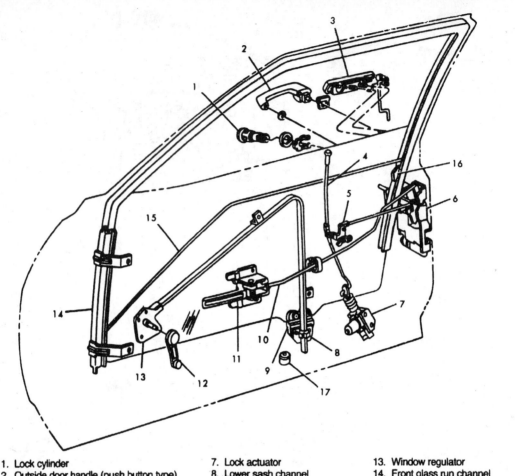

1. Lock cylinder
2. Outside door handle (push button type)
3. Outside door handle (lift bar type)
4. Inside locking rod
5. Locking rod bell crank
6. Door lock
7. Lock actuator
8. Lower sash channel
9. Regulator sash
10. Inside handle connecting rod
11. Inside remote handle
12. Window regulator handle
13. Window regulator
14. Front glass run channel
15. Door glass
16. Plastic guide clip
17. Rubber down stop

85840053

**Fig. 51 Front door glass and operating hardware**

## Electric Window Motor

### REMOVAL & INSTALLATION

➡To perform this operation, you will need a drill, ³/₁₆ in. drill bit and ³/₁₆ in. rivets.

1. Disconnect the negative battery cable. Remove the door trim panel as described above.
2. Remove the interior pad and peel the water deflector off the soft sealer.
3. With the glass up all the way, tape the glass to the upper door frame.
4. Remove the regulator and glass as described above.
5. Disconnect the electrical connector. Drill out the rivets that attach the motor to the door and then remove it.
   **To install:**
6. Install the motor, and then mount it with the new rivets. Reconnect the electrical connector.

7. Install the window and regulator as described above.

## Tailgate Electric Window Motor

### REMOVAL & INSTALLATION

▶ See Figures 53 and 54

**Glass Attached to Regulator and Intact**

### ✳✳CAUTION

This procedure can be used only if the window is intact and attached to the regulator. The regulator lift arms are under tension and the weight of the window is required to neutralize the tension during motor removal to prevent serious injury. If the glass is not attached or is broken, refer to the appropriate procedure.

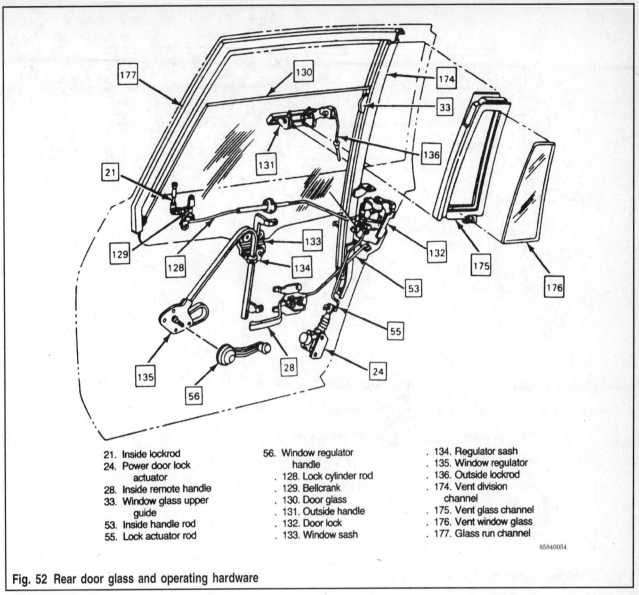

| | | |
|---|---|---|
| 21. Inside lockrod | 56. Window regulator | . 134. Regulator sash |
| 24. Power door lock | handle | . 135. Window regulator |
| actuator | . 128. Lock cylinder rod | . 136. Outside lockrod |
| 28. Inside remote handle | . 129. Bellcrank | . 174. Vent division |
| 33. Window glass upper | . 130. Door glass | channel |
| guide | . 131. Outside handle | . 175. Vent glass channel |
| 53. Inside handle rod | . 132. Door lock | . 176. Vent window glass |
| 55. Lock actuator rod | . 133. Window sash | . 177. Glass run channel |

85840054

**Fig. 52 Rear door glass and operating hardware**

1. Open the tailgate as a door with the window in the full-up position.

2. Remove the inside handle, inner trim panel, water deflector and the left access hole cover.

3. Disconnect the wire harness from the motor.

4. Drive the center pin out of the motor rivet with a punch, then drill the rivet out with a ¼ inch drill bit.

5. Remove the bolts attaching the motor by working through the left access hole.

6. Remove the motor through the left access hole.

**To install:**

7. Lubricate the drive gears with white lithium soap grease that is approved to -20° F (-29° C).

8. Attach the motor to the window regulator, make sure the drive gear properly engages the sector gear teeth before installing the attaching bolts.

9. Install the motor to the tailgate inner panel using a U-nut and a ¼-20· ½ inch screw in place of the rivet drilled out.

10. Reconnect the motor wiring harness and reinstall the access hole cover, water deflector, inner trim panel and handle.

**Glass Not Attached to Regulator or Broken**

**❊❊CAUTION**

This procedure must be used if the glass is broken or is not attached to the regulator. The regulator sector gear must be locked in position before removing the motor from the window regulator. The lift arms are under tension and can cause serious injury if the motor is removed without locking the sector gear in position.

1. Remove the tailgate window regulator and motor as an assembly.

2. Drill a ⅛in. (3.2 mm) hole through the regulator sector gear and back plate. Do not drill the hole closer than ½ in (13 mm) to the edge of the sector gear or back plate.

3. Install a 10-12 · ¾ inch pan head sheet metal screw in the drilled hole to lock the sector gear in position.

4. Remove the motor attaching bolts and remove the motor.

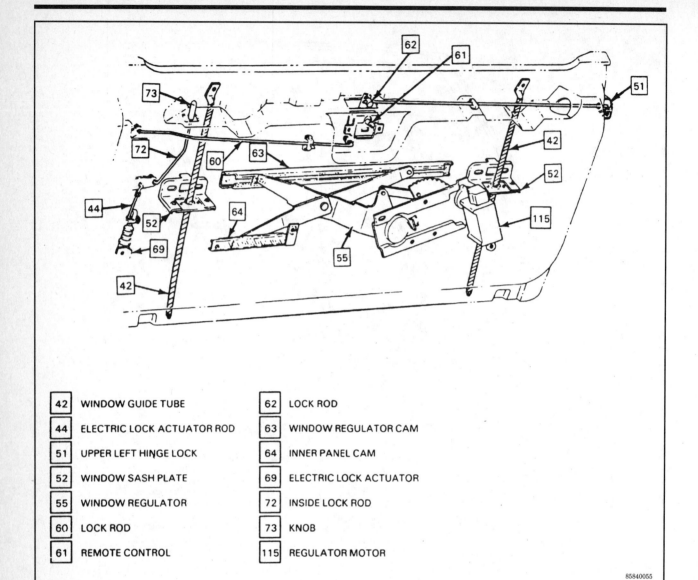

| | | | |
|---|---|---|---|
| 42 | WINDOW GUIDE TUBE | 62 | LOCK ROD |
| 44 | ELECTRIC LOCK ACTUATOR ROD | 63 | WINDOW REGULATOR CAM |
| 51 | UPPER LEFT HINGE LOCK | 64 | INNER PANEL CAM |
| 52 | WINDOW SASH PLATE | 69 | ELECTRIC LOCK ACTUATOR |
| 55 | WINDOW REGULATOR | 72 | INSIDE LOCK ROD |
| 60 | LOCK ROD | 73 | KNOB |
| 61 | REMOTE CONTROL | 115 | REGULATOR MOTOR |

85840055

**Fig. 53 Tailgate window regulator and motor assembly**

**To install:**

5. Lubricate the drive gears with white lithium soap grease that is approved to -20° F (-29° C).

6. Attach the motor to the window regulator, make sure the drive gear properly engages the sector gear teeth before installing the attaching bolts.

7. Remove the screw locking the sector gear in a fixed position.

8. Install the tailgate window regulator and motor as an assembly.

## Windshield

### REMOVAL & INSTALLATION

▶ **See Figures 55, 56, 57, 58 and 59**

➡ To install a new windshield, you will have to use an adhesive service kit. The GM part No. is 9636067 or you can shop for an equivalent. You will also need: an alcohol

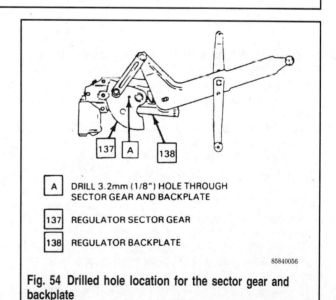

| | |
|---|---|
| A | DRILL 3.2mm (1/8") HOLE THROUGH SECTOR GEAR AND BACKPLATE |
| 137 | REGULATOR SECTOR GEAR |
| 138 | REGULATOR BACKPLATE |

85840056

**Fig. 54 Drilled hole location for the sector gear and backplate**

base solvent; an adhesive dispensing gun GM part No. J 24811 or equivalent; a commercial type of razor knife; a hot knife; black weatherstrip adhesive; two side support spacers; if the windshield has an embedded antenna, a butyl strip; lower support spacers; masking tape. The area in which you work must be at room temperature to ensure timely curing of adhesive.

1. Place protective coverings around the areas of the body around the glass.

2. Remove the trim moldings around the windshield. These are retained by wire clips. You can carefully pry these moldings out until the clip ends are visible. The ends can be pried away from retaining grooves in the body to free them and permit removal of the moldings.

3. Remove the windshield wiper arms as described in Section 6. If it looks like lower glass stops will interfere with removal of the windshield, remove them too.

4. If the vehicle has an embedded antenna, disconnect the wiring connector at the bottom center of the windshield.

5. With the razor knife, cut the adhesive material built up along the edge of the windshield all around. Run the knife right along the edge of the windshield to do this, cutting as close as possible.

6. Install the foam sealing strip to the new windshield, as follows:

a. Remove the backing paper from the sticky side of the strip.

b. Apply the strip to the windshield, using the original windshield as a guide. Check to make sure that the new strip will not obscure the view of the serial number mounted to the top of the dash.

c. Trim the strip as necessary with a sharp knife to remove excess.

7. Inspect all the retaining clips which fasten the moldings to the body. Clips must not be bent away from the body more than    in. (1.6mm). If possible, bend the clips back into the proper configuration; otherwise, replace them.

8. Locate the lower support spacers for the glass as shown in the illustration. Then, carefully position the new glass on these spacers, resting on the original adhesive. See Step 15 for pointers on getting the glass safely into the right position. Check the relationship between the glass and adhesive mounting material on the pinchweld flange. Mark these areas so that later, when you apply additional adhesive, you can fill in any gaps and ensure proper mounting and sealing of the glass. Gaps must not exceed ⅛ in. (3mm).

9. Now, apply masking tape to both sides of the windshield with the inside edge on the glass and the outside edge on the adjacent body pillar. Then, slit the tape with the knife. (This will provide a guide for proper positioning of the windshield later).

10. If the vehicle has an imbedded antenna, mark the location of either end of the butyl strip, mark the location of either end of the strip with the masking tape. On vehicles with this type antenna only, after the glass is removed in the next step, replace the butyl strip originally used to fill the gap between the windshield and body in this area. It should be approximately 8 in. (203mm) long.

11. Now, remove the glass from the opening. Apply masking tape to the inside of the glass ¼ in. (6mm) inboard from the edge of the glass, across the top and down both sides. This

will make clean up easier. Make sure not to apply the tape farther in than this to keep it from being visible after installation.

12. Clean the glass around the edge of the inside surface by wiping it with a clean cloth dampened with the alcohol. Make sure the glass dries without application of heat before installation.

13. Apply the clear primer as follows, depending on the type of antenna used:

a. Normal antenna: Apply the primer around the entire periphery of the glass edge and ¼ in. (6mm) inboard on the inner surface. Allow the primer to dry five minutes.

b. Embedded antenna: Apply the clear primer just as for the plain windshield; around the entire periphery of the glass edge and ¼ in. (6mm) inboard on the inner surface. But, avoid getting any of the primer at all into the area marked by the tape. Allow the primer to dry five minutes.

14. Apply a smooth bead of adhesive material over the entire inside edge only of the glass where the primer was applied in the step above. Make sure the bead is continuous and smooth.

15. Make sure the front windows/windwings are open. Now, with a helper, carry the glass over to the vehicle. Put one hand on the inside of the glass and one on the outside. Tilt the glass until it is horizontal. One person at a time can hold one hand to support the inside of the glass while reaching around the body pillar to grab the glass with the other. Once the glass is held with both hands (one inside the pillar and the other outside), tilt the glass into position, position the glass on the lower supports and, using the tape markers made above, line the glass up in the right position and then drop it straight into place.

16. Press the glass down firmly to squeeze the adhesive material slightly. Avoid too much squeeze-out, as this will cause an ugly appearance. Paddle on additional adhesive, if necessary, to ensure a full and effective seal, utilizing marks made in Step 8 and inspecting for any other areas of poor seal, as well. If the vehicle has an embedded antenna, one place additional material must be applied is at the edges of the butyl sealing strip.

17. Water test the windshield with a gentle spray from a garden hose. A hard spray will disturb adhesive. Use warm water, if you can (it finds leaks more readily). Paddle extra adhesive in to seal any areas that leak and then retest the area.

18. Once all leaks have been stopped, cement a rubber spacer between both the right and left sides of the windshield and the body metal to retain the windshield tightly in its present position as the adhesive cures.

19. Install the moldings. Remove clean-up masking tape from the inner surface of the glass and install/connect any remaining parts. Make sure the vehicle sits for six hours at room temperature before moving it so that the adhesive is properly cured.

## Stationary Glass

Since the glass is bonded and sealed in the same manner with the same adhesives, proceed exactly as described above, with one exception. On many rear window installations, you cannot reach around inside the vehicle with one hand in order

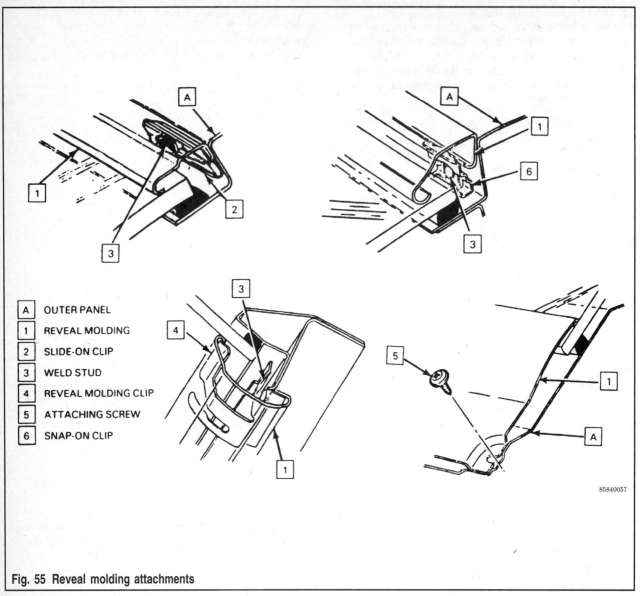

| | |
|---|---|
| **A** | OUTER PANEL |
| **1** | REVEAL MOLDING |
| **2** | SLIDE-ON CLIP |
| **3** | WELD STUD |
| **4** | REVEAL MOLDING CLIP |
| **5** | ATTACHING SCREW |
| **6** | SNAP-ON CLIP |

**Fig. 55 Reveal molding attachments**

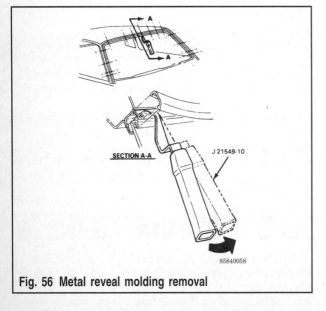

**Fig. 56 Metal reveal molding removal**

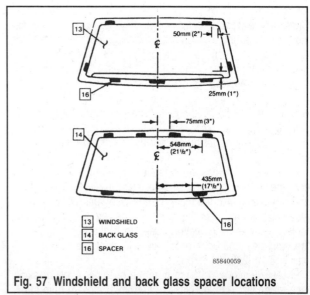

| | |
|---|---|
| **13** | WINDSHIELD |
| **14** | BACK GLASS |
| **16** | SPACER |

**Fig. 57 Windshield and back glass spacer locations**

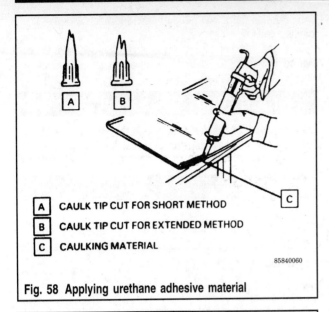

| | |
|---|---|
| **A** | CAULK TIP CUT FOR SHORT METHOD |
| **B** | CAULK TIP CUT FOR EXTENDED METHOD |
| **C** | CAULKING MATERIAL |

85840060

**Fig. 58 Applying urethane adhesive material**

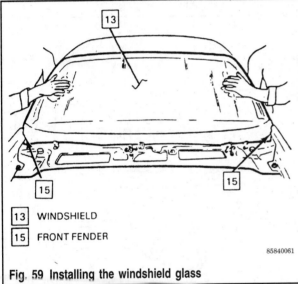

| | |
|---|---|
| **13** | WINDSHIELD |
| **15** | FRONT FENDER |

85840061

**Fig. 59 Installing the windshield glass**

to support and handle the glass. In these cases, you will have to use special suction cup devices to handle the glass. Be careful to ensure adequate seal of the cups for safe handling.

## Tailgate Window

### REMOVAL & INSTALLATION

▶ **See Figures 60, 61, 62 and 63**

1. Open the tailgate as a gate.
2. Remove the inside handle, inner trim panel, water deflector and the access hole covers. If equipped with a heated glass option, disconnect the wire harness.
3. Mark the location of the up-travel stop attaching bolts and remove them.

4. Mark the location of the belt trim support retainers and slide them away from the window.

### ✳✳CAUTION

**With the tailgate open in the gate position and the left upper lock manually engaged, the tailgate has been placed in a vulnerable position and could drop from the right lower lock if the locking rod or the outside handle is activated. Personal injury or damage to the tailgate could result if either the handle or rods are activated.**

5. Manually latch the left upper hinge lock.
6. Operate the window to a point where the regulator cam nuts are visible through the holes in the inner panel and remove the nuts.
7. Remove the sash plate attaching nuts working through the access holes.
8. Remove the window through the belt opening.

**To install:**

9. Always use new window hardware when installing new windows. Install the window through the belt opening and install the sash attaching nuts.
10. Install the regulator cam attaching nuts.
11. Operate the window to the full down position.
12. Unlatch the left upper hinge lock by temporarily installing the handle without the screw and operating it.
13. Install the belt trim support retainers into the original position and tighten the bolts.
14. Install the up travel stop and reconnect the window heater wire connector, if equipped.
15. Check the window for proper alignment before installing the trim, adjust if necessary.
16. Install the access hole covers, water deflector, inside trim panel and handle.

## Inside Rear View Mirror

### REPLACEMENT

▶ **See Figure 64**

The rearview mirror is attached to a support which is secured to the windshield glass. A service replacement windshield glass has the support bonded to the glass assembly. To install a detached mirror support or install a new part, use the following procedures to complete the service.

1. Locate the support position at the center of the glass 22 in. (557mm) from the bottom of the glass to the bottom of the support.
2. Circle the location on the outside of the glass with a wax pencil or crayon. Draw a large circle around the support circle.
3. Clean the area within the circle with household cleaner and dry with a clean towel. Repeat the procedures using rubbing alcohol.
4. Sand the bonding surface of the support with fine grit (320-360) emery cloth or sandpaper. If the original support is being used, remove the old adhesive with rubbing alcohol and a clean towel.
5. Apply the adhesive as outlined in the kit instructions.

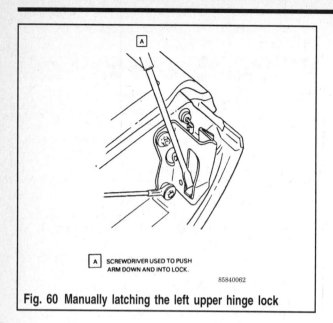

A SCREWDRIVER USED TO PUSH ARM DOWN AND INTO LOCK.

85840062

**Fig. 60 Manually latching the left upper hinge lock**

6. Position the support to the marked location with the rounded end UP.

7. Press the support to the glass for 30-60 seconds. Excessive adhesive can be removed after five minutes with rubbing alcohol.

## ✳✳CAUTION

**DO NOT apply excessive pressure to the windshield glass. The glass may break, causing personal injury.**

## Seats

### REMOVAL & INSTALLATION

◆ See Figures 65, 66 and 67

**Front**

1. Disconnect the negative battery cable.

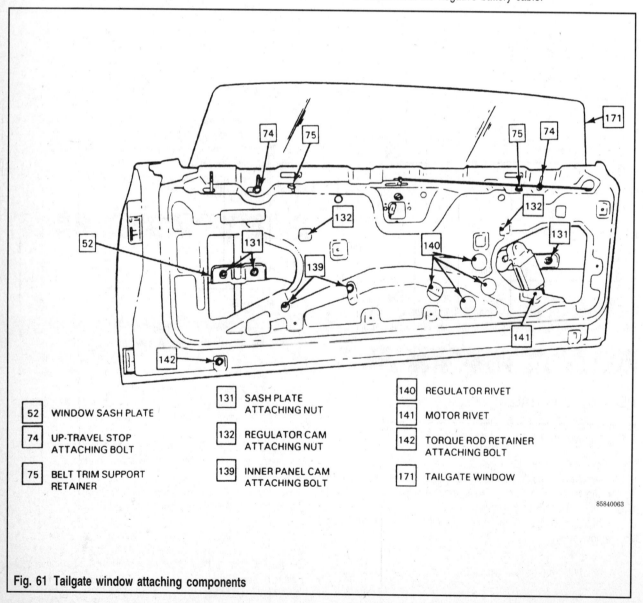

| 52 | WINDOW SASH PLATE |
| 74 | UP-TRAVEL STOP ATTACHING BOLT |
| 75 | BELT TRIM SUPPORT RETAINER |

| 131 | SASH PLATE ATTACHING NUT |
| 132 | REGULATOR CAM ATTACHING NUT |
| 139 | INNER PANEL CAM ATTACHING BOLT |

| 140 | REGULATOR RIVET |
| 141 | MOTOR RIVET |
| 142 | TORQUE ROD RETAINER ATTACHING BOLT |
| 171 | TAILGATE WINDOW |

85840063

**Fig. 61 Tailgate window attaching components**

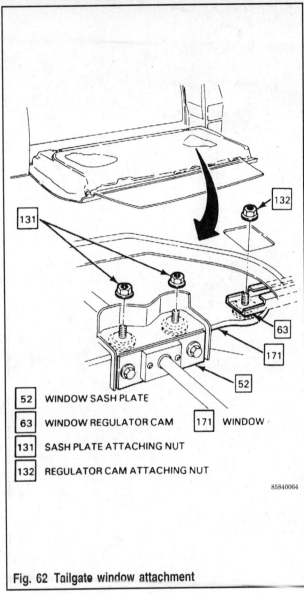

Fig. 62 Tailgate window attachment

| 52 | WINDOW SASH PLATE | | |
| 63 | WINDOW REGULATOR CAM | 171 | WINDOW |
| 131 | SASH PLATE ATTACHING NUT | | |
| 132 | REGULATOR CAM ATTACHING NUT | | |

85840064

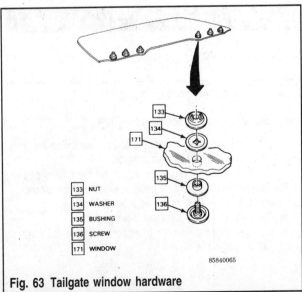

| 133 | NUT |
| 134 | WASHER |
| 135 | BUSHING |
| 136 | SCREW |
| 171 | WINDOW |

85840065

Fig. 63 Tailgate window hardware

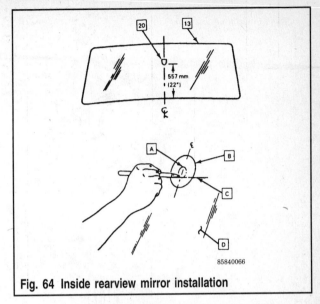

Fig. 64 Inside rearview mirror installation

2. Operate the front seat to the full forward position.

3. Remove the screws, rear support covers and adjuster hold down nuts.

4. Remove the seat belt cover.

5. Operate the seat to the full rearward position.

6. Remove the screws, front support covers and adjuster hold down nuts.

7. Remove the seat belt anchor bolt using a Torx® socket J 29843 9.

8. Disconnect and electrical connections to the seat.

9. Before removing the seat, place paint protection over the trim to prevent damage.

10. With an assistant, remove the seat assembly with adjusters attached.

**To install:**

11. With an assistant, install the seat assembly onto the mounting studs.

12. Connect all electrical connections and seat belts. Torque the seat belt anchor to 31 ft. lbs. (42 Nm).

13. Install and torque the front nuts to 22 ft. lbs. (30 Nm). Install the support covers.

14. Move the seat to the full forward position.

15. Install the seat belt cover, rear nuts and torque to 22 ft. lbs. (30 Nm).

16. Install the support covers, connect the negative battery cable and check operation.

**Rear**

*SEAT BOTTOM*

1. The seatbottom is held in place by dome stops located on the floor pan. The dome stops hook over the frame wires on the seatbottom.

2. To disengage, push the lower front edge of the seatbottom rearward, lift up and pull forward to disengage the dome stops.

**To install:**

3. Slide the bottom rearward, press down and pull forward. The frame wire in the bottom should slide into the dome stops.

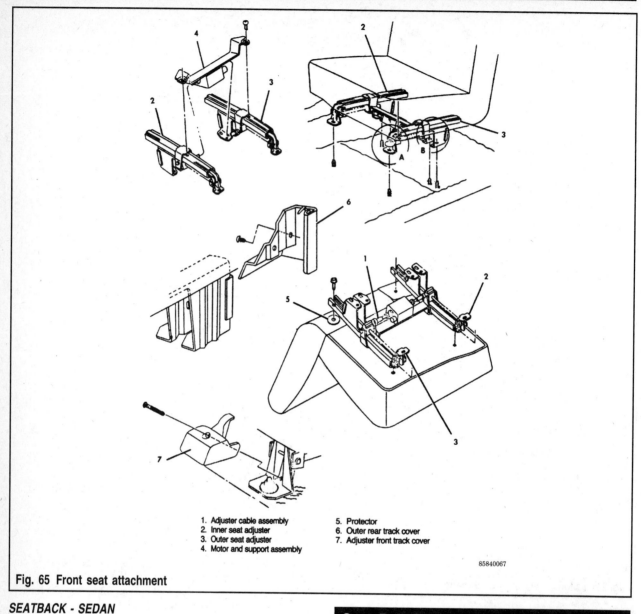

1. Adjuster cable assembly
2. Inner seat adjuster
3. Outer seat adjuster
4. Motor and support assembly
5. Protector
6. Outer rear track cover
7. Adjuster front track cover

85840067

**Fig. 65 Front seat attachment**

## SEATBACK - SEDAN

1. Remove the two retaining bolts in the lower corners.
2. Lift the rear seatback off the hooks on the seat panel.
3. Hang the seatback over the hooks on the panel and install the two bolts.

## SEATBACK - WAGON

1. Lower the second seat and remove the bolts from each side of the seatback.
2. Remove the screws from the bottom edge of the seat.
3. Raise the seat enough to pull the lower edge forward.
4. Lift upward to release the upper edge of the seat from the hooks on the seat panel and remove the seatback.

**To install:**

5. Hang the seatback over the hooks on the seat panel.
6. Install the screws and bolts.
7. Raise the seat and check operation.

## Seat Belt Systems

### REMOVAL & INSTALLATION

▶ See Figures 68, 69, 70, 71, 72 and 73

**Lap Belts and Floor Attachments**

1. For the front seats, move the seat forward. For the rear and third seats remove the seat cushion.
2. Disconnect the electrical connector on the drivers belt.
3. Remove the anchor bolt cover and remove the anchor bolt using tool J 29843-9 or it's equivalent.
4. Remove the safety belt and sleeve.
5. Installation is the reverse of removal. Torque the anchor bolt to 31 ft. lbs (42 Nm).

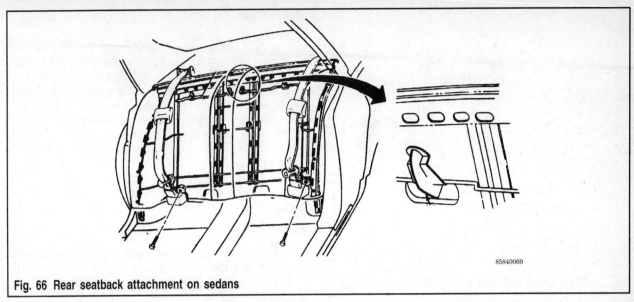

Fig. 66 Rear seatback attachment on sedans

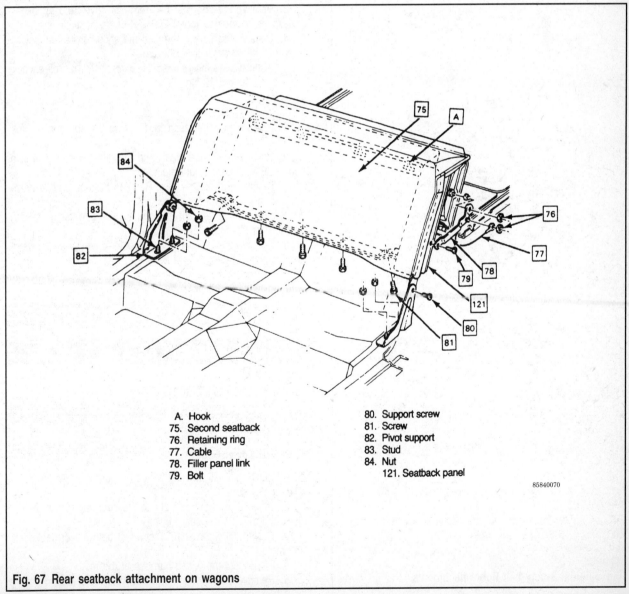

A. Hook
75. Second seatback
76. Retaining ring
77. Cable
78. Filler panel link
79. Bolt
80. Support screw
81. Screw
82. Pivot support
83. Stud
84. Nut
121. Seatback panel

Fig. 67 Rear seatback attachment on wagons

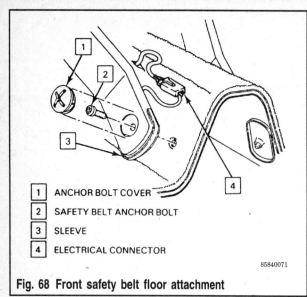

| 1 | ANCHOR BOLT COVER |
| 2 | SAFETY BELT ANCHOR BOLT |
| 3 | SLEEVE |
| 4 | ELECTRICAL CONNECTOR |

85840071

**Fig. 68 Front safety belt floor attachment**

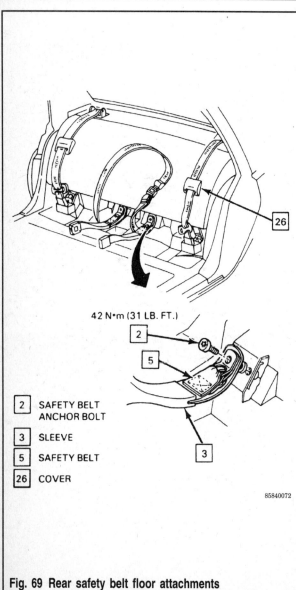

42 N•m (31 LB. FT.)

| 2 | SAFETY BELT ANCHOR BOLT |
| 3 | SLEEVE |
| 5 | SAFETY BELT |
| 26 | COVER |

85840072

**Fig. 69 Rear safety belt floor attachments**

### Shoulder Belts

#### FRONT SEATS

1. Remove the guide cover and remove the guide anchor bolt using tool J 29843-9 or it's equivalent.
2. Remove the center upper and lower pillar panel. Refer to appropriate procedure in this section.
3. Remove the retractor anchor bolt using tool J 29843-9 or it's equivalent and remove the retractor.
4. Remove the safety belt anchor bolt using tool J29843-9 or it's equivalent.
5. Remove the safety belt from the center pillar trim panels.
6. Installation is the reverse of removal. Torque all anchor bolts to 31 ft. lbs (42 Nm).

#### REAR SEAT

1. Remove the seat cushion. Refer to the appropriate procedure in this section.
2. Remove the lap belt retractor anchor bolt using tool J 29843-9 or it's equivalent.
3. Remove the shoulder belt retractor cover and remove the anchor bolt using tool J 29843-9 or it's equivalent.
4. Remove the safety belt with the shoulder belt retractor and lap belt retractor from the vehicle.
5. Installation is the reverse of removal. Torque all anchor bolts to 31 ft. lbs (42 Nm).

#### SECOND SEAT

1. Remove the seat cushion. Refer to the appropriate procedure in this section.
2. Remove the guide cover and the guide anchor bolt using tool J 29843-9 or it's equivalent.
3. Remove the quarter trim. Refer to the appropriate procedure in this manual.
4. Remove the lap belt retractor anchor bolt using tool J 29843-9 or it's equivalent.
5. Remove the shoulder belt retractor cover and remove the anchor bolt using tool J 29843-9 or it's equivalent.
6. Remove the safety belt with the shoulder belt retractor and lap belt retractor from the vehicle.
7. Installation is the reverse of removal. Torque all anchor bolts to 31 ft. lbs (42 Nm).

## Power Seat Motor

### REMOVAL & INSTALLATION

▶ See Figure 74

#### Two-Way Power Seats

1. If the seat will move, shift it to a position near the middle of it travel.
2. Remove the nuts that attach the seat adjuster to the floor and then tilt the seat forward for access.
3. On the full width seat, disconnect both power cables at the motor.
4. Disconnect the wiring harness at the motor.
5. Remove the screws that secure the motor support to the seat frame. Remove the motor with the support attached.

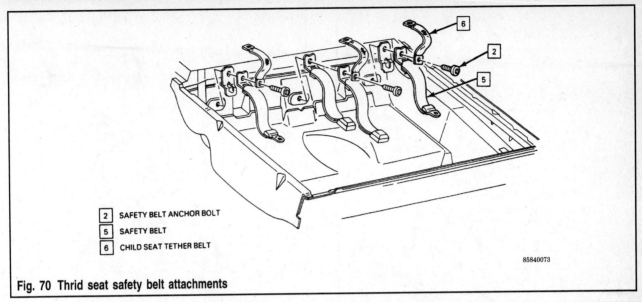

2   SAFETY BELT ANCHOR BOLT

5   SAFETY BELT

6   CHILD SEAT TETHER BELT

85840073

**Fig. 70  Thrid seat safety belt attachments**

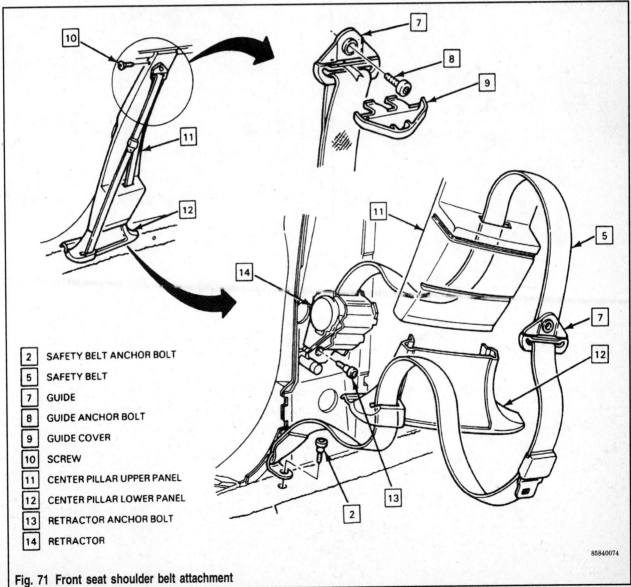

2   SAFETY BELT ANCHOR BOLT

5   SAFETY BELT

7   GUIDE

8   GUIDE ANCHOR BOLT

9   GUIDE COVER

10   SCREW

11   CENTER PILLAR UPPER PANEL

12   CENTER PILLAR LOWER PANEL

13   RETRACTOR ANCHOR BOLT

14   RETRACTOR

85840074

**Fig. 71  Front seat shoulder belt attachment**

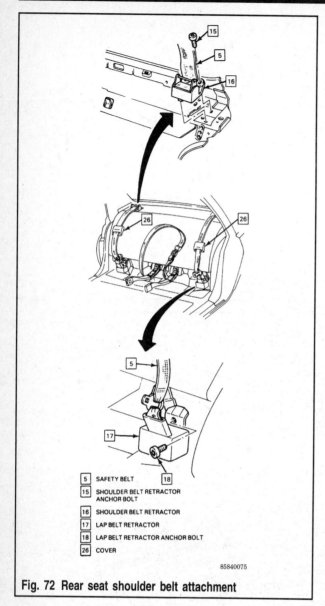

5   SAFETY BELT
15  SHOULDER BELT RETRACTOR
    ANCHOR BOLT
16  SHOULDER BELT RETRACTOR
17  LAP BELT RETRACTOR
18  LAP BELT RETRACTOR ANCHOR BOLT
26  COVER

85840075

**Fig. 72 Rear seat shoulder belt attachment**

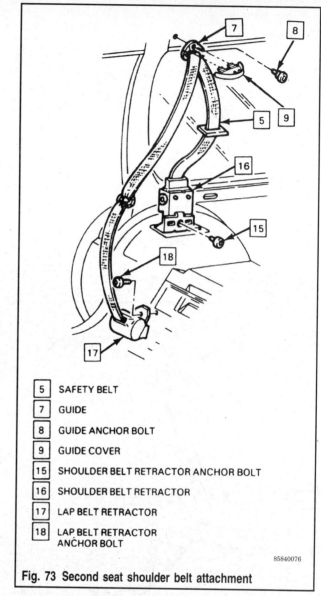

5   SAFETY BELT

7   GUIDE

8   GUIDE ANCHOR BOLT

9   GUIDE COVER

15  SHOULDER BELT RETRACTOR ANCHOR BOLT

16  SHOULDER BELT RETRACTOR

17  LAP BELT RETRACTOR

18  LAP BELT RETRACTOR
    ANCHOR BOLT

85840076

**Fig. 73 Second seat shoulder belt attachment**

Then, remove the screws that attach the motor to the support bracket and remove the motor from the bracket.

6. Installation is the reverse of removal. Make sure you test the motor for proper operation to the extremes of travel in both directions.

### Six-Way Power Seat Permanent Magnet Motor

1. Unbolt the seat from the floor of the vehicle. Place it upside down in a location where the upholstery is protected from dirt.

2. Disconnect the wires going to the motor at the motor control relay.

3. Remove the two mounting screws that attach the motor mounting support to the seat. Remove the three screws attaching the transmission to the motor.

4. Now, move the motor outboard or away from the transmission far enough to disengage it from the rubber coupling that connects it to the transmission, and remove it.

5. Installation is the reverse of removal.

## TORQUE SPECIFICATIONS

| Component | U.S. | Metric |
|---|---|---|
| Door hinge bolts | 15–21 ft. lbs. | 20–28 Nm |
| Hood mounting bolts | 20 ft. lbs. | 27 Nm |
| Trunk lid mounting bolts | 20 ft. lbs. | 27 Nm |
| Bumper retaining nuts | 18 ft. lbs. | 24 Nm |
| Seat belt anchor bolts | 31 ft. lbs. | 42 Nm |
| Seat attaching bolts | 22 ft. lbs. | 30 Nm |
| Sunroof | 7–10 ft. lbs. | 10–14 Nm |

85840c01

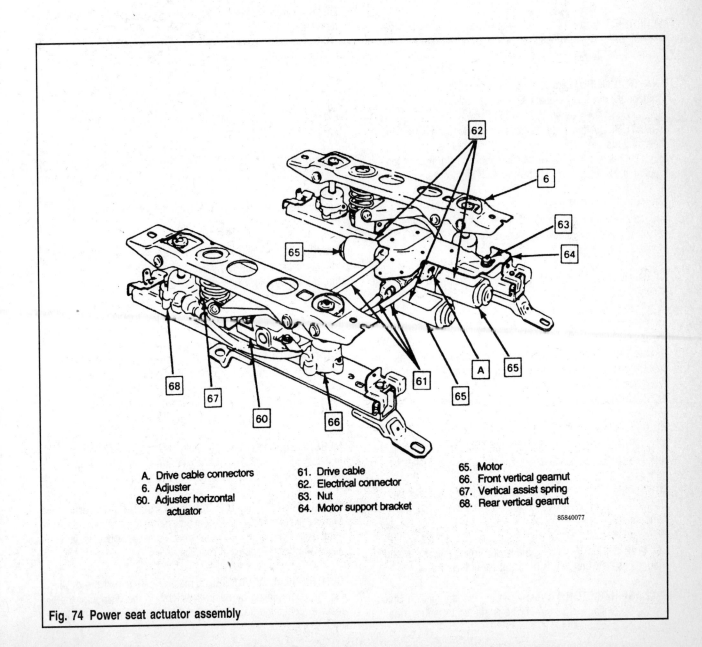

A. Drive cable connectors
6. Adjuster
60. Adjuster horizontal actuator
61. Drive cable
62. Electrical connector
63. Nut
64. Motor support bracket
65. Motor
66. Front vertical gearnut
67. Vertical assist spring
68. Rear vertical gearnut

85840077

**Fig. 74 Power seat actuator assembly**

## GLOSSARY

**AIR/FUEL RATIO:** The ratio of air to gasoline by weight in the fuel mixture drawn into the engine.

**AIR INJECTION:** One method of reducing harmful exhaust emissions by injecting air into each of the exhaust ports of an engine. The fresh air entering the hot exhaust manifold causes any remaining fuel to be burned before it can exit the tailpipe.

**ALTERNATOR:** A device used for converting mechanical energy into electrical energy.

**AMMETER:** An instrument, calibrated in amperes, used to measure the flow of an electrical current in a circuit. Ammeters are always connected in series with the circuit being tested.

**AMPERE:** The rate of flow of electrical current present when one volt of electrical pressure is applied against one ohm of electrical resistance.

**ANALOG COMPUTER:** Any microprocessor that uses similar (analogous) electrical signals to make its calculations.

**ARMATURE:** A laminated, soft iron core wrapped by a wire that converts electrical energy to mechanical energy as in a motor or relay. When rotated in a magnetic field, it changes mechanical energy into electrical energy as in a generator.

**ATMOSPHERIC PRESSURE:** The pressure on the Earth's surface caused by the weight of the air in the atmosphere. At sea level, this pressure is 14.7 psi at 32{248}F (101 kPa at 0{248}C).

**ATOMIZATION:** The breaking down of a liquid into a fine mist that can be suspended in air.

**AXIAL PLAY:** Movement parallel to a shaft or bearing bore.

**BACKFIRE:** The sudden combustion of gases in the intake or exhaust system that results in a loud explosion.

**BACKLASH:** The clearance or play between two parts, such as meshed gears.

**BACKPRESSURE:** Restrictions in the exhaust system that slow the exit of exhaust gases from the combustion chamber.

**BAKELITE:** A heat resistant, plastic insulator material commonly used in printed circuit boards and transistorized components.

**BALL BEARING:** A bearing made up of hardened inner and outer races between which hardened steel balls roll.

**BALLAST RESISTOR:** A resistor in the primary ignition circuit that lowers voltage after the engine is started to reduce wear on ignition components.

**BEARING:** A friction reducing, supportive device usually located between a stationary part and a moving part.

**BIMETAL TEMPERATURE SENSOR:** Any sensor or switch made of two dissimilar types of metal that bend when heated or cooled due to the different expansion rates of the alloys. These types of sensors usually function as an on/off switch.

**BLOWBY:** Combustion gases, composed of water vapor and unburned fuel, that leak past the piston rings into the crankcase during normal engine operation. These gases are removed by the PCV system to prevent the buildup of harmful acids in the crankcase.

**BRAKE PAD:** A brake shoe and lining assembly used with disc brakes.

**BRAKE SHOE:** The backing for the brake lining. The term is, however, usually applied to the assembly of the brake backing and lining.

**BUSHING:** A liner, usually removable, for a bearing; an anti-friction liner used in place of a bearing.

**CALIPER:** A hydraulically activated device in a disc brake system, which is mounted straddling the brake rotor (disc). The caliper contains at least one piston and two brake pads. Hydraulic pressure on the piston(s) forces the pads against the rotor.

**CAMSHAFT:** A shaft in the engine on which are the lobes (cams) which operate the valves. The camshaft is driven by the crankshaft, via a belt, chain or gears, at one half the crankshaft speed.

**CAPACITOR:** A device which stores an electrical charge.

**CARBON MONOXIDE (CO):** A colorless, odorless gas given off as a normal byproduct of combustion. It is poisonous and extremely dangerous in confined areas, building up slowly to toxic levels without warning if adequate ventilation is not available.

**CARBURETOR:** A device, usually mounted on the intake manifold of an engine, which mixes the air and fuel in the proper proportion to allow even combustion.

**CATALYTIC CONVERTER:** A device installed in the exhaust system, like a muffler, that converts harmful byproducts of combustion into carbon dioxide and water vapor by means of a heat-producing chemical reaction.

**CENTRIFUGAL ADVANCE:** A mechanical method of advancing the spark timing by using flyweights in the distributor that react to centrifugal force generated by the distributor shaft rotation.

**CHECK VALVE:** Any one-way valve installed to permit the flow of air, fuel or vacuum in one direction only.

**CHOKE:** A device, usually a moveable valve, placed in the intake path of a carburetor to restrict the flow of air.

**CIRCUIT:** Any unbroken path through which an electrical current can flow. Also used to describe fuel flow in some instances.

**CIRCUIT BREAKER:** A switch which protects an electrical circuit from overload by opening the circuit when the current flow exceeds a predetermined level. Some circuit breakers must be reset manually, while most reset automatically

**COIL (IGNITION):** A transformer in the ignition circuit which steps up the voltage provided to the spark plugs.

**COMBINATION MANIFOLD:** An assembly which includes both the intake and exhaust manifolds in one casting.

**COMBINATION VALVE:** A device used in some fuel systems that routes fuel vapors to a charcoal storage canister instead of venting them into the atmosphere. The valve relieves fuel tank pressure and allows fresh air into the tank as the fuel level drops to prevent a vapor lock situation.

**COMPRESSION RATIO:** The comparison of the total volume of the cylinder and combustion chamber with the piston at BDC and the piston at TDC.

**CONDENSER:** 1. An electrical device which acts to store an electrical charge, preventing voltage surges.
2. A radiator-like device in the air conditioning system in which refrigerant gas condenses into a liquid, giving off heat.

**CONDUCTOR:** Any material through which an electrical current can be transmitted easily.

**CONTINUITY:** Continuous or complete circuit. Can be checked with an ohmmeter.

**COUNTERSHAFT:** An intermediate shaft which is rotated by a mainshaft and transmits, in turn, that rotation to a working part.

**CRANKCASE:** The lower part of an engine in which the crankshaft and related parts operate.

**CRANKSHAFT:** The main driving shaft of an engine which receives reciprocating motion from the pistons and converts it to rotary motion.

**CYLINDER:** In an engine, the round hole in the engine block in which the piston(s) ride.

**CYLINDER BLOCK:** The main structural member of an engine in which is found the cylinders, crankshaft and other principal parts.

**CYLINDER HEAD:** The detachable portion of the engine, fastened, usually, to the top of the cylinder block, containing all or most of the combustion chambers. On overhead valve engines, it contains the valves and their operating parts. On overhead cam engines, it contains the camshaft as well.

**DEAD CENTER:** The extreme top or bottom of the piston stroke.

**DETONATION:** An unwanted explosion of the air/fuel mixture in the combustion chamber caused by excess heat and compression, advanced timing, or an overly lean mixture. Also referred to as "ping".

**DIAPHRAGM:** A thin, flexible wall separating two cavities, such as in a vacuum advance unit.

**DIESELING:** A condition in which hot spots in the combustion chamber cause the engine to run on after the key is turned off.

**DIFFERENTIAL:** A geared assembly which allows the transmission of motion between drive axles, giving one axle the ability to turn faster than the other.

**DIODE:** An electrical device that will allow current to flow in one direction only.

**DISC BRAKE:** A hydraulic braking assembly consisting of a brake disc, or rotor, mounted on an axle, and a caliper assembly containing, usually two brake pads which are activated by hydraulic pressure. The pads are forced against the sides of the disc, creating friction which slows the vehicle.

**DISTRIBUTOR:** A mechanically driven device on an engine which is responsible for electrically firing the spark plug at a predetermined point of the piston stroke.

**DOWEL PIN:** A pin, inserted in mating holes in two different parts allowing those parts to maintain a fixed relationship.

**DRUM BRAKE:** A braking system which consists of two brake shoes and one or two wheel cylinders, mounted on a fixed backing plate, and a brake drum, mounted on an axle, which revolves around the assembly.

**DWELL:** The rate, measured in degrees of shaft rotation, at which an electrical circuit cycles on and off.

**ELECTRONIC CONTROL UNIT (ECU):** Ignition module, module, amplifier or igniter. See Module for definition.

**ELECTRONIC IGNITION:** A system in which the timing and firing of the spark plugs is controlled by an electronic control unit, usually called a module. These systems have no points or condenser.

**ENDPLAY:** The measured amount of axial movement in a shaft.

**ENGINE:** A device that converts heat into mechanical energy.

**EXHAUST MANIFOLD:** A set of cast passages or pipes which conduct exhaust gases from the engine.

**FEELER GAUGE:** A blade, usually metal, of precisely predetermined thickness, used to measure the clearance between two parts.

**FIRING ORDER:** The order in which combustion occurs in the cylinders of an engine. Also the order in which spark is distributed to the plugs by the distributor.

**FLOODING:** The presence of too much fuel in the intake manifold and combustion chamber which prevents the air/fuel mixture from firing, thereby causing a no-start situation.

**FLYWHEEL:** A disc shaped part bolted to the rear end of the crankshaft. Around the outer perimeter is affixed the ring gear. The starter drive engages the ring gear, turning the flywheel, which rotates the crankshaft, imparting the initial starting motion to the engine.

**FOOT POUND (ft.lb. or sometimes, ft. lbs.):** The amount of energy or work needed to raise an item weighing one pound, a distance of one foot.

**FUSE:** A protective device in a circuit which prevents circuit overload by breaking the circuit when a specific amperage is present. The device is constructed around a strip or wire of a lower amperage rating than the circuit it is designed to protect. When an amperage higher than that stamped on the fuse is present in the circuit, the strip or wire melts, opening the circuit.

**GEAR RATIO:** The ratio between the number of teeth on meshing gears.

**GENERATOR:** A device which converts mechanical energy into electrical energy.

**HEAT RANGE:** The measure of a spark plug's ability to dissipate heat from its firing end. The higher the heat range, the hotter the plug fires.

**HUB:** The center part of a wheel or gear.

**HYDROCARBON (HC):** Any chemical compound made up of hydrogen and carbon. A major pollutant formed by the engine as a byproduct of combustion.

**HYDROMETER:** An instrument used to measure the specific gravity of a solution.

**INCH POUND (in.lb. or sometimes, in. lbs.):** One twelfth of a foot pound.

**INDUCTION:** A means of transferring electrical energy in the form of a magnetic field. Principle used in the ignition coil to increase voltage.

**INJECTOR:** A device which receives metered fuel under relatively low pressure and is activated to inject the fuel into the engine under relatively high pressure at a predetermined time.

**INPUT SHAFT:** The shaft to which torque is applied, usually carrying the driving gear or gears.

**INTAKE MANIFOLD:** A casting of passages or pipes used to conduct air or a fuel/air mixture to the cylinders.

**JOURNAL:** The bearing surface within which a shaft operates.

**KEY:** A small block usually fitted in a notch between a shaft and a hub to prevent slippage of the two parts.

**MANIFOLD:** A casting of passages or set of pipes which connect the cylinders to an inlet or outlet source.

**MANIFOLD VACUUM:** Low pressure in an engine intake manifold formed just below the throttle plates. Manifold vacuum is highest at idle and drops under acceleration.

**MASTER CYLINDER:** The primary fluid pressurizing device in a hydraulic system. In automotive use, it is found in brake and hydraulic clutch systems and is pedal activated, either directly or, in a power brake system, through the power booster.

**MODULE:** Electronic control unit, amplifier or igniter of solid state or integrated design which controls the current flow in the ignition primary circuit based on input from the pick-up coil. When the module opens the primary circuit, the high secondary voltage is induced in the coil.

**NEEDLE BEARING:** A bearing which consists of a number (usually a large number) of long, thin rollers.

**OHM:**($\Omega$) The unit used to measure the resistance of conductor to electrical flow. One ohm is the amount of resistance that limits current flow to one ampere in a circuit with one volt of pressure.

**OHMMETER:** An instrument used for measuring the resistance, in ohms, in an electrical circuit.

**OUTPUT SHAFT:** The shaft which transmits torque from a device, such as a transmission.

**OVERDRIVE:** A gear assembly which produces more shaft revolutions than that transmitted to it.

**OVERHEAD CAMSHAFT (OHC):** An engine configuration in which the camshaft is mounted on top of the cylinder head and operates the valve either directly or by means of rocker arms.

**OVERHEAD VALVE (OHV):** An engine configuration in which all of the valves are located in the cylinder head and the camshaft is located in the cylinder block. The camshaft operates the valves via lifters and pushrods.

**OXIDES OF NITROGEN (NOx):** Chemical compounds of nitrogen produced as a byproduct of combustion. They combine with hydrocarbons to produce smog.

**OXYGEN SENSOR:** Used with the feedback system to sense the presence of oxygen in the exhaust gas and signal the computer which can reference the voltage signal to an air/fuel ratio.

**PINION:** The smaller of two meshing gears.

**PISTON RING:** An open ended ring which fits into a groove on the outer diameter of the piston. Its chief function is to form a seal between the piston and cylinder wall. Most automotive pistons have three rings: two for compression sealing; one for oil sealing.

**PRELOAD:** A predetermined load placed on a bearing during assembly or by adjustment.

**PRIMARY CIRCUIT:** Is the low voltage side of the ignition system which consists of the ignition switch, ballast resistor or resistance wire, bypass, coil, electronic control unit and pick-up coil as well as the connecting wires and harnesses.

**PRESS FIT:** The mating of two parts under pressure, due to the inner diameter of one being smaller than the outer diameter of the other, or vice versa; an interference fit.

**RACE:** The surface on the inner or outer ring of a bearing on which the balls, needles or rollers move.

**REGULATOR:** A device which maintains the amperage and/or voltage levels of a circuit at predetermined values.

**RELAY:** A switch which automatically opens and/or closes a circuit.

**RESISTANCE:** The opposition to the flow of current through a circuit or electrical device, and is measured in ohms. Resistance is equal to the voltage divided by the amperage.

**RESISTOR:** A device, usually made of wire, which offers a preset amount of resistance in an electrical circuit.

**RING GEAR:** The name given to a ring-shaped gear attached to a differential case, or affixed to a flywheel or as part a planetary gear set.

**ROLLER BEARING:** A bearing made up of hardened inner and outer races between which hardened steel rollers move.

**ROTOR:** 1. The disc-shaped part of a disc brake assembly, upon which the brake pads bear; also called, brake disc.
2. The device mounted atop the distributor shaft, which passes current to the distributor cap tower contacts.

**SECONDARY CIRCUIT:** The high voltage side of the ignition system, usually above 20,000 volts. The secondary includes the ignition coil, coil wire, distributor cap and rotor, spark plug wires and spark plugs.

**SENDING UNIT:** A mechanical, electrical, hydraulic or electromagnetic device which transmits information to a gauge.

**SENSOR:** Any device designed to measure engine operating conditions or ambient pressures and temperatures. Usually electronic in nature and designed to send a voltage signal to an on-board computer, some sensors may operate as a simple on/off switch or they may provide a variable voltage signal (like a potentiometer) as conditions or measured parameters change.

**SHIM:** Spacers of precise, predetermined thickness used between parts to establish a proper working relationship.

**SLAVE CYLINDER:** In automotive use, a device in the hydraulic clutch system which is activated by hydraulic force, disengaging the clutch.

**SOLENOID:** A coil used to produce a magnetic field, the effect of which is produce work.

**SPARK PLUG:** A device screwed into the combustion chamber of a spark ignition engine. The basic construction is a conductive core inside of a ceramic insulator, mounted in an outer conductive base. An electrical charge from the spark plug wire travels along the conductive core and jumps a preset air gap to a grounding point or points at the end of the conductive base. The resultant spark ignites the fuel/air mixture in the combustion chamber.

**SPLINES:** Ridges machined or cast onto the outer diameter of a shaft or inner diameter of a bore to enable parts to mate without rotation.

**TACHOMETER:** A device used to measure the rotary speed of an engine, shaft, gear, etc., usually in rotations per minute.

**THERMOSTAT:** A valve, located in the cooling system of an engine, which is closed when cold and opens gradually in response to engine heating, controlling the temperature of the coolant and rate of coolant flow.

**TOP DEAD CENTER (TDC):** The point at which the piston reaches the top of its travel on the compression stroke.

**TORQUE:** The twisting force applied to an object.

**TORQUE CONVERTER:** A turbine used to transmit power from a driving member to a driven member via hydraulic action, providing changes in drive ratio and torque. In automotive use, it links the driveplate at the rear of the engine to the automatic transmission.

**TRANSDUCER:** A device used to change a force into an electrical signal.

**TRANSISTOR:** A semi-conductor component which can be actuated by a small voltage to perform an electrical switching function.

**TUNE-UP:** A regular maintenance function, usually associated with the replacement and adjustment of parts and components in the electrical and fuel systems of a vehicle for the purpose of attaining optimum performance.

**TURBOCHARGER:** An exhaust driven pump which compresses intake air and forces it into the combustion chambers at higher than atmospheric pressures. The increased air pressure allows more fuel to be burned and results in increased horsepower being produced.

**VACUUM ADVANCE:** A device which advances the ignition timing in response to increased engine vacuum.

**VACUUM GAUGE:** An instrument used to measure the presence of vacuum in a chamber.

**VALVE:** A device which control the pressure, direction of flow or rate of flow of a liquid or gas.

**VALVE CLEARANCE:** The measured gap between the end of the valve stem and the rocker arm, cam lobe or follower that activates the valve.

**VISCOSITY:** The rating of a liquid's internal resistance to flow.

**VOLTMETER:** An instrument used for measuring electrical force in units called volts. Voltmeters are always connected parallel with the circuit being tested.

**WHEEL CYLINDER:** Found in the automotive drum brake assembly, it is a device, actuated by hydraulic pressure, which, through internal pistons, pushes the brake shoes outward against the drums.

**MASTER INDEX**